Entrepreneurship: A Custom Text

We work with leading authors to develop the strongest educational materials bringing cutting-edge thinking and best learning practice to a global market.

Under a range of well-known imprints, including Financial Times/Prentice Hall, Addison Wesley and Longman, we craft high quality print and electronic publications which help readers to understand and apply their content, whether studying or at work.

Pearson Custom Publishing enables our customers to access a wide and expanding range of market-leading content from world-renowned authors and develop their own tailor-made book. You choose the content that meets your needs and Pearson Custom Publishing produces a high-quality printed book.

To find out more about custom publishing, visit www.pearsoncustom.co.uk

A Pearson Custom Publication

Entrepreneurship: A Custom Text

Compiled from:

Entrepreneurship: Successfully Launching New Ventures
Second Edition
by Bruce R. Barringer and R. Duane Ireland

Marketing and Entrepreneurship in SMEs: An Innovative Approach
by David Carson, Stanley Cromie, Pauric McGowan and Jimmy Hill

Selling and Sales Management Seventh Edition
by David Jobber and Geoff Lancaster

Entrepreneurship Fourth Edition
by Peggy A. Lambing and Charles R. Kuehl

Strategic Entrepreneurship Fourth Edition
by Philip A. Wickham

Essentials of Entrepreneurship and Small Business Management Fifth Edition
by Thomas W. Zimmerer and Norman M. Scarborough with Doug Wilson

Articles from International Journal of Entrepreneurial Behaviour & Research 2001

Pearson Education Limited
Edinburgh Gate
Harlow
Essex CM20 2JE

And associated companies throughout the world

Visit us on the World Wide Web at:
www.pearsoned.co.uk

First published 2008

Compiled from:

Entrepreneurship: Successfully Launching New Ventures Second Edition
by Bruce R. Barringer and R. Duane Ireland
ISBN 978 0 13 224057 4

Marketing and Enrepreneurship in SMEs: An Innovative Approach
by David Carson, Stanley Cromie, Pauric McGowan and Jimmy Hill
ISBN 978 0 13 150970 2

Selling and Sales Management Seventh Edition
by David Jobber and Geoff Lancaster
ISBN 978 0 273 69579 0

Entrepreneurship Fourth Edition
by Peggy A. Lambing and Charles R. Kuehl
ISBN 978 0 13 228174 4

Strategic Entrepreneurship Fourth Edition
by Philip A. Wickham
ISBN 978 0 273 70642 7

Essentials of Entrepreneurship and Small Business Management Fifth Edition
by Thomas W. Zimmerer and Norman M. Scarborough with Doug Wilson
ISBN 978 0 13 229438 6

ISBN 978 1 846776 123 1

Printed and bound in Great Britain by Henry Ling Limited at the Dorset Press, Dorchester, DT1 1HD

Contents

Chapter 1	The Challenge of Entrepreneurship	1
Readings	Chapter 1 'Marketing and entrepreneurship: an overview' in *Marketing and Entrepreneurship in SMEs: An Innovative Approach* David Carson, Stanley Cromie, Pauric McGowan and Jimmy Hill	3
	Chapter 4 'The concept of entrepreneurship' in *Marketing and Entrepreneurship in SMEs: An Innovative Approach* David Carson, Stanley Cromie, Pauric McGowan and Jimmy Hill	13
	Chapter 1 'The Foundations of Entrepreneurship' in *Essentials of Entrepreneurship and Small Business Management* Fifth Edition Thomas W. Zimmerer and Norman M. Scarborough with Doug Wilson	25
Chapter 2	Inside the Entrepreneurial Mind: From Ideas to Reality	65
Readings	Chapter 2 'Recognizing Opportunities and Generating Ideas' in *Entrepreneurship: Successfully Launching New Ventures* Second Edition Bruce R. Barringer and R. Duane Ireland	66
	Chapter 2 'Inside the Entrepreneurial Mind: From Ideas to Reality' in *Essentials of Entrepreneurship and Small Business Management* Fifth Edition Thomas W. Zimmerer and Norman M. Scarborough with Doug Wilson	99
Chapter 3	Intrapreneurship: Developing Corporate Entrepreneurship	141
Reading	Chapter 14 'Intrapreneurship' in *Strategic Entrepreneurship* Fourth Edition Philip A. Wickham	143

Chapter 4 **Strategic Management and the Entrepreneur** 155

Readings
Chapter 5 'Industry and Competitor Analysis' in *Entrepreneurship: Successfully Launching New Ventures* Second Edition
Bruce R. Barringer and R. Duane Ireland 156

Chapter 3 'Designing a Competitive Business Model and Building a Solid Strategic Plan' in *Essentials of Entrepreneurship and Small Business Management* Fifth Edition
Thomas W. Zimmerer and Norman M. Scarborough with Doug Wilson 187

Chapter 5 **Forms of Business Ownership and Franchising** 227

Readings
Chapter 15 'Franchising' in *Entrepreneurship: Successfully Launching New Ventures*
Second Edition
Bruce R. Barringer and R. Duane Ireland 228

Chapter 5 'Franchising and Other Alternatives' in *Entrepreneurship*
Fourth Edition
Peggy A. Lambing and Charles R. Kuehl 265

Chapter 6 **Buying an Existing Business** 283

Reading
Chapter 7 'Buying an Existing Business' in *Essentials of Entrepreneurship and Small Business Management* Fifth Edition
Thomas W. Zimmerer and Norman M. Scarborough with Doug Wilson 284

Chapter 7 **Building a Powerful Marketing Plan** 327

Readings
'A multidimensional study of the key determinants of effective SME marketing activity: Part 1' by Jimmy Hill
International Journal of Entrepreneurial Behaviour & Research, Vol 7 No. 5, 2001 329

'A multidimensional study of the key determinants of effective SME marketing activity: Part 2' by Jimmy Hill
International Journal of Entrepreneurial Behaviour & Research, Vol 7 No. 6, 2001 363

Chapter 13 'Marketing competencies for entrepreneurs' in *Marketing and Entrepreneurship in SMEs: An Innovative Approach*
David Carson, Stanley Cromie, Pauric McGowan and Jimmy Hill 388

Chapter 2 'Sales Strategies' in *Selling and Sales Management*
Seventh Edition
David Jobber and Geoff Lancaster 402

Chapter 8 **E-Commerce and the Entrepreneur** 435

Reading
Chapter 12 'Internet and IT Applications in Selling and Sales Management' in *Selling and Sales Management*
Seventh Edition
David Jobber and Geoff Lancaster 436

Chapter 9 — Integrated Marketing Communications and Pricing Strategies — 467

Readings
Chapter 15 'The entrepreneurial marketing plan' in *Marketing and Entrepreneurship in SMEs: An Innovative Approach* — 468
David Carson, Stanley Cromie, Pauric McGowan and Jimmy Hill

Chapter 10 'Pricing Strategies' in *Essentials of Entrepreneurship and Small Business Management* Fifth Edition — 481
Thomas W. Zimmerer and Norman M. Scarborough with Doug Wilson

Chapter 10 — Crafting a Winning Business Plan — 509

Readings
Chapter 19 'The business plan: an entrepreneurial tool' in *Strategic Entrepreneurship* Fourth Edition — 510
Philip A. Wickham

Chapter 4 'Conducting a Feasibility Analysis and Crafting a Winning Business Plan' in *Essentials of Entrepreneurship and Small Business Management* Fifth Edition — 534
Thomas W. Zimmerer and Norman M. Scarborough with Doug Wilson

Chapter 11 'Creating a Successful Financial Plan' in *Essentials of Entrepreneurship and Small Business Management* Fifth Edition — 571
Thomas W. Zimmerer and Norman M. Scarborough with Doug Wilson

Chapter 11 — Managing Entrepreneurial Growth — 613

Reading
Chapter 11 'Entrepreneurial management' in *Marketing and Entrepreneurship in SMEs: An Innovative Approach* — 615
David Carson, Stanley Cromie, Pauric McGowan and Jimmy Hill

Chapter 12 — Contemporary Issues in Entrepreneurship — 627

Readings
Chapter 14 'Networks for entrepreneurs and entrepreneurial marketers' in *Marketing and Entrepreneurship in SMEs: An Innovative Approach* — 628
David Carson, Stanley Cromie, Pauric McGowan and Jimmy Hill

Chapter 1 'Entrepreneurship Today' in *Entrepreneurship* Fourth Edition — 651
Peggy A. Lambing and Charles R. Kuehl

Chapter 1
The Challenge of Entrepreneurship

- Explaining the importance of entrepreneurs to economic growth
- Introducing the concept of an entrepreneurial perspective within individuals
- Examining the contemporary entrepreneurial revolution
- Illustrating the entrepreneurial environment
- Explaining the cultural diversity of entrepreneurship
- Putting failure into proper perspective

Chapter 1

Marketing and entrepreneurship: an overview

Objectives 3
Introduction 3
Entrepreneurship and management 5
Marketing and management 6
Marketing, entrepreneurship and SMEs 7
Marketing and entrepreneurship: separate or integrated? 8
The domain of marketing and entrepreneurship 9
Summary 11
Learning questions 12

Objectives

After reading this chapter the reader will have an understanding of the origins, evolution and progression of the concepts of marketing and entrepreneurship. The chapter reviews the broad domains of these distinct disciplines in the context of small and medium-sized enterprises (SMEs).

Introduction

What does marketing and entrepreneurship in SMEs mean? This is an intriguing question from many perspectives, especially so when one considers that marketing as a discipline is long established and has a strong empirical base founded on management concepts. Further, entrepreneurship has long been recognized as the catalyst for business development, innovation and growth. And in the broader sense, SMEs as an entity are generally acknowledged as the seedcorn for industrial and commercial development in most capitalist economies. So we have three strong, well-established components to answer the question posed above. This suggests that a mix of these components will yield a powerful approach to doing business. But this will only be true if we can harness the strengths of these dimensions and organize them into a cohesive mechanism. To this end we must consider what is actually meant by each of the dimensions. This involves examining the origins and evolution of the dimensions, thereby evaluating their characteristics. We can then determine the context in which they can be brought together for effective business development.

At first glance there seems little in common between marketing and entrepreneurship. In general, they can be seen as two distinct areas of study, both with a wide spectrum of specific interest topics. Indeed, the research history and origin of marketing and entrepreneurship have been traced back to what is primarily marketing on the one hand, and what is primarily entrepreneurial management on the other. Marketing and entrepreneurship have two quite different and distinct origins, and as a consequence, it could be argued that there is an inherent dichotomy between them.

Let us consider, by way of example, marketing planning. The nature of marketing planning is essentially that of a managerial process, which explores what marketing actually does, the process by which marketing operates. But how can marketing planning be described and explained? The principal stages in the process involve companies conducting an internal audit of all their activities relating to marketing and an external audit of all factors impacting on marketing activity; devising a strategy; and implementing and controlling the marketing activities. This definition suggests that planning is a formal process.

The importance of marketing planning is a point that is well made in much of the literature. The broad characteristics of formal marketing planning can be listed and described as follows:

- *Structured*, in that it adheres to rigid frameworks and processes designed to generate knowledge and known outcomes.
- *Sequential*, in that the structure will follow sequential steps designed to move progressively along a clear course of action.
- *Disciplined*, whereby adherence to the sequential structure is essential to the successful completion of the activity.
- *Systems-oriented*, because formal marketing needs to be built around systems, so that all those involved in using it know where their actions fit within the overall system.
- *Short-, medium- and long-term* decisions in marketing, like any other business discipline, require to be taken over time. The time-scales involved are not only short-term but, by necessity, must also include medium- and long-term time dimensions for certain courses of action to come to fruition.

Some measure of the dichotomy between formal marketing planning and entrepreneurship is highlighted by considering some of the fundamental characteristics of entrepreneurs. It is generally accepted that entrepreneurs are generalists rather than focused individuals, task-oriented, ambitious, domineering, inspirational and adaptive, autocratic and charismatic, creative and opportunistic, with a high degree of self-esteem and self-fulfilment. These traits obviously have an impact on small firms in a wide variety of ways, but particularly in relation to marketing. But this impact is often at odds with the formality of the process outlined above.

However, even though we can demonstrate a clear dichotomy between the two disciplines, there is a stronger argument for considering marketing and entrepreneurship as closely related. After all, both are inherently and explicitly concerned with doing business. By this we mean that essentially they are about making things happen for the benefit of all parties involved in an exchange. Both are concerned with identifying opportunities in the marketplace and determining the feasibility of finding, making or procuring the components or parts necessary for an end-product that satisfies the perceived opportunity.

So what is the catalyst or linkage? Both will involve strong elements of *management* in the form of decision-making activities. As we shall see later, such management can span a spectrum of styles, which may be extremely informal and flexible at one end – typically that which pertains in very small firms – and extremely formal and rigid at the other – typically where larger firms operate.

Let us first consider management in the context of entrepreneurship.

Entrepreneurship and management

The literature originating from both these areas can be grouped into two categories. The first category can be described as historical and conventional, and describes research concerned with validity and confirmation. Research here will carry out reciprocal and replicating studies designed to validate previous research studies. Research topics within this category are likely to focus on the managerial dimensions of entrepreneurship by considering principles of management and decision-making, structures of management and organization, and managerial processes. Research is focused on the formal aspects of management as the dominant perspective on entrepreneurship.

The second broad category tends to be more progressive, with a primary focus on new concepts applicable to the area. The research activity is concerned with the micro-dimensions of entrepreneurship. That is, the understanding of what happens within the firm in relation to entrepreneurship. Research topics are likely to focus on the characteristics and style of decision-making, behaviour and relationships, personal contact networks and entrepreneurial competencies – indeed, any new concepts applicable to the area. This outline is illustrated as a broad continuum in Figure 1.1

This research perspective can of course apply equally to the marketing domain, so let us now consider management from the perspective of marketing.

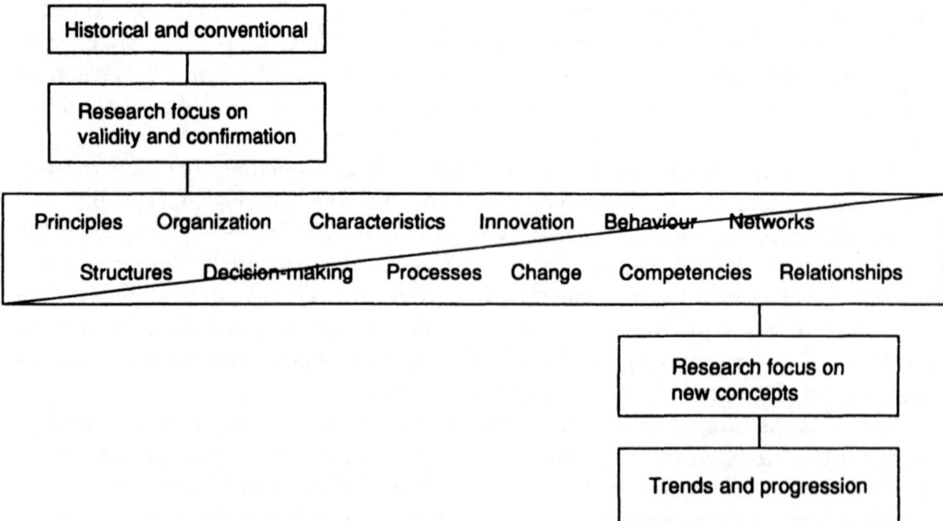

Figure 1.1 Research linkages and emphasis; marketing management and entrepreneurship.

Marketing and management

The marketing function, especially in larger organizations, can be seen as an adjunct of the broader management function of any enterprise that involves elements of organization and planning. The organization structures of management in an enterprise are most likely to be reflected in its marketing function. Indeed, the management processes, style and culture of a marketing function or department will reflect that of the enterprise as a whole.

Research in relation to management and marketing has traditionally centred on larger organizations in a variety of market sectors, although, generally, management thought and theory in the past have tended to centre on large *industrial* organizations, while marketing thought and theory have centred on large *consumer* organizations as a result of the interest in consumer behaviour.

Marketing also attracts researchers from many disciplines. Much of the focus is on the definitions and understanding of the marketing process, the managerial dimensions of marketing decision-making, the interaction between organization and customer and consumer satisfaction. It is easy to see the relationship between marketing and management. But if management is central to considerations of marketing and entrepreneurship, it is not difficult to see a connection between marketing and entrepreneurship.

We have suggested that management approaches can be informal and flexible, or formal and rigid. We can also consider management in two other ways: first, as a system for doing business, and second, as a context in which business will be performed. Management systems involve *organizing* work through the coordination and integration of activities and *formalizing* organization systems into hierarchical superior/subordinate positions and relationships. As management activities have been organized and formalized, and as this will mean that they must occur in the right sequence over time, management must incorporate the notions of *sequentiality* and *progression*. That is, management systems tend to be organized and ordered in such a way that they have a clear order in which they occur, and the sum total of these events progresses towards a cumulative whole end-result.

As an organization grows and develops, it begins to create *specialist* functions, activities and tasks. Individuals become specialized in one function, activity or task to the point where they become experts in that area. But they must still perform to a management system. Our earlier description of marketing planning serves to illustrate this process within a specialist function.

So far we have described the internal systems of management, but we must also recognize that management will be performed in some kind of *context*. Obvious management contexts are represented by the strong environmental influences of the market, in terms of geographical specificity or market segment. Such environmental influences, in fact, determine the focus and resources of management within an enterprise. For example, an enterprise that is solely concerned with a domestic market will have different management and marketing needs from an enterprise that has a wider international focus. Equally, an enterprise that is concerned with industrial markets will perform in a different context from an enterprise that is concerned with providing a service.

Marketing, entrepreneurship and SMEs

The concept of *context* allows us to bring into consideration the important context of small business. There is a substantial literature on the principal managerial component of SMEs, namely, entrepreneurs and entrepreneurship. Entrepreneurship attracts researchers from many disciplines. Much of the focus is on the concept of small business management and entrepreneurship, the characteristics of entrepreneurship, the characteristics of small business and management and entrepreneurship. The central dimension to this interface between small business and entrepreneurship is management, in the broad sense of the term.

While it is acknowledged that marketing and entrepreneurship are often seen as two distinct disciplines, it is important to emphasize that the emergence of marketing and entrepreneurship into a single discipline stems from strong common roots. As we have stated earlier, this commonality is inherent in *management* dimensions. Let us consider some of these in more detail from the perspective of *marketing management*, and then consider how this leads naturally to the context in which entrepreneurship thrives most; that is, in small firms.

Perhaps the strongest link between marketing and entrepreneurship is that they both have markets and customers as their central focus. It is generally recognized that the greatest difference between the marketing function and other functions within an organization (e.g. finance and personnel) is that marketing must perform *outside* the organization, that is, in the marketplace. The marketing function is the organization's interface between its internal systems and its customers; it is the bridge between the organization perspective and the market and customer perspective. This external focus is a natural dimension of entrepreneurship, since entrepreneurship is essentially about exploiting the market. An entrepreneur is only marginally concerned with mechanisms internal to the organization, and only then in terms of making change happen within the internal systems. An entrepreneur's interest will naturally be stimulated by what is perceived as a market opportunity which offers exploitation of a circumstance and/or stealing a march over competitors.

Marketing and entrepreneurship: separate or integrated?

The separate perspective

Marketing and entrepreneurship attract scholars from common backgrounds – psychology, organization behaviour and behavioural sciences in general. Currently, however, the research outputs of the combined area of marketing and entrepreneurship are only of general, if not peripheral interest to existing disciplines from any of these areas. That is, the entrepreneurial discipline is only marginally interested in the specifics of marketing. The majority of researchers are more interested in the *management* of entrepreneurship as it affects the *whole* of a business operation; few researchers are interested in the marketing dimensions of entrepreneurship. Entrepreneurship is viewed as an all-encompassing business activity and as such, it is seen as not belonging to any one business discipline or function. Entrepreneurs are generally viewed as not being good at, and therefore not getting involved in, organizing, planning, etc.; rather, they are seen as concentrating on issues more concerned with business opportunities and development.

Equally, most marketers, who may be interested in marketing dimensions of entrepreneurship, are unlikely to consider current entrepreneurial literature and research as a main source of information; their attention will more probably focus on the mainstream marketing discipline. Marketers have a strong base in processes and techniques. There are proven and accepted ways by which marketers can carry out their marketing activities. Often, these approaches and techniques seem to have no correspondence with entrepreneurship. Indeed, for the reasons outlined above, entrepreneurial literature makes little reference to marketing as a discipline or function. Consequently, marketers interested in entrepreneurship are frustrated by having to trawl a largely peripheral literature on entrepreneurship to find only occasional useful references.

The combined perspective

As we have indicated, however, marketing can be viewed as an integral part of entrepreneurial activity; in this context, the importance of marketing to entrepreneurship – or, indeed, entrepreneurial marketing – is obvious. All firms need to grow or adapt in order to survive and growth and change are marketing-led dimensions, since both rely on new sales, either of new products or from new customers. Entrepreneurial style, activities and concepts, such as innovation, creativity and idea generation, are all fundamentally intrinsic to and compatible with marketing philosophies. Consequently, the importance of marketing within entrepreneurship is inherent.

The domain of marketing and entrepreneurship

What are the implications for SMEs in applying marketing through entrepreneurship? To what extent do the tried-and-tested methods used by professional managers from larger companies need to be adapted? Is adaptation sufficient, or is a totally new and different approach required? These are the issues that management in SMEs needs to address and has been addressing over the past few years, though with varying degrees of success. Much of the early initiative has been in general management, but increasingly the problems of decision-making in specific business functions, such as finance and marketing, in the context of SMEs have become a focus.

However, when it comes to an understanding and knowledge of *marketing planning*, there is still some way to go. Indeed, it has been noted that SME owners/managers have a limited knowledge of marketing planning practices. Any attempts at formulating marketing plans using recognized marketing theory and terminology would seem to be limited and dependent on the depth of experience and knowledge of the owner or manager. In many SMEs, marketing planning activity may be limited to planning for selling within a narrow industry perspective. The broader scope of marketing planning seldom features understanding or relevance, perhaps because of lack of knowledge. Inadequate marketing is a commonly identified reason for SME failure and is recognized as a weakness of SMEs generally. Typically, inadequacies in marketing can be traced to the lack of a planned marketing approach.

If these assertions are accepted, then there is a real need to increase the awareness of SME owners/managers to the importance of a planned approach to marketing. Equally, there is a need to consider how marketing in SMEs can be improved. Arising from these considerations, marketing planning might be concerned with the practical implications of how SMEs plan their marketing. In understanding *how* SMEs do this it might be useful to explore in depth marketing in SMEs on the basis that marketing has, for a number of years, been focused on what to do in a given marketing situation, and has largely ignored how to do it within company, competitor and customer constraints.

Over the past decade significant research in the area of marketing and entrepreneurship has been situated on some kind of continuum between two categories (see Figure 1.1), that is, as represented by historical and conventional approaches on the one side and new concepts on the other. To consider this further, Figure 1.2 indicates that specific interest has occurred in some aspects of the following:

- *Base perspectives, overviews and insights.* Theorists and practitioners have begun to examine the suitability of some theories and techniques from the joint perspective of marketing and entrepreneurship. In addition, there is an examination of broad descriptions and definitions and analysis of their meaning in the joint context and its likely future direction.
- *Research issues.* There is much work concerning the appropriateness of research approaches and whether more innovative research techniques should be employed. There is some indication of this in the continuum outlined in Figure 1.1
- *Technology, growth and innovation.* Considerations in this area stem largely from historical research in entrepreneurship.
- *International issues and viewpoints.* There is a growing realization that the domain of marketing and entrepreneurship is international in perspective and that it does not belong to any one country or culture.
- *Marketing operations, forecasts and trends.* Considerations in this area stem largely from historical research in marketing.
- *Strategic issues and management decisions.* Considerations in this area stem largely from historical research in management.
- *Education and training.* Educators and trainers have long grappled with the difficulties of addressing marketing concepts to entrepreneurs and entrepreneural concepts to students of marketing.

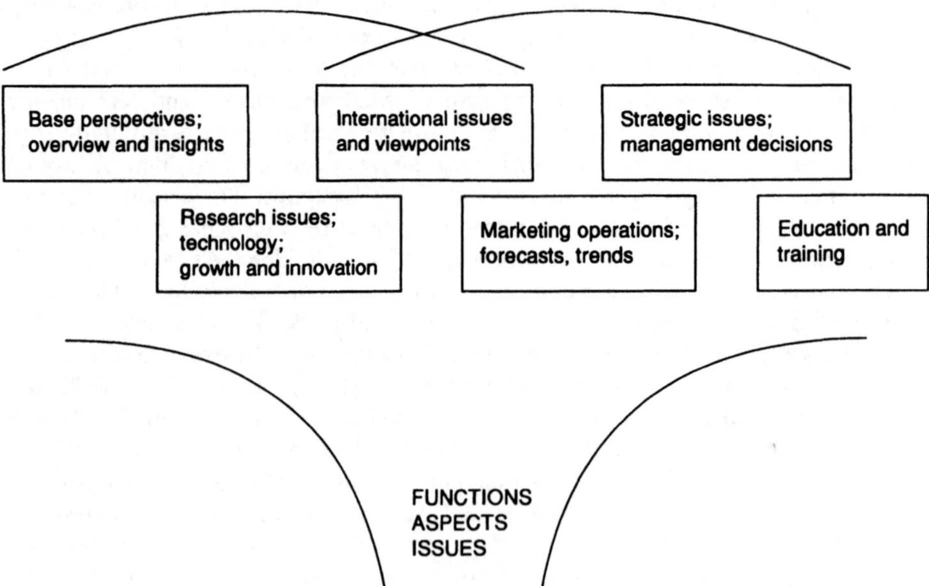

Figure 1.2 Significant research in marketing management and entrepreneurship.

Much of the research has examined the management functions of SMEs, the aspects of marketing and entrepreneurship and issues of marketing and entrepreneurship. In future, it is likely that these distinctive categories will continue to develop as the research area as a whole matures. It can also be expected that there will be increasing cross-fertilization between the two categories as well as further new concepts such as marketing and business or enterprise development and entrepreneurial cultures, and so on.

As stated in the introduction to this chapter, marketing and entrepreneurship in SMEs represents three strong, well-established components. This chapter has shown that, together, they have the potential to yield a powerful approach to doing business, but there are significant problems to be faced.

Established marketing approaches and techniques are built on operating systems that are framed around relatively rigid, progressive and sequential processes. That is, they tend to follow conventional management approaches. This standard marketing does not seem compatible with entrepreneurship when it is considered that entrepreneurs are inherently flexible, *ad hoc* and informal in their decision-making. To this must be added the limited resources of SMEs both in financial and human terms. These limitations mean that much of the standard management and marketing approaches are inappropriate for SMEs. The problem is compounded by the strong entrepreneurial influence in the decision-making, since entrepreneurship is equally incompatible with formal approaches.

It is these issues that are addressed in this text. That is, how to overcome the incompatibilities, gel the strengths of all three components and, by so doing, offer an innovative approach to harnessing these strengths successfully to create more effective entrepreneurial marketing in SMEs.

Summary

Research and the ensuing literature on marketing and entrepreneurship have seldom overlapped. As a result both have evolved along distinct paths and those interested in marketing have been concerned about issues of marketing and those interested in entrepreneurs have been concerned about issues of entrepreneurship. It is possible to think of marketing and entrepreneurship as two quite distinct disciplines, even to the point of there being a divergence between their fundamental characteristics. Where thought processes have converged it has been on aspects of management, that is managing marketing and managing entrepreneurship. When considering management aspects such as decision-making and exploitation of opportunities and making a profit, it is easy to see the common perspectives of marketing and entrepreneurship. These perspectives are seen most often in SMEs and here the notion of entrepreneurial marketing can be perceived.

Learning questions

After reading this chapter, the reader should be able to answer the following questions:

1. What are the research linkages between marketing and entrepreneurship?
2. What are the common areas of research of both disciplines?
3. Why is there a dichotomy between marketing and entrepreneurship?
4. What is the primary common focus of marketing and entrepreneurship?

Chapter 4

The concept of entrepreneurship

Objectives 13
An overview 13
Trait approaches to understanding entrepreneurship 14
The social psychological approach 17
Behaviourial approaches 18
Entrepreneurship as a process 18
Entrepreneurial managers 19
Summary 22
Learning questions 22

Objectives

After reading this chapter, the reader will be familiar with a number of approaches to understanding the concept of entrepreneurship, and will have an appreciation of the significance of entrepreneurship in determining a context for management. The reader will also have an insight into the appropriate management response to the challenge of managing an entrepreneurial SME.

An overview

Entrepreneurship is about change and the roles people play to bring it about. It is about innovation and doing new things to improve the circumstances of the enterprise. It is best understood as a process, the constituents of which are entrepreneurs, their persistent search for opportunities and their efforts to marshall the resources needed to exploit them. It can occur in either a new venture start-up or within an established enterprise. Developments in the social, technological and economic circumstances in which the entrepreneurial enterprise operates have an impact on it. The lead entrepreneur is prompted as a consequence to instigate and carry through such changes in the enterprise as are necessary in response. We need to consider and understand what type of person might make that response and how.

The entrepreneur is central to the entrepreneurial process, s/he is the driving force behind it. Without the entrepreneur's commitment, energy and ambition it would not happen. However, given the central role the entrepreneur plays in it, there is a notable lack of any agreed definition or clear understanding in the literature of who the entrepreneur is or what s/he does. It depends, it seems, on the individual researchers personal perspective and approach as to how the entrepreneur and entrepreneurship are ultimately interpreted and defined.

One approach, taken from psychology, is to develop an understanding of who the entrepreneur is by focusing on a set of personality traits and characteristics. Another approach is to consider the social context in which the entrepreneur is embedded and which will have an influence on her/his potential for success in venture creation and development. Entrepreneurship is not an activity conducted in isolation but is practised in the midst of an often dynamic environment which impacts on the entrepreneurial effort. The behavioural approach provides us with yet another way of understanding the entrepreneur and entrepreneurship. This approach views the entrepreneur in terms of a set of activities associated with venture creation and development. In this instance the focus is more on what entrepreneurial managers do than how well they do it.

The debate on the supremacy of the different approaches continues and each approach has its champions. The position in this chapter is that all three approaches contribute significantly, in their own way, to enhancing our understanding of who the entrepreneur is and what s/he does. No one approach has the definitive answer, but together they bring us close to some greater degree of clarity. In the following sections we shall consider contributions from each approach to a definition of entrepreneurship. We shall conclude with a definition of entrepreneurial management.

Trait approaches to understanding entrepreneurship

Who is the entrepreneur?

The approaches offered by trait theorists to understanding entrepreneurship focus on the personality or psychological makeup of the individual entrepreneur. The presumption is that s/he projects a particular personality type.[1] Researchers in the area have therefore sought to identify and extract those personality traits which might be considered to be uniquely entrepreneurial. They then seek to categorize and organize them like pieces of a jigsaw puzzle that comes together over a period and in a way that ultimately reveals a person who at first glance seems a larger-than-life character, a superhero, a 'do anything, go anywhere' type. They emerge as people who see what others cannot and do what others would not dare. Successive research projects, by applying personality theory, have sought to identify and measure the personality traits of entrepreneurs and have highlighted a number of factors as typically entrepreneurial. Factors such as a high need for achievement, beliefs about locus of control, a propensity to take calculated risks, a high tolerance of uncertainty and ambiguity in addition to other personal values such as honesty, integrity, duty and responsibility.[2]

Table 4.1 lists some of the key characteristics of successful entrepreneurs taken from the growing literature in this area.

Table 4.1 Key characteristics of successful entrepreneurs

Personality traits
Calculated risk-taking and risk sharing propensity Need for achievement Locus of control Personal values, integrity Need for power Need for affiliation Commitment, determination and perseverance Assuming personal responsibility A grip on reality Sense of humour Tolerance of ambiguity, stress and uncertainty Decisive, urgent Tolerance of failure.

Limitations of trait approaches

A good deal of criticism has been levelled against trait approaches for a number of reasons. One problem is their apparent inability to differentiate clearly between entrepreneurial small business owners and equally successful professional executives in more established organizations. This latter group has demonstrated comparable levels of achievement motivation or risk-taking propensity, two apparently distinctive entrepreneurial traits. This raises questions about the value of trait approaches in identifying what is particularly entrepreneurial.

A further criticism against trait theorists relates to the emphasis they have placed on identifying the supposed key trait that is most characteristic of the entrepreneur. The single trait approach seeks to identify and prioritize the aspects of a person's personality that are deemed to be particularly entrepreneurial.

Third, it is suggested that trait theories need to recognize that entrepreneurship is a dynamic, constantly changing process. As the venture develops and grows over its lifecycle new challenges with attendant levels of instability and lack of predictability emerge. These have implications for the entrepreneurial personality. The entrepreneur will be required to adapt continuously and change his/her psychological frame of mind and outlook as the enterprise itself grows and changes. There is clearly a need to define and redefine entrepreneurial characteristics according to the stage of development the entrepreneur and the enterprise have reached.

A further problem with the trait theorists' approach is the apparent implication that one either already has entrepreneurial traits or one has not, as a result of one's upbringing and a lifetime's influence from education, religion, socialization and culture. The argument appears to be that the fundamental building blocks of one's personality are formed during the early, more formative years of one's life. These values and attitudes remain constant during later life, even in the face of subsequent changes in circumstances. Having been inculcated in the individual over a lifetime it is unlikely that they can or will be developed at some later stage in any effective way.

Part of the problem with trait approaches arises from how the entrepreneur and entrepreneurship are defined. In the first instance a focus only on the individual who establishes a new venture is arguably too narrow. It fails to recognize sufficiently the entrepreneurial potential of people who work to develop and grow established enterprises. In addition, there is the difficulty raised by the fact that entrepreneurs are not an easily identifiable, homogeneous group. Entrepreneurs, it appears, come in all shapes and sizes, from different backgrounds, with varying motivations and aspirations. They are variously represented and addressed in the literature as opportunists or craftworkers, technical entrepreneurs or so-called intrapreneurs.

However, recognizing that entrepreneurs are a fundamentally heterogeneous population, coming from various backgrounds and circumstances, frees the researcher from the restrictions imposed in trying to define 'the entrepreneurial personality'.[3] The view is emerging that psychological variables might be more usefully studied in clusters or constellations of traits. This does much to defuse some of the criticism-levelled at trait approaches and allows more people to be seen as potential entrepreneurs. Timmons[4] offers an example of such clustering of what he calls 'desirable and acquirable attitudes and behaviours' for entrepreneurs. They include commitment and determination, an opportunity focus, a tolerance of risk, ambiguity and uncertainty, creativity, self-reliance and adaptability, motivation to excel and leadership.

A point of importance to note is that aspects of the entrepreneurial personality can be developed in order to improve the prospects of greater entrepreneurial success. One view is that personalities do continue to change and develop as a consequence of personal experiences and the changing nature of social relationships. It is recognized that basic traits may well be formed in early life, but it is also acknowledged that experiences in later life can play a role in shaping the personality and influencing a person's ideas and ambitions for an entrepreneurial career.

The value of trait approaches, while the subject of continuing debate, must be recognized. It is clear that the psychological perspective of entrepreneurship research, in emphasizing the intrinsic personality characteristics of entrepreneurs, has made and continues to make valuable contributions to our current understanding of entrepreneurs and their distinct role in new venture creation.

The social psychological approach

The origins of the entrepreneur

The social psychological perspective defines those external factors that act as potential stimulants to entrepreneurial activity. This approach places entrepreneurship within the wider social environment. It acknowledges the influence of numerous social factors on the propensity of an individual to behave entrepreneurially and to do so continuously. Examples of such factors are family and social background, education, religion, culture, work and general life experiences. As a widening of the psychological perspective this approach sees the entrepreneur as being embedded in a complex set of social networks. These will either facilitate or hinder the potential of the individual to launch new ventures or further develop an existing one.

They will do this in a number of ways. In the first instance the social background in which the individual is embedded will be a key determining factor of her/his personality as discussed earlier. In addition the social context of the entrepreneur provides the link between the entrepreneur, the opportunity identified and the resources needed to exploit it. This development of skills and use of social networking allows the entrepreneur to build an appropriate profile within society for the entrepreneurial role s/he wishes to play.

Social marginality theory suggests that when inconsistency exists between an individual's personality and the role s/he plays in society, s/he may be prompted to act to resolve that inconsistency. The pull of assuming a more attractive role in society and the push to do something about the inconsistency acts like a catalyst. Such effort to acquire a desired profile or role in society, however, may well act ultimately as a brake on continued entrepreneurial effort. The possibility of compromising one's hard-earned standing in society may prompt the individual to adopt a style of entrepreneurship that is less growth-focused, with all the risk and uncertainty that attends it.

An example in the literature which sees entrepreneurs very much as a product of their upbringing is offered by Kets de Vries.[5] His entrepreneurial individual emerges as a deviant personality – rebellious, insecure, a person of low self-esteem, one who could not work in a structured environment, who resents authority and almost as an act of defiance establishes, by extraordinary effort and fear of failure, a commercial enterprise. As a product of her/his upbringing, s/he then runs this venture with great energy and determination and high self-reliance and thus low dependence on others. This approach can have a number of outcomes. Either the enterprise will continue to grow until it becomes too large to be managed effectively by one person, when it will ultimately collapse or be forcefully taken over by others. Or the entrepreneur will undergo what is in effect a difficult personality change and learn to trust and share.

Behavioural approaches

What the entrepreneur does

The third pillar to our understanding of the entrepreneur and entrepreneurship is outlined by the behaviourial approaches. In addition to having some idea of who the entrepreneur is and the factors in her/his background that influence her/his personal development and decisions, we need to ask: What do entrepreneurs do? We need some insight into how they think, what actions they take and how they go about creating and developing a new venture. The focus is on understanding how attitudes, behaviours, management skills and know-how, past experience, and so on, all combine in determining entrepreneurial success.

Timmons suggests that successful entrepreneurs share a number of common behaviours and attitudes: they work extremely hard, apparently with unlimited energy; they work with commitment and determination; and they work with a competitive zeal and an ambition to excel and win. They thrive in situations of constant change, the more radical the better. It is after all in change that opportunities for new ideas are hidden for those with the vision to see their potential. They work to succeed, and in every setback there are lessons to be learned for the future. They move with the certainty of people who know that they are making the difference in the ultimate outcome of their ventures and the lives of those involved in it with them.

So, successful entrepreneurs are individuals who have a flair for creativity and innovation and are primarily driven by opportunity and its attendant change. The ability to exploit opportunities and cope with change will depend on the entrepreneurs' ability to take decisions and to judge the value of these decisions. Consequently, entrepreneurs require a broad portfolio of general management competencies and access to a wide network of personal contacts. (Competencies and networking will be the subject of later chapters.)

Entrepreneurship as a process

The entrepreneurial process is an action-oriented way of thinking and behaving which determines the way in which individuals approach their jobs and responsibilities, how they acquire resources, manage people, market their enterprise or produce products. It reflects the efforts and activities of the lead entrepreneur in any given venture somehow to make and manage a fit between an opportunity identified in the marketplace and the resources needed to exploit it.

The background to this effort will be one of environmental turbulence and uncertainty, and this highlights the need for a particularly entrepreneurial type of management response.

Entrepreneurial managers

What managers do to become and remain successful as entrepreneurs is that they are consistently innovative and committed to change; they are opportunity-focused, constantly on the lookout for new ideas, they take well thought out, calculated risks; they give leadership, energizing people who work with them, building them into cohesive, motivated entrepreneurial teams; they negotiate and persuade those with the necessary resources (financial, capital and human) to support the opportunity that they have identified. However subconsciously, they are forever networking, gathering information, confirming decisions made.

The entrepreneurial manager as an innovator and change agent

The classical school of entrepreneurship is the essence of this approach. The focus is on creativity, innovation and the constant search for new product or process ideas. The focus is essentially on opportunities and their successful development and management through to implementation. As change is the ultimate outcome of such activity to do new things, the entrepreneur must be seen as one who deals in change and change episodes. This approach to understanding entrepreneurship highlights the entrepreneurs' role in bringing about change in what might be called 'the established order of things'. Whether establishing a new enterprise or renewing an existing one, they are challenging the status quo.

The entrepreneur as an opportunity-focused manager

A major constituent of the entrepreneurial process is the opportunity. An entrepreneurial manager will be steeped in and committed to the search for new ideas which have real potential for future development. In the dynamics of an entrepreneurial marketplace an opportunity might be a new market opened up or a new product identified. It might be a new production process developed or a more efficient source of supply of raw materials identified. It might even be the introduction of new structures into the enterprise as it grows and develops. What the entrepreneurial manager seeks is that one idea on which the window of opportunity is opening and which offers the prospects of a worth while return on effort and resources invested, for some time to come.

We have considered entrepreneurial managers to be agents for change. The current entrepreneurial environment in which they operate may also be described as one of constant dynamic change. It is characterized by chaos, ambiguity, inconsistencies and substantial knowledge and information gaps. Entrepreneurial managers, though, will be steeped in the market for their chosen industry's goods and services. They will know (or make it their business to find out) what their customers want and what challenges the marketplace is likely to present to their ambitions. Entrepreneurs will combine their skill for creative thinking with their relatively keen vision for an opportunity which has its origins in what customers and the marketplace want. Successful entrepreneurial managers understand the marketplace as a source of opportunities and never forget it.

The entrepreneurial manager as a calculated risk-taker

Rapid changes in technology, in social and cultural norms, in economic circumstances, in people's lifestyles and the rapid emergence and decline of different markets and products create not only opportunity, but increasing levels of uncertainty in the environment. In the wake of such uncertainty comes what is for most of us unacceptable and debilitating levels of ambiguity and risk. For the action-oriented entrepreneurial manager, however, in such dynamic change lies opportunity. But the potential of those possibilities must be worked out or calculated, in a bid to keep that risk at a level that is acceptable to the entrepreneurial manager. Entrepreneurs demonstrate time and again a combination of a strong positive outlook with a higher tolerance of uncertainty, risk and ambiguity than most.

Entrepreneurial managers rarely own the financial resources they invest in their enterprises. What they risk, primarily, is their personal standing and reputation – not only in their own eyes but in the eyes of their social peers. Entrepreneurial managers are drawn from and work in a social context that strongly influences, if not actually determines, the roles they play, their outlook and career. Building and maintaining a reputation demands a level of caution and a calculation of the risk element involved in entrepreneurial decision-making.

The entrepreneurial manager as an entrepreneurial team builder

Successful entrepreneurial managers compete with themselves, setting personal standards to achieve and excel. They drive themselves, managing the stresses and strains that appear to be endemic in entrepreneurial life, in pursuit of their own self-imposed standards and goals. They are energetic self-starters who, uncomfortably for some, seek as much energy and effort from those who work with them as they do of themselves.

They know that they do not have all the knowledge and skills needed to run an entrepreneurial enterprise successfully. They appreciate their own strengths and weaknesses when it comes to managing the business and understand that its future prospects depend on their addressing the existing skills and knowledge deficit. Developing an entrepreneurial team as a means of doing so means finding and recruiting people into the enterprise, either on a full-time or part-time basis. In addition, they need to establish contacts with those outside the enterprise who can contribute, by their knowledge and skills, to the development of the venture. They recognize that if they are to build a successful entrepreneurial firm, they cannot do so alone. Building and developing the internal team requires leadership and vision.

The entrepreneurial manager as an entrepreneurial leader

The leadership style of the entrepreneurial SME will reflect the personality of the lead entrepreneur. Conventionally, it is seen as highly personalized, centralized, essentially autocratic. However, successful entrepreneurs know that if their small, potentially entrepreneurial firms are to develop and grow, they ultimately need to be able to recruit and retain people with the necessary skills and knowledge to help them to do it; people who, not unlike themselves, enjoy the prospect of and are competent in new ideas generation and change.

Owner managers who would be successful as entrepreneurs will seek to adapt their style of leadership to encourage the creation of an environment within their enterprise that is and will remain broadly attractive to such people. Without surrendering ultimate authority (there must always be a lead entrepreneur), the emphasis will be on a greater degree of participation. The lead entrepreneur will seek to exercise influence rather than formal control or direction, on motivating and empowering people within the enterprise to excel, on selling a vision of how the firm might develop and grow, on conflict resolution through persuasion, mediation and negotiation, on making heroes out of people, on sharing credit for achievement. The facts are that any dictatorial and adversarial management style which seeks to dominate people in the enterprise will lead ultimately to difficulties which will rob it of access to people of high calibre who will make the difference between being truly entrepreneurial or not.

The entrepreneurial manager as a negotiator

Acquiring the necessary resources to exploit a potential opportunity is a key part of the entrepreneurial process. The successful exploitation of any opportunity, however, requires sufficient funding, materials, equipment and labour. Since entrepreneurs rarely own resources in adequate quantities, they need to build effective relationships with investors, creditors and suppliers. They also need to create a large network of direct and indirect contacts who will keep them informed of possible supplies of necessary resources. Persuading those who own those resources to make them available, though, requires that entrepreneurs be particularly skilful in negotiating. They may be selling an idea for an opportunity which may have no tangible characteristics beyond that of a business plan.

The entrepreneurial manager as a networker

The management of personal contact networks is developed in Chapter 14. However, its importance as a particularly entrepreneurial activity and competency deserves recognition here. The entrepreneurial small firm is characterized by its need continually to identify opportunities and its limited access to the necessary resources to exploit them. In circumstances of constant, often radical, change, characterized by great risk and uncertainty, entrepreneurs must make decisions and take action, the consequences of which can have extremely lucrative or disastrous results for the enterprise. The importance of being able to gain access to rich supplies of focused, concise and current intelligence and be able, through good contacts, to confirm the validity of decisions made, preferably before implementation goes too far, could hardly be overstated. Such information and confirmation is possible through the peculiarly entrepreneurial activity of using personal contact networks.

Summary

Entrepreneurship is best understood as a process, an action-oriented way of thinking and behaving, the focus of which is innovation and change. Key constituents of the process are the entrepreneur, the opportunity and the acquisition and management of resources. The entrepreneur plays the central role in managing a good fit between the opportunity and the resources needed to exploit it.

Understanding entrepreneurship is made difficult by the apparent lack of clarity about how the entrepreneur should be defined. Trait theorists, social psychologists and behaviourialists all have contributions to make. An effective understanding of the entrepreneur can be distilled from the contributions of all three.

Managing the entrepreneurial process is the ultimate challenge confronting the entrepreneur. A consideration of this challenge gives us a brief insight into the profile of the entrepreneurial manager. The central core of entrepreneurial management is *change* and *growth*, and *continuous commitment to it*.

Learning questions

1. How might entrepreneurship be best understood?
2. What is your understanding of the entrepreneurial process? What are its key constituents?
3. What role does the entrepreneur play in the entrepreneurial process?
4. Comment on the contributions of trait theorists, social psychologists and behaviouralists to our understanding of the entrepreneur.
5. What is a useful and workable definition of the entrepreneur?
6. Discuss the implications for the entrepreneur of managing the entrepreneurial process.

Notes and references

1. Gartner, W. B. (1989) '"Who is the entrepreneur?" is the wrong question', *Journal of Entrepreneurship Theory and Practice* 13, (4), Summer, pp. 47–68.
2. Chell, E. and Haworth, J. M. (1992) 'The development of a research paradigm for the investigation of entrepreneurship: Some methodological issues', *Proceedings of the UIC/*

AMA Research Symposium on Marketing and Entrepreneurship, INSEAD, France, June, pp. 1–15.
3. Chell, E., Haworth, J. M. and Brearley, S. A, (1991) *The Entrepreneurial Personality: Concepts, Cases and Categories*, London: Routledge.
4. Timmons, J. A. (1990) *New Venture Creation*, 3rd edition, Chicago: Richard Irwin.
5. Kets de Vries, M. F. R. (1977) 'The entrepreneurial personality: A person at the crossroads', *Journal of Management Studies* **14**, pp. 34–57.

Further reading

Adam, E. and Chell, E. (1993) 'The successful international entrepreneur: A profile', *The Proceedings of the European Foundation for Management Development's 23rd European Small Business Seminar*, Northern Ireland, pp. 147–65.

Brockhaus, R. H. (1982) 'The psychology of the entrepreneur', in C. A. Kent, D. L. Sexton and K. H. Vesper (eds.), *Encyclopaedia of Entrepreneurship*, Englewood Cliffs, NJ: Prentice Hall, pp. 39–57.

Carsrud, A. L. and Johnson, R. N. (1989) 'Entrepreneurship: A social psychological perspective', *Journal of Entrepreneurship and Regional Development*, **1**, pp. 21–31.

Chell, E. (1985) 'The entrepreneurial personality: A few ghosts laid to rest?' *International Small Business Journal* 3 (3), pp. 43–54.

Cromie, S. and Johns, S. (1983) 'Irish entrepreneurs: some personal characteristics', *Journal of Occupational Behaviour*, **4**, pp. 317–24.

Cunningham, J. B. and Lischeron, J. (1991) 'Defining entrepreneurship', *Journal of Small Business Management* **29** (1), pp. 45–61.

Gibb, A. and Ritchie, J. (1981) 'Influences on entrepreneurship: A study over time', in *Bolton Ten Years On – Proceedings of the UK Small Business Research Conference*, 20–21 Polytechnic of Central London.

Hornaday, J. A. (1970) 'The nature of the entrepreneur', *Personnel Psychology* **23**, pp. 47–54.

Hornaday, J. A. and Aboud, J. (1971) 'Characteristics of successful entrepreneurs', *Personnel Psychology* **24**, pp. 141–53.

Lynn, R. (1969) 'Personality characteristics of a group of entrepreneurs', *Occupational Psychology* **43**, pp. 151–2.

McClelland, D. C. (1961) *The Achieving Society*, Princeton, NJ: Van Nostrand.

Stanworth, J. and Curran, J. (1973) 'Growth and the small firm – an alternative view', in *Management Motivation in the Smaller Business*, Aldershot: Gower Press, pp. 171–6.

The Challenge of Entrepreneurship

1 | The Foundations of Entrepreneurship

Small opportunities are often the beginning of great enterprises. —Demosthenes

Pain is temporary; quitting lasts forever. —Lance Howard

Learning Objectives

On completion of this chapter, you will be able to:

1. Define the role of the entrepreneur in business in the United States and across the world.
2. Describe the entrepreneurial profile and evaluate your potential as an entrepreneur.
3. Describe (A) the benefits and (B) the drawbacks of entrepreneurship.
4. Explain the forces that are driving the growth of entrepreneurship.
5. Explain the cultural diversity of entrepreneurship.
6. Describe the important role small businesses play in our nation's economy.
7. Describe the 10 deadly mistakes of entrepreneurship and how to avoid them.
8. Put failure into proper perspective.
9. Explain how an entrepreneur can avoid becoming another failure statistic.

LEARNING OBJECTIVES
1. Define the role of the entrepreneur in business in the United States and across the world.

The World of the Entrepreneur

Welcome to the world of the entrepreneur! Across the globe, growing numbers of people are realizing their dreams of owning and operating their own businesses. Although the level of entrepreneurial activity in the United States is down from record levels a few years ago, entrepreneurship continues to thrive in our nation. Every year, American entrepreneurs launch more than 850,000 new businesses, and the level of interest in pursuing entrepreneurship as a career remains high among people in all age groups.[1] Eighty-four percent of those who launch businesses are doing so for the first time.[2] This entrepreneurial spirit is the most significant economic development in recent business history. Around the globe, these heroes of the new economy are reshaping the business environment, creating a world in which their companies play an important role in the vitality of the global economy. With amazing vigor, their businesses have introduced innovative products and services, pushed back technological frontiers, created new jobs, opened foreign markets, and, in the process, provided their founders with the opportunity to do what they enjoy most.

Interest in entrepreneurship has never been higher. The future of entrepreneurial activity looks incredibly bright, given that the last two decades have seen record numbers of entrepreneurs launching businesses. Many of the world's largest companies continue to engage in massive downsizing campaigns, dramatically cutting the number of employees on their payrolls. This flurry of "pink slips" has spawned a new population of entrepreneurs: "castoffs" from large corporations (in which many of these individuals thought they would be lifetime ladder-climbers) with solid management experience and many productive years left before retirement. Small business researcher David Birch reports that over a recent five-year period, the largest companies in the United States shed 2 million jobs; during the same period, small businesses created 10 million jobs![3]

One casualty of this downsizing has been the long-standing notion of job security in large corporations. As a result, members of Generation X (people born between 1965 and 1981) and Generation Y (people born between 1982 and 1995) no longer see launching a business as being a risky career path. Having watched large companies lay off their parents after many years of service, these young people see entrepreneurship as the ideal way to create their own job security and success. They are eager to control their own destinies.

The downsizing trend among large companies has created a more significant philosophical change. It has ushered in an age in which "small is beautiful." Twenty-five years ago, competitive conditions favored large companies with their hierarchies and layers of management; today, with the pace of change constantly accelerating, fleet-footed, agile, small companies have the competitive advantage. These nimble competitors can dart into and out of niche markets as they emerge and recede; they can move faster to exploit market opportunities; and they can use modern technology to create within a matter of weeks or months products and services that once took years and all of the resources a giant corporation could muster. The balance has tipped in favor of small, entrepreneurial companies. Howard Stevenson, Harvard's chaired professor of entrepreneurship, says, "Why is it so easy [for small companies] to compete against giant corporations? Because while they [the giants] are studying the consequences, [entrepreneurs] are changing the world."[4]

One of the most comprehensive studies of global entrepreneurship, conducted by the Global Entrepreneurship Monitor (GEM), shows significant variation in the rate of new business formation among the nations of the world when measured by total entrepreneurial activity, or TEA (see Figure 1.1). The study found that 11.3 percent of the adult population in the United States—roughly one in nine people—is working to start a business. Nations in the Americas—North, South, and Latin—led the world in entrepreneurial activity, with Asian countries posting the lowest levels of entrepreneurship. The study also concluded that these different rates of entrepreneurial activity may account for as much as one-third of the variation in the rates of economic growth among these nations.[5] The GEM study also reports that globally men are twice as likely to start a business as women (although that trend is exactly the *opposite* in the United States), that the majority of

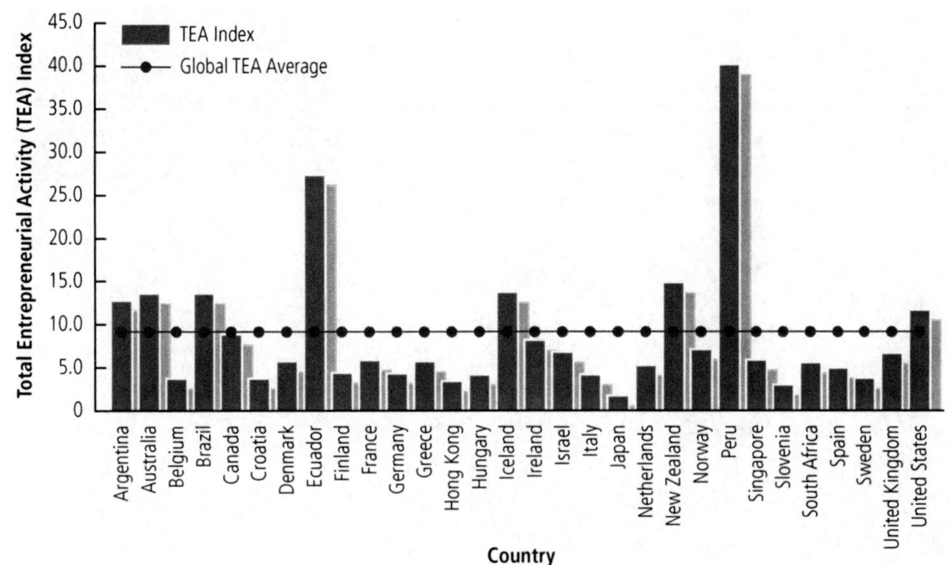

FIGURE 1.1

Entrepreneurial Activity across the Globe: Persons per 100 Adults Aged 18 to 64 Years Old Engaged in Entrepreneurial Activity

Source: 2004 Global Entrepreneurship Monitor Executive Report, http://www.gemconsortium.org/download/1123522826468/GEM_2004_Exec_Report.pdf. p.17.

entrepreneurs turn to family members and informal investors for external capital, and that nearly one-third of global entrepreneurs are between the ages of 25 and 44 years.[6]

The United States and many other nations are benefiting from this surge in global entrepreneurial activity. Eastern European countries, China, Vietnam, and many other nations whose economies were state controlled and centrally planned are now fertile ground for growing small businesses. Even in Japan, where the total entrepreneurial activity index is a meager 1.5, entrepreneurs are hard at work.

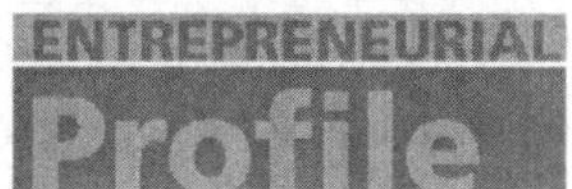

Risa Koyanagi

For instance, Risa Koyanagi convinced the president of a clothing company in Harajuku, Tokyo, one of Japan's most important fashion centers, to invest $25,000 so she could launch her own clothing line, which specializes in sporty, somewhat revealing garments for petite women. (Koyanagi is 5 feet, 1 inch tall and weighs 92 pounds.) To create buzz for her new company, Koyanagi convinced some well-connected friends to give some of her designs to Japanese pop stars such as Ayumi Hamazaki, and soon Koyanagi's clothes, which range in price from $35 to $400, were adorning celebrities appearing in newspapers and on television. Koyanagi's company, which she says is growing at "well over 100 percent a year," generates annual sales of more than $6 million and is quite profitable. Perhaps the most significant indication of her company's success is the fact that other design companies, including a few large ones, have begun knocking off some of Koyanagi's designs. She says her next move will be to expand her designs into accessories such as shoes and jewelry, and she plans to begin selling her line in the United States.[7]

Wherever they may choose to launch their companies, these business builders continue to embark on one of the most exhilarating—and one of the most frightening—adventures ever known: launching a business. It's never easy, but it can be incredibly rewarding, both financially and emotionally. It can be both thrilling and dangerous, like living life without a safety net. Still, true entrepreneurs see owning a business as the real measure of success. Indeed, entrepreneurship often provides the only avenue for success to those who otherwise might have been denied the opportunity.

Who are these entrepreneurs, and what drives them to work so hard with no guarantee of success? What forces lead them to risk so much and to make so many sacrifices in an attempt to achieve an ideal? Why are they willing to give up the security of a steady paycheck working for someone else to become the last person to be paid in their own companies? This chapter will examine the entrepreneur, the driving force behind the American economy.

You Be the Consultant

From Entrepreneur to Celebrity and from Celebrity to Entrepreneur

Pimp My Ride

At age 14, Ryan Friedlinghaus became enamored with the custom car show circuit and was soon customizing cars that were so good that they appeared on numerous magazine covers. To achieve the custom looks he wanted in the cars he worked on, however, he had to deal with a multitude of specialty shops for parts and services. One day, he vowed, he would start his own total-service customizing shop that offered all components in-house. In 1994, Friedlinghaus, just 20 years old, borrowed $5,000 from his grandfather to start West Coast Customs (WCC), a groundbreaking company in the customizing business. WCC's creative designs often are a pleasant surprise for car owners, who range from young adults with modest budgets to high-end clients that include a who's who list of athletes and movie stars. Friedlinghaus and WCC are stars in their own right, best known as the magicians behind MTV's hit show *Pimp My Ride*, which transforms clunker cars into one-of-a-kind show-stoppers. Because of the celebrity status the show has given Friedlinghaus and his company of automotive artists, WCC's calendar is booked months in advance. "There are no limits to what we can do," he says. "We like challenges."

P. Did It

Sean Combs was born in Harlem and was raised by his mother after his father was murdered when Sean was just two years old. Better known by his nickname, P. Diddy, Combs went on to become a successful rap star and actor. Today, Combs is an entrepreneur who heads Bad Boy Worldwide, a conglomerate that generates $300 million a year in sales from a record label, restaurants, a marketing company, and the Sean John clothing line, for which he recently won the Best Menswear Designer Award (the fashion industry's equivalent of an Oscar). Not just another star who licensed his name for a line of clothing, Combs recently opened a Sean John boutique on toney Fifth Avenue in New York City. Combs is very much a "hands-on" business owner, even spending some time teaching Bad Boy's summer interns himself. Combs also makes sure his company lives up to its social responsibility. He has given generous gifts to his alma mater, Howard University, and to numerous charities, including one he established called Daddy's House Social Programs. Recently, Combs ran in the New York City Marathon to raise $4 million for New York City public schools.

From Sit-Com to Entrepreneur

Many people remember Suzanne Somers as Chrissy, the ditzy blonde on the 1980's sit-com *Three's Company*, but there is much more to this former television star, who now manages her own company, ELO Somers Licensing (ELO stands for her business philosophy: Extraordinarily Low Overhead). From ELO's headquarters in Calabasas, California, Somers sells clothing, jewelry, skin-care products, diet food, fitness equipment, and others—300 different products in all—mostly through the Home Shopping Network (HSN). In fact, Somers' has sold more than $30 million of her Trilliant bracelet, making it the best-selling piece of jewelry in the history of the HSN. In the last three years, ELO's revenues have grown 100 percent a year thanks to Somers' sincerity and openness as she talks about the challenges she has faced in life and how she uses the products she sells. "She's able to talk to people about how life isn't perfect," says Marty Mealon, president of HSN US. One of her company's most successful products is the Thighmaster, which Somers created as a way to keep her legs in shape. "Ten million Thighmasters later," she quips, "mine turned out to be a good idea." These days, Somers stays busy writing books (11 so far with contracts for 7 more), but she is always looking for new ideas. She is trying to sell her husband and business partner, Alan Hamel, on the concept of Somersize Cafés, a chain of restaurants that will serve healthy meals. "My husband rolls his eyes," she laughs, "but I've got to make this happen."

Newman's Own

In 1982, movie star Paul Newman and writer A. E. Hotchner decided to launch a business and donate 100 percent of its after-tax profits to charities. The result was Newman's Own, a business that began by selling salad dressings and has expanded into steak sauces, beverages, salsa, pasta sauces, and popcorn. (The popcorn took two years and 70 different blends to perfect.) Not only have Newman and Hotchner had a great deal of fun running the company, but they also have made a difference in the lives of many people. Since the company's beginning, Newman's Own has donated more than $150 million to thousands of worthy charities that operate on low overhead.

From Supermodel to Entrepreneur

Former supermodel Kathy Ireland once made her living by selling her good looks. Her photo appeared in 13 issues of the famous *Sports Illustrated* swimsuit edition. The typical supermodel's career is quite short, however. What's a supermodel to do when the cameras stop clicking? For Ireland, the answer was "launch my own business," Kathy Ireland Worldwide, a company that brings in more than $1 billion in sales of clothing and home furnishings, much of it for K-Mart. "When I was modeling," says Ireland, "I would always look at the client and think, 'That's what I want to do.' I wanted to be the client." She started realizing that dream in 1993 when she put her name on a line of socks. K-Mart decided to market them and eventually sold 1 million pairs! Today, Ireland is the CEO and chief designer of her 37-person company, yet she devotes time to raising her three children, helping several charities, teaching Sunday school, and writing books, including *Powerful Inspirations*, now in its third printing. Because she is a busy working mother, many of Ireland's designs are aimed at other busy moms, and the products have proved to be very successful. Building a brand "requires infrastructure, leadership, and a strong, committed sales and distribution force," she says. "We've built our brand from the ground up."

1. In addition to the normal obstacles of starting a business, what barriers do celebrity entrepreneurs face?
2. What advantages do celebrity entrepreneurs have when launching a business?
3. Use the Internet to research other celebrities who have become entrepreneurs or entrepreneurs who have become celebrities and prepare a one-page report on his or her entrepreneurial story.

Sources: April Y. Pennington, "Custom Made," *Entrepreneur*, July 2005, p. 37; Elyssa Lee and Rob Turner, "Celebrity Entrepreneurs," *Inc.*, December 2004, pp. 70–81; Julia Boorstin, "For Suzanne Somers, the Thigh's Not the Limit," *Fortune*, June 14, 2004, p. 44; Kiri Blakeley, "The Model Mogul," *Forbes*, July 5, 2004, p. 116.

What Is an Entrepreneur?

LEARNING OBJECTIVES
1. Describe the entrepreneurial profile and evaluate your potential as an entrepreneur.

An **entrepreneur** is one who creates a new business in the face of risk and uncertainty for the purpose of achieving profit and growth by identifying significant opportunities and assembling the necessary resources to capitalize on them. Although many people come up with great business ideas, most of them never act on their ideas. Entrepreneurs do. The process of creative destruction, in which entrepreneurs create new ideas and new businesses that make existing ones obsolete, is a sign of a vibrant economy. Although this constant churn of businesses—some rising, others sinking, and many failing—concerns some people, in reality it is an indication of a healthy, growing, economic system that is creating new and better ways of serving people's needs and improving their quality of life and standard of living.

entrepreneur
one who creates a new business in the face of risk and uncertainty for the purpose of achieving profit and growth by identifying significant opportunities and assembling the necessary resources to capitalize on them.

Researchers have invested a great deal of time and effort over the last few decades trying to paint a clear picture of "the entrepreneurial personality." Although these studies have identified several characteristics entrepreneurs tend to exhibit, none of them has isolated a set of traits required for success. We now turn to a brief summary of the entrepreneurial profile.[8]

1. ***Desire for responsibility.*** Entrepreneurs feel a deep sense of personal responsibility for the outcome of ventures they start. They prefer to be in control of their resources, and they use those resources to achieve self-determined goals.
2. ***Preference for moderate risk.*** Entrepreneurs are not wild risk takers but are instead calculating risk takers. A study of the founders of the businesses listed as *Inc.* magazine's fastest-growing companies found no correlation between risk tolerance and entrepreneurship. "The belief that entrepreneurs are big risk takers just isn't true,"

says researcher and former *Inc.* 500 CEO Keith McFarland.[9] Unlike "high-rolling, riverboat" gamblers, entrepreneurs rarely gamble. Their goals may appear to be high—even impossible—in others' eyes, but entrepreneurs see the situation from a different perspective and believe that their goals are realistic and attainable. They usually spot opportunities in areas that reflect their knowledge, backgrounds, and experiences, which increases their probability of success. One writer observes

> Entrepreneurship is not the same thing as throwing darts and hoping for the best. It is about planning and taking calculated risks based upon knowledge of the market, the available resources or products, and a predetermined measure of the potential for success.[10]

In other words, successful entrepreneurs are not as much risk takers as they are risk eliminators, removing as many obstacles to the successful launch of their ventures as possible. One of the most successful ways of eliminating risks is to build a solid business plan for a venture.

3. ***Confidence in their ability to succeed.*** Entrepreneurs typically have an abundance of confidence in their ability to succeed. They tend to be optimistic about their chances for success. In a recent National Small Business Poll, the National Federation of Independent Businesses (NFIB) found that business owners rated the success of their companies quite high—an average of 7.3 on a scale of 1 (a total failure) to 10 (an extreme success).[11] This high level of optimism may explain why some of the most successful entrepreneurs have failed in business—often more than once—before finally succeeding. "I don't believe in luck," says Kerri Evans, owner of a mobile pet grooming business. "I believe in myself."[12]
4. ***Desire for immediate feedback.*** Entrepreneurs enjoy the challenge of running a business, and they like to know how they are doing and are constantly looking for feedback. "I love being an entrepreneur," says Nick Gleason, co-founder of CitySoft Inc., a Web-page design firm based in Cambridge, Massachusetts. "There's something about the sheer creativity and challenge of it that I like."[13]
5. ***High level of energy.*** Entrepreneurs are more energetic than the average person. That energy may be a critical factor, given the incredible effort required to launch a start-up company. Long hours and hard work are the rule rather than the exception, and the pace can be grueling.

iRobot

When Colin Angle and Helen Greiner, MIT graduates whose joint interest in robotics brought them together, formed a business venture, iRobot, they and their six employees routinely spent 18 hours a day creating software and assembling prototype robots. Their hard work paid off; their company has become the leader in the field of robotics. iRobot has developed a multitude of robots for a wide variety of market segments, ranging from My Real Baby ("an interactive, robotic, artificially-intelligent, emotionally-responsive baby doll") for kids and Roomba (an automatic vacuum cleaner) for busy homeowners to the MicroRig (a device that takes sensors to the bottom of oil wells) for industry and Ariel (a robot capable of removing obstacles on land and underwater) for the military.[14]

6. ***Future orientation.*** Entrepreneurs have a well-defined sense of searching for opportunities. They look ahead and are less concerned with what they did yesterday than with what they might do tomorrow. Not satisfied to sit back and revel in their success, real entrepreneurs stay focused on the future. Tom Stemberg, founder of the Staples office supply chain, went on to start Zoots, a 54-store dry cleaning chain (he came up with the idea after a dry cleaners lost one of his Brooks Brothers dress shirts), and Olly Shoes, a small chain of children's shoe stores (he came up with the idea after a frustrating experience shopping for shoes for his four boys).

   Entrepreneurs see potential where most people see only problems or nothing at all, a characteristic that often makes them the objects of ridicule (at least until their ideas become huge successes). Whereas traditional managers are concerned with managing available *resources*, entrepreneurs are more interested in spotting and capitalizing on *opportunities*. The United States leads the world in the percentage of opportunity entrepreneurs, those who start businesses because they spot an opportunity in the marketplace, compared to necessity entrepreneurs, those who start businesses because they cannot find work any other way.[15]

Serial entrepreneurs, those who repeatedly start businesses and grow them to a sustainable size before striking out again, push this characteristic to the maximum. The majority of serial entrepreneurs are leapfroggers, people who start a company, manage its growth until they get bored, and then sell it to start another. A few are jugglers (or parallel entrepreneurs), people who start and manage several companies at once.

serial entrepreneurs entrepreneurs who repeatedly start businesses and grow them to a sustainable size before striking out again.

Ron Berger

Ron Berger is a classic leapfrogging serial entrepreneur, having started five companies, one right after the other. Berger's business ventures include a camera retailer that grew to 54 stores before it folded, a company that managed the system by which video stores pay fees to movie studios, and his current business, Figaro's, a take-and-bake pizza restaurant that generates more than $24 million a year in sales.[16]

It's almost as if serial entrepreneurs are addicted to launching businesses. "Starting a company is a very imaginative, innovative, energy-driven, fun process," says Dick Kouri, who has started 12 companies in his career and now teaches entrepreneurship at the University of North Carolina. "Serial entrepreneurs can't wait to do it again."[17]

7. ***Skill at organizing.*** Building a company "from scratch" is much like piecing together a giant jigsaw puzzle. Entrepreneurs know how to put the right people together to accomplish a task. Effectively combining people and jobs enables entrepreneurs to transform their visions into reality.
8. ***Value of achievement over money.*** One of the most common misconceptions about entrepreneurs is that they are driven wholly by the desire to make money. To the contrary, *achievement* seems to be entrepreneurs' primary motivating force; money is simply a way of "keeping score" of accomplishments—a symbol of achievement. One business researcher says, "What keeps the entrepreneur moving forward is more complex—and more profound—than mere cash. It's about running your own show. It's about doing what is virtually impossible."[18]

Other characteristics frequently exhibited by entrepreneurs include the following:

High degree of commitment. Entrepreneurship is hard work, and launching a company successfully requires total commitment from an entrepreneur. Business founders often immerse themselves completely in their companies. Most entrepreneurs have to overcome seemingly insurmountable barriers to launch a company and to keep it growing. That requires commitment.

Tolerance for ambiguity. Entrepreneurs tend to have a high tolerance for ambiguous, ever-changing situations, the environment in which they most often operate. This ability to handle uncertainty is critical because these business builders constantly make decisions using new, sometimes conflicting information gleaned from a variety of unfamiliar sources. Based on his research, entrepreneurial expert Amar Bhidé says that entrepreneurs exhibit "a willingness to jump into things when it's hard to even imagine what the possible set of outcomes will be."[19]

Flexibility. One hallmark of true entrepreneurs is their ability to adapt to the changing demands of their customers and their businesses. In this rapidly changing global economy, rigidity often leads to failure. As our society, its people, and their tastes change, entrepreneurs also must be willing to adapt their businesses to meet those changes. When their ideas fail to live up to their expectations, successful entrepreneurs change them!

S.O.S. Pads

In 1917, Ed Cox invented a pre-soaped steel-wool scouring pad that was ideal for cleaning pots and used it as a "calling card" in his sales calls. Although his efforts at selling pots proved futile, Cox noticed how often his prospects asked for the soap pads. He quickly forgot about selling pots and shifted his focus to selling the scouring pads, which his wife had named S.O.S. ("Save Our Saucepans"), and went on to start a business that still thrives.[20]

Tenacity. Obstacles, obstructions, and defeat typically do not dissuade entrepreneurs from doggedly pursuing their visions. They simply keep trying.

Snocap

Shawn Fanning, who unleashed the downloaded digital music wars when he created Napster, a program that allowed users to download songs over the Internet without paying for them, lost the legal battle to keep his company going in 2002 over copyright infringement. One week after Napster closed, Fanning began planning his next entrepreneurial venture, a company called Snocap that works with major companies in the recording industry to operate a music file-sharing database that allows authorized users to download legally the songs for which they have paid.[21]

What conclusion can we draw from the volumes of research conducted on the entrepreneurial personality? Entrepreneurs are not of one mold; no one set of characteristics can predict who will become entrepreneurs and whether or not they will succeed. Indeed, *diversity* seems to be a central characteristic of entrepreneurs. One researcher of the entrepreneurial personality explains, "Entrepreneurs don't fit any statistical norm . . . . Most are aberrant or a bit odd by nature."[22] Entrepreneurs tend to be nonconformists, a characteristic that seems to be central to their views of the world and to their success.

As you can see from the examples in this chapter, *anyone*, regardless of age, race, gender, color, national origin, or any other characteristic, can become an entrepreneur (although not everyone should). There are no limitations on this form of economic expression. Entrepreneurship is not a mystery; it is a practical discipline. Entrepreneurship is not a genetic trait; it is a skill that most people can learn. The editors of *Inc.* magazine claim, "Entrepreneurship is more mundane than it's sometimes portrayed. . . . You don't need to be a person of mythical proportions to be very, very successful in building a company."[23]

LEARNING OBJECTIVES
3-A. Describe the benefits of entrepreneurship.

The Benefits of Entrepreneurship

Surveys show that owners of small businesses believe they work harder, earn more money, and are more satisfied than if they worked for someone else. Indeed, a study by the Gallup Organization found that 86 percent of small business owners would choose to own their own companies if they had it to do all over.[24] Before launching any business venture, every potential entrepreneur should consider the benefits of small business ownership.

Opportunity to Create Your Own Destiny

Owning a business provides entrepreneurs the independence and the opportunity to achieve what is important to them. Entrepreneurs want to "call the shots" in their lives, and they use their businesses to make that desire a reality.

Doug Danforth

After spending years in the construction business, Doug Danforth decided to pursue his dream of opening a flower shop in his hometown of Green Bay, Wisconsin. "I had managed two floral shops years before I went into the construction business, and I liked it a lot," he says. Danforth scraped together $900 of his own money, convinced family members to put up a small amount of cash, and launched his shop, which he has built into a thriving business. "I wanted to control my own destiny," he says. "I knew I wanted to be my own boss."[25]

Like Doug Danforth, entrepreneurs reap the intrinsic rewards of knowing they are the driving forces behind their businesses.

Opportunity to Make a Difference

Increasingly, entrepreneurs are starting businesses because they see an opportunity to make a difference in a cause that is important to them. Whether it is providing low-cost, sturdy housing for families in developing countries or establishing a recycling program to preserve Earth's limited resources, entrepreneurs are finding ways to combine their concerns for social issues and their desire to earn a good living.

CleanAirGardening.com

Concerned about protecting the environment, gardening enthusiast Lars Hundley launched a Web-based company, CleanAirGardening.com, which sells environmentally friendly lawn care and gardening products, from a spare room in his apartment. Hundley, who now operates his business from an office in his three-bedroom home, is constantly adding new products to the Web site, which also includes a comprehensive list of links that teach visitors about environmentally safe gardening and lawn care. Based on the responses from his growing list of customers, "I think I am certainly making a difference," says Hundley.[26]

Opportunity to Reach Your Full Potential

Too many people find their work boring, unchallenging, and unexciting. But not entrepreneurs! To them, there is little difference between work and play; the two are synonymous. Entrepreneurs' businesses become their instruments for self-expression and self-actualization. They know that the only boundaries on their success are those imposed by their own creativity, enthusiasm, and vision. Owning a business gives them a sense of empowerment. Barbie Dallman, who left the security (and the hassles) of corporate life at age 30 to start a résumé service, says, "Starting my own business was a spiritual awakening. I found out what was important to me—being able to follow my own interests."[27]

Opportunity to Reap Impressive Profits

Although money is not the primary force driving most entrepreneurs, the profits their businesses can earn are an important motivating factor in their decisions to launch companies. Most entrepreneurs never become super-rich, but many of them do become quite wealthy. In fact, nearly 75 percent of those on the *Forbes* list of the 400 richest Americans are first-generation entrepreneurs![28] According to research by Thomas Stanley and William Danko, self-employed business owners make up two-thirds of American millionaires. "Self-employed people are four times more likely to be millionaires than people who work for others," says Danko.[29] The typical millionaire's business is not a glamorous, high-tech enterprise; more often, it is something much less glamorous—scrap metal, welding, auctioneering, garbage collection, and the like.

Sam Walton

When Sam Walton launched Wal-Mart near his hometown of Bentonville, Arkansas, reaching the list of the wealthiest people in the United States wasn't even imaginable to him. Walton died in 1992, and his family business has grown into the largest company in the world; the 39 percent of Wal-Mart stock that the Walton family controls is worth $90 billion (an amount equivalent to the Gross Domestic Product of Singapore!), making them the richest family in the United States.[30]

Table 1.1 offers a brief profile of some of the wealthiest Americans in history.

Opportunity to Contribute to Society and Be Recognized for Your Efforts

Often, small business owners are among the most respected and most trusted members of their communities. Business deals based on trust and mutual respect are the hallmark of many established small companies. These owners enjoy the trust and recognition they receive from the customers they have served faithfully over the years. A study by the National Federation of Independent Businesses found that 78 percent of Americans believe that small business exerts a positive influence on the country's direction, a ranking exceeded only by science and technology.[31]

TABLE 1.1 Wealthiest Americans in History

Who	Comment	Business	Wealth as a Percentage of the U.S. Economy*
John D. Rockefeller (1839–1937)	America's first billionaire. Created America's most powerful monopoly, the Standard Oil Company.	Oil	1.53%
Sam Walton (1918–1992)	Launched Wal-Mart near his hometown of Bentonville, Arkansas, and built it into the largest company in the world.	Retail	1.30%
Cornelius Vanderbilt (1794–1877)	Known as the "Commodore." Borrowed $100 from his mother at age 12 to start what became the Staten Island Ferry.	Railroad and shipping	1.15%
John Jacob Astor (1763–1848)	A German-born immigrant who began as a for trader	New York real estate	0.93%
Stephen Girard (1750–1831)	Largest investor in the First Bank of the United States. Loaned the U.S. Treasury $8 million to finance the War of 1812.	Shipping and banking	0.67%
Andrew Carnegie (1835–1919)	A "rags to riches" story. Started as a bobbin boy and went on to found U.S. Steel.	Steel	0.60%
Alexander Turney Stewart (1803–1876)	Founded the first department store in the United States.	Retail	0.56%
Frederick Weyerhauser (1834–1914)	Made his fortune as American's demand for lumber exploded.	Timber	0.55%
Bill Gates (1955–)	Dropped out of Harvard and launched Microsoft Corporation with Paul Allen. Wealthiest man in the world today.	Computer software	0.43%
Larry Ellison (1944–)	Started Oracle Corporation with $2,000 of his own money. Now the second-largest maker of computer software behind Microsoft.	Computer software	0.15%
Michael Dell (1965–)	Started Dell Computer from his dormitory room at the University of Texas. Sales now exceed $56 billion a year.	Computers	0.11%

*Calculated by dividing person's total wealth by the U.S. GDP at the time of death, or if person is still living, by 2001 GDP.
Source: Adapted from "The World's Richest People," *Forbes,* February 26, 2003, http://www.forbes.com/lists/2003/02/26/billionaireland.html; "Richest Americans in History," *Forbes ASAP,* August 24, 1998, p. 32; Rachel Emma Silverman, "Rich & Richer: Fifty of the Wealthiest People of the Past 1,000 Years," *Wall Street Journal Reports: The Millenium,* January 11, 1999, pp. R6–R10.

Playing a vital role in their local business systems and knowing that their work has a significant impact on how smoothly our nation's economy functions is yet another reward for small business managers. One survey reports that 72 percent of business owners say that what they enjoy most about being a business owner is contributing to the local community.[32]

Opportunity to Do What You Enjoy and Have Fun at It

A common sentiment among small business owners is that their work really isn't work. Most successful entrepreneurs choose to enter their particular business fields because they have an interest in them and enjoy those lines of work. They have made their avocations (hobbies) their vocations (work) and are glad they did. These entrepreneurs are living Harvey McKay's advice: "Find a job doing what you love, and you'll never have to work a day in your life." The journey rather than the destination is the entrepreneur's greatest reward.

"Starting a company is very hard to do," says entrepreneur and small business researcher David Birch. "The risks are enormous; the anxiety is enormous. The only business you should start is one in which you have a huge interest, or else you won't have the persistence to stick with it. Get into [a business] because you're fanatically interested in it."[33]

Surf Diva

Sisters Izzy and Coco Tihany, founders of Surf Diva, a company that teaches women the joys of surfing and sells casual clothing, have transformed their lifelong passion for surfing into a successful business. The only problem: Their office chairs are always wet!

In 1996, twins Izzy and Coco Tihanyi decided to quit their desk jobs to transform their passion for surfing into a business venture. The Tihanyi sisters took $328 in savings and Izzy's surfboard collection and launched Surf Diva, a school that teaches women to surf. Since then, thousands of women, including the actress Minnie Driver, have learned the finer points of surfing at one of Surf Diva's three locations in California. In addition to the surfing school, the Tihanyis also sell surf boards and apparel under the Surf Diva brand through a company-owned boutique and 50 retailers in the United States, Japan, and England. Company headquarters in La Jolla is less than a block away from the beach, but the sisters' work seems more like play to them. "A big problem is keeping the office chairs dry," says Izzy. "We just put towels on them, but maybe we should buy vinyl chairs or something."[34]

Not only have the Tihanyi twins found a way to make a living, but what is more important, they are doing something they love!

You Be the Consultant

These Boots Are Made for Riding

In the late 1980s, Beth Cross was a management consultant for Bain and Company, where she worked with rising athletic shoe companies such as Reebok to incorporate the latest materials and technology such as gel padding, air pockets, and carbon fiber. Cross, who had grown up on a horse farm outside Swarthmore, Pennsylvania, soon recognized a market opportunity that she could capitalize on using her equestrian background and business experience: riding boots. At the time, the market for leather riding boots was dominated by two brands that had been around since the days of Wyatt Earp and were owned by business tycoon Warren Buffett: Justin Boots and Tony Lama.

Beth Cross left her job as a management consultant and with her friend Pam Parker launched Ariat, a company that provides the most technologically advanced boots in the market to the world's top equestrians. Ariat's ability to integrate athletic shoe technology and comfort into riding boots is a key ingredient in its rapid growth.

Cross's market research confirmed that the riding boot market had substantial purchasing power; some 20 million riders participated in equestrian sports worldwide. She also discovered that the market had seen no real innovations in a century and that a common customer complaint was that existing models of riding boots, whether Western or English, were not well designed and were very uncomfortable, at least until the rider was able to break them in, a process that could mean months of aching feet and blisters. In 1992, Cross quit her consulting job, and working from her home with her friend Pam Parker, created a business plan so that the two could take on the established companies in the riding boot market with a new boot that was as ranch-ready as any cowboy boot but was as comfortable as an athletic shoe. They launched their company, Ariat International, with $250,000 Cross assembled from her own pockets and from family and friends and with the help of Reebok's head of business development, Angel Martinez, whose daughter is an equestrian. (The company's name is derived from the Italian "aria," a perfect solo performance.) Ariat introduced riding boots that featured patented technology designed to deliver stability, durability, and comfort. Cross and Parker assembled a team of footwear engineers and designers and turned them loose to create an innovative performance riding boot. They started by redesigning the outsole, developing a new arch support system, and transforming the shape and fit of the boot to emulate modern athletic shoes. Indeed, Ariat is known as the pioneer of integrating athletic shoe technology into equestrian footwear. Throughout the process, Cross, Parker, and their team of footwear engineers included the opinions and feedback from hundreds of riders who field-tested their designs. The result was a boot that combined the comfort, fit, and performance of athletic shoes with the stylish look of a classic riding boot.

Cross convinced Reebok's Martinez to join the Ariat board of directors, which gave the young company credibility in the industry and helped it to land a $9 million investment from a venture capital firm in 1996. Ariat keeps its operations lean, operating with just 100 employees, most of whom are in sales and service. Cross has forged relationships with suppliers of high-quality leather in Europe and with contract manufacturers in China experienced in making shoes and boots. Ariat has won patents on a variety of boot features, including gel and carbon fiber components that reduce weight and lower costs.

Ariat shipped its first pair of boots in 1993, and serious equestrians recognized the difference in fit and performance almost immediately. With only a small marketing budget, Cross had to be creative. She hauled Ariat boots to horse shows in her car. Although the company could not afford to sponsor professional riders, she decided to give away Ariat boots to up-and-coming riders for publicity. Seeding the market this way paid off as growing numbers of customers began requesting the brand at tack stores, from catalogs, and from online retail outlets, all of which began to carry the Ariat brand. Today the company offers a full range of Western and English riding boots, work boots, casual footwear, and riding apparel. Ariat International, a privately held company, generates sales of more than $80 million a year and controls about 17 percent of the U.S. market for Western wear. With revenues climbing at an impressive 25 percent a year, the company leads the industry in sales growth. Ariat's international sales are climbing even faster—at a rate of 75 percent a year. Cross sees a bright future for her company and has set ambitious goals for it over the next decade. "I believe we are well positioned to achieve our goal of becoming the number one equestrian brand in the world," she says.

1. Explain how Beth Cross exhibits the entrepreneurial spirit.
2. How did Cross discover the business opportunity around which she built Ariat International? Do you think this process is typical of entrepreneurs? Explain.

Sources: Adapted from Michael V. Copeland, "These Boots Really Were Made for Walking," *Business 2.0*, October 2004, pp. 72–74; "A Sure Thing: Ariat International," Ariat International Press Kit, http://www.ariat.com/about_media_presskit.aspx; "The History of Ariat," Ariat International, http://www.ariat.com/about_history.aspx.

LEARNING OBJECTIVES
3-B. Describe the drawbacks of entrepreneur ship.

The Potential Drawbacks of Entrepreneurship

Although owning a business has many benefits and provides many opportunities, anyone planning to enter the world of entrepreneurship should be aware of its potential drawbacks. Individuals who prefer the security of a steady paycheck, a comprehensive benefits package, a two-week paid vacation, and the support of a corporate staff probably should not go into business for themselves. Some of the disadvantages of entrepreneurship include the following:

Uncertainty of Income

Opening and running a business provides no guarantee that an entrepreneur will earn enough money to survive. Some small businesses barely earn enough to provide the owner-manager with an adequate income. In a business's early days the owner often has trouble meeting financial obligations and may have to live on savings. The steady income that comes with working for someone else is absent. The owner is always the last one to be paid. One California couple left their corporate jobs that together brought in $120,000 a year to start a small vineyard; their combined income in their first year of business: $30,000.

Risk of Losing Your Entire Investment

The small business failure rate is relatively high. According to recent research, 35 percent of new businesses fail within two years, and 54 percent shut down within four years. Within six years, 64 percent of new businesses will have folded. Studies also show that when a company creates at least one job in its early years, the probability of failure after six years plummets to 35 percent![35]

Before "reaching for the golden ring," entrepreneurs should ask themselves if they can cope psychologically with the consequences of failure:

- What is the worst that could happen if I open my business and it fails?
- How likely is the worst to happen? (Am I truly prepared to launch my business?)
- What can I do to lower the risk of my business failing?
- If my business were to fail, what is my contingency plan for coping?

Long Hours and Hard Work

Business start-ups often demand that owners keep nightmarish schedules. According to a recent Dun & Bradstreet survey, 65 percent of entrepreneurs devote more than 40 hours per week to their companies (see Figure 1.2). In many start-ups, six- or seven-day workweeks with no paid vacations are the norm. In fact, one study by American Express found that 29 percent of small business owners had no plans to take a summer vacation. The primary reason? "Too busy."[36] These owners feel the pressure because they know that when the business closes, the revenue stops coming in, and customers go elsewhere. "You must have stamina to see it through," says Chantelle Ludski, founder of London-based fresh!, an organic food company. "I put in many 16-hour workdays. Holidays and time off are things that go out the window!"[37]

Lower Quality of Life until the Business Gets Established

The long hours and hard work needed to launch a company can take their toll on the other aspects of the entrepreneur's life. Business owners often find that their roles as husbands or wives and fathers or mothers take a back seat to their roles as company founders. Holly Dunlap, a 32-year-old designer of women's shoes, handbags, and party dresses that she

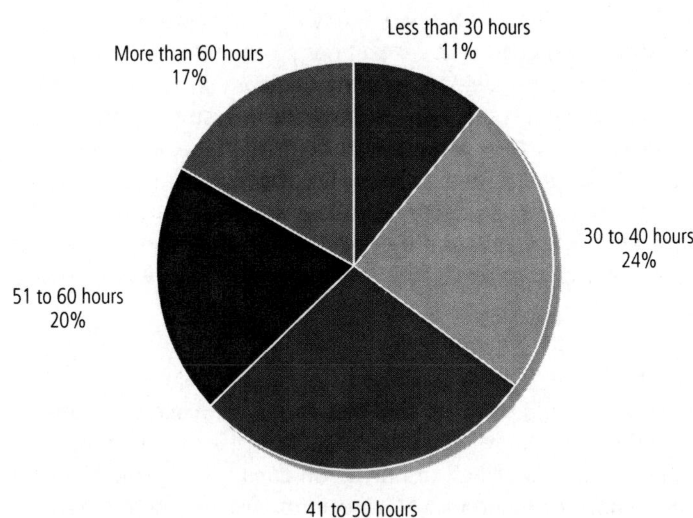

FIGURE 1.2

Number of Hours per Week Entrepreneurs Devote to Their Businesses.

Source: Adapted from Dun & Bradstreet, *21st Annual Small Business Survey Summary Report*, 2002, p. 35.

FIGURE 1.3

Entrepreneur Age When Business Was Formed

Source: Global Entrepreneurship Monitor, 2004.

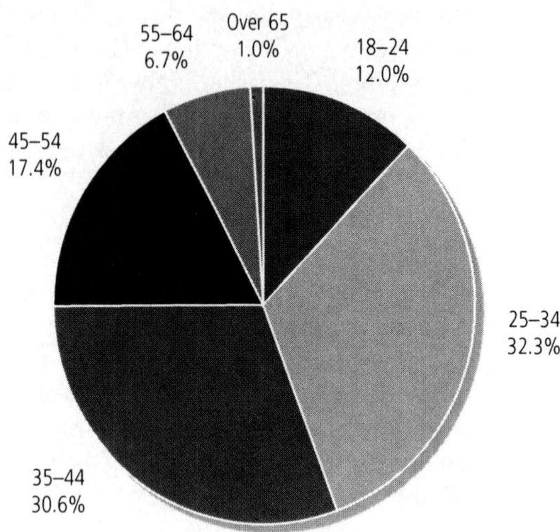

sells through Hollywould, the boutique she founded with locations in New York City and Palm Beach, Florida, admits that she is married to her business. Her 14-hour workdays leave little time for lunch most days or for a quiet evening with friends. "As my mother has pointed out," she says, "businesses do not produce grandchildren."[38] Part of the problem is that half of all entrepreneurs launch their businesses between the ages of 25 and 39 years, just when they start their families (see Figure 1.3). As a result, marriages, families, and friendships are too often casualties of small business ownership. "The traits that make you a successful entrepreneur are not the things you can turn off when you walk in the door at home," says one entrepreneurial researcher, describing how owning a business often conflicts with one's family and social life.[39]

High Levels of Stress

Starting and managing a business can be an incredibly rewarding experience, but it also can be a highly stressful one. Entrepreneurs often have made significant investments in their companies, have left behind the safety and security of a steady paycheck, and have mortgaged everything they own to get into business. Failure may mean total financial ruin, and that creates intense levels of stress and anxiety. Sometimes entrepreneurs unnecessarily bear the burden of managing alone because they cannot bring themselves to delegate authority and responsibility to others in the company, even though their employees are capable.

DeMars and Associates

Jo DeMars, founder of DeMars and Associates, a company that manages warranty disputes and arbitration for automakers, guided her company's growth for 13 years by micromanaging every aspect of it. Both DeMars and the company paid a price, however. "I was burned out and exhausted," she says. Because she was so focused on day-to-day issues, DeMars was neglecting the company's strategic management. Her solution was to take a four-month sabbatical and to allow her management team (and a trusted consultant) to run the company, which thrived in her absence. Now back at the helm, DeMars encourages employees to make daily decisions while she focuses on broader issues, such as writing the company's first comprehensive business plan and creating a new division.[40]

Complete Responsibility

It's great to be the boss, but many entrepreneurs find that they must make decisions on issues about which they are not really knowledgeable. Many business owners have difficulty finding advisors. A recent national small business poll conducted by the National Federation of Independent Businesses found that 34 percent of business owners have no one person to turn to for help when making a critical business decision.[41] When there is no one to ask, the pressure can build quickly. The realization that the decisions they make are the cause of success or failure has a devastating effect on some people. Small business owners discover quickly that *they* are the business.

Discouragement

Launching a business is a substantial undertaking that requires a great deal of dedication, discipline, and tenacity. Along the way to building a successful business, entrepreneurs will run headlong into many different obstacles, some of which appear to be insurmountable. In the face of such difficulties, discouragement and disillusionment are common emotions. Successful entrepreneurs know that every business encounters rough spots along the way, and they wade through difficult times with lots of hard work and an abundant reserve of optimism.

Behind the Boom: What's Feeding the Entrepreneurial Fire

LEARNING OBJECTIVES
4. Explain the forces that are driving the growth of entrepreneurship

What forces are driving this entrepreneurial trend in our economy? Which factors have led to this age of entrepreneurship? Some of the most significant ones include the following:

Entrepreneurs as heroes. An intangible but very important factor is the attitude that Americans have toward entrepreneurs. As a nation we have raised them to hero status and have held out their accomplishments as models to follow. Business founders such as Bill Gates (Microsoft Corporation), Mary Kay Ash (Mary Kay Cosmetics), Jeff Bezos (Amazon.com), Michael Dell (Dell Computer Corporation), and Ben Cohen and Jerry Greenfield (Ben & Jerry's Homemade Inc.) are to entrepreneurship what Tiger Woods and Kevin Garnett are to sports.

Entrepreneurial education. Colleges and universities have discovered that entrepreneurship is an extremely popular course of study. Disillusioned with corporate America's downsized job offerings and less promising career paths, a rapidly growing number of students sees owning a business as an attractive career option. Today more than 2,100 colleges and universities offer courses in entrepreneurship and small business to some 200,000 students. Many colleges and universities have difficulty meeting the demand for courses in entrepreneurship and small business.

Demographic and economic factors. Nearly two-thirds of entrepreneurs start their businesses between the ages of 25 and 44 years, and much of our nation's population falls into that age range. In addition, the economic growth that spanned most of the 1980s and 1990s created a significant amount of wealth among people of this age group and many business opportunities on which they can capitalize.

Shift to a service economy. The service sector produces 80 percent of the jobs and 64 percent of the Gross Domestic Product (GDP) in the United States, which represents a sharp rise from just a decade ago. Because of their relatively low start-up costs, service businesses have become very popular among entrepreneurs. The booming service sector continues to provide many business opportunities, and not all of them are in high-tech fields.

CharterAuction.com

Nathan McKelvey used his experience as a pilot and a manager of private jets for another company to launch CharterAuction.com, a business that locates private jets for clients through an online auction format. Before taking the entrepreneurial plunge, McKelvey conducted extensive research on the private jet industry and made a thorough analysis of his competition. "This was a $2 billion industry that was underserved," says McKelvey. His research proved to be accurate; McKelvey's company, which he started in 1999, now has 25 employees and generates $15 million in annual sales.[42]

FIGURE 1.4

U.S. Retail e-Commerce Revenues

Source: eMarketer, 2005.

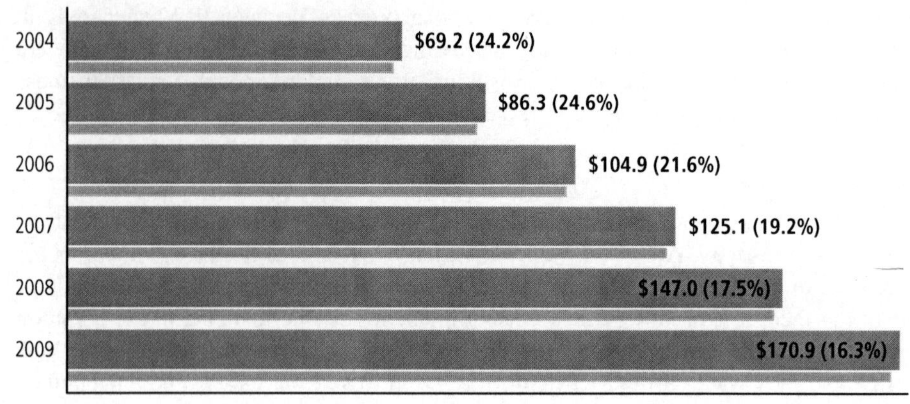

Technological advances. With the help of modern business machines such as personal computers, laptop computers, fax machines, copiers, color printers, answering machines, and voice mail, even one person working at home can look like a big business. At one time, the high cost of such technological wizardry made it impossible for small businesses to compete with larger companies that could afford the hardware. Today, however, powerful computers and communication equipment are priced within the budgets of even the smallest businesses. Although entrepreneurs may not be able to manufacture heavy equipment in their spare bedrooms, they can run a service- or information-based company from their homes very effectively and look like any Fortune 500 company to customers and clients.

Independent lifestyle. Entrepreneurship fits the way Americans want to live—independent and self-sustaining. People want the freedom to choose where they live, the hours they work, and what they do. Although financial security remains an important goal for most entrepreneurs, many place top priority on lifestyle issues such as more time with family and friends, more leisure time, and more control over work-related stress.

World Wide Web
the vast network that links computers around the globe via the Internet and opens up oceans of information to its users and a major business opportunity for entrepreneurs.

e-Commerce and the World Wide Web. The proliferation of the **World Wide Web,** the vast network that links computers around the globe via the Internet and opens up oceans of information to its users, has spawned thousands of entrepreneurial ventures since its beginning in 1993. Online commerce is growing rapidly (see Figure 1.4), creating many opportunities for Web-savvy entrepreneurs. Travel services, computer hardware and software, books, music, videos, and consumer electronics are among the best-selling items on the Web, but entrepreneurs are learning that they can use this powerful tool to sell just about anything! Approximately 57 percent of small businesses use the Internet for business-related purposes, and 70 percent have Web sites. Those that do have Web sites reap benefits quickly. The most commonly cited benefit of launching a Web site is additional customers; in fact, after launching a site, 41 percent of small companies reported an increase in sales. Fifty-five percent- of small companies with Web sites report that their sites are either breaking even or are earning a profit.[43] These "netpreneurs" are using their Web sites to connect with their existing customers and, ultimately, to attract new ones. "Small businesses that use the Web to market their products and services outperform those that don't," says an executive at Verizon, which sponsors an annual small business Internet survey. "The promise of the Internet is starting to pay off."[44]

ShavingCream.com

After spending more than 30 years in sales and marketing for a variety of companies, Mark Williams took a leap of faith and went into business for himself, launching ShavingCream.com after spending several months researching the concept and preparing a business plan. "The chance to work for myself, to put my ideas into play, to answer only to myself are what drove me to start my own business," says Williams. As its name suggests, Williams' company sells a wide selection of shaving creams as well as skin and hair care products online. Williams decided to create an e-commerce company because he realized that the Web was the "new sales frontier" and that it offered a much lower cost of entry for a retail operation than establishing a brick-and-mortar store. Williams launched his company in time to capitalize on the busy Christmas season, and the company's customer base—and its sales, thanks to repeat customers—have grown rapidly since its opening. Shaving Cream.com "has created a very healthy lifestyle for me and my family," says Williams. "I can work from home if I want, enjoy flexible working hours, spend quality time with my family and friends, exercise, and work with my wife."[45]

International opportunities. No longer are small businesses limited to pursuing customers within their own national borders. The shift to a global economy has opened the door to tremendous business opportunities for entrepreneurs willing to reach across the globe. Although the United States is an attractive market for entrepreneurs, approximately 95 percent of the world's population lives outside its borders. World-altering changes such as the crumbling of the Berlin Wall, the collapse of Communism, and the breaking down of trade barriers through trade agreements have changed the world order and have opened more of the world market to entrepreneurs. Today, small businesses can have a global scope from their inception. Small companies comprise 97 percent of all businesses engaged in exporting, yet they account for only 30 percent of the nation's export sales.[46] Most small companies do not take advantage of export opportunities, often because their owners don't know how or where to start an export initiative. Although terrorism and global recessions have slowed the growth of international trade somewhat, global opportunities for small businesses have a long-term positive outlook.

Although going global can be fraught with dangers and problems, many entrepreneurs are discovering that selling their products and services in foreign markets is really not so difficult. Small companies that have expanded successfully into foreign markets tend to rely on the following strategies:

- Researching foreign markets thoroughly.
- Focusing on a single country initially.
- Utilizing government resources designed to help small companies establish an international presence.
- Forging alliances with local partners.

Hibco Plastics

For nearly all of the nearly five decades it has existed, Hibco Plastics, a small maker of foam packaging based in Yadkinville, New York, sold its products strictly in the United States. In 1993, however, the company lost its largest customer, IBM, and sales immediately dropped 30 percent. Just as the company was beginning to recover, it was hit by an economic recession, and once again sales fell precipitously from $13.3 million to $10 million, forcing its owners, the Pavlanskey brothers Mark, Jon, and Keith, to lay off 40 percent of its workforce. Hibco's management team was forced to be creative, weighing options they had never before considered, including developing new products and exporting. In 2003, the Pavlanskeys took a crash course in global business, and Hibco began exporting to Mexico foam packaging and a synthetic soil ("rubber dirt") used for shipping plants. Building on its early exporting success, Hibco is entering export markets for foam roofing and insulation material and specialty packaging for the medical industry. Sales have recovered to $14 million, and the workforce is back to 100 employees. The Pavlanskeys say that exporting has transformed Hibco's entire culture from a once-complacent operation into a thriving, dynamic business. Exporting "keeps us on our toes in our core business," says Mark.[47]

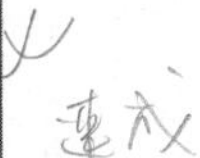

You Be the Consultant

Collegiate Entrepreneurs

For growing numbers of students, college is not just a time of learning, partying, and growing into young adulthood; it is fast becoming a place for building a business. More than 2,100 colleges and universities offer courses in entrepreneurship and small business management, and many of them have trouble keeping up with demand for these classes. "Students used to come to college and assume that five to ten years down the road, they'd start a business," says Gerry Hills, co-founder of the Collegiate Entrepreneurs Organization (CEO). Today, "they come in preparing to get ideas and launch."

Many of these collegiate entrepreneurs' ideas come from their college experiences. As a freshman enrolling in Santa Clara University in California, Ryan Garman faced the stereotypical moving day woes, struggling to pack and haul his belongings from his parents' home in Las Vegas to his dorm room in Santa Clara. Hoping to get an early start, he arrived on campus at 5 a.m., only to end up waiting in line with 2,400 other students who also were moving in. "It was miserable," he recalls. "I thought, 'There has to be a better way.'" What if college students could buy furnishings designed for small dorm spaces and then have the items shipped directly to their dorms so that they are waiting there when the students arrive? Garman began developing a business plan for his idea and discovered that students and their parents spend $2.6 billion a year on college dorm and apartment furnishings. By his sophomore year, Garman had convinced three friends—Kevon Saber, Chad Arimura, and Ivan Dwyer—to join in launching the business venture, which Garman named AllDorm Inc.

Although they were still in college when they launched AllDorm.com, Garman, Saber, Arimura, and Dwyer knew that they needed input from students in other parts of the country. They developed a network of contacts at other colleges and universities and asked them for input on various types of dorm furnishings and decorations. Now several years past graduation, the AllDorm founders recognize the need to stay in close contact with the ever-changing tastes of the college market. They always have two student interns on their staff whose input they find to be extremely valuable. The interns also get to test new product ideas and offer feedback on them. Early on, the entrepreneurs also made the wise decision to recruit several experienced business owners and experts to serve on the AllDorm advisory board. The network of contacts that advisory board members have provided the company has proved to be another important resource.

AllDorm offers customers more than 6,000 items, ranging from beanbag chairs and mini-refrigerators to shower sandals and shelving, but the company keeps costs low by stocking no inventory. Instead, it uses proprietary e-commerce software to link to its suppliers, who then ship the items ordered directly to AllDorm's customers. The company also coordinates delivery dates with each college and university to make sure shipments don't arrive too early and are returned. "When you're in college," says Garman, "you can study, you can party, or you can start a company. We chose to start a company."

Jeffrey Betz, Cecilia Domingos, and Michael Lobsinger, MBA students at Rensselaer Polytechnic Institute, also started their company, Orca Gear Inc., while in college. However, their idea came from a different source of inspiration: a class assignment. They recognized the market potential of a product that resulted from a year-long assignment in one of their entrepreneurship classes and decided to build a company around it: a stylish inflatable life jacket that looks like a regular jacket "that people will want to wear," says Betz, unlike the standard bulky orange life jackets that have been around for years. The company's mission is to revolutionize the life-jacket market with its cutting-edge, Float Tech™ life jacket.

The entrepreneurs earned most of their seed capital to launch the business by winning business plan competitions, tapping their professors for free consulting advice, and convincing local companies to help them perfect the product design—for free. "For the first two years, no one really charged us anything," recalls Betz. Sales for their company, now called Float Tech, have passed the $1 million mark, and the co-founders, who say their success is proof that entrepreneurship can be taught, are aiming for annual sales of $15 to $20 million within five years.

Budding entrepreneurs at a growing number of colleges can take advantage of special programs designed to create a culture for entrepreneurship. For instance, the University of Maryland's Hinman Campus Entrepreneurship Opportunities program provides space in a specially outfitted dormitory for 100 students who want to build their own companies. Students not only share living space with like-minded entrepreneurial types—an ideal setting for encouraging start-ups—but they also have access to amenities such as a professionally appointed conference room, wireless Internet access, smart whiteboards, ample computer facilities, video-conferencing equipment, copiers, and a phone system that simultaneously rings home and cellular phones so that no one misses an important business call. Weekly presentations from entrepreneurs, venture capitalists, attorneys, and others help students to define their business ideas and develop their business plans. Two hundred students recently applied for the 100 available spots in the dorm with its incubator-like business environment. The program, which won the Price Institute Innovative Entrepreneurship Educators Award, is working. Twenty of the students already have launched companies, including a medical software company and a textbook sales business. "It's often over those late-night pizzas where the best ideas are born," says one official. One student entrepreneur in the program agrees, "A lot of it is the community. Being around people in the program inspires one to think about other opportunities out there. What I've learned here is how to plan, how to make a business actually work."

1. In addition to the normal obstacles of starting a business, what other barriers do collegiate entrepreneurs face?
2. What advantages do collegiate entrepreneurs have when launching a business?
3. What advice would you offer a fellow college student about to start a business?
4. Work with a team of your classmates to develop ideas about what your college or university could do to create a culture of entrepreneurship on your campus or in your community.

Sources: Mark Henricks, "Honor Roll," *Entrepreneur*, April 2005, pp. 68–73; Nichole L. Torres, "Big Biz on Campus," *Entrepreneur B.Y.O.B.*, December 2004, p. 130; Nichole L. Torres, "Hit the Floor," *Entrepreneur*, May 2005, p. 122; Nichole L. Torres, "Inside Job," *Entrepreneur*, March 2005, p. 132; Michael Myser, "Giving College Kids a Smoother Move," *Business 2.0*, June 2004, p. 82; Nichole L. Torres, "Class Acts," *Entrepreneur*, June 2003, http://www.entrepreneur.com/article/print/0,2361,309005,00.html; Ellen McCarthy, "A Dorm for Dreamers," *Washington Post*, October 30, 2002, p. E1; "Hinman CEOs Living-Learning Entrepreneurship Program," http://www.hinmanceos.umd.edu/.

The Cultural Diversity of Entrepreneurship

LEARNING OBJECTIVES
5. Explain the cultural diversity of entrepreneurship.

As we have seen, virtually anyone has the potential to become an entrepreneur. Indeed, diversity is a hallmark of entrepreneurship. We now explore the diverse mix of people who make up the rich fabric of entrepreneurship.

Young Entrepreneurs

Young people are setting the pace in starting businesses. Disenchanted with their prospects in corporate America and willing to take a chance at controlling their own destinies, scores of young people are choosing entrepreneurship as their primary career path. A study by Babson College found that members of Generation X (people born between 1965 and 1981) are three times more likely than those in other age groups to launch businesses. Members of this generation are responsible for about 80 percent of all business start-ups, making Generation X the most entrepreneurial generation in history![48] There is no slowdown in sight as this generation flexes its entrepreneurial muscle. "Generation X" might be more appropriately called "Generation E."

Even teenagers and those in their early 20s (the Millennium Generation, born after 1982), show high levels of interest in entrepreneurship. Young entrepreneur camps are popping up all around the country to teach youthful business-building "wannabes" how to launch and run a business, and many of them are fulfilling their dreams. When she was just a sophomore in high school, Natalie Morris created a line of custom-made purses and handbags. Morris, who sells her stylish purses and bags at salons and boutiques across upstate South Carolina, recently received the South Carolina Young Entrepreneur of the

FIGURE 1.5

Reasons Women Give for Starting Businesses

Source: Center for Women's Business Research.

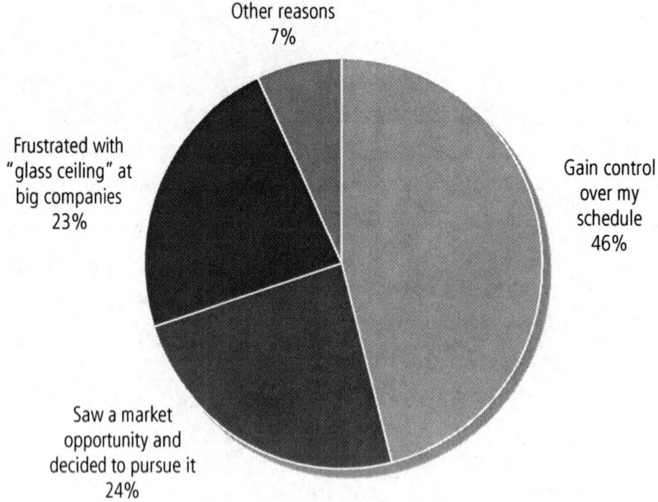

Year Award from Merrill Lynch.[49] Because of young people such as Morris, the future of entrepreneurship looks very bright.

Women Entrepreneurs

Despite years of legislative effort, women still face discrimination in the work force. However, small business has been a leader in offering women opportunities for economic expression through employment and entrepreneurship. Increasing numbers of women are discovering that the best way to break the "glass ceiling" that prevents them from rising to the top of many organizations is to start their own companies. In fact, women are opening businesses at a rate about twice that of the national average.[50] Women entrepreneurs have even broken through the comic strip barrier. Blondie Bumstead, long a typical suburban housewife married to Dagwood, now owns her own catering business with her best friend and neighbor Tootsie Woodley. Although about 69 percent of women-owned businesses are concentrated in retailing and services (as are most businesses), female entrepreneurs are branching out rapidly into previously male-dominated industries. According to the Center for Women's Business Research, the fastest-growing industries for women-owned companies are construction, transportation, communications, utilities, and agribusiness.[51] Figure 1.5 shows the reasons women give for starting businesses.

Although the businesses women start tend to be smaller than and require half as much start-up capital as those men start, their impact is anything but small. The nearly 11 million women-owned companies in the United States employ more than 19.1 million workers and generate sales of more than $2.5 trillion a year! Women now own about 48% of all privately-held businesses in the United States.[52] Although their businesses tend to grow more slowly than those owned by men, women-owned businesses have a higher survival rate than U.S. businesses overall. Female entrepreneurs today are more likely than ever to be highly educated and to have managerial experience in the industries in which they start their companies.[53]

Tennessee Bun Company

Cordia Harrington, a former real estate agent, wanted more control over her work hours and decided to open a McDonald's franchise. This single mother of three children was very successful and went on to own three McDonald's restaurants. While serving on a supplier audit committee for McDonald's, Harrington saw a business opportunity when she realized that the franchiser's two suppliers of hamburger buns could not keep up with demand. She sold her McDonald's franchises and built the world's most automated bakery, the Tennessee Bun Company (TBC), which is capable of turning out 60,000 buns an hour. Four years and 30 interviews later, Harrington finally convinced McDonald's to become a customer. Today, McDonald's is her largest customer, and TBC supplies buns and muffins to more than 600 McDonald's restaurants in the southeastern United States. As TBC's customer list expanded to include other large restaurant chains, Harrington saw the chance to launch a trucking business called Bun Lady Transport to speed the delivery of her baked products.[54]

Minority Entrepreneurs

Another rapidly growing segment of the small business population is minority-owned businesses. Hispanics, Asians, and African-Americans, are the minority groups most likely to become entrepreneurs, and minority entrepreneurs are launching businesses at a rate that is 1.5 times the national average.[55] Like women, minorities cite discrimination as a principal reason for their limited access to the world of entrepreneurship. Minority-owned businesses have come a long way in the last decade, however, and their success rate is climbing.

COMPANY Profile

Dash Ventures

After launching Roc-A-Fella Records with rapper Jay-Z and Kareem "Biggs" Burke, entrepreneur Damon Dash launched several other business ventures including film making, an urban lifestyle magazine, watches, a line of MP3 players, and a clothing line called Rocawear, which alone generates $350 million in annual sales for Dash Ventures. "Don't accept 'no' for an answer," Dash advises other entrepreneurs. "No one wanted to give me an opportunity, so I had to do it my own way."[56]

A study by the Small Business Administration reported that minorities now own 15 percent of all businesses.[57] Minority-owned businesses generate $591 billion in annual revenues and employ more than 4.51 million workers with a payroll of more than $96 billion.[58] The future is promising for this new generation of minority entrepreneurs, who are better educated, have more business experience, and are better prepared for business ownership than their predecessors.

Immigrant Entrepreneurs

The United States has always been a melting pot of diverse cultures, and many immigrants have been drawn to this nation by its promise of economic freedom. Unlike the unskilled "huddled masses" of the past, today's immigrants arrive with more education and experience. Although many of them come to the United States with few assets, their dedication and desire to succeed enable them to achieve their entrepreneurial dreams.

Newcrafters Nesting Dolls

After emigrating from Ukraine, Dr. Alexander Krilov became the business manager for Los Angeles Lakers basketball star Stanislav Medvedenko. That experience gave Krilov and his wife, Julia Butler, the idea to take traditional Russian nested dolls and put the images of famous National Basketball Association (NBA) players on them. Getting approval from the NBA took time, but Krilov and Butler persevered and won the rights to create nested dolls with portrait-quality images of many NBA stars. Since then, their company, Newcrafters Nesting Dolls, has forged similar deals with Major League Baseball and the National Hockey League as well as Elvis Presley and I Love Lucy properties and generates more than $1 million in annual sales.[59]

Part-Time Entrepreneurs

Starting a part-time business is a popular gateway to entrepreneurship. Part-time entrepreneurs have the best of both worlds: They can ease into business for themselves without sacrificing the security of a steady paycheck and benefits. Approximately 15 million Americans are self-employed part-time. A major advantage of going into business part-time is the lower risk in case the venture flops. Many part-timers are "testing the entrepreneurial waters" to see whether their business ideas will work, whether there is sufficient demand for their products and services, and whether they enjoy being self-employed. As they grow, many part-time enterprises absorb more of the entrepreneur's time until they become full-time businesses.

StringThis! Inc.

Joe Carmen decided to keep his job at a technology firm when he started his online guitar string company, String This! Inc. Carmen created a Web site and filled customer orders in the evenings and on weekends. Two years after start-up, however, Carmen transformed his business into a full-time venture when his company downsized and he was laid off.

Carmen rewrote his business plan and made a few adjustments in the way he ran the business. Within a year, he received a lucrative offer to sell the business, and he accepted it. He is now planning the launch of his next business, which will be a full-time venture.[60]

Home-Based Businesses

Home-based businesses are booming! Fifty-three percent of all businesses are home-based, but about 91 percent of them are very small with no employees other than the principal.[61] Several factors make the home the first-choice location for many entrepreneurs:

- Operating a business from home keeps start-up and operating costs to a minimum.
- Home-based companies allow owners to maintain a flexible lifestyle and workstyle. Many home-based entrepreneurs relish being part of the "open-collar workforce."
- Technology, which is transforming many ordinary homes into "electronic cottages," allows entrepreneurs to run a wide variety of businesses from their homes.
- Many entrepreneurs use the Internet to operate e-commerce businesses from their homes that literally span the globe.

In the past, home-based businesses tended to be rather unexciting cottage industries such as crafts or sewing. Today's home-based businesses are more diverse; modern home-based entrepreneurs are more likely to be running high-tech or service companies with millions of dollars in sales. The average home-based entrepreneur works 61 hours a week and earns an income of $63,000.[62] Studies by Link Resources Corporation, a research and consulting firm, suggest that the success rate for home-based businesses is high: 85 percent of such businesses are still in operation after three years.[63]

MusicStack

Dave Stack operates a Web site from his home for his company, MusicStack, which combines the inventory of more than 3,000 music and record stores that compete on price and selection. MusicStack, which generates more than $5 million in annual sales, allows the 3,000 individual stores to manage their own inventories and prices and offers customers more than 15 million items ranging from CDs, mini-discs, vinyl records, and eight-track tapes—more than online giants eBay and Amazon.com. "Fresh inventory is not a problem," says Stack. "The sheer volume of the site makes [MusicStack] different."[64]

Table 1.2 offers 18 "rules" home-based entrepreneurs should follow to be successful.

TABLE 1.2 Follow These Rules for a Successful Home-Based Business

Rule 1. Do your homework. Much of a home-based business's potential for success depends on how much preparation an entrepreneur makes *before* ever opening for business. The public library is an excellent source for research on customers, industries, competitors, and the like.

Rule 2. Find out what your zoning restrictions are. In some areas local zoning laws make running a business from home illegal. Avoid headaches by checking these laws first. You can always request a variance.

Rule 3. Choose the most efficient location for your office. About half of all home-based entrepreneurs operate out of spare bedrooms. The best way to determine the ideal office location is to examine the nature of your business and your clients. Avoid locating your business in your bedroom or your family room.

Rule 4. Focus your home-based business idea. Avoid the tendency to be "all things to all people." Most successful home-based businesses focus on a particular customer group or on some specialty.

Rule 5. Discuss your business rules with your family. Running a business from your home means you can spend more time with your family . . . and that your family can spend more time with you. Establish the rules for interruptions up front.

Rule 6. Select an appropriate business name. Your first marketing decision is your company's name, so make it a good one! Using your own name is convenient, but it's not likely to help you sell your product or service.

TABLE 1.2 *Contiunued*

Rule 7. Buy the right equipment. Modern technology allows a home-based entrepreneur to give the appearance of any *Fortune* 500 company, but only if you buy the right equipment. A well-equipped home office should have a separate telephone line, a computer, a laser or inkjet printer, a fax machine (or board), a copier, a scanner, and an answering machine (or voice mail), but realize that you don't have to have everything from Day One.

Rule 8. Dress appropriately. Being an "open-collar worker" is one of the joys of working at home. But when you need to dress up (to meet a client, make a sale, meet your banker, close a deal), do it! Avoid the tendency to lounge around in your bathrobe all day.

Rule 9. Learn to deal with distractions. The best way to fend off the distractions of working at home is to create a business that truly interests you. Budget your time wisely. Your productivity determines your company's success.

Rule 10. Realize that your phone can be your best friend . . . or your worst enemy. As a home-based entrepreneur, you'll spend lots of time on the phone. Be sure you use it productively.

Rule 11. Be firm with friends and neighbors. Sometimes friends and neighbors get the mistaken impression that because you're at home, you're not working. If one drops by to chat while you're working, tactfully ask them to come back "after work."

Rule 12. Take advantage of tax breaks. Although a 1993 Supreme Court decision tightened considerably the standards for business deductions for an office at home, many home-based entrepreneurs still qualify for special tax deductions on everything from computers to cars. Check with your accountant.

Rule 13. Make sure you have adequate insurance coverage. Some homeowner's policies provide adequate coverage for business-related equipment, but many home-based entrepreneurs have inadequate coverage on their business assets. Ask your agent about a business owner's policy (BOP), which may cost as little as $300 to $500 per year.

Rule 14. Understand the special circumstances under which you can hire outside employees. Sometimes zoning laws allow in-home businesses but they prohibit hiring employees. Check zoning laws carefully.

Rule 15. Be prepared if your business requires clients to come to your home. Dress appropriately (no pajamas!). Make sure your office presents a professional image.

Rule 16. Get a post office box. With burglaries and robberies on the rise, you're better off using a "P.O. Box" address rather than your specific home address. Otherwise you may be inviting crime.

Rule 17. Network, network, network. Isolation can be a problem for home-based entrepreneurs, and one of the best ways to combat it is to network. It's also a great way to market your business.

Rule 18. Be proud of your home-based business. Merely a decade ago there was a stigma attached to working from home. Today, home-based entrepreneurs and their businesses command respect. Be proud of your company!

Sources: Lynn Beresford, Janean Chun, Cynthia E. Griffin, Heather Page, and Debra Phillips, "Homeward Bound," *Entrepreneur*, September 1995, pp. 116–118; Jenean Huber, "House Rules," *Entrepreneur,* March 1993, pp. 89–95; Hal Morris, "Home-Based Businesses Need Extra Insurance," *AARP Bulletin,* November 1994, p. 16; Stephanie N. Mehta, "What You Need," *Wall Street Journal,* October 14, 1994, p. R10; Jeffery Zbar, "Home Free," *Business Start-Ups,* June 1999, pp. 31–37.

Family Businesses

family-owned business one that includes two or more members of a family with financial control of the company.

A **family-owned business** is one that includes two or more members of a family with financial control of the company. Family businesses are an integral part of our economy. Of the 25 million businesses in the United States, 90 percent are family-owned and managed. These companies account for 60 percent of total U.S. employment and 78 percent of all new jobs, pay 65 percent of all wages, and generate 50 percent of the nation's GDP. Not all of them are small; 37 percent of the *Fortune* 500 companies are family businesses.[65]

"When it works right," says one writer, "nothing succeeds like a family firm. The roots run deep, embedded in family values. The flash of the fast buck is replaced with long-term plans. Tradition counts."[66] Despite their magnitude, family businesses face a major threat, a threat from within: management succession. Only 30 percent of family businesses survive to the second generation, just 12 percent make it to the third generation, and only 3 percent survive into the fourth generation and beyond. Business periodicals are full of stories describing bitter disputes among family members that have crippled or destroyed once-thriving businesses.

To avoid such senseless destruction of valuable assets, founders of family businesses should develop plans for management succession long before retirement looms before them.

D&D Motors

After he underwent quadruple heart bypass surgery at age 42, George Davenport, second-generation owner of D&D Motors, a successful auto dealership in Greer, South Carolina, established by Davenport's father in 1937, decided it was time to develop a management succession plan for the family business. "I've spent my whole life building this business," he says. "I'd roll over in my grave if they shut it down after I die." With the help of a family business consultant, the family created a comprehensive succession plan that addressed management as well as estate planning issues. Today, all three of Davenport's children hold offices in the company, each in charge of the area that best suits his or her skills.[67]

Copreneurs

copreneurs
entrepreneurial couples who work together as co-owners of their businesses.

"Copreneurs" are entrepreneurial couples who work together as co-owners of their businesses. Unlike the traditional "Mom and Pop" team (Pop as "boss" and Mom as "subordinate"), copreneurs "are creating a division of labor that is based on expertise as opposed to gender," says one expert.[68] Studies show that companies co-owned by spouses represent one of the fastest-growing business sectors.

Managing a small business with a spouse may appear to be a recipe for divorce, but most copreneurs say otherwise. "There is nothing more exciting than nurturing a business and watching it grow with someone you love," says Marcia Sherrill, who, with her husband, William Kleinberg, runs Kleinberg Sherrill, a leather goods and accessories business.[69] Successful copreneurs learn to build the foundation for a successful working relationship before they ever launch their companies. Some of the characteristics they rely on include the following:

- An assessment of whether their personalities will mesh—or conflict—in a business setting.
- Mutual respect for each other and one another's talents.
- Compatible business and life goals—a common vision.
- A view that they are full and equal partners, not a superior and a subordinate.
- Complementary business skills that each acknowledges and appreciates and that lead to a unique business identity for each spouse.
- The ability to keep lines of communication open, talking and listening to each other about personal as well as business issues.
- A clear division of roles and authority, ideally based on each partner's skills and abilities, to minimize conflict and power struggles.
- The ability to encourage each other and to lift up a disillusioned partner.
- Separate workspaces that allow them to escape when the need arises.
- Boundaries between their business life and their personal life so that one doesn't consume the other.
- A sense of humor.
- The realization that not every couple can work together.

Although copreneuring isn't for everyone, it works extremely well for many couples and often leads to successful businesses. "Both spouses are working for a common purpose but also focusing on their unique talents," says a family business counselor. "With all these skills put together, one plus one equals more than two."[70]

Great Harvest

In 1995, Dennis and Susie Thompson left the security of their well-paying corporate jobs to operate a Great Harvest bakery franchise. Their jobs kept them so busy that they "never saw each other," says Susie, so they decided to run the bakery together. Early on, while the Thompsons were defining their roles and settling in to them, disagreements were common. Their business succeeded, partly because the copreneurs established a clear division of responsibilities and stuck to it. Dennis handles production and operations; Susie is responsible for marketing and management. The couple has since opened a second franchise, and they credit their joint efforts for their success. "A lot of husbands and wives can't work together," says Dennis, "but for us it worked out great."[71]

Corporate Castoffs

Concentrating on shedding the excess bulk that took away their flexibility and speed, many large American corporations have been downsizing in an attempt to regain their competitive edge. For decades, one major corporation after another has announced layoffs, and not just among blue-collar workers. Companies are cutting back their executive ranks as well. Millions of people have lost their jobs, and these corporate castoffs have become an important source of entrepreneurial activity. Some 20 percent of these discharged corporate managers have become entrepreneurs, and many of those left behind in corporate America would like to join them.

Many corporate castoffs are deciding that the best defense against future job insecurity is an entrepreneurial offense.

BB International

Barry Brinker was in his mid-30s when the large company in which he served as director of new product development was bought by an even larger business. Brinker was one of hundreds of employees whose jobs were eliminated. Rather than risk becoming the victim of another layoff at a large company, Brinker decided to start his own business. Today, Brinker operates BB International, a million-dollar-a-year business that designs and sells jewelry to upscale retailers across the United States ranging from small boutiques to Saks Fifth Avenue and Neiman Marcus. "Being fired was the best thing that ever happened to me," says Brinker, who claims that he would not have accomplished all he has without the push from the corporate nest.[72]

Corporate Dropouts

The dramatic downsizing of corporate America has created another effect among the employees left after restructuring: a trust gap. The result of this trust gap is a growing number of dropouts from the corporate structure who then become entrepreneurs. Although their workdays may grow longer and their incomes may shrink, those who strike out on their own often find their work more rewarding and more satisfying because they are doing what they enjoy. Other entrepreneurs are inspired to launch their companies after being treated unfairly by large, impersonal corporate entities.

Marion Laboratories

In the 1950s, Marion Kauffman was so successful as a salesman for a pharmaceutical company that his pay exceeded that of the company president, who promptly cut Kauffman's sales territory. Kauffman managed to rebuild sales so that he once again earned more than the boss, who then cut Kauffman's commission rate. Outraged, Kauffman left to start his own business, Marion Laboratories, which he sold to Dow Chemical Company in 1989 for $5.2 billion! Before his death in 1993, Kauffman established the Ewing Marion Kauffman Foundation in Kansas City, Missouri, to promote entrepreneurship.[73]

Because they have college degrees, a working knowledge of business, and years of management experience, both corporate dropouts and castoffs may ultimately increase the small business survival rate. A recent survey by Richard O'Sullivan found that 64 percent of people starting businesses have at least some college education, and 14 percent have advanced degrees.[74] Better-trained, more experienced entrepreneurs are less likely to fail.

social entrepreneurs
entrepreneurs who use their skills not only to create profitable businesses, but also to achieve social and environmental goals for the common good.

Social Entrepreneurs

Social entrepreneurs use their skills not only to create profitable business ventures, but also to achieve social and environmental goals for the common good. Their businesses often have a triple bottom line that encompasses economic, social, and environmental objectives. These entrepreneurs see their businesses as mechanisms for achieving social goals that are important to them as individuals.

Charlie Trotter's

Charlie Trotter, owner of the award-winning Chicago restaurant that bears his name, draws crowds of patrons willing to pay $135 or more per person for a world-class dining experience and to wait three months for a reservation. In addition to achieving his goal of operating a profitable restaurant, Trotter also works hard to make sure his business makes a difference to the people of Chicago. Every weeknight, Trotter devotes one of his restaurant's magnificent eight-course seatings to local high school students as part of his Excellence Initiative, which is designed not only to allow students to enjoy a stellar meal, but also to tour the restaurant and hear staff members talk about their passion for their work and their commitment to excellence. "This is about showing them what intensity is and what exuberance is," says Trotter. In addition to the Excellence Initiative, Trotter donates some of the company's profits to local charities. He also has raised $450,000 to fund scholarships for worthy students at culinary schools. "Anyone can raise money and give it away," says Trotter. "What's most interesting to me is having the young folks here in the restaurant and spreading the idea that you get what you give."[75]

LEARNING OBJECTIVES
6. Describe the important role small businesses play in our nation's economy.

The Power of "Small" Business

small business
one that employs fewer than 100 people.

Of the 25 million businesses in the United States, approximately 24.92 million, or 99.7 percent, are considered "small." Although there is no universal definition of a small business (the U.S. Small Business Administration has more than 800 definitions of a small business based on industry categories), a common delineation of a **small business** is one that employs fewer than 100 people. They thrive in virtually every industry, although the majority of small companies are concentrated in the service and retail industries (see Figure 1.6). Although they may be small businesses, their contributions to the economy are anything but small. For example, small companies employ 51 percent of the nation's private sector work force, even though they possess less than one-fourth of total business assets. Almost 90 percent of small businesses employ fewer than 20 workers. Because they are primarily labor intensive, small businesses actually create more jobs than do big businesses. In fact, small companies have created two-thirds to three-fourths of the net new jobs in the U.S. economy.[76]

David Birch, president of the research firm Arc Analytics, says, however, that the ability to create jobs is not distributed evenly across the small business sector. His research shows that just 3 percent of these small companies created 70 percent of the net new jobs in the economy, and they did so across all industry sectors, not just in "hot" industries.

FIGURE 1.6

Small Businesses by Industry

Source: U.S. Small Business Administration, 2005.

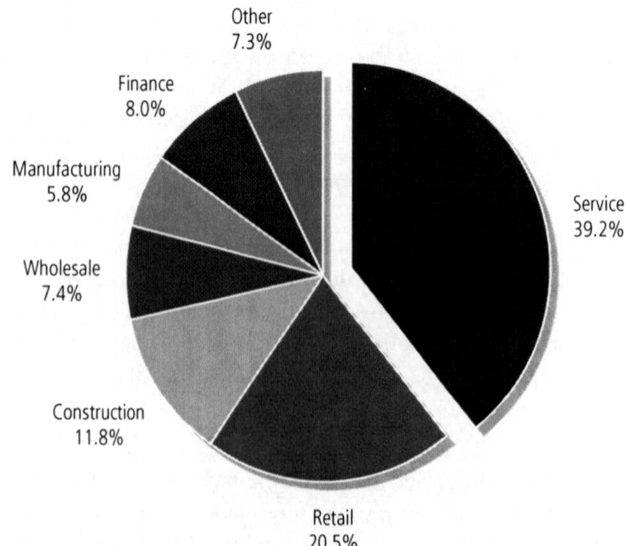

Birch calls these job-creating small companies "**gazelles**," those growing at 20 percent or more per year for four years with at least $100,000 in annual sales. His research also identified "mice," small companies that never grow much and don't create many jobs. The majority of small companies are "mice." Birch tabbed the country's largest businesses "elephants," which have continued to shed jobs for several years.[77]

gazelles
small companies that are growing at 20 percent or more per year with at least $100,000 in annual sales; they create 70 percent of net new jobs in the economy.

Not only do small companies lead the way in creating jobs, but they also bear the brunt of training workers for them. One study by the Small Business Administration concluded that small businesses are the leaders in offering training and advancement opportunities to workers. Small companies offer more general skills instruction and training than large ones, and their employees receive more benefits from the training than do those in larger firms. Although their training programs tend to be informal, in-house, and on-the-job, small companies teach employees valuable skills, from written communication to computer literacy.[78]

Small businesses also produce 51 percent of the country's private GDP and account for 47 percent of business sales.[79] In fact, the U.S. small business sector is the world's third-largest "economy," trailing only the entire U.S. economy and China![80] Small companies also are incubators of new ideas, products, and services. Small firms actually create 13 to 14 times more innovations per research employee than large companies.[81] Traditionally, small businesses have played a vital role in innovation, and they continue to do so today. Many important inventions trace their roots to an entrepreneur, including the zipper, FM radio, the laser, air conditioning, the escalator, the light bulb, the personal computer, and the automatic transmission.

Hands on ... How to

Transform Your Great Business Idea into Reality

It happens thousands of times every day: Someone comes up with a great idea for a new product, a modification of an existing product, or a new service. He or she is absolutely certain that the idea is going to be "the next big thing." Indeed, the U.S. Patent and Trademark Office (USPTO) receives more than 366,000 patent applications a year (but issues only about 187,000 patents a year). Technological advances, the Internet, faster communication tools, increased global interconnectivity, and computer-aided-design tools that allow inventors to go from the idea stage to creating a prototype faster than ever have made transforming a great idea into reality much easier than at any point in the past.

Does a "great idea" necessarily transfer into a successful business? Not always. So . . . what can a creative genius with a great idea do to put it to the test of business viability?

Step 1: Put your vision down on paper. You can draw a sketch of your concept by hand, use one of the many computer programs such as Adobe Illustrator to help you, or hire a freelance artist (perhaps from a local college or university) to help you. Getting a sketch and a description of your idea forces you to think about the total concept as well as the features of the product or service. It also makes it easier for you to explain your idea to others and to move on to Step 2.

Step 2: Test it to see if it really is a good idea. The reality is that transforming an idea into a successful business concept is much like the television show *American Idol*. For every person who really is a great singer, there are 99 people who can't stay on key but who *think* they are great singers. (Remember how bad a singer William Hung was, despite the fact that he actually made it onto television?) This step involves getting a reality check from other people—and not just friends and relatives who may not tell you what they really think about your idea because they don't want to hurt your feelings. One key is to involve potential customers and people who are knowledgeable about the particular industry into which your idea fits in evaluating your idea.

This step requires potential entrepreneurs to maintain a delicate balance between getting valuable feedback on their idea and protecting it from those who might steal it. Before they reveal their ideas to other people, some would-be entrepreneurs rely on nondisclosure agreements, contracts in which the other party promises not to use the idea for his or her own gain or to reveal it to others. Typically, the feedback, input, and advice entrepreneurs get at this phase far outweigh the risks of disclosing their ideas to others. "If you are on a mission, your first concern shouldn't be what someone takes from you but to be aggressive in refining [your idea]," says Rich Sloan, co-host with his brother Jeff of StartupNation.com and a nationally syndicated radio show designed to offer advice to entrepreneurs and inventors.

Sometimes entrepreneurs discover that Step 2 is as far as they should go; otherwise, they would be wasting time, talent, and resources. For instance, one venture capital investor recalls listening as an inventor excitedly described how he had figured out a creative way to speed the signal that passed from the keyboard of a computer to the processor so that text would appear on the screen faster. The only problem: Text already appears on a computer screen much faster than the human eye can blink! Who would notice the difference? "He'd created an elegant technical solution to a problem that didn't exist," says the venture capitalist.

Other entrepreneurs receive confirmation that they really are on to something in Step 2. While driving a long stretch of Western highway, truck driver Jeremiah Hutchins was listening to news reports and talk shows about a missing California girl. "All [of] the shows kept saying, 'If only they'd had better information about her,'" he recalls. Hutchins, together with a friend who was a security guard for the same trucking firm, had been toying with the idea of producing business cards on mini-CDs. He thought, "Why not apply the same concept to children's identification information?"

The next morning, Hutchins contacted a police investigator whom his wife knew to get feedback on his idea from a potential user of his idea. The police officer expressed a great deal of interest in the idea and encouraged Hutchins to pursue it. His next stop was the Internet, on which he conducted searches on "children identification." When his searches turned up very few leads, Hutchins concluded that there was very little competition in this market niche. Hutchins then went back to the police investigator to ask about the types of information police would need in a missing child case and then figured out how to put it on a mini-CD that parents could keep.

Using the information from the police investigator, Hutchins and his partner began developing a prototype mini-CD, testing everything from different types of digital cameras, CD burners, and ink to see which ones resisted smudges. Within 10 days, with prototype in hand, they made a presentation to Hutchins' police contact, who was so impressed that she invited the entrepreneurs to a local safety fair, where they had the chance to interact with real paying customers. Just three weeks after his initial brainstorm, Safe Kids Card Inc. sold 150 IDs to parents for $20 each. More important, the safety fair gave the entrepreneurs a solid gauge of the potential their idea had in the marketplace. Today, Safe Kids Card Inc. generates more than $1 million in revenue and has 44 franchises across the United States and three international operations selling children's ID cards for $13 each.

Step 3: Decide how serious you are about pursuing your idea and turning it into a business venture. As you have seen in this chapter, building a business is not for the faint-hearted. It requires a serious commitment of time, talent, energy, and resources. Taking the time to evaluate honestly the advantages and the disadvantages of owning your own business will help you to decide whether you should take the first step toward entrepreneurship.

Sources: Adapted from "U.S. Patent Statistics Chart," U.S. Patent and Trademark Office, http://www.uspto.gov/web/offices/ac/ido/oeip/taf/us_stat.htm; Gwendolyn Bounds, "You Have a Great Idea. Now What?" *Wall Street Journal*, May 9, 2005, pp. R1, R3; Michael V. Copeland and Andrew Tilin, "The New Instant Companies," *Business 2.0*, June 2005, pp. 82–94; Daniel Roth, "The Amazing Rise of the Do-It-Yourself Economy," *Fortune*, May 30, 2005, pp. 45–46.

LEARNING OBJECTIVES
7. Describe the 10 deadly mistakes of entrepreneurship, and explain how to avoid them.

The Ten Deadly Mistakes of Entrepreneurship

Because of their limited resources, inexperienced management, and lack of financial stability, small businesses suffer a mortality rate significantly higher than that of larger, established businesses. Figure 1.7 illustrates the small business survival rate over a 10-year period. Exploring the circumstances surrounding business failure may help you to avoid it.

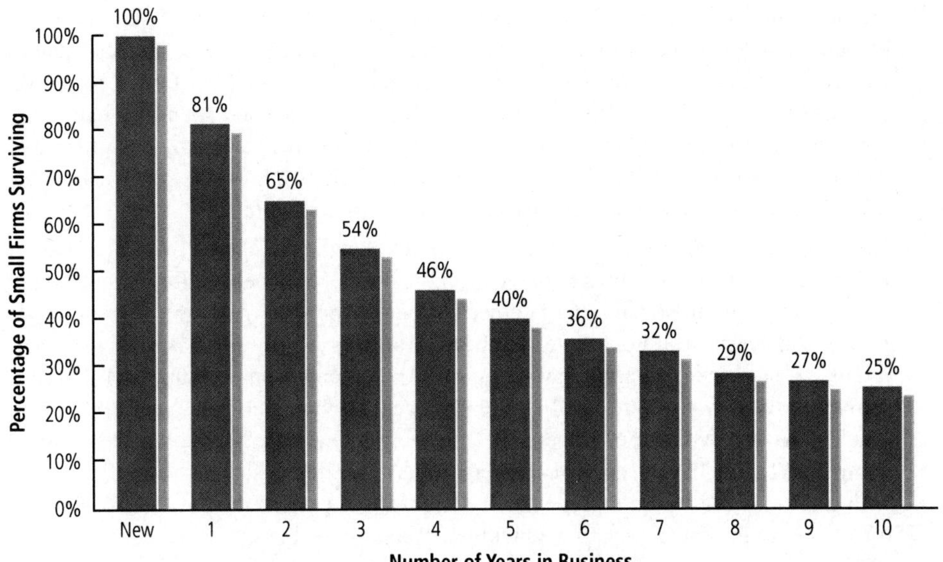

FIGURE 1.7

Small Business Survival Rate

Source: *NFIB Small-Business Policy Guide*, 2003, http://www.nfib.com/object/2753115.html, p. 16.

1. ***Management mistakes.*** In most small businesses, poor management is the primary cause of business failure. Sometimes the manager of a small business does not have the capacity to operate it successfully. The owner lacks the leadership ability, sound judgment, and knowledge necessary to make the business work. Many managers simply do not have what it takes to run a small enterprise. "What kills companies usually has less to do with insufficient money, talent, or information than with something more basic: a shortage of good judgment and understanding at the very top," says one business researcher.[82]

2. ***Lack of experience.*** Small business managers need to have experience in the field they want to enter. For example, if an entrepreneur wants to open a retail clothing business, he or she should first work in a retail clothing store. This will provide practical experience as well as knowledge about the nature of the business, which can spell the difference between failure and success. One aspiring entrepreneur who wanted to launch a restaurant went to work for a national chain known for its high-quality management training program after he graduated from college. After completing the training program, he took on a variety of tasks, from cook to manager, in one of the chain's restaurants. He took advantage of every subsequent training opportunity the company offered and asked lots of questions. He began developing a business plan based on his idea for a restaurant, and after nearly five years, he left to start his own restaurant. He credits the knowledge and experience he gained during that time for much of his success in the business.

   Ideally, a prospective entrepreneur should have adequate technical ability (a working knowledge of the physical operations of the business and sufficient conceptual ability); the power to visualize, coordinate, and integrate the various operations of the business into a synergistic whole; and the skill to manage the people in the organization and motivate them to higher levels of performance.

3. ***Poor financial control.*** Sound management is the key to a small company's success, and effective managers realize that any successful business venture requires proper financial control. Business success also requires having a sufficient amount of capital on hand at start-up. Undercapitalization is a common cause of business failure because companies run out of capital before they are able to generate positive cash flow. Many small business owners make the mistake of beginning their businesses on a "shoestring," which can be a fatal error. Entrepreneurs tend to be overly optimistic and often misjudge the financial requirements of going into business. As a result, they start off undercapitalized and can never seem to catch up financially as their companies consume increasing amounts of cash to fuel their growth.

   Another aspect of adequate financial control is implementing proper cash management techniques. Many entrepreneurs believe that profit is what matters most in a new venture, but cash is the most important financial resource a company owns.

Maintaining adequate cash flow to pay bills on time is a constant challenge for entrepreneurs, especially those in the turbulent start-up phase or for established companies experiencing rapid growth. Fast-growing companies devour cash fast! Poor credit screening, sloppy debt collection practices, and undisciplined spending habits are common factors in many business bankruptcies. One Internet company that ultimately went bust spent valuable cash on frivolous items such as a $40,000 conference table and a huge office aquarium that cost $4,000 a month to maintain.[83]

4. ***Weak marketing efforts.*** Sometimes entrepreneurs make the classic "*Field of Dreams* mistake." Like Kevin Costner's character in the movie, they believe that if they "build it," customers automatically "will come." Although the idea makes for a great movie plot, in business, it almost never happens. Building a growing base of customers requires a sustained, creative marketing effort. Keeping them coming back requires providing them with value, quality, convenience, service, and fun—and doing it all quickly. As you will see in Chapter 6, "Building a Guerrilla Marketing Plan," small companies do not have to spend enormous sums of money to sustain a successful marketing effort. Creative entrepreneurs find innovative ways to market their businesses effectively to their target customers without breaking the bank.
5. ***Failure to develop a strategic plan.*** Too many small business managers neglect the process of strategic planning because they think that it is something that benefits only large companies. "I don't have the time" or "We're too small to develop a strategic plan," they rationalize. Failure to plan, however, usually results in failure to survive. Without a clearly defined strategy, a business has no sustainable basis for creating and maintaining a competitive edge in the marketplace. Building a strategic plan forces an entrepreneur to assess *realistically* a proposed business's potential. Is it something customers are willing and able to purchase? Who is the target customer? How will the business attract and keep those customers? What is the company's basis for serving customers' needs better than existing companies? How will the business gain a sustainable edge over its rivals? We will explore these and other vital issues in Chapter 3, "Designing a Competitive Business Model and Building a Solid Strategic Plan."
6. ***Uncontrolled growth.*** Growth is a natural, healthy, and desirable part of any business enterprise, but it must be planned and controlled. Management expert Peter Drucker says that start-up companies can expect to outgrow their capital bases each time sales increase 40 to 50 percent.[84] Ideally, expansion should be financed by the profits they generate ("retained earnings") or by capital contributions from the owners, but most businesses wind up borrowing at least a portion of the capital investment.

   Expansion usually requires major changes in organizational structure, business practices such as inventory and financial control procedures, personnel assignments, and other areas. The most important change, however, occurs in managerial expertise. As the business increases in size and complexity, problems increase in magnitude, and the entrepreneur must learn to deal with them. Sometimes entrepreneurs encourage rapid growth, only to have the business outstrip their ability to manage it.

Avico and Prizm

Robert Schell, whose e-commerce consulting company, Avico, was growing fast enough to make *Inc.* magazine's list of the 500 fastest-growing companies in the United States, discovered too late the perils of rapid growth. Expanding too rapidly stretched the company's resources beyond their capacity and Schell's ability to control the business, and he was forced to lay off all of his employees and close the company. Schell, who now owns another company, Prizm, that also has made it to the *Inc.* 500 list, has used what he learned from his previous failure to avoid making the same mistakes again. "If a company doesn't have the right foundation, it can fall apart like a house of cards," he says.[85]

7. ***Poor location.*** For any business, choosing the right location is partly an art and partly a science. Too often, business locations are selected without proper study, investigation, and planning. Some beginning owners choose a particular location just because they noticed a vacant building. The location question is much too critical to leave to chance. Especially for retailers, the lifeblood of the business—sales—is influenced heavily by choice of location.

Mailboxes, Etc.

Before Dylan and Elise Fager bought their Mailboxes, Etc. (MBE) franchise, they invested a great deal of time researching the ideal site. Their final choice was a site across the street from a major shopping mall, which generated lots of customer traffic every day. The Fagers' research also showed them that the site was within five miles of 2 to 3 million square feet of office space, providing prime access to large numbers of potential customers. The Fagers' franchise was so successful that they quickly opened a second MBE franchise in the downtown district. A major advantage of that site was a complete lack of nearby competition.[86]

8. ***Improper inventory control.*** Normally, the largest investment a small business owner makes is in inventory, yet inventory control is one of the most neglected managerial responsibilities. Insufficient inventory levels result in shortages and stockouts, causing customers to become disillusioned and leave. A more common situation is that the manager has not only too much inventory, but also too much of the *wrong type* of inventory. Many small firms have an excessive amount of cash tied up in an accumulation of useless inventory. Computerized point-of-sale systems are now priced low enough to be affordable for small businesses, and they can track items as they come in and go out, allowing business owners to avoid inventory problems.
9. ***Incorrect pricing.*** Establishing prices that will generate the necessary profits means that business owners must understand how much it costs to make, market, and deliver their products and services. Too often, entrepreneurs simply charge what competitors charge or base their prices on some vague idea of "selling the best product at the lowest price," both of which approaches are dangerous. Small business owners usually underprice their products and services. The first step in establishing accurate prices is to know what a product or service costs to make or to provide. Then, business owners can establish prices that reflect the image they want to create for their companies, always, of course, with an eye on the competition.
10. ***Inability to make the "Entrepreneurial Transition."*** Making it over the "entrepreneurial start-up hump" is no guarantee of business success. After the start-up, growth usually requires a radically different style of management, one that entrepreneurs are not necessarily good at. The very abilities that make an entrepreneur successful often lead to managerial ineffectiveness. Growth requires entrepreneurs to delegate authority and to relinquish hands-on control of daily operations, something many entrepreneurs simply cannot do. Growth pushes them into areas where they are not capable, yet they continue to make decisions rather than involve others.

Table 1.3 explains some of the symptoms of these 10 deadly mistakes.

TABLE 1.3 Symptoms of the 10 Deadly Mistakes of Entrepreneurship

Entrepreneurs whose businesses fail usually can look back on their experiences and see what they did wrong, vowing never to make the same mistake again. If you find yourself making any of the following statements as you launch your business, look out! You may become a victim of one of the 10 deadly mistakes of entrepreneurship.

"We've got a great product (or service)! It will sell itself." Don't get so caught up in your product or service that you forget to evaluate whether real, live customers are willing and able to pay for it. Oh ... and no product or service has ever "sold itself."

"With a market this big, we only need a tiny share of it to become rich." Entrepreneurs tend to be overly optimistic in their sales, profits, and cash flow estimates, especially in the beginning. Most don't realize until they get into business how tough it really is to capture even a tiny share of the market.

"Strategic plan?! We don't need a strategic plan. That's only for big corporations." One of the quickest and surest paths to failure is neglecting to build a strategic plan that defines some point of distinction for your company. A plan helps you focus on what you can do for your customers that your competitors cannot.

"What a great business idea! It's cheap, easy to start, and it's the current rage," Because a business idea is so cheap and easy to start does not necessarily make it attractive. Too many entrepreneurs get clobbered in such businesses once the market matures and the competition gets stiff or the fad passes.

TABLE 1.3 *Contiunued*

"We may not know what we're doing yet, but we've got enough capital to last us until we do. We'll figure it out as we go" Everything—especially launching a business—takes longer and costs more than you think. Experienced entrepreneurs call it "the rule of two and three," Start-ups take either twice as long or need three times as much money (or both) to get off the ground as the founders forecast. Plan accordingly.

"Our forecast shows that we'll be making profits within three months; and that's very conservative ... really," Everyone expects entrepreneurs to be optimistic about their ventures' future, but you have to temper your optimism with reality. Launching a business on the basis of one set of forecasts is asking for trouble. Make sure you develop at least three sets of forecasts—pessimistic, most likely, and optimistic—and have contingency plans for all three.

"It's a good thing that we've got enough capital to last us the few months until we hit our break-even point." Attracting adequate start-up financing is essential to launching your business, but you also have to have access to *continuing* sources of funding. Growing businesses consume cash, and fast-growing businesses consume cash even faster. Don't become a victim of your own success; make sure you establish reliable sources of capital once your business is up and running.

"We'll make it easy for customers to buy from us. We'll extend credit to almost anyone to make a sale. One of the shortest routes to cash flow problems is failing to manage customer credit. It's easy to make a sale, but remember: Sales don't count unless you actually collect the payments for them. Watch for slow-paying customers.

"We're in the big time now. Our largest customer is [insert name of large customer here]." Landing a big customer is great, but it's dangerous to become overly dependent on a single customer for most of your sales. What happens if they decide to squeeze you for price concessions or to go to a competitor?

"Let's have our annual meeting in the Cayman Islands. We're the only 'stockholders,' and, besides, we deserve it. We've worked hard." Avoid the tendency to drain cash out of your business unnecessarily. A good rule of thumb: Don't start your business unless you have enough savings to support yourself (without taking cash from it) until the business breaks even.

"Let's go with this location. I know it's 'off the beaten path,' but it's so much cheaper!" For some businesses, choice of location is not a crucial issue. However, if your company relies on customers coming into your place of business to make sales, do not settle for the cheapest location. There's a reason such places are cheap! It's better to pay a higher price for a location that produces adequate sales volume.

"We're so small here. Everybody knows what our goals and objectives are." Just because a business is small doesn't necessarily mean that everyone who works there understands where you are trying to take the company. Do not assume that people will read your mind concerning your company's mission, goals, and objectives. You must communicate your vision for the business to everyone involved in it.

"This business is so easy it can run itself." Don't fool yourself. The only place a business will run itself is downhill! You must manage your company, and one of the most important jobs you have as leader is to prioritize your business's objectives.

"Of course our customers are satisfied! I never hear them complain." Most customers never complain about poor service or bad quality. They simply refuse to do business with you again. More often than not, the service and level of "personal treatment" that customers receive is what allows many small businesses to gain an edge over their larger rivals. Unfortunately, it's also one of the most overlooked aspects of a business. Set up a system to get regular feedback from your customers.

"What do you mean we're out of cash? We've been making a profit for months now, and sales are growing." Don't confuse cash and profits. You cannot spend profits—just cash. Many businesses fail because their founders mistakenly assume that if profits are rising, so is the company's cash balance. To be successful, you must manage both profits and cash!

Sources: Adapted from Ram Charan and Jerry Useem, "Why Companies Fail," *Fortune,* May 27, 2002, pp. 50–62; Frederick J. Beste III, "Avoiding the Traps Set for Small Firms," *Nation's Business,* January 1999, p. 10; Mel Mandell, "Fifteen Start-Up Mistakes," *Business Start-Ups,* December 1995, p. 22; Kenneth Labich, "Why Companies Fail," *Fortune,* November 14, 1994, pp. 52–68; Sharon Nelton, "Ten Key Threats to Success," *"Nation's Business,* June 1992, pp. 22–30; Robert J. Cook, "Famous Last Words," *Entrepreneur,* June 1994, pp. 122–128; David M. Anderson, "Deadly Sins," *Entrepreneur B.Y.O.B.,* August 2001, pp. 107–109; Geoff Williams, "109 Million Dollars Baked in a Pie," *Entrepreneur, B.Y.O.B.,* September 2001, pp. 107–109.

The first time Jerry Seinfeld walked onto the stage as a professional comedian, he looked at the audience and froze. He managed to stumble through a minute-and-a-half of his material before being booed off the stage. Like true entrepreneurs, however, Seinfeld refused to give up in the face of failure and went on to create one of the most successful television series of all time based on his standup comedy routines.

Putting Failure into Perspective

LEARNING OBJECTIVES
8. Put failure into the proper perspective.

Because they are building businesses in an environment filled with uncertainty and shaped by rapid change, entrepreneurs recognize that failure is likely to be part of their lives, but they are not paralyzed by that fear. "The excitement of building a new business from scratch is greater than the fear of failure," says one entrepreneur who failed in business several times before finally succeeding.[87] Entrepreneurs use their failures as a rallying point and as a means of refocusing their business ventures for success. They see failure for what it really is: an opportunity to learn what does not work. Successful entrepreneurs have the attitude that failures are simply stepping stones along the path to success

Failure is a natural part of the creative process. The only people who never fail are those who never do anything or never attempt anything new. Baseball fans know that Babe Ruth held the record for career home runs (714) for many years, but how many know that he also held the record for strikeouts (1,330)? Successful entrepreneurs know that hitting an entrepreneurial home run requires a few strikeouts along the way, and they are willing to accept them. Failure is an inevitable part of being an entrepreneur, and true entrepreneurs don't quit when they fail. One entrepreneur whose business burned through $800 million of investors' money before folding says, "If you're an entrepreneur, you don't give up when times get tough."[88]

One hallmark of successful entrepreneurs is the ability to fail *intelligently*, learning why they failed so that they can avoid making the same mistake again. They know that business success does not depend on their ability to avoid making mistakes but on their ability to be open to the lessons each mistake teaches. They learn from their failures and use them as fuel to push themselves closer to their ultimate target. Entrepreneurs are less worried about what they might lose if they try something and fail than about what they might lose if they fail to try.

Entrepreneurial success requires both persistence and resilience, the ability to bounce back from failure. Thomas Edison discovered about 1,800 ways not to build a light bulb before hitting on a design that worked. Walt Disney was fired from a newspaper job because, according to his boss, he "lacked imagination and had no good ideas." Disney also went bankrupt several times before he created Disneyland. R. H. Macy failed in business seven times before his retail store in New York City became a success. In the spirit of true entrepreneurship, these visionary business leaders refused to give up in the face of failure; they simply kept trying until they achieved success.

You Be the Consultant

If at First You Don't Succeed, So What!?

> **"Would you like for me to give you a formula for success? It's quite simple, really: Double your rate of failure. You are thinking of failure as the enemy of success. But it isn't at all. You can be discouraged by failure, or you can learn from it. So go ahead and make mistakes. Make all you can. Because remember, that's where you will find success."**
>
> **—Thomas J. Watson**
> **Founder, IBM**

Thomas Watson understood what true entrepreneurs know: that failure is a necessary and important part of the entrepreneurial process and that it does not have to be permanent. Some of the world's greatest entrepreneurs failed (some of them many times) before they finally succeeded. Henry Ford's first business, the Detroit Automobile Company, failed less than two years after Ford and his partners started it. Ford's second auto company also failed, but his third attempt in the then-new auto manufacturing business was, of course, a huge success. The Ford Motor Company, which is still controlled by the Ford family, is a major player in the automotive industry and is one of the largest companies in the world. Milton Hershey launched his first candy shop at age 18 in Philadelphia; it failed after six years. Four more attempts at building a candy business also failed before Hershey finally hit on success with the Lancaster Caramel Company, the business that was the parent of the famous Hershey Foods Corporation. Today, Hershey is the leading manufacturer of chocolate products in the United States and exports to more than 90 countries.

In post–World War II Japan, Masaru Ibuka and Akio Morita formed a partnership to produce an automatic rice cooker. Unfortunately, their machine burned the rice and was a flop. Their company sold just 100 cookers. Ibuka and Morita refused to give up, however, and created another company to build an inexpensive tape recorder that they sold to schools. Their tape recorder proved to be successful, and the company eventually became the consumer electronics giant Sony Corporation.

Rick Rosenfield and Larry Flax wrote a screenplay that never sold, started an Italian restaurant that went bankrupt, and developed a mobile skateboard park that quickly flopped. Then, in 1984, they tried the restaurant business again, launched the California Pizza Kitchen, and struck pay dirt. The California Pizza Kitchen is now a successful and well-recognized chain.

Over the course of his career, Dick Enrico has launched 20 companies that have either failed or been sold at fire sale prices, but Enrico took the lessons learned from his many failures and used them to build an exercise equipment business into a highly successful chain of 33 stores that generates more than $50 million in annual sales. Dick's brother, Roger, who achieved success in the corporate world by working his way to the top spot at soft drink giant Pepsico, admires Dick's business acumen. "He is the quintessential man of perseverance," says Roger. "It is that ability to persevere and to stay with it that makes really good business leaders."

Gail Borden (1801–1874) also knew about failure because he had a great deal of experience with it. One of his first inventions, the Terraqueous Wagon, a combination of wagon and sailboat that was designed to travel on both land and water, sank on its first trial run. Several years later, after returning to the United States from London where he had been promoting another invention, the condensed meat biscuit (a concoction of dehydrated meat and flour), Borden saw four babies die from tainted milk. He dropped the meat biscuit to focus on making milk safer for human consumption. He knew that the key was to remove the water from the milk, but the challenge was to do so without affecting its taste. For two years, he worked without success, always ending up with scorched milk. Ultimately Borden developed a vacuum condensation process that successfully removed the water from milk without adversely affecting its flavor. After three unsuccessful attempts, Borden finally won a patent for his process in 1856 and set up a manufacturing plant. It failed. A second attempt to produce condensed milk also failed. Undaunted, Borden convinced New York financier Jeremiah Milbank to invest in a new milk-processing venture, and this one succeeded. The New York Condensed Milk Company supplied much-needed nourishment to troops during the Civil War before becoming a staple in American households. Today, Borden Inc. is a multibillion-dollar conglomerate that still manufactures condensed milk using the same process that Borden developed 150 years ago. When he died in 1874, Gail Borden was buried beneath a tombstone that read, "I tried and failed; I tried again and succeeded."

1. Do the entrepreneurs described above exhibit the true entrepreneurial spirit? If so, how?
2. How do these entrepreneurs view failure? Is their view typical of most entrepreneurs?
3. James Joyce said, "Mistakes are the portals of discovery." What did he mean? Do you agree? Why is Joyce's idea important to entrepreneurs?

Sources: Adapted from Janet Adamy, "Try, Try Again," *Wall Street Journal*, July 12, 2004, p. R9; "Gail Borden," http://www.famoustexans.com/GailBorden.htm; Jeffrey Shuman and David Rottenberg, "Famous Failures," *Business Start-Ups*, February 1999, pp. 32–33; Francis Huffman, "A Dairy Tail," *Entrepreneur*, August 1993, p. 182; Bob Gatty, "Building on Failure," *Nation's Business*, April 1987, pp. 50–51.

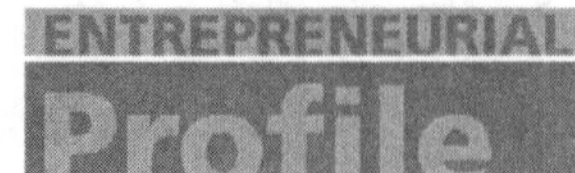

Frank Giotto

Frank Giotto operates three successful businesses, including Fiber Instrument Sales, a fiber-optic cable business, but Giotto would not be a successful entrepreneur today if he had let failure stop him. Giotto started five other companies that failed before he achieved his current success. One business delivered pickles and olives to grocery stores, another sold pizza to supermarket deli counters, and one offered guided tours of Utica, New York. Despite his failures, Giotto kept trying. When it comes to failure, entrepreneurs' motto seems to be: Failure is temporary; quitting is permanent.[89]

How to Avoid the Pitfalls

LEARNING OBJECTIVES
9. Explain how an entrepreneur can avoid becoming another failure statistic.

We have seen the most common reasons behind many small business failures. Now we must examine the ways to avoid becoming another failure statistic and gain insight into what makes a successful business. The suggestions for success follow naturally from the causes of business failure.

Know Your Business in Depth

We have already emphasized the need for the right type of experience in the business you plan to start. Get the best education in your business area you possibly can *before* you set out on your own. Become a serious student of your industry. Read everything you can that relates to your industry—trade journals, business periodicals, books, research reports—and learn what it takes to succeed in it. Personal contact with suppliers, customers, trade associations, and others in the same industry is another excellent way to get that knowledge. Smart entrepreneurs join industry trade associations and attend trade shows to pick up valuable information and to make key contacts before they open their doors for business.

COMPANY Profile

Executive Temporaries

Before she launched Executive Temporaries, Suzanne Clifton contacted other entrepreneurs in the temporary personnel services business (far enough away from her home base to avoid competitors) to find out "what it takes to operate this kind of business." She picked up many valuable tips and identified the key factors required for success. Today her company is a highly respected leader in the industry.[90]

Successful entrepreneurs are like sponges, soaking up as much knowledge as they can from a variety of sources.

Develop a Solid Business Plan

For any entrepreneur, a well-written business plan is a crucial ingredient in preparing for business success. Without a sound business plan, a firm merely drifts along without any real direction. Yet entrepreneurs, who tend to be people of action, too often jump right into a business venture without taking time to prepare a written plan outlining the essence of the business. Unfortunately, most entrepreneurs never take the time to develop a solid business plan. Not only does a plan provide a pathway to success, but it also creates a benchmark against which an entrepreneur can measure actual company performance. Resources to create a business plan, including software such as Business Plan Pro™, which may accompany this book, are available to help aspiring and current business owners create their business plans. Building a successful business begins with implementing a sound business plan with laser-like focus.

A business plan allows entrepreneurs to replace sometimes-faulty assumptions with facts before making the decision to go into business. The planning process forces entrepreneurs to ask and then answer some difficult, challenging, and crucial questions.

TerraCycle International

In his freshman year at Princeton, Tom Szaky created a business plan that helped him to launch TerraCycle International, a company that uses red worms to compost food waste into nutrient-rich soil. Szaky's ingenious plan was to sell waste disposal services to restaurants, schools, penitentiaries, and other institutions; the worms transform the waste into organic soil, which the company sells at premium prices to garden centers, nurseries, supermarkets, and other retail outlets. Because many of its key "employees" are worms and because the company can sell the organic soil they produce at premium prices, TerraCycle offers waste disposal fees that are 25 percent below those of traditional waste-disposal companies. Szaky's research told him that the organic segment of the potting soil industry is a multi-billion-dollar business and has been growing at double-digit rates for the last several years. TerraCycle recently signed a contract with clients across northern New Jersey to process 130 tons of food waste a day. Szaky's plans include expansion into the global market, and the company already has inquiries from potential partners in four countries.[91]

We will discuss the process of developing a business plan in Chapter 4, "Conducting a Feasibility Analysis and Crafting a Winning Business Plan."

Manage Financial Resources

The best defense against financial problems is to develop a practical information system and then use this information to make business decisions. No entrepreneur can maintain control over a business unless he or she is able to judge its financial health.

The first step in managing financial resources effectively is to have adequate start-up capital. Too many entrepreneurs begin their businesses with too little capital. One experienced business owner advises, "Estimate how much capital you need to get the business going and then double that figure." His point is well taken; it almost always costs more to launch a business than any entrepreneur expects.

The most valuable financial resource to any small business is *cash.* Although earning a profit is essential to its long-term survival, a business must have an adequate supply of cash to pay its bills and obligations. Some entrepreneurs count on growing sales to supply their company's cash needs, but this almost never happens. Growing companies usually consume more cash than they generate, and the faster they grow, the more cash they gobble up! Business history is littered with failed companies whose founders had no idea how much cash their businesses were generating and were spending cash as if they were certain there was "plenty more where that came from." We will discuss cash management techniques in Chapter 11, "Managing Cash Flow."

Understand Financial Statements

Every business owner must depend on records and financial statements to know the condition of her or his business. All too often entrepreneurs use these only for tax purposes and not as vital management control devices. Truly to understand what is going on in the business, an owner must have at least a basic understanding of accounting and finance.

When analyzed and interpreted properly, these financial statements are reliable indicators of a small firm's health. They can be quite helpful in signaling potential problems. For example, declining sales, slipping profits, rising debt, and deteriorating working capital are all symptoms of potentially lethal problems that require immediate attention. We will discuss financial statement analysis in Chapter 10, "Creating a Successful Financial Plan."

Learn to Manage People Effectively

No matter what kind of business you launch, you must learn to manage people. Every business depends on a foundation of well-trained, motivated employees. No business owner can do everything alone. The people an entrepreneur hires ultimately determine the heights to which the company can climb—or the depths to which it can plunge. Attracting and retaining a corps of quality employees is no easy task, however. It remains a challenge for every small business owner. "In the end, your most dominant sustainable resource is the quality of the people you have," says one small business expert.[92] We will discuss the techniques of managing and motivating people effectively in Chapter 15, "Building a New Venture Team and Planning for the Next Generation."

Keep in Tune with Yourself

"Starting a business is like running a marathon. If you're not physically and mentally in shape, you'd better do something else," says one business consultant.[93] The success of your business will depend on your constant presence and attention, so it is critical to monitor your health closely. Stress is a primary problem, especially if it is not kept in check.

Successful entrepreneurs recognize that their most valuable asset is their time, and they learn to manage it effectively to make themselves and their companies more productive. None of this, of course, is possible without passion—passion for their businesses, their products or services, their customers, their communities. Passion is what enables a failed entrepreneur to get back up, try again, and make it to the top.

Chapter Summary by Learning Objectives

1. Define the role of the entrepreneur in business in the United States and around the world.

Entrepreneurship is thriving in the United States, but the current wave of entrepreneurship is not limited to this country; many nations across the globe are seeing similar growth in their small business sectors. A variety of competitive, economic, and demographic shifts have created a world in which "small is beautiful."

Capitalist societies depend on entrepreneurs to provide the drive and risk taking necessary for the system to supply people with the goods and services they need.

2. Describe the entrepreneurial profile and evaluate your potential as an entrepreneur.

Entrepreneurs have some common characteristics, including a desire for responsibility, a preference for moderate risk, confidence in their ability to succeed, desire for immediate feedback, a high energy level, a future-directed orientation, skill at organizing, and a valuing of achievement over money. In a phrase, they are tenacious high achievers.

3A. Describe the benefits of entrepreneurship.

Driven by these personal characteristics, entrepreneurs establish and manage small businesses to gain control over their lives, make a difference in the world, become self-fulfilled, reap unlimited profits, contribute to society, and do what they enjoy doing.

3B. Describe the drawbacks of entrepreneurship.

Entrepreneurs also face certain disadvantages, including uncertainty of income, the risk of losing their investments (and more), long hours and hard work, a lower quality of life until the business gets established, high stress levels, and complete decision-making responsibility.

4. Explain the forces that are driving the growth of entrepreneurship.

Several factors are driving the boom in entrepreneurship, including the portrayal of entrepreneurs as heroes, better entrepreneurial education, economic and demographic factors, a shift to a service economy, technological advances, more independent lifestyles, and increased international opportunities.

5. Explain the cultural diversity of entrepreneurship.

Several groups are leading the nation's drive toward entrepreneurship: women, minorities, immigrants, part-timers, home-based business owners, family business owners, copreneurs, corporate castoffs, and corporate dropouts.

6. Describe the important role small businesses play in our nation's economy.

The small business sector's contributions are many. They make up 99 percent of all businesses, employ 51 percent of the private sector workforce, have created two-thirds to three-fourths of the net new jobs in the economy, produce 51 percent of the country's private gross domestic product, and account for 47 percent of all business sales.

7. Describe the 10 deadly mistakes of entrepreneurship.

There are no guarantees that the business will make a profit or even survive. Small Business Administration statistics show that 64 percent of new businesses will fail within six years. The 10 deadly mistakes of entrepreneurship include management mistakes, lack of experience, poor financial control, weak marketing efforts, failure to develop a strategic plan, uncontrolled growth, poor location, lack of inventory control, incorrect pricing, and inability to make the "entrepreneurial transition."

8. Put failure into the proper perspective.

Entrepreneurs recognize that failure is a natural part of the creative process. Successful entrepreneurs have the attitude that failures are simply stepping stones along the path to success, and they refuse to be paralyzed by a fear of failure.

9. Explain how an entrepreneur can avoid becoming another business failure statistic.

Entrepreneurs can employ several general tactics to avoid these pitfalls. They should know their businesses in depth, prepare a solid business plan, manage financial resources effectively, understand financial statements, learn to manage people, and try to stay healthy.

Discussion Questions

1. What forces have led to the boom in entrepreneurship in the United States and across the globe?
2. What is an entrepreneur? Give a brief description of the entrepreneurial profile.
3. *Inc.* magazine claims, "Entrepreneurship is more mundane than it's sometimes portrayed . . . you don't need to be a person of mythical proportions to be very, very successful in building a company." Do you agree? Explain.
4. What are the major benefits of business ownership?
5. Which of the potential drawbacks to business ownership are most critical?
6. Briefly describe the role of the following groups in entrepreneurship: women, minorities, immigrants, "part-timers," home-based business owners, family business owners, copreneurs, corporate castoffs, and corporate dropouts.
7. What is a small business? What contributions do they make to our economy?
8. Describe the small business failure rate.
9. Outline the causes of business failure. Which problems cause most business failures?
10. How does the typical entrepreneur view the possibility of business failure?
11. How can the small business owner avoid the common pitfalls that often lead to business failures?
12. Why is it important to study the small business failure rate and the causes of business failures?
13. Explain the typical entrepreneur's attitude toward risk.
14. Are you interested in someday launching a small business? If so, when? What kind of business? Describe it. What can you do to ensure its success?

Business Plan Pro

Business PlanPro

This book may include the best-selling business planning software Business Plan Pro™ by Palo Alto Software, Inc. This software can assist you in four ways as you begin to build your business plan.

1. *Structure.* Business Plan Pro provides a structure for the process of creating a business plan. There are general business plan standards and expectations, and Business Plan Pro has a recognized and well-received format that lends credibility to your plan. A comprehensive plan that follows a generally recognized outline adds credibility and, if it is a part of the plan's purpose, of being funded.
2. *Efficiency.* Business Plan Pro will save you time. Once you become familiar with the interface, Business Plan Pro creates all of the essential financial statements for you based on the information the software prompts you to enter. The income statement, balance sheet, and your profit and loss statement are formatted for you once the data are there.
3. *Examples.* Business Plan Pro includes dozens of example business plans. Seeing examples of other plans can be a helpful learning tool as you create a plan that is unique based on *your* product or service and *your* market.

4. *Appearance.* Business Plan Pro automatically incorporates relevant tables and graphs into your text. The result is a cohesive business plan that combines text, tables, and charts and enhances the impact of your document.

Writing a business plan is more than just creating a document. The process can be the most valuable benefit of all. A business plan requires you to "tell your story" about your business. It addresses why your business concept is viable, who your market is, what you offer that market, why you believe your offer represents a unique value, how you are going to reach your market, and how your business is going to be funded and, based on your projections, financially successful.

Creating a business plan is a learning process. For the start-up business, completing a business plan allows you better to understand what to do before you start writing checks and seek funding to open the doors of your business. The current business owner can benefit from writing a business plan to better address challenges and optimize opportunities. Business Plan Pro is a tool that assists you with this process. The software guides you through the process by asking a series of questions with software "wizards" to help you to build your business plan as you bring the vision of your business to paper.

At the end of each chapter in this book you will find a Business Plan Pro activity that applies the concepts discussed. These activities will enable you to build your plan one step at a time in manageable components. You will be able to assemble your plan in a way that captures the information you know about your business and also raise key questions that will push you to learn more in areas you may not have considered. Business Plan Pro will guide you through each step to complete your plan as you progress through this book. This combination of learning concepts and then applying them in your business plan can be powerful. It represents a critical step toward launching a business or establishing a better understanding of the business you now own.

The following exercises will lead you through the process of creating your own business plan. If you or your group does not have a business concept in mind, select a business idea and work through these steps. Future chapters will ask you to validate and change this concept as needed.

The EasyPlan Wizard™ within Business Plan Pro is another optional resource that will guide you through the process of creating your business plan, and, just as you follow the guidance each chapter offers, this will not proceed chronologically through the outline. Instead, it will skip from section to section as you build concepts about your business, the products and services you offer, the markets you will serve, and your financial information. You can use the wizard or follow the sections of the outline based on the guidance from each chapter. Both options will lead you through the entire process and help you to create a comprehensive business plan.

Business Plan Exercises

On the Web

First, visit the Web site designed for this book at www.prenhall.com/scarborough. Look for the Business Plan Resource tab at the top along with the chapters, and review the information that is provided in that section. The information and links here will be a resource for you as you progress through each chapter and as you develop your business plan.

In the Software

Follow the instructions included on the CD to install Business Plan Pro. After you first open Business Plan Pro—preferably on a PC with an Internet connection—open the Sample Plan Browser. The Sample Plan Browser allows you to preview a library of sample business plans. You will find numerous business plan examples ranging from restaurants to accounting firms to non-profit organizations. A tool will help you to sort through these plans based on a specific industry or key words. Don't be concerned about finding a plan that is identical to your business concept. Instead, look for plans that contain parallel characteristics, such as a product or service plan, or one that is targeted to consumers versus business customers. Review several of these plans to get a better idea of the outline and content. This may give you a clearer vision of what *your* finished business plan will look like.

Sample Plans

Click on the Sample Plan Browser within the software and review these two plans: The Daily Perc and Corporate Fitness.

1. Compare the table of contents of each plan. What differences do you notice?
2. Review the executive summary of each plan. What is the key difference in these two business concepts?
3. What similarities do the plans share regarding the reasons they were written?
4. As you look through the plans, what are some common tables and charts you find embedded into the text? What value do these tables and charts offer the reader?

Building Your Business Plan

Open Business Plan Pro and select the choice that allows you to start a new plan. You may want to view the movie, which will give you an animated and audio overview of the software. Then allow the EasyPlan Wizard to "ask" you about your start date, the title of your plan, and other basic information including the following:

1. Do you sell products or services?
2. Is your business a profit or a nonprofit organization?
3. Is your business a start-up operation or an ongoing business?

4. What kind of business plan do you want to create? Choose "complete business plan" here.
5. Do you want to include the SWOT (strengths, weaknesses, opportunities, and threats) analysis—check this box—and will you have a Web site?
6. A series of financial questions to structure the financial aspects of your plan with assistance throughout.
7. Do you want to prepare a plan for three years (a standard plan) or a longer-term plan of five years, both with a one-year monthly breakdown?

Save these decisions by using the drop-down menu under File and clicking on Save or by clicking on the Save icon at the top right of the menu bar. You can change your response to these decisions at any time as you build your plan.

Review the outline of your plan by clicking on the Preview icon on the top of your screen or by clicking on File, Print, and then Preview within the Print window. Based on your responses to the Wizard questions, you will now see the outline of your business plan. The software will enable you to change and modify the plan outline in any way you choose at any time. Business Plan Pro will help you to build your plan one step at a time as you progress through each chapter.

Beyond the Classroom . . .

1. Choose an entrepreneur in your community and interview him or her. What's the "story" behind the business? How well does the entrepreneur fit the entrepreneurial profile described in this chapter? What advantages and disadvantages does the owner see in owning a business? What advice would he or she offer to someone considering launching a business?
2. Select one of the categories under the section "The Cultural Diversity of Entrepreneurship" in this chapter and research it in more detail. Find examples of business owners in that category. Prepare a brief report for your class.
3. Search through recent business publications (especially those focusing on small companies) and find an example of an entrepreneur, past or present, who exhibits the entrepreneurial spirit of striving for success in the face of failure. Prepare a brief report for your class.

Chapter 2
Inside the Entrepreneurial Mind: From Ideas to Reality

- Explaining the differences between creativity, innovation and entrepreneurship
- Describing why creativity and innovation are such an integral part of entrepreneurship
- Understanding the two hemispheres of the human brain function and what role they play in creativity
- Explaining the 10 'mental locks' that limit creativity
- Understanding how entrepreneurs can enhance their own creativity and that of their employees aswell
- Describing the steps in the creative process
- Discussing the techniques for improving the creative process

CHAPTER 2

recognizing *opportunities* and generating ideas

Getting Personal *with* ANAND V. CHHATPAR

Best advice I've received

Make as many friends as you can as quickly as possible

First entrepreneurial experience

Web development company in high school!

Currently in my iPod

"Winning" by Jack Welch (audiobook)

Opening Profile

BrainReactions:

Bringing an External Perspective to Business Organizations

Anand V. Chhatpar, who grew up in India, always aspired to be an entrepreneur. As a teenager, he started a software and Web development company before moving to the United States to pursue an engineering degree at the University of Wisconsin. Shortly after starting classes, Chhatpar met Osman Ozcanil, an international student from Turkey, who he credits with changing his thinking. Ozcanil's imagination and "everything is possible" attitude were very inspiring to Chhatpar.

The engineering college at Wisconsin sponsors a number of contests that provide students an opportunity to try their hand at inventing and writing business plans. Early on, Chhatpar and Ozcanil entered several contests, based on different inventions they had worked on together. In 2002, after several unsuccessful tries, the two won the Tong Prototype Prize for an ergonomically designed stationery binder they had invented. For a short period, Chhatpar and Ozcanil actually produced and sold the binder through a chain of office supply stores in the upper Midwest.

During the summer between his sophomore and junior year in college, Chhatpar landed an internship with Pitney Bowes, the company that makes postal meters. Getting an internship with Pitney Bowes is no easy task, and Chhatpar believes that winning the Tong Prototype Prize sealed the deal. During his internship, Chhatpar was assigned to Pitney Bowes's "concept studio," which is a think tank inside the company that brainstorms new product ideas. The group included a highly diverse array of Pitney Bowes employees, including scientists, engineers, anthropologists, managers, and interns. One thing that struck Chhatpar during their brainstorming sessions was that it was the interns, who were all college students, who came up with the most new ideas. This observation caused Chhatpar to think that maybe people inside an organization are too constrained by conventional thinking to generate novel ideas. If this is a problem, then a solution might be to organize groups of college students to conduct brainstorming sessions on behalf of business organizations.

ANAND V. CHHATPAR
Founder & President,
BrainReactions
University of Wisconsin
BS, College of Engineering, 2004

To implement this idea, Chhatpar started working on a concept called BrainReactions, which would organize groups of college students to conduct brainstorming sessions on behalf of for-profit and not-for-profit business organizations. In Chhatpar's view, a carefully screened group of college

What I do when I'm not working

Hang out with people who inspire me in person or via their books or blogs

My advice for new entrepreneurs

Think about scalability: Make something once—get paid for it over and over

What I'd like to be doing in 10 years

Venture capitalist

After studying this chapter you should be ready to:

LEARNING Objectives

1. Explain why it's important to start a new firm when its "window of opportunity" is open.
2. Explain the difference between an opportunity and an idea.
3. Describe the three general approaches entrepreneurs use to identify opportunities.
4. Identify the four environmental trends that are most instrumental in creating business opportunities.
5. List the personal characteristics that make some people better at recognizing business opportunities than others.
6. Identify the five steps in the creative process.
7. Describe the purpose of brainstorming and its use as an idea generator.
8. Describe how to use surveys to generate new business ideas.
9. Explain the purpose of maintaining an idea bank.
10. Describe three steps for protecting ideas from being lost or stolen.

students could offer businesses something they'd never achieve in-house—a fresh perspective, no inhibitions, youthful enthusiasm, an understanding of the needs and wants of young people, and close proximity to new technologies. In addition, Chhatpar reasoned, half of the world's population is under the age of 25. By working with college students, businesses could see themselves through the lens of their future (young people), rather than their present and their past.

To validate his concept, Chhatpar partnered with another engineering student and entered BrainReactions into several business plan competitions. In 2003, the plan won fourth place in the G. Steven Burrill Technology Business Plan Competition at the University of Wisconsin. Inspired by the validation of his concept, Chhatpar decided to make BrainReactions his full-time vocation and launched it as a business when he graduated in the spring of 2004.

BrainReactions is now a for-profit entrepreneurial venture organizing brainstorming sessions for businesses. The company, which has developed a proprietary way of screening candidates to participate in the brainstorming sessions, has conducted sessions for a variety of organizations, including Intuit, Bank of America, Quantum Learning Network, the United Nations, and the U.S. Peace Corps. Through its online platform, BrainReactions is able to draw from campuses across the world to put together the ideal set of participants to tackle a company's specific needs. The participants have spanned a wide range of disciplines, including engineering, business, art, theater, music, political science, and journalism. In fact, in its brief history, the company has found that the simplest and most elegant ideas come from students outside engineering, which engineering students then further develop and build on. The deliverables to a participating company include an executive summary, a discussion of the most exciting ideas and themes that emerged from the brainstorming sessions, concept visualizations in the form of sketches and images, and a complete list of the ideas that were generated. The basic BrainReactions package costs $12,000, with an option to upgrade to a $19,800 premium package. The photo at the beginning of the chapter shows a typical BrainReactions brainstorming session. Anand V. Chhatpar is the person in the red shirt seated towards the middle of the group.

Chhatpar is enthused about the future of BrainReactions and the value it can provide to its clients. In terms of whether BrainReactions solves a legitimate business problem, the following client testimonial provides insight for your consideration:

> *You came up with some of the best ideas that we came up with during our brainstorms, plus you gave us lots of new ideas. Also, it's easy for me to get buy-in on these ideas because they're coming from our customers.*[1]
>
> –Zachary Lyons, Consumer Tax Product Development Team Intuit Inc.

Identifying and Recognizing Opportunities

Essentially, entrepreneurs recognize an opportunity and turn it into a successful business. An **opportunity** is a favorable set of circumstances that creates a need for a new product, service, or business. Most entrepreneurial ventures are started in one of two ways. Some ventures are externally stimulated. In this instance, an entrepreneur decides to launch a firm, searches for and recognizes an opportunity, and then starts a business, as Jeff Bezos did when he created Amazon.com. In 1994, Bezos quit his lucrative job at a New York City investment firm and headed for Seattle with a plan to find an attractive opportunity and launch an e-commerce company.[2] Other firms are internally stimulated. An entrepreneur

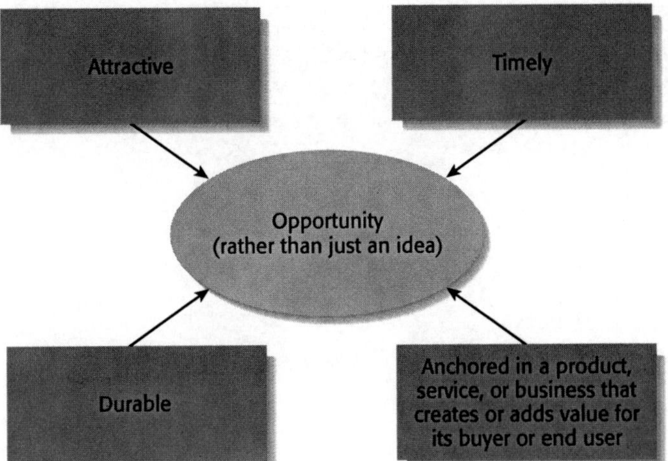

FIGURE 2.1

Four Essential Qualities of an Opportunity

recognizes a problem or an **opportunity gap** and creates a business to fill it. This was the case with BrainReactions.

Regardless of which of these two ways an entrepreneur starts a new business, opportunities are tough to spot. It is difficult to identify a product, service, or business opportunity that isn't merely a different version of something already available. A common mistake that entrepreneurs make in the opportunity recognition process is picking a currently available product or service that they like or are passionate about and then trying to build a business around a slightly better version of it. Although this approach seems sensible, such is usually not the case. The key to opportunity recognition is to identify a product or service that people need and are willing to buy, not one that an entrepreneur wants to sell.[3]

1. Explain why it's important to start a new firm when its "window of opportunity" is open.

As shown in Figure 2.1, an opportunity has four essential qualities: It is (1) attractive, (2) durable, (3) timely, and (4) anchored in a product, service, or business that creates or adds value for its buyer or end user.[4] For an entrepreneur to capitalize on an opportunity, its **window of opportunity** must be open.[5] The term *window of opportunity* is a metaphor describing the time period in which a firm can realistically enter a new market. Once the market for a new product is established, its window of opportunity opens. As the market grows, firms enter and try to establish a profitable position. At some point, the market matures, and the window of opportunity closes. This is the case with Internet search engines. Yahoo!, the first search engine, appeared in 1995, and the market grew quickly, with the addition of Lycos, Excite, Hotbot, AltaVista, and others. Google entered the market in 1998, sporting advanced search technology. Since then, the search engine market has matured, and the window of opportunity has essentially closed. Today, it would be very difficult for a new start-up search engine firm to be successful unless it was extraordinarily well funded and offered compelling advantages over already established competitors.

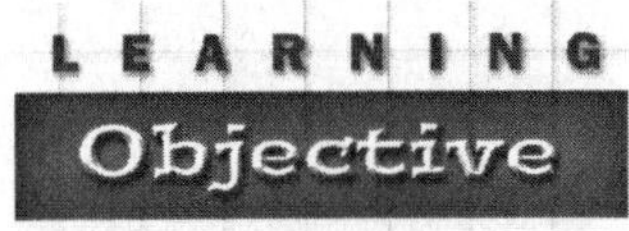

2. Explain the difference between an opportunity and an idea.

It is important to understand that there is a difference between an opportunity and an idea. An **idea** is a thought, an impression, or a notion.[6] An idea may or may not meet the criteria of an opportunity. This is a critical point because, as we noted in Chapter 1, many entrepreneurial ventures fail not because the entrepreneurs that launched them didn't work hard, but rather because there was no real opportunity to begin with. Before getting excited about a business idea, it is crucial to understand whether the idea fills a need and meets the criteria for an opportunity. When it doesn't, it can lead to a disappointing outcome, as illustrated in the boxed feature titled "What Went Wrong?"

Now let's look at the three ways to identify an opportunity, as depicted in Figure 2.2.

FIGURE 2.2

Three Ways to Identify an Opportunity

Observing Trends | Solving a Problem | Finding Gaps in the Marketplace

Planet Hollywood: An Idea Instead of an Opportunity

www.planethollywood.com

If a seemingly attractive new product or service idea consistently disappoints customers, it's almost sure to fail. The story of a Hollywood-themed restaurant that decided to focus on the lure of Hollywood rather than the quality of its food provides a vivid example of the importance of one of the four qualities of an attractive opportunity; namely, the opportunity must be anchored in a product or service that adds value for its buyer or end user.

In 1991, Planet Hollywood entered the restaurant industry. The idea was to create a Hollywood-themed restaurant chain, where visitors could catch a glimpse of their favorite movie stars. The initial investors, and presumably frequent diners at the restaurants, included Bruce Willis, Demi Moore, Whoopi Goldberg, Sylvester Stallone, and Arnold Schwarzenegger. The chain expanded rapidly and soon had 80 restaurants worldwide. Premier locations were secured in New York City, Chicago, and Los Angeles along with Paris, London, Sydney, and Tokyo.

Regrettably, the concept fell flat. The company has gone bankrupt twice. Although it is still on its feet, it has restaurants in only five U.S. cities. Interestingly, this concept seems to work better internationally in that there are about a dozen Planet Hollywood units located outside the United States. So how could a company with so much hype and so many famous people behind it flop so dramatically? Several things went wrong with Planet Hollywood, all tied to the basic notion that the concept may have been more of an idea than an opportunity to begin with.

First, there was the food. The company never advertised its food, and by most accounts, it was overpriced and average at best. Second, the lure of Planet Hollywood was to catch a glimpse of a movie star—if only for a moment. People would line up outside the restaurants and whisper to one another, "I wonder if Demi Moore or Whoopi Goldberg is inside?" But the stars rarely showed up—leaving guests disappointed. To compensate, the restaurants did display a lot of movie memorabilia. But this facet of Planet Hollywood's approach made it more of a one-time destination rather than a restaurant that people would frequent often.

So Planet Hollywood's customers would consistently overpay for average food and leave disappointed because they didn't see a movie star. As a result, in the end, the experience offered by the company failed one of the key tests of an opportunity: The idea wasn't anchored in a product that created enough value for its customers to represent a legitimate opportunity.

Questions for Critical Thinking

1. Evaluate Planet Hollywood's idea on all four dimensions of an opportunity. On a scale of 1 to 5 (5 is high), how does the idea that was launched as Planet Hollywood rate on each of the four dimensions?
2. If you have dined at a Planet Hollywood, describe your experience. What is your reaction to the food? Did your dining experience create value for you? If you have not dined at one of these units, find a friend who has done so and ask these questions.
3. When Planet Hollywood first started to struggle, what could the founders have done to try to revitalize the chain?
4. Are you surprised that Planet Hollywood turned out to be more of an idea than an opportunity? What, if anything, could the founders of the firm have done to create a different outcome?

Source: Planet Hollywood homepage, *www.planethollywood.com* (accessed June 5, 2006); Matt Haig, *Brand Failures* (London: Kogan Page, 2003).

Observing Trends

The first approach to identifying opportunities is to observe trends and study how they create opportunities for entrepreneurs to pursue. Economic factors, social factors, technological advances, and political action and regulatory statutes are the most important trends to follow. Changes in these areas often provide the impetus for a business opportunity. There are two ways entrepreneurs can get a handle on these trends. First, they can carefully study and observe them. Some entrepreneurs are better at this than others, depending on their personal characteristics and levels of motivation. Entrepreneurs who have industry experience, who have a well-established social network, who are creative, and who are, in general, alert are more likely to spot trends and interpret them correctly.[7] The second way entrepreneurs understand emerging trends is to purchase customized forecasts and market analyses from independent research firms. These tools allow for a fuller understanding of how specific trends create opportunities. Forrester Research, Gartner Group, and Yankee Group are some of the research firms that produce these reports, as illustrated in the boxed feature "Savvy Entrepreneurial Firm."

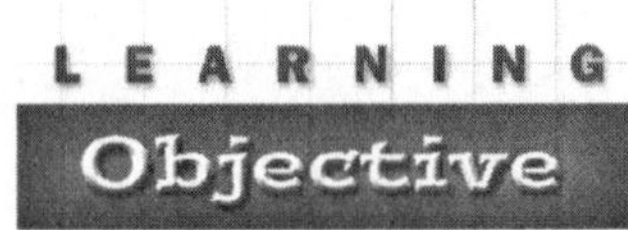

3. Describe the three general approaches entrepreneurs use to identify opportunities.

Getting High-Quality Advice on Emerging Trends

Savvy entrepreneurs realize they don't have the time and resources to know everything about emerging trends. This is particularly true of the entrepreneurs in the area of technology, where changes occur daily. So how do entrepreneurs keep up with the latest developments in their industry? Entrepreneurial firms can take advantage of the services offered by professional research firms, such as Forrester Research, Gartner, and Yankee Group. These companies provide conventional consulting services but also provide a variety of other products and services that may be more affordable to young entrepreneurial firms. For example, Forrester Research, which specializes in emerging technologies, offers the following:

- Annual memberships that provide access to research on specific business, industry, and technology topics
- Advisory and consulting services
- Access to global surveys pertaining to consumer attitudes toward and use of technology
- Peer-level executive program, forums, and hands-on boot camps

Other companies (e.g., Gartner) offer publications on emerging trends that can be downloaded from the Internet. The research is cutting-edge and may give a firm important insight that it never would have generated internally.

For entrepreneurial firms, an added benefit of using the services of consulting companies is getting an outside perspective on their current and potential operations. Prudent firms know that their time and field of vision is limited and that investing in a fresh perspective on business trends and developments can often be money well spent.

Questions for Critical Thinking

1. What disadvantages might an entrepreneurial firm experience by relying on outside firms for understanding emerging trends? Are some of these disadvantages more relevant in the short term while others are more relevant for the long term?
2. What options do entrepreneurs have for finding less expensive ways to collect the type of material supplied by a firm like Forrester Research or Gartner?
3. When might it be essential for entrepreneurs to rely on material prepared by an outside firm rather than on their own analysis?
4. Is it possible for aspiring entrepreneurs to become overwhelmed by the rapid pace of environmental changes? What advice would you offer to the person believing that change is too difficult to predict and understand?

Sources: Forrester Research homepage, www.forrester.com (accessed May 28, 2006); Gartner homepage, www.gartner.com (accessed May 28, 2006).

Figure 2.3 provides a summary of the relationship between the environmental factors mentioned previously and identifying opportunity gaps. Next, let's look at how each of these factors helps entrepreneurs spot business, product and service opportunity gaps.

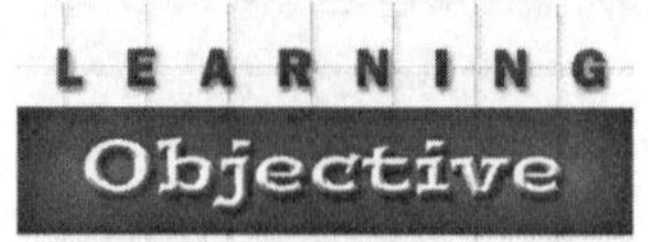

4. Identify the four environmental trends that are most instrumental in creating business opportunities.

Economic Forces Economic forces affect consumers' level of disposable income. When incomes are high, people are more willing to buy products and services that enhance their lives. Individual sectors of the economy have a direct impact on consumer buying patterns. For example, a drop in interest rates typically leads to an increase in new home construction and furniture sales. Conversely, a rapid decline in the stock market, such as the one in the late 1990s and early 2000s, may lead to a reduction in the demand for luxury goods.

When studying how economic forces affect opportunities, it is important to evaluate who has money to spend. For example, an increase in the number of women in the workforce and the subsequent increase in their disposable income is largely responsible for the number of boutique clothing stores targeting professional women that have opened in the past several years. Anne Fountaine and Tory Burch are examples of these boutiques competing on a national or international scale. Interestingly, a large number of boutiques are local entrepreneurial ventures with locations in a single community. Similarly, as more teens enter the workforce, demand increases for products they buy, such as designer clothing, MP3 players, and concert tickets. Sales of the Apple iPod, for example, took off so rapidly in part because teenagers have increasing levels of cash to spend.

Another trend that is affected by economic factors is pressure on firms to improve their economic performance. In a PricewaterhouseCoopers survey of fast-growth firms, which are companies identified in the media as the fastest-growing U.S. businesses over the past 5 years, 74 percent reported that cost control is one of their top priorities.[8] Many entrepreneurs have taken advantage of this trend by starting firms that help other firms control costs. In the chemical industry, for example, ChemConnect (founded in 1995) provides an online marketplace to make it less expensive for chemical companies to buy and sell chemicals on a global scale.[9]

FIGURE 2.3

Environmental Trends Suggesting Business or Product Opportunity Gaps

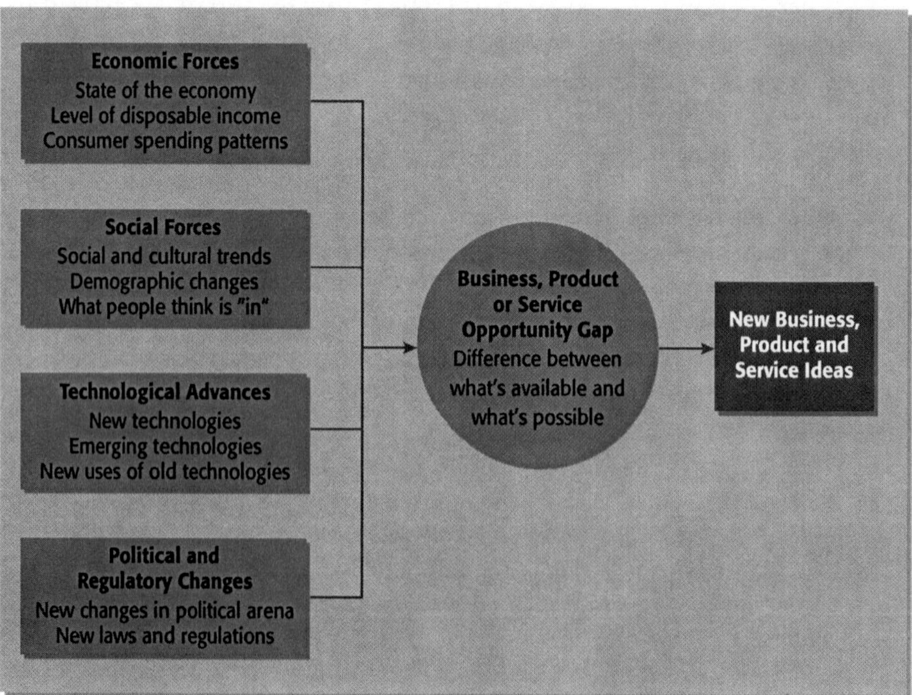

As baby boomers age, opportunities will grow for firms that provide unique products and services to this age group. Look for the resulting expansion of entrepreneurial opportunities in health care, organic food, insurance, travel and entertainment.

Social Forces An understanding of the impact of social forces on trends and how they affect new product, service, and business ideas is a fundamental piece of the opportunity recognition puzzle. The persistent proliferation of fast-food restaurants, for example, isn't due primarily to people's love of fast food but rather to the fact that people are busy—the number of households with both parents working remains high. Similarly, the Sony Walkman was developed not because consumers wanted smaller radios, but because people wanted to listen to music while on the move—while riding the subway, for example, and while exercising. The stress that many people experience while juggling work, family, and other activities provides opportunities for products and services that relieve stress. For example, the number of spa openings in the United States rose 12 percent from 2002 to 2004, with the fastest-growing segment being medical spas or wellness clinics. This increase is attributed to a jump in the number of people trying to deal with the stress in their daily lives, along with paying greater attention to mental health and wellness.[10] Additional recent social trends that allow for new opportunities are the following:

- Family and work patterns (e.g., the number of two-income households and the number of single-parent families)
- The aging of the population
- The increasing diversity in the workplace
- The globalization of industries
- The increasing focus on health care and fitness
- The proliferation of computers and the Internet
- The continual increase in the number of cell phone users
- New forms of music and other types of entertainment

There is an ebb and flow pertaining to how much each of these trends affects the availability of new opportunities. For example, although the number of households that have Internet access continues to grow, the window of opportunity to launch a new Internet search engine, as discussed previously, is essentially closed. Conversely, substantial opportunities may exist in other Internet-related areas, such as wireless Internet access, Web TV, and enhanced encryption software that secures the privacy of computer networks.

Technological Advances Advances in technology frequently dovetail with economic and social changes to create opportunities. For example, the creation of the cell phone is a technological achievement, but it was motivated by an increasingly mobile population that finds many advantages to having the ability to communicate with its co-workers, customers, friends, and families from anywhere and everywhere. Similarly, many e-commerce sites are technological marvels, allowing a customer to order products, pay for them, and choose how quickly they're shipped. But again, it isn't so much the technology that makes e-commerce attractive. The ultimate reason most people buy online is because they are busy and prefer to shop when they have free time rather than being restricted to traditional store hours and store locations.

In addition, technological advances often provide opportunities to help people satisfy basic needs in a better or more convenient way. In many areas people's needs don't change over time. For example, people who shave have always wanted to minimize the number of nicks and shaving time and get as close a shave as possible. These and other shaving-related desires will probably never change. What does change is the degree to which new technologies can better satisfy these needs and desires.

Another aspect of technological advances is that once a technology is created, products often emerge to advance it. For example, RealNetworks was launched to add video capabilities to the Internet, which took the Internet to the next level. The following quote from RealNetwork's Web site explains the impact that it is having on Internet users:

> In 1995, RealNetworks, Inc. pioneered the entire Internet media industry, and continues to fuel its exponential growth. Because the Internet was built to handle text-based information, not audio and video and other rich media, RealNetworks, Inc. foresaw the need for specific solutions that could handle the creation, delivery and consumption of media via the Internet. That led RealNetworks, Inc. to invent and release the RealPlayer and RealAudio in 1995. Today, hundreds of millions of RealPlayers that have been downloaded throughout the world take advantage of RealNetworks, Inc. world-class media creation, delivery and playback technology.[11]

Political Action and Regulatory Changes Political and regulatory changes also provide the basis for opportunities. For example, new laws create opportunities for entrepreneurs to start firms to help companies comply with these laws. RMS Systems, for example, designed a product called Compliance Suite, which helps its customers track their compliance with Environmental Protection Agency and Occupational Safety and Health Administration regulations. Many firms have benefited by helping others comply with the Sarbanes-Oxley Act of 2002, which requires certain companies to retain all business records, including electronic documents and messages, for at least 5 years. Since the act was put on the books, publicly held companies have spent millions of dollars to meet the new compliance rules. The beneficiaries have been software and hardware companies, which help companies store and manage this data.[12]

Political change also engenders new business and product opportunities. For example, global political instability and the threat of terrorism have resulted in many firms becoming more security conscious. These companies need new products and services to protect their physical assets and intellectual property as well as to protect their customers and employees. The backup data storage industry, for example, is expanding because of this new trend in the tendency to feel the need for data to be more protected than in the past. Companies such as Protect-Data.com and EMC provide data storage services that allow companies to back up their computer data in a secure off-site location.

Table 2.1 offers additional examples of changes in environmental trends that provided fertile soil for opportunities and subsequent concepts to take advantage of them.

Solving a Problem

The second approach to identifying opportunities is to recognize problems and find ways to solve them.[13] These problems can be recognized by observing the challenges that people encounter in their daily lives and through more simple means, such as intuition, serendipity, or chance.[14] There are many problems that have yet to be solved. Commenting

TABLE 2.1 Examples of How Changes in Environmental Trends Provide Openings for New Business and Product Opportunities

Changing Environmental Trend	Resulting New Business, Product, and Service Opportunities	Companies That Resulted
Economic Trends		
Teenagers with more cash and disposable income	Designer clothes, compact discs, MP3 players, games consoles, handheld computers	GAP, Banana Republic, MTV, Sega, Palm
Increased interest in the stock market	Online brokerage services, stock research services, magazines for investors	BuyAndHold.com, Motley Fool, The Street.com, *Business 2.0* magazine
Social Trends		
Increasing predominance of dual-income families leaves less time to cook at home	Restaurants, microwavable dinners, food delivery services	McDonald's, Stouffer's, Healthy Choice Frozen Dinners, Domino's Pizza, Dream Dinners
Increased interest in fitness, as the result of new medical information warning of the hazards of being overweight	Fitness centers, in-house exercise equipment, weight-loss centers, health food stores	Curves International, Stair Master Fitness Equipment, GNC Nutrition Center, Whole Foods Market, Wild Oats
Increased mobility of the population, as the result of better transportation and increased disposable incomes	Cell phones, laptop computers, handheld computers, phone cards	Nokia, Palm, Handspring, Research in Motion
Technological Trends		
Development of the Internet	E-commerce, improved supply chain management, improved communications	Yahoo!, Amazon.com, Google, Firefox, Travelocity, eBay, Overstock.com
Advances in biotechnology	Biotech-related pharmaceutical products, food products, veterinary products, information services	Genetech, Amgen, Genzyme, BioInform, Bio Online
Political and Regulatory Trends		
Increased EPA and OSHA standards	Consulting companies, software to monitor compliance, products to help ensure compliance	RMS Systems, PrimaTech, Compliance Consulting Services, Inc.

on this issue and how noticing problems can lead to the recognition of business ideas, Philip Kotler, a marketing expert, said:

> Look for problems. People complain about it being hard to sleep through the night, get rid of clutter in their homes, find an affordable vacation, trace their family origins, get rid of garden weeds, and so on. As the late John Gardner, founder of Common Cause, observed: "Every problem is a brilliantly disguised opportunity."[15]

Consistent with this observation, many companies have been started by people who have experienced a problem in their own lives, and then realized that the solution to the problem represented a business opportunity. For example, in 1991, Jay Sorensen dropped a cup of coffee in his lap because the paper cup was too hot. This experience led Sorensen to invent an insulating cup sleeve and to start a company to sell it. Since launching his venture, the company, Java Jacket, has sold over 1 billion cup sleeves.

Some business ideas are gleaned from the recognition of problems in emerging trends. For example, Symantec Corporation created Norton antivirus software to rid computers of viruses, and computer firewall firms such as McAfee developed software to secure computer systems and guard them against attack from hackers or unauthorized users. These companies took advantage of the problems that surface when new technology is introduced. At other times, the process is less deliberate. An individual may set out to solve a practical problem and realize that the solution may have broader market appeal. The most romantic example of this is the founding of Cisco Systems:

> The Cisco legend is the tale of two inhibited sweethearts at Stanford University in the late 1970s. Sandra Lerner of the Stanford University Business School and Leonard Bosack of the computer science department wanted to send love letters to each other via e-mail, but their respective departments used different computer networks. So Len and Sandy, impassioned and determined, invented the router—a mysterious black box consisting of a twist of cable and some agile software. Then they conceived Cisco (which is the last syllable in San Francisco, the city near where they lived). The router made Cisco the fastest-growing company ever. In 2004, 20 years after its founding, Cisco was worth $162 billion.[16]

At still other times, someone may simply notice a problem that others are having and think that the solution might represent an opportunity. Often, however, when you get the whole story, it turns out that the discovery wasn't quite so unanticipated. A **serendipitous discovery** is a chance discovery made by someone with a prepared mind.[17]

Newgistics, an entrepreneurial firm specializing in helping consumers return merchandise they order online and through catalogs is a good example of the serendipity that sometimes surrounds the launching of a new business. The firm was started by Phil Siegel, who had worked at Boston Consulting Group for a decade, where he had acquired a thorough understanding of consumer and retail businesses. Rod Adams, the venture capitalist who provided the early funding for the firm, tells of the auspicious conversation that led to the founding of Newgistics:

> Phil's idea for Newgistics grew out of a conversation with his wife, Lauren, a dedicated Internet and catalog shopper who relished the convenience of online buying. She'd just ordered a blouse from a well-known Internet retailer, and it didn't fit. Now, she'd have to e-mail the site, pack and ship the blouse, and wait until the merchant received it before getting credit toward another order. Why, Lauren lamented, did returning or exchanging these goods have to be so inconvenient? Why wasn't there a way to do it as easily as with a bricks-and-mortar retailer? Phil had a hunch that millions of online and catalog shoppers would second her concern. He resolved to start a company that would streamline the complex product return process—not just for the end consumer but for online and catalog retail merchants as well.[18]

There's no denying that Cartridge World helps solve a problem. Who hasn't cringed at the price of a new ink printer cartridge? A consumer can bring an empty ink cartridge to a Cartridge World store, wait while the cartridge is professionally refilled, and leave with a full cartridge at about half the price of a new one.

Newgistics offers Intelligent Returns Management, a service that provides catalog and Internet shopping customers a simple process for returning items by mail and getting credit for them. Among the first retailers to sign up for the service were Eddie Bauer, Spiegel, and J. Crew.

Newgistics received funding primarily because the company solves a specific problem. Many other colorful examples of people who launched businesses to solve problems are shown in Table 2.2.

There are opportunities that result from a combination of solving a problem and environmental trends. For example, in the mid-1980s, baby boomers (people born between 1945 and 1963) helped create a demand for golf-related products in the United States. This demographic group has been largely responsible for the popularity of golf in the 1980s, 1990s, and early 2000s. The first wave of baby boomers is now in their late 50s and early 60s, and research shows that golfers not only play more as they get older but that their overall spending on golf-related products increases.[19] This suggests that additional opportunities may be available for golf-related products—particularly those that are attractive to older golfers. Radar Golf, the subject of the "You Be the VC 2" feature at the end of the chapter, makes golf balls that have small electronic tags inside making them easy to find when lost. This is an example of a company that not only solves a problem—finding lost golf balls—but capitalizes on a societal trend—aging baby boomers and their interest in golf.

Finding Gaps in the Marketplace

The third approach to identifying opportunities is to recognize a need that customers have that is not being satisfied—by either large, established firms or entrepreneurial ventures. Large retailers like Wal-Mart, Costco, and Home Depot compete primarily on price by serving large groups of customers with similar needs. They do this by offering the most popular items targeted toward mainstream consumers. While this approach allows the large retailers to achieve economies of scale, it leaves gaps in the marketplace. This is the reason that small clothing boutiques and specialty shops exist. The small boutiques, which often sell designer

TABLE 2.2 Businesses Created to Solve a Problem

Entrepreneur(s)	Year	Problem	Solution	Name of Business That Resulted
Julie Aigner-Clark	1997	No method for exposing young children (six months to three years old) to arts and sciences	Created a company to produce videos designed to capture the attention and stimulate the minds of young children	Baby Einstein
Scott Cook	1982	Frustration over traditional process of paying bills and keeping track of personal finances	Developed a software program (Quicken) to make the task easier	Intuit
Lisa Druxman	2002	No fitness routine available to help new mothers stay fit and be with their newborns at the same time	Created a franchise organization that promotes a workout routine (which involves a 45-minute power walk with strollers) that mothers and their newborns can do together	Stroller Strides
Rob Glaser	1995	No way to play audio and video on the Internet	Developed software to play audio and video on the "Net"	RealNetworks
Fred Smith	1973	Inability to get spare parts delivered on a timely basis for his company, a jet aircraft sales firm	Started a new company to help others get packages delivered in a timely manner	Federal Express (now called FedEx)
Jerry Yang and David Filo	1994	No method to find or organize favorite Web sites	Created online directories to find and store favorites	Yahoo!

clothes or clothing for hard-to-fit people, are willing to carry merchandise that doesn't sell in large enough quantities for Wal-Mart or JC Penney to carry. For example, Adelita, a clothing boutique in Seattle, carries eclectic offerings from hard-to-find designers along with stylish handbags, lingerie, yoga wear, and upscale baby clothing. Adelita fills a gap in the marketplace by offering people with particular tastes a line of clothing they would be unlikely to find at a larger store that targets the needs of mainstream customers.

There are also gaps in the marketplace that represent consumer needs that aren't being met by anyone. These gaps are hard to recognize but offer potentially large rewards for those able to fill them. An example of a firm that recognized a gap that fits this profile is Curves International, which is the subject of Case 6.2 later in the book. Curves, which was founded in 1992 by Gary Heavin, is a fitness center just for women. At the time Curves was founded, most fitness centers targeted fitness enthusiasts and included a number of amenities, ranging from showers and towel service to swimming pools. Rather than compete head-to-head against these centers, Heavin opened a fitness center targeted towards an ignored part of the market: overweight women, 30 years old and older, who had never worked out before. Heavin believed that many women in this age group cared deeply about their health and appearance but didn't want to join a fitness center full of people who were already fit. He also felt that if he made the center affordable, which he did by cutting out many of the amenities, it would inspire women to give fitness a try. Heavin's idea was on the mark in that it represented a true opportunity. By targeting a market that had never been served before, Curves captured the attention of a large number of women and generated tremendous positive word of mouth. In fact, until recently, the company spent very little on advertising. Most of its new members come from referrals.[20]

Personal Characteristics of the Entrepreneur

LEARNING Objective

5. List the personal characteristics that make some people better at recognizing business opportunities than others.

How did Michael Dell come up with the idea of a "build it yourself" computer company? How did Howard Schultz, the founder of Starbucks, figure out how to turn a 50-cent cup of coffee and a little skimmed milk into a $3 plus cappuccino?

Researchers have identified several characteristics that tend to make some people better at recognizing opportunities than others. Before we talk about them, there is an important yet subtle difference between two key terms pertaining to this topic. We've already defined opportunity: a favorable set of circumstances that create the need for a new product, service, or business. But, the term **opportunity recognition** refers to the process of *perceiving* the possibility of a profitable new business or a new product or service. That is, an opportunity cannot be taken until it's *recognized*. Now let's look at some specific characteristics shared by those who excel at recognizing an opportunity.

Prior Experience Several studies show that prior experience in an industry helps entrepreneurs recognize business opportunities.[21] For example, a report of the *Inc.* 500 founders revealed that 43 percent of those studied got the idea for their new businesses while working for companies in the same industries.[22] This finding is consistent with research conducted by the National Federation of Independent Businesses.[23] There are several explanations. By working in an industry, an individual may spot a market niche that is underserved. It is also possible that while working in a particular area, an individual builds a network of social contacts in that industry that may provide insights that lead to opportunities.

Once an entrepreneur starts a firm, new venture opportunities become apparent. This is called the **corridor principle**, which states that once an entrepreneur starts a firm, he or she begins a journey down a path where "corridors" leading to new venture opportunities become apparent.[24] The insight provided by this principle is simply that once someone starts a firm and becomes immersed in an industry, it's much easier for that person to see new opportunities in the industry than it is for someone looking in from the outside.

Cognitive Factors Opportunity recognition may be an innate skill or a cognitive process.[25] There are some who think that entrepreneurs have a "sixth sense" that allows them to see opportunities that others miss. This sixth sense is called **entrepreneurial**

alertness, which is formally defined as the ability to notice things without engaging in deliberate search.[26] Most entrepreneurs see themselves in this light, believing they are more "alert" than others.[27] Alertness is largely a learned skill, and people who have more knowledge of an area tend to be more alert to opportunities in that area than others. A computer engineer, for example, would be more alert to needs and opportunities within the computer industry than a lawyer would be.

The research findings on entrepreneurial alertness are mixed. Some researchers conclude that alertness goes beyond noticing things and involves a more purposeful effort.[28] For example, one scholar believes that the crucial difference between opportunity finders (i.e., entrepreneurs) and nonfinders is their relative assessments of the marketplace.[29] In other words, entrepreneurs may be better than others at sizing up the marketplace and inferring the likely implications.

Social Networks The extent and depth of an individual's social network affects opportunity recognition.[30] People who build a substantial network of social and professional contacts will be exposed to more opportunities and ideas than people with sparse networks.[31] This exposure can lead to new business starts.[32] In a survey of 65 start-ups, half the founders reported that they got their business ideas through social contacts.[33] A similar study examined the differences between **solo entrepreneurs** (those who identified their business ideas on their own) and **network entrepreneurs** (those who identified their ideas through social contacts). The researchers found that network entrepreneurs identified significantly more opportunities than solo entrepreneurs but were less likely to describe themselves as being particularly alert or creative.[34]

An important concept that sheds light on the importance of social networks to opportunity recognition is the differential impact of strong-tie versus weak-tie relationships. Relationships with other people are called "ties." We all have ties. **Strong-tie relationships** are characterized by frequent interaction and ties between co-workers, friends, and spouses. **Weak-tie relationships** are characterized by infrequent interaction and ties between casual acquaintances. According to research in this area, it is more likely that an entrepreneur will get a new business idea through a weak-tie than a strong-tie relationship[35] because strong-tie relationships, which typically form between like-minded individuals, tend to reinforce insights and ideas the individuals already have. Weak-tie relationships, on the other hand, which form between casual acquaintances, are not as apt to be between like-minded individuals, so one person may say something to another that sparks a completely new idea.[36] An example might be an electrician explaining to a restaurant owner how he solved a business problem. After hearing the solution, the restaurant owner might say, "I would never have heard that solution from someone in my company or industry. That insight is completely new to me and just might help me solve my problem."

Creativity **Creativity** is the process of generating a novel or useful idea. Opportunity recognition may be, at least in part, a creative process.[37] On an anecdotal basis, it is easy to see the creativity involved in the formation of many products, services, and businesses.

For an individual, the creative process can be broken into five stages, as shown in Figure 2.4.[38] Let's examine how these stages relate to the opportunity recognition process.[39] In the figure, the horizontal arrows that point from box to box suggest that the creative process progresses through five stages. The vertical arrows suggest that if at any stage an individual (such as an entrepreneur) gets "stuck" or doesn't have enough information or insight to continue, the best choice is to return to the preparation stage—to obtain more knowledge or experience before continuing to move forward.

6. Identify the five steps in the creative process.

Preparation. Preparation is the background, experience, and knowledge that an entrepreneur brings to the opportunity recognition process. Just as an athlete must practice to excel, an entrepreneur needs experience to spot opportunities. Studies show that 50 to 90 percent of start-up ideas emerge from a person's prior work experience.[40]

FIGURE 2.4

Five Steps to Generating Creative Ideas

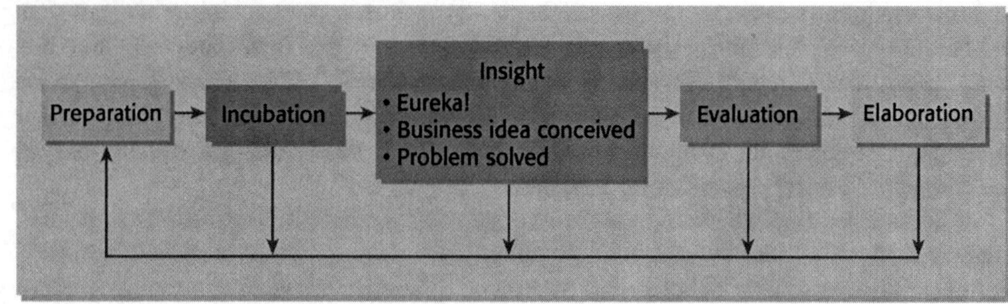

Incubation. Incubation is the stage during which a person considers an idea or thinks about a problem; it is the "mulling things over" phase. Sometimes incubation is a conscious activity, and sometimes it is unconscious and occurs while a person is engaged in another activity. One writer characterized this phenomenon by saying that "ideas churn around below the threshold of consciousness."[41]

Insight. Insight is the flash of recognition—when the solution to a problem is seen or an idea is born. It is sometimes called the "eureka" experience. In a business context, this is the moment an entrepreneur recognizes an opportunity. Sometimes this experience pushes the process forward, and sometimes it prompts an individual to return to the preparation stage. For example, an entrepreneur may recognize the potential for an opportunity but may feel that more knowledge and thought is required before pursuing it.

Evaluation. Evaluation is the stage of the creative process during which an idea is subjected to scrutiny and analyzed for its viability. Many entrepreneurs mistakenly skip this step and try to implement an idea before they've made sure it is viable. Evaluation is a particularly challenging stage of the creative process because it requires an entrepreneur to take a candid look at the viability of an idea.[42] The process of evaluating the feasibility of new business ideas is discussed in Chapter 3.

Elaboration. Elaboration is the stage during which the creative idea is put into a final form: The details are worked out and the idea is transformed into something of value, such as a new product, service, or business concept. In the case of a new business, this is the point at which a business plan is written.

Figure 2.5 illustrates the opportunity recognition process. As shown in the figure, there is a connection between an awareness of emerging trends and the personal characteristics of

FIGURE 2.5

The Opportunity Recognition Process

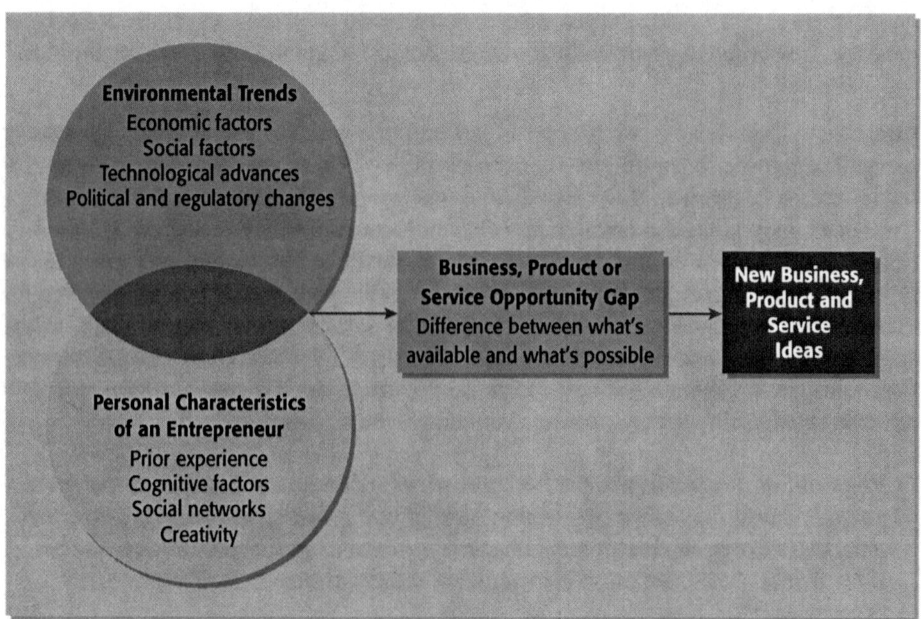

the entrepreneur because the two facets of opportunity recognition are interdependent. For example, an entrepreneur with a well-established social network may be in a better position to recognize emerging technological trends than an entrepreneur with a poorly established social network. Or the awareness of an emerging technology trend, such as digitization, may prompt an entrepreneur to attend conferences or workshops to learn more about the topic, expanding the social network.

Techniques for Generating Ideas

In general, entrepreneurs identify more ideas than opportunities[43] because many ideas are typically generated to find the best way to capitalize on an opportunity. Several techniques can be used to stimulate and facilitate the generation of new ideas for products, services, and businesses. Let's take a look at some of them.

Brainstorming

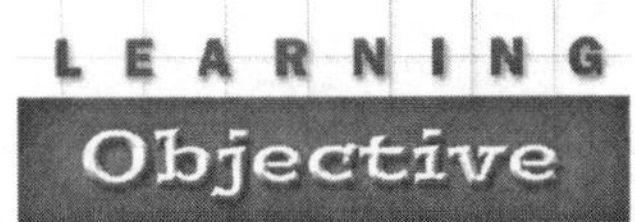

7. Describe the purpose of brainstorming and its use as an idea generator.

Brainstorming is used to generate a number of ideas quickly. It is not used for analysis or decision making—the ideas generated during a brainstorming session need to be filtered and analyzed, but this is done later. A brainstorming "session" is targeted to a specific topic about which a group of people are instructed to come up with ideas. The leader of the group asks the participants to share their ideas. One person shares an idea, another person reacts to it, another person reacts to the reaction, and so on. A flip chart or an electronic whiteboard is typically used to record all the ideas.

A productive session is freewheeling and lively. The main objective is to create an atmosphere of enthusiasm and originality where lots of ideas are generated.[44] However, there are four strict rules for conducting brainstorming sessions. If they are not adhered to, it is unlikely that the participants will feel comfortable openly sharing ideas:

- No criticism is allowed, including chuckles, raised eyebrows, or facial expressions that express skepticism or doubt. Criticism stymies creativity and inhibits the free flow of ideas.
- Freewheeling, which is the carefree expression of ideas free of rules or restraints, is encouraged; the more ideas, the better. Even crazy or outlandish ideas may lead to a good idea or a solution to a problem.

An increasing number of firms are using whiteboards to record ideas and conduct ongoing bronstorming sessions. Here, a Google employee adds a thought or suggestion to a permanent whiteboard at Google's headquarters.

- The session moves quickly, and nothing is permitted to slow down its pace. For example, it is more important to capture the essence of an idea than to take the time to write it down neatly.
- Leapfrogging is encouraged. This means using one idea as a means of jumping forward quickly to other ideas. (The word *leapfrogging* comes from the child's game of leapfrog, in which one player kneels down while the next in line leaps over him or her.)

There are two reasons brainstorming generates ideas that might not arise otherwise. First, because no criticism is allowed, people are more likely to offer ideas than they would in a traditional setting. Criticism is the act of passing judgment and typically stems from intolerance. For example, the manager of a retail store may be skeptical of the Internet. In a normal meeting, he might criticize any suggestion regarding its use. But if the store held a brainstorming session focused on ways to improve customer service, ideas about ways to use the Internet may surface and be discussed. Of course, an employee may be reluctant to suggest an idea that is directly counter to a known position of the boss even though no criticism in the brainstorming session is permitted. To avoid this complication, some firms conduct electronic brainstorming sessions by means of **group support system (or GSS) software**, which allows participants to submit ideas anonymously.

Second, brainstorming sessions can generate more ideas than a traditional meeting because brainstorming focuses on creativity rather than evaluation. Think about a typical meeting. One person suggests an idea, and immediately the rest of the group begins to evaluate it. This happens because most people are better at criticizing ideas than they are at suggesting new ones. The sole purpose of a brainstorming session is to generate ideas, with no evaluation permitted. So if a 2-hour brainstorming session is held, the group will spend 2 hours generating ideas, which almost never happens outside a brainstorming context.[45]

Most brainstorming sessions involve the employees of an organization, but Kodak, for example, hosts pizza-video parties where groups of customers meet with the company's technical people to discuss problems and needs and to brainstorm potential solutions. Similarly, some companies make brief brainstorming sessions a routine part of facility tours.[46]

Focus Groups

A **focus group** is a gathering of 5 to 10 people who are selected because of their relationship to the issue being discussed. Although focus groups are used for a variety of purposes, they can be used to help generate new business ideas.

The strength of focus groups is that they help companies uncover what's on their customers' minds through the give-and-take nature of a group discussion.[47] The weakness is because the participants do not represent a random sample, the results cannot be generalized to larger groups. Usually, focus groups are conducted by trained moderators. The moderator's primary goals are to keep the group "focused" and to generate lively discussion. It is also important that the moderator fully understand the underlying objectives of the study. Much of the effectiveness of a focus group session depends on the moderator's ability to ask questions and keep the discussion on track. For example, a retail establishment in which coffee is sold, such as Starbucks, might conduct a focus group consisting of 7 to 10 frequent customers and ask the group, "What is it that you *don't* like about our coffee shop?" A customer may say, "You sell 1-pound bags of your specialty ground coffees for people to brew at home. That's okay, but I often run out of the coffee in just a few days. Sometimes it's a week before I get back to the shop to buy another bag. If you sold 3-pound or 5-pound bags, I'd actually use more coffee because I wouldn't run out so often. I guess I could buy two or three 1-pound bags at the same time, but that gets a little pricey. I'd buy a 3- or 5-pound bag, however, if you'd discount your price a little for larger quantities." The moderator may then ask the group, "How many people here would buy 3-pound or 5-pound bags of our coffee if they were available?" If five hands shoot up, the coffee shop may have just uncovered an idea for a new product line.

partnering for *success*

The Growing Role of College Students in Helping Businesses Generate New Ideas

As firms of all sizes continue to search for new business ideas, one trend that is particularly interesting is the growing role of college students in helping businesses formulate new business ideas. This trend is exemplified by BrainReactions, the company featured in this chapter's Opening Profile. As you will recall, BrainReactions helps companies innovate new products, services, and marketing concepts by conducting brainstorming sessions with college students. The idea is that college students are enthused, creative, uninhibited, and understand the needs and wants of younger people—an important target customer group for many firms. College students are also up-to-date on new technologies and observe on a daily basis how technology affects people's lives.

While BrainReactions reaches out to companies to offer its services, companies also reach out to colleges and universities to accomplish the same objective. An example is Bold Furniture, a 2000 start-up. This venture is dedicated to designing office furniture that reflects its client's attitudes and cultures. Because the company is fairly young, it doesn't have the deep pockets needed to retain the help of professional design studios when developing new furniture lines. As a result, when the company wanted to design a new line of contemporary office furniture recently, instead of hiring professional help, it partnered with the University of Cincinnati's School of Design. Working with students to help generate new ideas turned out to be a good solution for the company. Commenting on the initiative, Bold Furniture co-owner Todd Folkert, 27, said:

> *Many designers require retainer fees, and that can be anywhere from a few thousand dollars a month to $10,000 a month. In addition, they'll look for royalties between one percent and five percent of sales. Working with the students, there's really not that significant of an up-front cost. It's pretty much all variable, tied to the success of the product.*

To compensate the university and the students for their work, Bold provides internship opportunities and future cash and royalties if the designs pan out.

Other companies are taking similar active roles in partnering with colleges and their students to generate design and product ideas. Recently, Ford Motor Company partnered with students at Carnegie Mellon University, which offers a master's degree in product development, to design interior features for the Ford Escape SUV. BodyMedia, an entrepreneurial start-up that makes body-monitoring devices for medical patients, has worked with several student design programs, including Carnegie Mellon's program. Commenting on his company's experience working with students on design projects, Chris Kasaback, BodyMedia's cofounder, said:

> *They (college design students) may not necessarily give you the next idea. But they help corroborate ideas you may have already been gravitating (toward), or help prove certain ideas aren't useful.*

Questions for Critical Thinking

1. In what ways do you think college students are uniquely capable of helping businesses innovate and come up with new product and service ideas? If you were the CEO of a company like Bold Furniture, would you consider partnering with a university college of design to help develop a new furniture line? What, if any, factors would have a bearing on your decision?
2. Many universities have internship programs that place students in businesses for the purpose of gaining practical experience. How can businesses use their interns to help generate new product and service ideas?
3. Go online and find another example of a business that partners with a college or university in a fashion similar to the companies described in the feature. Describe the partnership.
4. Find out if any of the academic units in your college or university partner with business organizations. Describe the nature of the partnerships and whether they help businesses, even in part, develop new product or service ideas.

Source: Chris Penttila, "Back to School," *Entrepreneur*, January 2006.

Some companies utilize hybrid focus group methodologies to achieve specific insights and goals. An example is "college drop-ins." This approach involves paying a pair of college students to host a party at their campus and providing them a budget to buy food and snacks. During the party, the hosts interview and videotape other students about specific market issues. Everything is up-front—the partygoers are told that the information is being collected for a market research firm (on behalf of a client). Most students are cooperative. One student, commenting on a college drop-in party he attended, said, "Everybody knows it costs a lot to throw a party and if all they have to do is give up 10 minutes of time to offer their opinions, it's a no-brainer!"[48]

Along with college drop-in parties, companies, across a wide spectrum are increasingly turning to college students to help generate new ideas. This subject is the focus of the "Partnering for Success" feature shown nearby.

Surveys

8. Describe how to use surveys to generate new business ideas.

A **survey** is a method of gathering information from a sample of individuals. The sample is usually just a fraction of the population being studied. Surveys can be conducted over the telephone, by mail, online, or in person. The most effective surveys sample a "random" portion of the population, meaning that the sample is not selected haphazardly or only from people who volunteer to participate. Instead, the sample is chosen in a way that ensures that everyone in the population has an equal chance of being selected, making the results of the survey generalizable to the larger population.

Surveys are taken in a standardized way so that every participant is asked the same questions in the same manner. The intention of a survey is not to describe the experiences or opinions of a particular individual, but rather to obtain a composite profile of the entire population. The quality of survey data is determined largely by the purpose of the survey and how it is conducted. For example, most call-in television surveys or magazine write-in polls are highly suspect because the participants represent what's called a **self-selected opinion poll**. Most people who take the time to participate in a self-selected opinion poll do so because they have either strong positive or strong negative feelings about a particular product or topic.[49]

Surveys generate new product, service, and business ideas because they ask specific questions and get specific answers. For example, a company such as Palm might administer a survey to a randomly selected sample of owners of Palm Pilots and ask the participants which of the following enhancements they would pay extra for if they were added to Palm Pilots: voice capabilities (e.g., a cell phone), text messaging, Internet access, paging, GPS capability, and so on. The survey might also ask how much extra the participants would be willing to pay for each enhancement and how likely it is that they would buy an enhanced product. Some surveys also include open-ended questions to provide the participants an opportunity to add information. For example, at the end of the survey, Palm might ask, "Is there any other product that our company might be uniquely capable of providing that we currently don't provide?" Although the answers to this question won't represent a scientific sample, they sometimes produce interesting leads to new product or service ideas.

Other Techniques

Firms use a variety of other techniques to generate ideas. Some companies set up **customer advisory boards** that meet regularly to discuss needs, wants, and problems that may lead to new ideas. For example, Johnson Controls, a global automotive systems and facility and management control systems company holds an annual event called the "Summit on Building Performance" to bring together customers and industry experts to better understand the impact of building performance on employee productivity.[50] Some advisory boards are conducted online to make it easier for the participants to meet. Other companies conduct varying forms of anthropological research, such as **day-in-the-life research**. A company that practices a variation of this technique is Chaparral Steel, which is an entrepreneurial-minded steel mini-mill. To make sure its customers are satisfied and to probe for new product ideas, the company routinely sends employees to the facilities of their customers.[51] A less expensive tool that some companies use to gain insights into their customer's lives and come up with new product ideas is IDEO Method Cards. IDEO is a design firm in California's Silicon Valley. IDEO Method Cards (which look like a deck of playing cards) show 51 of the methods that IDEO uses to come up with new product and service ideas. Each card has a picture on the front and a corresponding method for coming up with a new idea on the back. The cards are divided into four categories: learn, look, ask, and try. For example, one of the cards (in the look category) pictures an ordinary man on the front. The reverse side of the card, which provides instructions for how to use it, reads as follows:

> A DAY IN THE LIFE (REFERRING TO THE MAN IN THE PICTURE OR ANY OTHER USER OF A COMPANY'S PRODUCTS OR SERVICES)
>
> How: Catalog the activities and contexts that users (of your product) experience throughout an entire day.
>
> Why: This is a useful way to reveal unanticipated issues inherent in the routines and circumstances people experience every day.
>
> Example: IDEO asked potential wearers (or users) of a drug-delivery patch to document their daily behaviors including those that might affect the function of the patch—getting wet, snagging on clothing, etc.[52]

In addition to the techniques described above, some companies approach attendance at trade shows, conferences, and gatherings of industry personnel as intelligence missions to learn what their competition is doing and then use the information to stimulate new product and service ideas. Another technique for generating ideas is to set up an idea or suggestion program for employees. Important attributes of successful suggestion programs are processing suggestions rapidly, giving quality feedback, reacting to useful suggestions and ideas, and offering cash incentives. Suggestion programs vary in terms of their complexity, ranging from simple suggestion boxes to complex programs where ideas are placed in an idea bank for peer review and evaluation.

Encouraging and Protecting New Ideas

In many firms, idea generation is a haphazard process. However, entrepreneurial ventures can take certain concrete steps to build an organization that encourages and protects new ideas. Let's see what these steps are.

Establishing a Focal Point for Ideas

9. Explain the purpose of maintaining an idea bank.

Some firms meet the challenge of encouraging, collecting, and evaluating ideas by designating a specific person to screen and track them—for if it's everybody's job, it may be no one's responsibility.[53] Another approach is to establish an **idea bank** (or vault), which is a physical or digital repository for storing ideas. An example of an idea bank would be a password-protected location on a firm's **intranet** that is available only to qualified employees. It may have a file for ideas that are being actively contemplated and a file for inactive ideas. Other firms do not have idea banks but instead encourage employees to keep journals of their ideas.

Encouraging Creativity at the Firm Level

There is an important distinction between creativity and innovation. Innovation, as mentioned in Chapter 1, refers to the successful introduction of new outcomes by a firm. In contrast, creativity is the process of generating a novel or useful idea but does not require implementation. In other words, creativity is the raw material that goes into innovation. A team of employees may come up with a hundred legitimate creative ideas for a new product or service, but only one may eventually be implemented. Of course, it may take a hundred creative ideas to discover the one that ideally satisfies an opportunity.

An employee may exhibit creativity in a number of ways, including solving a problem or taking an opportunity and using it to develop a new product or service idea. Although creativity is typically thought of as an individual attribute, it can be encouraged or discouraged at the firm level.[54] The extent to which an organization encourages and rewards creativity affects the creative output of its employees.[55] Table 2.3 provides a list of actions and behaviors that encourage and discourage creativity at both the organizational level and the individual supervisor level.

Protecting Ideas from Being Lost or Stolen

Intellectual property is any product of human intellect that is intangible but has value in the marketplace. It can be protected through tools such as patents, trademarks, copyrights, and trade secrets, which we'll discuss in depth in Chapter 12. As a rule, a mere idea or concept does not qualify for intellectual property protection; that protection comes later when the idea is translated into a more concrete form. At the opportunity recognition stage, however, there are three steps that should be taken when a potentially valuable idea is generated:

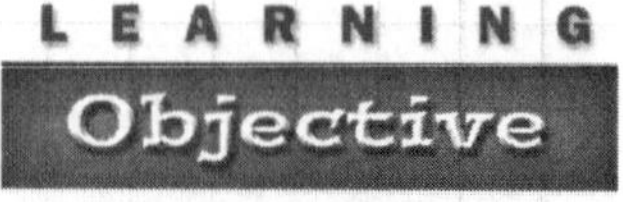

10. Describe three steps for protecting ideas from being lost or stolen.

Step 1 The idea should be put into a tangible form—either entered into a physical idea logbook or saved on a computer disk—and dated. When using a physical logbook, be sure that it is bound so that it cannot be alleged that a page was added. Make all entries in ink and have them witnessed. If an idea has significant potential, the signature of the person who entered the idea into the logbook and the witness should be notarized.

Putting the idea into tangible form is important for two reasons. First, if the idea is in concrete form, is original and useful, and is kept secret or is disclosed only in a situation where compensation for its use is contemplated, the idea may qualify as a "property right" or "trade secret" and be legally protected under a variety of statutes.

Second, in the case of an invention, if two inventors independently come up with essentially the same invention, the right to apply for the patent belongs to the first person who invented the product. A properly maintained idea log provides evidence of the date that the idea for the invention was first contemplated.

TABLE 2.3 Actions and Behaviors That Encourage and Discourage Creativity

Creativity Enhancers	
Organizational Level	Individual Supervisory Level
• Elevating creativity's importance throughout the organization • Offering tangible rewards to those generating new ideas • Investing in resources that help employees sharpen their creative skills • Hiring people different from those currently working in the company	• Listening attentively in order to acknowledge and provide early support to ideas • Dealing with employees as equals to show that status isn't very important • Speculate, be open, and build on others' ideas • Protecting people who make honest mistakes and are willing to learn from them
Creativity Detractors	
Organizational Level	Individual Supervisory Level
• Not attempting to hire creative people • Maintaining a "stiff" organizational culture with no room for different behaviors • Pigeonholing employees; keeping them in the same job for years • Promoting a mentality suggesting that the best solutions to all problems have already been found	• Being pessimistic, judgmental, and critical • Punishing mistakes or failed ideas • Being cynical or negative and insisting on early precision • Being inattentive, acting distant, and remaining silent when employees want to discuss new ideas

Source: Adapted from I. S. Servi, *New Product Development and Marketing* (New York: Praeger, 1990).

Once an invention demonstrates feasibility, a form called a "Disclosure Document," which describes an invention, can be filed with the U.S. Patent and Trademark Office. The purpose of the form is to provide evidence of the date of an invention's conception.[56]

Step 2 The idea, whether it is recorded in a physical idea logbook or saved in a computer file, should be secured. This may seem like an obvious step but is one that is often overlooked. The extent to which an idea should be secured depends on the circumstances. On the one hand, a firm wants new ideas to be discussed, so a certain amount of openness in the early stages of refining a business idea may be appropriate. On the other hand, if an idea has considerable potential and may be eligible for patent protection, access to the idea should be restricted. In the case of ideas stored on a computer network, access to the ideas should be at a minimum password protected.

Step 3 Avoid making an inadvertent or voluntary disclosure of an idea in a way that forfeits your claim to its exclusive rights. In general, the intellectual property laws seek to protect and reward the originators of ideas as long as they are prudent and try to protect the ideas. For example, if two co-workers are chatting about an idea in an elevator in a public building and a competitor overhears the conversation, the exclusive rights to the idea are probably lost.

In summary, opportunity recognition is a key part of the entrepreneurial process. As mentioned, many firms fail not because the entrepreneurs didn't work hard, but because there was no real opportunity to begin with.

Chapter Summary

1. Once an opportunity is recognized, a window opens, and the market to fill the opportunity grows. At some point, the market matures and becomes saturated with competitors, and the window of opportunity closes.
2. An idea is a thought, an impression, or a notion. An opportunity is an idea that has the qualities of being attractive, durable, and timely and is anchored in a product or service that creates value for its buyers or end users. Not all ideas are opportunities.
3. Observing trends, solving a problem, and finding gaps in the marketplace are the three general approaches entrepreneurs use to identify an opportunity.
4. Economic forces, social forces, technological advances, and political action and regulatory changes are the four environmental trends that are most instrumental in creating opportunities.
5. Prior experience, cognitive factors, social networks, and creativity are the personal characteristics that researchers have identified that tend to make some people better at recognizing business opportunities than others.
6. For an individual, the five steps in the creative process are preparation, incubation, insight, evaluation, and elaboration.
7. Brainstorming is a technique used to quickly generate a large number of ideas and solutions to problems. One reason to conduct a brainstorming session is to generate ideas that might represent product, service, or business opportunities.
8. A focus group is a gathering of 5 to 10 people who have been selected on the basis of their common characteristics relative to the issue being discussed. One reason to conduct a focus group is to generate ideas that might represent product or business opportunities.
9. An idea bank is a physical or digital repository for storing ideas.
10. The three main steps that can be taken to protect ideas from being lost or stolen are putting the idea into tangible form by such means as entering it in a logbook or saving it in a computer file, securing the idea, and avoiding making an inadvertent or voluntary disclosure of an idea in a manner that forfeits the right to claim exclusive rights to it if it falls into someone else's hands.

Key terms

Brainstorming
Corridor principle
Creativity
Customer advisory boards
Day-in-the-life research
Entrepreneurial alertness
Focus group
Group support system (or GSS) software
Idea
Idea bank
Intellectual property
Intranet
Network entrepreneurs
Opportunity
Opportunity gap
Opportunity recognition
Self-selected opinion poll
Serendipitous discovery
Solo entrepreneurs
Strong-tie relationships
Survey
Weak-tie relationships
Window of opportunity

Review Questions

1. What is a product opportunity gap? How can an entrepreneur tell if a product opportunity gap exists?
2. What is an opportunity? What are the qualities of an opportunity, and why is each quality important?
3. What four environmental trends are most instrumental in creating business opportunities? Provide an example of each environmental trend and the type of business opportunity that it might help create.
4. Explain how "solving a problem" can create a business opportunity. Provide an example that was not mentioned in the chapter of a business opportunity that was created in this way.
5. Explain how finding a gap in the marketplace can create a business opportunity.
6. What is meant by opportunity recognition?
7. In what ways does prior industry experience provide an entrepreneur an advantage in recognizing business opportunities?
8. What is the corridor principle? How does this corridor principle explain why the majority of business ideas are conceived at work?
9. What is entrepreneurial alertness?
10. In what ways does an extensive social network provide an entrepreneur an advantage in recognizing business opportunities?
11. Describe the difference between strong-tie relationships and weak-tie relationships. Is an entrepreneur more likely to get new business ideas through strong-tie or weak-tie relationships? Why?
12. Define creativity. How does creativity contribute to the opportunity recognition process?
13. Briefly describe the five stages of the creative process.
14. Explain the difference between an opportunity and an idea.
15. Describe the brainstorming process. Why is "no criticism" the number one rule for brainstorming?
16. Describe how a focus group is set up and how it is used to generate new business ideas.
17. Describe how surveys can be used to generate new business ideas.
18. What is a self-selected opinion poll? Are self-selected opinion polls an effective or an ineffective way to collect data to help generate new business ideas?
19. What is the purpose of an idea bank? Describe how an idea bank can be set up in a firm.
20. What are the three main steps to protect ideas from being lost or stolen?

Application Questions

1. Kevin, a software engineer, plans to write a memo to his boss describing an idea he has for a new software product. Kevin wants to convince his boss that his idea represents an opportunity the firm should pursue. In your opinion, what should Kevin put in the memo?

2. Melanie is very perceptive and believes she has identified an opportunity for a new business in the fashion industry. She wants to make sure, however, that she isn't just following a hunch—that the opportunity is sound. What criteria can Melanie use to determine whether she has identified an attractive opportunity?
3. Matrix Industries is interested in producing handheld devices similar to the products sold by Palm and Research In Motion. Jim Ryan, the founder of Matrix, remembers hearing about a concept called "window of opportunity." He asks you to explain the concept and how he can use it to help him make his decision. What do you tell him?
4. The "You Be the VC 1" feature focuses on Jingle Networks, a free 411 (directory assistance) service. Does Jingle Networks meet the tests of an opportunity (as opposed to an idea)? Justify your answer.
5. Kim is the founder of a small firm that produces highly specialized components for the semiconductor industry. Sales reps from both Forrester Research and Gartner have called to set up appointments with her to explain how their firms could help identify emerging opportunities that might translate into new product ideas for Kim's company. Keeping on top of emerging trends is important to Kim, and she knows that new product ideas are the lifeblood of high-tech firms. However, her busy schedule makes her reluctant to sit through two sales pitches. Kim explains this dilemma to you and asks whether you think she should take the time to meet with the sales reps. What is your answer?
6. Marshall Hanson, the founder of Santa Fe Hitching Rail, a chain of nine steak restaurants in New Mexico, is considering expanding his menu, which is currently restricted to steak, hamburger, potatoes, and fries. He has just read a book about entrepreneurship and learned that entrepreneurs should study social trends to help identify new product opportunities. List the social trends that might help Martin choose items to add to his menu. Given the trends you list, what items do you suggest Martin add?
7. Make a list of the three to five most compelling "technological advances" that have occurred in the United States or the world since you entered college. Think of at least two new product ideas that have emerged from each of these advances. To what extent do you believe each of these advances will continue to spawn new product ideas?
8. Recognizing a problem and proposing a solution to it is one way entrepreneurs identify opportunities. Think about your current activities as well as others in which you have an interest. Identify a problem with the activity you are considering and recommend a business to solve the problem.
9. Provide an example of a company that was started to fill a gap in the marketplace. Explain the nature of the gap that the company identified and describe how it is filling it.
10. Megan Jones owns a small chain of fitness centers in Kansas City. In general, her centers are successful, but she feels they are getting "stale" and could benefit from new ideas. Suggest to Megan some ways she could generate new ideas for her centers.
11. As mentioned in the chapter, "prior experience" in an industry helps entrepreneurs recognize business opportunities. This concept extends to prior experience in any aspect of life—whether it is in sports, music, or a volunteer activity. In what area or areas do you have a good amount of "prior experience"? How could this position you to start a business drawing on your experiences?
12. Make a list of your strong-tie and weak-tie relationships. (Include at least five names on each list.) Select two names from your list of weak-tie relationships, and speculate on the types of new business ideas that you think these individuals would be uniquely qualified to assist you with.
13. Tom Garrett, the manager of a midsize advertising agency, is planning to conduct several brainstorming sessions to identify new ideas for products and services to offer his clients. The first session is tomorrow, and Tom remembers from your résumé that you took an entrepreneurship class. He calls you into his office to ask whether you know anything about how to conduct brainstorming sessions. Using materials in this chapter, prepare an answer to Tom's question.
14. Delores Jones owns a company that produces a fat-free peanut butter named "Best Choice Peanut Butter." To learn of people's feelings about her product, she stamps an

invitation on each jar that reads, "If you'd like to tell me your opinion of Best Choice, send me a message at the following e-mail address." Is this an effective way to receive quality feedback from customers? In addition, Delores wants to know what other fat-free products her customers would be interested in and is considering sending a survey to 100 of her customers. Provide Delores advice about how to structure and administer the survey.

15. Freedom Electronics is a start-up with about 20 sales representatives. The company has a solid product line but knows that to remain competitive, it must continue recognizing opportunities for new products and services. The firm has not developed a systematic way for its sales staff to report new ideas. Suggest some ways that Freedom can record and protect the idea of its sales representatives.

you be the VC 2.1 Jingle Networks

www.jinglenetworks.com

Business Idea: Launch the first free national directory assistance service.

Pitch: As we write this "You be the VC" feature, placing a 411 (directory assistance) call costs you $1.25 if you are a Verizon customer. The same service costs $1.75 with T-Mobile and $3.49 if MCI is your carrier. Regardless of the carrier you are using, directory assistance is expensive.

Not anymore. Jingle Networks, through a service aptly named 1-800-FREE-411, is pioneering the first free to the consumer national directory assistance service. There are currently 6 billion 411 calls made every year in the United States, which represents an $8 billion market. What Jingle Networks has done is taken Google's advertising model and moved it to the telephone. The attractive thing about Google's advertising model is that it directs ads to people at the "point-of-sale." So, if you type "pizza" into the Google search engine, you'll see text ads for pizza restaurants in your area to the right of the search results.

To demonstrate how 1-800-FREE-411 works, here's a transcript of a 411 call you might place through the service. This short example illustrates how the service works for you, the consumer, and the company. Don't worry about manners—remember, you're talking to a computer!

1-800-FREE-411: Welcome to 1-800-FREE-411. What city and state please?

You: Chapel Hill, North Carolina

1-800-FREE-411: Are you looking for a business, government or residential listing?

You: Business

1-800-FREE-411: O.K. What listing?

You: Papa John's Pizza

1-800-FREE-411: While we search for your listing, I'd like to tell you about a great offer from Dominos. Connect now and you get three medium one-topping pizzas for just $5 each. To get connected to Dominos free of charge, press 1, to hear the number you originally requested, press 2.

Jingle Networks calls this short ad a "switch pitch." In early tests, callers have taken the switch pitch offer 6.2 percent of the time. In the cases where a caller asks for the name of a business and there aren't any 1-800-FREE-411 advertisers in the area to build a switch pitch around, the caller is put through to the business, free of charge, with a slight twist. When the call is connected, the person answering the phone hears a brief message that says, "You are receiving a call from 1-800-FREE-411." After the call is completed, someone from Jingle Network's telesales group calls the business to explain how the service works. In early trials, 13 percent of businesses that received a directory assistance call through the 1-800-FREE-411 service and were then contacted by Jingle Networks, eventually became advertisers on the network.

So take a few seconds right now and program 1-800-FREE-411 into your cell phone and give the service a try. With Jingle Networks, you'll never pay for directory assistance again.

Q&A: Based on the material covered in this chapter, what questions would you ask the firm's founders before making your funding decision? What answers would satisfy you?

Decision: If you had to make your decision on just the information provided in the pitch and on the company's Web site, would you fund this firm? Why or why not?

you be the VC 2.2 Radar Golf
www.radargolf.com

Business Idea: Place a tiny electronic tag inside golf balls to make them easy to find when lost.

Pitch: What is more frustrating than losing a ball during a round of golf? Not only does a lost ball cost a player a two-stroke penalty but looking for a ball slows down play on a golf course. Slow play is frustrating for all and reduces everyone's enjoyment of the game.

Radar Golf offers a solution to these problems. The company has developed a small electronic tag that can be built into a golf ball during the manufacturing process. The tagged ball looks, feels, and performs like a regular golf ball. When a ball is difficult to find, the golfer pulls out a handheld unit (that has also been developed by Radar Golf), turns it on, points it in the direction of interest, and begins walking toward the ball. Depending on the terrain, it works from up to 100 feet away. By moving the unit from left to right, a pulsed audio tone (from the handheld unit) provides information on ball location and distance. The golfer quickly walks in the direction of the ball, allowing it to be located within seconds. The system can be adapted to any brand of golf ball. Rather than manufacturing its own balls, Radar Golf plans to license its technology to golf ball manufacturers.

Radar Golf's system is intended to speed up play, improve the golfer's score, and provide an exciting new product to the $44 billion worldwide golf industry. It may also relieve a little of the frustration that most golfers experience on the golf course.

Q&A: Based on the material covered in this chapter, what questions would you ask the firm's founders before making your funding decision? What answers would satisfy you?

Decision: If you had to make your decision on just the information provided in the pitch and on the company's Web site, would you fund this firm? Why or why not?

CASE 2.1 Type 1 and Type 2 Tools and Flavorx: How Solving a Personal Problem Can Trigger the Recognition of a Promising Business Opportunity
www.type1tools.com; www.flavorx.com

Bruce R. Barringer,
University of Central Florida
R. Duane Ireland,
Texas A&M University

Introduction
Many business opportunities are recognized by people who are trying to find a way to solve a personal problem. The problem can arise in a person's job, because of financial issues, while participating in recreational and/or volunteer activities, or because of an issue affecting family. As many of us would agree, when a problem arises in a person's family for which there isn't an obvious solution, the need to find a solution can become urgent. In these instances, if a creative solution is found, it often represents a solution that other families, facing the same problem, might find useful. In some instances, the solution is compelling enough that it represents the basis for launching a new entrepreneurial venture.

This case provides examples of two firms that were started in this manner. In each case, the recognition of the business opportunity was triggered by a set of parents urgently trying to solve a problem for a member of their family.

Type 1 and Type 2 Tools
Doug and Lisa Powell, who are both graphic designers, live in the Minneapolis area with their two children. The Powells were a typical family until 2004, when their daughter Maya, who was seven at the time, got sick. The Powells took Maya to a doctor, who ran a few tests. Minutes later they were given heart-sinking news: Maya had Type 1 diabetes. Type 1 diabetes, formerly called "insulin-dependent" or "juvenile-onset" diabetes, develops in a very small percentage of children and young adults. A person with Type 1 diabetes has a pancreas that does not produce insulin, a hormone necessary to sustain life. Without insulin, food cannot be utilized by the body. To treat her condition, little Maya would have to prick her finger to test her blood and take insulin one or more times a day for the rest of her life. The reason for the permanent

Tools That Make it Easier for Young Diabetics to Embrace Healthy Eating Habits

FlashCarbs	FlashCarb Magnets	CarbWise Meal Worksheets
Colorful flashcards help kids and parents learn the carbohydrate counts of common food, making it easier to choose foods wisely	Colorful refrigerator magnets make it fun and easy to learn the carb counts of common foods and provide a quick reference while cooking	Preprinted Post-It notes simplify the process of counting carb choices and calculating the proper insulin dosages at mealtimes
Carb Count Stickers	**DataWise Logbook Set**	**Care Plan Worksheets**
Stickers can be used for labeling leftovers, school lunch items, or any foods packaged without nutritional information	Handy logbooks set contains a year's supply of books that can help parents record and track all diabetes-related data	Preprinted and customized worksheets help parents relay critical information and care directions to adults in charge

need to take insulin is that although taking it allows a person with diabetes to stay alive, it does not cure the disease.

As you can imagine, Doug and Lisa Powell initially felt overwhelmed. As the parents of a seven-year-old Type 1 diabetic, they needed to quickly learn how to calculate insulin dosages, administer shots, calculate the carbohydrate content in foods (which helps a diabetic regulate diet), understand the warning signs of possible trouble, and educate their family and friends about Maya's needs and daily regimens. At the same time, they tried to stay upbeat and reassuring in order to help Maya deal with her condition in a positive manner. They also tried to collect as much information as possible to share with Maya. They wanted their daughter to remain an independent, happy child who was able to care for herself.

To accomplish their goals, the Powells set out to try every device available to help Maya understand her condition and to help her cope with her daily regimen. They tried books, alarms, toys, games, medical alert bracelets, and other devices. After trying all of these items, they were struck by two things. First, almost everything they found related to Type 2 rather than Type 1 diabetes. Type 2 diabetes is more common in adults and represents about 90 percent of diabetes patients. Although the names "Type 1 diabetes" and "Type 2 diabetes" sound similar, they are distinctly different diseases. Many of the tools available for Type 2 diabetics don't work well for people with Type 1 diabetes. The second thing that the Powells noticed was that the vast majority of the material and devices they tried were emotionally cold and intimidating—particularly for a young child. They didn't see how using one or more of the various items could uplift Maya's spirits while teaching her about her disease.

Given what they had discovered, the Powells decided to take action. Using their skills as graphic designers, they started developing their own material to educate and encourage Maya. They developed prototypes of colorful and inviting flash cards, meal worksheets, forms, and charts. As Maya started using the material, the Powells observed how much the material helped her, both physically and emotionally. They started sharing the material with care providers, friends, and other parents whose children had Type 1 diabetes. The Powells were surprised by how positive the feedback was. As a result, they decided to launch their own firm, named Type 1 Tools, in order to share their materials with others on a more organized basis.

A sample of the types of products that Type 1 Tools sells is shown in the figure pictured above Word about the products quickly got out, and people with Type 2 diabetes started asking the Powells for similar material. The Powells obliged and refocused their company, renaming it Type 1 and Type 2 Tools, to help children and adults with both types of diabetes. The result—the company sold over $500,000 of Type 1 and Type 2 diabetes educational and motivational tools in 2005.

Flavorx

In 1992, Kenny Kramm's second daughter, Hadley, was born premature. As an infant, she developed a medical disorder that required her to take medicine four times a day. The medicine tasted awful, and it was difficult for Kramm and his wife to help Hadley keep it down. The Kramms grew increasingly concerned about this situation. Every time Hadley had a hard time keeping the medicine down, her conditioned worsened. "We were ending up in the emergency room on a weekly basis," Kramm recalls. The situation worsened. There was literally nothing that Hadley's doctors or nurses could do other than to urge the Kramms to help Hadley keep her medicine down—in any way they could.

In a funny twist of fate, Kenny Kramm worked in his parent's pharmacy. To help Hadley, Kenny and his father (a pharmacist for 40 years) started experimenting with concentrated flavors that could be mixed with Hadley's medicine to mask its bitter taste. Eventually, they produced a banana flavor concentrate that they were able to safely mix with the medicine; they were elated when Hadley started accepting the flavored medicine in its entirety. Almost immediately her condition stabilized, both medically and emotionally. Imagine the relief that Kramm and his wife also felt as a result of this positive turn of events.

Over the next 3 years, Kramm and his father continued to experiment with adding flavors to Hadley's various medicines. There were other medicine flavoring products available at the time, but none of them worked well enough to cover the bitter taste of most children's medications. Gradually, Kramm started seeing his pursuit as a business idea. Surely many others parents faced the same challenge that he and his wife had faced with Hadley, he thought. In 1995, he decided to incorporate and named the business Flavorx. To move the business forward, he partnered with one of the largest flavoring companies in the world to help develop custom flavors that could be safely mixed with medicines. After months of testing, Flavorx's first flavor additives were formally approved.

Flavorx's additives are now available in most pharmacies in the United States and are frequently used to improve the taste of both child and adult medicines. Medicines mixed with Flavorx's formulas not only taste better; they improve medicinal compliance and make it possible for some people to take their entire prescribed dosage. Not all Flavorx-treated medicines taste like candy, but they all make medicine taste better. Today, Flavorx offers over 40 flavors. In 2002, *Inc.* magazine reported that in 2001 Flavorx's sales were in the $1.8 million range. Flavorx is a private company and doesn't report its yearly earnings.

As for Hadley, her father's solution was just what she needed. From the time she took her first dose of banana-flavored medicine, she has never had another medicine-related hospital visit.

Discussion Questions

1. What similarities, other than the fact that they both involved medical challenges and children, do you see between the Flavorx and the Type 1 and Type 2 Tools' examples? What does each of these stories teach you about the opportunity recognition process?
2. In the chapter, an opportunity is defined as having the qualities of being (1) attractive, (2) durable, (3) timely, and (4) anchored in a product or service that creates value for its buyer or end user. To what extent do Type 1 and Type 2 Tools and Flavorx meet each of these tests of an opportunity?
3. Refer to the figure titled "Dream Dinners Recipe for Success: Passion, Market Opportunity, and the Skills to Make It Happen" that is pictured in Case 1.1 in the book's first chapter. Think about the point made in that case that resulted in the drawing of the figure—namely, that new businesses typically happen when three things converge: someone is passionate about an idea, a market opportunity for the idea exists, and the person with the idea has the skills to implement it. To what extent were all three of these factors present in the founding of Type 1 and Type 2 Tools and of Flavorx?
4. Why do you think that the types of products that Doug and Lisa Powell developed for Type 1 and Type 2 Tools weren't developed years earlier by a company that sells traditional diabetes treatment supplies? Similarly, why do you think that the products developed by Kenny Kramm weren't developed years earlier by an established drug company?

Application Questions

1. How could Type 1 and Type 2 Tools effectively use focus groups to develop additional diabetes-related products?
2. Think about a challenge in your own life that might represent a business opportunity. If you don't think of something right away, don't give up. Think about the challenges and problems that you have. All of us encounter problems and challenges in our everyday lives that might represent the basis of a promising business opportunity. Be prepared to describe to others the challenge and the business opportunity it presents.

Source: Type 1 Tools homepage (2006) (accessed May 10, 2006); Flavorx homepage (2006) (accessed May 10, 2006); *Minneapolis Star Tribune*. "Type 1 Tools: Helpful Resources for Families Struggling with Diabetes," January 18, 2004.

Intellifit: Is This an Opportunity or Just an Interesting Idea?
www.intellifit.com

Bruce R. Barringer,
University of Central Florida
R. Duane Ireland,
Texas A&M University

Introduction

What do great-fitting clothes and security scanning have in common? The answer: Small companies in both industries are licensing the same technology—the Millimeter Wave Holographic Scanning device. The technology, developed by the Pacific Northwest National Laboratory in Richland, Washington, provides a full-body, 360-degree imagery of a person in real time. *R&D* magazine named this technology the most promising innovation of 2004. The technology has many potential applications, such as security screening. In fact SafeView, a security company, has licensed the technology to build a glass booth that people can be asked to step into, and while standing in the booth, the technology can detect whether the person is carrying any weapons, explosives, plastics, or metals. The subject of this case, Intellifit, licensed the technology for an entirely different purpose. People can step into an Intellifit glass booth, and in 10 seconds, a scanner captures their exact body measurements. The measurements can then be compared to garment-sizing data from participating retailers, and in an instant, a person can know exactly what size of jeans will fit best at each retailer. Among other positive benefits, having this knowledge can save a great deal of time for the individual shopper.

Intellifit is currently deploying its system. Its potential customers include malls, large retailers like Levi's and Gap, and specialty retailers like bridal shops and plus-sized stores. Intellifit sees its system as the solution to a major source of frustration for shoppers—poor-fitting clothes. It also sees its system as a solution to a major problem for retailers—returns. The question, which at this point is too early to answer, is whether shoppers and retailers will actually use Intellifit's machines. In addition, the company can't be sure that the problem the firm has identified is compelling enough that shoppers and retailers, in large numbers, will take notice.

So, has Intellifit uncovered a genuine opportunity or does it just have some neat technology and an interesting idea? After reading the case, you decide.

Intellifit

Intellifit was launched in 1999 as Made4Me, a custom-clothing maker. The founder, Albert Charpentier, who is now Intellifit's CEO, felt there was a demand for custom-made clothing. To acquire customers, he sent out 4,000 kits, which included a tape measure, instructions for how to measure yourself, and instructions for how to order custom clothes. Only 40 kits were returned with measurements and orders for custom clothes, so the idea was dropped. In 2002, Charpentier changed the name of his company to Intellifit. Intellifit briefly pilot-tested, at David's Bridal chain and plus-size retailer Catherines, another approach for helping people get better-fitting clothes. This approach required a store's salesperson to use a tape measure to take 38 measurements of a customer's body and feed the measurements into a computer. The computer would then give customers a printout of their exact measurements. This approach was dropped, as retailers reported they didn't have enough salespeople to do the job and they were hesitant to put their customers through such a tedious ordeal. The next year, the scanning technology from the Pacific Northwest National Laboratory was acquired, and work on Intellifit's current measuring system was started.

Interestingly, Charpentier found out about the Pacific Northwest National Lab's technology while he was surfing the Internet one day looking for alternative body-scanning technologies he might use in his business. Intellifit's machine, named The Body Scanner took about 18 months to build and test.

The Body Scanner

The Body Scanner is a fairly generously sized glass booth that a person steps into fully clothed. All a person has to do is remove metal objects, like keys, coins, and cell phones, from pockets before being scanned. The scanner, which is no more invasive than going through a security scanner at an airport, uses safe, low-power radio waves to capture about 200,000 data points on a person's body. A computer in the booth then condenses and analyzes the data and prints out measurements that are accurate to within a quarter-inch. Depending on the retailers that participate, a young woman that gets scanned and is interested in buying jeans might get a printout that says she is a size 4 at Gap, a size 5 at American Eagle, a size 5 at Levi's, and a size 4 at Internet retailer Lands' End.

The technology utilized by Intellifit's system is much less cumbersome than other systems that have been developed to help people get a good fit. Some scanners require shoppers to enter a private booth and partially undress. These machines have never gained traction. Lands' End, the Internet and catalog retailer, introduced a virtual model in 1998. It lets customers try on clothes in a virtual environment (meaning a computer model of a person's body is made and the computer tries clothes on the model). It also lets people see how clothes would fit if they were thinner. To its credit, Lands' End reports that tens of thousands of people have utilized the service. Intellifit sees Lands' End's success as a validation that people will spend time trying to get a better fit. Of course, it also believes that its system is superior to what Lands' End uses.

Markets for Intellifit's Body Scanner

Intellifit has identified three potential market spaces for its Body Scanner.

1. *Malls.* Placing Body Scanners in common areas in malls and manning them with Intellifit employees is the first potential market space. The service would be free to consumers, but retailers would pay Intellifit a monthly fee to have their clothing measurements appear on the printouts. Intellifit could also use this service to collect "blind" data (meaning the data are only reported in aggregate form, no individual measurements are shown) to sell to retailers to help them better understand the most common sizes of shoppers, by age group or some other characteristic, in their areas.
2. *Retail chains.* Another potential market is to sell Body Scanners, which price out at about $50,000 a piece, to retail chains like Levi's and Gap. The chains could use the machines to help shoppers get a good fit and to differentiate themselves from their competitors. If the machines are heavily used, they could also help a retail chain control inventory, improve full-margin sell-through rates, and increase customer satisfaction by providing them with clothing items that fit properly.

3. *Specialty retailers.* The most realistic market, at the outset, may be specialty retailers, like bridal shops, plus-sized retailers, and tall-men clothing stores. These retailers serve people who are particularly concerned about a good fit. A specialty retailer like David's Bridal could advertise that it uses the Intellifit Body Scanning system so brides will be able to have their perfect dress fit perfectly!

An Idea or an Opportunity?

It's too early to tell how successful Intellifit will be. According to an Intellifit press release, Intellifit systems were purchased and placed into select Lane Bryant stores, Catherines stores, David's Bridal stores, and After Hours Formalware stores in late 2004. In fall 2005, Intellifit Body Scanning machines were placed in six malls in Pennsylvania. The first mall to receive the machine was the Willow Grove Park mall, just north of Philadelphia. An article in the *Philadelphia Inquirer* in September 2005 reported the comments of some shoppers who used the service in the mall—with mixed results. One teenager said, "American Eagle gave me too small of a size. It said I'm a double zero. I'm not a double zero, I'm a 2." Another shopper, the mother of a 15-year-old girl who was scanned by the Intellifit machine, said she hopes the data will help her minimize the number of items she buys for her daughter and has to return. Her only complaint was that many of her favorite retailers were not yet participating in the service. Having more stores carry the Intellifit machine would solve this complaint. In mid-2006, additional stores (such as Levi Stores in Washington D.C. and Dallas, Texas) were carrying Intellifit's product.

Discussion Questions

1. According to the chapter, what are the attributes of an opportunity? Use these attributes to evaluate Intellifit. Based on your evaluation, is Intellifit an opportunity or just an interesting idea?
2. What environmental trends are working in Intellifit's favor? If Intellifit has uncovered a promising business opportunity, what environmental trends have made Intellifit's system possible and potentially attractive to consumers?
3. On two previous occasions, Intellifit (as Intellifit and Made4Me) developed approaches for helping people get better-fitting clothes that didn't work out. What is different about Intellifit's current approach? What, if anything, gives Intellifit's current approach a better chance of succeeding?
4. Which of the three potential markets that Intellifit has identified for its device do you believe is the most promising? Which is the least promising? If Intellifit decides to place a large number of its machines in malls, how important is it that a large percentage of the retailers in the mall participate?

Application Questions

1. Think about the scanning technology that Intellifit licensed from the Pacific Northwest National Laboratory. To what uses, other than security scanning and helping people find better-fitting clothing, could this technology be applied?
2. Look at the "You Be the VC 2" feature, which focuses on Radar Golf, a company that helps people find golf balls. In your judgment, is Radar Golf a promising business opportunity? Explain the basis for your answer.

Sources: Intellifit homepage (accessed May 10, 2006); J. Graybeal, "Fit a Suit, Screen For Weapons," *Innovation: America's Journal of Technology Communications*, February/March, 2005; W. Tanaka, "Fit To Be Tried," *The Philadelphia Inquirer*, September 12, 2005; D. Clark, "Tech Devices Add Oomph to TV, Cars, Games," *The Wall Street Journal*, February 14, 2005.

Endnotes

1. BrainReactions homepage, www.brainreactions.com, (accessed May 30, 2006).
2. Amazon.Com Company Report, *Standard and Poor's Stock Report*, May 27, 2006; *Time*, "Amazing Person.com," December 27, 1999.
3. A. Ulwich, *What Customers Want* (New York: McGraw-Hill, 2005).
4. J. E. Cliff, P. D. Jennings, and R. Greenwood, "New to the Game and Questioning the Rules: The Experiences and Beliefs of Founders Who Start Imitative versus Innovative Firms," *Journal of Business Venturing* 21: (2006): 633–63; J. A. Timmons, "Opportunity Recognition," in *The Portable MBA in Entrepreneurship*, ed. W. D. Bygrave (New York: John Wiley & Sons, 1997), 27.
5. D. N. Sull, "The Three Windows of Opportunity," *Harvard Business School Working Knowledge*, June 6, 2005.
6. D. B. Audretsch and E. Lehmann, "Entrepreneurial Access and Absorption of Knowledge Spillovers: Strategic Board and Managerial Composition for Competitive Advantage," *Journal of Small Business Management* 44, no. 2, (2006): 155–166; *New Webster's Dictionary* (New York: Delair Publishing, 1981).
7. A. Ardichvili, R. Cardozo, and S. Ray, "A Theory of Entrepreneurial Opportunity Identification and Development," *Journal of Business Venturing* 18, no. 1 (2003): 105–23.
8. PricewaterhouseCoopers, "Fast Growth Companies Have Two Big Priorities, PricewaterhouseCoopers Finds," in *Trendsetter Barometer* (New York: PricewaterhouseCoopers, 2000).
9. M. Perin, "ChemConnect to Provide Energy Closing Prices to Dow Jones," *Houston Business Journal Online*, www.houston.bizjournals.com, February 15, 2006; S. H. Diorio, *Beyond "e": 12 Ways Technology Is Transforming Sales and Marketing Strategy* (New York: McGraw-Hill, 2002).
10. H. K. Kinnersley, "Searching for a Stress Buster," *The Wall Street Journal*, March 30, 2006, D6.
11. RealNetwork homepage, www.realnetworks.com (accessed June 5, 2006).
12. J. L. Koehn and S. C. DelVecchio, "Revisiting the Ripple Effects of the Sarbanes-Oxley Act," *The CPA Journal*, www.nysscpa.org, May 2006; Donna Fuscaldo, "For Tech Firms, Sarbanes-Oxley Provides Revenue Opportunities." *The Wall Street Journal*, December 1, 2004, B2A.
13. D. Smagalla, "The Truth About Software Startups," *MIT Sloan Management Review* (Winter 2004): 7.
14. D. A. Shepherd and D. R. DeTienne, "Prior Knowledge, Potential Financial Reward, and Opportunity Identification," *Entrepreneurship Theory and Practice* 29, no. 1 (2005): 91–112.
15. P. Kotler, *Marketing Insights from A to Z* (New York: John Wiley & Sons, 2003), 128.
16. Hoovers, www.hoovers.com (accessed June 24, 2004).
17. C. M. Crawford and C. A. Di Benedetto, *Product Management*, 6th ed. (Boston: Irwin McGraw-Hill, 2000).
18. R. Adams, *A Good Hard Kick in the Ass* (New York: Crown Business, 2002), 76.
19. C. Malta and L. Suttora *What to Sell on eBay* (New York: McGraw-Hill, 2006).
20. Curves homepage, www.curves.com (accessed May 22, 2006).
21. G. D. Markham and R. A. Baron, "Person–Entrepreneurship Fit—Why Some People Are More Successful as Entrepreneurs Than Others," *Human Resource Management Review* 13, no. 2 (2003): 281–301.
22. J. Case, "The Origins of Entrepreneurship," *Inc.*, June 1989.
23. A. C. Cooper, W. Dunkelberg, C. Woo, and W. Dennis, *New Business in America: The Firms and Their Owners* (Washington, DC: National Federation of Independent Business, 1990).
24. R. Ronstadt, "The Educated Entrepreneurs: A New Era of Entrepreneurial Education Is Beginning," *American Journal of Small Business* 10, no. 1 (1985): 7–23.
25. G. T. Lumpkin and B. B. Lichtenstein, "The Role of Organizational Learning in the Opportunity-Recognition Process," *Entrepreneurship Theory and Practice* 29, no. 4 (2005): 451–72.
26. I. M. Kirzner, *Perception, Opportunity, and Profit: Studies in the Theory of Entrepreneurship* (Chicago: University of Chicago Press, 1979).
27. S. A. Alvarez and J. B. Barney, "Entrepreneurial Alertness," in *The Blackwell Encyclopedia of Management—Entrepreneurship,* eds. M. A. Hitt and R. D. Ireland, (Malden, MA: Blackwell Publishing, 2005), 63–64.
28. C. M. Gaglio and J. A. Katz, "The Psychological Basis of Opportunity Identification: Entrepreneurial Alertness," *Small Business Economics* 16, no. 2 (2001): 95–111.

29. I. M. Kirzner, "The Primacy of Entrepreneurial Discovery," in *The Prime Mover of Progress*, ed. A. Seldon (London: Institute of Economic Affairs, 1980), 5–30.
30. G. Kingsley and E. J. Malecki, "Networking for Competitiveness," *Small Business Economics* 23, no. 1 (2004): 71–84.
31. A. C. Cooper and X. Yin, "Entrepreneurial Networks," in *The Blackwell Encyclopedia of Management—Entrepreneurship*, eds. M. A. Hitt and R. D. Ireland (Malden, MA: Blackwell Publishing, 2005), 98–100.
32. P. Davidsson and B. Honig, "The Role of Social and Human Capital among Nascent Entrepreneurs," *Journal of Business Venturing* 18, no. 3 (2003): 301–31.
33. R. H. Koller, "On the Source of Entrepreneurial Ideas," in *Frontiers of Entrepreneurship Research* (Wellesley, MA: Babson College, 1988), 194–207.
34. Hills et al., "Opportunity Recognition,"168–72.
35. R. P. Singh, G. E. Hills, R. C. Hybels, and G. T. Lumpkin, "Opportunity Recognition through Social Network Characteristics of Entrepreneurs," in *Frontiers of Entrepreneurship Research* (Wellesley, MA: Babson College, 1999), 228–38.
36. C. J. Medlin, "Self and Collective Interests in Business Relationships," *Journal of Business Research* 59, no. 7 (2006): 858–65; M. Granovetter, "The Strength of Weak Ties," *American Journal of Sociology* 78, no. 6 (1973): 1360–80.
37. A. Ardichvili, R. Cardozo, and S. Ray, "A Theory of Entrepreneurial Opportunity Identification and Development," *Journal of Business Venturing* 18, no. 1 (2003): 105–23.
38. J. J. Kao, *Entrepreneurship, Creativity, and Organization* (Upper Saddle River, NJ: Prentice Hall, 1989).
39. G. E. Hills, R. C. Shrader, and G. T. Lumpkin, "Opportunity Recognition as a Creative Process," in *Frontiers of Entrepreneurship Research* (Wellesley, MA: Babson College, 1999), 216–27.
40. W. Bygrave, "The Entrepreneurial Process," in *The Portable MBA in Entrepreneurship,* ed. William B. Bygrave (New York: John Wiley & Sons, 1997), 1–26.
41. M. Csikszentmihalyi, *Creativity* (New York: HarperCollins, 1996).
42. E. Edmonds and L. Candy, "Creativity, Art Practice, and Knowledge," *Communications of the ACM* 4, no. 10 (2002): 91–95.
43. J. S. Park, "Opportunity Recognition and Product Innovation in Entrepreneurial High-Tech Start-Ups: A New Perspective and Supporting Case Study," *Technovation* 2, no. 7 (2005): 739–52; R. P. Singh, *Entrepreneurial Opportunity Recognition* (New York: Garland Publishing, 2000).
44. E. F. Rietzschel, B. A. Nijstad, and W. Stroebe, "Productivity is Not Enough: A Comparison of Interactive and Nominal Brainstorming Groups on Idea Generation and Selection," *Journal of Experimental Social Psychology* 42, no. 2 (2006): 244–51.
45. R. G. Cooper, *Winning at New Products: Accelerating the Process from Idea to Launch*, 2nd ed. (Reading, MA: Addison-Wesley, 1993).
46. R. G. Cooper and S. J. Edgett, *Product Development for the Service Sector* (Cambridge, MA: Perseus Books, 1999).
47. American Statistical Association, *What Are Focus Groups?* (Alexandria, VA: American Statistical Association, 1997), 1.
48. S. Gold, "Have Insights, Will Party," *The Hub Magazine*, November 9, 2005, p. 18.
49. American Statistical Association, Web site section on survey research methods, www.bios.unc.edu/~kalsbeek/asa/survpamphlet.html (accessed June 3, 2002).
50. Johnson Controls homepage, www.johnsoncontrols.com (accessed June 5, 2006).
51. T. S. Foster, *Managing Quality: An Integrative Approach* (Upper Saddle, NJ: Prentice Hall, 2001).
52. IDEO homepage, www.ideo.com (accessed May 25, 2006).
53. A. Majchrzak, D. Logan, R. McCurdy, and M. Kirchmer, "Four Keys to Managing Emergence," *MIT Sloan Management Review* 47, no. 2 (2006): 14–18.
54. J. A. Goncalo and B. M. Staw, "Individualism-Collectivism and Group Creativity," *Organizational Behavior and Human Decision Processes* 100 (May 2006): 96–109.
55. S. H. Thomke, "Capturing the Real Value of Innovation Tools," *MIT Sloan Management Review* 47, no.2 (2006): 24–32; A. Cummings and G. R. Oldham, "Enhancing Creativity: Managing Work Contexts for the High Potential Employee," *California Management Review* 40, no. 1 (1997): 22–38.
56. United States Patent and Trademark Office, "Disclosure Document Program," www.uspto.gov/web/offices/pac/disdo.html (accessed June 4, 2002).

2 | Inside the Entrepreneurial Mind: From Ideas to Reality

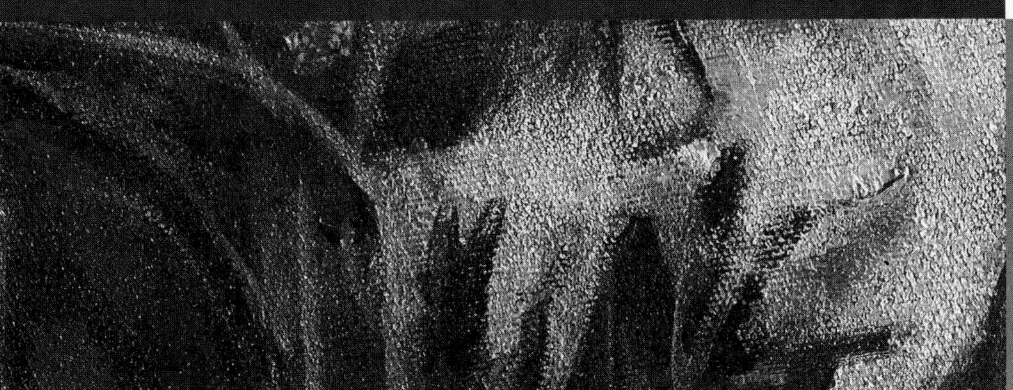

Imagination is the highest kite one can fly. —Lauren Bacall

Think left and think right and think low and think high. Oh, the thinks you can come up with if only you try. —Theodor Geisel (Dr. Suess)

Learning Objectives

On completion of this chapter, you will be able to do the following:

1. Explain the differences among creativity, innovation, and entrepreneurship.
2. Describe why creativity and innovation are such integral parts of entrepreneurship.
3. Understand how the two hemispheres of the human brain function and what role they play in creativity.
4. Explain the 10 "mental locks" that limit individual creativity.
5. Understand how entrepreneurs can enhance their own creativity and that of their employees as well.
6. Describe the steps in the creative process
7. Discuss techniques for improving the creative process.
8. Describe the protection of intellectual property through patents, trademarks, and copyrights.

One of the tenets of entrepreneurship is the ability to create new and useful ideas that solve the problems and challenges people face every day. Entrepreneurs achieve success by creating value in the marketplace when they combine resources in new and different ways to gain a competitive edge over rivals. From Alexander Fleming's pioneering work that resulted in a treatment for infections (penicillin) and the founders of the Rocket Chemical Company's fortieth try to create an industrial lubricant (WD-40) to Jeff Bezos' innovative use of the World Wide Web in retailing (Amazon.com) and Ted Turner's unique approach to the availability of television news (CNN), entrepreneurs' ideas have transformed the world.

As you learned in Chapter 1, entrepreneurs can create value in a number of ways—inventing new products and services, developing new technology, discovering new knowledge, improving existing products or services, finding different ways of providing more goods and services with fewer resources, and many others. Indeed, finding new ways of satisfying customers' needs, inventing new products and services, putting together existing ideas in new and different ways, and creating new twists on existing products and services are hallmarks of the entrepreneur!

Freitag Bags

Needing a waterproof bag to transport his art to class, Markus Freitag invited his brother Daniel to help design one. Using recycled truck tarpaulins, seatbelts, bicycle inner tubes, and airbags, the Freitags came up with a sturdy, creative product, one that has won numerous design awards and is sold worldwide.

Twenty-two-year-old Markus Freitag, who was studying in Zurich, Switzerland, rode his bike to art class every day. Because Zurich averages 127 rainy days a year, Freitag's sketches often got soaked on the trip. He searched for a messenger bag like the ones bicycle messengers in New York City use but could not find one. Recognizing a business opportunity, Markus and his brother Daniel, a graphic designer, sat down one evening to brainstorm ideas for a new waterproof messenger bag made from recycled materials. They decided to use seat belts as straps and bicycle inner tubes to insulate the bag's seams. "But we had no idea what to use for the bag itself," recalls Markus. As they talked, Markus looked out the kitchen window that overlooked autobahn A3 and saw trucks carrying cargo from Germany to Italy tucked safely underneath waterproof vinyl tarpaulins imprinted with bright logos. "How about those?" he asked, pointing to a passing truck. A short time later, Markus rode his bike to a Zurich truck depot, where he convinced the manager to let him have 30 square feet of discarded tarps, which he took home and soaked in the bathtub to remove the grime. He stitched together a bag on an industrial sewing machine he borrowed and sent the prototype to Daniel, who had moved to San Francisco. Daniel soon returned to Zurich, and the brothers transformed their apartment into a factory and warehouse for their bags. When their roommates began to complain, they decided to rent an actual warehouse. Demand for their bags took off when a Swiss newspaper printed a story on the Freitags and named their bags the cool product of the week. Today, the Freitags sell their messenger bags from their Web site and in 250 stores worldwide at prices ranging from $70 to $220. In addition to the satisfaction of building a successful business, the Freitags take pride in knowing that their first bag, the Top Cat, is on display in New York's Museum of Modern Art with the Apple iPod and other design classics.[1] Like many innovators, the Freitags created a successful business by taking several everyday items that had existed for many years and combining them in a different way.

Creativity, Innovation, and Entrepreneurship

LEARNING OBJECTIVES

1. Explain the differences among creativity, innovation, and entrepreneurship.

A recent study by the Small Business Administration found that small firms produce more economically and technically important innovations than larger firms.[2] What is the entrepreneurial "secret" for creating value in the marketplace? In reality, the "secret" is no secret at all: it is applying creativity and innovation to solve problems and to exploit opportunities that people face every day. **Creativity** is the ability to develop new ideas and to discover new ways of looking at problems and opportunities. **Innovation** is the ability to *apply* creative solutions to those problems and opportunities to enhance or to enrich people's lives. Harvard's Ted Levitt says that creativity is *thinking* new things, and innovation is *doing* new things. In short, entrepreneurs succeed by *thinking and doing* new things or old things in new ways. Simply having a great new idea is not enough; transforming the idea into a tangible product, service, or business venture is the essential next step. Management legend Peter Drucker says, "Innovation is the specific instrument of entrepreneurs, the means by which they exploit change as an opportunity for a different business or a different service."[3]

creativity
the ability to develop new ideas and to discover new ways of looking at problems and opportunities.

innovation
the ability to apply creative solutions to problems and opportunities to enhance or to enrich people's lives.

Successful entrepreneurs come up with ideas and then find ways to make them work to solve a problem or to fill a need. In a world that is changing faster than most of us ever could have imagined, creativity and innovation are vital to a company's success—and survival. That is true for businesses in every industry—from automakers to tea growers—and for companies of all sizes. However, creativity and innovation are the signatures of small, entrepreneurial businesses. Creative thinking has become a core business skill, and entrepreneurs lead the way in developing and applying that skill. In fact, creativity and innovation often lie at the heart of small companies' ability to compete successfully with their larger rivals. Even though they cannot outspend their larger rivals, small companies can create powerful, effective competitive advantages over big companies by "out-creating" and "out-innovating" them! If they fail to do so, entrepreneurs don't stay in business very long. Leadership expert Warren Bennis says, "Today's successful companies live and die according to the quality of their ideas."[4]

Sometimes innovation involves generating something from nothing. However, innovation is more likely to result from elaborating on the present, from putting old things together in new ways, or from taking something away to create something simpler or better. An experiment designed to improve the adhesive on tape resulted in a glue that hardly stuck at all. Although most researchers might have considered the experiment a total failure and scrapped it, this researcher asked a simple, creative question: What can you do with a glue when you take away most of its stickiness? The answer led to the invention of one of the most popular office products of all time: 3M's Post-it note™.

In many cases, creative ideas spring up from the most unexpected places. Edwin Land, one of America's most prolific inventors, credits his three-year-old daughter with the idea of the Polaroid camera. On a vacation trip in 1943, she asked why she couldn't see the photograph Land had just taken of her. During the next hour, as he walked around with his family, Land's mind was at work on his daughter's question. Before long, he had worked out the concept of building the camera that launched the era of instant photography, "The camera and the film became clear to me," Land recalls. "In my mind they were so real that I spent several hours describing them." Land's invention—instant photography—was so outlandish that only a child could conceive of it![5]

More often, creative ideas arise when entrepreneurs look at something old and think of something new or different. Legendary Notre Dame football coach Knute Rockne, whose teams dominated college football in the 1920s, got the idea for his constantly shifting backfields while watching a burlesque chorus routine! Rockne's innovations in the backfield (which included the legendary "Four Horsemen") and his emphasis on the forward pass (a legal but largely unused tactic in his era) so befuddled opposing defenses that his teams compiled an impressive 105-12-5 record. Similarly, military tacticians, needing better camouflage designs to protect troops and equipment in World War I, borrowed ideas from the "cubist" art of Picasso and Braque. Their improved camouflage patterns helped the Allies win the war.[6] More recently, one entrepreneur helped solve a problem that plagued U.S. troops in the deserts of Saudi Arabia and Kuwait during Desert Storm. U.S. military experts discovered that enemy aircraft were able to detect the location of troops and equipment by looking for the repeating patterns in the camouflage used to hide them. The entrepreneur began selling the military a special camouflage whose pattern never repeated. He developed it using technology he was already employing to produce multicolored, multipatterned area rugs (each one unique) for the home market.

Entrepreneurs also create innovations to solve problems they observe, often problems they face themselves.

Accentra

Running late for an important meeting with a venture capital firm where he was to make a pitch for $5 million for a chain of restaurants, Todd Moses picked up a stapler to staple the copies of his 19-page plan. On the first copy, the staple went only halfway through, and then it jammed completely, tearing the pages of the second copy. Trying to pull out the staple, Moses cut his finger and bled on the several other copies. Furious, he threw the stapler against the wall and went to his meeting where he apologized not only for being late, but also for being short of copies. That night, Moses thought back to the stapler. Because he once had worked for a hardware manufacturer, he recalled a reliable, easy-to-use, heavy-duty staple gun used in construction. Unable to sleep, he searched the Internet to see if anyone had invented a similar office stapler but found nothing. In the world of desktop staplers, "there wasn't much innovation," he says. The next morning, Moses tracked down Joel Marks, the designer of the spring-loaded mechanism used in the heavy-duty construction stapler, and convinced him to collaborate with Moses on an office version. Before long, they had designed a compact model that used less than one-fourth the force that a traditional office stapler required and was more reliable. Moses and Marks found a Taiwanese manufacturer to produce the new stapler and formed a company called Accentra to market the device, which they named the PaperPro. In just 40 days, Moses met with 120 distributors and convinced 119 of them, including industry giant Staples, to carry the PaperPro. Accentra now sells the PaperPro in more than 60 countries worldwide, generates $50 million in annual sales, and is preparing to introduce a new and improved hole puncher.[7]

Entrepreneurship is the result of a disciplined, systematic process of applying creativity and innovation to needs and opportunities in the marketplace. It involves applying focused strategies to new ideas and new insights to create a product or a service that satisfies customers' needs or solves their problems. It is much more than random, disjointed tinkering with a new gadget. Millions of people come up with creative ideas for new or different products and services; most of them, however, never do anything with them. Entrepreneurs are people who connect their creative ideas with the purposeful action and structure of a business. Thus, successful entrepreneurship is a constant process that relies on creativity, innovation, and application in the marketplace.

Innovation must be a constant process because most ideas don't work and most innovations fail. One writer explains, "Trial—and lots of error—is embedded in entrepreneurship."[8] Karen Anne Zien, co-founder of Polaroid Corporation's Creativity and Innovation Lab, estimates that for every 3,000 new product ideas, 4 make it to the development stage, 2 are actually launched, and only 1 becomes a success in the market. These new products are crucial to companies' success, however. According to Robert Cooper, a researcher who has analyzed thousands of new product launches, new products on average account for a whopping 40 percent of companies' sales.[9] Still, successful entrepreneurs recognize that many failures will accompany innovations, and they are willing to accept their share of failures because they know that failure is merely part of the creative process. Entrepreneurship requires business owners to be bold enough to try their new ideas, flexible enough to throw aside those that do not work, and wise enough to learn about what will work based on their observations of what did not. We now turn our attention to creativity, the creative process, and methods of enhancing creativity.

Creativity—A Necessity for Survival

LEARNING OBJECTIVES
2. Describe why creativity and innovation are such an integral part of entrepreneurship.

In this fiercely competitive, fast-faced, global economy, creativity is not only an important source for building a competitive advantage, but it also is a necessity for survival. When developing creative solutions to modern problems, entrepreneurs must go beyond merely relying on what has worked in the past. "A company that's doing all the things that used to guarantee success—providing quality products backed by great service, marketing with flair, holding down costs, and managing cash flow—is at risk of being flattened if it fails to become an engine of innovation," says one business writer.[10] Transforming their organizations into engines of innovation requires entrepreneurs to cast off the limiting assumptions, beliefs, and behaviors and to develop new insights into the relationship among resources, needs, and value. In other words, they must change their perspectives, looking at the world in new and different ways.

Entrepreneurs must always be on guard against traditional assumptions and perspectives about how things out to be because they are certain killers of creativity. Such self-imposed mental constraints and other paradigms that people tend to build over time push creativity right out the door. A **paradigm** is a preconceived idea of what the world is, what it should be like, and how it should operate. These ideas become so deeply rooted in our minds that they become immovable blocks to creative thinking, even though they may be outdated, obsolete, and no longer relevant. In short, they act as logjams to creativity. Look, for example, at the following illustrations and read the text aloud:

paradigm
a preconceived idea of what the world is, what it should be like, and how it should operate.

Paris	Once	A Bird
in the	in a	in the
the Spring time	a Lifetime	the Hand

If you're like most people, you didn't notice the extra word in each phrase ("Paris in the the spring time"). Why? Part of the reason is that we see what we expect to see! Past experiences shape the ways in which we perceive the world around us ("We've always done it this way"). That is why children are so creative and curious about new possibilities; society has not yet brainwashed them into an attitude of conformity, nor have they learned to accept *traditional* solutions as the *only* solutions. Retaining their creative "inner child," entrepreneurs are able to throw off the shackles on creativity and see opportunities for creating viable businesses where most people see what they've always seen (or, worse yet, see nothing).

Source: © 2002 Randy Glasbergen. www.glasbergen.com

Many years ago, during an international chess competition, Frank Marshall made what has become known as one of the most beautiful—and one of the most creative—moves ever made on a chess board. In a crucial game in which he was evenly matched with a Russian master player, Marshall found his queen under serious attack. Marshall had several avenues of escape for his queen available. Knowing that the queen is one of the most important offensive players on the chessboard, spectators assumed that Marshall would make a conventional move and push his queen to safety.

Using all the time available to him to consider his options, Marshall picked up his queen—and paused—and put it down on the most *illogical* square of all, a square from which the queen could easily be captured by any one of three hostile pieces. Marshall had done the unthinkable! He had sacrificed his queen, a move typically made only under the most desperate of circumstances. All the spectators—even Marshall's opponent—groaned in dismay. Then, the Russian, and finally the crowd, realized that Marshall's move was, in reality, a brilliant one. No matter how the Russian opponent took the queen, he would eventually be in a losing position. Seeing the inevitable outcome, the Russian conceded the game. Marshall had won the match in a rare and daring fashion: he had won by sacrificing his queen![11]

What lesson does this story hold for entrepreneurs? By suspending conventional thinking long enough to even consider the possibility of such a move, Marshall was able to throw off the usual paradigms constraining most chess players. He had looked beyond the traditional and orthodox strategies of the game and was willing to take the risk of trying an unusual tactic to win. The result: he won. Although not every creative business opportunity that entrepreneurs take will be successful, many who, like Frank Marshall, are willing to go beyond conventional wisdom will be rewarded for their efforts. Successful entrepreneurs, those who are constantly pushing technological and economic boundaries forward, constantly ask, "Is it time to sacrifice the queen?"

Merely generating one successful creative solution to address a problem or a need, however, usually is not good enough to keep an entrepreneurial enterprise successful in the long run. Success—even survival—in this fiercely competitive, global environment requires entrepreneurs to tap their creativity (and that of their employees) constantly. Entrepreneurs can be sure that if they have developed a unique, creative solution to solve a problem or to fill a need, a competitor (perhaps one six times zones away) is hard at work developing an even more creative solution to render theirs obsolete. This extremely rapid and accelerating rate of change has created an environment in which staying in a leadership position requires constant creativity, innovation, and entrepreneurship. A company that has achieved a leadership position in an industry but then stands still creatively is soon toppled from its perch as number one.

Can Creativity Be Taught?

For many years, conventional wisdom held that a person was either creative—imaginative, free-spirited, and entrepreneurial—or he or she was not. Therefore, some people were considered to be at the other end of the spectrum and were restrictively logical, narrow-minded, and rigid. Today, we know better. Research shows that *anyone* can learn to be creative. "Every person can be taught techniques and behaviors that help them generate more ideas," says Joyce Wycoff, author of several books on creativity.[12] The problem is that in most organizations, employees have never been expected to be creative. In addition, many businesses fail to foster an environment that encourages creativity among employees. Restricted by their traditional thinking patterns, most people never tap into their pools of innate creativity, and the company becomes stagnant. Creative exercises such as the one illustrated in Figure 2.1 can help adults to reconnect with the natural creativity they exhibited so willingly as children.

Not only can entrepreneurs and the people who work for them learn to think creatively, but they must for their companies' sake! "Innovation and creativity are not just for artists," says Wycoff. "These are skills with a direct, bottom-line payoff."[13]

COMPANY Profile

Capitol Concierge

For instance, Mary Naylor, owner of Capitol Concierge, a company that provides concierge services in office building lobbies, looks to an unusual source for new ideas about how to promote her business: junk mail. "I collect junk mail and keep it in a box I call 'Mary's Ideas,'" says Naylor. "I get inspiration from things most people throw away. When I want to kick start my creative processes, I go to my box and see what's new."[14]

Chun Hundred Chun Hundred Chun Hundred Chun Hundred Hundred	1111111 Lightly	Umph Umph Umph Of the Spirit	Grace.
Scholar	The Month Due	SPR ING	pitching
cucucucu	History, History, History, History, History, History, History, History, History, History,	Cover Agent	S H E E T
evil EVIL	1. C 6. C 2. O 7. R 3. U 8. I 4. N 9. S 5. T 10. T 11. O	Purchase	EQUITY
Tax]	Go It It It It	Blouse	Trehidasure
√Labor	_____ Cadet	A+AA-B+BB-C+CC-D+DD-E	W E B
B U R N B U R N	Roll Beethoven	KICKING Idea	0 B.S. M.S. Ph.D.
S T ONE	THAN life	Objection Ruled	Tomb of 210, N

FIGURE 2.1

How Creative Are You? Can You Recognize the Well-Known Phrases These Symbols Represent?

Before entrepreneurs can draw on their own creative capacity or stimulate creativity in their own organizations, they need to understand creative thinking.

Creative Thinking

LEARNING OBJECTIVES
3. Understand how the two hemispheres of the human brain function and what role they play in creativity.

Research into the operation of the human brain shows that each hemisphere of the brain processes information differently and that one side of the brain tends to be dominant over the other. The human brain develops asymmetrically, and each hemisphere tends to specialize in certain functions. The left-brain is guided by linear, vertical thinking (from one logical conclusion to the next), whereas the right-brain relies on kaleidoscopic, lateral thinking (considering a problem from all sides and jumping into it at different points). The left-brain handles language, logic, and symbols; the right-brain takes care of the body's emotional, intuitive, and spatial functions. The left-brain processes information in a step-by-step fashion, but the right-brain processes it intuitively—all at once, relying heavily on images.

Left-brained, vertical thinking is narrowly focused and systematic, proceeding in a highly logical fashion from one point to the next. Right-brained, lateral thinking, on the other hand, is somewhat unconventional, unsystematic, and unstructured, much like the image of a kaleidoscope whirling around to form one pattern after another. Right-brain driven, lateral thinking lies at the heart of the creative process. Those who have learned to develop their right-brained thinking skills tend to:

- Always ask the question, "Is there a better way?"
- Challenge custom, routine, and tradition.
- Be reflective, often staring out windows, deep in thought. *(How many traditional managers would stifle creativity by snapping these people out of their "daydreams," chastise them for "loafing," and admonish them to "get back to work?")*
- Be prolific thinkers. They know that generating lots of ideas increases the likelihood of coming up with a few highly creative ideas.
- Play mental games, trying to see an issue from different perspectives.
- Realize that there may be more than one "right answer."
- See mistakes and failures as mere "pit stops" on the way to success.
- See problems as springboards for new ideas.
- Relate seemingly unrelated ideas to a problem to generate innovative solutions.
- Have "helicopter skills," the ability to rise above the daily routine to see an issue from a broader perspective and then swoop back down to focus on an area in need of change.

Energy Conversion Devices

Stanford Ovshinsky, now 80, has used right-brained thinking to generate the ideas that have led him to earn an amazing 274 patents. Ovshinsky, who skipped college to become a tool-maker and machinist, used his first-hand knowledge of machinery to earn his first patent in the 1940s for a high-speed, automated machine tool he designed. His curiosity led him to study neurophysiology, from which he branched into a field known as disordered materials physics. In 1960, he founded a company, Energy Conversion Devices, that has produced low-cost solar-powered batteries, a rechargeable battery that powers hybrid-electric cars, rewritable CDs and DVDs, and many other important inventions. Most of his patents and his company's products derive from Ovshinsky's ability to translate his knowledge of unstructured elements and superconductivity into useful products that produce clean energy. "Most people think in two dimensions," says a long-time colleague. "Stan thinks not only in three dimensions but also in different colors."[15]

Although each hemisphere of the brain tends to dominate in its particular functions, the two halves normally cooperate, with each part contributing its special abilities to accomplish those tasks best suited to its mode of information processing. Sometimes, however, the two hemispheres may even compete with each other, or one half may choose not to participate. Some researchers have suggested that each half of the brain has the capacity to keep information from the other! The result, literally, is that "the left hand doesn't know what the right hand is doing." Perhaps the most important characteristic of this split-brain phenomenon is that an individual can learn to control which side of the brain is dominant in a given situation. In other words, a person can learn to "turn down" the dominant left hemisphere (focusing on logic and linear thinking) and "turn up" the right hemisphere (focusing on intuition and unstructured thinking) when a situation requiring creativity arises.[16] To get a little practice at this "shift," try the visual exercises presented in Figure 2.2. When viewed from one perspective, the picture in the middle portrays an attractive young lady with a feather in her hair and a boa around her shoulders. Once you shift your perspective, however, you will see an old woman with a large nose wearing a scarf on her head! This change in the image seen is the result of a shift from one hemisphere in the viewer's brain to the

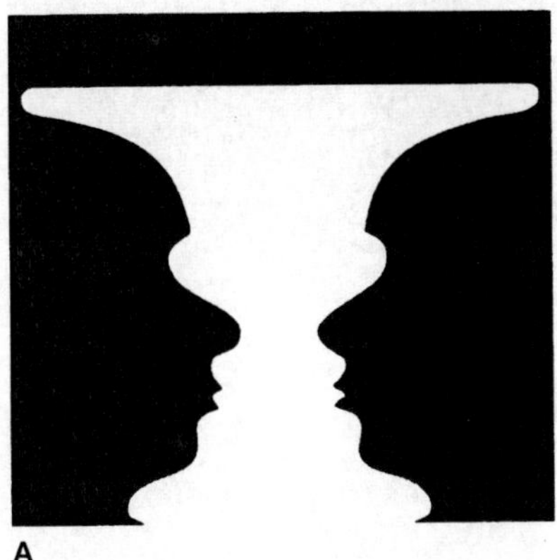

A

B

C

FIGURE 2.2

What Do You See?

Source: Thomas W. Zimmerer and Norman M. Scarborough, *Entrepreneurship and New Venture Formation*, © 1995. Reprinted by permission of Prentice Hall, Inc., Upper Saddle River, NJ.

other. With practice, a person can learn to control this mental shift, tapping the pool of creativity that lies hidden within the right side of the brain. This ability has tremendous power to unleash the creative capacity of entrepreneurs. The need to develop this creative ability means that exploring inner space (the space within our brains)—not outer space—becomes the challenge of the century.

Successful entrepreneurship requires both left- and right-brained thinking. Right-brained thinking draws on the power of divergent reasoning, which is the ability to create a multitude of original, diverse ideas. Left-brain thinking counts on convergent reasoning, the ability to evaluate multiple ideas and choose the best solution to a given problem. Entrepreneurs need to rely on right-brain thinking to generate innovative product, service, or business ideas. Then, they must use left-brain thinking to judge the market potential of the ideas they generate. Successful entrepreneurs have learned to coordinate the complementary functions of each hemisphere of the brain, using their brain's full creative power to produce pragmatic innovation. Otherwise, entrepreneurs, who rarely can be accused of being "half-hearted" about their business ideas, run the risk of becoming "half-headed."

How can entrepreneurs learn to tap their innate creativity more readily? The first step is to break down the barriers to creativity that most of us have erected over the years. We now turn our attention to these barriers and some suggested techniques for tearing them down.

You Be the Consultant

The Spirit of Entrepreneurship in the Olympics

With his innovative high jumping technique that became known as the Fosbury Flop, Dick Fosbury won an Olympic gold medal, set a new world record, and invented a new style of high jumping that athletes still use today.

Entrepreneurs aren't the only ones who use creativity to create competitive advantages for themselves. Throughout history, Olympic athletes have pushed back the frontiers of their sports by developing new techniques, improved training methods, and innovative solutions to existing problems. Two of the best examples of applying creativity to their sports are figure skater Sonja Henie and high jumper Dick Fosbury. Although their sports are at different extremes of the Olympic spectrum, both of these athletes relied on the creative process to throw off the paradigms that bound the other athletes competing in these sports.

Before Sonja Henie came along, figure skating routines were exactly that—routine. In competitions, skaters performed a series of precise moves that emphasized accuracy and control. But when the young Norwegian glided onto the ice, skating changed forever. Bringing the beauty and movement of ballet to the skating rink, Henie transformed the sport into the graceful combination of motion, music, and muscle that it remains today. From 1927 to 1936, Henie dominated ice skating by creatively blending her graceful ballet skills with her strength on the ice. She won 10 straight world championships, eight European titles, and a record three Olympic gold medals. Trained in both dance and ballet as a child, Henie cast aside the existing paradigms of what ice skating was as she recognized the possibilities of transferring dance movements onto the ice.

After winning her last world championship in 1936, Henie used her dance and skating skills to get into show business. She became an international star in movies and in traveling ice shows that gave her the freedom to use her creative genius on the ice. Even her glamorous and daring (for the 1930s) costumes proved to be an exciting innovation in ice skating as they emphasized the grace and flow of her movements. Later generations of ice skaters would push the sport even farther. Tenley Albright (1956 Olympics) and Peggy Fleming (1968 Olympics) introduced spins, twirls, and leaps. More recently, Tara Lipinsky, Kristi Yamaguchi, Nancy Kerrigan, Katarina Witt, and others have injected an element of gymnastics to ice skating, performing triple jumps and double and triple Axels. Yet every one of these champions owes a debt of gratitude to Sonja Henie, the daring young skater who had the creativity and the courage to make innovations on the ice.

Until 1968, much like ice skating, the sport of high jumping had changed little since its origins in ancient Greece. Athletes sprinted toward the bar and then leaped forward and upward, rolling over the bar face down. In the 1968 Olympics in Mexico City, Dick Fosbury revolutionized the sport with his innovative style of high jumping. He approached the bar at a different angle and then curved his body over the bar face *up*, kicking his legs over the end of the jump. Based on the principles of biomechanics, the "Fosbury Flop," as the style became known, transfers the weight of the jumper over the bar in stages. It also requires less energy and is more efficient. The result of Fosbury's innovation? An Olympic gold medal, a new world high jump record (Fosbury broke the old record by 6 cm), and the satisfaction of creating a new style of high jumping used by athletes across the world even today.

Sonja Henie and Dick Fosbury became champions by applying creativity and innovation to the sports they loved so much. Similarly, entrepreneurs can become "champions" in their industries by using their creative spirits to come up with new ideas, better products and services, and innovative techniques. Successful entrepreneurs rely on their ability to see the same things everyone else sees and to dream what no one else dreams.

1. What is a paradigm? How does a paradigm stifle creativity?
2. Work with a small group of your classmates to identify a local business that is bound by a paradigm. What impact is this paradigm having on the business? Identify the paradigm and then generate as many creative suggestions as you can in 20 minutes that would change this paradigm.
3. What can entrepreneurs do to throw off existing paradigms?

Source: "Innovations of the Olympic Games," *Fortune*, January 27, 1992, pp. 28–29.

Barriers to Creativity

LEARNING OBJECTIVES
4. Understand the 10 "mental locks" that limit individual creativity.

The number of potential barriers to creativity is virtually limitless—time pressures, unsupportive management, pessimistic co-workers, overly rigid company policies, and countless others. Perhaps the most difficult hurdles to overcome, however, are those that individuals impose on themselves. In his book *A Whack on the Side of the Head*, Roger von Oech identifies 10 "mental locks" that limit individual creativity[17]:

1. ***Searching for the one "right" answer.*** Deeply ingrained in most educational systems is the assumption that there is one "right" answer to a problem. The average student who has completed four years of college has taken more than 2,600 tests; therefore, it is not unusual for this one-correct-answer syndrome to become an inherent part of our thinking. In reality, however, most problems are ambiguous. Depending on the questions one asks, there may be (and usually are) several "right" answers.

COMPANY Profile

Jacksonville, Florida

When Jacksonville, Florida, city officials bid to host Super Bowl XXXIX, they knew that they had to overcome a huge obstacle: a lack of high-end hotel rooms. Their creative solution was to dock cruise ships along the St. Johns River to serve as floating hotels. The result of their creative thinking? Jacksonville became the smallest city ever to host a Super Bowl game.

When representatives from Jacksonville, Florida, made a proposal to the National Football League (NFL) to host the 2005 Super Bowl, they knew that they had to overcome one major disadvantage: a lack of high-end hotel space, always a key factor in the NFL's bid requirements. The team's approach was based on the assumption that there was more than one right answer to providing upscale hotel space, and they came up with an innovative solution: they would dock cruise ships along the St. Johns River that would serve as floating hotels, putting guests within easy walking distance of the football stadium! Shortly after the meeting, NFL officials named Jacksonville the host city for the 2005 Super Bowl, making it the smallest city ever to host the big game.[18]

2. ***Focusing on "being logical."*** Logic is a valuable part of the creative process, especially when evaluating ideas and implementing them. However, in the early imaginative phases of the process, logical thinking can restrict creativity. Focusing too much effort on being logical also discourages the use of one of the mind's most powerful creations: intuition. Von Oech advises us to "think something different" and to use nonlogical thinking freely, especially in the imaginative phase of the creative process. Intuition, which is based on the accumulated knowledge and experiences a person encounters over the course of a lifetime and resides in the subconscious, can be unlocked. It is a crucial part of the creative process because using it often requires one to tear down long-standing assumptions that limit creativity and innovation.

Charles Arntzen

Charles Arntzen is an entrepreneur who challenges traditional assumptions, and his efforts may revolutionize the concept of immunization and save millions of lives around the world. Arntzen, who grew up on a farm before earning his Ph.D. in molecular biology at Purdue University and working at DuPont and the U.S. Department of Agriculture, traveled to Bangkok, Thailand, where he was touring the city's famous floating market. As he watched hundreds of farmers selling their harvest from wooden boats in the Klong canals, he noticed a mother feeding her infant a banana. From his travels, Arntzen knew that worldwide 30 million infants go without basic immunizations each year and that 3 million of those children die from preventable diseases. As he watched the infant eat the banana, Arntzen thought: What if that banana could immunize the infant against disease? When he returned home, Arntzen began to work on his idea of incorporating vaccines into food. If he could engineer plants to produce specific proteins that would cause the human body to produce protective antibodies, he could eliminate the need to acquire, refrigerate, and transport fragile vaccines, an especially critical problem for poor nations. Within weeks, Arntzen had uncovered enough supporting research to prove that his idea could work. "I was looking for a way to combine my agricultural expertise with human medicine," he says. Arntzen has invested $5 million to develop potatoes and tomatoes that can serve as vaccines and is searching for the $20 million more he needs to finance the clinical trials required by the Food and Drug Administration. "We're trying to create a new paradigm [that] could save millions of lives," he says.[19]

3. ***Blindly following the rules.*** We learn at a very early age not to "color outside the lines," and we spend the rest of our lives blindly obeying such rules. Sometimes, creativity depends on our ability to break the existing rules so that we can see new ways of doing things. Consider, for example, the top row of letters on a standard typewriter or computer keyboard:

Qwertyuiop

In the 1870s, Sholes & Company, a leading manufacturer of typewriters, began receiving numerous customer complains about its typewriter keys sticking together when typists' fingers were practiced enough to go really fast. Company engineers came up with an incredibly creative solution to eliminate the problem of sticking keys. They designed a less efficient keyboard configuration, placing the letters O and I (the third- and sixth-most-commonly used letters of the alphabet) so that the weakest fingers (the ring and little fingers) would strike them. By slowing down typists with this inefficient keyboard, the engineers solved the sticking-keys problem. Today, despite the fact that computer technology has eliminated all danger of sticking keys, this same inefficient keyboard configuration remains the industry standard!

4. ***Constantly being practical.*** Imagining impractical answers to "what if" questions can be powerful stepping stones to creative ideas. Suspending practicality for a while frees the mind to consider creative solutions that otherwise might never arise. Whenever Thomas Edison hired an assistant to work in his creative laboratory, he would tell the new employee, "Walk through town and list 20 things that interest you." When the worker returned, Edison would ask him to split the list into two columns. Then he would say, "Randomly combine objects from column A and column B and come up with as many inventions as you can." Edison's methods for stimulating creativity in his lab proved to be successful; he holds the distinction of being the only person to have earned a patent every year for 65 consecutive years![20]

   Periodically setting aside practicality allows entrepreneurs to consider taking a product or a concept from one area and placing it in a totally different application.

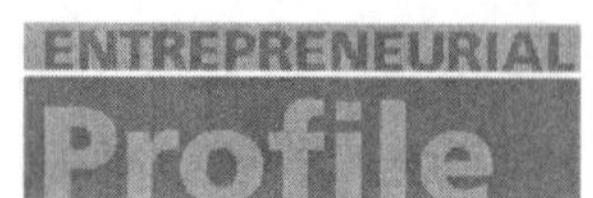

Richard Rawls

Richard Rawls, who once owned a company that sold firefighting foam, recognized that fire-retardant foams sometimes failed to work because they evaporated or slid off the vertical surfaces of the buildings they were designed to protect from flames. He began exploring the possibility of using fire-retardant gels to solve the problem, eventually settling on a gel made from a superabsorbent plastic called polyacrylate. He got the idea from a disposable diaper! The fibrous material in those diapers, which can hold as much as 1,000 times its weight in water, turns into a thick goo when it gets wet—the perfect way to protect a structure from fire. Experimenting in his backyard, Rawls modified the mixture to come up with the right gel consistency. Fire departments across the country have added the fire-retardant gel to their arsenal of fire-fighting weapons.[21]

5. ***Viewing play as frivolous.*** A playful attitude is fundamental to creative thinking. There is a close relationship between the "haha" of humor and the "aha" of discovery. Play gives us the opportunity to reinvent reality and to reformulate established ways of doing things. Children learn when they play, and so can entrepreneurs. Watch children playing and you will see them invent new games, create new ways of looking at old things, and learn what works (and what doesn't) in their games.

   Entrepreneurs can benefit from playing in the same way that children do. They, too, can learn to try new approaches and discover what works and what doesn't. Creativity results when entrepreneurs take what they have learned at play, evaluate it, corroborate it with other knowledge, and put it into practice. Encourage employees to have fun when solving problems; they are more likely to push the boundaries and come up with a genuinely creative solution if they do. What kind of invention would Wile E. Coyote, who seems to have an inexhaustible supply of ideas for catching Road Runner in those cartoons, create in this situation? How might the Three Stooges approach this problem? What would Seinfeld's Kramer suggest? A group of fundraisers was discussing the plans for an upcoming annual fund-raising banquet, which had been the organization's primary source of income for many years. Lamenting the declining turnout over the last several years and the multitude of other organizations that were using banquets as a source of revenue, one officer jokingly said, "Maybe we should have a 'nonbanquet,' where people pay not to tie up several hours, eat rubber chicken, and listen to some dull speaker talk about a topic they'd rather not hear about." The other officers laughed at the idea initially and then began throwing in humorous ideas of their own. The group mustered the courage to try out their creative solution, and their "nonbanquet" was a tremendous success. It raised more money than the organization had ever generated before, and no one had to attend!

6. ***Becoming overly specialized.*** Defining a problem as one of "marketing" or "production" or some other area of specialty limits the ability to see how it might be related to other issues. Creative thinkers tend to be "explorers," searching for ideas outside their areas of specialty. The idea for the roll-on deodorant stick came from the ballpoint pen. The famous Mr. Potato Head toy was invented by a father sitting with his family at the dinner table who noted how much fun his children had playing with their food. Velcro was invented by a man who, while hiking one day to take a break from work, had to stop to peel sticky cockleburs from his clothing. As he picked them off, he noticed how their hooked spines caught on and held tightly to the cloth. When he resumed his hike, he began to think about the possibilities of using a similar design to fasten objects together. Thus was born Velcro!

Liquid Paper Company

Betty Nesmith Graham wanted to become an artist, but after a divorce left her with her young son to raise alone, Graham took a job as an executive secretary shortly after World War II. A dedicated employee, Graham began searching for a way to correct her typing mistakes. (Remember that this was before computers were commonplace, and typewriters were the only "word processors.") Recalling how artists often paint over their mistakes, Graham thought that typists might be able to paint over their errors as well. At home, she mixed up a batch of tempera water-based paint to match the stationery her company used and used it to paint over her typing mistakes. Her boss never noticed, but another secretary did and asked for a bottle of the mixture. Graham found a green bottle at home, put some of the correcting fluid in it, and labeled it "Mistake Out." Soon other secretaries were clamoring for the product, and from her north Dallas home, Graham started the Mistake Out Company (later changing the name to the Liquid Paper Company). She turned her kitchen into a small factory, where her son Michael (who went on to be a star in the 1960s music group, The Monkees) helped her pour the concoction into small bottles. When her boss fired her, Graham turned her part-time, home-based business into a full-time venture, eventually selling it in 1980 for $47.5 million.[22]

7. ***Avoiding ambiguity.*** Ambiguity can be a powerful creative stimulus; it encourages us to "think something different." Being excessively detailed in an imaginative situation tends to stifle creativity. Ambiguity, however, requires us to consider at least two different, often contradictory notions at the same time, which is a direct channel to creativity. Ambiguous situations force us to stretch our minds beyond their normal boundaries and to consider creative options we might otherwise ignore. Although ambiguity is not a desired element when entrepreneurs are evaluating and implementing ideas, it is a valuable tool when they are searching for creative ideas and solutions. Entrepreneurs are famous for asking a question and then going beyond the first answer to explore other possible answers. The result is that they often find business opportunities by creating ambiguous situations.

Tom and Sally's Handmade Chocolates

Copreneurs Tom and Sally Fegley, owners of Tom and Sally's Handmade Chocolates, considered the possibility of other answers to the question, "What uses exist for chocolate sauce?" Although most people see chocolate sauce merely as a topping for ice cream or other desserts, their friend Larry (whom they have nicknamed "Dirty Larry") came up with a different idea. The Fegleys were trying to come up with an innovative recipe that would keep going their string of awards at a local fund-raising event devoted to celebrating chocolate, the Brown-Out. Their fun-loving friend suggested they shoot for the Most Decadent Award. "I'll go naked," he said. "You paint melted chocolate all over my body, and you'll win!" Although the Fegleys declined Larry's offer, his suggestion got them thinking. Before long, Tom had whipped up a batch of chocolate dessert topping, labeled it "Chocolate Body Paint," and included the following directions on the bottle: "Heat to 98.6 degrees, apply liberally, and let your imagination run wild." Today, Chocolate Body Paint is the Fegley's best-selling product, and it has won awards and has been featured in publications ranging from the *Wall Street Journal* to *Playboy* magazine. "Never judge an idea by its source," advises Sally.[23]

8. ***Fearing looking foolish.*** Creative thinking is no place for conformity! New ideas rarely are born in a conforming environment. People tend toward conformity because they don't want to look foolish. The fool's job is to whack at the habits and rules that keep us thinking in the same old ways. In that sense, entrepreneurs are top-notch "fools." They are constantly questioning and challenging accepted ways of doing things and the assumptions that go with them. The noted entrepreneurship theorist Joseph Schumpeter wrote that entrepreneurs perform a vital function—"creative destruction"— in which they rethink conventional assumptions and discard those that are no longer useful. According to Schumpeter, "The function of entrepreneurs is to reform or revolutionize the pattern of production by exploiting an invention or, more generally, an untried technological possibility for producing a new commodity or producing an old one in a new way, by opening up a new source of supply of materials or a new outlet for products, by reorganizing an industry or so on."[24] In short, entrepreneurs look at old ways of doing things and ask, "Is there a better way?" By destroying the old, they create the new.

    One way in which entrepreneurs often engage in creative destruction is by reversing their thinking. For example, one agricultural entrepreneur had been trying to solve a common problem that automatic picking machines have when picking the fruit from apple trees. The machines, which are quite efficient at picking apples growing on the outer limbs of the trees, often miss or damage the fruit growing on the inner limbs. For years, he worked to develop a machine with the dexterity to pick apples in both locations but to no avail. Finally, this entrepreneur reversed his thinking and began to focus his efforts, not on the picking machine, but *on the apple tree*! Working with horticulturists, he was able to develop a new breed of tree whose fruit grew only on the outer limbs, where standard picking machines could easily get to it! By reversing his thinking, he solved the problem and created a new business opportunity.

9. ***Fearing mistakes and failure.*** Creative people realize that trying something new often leads to failure; however, they do not see failure as an end. It represents a learning experience on the way to success. As you learned in Chapter 1, failure is an important part of the creative process; it signals entrepreneurs when to change their course of action. Entrepreneurship is all about the opportunity to fail! Many entrepreneurs failed numerous times before they succeeded. Despite their initial setbacks, they were able to set aside the fear of failure and kept trying.

   The key, of course, is to see failure for what it really is: a chance to learn how to succeed. Entrepreneurs who willingly risk failure and learn from it when it occurs have the best chance of succeeding at whatever they try. Charles F. Kettering, a famous inventor (he invented the lighting and ignition systems in automobiles, among other things), explains, "You fail because your ideas aren't right, but you should learn to fail intelligently. When you fail, find out *why* you failed and each time it will bring you nearer to the goal."[25] Successful entrepreneurs equate failure with innovation rather than with defeat.

10. ***Believing that "I'm not creative."*** Some people limit themselves because they believe creativity belongs only to the Einsteins, Beethovens, and da Vincis of the world. Unfortunately, this belief often becomes a self-fulfilling prophecy. A person who believes he or she is not creative will, in all likelihood, behave that way and will make that belief come true. Many people who are considered geniuses, visionaries, and inventors actually are no smarter and have no more innate creative ability than the average person; however, they have learned how to think creatively and are persistent enough to keep trying until they succeed.

    Successful entrepreneurs recognize that "I'm not creative" is merely an excuse for inaction. *Everyone* has within him or her the potential to be creative; not everyone will tap that potential, however. Successful entrepreneurs find a way to unleash their creative powers on problems and opportunities.

    By avoiding these 10 mental locks, entrepreneurs can unleash their own creativity and the creativity of those around them as well. Successful entrepreneurs are willing to take some risks, explore new ideas, play a little, ask "What if?" and learn to appreciate ambiguity. By doing so, they develop the skills, attitudes, and motivation that make them much more creative—one of the keys to entrepreneurial success. Table 2.1 lists some questions designed to spur imagination.

How to Enhance Creativity

LEARNING OBJECTIVES
5. Understand how entrepreneurs can enhance their own creativity and that of their employees as well.

Enhancing Organizational Creativity

Creativity doesn't just happen in organizations; entrepreneurs must establish an environment in which creativity can flourish for themselves and for their workers. New ideas are fragile creations, but the right company culture can encourage people to develop and cultivate them. Ensuring that workers have the freedom and the incentive to be creative is one of the best ways to achieve innovation. "Developing a corporate culture that both fosters and rewards creativity . . . is critical because companies must be able to churn out innovations at a fast pace since technology has shortened product life cycles," says Geoff Yang, successful entrepreneur and venture capitalist.[26] Entrepreneurs can stimulate their own creativity and encourage it among workers by following these suggestions, which are designed to create a culture of innovation.

Include Creativity as a Core Company Value Entrepreneurs have the responsibility of establishing an innovative culture in their companies, and setting a creative tone in an organization begins with the company's mission statement. Entrepreneurs should incorporate creativity and innovation into their companies' mission statements and affirm their commitment to them in internal communications. If creativity and innovation are vital to a company's success (and they usually are!), they should be a natural part of the performance appraisal process.

TABLE 2.1 Questions to Spur the Imagination

People learn at an early age to pursue answers to questions. Creative people, however, understand that good *questions* are extremely valuable in the quest for creativity. Some of the greatest breakthroughs in history came as a result of creative people asking thought-provoking questions. Bill Bowerman, contemplating a design for the soles of running shoes over a breakfast of waffles, asked, "What would happen if I poured rubber into my waffle iron?" He did, and that's how Nike shoes came to be. (The Bowerman's rubber-coated waffle iron is on display in the Nike Town superstore and museum in Chicago.) Albert Einstein, creator of the theory of relativity, asked, "What would a light wave look like to someone keeping pace with it?" Masura Ibuka, who created the Sony Walkman, asked, "Why can't we remove the recording function and speaker and put headphones on the recorder?" William Riblich, CEO of Foster-Miller Inc., a company that develops production equipment for businesses, says his company routinely asks, "In what other ways can we use this particular technology?" Answering that question enabled Foster-Miller to adapt a metallurgical heat-treating technology for use in a candy manufacturing process.

The following questions can help spur your imagination:

1. Is there a new way to do it?
2. Can you borrow or adapt it?
3. Can you give it a new twist?
4. Do you merely need more of the same?
5. Less of the same?
6. Is there a substitute?
7. Can you rearrange the parts?
8. What if you do just the opposite?
9. Can you combine ideas?
10. Can you put it to other uses?
11. What else could we make from this?
12. Are there other markets for it?
13. Can you reverse it?
14. Can you rearrange it?
15. Can you put it to another use?
16. What idea seems impossible but, if executed, would revolutionize your business?

Sources: Adapted from: David Lidsky, "Brain Calisthenics," *Fast Company,* December 2004, p. 95; Thea Singer, Christopher Caggiano, Ilan Mochari, and Tahl Raz"If You Come, They Will Build It," *Inc.*, August 2002, p. 70; Creativity Web, "Question Summary," http://www.ozemail.com/au/~caveman/Creative/Techniques/ost_quest.html; *Bits & Pieces,* February 1990, p. 20; *Bits & Pieces,* April 29, 1993, "Creativity Quiz," *In Business,* November/December 1991, p. 18, Doug Hall, *Jump Start Your Brain* (New York: Warner Books, 1995), pp. 86–87; Christine Canabou, "Imagine That," *Fast Company,* January 2001, p. 56.

Embracing Diversity One of the best ways to cultivate a culture of creativity is to hire a diverse workforce. When people solve problems or come up with ideas, they do so within the framework of their own experience. Hiring people from different backgrounds, cultural experiences, hobbies, and interests provides a company with a crucial raw material needed for creativity. Smart entrepreneurs enhance organizational creativity by hiring beyond their own comfort zones.

Expecting Creativity Employees tend to rise—or fall—to the level of expectations entrepreneurs have of them. One of the best ways to communicate the expectation of creativity is to give employees permission to be creative. At one small company that manufactures industrial equipment, the owner put a "brainstorming board" in a break area. Anyone facing a sticky problem simply posts it on a brightly colored piece of paper on the board. Other workers are invited to share ideas and suggestions by writing them on white pieces of paper and posting them around the problem. The board has generated many creative solutions that otherwise would not have come up.

Expecting and Tolerating Failure Creative ideas will produce failures as well as successes. People who never fail are not being creative. Creativity requires taking chances, and managers must remove employees' fear of failure. The surest way to quash creativity throughout an organization is to punish employees who try something new and fail.

Encouraging Curiosity Entrepreneurs and their employees constantly should ask "what if . . ." questions and to take a "maybe we could . . ." attitude. Doing so allows them to break out of assumptions that limit creativity.

Creating a Change of Scenery Periodically The physical environment in which people work has an impact on their level of creativity. The cubicles made so famous in the *Dilbert* cartoon strip can suck the creativity right out of a workspace. Transforming a typical office space—even one with cubicles—into a haven of creativity does not have to be difficult or expensive. Covering bland walls with funny posters, photographs, murals, or other artwork, adding splashes of color and incorporating live plants can enliven a workspace and enhance creativity. When Michael Sachs, founder of Sg2, a health care consulting company, conducts routine business meetings, he assembles the group in the company's boardroom in the company's Evanston, Illinois, headquarters. However, when he needs a creative solution or wants to stimulate innovation, he takes his team offsite to the Catalyst Ranch, a unique meeting space in downtown Chicago. The room's walls are decorated in bright colors, rich fabrics, and paper cuttings. Brightly colored furnishings abound, and mixed in with the plentiful supply of whiteboards and markers are toys—from Hula-Hoops and Play-Doh to Slinkies and sailboats. Natural light floods the space, where teams of workers can escape the pressures of the office and feel free to relax and let their creativity flow freely.[27] Even if going to an offsite location is not practical, entrepreneurs can still stimulate creativity by starting meetings with some type of short, fun exercise designed to encourage participants to think creatively.

Viewing Problems as Challenges Every problem offers the opportunity for innovation. Entrepreneurs who allow employees to dump all of their problems on their desks to be "fixed" do nothing to develop creativity within those employees.

Providing Creativity Training Almost everyone has the capacity to be creative, but developing that capacity requires training. One writer claims, "What separates the average person from Edison, Picasso, or even Shakespeare isn't creative capacity—it's the ability to tap that capacity by encouraging creative impulses and then acting upon them."[28] Training accomplished through books, seminars, workshops, and professional meetings can help everyone learn to tap their creative capacity.

Providing Support Entrepreneurs must give employees the tools and the resources they need to be creative. One of the most valuable resources is time. Cambridge Consultants, a company that creates products for clients in five industries, allows employees to spend a portion of their time working on "pet projects" that they find exciting and believe have potential. In addition, Cambridge sets aside 10 percent of its annual revenue to provide seed capital for spin-off companies based on employees' most promising ideas. If the spin-off succeeds, the employee gets to operate it and enjoy the profits, in which Cambridge shares. If it fails, the employee gets his or her old job back, and Cambridge simply writes off the investment as a loss.[29] Entrepreneurs should remember that creativity often requires nonwork phases, and allowing employees the time to "daydream" is an important part of the creative process.

Developing a Procedure for Capturing Ideas Workers in every organization come up with creative ideas; however, not every organization is prepared to capture those ideas. The unfortunate result is that ideas that might have vaulted a company ahead or made people's lives better simply evaporate. Without a structured approach for collecting of employees' creative concepts, a business leaves its future to chance. Clever entrepreneurs establish processes within their companies that are designed to harvest the results of employees' creativity. George Calhoun, Chairman of Isco International, a company that makes wireless communications products, routinely sends employees to work with customers all over the globe, knowing that they will come back with insights and ideas they otherwise might never have had. The company captures those ideas in "trip reports" that employees make on their return.[30]

Talking with Customers Innovative companies take the time to get feedback about how they use the companies' products or services, listening for new ideas. CLAAS KGaA, a German manufacturer of agricultural equipment, operates practice centers in each of its principal markets. These centers serve as model farms where farmers can test new equipment and company officials can observe farmers first hand as they use CLAAS products, sometimes in ingenious ways that company employees never could have imagined.[31]

Looking for Uses for Your Company's Products or Services in Other Markets Focusing on the "traditional" uses of a product or service limits creativity—and a company's sales. Entrepreneurs can boost sales by finding new applications, often in unexpected places, for their products and services.

QuVIS

QuVIS, a small company based in Topeka, Kansas, had developed a technique for transmitting digital pictures faster and without the distortion and blurring that typically plagues high-resolution images when they are compressed. The company had established customers in the film-making industry, in which editors used the system to touch up video images, and at theme parks, where animators created special effects for high-tech rides. After watching the space shuttle Columbia disaster in 2003, in which a piece of falling foam breached the integrity of the spaceship and caused it to break up on reentry, a creative group of workers realized that the small company's high-definition digital imaging system could help NASA monitor the safety of the launch of the space shuttle Discovery on its "Return to Flight" mission, the first since the Columbia disaster. After many months of testing, NASA installed more than 100 cameras equipped with QuVIS's Acuity system, which allowed engineers to beam launch photos with much less distortion to labs for analysis much faster. When another piece of foam broke loose during the Discovery launch, NASA engineers were able to use the photos from QuVIS's Acuity system to determine that the astronauts could return to earth safely.[32]

Rewarding Creativity Entrepreneurs can encourage creativity by rewarding it when it occurs. Financial rewards can be effective motivators of creative behavior, but nonmonetary rewards such as praise, recognition, and celebration, usually offer more powerful incentives for creativity.

Digital Communications Corporation

Digital Communications Corporation, a small company that develops advanced wireless technologies, recognizes employees who develop patentable inventions with stock options, cash awards, and honors at an Inventors' Dinner. The reward system works; within two years after implementing it, the number of patent applications Digital Communications filed increased by a factor of five![33]

Modeling Creative Behavior Creativity is "caught" as much as it is "taught." Companies that excel at innovation find that the passion for creativity starts at the top. Entrepreneurs who set examples of creative behavior, taking chances, and challenging the status quo will soon find their employees doing the same.

Lush Cosmetics

At Lush Cosmetics, a fast-growing maker of soaps, shampoos, lotions, and moisturizers, founder Mark Constantine understands that a constant stream of innovative new products is one key to his company's success. That's why he holds annual "Mafia meetings," at which Constantine and his staff mark one-third of the company's products for elimination. Although dropping one-third of Lush's product line every year is risky and means that the product development team must come up with at least 100 new products annually, it gives team members incredible freedom and fearlessness to dream. CEO Constantine himself works on new product development for Lush, and most of his ideas, like those of other team members, never make into finished products. By modeling creative behavior, Constantine encourages creativity among his staff.[34]

TABLE 2.2 Ten "Secrets" for Leading Creativity

Leaders at innovative companies know that their roles in stimulating creativity and establishing a culture that embraces and encourages creativity are vital. Katherine Catlin, founder of a consulting firm specializing in leadership and innovation, has identified the following characteristics exhibited by leaders of innovation.

1. *They think.* These leaders invest time in thinking because they recognize the power of their own creativity and the ideas it generates.
2. *They are visionaries.* These people are totally focused on the values, vision, and mission of their companies and express them through their companies' products and services as well as through its culture. They are able to communicate to others exactly what they want to accomplish.
3. *They listen to customers.* They recognize that customers or potential customers can be a valuable source of new ideas for product or service development and improvement, sales techniques, and market positioning.
4. *They understand how to manage ideas.* As they search for new ideas and creative solutions, these managers look to a variety of sources—customers, employees, the board of directors, and even their own dreams.
5. *They are people-centered.* These leaders hire people for their creative abilities and then place them in a setting that enables that creativity to blossom. They see their employees and their employees' ideas as an important part of their companies' competitive edge.
6. *They maintain a culture of "change."* These leaders do not simply manage change; they embrace it. They seek out change, recognizing that there is a constant need to improve.
7. *They maximize team synergy, balance, and focus.* Realizing that teamwork fosters creativity and innovation, these leaders bring together people from diverse backgrounds into teams to maximize their companies' creative output.
8. *They hold themselves and others accountable for extremely high standards of performance.* These leaders demand results of the highest quality from themselves and their employees and are unwilling to settle for anything less.
9. *They refuse to take "no" for an answer.* These leaders persist in the face of adversity even when others say it cannot be done.
10. *They love what they do and have fun doing it.* These leaders' passion for their work is contagious, empowering everyone in the organization to accomplish everything they possibly can.

Source: Katherine Catlin, "10 Secrets to Leading Innovation," *Entrepreneur,* September 2002, p. 72.

Table 2.2 describes 10 "secrets" for leading innovation in an organization.

Building a creative environment takes time, but the payoffs can be phenomenal. 3M, a company that is famous for cultivating a creative environment, estimates that 70 percent of its annual sales comes from creative ideas that originated from its workforce. As one creativity consultant explains, "For your employees to be more creative, you have to create an environment that values their creativity."[35]

Enhancing Individual Creativity

Just as entrepreneurs can cultivate an environment of creativity in their organizations by using the techniques described above, they can enhance their own creativity by using the following techniques:

Allow yourself to be creative. As we have seen, one of the biggest obstacles to creativity occurs when a person believes that he or she is not creative. Giving yourself the permission to be creative is the first step toward establishing a pattern of creative thinking. Refuse to give in to the temptation to ignore ideas simply because you fear that someone else may consider them "stupid." When it comes to creativity, there are no stupid ideas!

- ***Give your mind fresh input every day.*** To be creative, your mind needs stimulation. Do something different each day—listen to a new radio station, take a walk through a park or a shopping center, pick up a magazine you never read.

Agenda Dynamics Inc.

When Janet Harris-Lange, founder of Agenda Dynamics Inc., a meeting and event management company, needs a fresh idea for an upcoming event, she makes an effort to expose her mind to new stimuli. In the past, she has walked through a second-hand thrift shop, shopped in a dime store, talked with children, and put on funny hats to generate creative ideas for her clients' events, something that is vital to her company's success. "To be better than the competition, I have to employ creative thinking," she says.[36]

- ***Observe the products and services of others companies, especially those in completely different markets.*** Creative entrepreneurs often borrow ideas from companies that are in businesses totally unrelated to their own. In the 1950s, Ruth and Elliott Handler, co-founders of Mattel Inc., drew the inspiration for the best-selling doll of all time, Barbie (named after the Handler's daughter), from a doll called Lilli that was based on a shapely character in a German comic strip and then borrowed the idea of dressing her in stylish outfits from cardboard cut-out games that were popular in that era. Another example of borrowing an idea occurred when Jean Nidetech made Weight Watchers a major force in the weight loss industry by applying the support group technique from Alcoholics Anonymous to the diet plan she had developed.[37]
- ***Recognize the creative power of mistakes.*** Innovations sometimes are the result of serendipity, finding something while looking for something else, and sometimes they arise as a result of mistakes. Creative people recognize that even their errors may lead to new ideas, products, and services. Charles Goodyear worked for five years trying to combine rubber with a variety of chemicals to prevent it from being too soft in hot weather and too brittle in cold weather. One cold night in 1839, Goodyear was combining rubber, sulfur, and white lead when he accidentally spilled some of the mixture on a work stove. The substances melted together to form a new compound that had just the properties Goodyear was looking for! Goodyear named the process he discovered accidentally "vulcanization," and today practically every product made from rubber depends on it.[38]
- ***Keep a journal handy to record your thoughts and ideas.*** Creative ideas are too valuable to waste, so always keep a journal nearby to record them as soon as you get them. Leonardo Da Vinci was famous for writing down ideas as they struck him. Patrick McNaughton invented the neon blackboards restaurants use to advertise their specials, as well as more than 30 other products, many of which are sold through the company that he and his sister, Jamie, own. McNaughton credits much of his creative success to the fact that he writes down every idea he gets and keeps it in a special folder. "There's no such thing as a crazy idea," he insists.[39]
- ***Listen to other people.*** No rule of creativity says that an idea has to be your own! Sometimes the best business ideas come from someone else, but entrepreneurs are the ones to act on them.

Ranchmark

While celebrating his friend Robert Lewis' birthday, Thomas Perlmutter presented Lewis with a gift, a Montblanc fountain pen packaged in a hard plastic case known as a "clamshell." Unable to pry open the clamshell, Lewis simply gave up and began teasing Perlmutter, whose company designed inserts for those obnoxious clamshells. Half-jokingly, his wife said, "You should invent something to open those things." Before their dinner was finished, Perlmutter and Lewis had sketched a design of a safe, easy-to-use tool that would crack open even the toughest clamshell. Within two months, they had forged a prototype, which they named the OpenX. The entrepreneurs worked with a factory in Taiwan to produce the OpenX and launched a company called Ranchmark to market the device. Ranchmark sells the OpenX from its Web site and through retailers across the United States for $9.95. The day after the popular blog Gizmodo said that the OpenX was "a great solution to an infuriating problem," Ranchmark sold 1,110 units. "I was part of the problem," laughs Perlmutter, "and now I have created the solution."[40]

Listen to customers. Some of the best ideas for new products and services or new applications of an existing product or service come from a company's customers. Entrepreneurs who take the time to listen to their customers often receive ideas they may never have come up with on their own. At Lush Cosmetics, founder Mark Constantine routinely draws ideas for new products or product names from the company's loyal customers (affectionately known as "Lushies") in the company's chat room.[41]

Talk to a child. As we grow older, we learn to conform to society's expectations about many things, including creative solutions to problems. Children place very few limitations on their thinking; as a result, their creativity is practically boundless. (Remember all of the games you and your friends invented when you were young?) Frustrated at not being able to use the small pieces of broken crayons, 11-year-old Cassidy Goldstein invented a plastic crayon holder now sold in stores across the United States. Inspired by the plastic tubes that keep roses fresh in transport, Goldstein developed a plastic device capable of holding a crayon, no matter how small it is.[42]

Keep a toy box in your office. Your box might include silly objects such as wax lips, a yo-yo, a Slinky, fortune cookie sayings, feathers, a top, a compass, or a host of other items. When you are stumped, pick an item at random from the toy box and think about how it relates to your problem.

Read books on stimulating creativity or take a class on creativity. Creative thinking is a technique that anyone can learn. Understanding and applying the principles of creativity can improve dramatically the ability to develop new and innovative ideas.

Take some time off. Relaxation is vital to the creative process. Getting away from a problem gives the mind time to reflect on it. It is often during this time, while the subconscious works on a problem, that the mind generates many creative solutions. One creativity expert claims that fishing is the ideal activity for stimulating creativity. "Your brain is on high alert in case a fish is around," he says, "but your brain is completely relaxed. This combination is the time when you have the 'Aha!' moment."[43]

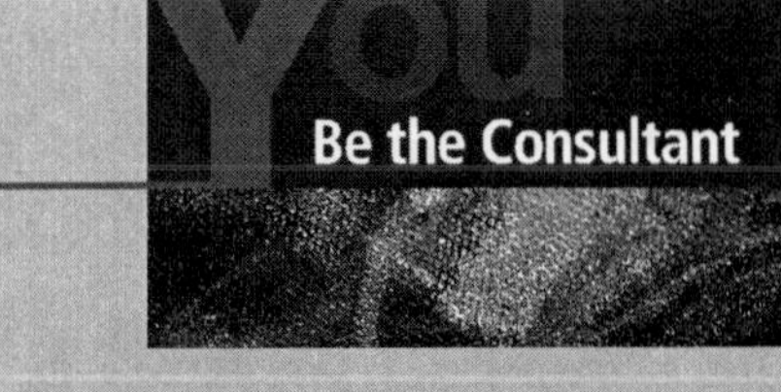

The Creative Side of Entrepreneurship

When St. Petersburg, one of the most splendid, harmonious cities in Europe, was being laid out early in the eighteenth century, many large boulders brought by a glacier from Finland had to be removed. One particularly large rock was in the path of one of the principal avenues that had been planned, and bids were solicited for its removal. The bids submitted were very high. This was understandable because at that time modern equipment did not exist and there were no high-powered explosives. As officials pondered what to do, a peasant presented himself and offered to get rid of the boulder for a much lower price than those submitted by other bidders. Since they had nothing to lose, officials gave the job to the peasant.

The next morning he showed up with a crowd of other peasants carrying shovels. They began digging a huge hole next to the rock. They propped up the rock with timbers to prevent it from rolling into the hole. When the hole was deep enough, the timber props were removed and the rock dropped into the hole below the street level. Then they covered it with dirt and carted the excess dirt away.

This is an early example of what creative thinking can do to solve a problem. The unsuccessful bidders only thought about moving the rock from one place to another on the city's surface. The peasant looked at the problem from another angle. He considered another dimension—up and down. He couldn't lift it up, so he put it underground!

Managers at the Cleveland Museum used a similar kind of creative thinking to ensure the success of a dazzling exhibit of ancient Egyptian treasures. Taking a different marketing approach, museum managers held a free private showing for the city's taxi drivers. Some of the museum's snooty, blue-blood patrons scoffed at the idea and dismissed it as an exercise in foolishness. After all, they said, taxi drivers aren't known for their polish or their culture. But the museum managers persisted. Impress the cab drivers, they reasoned, and the "cabbies" would be more likely to recommend the new exhibit to their customers, who would, in turn, flock to the museum. That's exactly what happened. During the exhibit's run in Cleveland, the museum enjoyed shoulder-to-shoulder attendance, thanks to talkative cab drivers and creative museum managers!

The principal at one Oregon middle school used creativity to solve a maintenance problem. Girls would put on lipstick in the bathrooms and then press their lips to the mirror, leaving dozens of sticky lip prints that the maintenance crew had to scrub off. The principal invited all of the girls to the bathroom, where she explained the problem and the time and cost associated with cleaning the mirrors every day. She then asked the maintenance man to demonstrate how difficult it was to scrub off the lipstick. He took out a long-handled squeegee, dipped it in a toilet, and proceeded to clean the mirror with it. Since then, no lip prints have appeared on the mirrors in the girls' bathrooms!

1. Contact a local small business owner and ask him or her about a problem his or her company is facing. Work with a small team of your classmates and use the type of creative thinking described above to generate potential solutions to the problem. Remember to think creatively!

Sources: Bernard Percy and Marina Leight, "Side by Side," *Converge*, April–May 2002, p. 11; Charles R. Davey, "Oddball Ideas Aren't So Odd," *Industry Week*, August 3, 1992, p. 7; *Bits & Pieces*, October 15, 1992, pp. 8–10.

LEARNING OBJECTIVES
6. Describe the steps in the creative process.

The Creative Process

Although creative ideas may appear to strike as suddenly as a bolt of lightning, they are actually the result of the creative process, which involves seven steps:

1. Preparation
2. Investigation
3. Transformation
4. Incubation
5. Illumination
6. Verification
7. Implementation

Step 1. Preparation This step involves getting the mind ready for creative thinking. Preparation might include a formal education, on-the-job training, work experience, and taking advantage of other learning opportunities. This training provides a foundation on which to build creativity and innovation. As one writer explains, "Creativity favors the prepared mind."[44] For example, Dr. Hamel Navia, a scientist at tiny Vertex Pharmaceuticals, recently developed a promising new drug to fight the AIDS virus. His preparation included earning an advanced degree in the field of medicine and learning to use computers to create three-dimensional images of the protein molecules he was studying.[45] How can you prepare your mind for creative thinking?

- Adopt the attitude of a lifelong student. Realize that educating yourself is a never-ending process. Look at every situation you encounter as an opportunity to learn.

Orbital Research Inc.

Ravi Vaidyanathan, a research scientist at Orbital Research Inc., a small high-tech firm based in Cleveland, began studying the reflexes of the cockroach after observing its uncanny ability to escape an approaching shoe. Vaidyanathan used what he learned from the insect to create a neural network called BioAVERT based on a mathematical algorithm for the company that promises to improve the navigation systems in cars, ships, airplanes, and other methods of transportation. "By mimicking a cockroach," he says, "we're able to come up with a neural network for very fast responses."[46]

- Read . . . a lot . . . and not just in your field of expertise. Many innovations come from blending ideas and concepts from different fields in science, engineering, business, and the arts. Reading books, magazines, and papers covering a variety of subject matter is a great way to stimulate your creativity.
- Clip articles of interest to you and create a file for them. Over time, you will build a customized encyclopedia of information from which to draw ideas and inspiration.
- Take time to discuss your ideas with other people, including those who know little about it, as well as experts in the field. Sometimes, the apparently simple questions an "unknowledgeable" person asks lead to new discoveries and to new approaches to an old problem.

American Wilderness Experience Inc.

Dave Wiggins, president of American Wilderness Experience, Inc., an adventure travel company, gets valuable ideas from his wife, Carol, a network of business advisors, and his employees. The idea for the company's most popular trip, snowmobiling in Yellowstone National Park, came from one of the company's guides. "I find it extremely helpful to get different perspectives from people I respect and trust," says Wiggins.[47]

- Join professional or trade associations and attend their meetings. There you have the chance to brainstorm with others who have similar interests. Learning how other people have solved a particular problem may give you fresh insight into solving it.
- Invest time in studying other countries and their cultures; then travel there. Our global economy offers incredible business opportunities for entrepreneurs with the necessary knowledge and experience to recognize them. One entrepreneur began a lucrative business exporting a variety of consumer products to Latvia after he accompanied his daughter there on a missionary trip. He claims that he never would have seen the opportunity had he not traveled to Latvia with his daughter.
- Develop listening skills. It's amazing what you can learn if you take the time to listen to other people, especially those who are older and have more experience. Try to learn something from everyone you meet.
- Eliminate creative distractions. Interruptions from telephone calls, e-mails, and visitors can crush creativity. Allowing employees to escape to a quiet, interruption-free environment enhances their ability to be creative.

Step 2. Investigation This step requires one to develop a solid understanding of the problem, situation, or decision at hand. To create new ideas and concepts in a particular field, an individual first must study the problem and understand its basic components. Creative thinking comes about when people make careful observations of the world around them and then investigate the way things work (or fail to work). For example, Dr. Navia and another scientist at Vertex had spent several years conducting research on viruses and on a protein that blocks a type of virus enzyme called a protease. His exploration of the various ways to block this enzyme paved the way for his discovery.

Endocyte

After earning his Ph.D. in chemistry, Christopher Leamon began researching targeted anticancer therapy using molecules that tumors absorb as "Trojan horses" to deliver drugs that are lethal to them. Initially, Leamon had focused on the vitamin biotin, but after nine months of research and hard work, "it was a total failure," he says. One morning while sitting at the breakfast table with his wife, Leamon, a long-time cereal lover, was reading the ingredients on the nutrition panel of his box of Kellogg's Frosted Flakes. One of the items, folic acid, caught his attention. Leamon dashed off to the library and found a research paper on how folic acid enters a human cell. "I knew this was it," he recalls. Before long, Leamon had developed a technique for attaching cancer drugs to folic acid so that they would be absorbed and enable the cells to fight the disease in much the same way they battle infections. Leamon has licensed the promising therapy to a company called Endocyte, which plans to have drugs on the market within a few years. "There are lots of 'Eureka' moments in the lab," says Leamon. "None as great as the one with the folic acid though. That breakfast redefined my career and my life."[48]

convergent thinking
the ability to see similarities and the connections among various data and events.

Step 3. Transformation Transformation involves viewing the similarities and the differences among the information collected. This phase requires two types of thinking: convergent and divergent. **Convergent thinking** is the ability to see the *similarities* and the connections among various and often diverse data and events.

SBI Enterprises

Physicist Bruce Middleton used convergent thinking to develop the idea for the award-winning Flybar, the highest flying pogo stick in the world.

While pedaling his daughters to school on a bicycle, physicist Bruce Middleton was annoyed by a stop sign at the bottom of a hill. "You lose your momentum," he explains. Middleton began to ponder a bike's ability to store kinetic energy, thinking how a steel spring could capture the energy released during braking and release it later. His calculations, however, showed that the spring would have to weigh 150 pounds. One day while in a hardware store, Middleton noticed a display rack of slingshots and his mind returned to the kinetic energy problem. He calculated that rubber's energy-storing capacity is 10 to 20 times greater than steel's. "That was the real breakthrough," he says. Thinking back to his childhood days, Middleton had the idea of replacing the steel springs in a pogo stick with rubber. To test his idea, he bought surgical tubing from a medical supply store but quickly realized that it was too bulky. Later, while walking through a thrift store, Middleton noticed a pair of "moon boots," shoes fitted with rubber bands that allow the wearer to bounce as if on a trampoline. Inspired, he purchased industrial-strength rubber bands and used the planks from his IKEA couch to build a pogo stick prototype. Eureka! The prototype bounced four feet off the ground. "The limiting factor was courage rather than mechanics," he recalls. Middleton then worked with SBI Enterprises, the world's oldest pogo stick manufacturer, to create the Flybar pogo stick. Eight-time World Cup skateboarding champion Andy MacDonald is working with SBI and Middleton to market the world's highest-flying pogo stick.[49]

divergent thinking
the ability to see the differences among various data and events.

Divergent thinking is the ability to see the *differences* among various data and events. While developing his AIDS-fighting drug, Dr. Navia studied the work of other scientists whose attempts at developing an enzyme-blocking drug had failed. He was able to see the similarities and the differences in his research and theirs and to build on their successes while avoiding their failures.

How can you increase your ability to transform the information collected into a purposeful idea?

- Evaluate the parts of the situation several times, trying to grasp the "big picture." Getting bogged down in the details of a situation too early in the creative process can diminish creativity. Look for patterns that emerge.
- Rearrange the elements of the situation. By looking at the components of an issue in a different order or from a different perspective, you may be able to see the similarities and the differences among them more readily. Rearranging them also may help uncover a familiar pattern that had been masked by an unfamiliar structure.
- Try using synectics (a term derived from the Greek words for "to bring together" and "diversity"), taking two seemingly nonsensical ideas and combining them. For instance, why not launch a bookstore with no physical storefront and no books—an

accurate description of what Jeff Bezos did when he came up with the idea for Amazon.com.[50]

- Before locking into one particular approach to a situation, remember that several approaches might be successful. If one approach produces a dead end, don't hesitate to jump quickly to another. Considering several approaches to a problem or opportunity simultaneously would be like rolling a bowling ball down each of several lanes in quick succession. The more balls you roll down the lanes, the greater is the probability of hitting at least one strike. Resist the temptation to make snap judgments on how to tackle a problem or opportunity. The first approach may not be the best one.

Step 4. Incubation The subconscious needs time to reflect on the information collected. To an observer, this phase of the creative process would be quite boring; it looks as though nothing is happening! In fact, during this phase, it may appear that the creative person is *loafing*. Incubation occurs while the individual is away from the problem, often engaging in some totally unrelated activity. Dr. Navia's creative powers were working at a subconscious level even when he was away from his work, not even thinking about his research on AIDS-fighting drugs.

How can you enhance the incubation phase of the creative process, letting ideas marinate in your mind?

- Walk away from the situation. Time away from a problem is vital to enhancing creativity. A study by Wilson Brill, an expert on creativity, of how 350 great ideas became successful products shows that two-thirds of the ideas came to people while they were *away* from work—in the shower, in their cars, in bed, on a walk, and other nonwork situations.[51] Doing something totally unrelated to the problem gives your subconscious mind the chance to work on the problem or opportunity. Indeed, the "three b's"—bath, bed, and bus—are conducive to creativity. "I do some of my best thinking in my hot tub at home," says American Wilderness Experience's Dave Wiggins. "I sit there, look at the stars, and come up with some pretty good ideas."[52]
- Take the time to daydream. Although it may *look* as if you're doing nothing, daydreaming is an important part of the creative process. That's when your mind is most free from paradigms and other self-imposed restrictions on creativity. Feel free to let your mind wander, and it may just stumble onto a creative solution.
- Relax —and play—regularly. Perhaps the worst thing you can do for creativity is to work on a problem or opportunity constantly. Soon enough, fatigue walks in, and creativity walks out! Great ideas often are incubated on the golf course, on the basketball court, in the garden, or in the hammock.
- Dream about the problem or opportunity. Although you may not be able to dream on command, thinking about an issue just before you drift off to sleep can be an effective way to encourage your mind to work on it while you sleep, a process called lucid dreaming. When he gets in bed, prolific inventor, serial entrepreneur, and author Ray Kurzweil focuses on a particular problem, sometimes imagining that he is giving a speech about his success at solving it. "This has the purpose of seeding your subconscious to influence your dreams," he explains. Often, while he is asleep, ideas and potential solutions to the problem drift into his dreams. When he begins to awaken but is still in that nether land of semi-sleep, Kurzweil merges the logic of conscious thought with the content of his dreams. The process often produces astonishing insights that Kurzweil says he otherwise might have missed.[53]

Beach'N Billboard

Patrick Dori came up with the idea for his business from an intense dream in which he was floating in midair over a beach watching a contraption made of iron roll across the sand. "You could put advertising on that machine," he remembers dreaming. Today, Dori is the owner of Beach'N Billboard, a New Jersey company that imprints beach sand with advertisements for products including Snapple and Skippy Peanut Butter![54]

- Work on the problem or opportunity in a different environment—somewhere other than the office. Take your work outside on a beautiful fall day or sit on a bench in a mall. The change of scenery will likely stimulate your creativity.

Step 5. Illumination This phase of the creative process occurs at some point during the incubation stage when a spontaneous breakthrough causes "the light bulb to go on." It may take place after five minutes—or five years. In the illumination stage, all of the previous stages come together to produce the "Eureka factor"—the creation of the innovative idea. In one study of 200 scientists, 80 percent said that at least once a solution to a problem had "just popped into their heads"—usually when they were away from the problem.[55] For Dr. Navia, the illumination stage occurred one day while he was reading a scientific journal. As he read, Dr. Navia says he was struck with a "hallucination" of a novel way to block proteases.

Although the creative process itself may last for months or even years, the suddenness with which the illumination step occurs can be deceiving. For example, one night, Kent Murphy, an electrical engineer, began dreaming about what it would be like to be a photon of light. "I was riding a ray of light moving through the fiber," he recalls about his dream. Murphy, who holds 30 patents, used the insight from his dream to invent a fiber-optic gauge that monitors on a real-time basis the structural wear in airplanes.[56] Barry Kemp says that the idea for the TV series *Coach* popped into his head—characters, plotline, and all—at 3 o'clock in the morning. He got up and scribbled seven pages of notes that became the foundation for the successful sit-com. A professor of mathematical sciences came up with an important new theory to explain how gravity works in the rotation of spiral galaxies, a problem that has perplexed physicists and astronomers for decades, while gazing at a ceiling fan in a restaurant. Like a point on the blade of a ceiling fan, he thought (he was daydreaming at the time), the speed of a star in a spinning galaxy is slower if it lies closer to the axis. He developed an equation to test his theory and then compared its results to various measurements of galactic rotation. The results were consistent with reality, and the theory worked![57]

Step 6. Verification For entrepreneurs, validating an idea as accurate and useful may include conducting experiments, running simulations, test marketing a product or service, establishing small-scale pilot programs, building prototypes, and engaging in many other activities designed to verify that the new idea will work and is practical to implement. The goal is to subject the innovative idea to the test of cold, hard reality. At this phase, appropriate questions to ask include the following:

- Is it *really* a better solution to a particular problem or opportunity? Sometimes an idea that appears to have a bright future in the lab or on paper dims considerably when put to the test of reality.
- Will it work?
- Is there a need for it?
- If so, what is the best application of this idea in the marketplace?
- Does this product or service idea fit into our core competencies?
- How much will it cost to produce or to provide?
- Can we sell it at a reasonable price that will produce adequate sales, profit, and return on investment for our business?

Ramtron International Corporation, a maker of memory chips, uses a "product justification form" to collect information from the idea generator as well as from other departments in the company so it can verify the potential of each idea.[58] To test the value of his new drug formulation, Dr. Navia used powerful computers at Vertex Pharmaceuticals to build three-dimensional Tinkertoy-like models of the HIV virus and then simulated his new drug's ability to block the protease enzyme. Subsequent testing of the drug verified its safety. "I was convinced that I had an insight that no one else had," he recalls.[59]

Step 7. Implementation The focus of this step is to transform the idea into reality. Plenty of people come up with creative idea for promising new products or services, but most never take them beyond the idea stage. What sets entrepreneurs apart is that they *act* on their ideas. An entrepreneur's philosophy is "Ready, aim, fire," not "Ready, aim, aim, aim, aim, ..."

COMPANY Profile

NCT Group and Cygnus Inc.

NCT Group, a small company, had developed a system that sent mirror images of sound waves through ceramic tiles to cancel out noise. One day, an engineer wondered what would happen if he sent music instead of "anti-noise" through the tiles. He connected a radio to the unit, and from the flat tiles came the sound of the Beatles! The company took the engineer's discovery and developed two-inch-thick wall-mounted speakers that produce high-quality audio for the consumer market! Another small business, Cygnus Inc., had created a patch that was designed to deliver drugs through the wearer's skin. While taking apart a patch one day, a researcher realized that not only did it deliver drugs, but it also absorbed material from the body. Cygnus transformed the discovery into a line of watch-like devices that monitor the glucose levels of diabetic patients.[60]

The key to both companies' success was their ability to take a creative idea for a useful new product and turn it into a reality. As one creativity expert explains, "Becoming more creative is really just a matter of paying attention to that endless flow of ideas you generate, and learning to capture and act upon the new that's within you."[61]

For Dr. Navia and Vertex Pharmaceuticals, the implementation phase required testing the drug's ability to fight the deadly virus in humans. If it proved to be effective, Vertex would complete the process by bringing the drug to market. In this final phase of testing, Navia was so certain that he was on the verge of a major breakthrough in fighting AIDS that he couldn't sleep at night. Unfortunately the final critical series of tests proved that Dr. Navia's flash of creativity was, as he now says, "completely, totally, and absolutely incorrect." Although his intuition proved to be wrong this time, Dr. Navia's research into fighting AIDS continues. Much of the current work at Vertex is based on Dr. Navia's original idea. Although it proved to be incorrect, his idea has served a valuable purpose: generating new ideas. "We are now applying a powerful technology in HIV research that wasn't used before, one inspired by a hunch," he says.[62]

Hands on ... How to

Create a Culture of Innovation

Creating a culture in which creativity and innovation thrive is no easy task for an entrepreneur and requires a well-balanced management approach. A heavy-handed management style stifles creativity and invites high turnover rates among creative types. An approach that is too laissez-faire can lead to lapses in productivity and chaos. "The workplace of today isn't set up to manage creative people," says Richard Florida, author of *The Rise of the Creative Class*. "It's a recipe for competitive disaster to manage creative people like they're industrial workers." What can entrepreneurs do to build a culture of innovation that encourages and supports daily creativity among employees?

Step 1. Recognize that creativity comes from everywhere in your company. A common misconception is that only certain types of people have creative ability and that most people lack it. Research shows that *anyone* with normal intelligence has the capacity to be creative; it's up to business owners to unleash employees' creativity for the benefit of the company and society as a whole. The goal is to get everyone in the organization—from the factory floor to the finance department—involved in generating creative solutions.

Step 2. Don't count on money as the primary motivator of creativity. Money can be an important motivator for some employees, but research suggests that it is not the primary motivator of creative behavior. Far more important as motivators are recognition and appreciation of creativity and the freedom and the autonomy to pursue creative solutions. In fact, when it comes to creativity, pay-for-performance systems may not be the best solutions because they encourage employees to avoid taking chances to develop creative solutions. (Remember that failure is a natural part of the creative process.) To encourage creativity among employees, entrepreneurs must create a work environment that supports, values, recognizes, and encourages creative behavior. In addition, assigning people projects based not only on their experience and education but also on their interests can stimulate creativity. People tend to be more creative when they genuinely care about their work and are learning new skills. That's why Google allows employees to spend up to 20 percent of their time working on "Googlettes," projects in which the employees are interested and see potential for business development.

Step 3. Let employees know that taking chances—and the failure that sometimes results—are acceptable outcomes. For creativity to blossom, employees have to know that it is safe to take chances that might result in failure. They have to know that they won't be punished for an innovative solution that fails, even if it costs the company money. The fastest way to snuff out creativity is to punish those who dare to take creative chances and fail.

Step 4. Provide the necessary resources, especially time, for employees to be creative. To be productive in their "regular" work, employees must have the proper resources. The same is true for their creative work. Creativity-training programs, a work environment that allows employees to interact freely (as opposed to staying locked up in their offices or, worse, cubicles), a diverse group of co-workers, and physical surroundings that are comfortable, relaxed, and pleasant are just some to the factors that can enhance creativity.

Step 5. Protect them from creativity killers. Protecting employees from creativity killers such as interruptions allows them to focus on the task at hand and to be more creative. Perhaps the most important resource entrepreneurs can give employees is *time*. Research shows that people are least creative when they are under intense pressure to meet a short deadline. Time pressure short-circuits the creative process you learned about in this chapter. Although emergencies will pop up in business periodically, a business owner who plans and schedules work in advance can remove much of the time pressure that erodes creativity.

Step 6. Allow time for dreaming and creative thinking. Although employees must stay focused on the problem at hand to produce results, creativity demands that they have time to step away from it so that the incubation process can take place. Just because a worker is staring out of a window does not meant that he or she is loafing. Sometimes the most creative ideas come about when, to a casual observer, employees look as if they are daydreaming.

Step 7. Eliminate bureaucratic procedures that add no value. There is no room for punch clocks in businesses that count on creative genius for survival. Where possible, smart entrepreneurs allow employees to establish policies and procedures within certain boundaries. Jobs designed around flextime, job sharing, telecommuting, and other techniques that accommodate the busy lifestyles of modern workers go a long way toward enhancing creativity.

Step 8. Encourage collaboration rather than competition for the best creative results. Many managers believe that the best way to stimulate creativity is to use the "*Survivor*" approach, establishing competition among teams of workers. It's just not true! Although competition may result in a hit reality television show, research shows that creativity actually *suffers* when competition is introduced. When it comes to creativity, competition shuts off information and idea sharing, both essential parts of the creative process.

Step 9. Let employees have fun! Creativity thrives where employees are having fun. That doesn't mean that employees should spend most of their time playing games, but they should be able to enjoy their work and their work environment. Smart entrepreneurs know that the Nerf basketball hoop can be just as important a business tool as a fax machine. Providing a physical workspace that includes light (natural, if possible), offbeat, inspiring artwork, plants, goofy toys, the occasional office pizza, and whiteboards are excellent ways to create an environment primed for creativity.

Sources: Adapted from Linda Tischler, "The Care and Feeding of the Creative Class," *Fast Company*, December 2004, pp. 93–95; Chris Pentilla, "An Art in Itself," *Entrepreneur*, December 2003, pp. 96–97; Juanita Weaver, "Under Pressure," *Entrepreneur*, August 2003, pp. 68–69; Bill Breen, "The 6 Myths of Creativity," *Fast Company*, December 2004, pp. 75–78; Anne Fisher, "How to Encourage Bright Ideas," *Fortune*, May 3, 2004, p. 70.

LEARNING OBJECTIVES
7. Discuss techniques for improving the creative process.

Techniques for Improving the Creative Process

Teams of people working together usually can generate more and more-creative ideas. Four techniques that are especially useful for improving the quality of creative ideas from teams are brainstorming, mind-mapping, TRIZ, and rapid prototyping.

Brainstorming

A creative process in which a small group of people interact with very little structure with the goal of producing a large *quantity* of novel and imaginative ideas is called **brainstorming.** The goal is to create an open, uninhibited atmosphere that allows members of the group to "free-wheel" ideas. Participants should suggest any ideas that come to mind *without evaluating or criticizing them.* As group members interact, each idea sparks the thinking of others, and the spawning of ideas becomes contagious. For a brainstorming session to be successful, entrepreneurs should use the following guidelines:

brainstorming
a process in which a small group of people interact with very little structure with the goal of producing a large quantity of novel and imaginative ideas.

- Keep the group small—just five to eight members. Amazon founder Jeff Bezos uses the "two-pizza rule"—if a brainstorming group can eat two pizzas, it's too big.[63]
- Make the group as diverse as possible. Include people with different backgrounds, disciplines, and perspectives. At Joe Design Inc., a successful design firm, every employee in the small firm takes part in brainstorming sessions. "We bring in everybody from the bookkeeper to the office manager because they see things completely differently than we do," says co-founder Joe Rai.[64]
- Company rank and department affiliation are irrelevant. Every member of the brainstorming team is on equal ground.
- Have a well-defined problem for the group to address but don't reveal it ahead of time. Otherwise, participants will discuss their ideas, criticize them, and engage in other creativity-limiting activities. Stating the problem in the form of a "Why," "How," or "What" question often helps.
- Limit the session to 40 to 60 minutes. Beyond that, participants grow weary, and creativity flags because brainstorming is an intense activity.
- Take a field trip. Visit the scene of the problem, if possible. Research shows that brainstorming teams that go "onsite" actually come up with more and better ideas.[65]
- Appoint someone (preferably not a brainstorming participant) the job of recorder. The recorder should write every idea on a flip chart or board so that everyone can see it.
- Use a seating pattern that encourages communication and interaction (e.g., circular or U-shaped arrangements).
- Throw logic out the window. The best brainstorming sessions are playful and anything but logical.
- Encourage *all* ideas from the team, even wild and extreme ones. Discourage participants from editing their ideas. Not only can ideas that initially seem crazy get the group's creative juices flowing, but they also can spread creativity like wildfire. In addition, the group often can polish some of these wild ideas into practical, creative solutions!
- Establish a goal of *quantity* of ideas over *quality* of ideas. There will be plenty of time later to evaluate the ideas generated. At Ideo Inc., a Silicon Valley design firm, brainstorming teams shoot for at least 150 ideas in a 30- to 45-minute session.[66] When chemist Linus Pauling received his second Nobel Prize, someone asked him how he came up with so many great ideas. Pauling replied simply, "I come up with lots of ideas."[67]
- *Forbid* evaluation or criticism of any idea during the brainstorming session. No idea is a bad idea. Criticism slams the brakes on the creative process instantly!
- Encourage participants to use "idea hitch-hiking," building new ideas on those already suggested. Often, some of the best solutions are those that are piggybacked on others.
- Dare to imagine the unreasonable. Creative ideas often arise when people suspend conventional thinking to consider far-fetched solutions.

Digital River

Digital River is a company based in Eden Prairie, Minnesota, that provides e-commerce solutions for businesses and counts on a fresh supply of ideas to maintain a competitive edge. Every Friday morning at 8 a.m., CEO Joel Ronning assembles the 45 members of the company's "entrepreneurial council" to brainstorm ways to enhance customer service, boost revenues, or cut costs. In just three years, the team has generated ideas for everything from better ways to train new employees to more effective sales techniques, and, according to Ronning, has saved or made Digital River hundreds of thousands of dollars. As an added incentive for creativity, Ronning awards $2,500 every quarter for the best idea generated.[68]

Mind-Mapping

mind-mapping
a graphical technique that encourages thinking on both sides of the brain, visually displays the various relationships among ideas, and improves the ability to view a problem from many sides.

Another useful tool for jump-starting creativity is mind-mapping, an extension of brainstorming. One strength of mind-mapping is that it reflects the way the brain actually works. Rather than throwing out ideas in a linear fashion, the brain jumps from one idea to another. In many creative sessions ideas are rushing out so fast that many are lost if a person attempts to shove them into a linear outline. Creativity suffers. **Mind-mapping** is a graphical technique that encourages thinking on both sides of the brain, visually displays the various relationships among ideas, and improves the ability to view a problem from many sides.

The mind-mapping process works in the following way:

- Start by writing down or sketching a picture symbolizing the problem or area of focus in the center of a large blank page. Tony Buzan, originator of the mind-mapping technique, suggests using ledger paper or covering an entire wall with butcher paper to establish a wide open attitude toward creativity.
- Write down *every* idea that comes into your mind, connecting each idea to the central picture or words with a line. Use key words and symbols to record ideas in shorthand. Work as quickly as possible for no more than 20 minutes, doing your best to capture the tide of ideas that flows from your brain. Just as in brainstorming, do not judge the quality of your ideas; just get them onto the paper. Build new ideas on the backs of existing ones. If you see a connection between a new idea and one already on the paper, connect them with a line. If not, simply connect the idea to the center symbol. You will organize your ideas later in the process.
- When the flow of ideas slows to a trickle, stop! Don't try to force creativity.
- Allow your mind to rest for a few minutes and then begin to integrate the ideas on the page into a mind map. Use colored pens and markers to connect ideas with similar themes or to group ideas into related clusters. As you organize your thoughts, look for new connections among your ideas. Sometimes the brain needs time to process the ideas in a mind map. (Recall the incubation stage of the creative process.) Walking away from the mind map and the problem for a few minutes or a few hours may lead to several new ideas or to new relationships among ideas. One entrepreneur created the format for his company's business plan with a mind map rather than with a traditional linear outline. When he finished, he not only knew what he should include in his plan, but he also had a clear picture of the order in which to sequence the elements.

Source: Copyright 2002 by Randy Glasbergen. www.glasbergen.com

"My boss sent me to a mind mapping workshop and now I can't refold my brain!"

TRIZ

In 1946, Genrich Altshuller, a 22-year-old naval officer in the former Soviet Union, developed a process with a name derived from the acronym for the Russian phrase that translates as "theory of inventive problem solving" or TRIZ (pronounced "trees"). TRIZ is a systematic approach designed to help solve any technical problem, whatever its source. Unlike brainstorming and mind-mapping, which are right-brained activities, TRIZ is a left-brained, scientific, step-by-step process that is based on the study of hundreds of the most innovative patents across the globe. Altshuller claimed that these innovations followed a particular set of patterns. Unlocking the principles behind those patterns allows one not only to solve seemingly insurmountable problems, but also to predict where the next challenges would arise.

Altshuller and his colleagues developed 40 principles underlying these innovative patents and then developed the "TRIZ contradiction matrix," a tool that combines these principles to solve a problem. They recognized that innovations come about when someone is able to overcome the inherent contradictions in a process. For instance, in the packaging industry, a contradiction exists between the effectiveness of child-proof safety caps for medicine containers and making those containers easy for authorized users to open. Manufacturers of mattresses face the contradiction of making mattresses that are both hard and soft. Too often, companies rely on a very unimaginative solution to contradictions such as these; they compromise. Rather than settle for a mediocre compromise, the TRIZ contradiction matrix is designed to *resolve* these conflicts using the 40 principles Altshuller developed. One axis of the matrix displays the characteristic of the process to be improved, and the other axis displays the conflicting characteristic that is becoming worse.

For example, suppose that a candy maker wants to make syrup-filled, bottle-shaped chocolates by molding the chocolate bottles and then pouring syrup into the mold. To speed production of the finished product to meet demand, the business owner tries heating the syrup to allow for faster pouring, but the heated syrup melts the molded chocolate bottles and distorts their shape (the contradiction; see Figure 2.3). Using the TRIZ contradiction matrix, the candy maker recognizes the problem as a conflict between speed and shape. Speed is the characteristic to be improved, and shape is the characteristic that is getting worse. The principles that the matrix suggests for solving this problem include the following:

1. Changing the dynamics of the object or the environment (e.g., making a rigid part flexible).
2. Discarding or recovering parts of an object (e.g., dissolving a protective case when it is no longer needed).
3. Causing an object to vibrate or oscillate (e.g., transforming a standard knife into an electric knife by introducing oscillating blades).
4. Changing the properties of the object (e.g., freezing the chocolate syrup and then molding the bottles around the syrup).

Choosing principle number 4, the candy maker decides to change the properties of the chocolate syrup by adding a compound that causes it to solidify when exposed to air, making it easier and faster to coat with chocolate. Once enclosed inside the chocolate, the syrup once again becomes a liquid. Problem solved![69]

Rapid Prototyping

Generating creative ideas is a critical step in the process of taking an idea for a product or a service successfully to the market. However, entrepreneurs find that most of their ideas won't work, and that is where rapid prototyping plays an important part in the creative process. The premise behind **rapid prototyping** is that transforming an idea into an actual model will point out flaws in the original idea and will lead to improvements in its design. "If a picture is worth a thousand words, a prototype is worth ten thousand," says Steve Vassallo of Ideo Inc.[70]

rapid prototyping the process of creating a model of an idea, enabling an entrepreneur to discover flaws in the idea and to make improvements in the design.

The three principles of rapid prototyping are the three R's: rough, rapid, and right. Models do not have to be perfect; in fact, in the early phases of developing an idea, perfecting a model usually is a waste of time. The key is to make the model good enough to

FIGURE 2.3

TRIZ Contradiction Matrix

Characteristic to be improved	Characteristic that is getting worse: Volume of stationary object	Speed	Force	Stress or pressure	Shape	Stability of the object
Volume of stationary object	—	*	Taking out Mechanical vibration Thermal expansion	Intermediary Parameter changes	Nested doll Taking out Parameter changes	Discarding and recovering Mechanics substitution Parameter changes Composite materials
Speed	*	—	The other way round Mechanics substitution Dynamics Periodic action	Universality Mechanical vibration Strong oxidants Composite materials	Dynamics Discarding and recovering Mechanical vibration Parameter changes	Mechanics substitution Homogeneity Segmentation Mechanical vibration
Force	Taking out Phase transitions Mechanical vibration Thermal expansion	The other way round Mechanics substitution Dynamics Equipotentiality	—	Mechanical vibration Skipping Beforehand cushioning	Preliminary action Parameter changes Composite materials Discarding and recovering	Parameter changes Preliminary action Skipping
Stress or pressure	Parameter changes Intermediary	Universality Parameter changes Phase transitions	Phase transitions Parameter changes Skipping	—	Parameter changes Asymmetry Dynamics Preliminary action	Parameter changes Homogeneity Taking out Composite materials
Shape	Nested doll Taking out Parameter changes	Parameter changes Discarding and recovering Mechanical vibration	Parameter changes Preliminary action Thermal expansion Composite materials	Discarding and recovering Dynamics Preliminary action Spheroidality and curvature	—	Homogeneity Segmentation Mechanical vibration Asymmetry

Source: TRIZ 40, http://www.triz40.com/aff_Matrix.htm.

determine what works and what does not. Doing so allows an entrepreneur to develop prototypes rapidly, moving closer to a successful design with each iteration. The final R, right, means building lots of small models that focus on solving particular problems with an idea. "You're not trying to build a complete model," says Vassallo. "You're just focusing on a small section of it."[71]

Evaluating Ideas for Their Market Potential

Legend has it that in 1899, Charles H. Duell, U.S. Commissioner of Patents, advised President McKinley to close the U.S. Patent Office because "Everything that can be invented has been invented." Duell was way off the mark, of course; the U.S. Patent and Trademark Office has issued more than 7 million patents since

1899. However, does a great idea that earns a patent mean that the inventor has the foundation for a successful business?

Not necessarily. Alden McMurtry, a Connecticut tinkerer, in 1911 rushed to the U.S. Patent Office with his immortal design for the bubble-hat. It used a hidden gas canister to send soap bubbles out of a hat—perfect, Mr. McMurtry thought, for show-stopping chorus numbers. It never became a commercial success. Other patents that demonstrate Americans' creative if not always marketable ideas include the underwater airplane, protective glasses for chickens, a 12-foot-long TV remote control, bird diapers, and a dog-shaped vacuum cleaner.

How can an entrepreneur evaluate the market potential of a new product or service idea? The following questions can help any entrepreneur or inventor assess the profit potential of a creative idea:

- What benefits does the product or service offer customers? Is there a real need for it?
- Have you pinpointed the exact problems or difficulties your idea aims to solve? Have you considered the problems or difficulties it might create?
- On a scale of 1 to 10, how difficult will it be to execute the idea and sell it commercially?
- Does the product or service have natural sales appeal? Can customers afford it? Will they buy it? Why?
- What existing products or services would compete with your idea? Is your product or service superior to these competing products or services? If so, in what way?
- On a scale of 1 to 10, how easily can potential customers understand the benefits of your new product or service idea? Are they obvious?
- On a scale of 1 to 10, how complex is the product or service? If it is a product, can you make a prototype of it yourself?
- On a scale of 1 to 10, how complex is the distribution or delivery system necessary to get the product or service into customers' hands?
- How unique is your product or service? How easily can other companies imitate your idea?
- How much will it cost to produce or provide the product or service? To distribute it?

To evaluate creative ideas for their commercial potential, Mail Boxes Etc. relies on a set of 20 criteria, each weighted to reflect its importance, and a scoring scale of minus 2 to plus 2. By multiplying an idea's score on each criterion by the criterion's weight, managers calculate a total score that gives them a sense of an idea's market potential. Michael Michalko, author of *Cracking Creativity: The Secrets of Creative Geniuses*, suggests using the PMI (Plus, Minus, Interesting) technique. "First, list all of the positive (plus) aspects of the idea," he says. "Then list all of the negative (minus) aspects of the idea. Last, list everything that's interesting [about it], but you're not sure if it's a plus or a minus." Evaluating an idea in this way will lead to one of three results. "You'll decide it's a bad idea, you'll decide it's a good idea, or you'll recycle it into something else," says Michalko.

Try your hand at this process. Assume the role of consultant and help Randi Altschul evaluate the market potential of her business idea. One day, Randi was trying to use her malfunctioning cellular phone in her car when she became so frustrated that she was tempted to throw the expensive phone out the window. That's when the idea of a disposable cellular phone came to her. Using her background in inventing board games, Randi worked with engineers to design an ultrathin (the equivalent in size to three credit cards), inexpensive phone whose circuitry is printed in with conductive ink. The two-inch by three-inch phone gives users 60 minutes of calling time (outgoing calls only) and a hands-free attachment, all for an estimated average price of $20 (and a $2 to $3 rebate for returning the phone instead of tossing it). Randi and partner Lee Volte are working through their company, Dieceland Technologies, to apply the same technology used in the cell phone to create a paper laptop computer that they expect to serve as an Internet access device that will sell for $20.

1. Use the resources on the World Wide Web and your library to explore the prospects for Randi Altschul's cell phone.
2. Use the information you collect to answer as many of the questions listed above as possible. Conduct a PMI (plus, minus, interesting) analysis for Randi's idea.

Sources: Adapted from Mary Bellis, "Disposable Cell Phone–Phone Card Phone," *Inventors*, http://inventors.about.com/library/weekly/aa22801b.htm; Joshua Hyatt, "Inside an Inventive Mind," *FSB*, March 2002, p. 26; Jane Bahls, "Got a Winner?" *Business Start-Ups*, March 1999, pp. 6–7; Patricia L. Fry, "Inventor's Workshop," *Business Start-Ups*, August 1997, pp. 34–37; Peter Carbonara, "What Do You Do with a Great Idea?" *Business Start-Ups*, August/September, pp. 28–58; Michael W. Miller, "It Seemed Like a Good Idea," *Wall Street Journal*, May 24, 1993, p. R24; Don Debelak, "Ready or Not?" *Business Start-Ups*, January 1998, pp. 62–65; Karen Axelton, "Imagine That!" *Business Start-Ups*, April 1998, p. 96; Susan Greco, "Where Great Ideas Come From," *Inc.*, April 1998, pp. 76–86; Ross McDonald, "Patent Office Gold," *Kiplinger's Personal Finance Magazine*, June 2002, p. 124; Michael S. Malone, "The Smother of Invention," *Forbes ASAP*, June 24, 2002, pp. 32–40.

LEARNING OBJECTIVES
8. Describe the protection of intellectual property rights through patents, trademarks, and copyrights.

Intellectual Property: Protecting Your Ideas

Once entrepreneurs come up with innovative ideas for a product or service that has market potential, their immediate concern should be to protect it from unauthorized use. The U.S. Chamber of Commerce estimates that intellectual property theft and piracy and counterfeiting of goods cost businesses $250 billion a year.[72] Entrepreneurs must understand how to put patents, trademarks, and copyrights to work for them.

Patents

patent
a grant from the federal government's Patent and Trademark Office to the inventor of a product, giving the exclusive right to make, use, or sell the invention in this country for 20 years from the date of filing the patent application.

A **patent** is a grant from the United States Patent and Trademark Office (PTO) to the inventor of a product, giving the exclusive right to make, use, or sell the invention in this country for 20 years from the date of filing the patent application. The purpose of giving an inventor a 20-year monopoly over a product is to stimulate creativity and innovation. After 20 years, the patent expires and cannot be renewed. Most patents are granted for new product inventions (called utility patents), but *design patents*, extending for 14 years beyond the date the patent is issued, are given to inventors who make new, original, and ornamental changes in the design of existing products that enhance their sales. Inventors who develop a new plant can obtain a ***plant patent***, provided they can reproduce the plant asexually (e.g., by grafting or cross-breeding rather than planting seeds). To be patented, a device must be new (but not necessarily better!), not obvious to a person of ordinary skill or knowledge in the related field, and useful. A device *cannot* be patented if it has been publicized in print anywhere in the world or if it has been used or offered for sale in this country prior to the date of the patent application. A U.S. patent is granted only to the true inventor, not a person who discovers another's invention, and is effective only in the United States and its territories. Inventors who want to sell their inventions abroad must file for patents in each country in which they plan to do business. Once a product is patented, no one can copy or sell it without getting a license from its creator. A patent does not give one the right to make, use, or sell an invention, but the right to exclude others from making, using, or selling it.

Although inventors are never assured of getting a patent, they can enhance their chances considerably by following the basic steps suggested by the PTO. Before beginning the often lengthy and involved procedure, inventors should obtain professional assistance from a patent practitioner—a patent attorney or a patent agent—who is registered with the PTO. Only those attorneys and agents who are officially registered may represent an inventor seeking a patent. A list of registered attorneys and agents is available at the PTO's Web site. Approximately 98 percent of all inventors rely on these patent experts to steer them through the convoluted process. Legal fees for filing a patent application range from $5,000 to $20,000, depending on the complexity of the product.[73] One study reports that for the typical small business, obtaining a patent and maintaining it for 20 years cost about $10,000.[74]

The Patent Process Since George Washington signed the first patent law in 1790, the U.S. Patent and Trademark Office (http://www.uspto.gov) has issued patents on everything imaginable (and some unimaginable items, too), including mouse traps (of course!), Robert Fulton's steamboat, animals (genetically engineered mice), Thomas Edison's light bulb, golf tees (764 different patents), games, and various fishing devices. The J. M. Smucker Company even holds a patent issued in 1999 on a "sealed, crustless sandwich," a peanut butter and jelly sandwich it markets very successfully under the name "Uncrustables."[75] The PTO also has issued patents on business processes—methods of doing business—including Amazon.com's controversial patent on its "1-Click" technology, which allows users to store their customer information in a file and then recall it with one mouse click at checkout. To date the PTO has issued more than 7 million patents, and it receives more than 360,000 new applications each year (see Figure 2.4)![76] To receive a patent, an inventor must follow these steps:

Establish the invention's novelty. An invention is not patentable if it is known or has been used in the United States or has been described in a printed publication in this or a foreign country.

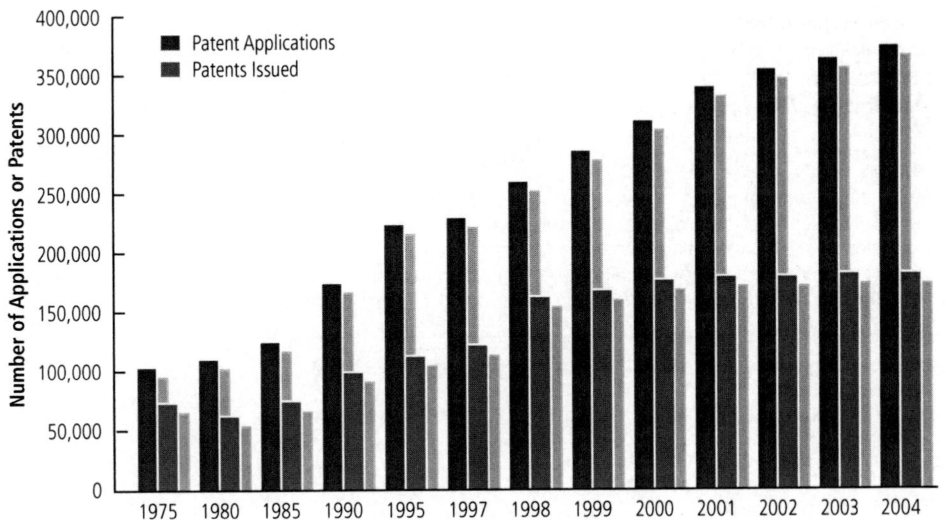

FIGURE 2.4

Number of Patent Applications and Patents Issued

Source: U.S. Patent and Trademark Office, 2005.

Document the device. To protect their patent claims, inventors should be able to verify the date on which they first conceived the idea for their inventions. Inventors can document a device by keeping dated records (including drawings) of their progress on the invention and by having knowledgeable friends witness these records. Inventors also can file a disclosure document with the PTO, a process that includes writing a letter describing the invention and sending a check for $10 to the PTO. A disclosure document is *not* a patent application, but it does provide evidence of the date an inventor conceived an invention.

Search existing patents. To verify that the invention truly is new, not obvious, and useful, an inventor must conduct a search of existing patents on similar products. The purpose of the search is to determine whether the inventor has a chance of getting a patent. Most inventors hire professionals trained in conducting patent searches to perform the research. Inventors themselves can conduct an online search of all patents granted by the PTO since 1976 from the office's Web site. An online search of these patents does not include sketches; however, subscribers to Delphion's Research Intellectual Property Network can access patents, including sketches, as far back as 1971 at http://www.delphion.com/.

Study search result. Once the patent search is finished, inventors must study the results to determine their chances of getting a patent. To be patentable, a device must be sufficiently different from what has been used or described before and must not be obvious to a person having ordinary skill in the area of technology related to the invention.

Submit the patent application. If an inventor decides to seek a patent, he or she must file an application describing the invention with the PTO. The typical patent application runs 20 to 40 pages, although some, especially those for biotech or high-tech products are tens of thousands of pages long. The longest patent application to date is one for a gene patent that was 6 million pages long![77] Most inventors hire patent attorneys or agents to help them complete their patent applications. Figure 2.5 shows a portion of the application for a rather unusual patent, number 5,971,829.

Prosecute the patent application. Before the PTO will issue a patent, one of its examiners studies the application to determine whether the invention warrants a patent. Approval of a patent normally takes about two and one-half years from the date of filing. If the PTO rejects the application, the inventor can amend the application and resubmit it to the PTO.

Defending a patent against "copycat producers" can be expensive and time-consuming but often is necessary to protect an entrepreneur's interest. The median cost of a patent infringement lawsuit seeking less than $1 million is about $500,000 if the case goes to trial (about half that if the parties settle before going to trial), but the odds of winning are

FIGURE 2.5

Patent Number 5,971,829

United States Patent | *5,971,829*
Hartman | **October 26, 1999**

Motorized ice cream cone

Abstract

A novelty amusement eating receptacle for supporting, rotating and sculpting a portion of ice cream or similarly malleable food while it is being consumed comprising: a hand-held housing, a cup rotatably supported by the hand-held housing and adapted to receive and contain a portion of ice cream or food product of similar consistency, and a drive mechanism in the hand-held housing for imparting rotation upon the cup and rotationally feeding its contents against a person's outstretched tongue.

Inventors: **Hartman; Richard B.** (P.O. Box 228, Issaquah, WA 98027)
Appl. No.: **036398**
Filed: **March 6, 1998**

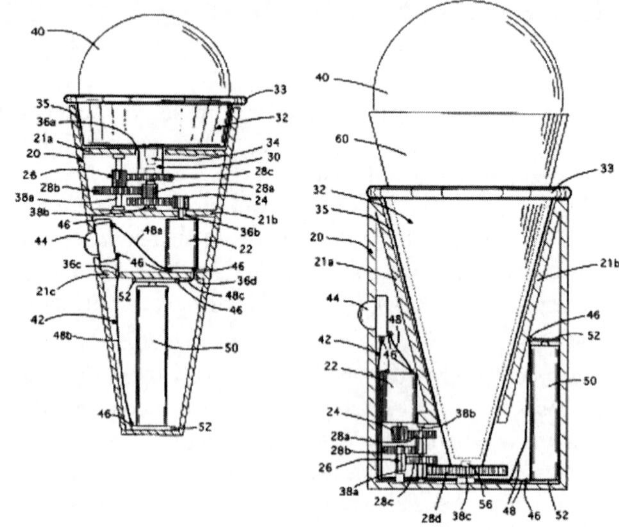

in the patent holder's favor. More than 60 percent of those holding patents win their infringement suits.[78]

Calla Way Golf Company

Knockoffs of its famous "Big Bertha" golf club have kept Callaway Golf Company busy defending its patents against counterfeiters. The company once discovered a competitor making a look-alike driver it called the "Big Bursa." Experts estimate that in some cases, the knockoffs, with their steeply discounted prices, actually outsell the original clubs![79]

With its global reach and speedy convenience, the World Wide Web has only compounded the problem of counterfeit sales, especially among luxury items such as Luis Vuitton and Coach bags, Cartier jewelry, and Chanel perfumes.

trademark
any distinctive word, phrase, symbol, design, name, logo, slogan, or trade dress that a company uses to identify the origin of a product or to distinguish it from other goods on the market.

service mark
offers the same protection as a trademark but identifies and distinguishes the source of a service rather than a product.

Trademarks

A **trademark** is any distinctive word, phrase, symbol, design, name, logo, slogan, or trade dress that a company uses to identify the origin of a product or to distinguish it from other goods on the market. (A **service mark** is the same as a trademark except that it identifies and distinguishes the source of a service rather than a product.) A trademark serves as a company's "signature" in the marketplace. A trademark can be more than just a company's logo, slogan, or brand name; it can also include symbols, shapes, colors, smells, or sounds. For instance, Coca Cola holds a trademark on the shape of its bottle, and NBC owns a trademark on its three-toned chime. Motorcycle maker Harley-Davidson has applied for trademark protection for the shape of its oil tanks and the throaty rumbling sound its engines make![80]

Cheeseburger in Paradise

While they were vacationing in Hawaii, Lauren Gartner and Edna Bayliff craved a cheeseburger but had trouble finding one, so they decided to open a restaurant that specialized in burgers. The name they chose for a burger restaurant located in Maui was, of course, "Cheeseburger in Paradise"—a phrase borrowed from Jimmy Buffet's song of the same name. They hired an attorney to acquire the service mark for the name. The restaurant thrived, and Buffet filed a lawsuit claiming that he owned the rights to the song title for all commercial uses. Gartner and Bayliff defended their right to use the name, pointing to their service mark. As the lawsuit dragged on, the entrepreneurs opened a second Cheeseburger in Paradise location in Waikiki. Several years after the legal battle began, Gartner and Bayliff conceded the rights to the name—excluding their two existing locations—to Buffet, who launched his own chain of restaurants called "Margaritaville" after another one of his songs. Gartner and Bayliff have since opened several more restaurants in Hawaii and on the West Coast under the name "Cheeseburgers, Mai Tais, and Rock-n-roll."[81]

Components of a product's identity such as these are part of its **trade dress,** the unique combination of elements that a company uses to create a product's image and to promote it. For instance, a Mexican restaurant chain's particular décor, color schemes, design, and overall "look and feel" would be its trade dress. To be eligible for trademark protection, trade dress must be inherently unique and distinctive to a company, and another company's use of that trade dress must be likely to confuse customers.

trade dress the unique combination of elements that a company uses to create a product's image and to promote it.

Zippo Manufacturing Company

The Zippo Manufacturing Company, which has been making its distinctive metal cigarette lighter since 1932, has trademarked the shape of its classic lighter with the PTO to protect it from an onslaught of cheap imitations. Every year, the company sells more than 12 million lighters with their gently curved metal case, beveled edges, and distinctive flip-top. Zippo estimates that look-a-like knockoffs, many of which are made in China, have been skimming off as much 30 percent of the company's sales by infringing on its trade dress.[82]

There are 1.5 million trademarks registered in the United States, 900,000 of which are in actual use (see Figure 2.6). Federal law permits a manufacturer to register a trademark, which prevents other companies from employing a similar mark to identify their goods. Before 1989, a business could not reserve a trademark in advance of use. Today, the first party who either uses a trademark in commerce or files an application with the PTO has the ultimate right to register that trademark. Unlike patents and copyrights,

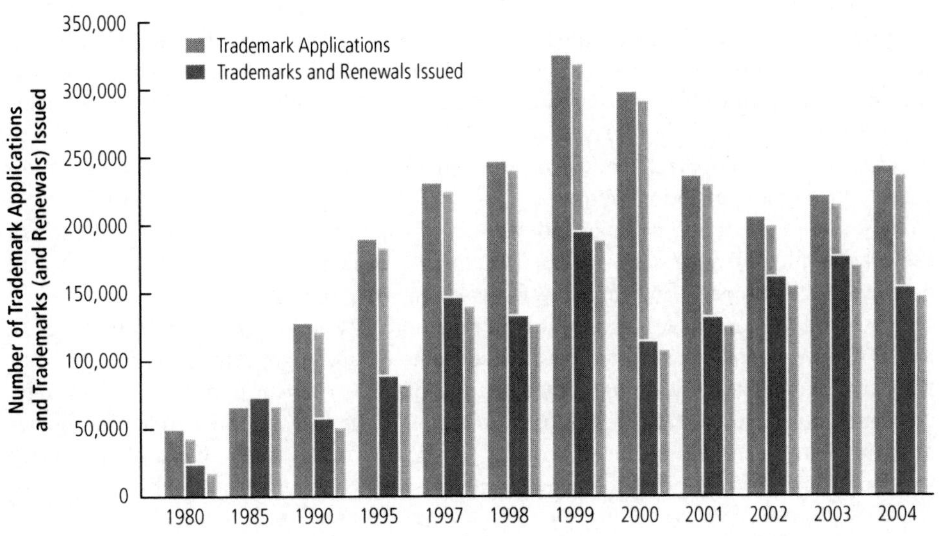

FIGURE 2.6

Number of Trademark Applications and Trademarks Issued

Source: U.S. Patent and Trademark Office, 2005.

which are issued for limited amounts of time, trademarks last indefinitely as long as the holder continues to use it. (Five years after a trademark's registration date, the entrepreneur must file an affidavit of use with the PTO.) However, a trademark cannot keep competitors from producing the same product and selling it under a different name. It merely prevents others from using the same or confusingly similar trademark for the same or similar products.

Many business owners are confused by the use of the symbols "TM" and "®." Anyone who claims the right to a particular trademark (or service mark) can use the "TM" (or "SM") symbols without having to register the mark with the PTO. The claim to that trademark or service mark may or may not be valid, however. Only those businesses that have registered their marks with the PTO can use the "®" symbol. Entrepreneurs do not have to register trademarks or service marks to establish their rights to those marks; however, registering a mark with the PTO does give entrepreneurs greater power to protect their marks. Filing an application to register a trademark or service mark is relatively easy, but it does require a search of existing names.

Cosmic Debris, Etc.

Cosmic Debris, Etc., a 25-employee company based in Oakland, California, created a popular character known as Emily the Strange, a girl who dresses in black and whose favorite phrase is "Get lost!." The company generates $5 million in annual sales marketing a variety of products such as T-shirts and backpacks bearing the image of Emily the Strange. Unfortunately, knock-off artists around the world have been stealing the company's trademarked images and putting them on unlicensed garments. To cope with the threat of millions in lost sales, Cosmic Debris managers hired a private investigator, tracked some of the worst perpetrators to Taiwan, and worked with police there to confiscate cartons of counterfeit product.[83]

An entrepreneur may lose the exclusive right to a trademark if it loses its unique character and becomes a generic name. Aspirin, escalator, thermos, brassiere, super glue, yo-yo, and cellophane all were once enforceable trademarks that have become common words in the English language. Such generic terms can no longer be licensed as trademarks.

Copyrights

copyright
an exclusive right that protects the creators of original works of authorship such as literary, dramatic, musical, and artistic works.

A **copyright** is an exclusive right that protects the creators of original works of authorship such as literary, dramatic, musical, and artistic works (e.g., art, sculptures, literature, software, music, videos, video games, choreography, motion pictures, recordings, and others). The internationally recognized symbol "©" denotes a copyrighted work. A copyright protects only the form in which an idea is expressed, not the idea itself. A copyright on a creative work comes into existence the moment its creator puts that work into a tangible form. Just as with a trademark, obtaining basic copyright protection does *not* require registering the creative work with the U.S. Copyright Office (http://lcweb.loc.gov/copyright).

Registering a copyright, however, does give creators greater protection over their work. Copyright applications must be filed with the Copyright Office in the Library of Congress for a fee of $30 per application. A valid copyright on a work lasts for the life of the creator plus 70 years after his or her death. When a copyright expires, the work becomes public property and can be used by anyone free of charge.

Because they are so easy to duplicate, computer software programs, videotapes, CDs, and DVDs are among the most-often pirated items by copyright infringers. Experts estimate that the global software industry loses $12 billion each year to pirates who illegally copy programs and that Hollywood loses $2 billion to those who forge counterfeit movies and sell them. Because they are so adept at plying their trade, video pirates often manage to beat genuine distributors to the market with movies![84]

TABLE 2.3 Characteristics of Patents, Trademarks, and Copyrights

Type of Protection	What It Covers	Time Required	Cost
Copyright	Works of original authorship such as books or software	About two weeks	About $30
Trademark	Logos, names, phrases	Six months to one year	$900 to $1,500
Design patent	The look of an original product	Up to two years	$5,000 to $20,000
Utility patent	How an original product works	Two to five years	$5,000 to $20,000
Business method patent	A business process or procedure	Two to five years	$5,000 to $20,000

Source: Anne Field, "How to Knock Out Knock Offs," *Business Week,* March 14, 2005, http://www.businessweek.com/@@7oPzclQQnlwLqxsA/magazine/content/05_11/b3924446.htm.

Thimbleberries

Thimbleberries, a small company that sells designs and fabrics to quilters and generates $2 million in annual sales, copyrights every one of its designs, and the company's name is a registered trademark. When CEO Lynette Jensen discovered that 20 eBay sellers were listing what they claimed were Thimbleberries quilting kits—a product the company has never made—she took immediate action, sending letters to the offenders threatening legal action if they did not stop immediately. The Thimbleberries name quickly disappeared from the products listed on the eBay auction site.[85]

Table 2.3 provides a summary of the characteristics of patents, trademarks, and copyrights.

Protecting Intellectual Property

Acquiring the protection of patents, trademarks, and copyrights is useless unless an entrepreneur takes action to protect those rights in the marketplace. Unfortunately, not every businessperson respects others' rights of ownership to products, processes, names, and works, and some infringe deliberately on those rights with impunity. In other cases, the infringing behavior simply is the result of a lack of knowledge about others' rights of ownership. After acquiring the proper legal protection through patents, copyrights, or trademarks, entrepreneurs must monitor the market (and the World Wide Web in particular) for unauthorized, copycat users. If an entrepreneur has a valid patent, trademark, or copyright, stopping an infringer usually requires nothing more than a stern "cease and desist" letter from an attorney. Often, offenders do not want to get into expensive legal battles and agree to stop their illegal behavior. If that tactic fails, the entrepreneur may have no choice but to bring an infringement lawsuit, many of which end up being settled out of court.

The primary weapon an entrepreneur has to protect patents, trademarks, and copyrights is the legal system. The major problem with relying on the legal system to enforce ownership rights, however, is the cost and time of infringement lawsuits, which can quickly exceed the budget of most small businesses and occupy huge blocks of managers' time. Lawsuits always involve costs. Before pursuing what could become an expensive and drawn-out legal battle, an entrepreneur must consider the following issues:

- Can your opponent afford to pay if you win?
- Do you expect to get enough from the suit to cover the costs of hiring an attorney and preparing a case?
- Can you afford the loss of time, money, and privacy from the ensuing lawsuit?

Chapter Summary by Learning Objectives

1. Explain the differences among creativity, innovation, and entrepreneurship.

The entrepreneur's "secret" for creating value in the marketplace is applying creativity and innovation to solve problems and to exploit opportunities that people face every day. Creativity is the ability to develop new ideas and to discover new ways of looking at problems and opportunities. Innovation is the ability to apply creative solutions to those problems and opportunities to enhance or to enrich people's lives. Entrepreneurship is the result of a disciplined, systematic process of applying creativity and innovation to needs and opportunities in the marketplace.

2. Describe why creativity and innovation are such integral parts of entrepreneurship.

Entrepreneurs must always be on guard against paradigms—preconceived ideas of what the world is, what it should be like, and how it should operate—because they are logjams to creativity. Successful entrepreneurs often go beyond conventional wisdom as they ask "Why not . . .?"

Success—even survival—in this fiercely competitive, global environment requires entrepreneurs to tap their creativity (and that of their employees) constantly.

3. Understand how the two hemispheres of the human brain function and what role they play in creativity.

For years, people assumed that creativity was an inherent trait. Today, however, we know better. Research shows that almost anyone can learn to be creative. The left hemisphere of the brain controls language, logic, and symbols, processing information in a step-by-step fashion. The right hemisphere handles emotional, intuitive, and spatial functions, processing information intuitively. The right side of the brain is the source of creativity and innovation. People can learn to control which side of the brain is dominant in a given situation.

4. Explain the 10 "mental locks" that limit individual creativity.

The number of potential barriers to creativity is limitless, but entrepreneurs commonly face 10 "mental locks" on creativity: Searching for the one "right" answer; focusing on "being logical;" blindly following the rules; constantly being practical; viewing play as frivolous; becoming overly specialized; avoiding ambiguity; fearing looking foolish; fearing mistakes and failure; and believing that "I'm not creative."

5. Understand how entrepreneurs can enhance their own creativity and that of their employees as well.

Entrepreneurs can stimulate creativity in their companies by expecting creativity; expecting and tolerating failure; encouraging curiosity; viewing problems as challenges; providing creativity training; providing support; rewarding creativity; and modeling creativity. Entrepreneurs can enhance their own creativity by using the following techniques: allowing themselves to be creative; giving their minds fresh input every day; keeping a journal handy to record their thoughts and ideas; reading books on stimulating creativity or taking a class on creativity; taking some time off to relax.

6. Describe the steps in the creative process.

The creative process consists of seven steps: Step 1. Preparation—involves getting the mind ready for creative thinking; Step 2. Investigation—requires the individual to develop a solid understanding of the problem or decision; Step 3. Transformation—involves viewing the similarities and the differences among the information collected; Step 4. Incubation—allows the subconscious mind to reflect on the information collected; Step 5. Illumination—occurs at some point during the incubation stage when a spontaneous breakthrough causes "the light bulb to go on;" Step 6. Verification—involves validating the idea as accurate and useful; and Step 7. Implementation—involves transforming the idea into a business reality.

7. Discuss techniques for improving the creative process.

Four techniques that are especially useful for improving the creative process are as follows:

- Brainstorming is a process in which a small group of people interact with very little structure with the goal of producing a large *quantity* of novel and imaginative ideas.
- Mind-mapping is a graphical technique that encourages thinking on both sides of the brain, visually displays the various relationships among ideas, and improves the ability to view a problem from many sides.
- TRIZ is a systematic approach designed to help solve any technical problem, whatever its source. Unlike brainstorming and mind-mapping, which are right-brained activities, TRIZ is a left-brained, scientific, step-by-step process that is based on the study of hundreds of the most innovative patents across the globe.
- Rapid prototyping is based on the premise that transforming an idea into an actual model will point out flaws in the original idea and will lead to improvements in its design.

8. Describe the protection of intellectual property through patents, trademarks, and copyrights.

A patent is a grant from the federal government that gives an inventor exclusive rights to an invention for 20 years.

A trademark is any distinctive word, symbol, or trade dress that a company uses to identify its product and to distinguish it from other goods. It serves as a company's "signature" in the marketplace.

A copyright protects original works of authorship. It covers only the form in which an idea is expressed and not the idea itself and lasts for 70 years beyond the creator's death.

Discussion Questions

1. Explain the differences among creativity, innovation, and entrepreneurship.
2. How are creativity, innovation, and entrepreneurship related?
3. Why are creativity and innovation so important to the survival and success of a business?
4. One entrepreneur claims, "Creativity unrelated to a business plan has no value." What does he mean? Do you agree?
5. What is a paradigm? What impact do paradigms have on creativity?
6. Can creativity be taught or is it an inherent trait? Explain.
7. How does the human brain function? What operations does each hemisphere specialize in? Which hemisphere is the "seat" of creativity?
8. Briefly outline the 10 "mental locks" that can limit individual creativity. Give an example of a situation in which you subjected yourself to one of these mental locks.
9. What can entrepreneurs do to stimulate their own creativity and to encourage it among workers?
10. Explain the steps of the creative process. What can an entrepreneur do to enhance each step?
11. Explain the differences among a patent, a trademark, and a copyright. What form of intellectual property does each protect?

Business Plan Pro

Business PlanPro

The creative process can help you to develop your business concept and add dimension to an existing business venture. The process of creating your business plan will enable you to refine and test your creative ideas.

Business Plan Exercises

Select one of the creative processes mentioned in this chapter. You may want to consider mind-mapping, TRIX, or brainstorming if you are in a group. Apply this technique to your business concept. If your business idea is in the embryonic stage, use this exercise to bring focus to the business. If you have a solid grasp on your business concept, use one of these creative techniques to address a specific business challenge or to explore a potential opportunity for your business.

On the Web

Identify at least three key words or phrases that you associate with your business concept. For example, if your business is a specialty retail and online store selling wakeboards, you may consider the terms "wakeboards," "water sports," and "boards." Enter terms relevant to your business in your favorite search engine and see what information appears.

1. What companies advertise under those terms?
2. What are the top three listings?
3. How is your business unique from those businesses listed, including the fact that your business may offer a local presence?
4. What other attributes set your business apart from what you see on the Web?

Make note of anything that you learned or observed from what you saw online.

In the Software

Open Business Plan Pro and the business plan you began in Chapter 1. If this exercise has changed any of your initial concepts or produced an entirely different business concept, think about why the exercise led you down a different path. If that venture is different, select the Create a new business plan option and work through the wizards as you did before. Once again, you can view the outline created based on those responses by clicking on the Preview icon or going to File, Print, and then Print Preview.

Sample Plans

Open the Sample Plan Browser in Business Plan Pro; it will be helpful to have an Internet connection when you do. Enter one or more of the search terms you selected in the exercise in the search window of the Sample Plan Browser. Do any sample plans appear based on the term you entered? If so, review those plans. Will one of those plans be a potential resource for you as create your business plan? Remember, the sample plan does not have to be identical to your business concept. With even distant similarities, sample plans may be a resource for you based on its general content or layout.

Building Your Business Plan

Open your business plan and go to the section titled "Product and Service Description." You can do that by clicking on the Plan Outline icon at the top of your screen or clicking on View and selecting Outline from the dropdown menu. Within that section, begin to describe the products or services your business will offer. Notice that you have the option to view that section of a sample plan by clicking on Examples in the upper right hand section of the screen. Now, go to the "Market Needs" section of the plan. Make a few notes here regarding the needs that your products and services satisfy. We will revisit these sections, so just make comments that will help you develop your thoughts as you progress through the chapters.

Beyond the Classroom . . .

1. Your dinner guests are to arrive in five minutes, and you've just discovered that you forgot to chill the wine! Wanting to maintain your reputation as the perfect host/hostess, you must tackle this problem with maximum creativity. What could you do? Generate as many solutions as you can in five minutes working alone. Then, work with two or three students in a small group to brainstorm the problem.
2. Work with a group of your classmates to think of as many alternative uses for the commercial lubricant WD-40 as you can. Remember to think *fluidly* (generating a quantity of ideas) and *flexibly* (generating unconventional ideas).
3. Review the following list of household appliances. Working with a small group of your classmates, select one and use the brainstorming technique to develop as many alternative uses for the appliance as you can in 15 minutes. Remember to abide by the rules of brainstorming! The appliances: dishwasher, clothes dryer, curling iron, toaster oven, iron, microwave oven, coffeemaker, and any others you want to use.
4. A major maker of breakfast cereals was about to introduce a new multigrain cereal. Its principal selling point is that it features "three great tastes" in every bowl: corn, rice, and wheat. Because a cereal's name is an integral part of its marketing campaign, the company hired a very costly consulting firm to come up with the right name for the new product. The consulting firm tackled the job using "a combination of structural linguistics and personal creativity." One year and many dollars later, the consulting firm gave its recommendation.

   Take 20 minutes to list names that you think would be appropriate for this cereal. Make brief notes about why you think each name is appropriate.

   Your professor may choose to prepare a list of names from all of the members of your class and may take a vote to determine the "winner."
5. Each hemisphere of the brain processes information differently, and one hemisphere tends to dominate the other. Consider the following lists of words and decide which one best describes the way you make decisions and solve problems:

Metaphor	Logic
Dream	Reason
Humor	Precision
Ambiguity	Consistency
Play	Work
Approximate	Exact
Fantasy	Reality
Paradox	Direct
Diffuse	Focused
Hunch	Analysis
Generalization	Specific
Child	Adult

   If you chose the list on the left, you tend to engage in "soft" thinking, which suggests a right-brain orientation. If you chose the list on the right, you tend to engage in "hard" thinking, which suggests a left-brain orientation.

   Creativity relies on both "soft" and "hard" thinking. Each plays an important role in the creative process but at different phases.

   A. Identify which type of thinking—"soft" or "hard"—would be most useful in each of the seven stages of the creative process.

   B. List five things you can do to develop your thinking skills in the area ("soft" or "hard") that least describes your decision-making style.
6. Interview at least two entrepreneurs about their experiences as business owners. Where did their business ideas originate? How important are creativity and innovation to their success? How do they encourage an environment of creativity in their businesses?

Chapter 3
Intrapreneurship: Developing Corporate Entrepreneurship

- Defining the term 'intrapreneurship'
- Illustrating the important role of corporate entrepreneuring
- Describing the corporate obstacles preventing innovation from existing in corporations
- Describing the elements of an intrapreneurial strategy
- Profiling intrapreneurial characteristics and myths
- Illustrating the interactive process of intrapreneurship

CHAPTER 14

Intrapreneurship

Chapter overview

Intrapreneurship is something of a holy grail for management: the promise of entrepreneurial dynamism, agility and adeptness in exploiting opportunities combined with the stability, market power and low risk of the established business. However, there are problems in combining the two.

14.1 The nature of intrapreneurship

Key learning outcome

An appreciation of the potential and role of intrapreneurship in established organisations.

In recognising the power of the entrepreneurial organisation, it is important not to be too dismissive of what the established 'non-entrepreneurial' organisation has to offer its stakeholders. After all, an established business is only established because it has enjoyed success. The entrepreneurial organisation and the established organisation both have advantages. The entrepreneurial shows an acceptance of (even a need for) change and an ability to exploit new opportunity. The established demonstrates an ability to consolidate around success, manage risk and control resource flows.

A combination of the two, that is, an organisation which recognised the basis of its success and was able to manage it to reduce risk and yet at the same time was flexible to the shifting needs of its stakeholders, remained attuned to new market opportunities and responsive to the need for change, would suggest itself as an ideal type of business. The *intrapreneur* provides a means of achieving the established–entrepreneurial synthesis.

The intrapreneur is a role defined by Pinchot (1985) in his book, *Intrapreneuring*. In essence, the intrapreneur is an entrepreneur who works within the confines of an established organisation. The intrapreneur's role would parallel that of the entrepreneur. In particular he or she would be responsible for developing and communicating organisational vision; identifying new opportunities for the organisation; generating innovative strategic options; creating and offering an organisation-wide perspective; facilitating and encouraging change within the organisation; challenging existing ways of doing things and breaking down bureaucratic inertia. This role has also been described as that of a 'change master' (Kanter, 1985).

Intrapreneurial activity can be directed at four levels within and outside the organisation. These differ in the impact they will have on the organisation and its surroundings, their effect on the venture's stakeholders, the resources they will require and the level of risk they entail.

- *The management of specific projects.* All businesses engage in new projects of some type. Projects such as new product development, the exploitation of a new market opportunity (perhaps international through exporting or strategic alliance), the integration of a new technology into the firm's operations or the acquiring of new funding are especially important to the maturing entrepreneurial venture that wants to keep its competitive edge. Such projects may be best managed in an entrepreneurial way that cuts across conventional organisational boundaries. They may be made the responsibility of a particular cross-disciplinary team that operates with intrapreneurial flair. Ahuja and Lampert (2001) develop a model of how intrapreneurism helps large firms to achieve breakthrough inventions.
- *The setting up of new business units.* As the venture becomes larger, new and distinct business functions and units come into their own. A particular part of the business may operate best if it has a distinct character and a degree of independence. The setting up of new business units is a demanding project. Not only must the structural and external strategic issues be considered, but there are also the resourcing issues (including human), and the relationship with the parent business to be taken into account. Again, an intrapreneurial team, the members of which may have a future role in the new unit, may best manage this sort of project.
- *Reinvigorating the whole organisation.* The success of entrepreneurial ventures is largely based on their flexibility and responsiveness to new and unmet customer demands. Such flexibility can be lost as the business grows and its attention is drawn to internal concerns. Reintroducing the inventive spirit back into the business may be a radical process. Making the organisation entrepreneurial again is clearly an intrapreneurial project. An intrapreneur must lead such a project with entrepreneurial vision for the organisation's future, with an entrepreneurial approach to using power, leadership and motivation and an ability to overcome organisational resistance to change.
- *Reinventing the business's industry.* Entrepreneurs make a difference. The world is not the same after they have built their venture. The most successful entrepreneurs do not just enter a market: they reinvent the industry in which they operate by introducing new technology, delivering new products or operating in a new, more effective way. There is no reason why the maturing entrepreneurial venture should not hold on to this ambition. A business can win by playing to the rules well; but it can also win by changing the rules to suit itself. Clearly though, such a project is wide in its scope and challenging to implement. It demands an eye on the future, strategic vision, comfort with risk and an ability to lead people forward. It is at this level that intrapreneurship meets up with and becomes entrepreneurship.

Intrapreneurism offers an exciting option for the consolidating entrepreneurial venture. It promises a way to build on success while retaining the original dynamism of the venture. It suggests a way to reduce risk while still pursuing fleeting opportunities. However, any organisational form which promises such high rewards must also present some challenges. There are limitations to intrapreneurship, a point developed by Ross (1987).

14.2 The challenges to intrapreneurship

Key learning outcome

A recognition that the potential for intrapreneurship may be limited.

Existing managers' comfort

Allowing a role for the intrapreneur to develop demands that the existing senior managers must create space for the intrapreneur to operate. That means letting go of some degree of control. Existing senior (and not so senior) managers may not feel comfortable with this. In effect, allowing the intrapreneur to operate means that senior managers must give up, or at least share a part of their power at a core rather than a peripheral level. After all, as Young (1999) points out, intrapreneurial management is about breaking rules. And this means the rules that existing managers see as their role to protect and may even have created in the first place.

Decision-making control

Entrepreneurs exist to challenge orthodoxies. They seek a better way of doing things. They must be dissatisfied with the status quo. This same dissatisfaction must also motivate the intrapreneur. Unlike the entrepreneur, however, the intrapreneur must operate within some sort of organisational decision-making framework. If they did not, then they would not actually be working for the organisation at all. The question here is to what extent the intrapreneur can be allowed to challenge existing decision-making procedures and to what extent they must be bound by them. A balance must be created between allowing the intrapreneur freedom to make their own moves and the need to keep the business on a constant strategic path.

Internal politics

The intrapreneur must question the existing order and drive change within the organisation. For many individuals and groups within the organisation, such change will present a challenge. As a result, the intrapreneur is likely to meet resistance, both active and passive, to the ideas they bring along. An ability to predict and understand that resistance, and developing the leadership skills necessary to overcome it, present a considerable challenge to the manager. Intrapreneurs are a rare breed. Tom Peters (1989) has suggested that intrapreneurs must be able to 'thrive on chaos'.

Rewards for the intrapreneur

The intrapreneur, if they are to be effective, must bring along the same type and level of skills that entrepreneurs themselves offer. The question is, can the organisation *really* offer the intrapreneur the rewards (economic, social and developmental) they might come to expect in return for using them? In short, if someone is an effective intrapreneur, how long will it be before the temptation of full-blown entrepreneurship is felt and they move off to start a venture of their own?

Clearly, intrapreneurship presents itself as a spectrum which, as a style of management, acts to connect 'conventional' management with entrepreneurial management. It offers a way to bring the advantages of both types of management together. In this it is a compromise. The entrepreneur can only facilitate intrapreneurship within the business by recognising the nature of this compromise and making decisions in relation to it. The central question relates to how much latitude the venture's strategy gives individuals to make their own decisions. The question is not just strategic. An entrepreneur must decide to what extent they will be willing to accept dissent from the intrapreneur. Will it be received as a challenge? How does active dissent fit with the leadership strategy the entrepreneur has nurtured?

Entrepreneurs must also ask how the reward structure they have set up encourages and discourages individual decision making. What does the individual get in return for venturing on behalf of the business? What sanctions come into force if things go wrong? The entrepreneur must remember that such rewards and sanctions are not always formal and explicit. Further, the entrepreneur must recognise the level of resistance that agents driving change meet from the organisation and accept responsibility for helping the intrapreneur to overcome this. No less than any other member of the organisation, the intrapreneur needs support, encouragement and leadership.

Summary of key ideas

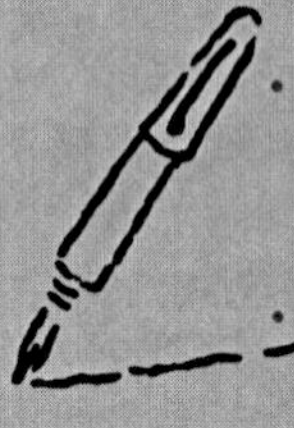

- Intrapreneurship – the entrepreneur in the established organisation – would seem to offer a great prize: the possibility of entrepreneurial dynamism with the stability and market power of the proven firm.
- Intrapreneurs can operate at several levels:
  - managing specific projects;
  - setting up new business units;
  - reinvigorating the organisation;
  - reinventing industries.
- However, the potential for intrapreneurship is limited by:
  - existing managers' comfort with rule-breaking intrapreneurs;
  - keeping the intrapreneur aligned with the organisation's strategy;
  - the ability to provide the effective intrapreneur with sufficient rewards (financial and developmental).

Research themes

Defining the intrapreneur

Refer back to the discussion of defining the entrepreneur in Chapter 1. Consider the two studies undertaken by Gartner (1988, 1990) to ascertain the definitions of the entrepreneur that various people (politicians, managers, experts) suggested and how the responses were analysed.

Repeat the study (or at least using a similar methodology) focusing in on the terms 'entrepreneur' and 'intrapreneur'. You may find human resource and development managers within established firms to be a good response group. (You will find that by using e-mail your study will not be as expensive to conduct as Gartner's!)

Compare your findings to those of Gartner. Is there a greater consensus on what an intrapreneur is? How is the intrapreneur distinguished from the entrepreneur?

Conceptualising the intrapreneur

Review the discussion about economic approaches to the entrepreneur in Chapter 7. To what extent can the points made from various economic perspectives be said to apply to the intrapreneur as much as to the entrepreneur? Can any of them distinguish the intrapreneur from the entrepreneur? Attempt to relate your conclusions in the form of some diagram or conceptual map.

Key readings

Two contrasing readings, the first emphasising the opportunity of intrapreneurship, the second emphasising its limitations, are:

Stopford, J.M. (1994) 'Creating corporate entrepreneurship', *Strategic Management Journal*, Vol. 15, pp. 521–36.

Wesley Morse, C. (1986) 'The delusion of intrapreneurship', *Long Range Planning*, Vol. 19, No. 6, pp. 92–5.

Suggestions for further reading

Ahuja, G. and Lampert, C.M. (2001) 'Entrepreneurship in the large corporation: a longitudinal study of how established firms create breakthrough inventions', *Strategic Management Journal*, Vol. 22, pp. 521–43.

Coulson-Thomas, C. (1999) 'Individuals and enterprise: developing intrapreneurs for the new millennium', *Industrial and Commercial Training*, Vol. 31, No. 7.

Gartner, W.B. (1998) '"Who is an entrepreneur?" is the wrong question', *American Journal of Small Business*, Spring, pp. 11–32.

Gartner, W.B. (1990) 'What are we talking about when we talk about entrepreneurship?', *Journal of Business Venturing*, Vol. 5, pp. 15–28.

Jennings, R., Cox, C. and Cooper, G.L. (1994) *Business Elites: The Psychology of Entrepreneurs and Intrapreneurs*. New York: Routledge.

Johnson, D. (2001) 'What is innovation and entrepreneurship? Lessons for larger organizations', *Industrial and Commercial Training*, Vol. 13, No. 4, pp. 135–40.

Kanter, R.M. (1985) *The Change Masters*. London: Unwin Hyman.

Koon, P.A. (2000) 'Developing corporate intrapreneurs', *Engineering Management Journal*, Vol. 12, No. 2, pp. 3–7.

Moon, M.J. (1999) 'The pursuit of managerial entrepreneurship: does organization matter?', *Public Administration Review*, Vol. 59, No. 1, pp. 31–43.

Morris, M.H. and Jones, F.F. (1999) 'Entrepreneurhip in established organizations: the case of the public sector', *Entrepreneurship: Theory and Practice*, Vol. 24, No. 1, pp. 71–91.

Pearson, G.J. (1989) 'Promoting entrepreneurship in large companies', *Long Range Planning*, Vol. 22, No. 3, pp. 87–97.

Peters, T. (1989) *Thriving on chaos*. London: Macmillan.

Pinchot, III, G. (1985) *Intrapreneuring*. New York: Harper & Row.

Prassad, L. (1993) 'The etiology of organizational politics: implications for the intrapreneur', *SAM Advanced Management Journal*, Vol. 58, No. 3, pp. 35–41.

Robinson, M. (2001) 'The ten commandments of intrapreneurs', *New Zealand Management*, Vol. 48, No. 11, pp. 95–7.

Ross, J. (1987) 'Corporations and entrepreneurs: paradox and opportunity', *Business Horizons*, July/Aug., pp. 76–80.

Stopford, J.M. (1994) 'Creating corporate entrepreneurship', *Strategic Management Journal*, Vol. 15, pp. 521–36.

Wesley Morse, C. (1986) 'The delusion of intrapreneurship', *Long Range Planning*, Vol. 19, No. 6, pp. 92–5.

Young, A.P. (1999) 'Rule breaking and a new opportunistic managerialism', *Management Decision*, Vol. 37, No. 7, pp. 582–8.

Selected case material

CASE 14.1 25 July 2005 FT

Smart companies take an 'intrapreneurial' spirit

PAUL TYRELL

How do large companies such as Apple Computer continue to innovate and respond rapidly to new opportunities, as if they were start-ups?

Apple seemed to produce the iPod out of thin air in 2001 – at the time, a personal digital music player was not regarded as the obvious progeny of a personal computer manufacturer. Yet the company has since re-entered the FT Global 500 ranking of the world's largest companies after a four-year absence.

The iPod now accounts for one-third of Apple's revenues and its 'halo effect' has contributed to a 35 per cent increase in sales of the company's Macintosh computers over the past year.

The iconic music player has also given critical mass to an entirely new market – the selling of digital music online. Even with his expertise in marketing, Steve Jobs, Apple chief executive, could never have predicted such success. Yet he was prepared for it in part thanks to a company culture in which innovative opportunities are spotted, nurtured and championed in an entrepreneurial manner – in short, a culture that is 'intrapreneurial'.

The term has its roots in an *Economist* article of 1976 by its then-deputy editor, Norman Macrae. Among other things, Mr Macrae argued that 'dynamic corporations of the future should simultaneously be trying alternative ways of doing things in competition with themselves.'

In a follow-up article, published in 1982, he suggested large organisations should form internal markets in which groups of staff would compete for modules of work and proportionate remuneration, rather than simply being paid for attendance.

The term 'intrapreneur' was coined at about the same time by a husband-and-wife team, Gifford and Elizabeth Pinchot, who cited Macrae's 1976 article as their inspiration.

Both entrepreneurs and business consultants, the Pinchots suggested individuals could act like entrepreneurs within a large organisation to the benefit of both employee and employer, provided they were willing to risk something of value to themselves – a portion of their salary, for example. Such intrapreneurs could exchange a completed project for a cash bonus or capital to invest internally in future projects.

The idea of setting up semi-autonomous units dedicated to innovation had a famous precedent.

Lockheed Martin, the US aerospace company, set up its 'Advanced Development Projects Unit', nicknamed 'Skunk Works', during the Second World War. A small facility, it was given huge resources and top personnel to develop cutting-edge technology in secret.

Some of the world's most famous military aircraft – such as the SR-71 Blackbird, the high-speed and radar-resistant reconnaissance aircraft – emerged from its hangars. Still operating from an Air Force base in California, Skunk Works is now a registered trademark and a widely used term for any secret innovation-led project.

During the 1970s, similar units were set up inside many organisations to think 'disruptively' – to look at products or markets outside their usual offering.

One of the most famous was 'Project Chess', the twelve-man team at IBM that developed the first personal computer in 1981. Similarly, after the Macintosh computer was launched in 1984, Steve Jobs described its development as an 'intrapreneurial venture' within Apple – since the machine would compete with the Apple II, previously the company's core product.

Today the term intrapreneurship encompasses two main concepts: first, 'corporate venturing', which usually describes the search for spin-off opportunities; and second, the fostering of an entrepreneurial culture in large organisations, with the main objective of innovation.

The first of these has a dismal track record. Recent research by Ashridge and London business schools concluded that less than 5 per cent of corporate venturing units created new businesses that were taken up by a parent company.

Nevertheless, Julian Birkinshaw, a professor at London Business School, suggests that in certain conditions large companies can create value by acting like venture capitalists.

These include 'harvest venturing', where surplus resources are used in commercial ventures, and 'ecosystem venturing', where the company supports entrepreneurial moves

CASE 14.1 CONT.

among its stakeholders – investing in its suppliers, for example, to ensure that components are always available.

Evidence suggests that an 'intrapreneurial' culture may be more powerful. Professor Birkinshaw says that companies now treat the generation of ideas as a vital task.

'If you went back 50 years and asked someone on the production line who was responsible for quality, they'd point to the quality assurance guy at the end of the line,' he says. 'Now quality is everyone's responsibility. Similarly, when you ask someone in a large organisation today who is responsible for new ideas, the venturing laboratory is no longer a satisfactory solution. You need to get everybody alert to opportunities and acting on them.'

Corporations should aim to be 'ambidextrous', Prof. Birkinshaw says. In other words, 'good at both traditional, boring, efficiency-oriented functions and at spotting and acting on sexy new ideas'.

A sales manager, for example, may sell to a specific group of clients, but through their awareness of others they may identify an entirely untapped group, or even a new line of business. In such a situation, the successful company will have a culture that supports them – one that is 'empowering as well as aggressively performance-oriented'.

Moreover, such a company is more likely to have a culture that supports learning, says Dylan Jones-Evans, director of the newly formed National Entrepreneurship Observatory for Wales.

Professor Jones-Evans was part of a team that recently surveyed the 120 most innovative companies in South Korea, as classified by the government. He found that the most successful were those that continually tried to learn from their competitors and other external sources of information about their markets.

'As organisations grow out of their entrepreneurial stage, many suffer from what we call founders' disease,' he says. 'They develop their core competence to such an extent that it becomes all they concentrate on. As a result, they're left behind by the dynamic environment around them.'

Recent research by Clark Gilbert, a professor at Harvard Business School, suggests the best innovations result from thinking about external forces.

'Intrapreneurial' ventures should be 'opportunity-based rather than resource-based', he says, explaining that most large organisations try unsuccessfully to develop new ideas from their existing resources and competencies, rather than look outside for ideas. 'The problem in so many existing markets is that product lines have already overshot what most consumers can absorb,' he adds.

In such an environment, companies should be aiming for 'disruptive' ideas of the sort described by economist Joseph Schumpeter when, in 1934, he described the 'creative destruction' of established businesses by entrepreneurs.

'We find big firms are interested in disruption only when they think it will overlap or attack their business,' says Prof. Gilbert. 'Yet it always leads to growth in the overall market. The personal computer did disrupt the mainframe but it caused the total market for hardware to grow.

'Easyjet is disrupting the airline industry but it's also bringing growth in the consumption of air travel. Often, big firms are so worried about cannibalising that they fail to realise they're poised on the edge of huge growth opportunities.'

Source: Paul Tyrell, 'Smart companies take an "intrapreneurial" spirit', *Financial Times*, 25 July 2005, p. 11.

CASE 14.2

9 August 2004 

Know the limits of corporate venturing

JULIAN BIRKINSHAW AND ANDREW CAMPBELL

With growth back on the agenda after a period of austerity and cost cutting, it is worth reflecting on the lessons arising from similar periods in the past.

In the late 1990s, more than three-quarters of companies in the Fortune 100 and an equivalent number of FTSE 100 companies set up corporate venturing units as part of their search for growth. For example, BAT, the tobacco company, set up two units: Imagination, to search for new ideas, and Evolution, to develop the ideas into new businesses. While these units helped the company explore a number of areas, they failed to develop any significant new businesses.

Recent research into corporate venturing units and corporate incubators by both Ashridge and London business schools concluded that less than 5 per cent of corporate venturing units created new businesses that were taken up by the parent company. Moreover, many failed to make any positive contribution.

So why do corporate venturing units fail to help their parent companies find new legs? There are three reasons.

First, early stage venturing is a tough job, even for professional, independent venture capital (VC) companies. Many VC companies earn less than their cost of capital unless they are fortunate enough to invest in one of the rare big winners. Angels, another form of independent investor in early stage ventures, also frequently fail to earn a good return on their investments. Without some advantage, corporate venturers are unlikely to beat these odds.

Second, corporate venturers rarely have an advantage over the professionals. Those business opportunities where the company does have a clear advantage are normally dealt with through the strategic planning process. At BAT, for instance, acquisitions of tobacco companies in new regions would not be allocated to a corporate venturing unit. Instead, BAT's venturing focused on areas such as e-commerce, where its sources of advantage were questionable.

Further, individuals in a corporate venturing unit rarely match their independent competitors. They may include some of the most entrepreneurial managers in the company, but they do not usually have the accumulated experience of seasoned venture capitalists.

Third, the new ventures that start up within a corporate venturing unit often attract little attention or commitment from the core of the company. Because they are developed within a separate unit, they are not part of the strategic planning discussions that drive resource allocation.

When the parent company is short of resources, either because of an economic downturn or because the new activities begin to compete with existing businesses, the new ventures lose out. Since it takes longer to nurture a new venture than most business cycles, competition for resources is almost inevitable.

These obstacles to corporate venturing appear to be insurmountable. In our research, we could find no examples of new legs being developed from a venturing unit that passed the test of being 'significant, permanent new businesses' – meaning that they are profitable, are part of the parent company's portfolio and amount to 20 per cent of sales or $1bn in value. Even when the research was extended

▶

CASE 14.2 CONT.

back to venturing units set up in the 1970s or 1980s, none of them spawned a new business that passed our significance and permanence tests. Corporate venturing units do not, it appears, deliver growth.

Managements looking for new growth have two routes: strategic planning (thinking through the options and choosing one or more with reasonable chances of success), or opportunistic investments (reacting to events or external proposals when they appear sufficiently promising).

In a separate strand of research, we assembled a database of companies that had created new businesses that passed the significance and permanence tests. In only one of these cases did the new business begin its life in a corporate venturing unit or corporate incubator. Two-thirds were the result of carefully considered strategic decisions and one-third were more opportunistic.

So, if corporate venturing does not create new businesses, does it have any place within large companies? The answer is yes. The techniques of corporate venturing can be harnessed for four purposes:

- **Harvest venturing** – This is appropriate when some corporate resources, such as technology, managerial skills, brands and even fixed assets, are surplus to requirements. It uses the techniques of venturing to convert existing corporate resources into commercial ventures, and then into cash.

  Lucent New Ventures Group was an example of harvest venturing before it was sold to Coller Capital. Set up to exploit Lucent's technology, the unit evaluated over 300 opportunities, started 35 ventures and drew in $350m (£192m) of external venture capital.

- **Ecosystem venturing** – This is appropriate when the success of a business unit depends on a community of connected businesses, such as suppliers, agents, distributors, franchisees, technology entrepreneurs or manufacturers of complementary products.

  If this ecosystem is short of venture capital funds there is an opportunity for the company to act as a support to entrepreneurs in the community. The benefit to the company is the vibrancy of the community and the impact this has on its core businesses, rather than the prospect of capital gain from the investments.

  Intel Capital and Microsoft both use corporate venturing to stimulate their ecosystems. Intel Capital's early investments were made in suppliers, often to guarantee availability of components. As the component industry matured, Intel switched to investing in software companies and supercomputer makers to promote the use of Intel technology.

- **Innovation venturing** – This is appropriate when an existing function within a business unit, normally research or new product development, is underperforming because there is insufficient energy directed towards innovation. There must also be some belief that entrepreneurial energy is latent inside the company and can be fostered by stimulating 'intrapreneurs' or by tapping into external entrepreneurs.

  A unit with a venturing approach is set up to take on part of the function that is underperforming. By providing the right conditions, internal or external managers with entrepreneurial instincts will take more risks and invest more energy in developing new technologies or ways of working. Shell's GameChanger programme was set up in 1996 to increase innovation in the technical function of Shell's exploration business. The idea was to take 10 per cent of the technical budget and spend it in a 'venturing' way. This new approach to innovation was taken up by other divisions in Shell and is viewed as having produced a step-change in some areas.

- **Private equity venturing** – This is appropriate under rather limited circumstances. It is equivalent to a diversification into the private equity business, so the company needs to believe that it has better access to a flow of good deals than independent private equity companies. Also, managers must be confident that the deal flow they are tapping into is in the early stages of an upswing. To make money in the cycle of boom and bust, managers need to invest early and exit before the shakeout.

Nokia Venture Partners was set up to make minority investments in wireless internet projects. As one of the partners explained: 'We do not do strategic investments [for Nokia] but the reason we exist is strategic for Nokia.'

Managers planning any kind of venturing unit need to be clear about which type they are setting up and why. 'New leg venturing' and units with mixed objectives do not work. Unless managers are clear about which of the four types they want, they will not build the necessary business model or skills to be successful. Companies wanting to do more than one kind of venturing need more than one type of venturing unit.

Source: Julian Birkinshaw and Andrew Campbell, 'Know the limits of corporate venturing', *Financial Times*, 9 August 2004, p. 11.

Discussion points

1. Sketch the outline of a compensation and reward package for an 'intrapreneur'. (Think in terms of fixed salary, performance bonuses and non-financial rewards.)
2. What parallels and distinctions might be drawn between the intrapreneur as innovator and the intrapreneur as the establisher of new business units? How might these two roles be compared with those of the traditional entrepreneur?

Chapter 4
Strategic Management and the Entrepreneur

- Understanding the importance of strategic management to a small business
- Explaining why and how a small business must create a competitive advantage in the market
- Developing a strategic plan for a business using the nine steps in the strategic planning process
- Discussing the characteristics of low-cost differentiation and focus strategies and knowing when to employ them
- Understanding the importance of controls such as the balanced scorecard in the planning process

CHAPTER 5

industry and competitor *analysis*

Getting Personal *with* **EVAN SHAPIRO**

What I do when I'm not working

Playing my guitar or basketball or hang out with my girlfriend

My advice to new entrepreneurs

Be persistent on your path, but open to new ideas

Best part of being a student

It's easier than being an entrepreneur

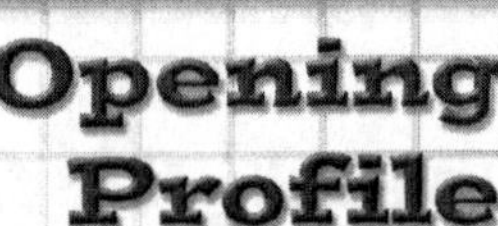

Blue Maze Entertainment:

Occupying a Unique Position in a Difficult Industry—and Thriving

The music industry may be one of the worst industries in which to start a new firm. It is plagued by low-profit margins, fierce competition, and piracy—factors that have created a poor environment for start-ups. It is also in the midst of change, and has been since music was digitized and the Internet has enabled people to share music online. The emergence of Apple's iTunes Music Store and similar services that allow people to buy individual songs has also been a big change.

In the midst of all of these changes, Evan Shapiro and Mitch Towbin, two business students at Emory University in Atlanta, started a music company. Their company, Blue Maze Entertainment, was launched in 2000 while Shapiro, who is shown in the picture, was still in college. The initial plan was to build an all-purpose music company, with elements of production, promotion, and distribution. That plan never fully panned out. By 2003, Shapiro and Towbin repositioned Blue Maze, and it is now a profitable, branded music company.

EVAN SHAPIRO
Cofounder, Blue Maze Entertainment
Goizueta Business School
Emory University, 2003

MITCH TOWBIN
Cofounder, Blue Maze Entertainment
Goizueta Business School
Emory University, 2003

EMORY UNIVERSITY

To understand how Blue Maze reached its current stage of development, a little background information is in order. In 1999, Evan Shapiro, who was then a junior, took a break from his studies at Emory and interned at a record label in New York City. That was a pivotal experience for Shapiro. It exposed him to the music industry and gave him the desire to start a music company of his own.

Back at Emory, it didn't take Shapiro long to follow through on his ambition. In 2000, he started Blue Maze with recent graduate Mitch Towbin. The initial plan to make Blue Maze an all-purpose music company turned out to be a

Currently in my iPod	My biggest surprise as an entrepreneur	First entrepreneurial experience
Incubus, Chili Peppers and Atmosphers	*How quickly markets can change*	*Trading baseball cards*

After studying this chapter you should be ready to:

LEARNING

Objectives

1. Explain the purpose of an industry analysis.
2. Identify the five competitive forces that determine industry profitability.
3. Explain the role of "barriers to entry" in creating disincentives for firms to enter an industry.
4. Identify the nontraditional barriers to entry that are especially associated with entrepreneurial firms.
5. List the four industry-related questions to ask before pursuing the idea for a firm.
6. Identify the five primary industry types and the opportunities they offer.
7. Explain the purpose of a competitor analysis.
8. Identify the three groups of competitors a new firm will face.
9. Describe ways a firm can ethically obtain information about its competitors.
10. Describe the reasons for completing a competitive analysis grid.

tough go. Although Blue Maze experienced some success, 2001 and 2002 were difficult years in the industry, and there wasn't a clear need for another all-purpose music company. Rather than give up, the two decided to reposition Blue Maze as a branded music company—an area in which they had had good success. Branded music is a fairly new concept that combines music with a company's brand to create a unique promotional product. An example is a clothing company that attaches a tag to every pair of blue jeans that it sells. The tag contains a music download card that allows the buyer to download one or more songs for free. The songs are carefully selected to enhance the company's brand and create buzz surrounding its products.

Blue Maze is now in the business of creating branded music products and managing branded music campaigns. Its clients set up their campaigns as either branded, value-added incentives (like the blue jeans example just mentioned) or as memorable gift-with-purchase programs. The music is distributed via a limited run of CDs or DVDs or through music download cards. The recipients of the music vary depending on the nature of the campaign. In some instances, the music is distributed to everyone who attends an event or buys a product. In other cases, it is limited to contest winners, opinion leaders, or trendsetters. One competitive advantage that Blue Maze maintains is its access to the freshest progressive urban sounds. It is the latest music that cannot yet be found on the radio or in a record store. For example, Blue Maze produced a CD titled *21st Century Style.* This product featured tracks from today's top emerging and established progressive-urban artists and was used as a free promotional incentive and branding vehicle at retail and live fashion and music events. The CDs were cobranded by Blue Maze and Enyce, a designer of men's and women's urban fashions and one of Blue Maze's customers. Blue Maze makes money by producing branded music on an a-la-carte basis or by managing entire campaigns.

Another differentiator for Blue Maze, and a particularly promising product that the company has created, is called The Virtual CD (VCD). It is a digital representation of a CD, which emulates the process of opening a CD and flipping through the booklet inside. It is placed on a Web site and contains both streaming music and music downloads, as well as links to e-commerce opportunities. By presenting a robust, self-contained format, The Virtual CD provides innovative product placement opportunities while associating the presenting brand with the hottest music. It also includes a "Send VCD to a Friend" feature, which allows users to share the application with friends, in a viral manner. A sample of a Virtual CD is shown on Blue Maze's Web site.[1]

Today, Shapiro and Towbin feel Blue Maze is well positioned for the future. Rather than slugging it out with the major record labels, as they intended to do when their company was founded as an all-purpose music company, Blue Maze is now firmly positioned in a growing niche in the music industry. As such, Blue Maze is able to service both brands and record labels in a harmonious fashion.

Blue Maze Entertainment is a success in part because of Shapiro's ability to analyze the music industry and precisely position Blue Maze within it. In this chapter, we'll look at industry analysis and competitor analysis. The first section of the chapter considers **industry analysis**, which is business research that focuses on the potential of an industry. An **industry** is a group of firms producing a similar product or service, such as music, fitness drinks, or electronic games. Once it is determined that a new venture is feasible in regard to the industry and market in which it will compete, a more in-depth analysis is needed to learn the ins and outs of the industry the firm plans to enter. This analysis helps a firm determine if the niche or vertical markets it identified during its feasibility analysis are accessible and which ones represent the best point of entry for a new firm.

The second section of the chapter focuses on competitor analysis. A **competitor analysis** is a detailed evaluation of a firm's competitors. Once a firm decides to enter an industry and chooses a market in which to compete, it must gain an understanding of its competitive environment. We'll look at how a firm identifies its competition and the importance of completing a competitive analysis grid.

Industry Analysis

1. Explain the purpose of an industry analysis.

When studying an industry, an entrepreneur must answer three questions before pursuing the idea of starting a firm. First, is the industry accessible—in other words, is it a realistic place for a new venture to enter? Second, does the industry contain markets that are ripe for innovation or are underserved? Third, are there positions in the industry that will avoid some of the negative attributes of the industry as a whole? It is useful for a new venture to think about its **position** at both the company level and the product or service level. At the company level, a firm's position determines how the entire company is situated relative to its competitors. For example, Blue Maze Entertainment has positioned itself as a company that produces branded music products and manages branded music campaigns. This is a much different position than Warner Music or EMI, which are all-purposes music companies. Sometimes, through savvy positioning, a firm can enter an unattractive industry and do well. Because it found an attractive niche market and has nicely positioned itself in that market, Blue Maze is profitable even though it competes in a moderately unattractive industry.

The importance of knowing the competitive landscape, which is what an industry is, may have been first recognized in the fourth century B.C. by Sun-tzu, a Chinese philosopher. Reputedly he wrote *The Art of War* to help generals prepare for battle. However, the ideas in the book are still used today to help managers prepare their firms for the competitive wars of the marketplace. The following quote from Sun-tzu's work points out the importance of industry analysis:

> We are not fit to lead an army on the march unless we are familiar with the face of the country—its pitfalls and precipices, its marshes and swamps.[2]

These words serve as a reminder to entrepreneurs that regardless of how eager they are to start their businesses, they are not adequately prepared until they are "familiar with the face of the country"—that is, until they understand the industry or industries they plan to enter.

The Importance of Industry Versus Firm-Specific Factors

To illustrate the importance of the industry a firm chooses to enter, research has shown that both firm- and industry-specific factors contribute to a firm's profitability.[3] Firm-level factors include a firm's assets, products, culture, teamwork among its employees, reputation, and other resources. Industry-specific factors include the threat of new entrants, rivalry among existing firms, the bargaining power of suppliers, and other factors discussed in this chapter. A number of studies have tried to determine whether firm-specific or industry-specific factors are more important when it comes to affecting a firm's potential to generate profits. Virtually all the studies have concluded that firm-specific factors are the most important, although the industry a firm chooses is important too.[4] In various studies, researchers have found that from 8 to 30 percent of the variation in firm profitability is directly attributable to the industry in which a firm competes. In a recent study, two researchers, including Harvard University professor Michael Porter, the author of the five competitive forces framework discussed in the next section, found that 19 percent of the variation in firm profitability is attributable to stable industry effects. Commenting on the 19 percent figure, Porter concluded, "This result provides strong support for the idea that industry membership has an important influence on [firm] profitability."[5] The industry a firm is in may matter even more for firms that are not well positioned in their industries

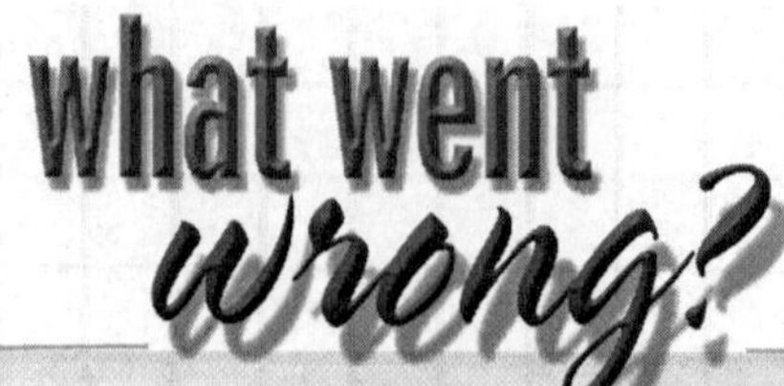

Bath & Body Works: How One Company Lost a Favorable Position in an Industry

www.bathandbodyworks.com

Once a company establishes a favorable position in an industry, it must remain vigilant or its position can be lost. This is what happened to Bath & Body Works in the early 2000s. For over 10 years, the company had been selling, with great success, midprice body and personal care products, primarily through stores in malls. From 1993 to 2000, the company grew at an incredible rate of 51 percent per year, soaring to nearly $2 billion in annual sales. But then the bottom fell out. The company's revenues dropped 19 percent from 2000 to 2002, and it lost nearly 40 percent of its pretax income. What went wrong? The company simply lost its favorable position in the marketplace. Here's how it happened.

Bath & Body Works was launched in 1990 by Leslie Wexner, founder of The Limited. The hunch was that there was a favorable position in the health and beauty products market just waiting to be filled—a position just above the drug store and just below the department store in terms of pricing. Bath & Body Works moved into this position and opened a chain of cheerful and wholesome stores, brimming over with fruit- and flower-scented soaps, creams, oils, scented candles, and other accessories. For millions of shoppers, Bath & Body Works' positioning was just right. It offered attractive and fun products at a price that was high enough to be enticing but low enough to be affordable. The company grew from 15 stores in 1990 to more than 1,300 in 2000.

By the year 2000, however, things had turned sour. Competing retailers, such as Aveda, Sephora, and Origins began opening stores in malls—Bath & Body Works' turf—and started offering fresh new products, like all-natural and organic compounds. Their stores were well organized and pleasant, with signature music always playing. More importantly, they offered a different approach to beauty than the homey approach offered by Bath & Body Works. Their product lines wove together elements of science, design, fitness, relaxation, and psychology, which resonated with consumers. People were willing to spend a little more for their fresher and more sophisticated offerings, particularly in the area of facial creams and makeup. At the same time this was happening, Target, Wal-Mart, and the other big-box retailers were nipping at Bath & Body Works from the low end, particularly in the area of body lotions, soaps, and accessories. The big boxes started carrying products that looked just like those sold at Bath & Body Works, but were cheaper.

As the result of these factors, which unfolded quickly, Bath & Body Works lost its edge and was no longer seen as distinctive and special. The company was outflanked by Aveda, Sephora, and others at the top end of the market and by Target, Wal-Mart, and others at the bottom end. To counter its slipping sales, Bath & Body Works started to rely more and more on discounts, promotions, and sales. According to Neil Fiske, the company's newly hired CEO, "In 2002, during our critical holiday time period, there were twenty-two in-store deals at Bath & Body Works. It was like a garage sale with deal signs all over." Stated plainly, Bath & Body Works lost the favorable position it had occupied in the bath and beauty products industry for over 10 years. It was essentially stuck in the middle, with no discernible competitive advantage.

Fortunately, Bath & Body Works' leaders recognized its rapidly deteriorating plight and hired Neil Fiske, a Boston Consulting Group veteran, to revive the company and reestablish its position in the marketplace. Fiske started by reconnecting the company with its customers and refashioning its product line based on more contemporary customer preferences and tastes. As a result, over time, a bevy of new partners have been brought on board, enabling the company to enhance its product offerings and update its stores. Shoppers may now purchase many non-Bath & Body Works brands in the stores, which has created a marketplace that brings together all kinds of offerings at many price points, to appeal to a broad cross section of mall shoppers. This new strategy seems to be working. The company is growing again and has returned to profitability.

Questions for Critical Thinking

1. What steps, if any, could Bath & Body Works have taken to prevent the loss of its favorable position in the bath and beauty products marketplace in the early 2000s?
2. Look at the Web sites of Bath & Body Works and Sephora, one of the other firms mentioned in the feature. How would you describe the positioning

differences between Bath & Body Works and Sephora today? Which firm do you think has the most distinct positioning strategy?

3. Why do you think Bath & Body Works seemed to get caught off-guard by emerging competition at the top end from Sephora and others and the bottom end from Target and Wal-Mart?

4. Use Table 5.2 to complete an industry analysis on the bath and beauty products industry today. Is it an attractive industry? Would it be a good or poor industry for a start-up firm to enter?

Sources: Bath & Body Works homepage, www.bathandbodyworks.com, (accessed August 8, 2006); M. J. Silverstein and J. Butman, *Treasure Hunt* (New York: Portfolio).

and do not have products or services that are clearly differentiated from the pack—an unenviable position on both counts. In these instances, the firms involved basically ride the tide of an industry's economic fortunes, because they are not able to insulate themselves from an industry's ups and downs.[6] An example of firm that lost a favorable position in its industry, and the consequences it suffered as a result, is provided in the "What Went Wrong" feature nearby.

Because both firm- and industry-level factors are important in determining a firm's profitability, there are firms that do well in unattractive or moderately attractive industries, as illustrated in the Blue Maze case, if they are well positioned. Still, the overall attractiveness of an industry should be part of the equation when an entrepreneur decides whether to pursue a particular business opportunity. A new venture can use the five forces model shown below to assess the overall attractiveness of the industry it plans to enter and to determine if a favorable position to occupy exists in that industry.

The Five Competitive Forces That Determine Industry Profitability

2. Identify the five competitive forces that determine industry profitability.

The five competitive forces model is a framework for understanding the structure of an industry and was developed by Harvard professor Michael Porter. Shown in Figure 5.1, the framework is comprised of the forces that determine industry profitability.[7] These forces—the threat of substitutes, the entry of new competitors, rivalry among existing firms, the bargaining power of suppliers, and the bargaining power of buyers—determine the average rate of return for the firms in an industry.

Each of Porter's five forces impacts the average rate of return for the firms in an industry by applying pressure on industry profitability. Well-managed companies try to position their firms in a way that avoids or diminishes these forces—in an attempt to beat the average rate of return for the industry. For example, the rivalry among existing firms in the music industry is high. Blue Maze diminished the impact of this threat to its profitability by avoiding head-to-head competition with the major record labels.

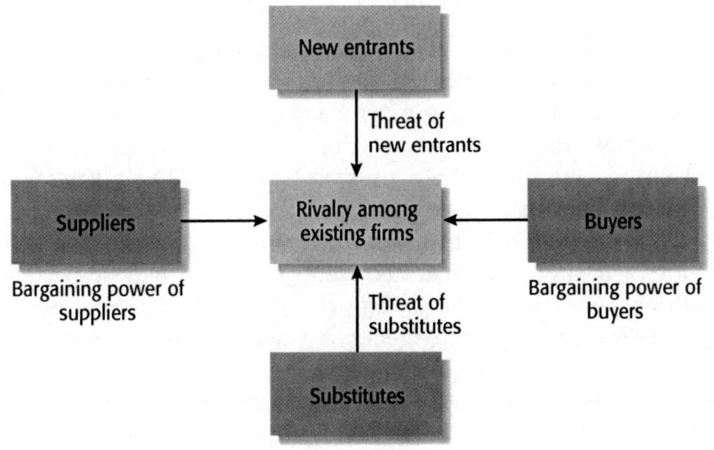

FIGURE 5.1

Forces That Determine Industry Profitability

Source: M. Porter, *Competitive Strategy: Techniques for Analyzing Industries and Competitors* (New York: Free Press, 1980).

In his book *Competitive Advantage*, Porter points out that industry profitability is not a function of *only* a product's features. Although it was written in 1985 and the dynamics of the industries mentioned have changed, Porter's essential point remains correct:

> Industry profitability is not a function of what the product looks like or whether it embodies high or low technology but of industry structure. Some very mundane industries such as postage meters and grain trading are extremely profitable, while some more glamorous, high-technology industries such as personal computers and cable television are not profitable for many participants.[8]

The five competitive forces that determine industry profitability are described next.

Threat of Substitutes In general, industries are more attractive when the threat of substitutes is low. This means that products or services from other industries can't easily serve as substitutes for the products or services being made and sold in the focal firm's industry. For example, there are few if any substitutes for prescription medicines, which is one of the reasons the pharmaceutical industry is so profitable. When people are sick, they typically don't quibble with the pharmacist about the price of a medicine. In contrast, when close substitutes for a product do exist, industry profitability is suppressed because consumers will opt not to buy when the price is too high. Consider the price of movie tickets. If the price gets too high, consumers can easily switch to watching rented videos or pay-per-view. Similarly, if the price of glass bottles gets too high, manufacturers can easily switch to aluminum cans, plastic bottles, or other alternatives.[9]

The extent to which substitutes suppress the profitability of an industry depends on the propensity for buyers to substitute alternatives. This is why the firms in an industry often offer their customers amenities to reduce the likelihood of their switching to a substitute product, even in light of a price increase. Let's look at the coffee restaurant industry as an example of this. The coffee sold at Starbucks is relatively expensive. A consumer could easily find a less expensive cup of coffee at a convenience store or brew coffee at home rather than pay more at Starbucks. To decrease the likelihood that customers will choose either of these alternatives, Starbucks offers high-quality fresh coffee, a pleasant atmosphere, and good service. Some Starbucks restaurants even offer their customers access to computers and the Internet as a way of motivating them to remain loyal to Starbucks. Starbucks doesn't do this just so its customers don't go to a different coffee restaurant. It offers the service so its customers won't switch to substitute products as well.

LEARNING Objective

3. Explain the role of "barriers to entry" in creating disincentives for firms to enter an industry.

Threat of New Entrants In general, industries are more attractive when the threat of entry is low. This means that competitors cannot easily enter the industry to copy what the industry incumbents are doing. There are a number of ways that firms in an industry can keep the number of new entrants low. These techniques are referred to as barriers to entry. A **barrier to entry** is a condition that creates a disincentive for a new firm to enter an industry.[10] Let's look at the six major sources of barriers to entry:

- ***Economies of scale:*** Industries that are characterized by large economies of scale are difficult for new firms to enter, unless they are willing to accept a cost disadvantage. **Economies of scale** occur when mass-producing a product results in lower average costs. For example, Intel has huge microchip factories that produce vast quantities of chips, thereby reducing the average cost of a chip. It would be difficult for a new entrant to match Intel's advantage in this area.
- ***Product differentiation:*** Industries such as the soft-drink industry that are characterized by firms with strong brands are difficult to break into without spending heavily on advertising. For example, imagine how costly it would be to compete head-to-head against Pepsi or Coca-Cola. Another way of achieving differentiation is through exclusive licensing agreements. For example, in 2004, Electronic Arts inked a 5-year exclusive deal with the National Football League, making it the only company that can produce electronic games involving NFL players, teams, or stadiums.[11]

- ***Capital requirements:*** The need to invest large amounts of money to gain entrance to an industry is another barrier to entry. The airline industry is characterized by large capital requirements, although JetBlue, which launched in 1999, was able to overcome this barrier and raise substantial funds by winning the confidence of investors through the strength of its business model and its management team. Similarly, it currently takes about 2 years and $4 million to develop a single electronic game (such as those sold by Electronic Arts and Activision).[12] Many new firms do not have the capital to compete at this level.
- ***Cost advantages independent of size:*** Entrenched competitors may have cost advantages not related to size that are not available to new entrants. Commonly, these advantages are grounded in the firm's history. For example, the existing competitors in an industry may have purchased land and equipment in the past when the cost was far less than new entrants would have to pay for the same assets at the time of their entry.
- ***Access to distribution channels:*** Distribution channels are often hard to crack. This is particularly true in crowded markets, such as the convenience store market. For a new sports drink to be placed on a convenience store shelf, it typically has to displace a product that is already there.
- ***Government and legal barriers:*** In knowledge-intensive industries, such as biotechnology and software, patents, trademarks, and copyrights form major barriers to entry. Other industries, such as banking and broadcasting, require the granting of a license by a public authority.

When a new firm tries to enter an industry with powerful barriers to entry, it must have a plan to overcome those barriers. Scott McNealy, the cofounder of Sun Microsystems, says that Sun was able to overcome the barriers to entry in many of its industries primarily through a program of partnering with other firms:

> Initially, Sun's business model was no different from that of its rivals. We wanted to beat our competitors, grow internally, build manufacturing plants, create new distribution channels, acquire promising new start-ups, and so on. What happened was that we realized we couldn't do it alone. The markets were vast, our competitors were huge, barriers to entry to some segments were overwhelming, we didn't have

Starbucks doesn't just sell coffee. It also offers its patrons a convenient and pleasant place to meet, socialize, and study. Starbucks offers these amenities in part to decrease the likelihood that its customers will "substitute" their Starbucks coffee for a less expensive alternative.

enough cash, and the pace of change in the industry was too fast. What we did was purely instinctive. We reached out to other companies that could help us. We leveraged their expertise and specialty products by forming strategic alliances.[13]

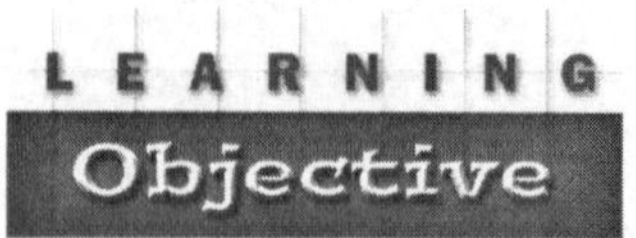

4. Identify the nontraditional barriers to entry that are especially associated with entrepreneurial firms.

When start-ups create their own industries or create new niche markets within existing industries, they must create barriers to entry of their own to reduce the threat of new entrants. It is difficult for start-ups to create barriers to entry that are expensive, such as economies of scale, because money is usually tight. The biggest threat to a new firm's viability, particularly if it is creating a new market, is that larger, better-funded firms will step in and copy what it is doing. The ideal barrier to entry is a patent, trademark, or copyright, which prevents another firm from duplicating what the start-up is doing. Apart from these options, however, start-ups have to rely on nontraditional barriers to entry to discourage new entrants, such as assembling a world-class management team that would be difficult for another company to replicate. A list of nontraditional barriers to entry, which are particularly suited to start-up firms, is provided in Table 5.1.

Rivalry Among Existing Firms In most industries, the major determinant of industry profitability is the level of competition among the firms already competing in the industry. Some industries are fiercely competitive to the point where prices are pushed below the level of costs. When this happens, industry-wide losses occur. In other industries, competition is much less intense and price competition is subdued. For example, the personal computer industry is so competitive that profit margins are extremely thin. In contrast, the market for specialized medical equipment is less competitive, and profit margins are higher.

There are four primary factors that determine the nature and intensity of the rivalry among existing firms in an industry:

- ***Number and balance of competitors:*** The more competitors there are, the more likely it is that one or more will try to gain customers by cutting its prices. Price-cutting causes problems throughout the industry and occurs more often when all the competitors in an industry are about the same size and when there is no clear market

TABLE 5.1 Nontraditional Barriers to Entry

Barrier to Entry	Explanation	Example
Strength of management team	If a start-up puts together a world-class management team, it may give potential rivals pause in taking on the start-up in its chosen industry.	JetBlue
First-mover advantage	If a start-up pioneers an industry or a new concept within an existing industry, the name recognition the start-up establishes may create a formidable barrier to entry.	Facebook
Passion of management team and employees	If the key employees of a start-up are highly motivated by its unique culture, are willing to work long hours because of their belief in what they are doing, and anticipate large financial gains through stock options, this is a combination that cannot be replicated by a larger firm. Think of the employees of a biotech firm trying to find a cure for a disease.	Amgen
Unique business model	If a start-up is able to construct a unique business model and establish a network of relationships that make the business model work, this set of advantages creates a barrier to entry.	Dell
Internet domain name	Some Internet domain names are so "spot-on" in regard to a specific product or service that they give a start-up a meaningful leg up in terms of e-commerce opportunities. Think of www.1800flowers.com, www.1800gotjunk.com, and www.bodybuilding.com.	www.1800contacts.com
Inventing a new approach to an industry and executing the idea in an exemplary fashion	If a start-up invents a new approach to an industry and executes it in an exemplary fashion, these factors create a barrier to entry for potential imitators.	Wikipedia

leader. In industries where there is a clear market leader, such as Intel in the semiconductor industry, the leader maintains price discipline and keeps the industry from engaging in destructive price wars.

- ***Degree of difference between products:*** The degree to which products differ from one producer to another affects industry rivalry. For example, commodity industries such as paper products producers tend to compete on price because there is no meaningful difference between one manufacturer's products and another's.
- ***Growth rate of an industry:*** The competition among firms in a slow-growth industry is stronger than among those in fast-growth industries. Slow-growth industry firms, such as insurance, must fight for market share, which may tempt them to lower prices or increase quality to get customers. In fast-growth industries, such as pharmaceutical products, there are enough customers to go around to fill the capacity of most firms, making price-cutting less likely.
- ***Level of fixed costs:*** Firms that have high fixed costs must sell a higher volume of their product to reach the break-even point than firms with low fixed costs. Once the break-even point is met, each additional unit sold contributes directly to a firm's bottom line. Firms with high fixed costs are anxious to fill their capacity, and this anxiety may lead to price-cutting.

Bargaining Power of Suppliers In general, industries are more attractive when the bargaining power of suppliers is low. In some cases, suppliers can suppress the profitability of the industries to which they sell by raising prices or reducing the quality of the components they provide. If a supplier reduces the quality of the components it supplies, the quality of the finished product will suffer, and the manufacturer will eventually have to lower its price. If the suppliers are powerful relative to the firms in the industry to which they sell, industry profitability can suffer.[14] For example, Intel, with its Pentium chip, is a powerful supplier to the PC industry. Because most PCs feature Pentium chips, Intel can command a premium price from the PC manufacturers, thus directly affecting the overall profitability of the PC industry. Several factors have an impact on the ability of suppliers to exert pressure on buyers and suppress the profitability of the industries they serve. These include the following:

- ***Supplier concentration:*** When there are only a few suppliers to provide a critical product to a large number of buyers, the supplier has an advantage. This is the case in the pharmaceutical industry, where relatively few drug manufacturers are selling to thousands of doctors and their patients.
- ***Switching costs:*** Switching costs are the fixed costs that buyers encounter when switching or changing from one supplier to another. If switching costs are high, a buyer will be less likely to switch suppliers. For example, suppliers often provide their largest buyers with specialized software that makes it easy to buy their products. After the buyer spends time and effort learning the supplier's ordering and inventory management systems, it will be less likely to want to spend time and effort learning another supplier's system.
- ***Attractiveness of substitutes:*** Supplier power is enhanced if there are no attractive substitutes for the products or services the supplier offers. For example, there is little the computer industry can do when Microsoft and Intel raise their prices, as there are relatively few if any practical substitutes for these firms' products.
- ***Threat of forward integration:*** The power of a supplier is enhanced if there is a credible possibility that the supplier might enter the buyer's industry. For example, Microsoft's power as a supplier of computer operating systems is enhanced by the threat that it might enter the PC industry if PC makers balk too much at the cost of its software or threaten to use an operating system from a different software provider.

Bargaining Power of Buyers In general, industries are more attractive when the bargaining power of buyers (a start-up's customers) is low. Buyers can suppress the profitability of the industries from which they purchase by demanding price concessions or increases in quality. For example, the automobile industry is dominated by a handful of large automakers that buy products from thousands of suppliers in different industries. This enables the automakers to suppress the profitability of the industries from which they buy by demanding price reductions. Similarly, if the automakers insisted that their suppliers provide better-quality parts for the same price, the profitability of the suppliers would suffer. Several factors affect buyers' ability to exert pressure on suppliers and suppress the profitability of the industries from which they buy. These include the following:

- ***Buyer group concentration:*** If the buyers are concentrated, meaning that there are only a few large buyers, and they buy from a large number of suppliers, they can pressure the suppliers to lower costs and thus affect the profitability of the industries from which they buy.
- ***Buyer's costs:*** The greater the importance of an item is to a buyer, the more sensitive the buyer will be to the price it pays. For example, if the component sold by the supplier represents 50 percent of the cost of the buyer's product, the buyer will bargain hard to get the best price for that component.
- ***Degree of standardization of supplier's products:*** The degree to which a supplier's product differs from its competitors' affects the buyer's bargaining power. For example, a buyer who is purchasing a standard or undifferentiated product from a supplier, such as the corn syrup that goes into a soft drink, can play one supplier against another until it gets the best combination of features such as price and service.
- ***Threat of backward integration:*** The power of a buyer is enhanced if there is a credible threat that the buyer might enter the supplier's industry. For example, the PC industry can keep the price of computer monitors down by threatening to make its own monitors if the price gets too high.

The bargaining power of buyers is such a pervasive threat that some new ventures opt out of particular industries when the extent of the bargaining power of buyers becomes clear. This scenario changed the course of history for the Sony Corporation, as explained in the boxed feature titled "Savvy Entrepreneurial Firm."

The Value of the Five Forces Model

Along with helping a firm understand the dynamics of the industry it plans to enter, the five forces model can be used in two ways: (1) to help a firm determine whether it should enter a particular industry and (2) whether it can carve out an attractive position in that industry. Let's examine these two positive outcomes.

First, the five forces model can be used to assess the attractiveness of an industry or a specific position within an industry by determining the level of threat to industry profitability for each of the forces, as shown in Table 5.2. This analysis of industry attractiveness should be more in-depth than the cursory analysis conducted during feasibility analysis. For example, if a firm filled out the form shown in Table 5.2 and several of the threats to industry profitability were high, the firm may want to reconsider entering the industry or think carefully about the position it will occupy in the industry. In the restaurant industry, for example, the threat of substitute products, the threat of new entrants, and the rivalry among existing firms are high. For certain restaurants, such as fresh-seafood restaurants, the bargaining power of suppliers may also be high (the number of seafood suppliers is relatively small compared to the number of beef and chicken suppliers). Thus, a firm that enters the restaurant industry has several forces working against it simply because of the nature of the industry. To help sidestep or diminish these threats, it must establish a favorable position. One firm that has accomplished this is Panera Bread, as discussed in Case 5.1 in this chapter. By studying the restaurant industry, Panera found that some consumers have tired of fast food but don't

How the Bargaining Power of Buyers Changed the Fate of Sony in Its Start-Up Years

www.sony.com

There are many variables that shape a company in its start-up years, but perhaps none are as powerful as Porter's five forces. Many companies, for example, establish strong brands or differentiate themselves in creative ways, primarily to establish barriers to entry and stem the tide of new entrants. Other companies, such as Starbucks, offer amenities in their places of business to discourage customers from switching to less expensive substitute products. The story of Sony, however, tops them all. When Sony was a start-up, it changed its entire approach to doing business as the result of the bargaining power of buyers. In fact, if Sony hadn't responded to this threat in the way it did, it wouldn't be a household name today.

Sony was established in 1946 by Masaru Ibuka and Akio Morita, two Japanese businessmen, to make communication equipment for the reconstruction of Japan after World War II. One thing Ibuka and Morita learned quickly was that to make a sale, they had to win the confidence of the purchasing officers in the government agencies with whom they were dealing. This task often proved difficult, but their hard work typically paid off in orders from these purchasing officers. One day, however, early in the life of Sony, a purchasing agent who Morita had worked particularly hard to win over was transferred to a new position. This was frustrating to Morita because he had to start from square one to win the confidence of the purchasing officer's replacement.

After this scenario repeated itself several times, Morita considered the problem. While he liked the fact that large orders could be granted by the purchasing agents of government agencies and large firms, he was leery of the fact that Sony's sales hinged on the decisions of such a small number of people. After discussing this concern with Ibuka, Morita decided to take Sony in a different direction. Instead of placing the future of Sony in the hands of a few purchasing agents, Morita decided that Sony would go after the consumer market. "In other words, we decided to do business with unspecified millions of individuals instead of with a specific few. On this basis we started to produce the first tape recorders and tapes in Japan," Morita later recalled.

This remarkable story illustrates the compelling nature of the real bargaining power of buyers. This clout is most formidable when there are only a few buyers and many sellers. Morita redirected Sony's entire future to avoid this threat. Today, as it has throughout the majority of its history, Sony's future lies in the hands of the millions of people who buy its products rather than in the hands of just a few powerful buyers.

Questions for Critical Thinking

1. Analyze the electronics industry using Porter's five forces model. What do you think are the biggest threats to the electronics industry today? What is Sony doing to try to deter these threats?
2. Think of examples of at least two other companies that are in industries that are subject to the strong bargaining power of buyers. Do you think the profitability of these firms is being suppressed by the strong bargaining power of their buyers? What, if anything, can these firms do to neutralize this threat?
3. How would you describe Sony's positioning strategy in the electronics industry?
4. What single industry do you think suffers the most from the bargaining power of buyers? How about the bargaining power of suppliers? Are entrepreneurial start-ups able to enter these industries? If so, how?

Source: A. Morita, "Moving Up in Marketing by Getting Down to Basics," in *The Book of Entrepreneurs' Wisdom*, ed. Peter Krass (New York: John Wiley & Sons, 1999), 315–23.

always have the time to patronize a sit-down restaurant. To fill the gap, Panera helped to pioneer a new category called "fast casual," which combines relatively fast service with high-quality food. Panera has been very successful in occupying this unique position in the restaurant industry. You'll learn more about Panera Bread's success while reading Case 5.1.

Panera Bread offers a variety of alternatives to the typical burger and fries offered at many fast-food restaurants. In addition to a selection of fresh baked bread, Panera is also known for bagels, pastries, soups, sandwiches, salads, and coffee.

The second way a new firm can apply the five forces model to help determine whether it should enter an industry is by using the model pictured in Figure 5.2 to answer several key questions. By doing so, a new venture can assess the thresholds it may have to meet to be successful in a particular industry:

5. List the four industry-related questions to ask before pursuing the idea for a firm.

Question 1: Is the industry a realistic place for our new venture to enter? This question can be answered by looking at the overall attractiveness of an industry, as depicted in Table 5.2, and by assessing whether the window of opportunity is open. It is up to the entrepreneur to determine if the window of opportunity for the industry is open or closed.

TABLE 5.2 Determining the Attractiveness of an Industry Using the Five Forces Model

	Threat to Industry Profitability		
Competitive Force	Low	Medium	High
Threat of substitutes			
Threat of new entrants			
Rivalry among existing firms			
Bargaining power of suppliers			
Bargaining power of buyers			

Instructions:

Step 1 Select an industry.

Step 2 Determine the level of threat to industry profitability for each of the forces (low, medium, or high).

Step 3 Use the table to get an overall feel for the attractiveness of the industry.

Step 4 Use the table to identify the threats that are most often relevant to industry profitability.

FIGURE 5.2

Using the Five Forces Model to Pose Questions to Determine the Potential Success of a New Venture

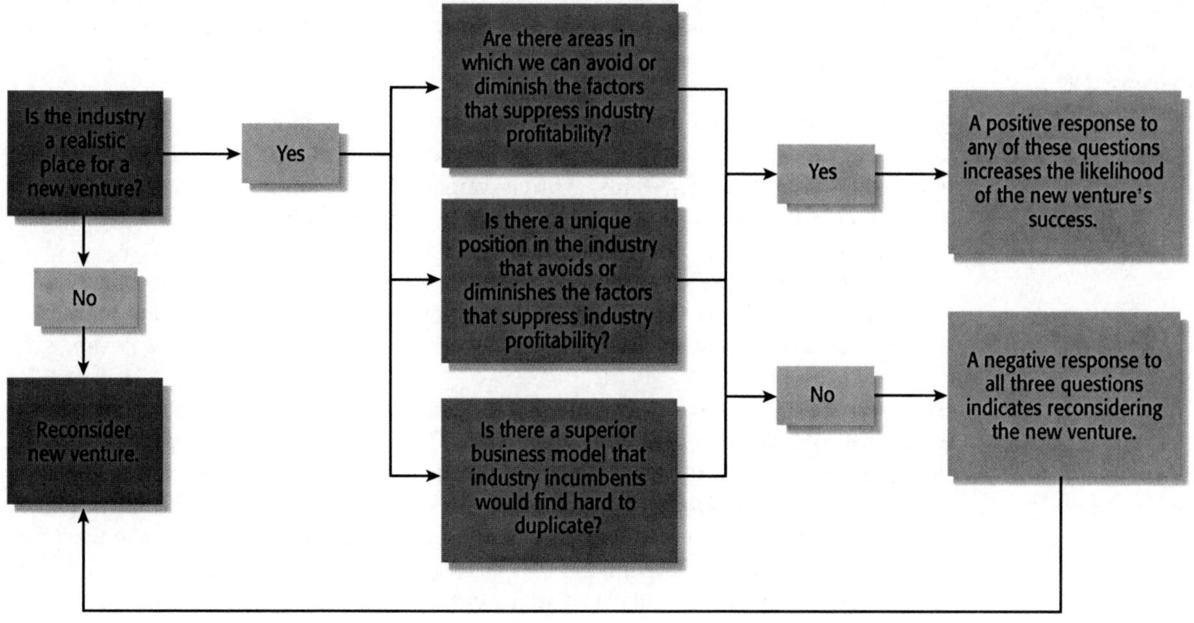

Question 2: If we do enter the industry, can our firm do a better job than the industry as a whole in avoiding or diminishing the impact of the forces that suppress industry profitability? A new venture can enter an industry with a fresh brand, innovative ideas, and a world-class management team and perform better than the industry incumbents. This was the case when Google entered the Internet search engine industry and displaced Yahoo! as the market leader. Outperformance of industry incumbents can also be achieved if a new venture brings an attractive new product to market that is patented, preventing others from duplicating it for a period of time.

Question 3: Is there a unique position in the industry that avoids or diminishes the forces that suppress industry profitability? As we've described, this is the advantage that both Blue Maze Entertainment and Panera Bread have captured.

Question 4: Is there a superior business model that can be put in place that would be hard for industry incumbents to duplicate? Keep in mind that the five forces model provides a picture of an industry "as is," which isn't necessarily the way a new venture has to approach it. Sometimes the largest firms in an industry are trapped by their own strategies and contractual obligations, providing an opening for a start-up to try something new. For example, when Dell started selling computers directly to consumers, its largest rivals—Hewlett-Packard, Compaq, and IBM—were not able to respond. They were locked into a strategy of selling through retailers. If they had tried to mimic Dell and sell directly to end users or customers, they would have alienated their most valuable partners—retailers such as Sears, Circuit City, and Best Buy.

The steps involved in answering these questions are pictured in Figure 5.2. If the founders of a new firm believe that a particular industry is a realistic place for their new venture, a positive response to one or more of the questions posed in Figure 5.2 increases the likelihood that the new venture will be successful.

6. Identify the five primary industry types and the opportunities they offer.

Industry Types and the Opportunities They Offer

Along with studying the factors discussed previously, it is helpful for a new venture to study industry types to determine the opportunities they offer.[15] The five most prevalent industry types, depicted in Table 5.3, are emerging industries, fragmented industries, mature industries, declining industries, and global industries.[16] There are unique opportunities offered by each type of industry.

Emerging Industries An **emerging industry** is a new industry in which standard operating procedures have yet to be developed. The firm that pioneers or takes the leadership of an emerging industry often captures a first-mover advantage, which is a sometimes insurmountable advantage gained by the firm initiating the first significant move into a new market, as explained in Chapter 3.

Because a high level of uncertainty characterizes emerging industries, any opportunity that is captured may be short-lived. Still, many new ventures enter emerging industries because barriers to entry are usually low and there is no established pattern of rivalry.

Fragmented Industries A **fragmented industry** is one that is characterized by a large number of firms of approximately equal size. The primary opportunity for start-ups in fragmented industries is to consolidate the industry and establish industry leadership as a result of doing so. In **industry consolidation**, the smaller companies are typically acquired or go out of business to give way to a handful of larger companies that take over the majority of the business. This is what Blockbuster did in the video rental industry. Prior to Blockbuster's arrival, thousands of small video stores were scattered throughout the United States. Through internal growth and acquisitions, Blockbuster grew quickly, consolidating a previously fragmented industry.

Mature Industries A **mature industry** is an industry that is experiencing slow or no increase in demand, has numerous repeat (rather than new) customers, and has limited product innovation. Occasionally, entrepreneurs introduce new product innovations to mature industries, surprising incumbents who thought nothing new was possible in their industries. An example is Steve Demos, the founder of White Wave, a company that

TABLE 5.3 Industry Structure and Opportunities

Industry Type	Industry Characteristics	Opportunities	Examples of Entrepreneurial Firms Exploiting These Opportunities
Emerging industries	Recent changes in demand or technology; new industry standard operating procedures have yet to be developed	First-mover advantage	• Apple with its iTunes Music Store • XM Satellite Radio with its satellite radio service • MySpace.com with its online social networking Web site
Fragmented industries	Large number of firms of approximately equal size	Consolidation	• Starbucks in coffee restaurants • Movie Gallery in video rentals • Geeks on Call in home computer repairs
Mature industries	Slow increases in demand, numerous repeat customers, and limited product innovation	Process and after-sale service innovation	• Whole Foods Markets in groceries • 1-800-GOT-JUNK? in trash and junk removal • ProFlowers in flower delivery
Declining industries	Consistent reduction in industry demand	Leadership, niche, harvest, and divest	• Nucor in steel • JetBlue in airlines • Circus du Soleil in circuses
Global industries	Significant international sales	Multidomestic and global	• Nike in athletic shoes • Electronic Arts in electronic games

makes vegetarian food products and is further described in Case 11.1. In 1996, the company introduced Silk Soymilk, which has quickly become the best-selling soymilk in the country. Soymilk isn't really milk at all—it's a soybean-based beverage that looks like milk and has a similar texture. Still, it has made its way into the dairy section of most supermarkets in the United States and has positioned itself as a healthy substitute for milk. Who would have thought that a major innovation was possible in the milk industry?

Declining Industries A **declining industry** is an industry that is experiencing a reduction in demand. Typically, entrepreneurs shy away from declining industries because the firms in the industry do not meet the tests of an attractive opportunity, described in Chapter 2. There are occasions, however, when a start-up will do just the opposite of what conventional wisdom would suggest and, by doing so, stakes out an industry position that isn't being hotly contested.

Entrepreneurial firms employ three different strategies in declining industries. The first is to adopt a **leadership strategy**, in which the firm tries to become the dominant player in the industry. This is a rare strategy for a start-up in a declining industry. The second is to pursue a **niche strategy**, which focuses on a narrow segment of the industry that might be encouraged to grow through product or process innovation. The third is a **cost reduction strategy**, which is accomplished through achieving lower costs than industry incumbents through process improvements. Nucor Steel, a small steel company that revolutionized the steel industry through the introduction of the "minimill" concept, is an example of an entrepreneurially minded firm that pursued this strategy. Most steel mills in the United States use large blast furnaces that produce a wide line of products and require enormous throughput in order to be profitable. Nucor's minimills are smaller and produce a narrower range of products. They are, however, energy efficient and make high-quality steel.[17] Nucor proved its concept and quickly found growth markets within the largely declining U.S. steel industry.

Global Industries A **global industry** is an industry that is experiencing significant international sales. Many start-ups enter global industries and from day one try to appeal to international rather than just domestic markets. The two most common strategies pursued by firms in global industries are the multidomestic strategy and the global strategy. Firms that pursue a **multidomestic strategy** compete for market share on a country-by-country basis and vary their product or service offerings to meet the demands of the local market. In contrast, firms pursuing a **global strategy** use the same basic approach in all foreign markets. The choice between these two strategies depends on how similar consumers' tastes are from market to market. For example, food companies typically are limited to a multidomestic strategy because food preferences vary significantly from country to country. Firms that sell more universal products, such as athletic shoes, have been successful with global strategies. A global strategy is preferred because it is more economical to sell the same product in multiple markets.[18]

Competitor Analysis

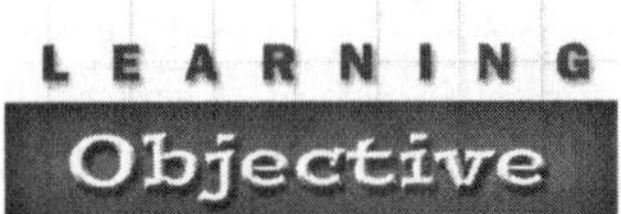

7. Explain the purpose of a competitor analysis.

After a firm has gained an understanding of the industry and the market in which it plans to compete, the next step is to complete a competitor analysis. A competitor analysis is a detailed analysis of a firm's competition. It helps a firm understand the positions of its major competitors and the opportunities that are available to obtain a competitive advantage in one or more areas. These are important issues, particularly for new ventures.[19] In the words of Sun-tzu, quoted earlier in this chapter, "Time spent in reconnaissance is seldom wasted."

First we'll discuss how a firm identifies its major competitors, and then we'll look at the process of completing a competitive analysis grid, which is a tool for organizing the information a firm collects about its primary competitors.

8. Identify the three groups of competitors a new firm will face.

Identifying Competitors

The first step in a competitive analysis is to determine who the competition is. This is more difficult than one might think. For example, take a company such as 1-800-FLOWERS. Primarily, the company sells flowers. But 1-800-FLOWERS is not only in the flower business. Because flowers are often given for gifts, the company is also in the gift business. If the company sees itself in the gift business rather than just the flower business, it has a broader set of competitors—and opportunities—to consider.

The different types of competitors a business will face are shown in Figure 5.3. The challenges associated with each of these groups of competitors are described here:

- ***Direct competitors:*** These are businesses that offer products identical or similar to the products of the firm completing the analysis. These competitors are the most important because they are going after the same customers as the new firm. A new firm faces winning over the loyal followers of its major competitors, which is difficult to do, even when the new firm has a better product.
- ***Indirect competitors:*** These competitors offer close substitutes to the product the firm completing the analysis sells. These firms' products are also important in that they target the same basic need that is being met by the new firm's product. For example, when people told Roberto Goizueta, the late CEO of Coca-Cola, that Coke's market share was at a maximum, he countered by saying that Coke accounted for less than 2 percent of the 64 ounces of fluid that the average person drinks each day. "The enemy is coffee, milk, tea [and] water," he once said.[20]
- ***Future competitors:*** These are companies that are not yet direct or indirect competitors but could move into one of these roles at any time. Firms are always concerned about strong competitors moving into their markets. For example, think of how the world has changed for Barnes & Noble since Amazon.com was founded.

It is impossible for a firm to identify all its direct and indirect competitors, let alone its future competitors. However, identifying its top 5 to 10 direct competitors and its top 5 to 10 indirect and future competitors makes it easier for the firm to complete its competitive analysis grid.

If a firm does not have a direct competitor, it shouldn't forget that the status quo can be the toughest competitor of all. In general, people are resistant to change and can always keep their money rather than spend it.[21] A product or service's utility must rise above its cost, not only in monetary terms but also in terms of the hassles associated with switching or learning something new, to motivate someone to buy a new product or service.[22]

Although most of the time the firms in an industry compete against one another, there are occasions when competitors unite for the good of the industry as a whole. On these occasions, it is typically to the advantage of a new venture to cooperate. If it doesn't, it may find itself trying to sell a product or service that doesn't comply with evolving industry norms. The chapter's "Partnering for Success" feature offers an example of this scenario. As you'll see, this segment deals with an organization called Digital Living Network Alliance.

FIGURE 5.3

Types of Competitors New Ventures Face

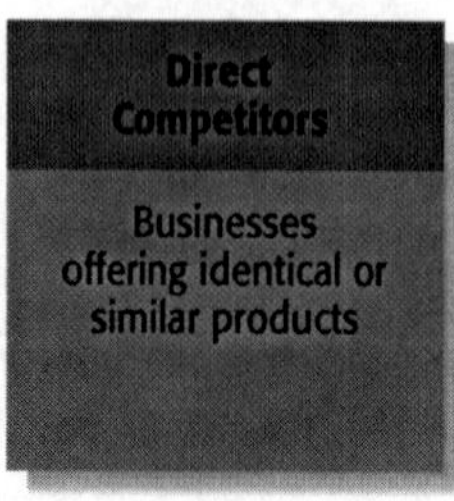

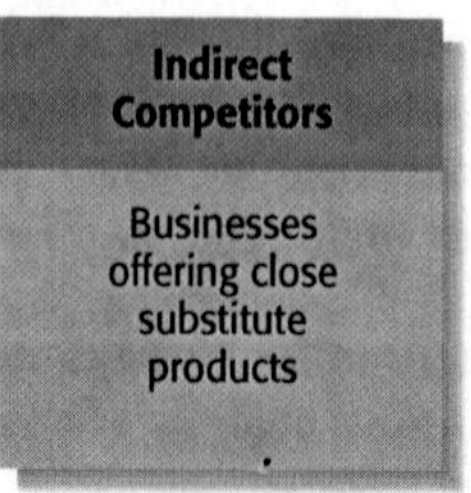

partnering for success

Tech Industry Unites to Create Common Standards for Home Networks

www.dlna.org

Although most of the time firms in an industry compete with one another, there are occasions when firms unite for the good of the industry as a whole. An example is the creation of the Digital Living Network Alliance (DLNA), which is a nonprofit organization founded to create a set of rules aimed at making gadgets communicate better with each other through home networks. Gateway, Hewlett-Packard, Intel, Microsoft, Sony, Nokia, and 11 other firms that create products for home networks created the organization. Today, the organization has over 250 members.

Many people have a growing collection of electronic devices in their homes and would like to network them together. They want to share music, pictures, and video, for example, among their PCs, televisions, sound systems, and mobile devices. However, it is often difficult to network these different devices together because they are seldom perfectly compatible. To make the problem more difficult, many forms of digital music and movies are based on proprietary formats that work on some devices but not on others.

The purpose of the Digital Living Network Alliance is to solve this problem. The belief is that all technology-intensive firms will benefit if their devices easily network with each other and if consumers can feel confident that when they buy a new device, it will seamlessly integrate with the other devices in their homes. The Digital Living Network Alliance has established guidelines to ensure that these goals will be met. For example, a cell phone with a digital camera that adheres to the guidelines will be able to transmit pictures wirelessly to PCs or television sets.

Philip Kotler, a marketing expert and highly respected business professor,, has made the statement that for a firm to be an effective competitor, it must also be "an effective cooperator." The firms that established the Digital Living Network Alliance adhere to the spirit of Professor Kotler's observation.

Questions for Critical Thinking

1. What do you think Professor Kotler means when he says that "firms must be effective cooperators to be effective competitors"? Given what you've read in this book and learned from your other courses, do you agree with Kotler's statement? Why or why not?
2. In general, is it easier for direct competitors or indirect competitors to cooperate? Explain your answer.
3. Do you think the adoption of uniform standards that will enable electronic devices used in homes to better network with one another will make it easier or harder for new firms to enter the industries that make electronic devices for homes? Explain your answer.
4. Research the term *open standards* as it applies to electronics and firm competitiveness. What does "open standards" mean in the context of this feature? In your judgment, are open standards a good thing for consumer electronic firms? Do you think we are likely to see more or less open standards in the electronics industry in the future?

Sources: Digital Living Network Alliance homepage, www.dlna.org (accessed August 8, 2006); P. Kotler, *Marketing Insights from A to Z* (New York: John Wiley & Sons, 2002), 24, and "Tech Giants Unite on Gadget Standard for Home Networks," *The Wall Street Journal*, 2003, B4.

Sources of Competitive Intelligence

9. Describe ways a firm can ethically obtain information about its competitors.

To complete a meaningful competitive analysis grid, a firm must first understand the strategies and behaviors of its competitors. The information that is gathered by a firm to learn about its competitors is referred to as **competitive intelligence**. Obtaining sound competitive intelligence is not always a simple task. If a competitor is a publicly traded firm, a description of the firm's business and its financial information is available through annual reports filed with the Securities and Exchange Commission (SEC). These reports are public records and are available at the SEC's Web site (www.sec.gov). If one or more of the competitors is a private company, the task is more difficult. Private companies are

Many companies attend trade shows to display their products and see what their competitors are up to. This is a shot of the Consumer Electronics Trade Show, held in Las Vegas, which is America's largest annual trade show of any kind.

not required to divulge information to the public. There are a number of ways that a firm can ethically obtain information about its competitors:

- ***Attend conferences and trade shows:*** Most industries have conferences and trade shows at which firms talk about the latest trends in the industry and display their products.
- ***Read industry-related books, magazines, and Web sites, along with general business magazines, such as Inc. and BusinessWeek:*** In addition, many industries and associations publish magazines and newsletters that contain information about competitors.
- ***Talk to customers about what motivated them to buy your product as opposed to your competitors':*** Customers can provide a wealth of information about the advantages and disadvantages of competing products.
- ***Purchase competitors' products to understand their features, benefits, and shortcomings:*** The process of purchasing the product will also provide data about how the competitor treats its customers.
- ***Study competitors' Web sites:*** Many companies put a lot of information on their Web sites, including their company's history, profiles of their management teams, product information, and the latest news about the company.

There are a number of additional resources available to help entrepreneurs collect competitive intelligence. A sample of these resources in shown in Table 5.4.

Completing a Competitive Analysis Grid

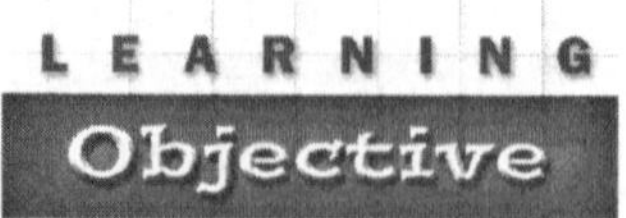

10. Describe the reasons for completing a competitive analysis grid.

As we mentioned previously, a **competitive analysis grid** is a tool for organizing the information a firm collects about its competitors. It can help a firm see how it stacks up against its competitors, provide ideas for markets to pursue, and, perhaps most importantly, identify its primary sources of competitive advantage. To be a viable company, a new venture must have at least one clear competitive advantage over its major competitors.

An example of a competitive analysis grid is provided in Table 5.5. This grid is for Activision, a company that makes electronic games. The company's products cover the action, adventure, action sports, racing, role-playing, simulation, and strategy games categories. These products operate on both PCs and game consoles such as the Nintendo GameCube. According to Activision, the main competitive factors in the electronics games industry are product features and playability, brand-name recognition, compatibility of

TABLE 5.4 Resources to Help Entrepreneurs Complete a Competitor Analysis

Source	Description	Cost
Hoover's Online (www.hoovers.com)	Provides a brief history, financial information, and list of competitors for each company in its vast database. For publicly traded firms, a detailed comparison of the company's financial results to industry averages is also provided.	Typically free if accessed from a college, university, or public library.
InfoUSA (www.infousa.com)	InfoUSA, a publicly traded company, provides access to lists of companies within industries. A leading supplier of information for ethical competitive intelligence.	Fee-based
LexisNexis (www.lexisnexis.com)	Offers subscribers access to thousands of sources—including newspapers, magazines, journal articles, and public records—that can be used to gather information on companies and individuals.	Portions of LexisNexis are typically free if accessed from a college, university, or public library. Full access available on a subscription basis.
LookSmart Find Articles (www.findarticles.com)	A search engine specifically designed to find articles on businesses. Links to the articles are provided.	Free
Wall Street Journal Online (www.wsj.com)	Very powerful search engine for searching for company performance within a particular industry.	You need to subscribe to *The Wall Street Journal*
ZapData (www.zapdata.com)	ZapData is a Dun & Bradstreet service that, like InfoUSA, allows you to create lists of companies within industries. The lists can be used to generate sales leads or to research competitors.	Fee-based

products with popular platforms (e.g., Microsoft's Xbox), access to distribution channels, quality of products, ease of use, price, marketing support, and quality of customer service.[23] These factors are placed on the vertical axis of Activision's competitive analysis grid. The horizontal axis contains Activision and its five main competitors. In each box, Activision would rate itself compared to its main competitors. The purpose of this exercise is for a company to see how it stacks up against its competitors and to determine if any opportunities exist that it may have overlooked. For example, if Activision judged itself superior to its competitors in the category "ease of use," it might use this knowledge to highlight this advantage in its advertising and promotions.

In summary, it is extremely important for a new venture to have a firm grasp of the industry it plans to enter and of the companies it will be competing against on a day-to-day basis. By carefully studying these important areas, a new venture can position itself correctly in its industry and be fully aware of its competitors' strengths and weaknesses as its makes its own decisions about the best way to compete against those competitors.

TABLE 5.5 Competitive Analysis Grid for Activision

Name	Activision	Electronic Arts	Take-Two	LucasArts	Eidos	THQ
Product features and playability						
Brand-name recognition						
Compatibility of products with popular platforms						
Access to distribution channels						
Quality of products						
Ease of use						
Price						
Marketing support						
Quality of customer service						

Chapter Summary

1. Industry analysis is business research that focuses on an industry's potential. The knowledge gleaned from an industry analysis helps a firm decide whether to enter an industry and if it can carve out a position in the industry that will provide it a competitive advantage.
2. The threat of substitutes, the threat of new entrants, rivalry among existing firms, the bargaining power of suppliers, and the bargaining power of buyers are the five competitive forces that determine an industry's profitability.
3. The threat of new entrants is one of the five forces that determine industry profitability. Firms try to keep other firms from entering their industries by erecting barriers to entry. A barrier to entry is a condition that creates a disincentive for a new firm to enter an industry. Economies of scale, product differentiation, capital requirements, cost advantages independent of size, access to distribution channels, and government and legal barriers are examples of barriers to entry.
4. The nontraditional barriers to entry that are particularly well suited to entrepreneurial firms include strength of the management team, first-mover advantage, passion of the management team and employees, unique business model, special internet domain name, and inventing a new approach to an industry and executing the approach in an exemplary manner.
5. The four industry-related questions that a firm should ask before entering an industry are the following: Is the industry a realistic place for a new venture? If we do enter the industry, can our firm do a better job than the industry as a whole in avoiding or diminishing the threats that suppress industry profitability? Is there a unique position in the industry that avoids or diminishes the forces that suppress industry profitability? Is there a superior business model that can be put in place that would be hard for industry incumbents to duplicate?
6. The five primary industry types and the opportunities they offer are as follows: emerging industry/first-mover advantage; fragmented industry/consolidation; mature industry/emphasis on service and process innovation; declining industry/leadership, niche, harvest, and divest; and global industry/multidomestic strategy or global strategy.
7. A competitor analysis is a detailed analysis of a firm's competition. It helps a firm understand the positions of its major competitors and the opportunities that are available to obtain a competitive advantage in one or more areas.
8. The three groups of competitors a new firm will face are direct competitors, indirect competitors, and future competitors.
9. There are a number of ways a firm can ethically obtain information about its competitors, including attending conferences and trade shows; reading industry-related books, magazines, and publications; talking to customers about what motivated them to buy your product as opposed to those of your competitors; purchasing competitors' products to understand their features, benefits, and shortcomings; and studying competitors' Web sites.
10. A competitive analysis grid is a tool for organizing the information a firm collects about its competitors. This grid can help a firm see how it stacks up against its competitors, provide ideas for markets to pursue, and, perhaps most importantly, identify its primary sources of competitive advantage.

Key Terms

barrier to entry
competitive analysis grid
competitive intelligence
competitor analysis
cost reduction strategy
declining industry
economies of scale
emerging industry
fragmented industry
global industry
global strategy
industry

industry analysis
industry consolidation
leadership strategy
mature industry
multidomestic strategy
niche strategy
position

Review Questions

1. What is an industry? Provide an example of an industry and several firms in it.
2. What is the purpose of industry analysis?
3. Identify the five competitive forces that determine industry profitability.
4. Describe how the threat of substitute products has the potential to suppress an industry's profitability.
5. How does the threat of new entrants have the potential to suppress an industry's profitability?
6. What is meant by the term *barrier to entry*? Describe the six major sources of barriers to entry that firms use to restrict entry into their markets.
7. Identify the nontraditional barriers to entry that are particularly suitable for entrepreneurial firms.
8. Describe the four primary factors that play a role in determining the nature and intensity of rivalry among an industry's existing firms. How does rivalry among existing firms have the potential to suppress an industry's profitability?
9. Describe how the bargaining power of suppliers has the potential to suppress an industry's profitability.
10. Describe the four major factors that affect suppliers' ability to exert pressure on buyers and suppress the profitability of the industries to which they sell.
11. In what way does the bargaining power of buyers have the potential to suppress an industry's profitability?
12. Describe the four major factors that affect buyers' ability to exert pressure on suppliers and suppress the profitability of the industries from which they buy materials.
13. Describe the characteristics of a fragmented industry. What is the primary opportunity for new firms in fragmented industries?
14. Describe the characteristics of a mature industry. What is the primary opportunity for new firms in a mature industry?
15. What is a global industry? Describe the two most common strategies pursued by firms in global industries.
16. Describe the purpose of a competitor analysis. Make your answer as complete as possible.
17. Describe the differences between direct competitors, indirect competitors, and future competitors.
18. What is meant by the term *competitive intelligence*? Why is it important for firms to collect intelligence about their competitors?
19. Identify three sources of competitive intelligence.
20. What is the purpose of completing a competitive analysis grid?

Application Questions

1. Linda Williams is thinking about starting a firm in the electronic games industry. When asked by a potential investor if she had studied the industry, Linda replied, "The electronic games industry is so full of potential, it doesn't need formal analysis." Will Linda's answer satisfy the investor? In what ways will Linda limit her potential if her current attitude about the importance of industry analysis doesn't change?

2. The "You Be the VC 2" feature in this chapter focuses on DayJet. Spend some time studying DayJet's Web site and other information about the company. How would you describe DayJet's positioning strategy? What steps is the company taking to avoid some of the negative attributes of the airline industry?
3. Your friend Lisa Ryan is opening a smoothie shop that will sell a variety of smoothie drinks in the $3 to $4 price range. When you ask her if she is worried that the steep price of smoothies might prompt potential customers to buy a soda or a sports drink instead of a smoothie, Lisa answers, "You're right. Someone could substitute a soda or a sports drink for a smoothie and save a lot of money. Is there anything I can do to discourage that?" What do you tell her?
4. Jose Gonzales has been investigating the possibility of starting a package delivery service but is frustrated by the amount of money it takes to get into the industry. He is particularly concerned about getting the cash to buy the trucks he would need. Which of the five forces in Porter's five forces model is strongly affecting Jose's potential business? How can Jose overcome this obstacle?
5. Peter Jones is in the process of starting a business in the restaurant industry. In a recent *Fortune* magazine article, he read that in industries where the bargaining power of suppliers is high, industry profitability suffers. What criteria can Peter use to determine if the bargaining power of suppliers is high in the industry in which he has an interest?
6. Look at Table 5.1 in the chapter and read Case 5.2, which focuses on Cirque du Soleil and Curves International. Which of the nontraditional barriers to entry have been the most helpful to Cirque du Soleil and Curves in terms of deterring new entrants into their industries?
7. Think of at least three entrepreneurial firms, not listed in Table 5.1, that benefit greatly from their Internet domain names. In each case, to what extent do you think the strength of their Internet domain names is instrumental to their ability to limit the number of new entrants in their industries?
8. As mentioned in this chapter, White Wave Inc. produces Silk Soymilk, a product that has done surprisingly well in the mature milk industry. Based on the material we've covered so far, why do you think Silk Soymilk has been so successful?
9. Troy Pearson is starting a medical products business in Albany, New York. He knows he should put together a competitor analysis but doesn't know how to go about it. If Troy turned to you for advice, what would you tell him?
10. Susan Willis is planning to launch an advertising agency in Tampa, Florida. She knows that she needs to complete a competitor analysis but doesn't know where to obtain information about her competitors. Provide Susan with several suggestions on how to proceed.
11. M. B. Jenkins is the founder of a new firm in the electronics industry. A friend of his owns an electronic business in a neighboring state and has invited him to be his guest at a large electronics industry trade show. M. B. can't decide whether to take the time to attend the trade show. In the context of the material presented in this chapter, what are the arguments in favor of attending the trade show?
12. Dana Smith will soon be opening a fitness club in Tucson, Arizona. Having identified his competitors, he wants to display the information he has collected in a way that will help him determine how he'll stack up against his competitors and pinpoint his sources of competitive advantage. Describe to Dana a technique that he could use to help achieve his objectives.
13. Look at Table 5.4 in the chapter. Describe how a company could use a service like InfoUSA to conduct ethical competitive intelligence.
14. Complete Activision's competitive analysis grid, which is pictured in Table 5.5.
15. Access Panera Bread's most recent 10-K report (www.sec.gov/edgar.searchedgar.companysearch.html). Determine from the report what Panera believes are the primary competitive factors in its industry. Complete a competitive analysis grid for Panera Bread. (See Case 5.1 for additional information on Panera.)

you be the VC 5.1 Eclipse Aviation
www.eclipseaviation.com

Business Idea: Build a jet airplane that is so small and inexpensive to operate that a new class of air taxi services will emerge to make private jet travel more readily accessible to middle-class individuals and companies.

Pitch: Private jet service is safe and convenient but is also very expensive. To remedy this problem, Eclipse Aviation, a start-up in Albuquerque, New Mexico, has designed and constructed a six-passenger jet that has been successfully flown and tested. Eclipse plans to sell the jet for approximately $1 million, which is about one-fourth the cost of the least expensive corporate jet on the market. And it's engineered to be very cheap to operate: less than $1 per mile, which is one-third to one-fifth what it costs to fly other small jets. Eclipse's first jet is dubbed the Eclipse 500 Very Light Jet (VLJ). Eclipse hopes to sell the jet to individuals, corporations, and regional airlines or "taxi services" that will use it to shuttle individuals to and from municipal airports. An advantage of the Eclipse 500 is that it can land on a runway as short as 3,000 feet, compared to 4,000 to 5,000 feet needed by the smallest jets now in service. This advantage will allow the Eclipse 500 to service many of the small airports that currently can't accommodate jets. The Eclipse 500 is expected to be certified for commercial flight by the FAA in the near future.

The way Eclipse is able to keep the sale price of the Eclipse 500 so low is through ultra-efficient manufacturing techniques that reduce costs and allow for high-volume manufacturing. An individual jet is made in 5 days and can be delivered 10 days later.

As an added bonus, the Eclipse 500 will boast an optional safety feature no jetliner can match: a parachute big enough to float the plane gently down to the ground. The parachute is made by Ballistic Parachute Systems (www.brsparachutes.com), which is a company that develops and deploys parachute systems for small aircraft.

Q&A: Based on the material covered in this chapter, what questions would you ask the firm's founders before making your funding decision? What answers would satisfy you?

Decision: If you had to make your decision on just the information provided in the pitch and on the company's Web site, would you fund this firm? Why or why not?

you be the VC 5.2 DayJet
www.dayjet.com

Business Idea: Offer a new and affordable form of air travel that provides "air-taxi" services to individuals and groups that accommodate their schedules and is able to reach out-of-the way places.

Pitch: Busy individuals and business travelers have two choices when it comes to air travel: booking a flight on a commercial airline or owning or chartering a private jet. Neither of these choices is very attractive. Commercial airline travel comes with lots of hassles, like checking bags, standing in line at security, crowded airplanes, and either no food at all, food that often just doesn't taste very good, or food offered at a high cost to the customer. At the same time, only the superrich and large companies can afford to charter or own a private jet. To further complicate matters, it's hard to get to and from places that have small airports. For example, take the challenge of trying to travel by air from Columbia, South Carolina, to Gainesville, Florida, in an efficient manner.

DayJet's mission is to fill this void. The company, made possible largely by the emergence of affordable "very light jets," like the Eclipse 500, is rolling out an air-taxi service unlike any service currently available. The service will be a "per-seat, on-demand" service, which will resemble a taxicab service but will take travelers from point to point on very light jets. The service will operate between specific airports called DayPorts. DayPorts are mostly regional and community airports that have little or no scheduled airline service. And customers will pay only for the seats they require, not the whole plane.

The cost of a flight on DayJet will range from $1 to $3 per mile. That compares to 50 cents per mile on a commercial airline and $10 per mile on a chartered jet. The big advantage of DayJet will be time savings and convenience. A business executive who flies from South Florida to Raleigh, North Carolina, to visit a client could easily make the round-trip in a single day using DayJet's service.

The same trip on a commercial airline could take parts of three days, and require two nights in a hotel room, if the executive had to leave the night before the visit and return the morning after.

Q&A: Based on the material covered in this chapter, what questions would you ask the firm's founders before making your funding decision? What answers would satisfy you?

Decision: If you had to make your decision on just the information provided in the pitch and on the company's Web site, would you fund this firm? Why or why not?

Panera Bread: Occupying a Favorable Position in a Highly Competitive Industry

www.panera.com

Bruce R. Barringer,
University of Central Florida
R. Duane Ireland,
Texas A&M University

Introduction

If you analyzed the restaurant industry using Porter's five forces model, you wouldn't be favorably impressed. Three of the threats to profitability—the threat of substitutes, the threat of new entrants, and rivalry among existing firms—are high. Despite these threats to industry profitability, one restaurant chain is moving forward in a very positive direction. St. Louis–based Panera Bread Company, a chain of specialty bakery-cafés, has grown from 602 company owned and franchised units in 2003 to over 877 today. In 2005 alone, its sales increased by 33.6 percent and its net income increased by 35.2 percent. So what's Panera's secret? How is it that this company flourishes while its industry as a whole is experiencing difficulty? As we'll see, Panera Bread's success can be explained in two words: positioning and execution.

Changing Consumer Tastes

Panera's roots go back to 1981, when it was founded under the name of Au Bon Pain Co. and consisted of three Au Bon Pain bakery-cafés and one cookie store. The company grew slowly until the mid-1990s, when it acquired Saint Louis Bread Company, a chain of 20 bakery-cafes located in the St. Louis area. About that time, the owners of the newly combined companies observed that people were increasingly looking for products that were "special"—that were a departure from run-of-the-mill restaurant food. Second, they noted that although consumers were tiring of standard fast-food fare, they didn't want to give up the convenience of quick service. This trend led the company to conclude that consumers wanted the convenience of fast food combined with a higher-quality experience. In slightly different words, they wanted good food served quickly in an enjoyable environment.

The Emergence of Fast Casual

As the result of these changing consumer tastes, a new category in the restaurant industry, called "fast casual," emerged. This category provided consumers the alternative they wanted by capturing the advantage of both the fast-food category (speed) and the casual dining category (good food), with no significant disadvantages. The owners of Au Bon Pain and Saint Louis Bread Company felt that they could help pioneer this new category, so they repositioned their restaurants and named them Panera Bread. The position that Panera moved into is depicted in the graphic titled "Positioning Strategy of Various Restaurant Chains." A market positioning grid provides a visual representation of the positions of various companies in an industry. About Panera's category, industry expert T. J. Callahan said, "I don't think fast casual is a fad; I think it's a structural change starting to happen in the restaurant industry."

Panera's Version of Fast Casual

To establish itself as the leader in the fast-casual category and to distinguish itself from its rivals, Panera (which is Latin for "time for bread") added a bonus to the mix—specialty food. The company has become known as the nation's bread expert and offers a variety of artisan and other specialty breads, along with bagels, pastries, and baked goods. Panera Bread's restaurants are open for breakfast, lunch, and dinner and also offer hand-tossed salads, signature sandwiches, and hearty soups served in edible sourdough bread bowls, along with hot and cold coffee drinks. The company also provides catering services through its Via Panera catering business. Its restaurants provide an inviting neighborly atmosphere, adding to their appeal. Panera even suggests a new time of day to eat specialty foods, calling the time between lunch and dinner "chill-out" time.

Positioning Strategy of Various Restaurant Chains

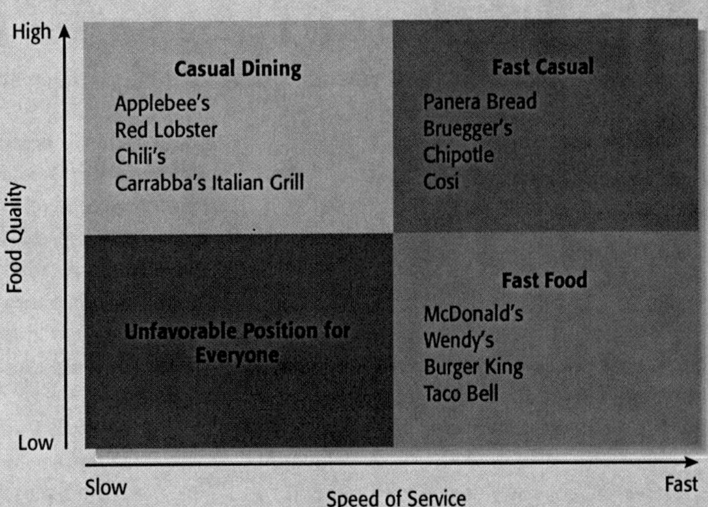

With high hopes for future expansion, Panera Bread is now the acknowledged leader in the fast-casual category. Systemwide sales were $640 million in 2005. Its unique blend of fast-casual service and specialty foods also continues to gain momentum. This sentiment is captured in the following quote from Mark von Waaden, an investor and restaurateur who recently signed an agreement to open 20 Panera Bread restaurants in the Houston, Texas, area. Commenting on why he was attracted to Panera Bread as opposed to other restaurant chains, Mr. von Waaden said,

> My wife, Monica, and I fell in love with the fresh-baked breads and the beautiful bakery-cafés. We think the Panera Bread concept of outstanding bread coupled with warm, inviting environment is a natural fit with the sophistication that the Houston market represents.

The spirit of von Waaden's statement captures the essence of Panera's advantage. It isn't just another restaurant. By observing trends and listening to customers, its leaders helped the firm carve out a unique and favorable position in a difficult industry.

Present Status and Goal for the Future

Panera's leadership in the fast-casual category and its financial performance has drawn considerable attention to the company. As evidence of this, in early 2006 Panera was recognized by the *Wall Street Journal*'s Shareholder Scorecard as the top performer in the restaurant category for one-, five-, and ten-year returns to shareholders.

The company's goal remains to make Panera a leading national brand. The company is counting on its unique positioning strategy, its signature foods, and savvy execution to make this goal a reality.

Discussion Questions

1. How has Panera Bread establish a unique position in the restaurant industry? How has this unique position contributed to its success? Do you think Panera Bread will reach its goal of becoming a leading national brand in the restaurant industry? Why or why not?
2. Analyze the restaurant industry using Porter's five forces model. In what ways has Panera Bread successfully positioned itself against the forces that are suppressing the profitability of the restaurant industry as a whole?
3. What barriers to entry has Panera Bread created for potential competitors? How significant are these barriers?
4. What are Panera Bread's primary sources of competitive advantage? In your judgment, are these sources of advantage sustainable? Why or why not?

Application Questions

1. What are the ways that Panera Bread can conduct ethical and proper forms of competitive analysis to learn about potential competitors entering the fast-casual category?
2. Think of at least two other businesses that have established unique positions in their industries. How have their unique positions contributed to their success?

Sources: Panera Bread homepage, www.panera.com, (accessed May 18, 2006); Panera Bread Annual Report (2005); "Industry by Industry: A Look at the Start, Their Stocks—and Their Latest Picks, *The Wall Street Journal*, May 12, 2003, R8.

Cirque du Soleil and Curves International: Succeeding in Unattractive Industries Via Blue Ocean Strategies

www.cirquedusoleil.com, www.curves.com

Bruce R. Barringer,
University of Central Florida
R. Duane Ireland,
Texas A&M University

Introduction

At first glance, Cirque du Soleil and Curves International have little in common. One is a high-end entertainment company with only five permanent locations. The other is a fitness center for women, with close to 10,000 locations worldwide. But when it comes to this chapter's topic, industry and competitor analysis, the two have similar start-up stories as well as current performance-related outcomes. Indeed, although both companies were launched in what would be called unattractive industries, both are thriving today, primarily by attracting new customers to their industries and by changing the rules of competition in their respective industries.

Examining these firms shows that both Cirque du Soleil and Curves have started companies in what W. Chan Kim and Renee Mauborgne call "blue oceans." In their book *Blue Ocean Strategy*, Kim and Mauborgne ask their readers to imagine a market universe composed of two types of oceans: blue oceans and red oceans. In the red oceans, industry boundaries are well defined and the rules of the game are known. Companies slug it out for market share, and as the market gets increasingly crowded, prospects for growth and profits diminish, and cutthroat competition turns the oceans red. In contrast, blue oceans are defined by untapped market space and the opportunity for highly profitable growth. Most blue oceans are actually created within red oceans by expanding existing industry boundaries. When this happens, the industries experience a flood of new customers that rarely, if ever, participated before.

Although not all industries are ripe for blue ocean strategies, Cirque du Soleil and Curves are extraordinary examples of firms that rejuvenated unattractive industries by changing the rules of the game. They have succeeded *not* by taking customers away from their rivals, but by unlocking huge untapped markets in previously unattractive industries. Read on to see how they did it.

Cirque du Soleil

Cirque du Soleil (French for "circus of the sun") was started in Montreal, Canada, in 1984 by Guy Lailberte, a 23-year-old Montreal fire breather, and Daniel Gauthier, a 24-year-old hotel manager. At the time the circus industry was in decline. There was a growing sentiment against the use of animals in circuses and alternative forms of entertainment were increasing. The existing circus companies were focused on maximizing their share of the existing demand by tweaking their acts. This meant hiring more famous clowns and more spectacular circus acts, which resulted in higher costs with little or no corresponding increase in revenue and, subsequently, income.

Rather than trying to create a circus with better fun and more thrilling acts, Cirque du Soleil decided to redefine the boundaries of the circus by offering people at the same time (1) the thrill of the circus and (2) the artistic richness and the intellectual sophistication of the theater. By adopting this approach, Cirque du Soleil was able to eliminate many of the negatives associated with traditional circuses and add the positives associated with more upscale theater productions. In the process, it did away with animal shows, hiring star performers, aisle concession sales, and the "three rings" of the three-ring circus. Animals are expensive to maintain and are controversial in a circus setting. The so-called "circus stars" paled in popularity to movie stars and professional athletics. And the "three rings" of the three-ring circus not only created angst among spectators, who rapidly switched their attention from one ring to another, but drove costs up as well.

To the founders of Cirque du Soleil, the lasting allure of the circus came down to three essential elements: the tent, the clowns, and the acrobatic acts. So they retained these elements and dressed them up. To expand the richness and the boundaries of the circus, they added new elements, such as a story line, a refined environment, artistic music and dance, and permanent venues. In addition, a key decision made early in the life of the company set its direction in terms of quality. As word spread about Cirque du Soleil's early success, offers flooded in from agents and production companies wanting to finance touring renditions of the show. But the founders refused. The supply of world-class circus performers was just too limited, they reasoned, to put dozens of Cirque du Soleil–branded shows on the road. Instead, they decided to strictly limit the number of shows they produced to avoid diluting their talent.

To visually see how Cirque du Soleil redefined the circus industry, refer to the figure titled "How Cirque du Soleil and Curves International Redefined the Industries in Which They Compete." This figure shows the factors that Cirque du Soleil eliminated from the traditional circus and

How Cirque du Soleil and Curves Redefined the Industries in Which They Compete

Cirque du Soleil

Eliminated from Traditional Circuses	Unique Additions to the Circus Concept
• Star performers • Animal shows • Aisle concession sales • Multiple show arenas	• Theme • Refined environment • Artistic music and dance • Multiple productions

Curves International

Eliminated from Traditional Fitness Centers	Unique Additions to the Fitness Center Concept
• Full range of aerobic and strength machines • Locker room and showers • Aerobic classes • Juice bars	• Just for women • A tightly structured 30-minute workout • Affordable prices • Advocacy for women

the factors that it added. The company presently has five permanent venues, four in Las Vegas and one in Orlando, and five touring shows. Each venue features a unique show, which includes a distinct story line, an original musical score, and a masterfully choreographed series of acrobatic acts and spiritual dances. By offering the best of both the circus and the theater, the company has drawn people to its performances that would never have considered attending a traditional circus. Its prices, which range from $40 to $125 per ticket, are comparable to Broadway shows.

Cirque de Soleil's unique approach has created a blue ocean and a new form of live entertainment—which is neither circus nor theater. In just over 20 years, the company has brought in as much revenue as it took Barnum & Bailey and Ringling Brothers a combined 100 years to obtain. To date, its shows have been seen by over 40 million people in 90 cities around the world.

Curves International

In the early 1990s, most fitness centers in the United States targeted people between the ages of 20 and 30. They focused on fitness and sports and typically offered exercise equipment and classes such as aerobics. Amenities ranged from towel service and showers to massages, swimming pools, and child care. Most centers sold annual or monthly memberships. Some of these memberships were expensive, running at high as $1,800 per year.

Like the founders of Cirque du Soleil, Gary and Diane Heavin, who founded Curves in 1992, had a different idea. They wanted to open a fitness center targeted at an underserved part of the market: overweight women who had never worked out before. The Heavins believed that many women 30 and older cared deeply about their health and appearance but didn't want to join a fitness center full of people who were already fit. They also figured that if they made the center convenient and affordable, and restricted it to females, it would inspire middle-aged women to give fitness a try.

To implement their idea, the Heavins stripped the fitness center concept down to what they felt would appeal to the emotional and physical needs of women and would fit into their budgets and busy lives. They started by eliminating many of the factors that drive up the cost of a fitness club membership and provide little value to many women: multiple aerobic and strength machines, locker rooms and showers, aerobic classes and juice bars. In their place, they implemented a tightly structured 30-minute workout on 8 to 12 exercise machines. The machines are located in a circle, and a recorded voice tells a member when to move from one machine to another. A member walks in, works out, and walks out, all in just over half an hour. This approach gives busy women the ability to participate without sacrificing a large portion of their day. It also allows them to shower and dress in the privacy of their homes.

What Curves has eliminated, and has uniquely added to the fitness center concept, is shown in the figure referred to earlier. As shown in the figure, the additions go beyond the workout itself. By creating a fitness center designed specifically for women, the company explicitly and implicitly told this group, "We know how you feel. We know it is not easy to go to a fitness center if you're a little embarrassed about how you look. You're important enough that we've created a company just for you. We care." By positioning itself in this way, Curves became an advocate for women 30 and older and expanded the boundaries of the fitness industry. "What Curves has done is broken through the perception that you have to be fit, coordinated and thin to go to a gym," says Bill Howland, director of research for the International Health, Racquet and Sports Association. "They've carved out a niche within the population that had never been served." In different words, Curves has created a blue ocean out of an existing red ocean.

There are now close to 10,000 Curves locations worldwide with sales exceeding the $1 billion mark. Through its unique approach, Curves has attracted a large number of women to the fitness industry who would never have joined a fitness center before. Its unique approach has also made the opening of a Curves franchise affordable for a wider range of potential franchisees. A curves franchise can be opened for between $35,000 and $50,000. By comparison, a full-service fitness center can cost up to $1 million to build and fully equip.

Discussion Questions

1. What are the primary lessons learned from the Cirque du Soleil and the Curves cases? How do these lessons help the founders of a start-up better appreciate and understand the dynamics of the industry that they are about to enter?
2. What barriers to entry have both Cirque du Soleil and Curves established to deter competitors? Has capturing a first-mover advantage helped these firms deter new entrants from expanding their respective industries in the same ways that Cirque du Soleil and Curves did? Which company has established stronger barriers to entry—Cirque du Soleil or Curves?
3. Which of the nontraditional barriers to entry, shown in Table 5.1, were utilized by Cirque du Soleil and which were utilized by Curves? To what extent have these nontraditional barriers to entry contributed to each company's success?
4. Develop a competitive analysis grid for Curves. Replicate the grid shown in Table 5.4, replacing the information provided for Activision with similar information for Curves.

Application Questions

1. Provide an example of a company, other than Cirque du Soleil or Curves, that has expanded the market boundaries (that is, that has created a blue ocean) out of an unattractive industry (that is, from a red ocean). Briefly tell this company's story.
2. Do you think a fitness center designed specifically for men could be as successful in drawing new people into the fitness center industry as Curves has been with its fitness centers designed specifically for women? Explain your answer.

Sources: W. C. Kim and R. Mauborge, *Blue Ocean Strategy* (Boston: Harvard Business School Press, 2005); Cirque du Soleil homepage, www.cirquedusoleil.com (accessed May 8, 2006); Curves International homepage, www.curves.com (accessed May 8, 2006); H. W. Tesoriero, "A Slim Gym's Fat Success," *Time*, June, 2003.

Endnotes

1. Personal Interview with Evan Shapiro, July 25, 2006.
2. Sun-tzu, *The Art of War* (Mineola, NY: Dover Publications, 2002), chap. 7.
3. R. P. Rumelt, "How Much Does Industry Matter?" *Strategic Management Journal* 12, no. 3 (1991): 167–85.
4. Y. E. Spanos, G. Zaralis, and S. Lioukas, "Strategy and Industry Effects on Profitability: Evidence From Greece," *Strategic Management Journal* 25 (2004), 139–65.
5. A. M. McGahan and M. Porter, "How Much Does Industry Matter, Really?" *Strategic Management Journal* 18, special issue (1997): 15–30.
6. G. Hawawini, V. Subramanian, and P. Verdin, "Is Performance Driven By Industry Or Firm-Specific Factors? A Reply to McNamara, Aime, and Vaaler," *Strategic Management Journal* 26 (2006), 1083–86.
7. M. Porter, *Competitive Strategy: Techniques for Analyzing Industries and Competitors* (New York: Free Press, 1980).
8. Porter, *Competitive Strategy.*
9. J. W. Mullins, *The New Business Road Test* (London: Financial Times Prentice Hall, 2003).
10. Porter, *Competitive Strategy.*
11. T. Surette and C. Feldman, "Big Deal: EA and NFL Ink Exclusive Licensing Agreement," *Gamespot News*, www.gamespot.com (accessed December 13, 2004).
12. G. Keighley, "Could This Be the Next Disney?" *Business 2.0*, December 2002.

13. S. McNealy, "A Winning Business Model," in *The Book of Entrepreneurs' Wisdom*, ed. Peter Krass (New York: John Wiley & Sons, 1999), 171–89.
14. M. Porter, "How Competitive Forces Shape Strategy," *Harvard Business Review* 57, no. 2, (1979), 137–45.
15. Geoffrey A. Moore, *Dealing With Darwin* (New York: Portfolio, 2005).
16. J. A. Barney and W. Hesterly, "Organizational Economics: Understanding the Relationship Between Organizations and Economic Analysis," in *Handbook of Organization Studies*, eds. Steward R. Clegg, Cynthia Hardy, and Walter R. Nord (London: Sage, 1996), 115–47.
17. J. Rodengen, *The Legend of Nucor Corporation* (Ft. Lauderdale, FL: Write Stuff Enterprises, 1997).
18. T. Levitt, *The Marketing Imagination* (New York: Free Press, 1986).
19. M-J. Chen, "Competitor Analysis and Inter-Firm Rivalry: Toward a Theoretical Integration," *Academy of Management Review* 21, no. 1 (1996): 100–34.
20. P. Kotler, *Marketing Insights from A to Z* (Hoboken, NJ: Wiley, 2003), 23.
21. P. Coburn, *The Change Function* (New York: Portfolio, 2006).
22. J. L. Nesheim, *The Power of Unfair Advantage* (New York: Free Press, 2005).
23. Activision 10-K Report for the Fiscal Year Ending March 31, 2006.

3 | Designing a Competitive Business Model and Building a Solid Strategic Plan

If you aim at nothing, you'll hit it every time. —Zig Ziglar

The best way to predict the future is to invent it. —Alan Kay

Learning Objectives

On completion of this chapter, you will be able to:

1. Understand the importance of strategic management to a small business.
2. Explain why and how a small business must create a competitive advantage in the market.
3. Develop a strategic plan for a business using the nine steps in the strategic planning process.
4. Discuss the characteristics of three basic strategies—low cost, differentiation, and focus—and know when and how to employ them.
5. Understand the importance of controls such as the balanced scorecard in the planning process.

LEARNING OBJECTIVES
1. Understand the importance of strategic management to a small business.

Few activities in the life of a business are as vital—or as overlooked—as that of developing a strategy for success. Too often, entrepreneurs brimming with optimism and enthusiasm launch businesses destined for failure because their founders never stop to define a workable strategy that sets them apart from their competition. Because they tend to be people of action, entrepreneurs often find the process of developing a strategy dull and unnecessary. Their tendency is to start a business, try several approaches, and see what works. Without a cohesive plan of action, however, these entrepreneurs have as much chance of building a successful business as a defense contractor attempting to build a jet fighter without blueprints. Companies lacking clear strategies may achieve some success in the short run, but as soon as competitive conditions stiffen or an unanticipated threat arises, they usually "hit the wall" and fold. Without a basis for differentiating itself from a pack of similar competitors, the best a company can hope for is mediocrity in the marketplace.

In today's global competitive environment, any business, large or small, that is not thinking and acting strategically is extremely vulnerable. Every business is exposed to the forces of a rapidly changing competitive environment, and in the future small business executives can expect even greater change and uncertainty. From sweeping political changes around the planet and rapid technological advances to more intense competition and newly emerging global markets, the business environment has become more turbulent and challenging to business owners. Although this market turbulence creates many challenges for small businesses, it also creates opportunities for those companies that have in place strategies to capitalize on them. Historically important, entrepreneurs' willingness to adapt, to create change, to experiment with new business models, and to break traditional rules has become more important than ever. "It's not the strongest or the most intelligent [companies that] survive," says American Express CEO Ken Chenault, "but those most adaptive to change."[1]

Perhaps the biggest change business owners face is unfolding now: the shift in the world's economy from a base of *financial* to *intellectual* capital. "Knowledge is no longer just a factor of production," says futurist Alvin Toffler. "It is the *critical* factor of production."[2] Today, a company's intellectual capital is likely to be the source of its competitive advantage in the marketplace. **Intellectual capital** comprises three components:[3]

intellectual capital
a key source of a company's competitive advantage that comprises (1) human capital, (2) structural capital, and (3) customer capital.

1. *Human capital*, the talents, creativity, skills, and abilities of a company's workforce, shows up in the innovative strategies, plans, and processes that the people in an organization develop and then passionately pursue.
2. *Structural capital*, the accumulated knowledge and experience that a company possesses, can take many forms including processes, software, patents, copyrights, and, perhaps most important, the knowledge and experience of the people in a company.
3. *Customer capital* is the established customer base, positive reputation, ongoing relationships, and goodwill that a company builds up over time with its customers.

Increasingly, entrepreneurs are recognizing that the capital stored in these three areas forms the foundation of their ability to compete effectively and that they must manage this intangible capital base carefully. Every business uses all three components in its strategy, but the emphasis they place on each one varies.

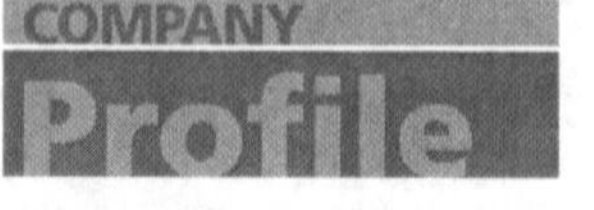

Whole Foods

Whole Foods, a highly successful retailer of natural and organic foods with 172 stores in North America and the United, relies heavily on human capital as the basis for its competitive advantage in the marketplace. The company subjects all job applicants to a thorough screening process, carefully selecting only those who demonstrate a passion for what lies at the heart of its competitive edge: a love of food and dedication to customer service. Unlike most of its competitors in the supermarket industry, Whole Foods invests heavily in training its workers (called Team Members inside the company) so that they can demonstrate and explain to customers the features and the benefits of the company's natural foods. In addition, managers recognize that food preferences vary from one region of a nation to another, and they give Team Members at the local level a great deal of autonomy in the selection of foods they stock. Because of its recognition of the role Team

Members play in the company's success and its employee-friendly policies, Whole Foods is consistently listed on *Fortune's* "100 Best Companies to Work For" list. Even though its cost structure is not the lowest in the industry, the company is growing rapidly because owners know that its loyal customers do not shop there searching for the lowest prices.[4]

This knowledge shift will create as much change in the world's business systems as the Industrial Revolution did in the agriculture-based economies of the 1800s. The Knowledge Revolution will spell disaster for those companies who are not prepared for it, but it will spawn tremendous opportunities for those entrepreneurs equipped with the strategies to exploit these opportunities. Management legend Jack Welch, who masterfully guided General Electric for many years, says, "Intellectual capital is what it's all about. Releasing the ideas of people is what we've got to do if we are going to win."[5] However, in practice, releasing people's ideas is much more difficult than it appears. The key is to encourage employees to generate a large volume of ideas, recognizing that only a few (the best) will survive. According to Gary Hamel, author of *Inside the Revolution*, "If you want to find a few ideas with the power to enthrall customers, foil competitors, and thrill investors, you must first generate hundreds and potentially thousands of unconventional strategic ideas. Put simply, you have to crush a lot of rock to find a diamond."[6] In other words, small companies must use the creative techniques discussed in Chapter 2 as one source of competitive advantage over their rivals.

The rules of the competitive game of business are constantly changing. To be successful, entrepreneurs can no longer do things in the way they've always done them. Fortunately, successful entrepreneurs have at their disposal a powerful weapon to cope with a hostile, ever-changing environment: the process of strategic management. **Strategic management** involves developing a game plan to guide a company as it strives to accomplish its vision, mission, goals, and objectives and to keep it from straying off its desired course. The idea is to give an entrepreneur a blueprint for matching the company's strengths and weaknesses to the opportunities and threats in the environment.

strategic management
the process of developing a game plan to guide a company as it strives to accomplish its vision, mission, goals, and objectives and to keep it from straying off course.

Building a Competitive Advantage

LEARNING OBJECTIVES
2. Explain why and how a small business must create a competitive advantage in the market.

The goal of developing a strategic plan is to create for the small company a **competitive advantage**—the aggregation of factors that sets a small business apart from its competitors and gives it a unique position in the market that is superior to its competition. From a strategic perspective, the key to business success is to develop a unique competitive advantage, one that creates value for customers and is difficult for competitors to duplicate. A company that gains a competitive advantage becomes a leader in its market and can achieve above-average profits.

competitive advantage
the aggregation of factors that sets a small business apart from its competitors and gives it a unique position in the market superior to its competition.

Blockbuster Video

Early in its existence, the Blockbuster Video chain gained a significant advantage over rival video rental stores when it negotiated a deal with the major movie studios to purchase videos for just $6 each, plus a revenue sharing agreement of 40 percent of the rental fees. The agreement meant that Blockbuster could lower the cost of its inventory to less than one-tenth of that of its competitors, who were still paying an average of $65 per video! Blockbuster's significantly lower costs meant that it could stock thousands more video titles than any of its rivals, enabling the company to offer customers a tangible benefit (greater selection and in-stock guarantees) while creating a sizeable competitive advantage in the market.[7]

Building a competitive advantage alone is not enough; the key to success over time is building a *sustainable* competitive advantage. In the long run, a company gains a sustainable competitive advantage through its ability to develop a set of core competencies that enable it to serve its selected target customers better than its rivals. **Core competencies** are a unique set of capabilities that a company develops in key areas, such as superior quality,

core competencies
a unique set of capabilities that a company develops in key operational areas that allow it to vault past competitors.

FIGURE 3.1

Building a Sustainable Competitive Advantage

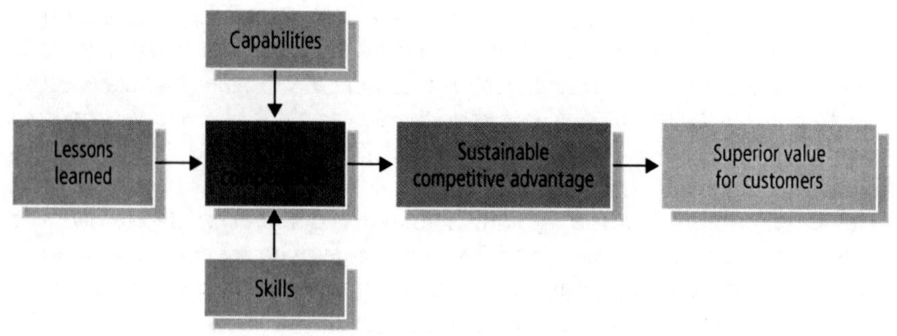

customer service, innovation, team-building, flexibility, responsiveness, and others, that allow it to vault past competitors. As the phrase suggests, they are central to a company's ability to compete successfully and are usually the result of important skills and lessons a business has learned over time. Two of the Disney Company's core competencies are animation and the ability to create magical experiences for guests at its theme parks through superior customer service. After company founder Walt Disney died, however, the company lost its focus, moved away from these core competencies, and struggled as its competitive edge in animated films slipped away to smaller competitors such as Pixar.

Typically, a company develops core competencies in no more than five or six (often fewer) areas. These core competencies become the nucleus of a company's competitive advantage and are usually quite enduring over time. Markets, customers, and competitors may change, but a company's core competencies are more durable, forming the building blocks for everything a company does. To be effective strategically, these competencies should be difficult for competitors to duplicate, and they must provide customers with an important perceived benefit. Small companies' core competencies often have to do with the advantages of their size—such as agility, speed, closeness to their customers, superior service, or the ability to innovate. In short, their small size is an advantage, allowing them to do things that their larger rivals cannot. The key to success is building the company's strategy on these core competences and concentrating them on providing superior service and value for its target customers (see Figure 3.1).

Netflix

Reed Hastings, founder of Netflix, transformed the video rental industry when he created a Web-based model that allows customers to make their video selections online and to avoid having to pay late fees. Hastings' next innovation is to deliver movies over the Internet without having to ship DVDs through its distribution centers.

Blockbuster Video's early market dominance in the video rental business did not go unchallenged, and its competitive advantage proved to be unsustainable over time. The most serious challenge comes from Netflix, a small company that has created a unique online DVD rental service. Software entrepreneur Reed Hastings saw the Web as a way to revolutionize the delivery of videos to consumers and launched the company in 1997 by investing his own money and raising $120 million in equity capital. For a monthly subscription fee, customers log onto the Netflix Web site and pick the movies they want to rent and the order in which they want to receive them. The order goes to one of the 35 Netflix regional distribution centers that is closest to the customer, where employees fill the order. Customers can keep a DVD as long as they want without incurring any late fees, and shipping (both ways) is free. When a customer returns a DVD, a computer scans it, looks up the next video on the customer's order, and sends it out. About 90 percent of DVDs come in and go out on the same day. Netflix is building its competitive advantage on several core competencies. Hastings created the business system that drives Netflix using his extensive knowledge of computer software. One venture capitalist says Netflix's "film recommendation software, its merchandising, and the inventory control systems are so sophisticated. It isn't that they couldn't be replicated, but they're hard to do, and it'll take a lot of money, time, and commitment to get it right as Netflix has." CineMatch, the company's proprietary film suggestion software (29,000 lines of code), uses customers' ratings from past films they have rented to suggest new ones. The CineMatch system works so well that its recommendations account for 70 percent of the movies Netflix customers rent! Netflix also has entered into revenue-sharing deals with 50 film distributors, including most of the major studios, giving it an inventory of more than 50,000 titles, including lesser-known, niche films as well as box office hits. The largest Blockbuster Video stores have 7,000 to 8,000 titles. Netflix's strategy of offering customers maximum convenience—free in-home delivery, no due dates, no late fees, and no return shipping charges—has enabled it to increase its customer base to 3 million people. Once the industry leader, Blockbuster is now relentlessly pursuing Netflix with an online DVD rental service of its own and has attracted 1 million customers. Amazon, which has launched a similar service in England as a test run for entering the U.S. market, also promises to be a formidable competitor. Hastings, however, is not standing still; his goal is to have 20 million subscribers by 2010. How? His next innovation involves working in a strategic alliance with TiVo to allow customers of both services to download movies over the Internet. In fact, Hastings projects that by 2010, Netflix will deliver most of its movies over the Internet rather than shipping DVDs through its distribution centers.[8]

No business can be everything to everyone. In fact, one of the biggest pitfalls many entrepreneurs stumble into is failing to differentiate their companies from the crowd of competitors. Entrepreneurs often face the challenge of setting their companies apart from their larger, more powerful competitors (who can easily outspend them) by using their creativity and the special abilities their businesses offer customers. Developing core competencies does *not* necessarily require a company to spend a great deal of money. It does, however, require an entrepreneur to use creativity, imagination, and vision to identify those things that it does best and that are most important to its target customers. Businesses have a huge number of ways to create a competitive edge, but building strategy around a company's core competencies allows it to gain a sustainable competitive edge based on what it does best.

Tom's of Maine

Tom's of Maine has built its reputation over the last 35 years as a back-to-nature company that sells a line of more than 90 all-natural personal care products with environmentally friendly packaging and donates 10 percent of its pre-tax profits to charity. Founder Tom Chappell's company competes in the same industry as giants such as Unilever, Colgate-Palmolive, and Procter & Gamble by focusing on its base of environmentally conscious customers and by promoting itself as a company "working with nature to make a difference." Gearing up for growth, Tom's of Maine has introduced a line of herbal remedy products as well as a line of toothpastes for adults and children. Like all of its other products, the new toothpastes contain no artificial flavors, dyes, sweeteners, or preservatives, nor are they tested on animals. Tom's of Maine is the only company to have a complete line of all-natural fluoride toothpastes that are approved by the American Dental Association. The toothpastes and all of the company's product extensions are based on its core competency of developing and manufacturing all-natural, environmentally friendly products that meet the highest standards of quality and safety, something that enables Tom's products to sell at a premium. Another core competency is the company's stellar reputation among a loyal customer base as a business with a deep sense of ethics and environmental and social responsibility. (Chappell is the only CEO to have earned a master's degree at the Harvard Divinity School.) Explaining the company's enduring success, Gwynne Rogers of the Natural Marketing Institute says, "Lots of companies foster sustainable business practices, but they don't make them relevant to consumers. Tom's has positioned its mission right at the point of sale."[9]

When it comes to developing a strategy for establishing a competitive advantage, small companies such as Tom's of Maine have a variety of natural advantages over their larger competitors. Small businesses often have narrower product lines, more clearly defined customer bases, a special connection with their customers, and specific geographic market areas. Entrepreneurs usually are in close contact with their markets, giving them valuable knowledge on how to best serve their customers' needs and wants. Because of the simplicity of their organization structures, small business owners are in touch with employees daily, often working side by side with them, allowing them to communicate strategic moves first-hand. Consequently, small businesses find that strategic management comes more naturally to them than to larger companies with their layers of bureaucracy and far-flung operations.

Strategic management can increase a small company's effectiveness, but entrepreneurs first must have a process designed to meet their needs and their business's special characteristics. It is a mistake to attempt to apply a big business's strategic development techniques to a small business because a small business is not merely "a little big business." Because of their size and their particular characteristics—small resource base, flexible managerial style, informal organizational structure, and adaptability to change—small businesses need a different approach to the strategic management process. The strategic management procedure for a small business should include the following features:

LEARNING OBJECTIVES
3. Develop a strategic plan for a business using the nine steps in the strategic planning process.

- Use a relatively short planning horizon—two years or less for most small companies.
- Be informal and not overly structured; a shirtsleeve approach is ideal.
- Encourage the participation of employees and outside parties to improve the reliability and creativity of the resulting plan.
- Do not begin with setting objectives because extensive objective setting early on may interfere with the creative process of strategic management.
- Maintain flexibility; competitive conditions change too rapidly for any plan to be considered permanent.
- Focus on strategic *thinking*, not just planning, by linking long-range goals to day-to-day operations.
- Let planning be an ongoing process because businesses and the competitive environment in which they operate constantly change.

You Be the Consultant

Who Says Shopping for Groceries Can't Be Fun?

In an industry famous for razor-thin profit margins, high levels of employee turnover, and intense competition usually based on price, Wegmans, a family-owned chain of 67 supermarkets in New York, New Jersey, Pennsylvania, and Virginia, is quite unique. It has to be. Traditional grocers are under attack on many fronts. Mass merchandisers such as Wal-Mart with its superstore concept are taking customers, sales, and market share from traditional grocers. Mass merchandisers' now control one-third of the grocery market, and experts predict that their market share will continue to rise, hitting about 40 percent in 2008. Customers say they are bored with the shopping experience at most traditional grocers. One recent study reports that 84 percent of shoppers say that traditional grocery stores are all alike. Over the past several years, several chains have struggled to survive, and some have declared bankruptcy or were bought out by competitors.

How does this relatively small chain of grocery stores founded in 1930 by brothers John and Walter Wegman manage not only to survive, but also to claim a spot near the top of the industry? Although the answer to that question involves as many components as the number of brands on the cereal aisle in one of the Wegmans stores, much of the credit goes to the company's clever retail strategy and the way it treats employees. That strategy took root early in the company's existence when its founding brothers built a 300-seat café in their first store in Rochester, New York, a concept that was unheard of in 1930. When Robert Wegman, son of one of the founders, took over the company in 1950, he instituted a host of employee-friendly benefits such as profit-sharing and full medical coverage long before benefits of this type were popular. When asked why he made such a bold move, Robert, now chairman of the company, says simply, "I was no different from them."

Wegmans' annual salaries for full-time workers and hourly wages for part-time workers are among the highest in the industry. Not only do the higher wages discourage labor unions from setting up shop, but they also keep the employee turnover rate—and the resulting costs of constantly having to hire and train new workers—well below the industry average. Wegmans' generous pay scale and its consistent listing as one of the 100 best companies to work for also attracts quality workers. In fact, the sous chef at its Pittsford, New York, store previously worked at the French Laundry, the famous Napa Valley restaurant that is consistently voted as the best in the United States.

In addition to excellent pay, Wegmans also offers college scholarships for both its full- and part-time employees. Over the last two decades, the company has awarded more than $54 million in scholarships to some 17,500 workers. Wegmans also sends many of its employees to locations around the world to learn about or to locate new and unique sources of foods—from wine and cheese to mushrooms and sushi. After all, reasons Robert's son, Danny, who now manages Wegmans, what good is it to offer 500 varieties of cheese if employees can't explain to customers the best way to serve them, which types of crackers to serve them on, and which wines go best with them?

Although Wegmans approach to managing people pushes its labor cost to 15 to 17 percent of sales (compared with 12 percent of sales for the average supermarket), its annual turnover rate for full-time employees is just 6 percent, less than one-third the industry average of 19 percent. More than 20 percent of Wegmans' employees have 10 years or more of service, and this shows up in the wealth of knowledge about the company's products that they enthusiastically share with customers. "It's our [employees'] knowledge that can help the customer," says Danny. "So the first pump we have to prime is our own people."

Almost everyone Wegmans hires has a keen interest in food, but the real acid test for new hires is a passion for taking care of customers. Indeed, Wegmans' focus on customer service is another component of its strategy for success. Every employee in the store has the power to do whatever it takes to keep customers happy without having to involve a manager higher up the chain of command. One worker even cooked a customer's Thanksgiving turkey for her in the store when the bird proved to be too big to fit in her oven. Why does Wegmans go to such lengths for its customers? Because it pays big dividends! The Wegmans know that satisfied customers keep coming back and that they spend more when they do. However, Wegmans' wants to do more than satisfy customers; the goal is to build an emotional connection with them. One Gallup survey finds that shoppers who were emotionally connected to a supermarket spent 46 percent more than shoppers who were satisfied but lacked an emotional bond with the store.

Wegmans' retail strategy involves offering customers superior service and the convenience of one-stop shopping. Each store—the new ones are 130,000 square feet, three times the size of the typical supermarket—provides shoppers with a huge selection of top-quality products ranging from national brands such as Cocoa Puffs to upscale organic produce, all displayed with the flair and style of an upscale retail boutique. Each store also boasts a bookstore, child play centers, a dry cleaner, a photo processing lab, a video rental center, a wine shop, a pharmacy, a florist, international newspapers, and an $850 espresso maker. "Going there is not just shopping," says one industry consultant. "It's an event." The result is that Wegmans' sales per square foot of store space is 50 percent higher than the industry average of $9.29.

The Wegman family intentionally follows a methodical growth strategy, opening only two new stores a year. To make sure each new store is a success, the company puts some of the best and brightest workers from its existing stores to work in its new ones. After earning an undergraduate degree in mechanical engineering and an MBA, Heather Pawlowski decided to enter Wegmans management training program, in which she learned all of the aspects of store operations first-hand. When asked about the company's consistent track record of success, Pawlowski, now one of the company's vice presidents, says, "We're taking customers to a place they have not been before."

1. Explain the core competencies that Wegmans has built. What is the source of its core competencies?
2. Identify Wegmans' strengths, weaknesses, opportunities, and threats. (You may want to use the Web or your library to read more about this interesting company.)
3. How has Wegmans' strategy created a competitive edge for the company in its markets? How does the company sustain its competitive edge? What suggestions can you offer for ensuring that Wegmans maintains its competitive edge?

Sources: Matthew Boyle, "The Wegmans Way," *Fortune*, January 24, 2005, pp. 62–68; "About Us," Wegmans, http://www.wegmans.com/about.

The Strategic Management Process

Strategic management is a continuous process that consists of nine steps:

Step 1 Develop a clear vision and translate it into a meaningful mission statement.
Step 2 Assess the company's strengths and weaknesses.
Step 3 Scan the environment for significant opportunities and threats facing the business.
Step 4 Identify the key factors for success in the business.
Step 5 Analyze the competition.
Step 6 Create company goals and objectives.
Step 7 Formulate strategic options and select the appropriate strategies.
Step 8 Translate strategic plans into action plans.
Step 9 Establish accurate controls.

Step 1. Develop a Clear Vision and Translate It into a Meaningful Mission Statement

Vision Throughout history, the greatest political and business leaders have been visionaries. Whether the vision is as grand as Martin Luther King Jr.'s "I have a dream" speech or as simple as Ray Kroc's devotion to quality, service, cleanliness, and value at McDonald's, the purpose is the same: to focus everyone's attention on the same target and to inspire them to reach it. The vision is future-oriented and touches everyone associated with the company—employees, investors, lenders, customers, and the community. It is an expression of what an entrepreneur stands for and believes in. Highly successful entrepreneurs are able to communicate their vision and their enthusiasm about that vision to those around them.

A vision is the result of an entrepreneur's dream of something that does not exist yet and the ability to paint a compelling picture of that dream for everyone to see. It answers the question "Where are we going?" A clearly defined vision helps a company in three ways:

1. ***Vision provides direction.*** Entrepreneurs who spell out the vision for their company focus everyone's attention on the future and determine the path the business will take to get there.
2. ***Vision determines decisions.*** The vision influences the decisions, no matter how big or how small, that owners, managers, and employees make every day in a business. This influence can be positive or negative, depending on how well defined the vision is.
3. ***Vision motivates people.*** A clear vision excites and ignites people to action. People want to work for a company that sets its sights high.

Vision is based on an entrepreneur's values. Explaining how an entrepreneur's values are the nucleus around which a company grows, author and consultant Ken Blanchard says, "Winning companies first emphasize values—the beliefs that you, as the business owner, have about your employees, customers, quality, ethics, integrity, social responsibility, growth, stability, innovation, and flexibility. Managing by values—not by profits—is a powerful process."[10] Successful entrepreneurs build their businesses around a set of three to six core values, which might range from respect for the individual and innovation to creating satisfied customers and making the world a better place.

Hewlett Packard

In 1957, 18 years after they had launched the company bearing their names, Bill Hewlett and Dave Packard were pleased with their company's rapid growth but were concerned that the business might lose its "small company atmosphere." The cofounders took 20 of their best employees to an upscale resort in California's wine country (on one of the first recorded corporate retreats) to define the type of culture Hewlett Packard would foster. By the end of the retreat, the team had drafted a set of values that ultimately became the basis of "the HP Way," the highly admired culture the company retained long after the death of its founders.[11]

Indeed, truly visionary entrepreneurs see their companies' primary purpose as more than just "making money." One writer explains, "Almost all workers are making decisions, not just filling out weekly sales reports or tightening screws. They will do what they think best. If you want them to do as the company thinks best too, then you must [see to it that] that have an inner gyroscope aligned with the corporate compass."[12] That gyroscope's alignment depends on the entrepreneur's values and how well he or she transmits them throughout the company.

The best way to put values into action is to create a written mission statement that communicates those values to everyone the company touches.

Mission Statement The **mission statement** addresses another basic question of any business venture: "What business are we in?" Establishing the purpose of the business in writing must come first in order to give the company a sense of direction. "If you don't reduce [your company's purpose] to paper, it just doesn't stick," says the owner of an architecture firm. "Reducing it to paper really forces you to think about what you are doing."[13] As an enduring declaration of a company's purpose, a mission statement is the mechanism for making it clear to everyone the company touches "why we are here" and "where we are going."

mission statement
an enduring declaration of a company's purpose that addresses the first question of any business venture: What business am I in?

Chick-fil-A

Truett Cathy, founder of the highly successful restaurant chain Chick-fil-A, recalls a time when his business was struggling because of intensifying competition from big hamburger chains. The company, with 200 outlets at the time, was struggling to keep operating costs under control as inflation threatened to push them ever higher. Cathy scheduled an executive retreat at a lake outside of Atlanta, where managers could relax and talk about their concerns and ideas for the company. His oldest son, Dan, director of operations, asked, "Why are we in business? Why are we here?" Cathy was about to tell his son that this retreat was no time to dwell on philosophical issues because there were bigger problems to solve. "Then," recalls Cathy, "I realized he was serious. His question both challenged and inspired us." In the ensuing brainstorming session, the group defined values that became Chick-fil-A's mission statement: "To glorify God by being faithful stewards of all that is entrusted to us. To have a positive influence on all who come in contact with Chick-fil-A." With their purpose clearly defined, the management team went on to lead the company in a growth spurt in which sales climbed 30 percent a year. Today, the company has more than 1,000 restaurants across the country (none of which are open on Sundays).[14]

Without a concise, meaningful mission statement, a small business risks wandering aimlessly in the marketplace, with no idea of where to go or how to get there. The mission statement sets the tone for the entire company and focuses its attention on the right direction.

Elements of a Mission Statement A sound mission statement need not be lengthy to be effective. Three key issues entrepreneurs and their employees should address as they develop a mission statement for their businesses include the following:

- The *purpose* of the company: What are we in business to accomplish?
- The *business* we are in: How are we going to accomplish that purpose?
- The *values* of the company: What principles and beliefs form the foundation of the way we do business?

A company's mission statement may be the most essential and basic communications that it puts forward. If the people on the plant, shop, retail, or warehouse floor don't know what a company's mission is, then, for all practical purposes, it does not have one! The mission statement expresses a company's character, identity, and scope of operations, but writing it is only half the battle, at best. The most difficult part is *living* that mission every day. *That's* how employees decide what really matters. To be effective, a mission statement must become a natural part of the organization, embodied in the minds, habits, attitudes, and decisions of everyone in the company every day. According to the Workplace 2000

Source: Copyright 2004 by Randy Glasbergen. www.glasbergen.com

"It's not a great mission statement, but we'll revise it if things get better."

Employee Insight Survey, 89 percent of employees say their companies have mission statements. Unfortunately, only 23 percent of workers believe their company's mission statement has become a way of doing business![15] One business writer claims, "If what you say about your firm's values and mission isn't true, you're in worse trouble than if you'd never articulated it in the first place."[16] Five years after founding Field Trip Factory Inc., a business that organizes life skill educational field trips for students, Susan Singer saw the need to update the company's mission statement. At a company retreat, she and her employees decided that their existing mission statement no longer reflected what the company actually stood for and did. A brainstorming session yielded a new mission statement that Singer says is helping her company improve its bottom line. "It became so clear what we do vs. what we want to be," she says.[17]

Starbucks

A well-used mission statement serves as a strategic compass for a small company. In its mission statement, Starbucks commits not only to building a successful coffee business, but also to strengthening the communities in which the company operates and to protecting the environment. Consider the message that Starbucks' two-part mission statement sends to company stakeholders:

> Starbucks Mission: Establish Starbucks as the premier purveyor of the finest coffee in the world while maintaining our uncompromising principles while we grow. The following six guiding principles will help us measure the appropriateness of our decisions:
>
> - Provide a great work environment and treat each other with respect and dignity.
> - Embrace diversity as an essential component of the way we do business.
> - Apply the highest standards of excellence to the purchasing, roasting, and fresh delivery of our coffee.
> - Develop enthusiastically satisfied customers all of the time.
> - Contribute positively to our communities and our environment.
> - Recognize that profitability is essential to our future success.
>
> Environmental Mission Statement: Starbucks is committed to a role of environmental leadership in all facets of our business.

We fulfill this mission by a commitment to:

- Understanding of environmental issues and sharing information with our partners.
- Developing innovative and flexible solutions to bring about change.
- Striving to buy, sell and use environmentally friendly products.
- Recognizing that fiscal responsibility is essential to our environmental future.
- Instilling environmental responsibility as a corporate value.[18]

A company may have a powerful competitive advantage, but it is wasted unless (1) the owner communicates that advantage to workers, who, in turn, work hard to communicate it to customers and potential customers and (2) customers recommend the company to their friends because they understand the benefits they are getting from it that they cannot get elsewhere. *That's* the real power of a mission statement. Table 3.1 offers some useful tips on writing a mission statement.

Step 2. Assess the Company's Strengths and Weaknesses

Having defined the vision that he or she has for the company and translated that vision into a meaningful mission statement, an entrepreneur can turn his or her attention to assessing company strengths and weaknesses. Building a successful competitive strategy requires a business to magnify its strengths and overcome or compensate for its weaknesses. **Strengths** are positive internal factors that a company can draw on to accomplish its mission, goals, and objectives. They might include special skills or knowledge, a positive public image, an experienced sales force, an established base of loyal customers, and many other factors. **Weaknesses** are negative internal factors that inhibit a company's ability to accomplish its mission, goals, and objectives. A lack of capital, a shortage of skilled workers, the inability to master technology, and an inferior location are examples of weaknesses.

strengths
positive internal factors that a company can use to accomplish its mission, goals, and objectives.

weaknesses
negative internal factors that inhibit the accomplishment of a company's mission, goals, and objectives.

Identifying strengths and weaknesses helps owners to understand their businesses as they exist (or, for start-ups, will exist). An organization's strengths should originate in the core competencies that are essential to gaining an edge in each of the market segments in which the firm competes. The key to building a successful strategy is using the company's underlying strengths as its foundation and matching those strengths against competitors' weaknesses.

One effective technique for taking this strategic inventory is to prepare a balance sheet of the company's strengths and weaknesses (see Table 3.2). The positive side should reflect important skills, knowledge, or resources that contribute to the firm's success. The negative side should record honestly any limitations that detract from the company's ability to compete. This balance sheet should analyze all key performance areas of the business—human resources, finance, production, marketing, product development, organization, and others. This analysis should give owners a more realistic perspective of their businesses, pointing out foundations on which they can build future strengths and obstacles that they must remove for the business to progress. This exercise can help entrepreneurs move from their current position to future actions.

Step 3. Scan the Environment for Significant Opportunities and Threats Facing the Business

Opportunities Once entrepreneurs have taken an internal inventory of company strengths and weaknesses, they must turn to the external environment to identify any opportunities and threats that might have a significant impact on the business. **Opportunities** are positive external options that a firm can exploit to accomplish its mission, goals, and objectives. The number of potential opportunities is limitless, so entrepreneurs need to analyze only those factors that are most significant to the business

opportunities
positive external options that a firm can exploit to accomplish its mission, goals, and objectives.

TABLE 3.1 Tips for Writing a Powerful Mission Statement

A mission statement is a useful tool for getting everyone fired up and heading in the same direction, but writing one is not as easy as it may first appear. Here are some tips for writing a powerful mission statement:

- *Keep it short.* The best mission statements are just a few sentences long. If they are short, people will tend to remember them better.
- *Keep it simple.* Avoid using fancy jargon just to impress outsiders such as customers or suppliers. The first and most important use of a mission statement is inside a company.
- *Take a broad view, but not too broad.* If it is too specific, a mission statement can limit a company's potential. Similarly, a mission statement is too broad if it applies to any company in the industry. When asked what business his company was in, Rob Carter, a top manager at FedEx, did not mention shipping packages quickly; instead, his response was, "We're in the business of engineering time."
- *Get everyone involved.* If the boss writes the company mission statement, who is going to criticize it? Although the entrepreneur has to be the driving force behind the mission statement, everyone in the company needs the opportunity to have a voice in creating it. Expect to write several drafts before you arrive at a finished product.
- *Keep it current.* Mission statements can get stale over time. As business and competitive conditions change, so should your mission statement. Make a habit of evaluating your mission periodically so that it stays fresh.
- *Make sure that your mission statement reflects the values and beliefs you hold dear.* They are the foundation on which your company is built.
- *Make sure your mission includes values that are worthy of your employees' best efforts.* One entrepreneur says that a mission statement should "send a message to employees, suppliers, and customers as to what the purpose of the company is aside from just making profits."
- *Make sure your statement reflects a concern for the future.* Business owners can get so focused on the present that they forget about the future. A mission statement should be the first link to the company's future.
- *Keep the tone of the statement positive and upbeat.* No one wants to work for a business with a pessimistic outlook of the world.
- *Consider using your mission statement to lay an ethical foundation for your company.* This is the ideal time to let employees know what you company stands for—and what it won't stand for.
- *Look at other companies' mission statements to generate ideas for your own.* Two books, *Say It and Live It: The 50 Corporate Mission Statements That Hit the Mark,* by Patricia Jones and Larry Kahaner (New York: Currency/Doubleday, 1995), and *Mission Statements: A Guide to the Corporate and Nonprofit Sectors,* by John W. Graham and Wendy C. Havlick (New York: Garland, 1994), are useful resources.
- *Make sure that your mission statement is appropriate for your company's culture.* Although you should look at other companies' missions, do not make the mistake of trying to copy them. Your company's mission is unique to you and your company.
- *Use it.* Don't go to all of the trouble of writing a mission statement just to let it collect dust. Post it on bulletin boards, print it on buttons and business cards, stuff it into employees' pay envelopes. Talk about your mission often, and use it to develop your company's strategic plan. That's what it's for!

Sources: Adapted from Ken Blanchard, "The New Bottom Line," *Entrepreneur,* February 1998, pp. 127–131; Alan Farnham, Brushing Up Your Vision Thing," *Fortune,* May 1, 1995, p. 129; Sharon Nelton, "Put Your Purpose in Writing," *Nation's Business,* February 1994, pp. 61–64; Jacquelyn Lynn, "Single-Minded," *Entrepreneur,* January 1996, p. 97.

(probably two or three at most). The key is to focus on the most promising opportunities that fit most closely with the company's strengths and core competencies.

When identifying opportunities, an entrepreneur must pay close attention to new potential markets. Are competitors overlooking a niche in the market? Is there a better way to reach customers? Can we develop new products that offer customers better value? What opportunities are trends in the industry creating?

TABLE 3.2 Identifying Company Strengths and Weaknesses

Strengths (Positive Internal Factors)	Weaknesses (Negative Internal Factors)

COMPANY **Profile**

Aviation Partners

Rising fuel prices have created problems for many businesses, but few have felt the impact as directly as those in the airline industry. Yet rising energy prices have produced a significant opportunity for Aviation Partners, a small company founded by a group of retired aeronautic engineers. Noting that birds' wings turn up at the tips to provide more lift and less drag (hence requiring birds to use less energy), the founders of Aviation Partners developed "winglets," small fins attached to the ends of wings that extend upward, for use on commercial jets. Tests indicated that jets using the winglets were far more fuel-efficient than those without them. In the late 1990s, however, the small company found it difficult to market the winglets because jet fuel prices were just 50 cents a gallon. As jet fuel prices climbed significantly over the next several years, Aviation Partners, now partnering with Boeing Company, found airlines much more interested in their product. Although the cost to install the winglets can run as high as $700,000 per plane, the savings in fuel costs add up to the millions over the life of a jet. Aviation Partners is capitalizing on this opportunity and counts among its customers virtually every airline in operation today.[19]

As Aviation Partners' experience illustrates, opportunities arise as a result of factors that are beyond entrepreneurs' control. Constantly scanning for those opportunities that best match their companies' strengths and core competencies and then pouncing on them ahead of competitors is the key to success.

M Cubed

When demand for the composite materials manufactured by Steve Warshaw's company M Cubed declined as the semiconductor market slumped, he began searching for opportunities to apply the company's expertise in other industries. As the United States stepped up its efforts in the war of terrorism, Warshaw spotted an opportunity to produce the ceramic plates used in bulletproof vests. Although the finished product was quite different from semiconductors, M Cubed found it quite easy to adapt its techniques and technology to produce strong yet lightweight panels capable of stopping even armor-piercing bullets. Shifting to this new market has accelerated M Cube's sales, and Warshaw sees tremendous potential for future growth as both law enforcement and military officials increase their purchases of bulletproof vests.[20]

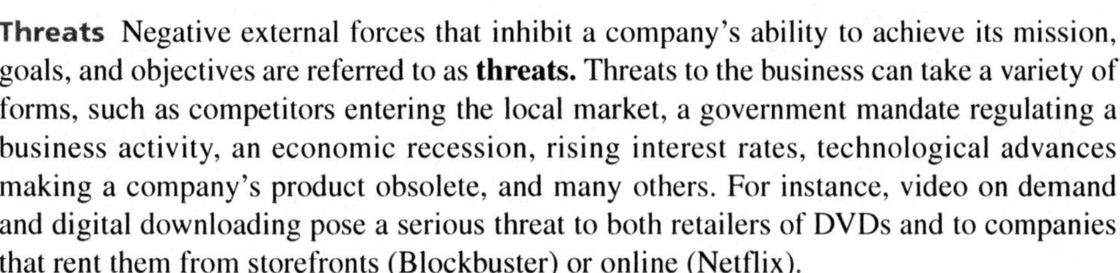

Threats Negative external forces that inhibit a company's ability to achieve its mission, goals, and objectives are referred to as **threats.** Threats to the business can take a variety of forms, such as competitors entering the local market, a government mandate regulating a business activity, an economic recession, rising interest rates, technological advances making a company's product obsolete, and many others. For instance, video on demand and digital downloading pose a serious threat to both retailers of DVDs and to companies that rent them from storefronts (Blockbuster) or online (Netflix).

threats
negative external forces that inhibit a company's ability to achieve it mission, goals, and objectives.

Many small retailers face a threat from "big box" retailers such as Wal-Mart, Home Depot, Circuit City, and others offering lower prices because of their high-volume purchasing power, huge advertising budgets, and mega-stores that attract customers for miles around.

FIGURE 3.2

The Power of External Market Forces

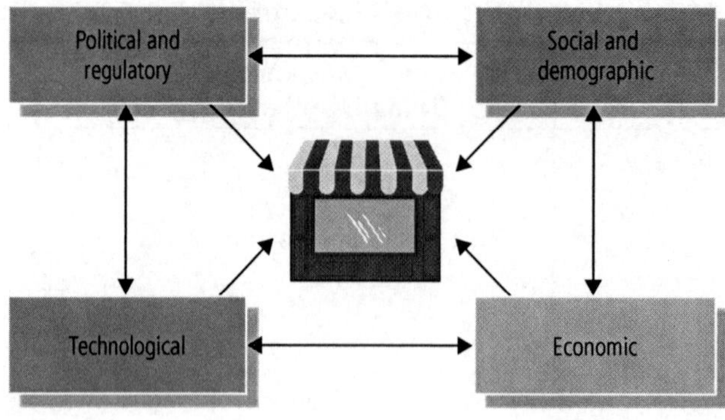

Kenneth Stone, a professor at Iowa State University and a leading researcher on Wal-Mart's impact on small companies, says that after Wal-Mart entered Iowa in 1983, 23 percent of drugstores and 45 percent of hardware stores disappeared.[21] However, small businesses with the proper strategies in place do *not* have to fold in the face of intense competition.

Dobson's Gifts and General Hardware

After Wal-Mart, Home Depot, Tractor Supply Company, and Lowe's opened next to their second-generation small hardware store in Greenville, South Carolina, Terry and Debbie Dobson changed their competitive strategy and refocused their business, Dobson's Gifts and General Hardware, more on gifts and less on the standard hardware items their larger rivals sold. The Dobsons now rely on a focus strategy that emphasizes unique gifts and home décor items with a distinctively local flavor and specialty hardware items such as loose nuts and bolts, pocket knives, and Radio Flyer wagons that their big box competitors overlook. The Dobsons continue to set their business apart by offering a high level of personal service, including knowledgeable, long-time employees and a home delivery service that customers love. "I'm within a rock's throw of my two major competitors," says Terry, "and actually we're glad they're here now. They bring in traffic, and we draw off that traffic."[22]

Although they cannot control the threats themselves, entrepreneurs such as the Dobsons must prepare a plan for shielding their businesses from these threats.

Figure 3.2 illustrates that opportunities and threats are products of the interactions of forces, trends, and events outside the direct control of the business. These external forces have direct impact on the behavior of the markets in which the business operates, the behavior of competitors, and the behavior of customers. Table 3.3 provides a form that allows business owners to take a strategic inventory of the opportunities and threats facing their companies.

The interactions of strengths and weaknesses and opportunities and threats can be the most revealing aspects of using a SWOT analysis as part of a strategic plan. This analysis also requires entrepreneurs to take an objective look at their businesses and the environment in which they operate as they address many issues fundamental to their companies' success in the future.

TABLE 3.3 Identifying Opportunities and Threats

Opportunities (Positive External Factors)	Threats (Negative External Factors)

Tunes for the Taking

Before music downloading became so popular, music lovers often bought a single CD for just one song. Given the attitude, "Who wants to pay nearly $20 for one song?" it is little wonder that customers embraced "free" music download services such as Napster (the original), KaZaA, and Grokster. Still, those downloading music without paying for it had to feel a twinge of guilt about the ethics of their actions. Then there were all of those lawsuits that the Recording Industry Association of America (RIAA) was filing against heavy downloaders, many of them college students. Who wants to be sued for downloading music, especially when damages can range from $750 to $150,000 per copyright violation? Representing the five major music companies, the RIAA filed 261 lawsuits against individuals it claimed had illegally used file-sharing software to distribute vast numbers of copyrighted songs. The suits claim that illegal file sharing is responsible for falling sales of recorded music and for robbing artists of their royalties. In addition, modern technology makes it quite easy for computer users to "rip and burn" tracks from CDs to create their own favorites or to store on their MP3 players. Indeed, shipments of recorded music have fallen 26 percent since 1999, and sales of blank CDs now exceed those of prerecorded CDs. "Our industry is being ravaged by piracy," says a top executive at one music company.

To combat declining sales, the recording industry is attempting to create new business models that incorporate the legitimate sale of recorded music online. All of the major music companies are cooperating with Apple Computer Inc.'s industry-leading iTunes Music Store, which allows users to download songs *legally* for just 99 cents each. (Music companies receive roughly 65 cents for every downloaded song.) Users can listen to a 30-second preview of any song and, if they like it, can purchase a high-quality legal download with just one mouse-click. There is no subscription fee, and the iTunes library contains more than 1.5 million songs from the major music companies and more than 1,000 independent record companies as well as 10,000 audiobooks. Shoppers can browse titles by artist, song title, or genre. Because of the many benefits it offers, industry analysts predict that by 2010, digitally downloaded music will comprise between one-fourth to one-third of the recording industry's sales. "It pained us to see the music companies and the technology companies threatening to take each other to court," says Apple founder Steve Jobs. "We thought that rather than sit around and throw stones, we'd actually do something about this."

Throughout its history, the music industry has benefited from introducing new musical formats, from 78 rpm singles to the 33 rpm vinyl LP album to the eight-track tape to the Compact Disc. The transformation to digitally downloaded music, however, may be the most significant change of all. Not only would it be more convenient for customers, but the switch also would cut costs for all of the music companies by virtually eliminating manufacturing and distribution costs.

Music artists themselves see downloading as a double-edged sword. One survey reports that only three percent of music artists say that the Internet has hurt their ability to protect their creative work. Forty-seven percent agreed that peer-to-peer networks prevented them from earning royalties from their songs, but 43 percent said that those same networks helped artists promote and distribute their material. Two-thirds of the survey's respondents said that file-sharing posed little threat to them.

It's ironic that the music industry is struggling in an era when people are listening to music more than ever before. They simply aren't paying for the privilege of listening the way they used to. Downloading, file sharing, and ripping and burning also pose a serious threat to music retailers, most of which are stuck selling music in a format (CDs) customers seem to dislike. Many music retail chains have either filed for Chapter 11 bankruptcy protection (Wherehouse and Tower Records) or have simply closed (National Record Mart).

Entrepreneur Bob French thinks he may have discovered one way to preserve retail music outlets with his

Mix and Burn machine, a device that allows users to scroll through a database of songs, listen to the ones they choose, create a personal playlist, and then burn the songs to a CD. French's company, Mix and Burn, currently provides a library of 320,000 songs but offers additions weekly. French has established relationships with all five of the major music companies but has had difficulty signing independent record labels onto the company's service. "We really focused on getting those major labels done to make this a viable business," explains French. "Next year at this time, there will be more content from independent producers."

Jack Dennis, owner of the Earshot Music store in downtown Greenville, South Carolina, was one of the early adopters of the Mix and Burn technology. Still a traditional music store, Earshot has transformed itself with the addition of 12 Mix and Burn stations grouped together in an area of the store called "The Blender" that in just a short time has become one of the most popular spots in the store. There customers can download five songs for $9.99 and 99 cents for each subsequent song. "We wanted to be able to offer digital technology in a retail environment," says Dennis. You buy songs just like you would off the Internet, except you are here at our store."

1. One analyst says, "Many music listeners have shown little regard for the idea that downloading a song from a file-sharing service such as KaZaA is tantamount to shoplifting from Tower Records." Comment.
2. What strategic recommendations can you make to the music industry concerning the future of digital downloading?
3. What strategic recommendations can you make to music retailers concerning the future of digital downloading?

Sources: "Survey: Net File-Sharing Doesn't Hurt Most Musicians," CNN.com, December 6, 2004; Bruce Orwall, Martin Peers, and Ethan Smith, "Music Industry Presses 'Play' on Plan to Save Its Business," *Wall Street Journal*, September 9, 20003, pp. A1–A14; "Apple Kicks Off iTunes Music Store Countdown to Half a Billion Songs," http://www.Apple.com/pr/library/2005/jul/05itms_live.html; Devin Leonard, "Songs in the Key of Steve," *Fortune*, May 12, 2003, pp. 53–62; Alex Veiga, "Students Still Go for Hot Music, Despite Available Legal Options," *Greenville News*, August 20, 2005, p. 12A; Paul Keegan, "Is the Music Store Over?" *Business 2.0*, March 2004, pp. 115–119; Lilla Callum-Penso, "Technology Offers New Ways to Mix It Up," *Greenville News*, August 8, 2005, pp. 1D, 3D.

Step 4. Identify the Key Factors for Success in the Business

Key Success Factors Every business is characterized by controllable variables that determine the relative success of market participants. Identifying and manipulating these variables is how a small business gains a competitive advantage. By focusing efforts to maximize their companies' performance on these key success factors, entrepreneurs can achieve dramatic market advantages over their competitors. Companies that understand these key success factors tend to be leaders of the pack, whereas those that fail to recognize them become also-rans.

key success factors the factors that determine a company's ability to compete successfully in an industry.

Key success factors (KSFs) come in a variety of different patterns depending on the industry. Simply stated, they are the factors that determine a company's ability to compete successfully in an industry. Every company in an industry must understand the key success factors driving the industry; otherwise, they are likely to become industry "also-rans" like the horses trailing the pack in the Kentucky Derby. Many of these sources of competitive advantages are based on cost factors such as manufacturing cost per unit, distribution cost per unit, or development cost per unit. Some are less tangible and less obvious but are just as important, such as superior product quality, solid relationships with dependable suppliers, superior customer service, a highly trained and knowledgeable sales force, prime store locations, readily available customer credit, and many others. For example, one restaurant owner identified the following key success factors:

- Tight cost control (labor costs, 15 to 18 percent of sales and food costs, 35 to 40 percent of sales)
- Trained, dependable, honest in-store managers
- Close monitoring of waste
- Careful site selection (the right location)

TABLE 3.4 Identifying Key Success Factors

Key Success Factor	How Your Company Rates
1	Low 1 2 3 4 5 6 7 8 9 10 High
2	Low 1 2 3 4 5 6 7 8 9 10 High
3	Low 1 2 3 4 5 6 7 8 9 10 High
4	Low 1 2 3 4 5 6 7 8 9 10 High
5	Low 1 2 3 4 5 6 7 8 9 10 High
Conclusions:	

List the specific skills, characteristics, and core competencies that your business must possess if it is to be successful in its market segment.

- High food quality
- Consistency
- Cleanliness
- Friendly and attentive service from a well-trained wait staff

These controllable variables determine the ability of any restaurant in his market segment to compete. Restaurants lacking these KSFs are not likely to survive, but those that build their strategies with these factors in mind will prosper. However, before entrepreneurs can build a strategy around the industry's KSFs, they must identify them. Table 3.4 presents a form to help owners identify the most important success factors in the industry and their implications for their companies.

Identifying the KSFs in an industry allows entrepreneurs to determine where they should focus their companies' resources strategically. It is unlikely that a company, even a large one, can excel on every KSF it identifies. Therefore, as they begin to develop their strategies, most entrepreneurs focus on surpassing their rivals on one or two KSFs to build a sustainable competitive edge. As a result, KSFs become the cornerstones of a company's strategy.

John H. Daniel Company

John H. Daniel Company, a custom tailor of high-end men's suits in Knoxville, Tennessee, understands that attracting and retaining skilled master tailors is crucial to its success. The company, founded in 1928, produces 75,000 to 80,000 made-to-measure suits a year that retail at prices ranging from $800 to $3,000, and sells them under a variety of labels. Unfortunately, the number of master tailors in the United States is negligible, and the family-owned business dedicates a significant portion of its budget to searching them out in foreign countries such as Turkey, Italy, and Vietnam. Owners Richard and Benton Bryant send scouts on recruiting trips to these countries and then pay to relocate the master tailors they hire along with their families to Tennessee. The company provides low-interest loans to help families get settled, and a company attorney handles all of the paperwork necessary to get visas for the tailors and their families.[23]

Step 5. Analyze the Competition

Ask most small business owners to identify the greatest challenge their companies face and the most common response is *competition*. One study of small business owners by the National Federation of Independent Businesses (NFIB) reports that small business owners believe they operate in a highly competitive environment and that the level of competition is increasing.[24] The World Wide Web and e-commerce have increased the ferocity and the scope of the competition entrepreneurs face as well and have forced

FIGURE 3.3

How Small Businesses Compete

Source: William J. Dennis, Jr., *National Small Business Poll: Competition* (Washington, DC: National Federation of Independent Businesses, 2003), Vol. 3, Issue 8, p. 1.

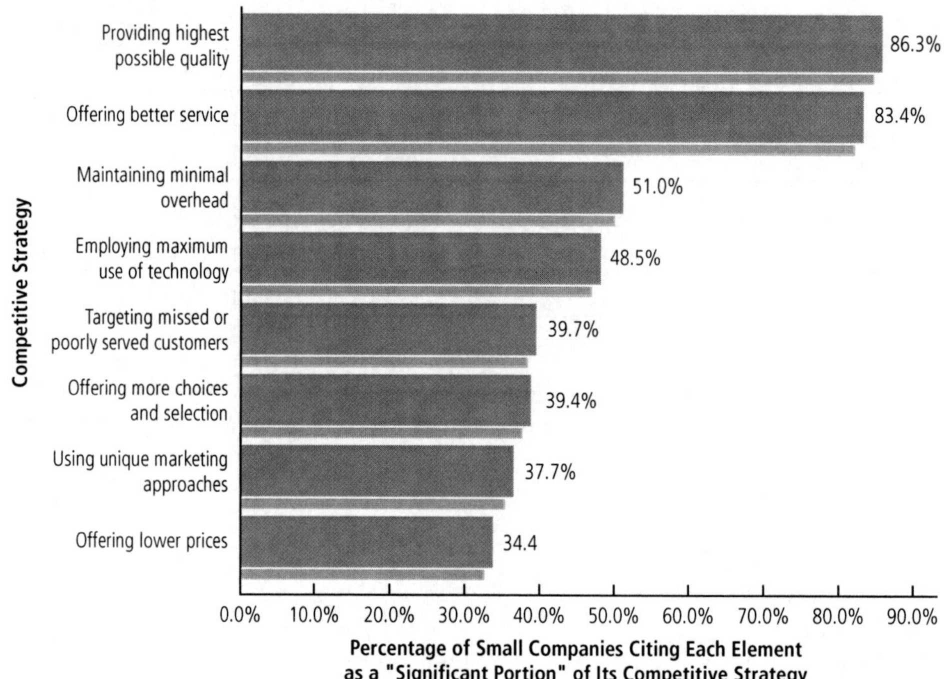

many business owners to reshape completely the ways in which they do business. Figure 3.3 shows the competitive strategies that small business owners rely on most heavily to compete with their rivals.

Joseph-Beth Booksellers

Neil Van Uum, owner of Joseph-Beth Booksellers, a small chain of six bookstores, faces intense competition from larger, more powerful rivals in an industry that has seen thousands of small booksellers close within the last decade. Yet, Joseph-Beth Booksellers manages not only to survive, but also to thrive in an industry where giants such as Barnes and Noble and Borders Books saturate local markets with retail outlets and Amazon blankets the market from its perch high atop the online food chain. "Either you have to be very niche[-oriented], or you need a physical presence that says you're significant," says Michael Powell, owner of Powell's Books, a legendary 70,000-square-foot bookstore in downtown Portland, Oregon. Like Powell, Van Uum has chosen to create a significant physical presence. His stores average 30,000 square feet, about 5,000 square feet larger than a typical Barnes and Noble store. Like most successful independent bookstores, Joseph-Beth emphasizes superior customer service, sponsors unique, in-store events (wine tastings, book signings, appearances by the Berenstain Bears for kids), and specializes in books that reflect local tastes. For instance, the Lexington, Kentucky, store located in the Mall at Lexington Green stocks more than 1,000 books by local authors, something national chain stores don't do. Going one better than Barnes and Noble's coffee bar and pastry shop, each Joseph-Beth store contains a full-service restaurant, each offering entrees inspired by cookbooks the company sells. Every store also includes a stationery department, a board game section, and a "health and well-being section" selling lotions, soaps, scented candles, and quilted tote bags. A store décor that includes cherry bookcases, comfortable couches, and fireplaces encourages shoppers to linger, and, of course, buy more. Dan Burstin, author of the popular *Secrets of the Code,* recently appeared in two Joseph-Beth stores to discuss his work. "What they've done," he says, "is turn these stores into cultural centers."[25]

Keeping tabs on rivals' movements through competitive intelligence programs is a vital strategic activity. "Business is like any battlefield. If you want to win the war, you have to know who you're up against," says one small business consultant.[26] Unfortunately, most businesses are not very good at competitive intelligence; 97 percent of U.S. businesses do not systematically track the progress of their key competitors.[27] The primary goals of a competitive intelligence program include the following:

- Avoiding surprises from existing competitors' new strategies and tactics.
- Identifying potential new competitors.
- Improving reaction time to competitors' actions.
- Anticipating rivals' next strategic moves.

Competitor Analysis Sizing up the competition gives a business owner a more realistic view of the market and his or her company's position in it. Yet not every competitor warrants the same level of attention in the strategic plan. *Direct competitors* offer the same products and services, and customers often compare prices, features, and deals from these competitors as they shop. *Significant competitors* offer some of the same products and services. Although their product or service lines may be somewhat different, there is competition with them in several key areas. *Indirect competitors* offer the same or similar products or services only in a small number of areas, but their target customers seldom overlap yours. Entrepreneurs should monitor closely the actions of their direct competitors, maintain a solid grasp of where their significant competitors are heading, and spend only minimal resources tracking their indirect competitors.

A competitive intelligence exercise enables entrepreneurs to update their knowledge of competitors by answering the following questions:

- Who are your primary competitors? Where are they located? (The *Yellow Pages* is a great place to start.)
- What distinctive competencies have they developed?
- How do their cost structures compare to yours? Their financial resources?
- How do they market their products and services?
- What do customers say about them? How do customers describe their products or services; their way of doing business; the additional services they might supply?
- What are their key strategies?
- What are their strengths? How can your company surpass them?
- What are their major weaknesses? How can your company capitalize on them?
- Are new competitors entering the business?

According to the Society of Competitive Intelligence, 95 percent of the competitive intelligence information is available from public sources that anyone can access—if they know how.[28] Gathering information on competitors does not require entrepreneurs to engage in activities that are unethical, illegal, or unsavory (such as dumpster diving). One expert says that competitive intelligence (CI) involves "taking information from the public domain, adding it to what you know about your company and your industry, and looking for patterns."[29] Entrepreneurs using the following low-cost competitive intelligence methods can collect a great deal of information about their rivals:

- Read industry trade publications for announcements and news stories about competitors.
- Ask questions of customers and suppliers on what they hear competitors may be doing. In many cases, this information is easy to gather because some people love to gossip.
- Regularly debrief employees, especially sales representatives and purchasing agents. Experts estimate that 70 to 90 percent of the competitive information a company needs already resides with employees who collect it in their routine dealings with suppliers, customers, and other industry contacts.[30]
- Attend trade shows and collect competitors' sales literature.
- Watch for employment ads and job postings from competitors; knowing what types of workers they are hiring can tell you a great deal about their future plans.
- Conduct patent searches (see Chapter 2) for patents that competitors have filed. This gives important clues about new products they are developing.
- Environmental Protection Agency reports can provide important information about the factories of manufacturing companies, including the amounts and the kinds of

emissions released. A private group, Environmental Protection, also reports emissions for specific plants.[31]

- Learn about the kinds and amounts of equipment and raw materials competitors are importing by studying the *Journal of Commerce* Port Import Export Reporting Service (PIERS) database. These clues can alert an entrepreneur to new products a competitor is about to launch.
- If appropriate, buy competitors' products and assess their quality and features. Benchmark their products against yours. The owner of a mail-order gourmet brownie business periodically places orders from her primary rivals and compares their packaging, pricing, service, and quality to her own.[32]
- Obtain credit reports on each of your major competitors to evaluate their financial condition. For as little as $122, Dun & Bradstreet and other research firms provide detailed credit reports of competitors that can be helpful in a strategic analysis.
- Publicly held companies must file periodic reports with the Securities and Exchange Commission (SEC), including quarterly 10-Q and annual 10-K reports. Information on publicly held companies is available at the Securities and Exchange Commission Web site (http://www.sec.gov).
- Investigate Uniform Commercial Code reports. Banks file these with the state whenever they make loans to businesses. These reports often include the amount of the loan and what it is for.
- Check out the resources of your local library, including articles, computerized databases, and online searches. Press releases, which often announce important company news, can be an important source of competitive intelligence. Many companies supply press releases through the PR Newswire. For local competitors, review back issues of the area newspaper for articles on and advertisements by competitors.
- Use the vast resources of the World Wide Web to learn more about your competitors. Visit their Web sites periodically to see what news is contained there. The Web enables small companies to uncover valuable competitive information at little or no cost. (Refer to our Web site at http://www.prenhall.com/scarborough for an extensive listing of more than 1,200 useful small business Web sites.)
- Visit competing businesses periodically to observe their operations. Tom Stemberg, CEO of Staples, a chain of office supply superstores, says, "I've never visited a store where I didn't learn something."[33]

competitive profile matrix a tool that allows a business owner to evaluate their companies against major competitors using the key success factors for that market.

Entrepreneurs can use the results of their competitive intelligence efforts to construct a competitive profile matrix for its most important competitors. A **competitive profile matrix** allows owners to evaluate their firms against the major competitor using the key success factors for that market segment. The first step is to list the key success factors identified in Step 4 of the strategic planning process (refer to Table 3.4) and to attach weights to them reflecting their relative importance. (For simplicity, the weights in this matrix sum add up to 1.00.) In this example, notice that product quality is weighted twice as heavily (twice as important) as is price competitiveness.

The next step is to identify the company's major competitors and to rate each one (and your company) on each of the key success factors:

If factor is a:	Rating is:
Major weakness	1
Minor weakness	2
Minor strength	3
Major strength	4

Once the rating is completed, the owner simply multiplies the weight by the rating for each factor to get a weighted score, and then adds up each competitor's weighted scores to get a total weighted score. Table 3.5 shows a sample competitive profile matrix for a small company. The results should show which company is strongest, which is weakest, and

TABLE 3.5 Sample Competitive Profile Matrix

		My Company		Competitor 1		Competitor 2	
Key Success Factor (from Step 4)	Weight	Score	Weighted Score	Score	Weighted Score	Score	Weighted Score
Quality	0.25	4	1.00	2	0.50	2	0.50
Customer Retention	0.20	3	0.60	2	0.40	3	0.60
Location	0.16	4	0.60	3	0.45	4	0.60
Perception of Value	0.20	4	0.80	2	0.40	3	0.60
Cost Control	0.20	3	0.60	1	0.20	4	0.80
Total	100%		3.60		1.95		3.10

which of the key success factors each one is best and worst at meeting. By carefully studying and interpreting the results, an entrepreneur can begin to envision the ideal strategy for building a competitive edge in her or his market segment.

Knowledge Management Unfortunately, many small companies fail to gather competitive intelligence because their owners mistakenly assume that it is too costly or simply unnecessary. In reality, the cost of collecting information about competitors and the competitive environment typically is minimal, but it does require discipline. Thanks in large part to the Internet, "all companies, large and small, have virtually the same access to information," says competitive intelligence consultant Leonard Fuld.[34] Identifying and organizing the information a company possesses and then getting it efficiently to those who need it when they need it is the real challenge. In an age in which knowledge is the primary source of a company's competitive edge, the key is learning how to *manage* the knowledge and information a company accumulates. A study by software firm Business Objects found that 90 percent of managers admit they make most of their decisions using instinct because they lack the right information when they need it![35]

Knowledge management is the practice of gathering, organizing, and disseminating the collective wisdom and experience of a company's employees for the purpose of strengthening its competitive position. "Knowledge management allows you to determine the explicit knowledge that is somewhere in your organization and that you can leverage rather than having to reinvent the wheel," says Dorothy Leonard-Barton, author of *Wellsprings of Knowledge*.[36] Unfortunately, a study by Accenture reports that nearly half of businesses have no formal process for capturing workers' knowledge so that it can be passed on to others.[37] As growing numbers of baby boomers retire and take their accumulated knowledge with them, these companies face the threat of a serious "brain drain" that could hurt their ability to compete. Business owners who do practice knowledge management realize that knowledge is power and that managing it can produce huge benefits. Because of their size and simplicity, small businesses have an advantage over large companies when it comes to managing employees' collective knowledge.

knowledge management the practice of gathering, organizing, and disseminating the collective wisdom and experience of a company's employees for the purpose of strengthening its competitive position.

The first step in creating a knowledge management program is to take an inventory of the special knowledge a company possesses that gives it a competitive advantage. This involves assessing the knowledge bank that employees at all levels of the organization have compiled over time. The second step is to organize the essential knowledge and disseminate it throughout the company to those who need it. High-tech solutions such as e-mail, computerized databases, document sharing, and special knowledge management software that allows many different employees to work on a project simultaneously are important tools, but low-tech methods such as whiteboards, Post-it notes, and face-to-face meetings can be just as effective in small companies. "To understand and respond to the kaleidoscopic patterns of new opportunities and potential dangers to its mission, an organization must mobilize the distributed intelligence of its members and listen to the collective knowledge of the whole," says one expert.[38]

eBay

As eBay, provider of the popular online marketplace, expanded its operations globally, managers began to assemble the collective knowledge from employees about what works—and what doesn't—and make it available to everyone in the company. The resulting playbooks—one for every function within the company, from product management to Web development—give managers and employees in every country how-to manuals for establishing the eBay model and expanding their divisions. They teach managers how to create the ideal conditions for electronic trading on eBay to flourish in a particular country. For instance, Gregory Boutte, country manager for France, learned from an eBay playbook that it doesn't make sense to spend money on television ads until the number of customers using the site reaches a critical mass. As new ideas arise throughout the company, managers make a concerted effort to capture them and incorporate them into each playbook.[39]

You Be the Consultant

Protect This Business!

Kevin Plank may not have been a star when he played college football at the University of Maryland, but he has become an entrepreneurial superstar because the success of Under Armour, the company he founded during his senior year in college. As a special teams captain, Plank grew weary of wearing a heavy, sweat-soaked cotton T-shirt under his football pads. He began to research the properties of various fabrics, and he produced sample shirts made with a polyester blend base layer that fit as snugly as Spiderman's suit and were extremely lightweight, durable, and capable of wicking away perspiration so that they stayed dry. He tested early prototypes himself, and, at first, his teammates laughed at him because the fabric resembled lingerie. Before long, however, those teammates were asking for shirts of their own!

After graduating, Plank received a trademark for the name Under Armour and launched a business from the basement of his grandmother's townhouse in Washington, D.C., which served as the company's first office, warehouse, distribution center—and bedroom. He started the company with $20,000 of his own money and $40,000 in credit card debt he ran up on five cards before landing a $250,000 loan guaranteed by the U.S. Small Business Administration. Plank used a network of contacts he had developed during his years of playing football to get Under Armour shirts into the hands of top college and professional football players such as Eddie George and Frank Wychek.

Sales for Plank's company started slowly, but he managed to land accounts with the football teams at the University of Arizona and Georgia Institute of Technology. Under Armour's first big break came in 1999, when its shirts appeared in the film *Any Given Sunday*. Before the film aired, Plank took out a $25,000 ad in *ESPN* magazine, counting on the movie to attract attention for the small company's products. It worked. Today, thousands of athletes in a variety of sports wear Under Armour clothing, generating more than $200 million in annual sales for the company. Under Armour has since developed distinct product lines for six different sports under every playing condition and every season. Athletes from little league to the pros are dedicated to their Under Armour clothing. Although Plank's company pays a few star athletes to wear Under Armour; most of its endorsements are unofficial. Yet the company gets tremendous amounts of publicity when Barry Bonds, Roger Clemens, Allen Iverson, LaVar Arrington, and other pros display Under Armour garments on national television.

The market for performance apparel, which Plank created almost single-handedly, is the fastest-growing segment of the athletic equipment market. Under Armour has extended its product line to include sports bras, batting gloves, loose-fitting shirts, sweat suits, boxers, and many others—for a total of 300 products. Succeeding against the odds, Plank's bold entrepreneurial moves, aggressive advertising and public relations campaign, and superior product quality have enabled Under Armour to capture about 75 percent of the market for compression performance apparel, far surpassing the "big three" industry giants, Nike, Reebok, and Adidas. Although Under Armour may have caught the industry giants napping, they have awakened and are fighting back. All three companies have introduced products similar to Under Armour and are promoting them aggressively. "We're not taking this lying down," declares Ken Barker, director of apparel at Adidas America. "It's a war." Nike, whose Nike Pro brand is second to Under Armour, launched an ad campaign aimed squarely at Under Armour. Its "For Warriors" campaign was one of the largest in the history of the company, whose $13 billion in annual sales dwarfs Under Armour's annual revenues.

Small companies such as Under Armour that surprise the established players in a market with an innovative approach soon find themselves facing what some experts call the "disrupter's dilemma." Although Under Armour took the lead when it jolted the industry with its innovative new products, Plank's small company has become the hunted in a high-stakes game of cat and mouse. The dilemma Plank's company faces is, "What do we do next?" With competition intensifying, Under Armour cannot bask in the glow of its past successes. "Most people are saying [that] we're going to trip up at some point—it's just a matter of when," says Plank. "Our job is to prove them wrong."

One of Under Armour's most recent moves was to aim its products at women, which also poses a challenge. Most of the company's early ads (which proved to be hugely successful) were testosterone-laden spots featuring his former teammate Eric Ogbogu from the National Football League with the tag line "Protect this house," a reference to sports teams winning on their home fields. The challenge the company faces is appealing to women without alienating its core customer base, which consists primarily of young male athletes. Ads featuring soccer star Heather Mitts wearing Under Armour garments made for women are designed to introduce the brand to women athletes, to many of whom the brand is new. Under Armour also has received exposure in some 50 movies, including the hit *Million Dollar Baby*, and on a dozen TV shows, including *The Apprentice*. After the ads and television and movie placements, Under Armour has seen sales to women climb from 13 percent of revenue to 19 percent.

Plank knows that his company is in a battle and that his competitors are much bigger and stronger. Yet he remains confident that his company's future is bright because he has been both a fierce competitor and an entrepreneur since he was a child. Ignored as a scholarship player in college, Plank made the team as a walk-on and then went on to become a starter and a team captain thanks to his persistence and dogged determination. Once, when he was assigned to block his friend, 6-foot, 4-inch, 269-pound Eric Ogbogu, the much smaller Planck undertook the task with such enthusiasm that Ogbogu ended up on the his back with a mild concussion. Can he do the same to Nike, Reebok, and Adidas?

1. What strategic challenges does the "disrupter's dilemma" pose for Under Armour?
2. What strategic recommendations can you make for Under Armour as the competition in the performance apparel heats up?
3. Work with a group of your classmates to develop a list of lessons you can learn from Kevin Plank and Under Armour about how small companies can compete successfully with much larger firms that have more resources.

Sources: Chuck Salter, "Protect This House," *Fast Company*, August 2005, pp. 70–75; Karen E. Spaeder, "Beyond Their Years: Kevin Plank," *Entrepreneur*, November 2003, p. 76; Kevin Plank and Mark Hyman, "How I Did It," *Inc.*, December 2003, pp. 102–104; "Company Overview," Under Armour, http://www.underarmour.com/ua2/biz/pages/company_overview.asp.

Step 6. Create Company Goals and Objectives

Before entrepreneurs can build a comprehensive set of strategies, they must first establish business goals and objectives, which give them targets to aim for and provide a basis for evaluating their companies' performance. Without them, it is impossible to know where a business is going or how well it is performing. The following conversation between Alice and the Cheshire Cat, taken from Lewis Carroll's *Alice in Wonderland*, illustrates the importance of creating meaningful goals and objectives as part of the strategic management process:[40]

> "Would you tell me please, which way I ought to go from here?" asked Alice.
>
> "That depends a good deal on where you want to get to," said the Cat.
>
> "I don't much care where . . . ," said Alice.
>
> "Then it doesn't matter which way you go," said the Cat.

A small business that "doesn't much care where" it wants to go (i.e., one that has no goals and objectives) will find that "it really doesn't matter which way" it chooses to go (i.e., its strategy is irrelevant).

goals
the broad, long-range attributes a business seeks to accomplish; they tend to be general and sometimes even abstract.

Goals Business **goals** are the broad, long-range attributes that a business seeks to accomplish; they tend to be general and sometimes even abstract. Goals are not intended to be specific enough for a manager to act on, but simply state the general level of accomplishment sought. Do you want to boost your market share? Does your cash balance need strengthening? Would you like to enter a new market or increase sales in a current one? Do you want to develop new products or services? Researchers Jim Collins and Jerry Porras studied a large group of businesses and determined that one of the factors that set apart successful companies from unsuccessful ones was the formulation of very ambitious, clear, and inspiring long-term goals. Collins and Porras call them BHAGs ("Big Hairy Audacious Goals," pronounced "bee-hags") and say that their main benefit is to inspire and focus a company on important actions that are consistent with its overall mission.[41]

Addressing these broad issues will help you focus on the next phase—developing specific, realistic objectives.

objectives
more specific targets of performance, commonly addressing areas such as profitability, productivity, growth, and other key aspects of a business.

Objectives Business **objectives** are more specific targets of performance. Common objectives concern profitability, productivity, growth, efficiency, markets, financial resources, physical facilities, organizational structure, employee welfare, and social responsibility. Because some of these objectives might conflict with one another, it is important to establish priorities. Which objectives are most important? Which are least important? Arranging objectives in a hierarchy according to their priority can help an entrepreneur resolve conflicts when they arise. Well-written objectives have the following characteristics:

They are specific. Objectives should be quantifiable and precise. For example, "to achieve a healthy growth in sales" is not a meaningful objective; however, "to increase retail sales by 12 percent and wholesale sales by 10 percent in the next fiscal year" is precise and spells out exactly what management wants to accomplish.

They are measurable. Managers should be able to plot the organization's progress toward its objectives; this requires a well-defined reference point from which to start and a scale for measuring progress.

They are assignable. Unless an entrepreneur assigns responsibility for an objective to an individual, it is unlikely that the company will ever achieve it. Creating objectives without giving someone responsibility for accomplishing it is futile.

They are realistic, yet challenging. Objectives must be within the reach of the organization or motivation will disappear. In any case, managerial expectations must remain high. In other words, the more challenging an objective is (within realistic limits), the higher the performance will be. Set objectives that will challenge your business and its employees.

They are timely. Objectives must specify not only what is to be accomplished, but also when it is to be accomplished. A time frame for achievement is important.

They are written down. This writing process does not have to be complex; in fact, the manager should make the number of objectives relatively small, from 5 to 15.

LEARNING OBJECTIVES
4. Discuss the three basic strategies—low cost, differentiation, and focus—and know when and how to employ them.

The strategic planning process works best when managers and employees are actively involved in setting goals and objectives together. Developing a plan is top management's responsibility, but executing it falls to managers and employees; therefore, encouraging them to participate broadens the plan's perspective and increases the motivation to make the plan work. In addition, managers and employees know a great deal about the organization and usually are willing to share their knowledge.

Step 7. Formulate Strategic Options and Select the Appropriate Strategies

By this point in the strategic management process, entrepreneurs should have a clear picture of what their businesses do best and what their competitive advantages are. They also should understand their firms' weaknesses and limitations as well as those of its competitors. The next step is to evaluate strategic options and then prepare a game plan designed to achieve the stated mission, goals, and objectives.

Strategy A **strategy** is a road map of the actions an entrepreneur draws up to achieve a company's mission, goals, and objectives. In other words, the mission, goals, and objectives spell out the ends, and the strategy defines the means for reaching them. A strategy is the master plan that covers all of the major parts of the organization and ties them together into a unified whole. The plan must be action oriented; it should breathe life into the entire planning process. An entrepreneur must build a sound strategy based on the preceding steps that uses the company's core competencies and strengths as the springboard to success. Joseph Picken and Gregory Dess, authors of *Mission Critical: The 7 Strategic Traps that Derail Even the Smartest Companies,* write, "A flawed strategy—no matter how brilliant the leadership, no matter how effective the implementation—is doomed to fail. A sound strategy, implemented without error, wins every time."[42]

strategy
a road map of the actions an entrepreneur draws up to fulfill a company's mission, goals, and objectives.

Grant Petersen

An avid bicyclist, Grant Petersen, quit his job at the bicycle division of Japanese conglomerate Bridgestone in 1994 to start his own specialty bicycle manufacturing business, Rivendell Bicycle Works. In an industry dominated by giant companies, Petersen and his eight workers, including his bookkeeper wife, succeed by implementing a well-planned niche strategy, selling "retro-bikes" that are made of old-fashioned steel rather than the latest carbon fiber composites and use manual derailleurs rather than modern sophisticated electronic gear shifters. "Our whole business is based on selling things that are unpopular," says Petersen. Rivendell sells just 600 bicycles a year, but they are all hand-built with exquisite attention to detail and sell for $1,700 to $4,000. To promote his business, Petersen sells subscriptions to a quarterly publication called the *Rivendell Reader* for $20 a year ($200 for 99 years) in which bicycle enthusiasts can read articles covering everything from "Bicycling 101" to "Comparing Centerpulls and Cantilevers." Of course, a catalog featuring the company's products accompanies every issue of the reader. Petersen says that the 6,200 subscribers purchase an average of $260 of merchandise through the catalog each year. Demand for Rivendell bicycles is so strong that customers wanting to purchase one of the high-end custom models are on a waiting list of 18 months. To fuel the company's growth, Petersen has introduced two new lower-priced models and has expanded his base of dealers. Moderate growth is fine with Petersen, but he still wants his company to remain small. He seems to enjoy the fact that he makes the beeswax lubricant for bolt threads in his kitchen and sells it in Dixie cups![43]

A successful strategy is comprehensive and well integrated, focusing on establishing the key success factors that the manager identified in Step 4. For instance, if maximum shelf space is a key success factor for a small manufacturer's product, the strategy must identify techniques for gaining more in-store shelf space (e.g., offering higher margins to distributors and brokers than competitors do, assisting retailers with in-store displays, or redesigning a wider, more attractive package).

Three Strategic Options Obviously, the number of strategies from which the small business owner can choose is enormous. When all the glitter is stripped away, however, three basic strategies remain. In his classic book *Competitive Strategy*, Michael Porter defines these strategies: (1) cost leadership, (2) differentiation, and (3) focus (see Figure 3.4).[44]

COST LEADERSHIP A company pursuing a **cost leadership strategy** strives to be the lowest-cost producer relative to its competitors in the industry. Low-cost leaders have a competitive advantage in reaching buyers whose primary purchase criterion is price, and they have the power to set the industry's price floor. This strategy works well when buyers are sensitive to price changes, when competing firms sell the same commodity products and compete on the basis of price, and when companies can benefit from economies of

cost leadership strategy
a strategy in which a company strives to be the lowest-cost producer relative to its competitors in the industry.

FIGURE 3.4

Three Strategic Options

Target Market	Competitive Advantage: Uniqueness perceived by the customer	Competitive Advantage: Low cost position
Industry	Differentiation	Low cost
Niche	Differentiation focus	Cost focus

scale. Not only is a low-cost leader in the best position to defend itself in a price war, but it also can use its power to attack competitors with the lowest price in the industry.

There are many ways to build a low-cost strategy, but the most successful cost leaders know where they have cost advantages over their competitors, and they use these as the foundation for their strategies. They also are committed to squeezing unnecessary costs out of their operations.

JetBlue Airways

Because its workforce is not unionized, JetBlue Airlines has a significant advantage over its rivals in labor costs, and it has more flexibility in job assignments for its cross-trained workers. Pilots even pitch in to help flight attendants clean cabins, which keeps flight turnaround times short. Reservation-takers work from their homes, creating significant cost savings for themselves and for the company. Because the company offers stock options to its workers, employees often are willing to work for lower salaries. The result is that JetBlue's labor cost is just 25 percent of revenues compared to 33 to 44 percent of revenues for its competitors, and the company uses this to deploy its fleet of planes more efficiently and more profitably than its competition. JetBlue also flies just two types of planes—Airbus A320s and Embraer 190s—to keep maintenance and training costs low. Every JetBlue seat is upholstered in leather, a luxury that costs $15,000 more per plane but sends an important signal to passengers. In addition, the leather surfaces are easier to maintain and last much longer, lowering JetBlue's costs. The net effect of this cost-leadership strategy is that JetBlue's operating cost is the lowest in the industry—just six cents per seat-mile compared with eight to twelve cents per seat-mile for older, "legacy" carriers. JetBlue and other low-cost carriers use their lower cost structures to put pressure on legacy carriers (many of which have declared bankruptcy), who find it increasingly difficult to raise fares in markets where they compete directly. "The low-cost airlines are now dictating pricing in our business," says a top manager at one legacy airline. "Every time the [legacy airlines] match the fares of the discounters, they lose money."[45]

Of course, there are dangers in following a cost leadership strategy. Sometimes, a company focuses exclusively on lower manufacturing costs, without considering the impact of purchasing, distribution, or overhead costs. Another danger is incorrectly identifying the company's true cost drivers. Although their approach to managing is characterized by frugality, companies that understand cost leadership are willing to invest in those activities that drive costs out of doing business, whether it is technology, preventive maintenance, or some other factor. Finally, a firm may pursue a low-cost leadership strategy so zealously that in its drive to push costs downward, it eliminates product or service features that customers consider to be essential.

Under the right conditions, a cost leadership strategy executed properly can be an incredibly powerful strategic weapon. Small discount retailers that live in the shadows of Wal-Mart and thrive even when the economy slows succeed by relentlessly pursuing low-cost strategies. Small chains such as Fred's, Dollar General, Family Dollar, and 99 Cents Only cater to low- and middle-income customers who live in inner cities or rural areas. They offer inexpensive products such as food, health and beauty products, cleaning supplies, clothing, and seasonal merchandise, and many of the items they stock are closeout buys (purchases made as low as 10 cents on the dollar) on brand name merchandise. These companies also strive to keep their overhead costs as low as possible. For instance, 99 Cents

Only, whose name describes its merchandising strategy, is housed in a no-frills warehouse in an older section of City of Commerce, California.[46] The success of these stores proves that companies pursuing a cost leadership strategy must emphasize cost containment in *every* decision, from where to locate the company headquarters to which items to stock.

DIFFERENTIATION A company following a **differentiation strategy** seeks to build customer loyalty by positioning its goods or services in a unique or different fashion. That, in turn, enables the business to command a higher price for its products or services than competitors. There are many ways to create a differentiation strategy, but the key is to be special at something that is important to the customer. In other words, a business strives to be better than its competitors at something customers value.

differentiation strategy a strategy in which a company seeks to build customer loyalty by positioning its goods or services in a unique or different fashion.

COMPANY Profile

Urban Outfitters

Urban Outfitters, a 75-store chain selling clothing for young people, has achieved success by implementing a contrarian strategy to distinguish itself from the cookie-cutter stores on which many of its national retail competitors rely. "Shopping here should be like a treasure hunt," says the company's general merchandising manager. Indeed, the company engages customers' sense of adventure by displaying one-of-a-kind vintage garments next to new fashions and unique, funky home décor items such as beaded curtains and cocktail shakers. Founder Richard Hayne encourages customers to return to Urban Outfitters outlets by stocking small batches of new merchandise and employing a visual arts staff to redesign its stores every two weeks. "Rather than relying on identical stores," says one industry analyst, "Urban creates an experience that's intellectually stimulating." Customers seem to enjoy the "organized clutter" layout because they shop for an average of 45 minutes per visit, twice as long as shoppers spend in a typical clothing store. In another clever move, every Urban Outfitters store places Xboxes and vintage video games in the men's section to keep bored boyfriends from pressuring female shoppers into leaving! To ensure that it sells the latest fashions, the company sends teams of buyers and designers on globe-hopping trips, where they look for design inspirations. The teams have come back with ideas for tunics from Stockholm and art deco jewelry from a Prague art museum. Urban Outfitters' differentiation strategy works well; its stores generate $596 in annual sales per square foot of space, 80 percent higher than its competitors.[47]

If a small company can improve a product's (or service's) performance, reduce the customer's cost and risk of purchasing it, or provide intangible benefits that customers value (such as status, prestige, a sense of safety, among others), it has the potential to be a successful differentiator. Companies that execute a differentiation strategy successfully can charge premium prices for their products and services, increase their market share, and reap the benefits of customer loyalty and retention. To be successful, a business must make its product or service truly different, at least in the eyes of its customers.

Ice Hotel

A stay at the Ice Hotel in Jukkasjärvi, Sweden, is like an evening in no other hotel in the world. *Everything* in the hotel—the walls, the beds, the bar, the glasses—is made of ice! Rebuilt every year from ice from the Torne River, the Ice Hotel is the ultimate example of a differentiation strategy.

Entrepreneur Yngve Bergqvist has no trouble setting his hotel in Jukkasjärvi, Sweden, apart from others. Located 125 miles above the Arctic Circle, the aptly named Ice Hotel offers travelers a unique experience. *Everything* in the hotel—walls, beds, night tables, chairs, cinema, bars—is made from 30,000 tons of snow and 10,000 tons of crystal clear ice harvested from the Torne River! Each of the 60 rooms is unique, designed by a different artist from around the world. Guests sleep in insulated sleeping bags on ice beds covered with thin mattresses and plenty of reindeer blankets. Because temperatures inside the hotel typically hover at 5 degrees below zero (centigrade), guests cannot take their luggage to their ice rooms; it will freeze! Amenities include an ice bar, an ice chapel, an ice cinema, and an ice art exhibition. The

30,000-square-foot Ice Hotel is open from December through April (it melts in the spring), but during its brief existence, it will accommodate some 5,000 guests at rates ranging from $200 to $500 per night! Countless rock groups, including Van Halen, have shot music videos at the Ice Hotel. It's not about comfort," says co-owner Arne Bergh. "It's a journey, an adventure."[48]

Although few businesses are innately as unique as the Ice Hotel, the goal for a company pursuing a differentiation strategy is to create that kind of uniqueness in the minds of its customers. The key to a successful differentiation strategy is to build it on a core competency, something a small company is uniquely good at doing in comparison to its competitors. Common bases for differentiation include superior customer service, special product features, complete product lines, instantaneous parts availability, absolute product reliability, supreme product quality, and extensive product knowledge. To be successful, a differentiation strategy must create the perception of value in the customer's eyes. No customer will purchase a good or service that fails to produce its perceived value, no matter how real that value may be. One business consultant advises, "Make sure you tell your customers and prospects what it is about your business that makes you different. Make sure that difference is on the form of a true benefit to the customer."[49]

Other small companies that are deploying a differentiation strategy successfully include the following:

- Woodentoys-and-more.com is an online store that sells upscale children's toys. Shoshana Bailey started the company when she had difficulty finding creative, educational toys for her grandchildren at mass merchandisers such as Wal-Mart and Toys-R-Us. Some of her company's best-selling items include a $147 hand-made wooden train set and a $420 cherry wood rocking horse made by a Tennessee craftsman. "Mass-market retailers can't stock all of these unique toys," explains one industry analyst. "Their job is to stock the most in-demand toys."[50]
- PrarieStone Pharmacy is using technology to offer fast service and individual attention to customers getting drug prescriptions filled. At locations inside Lund Food Holdings, a chain of upscale supermarkets in the Minneapolis-St. Paul area, PrarieStone stores drugs in a high-tech vertical container that saves space, dispenses the most often prescribed drugs automatically, and allows pharmacists to have more face-to-face time with customers. A system of bar-code scanners verifies the accuracy of every order and protects customers from medication errors. PrarieStone also was the first pharmacy in the nation to offer automated multidose packaging for customers taking multiple medications. A specialized machine organizes the various drugs and then packages them in a sealed sleeve marked with the time of day the patient should take the medication. Not only does the technology provide cost savings for PrarieStone, but it also speeds up transaction times, enhances safety for customers, and gives pharmacists more time to spend working with customers rather than counting pills manually.[51]

Small companies encounter risks when pursuing a differentiation strategy. One danger is trying to differentiate a product or service on the basis of something that does not boost its performance or lower its cost to customers. Another pitfall is trying to differentiate on the basis of something that customers do not see as important. Business owners also must consider how long they can sustain a product's or service's differentiation; changing customer tastes make the basis for differentiation temporary at best. Imitations and "knock-offs" from competitors also pose a threat to a successful differentiation strategy. For instance, entrepreneurs in Finland have built an ice hotel to compete with the original ice hotel in Sweden. Designers of high-priced original clothing see much cheaper knock-off products on the market shortly after their designs hit the market. Another pitfall is overdifferentiating and charging so much that the company prices its products out of the market. The final risk is focusing only on the physical characteristics of a product or service and ignoring important psychological factors such as status, prestige, and image, which can be powerful sources of differentiation.

FOCUS A **focus strategy** recognizes that not all markets are homogeneous. In fact, in any given market, there are many different customer segments, each having different needs, wants, and characteristics. The principal idea of this strategy is to select one or more market segments, identify customers' special needs, wants, and interests, and approach them with a good or service designed to excel in meeting these needs, wants, and interests. Focus strategies build on *differences* among market segments. For instance, most markets contains a population of customers who are willing and able to pay for premium goods and services, giving small companies the opportunity to follow a focus strategy aimed at the premium segment of the market.

focus strategy
a strategy in which a company selects one or more market segments, identifies customers' special needs, wants, and interests, and approaches them with a good or service designed to excel in meeting those needs, wants, and interests.

A successful focus strategy depends on a small company's ability to identify the changing needs of its targeted customer group and to develop the skills required to serve them. That means an entrepreneur and everyone in the organization must have a clear understanding of how to add value to the product or service for the customer. How does the product or service meet the customer's needs at each stage—from raw material to final sale?

Rather than attempting to serve the total market, the focusing firm specializes in serving a specific target segment or niche. A focus strategy is ideally suited to many small businesses, which often lack the resources to reach the overall market. Their goal is to serve their narrow target markets more effectively and efficiently than do competitors that pound away at the broad market. Common bases for building a focus strategy include zeroing in on a small geographic area, targeting a group of customers with similar needs or interests (e.g., left-handed people), specializing in a specific product or service (e.g., Batteries Plus, a store that sells and services every kind of battery imaginable), or selling specialized knowledge (e.g., restoring valuable works of art).

Cereality

David Roth (l) and Rick Bacher gave new meaning to the phrase "cereal bar" when they launched Cereality, a restaurant that specializes in cereal and cereal products. Initially targeting college students, Roth and Bacher are expanding their specialty stores into airports, train stations, office buildings, and other locations with high volumes of morning traffic.

After researching the $6.2 billion-a-year breakfast cereal industry, David Roth and Rick Bacher decided to start a restaurant dedicated to the popular breakfast food. (One of the factors that prompted Roth, a former marketing consultant, to come up with the idea was a meeting with an executive who kept a stash of Cocoa Puffs hidden in his briefcase.) Initially targeting college students ("They basically live on cereal," jokes Roth), the two friends launched Cereality in the Arizona State University food court in 2003. The pilot store was so successful that Roth and Bacher have opened stores in Philadelphia and Chicago and are planning to set up Cereality outlets in hospitals, airports, train stations, office buildings, and other college campuses. For about $4, customers can fill up their Cereality Chineses-food-like bucket with two scoops of any of the more than 30 brands of cereal on the menu (from Fruit Loops to Corn Chex), add one of more than 40 toppings, ranging from bananas or dried cherries to chocolate malt balls, and top it off with milk (several varieties here as well). "Cerealogists" dressed in pajama tops also sell cereal bars, Cereality Bites™ snack mixes and "Slurrealities®" (smoothies made with cereal) that account for one-third of a Cereality outlet's sales. "The idea is to become the Starbucks of cereal," says Roth.[52]

The most successful focusers build a competitive edge by concentrating on specific market niches and serving them better than any other competitor can. Essentially, this strategy depends on creating value for the customer either by being the lowest-cost producer or by differentiating the product or service in a unique fashion, but doing it in a narrow target segment. To be worth targeting, a niche must be large enough to be profitable, reasonably reachable through advertising media, and capable of sustaining a business over time (i.e., not a passing fad). Consider the following examples of companies that operate quite successfully in small, yet profitable, niches:

- The Flutter Fetti Fun Factory specializes in making—and dropping—confetti. The small company has dropped its patented product, Flutter Fetti ("The only party confetti that Flutters, Flies, and Floats"™), at a variety of high-profile events, including the Republican and Democratic national conventions, the Olympics, Mardi Gras, presidential inaugural balls, the Macy's Thanksgiving Day Parade, and music concerts by Shania Twain, Britney Spears, and Paul McCartney.[53]
- After his father, Joe, moved into his new Beverly Hills, California, home, Jeff Smith, a wine connoisseur, organized Joe's 5,000-bottle wine collection. When a family friend saw the result, he offered the younger Smith $500 to organize his wine cellar. "That's when the light bulb went off," says Smith, who then started his company, Carte du Vin, from a spare bedroom in his Hollywood Hills, California, home. A customized software package categorizes his clients' wine collections by type, vintage, critics' ratings, peak drinking date, and price. The database that he uses contains information on more than 10,000 wines, but Smith and his two part-time employees are constantly updating and expanding it. Once he organizes a client's wine cellar, Smith provides a leather-bound printout and a password-protected Web site customers can access anytime. Smith also performs monthly wine cellar maintenance for many of his clients after initially organizing their collections.[54]

Although it can be a highly profitable strategy, pursuing a focus strategy is not without risks. Companies sometimes must struggle to capture a large enough share of a small market to be profitable. If a small company is successful in a niche, there is also the danger of larger competitors entering the market and eroding it. Entrepreneurs following this strategy often face a constant struggle to keep costs down; the small volume of business that some niches support pushes production costs upward, making a company vulnerable to lower-cost competitors as their prices spiral higher. Sometimes a company with a successful niche strategy gets distracted by its success and tries to branch out into other areas. As it drifts farther away from its core strategy, it loses its competitive edge and runs the risk of confusing or alienating its customers. Muddying its image with customers puts a company in danger of losing its identity.

Strategy in Action The strategies a small business pursues depend on its competitive advantages in the market segments in which it competes. In some cases, the business will implement multiple strategies across several segments. When a business has a well-defined strategic advantage, it may pursue highly aggressive growth strategies in an attempt to increase its market share. This is especially true when a business achieves a "first-mover" advantage in a market with little direct competition. By being the first in the market, it establishes name recognition and a loyal customer base. Starbucks Coffee continues to reap the benefits of being the first company to establish a chain of upscale retail coffee houses in major markets after Howard Shultz traveled to Milan, Italy, and noticed the tremendous popularity of espresso bars. A year later, in 1984, Schultz launched his coffee bar concept as a test in Seattle, Washington. Today, the chain has nearly 6,000 locations around the globe! Aggressive strategies sometimes can backfire if larger competitors decide to fight back. In many cases, the old adage of being the "big frog in a small pond" allows a small business to earn a handsome profit in a market niche without attracting the attention of larger competitors.

Small companies must develop strategies that exploit all of the competitive advantages of their size by:

- Responding quickly to customers' needs.
- Remaining flexible and willing to change.
- Constantly searching for new, emerging market segments.
- Building and defending market niches.
- Erecting "switching costs," the costs a customer incurs by switching to a competitor's product or service, through personal service and loyalty.
- Remaining entrepreneurial and willing to take risks and act with lightning speed.
- Constantly innovating.

Hands on ... How to

Beat Big-Box Competitors

It's the news that sends shivers down the spines of small business owners everywhere: Wal-Mart (or any other "big-box" retailer) is coming to town. "How can my small business compete against the largest company in the world?" they wonder. "Can my business survive?"

Although no business owner welcomes a threat of this magnitude from a giant competitor with greater buying power, more name recognition, and a reputation for driving small companies out of business, it is no reason to fold up the tent and go home. Smart entrepreneurs know that, by formulating and executing the proper strategy, they not only can survive in the face of big box competitors, but they also can thrive in their presence.

Rule 1. Don't play their game. A fundamental concept in strategy is to avoid matching your company's weaknesses against a competitor's strengths. For instance, because Wal-Mart buys in such huge volume from its supplier, it can extract the lowest prices from them. Small companies purchasing from those same suppliers cannot; therefore, it makes little sense for small companies to try to compete with Wal-Mart and other giant retailers on the basis of price. Unless your small company has another, more significant cost advantage, competing on the basis of price is a recipe for disaster.

Rule 2. Hit 'em where they ain't. Jeff Brotman, founder of Costco, a discount warehouse that goes up against Wal-Mart's Sam's Club discount warehouses, has been competing in competition with the industry giant for two decades. "When [Wal-Mart] comes to town," he says, "it usually means death and destruction." By pursuing a niche, however, Costco has managed to grow despite Wal-Mart's power. Even though Costco has 218 fewer locations than Sam's Club, Costco manages to generate more sales and higher profits than its rival. Brotman's strategy is to target small business owners with more upscale products than Sam's Club typically offers. When he first launched the company, Brotman's research showed that small business owners were among the wealthiest people in a typical community, but, because of their business experience, they were always looking for a good bargain. "They want high-end merchandise that reflects their status, but they'd prefer it cheap," he says. That's just what Costco delivers. A Costco store carries only half as many items as a Sam's Club outlet, but the selection is quite different and is designed to appeal to upscale shoppers—Godiva chocolates, Coach handbags, Waterford crystal, Dom Perignon champagne, J. A. Henckels International cutlery, and others. Like Wal-Mart, Costco has developed a highly effective supply chain system to keep stores stocked with the best-selling items. "This business is a game of inches," says Brotman, "so we'll get a little better every year."

Rule 3. Hire the best . . . and train them. Costco pays its workers at rates well above the industry average, which keeps turnover rates low (in fact, the lowest in the industry) and productivity high, giving it another edge over Wal-Mart. Small companies cannot always afford to pay the highest wages in an area; however, because their companies are small, entrepreneurs have the opportunity to create a work environment in which employees can thrive. For instance, one small company attracts and retains quality workers by allowing them to use flexible work schedules that make it easier for them to manage their busy lives. The owner also invests heavily in training workers so that they can move up the organization—and the pay scale—faster. The training pays off, however, in the form of greater productivity, lower turnover, increased customer satisfaction, and higher sales per employee. Paying attention to seemingly small details such as more communication, frequent recognition for jobs well done, less bureaucracy, and flexible benefits enables small companies to build a loyal, motivated workforce that can outperform those at larger companies.

Rule 4. Bring back what the big boys have eliminated. Many companies in the supermarket industry have taken a beating as discount mass retailers have expanded their superstore concepts into more markets across the United States. Yet, many small supermarket chains have thrived by taking a completely different strategic approach, building small stores that allow shoppers to make their purchases quickly and conveniently. A Wal-Mart supercenter, for instance, adds about 40,000 grocery items to the already mind-boggling 116,000 items in its outlets. Customers have a wide selection of products at low prices, but many have grown weary of the time they have to invest to navigate these cavernous stores just to find the items they need. That's exactly what small grocers such as Save-a-Lot are counting on. Going back to the days of the old corner grocer, the St. Louis-based chain keeps its 1,250 stores small—operated by no more than 25 employees—and sells no more than 1,250 grocery items in each one. To keep its costs and prices low, Save-a-Lot carefully selects neighborhood locations and emphasizes private label items (in fact, private label items make up 75 percent of the company's inventory).

Rule 5. Beat them at the service game. In tennis, the serve is one of the most important parts of the game; so it is in the retail game. Small companies can differentiate themselves from their larger, more powerful rivals by emphasizing superior, friendly, personal service, something their size makes them uniquely capable of doing. For instance, Dick's Sporting Goods, a chain of 240 sporting goods stores, relentlessly trains its workers so they can share their knowledge of the company's products and how best to use them with customers. Despite the low prices they offer customers, giant chain stores are famous for failing to provide even basic customer service and product information, once again giving small companies the opportunity to outperform their giant rivals. "Customers today want information," says Dick's CEO, Ed Stack, whose father founded the company in 1948. "They're not going to go somewhere where they are ignored." At Dick's, customers in the golf shop are likely to work with a PGA golf pro, and hunters and fishermen can talk with sales people who are enthusiasts of those sports. The store layout encourages customers to test products—from bicycles and running shoes to golf clubs and tennis rackets—before they purchase them. Dick's stores also offer a wider selection of sporting goods than Wal-Mart does. When it comes to managing inventory and supplier relationships, the company has taken a page from Wal-Mart's playbook. The automated system keeps inventory very lean and operates on a just-in-time basis, enabling Dick's to boast an inventory turnover ratio of 3.7 times a year, far above the industry average of 2.7.

1. Why do many small businesses fail when a big discount retailer such as Wal-Mart becomes a competitor?
2. Work with a team of your classmates to identify a local small business that competes with a big discounter. Which of these strategies has the small company employed to become a stronger competitor? What other strategies would you recommend to the owner of this business?
3. Based on your work in Question 2, develop a one-page report summarizing your strategic suggestions.

Sources: Matthew Maier, "How to Beat Wal-Mart," *Business 2.0*, pp. 108–114; Rhonda Abrams, "Small Businesses Can Compete with the Big Guys," *Business*, September 26, 2004, p. 8; Ann Zimmerman, "Behind the Dollar-Store Boom: A Nation of Bargain Hunters," *Wall Street Journal*, December 13, 2004, pp. A1, A10; Barry Cotton, and Jean-Charles Cachon, "Resisting the Giants: Small Retail Entrepreneurs Against Mega-Retailers—An Empirical Study," Presented at the International Council for Small Business 2005 World Conference, June 2005; Amy Merrick, Gary McWilliams, Ellen Byron, and Kortney Stringer, "Targeting Wal-Mart," *Wall Street Journal*, December 1, 2004, pp. B1, B2.

Step 8. Translate Strategic Plans into Action Plans

No strategic plan is complete until it is put into action; planning a company's strategy and implementing it go hand in hand. Entrepreneurs must convert strategic plans into operating plans that guide their companies on a daily basis and become a visible, active part of the business. No small business can benefit from a strategic plan sitting on a shelf collecting dust. Unfortunately, failure to implement a strategy effectively is a common problem. In a recent survey conducted by Marakon Associates and the Economist Intelligence Unit, senior executives reported that their companies had achieved only 63 percent of the results expected in their strategic plans.[55] The lesson is that even sound strategies, unless properly implemented, will fail.

Implementing the Strategy Implementing a strategy successfully requires both a process that fits a company's culture and the right people committed to making that process work. Getting the right people in place starts with the selection process but includes every other aspect of the human resources function, from job design and training to motivational methods and compensation. To make their strategic plans workable, entrepreneurs should divide them into projects, carefully defining each one by the following:

Purpose. What is the project designed to accomplish?

Scope. Which areas of the company will be involved in the project?

Contribution. How does the project relate to other projects and to the overall strategic plan?

Resource requirements. What human and financial resources are needed to complete the project successfully?

Timing. Which schedules and deadlines will ensure project completion?

Once entrepreneurs assign priorities to projects, they can begin to implement the strategic plan. Involving employees and delegating adequate authority to them is essential because these projects affect them most directly. If an organization's people have been involved in the strategic management process to this point, they will have a better grasp of the steps they must take to achieve the organization's goals as well as their own professional goals. Early involvement of the work force in the strategic management process is a luxury that larger businesses cannot achieve. Commitment to reaching the company's objectives is a powerful force, but involvement is a prerequisite for achieving total employee commitment. The greater the level of involvement of those who will implement a company's strategy (often those at the lower levels of an organization) in the process of creating the strategy (often the realm of those at the top of an organization), the more likely it is that the strategy will be successful. Without a team of committed, dedicated employees, a company's strategy, no matter how precisely planned, usually fails.

LEARNING OBJECTIVES
5. Understand the importance of controls such as the balanced scorecard in the planning process.

Step 9. Establish Accurate Controls

So far, the planning process has created company objectives and has developed a strategy for reaching them, but rarely, if ever, will the company's actual performance match stated objectives. Entrepreneurs quickly realize the need to control actual results that deviate from plans.

Controlling the Strategy Planning without control has little operational value; therefore, a sound planning program requires a practical control process. The plans created in the strategic planning process become the standards against which actual performance is measured. It is important for everyone in the organization to understand—and to be involved in—the planning and controlling process.

Controlling plans and projects and keeping them on schedule means that an entrepreneur must identify and track key performance indicators. The source of these indicators is the operating data from the company's normal business activity; they are the guideposts for detecting deviations from established standards. Financial, production, sales, inventory, quality, customer service and satisfaction, and other operating records are primary sources of data managers can use to control activities. For example, on a customer service project, performance indicators might include the number of customer complaints, the number of orders returned, the percentage of on-time shipments, and a measure of order accuracy.

The most commonly used indicators of a company's performance are financial measures; however, judging a company's performance solely on the basis of financial measures can lead to strategic myopia. To judge the effectiveness of their strategies, many companies are developing a **balanced scorecard,** a set of multidimensional measurements that are unique to a company and that incorporate both financial and operational measures to give managers a quick yet comprehensive picture of the company's overall performance. One writer says that a balanced scorecard

balanced scorecard
a set of multidimensional measurements that are unique to a company and that incorporate both financial and operational measures to give managers a quick yet comprehensive picture of a company's overall performance.

> is a sophisticated business model that helps a company understand what's really driving its success. It acts a bit like the control panel on a spaceship—the business equivalent of a flight speedometer, odometer, and temperature gauge all rolled into

> one. It keeps track of many things, including financial progress and softer measurements—everything from customer satisfaction to return on investment—that need to be managed to reach the final destination: profitable growth.[56]

Rather than sticking solely to the traditional financial measures of a company's performance, the balanced scorecard gives managers a comprehensive view from *both* a financial and an operational perspective. The premise behind such a scorecard is that relying on any single measure of company performance is dangerous. Just as a pilot in command of a jet cannot fly safely by focusing on a single instrument, an entrepreneur cannot manage a company by concentrating on a single measurement. The complexity of managing a business demands that an entrepreneur be able to see performance measures in several areas simultaneously. "Knowing whether an enterprise is viable or not doesn't mean looking at just the bottom line," says one manager.[57] Scoreboards that combine relevant results from all aspects of the operation allow everyone in the organization to see how their job performance connects to a company's mission, goals, and objectives.

When creating a balanced scorecard for a company, an entrepreneur should establish goals for each critical indicator of company performance and then create meaningful measures for each one.

Certifiedmail.com

Court Coursey, founder of Certifiedmail.com, a company that delivers certified mail electronically, has developed a scorecard that encompasses measures on everything from financial performance to employee satisfaction. Every quarter, Coursey presents Certifiedmail.com's one-page scorecard to his 10 employees for review. "It's a good way to get a grasp on the company and how it's performing," he says. The scorecard gives Coursey important feedback that allows him to adjust his management style and the company's direction when necessary. The scorecard already has improved Certifiedmail.com's performance. One of Coursey's top priorities is cost control, and the scorecard recently pointed out a wasteful practice that he halted. The scorecard "showed me a way to save money," he says. "And it was something I may not have seen without this feedback."[58]

Ideally, a balanced scorecard looks at a business from four important perspectives (see Figure 3.5)[59]:

Customer Perspective: How do customers see us? Customers judge companies by at least four standards: time (how long it takes the company to deliver a good or service), quality (how well a company's product or service performs in terms of reliability, durability, and accuracy), performance (the extent to which a good or service performs as expected), and service (how well a company meets or exceeds customers' expectations of value). Because customer-related goals are external, managers must translate them into measures of what the company must do to meet customers' expectations.

Internal Business Perspective: At what must we excel? The internal factors on which managers should focus are those that have the greatest impact on customer satisfaction and retention and on company effectiveness and efficiency. Developing goals and measures for factors such as quality, cycle time, productivity, costs, and others that employees directly influence is essential.

Innovation and Learning Perspective: Can we continue to improve and create value? This view of a company recognizes that the targets required for success are never static; they are constantly changing. If a company wants to continue its pattern of success, it cannot stand still; it must continuously improve. A company's ability to innovate, learn, and improve determines its future. These goals and measures emphasize the importance of continuous improvement in customer satisfaction and internal business operations.

Financial Perspective: How do we look to shareholders? The most traditional performance measures, financial standards tell how much the company's overall strategy and its execution are contributing to its bottom line. These measures focus on such

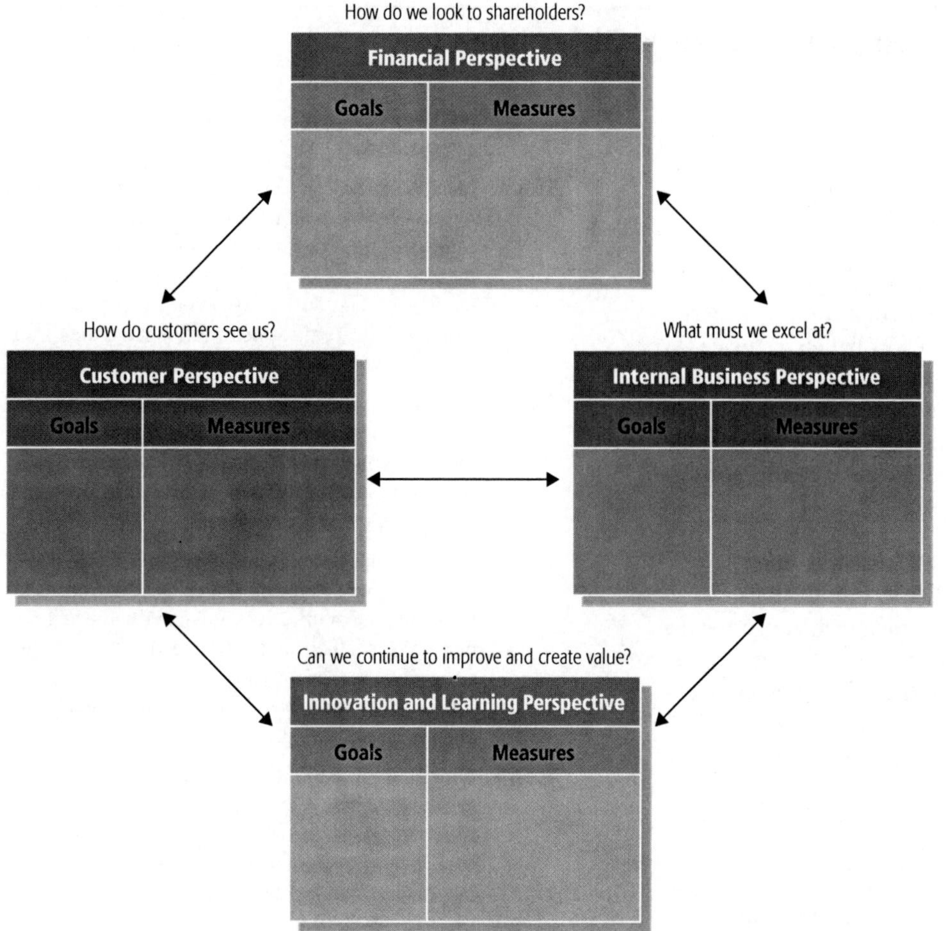

FIGURE 3.5

The Balanced Scorecard Links Performance Measures

factors as profitability, growth, and shareholder value. On balanced scorecards, companies often break their financial goals into three categories: survival, success, and growth.

Although the balanced scorecard is a vital tool that helps managers keep their companies on track, it is also an important tool for changing behavior in an organization and for keeping everyone focused on what really matters. Used properly, balanced scorecards allow managers to see how actions in each of the four dimensions of performance influence actions in the others. As competitive conditions and results change, managers can use the balanced scorecard to make corrections in plans, policies, strategies, and objectives to get performance back on track. A practical control system is also economical to operate. Most small businesses have no need for a sophisticated, expensive control system. The system should be so practical that it becomes a natural part of the management process.

Conclusion

The strategic planning process does *not* end with the nine steps outlined here; it is an ongoing procedure that entrepreneurs must repeat. With each round, managers and employees gain experience, and the steps become easier. The planning process outlined here is designed to be as simple as possible. No small business should be burdened with an elaborate, detailed formal planning process that it cannot easily use. Such processes require excessive amounts of time to operate, and they generate a sea of paperwork. Entrepreneurs need neither.

What does this strategic planning process lead to? It teaches business owners a degree of discipline that is important to business survival. It helps them to learn about their businesses, their core competencies, their competitors, and, most important, their customers. Although strategic planning cannot guarantee success, it does dramatically increase a small company's chances of survival in a hostile business environment.

Chapter Summary by Learning Objectives

1. Understand the importance of strategic management to a small business.

Small companies that lack clear strategies may achieve some success in the short run, but as soon as competitive conditions stiffen or an unanticipated threat arises, they usually "hit the wall" and fold. Without a basis for differentiating itself from a pack of similar competitors, the best a company can hope for is mediocrity in the marketplace. In today's intensely competitive global environment, entrepreneurs who are not thinking and acting strategically are putting their businesses at risk. Strategic management is the mechanism for operating successfully in a chaotic competitive environment.

2. Explain why and how a small business must create a competitive advantage in the market.

The goal of developing a strategic plan is to create for the small company a competitive advantage—the aggregation of factors that sets the small business apart from its competitors and gives it a unique position in the market. Every small firm must establish a plan for creating a unique image in the minds of its potential customers. A company builds a competitive edge on its core competencies, which are a unique set of capabilities that a company develops in key operational areas, such as quality, service, innovation, team building, flexibility, responsiveness, and others, that allow it to vault past competitors. They are what the company does best and are the focal point of the strategy. This step must identify target market segments and determine how to position the firm in those markets. Entrepreneurs must identify some way to differentiate their companies from competitors.

3. Develop a strategic plan for a business using the nine steps in the strategic planning process.

Small businesses need a strategic planning process designed to suit their particular needs. It should be relatively short, be informal and not structured, encourage the participation of employees, and not begin with extensive objective setting. Linking the purposeful action of strategic planning to an entrepreneur's ideas can produce results that shape the future.

Step 1 Develop a clear vision and translate it into a meaningful mission statement. Highly successful entrepreneurs are able to communicate their vision to those around them. The firm's mission statement answers the first question of any venture: What business am I in? The mission statement sets the tone for the entire company.

Step 2 Assess the company's strengths and weaknesses. Strengths are positive internal factors; weaknesses are negative internal factors.

Step 3 Scan the environment for significant opportunities and threats facing the business. Opportunities are positive external options; threats are negative external forces.

Step 4 Identify the key factors for success in the business. In every business, key factors that determine the success of the firms in it, and so they must be an integral part of a company's strategy. Key success factors are relationships between a controllable variable and a critical factor influencing the firm's ability to compete in the market.

Step 5 Analyze the competition. Business owners should know their competitors' business almost as well as they know their own business. A competitive profile matrix is a helpful tool for analyzing competitors' strengths and weaknesses.

Step 6 Create company goals and objectives. Goals are the broad, long-range attributes that the firm seeks to accomplish. Objectives are quantifiable and more precise; they should be specific, measurable, assignable, realistic, timely, and written down. The process works best when managers and employees are actively involved.

Step 7 Formulate strategic options and select the appropriate strategies. A strategy is the game plan the firm plans to use to achieve its objectives and mission. It must center on establishing for the firm the key success factors identified earlier.

Step 8 Translate strategic plans into action plans. No strategic plan is complete until the owner puts it into action.

Step 9 Establish accurate controls. Actual performance rarely, if ever, matches plans exactly. Operating data from the business assembled into a comprehensive scorecard serve as an important guidepost for determining how effective a company's strategy is. This information is especially helpful when plotting future strategies.

The strategic planning process does not end with these nine steps; rather, it is an ongoing process that an entrepreneur will repeat.

4. Discuss the characteristics of three basic strategies—low cost, differentiation, and focus—and know when and how to employ them.

Three basic strategic options are cost leadership, differentiation, and focus. A company pursuing a cost leadership strategy strives to be the lowest-cost producer relative to its competitors in the industry. A company following a differentiation strategy seeks to build customer loyalty by positioning its goods or services in a unique or different fashion. In other words, the firm strives to be better than its competitors at something that customers value. A focus strategy recognizes that not all markets are homogeneous. The principal idea of this strategy is to select one or more segments, identify customers' special needs, wants, and interests, and approach them with a good or service designed to excel in meeting these needs, wants, and interests. Focus strategies build on *differences* among market segments.

5. Understand the importance of controls such as the balanced scorecard in the planning process.

Just as a pilot in command of a jet cannot fly safely by focusing on a single instrument, a entrepreneur cannot manage a company by concentrating on a single measurement. The balanced scorecard is a set of measurements unique to a company that includes both financial and a balanced scorecard of financial and operational measures gives managers a quick yet comprehensive picture of the company's total performance.

Discussion Questions

1. Why is strategic planning important to a small company?
2. What is a competitive advantage? Why is it important for a small business to establish one?
3. What are the steps in the strategic management process?
4. "Our customers don't just like our ice cream," write Ben Cohen and Jerry Greenfield, co-founders of Ben and Jerry's Homemade Inc. "They like what our company stands for. They like how doing business with us makes them feel." What do they mean?
5. What are strengths, weaknesses, opportunities, and threats? Give an example of each.
6. Explain the characteristics of effective objectives. Why is setting objectives important?
7. What are business strategies?
8. Describe the three basic strategies available to small companies. Under what conditions is each most successful?
9. "It's better to be a company with a great strategy in a crummy business than to be a company with a crummy strategy in a great business," says one business expert. Do you agree? Explain.
10. Explain how a company can gain a competitive advantage using each of the three strategies described in this chapter: cost leadership, differentiation, and focus. Give an example of a company that is using each strategy.
11. How is the controlling process related to the planning process?
12. What is a balanced scorecard? What value does it offer entrepreneurs who are evaluating the success of their current strategies?

Business Plan Pro

Business PlanPro

We are now going to think about your business from a strategic perspective. This will involve first describing your business objectives, drafting your mission statement, identifying "keys to success," conducting a SWOT analysis, and making initial comments about your strategy and your competitive advantage.

Business Plan Exercises

On the Web

Visit http://www.prenhall.com/scarborough and click on the Business Plan Resources tab. Scroll down and find the information with the heading Standard Industry Classification Codes. Step through the process to find the Standard Industry Classification code associated with your industry. Then, review the information associated with the Competitor Analysis section. This information may provide insight into learning more about your industry competitors on a global, national, or even on a local basis.

In the Software

Open your business plan in Business Plan Pro. You are now going to add text to the strategic areas mentioned in this chapter. Don't worry about perfecting this information. You will want to capture your thoughts and ideas so you can come back to these topics, add detail, and make certain the sections are congruent with your entire plan. Before we do that, let's look at some examples of each of these sections in one or more of the sample plans that you had selected earlier.

Sample Plans

Review the following sections, as they appear, of one or more of the sample plans that you identified earlier:

- Mission Statement
- Objectives
- SWOT Analysis
- Keys to Success
- Competition, Buying Patterns, and Main Competitors
- Value Proposition
- Competitive Edge
- Strategy and Implementation Summary

Note the information captured in these sections of the plans. Some areas may be quite elaborate, whereas others might be brief and contain only bullet points. As you look at each plan, determine whether it provides the needed information under each topic and think about the type of information you will include in your plan.

Building Your Business Plan

Here are some tips you may want to consider as you tackle each of these sections:

Mission statement. Use your mission statement to establish your fundamental goals for the quality of your business offering. The mission statement represents the opportunity to answer the questions "What business are you in?" and "Why does your business exist?" This may include the value you offer and the role customers, employees and owners play in providing and benefiting from that value. A good mission statement can be a critical element in defining your business and communicating this definition to key stakeholders including investors, partners, employees, and customers.

Objectives. Objectives should be specific goals that are quantifiable and measurable. Setting measurable objectives will enable you to track your progress and measure your results.

SWOT analysis. What are the internal strengths and weaknesses of your business? As you look outside the organization, what are the external opportunities and threats? List these and then assess what this tells you about your business. How can you leverage your strengths to take advantage of the opportunities ahead? How can you further develop or minimize the areas of weaknesses?

Keys to success. Virtually every business has critical aspects that make the difference between success and failure. These may be brief bullet point comments that capture key elements that will make a difference in accomplishing your stated objectives and realizing you mission.

Competition, buying patterns, and main competitors. Discuss your ideal position in the market. Think about specific kinds of features and benefits your business offers and how that is unique compared to what is available to your market today. Why do people buy your services instead of other services your competitor offer? Discuss your primary competitor's strengths and weaknesses. Consider their service offering, pricing, reputation, management, financial position, brand awareness, business development, technology, and any other factors that may be important. What market segments do they occupy? What strategy to they appear to pursue? How much of a competitive threat do the present?

Value proposition. A value proposition is a clear and concise statement that describes the tangible value-based result a customer receives from using your product or service. The more specific and meaningful this statement is from a customer's perspective, the better. Once you have your value proposition, look at your organization—and your business plan—in terms of how well you communicate the service proposition and fulfill your promise to your customers or clients.

Your competitive edge. A competitive edge may build on your value proposition and seeks to capture the unique value—in whatever terms the customer defines that value—that your business offers. Your competitive edge may be through your product, customer service, method of distribution, pricing, or promotional methods. It describes how your business is uniquely different from all others in a way that is sustainable over time.

Strategy and implementation. This is a section that you will build on and, for now, make comments that capture your plans for the business. This describes the game plan and provides focus to realize your venture's objectives and mission. Based on your initial strategic analysis, which of the three business strategies—low cost, differentiation, or focus—will you use to give your company a competitive advantage? How will this strategy capitalize on your company's strengths and appeal to your customer's need? You will later build on this information as you formulate action plans to bring this strategic plan to life.

Capture your ideas in each of these sections and continually ask yourself about the relevance of this information. If it does not add value to your business plan, there is no need to include this information.

Beyond the Classroom . . .

1. Contact the owner of a small business that competes directly with an industry giant (such as Home Depot, Wal-Mart, Barnes & Noble, or others). What does the owner see as his or her competitive advantage? How does the business communicate this advantage to its customers? What competitive strategy is the owner using? How successful is it? What changes would you suggest the owner make?
2. In his book *The HP Way,* Dave Packard, co-founder of Hewlett Packard, describes the seven commitments of the HP Way:
   - Profit—the ultimate source of corporate strength.
   - Customers—constant improvement in the value of the products and services the company offers them.

- Field of interest—seeking new opportunities but limiting them to complementary products and services based on company core competences.
- Growth—a measure of strength and a requirement for survival.
- Employees—provide opportunities for advancement, share in their success, and offer job security based on performance.
- Organization—foster individual motivation, initiative, and creativity by giving employees the freedom to work toward established goals and objectives.
- Citizenship—contribute in a positive way toward the community and society at large.

In what ways do these values help HP to define its vision? Its competitive edge? How important is it for entrepreneurs to define a system of values to guide their companies?

3. Contact a local entrepreneur and help him or her devise a balanced scorecard for his or her company. What goals did you and the owner establish in each of the four perspectives? What measures did you use to judge progress toward those goals?
4. Use the strategic tools provided in this chapter to help a local small business owner discover his or her firm's strengths, weaknesses, opportunities, and threats; identify the relevant key success factors; and analyze its competitors. Help the owner devise a strategy for success for his or her business.
5. Choose an entrepreneur in your community and interview him or her. Does the company have a strategic plan? A mission statement? Why or why not? What does the owner consider the company's strengths and weaknesses to be? What opportunities and threats does the owner perceive? What image is the owner trying to create for the business? Has the effort been successful? (Do you agree?) Which of the generic competitive strategies is the company following? Who are the company's primary competitors? How does the owner rate his or her chances for success in the future (use a low [1] to high [10] scale). When you have completed the interview, use the evaluation questionnaire (1 = low to 10 = high) to rate the company's strategic orientation. Compare your evaluation with other classmates. What, if any, generalizations can you draw from the interview?

Chapter 5

Forms of Business Ownership and Franchising

- Explaining the advantages and disadvantages of the three major forms of business ownership
- Discussing the advantages and disadvantages of the S corporation
- Describing the three types of franchising
- Explaining the benefits and drawbacks of buying a franchise
- Discussing the right way to buy a franchise
- Outlining the major trends in franchising

CHAPTER 15

franchising

Getting Personal with JOSEPH KEELEY

Currently in my iPod

Michael Buble

Hardest part of getting funding

Outside pressures for return

My advice for new entrepreneurs

Be innovative, be nimble

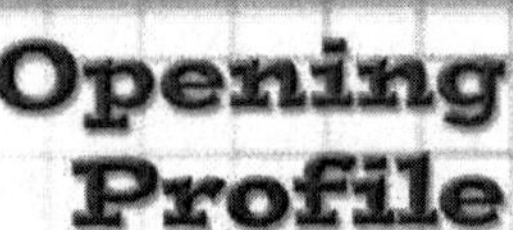

College Nannies & Tutors:

Franchising as a Form of Business Ownership and Growth

Joseph Keeley grew up in a small town in North Dakota. After graduating from high school in 2000, he moved to St. Paul, Minnesota, to attend St. Thomas University. One of Keeley's passions was hockey, which he fulfilled as a member of St. Thomas's varsity hockey team. While playing hockey, he became acquainted with a couple that had two young boys and a girl. As the summer following his freshman year approached, the couple asked him if he'd be interesting in watching their kids as a full-time summer job. Keeley jumped at the chance. While his two roommates spent the summer digging pools for a local contractor, Keeley engaged in fun activities with the children, and acted as their nanny and role model.

The summer job got Keeley to thinking about how young kids need positive role models and how college students are uniquely capable of filling that role. The idea was so compelling that during his sophomore year he launched a company called Summer College Nannies. Matching college students with families that needed part-time or full-time nanny services was the firm's core service. Early on he viewed himself more as a matchmaker than as a potential franchisor, and viewed his business primarily as a way to earn extra cash. But as time went on, two things struck Keeley. First, rather than just a means of earning extra money, he started to see real potential in the college nanny idea. For many parents, there wasn't a service available to help them find a safe and reliable nanny. He also liked the idea of making a positive difference in the lives of families and young children. Second, he found that having an actual business to work on enhanced his classroom experiences. "I feel I had 10 times the education that anyone else did because I had a working, living project everyday," Keeley said, reflecting on this point.[1]

JOSEPH KEELEY
Founder, College Nannies & Tutors
BS in Entrepreneurship
St. Thomas University, 2003

As the business picked up steam, St. Thomas provided Keeley with office space, and he turned Summer College Nannies into a self-made internship. To get advice, he started dropping in on St. Thomas entrepreneurship professors, who urged him to enroll in the entrepreneurship program—which he did. As time went on, Keeley entered and won several business plan competitions with the Summer College Nannies business idea. He also won the 2003 Global Student Entrepreneurship Award, which is presented by the Entrepreneurs' Organization and included a

What I do when I'm not working

Water & snow ski, ice hockey, enjoy time with my baby daughter and wife

First entrepreneurial experience

Custom car washing service

My biggest surprise as an entrepreneur

The many areas that one must be good at or willing to learn

After studying this chapter you should be ready to:

LEARNING

Objectives

1. Explain franchising and how it differs from other forms of business ownership.
2. Describe the differences between a product and trademark franchise and a business format franchise.
3. Explain the differences among an individual franchise agreement, an area franchise agreement, and a master franchise agreement.
4. Describe the advantages of establishing a franchise system as a means of firm growth.
5. Identify the rules of thumb for determining when franchising is an appropriate form of growth for a particular business.
6. Discuss the factors to consider in determining if owning a franchise is a good fit for a particular person.
7. Identify the costs associated with buying a franchise.
8. Discuss the advantages and disadvantages of buying a franchise.
9. Identify the common mistakes franchise buyers make.
10. Describe the purpose of the Uniform Franchise Offering Circular.

$20,000 prize. At the awards ceremony, Keeley met Peter Lytle, an angel investor and well-known Minneapolis entrepreneur. Although he had interviewed for traditional jobs, by this time Keeley had decided that following graduation he would devote his time and energy to his own business venture. Lytle was so impressed with Keeley and his business idea that he offered to invest, and Keeley accepted the offer. At this point, Lytle helped Keeley expand his vision for the business to include tutors, and College Nannies & Tutors was born.

Following graduation, the money Lytle invested provided Keeley the time and resources to more fully develop the College Nannies & Tutors business idea. The company started to generate some buzz, primarily through media coverage and word of mouth. One of the things that interested the media was the fact the Keeley, a male and a recent college graduate, was starting a company in an industry—childcare—that traditionally, females dominated. The first College Nannies & Tutors center was opened in Wayzata, a suburb of Minneapolis. In college, Keeley took a class in franchising, and as Keeley and Lytle fine-tuned their business idea over 2 long years of testing and planning, it became clear that College Nannies & Tutors was franchiseable. Interestingly, part of the firm's franchising process included proprietary ways for screening nannies through background checks, interviews, and psychological assessments and matching them with families. Commenting on the suitability of College Nannies & Tutors for franchising, Keeley remarked, "[And] there's value there as a franchise because we've figured it out. You (a potential franchisee) don't have to go through the learning curve."[2]

College Nannies & Tutors currently has seven franchise locations in three states, including Minnesota, Arizona, and Pennsylvania. The goal is to have 200 locations in 5 years.[3]

As with College Nannies & Tutors, many retail and service organizations find franchising to be an attractive form of business ownership and growth. In some industries, such as restaurants, hotels, and automobile service, franchising is a dominant business ownership form. Franchising is less common in other industries, although franchising is now being used in industries as diverse as Internet service providers, furniture restoration, cellular services, and senior care.

There are instances in which franchising is not appropriate. For example, new technologies are typically not introduced through franchise systems, particularly if the technology is proprietary or complex. Why? Because franchising, by its very nature, involves the sharing of knowledge between a franchisor and its franchisees, and this, in large franchise organizations, can involve thousands of people. The inventors of new technologies typically involve as few people as possible in the process of rolling out their new products or services because they want to keep their trade secrets secret. They typically reserve their new technologies for their own use or license them to a relatively small number of companies, with strict confidentiality agreements in place.[4]

Still, franchising is a common method of business expansion and is growing in popularity. In 1950, fewer than 100 franchisors existed in the United States. Today, there are roughly 2,500 franchise systems in the United States, collectively accounting for about one-third of all retail sales.[5] You can even go to a Web site (www.franchising.com) to examine the array of franchises available for potential entrepreneurs to consider. This Web site groups franchising opportunities by type (e.g., automotive, personal services, specialty retail, and so forth) as well as the total number of dollars a franchisee must invest to get started. These categorizations highlight the breadth of franchising opportunities now available for consideration.

Unfortunately, not all the news about franchising is positive. Because many franchise systems operate in competitive industries and grow quickly, the failure rate is relatively high. It is estimated that three-quarters of all franchise systems fail within 12 years of their founding.[6] Plus, despite its proliferation, franchising is a relatively poorly understood form of business ownership and growth. While most students and entrepreneurs generally know what franchising is and what it entails, franchising has many subtle aspects that can be learned only through experience or careful study.

We begin this chapter, which is dedicated to franchising as an important potential path to entrepreneurship and subsequent venture growth, with a description of franchising and when it is appropriate to use franchising. We then explore setting up a franchise system from the franchisor's perspective and buying a franchise from the franchisee's point of view. Next, we look at the legal aspects of franchising. We close this chapter by considering a few additional topics related to the successful use of franchising.

What Is Franchising and How Does It Work?

Franchising is a form of business organization in which a firm that already has a successful product or service (**franchisor**) licenses its trademark and method of doing businesses to other businesses (**franchisees**) in exchange for an initial franchise fee and an ongoing royalty.[7] Some franchisors are established firms; others are first-time enterprises being launched by entrepreneurs (this is the case for College Nannies & Tutors). This section explores the origins of franchising and how franchising works.

LEARNING Objective

1. Explain franchising and how it differs from other forms of business ownership.

What Is Franchising?

The word *franchise* comes from an old dialect of French and means "privilege" or "freedom." Franchising has a long history. In the Middle Ages, kings and lords granted franchises to specific individuals or groups to hunt on their land or to conduct certain forms of commerce. In the 1840s, breweries in Germany granted franchises to certain taverns to be the exclusive distributors of their beer for the region. Shortly after the U.S. Civil War, the Singer Sewing Machine Company began granting distribution franchises for its sewing machines and pioneered the use of written franchise agreements. Many of the most familiar franchises in the United States, including Kentucky Fried Chicken (1952), McDonald's (1955), Burger King (1955), Midas Muffler (1956), and H&R Block (1958), started in the post–World War II era of the 1940s and 1950s.

The franchise organization Comfort Keepers demonstrates how franchises are started. A year before the company was founded, Kristina Clum, a registered nurse, noticed that her parents were having trouble with ordinary daily chores. She wanted someone to come into their home to help them but was unable to find people willing to do so. So Kristina and her husband Jerry founded a business dedicated to helping seniors cope with everyday nonmedical tasks, such as meal preparation, light housekeeping, grocery shopping, laundry, and errands. The first Comfort Keepers office was opened in Springfield, Ohio, in March 1998, and the second was opened in Dayton a year later.

Smoothie franchises such as Planet Smoothie and Smoothie King are examples of business format franchises. Smoothie King has certainly used this approach to its advantage. It operates more than 425 locations in 38 states and 14 foreign countries and opens new stores on a weekly basis in the United States.

Comfort Keepers is a timely idea that addresses a need for a particular target market. As we've discussed in earlier chapters, having a solid business idea is critical to achieving firm growth. In mid-2005, there were 36.8 million people in the United States over the age of 65. That number is expected to exceed 70 million over the next two decades. The services offered by Comfort Keepers may provide some seniors the option of staying in their homes as opposed to entering more costly assisted living centers.[8] In August 1999, the company began franchising and by 2006 had over 540 franchise outlets. At a total franchise investment cost of between $44,000 and $66,000, Comfort Keepers claimed that it was one of the least expensive franchises available to investors/entrepreneurs.[9]

The Comfort Keepers business idea lends itself to franchising because the company has a good trademark and a good business method. Moreover, because the nature of the business keeps the cost of starting a Comfort Keepers franchise relatively low, there is a substantial pool of people available to purchase the franchise. For Comfort Keepers and its franchisees, franchising is a win–win proposition. Comfort Keepers wins because it is able to use its franchisees' money to quickly grow its business and strengthen its brand. The franchisees win because they are able to start a business in a growing industry relatively inexpensively and benefit by adopting the Comfort Keepers trademark and method of doing business.

How Does Franchising Work?

There is nothing magical about franchising. It is a form of growth that allows a business to get its products or services to market through the efforts of business partners or "franchisees." As described previously, a franchise is an agreement between a franchisor (the parent company, such as College Nannies & Tutors or Comfort Keepers) and a franchisee (an individual or firm that is willing to pay the franchisor a fee for the right to sell its product, service, and/or business method).[10] Subway, for example, is a very successful franchise system. The franchisor (Subway, Inc.) provides the rights to individual businesspersons (the local franchisees) to use the Subway trademark and business methods. The franchisees, in turn, pay Subway a franchise fee and an ongoing royalty for these privileges and agree to operate their Subway restaurants according to Subway, Inc.'s standards.

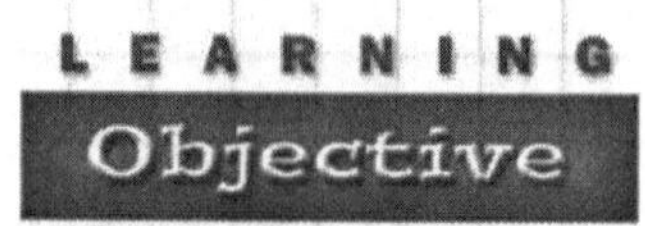

2. Describe the differences between a product and trademark franchise and a business format franchise.

There are two distinctly different types of franchise systems: the product and trademark franchise and the business format franchise. A **product and trademark franchise** is an arrangement under which the franchisor grants to the franchisee the right to buy its products and use its trade name. This approach typically connects a single manufacturer with a network of dealers or distributors. For example, General Motors has established a network of dealers that sell GM cars and use the GM trademark in their advertising and promotions. Similarly, British Petroleum (BP) has established a network of franchisee-owned gasoline stations to distribute BP gasoline. Product and trademark franchisees are typically permitted to operate in a fairly autonomous manner. The parent company, such as GM or BP, is generally concerned more with maintaining the integrity of its products than with monitoring the day-to-day activities of its dealers or station owners. Other examples of product and trademark franchise systems include agricultural machinery dealers, soft-drink bottlers, and beer distributorships. Rather than obtaining a royalty or franchise fee, the product and trademark franchisor obtains the majority of its income from selling its products to its dealers or distributors at a markup.

The second type of franchise, the **business format franchise**, is by far the more popular approach to franchising and is more commonly used by entrepreneurs and entrepreneurial ventures. In a business format franchise, the franchisor provides a formula for doing business to the franchisee along with training, advertising, and other forms of assistance. Fast-food restaurants, convenience stores, fitness centers, and tax preparation services are well-known examples of business format franchisees. While a business format franchise provides a franchisee a formula for conducting business, it can also be very rigid and demanding. For example, fast-food restaurants such as McDonald's and Burger King teach their franchisees every detail of how to run their restaurants, from how many seconds to cook french fries to the exact words their employees should use when they greet customers (such as "Will this be dining in or carry out?"). Business format franchisors obtain the majority of their revenues from their franchisees in the form of royalties and franchise fees.

For both product and trademark franchises and business format franchises, the franchisor–franchisee relationship takes one of three forms of a franchise agreement, which are depicted in Figure 15.1. The most common type of franchise arrangement is an individual franchise agreement. An **individual franchise agreement** involves the sale of a single franchise for a specific location. For example, an individual may purchase a CD Warehouse franchise to be constructed and operated at 901 Pearl Street in Boulder, Colorado. An **area franchise agreement** allows a franchisee to own and operate a specific number of outlets in a particular geographic area. For example, a franchisee may purchase the rights to open five CD Warehouse franchises within the city limits of Augusta, Georgia. This is a very popular franchise arrangement, because in most cases it gives the franchisee exclusive rights for a given area. Finally, a **master franchise agreement** is similar to an area franchise agreement, with one major

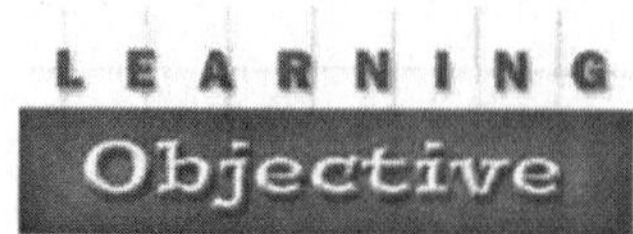

3. Explain the differences among an individual franchise agreement, an area franchise agreement, and a master franchise agreement.

FIGURE 15.1

Different Types of Franchise Systems

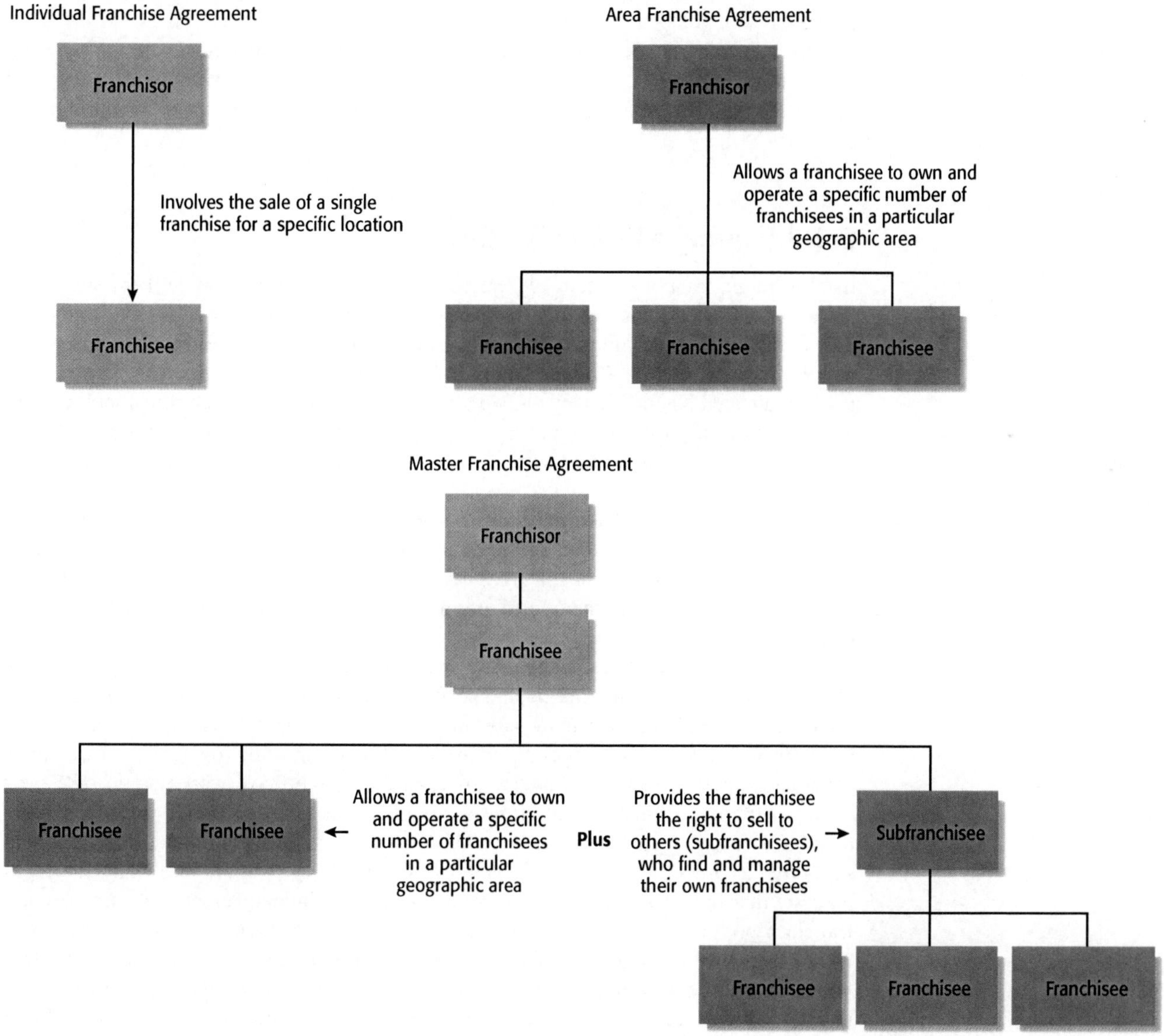

Individual Franchise Agreement

Franchisor

Involves the sale of a single franchise for a specific location

Franchisee

Area Franchise Agreement

Franchisor

Allows a franchisee to own and operate a specific number of franchisees in a particular geographic area

Franchisee | Franchisee | Franchisee

Master Franchise Agreement

Franchisor

Franchisee

Franchisee | Franchisee ← Allows a franchisee to own and operate a specific number of franchisees in a particular geographic area **Plus** Provides the franchisee the right to sell to others (subfranchisees), who find and manage their own franchisees → Subfranchisee

Franchisee | Franchisee | Franchisee

difference. A master franchisee, in addition to having the right to open and operate a specific number of locations in a particular area, also has the right to offer and sell the franchise to other people in its area. For example, Barnie's Coffee & Tea is a coffee restaurant franchise. The company sells master franchise agreements that provide a master franchisee the right to open a certain number of Barnie's Coffee & Tea outlets in a defined geographic area. After its own outlets have been opened, the master franchisee can then sell the rights to open additional Barnie's Coffee & Tea locations in the same area to other individuals. The people who buy franchises from master franchisees are typically called **subfranchisees**.

An individual who owns and operates more than one outlet of the same franchisor, whether through an area or a master franchise agreement, is called a **multiple-unit franchisee**. Multiple-unit franchisees are common in both small and large franchise chains, and this source of growth far outpaces the units added by new franchisees in most franchise organizations.[11] For the franchisee, there are advantages and disadvantages to multiple-unit franchising. By owning more than one unit, a multiple-unit franchisee can capture economies of scale and reduce its administrative overhead per unit of sale. The disadvantages of multiple-unit franchising are that the franchisor takes more risk and makes a deeper commitment to a single franchisor. In general, franchisors encourage multiple-unit franchising. By selling an additional franchise to an existing franchisee, a franchisor can grow its business without adding to the total number of franchisees with whom it must maintain a relationship to conduct its business.

An increasingly common practice among franchise organizations is to partner with one another through co-branding arrangements to increase systemwide sales and decrease costs. This practice is discussed in the "Partnering for Success" feature for this chapter.

Establishing a Franchise System

Establishing a franchise system should be approached carefully and deliberately. While the process is a familiar one to a company such as McDonald's, which as of mid-2006 had 18,420 franchised units worldwide, franchising is quite an unfamiliar process to new businesses, such as College Nannies & Tutors and Comfort Keepers. Franchising is a complicated business endeavor, which means that an entrepreneur must look closely at all of its aspects before deciding to franchise. Indeed, franchising often involves the managerially demanding tasks of training, supporting, supervising, and nurturing franchisees.

An entrepreneur should also be aware that over the years a number of fraudulent franchise organizations have come and gone and left financially ruined franchisees in their wake. Because of this, franchising is a fairly heavily regulated form of business expansion. Even with this regulation, though, caution is in order for those pursuing franchising as a business opportunity.

Despite the challenges, franchising is a popular form of growth. It is particularly attractive to new firms in retailing and services because it helps firms grow quickly and alleviates the challenge of raising substantial amounts of money. There is some anecdotal evidence, however, that many companies are hasty in putting together their franchise programs and as a result do a poorer job than they might have were they to take their time.[12] Although franchising is often touted as an easy way to rapidly expand a business, an effective franchise system needs to be as consciously initiated, managed, and supported as any other form of business expansion.[13] An example of a franchise organization that has gotten off to a good start via prudent management is Which Wich, a franchise with a new sandwich concept. Which Wich's unique twist is that customers "build their own sandwich" by checking off the ingredients they want on a paper bag with a Sharpie as they enter the restaurant. The company opened its first 12 restaurants in 2004 but didn't sell a franchise until 15 months later, preferring to wait until all the

partnering for success

Boosting Sales and Reducing Expenses Through Co-branding

Have you ever stopped at a gas station and caught a quick lunch of an Arbys or a Blimpie sub sandwich inside? Or have you ever noticed that Baskin-Robbins and Dunkin Donuts often share the same building? If either of these two scenarios applies to you, then you have witnessed co-branding first hand.

Co-branding takes place when two or more businesses are grouped together. It is becoming increasingly common among franchise organizations that are looking for new ways to increase sales and reduce expenses. As we describe next, there are two primary types of co-branding arrangement that apply to franchise organizations.

Two Franchises Operating Side by Side

The first type of co-branding arrangement involves two or more franchises operating side by side in the same building or leased space. This type of arrangement typically involves a franchise like a donut shop that is busiest in the morning and a taco restaurant that is the busiest at lunch and dinner. By locating side by side, these businesses can increase their sales by picking up some business from the traffic generated by their co-branding partner and can cut costs by sharing rent and other expenses.

Side-by-side co-branding arrangements are not restricted to restaurants. Sometimes the benefit arises from the complementary nature of the products involved, rather than time of day. For example, a franchise that sells exercise equipment could operate side by side with a business that sells vitamins. By locating side by side, these two businesses could realize the same types of benefits as the donut shop and the taco restaurant.

Two Franchises Occupying the Exact Same Space

The second type of co-branding arrangement involves two franchises occupying essentially the same space. For example, it is increasingly common to see sub shops inside gasoline stations and other retail outlets. The relationship is meant to benefit both parties. The sub shop benefits by opening another location without incurring the cost of constructing a freestanding building or leasing expensive shopping mall space. The gasoline station benefits by having a quality branded food partner to help it attract road traffic and by collecting lease income. Having a sub shop inside its store also helps a gasoline station become a "destination stop" for regular customers rather than simply another gas station serving passing cars.

Important Considerations

Although co-branding can be an excellent way for franchise organizations to partner for success, before a firm enters into a co-branding relationship, it should consider the following three questions:

- Will the co-branding arrangement maintain or strengthen my brand image?
- Do I have adequate control over how my partner will display or use my brand?
- Are their tangible benefits associated with attaching my brand to my partner's brand? For example, will my partner's brand have a positive effect on my brand and actually increase my sales?

If the answer to each of these questions is yes, than a co-branding arrangement may be a very effective way for a franchise organization to boosts sales and reduce expenses.

Questions for Critical Thinking

1. Do you think that co-branding will continue to gain momentum, or do you think it is a fad they will wane in terms of its popularity? Explain your answer.
2. What are the potential downsides of co-branding? What might make a franchise hesitant to enter into a co-branding relationship with another franchise organization?
3. Consider the College Nannies & Tutor's Opening Profile at the beginning of the chapter. Suggest some co-branding relationships that College Nannies & Tutors might consider forming.
4. Do some research in order to identify at least two additional examples of each of the two types of co-branding relationships just described. Explain how each co-branding relationship benefits the parties involved.
5. Make a list of the types of businesses that might work well together in a co-branding relationship. Several initial examples include: (1) quick oil change and tire store, (2) bakery and a coffee house, (3) and a florist and candy store.

kinks were worked out of its approach. Which Wich now has about 20 franchise outlets and is growing.[14]

Now let's look more closely at the issues to consider when an entrepreneur is trying to decide if franchising is an appropriate approach to growing a business.

When to Franchise

Retail firms grow when two things happen: first, when the attractiveness of a firm's products or services become well known, whether it is a new restaurant or a fitness center, and, second, when a firm has the financial capability to build the outlets needed to satisfy the demand for its products or services.

There are at least two options firms have as a means to grow. Building company-owned outlets is one of these options. However, this choice presents a company with the challenge of raising the money to fund its expansion. As discussed in Chapter 10, this option is typically pursued through debt, investment capital, or earnings, none of which is easy to achieve for a start-up venture.

Franchising is a second growth alternative available to firms. Franchising is perhaps especially attractive to young firms in that the majority of the money needed for expansion comes from the franchisees. Franchising is appropriate when a firm has a strong or potentially strong trademark, a well-designed business model, and a desire to grow. A franchise system will ultimately fail if the franchisee's brand doesn't create value for customers and its business model is flawed or poorly developed.

In some instances, franchising is simply not appropriate. For example, franchising works for Burger King but would not work for Wal-Mart. While Burger King has a large number of franchise outlets, each individual outlet is relatively small and has a limited menu, and policies and procedures can be written to cover almost any contingency. In contrast, although Wal-Mart is similar to Burger King in that it, too, has a strong trademark and thousands of outlets, Wal-Mart stores are much larger, more expensive to build, and more complex to run than Burger King restaurants. It would be nearly impossible for Wal-Mart to find an adequate number of qualified people who would have the financial capital and expertise to open and successfully operate a Wal-Mart store.

Steps to Franchising a Business

Let's assume that as an entrepreneur you have decided to use franchising as a means of growing your venture. What steps should you take to develop a franchise system? As illustrated in Figure 15.2, entrepreneurs should take nine steps in order to successfully set up a franchise system.

Step 1 **Develop a franchise business plan:** The franchise business plan should follow the format of a conventional business plan that we discussed in Chapter 4 and should fully describe the rationale for franchising the business and act as a blueprint for rolling out the franchise operation.

Step 2 **Get professional advice:** Before going too far, a potential franchisor should seek advice from a qualified franchise attorney, consultant, or certified public accountant. If the business is not realistically franchisable, then a qualified professional can save a potential franchisor a lot of time, money, and frustration by urging that the process be stopped. If the business is franchisable, then it is advisable to get professional advice to help direct the entire process.

Step 3 **Conduct an intellectual property audit:** As we discussed in Chapter 12, this step is necessary to determine the intellectual property a company owns and to ensure that the property is properly registered and protected. All original written, audio, and visual material, including operating manuals, training videos, advertising brochures, audiotapes, and similar matter, should be afforded copyright protection. If a firm has a unique business model that includes a unique business method, it should consider obtaining a patent for its

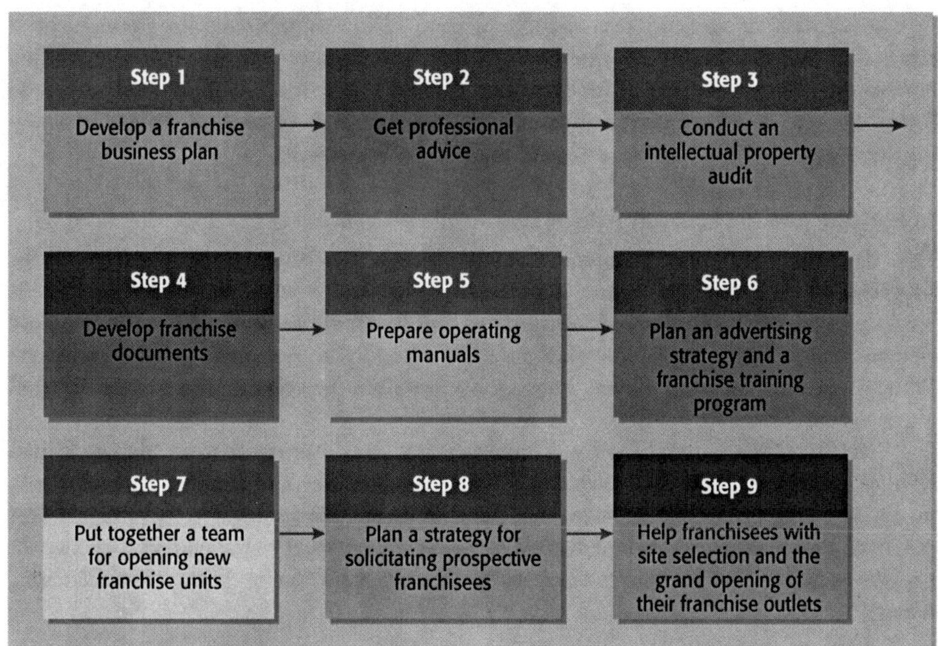

FIGURE 15.2

Nine Steps in Setting Up a Franchise System

business method. These protective measures are vital because once a company begins franchising, its trademarks and business model and any unique business methods are disseminated, making them more visible to customers and competitors. In addition, a franchisor should make sure that its trademark is not infringing on the trademark of any other firm.

Step 4 Develop franchise documents: We will discuss the documents that are required to franchise a business later in this chapter. Here, we can note that at the beginning of the franchise evaluation process, a prospective franchisor should prepare the Uniform Franchise Offering Circular (this circular is explained in detail later in this chapter) and the Franchise Agreement. A franchise attorney can provide specific information regarding the content and format of these documents.

Step 5 Prepare operating manuals: Businesses that are suitable for franchising typically have a polished business system that can be fairly easily taught to qualified franchisees. The franchisor should prepare manuals that document all aspects of its business model.

Step 6 Plan an advertising strategy and a franchisee-training program: Prospective franchisees will want to see an advertising strategy and a franchisee-training program in place. The scope of each program should match the speed at which the franchisor wants to grow its business.

Step 7 Put together a team for opening new franchise units: A team should be developed and prepared to help new franchisees open their franchise units. The team should be well trained and equipped to provide the franchisee a broad range of training and guidance.

Step 8 Plan a strategy for soliciting prospective franchisees: There are many channels available to franchisors to solicit and attract potential franchisees. Franchise trade fairs, newspaper ads, franchise publications, and Internet advertising are examples of these channels.

Step 9 Help franchisees with site selection and the grand opening of their franchise outlet: Location is very important to most businesses, so a franchisor should be heavily involved in the site selection of its franchisees' outlets. The franchisor should also help the franchisee with the grand opening of the franchise outlet.

Along with the specific steps shown in Figure 15.2, it is important for a franchisor to remember that the quality of relationships that it maintains with its franchisees often defines the ultimate success of the franchise system. It is to the franchisor's advantage to follow through on all promises and to establish an exemplary reputation. This is an ongoing commitment that a franchisor should make to its franchisees.

Selecting and Developing Effective Franchisees

The franchisor's ability to select and develop effective franchisees strongly influences the degree to which a franchise system is successful. For most systems, the ideal franchisee is someone who has good ideas and suggestions but is willing to work within the franchise system's rules. Bold, aggressive entrepreneurs typically do not make good franchisees. Franchisees must be team players to properly fit within the context of a successful franchise system.

Once franchisees are selected, it is important that franchisors work to develop their franchisees' potential. Table 15.1 contains a list of the qualities that franchisors look for in prospective franchisees and the steps that franchisors can take to develop their franchisees' potential. Personality tests are one method for screening prospective franchisees that is growing in popularity. This method is discussed in this chapter's "Savvy Entrepreneurial Firm" feature.

Advantages and Disadvantages of Establishing a Franchise System

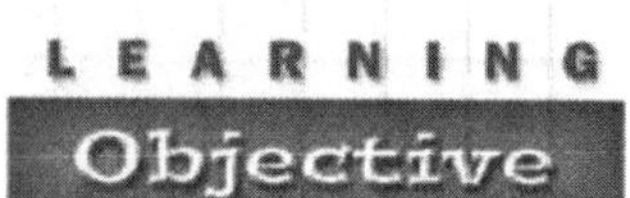

4. Describe the advantages of establishing a franchise system as a means of firm growth.

There are two primary advantages to franchising. First, early in the life of an organization, capital is typically scarce, and rapid growth is needed to achieve brand recognition and economies of scale. Franchising helps an organization grow quickly because franchisees provide the majority of the capital.[15] For example, if Comfort Keepers were growing via company-owned outlets rather than franchising, it would probably have only a handful of outlets rather than the more than 540 it has today. Many franchisors even admit that they would have rather grown through company-owned stores but that the capital requirements needed to grow their firms dictated franchising. This sentiment is affirmed by an executive at Hardee's, who wrote the following about the growth of this fast-food chain:

> Hardee's would have preferred not to have franchised a single location. We prefer company-owned locations. But due to the heavy capital investment required, we could only expand company-owned locations to a certain degree—from there we had to stop. Each operation represents an investment in excess of $100,000; therefore, we entered the franchise business.[16]

TABLE 15.1 Selecting and Developing Effective Franchisees

Qualities to Look for in Prospective Franchisees

- Good work ethic
- Ability to follow instructions
- Ability to operate with minimal supervision
- Team oriented
- Experience in the industry in which the franchise competes
- Adequate financial resources and a good credit history
- Ability to make suggestions without becoming confrontational or upset if the suggestions are not adopted
- Represents the franchisor in a positive manner

Ways Franchisors Can Develop the Potential of Their Franchisees

- Provide mentoring that supersedes routine training
- Keep operating manuals up-to-date
- Keep product, services, and business systems up-to-date
- Solicit input from franchisees to reinforce their importance in the larger system
- Encourage franchisees to develop a franchise association
- Maintain the franchise system's integrity

savvy entrepreneurial firm

Using Personality Tests to Identify High-Potential Franchisees

An increasingly common tool that franchisors are using to screen potential franchisees is personality tests. The idea is that each franchise system is unique, and people with certain personality characteristics represent the best fit for a particular franchise organization.

Here's how the process works. A franchisor, like College Nannies & Tutors or Comfort Keepers, contracts with a personality assessment company to develop a profile of an ideal franchisee. The profile is usually developed by assessing the personality characteristics of the franchisor's most successful franchisees. Potential franchisees are then administered a personality test, to show how they compare to the chain's ideal franchisee. There are no value judgments made in regard to a person's character. Instead, the tests are designed to predict how well a person will fit into a particular franchise system. For example, a person may be found to be "meticulous and reserved," which might be an ideal fit for a tax preparation service like Jackson Hewitt but a poor fit for a day care or a fitness franchise like Curves. Some tests also assess how a person's personality matches with the management characteristics that are required to lead a specific franchise. For instance, a person who is found to be "aggressive, assertive, ambitious, and goal oriented" may be an ideal candidate for a new franchise system that needs to prove the worth of its product to a skeptical clientele.

Despite their growing popularity, personality tests have their skeptics. Stephen Spinelli, a professor at Babson College and the author of a book on franchising, says, "I've never seen any academic analysis that shows that they [personality tests] work." Others worry that the tests will cause franchisors to pick franchisees who all resemble each other—missing out on the advantages of diversity. Commenting on this issue, Bob Kreisberg, president of Opus Marketing, said, "Franchise companies that say, 'We have one culture. If you don't fit, we don't want you,' are missing out on the advantages that different people bring to the table."

Still, there is mounting anecdotal evidence that personality tests are an effective tool for qualifying high-potential franchisees. In addition, franchisors are increasingly trying to become savvier in selecting franchisees, to maximize the potential of every franchise outlet. The International Franchise Association estimates that 30 percent to 40 percent of the group's 1,000 franchise members now use personality tests, and the number is growing.

Questions for Critical Thinking

1. If you were a franchisor, would you use personality tests to screen prospective franchisees? If you were a prospective franchisee, would you feel comfortable taking the type of test described here? Explain your answers.
2. In your judgment, how compelling are arguments against using personality tests to screen potential franchisees?
3. If you were a franchisor, what methods, other than personality tests, would you use to screen prospective franchisees? How important do you think the process of selecting franchisees is for the ultimate success of a franchise system? Make your answers as thoughtful and substantive as possible.
4. Do some research to determine the attrition rate for the average franchisee. In your view, what are the major factors contributing to franchise failures?

Sources: J. Bennett, "What It Takes to Be a Successful Franchisee," *StartupJournal*, www.startupjournal.com (accessed June 1, 2006); J. Bennett, "Do You Have What It Takes?" *The Wall Street Journal*, September 19, 2005, R11.

Second, a management concept called **agency theory**, which we discussed in Chapter 13, argues that for organizations with multiple units (such as restaurant chains), it is more effective for the units to be run by franchisees than by managers who run company-owned stores. The theory is that managers, because they are usually paid a salary, may not be as committed to the success of their individual units as franchisees, who are in effect the owners of the units they manage.[17]

The primary disadvantage of franchising is that an organization allows others to profit from its trademark and business model. For example, each time Comfort Keepers sells a franchise it gets a $23,200 franchise fee and an ongoing royalty, which is 3 to 5 percent of gross sales. However, if Comfort Keepers had provided its service itself in the same location, it would be getting 100 percent of the gross sales and net profits from the location. This is the main reason some organizations that are perfectly suitable for franchising grow through company-owned stores rather than franchising. An example is Darden Restaurants Inc., the parent company of Red Lobster, Olive Garden, Bahama Breeze, Smokey Bones BBQ, and Seasons 52. With over 1,400 locations, this firm is the world's largest publicly held casual dining restaurant chain.[18] All of Darden's units are company owned. Jamba Juice is another company that is suitable for franchising but does not have any franchise outlets. A more complete list of the advantages and disadvantages of franchising as a means of business expansion is provided in Table 15.2.

5. Identify the rules of thumb for determining when franchising is an appropriate form of growth for a particular business.

When a company decides to investigate franchising as a means of growth, it should ensure that it and its product or service meet several criteria. Businesses that fail to satisfy these criteria are less likely to make effective franchise systems. Before deciding to franchise, a firm should consider the following:

- ***The uniqueness of its product or service:*** The business's product or service should be unique along some dimension that customers value. Businesses with a unique product or service typically have the best potential to expand.

TABLE 15.2 Advantages and Disadvantages of Franchising as a Method of Business Expansion

Advantages	Disadvantages
Rapid, low-cost market expansion. Because franchisees provide most of the cost of expansion, the franchisor can expand the size of its business fairly rapidly.	**Profit sharing.** By selling franchises instead of operating company-owned stores, franchisors share the profits derived from their proprietary products or services with their franchisees. For example, before being acquired by FedEx, Kinko's did not sell franchises, allowing it to retain all its profits.
Income from franchise fees and royalties. By collecting franchise fees, the franchisor gets a fairly quick return on the proprietary nature of its products/services and business model. The franchisor also receives ongoing royalties from its franchisees without incurring substantial risk.	**Loss of control.** It is typically more difficult for a franchisor to control its franchisees than it is for a company to control its employees. Franchisees, despite the rules governing the franchise system, still often view themselves as independent businesspeople.
Franchisee motivation. Because franchisees put their personal capital at risk, they are highly motivated to make their franchise outlets successful. In contrast, the managers of company-owned outlets typically do not have their own capital at risk. As a result, these managers may not be prone to work as hard as franchisees or be as attentive to cost savings.	**Friction with franchisees.** A common complaint of franchisors is dealing with the friction that often develops between franchisors and franchisees. Friction can develop over issues such as the payment of fees, hours of operation, caveats in the franchise agreement, and surprise inspections.
Access to ideas and suggestions. Franchisees represent a source of intellectual capital and often make suggestions to their franchisors. By incorporating these ideas into their business model, franchisors can in effect leverage the ideas and suggestions of their individual franchisees.	**Managing growth.** Franchisors that are in growing industries and have a strong trademark often grow quickly. Although this might seem like an advantage, rapid growth can be difficult to manage. A franchisor provides each of its franchisees a number of services, such as site selection and employee training. If a franchise system is growing rapidly, the franchisor will have to continually add personnel to its own staff to properly support its growing number of franchisees.
Cost savings. Franchisees share many of the franchisors' expenses, such as the cost of regional and national advertising.	**Differences in required business skills.** The business skills that made a franchisor successful in the original business are typically not the same skills needed to manage a franchise system. For example, Sam Jones may be a very effective owner/manager of a seafood restaurant. That does not necessarily mean, however, that he will be an effective manager of a franchise system if he decided to franchise his seafood restaurant concept.
Increased buying power. Franchisees provide franchisors increased buying power by enlarging the size of their business, allowing them to purchase larger quantities of products and services when buying those items.	**Legal expenses.** Many states have specific laws pertaining to franchising. As a result, if a franchisor sells franchises in multiple states, legal expenses can be high to properly interpret and comply with each state's laws. Unfortunately, from the franchisor's point of view, some of the toughest laws are in the most populated states.

- ***The consistent profitability of the firm:*** The business should be consistently profitable, and the future profitability of the business should be fairly easy to predict. When developing a franchise system, a company should have several prototype outlets up and running to test and ensure the viability of the business idea. Remember, a franchisee is supposed to be buying a way of doing business (in the form of a business model) that is "proven"—at least to a certain extent. Franchisors that learn how to run their businesses through the trial and error of their franchisees have typically franchised their businesses prematurely (especially from the franchisees' point of view).
- ***The firm's year-round profitability:*** The business should be profitable year-round, not only during specific seasons. For example, a lawn and garden care franchise in North Dakota should be set up to provide the franchisee supplemental products and services to sell during off-peak seasons. Otherwise, owning the franchise may not be an attractive substitute for a full-time job. This issue is particularly problematic for some ice cream and smoothie franchises in northern states, which experience a significant decline in sales during winter months.
- ***The degree of refinement of the firm's business systems:*** The systems and procedures for operating the business should be polished and the procedures documented in written form. The systems and procedures should also be fairly easy to teach to qualified candidates.
- ***The clarity of the business proposition:*** The business proposition should be crystal clear so that prospective franchisees fully understand the business proposition to which they are committing. The relationship between the franchisor and the franchisee should be completely open, and communication between them should be candid.

After determining that the firm satisfies these criteria, the entrepreneur should step back and review all the alternatives for business expansion. No single form of business expansion is the best under all circumstances. For any entrepreneurial venture, the best form of expansion is the one that increases the likelihood that the venture will reach its objectives.

Buying a Franchise

Now let's look at franchising from the franchisee's perspective. Purchasing a franchise is an important business decision involving a substantial financial commitment. Potential franchise owners should strive to be as well informed as possible before purchasing a franchise and should be well aware that it is often legally and financially difficult to exit a franchise relationship. Indeed, an individual franchise opportunity should be meticulously scrutinized. Close scrutiny of a potential franchise opportunity includes activities such as meeting with the franchisor and reading the Uniform Franchise Offering Circular, soliciting legal and financial advice, and talking to former franchisees who have dropped out of the system one is considering. In particularly heavily franchised industries, such as fast food and automobile repair, a prospective franchisee may have 20 or more franchisors from which to make a selection. It is well worth franchisees' time to carefully select the franchisor that best meets their individual needs.[19]

Some franchise organizations are designed to provide their franchisees a part-time, rather than a full-time income, which is attractive to some people. An example is Stroller Strides, a company that gathers new mothers together to do 45-minute power walks with their babies in strollers. The initial franchise fee ranges between $2,500 and $5,000. Owing a Stroller Strides franchise is ideal for a woman who wants to work 2 to 3 hours a day rather than 8 and is passionate about fitness.

6. Discuss the factors to consider in determining if owning a franchise is a good fit for a particular person.

Is Franchising Right for You?

Entrepreneurs should weigh the possibility of purchasing a franchise against the alternatives of buying an existing business or launching their own venture from scratch. Answering the following questions will help determine whether franchising is a good fit for people thinking about starting their own entrepreneurial venture:

- Are you willing to take orders? Franchisors are typically very particular about how their outlets operate. For example, McDonald's and other successful fast-food chains are very strict in terms of their restaurants' appearance and how the unit's food is prepared. Franchising is typically not a good fit for people who like to experiment with their own ideas or are independent minded.
- Are you willing to be part of a franchise "system" rather than an independent businessperson? For example, as a franchisee you may be required to pay into an advertising fund that covers the costs of advertising aimed at regional or national markets rather than the market for your individual outlet. Will it bother you to have someone use your money to develop ads that benefit the "system" rather than only your outlet or store? Are you willing to lose creative control over how your business is promoted?
- How will you react if you make a suggestion to your franchisor and your suggestion is rejected? How will you feel if you are told that your suggestion might work for you but can be put in place only if it works in all parts of the system?
- What are you looking for in a business? How hard do you want to work?
- How willing are you to put your money at risk? How will you feel if your business is operating at a net loss but you still have to pay royalties on your gross income?

None of these questions is meant to suggest that franchising is not an attractive method of business ownership for entrepreneurs. It is important, however, that a potential franchisee be fully aware of the subtleties involved with franchising before purchasing a franchise outlet.

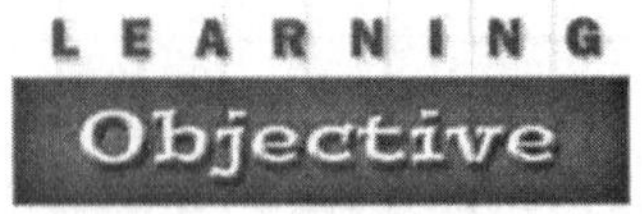

7. Identify the costs associated with buying a franchise.

The Cost of a Franchise

The initial cost of a business format franchise varies, depending on the franchise fee, the capital needed to start the business, and the strength of the franchisor. The average initial investment for about 8 of every 10 franchise units operating in the United States is less than $250,000 (excluding the cost of real estate).[20] Capital costs vary. For example, McDonald's typically provides the land and buildings for each franchisee's unit. In contrast, other organizations require their franchisees to purchase the land, buildings, and equipment needed to run their franchise outlets. Table 15.3 shows the total costs of buying

TABLE 15.3 Initial Costs to the Franchisee of a Sample of Franchise Organizations

Franchise Organization	Year Started Franchising	Company-Owned Units	Franchised Units	Franchise Fee	Ongoing Royalty Fee	Total Initial Investment
Comfort Keepers	1999	0	539	$23,200	3%–5%	$46,000–$69,000
Curves	1995	0	9,468	$35,900	5%–6%	$38,400–$53,500
General Nutrition Centers	1988	2,644	2,108	$35,000	6%	$132,700–$182,000
Gold's Gym	1965	38	679	$25,000	3%	$300,000–$2 million
McDonald's	1955	8,135	22,435	$45,000	12.5% +	$506,000–$1.6 million
Play It Again Sports	1988	0	414	$20,000	5%	$185,000–$354,000
Smoothie King	1988	1	389	$25,000	6%	$91,000–$239,000
Subway	1974	0	24,815	$12,500	8%	$70,000–$220,000

Source: Entrepreneur.com, www.entrepreneur.com (accessed June 1, 2006).

into several franchise organizations. As you can see, the total initial cost ranges from a low of $38,400 for a Curves International franchise to more than $2 million for a Gold's Gym franchise.

Also shown in Table 15.3 is a breakdown of the number of company-owned units and the number of franchise units maintained by different organizations. Company-owned units are managed and operated by company personnel, and there is no franchisee involved. Franchise organizations vary in their philosophies regarding company-owned versus franchised units. As we noted earlier in this chapter, some companies (e.g., Subway) are strictly franchisors and have no company-owned units. Other companies, such as General Nutrition Centers, maintain large numbers of both company-owned and franchised units.

When evaluating the cost of a franchise, prospective franchisees should consider all the costs involved. Franchisors are required by law to disclose all their costs in a document called the Uniform Franchise Offering Circular and send it to the franchisee. (We'll talk about this document in more detail later in this chapter.) To avoid making a hasty judgment, a franchisee may not purchase a franchise for 10 days from the time the circular is received. The following costs are typically associated with buying a business format franchise:[21]

- ***Initial franchise fee:*** The initial franchise fee varies, depending on the franchisor, as shown in Table 15.3.
- ***Capital requirements:*** These costs vary, depending on the franchisor, but may include the cost of buying real estate, the cost of constructing a building, the purchase of initial inventory, and the cost of obtaining a business license. Some franchisors also require a new franchisee to pay a "grand opening" fee for its assistance in opening the business.
- ***Continuing royalty payment:*** In the majority of cases, a franchisee pays a royalty based on a percentage of weekly or monthly gross income. Note that because the fee is typically assessed on gross income rather than net income, a franchisee may have to pay a monthly royalty even if the business is losing money. Royalty fees are usually around 5 percent of gross income.[22]
- ***Advertising fees:*** Franchisees are often required to pay into a national or regional advertising fund, even if the advertisements are directed at goals other than promoting the franchisor's product or service. (For example, advertising could focus on the franchisor's attempt at attracting new franchisees.) Advertising fees are typically less than 3 percent of gross income.
- ***Other fees:*** Other fees may be charged for various activities, including training additional staff, providing management expertise when needed, providing computer assistance, or providing a host of other items or support services.

Although not technically a fee, many franchise organizations sell their franchisee products that they use in their businesses, such as restaurant supplies for a restaurant franchise. The products are often sold at a markup and may be more expensive than those the franchisee could obtain on the open market.

There are some franchise organizations that use a more hybrid fee structure than the pricing formula shown here. An example is Candy Bouquet, which charges an initial franchise fee starting at $3,500 but has no ongoing royalty fee. Instead, the company charges its franchisees a monthly association fee of $35 to $200, which is not tied to store volume.[23]

The most important question a prospective franchisee should consider is whether the fees and royalties charged by a franchisor are consistent with the franchise's value or worth. If they are, then the pricing structure may be fair and equitable. If they are not, then the terms should be renegotiated or the prospective franchisee should look elsewhere.

Finding a Franchise

There are thousands of franchise opportunities available to prospective franchisees. The most critical step in the early stages of investigating franchise opportunities is for the entrepreneur to determine the type of franchise that is the best fit. For example, it is typically unrealistic for someone who is not a mechanic to consider buying a muffler repair franchise. A franchisor teaches a franchisee how to use the contents of a business model, not a trade. Before buying a franchise, a potential franchisee should imagine operating the prospective franchise or, better yet, should spend a period of time working in one of the franchisor's outlets. After working in a print shop for a week, for example, someone who thought she might enjoy running a print shop might find out that she hates it. This type of experience could help avoid making a mistake that is costly both to the franchisee and to the franchisor.

There are many periodicals, Web sites, and associations that provide information about franchise opportunities. Every Thursday, for example, ads for franchise opportunities appear in special sections of *The Wall Street Journal* and *USA Today*. Periodicals featuring franchise opportunities include *Inc.*, *Entrepreneur* (especially the January issues), *Nation's Business*, and franchise-specific magazines such as *The Franchise Handbook* and *Franchise Opportunities Guide*. Prospective franchisees should also consider attending franchise opportunity shows that are held periodically in major U.S. cities and the International Franchise Exposition, which is held annually in Washington, D.C. The U.S. Small Business Administration is another good source of franchise information.

8. Discuss the advantages and disadvantages of buying a franchise.

Because of the risks involved in franchising, the selection of a franchisor should be a careful, deliberate process. One of the smartest moves a potential franchise owner can make is to talk to current franchisees and inquire if they are making money and if they are satisfied with their franchisor. Reflecting on how this approach helped ease her inhibitions about buying a franchise, Carleen Peaper, the owner of a Cruise Planner franchise, said:

> I was really apprehensive about making an investment of my time and money into a franchise, so I e-mailed 50 Cruise Planner agents with a set of questions, asking for honest feedback. Everyone responded. That was a big thing and helped me determine that I wanted to join them.[24]

Table 15.4 contains a list of sample questions to ask a franchisor and some of its current franchisees before investing. Potential entrepreneurs can expect to learn a great deal by studying the answers they receive in response to these questions.

Advantages and Disadvantages of Buying a Franchise

There are two primary advantages to buying a franchise over other forms of business ownership. First, franchising provides an entrepreneur the opportunity to own a business using a tested and refined business model. This attribute lessens the probability of business failure. In addition, the trademark that comes with the franchise often provides instant legitimacy for a business.[25] For example, an entrepreneur opening a new Curves fitness center would likely attract more customers than an entrepreneur opening a new, independently owned fitness center because many women who are a part of the target market of Curves have already heard of the firm and have a positive impression of it. Second, when an individual purchases a franchise, the franchisor typically provides training, technical expertise, and other forms of support. For example, many franchise organizations provide their franchisees periodic training both at their headquarters location and in their individual franchise outlets.

The main disadvantage of buying a franchise is the cost involved. As mentioned earlier, the franchisee must pay an initial franchise fee. The franchisee must also pay the franchisor an ongoing royalty as well as pay into a variety of funds, depending on the franchise organization. Thus, franchisees have both immediate (i.e., the initial franchise fee) and long-term (i.e., continuing royalty payments) costs. By opening an independent business, an entrepreneur can keep 100 percent of the profits if it is successful.

TABLE 15.4 Questions to Ask before Buying a Franchise

Questions to Ask a Franchisor

- What is the background of the company and its performance record?
- What is the company's current financial status?
- What are the names, addresses, and phone numbers of existing franchisees in my trade area?
- Describe how you train and mentor your franchisees.
- If at some point I decide to exit the franchise relationship, how does the exit process work?
- In what ways do you work with a franchisee who is struggling?

Questions to Ask Current Franchisees

- How much does your franchise gross per year? How much does it net? Are the procedures followed to make royalty payments to the franchisee burdensome?
- Are the financial projections of revenues, expenses, and profits that the franchisor provided me accurate in your judgment?
- Does the franchisor give you enough assistance in operating your business?
- How many hours, on average, do you work?
- How often do you get a vacation?
- Have you been caught off-guard by any unexpected costs or expectations?
- Does your franchisor provide you ongoing training and support?
- If you had to do it all over again, would you purchase a franchise in this system? Why or why not?

Table 15.5 contains a list of the advantages and disadvantages to buying a franchise.

Steps in Purchasing a Franchise

Purchasing a franchise system is a seven-step process, as illustrated in Figure 15.3. The first rule of buying a franchise is to avoid making a hasty decision. Again, owning a franchise is typically costly and labor-intensive, and the purchase of a franchise should be a careful, deliberate decision. Once the decision to purchase a franchise has been nearly made, however, the following steps should be taken. If at any time prior to signing the franchise agreement the prospective franchisee has second thoughts, the process should be stopped until the prospective franchisee's concerns are adequately addressed.

Step 1 ***Visit several of the franchisor's outlets:*** Prior to meeting with the franchisor, the prospective franchisee should visit several of the franchisor's outlets and talk with their owners and employees. During the visits, the prospective franchisee should continually ask, "Is this the type of business I would enjoy owning and operating or managing?"

Step 2 ***Retain a franchise attorney:*** Prospective franchisees should have an attorney who represents their interests, not the franchisor's. The attorney should prepare the prospective franchisee for meeting with the franchisor and should review all franchise documents before they are signed. If the franchisor tries to discourage the prospective franchisee from retaining an attorney, this is a red flag.

Step 3 ***Meet with the franchisor and check the franchisor's references:*** The prospective franchisee should meet with the franchisor, preferably at the franchisor's headquarters. During the meeting, the prospective franchisee should compare what was observed firsthand in the franchised outlets with what the franchisor is saying. Additional references should also be checked. The Uniform Franchise Offering Circular is a good source for references. In section 20 of this document, there is a list of all the franchisees that have dropped out of the system in the past 3 years along with their contact information. Several of these should be called. Although it may seem to be overkill, the mantra for prospective franchisees is to check, double-check, and triple-check a franchisor's references.

Step 4 ***Review all franchise documents with the attorney:*** The franchise attorney should review all the franchise documents, including the Uniform Franchise Offering Circular and the franchise agreement.

TABLE 15.5 Advantages and Disadvantages of Buying a Franchise

Advantages	Disadvantages
A proven product or service within an established market. The most compelling advantage to buying a franchise is that the franchise offers a proven product or service within an established market.	**Cost of the franchise.** The initial cost of purchasing and setting up a franchise operation can be quite high, as illustrated in Table 15.3.
An established trademark or business system. The purchase of a franchise with an established trademark provides franchisees with considerable market power. For example, the purchaser of a McDonald's franchise has a trademark with proven market power.	**Restrictions on creativity.** Many franchise systems are very rigid and leave little opportunity for individual franchisees to exercise their creativity. This is an often-cited frustration of franchisees.
Franchisor's training, technical expertise, and managerial experience. Another important attribute of franchising is the training, technical expertise, and managerial experience that the franchisor provides the franchisee.	**Duration and nature of the commitment.** For a variety of reasons, many franchise agreements are difficult to exit. In addition, virtually every franchise agreement contains a noncompete clause. These clauses vary in terms of severity, but a typical clause prevents a former franchisee from competing with the franchisor for a period of 2 years or more.
An established marketing network. Franchisees who buy into a powerful franchise system are part of a system that has tremendous buying power and substantial advertising power and marketing prowess.	**Risk of fraud, misunderstandings, or lack of franchisor commitment.** Along with the many encouraging stories of franchise success, there are also many stories of individuals who purchase a franchise only to be disappointed by the franchisor's broken promises.
Franchisor ongoing support. One of the most attractive advantages of purchasing a franchise rather than owning a store outright is the notion that the franchisor provides the franchisee ongoing support in terms of training, product updates, management assistance, and advertising. A popular slogan in franchising is that people buy franchises to "be in business for themselves but not by themselves."	**Problems of termination or transfer.** Some franchise agreements are very difficult and expensive to terminate or transfer. Often, a franchisee cannot terminate a franchise agreement without paying the franchisor substantial monetary damages.
Availability of financing. Some franchisors offer financing to their franchisees, although these cases are the exception rather than the rule. This information is available in section 10 of the UFOC.	**Poor performance on the part of other franchisees.** If some of the franchisees in a franchise system start performing poorly and make an ineffective impression on the public, that poor performance can affect the reputation and eventually the sales of a well-run franchise in the same system.
Potential for business growth. If a franchisee is successful in the original location, the franchisee is often provided the opportunity to buy additional franchises from the same franchisor. For many franchisees, this prospect offers a powerful incentive to work hard to be as successful as possible.	**Potential for failure.** Some franchise systems simply fail to reach their objectives. When this happens, franchisees' wealth can be negatively affected. Indeed, when a franchise system fails, it commonly brings its franchisees down with it.

FIGURE 15.3

Seven Steps in Purchasing a Franchise

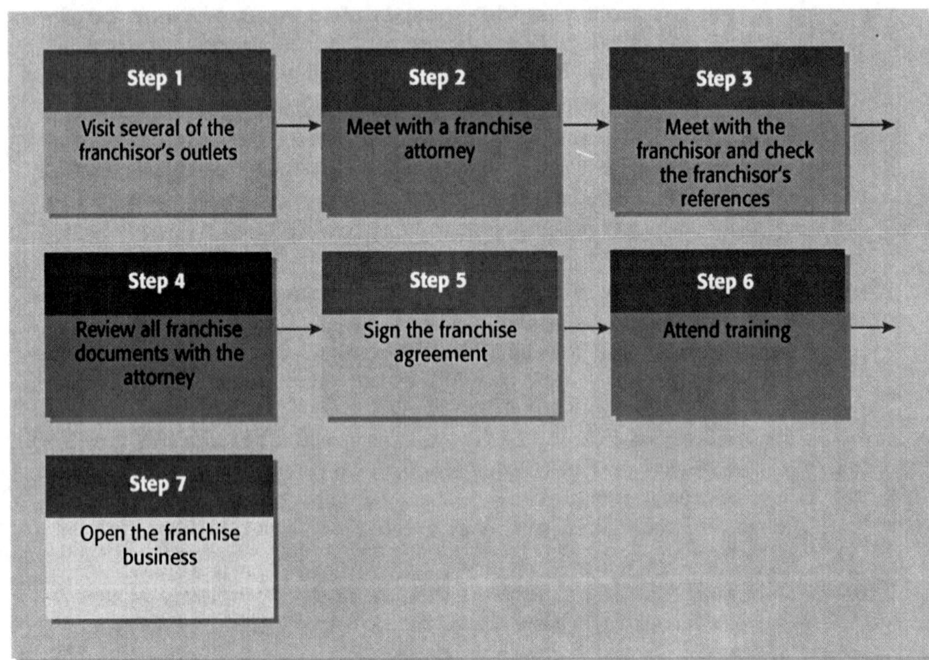

Step 5 ***Sign the franchise agreement:*** If everything is a go at this point, the franchise agreement can be signed. The franchise agreement is the document in which the provisions of the franchisor–franchisee relationship are outlined. We discuss this agreement in greater detail later in this chapter.

Step 6 ***Attend training:*** Almost all franchise organizations provide their franchisees training. For example, Comfort Keepers requires each of its new franchisees to attend an intensive 5-day training program at its corporate headquarters, and ongoing opportunities for training are made available.

Step 7 ***Open the franchise business:*** For many franchises, particularly restaurants, the first 2 to 3 weeks after the business is opened may be its busiest period, as prospective customers "try it out." This is why many franchise organizations send experienced personnel to help the franchisee open the business as smoothly as possible. One goal of a franchisee is generating positive word of mouth about the business right from the start.

Watch Out! Common Misconceptions About Franchising

Despite the abundance of advice available to them, many franchisees make false assumptions about franchising. Part of the explanation for this is that franchising has an attractive lure. It is easy to become enthralled with the promise of franchising and not spend an adequate amount of time examining the potential pitfalls. The following is a list of misconceptions that franchisees often have about franchising:

9. Identify the common mistakes franchise buyers make.

- ***Franchising is a safe investment:*** Franchising, in and of itself, is no safer an investment than any other form of business ownership.
- ***A strong industry ensures franchise success:*** Although it is generally important to operate in a growing industry, the strength of an industry does not make up for a poor product, a poor business model, poor management, or inappropriate advertising. There are many firms that fail in growing industries just as there are firms that succeed in unattractive ones.
- ***A franchise is a "proven" business system:*** A franchisor sells a franchisee the right to use a particular business model. Whether the model is proven or not is subject to the test of time. Obviously, companies such as Subway, Curves, and McDonald's are using models that are polished and that have worked well over time. Most prospective franchisees, however, cannot afford a McDonald's or a Subway unit and will be considering a lesser-known franchise. All too frequently, companies start selling franchises before their systems are anywhere close to being proven—a fact that should cause entrepreneurs to be wary.
- ***There is no need to hire a franchise attorney or an accountant:*** Professional advice is almost always needed to guide a prospective franchisee through the franchise purchase process. A prospective franchisee should never give in to the temptation to save money by relying solely on the franchisor's advice.
- ***The best systems grow rapidly, and it is best to be a part of a rapid-growth system:*** While some franchise systems grow rapidly because they have a good trademark and a polished business model, other franchise systems grow quickly because their major emphasis is on selling franchises. It is to a franchisee's benefit to be part of a system that has a solid trademark and business system—as that trademark and system will attract more customers—but some franchise systems grow so quickly that they outrun their ability to provide their franchisees adequate support.
- ***I can operate my franchise outlet for less than the franchisor predicts:*** The operation of a franchise outlet usually costs just as much as the franchisor predicts.
- ***The franchisor is a nice person—he'll help me out if I need it:*** Although it may be human nature to rely on the goodwill of others, don't expect anything from your franchisor that isn't spelled out in the franchise agreement.

Because these misconceptions are often hard to detect, some prospective franchisees attend seminars or franchise "boot camps" that teach them the ins and outs of franchising, including the things to watch out for when they talk to prospective franchisors. These types of seminars and boot camps are regularly offered by organizations such as Women in Franchising, the United States Hispanic Chamber of Commerce, and the International Franchising Organization.

Legal Aspects of the Franchise Relationship

According to the Federal Trade Commission, a franchise exists any time that the sale of a business involves (1) the sale of goods or services that bear a trademark, (2) the retention of significant control or assistance by the holder of the trademark on the operation of the business, and (3) royalty payments by the purchaser of the business to the owner of the trademark for the right to use the trademark in the business.

The legal and regulatory environment surrounding franchising is based on the premise that the public interest is served if prospective franchisees are as informed as possible regarding the characteristics of a particular franchisor. The offer and sale of a franchise is regulated at both the state and the federal level. The legal aspects of the franchise relationship are unique enough that some attorneys specialize in franchise law. One law firm, Wiggin & Dana, has even set up a blog that focuses on franchise law. The blog is available at www.FranchiseLawBlog.com.

Federal Rules and Regulations

Except for the automobile and petroleum industries, federal laws do not directly address the franchisor–franchisee relationship. Instead, franchise disputes are matters of contract law and are litigated at the state level. During the 1990s, Congress considered several proposals for federal legislation to govern franchise relationships, but none became law.

However, the offer and sale of a franchise is regulated at the federal level. According to Federal Trade Commission (FTC) Rule 436, franchisors must furnish potential franchisees with written disclosures that provide information about the franchisor, the franchised business, and the franchise relationship. The disclosures must be supplied at least 10 business days before a franchise agreement can be signed or the franchisee pays the franchisor any money.[26] In most cases, the disclosures are made through a lengthy document referred to as

The fitness industry represents one of the most rapidly growing areas of franchising because it caters to all ages and demographics. Here, a young man and a young woman chat while working out on stair-climbing exercise machines at a fitness center in California.

the Uniform Franchise Offering Circular, which is accepted in all 50 states and parts of Canada. The **Uniform Franchise Offering Circular** (UFOC) contains 23 categories of information that give a prospective franchisee a broad base of information about the background and financial health of the franchisor. A summary of the information contained in the UFOC is provided in Table 15.6. A prospective franchisee should fully understand all the information contained in the UFOC before a franchise agreement is signed.

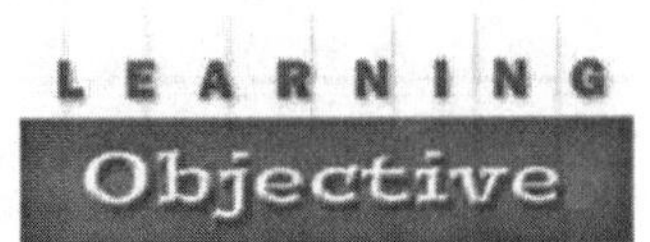

10. Describe the purpose of the Uniform Franchise Offering Circular.

The UFOC requires the franchisor to attach a copy of the franchise agreement and any other related contractual documents to the circular. The **franchise agreement**, or contract, is the document that consummates the sale of a franchise. Franchise agreements vary, but each agreement typically contains two sections: the purchase agreement and the franchise or license agreement. The purchase agreement typically spells out the price, the services to be provided by the franchisor to the franchisee, and the "franchise package," which refers to all the items the franchisee has been told to expect. The franchise or license agreement typically stipulates the rights granted to the franchisee (including the right to use the franchisor's trademark), the obligations and duties of the franchisor, the obligations and duties of the franchisee, trade restrictions, rights and limitations regarding the transfer or termination of the franchise agreement, and who is responsible for attorney fees if disputes arise. Most states have enacted a statute of frauds that requires franchise agreements to be in writing.

The federal government does not require franchisors to register with the Federal Trade Commission (FTC). The offer of a franchise for sale does not imply that the FTC has examined the franchisor and has determined that the information contained in the franchisor's UFOC is accurate. The franchisor is responsible for voluntarily complying with the law, and it is the responsibility of prospective franchisees to exercise due diligence in investigating franchise opportunities. Although most franchisor–franchisee relationships are conducted in an entirely ethical manner, it is a mistake to assume that a franchisor has a fiduciary obligation to its franchisees. What this means is that if a franchisor had a **fiduciary obligation** to its franchisees, it would always act in their best interest, or be on the franchisees' "side." Commenting on this issue, Robert Purvin, an experienced franchise attorney, wrote:

> While the conventional wisdom talks about the proactive relationship of the franchisor to its franchisees, virtually every court case decided in the U.S. has ruled that a franchisor has no fiduciary obligation to its franchisees. Instead, U.S. courts have agreed with franchisors that franchise agreements are "arms length" business transactions.[27]

This quote suggests that a potential franchisee should not rely solely on the goodwill of a franchisor when negotiating a franchise agreement. A potential franchisee should have a lawyer who is fully acquainted with franchise law and should closely scrutinize all franchise-related legal documents.

State Rules and Regulations

In addition to the FTC disclosure requirements, 17 states have laws providing additional protection to potential franchisees. California, Florida, Hawaii, Illinois, Indiana, Maryland, Michigan, Minnesota, New York, North Dakota, Rhode Island, South Dakota, Texas, Utah, Virginia, Washington, and Wisconsin are the states in which these laws have been established. In most of these states, a franchisor is required to file its UFOC with a designated state agency, making the UFOC public record. In these states, the agency typically reviews the UFOC for compliance with the law. In most of these 17 states, a franchisor can be prevented from selling a franchise if the state agency in charge is not satisfied that the UFOC is complete, understandable, and fully in compliance with FTC Rule 436.

By requiring franchisors to file their UFOCs with a state agency, these states provide franchise purchasers important legal protection, including the right to sue a franchisor for violation of state disclosure requirements (if the franchise purchaser feels that full disclosure in the offering circular was not made). For example, if someone purchased a franchise in one of the states fitting the profile described previously and 6 months later discovered that the franchisor did not disclose an issue required by the UFOC (and, as a result, felt that he had

TABLE 15.6 Information Contained in the Uniform Franchise Offering Circular (UFOC) Along with Explanations of Their Meanings

Section and Item	Explanation
1. The franchisor, its predecessors, and affiliates 2. Business experience of the franchisor 3. Litigation experience of the franchisor 4. Bankruptcy on the part of the franchisor	These items provide information about the franchisor's operating history, business affiliations, and past litigation and bankruptcy experience, if any. It is not uncommon for a large company to have experienced some litigation. It would be a red flag, however, if a disproportionate percentage of the litigation involved suits with current or former franchisees.
5. Initial franchise fee 6. Other fees 7. Initial investment	These items specify the fees that the franchisee is subject to along with the franchisees initial investment, which can be quite substantial. The "other fees" section should be carefully studied to avoid any surprises.
8. Restrictions on sources of products and services 9. Franchisee's obligations	These items stipulate the franchisee's obligations, along with restrictions pertaining to where the franchisee is permitted to purchase supplies and services. Some franchise agreements require the franchisee to purchase supplies from the franchisor.
10. Financing available 11. Franchisor's obligations	These items spell out the franchisor's obligations, along with a description of the financing (if any) that the franchisor offers to the franchisee. The franchisor's obligations typically include providing assistance in opening the franchise's unit, ongoing training, and advertising.
12. Territory 13. Trademarks 14. Patents, copyrights, and proprietary information	These items describe the territorial rights granted the franchisee (if any) and the franchisor's right to grant other franchises and open company-owned outlets. In addition, items 13 and 14 specify the principal trademarks, patents, and copyrights and other proprietary information owned by the franchisor and the extent to which these items can be used by the franchisee.
15. Obligation to participate in the actual operation of the franchise business	This section addresses the franchisee's obligation to participate personally in the operation of the franchise. Franchisors typically do not want absentee franchisees.
16. Restrictions on what the franchisee may sell 17. Renewal, termination, transfer, and dispute resolution	These sections deal with what the franchisee may sell and how the franchisor resolves disputes with its franchisees. Item 17 also contains important information about the manner in which franchisees can renew, terminate, and/or transfer their franchise.
18. Public figures	This section lists public figures affiliated with the franchise through advertising and other means.
19. Earnings claim	If a franchisor makes an earnings claim in connection with an offer of a franchise, then certain past and projected earnings information must be provided.
20. List of outlets	This section is quite exhaustive and contains (1) the number of franchises sold by the franchisor, (2) the number of company-owned outlets, (3) the names of all franchisees and the addresses and telephone numbers of all their outlets (within certain limitations), (4) an estimate of the number of franchises to be sold in the next year, and (5) a list of all franchisees (covering the past 3 years) who have dropped out of the system, including their last-known home addresses and telephone numbers.
21. Financial Statements	This section contains the franchisor's previous 2 years of independently audited financial statements.
22. Contracts	These last two sections contain copies of the documents that franchisees have to sign.
23. Receipt Attachments: Franchise Agreement (or contract) Equipment Lease Lease for Premises Loan Agreement	These are the common exhibits attached to the UFOC.

been damaged), that person could seek relief by suing the franchisor in state court. All 17 states providing additional measures of protection for franchisees also regulate some aspect of the termination process.[28] Although the provisions vary by state, they typically restrict a franchisor from terminating the franchise before the expiration of the franchise agreement, unless the franchisor has "good cause" for its action.

More About Franchising

There are a number of additional issues pertaining to the franchisor–franchisee relationship. Three important topics, for both franchisors and franchisees, are franchise ethics, international franchising, and the future of franchising as a method of business ownership and growth.

Franchise Ethics

The majority of franchisors and franchisees are highly ethical individuals who are interested only in making a fair return on their investment. In fact, according to a recent FTC report, instances of problems between franchisors and their franchisees tend to be isolated occurrences rather than prevalent practices.[29] There are certain features of franchising, however, that make it subject to ethical abuse. An understanding of these features can help franchisors and franchisees guard against making ethical mistakes. These features are the following:

- ***The get-rich-quick mentality:*** Some franchisors see franchising as a get-rich-quick scheme and become more interested in selling franchises than in using franchising as a legitimate means of distributing their product or service. These franchisors have a tendency to either oversell the potential of their franchise or overpromise the support they will offer to their franchisees.
- ***The false assumption that buying a franchise is a guarantee of business success:*** Buying a franchise, as is the case with all other business investments, involves risk. Any statement to the contrary is typically misleading or unethical. A franchisor must steer clear of claims that it has the "key" to business success, and a franchisee needs to be wary of all such claims.
- ***Conflicts of interest between franchisors and their franchisees:*** The structure of the franchise relationship can create conflicts of interest between franchisors and their franchisees. For example, franchisees benefit from the profits of a unit, while franchisors benefit from increased revenues (recall that a franchisor's royalty is typically paid on a percentage of gross profits rather than net profits). This anomaly in the franchise arrangement can motivate franchisors to take steps that boost revenues for the entire system but hurt profits for individual franchisees. For example, a franchisor might insist that a franchisee sell a product that has high revenue but low margins (or net income). Similarly, a franchisor might sell several franchises in a given geographic area to maximize the revenue potential of the area regardless of the effect on each individual franchisee's net income. These actions can at times be ethically questionable and can often lead to contentious conflicts of interests in franchise systems.

Despite the protection of law and the advocacy of franchise associations, individual franchisors and franchisees must practice due diligence in their relationships. "Buyer beware" is a good motto for franchisors selecting franchisees and prospective franchisees selecting franchisors. Entering into a franchise relationship is a major step for both parties and should be treated accordingly. The metaphor used frequently to describe the franchisor–franchisee relationship is marriage. Similar to marriage, the franchisor–franchisee relationship is typically close, long-term, and painful to terminate. Each side of the franchise partnership should scrutinize the past ethical behavior of the other before a franchise agreement is executed.

International Franchising

International opportunities for franchising are becoming more prevalent as the markets for certain franchised products in the United States have become saturated.[30] Indeed, heavily franchised companies, such as McDonald's, Kentucky Fried Chicken, and Century 21 Real

Estate, are experiencing much of their growth in international markets. For example, Century 21 currently has 1,384 offices in Europe and Asia, including 58 in Hong Kong, 19 in Spain, and 77 in the Belgium, Netherlands and Luxembourg region. The trend toward globalization in many industries is also hastening the trend toward international franchising. Regional initiatives, such as the North American Free Trade Agreement, are making it increasingly attractive for U.S. firms to offer franchises for sale in foreign countries. Many new franchise organizations have made international expansion part of their initial business plans. An example is WSI Internet, which is a U.S. company that was founded in 1995 and now has franchise outlets in 87 countries.

A U.S. citizen who is thinking about buying a franchise abroad may be confronted with the choice of buying from an American company or a foreign company regardless of the location in the world. For U.S. citizens, these are some of the steps to take before buying a franchise in a foreign country:

- ***Consider the value of the franchisor's name in the foreign country:*** There are very few franchise systems whose names are known worldwide. Beyond a select few—McDonald's, Coca-Cola, and Budweiser come to mind—the majority of trademarks well known to Americans may be known to only a small percentage of the population of a foreign country. When considering the purchase of a U.S.-based franchise in a foreign country, carefully evaluate the value of the trademark in that country.
- ***Work with a knowledgeable lawyer:*** Many of the legal protections afforded to prospective franchisees in the United States are unavailable in foreign countries, highlighting the need for the purchaser of a franchise in a foreign country to obtain excellent legal advice. All the hazards involved with purchasing a domestic franchise are magnified when purchasing a franchise in a foreign country.
- ***Determine whether the product or service is salable in a foreign country:*** Just because a product or service is desirable to Americans is no guarantee of success in a foreign culture. Before buying a franchise in a foreign country, determine if sufficient marketing research has been conducted to ensure that the product or service will have a sufficient market in the foreign country.
- ***Uncover whether the franchisor has experience in international markets:*** It is typically not a good idea to be a franchisor's "test case" to see if the franchisor wants to operate in foreign markets. Be leery of franchisors with aggressive expansion plans but little international experience.
- ***Find out how much training and support you will receive from the franchisor:*** If your franchise unit will be in a foreign country and the franchisor remains headquartered in the United States, make sure you fully understand the amount of training and support you can expect. Will the franchisor have an area representative in your country? If not, do you have to make an international phone call each time you want to talk to your franchisor? Will your franchisor be willing to travel to the foreign country to offer you training and support? Who pays for the international travel of the franchisor's training staff? Who is responsible for advertising in the foreign country, the franchisor or the franchisee?
- ***Evaluate currency restrictions:*** Evaluate any restrictions that the foreign country places on the convertibility of its currency into U.S. dollars.

To avoid some of the potential problems alluded to here, U.S. franchisors typically structure their expansion into a foreign country through the following:

- ***Direct franchising arrangement:*** Under a direct franchise arrangement, the U.S. franchisor grants the rights to an individual or a company (the developer) to develop multiple franchised businesses within a country or territory. For example, if Midas Muffler decided to sell franchises for the first time in Spain, Midas may grant the rights to a Spanish company to develop multiple Midas franchises there.
- ***Master franchise agreement:*** Under a master franchise arrangement, the U.S. firm grants the right to an individual or company (the master franchisee) to develop one or more franchise businesses and to license others to develop one or more franchise businesses within the country or territory.

- ***Other agreements:*** Combinations of other arrangements are also employed by franchisors expanding to foreign markets. Examples include joint-venture arrangements, direct-sales arrangements, or straight franchising agreements.

Even when a company adheres to these safeguards, there is plenty that can go wrong when opening franchise outlets overseas. This topic is addressed in this chapter's "What Went Wrong?" feature.

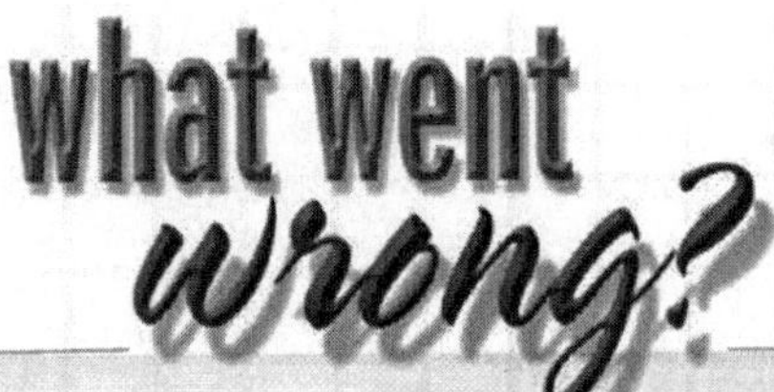

Watch Out: Plenty Can Go Wrong in Opening Franchise Outlets Overseas

Although the Internet, satellite television, and Hollywood movies have increased the demand for American products and services abroad, franchisors should take care not to rush into opening franchise outlets overseas. Because many of the easiest countries into which U.S. firms can export their products and services, such as Canada and England, are already saturated with U.S. franchised outlets, this leaves only more difficult foreign markets. Differences in language and the customs associated with a nation's culture are examples of factors making franchising very challenging in these more difficult foreign markets. Indeed, plenty can go wrong because of the complexities of operating overseas.

Sometimes, franchisors run into unique challenges in foreign markets, sometimes they simply make mistakes, and sometimes they insist on trying to impose American tastes on overseas markets, which doesn't always work. All of these complications result from a lack of familiarity with the foreign markets the companies are trying to enter. Here are some examples of mistakes U.S. franchisors have made when trying to enter foreign markets:

- Burger King didn't register its trademark in Australia before another restaurant group did. If you walk through the Sydney airport, you'll pass hamburger stands called Burger King and Hungry Jack's. Burger King is a local company—U.S. Burger King sandwiches are sold at Hungry Jack's.
- A donut concept failed in Brazil because people felt the hole meant they were being shortchanged.
- In Malaysia, a company put up a hotel, but no one would go inside because the door was on the wrong side of the building, violating the residents' religious norms.
- The Coca-Cola Company bought one of India's most successful soft-drink companies, which distributed the popular brand Thumbs Up, to get access to its distribution channels. Although this acquisition gave Coca-Cola immediate access to distribution channels, Thumbs Up remained more popular than Coke for many years. Most Indians thought that Coke wasn't fizzy enough.
- TCBY, the yogurt maker, found that it couldn't use its slogan "None of the guilt, all of the pleasure" in Japan because the Japanese culture does not have the same interpretation of the word *guilt* as American culture does.

Fortunately, many U.S franchisors are gaining experience and are making fewer mistakes in foreign countries. Flexibility is increasing too. For example, Domino's, which has almost 3,000 franchises overseas, is now encouraging its owner-operators to tweak menus according to local tastes. As a result, the company's overseas franchisees now offer pizzas topped with squid and peas in Taiwan, lamb and pickled ginger in India, and tuna in Iceland. Amazingly, Iceland is now home to three of Domino's four highest-grossing outlets. Similarly, in China, KFC outlets offer the chain's U.S. menu, plus "Duck Soup" and the "Old Beijing Twister," which is a wrap modeled on the way Peking duck is served, but with fried chicken inside.

Questions for Critical Thinking

1. In this feature, we considered a number of things that can go wrong when trying to pursue what appear to be franchising opportunities in some foreign markets. Using insights you've drawn from this chapter as well as your study of the book's first 14 chapters, prepare a list of reasons firms or entrepreneurs might be willing to accept the risks of establishing a franchise unit in a challenging foreign market. In slightly different words, what are the potential advantages of franchising in challenging international markets?

2. The examples of franchising mistakes made by Burger King and Coca-Cola, as described in this feature, may surprise you. Why is it that large organizations such as Burger King and Coca-Cola sometimes err when pursuing apparent franchising opportunities in difficult or challenging foreign markets? Prepare a list of factors you believe could cause large, long-lived organizations to make these types of mistakes.
3. Unlike Domino's Pizza, some restaurant chains sell the exact same food overseas as they sell in the United States. What are the pluses and the minuses of doing this?
4. Do some Internet research and identify a foreign-owned franchise organization that sells franchises in the United States. Do the company's U.S. franchises sell the same exact product as the company sells in its home country? If not, what types of changes or modification have been made to satisfy American consumers?

Sources: "Giving New Meaning to the Term 'Gross Revenue,'" *Business 2.0*, October 2005, 144; M. Haig *Brand Failures* (London: Kogan Page 2003); J. Bennett, "Some Franchises Don't Translate Well Overseas," *The Wall Street Journal*, www.startupjournal.com (accessed October 28, 2003); J. Bennett, "Why U.S. Franchises Face Problems Abroad," *The Wall Street Journal*, www.startupjournal.com (accessed October 28, 2003).

The Future of Franchising

The future of franchising appears bright. Franchise organizations represent a large and growing segment of the retail and service sectors of U.S. businesses and are in some cases replacing more traditional forms of small business ownership.[31] According to the International Franchise Association (IFA), franchising represents about $1 trillion in annual retail sales in the United States and involves 320,000 franchised outlets in 75 industries. In addition, the IFA estimates that a new franchise outlet opens somewhere in the United States every 8 minutes.[32] More and more college graduates are choosing careers in industries that are heavily dominated by franchising. The availability of digital business tools, which increase the effectiveness of franchise organizations in a variety of ways, is also making franchising more desirable. As franchising continues to become a more pervasive form of business, regulators and franchise associations are likely to intervene in ways that strengthen the viability of the franchise concept.[33]

Chapter Summary

1. A franchise is an agreement between a franchisor (the parent company, such as McDonald's), and a franchisee (an individual or firm that is willing to pay the franchisor a fee for the right to sell its product or service).
2. There are two distinctly different types of franchise systems: the product trademark franchise and the business format franchise. A product trademark franchise is an arrangement under which the franchisor grants to the franchisee the right to buy its products and use its trade name. Automobile dealerships and soft-drink distributorships are examples of product trademark franchises. In a business format franchise, the franchisor provides a formula for doing business to the franchisee along with training, advertising, and other forms of assistance. Curves, Comfort Keepers, and College Nannies & Tutors are examples of this type of franchise system.
3. An individual franchise agreement involves the sale of a single franchise for a specific location. An area franchise agreement allows a franchisee to own and operate a specific number of outlets in a particular geographic area. A master franchise agreement is similar to an area franchise agreement with one major exception. In addition to having the right to operate a specific number of locations in a particular area, the franchisee also has the right to offer and sell the franchise to other people in the area.
4. The advantages of setting up a franchise system include rapid, low-cost market expansion; income from franchise fees and royalties; franchisee motivation; access to ideas and suggestions; cost savings; and increased buying power. The disadvantages of setting up a franchise system include sharing profits with franchisees, loss of control, friction with franchisees, managing growth, differences in required business skills, and legal expenses.

5. The rules of thumb for determining whether franchising is a good choice for growing a business are as follows: The product or service the business sells should be unique; the business should be consistently profitable; the business should be profitable year-round, not only during a specific season; the business system and procedures should be polished; and the business proposition should be clear so that prospective franchisees fully understand the relationship to which they are committing.
6. Preparing answers to the following questions helps the entrepreneur determine if franchising is a good fit as a way to launch a venture: Are you willing to take orders? Are you willing to be part of a franchise system? How will you react if you make a suggestion to your franchisor and your suggestion is rejected? What are you looking for in a business? How willing are you to put your money at risk?
7. The following costs are typically associated with buying a business format franchise: initial franchise fee, capital requirements (such as land, buildings, and equipment), continuing royalty payment, advertising fee, and other fees (depending on the franchise system).
8. The advantages of buying a franchise include a proven product or service within an established market; an established trademark or business system; the franchisor's training, technical expertise, and managerial experience; an established marketing network; ongoing franchisor support; availability of financing; and potential for business growth. The disadvantages of buying a franchise include cost of the franchise; restrictions on creativity; duration and nature of commitment; risk of fraud, misunderstanding, or lack of franchisor commitment; problems of termination or transfer; and the possibility of poor performance on the part of other franchisees.
9. The common mistakes made by franchise buyers include believing that franchising is a completely safe investment, believing that a great industry ensures franchise success, putting too much faith in the idea that a franchise is a "proven" business system, believing that there is no need to hire a franchise attorney or accountant, being overly optimistic about how fast the franchise outlet will grow, believing that "I can operate my franchise outlet for less than the franchisor predicts," and believing that just because the franchisor is a nice person, he or she will always be there to help out when needed.
10. The Uniform Franchise Offering Circular (UFOC) is a document with 23 categories of information. This document provides a prospective franchisee a broad base of information about a franchisor's background and financial health. The UFOC must be provided by the franchisor to a prospective franchisee at least 10 business days before a franchise contract can be signed or the franchisee pays the franchisor any money.

Key Terms

agency theory
area franchise agreement
business format franchise
fiduciary obligation
franchise agreement
franchisees
franchising
franchisor
individual franchise agreement
master franchise agreement
multiple-unit franchisee
product and trademark franchise
subfranchisees
uniform franchisor offering circular

Review Questions

1. What is franchising? How does it differ from other forms of business ownership?
2. Describe the differences between a product and trademark franchise and a business format franchise. Provide an example of both types of franchise arrangements.
3. What is the difference among an individual franchise agreement, an area franchise agreement, and a master franchise agreement?
4. What are the nine basic steps in setting up a franchise system?
5. What are the advantages and disadvantages of establishing a franchise system?

6. What are the rules of thumb for determining whether franchising is a good choice for a particular business? Provide an example of a business that wouldn't be suitable for franchising.
7. What are some of the issues an entrepreneur should consider when answering the question "Is franchising a good choice for me?"
8. What are the costs involved in purchasing a business unit franchise? Are these costs similar across franchise systems, or do they vary widely?
9. Explain why it is to the franchisor's advantage to receive its royalty payment on the gross income rather than net income of its franchise outlets.
10. Describe some of the resources available to prospective franchisees to identify franchise opportunities.
11. What are the principal advantages and disadvantages of buying a franchise?
12. What are the seven steps involved in purchasing a franchise?
13. What are some of the common misconceptions franchisees often have about franchising?
14. What is the purpose of the Uniform Franchise Offering Circular (UFOC)? Are there any regulations regarding when the UFOC must be provided to a prospective franchisee? If so, what are they?
15. What is the purpose of a franchise agreement? Identify the two sections of the franchise agreement and describe the purpose of each one.
16. To date, every court case that has been adjudicated in the United States indicates that franchisors do not have a fiduciary responsibility to their franchisees. What do these rulings suggest to entrepreneurs considering the possibility of buying into a franchise system? Why?
17. What are some of the aspects of franchising that make it subject to ethical abuses?
18. For U.S. citizens, what are the main issues that should be considered before buying a franchise in a foreign country?
19. What are the main reasons that many U.S. franchise systems are expanding into global markets? Do you think this expansion will continue to gain momentum or will decline over time? Explain your answer.
20. Does franchising have a bright or a dim future in the United States? Make your answer as substantive and thoughtful as possible.

Application Questions

1. Reread the opening feature, which focuses on Joseph Keeley and the franchise organization that he founded—College Nannies & Tutors. Think of an activity, other than nanny and tutoring services, that you think college students might be particularly good at and has a defined need and is franchisable. Describe how that activity could be turned into a franchise organization.
2. Several executives from Coca-Cola have decided to leave their jobs to launch a new chain of a Dairy Queen type of restaurant called Thirst Burst Etc. They want to grow quickly. Under what conditions would franchising be a good choice for them?
3. Pick a franchise organization that you admire. Spend some time looking at the company's Web site. Describe how the company is set up. Is it a product and trademark franchise or a business format franchise? Does it sell individual franchise agreements, area franchise agreements, master franchise agreements, or some combination of the three? How many company-owned stores and how many franchise outlets are in the system? Report any particularly interesting or unusual things you learned about the system.
4. Up to this point, Comfort Keepers has not sold master franchise agreements. Would setting up master franchises be an effective course of action for Comfort Keepers? Explain your answer.
5. Select a franchise organization that is located on your campus or near the campus that isn't involved in any co-branding arrangements. Suggest several co-branding relationships that would make sense for this company.
6. Bill Watts has decided to buy a sub shop franchise called Deluxe Subs. He lives in Cedar Falls, Iowa, and will be the first Deluxe Subs franchisee in the state. Along with

buying a Deluxe Subs franchise, Bill would also like to purchase the rights to offer and sell Deluxe Subs franchises to other people in the Cedar Falls area. What type of franchise agreement should Bill negotiate with Deluxe Subs? For Bill, what are the advantages and disadvantages of this type of arrangement?

7. Sarah Gandy works for a computer consulting firm in Salt Lake City. For some time, she has been thinking about either starting her own computer consulting company or buying a computer consulting franchise. She knows that you have been taking a course in entrepreneurship and asks you to tell her a little bit about what a franchise costs and how to identify a good franchise system. What would you tell her?
8. Helen Partridge owns a very successful chain of Web site development businesses. She currently has 21 offices spread across Illinois, Indiana, and Ohio. She is thinking about franchising her business as a means of expanding beyond the Midwest. Helen has always believed in getting professional advice before making a major decision. Who should Helen talk to, and what types of questions should she ask before making the decision to franchise her business?
9. Jason Carpenski is a serial entrepreneur. Although he is only 35, he has already started three businesses. Jason loves launching businesses because he likes being his own boss and enjoys the independence an entrepreneurial career offers him. Recently, Jason sold his latest business, a communications equipment start-up, and is looking for a new opportunity. He just attended a franchise fair and is extremely interested in buying a printing and copying franchise. Do you think Jason is a good candidate to buy a franchise in an established franchise system? Why or why not?
10. Joan Wagner has worked for Walgreen's for several years as a photo processor. She just inherited a nice sum of money and has decided to purchase a Planet Smoothie franchise. Before she signs the franchise agreement, however, she wants to make sure that she fully understands the advantages and disadvantages of buying a franchise. What would you tell Joan if she asked you for this information?
11. Suppose you ran into an old friend who is just about to buy into a handheld computer accessories retail franchise. He tells you that he is excited about the opportunity because the system he is about to buy into (1) is in an industry that virtually guarantees its success, (2) has a "proven" business model, and (3) is operated by people who are so honest that he can skip the expense of hiring a franchise attorney to review the documents he has to sign. If your friend asked you, "Be honest with me now—am I being naive, or does this sound like a great opportunity?" what would you tell your friend? Why?
12. Suppose you saw an ad in your local newspaper for a franchise opportunity that caught your attention. You called the phone number listed in the ad and liked what you heard. As a result, you scheduled a time to meet with a representative of the franchise organization at a nearby Panera Bread restaurant. After learning more about the opportunity, you tell the representative that you're really interested and would like more information. If the opportunity is legitimate and the organization you are dealing with complies with the law, what should you expect from this point forward?
13. Sarah Saladino, a close high school friend, is thinking about buying into a franchise operation that sells expensive clothing that is targeted to middle-aged working women. Although interested in the possibility, Sarah is concerned by the franchisor's request that she take a personality test. "Why in the world should I take such a test?" Because you are a psychology major with a minor in entrepreneurship, Sarah believes that you be able to help her understand this request. What answer would you give to Sarah regarding her question about the use of personality tests by franchisors?
14. If College Nannies & Tutors decided to start selling franchises in Great Britain and France, which steps should it take to make sure that its concept is suitable for use in those countries? What types of mistakes should it be careful to avoid?
15. Suppose you are an American citizen living in England. You just lost your job with a telecommunications firm that merged with a French company. You would like to stay in England and are thinking about buying a franchise in an American cell phone retail company that is expanding to Europe. What are some of the issues you should evaluate before buying an outlet in an American franchise system that is selling franchises in England?

you be the VC 15.1 Velocity Sports Performance

www.velocitysp.com

Business Idea: Develop a business that helps athletes in every sport, at all ages and skill levels, realize their athletic potential through advanced sports performance training programs scientifically designed to maximize human sports performance.

Pitch: Many people are interested in becoming better athletes. The reasons vary and range from reaching a personal goal, to making the varsity team in high school, to getting a college scholarship. Regrettably, despite their aspirations, many people never reach their full potential as an athlete. The problem often centers on not having sufficient personal strength, speed, and overall athleticism to perform at a high level. Most people can't obtain these attributes on their own. They need fitness education, personal attention, and professional coaching to take themselves to the next level.

Velocity Sports Performance was founded to address this exact set of problems. The company is developing a national chain of training centers to equip athletes of all ages to reach their full potential. Each Velocity Sports Performance Center is a 10,000–30,000-square-foot, climate-controlled facility. Rather than teaching specific skills, like how to throw a football further or how to improve a golf swing, the centers focus on athleticism and fitness. A personal training program is established for each client, and the clients train in small groups, under the direction of coaches. All of Velocity's coaches have at least a bachelor's degree in exercise science or a related field and have coached at least at the collegiate level. The individual programs that most clients rotate through, with their small groups, are as follows:

- Speed, Agility, and Coordination
- Strength and Power
- Mobility and Flexibility
- Energy Systems
- Injury Prevention

Each program was carefully designed by Loren Seagrave, Velocity's founder and world-renowned speed and sports performance coach. To accommodate clients' personal interests, and to provide training facilities for drop-in college and pro athletes, each Velocity center includes athletic turf fields, running tracks, hard court basketball/volleyball surfaces, and Olympic-style weightlifting equipment.

One particularly fun aspect of the Velocity Sport Performance experience is that many top-notch college and professional athletes train at Velocity facilities, right alongside Velocity's other clients. Wouldn't it be fun to pace yourself against some of the world's finest while completing one or more exercise activities?

Q&A: Based on the material covered in this chapter, what questions would you ask the firm's founders before making your funding decision? What answers would satisfy you?

Decision: If you had to make your decision on just the information provided in the pitch and on the company's Web site, would you fund this firm? Why or why not?

you be the VC 15.2 ZENhome

www.zenhomecleaning.com

Business Idea: Provide unique housecleaning services while remaining conscious of environmental concerns by using only nontoxic, eco-friendly products.

Pitch: Many people pay professional housekeepers to clean their homes. A potential downside to this approach is that most housekeepers use traditional cleaning supplies to do their work. This situation poses a problem for people who prefer to use nontoxic, eco-friendly products in their homes. At the same time, most housecleaning companies are similar in terms of the services they provide. For instance, few if any housecleaning services view housecleaning as a holistic service that deals with both the physical act of housekeeping and the emotional and spiritual well-being of the client.

ZENhome offers a solution to this problem by changing humdrum cleaning into something special. The company uses only nontoxic, environmentally friendly cleaning products, which appeals to both ecologically aware customers and people with allergies. In addition, ZENhome cleaners burn essential oils while cleaning, spray linens with lavender mist, turn down beds, place organic chocolate bars on pillows, and leave small bowls of potpourri in their clients' homes. The entire effort is meant to help customers feel good about choosing an environmentally friendly cleaning service and feel good about themselves. Not only does ZENhome want its customers to come home to a clean house, they want them to come home to a peaceful, therapeutic setting as well.

ZENhome is currently operating in New York City. The company is thinking about using franchising to expand outside of the city.

Q&A: Based on the material covered in this chapter, what questions would you ask the firm's founders before making your funding decision? What answers would satisfy you?

Decision: If you had to make your decision on just the information provided in the pitch and on the company's Web site, would you fund this firm? Why or why not?

1-800-GOT-JUNK?: How to Turn People's Discards Into a Vibrant Franchise System

www.1800gotjunk.com

Bruce R. Barringer,
University of Central Florida
R. Duane Ireland,
Texas A&M University

Introduction

1-800-GOT-JUNK? advertises itself as the "world's largest junk removal service." If you have junk that needs to be removed from your home or business, all you have to do is call the company's toll-free number, and if you're in one of the markets the company serves, you can schedule an appointment for the junk to be removed at your convenience.

Sound pretty ordinary? It is—and it isn't. There is certainly nothing new about 1-800-GOT-JUNK?'s business idea. Junk removal services have always been around. What is new is the way the company has approached selling its services in the junk removal industry. Impressively, the company's approach has made it a profitable and rapidly growing franchise organization. Let's see how this has happened.

Brian Scudamore

Brian Scudamore started 1-800-GOT-JUNK? in 1989. He remembers the exact moment of inspiration that led to launching his venture. It was three days before his 19th birthday, and he was waiting his turn in a McDonald's drive-through lane. Just ahead of him was a beat-up old pickup truck, filled with old tires and twisted bicycle frames. The hand-painted sign on the door read MARK'S HAULING. Scudamore thought, "I could do that." He figured he could buy a beat-up old truck and haul junk for people as a way of paying for college education.

The next day, Scudamore bought a $700 truck and started a junk removal service. He named it Rubbish Boys. The business started slowly but picked up as time went on, and eventually Scudamore was so busy that he dropped out of college to pursue the business full-time. One of his favorite stories from that time in his life is telling his father that he dropped out of school to build a junk removal business. His father was, of all things, a liver transplant surgeon. He recalls that his father was not impressed—to say the least. He chuckles when he says that today in that his father is a member of the board of directors for the company his son founded.

In 1998, Scudamore changed the name of his company from Rubbish Boys to 1-800-GOT-JUNK? He wanted a name that was descriptive of his service and was easy for customers to use and remember. Scudamore decided to franchise the business, primarily to avoid having to borrow money to expand. Reflecting on his decision to become a franchisor Scudamore said:

> It's the ultimate leverage model. People pay you a fee up-front to help them grow. Rather than lose control of my vision by going public—I chose franchising. It's the ultimate growth model.

1-800-GOT-JUNK?'s Unique Approach to the Junk Industry

There are three aspects of the way 1-800-GOT-JUNK? has approached the junk industry that have helped the company differentiate itself in the marketplace and build a high-quality franchise organization.

1. Positioning. The company occupies a position in the junk industry that previously wasn't served adequately, if at all. 1-800-GOT-JUNK? fills the sweet stop between city-provided trash removal (provided to most homes for free) and companies like Waste Management, which serve businesses, factories, and apartment complexes. 1-800-GOT- JUNK?'s position is depicted in the figure titled 1-800-GOT-JUNK?'s Positioning Strategy: Occupying the Sweet Spot in the Middle. By occupying this position, the company is filling unmet needs. Think about it. All homeowners have larger items they need to get rid of from time to time, like an old refrigerator, sofa, or dishwasher. City trash collectors typically won't

1-800-GOT-JUNK's Positioning Strategy: Occupying the Sweet Spot in the Middle

Curbside Trash and Garbage Pickup for Homeowners	Larger Items Consumers Have that are Too Big for City Pickup but Too Small for Large Companies	Big Bins with Trash From Businesses, Factories, and Apartment Buildings
Removal Provided by City Governments	**Removal Provided by 1-800-GOT-JUNK** (The sweet spot in the middle)	Removal Provided by Large For-Profit Companies like Waste Management

take these types of items. 1-800-GOT JUNK? provides a pickup service to satisfy these types of needs.

2. Standardized, high-quality service. In communities where junk removal services are available, they are typically hit-and-miss. The services are run mostly by independent operators. Many of these operators are fine, but the consumer typically doesn't know what to expect. If a consumer picks a junk removal service out of the yellow pages, it's entirely possible that someone will show up late in a beat-up old truck that may or may not have the capacity to complete the customer's job. In contrast, 1-800-GOT-JUNK? provides a highly standardized, branded service. Its drivers show up on time, in late-model Ford F-450s, Nissan UD 1400s, or Isuzu NPR trucks. The trucks are all painted the same colors (blue and white) and have identical dump boxes. Franchisees are required to wash their trucks once a day. All of the company's employees wear uniforms. A 1-800-GOT-JUNK? employee wears navy slacks, a royal-blue golf shirt (tucked in) with logo, a baseball cap, belt, and boots, all of which must match.

   To illustrate Scudamore and his top-management team's commitment to providing customers a high-quality standardized service, CNNMoney.com reported in an article that Scudamore pulled the plug on a Canadian franchisee for driving a muddy truck with a peeling 1-800-GOT-JUNK? decal. According to the article, Scudamore reacted to the incident by saying, "Do you ever see a dirty FedEx truck? I mean, do you ever"?
3. A savvy mix of low-tech and high-tech. While hauling junk is a low-tech activity, the company is decidedly high-tech in its behind-the-scenes activities. All the calls that are placed to the company's toll-free number, which is the same as its name (1-800-GOT-JUNK?), are handled by a call center in Vancouver, Canada, which is where the company is headquartered. The requests for service are entered into a proprietary computer program called JunkNet, which is a program the company built from scratch for $500,000. To view a given day's schedule of jobs, all a franchisee has to do is log on to his or her JunkNet account. If a new job comes in during the day, the program automatically sends the applicable franchisee an alert. All of the franchisees are equipped with Web-enabled cell phones. JunkNet provides other back-end type functionality for the franchisees.

There is also a green, or environmentally friendly, aspect to 1-800-GOT-JUNK?'s business. Franchisees are encouraged to dispose of items at recycling centers, instead of county landfills, when appropriate. Along with helping the environment, this policy has a financial reward. Most landfills charge a fee; dropping items at recycling centers is typically free. Some recycling centers even pay for certain items, like scrap metal. There are also times when people dispose of things that have value. In these instances, the franchisees can take the items and resell them, if the effort is worth the gain.

One thing the company enjoys doing is maintaining a list of the most unusual things they have been asked to dispose of. The list currently includes:

- An 8-foot-long stuffed swordfish
- A ship's compass
- A prosthetic leg
- A Bill Clinton mask
- 18,000 cans of outdated sardines
- Antique rifles

What Lies Ahead

To Scudamore's credit, he has gotten his company off to a good start. The firm has 241 franchisees in the United States, Canada, and Australia, and is still growing. 1-800-GOT-JUNK?'s growth has been bootstrapped entirely from its own cash flow, and Scudamore remains the sole owner of the company. The question for 1-800-GOT-JUNK? now is "What lies ahead?"

Discussion Questions

1. What do you think lies ahead for 1-800-GOT-JUNK? What are some of the things that can go right and what are some of the things that can go wrong as this firm continues to expand?
2. What qualities do you think 1-800-GOT-JUNK? looks for in prospective franchisees? If you were a prospective franchisee, what questions would you ask the company as part of your own due diligence process?
3. Do you think 1-800-GOT-JUNK? is a business concept that lends itself to franchising, or do you think franchising

is inappropriate for this company? Justify your answer. What alternatives did Brian Scudamore have for growing 1-800-GOT-JUNK? other than franchising?

4. In your judgment, would 1-800-GOT-JUNK? be better off pursuing new markets via individual franchise agreements or area franchise agreements? Explain your answer.

Application Questions

1. Do you think 1-800-GOT-JUNK? will stay in its niche as it continues to grow, or do you think the company will eventually expand into markets pictured to the left and markets pictured to the right of its current position in the figure titled 1-800-GOT-JUNK's Positioning Strategy? (*Note*: Some city governments contract with private firms for curbside trash and garbage removal.)
2. Spend some time looking at 1-800-GOT-JUNK?'s Web site and doing some additional reading about the company. Make a list of what you believe are some of the firm's strengths and weaknesses. In addition, briefly describe what an average day would be like for a 1-800-GOT-JUNK? franchisee.

Sources: 1-800-GOT-JUNK? homepage, (accessed May 10, 2006); S. Allen, (2004). About homepage, "Entrepreneur Success Story: Brian Scudamore of 1-800-GOT-JUNK?" (accessed May 11, 2006); J. Martin, "Cash From Trash," CNNMoney.com (2003).

Cartridge World: How Bright Is the Outlook for the Company's Franchisees?

www.cartridgeworld.com

Bruce R. Barringer,
University of Central Florida
R. Duane Ireland,
Texas A&M University

Introduction

There is no denying that Cartridge World's service meets a need. The company, which is a franchise organization, sells franchises to individuals who operate small storefronts that refill ink cartridges. The idea behind the business is to offer consumers an affordable alternative to buying expensive printer replacement cartridges. Haven't you cringed over the prices as you buy a replacement cartridge for your printer?

Cartridge World's concept has caught on so quickly that the company recently passed the 1,000-store threshold worldwide. But there are two threats looming on Cartridge World's horizon that could have a major impact on the company and its franchisees' future. This case describes the history of Cartridge World and then presents the challenges that the company is facing.

Easing a Pain

Cartridge World was launched in Australia in 1988. From the outset, it has been a business that specializes in refilling empty printer cartridges. A consumer can bring an empty ink cartridge to a Cartridge World store, wait while the cartridge is professionally refilled, and leave with a full cartridge at about half the price of a new one. To spur its growth, the company starting selling franchises in 1997. Since then, its growth has taken off. Its roster of 1,000-plus franchised outlets is currently growing by more than one outlet every day.

The essence of Cartridge World's success is clear—the company eases a pain. There is one frustration that almost all computer printer owners have in common: the replacement cost cartridges. To illustrate just how expensive the ink in a printer cartridge is, Burt Yarkin, the CEO of Cartridge World's North American division, points out that the ink inside a new cartridge from Hewlett-Packard (HP), Lexmark, or Canon costs more per ounce than Chanel No. 5 (perfume) or Dom Perignon champagne. "People know they're getting ripped off," Yarkin recently told *BusinessWeek*. "We're giving consumers and businesses a choice."

Why Cartridge World Sells Franchises

The idea of refilling ink cartridges rather than buying replacements isn't new, but Cartridge World is the first company to set up retail stores that offer ink cartridge refills while you wait. The bet is that consumers will make a habit of getting their existing cartridges refilled, rather than buying new ones, if the process is cheaper, simple, and convenient. To make the process convenient, Cartridge World is selling franchises at an aggressive pace. "We want to be the McDonald's of ink and toner," Burt Yarkin said in a separate interview. "We're going right into people's neighborhoods and becoming part of their daily lives."

Cartridge World turned to franchising primarily as a means of accelerating its growth.

The cost of a Cartridge World franchise is between $105,000 and $175,000. These figures, which include a one-time franchise fee of $25,000 to $35,000 and the capital needed to start up the business, show the beauty of franchising for a company like Cartridge World. If Cartridge World sells 1,000 franchises in the United States in the next 10 years, the company will collect $25 million to $35 million in franchise fees, and its franchisees will invest between $75 million and $145 million for land and equipment to open their stores. This is money that the company would have had to raise through other means if it had decided to expand via company-owned stores rather than franchising.

With a focus on even more growth, Cartridge World offers a range of products, including new ink and laser cartridges, specialty papers for quality photographic prints, copy toners, fax supplies, and printer and cash register ribbons in addition to its core service of cartridge refilling. The idea behind adding products is to become a true one-stop shop for printer supplies.

Threats on the Horizon

Despite its positive momentum, there are two threats looming on Cartridge World's horizon. It is unclear how significant these threats are.

Threat #1: New Entrants.
In early 2006, Walgreens announced that it plans to enter the ink-replacement business and is currently pilot-testing its service. If Walgreens decides to offer the service nationwide, it will become available to customers in more than 1,500 of its stores. Similar offerings are in the works at OfficeMax and Office Depot, along with a number of smaller companies. At Walgreens, consumers will be able to have ink cartridges refilled within 15 minutes, which is similar to the time it takes at Cartridge World. Walgreens says that its price will be around 50 percent less than the price of a new cartridge, which provides it a slight price advantage over Cartridge World.

Along with larger companies offering a similar service, Cartridge World may also be facing new competition from smaller firms that plan to open their own storefronts or put ink-refill service in existing retail locations. For example, Rapid Refill, an Oregon-based franchise organization, presently has 40 cartridge-refill stores and is expanding.

Threat #2: The Cartridge Makers Are Fighting Back.
Obviously, the potential losers in Cartridge World's pursuit to provide consumers a more affordable way to refill their cartridges are the printer cartridge manufacturers. Analysts say that ink and toner supplies made up more than 50 percent of HP's 2004 profits, even though they brought in less than 25 percent of the company's $80 billion in sales. Similar types of proportions between revenue and profit are thought to exist at Canon and Lexmark. The impact of Cartridge World and its peers is being felt. According to a recent *New York Times* article, the migration by consumers to alternative ways of getting their printer cartridges refilled is the primary reason that Lexmark's net income dropped 47 percent in the fourth quarter of 2005.

In response to these developments, the cartridge makers are fighting back in two ways. First, they are using the courts to make sure that Cartridge World and similar firms don't use the same patented ink formulation that they do. For example, HP, which has over 4,000 patents in its printer supply business, went after Cartridge World in October 2005 for using ink that HP alleged infringed on its patents. Similarly, at roughly the same time, HP went after InkCycle, the company that makes cartridge refills under the Staples brand, saying that it had violated three HP patents covering fast-drying ink for paper and methods for preventing color from bleeding on paper. That dispute was settled when InkCycle changed its ink formulation.

The second way that the cartridge manufacturers are fighting back is by arguing that refilled cartridges produce lower-quality printing results and are more expensive for consumers in the long run. Some independent analysts agree that a tangible difference still exists between the results produced by a new cartridge and a refilled one, although many people have a hard time seeing the difference. In regard to costs, the manufacturers say that the original cartridges will print more pages than refilled cartridges, and that the per page cost is actually lower for new cartridges.

A potential third way that HP and the other manufacturers could fight back, but haven't pursued, is to engineer their cartridges in a way that would prevent them from being refilled. This possibility is seen as unlikely as a result of regulatory issues.

Cartridge World's Outlook for the Future

Cartridge World is continuing to aggressively expand and sell new franchises. Two important questions the company must now face are: to what extent should it be concerned about the competitive threats it is facing and what steps should it take to deal with them?

Discussion Questions

1. What do you think? How important are the two competitive threats that Cartridge World is facing? What steps, if any, should Cartridge World take to meet these threats?
2. Of the two major threats facing Cartridge World, which one do you think has the most potential to negatively affect this firm? Explain your answer.
3. Do you think the competitive threats mentioned in the case will slow the pace at which Cartridge World sells franchises? Should they?
4. Do you think that this is a good time or a poor time to start a new company in the cartridge-refill business? If you started a new company in this area, what types of competitive issues would be foremost in your mind?

Application Questions

1. Reflect back on Chapter 5 of this book. What does the Cartridge World case teach us with regard to the impact of Porter's five forces on an industry's profitability? Which of the five forces will be most adversely impacted (in terms of lowering the cartridge-refill industry's profitability) if Walgreens, Office Depot, and OfficeMax establish a significant presence in the market?
2. If Walgreens, Office Depot, and OfficeMax enter Cartridge World's business, how can Cartridge World differentiate itself from these larger firms? Think carefully about your answer. Brainstorm some ways that Cartridge World could remain vibrant by serving its customers in a different, a unique, or a more valuable way as compared to its larger competitors.

Sources: D. Darlin, "New Printer Cartridge or a Refill? Either Way, Ink Is Getting Cheaper," *The New York Times*, February 4, 2006, C1; Pui-Wing Tam, "A Cheaper Way to Refill Your Printer," *The Wall Street Journal*, January 26, 2006, p. D1; P. Burrows, "Ever Wonder Why Ink Costs So Much?" *BusinessWeek*, November 4, 2005, 42–44; Pui-Wing Tam, "Fill'er Up, with Color," *The Wall Street Journal*, August 3, 2004, B1.

Endnotes

1. L. Wolf, "Learning Curve," *Upsizemag.com*, www.upsizemag.com (accessed June 1, 2006).
2. Wolf, "Learning Curve."
3. Personal interview with Joseph Keeley, May 30, 2006.
4. V. K. Jolly, *Commercializing New Technologies* (Cambridge, MA: Harvard Business School Press, 1997).
5. www.franchise.com (accessed June 3, 2006); I. Alon, "The Use of Franchising by U.S.-Based Retailers," *Journal of Small Business Management* 39, no. 2 (2001): 111–22.
6. J. G. Combs, D. J. Ketchen, and R. D. Ireland, "Effective Managing Service Chain Organizations," *Organizational Dynamics* (2007, in press).
7. Wikipedia Encyclopedia, www.wikpedia.com (accessed June 3, 2006).
8. "Breaking the Silver Ceiling," U.S. Congress Report from the Committee on Aging, 2005; Start Your Own Business, "It Pays to Care," *Small Business Opportunities*, Spring 2002.
9. Comfort Keepers homepage, www.comfortkeepers.com (accessed June 1, 2006).
10. P. H. Rubin, "The Theory of the Firm and the Structure of the Franchise Contract," *Journal of Law and Economics* 21 (1978): 223–33.
11. Combs, Ketchen, and Ireland, "Effectively Managing Service Chain Organizations."
12. D. H. B. Welsh, I. Alon, and C. M. Falbe, "An Examination of Retail Franchising in Emerging Markets," *Journal of Small Business Management* 44, no. 1 (2006): 130–49.
13. B. Merrilees and L. Frazer, "Entrepreneurial Franchises Have Hidden Superior Marketing Systems, *Qualitative Market Research* 9, no. 1 (2006): 73–85.
14. R. Sloan, J. Sloan, and J. Sinelli, Startupnation Podcast, March 27, 2006.
15. G. J. Castrogiovanni, J. G. Combs, and R. T. Justis, "Shifting Imperatives: An Integrating View of Resource Scarcity and Agency Reasons for Franchising," *Entrepreneurship Theory and Practice* 39, no. 1 (2006): 23–40.
16. R. Bennett, "To Franchise or Not: How to Decide," in *Franchising Today: 1966–1967*, ed. C. L. Vaughn and D. B. Slater (New York: Matthew Bender and Company, 1967), 20.
17. J. Brickley and F. Dark, "The Choice of Organizational Form: The Case of Franchising," *Journal of Financial Economics* 18 (1987): 401–20.
18. "Darden Restaurants, Inc.," *Standard & Poor's Stock Report*, www.standardandpoors.com (accessed June 4, 2006).
19. J. E. Clarkin and S. M. Swavely, "The Importance of Personal Characteristics in Franchisee Selection," *Journal of Retailing and Consumer Services* 13, no. 2 (2006): 133–42.
20. International Franchising Association, "What Is Franchising?" www.franchise.org (accessed May 27, 2004).
21. Federal Trade Commission, *Consumers Guide to Buying a Franchise* (Washington, DC: U.S. Government Printing Office, 2002).
22. M. Grunhagen and M. Mittlestaedt, "Entrepreneurs or Investors: Do Multi-Unit Franchisees Have Different Philosophical Orientations?" *Journal of Small Business Management* 43, no. 3 (2005): 207–25.
23. Candy Bouquet homepage, www.candybouquet.com (accessed June 1, 2006).
24. J. Bennett, "Cruise Franchisee Says It's Been Smooth Sailing, *StartupJournal.com*, www.startupjournal.com (accessed May 30, 2006).
25. L. Altinay, "Selecting Partners in an International Franchise Organisation," *International Journal of Hospitality Management* 25, no. 1 (2006): 108–28.
26. Federal Trade Commission, "Guide to the FTC Franchise Rule," www.ftc.gov/bcp/franchise/netrule.html (accessed June 1, 2006).
27. R. L. Purvin, *The Franchise Fraud* (New York: John Wiley & Sons, 1994), 7.
28. American Bar Association, *Legal Guide for Small Business* (New York: Random House, 2000).
29. Federal Trade Commission, "Guide to the FTC Franchise Rule."
30. I. Alon and K. Bian, "Real Estate Franchising: The Case of Coldwell Banker Expansion into China," *Business Horizons* 48, no. 3 (2005): 223–31.
31. Federal Trade Commission, "Guide to the FTC Franchise Rule."
32. International Franchise Association, "How Widespread Is Franchising?" www.franchise.org (accessed March 29, 2002).
33. E. Pfister, B. Deffians, M. Doriant-Duban, and S. Saussier, "Institutions and Contracts: Franchising," *European Journal of Law and Economics* 21, no. 1 (2006): 53–78.

Chapter 5 Franchising and Other Alternatives

Learning Objectives

- $ To know why franchising has become an extremely popular way of going into business.
- $ To understand the many significant advantages to an entrepreneur being a part of a franchise chain.
- $ To know the franchisees' legal protection from being rushed into a premature decision by the franchisor.
- $ To be aware that despite government regulations, many individuals are cheated by unscrupulous sellers of franchises and business opportunities.
- $ To understand what the failure rate of franchises really is and what it means.

We have just examined two ways for an entrepreneur to go into business: by starting one or by buying one. In this chapter, we describe a third option—becoming franchised. We first define it as a concept; we next consider some of the reasons for its popularity, and we identify and explain some of the problems associated with the practice. Finally, we discuss the growing use of "business opportunities" as a means of entry into small business.

One of the more remarkable economic developments in the 20th century was been the growth in franchising as a way to do business. Much of the early activity in franchising was of a type known as *product franchising*.[1]

Under this arrangement, dealers were given the right to distribute goods for a manufacturer. For this right, the dealer (the franchisee) paid a fee for the right to sell the trademarked goods of the producer (the franchisor).

Perhaps the first important use of product franchising can be seen in the efforts of the Singer Corporation during the 1800s to distribute its sewing machines.[2] This practice then became common in the petroleum and automobile industries early in the 20th century.

Manufacturing franchising is commonly used in the soft-drink industry. Using this kind of franchising, the franchisor gives the dealer (bottler) the exclusive right to produce and distribute the product in a particular area.

The last type of franchising, business-format franchising, is what most people today mean when they use the term *franchising*. It is the most popular form, accounting for nearly 75 percent of all franchised outlets in the United States.[3] Business-format franchising is an arrangement under which the franchisor offers a wide range of services to the franchisee, including marketing, advertising, strategic planning, training, production of operations manuals and standards, and quality-control guidance. Because of the wide and growing popularity of this type of franchising, we focus on it in this chapter.

Franchising – a legal arrangement by which one company allow its products, services, or business format to be used by others for a fee.

Franchisee – a company or individual who pays for the legal right to use the product, service, or format of another.

Franchisor – the party that grants to a company or individual the legal right to use the franchisor's products, services, or format.

THE POPULARITY OF FRANCHISING

Franchising has made its mark not only in the United States but throughout the world. The logos of many retailing giants are seen in shopping centers around the globe, as are the logos of many small and moderate-sized establishments. This has not been the result of franchising practices exclusively, but clearly they have played a major role in the globalization of products.

Much of the vitality of franchising has come from U.S. firms looking for new markets and finding them on all the continents. But while the United States may still have the dominant role in the spread of franchising, the rest of the world is becoming increasingly active. There remains, however, great potential for expansion in franchising in the international arena; in the European economy, for example, to reach the same level of penetration as achieved by U.S. franchisers would require doubling the existing number of franchised outlets.

In the United States, the influence of franchising can be clearly seen in the results of a recent study, which found that franchised businesses accounted for more than $1 trillion in sales during 2000.[4] The same study showed that franchised outlets account for 40 percent of all retail sales.[5] To these impressive indicators of growth can be added important considerations concerning employment and job creation. More than 8 million people are employed by franchised establishments, and more than 170,000 new jobs are created each year by franchised businesses.[6] In summary, it is clear that franchising is an increasingly significant component in the U.S. economy. We now discuss some of the reasons why franchising has grown as it has.

ADVANTAGES FOR THE FRANCHISEE

Firms that use franchising as a means to expand do so because they believe the franchisor-franchisee relationship is a symbiotic one. That is, each party provides the other something beneficial it would not have been able to provide for itself. Both gain from the relationship and both must contribute. The two parties are interdependent. The franchisor's interests are best served by having each of its outlets succeed, and because this is so, the franchising firm provides a number of advantages to its franchisees.

Start-up Assistance

The franchisor will typically provide services intended to make the task of getting started easier. Among these services are site selection advice, facilities layout analysis, financial assistance (sometimes directly, but more often indirectly, by making it a bit easier to get other sources of capital due to the presence of the franchisor), management training, employee selection, and training assistance.

Basis for Judging Prospect of Success

In addition to these services, the franchising option provides a ready-made basis for assessing the possibilities for making money. The process by which future profitability of a new business is determined is always an uncertain one. Whenever a new undertaking is launched, no one can predict exactly how things will turn out. With the purchase of a franchise, however, making a projection of profit level becomes an easier task. A "Burger Heaven" in Peoria will probably do about as well as the one in Portland. The two towns are not the same, of course, so if you are interested in buying a franchise you will want to check the results of sister outlets in other cities as well. These stores provide as good a comparison as you will be able to find and they should be accessible and cooperative to you as a prospective franchise owner.

Instant Recognition

Well-established franchise chains bring with them the important advantage of recognition. Many new businesses experience lean months, or years, after start-up. Obviously, the longer the period the firm must endure this, the greater the chances of failure. With the right franchise this period of agony may last only weeks, or perhaps just days.

Purchasing Power

Being part of a large organization means paying less for a variety of things such as supplies, equipment, inventory, services, and insurance. It also can mean getting better service from suppliers because of the importance of the national account of which you are part.

Advertising Scope and Sophistication

Franchise companies are often national in scope, and because they are, they do national advertising. This advertising is not only less expensive on the basis of cost per contact than most locally produced and distributed material, it is usually far better. To pay for this, most franchisors levy a certain amount on each franchisee. This contribution brings quality and coverage beyond what that amount would pay for if it were used on its own.

Operational Improvements

In many industries, competition is so tough that the difference between success and failure can be the result of minor efficiency improvements. Because of the importance of the success of each franchised outlet to the franchisor, the organization will concentrate a great deal of its time and other resources on making methods more efficient. Once again, centralization of effort can lead to improvements that the individual units would not be able to accomplish. The improvements are made available as systemwide consulting services and are targeted toward areas such as financial and inventory control, use of custom-designed information systems, and maintenance and repair guidelines.

DISADVANTAGES FOR THE FRANCHISEE

Although there are some significant advantages to having a franchise as one starts into business, some disadvantages should also be acknowledged.

Restrictions

Many entrepreneurs start their own business because they believe there is a better way to operate and they have discovered it, or will soon do so. This kind of creative urge has no place in most franchised outlets. The interest in efficiency runs high in many franchisor headquarters. This efficiency and uniformity of operation mean that the individual operator faces numerous restrictions on how to go about managing the business. One classic example of regimentation in franchising can be found in the McDonald's restaurant organization. A McDonald's franchisee is given very little operational latitude; indeed, the operations manual attends to such minor details as when to oil the bearings on the potato slicer. The purpose of these regulations is not to frustrate the franchisee but to ensure that each outlet is run in a uniform, correct manner.

Restrictions are also found on the owner's decisions regarding the product line. It may be in the best interest of one particular PoFolks restaurant to add chocolate truffles to its product line, but the franchisor, who may be skeptical, has the last say and will make the determination on the basis of what is good for all the restaurants in the chain.

Costs

The costs associated with being a franchise member are an additional consideration. These costs include the original outlay to get the franchise, the share of profits that must go to the franchisor, and fees for advertising and other services.

Termination

Another disadvantage facing franchisees is the threat of termination of the franchise. Although some states have laws restricting franchisor actions that result in the loss of the franchise, many franchisees are vulnerable to this development.

Unrealistic Expectations

For years, we have heard claims that buying a franchise was far safer than trying to start a business. The industry's top group, the International Franchise Association (IFA), reports that 97 percent of all franchise units opened nationwide during the last five years are still in operation.[7] This figure is consistent with the 95 percent survival rate cited by the IFA and other industry observers in the past. The conclusion is obvious: Buying a franchise is not risky, and, compared to the hazards of opening your own business, it is clearly the better way to go.

What makes these figures believable is the logic behind the process: An idea that is a proven winner in one location is transplanted to another and then another. At each new place all of the old ideas, with refinements, that worked so well elsewhere are put to use. Add to this compelling idea all those important advantages mentioned earlier and you have the formula for success. The difference between the security offered by franchising and the risks of starting a new business is substantial, perhaps even dramatic when the commonly held, but mistaken, perception of small business mortality rates (that one-third fail the first year and that by year 5 the figure climbs to near 80 percent) is factored into the comparison.

With the available "information," it is no surprise that many people held the opinion that franchises were safe and start-ups were risky. Recent studies have cast a different light on the topic, however. One of the problems with information provided by industry groups like the IFA is the manner by which the data are collected. The 97 percent survival rate is based on a survey of franchisors only, to which less than 20 percent responded. If we assume that the most successful franchisees are the ones most likely to want to talk about their experience, the survival rate looks considerably different. Indeed, the bias is strong enough to make the results suspect, perhaps even meaningless. See Illustration Capsule 5-1 for a description of the disappointment encountered by a

Illustration Capsule 5-1

EXPECTATIONS NOT FULFILLED

The prospect of running his own business appealed to Gene Swanzy of Arlington, Maryland, so, at age 58, he bought two Mail Boxes Etc. franchises. He had just retired from a long career as a broadcasting executive and with $300,000 in savings, he and his wife, Mary Anna Severson, made the plunge. He regrets the move greatly. "It's been a horrendous experience, I blew my retirement money and now I'm trapped," he says. To add to his woes, he is in debt $250,000.

The couple and 29 other franchisees are suing the San Diego-based franchisor for fraud and misrepresentation. The company denies the charges and has filed a cross-complaint.

Source: Earl C. Gottschalk, Jr., "Tax Shop? Gym? Finding a Franchise without Losing Your Shirt," *The New York Times*, March 26, 1995, section F, 12.

franchisee who had high hopes for what franchising would mean for him upon his retirement.

A more recent survey was conducted among franchisees. The results are important because they differ so greatly from those of the IFA. The study, conducted by Timothy Bates of Wayne State University, found that of the people who had purchased their franchises in 1987, only 54 percent were still running the business in 1991, 8 percent had sold it, and 38 percent had lost their franchise.[8] This figure is substantially larger than anything we were given in the past. Moreover, the fate of independent entrepreneurs was better: 62 percent were still in business, 6 percent had sold, and 32 percent had lost their businesses.[9]

Do these new results mean that franchising is no longer a desirable way to go into small business? Certainly not; it is a proven concept. What they do mean, however, is that the security that some people associate with franchising is an illusion. Hard work, realistic expectations, and careful investigation are required if becoming a franchisee is to be a successful, satisfying experience. Our next section describes the process of evaluation.

EVALUATING THE FRANCHISE OPTION

The choice between buying a franchise and starting a business can be a difficult decision. It involves looking at yourself as a prospective franchisee, including reflection on such personal concerns as your interests, personality, and background. Then conduct a careful investigation and analysis of the franchisor. The process is frequently long and demanding, but the costs associated with a bad decision can be devastating.

You as a Franchisee

What are the requirements to be successful as a franchisee? A U.S. Department of Commerce publication, the *Franchise Opportunities Handbook*, cautions that anyone going into franchising must be willing to work long hours, engage in hard work, and face personal sacrifices.[10] Furthermore, the individual must enjoy working with others, be a good supervisor, and be an organized person. To this list could be added the ability to accept orders and policy as handed down by the franchisor and the willingness to be a team player.

Considering the entire list of "requirements" leads one to the conclusion that the ideal franchisee might be a blend of the entrepreneur and the corporate manager. This may, in fact, be a reasonable way to characterize the job of the franchisee. Much of what happens in the conduct of the franchised outlet's business is carefully programmed and therefore within the area covered by corporate policy. This activity, then, is similar to that engaged in by many managers in large companies. Life in a franchised business is by no means completely predictable, however, and the franchisee soon learns that he or she is on the firing line much the same as he or she would be if the business were independent.

A study reported in the April 1995 issue of the *Journal of Small Business Management* examined the determinants of franchisee satisfaction of 127 franchisee owner-managers in Australia.[11] The author provides the following observation: ". . . the finding that most franchisee characteristics were unrelated to their post-purchase satisfaction is a significant step towards differentiating the personal characteristics of franchisees from those of independent entrepreneurs." In other words, the results found in this study were contrary to those describing "conventional" entrepreneurs. This difference in personality underscores the significance of franchising as a route into business distinct from the independent start-up.

Beyond their psychological makeup, prospective franchisees are evaluated by franchisors as to their background. Knowing about the business can have a powerful influence on whether the undertaking succeeds. Although many franchisors provide operating directions that are carefully and precisely written, having actual experience is seen as an important advantage. A high school history teacher who hopes to operate an automobile paint and repair franchise may find the franchisor manual helpful but not enough to allow him to deal with all of the technical problems encountered in the shop. For this individual to prosper, or perhaps just survive, would require some rather dramatic changes. The best advice may be to build on the skills you already have, rather than try to develop a whole new set.

A final area of concern is whether you would enjoy the business you are thinking about entering. Suppose your investigation pointed to the muffler repair business as one that met all of your growth and profitability criteria nicely. Does this mean you should buy a franchise to get you into this line of work? No, not unless you know what it is like to inspect and replace mufflers. Try it, see if you like it by actually spending some time under the car, working with rusted nuts and bolts and occasionally coming into contact with a very hot muffler or exhaust pipe. It will be worth your time to invest a week or two getting this kind of introduction to the work, even if it means working for free at the kind of shop you are thinking about getting into.

The Industry

An important element in any prospective franchise agreement that you may enter into is the industry in which your business will compete. An exploration of the industry requires library research and data gathering with the goal of deepening your understanding of how the industry operates. Among the questions that should be addressed are the following:

- ❑ What are the industry's dominant economic characteristics? How big is it? What is its growth rate? How many competitors are there? How easy is it to enter or exit the industry?
- ❑ What is the competition like? Who are the major forces in the industry? Who buys the product? How much emphasis is there on price? Are new entrants likely?
- ❑ What changes are on the horizon? Are substitute products being marketed? Are there any big organizations that may enter? Are foreign competitors likely to emerge?
- ❑ What are the key factors for competitive success? Are they technological in nature? Marketing-related? Distribution-related? Manufacturing-related?

The concern here is to see how good the market or industry is and what it takes to compete successfully in it. The research will probably involve a great deal of time in the library, conversations with people who have experience in the industry, examination of company-provided materials, trade shows visits, and use of government information.

The Franchisor

Clearly, the most important single element for the prospective franchisee to investigate is his or her business partner, the franchisor. Whether the franchisor is fraudulent or just inept, making the wrong choice here can be catastrophic. Another reason for learning as much as possible about the company is that there are so many from which to choose.

The point is, you do not have to settle for any company that has the least question associated with it. If you have decided to explore the opportunities provided by franchising, many possibilities await. Let's look at http://www.franchise.org/, which provides a wide range of information. For those who are seeking a franchise, information is easily accessed. Let's use as an example here, the first category listed, "Accounting/Tax Services." In addition to the category we are asked to specify our investment range. For the lowest range, under $10,000, only one franchisor is given—ExpressTax. When we increase our range to $10,000 to $25,000 we get no hits; at $25,000 to $50,000, however, five appear. The only one above this investment is United Check Cashing in the $100,000 to $250,000 investment range. To illustrate the kinds of information available at the site, we have provided three company listings, from three different industries, each requiring an investment in the $25,000 to $50,000 range. They are listed as Options 1–3 in Figure 5-1. These are only three of many; go to the site, or the one that follows, and do your own investigation.

Another such Web site is http://opportunities.franchise.org/Public/Index.aspx, which lists 27 "industries" from Advertising to Wholesale/Distribution. Within each of the industries are "Industry Sectors." Within the industry "Home/Mobile Services" list are 28 industry sectors, including businesses such as Debt Consolidation, Air Purification, and Decoration/Remodeling. Finally within each sector are franchise listings; Air Purification yields 4 prospects, another "sector," Residential Cleaning has 11.

Another promising source of franchise prospect information is *The Wall Street Journal*. The Thursday edition of each week includes advertisements from companies looking for new franchisees. Local newspapers also carry ads for franchisors, as do many magazines.

By now it should be clear that there is no shortage of franchise opportunities. Selecting the one that is right for you will be considerably more demanding. After selecting the industry that looks most promising, the next step is to get in touch with its members who are franchising. A telephone call or letter will do it; chances are all of the firms you contact will provide everything you need to make some early cuts. Assemble the company materials so you can make a side-by-side comparison of what each offers and how much it costs. To help in this round of screening, use the checklist in Figure 5-2.

Read the material provided by each franchisor carefully and compare the details. Who seems to have the best training program? If that is of no concern to you because of your experience in the business, the amount of financial assistance may be. How much is the franchise fee? What kind of ongoing financial obligations are there? Is it a percentage of profit? Of sales? How much? Will you be assessed a fee for advertising and support services that you do not even want?

One piece of information that you probably will not be given is an estimate of what you can expect to earn with the franchise. Any franchisor making claims about sales or profitability is required by the federal government to provide substantiation for those claims. Review any claims carefully. Are they based on

OPTION 1 EXAMPLES OF FRANCHISE OPPORTUNITIES

Tedeschi Food Shops, Inc.
Company details
Description: We are a turnkey franchise convenience food store company operating in urban and suburban locations offering "fast and friendly" service. Provide groceries, beverages, general merchandise, dairy products, lottery. Deli and gasoline available in some locations.
Business established: 1962
Franchised since: 1972
# of franchised units: 87
Company owned: 114

Contact info.
Address: 14 Howard Street, Rockland, MA
ZIP code: 02370
Country: USA
No-800: (800)833-3724
Phone1: (781)878-8210
Fax: (781)878-0476
Primary contact name & title: Mike Ota - Director of franchising, Ext.2
Secondary contact name & title: –
Email: mota@tedeschifoodshops.com
Web site: http://www.tedeschifoodshops.com

Financial info.
Start-up cash required: $20,000 - $60,000
Investment required: $45,000 - $137,000
Financial comment: Financial assistance is available.

Training
Extensive 3 weeks in-store training. In-depth instructional seminars offered in accounting, merchandising, P&L reviews, sales. Field personnel counsel weekly to advise on operations and financial issues. Annual companywide trade show.

Qualifications
Commitment to excel, dedicated team player, positive personality, sales driven and motivated, financially stable. Experience is helpful but not required.

OPTION 2

Aire Serv Heating and Air Conditioning, Inc.
Company details
Description: Aire Serv is a residentail and commercial provider of heating, cooling and air quality related services and systems.
Business established: 1993
Franchised since: 1993
# of franchised units: 85
Company owned: 0

FIGURE 5–1 Examples of franchise opportunities.

Contact info.
Address: 1020 N. University Parks Drive, Waco, TX
ZIP code: 76707
Country: USA
No-800: (800)583-2662
Fax: (254)745-7546
Primary contact name & title: Doyle James - President
Secondary contact name & title: Tracy Brackeen - Executive Assistant
Email: djames@dwyergroup.com
Web site: http://www.aireserv.com

Financial info.
Start-up cash required: $31,595 - $119,500
Investment required: $31,595 - $119,500
Financial comment: Partial financing available to those who qualify.

Training
Training is provided for operations management, sales and administration functions of the business.

Qualifications
People with a strong desire to follow a proven system, with a previous background in business.

OPTION 3

Reality Sports Entertainment, Inc.
Company details
Description: Reality Sports Entertainment, creators of World Championship Armwrestling (WCA), established the sport of arm wrestling as a pervasive, professional and profitable entity.
Business established: 2002
Franchised since: 2003
# of franchised units: 1
Company owned: 2

Contact info.
Address: 303 Sondrol, P.O. Box 882, Ames, IA
ZIP code: 50010
Country: USA
No-800: (866)232-5023
Fax: (515)232-5036
Primary contact name & title: Donald W. Myers - Operations Manager
Secondary contact name & title: Jack Barringer - CEO
Email:
Web site: --NA--

Financial info.
Start-up cash required: $3,000 - $6,000
Investment required: $35,000 - $50,000
Financial comment: Third-party financing available.

FIGURE 5–1 Examples of franchise opportunities (*continued*).

Training
Franchisees receive an extensive three-day training program at national headquarters. After the initial three-day period, RSE will assist in conducting the first tournament, booking events, and sponsor relations.

Qualifications
Entrepreneurial spirit, sports minded, outgoing personality, sales background preferred. RSE interviews each franchisee extensively.

FIGURE 5–1 Examples of franchise opportunities (*continued*).

EVALUATING THE FRANCHISE OPTION

How many franchised units exist? How many company-owned stores?

When was the franchise founded?

What products and services are provided by the franchised outlets?

How much money is needed to start a franchise?

How much is the franchise fee?

How much is the monthly royalty fee?

Is there an advertising co-op fee?

Does the franchisor offer any financing for franchisees?

What type of ongoing assistance does the franchisor provide to the franchisees?

What type of training does the franchisor provide?

FIGURE 5–2 Checklist for evaluating the franchise option.

actual or projected results? Are they average figures for all franchisees or for a selected few? What assumptions were used in making any projections? Do the claims hold for first-year franchises or only for those that have been in existence for some time?

One last piece of advice: Prepare to be confused. Each company will be putting the best possible light on whatever package it offers, but beneath it all may be some unpleasant facts. It is your job to find out what they are and how bad they are.

Beyond the printed materials of the company and conversations with corporate officials, an important source of information is the franchisee group. Talk with both successful and marginal owner-managers. How satisfied are they? Has the company delivered on its promises? Is it continuing to push for market penetration, or is a sense of complacency setting in? If your contacts are not willing to share their views with you openly, be suspicious. People with success stories usually enjoy telling others about them. See Figure 5–3.

The efforts we have just recommended are intended to help you to protect yourself against making a bad decision. Some people in the franchising field have

---

The Franchise

1. Did your lawyer approve the franchise contract you are considering after he or she studied it paragraph by paragraph?
2. Does the franchise call on you to take any steps that are, according to your lawyer, unwise or illegal in your state, county, or city?
3. Does the franchise give you an exclusive territory for the length of the franchise, or can the franchisor sell a second or third franchise in your territory?
4. Is the franchisor connected in any way with any other franchise company handling similar merchandise or service?
5. If the answer to the last question is yes, what is your protection against this second franchisor organization?
6. Under what circumstances can you terminate the franchise contract and at what cost to you, if you decide for any reason at all that you wish to cancel it?
7. If you sell your franchise, will you be compensated for your goodwill or will the goodwill you have built into the business be lost by you?

The Franchisor

8. How many years has the firm offering you a franchise been in operation?
9. Has it a reputation for honesty and fair dealing among the local firms holding its franchise?
10. Has the franchisor shown you any certified figures indicating exact net profits of one or more going firms that you personally checked yourself with the franchisee?
11. Will the firm assist you with
    a. A management training program?
    b. An employee training program?
    c. A public relations program?
    d. Capital?
    e. Credit?
    f. Merchandising ideas?
12. Will the firm help you find a good location for your new business?
13. Is the franchising firm adequately financed so that it can carry out its stated plan of financial assistance and expansion?
14. Is the franchisor a one-person company or a corporation with an experienced management trained in depth (so that there would always be an experienced person at its head)?
15. Exactly what can the franchisor do for you that you cannot do for yourself?
16. Has the franchisor investigated you carefully enough to assure itself that you can successfully operate one of its franchises at a profit both to itself and to you?
17. Does your state have a law regulating the sale of franchises, and has the franchisor complied with that law?

FIGURE 5–3 Checklist for evaluating a franchise *(continued)*.

You—The Franchisee

18. How much equity capital will you have to have to purchase the franchise and operate it until your income equals your expenses? Where are you going to get it?
19. Are you prepared to give up some independence of action to secure the advantages offered by the franchise?
20. Do you really believe you have the innate ability, training, and experience to work smoothly and profitably with the franchisor, your employees, and your customers?
21. Are you ready to spend much or all of the remainder of your business life with this franchisor, offering its product or service to your public?

Your Market

22. Have you made any study to determine whether the product or service that you propose to sell under franchise has a market in your territory at the prices you will have to charge?
23. Will the population in the territory given to you increase, remain static, or decrease over the next five years?
24. Will the product or service you are considering be in greater demand, about the same, or less demand five years from now than today?
25. What competition exists in your territory already for the product or service you contemplate selling?
    a. Nonfranchise firms?
    b. Franchise firms?

Source: *Franchise Opportunities Handbook* (Washington, DC: U.S. Government Printing Office, 1988).

FIGURE 5–3 Checklist for evaluating a franchise (*continued*).

observed that many buyers investigate what make of car to get more thoroughly than they investigate the franchise purchase. Do not make that mistake; you are your own first-line and best defense against the wrong kind of franchisor. Some protection is provided by others, however; the federal government and many states have taken measures to limit corrupt practices by franchisors. These limits take the form of causing unscrupulous companies to stop doing business, but the people who were victimized are seldom made whole. Our next section discusses franchising law.

FRANCHISING AND THE LAW

Any activity in which so many people are involved with the exchange of so much money has great potential for abuse. Some franchisors are greedy and willing to mislead prospective franchisees; others will use the agreement as it fits their needs, often in clear violation of what it specifies. Because unfair tactics have so frequently found their way into franchisor-franchisee relations, many regulations have been put into place at both federal and state levels. We will discuss the more important means of protection provided by these regulations.

Because of the aggressiveness of some franchisors, the regulations provide protection starting with the first contact made by the company. If you are intrigued by what you have read or heard about a franchisor and decide to contact it, what happens next? Typically the response will be in the form of promotional material—lots of glossy promotional material. It is, of course, intended to entice you into thinking about what all those benefits of franchise ownership would mean to you. There will also likely be a follow-up of some kind, possibly by phone, and then there will be a letter, accompanied by an application blank. If you complete and return the application, expect some pressure from the sales group in the franchisor home office. Don't worry about the pressure you may get to make a quick decision. You are protected; the law precludes the franchisor from selling you anything or taking any money until 10 days after you have received two things: a copy of the franchise agreement and a copy of the disclosure statement.

The franchise agreement is the contract between franchisor and franchisee. It gives the vital details about the relationship between franchisees and the company. It is precise; unfortunately, it is also hard to read and is therefore probably best put in the hands of a lawyer. The items in the agreement include such important items as costs, terms, obligations of both parties, conditions governing termination of the franchise, and limitations of the franchisee. Remember that it is the franchisor's document; it was written by the franchisor and says what the company wants it to say. Read it very carefully and compare it to others.

The other important document that the regulations state you must be given is the disclosure statement, or, as it is officially called, the uniform franchise offering circular or prospectus. If there is a single most important source of information, this is it. The franchisor must provide information on the 23 topics in Figure 5-4.

Uniform franchise offering circular – a document, required of franchisors by federal law, that makes available to prospective franchisees information on a wide range of important topics.

The topics covered in the disclosure statement are intended to allow the prospective franchisee to determine whether the company is trustworthy and therefore someone with whom he or she wants to do business. A cautionary note should be added: The information given in the statement is vital, but bear in mind that it is information provided by the franchisor and not subject to independent verification. Furthermore, the Federal Trade Commission (FTC), the agency requiring this statement, makes no claim as to its authenticity. What if the company lies to you? It has broken the law and so is subject to penalties, but that may not help you if you have already given it your money. Typically, the FTC tries to have money returned to those who were victimized by fraudulent claims, but they often are not able to do so, and when they do, it is usually only a partial settlement.

Honesty questions aside, the information in the disclosure statement should provide the basis for judging the costs and benefits of franchise ownership. The chances of a comparison of these statements from several franchises leading to a clear winner are slim. That is, the very good franchises, those with excellent reputations and an impressive list of services for franchisees, are usually very expensive. If you want to spend less, you will probably have to settle for less.

In summary, the major thrust of the law is to prevent abuses by franchisors. The prospective franchisee has the legally protected right not to be rushed into doing something he or she otherwise would not have done. The franchisee also has the right to be given information that allows for an informed decision.

The relationship between the franchisor and the franchisee is specified in the franchise agreement. In it, the two parties agree to certain arrangements regarding such things as how the business is to be run, purchase of supplies, royalty levels, charges for management, and advertising and other corporate services.

Important variations exist in franchise agreements; it is a contract between the franchisee and the company and, as such, can be shaped to suit the needs of

1. Information identifying the franchisor and its affiliates and describing their business experience.
2. Information identifying and describing the business experience of each of the franchisor's officers, directors, and management personnel responsible for franchise services, training, and other aspects of the franchise program.
3. A description of the lawsuits in which the franchisor and its officers, directors, and management personnel have been involved.
4. Information about any previous bankruptcies in which the franchisor and its officers, directors, and management personnel have been involved.
5. Information about the initial franchise fee and other initial payments that are required to obtain the franchise.
6. A description of the continuing payments franchisees are required to make after the franchise opens.
7. Information about any restrictions on the quality of goods and services used in the franchise and where they may be purchased, including restrictions requiring purchases from the franchisor or its affiliates.
8. A description of any assistance available from the franchisor or its affiliates in financing the purchase of the franchise.
9. A description of restrictions on the goods or services that franchisees are permitted to sell.
10. A description of any restrictions on the customers with whom franchisees may deal.
11. A description of any territorial protection that will be granted to the franchisee.
12. A description of the conditions under which the franchise may be repurchased or refused renewal by the franchisor, transferred to a third party by the franchisee, and terminated or modified by either party.
13. A description of the training programs provided to franchisees.
14. A description of the involvement of any celebrities or public figures in the franchise.
15. A description of any assistance given by the franchisor in selecting a site for the franchise.
16. Statistical information about the present number of franchises, the number of franchises projected for the future, the number of franchises terminated, the number the franchisor has decided not to renew, and the number repurchased in the past.
17. The financial statements of the franchisor.
18. A description of the extent to which franchisees must personally participate in the operation of the franchise.
19. A complete statement of the basis for any earnings claims made to the franchisee, including the percentage of existing franchises that have actually achieved the results that are claimed.
20. A list of the names and addresses of other franchisees.
21. Copies of the franchisor's financial statements, which are audited and provided to give the prospective franchisee a view of the financial condition of the company.
22. Copies of the contracts the franchisee will be required to sign upon purchase of the franchise.
23. A receipt for the franchisee to sign and return as evidence of receipt of the UFOC.

FIGURE 5–4 Required information in uniform franchise offering circular.

both parties. The prospective franchisee can agree to it or try to negotiate a better deal. Anything unacceptable, or undesirable, should be regarded as something that would be reviewed for change. A large, powerful chain will seldom agree to such requests, but since the agreement specifies the conditions of the relationship, it is important to attempt to shape the document in the interests of the franchisee to the extent possible.

Among the most critical factors in the relationship are those having to do with termination of the contract. It is around this issue that the imbalance of bargaining power is most apparent. The franchisor can refuse to renew the contract, terminate it, or refuse to agree to a sale transferring it to a new owner. Any of these moves will simply mean one less outlet for the franchisor. For the franchisee, however, the decision has far greater significance: It can bring grievous financial loss and the loss of livelihood. Consequently, any prospective franchisee should examine carefully the franchisor's policy on termination of franchise, in light of both state and federal law.

OTHER ENTREPRENEURIAL OPTIONS

Business Opportunities

We have all seen the ads and wondered what they were all about: "Make Big Money"; "Get Rich in Your Spare Time"; "Be Your Own Boss"; and so on. These are doubtful claims, perhaps, but attractive to many people with entrepreneurial tendencies and interests but without sufficient capital, experience, and time for a long-term commitment. These people are turning to yet another route into small business: the business opportunity. While there is no formal definition of the term, it can be described as the sale of a product or service that the seller promises the buyer will provide a profit on the buyer's original investment.

The concept of franchising is based in large part on the trust and confidence that develop in the relationship between franchisee and franchisor. The two parties are interdependent in such a way that the success of one depends on, and fuels, the success of the other. This kind of relationship usually takes time to build. The business opportunity format has a "quickie" quality to it. Even in cases where both of the parties make money on the transaction, they may never see each other again. The short-term nature of the relationship between buyer and seller in a business opportunity is one of the things that distinguish it from franchising.

Another critical difference between the two is that of requirements or restrictions. The buyer is not required to pay fees and is not faced with operating restrictions of the kind usually imposed on franchisees. The flexibility given the buyer has its counterpart in the lack of service from the seller. Although many ads say there will be marketing materials, sales leads, exclusive territories, and the like, not all sellers deliver on these promises, and getting them to do so can be a discouraging undertaking.

To our knowledge, no scientific study of the safety of business opportunities has been conducted, but the anecdotal evidence points to the need for caution. While the business opportunity seller faces the same FTC restrictions that apply to franchisors, enforcement is difficult and spotty. Among the reasons for this ineffective protection is that only about one-half of the states have any regulation of sellers of business opportunities. In addition, there are the skill, methods, and determination of some of the sellers. Consider, for example, the case of a vending machine scam investigated for two years by the FTC. It involved 31 companies run by 16 individuals, including a man who had six aliases. In another incident, six people running 18 Florida-based companies were charged with deceptive business practices.[12]

With a web of businesses, fake identities, and multiple locations, some of the most aggressive and unscrupulous of these operators will be selling business opportunities for a long time to come. Can buyers protect themselves? Yes, at least partially, if they investigate thoroughly, are extremely skeptical, and do not believe any ads that offer anything that seems too good to be true. Even then, unpleasant surprises can occur. When a Seattle woman investigated a Denver company's offer of an exclusive territory (which it wasn't—there were 10 other dealers), she was given the name of a Kansas woman purported to be a satisfied dealer. The woman wasn't a dealer; she was paid to lie to prospects.[13]

Manufacturer's Representative

Another entrepreneurial option is to become a manufacturer's representative. In this arrangement, the entrepreneur represents a manufacturer or other supplier in dealings with customers. Typically, the representative is compensated only on the basis of actual sales on behalf of the company. Consequently, the entrepreneur takes on the expenses of the job with the prospect of a payoff, but only if a sale is made. This relationship is like that between a company and a salesperson who is paid on a commission-only basis, except that the salesperson is an employee and therefore eligible for benefits, possible promotion, reimbursement for travel, and so on. The manufacturer's representative relies on his or her sales ability to generate enough income to at least cover these kinds of items. In some "big-ticket" industries, such as expensive equipment and medical fixtures, an occasional sale is often enough to do just that. While the level of remuneration varies from one situation to another, the standard arrangement is for the manufacturer's representative to receive 10 percent of the sale.

Entrepreneurs who operate as manufacturer's representatives have a great deal of autonomy. They can set their own schedule, develop their own prospects, and decide which manufacturers to represent. This is considerably more freedom than the typical franchisee, but, like a franchisee, the manufacturer's representative must depend on the "parent" organization for support and the ability to serve customers effectively.

Manufacturer's representative – a firm or individual who represents a manufacturer or supplier in dealings with customers.

FRANCHISES AND THE BUSINESS PLAN

If the entrepreneur's business will be a franchise, it is important to include information on the franchise in the business plan. The history and financial stability of the franchisor are critical factors in assessing the viability of the new francise outlet. It is also important to include the amount and type of training that the franchisor will provide and if ongoing advice is available if the franchisee has problems. Because the franchise is often dependent on the franchisor, bankers and investors will be as concerned about the franchisor's information as the franchisee's. Any problems at the parent corporation are likely to impact all businesses in the system. Therefore, the questions listed in "Evaluating the Franchise Option" should be included in the business plan.

SUMMARY

For many people, the dreams of self-employment and financial independence have been realized through the purchase of a franchise. For many others, however, the purchase has brought grief and financial ruin. Buying a franchise is a move that must be painstakingly investigated. While legal protection is available, the best strategy for problem prevention is exhaustive information gathering. As alternatives to starting or buying a business or buying a franchise, business opportunities and manufacturers' representatives should be mentioned. Great caution should be used in responding to "business opportunities." This route to independent business affords far less legal protection than that of franchising and has been the source of many scams through the years. The role of manufacturer's representative is that of an independent salesperson who must make a living—and pay expenses—through commissions on sales.

DISCUSSION QUESTIONS

1. Why has franchising become so popular in recent years?
2. Describe the advantages franchising offers for an entrepreneur.
3. What is the level of risk of failure faced by the buyer of a franchise? How does it compare to the risk faced by entrepreneurs who start businesses?
4. What is the purpose of the franchise agreement?
5. What kind of protection is given by the disclosure statement?
6. Compare and contrast franchises and business opportunities.
7. Why is the regulation of the sellers of business opportunities so difficult?

ENDNOTES

1. Thomas S. Dicke, *Franchising in America* (Chapel Hill, NC: University of North Carolina Press, 1992), 3.
2. Gordon Storholm and Eberhard E. Scheuing, "Ethical Implications of Business Format Franchising," *Journal of Business Ethics*, March 1994, 181–188.
3. Andrew Kostecka, *Franchising in the Economy, 1986–1988* (Washington, DC: U.S. Government Printing Office), 4.
4. IFA Resource Center, "What Is Franchising?" http://www.franchise.org/resourcectr/faq/1.asp.
5. Ibid.
6. Ibid.
7. Arthur Andersen and Co., *Franchising in the Economy: 1989–1992* (Washington, DC: International Franchise Association, 1992).
8. Timothy Bates, "Look Before You Leap," *Inc.*, July 1995, 23–24.
9. Ibid.
10. *Franchise Opportunities Handbook* (Washington, DC: U.S. Department of Commerce, 1994), ix–xii.
11. Nerilee Hing, "Franchisee Satisfaction: Contributors and Consequences," *Journal of Small Business Management*, April 1995, 12–25.
12. Sana Siwolop, "Have I Got a Business Opportunity for You," *The New York Times*, August 27, 1995, section 3, 1, 8.
13. Ibid.

Chapter 6
Buying an Existing Business

- Understanding the advantages and disadvantages of buying an existing business
- Defining the steps involved in the right way to buy a business
- Explaining the process of evaluating an existing business
- Describing the various techniques for determining the value of a business
- Understanding the seller's side of the buyout decision and how to structure a deal
- Understanding how the negotiation process works and identifying the factors that affect the negotiation process

7 | Buying an Existing Business

Goodwill, like a good name, is gotten by many actions, and lost by one. —Lord Jeffrey

There is nothing so easy to learn as experience and nothing so hard to apply. —Josh Billings

Learning Objectives

On completion of this chapter, you will be able to:

1. Understand (A) the advantages and (B) the disadvantages of buying an existing business.
2. Define the steps involved in the right way to buy a business.
3. Explain the process of evaluating an existing business.
4. Describe the various techniques for determining the value of a business.
5. Understand the seller's side of the buyout decision and how to structure the deal.
6. Understand how the negotiation process works and identify the factors that affect it.

Rather than launch their own businesses or purchase a franchise, some entrepreneurs opt for a more direct route to business ownership: They buy an existing business. In fact, in a typical year, more than 500,000 businesses are bought and sold. Each circumstance is unique, but the process of evaluating a potential business acquisition is not. The "due diligence" process that involves analyzing and evaluating an existing business for possible purchase is no less time consuming than developing a comprehensive business plan for a start-up. Done correctly, this due diligence process will reveal both the negative and the positive aspects of an existing business. Skipping or glossing over the due diligence process is a huge mistake because a business that looks good on the surface may have serious flaws at its core. Investigating a business to discover its real condition and value requires time, dedication, and, as the name implies, diligence, but the process is worthwhile because it can prevent an entrepreneur from purchasing a business destined for failure. When considering purchasing a business, the first rule is, "Do not rush into a deal." Taking shortcuts when investigating a potential business acquisition almost always leads to nasty—and expensive—surprises. Prospective buyers must be sure that they discover the answers to the following fundamental questions:

- Is the right type of business for sale in a market in which you want to operate?
- What experience do you have in this particular business and the industry in which it operates? How critical to your ultimate success is experience in the business?
- What is the company's potential for success?
- What changes will you have to make—and how extensive will they be—to realize the business's full potential?
- What price and payment method are reasonable for you and acceptable to the seller?
- Will the company generate sufficient cash to pay for itself and leave you with a suitable rate of return on your investment?
- Should you be starting a business and building it from the ground up rather than buying an existing one?

Buying an Existing Business

LEARNING OBJECTIVES
1A. Understand the advantages of buying an existing business.

The Advantages of Buying an Existing Business

Over the next decade, entrepreneurs looking to buy existing businesses will have ample opportunities to consider. A recent study by PricewaterhouseCoopers reports that 50 percent of existing company owners plan to sell their businesses within the next decade.[1] Those who purchase an existing business may reap the following benefits.

A Successful Existing Business May Continue to Be Successful Purchasing a thriving business at an acceptable price increases the likelihood of success. The previous management team already has established a customer base, built supplier relationships, and set up a business system. The customer base inherited in a business purchase can carry an entrepreneur while he or she studies how the business has become successful and how to build on that success. Time spent learning about the business and its customers before introducing changes will increase the probability that any changes made will be successful. The new owner's objective should be to make those modifications that will attract new customers while retaining the company's existing customers. Maintaining the proper balance of old and new is not an easy task, however.

An Existing Business May Already Have the Best Location When the location of the business is critical to its success (as is often the case in retailing), it may be wise to purchase a business that is already in the right place. Opening in a second-choice location and hoping to draw customers may prove fruitless. In fact, an existing business's biggest asset may be its prime location. If this advantage cannot be matched by other locations, an entrepreneur may have little choice but to buy a business instead of launching one. As part of its expansion plans, one fast food chain recently purchased a smaller chain, not so much for its customer base or other assets as for its prime store locations.

Employees and Suppliers Are Established An existing business already has experienced employees who can help the new owner through the transition phase. Experienced employees enable a company to continue to earn money while a new owner learns the business. Many new owners find it valuable to solicit ideas from employees about methods for increasing sales or reducing costs. In many cases, the previous owner may not have involved employees in this fashion and never gained the advantages found in the wisdom of employees. Few people know a job better than the people who are performing it.

In addition, an existing business has an established set of suppliers with a history of business dealings. Those vendors can continue to supply the business while the new owner investigates the products and services of other suppliers. However, suppliers may want to ensure that the new owners are capable of running the business successfully.

Cole-Kramer Imports

When Reid Chase and Scott Semel purchased Cole-Kramer Imports, a high-end candy company that imported and distributed Swiss mint candies, they invested $100,000 of their own money and borrowed the remaining $500,000. The new owners soon discovered that the previous owners had no written contracts with its key suppliers. When Chase and Semel attempted to negotiate a formal supply contract, their suppliers refused, insisting that the new owners first prove their ability to operate the candy company successfully. Chase and Semel expanded their product line beyond mints and landed several major retail accounts in the process. Convinced that the new owners could manage the business, the Swiss suppliers forged long-term contracts with Cole-Kramer Imports, whose sales climbed from $600,000 to more than $40 million in just seven years.[2]

Equipment Is Installed and Productive Capacity Is Known Acquiring and installing new equipment exerts a tremendous strain on a fledgling company's financial resources. In an existing business, a potential buyer can determine the condition of the plant and equipment and its capacity before buying. The previous owner may have established an efficient production operation through trial and error, although the new owner may need to make modifications to improve it. In many cases, entrepreneurs can purchase physical facilities and equipment at prices significantly below their replacement costs.

Inventory Is in Place and Trade Credit Is Established The proper amount of inventory is essential to both controlling costs and generating adequate sales volume. If a business has too little inventory, it will not have the quantity and variety of products it needs to satisfy customer demand. However, if a business has too much inventory, it is tying up excessive capital unnecessarily, thereby increasing costs and reducing profitability. Owners of successful established businesses have learned the proper balance between these extremes. In addition, previous owners have established trade credit relationships with vendors that can benefit the new owner. No supplier wants to lose a good customer.

The New Business Owner Hits the Ground Running Entrepreneurs who purchase existing businesses avoid the time, costs, and energy required to launch a new business. The day they take over an ongoing business is the day their revenues begin. Entrepreneurs who buy existing successful businesses do not have to invest a lifetime building a company to enjoy its success.

Mannequin Service Company

Lania D'Agostino, a sculptor who moved from Michigan to Baltimore, Maryland, to attend the Maryland Institute College of Art, began working at Mannequin Service Company, a business that specializes in designing and creating custom mannequins for museums, special events, and entertainment companies. D'Agostino spent three years learning the business before buying it from the founder, who had built the business by making display mannequins for retail stores such as Sears. After buying the business,

D'Agostino shifted the strategy to focus on highly specialized, artistic projects. A big break came for the company when D'Agostino landed a contract with Lucasfilm Inc., the company that produced the Star Wars trilogies, to provide mannequins depicting the characters from the films, from Obi-Won Kenobi and Princess Leia to Padme and Chewbacca, the Wookiee. Requiring as many as 80 hours to create, the company's character mannequins sell for $7,500 and up.[3]

The New Owner Can Use the Experience of the Previous Owner Even if the previous owner is not around after the sale, the new owner will have access to all of the business's records to guide him or her until he or she becomes acclimated to the business and the local market. The new owner can trace the impact on costs and revenues of the major decisions that the previous owner made and can learn from his or her mistakes and profit from his or her achievements. In many cases, the previous owner spends time with the new owner during the transition period, giving the new manager the opportunity to learn about the policies and procedures in place and the reasons for them. Previous owners also can be extremely helpful in unmasking the unwritten rules of business in the area, including critically important intangibles such as how to keep customers happy and whom one can trust and cannot trust. After all, most owners who sell out want to see the buyer succeed in carrying on their businesses.

Easier Financing Attracting financing to purchase an existing business often is easier than finding the money to launch a company from scratch. Many existing businesses already have established relationships with lenders, which may open the door to financing through traditional sources such as banks. As we will see later in this chapter, many business buyers also have access to another important source of financing: the seller.

It's a Bargain Some existing businesses may be real bargains. The current owners may need to sell on short notice, which may lead them to sell the business at a low price. Many small companies operate in profitable but tiny niches, making it easy for potential buyers to overlook them. The more specialized a business is, the greater the likelihood is that a buyer can find a bargain. If special skill or training is required to operate a business, the number of potential buyers will be significantly smaller. If the seller wants a substantial down payment or the entire selling price in cash, few buyers may qualify; however, those who do may be able to negotiate a good deal.

Disadvantages of Buying an Existing Business

LEARNING OBJECTIVES
1B. Understand the disadvantages of buying an existing business.

It's a "Loser" A business may be for sale because it is struggling and the owner wants out. In these situations, a prospective buyer must be wary. Business owners sometimes attempt to disguise the facts and employ creative accounting techniques to make the company's financial picture appear much brighter than it really is. Few business sellers honestly state "It's losing money" as the reason for putting their companies up for sale. If there is one area of business where the maxim "let the buyer beware" still prevails, it is in the purchase of an existing business. Any buyer unprepared to do a complete and thorough analysis of a business may be stuck with a real loser.

Although buying a money-losing business is risky, it is not necessarily taboo. If an analysis of a company shows that it is poorly managed or suffering from neglect, a new owner may be able to turn it around. However, a prospective buyer who does not have well-defined plan for improving a struggling business should *not* consider buying it.

Workhorse Custom Chassis

Andrew Taitz spent three years searching for the right business to buy. After screening many options, Taitz and a group of investors purchased Union City Body Company in Union City, Indiana, a bankrupt division of General Motors that made bodies for delivery trucks. Renamed Workhorse Custom Chassis, the company has expanded its product line to make the frames that support the wheels, engine, fuel systems, brakes, and suspension for motor homes and delivery trucks. "I saw an excellent opportunity to turn a low-tech, nuts-and-bolts product into a growth market," says Taitz. Taitz and his investors spent $100 million, including the initial purchase price, revamping the entire plant to make it more flexible, efficient, and ergonomically sound. Today, Workhorse builds customized frames from more than 3,500 parts one right after another on the same assembly line. Taitz also implemented a host of changes in the company's management style, cutting the workweek to four 10-hour days (from five 8-hour days) and allowing employees to work in small teams and to practice job rotation. Taitz also set up a Web site that allows customers to design their own chassis online, and the company's FasTrack program delivers a chassis to a customer in just four weeks. The result is that Workhorse's revenues exceed $300 million per year, and the company is now profitable.[4]

The Previous Owner May Have Created Ill Will Just as ethical, socially responsible business dealings create goodwill for a company, improper business behavior creates ill will. The due diligence process may reveal that customers, suppliers, creditors, or employees may have extremely negative feelings about a company's reputation because of the unethical actions of its current owner. Business relationships may have begun to deteriorate, but their long-term effects may not yet appear in the business's financial statements. Ill will can permeate a business for years.

Employees Inherited with the Business May Not Be Suitable Previous managers may have kept marginal employees because they were close friends or because they started with the company. A new owner, therefore, may have to make some very unpopular termination decisions. For this reason, employees often do not welcome a new owner because they feel threatened by change. Some employees may not be able to adapt to the new owner's management style, and a culture clash may result. If the due diligence efforts reveals that existing employees are a significant cause of the problems a business faces, the new owner will have no choice but to terminate them and make new hires.

The Business Location May Have Become Unsatisfactory What was once an ideal location may have become obsolete as market and demographic trends change. Large shopping malls, new competitors, or highway re-routings can spell disaster for small retail shops. Prospective buyers should always evaluate the existing market in the area surrounding an existing business as well as its potential for expansion. Buyers must remember that they are buying the future of a business, not merely its past. A location in decline may never recover. If business success is closely linked to a good location, acquiring a business in a declining area or where demographic trends are moving downward is not a good idea. The value of the business will erode faster than the neighborhood surrounding it.

Equipment and Facilities May Be Obsolete or Inefficient Potential buyers sometimes neglect to have an expert evaluate a company's facilities and equipment before they purchase it. Only later do they discover that the equipment is obsolete and inefficient and that the business may suffer losses from excessively high operating costs. The equipment may have been well suited to the business they purchased, but not to the business they want to build. Modernizing equipment and facilities is seldom inexpensive.

Change and Innovation Are Difficult to Implement It is easier to plan for change than it is to implement it. Methods, policies, and procedures the previous owner used in a business may have established precedents that a new owner finds difficult to modify. Customers may resist changes the new owner wants to make to the business.

Esso Club

When Charles Usry purchased the Esso Club a legendary destination for sports fans in Clemson, South Carolina, he began making plans to upgrade the décor of the old cinderblock building. Usry changed his plans when loyal customers resisted the changes to their beloved Esso Club.

When Charles Usry purchased the landmark Esso Club in Clemson, South Carolina, he quickly discovered that the bar's regulars were skeptical of the changes he had planned to implement. Originally begun as a gas station/grocery store in 1935, the Esso Club eventually was converted into a bar and became a legendary destination for sports fans when *ESPN the Magazine* named it one of the top must-visit locations for sports fans. When Usry announced his plans to upgrade the décor of the no-frills, cinder-block building and to transform the club into a sports bar, long-time customers and loyal visitors howled in protest. "It's the ambiance of the place that really does it for us," says David Ford, an Esso Club regular, only half-joking. "The closest thing [to the Esso Club] is Cheers," says another long-time customer.[5]

Reversing a downward slide in an existing company's sales can be just as difficult as implementing change. Making changes that bring in new business and convince former clients to return can be an expensive, time-consuming, and laborious process. A business buyer must be aware of the effort, time, and expense it takes to change the negative momentum of a business in trouble. Before a business can go forward, it must stop going backward.

Inventory May Be Outdated or Obsolete Inventory is valuable only if it is salable. Smart buyers know better than to trust the inventory valuation on a firm's balance sheet. Some of it may actually appreciate in value in periods of rapid inflation, but inventory is more likely to depreciate. A prospective buyer must judge inventory by its market value, *not* by its book value.

Accounts Receivable May Be Worth Less Than Face Value Like inventory, accounts receivable rarely are worth their face value. The prospective buyer should age the company's accounts receivable (a breakdown of accounts 30, 60, 90, and 120 days old and beyond) to determine their collectibility. The older the receivables are, the less likely they are to be collected, and, consequently, the lower their value is. Table 7.1 shows a simple but effective method of evaluating accounts receivable once they have been aged, using the estimated probabilities of collecting the accounts.

TABLE 7.1 Valuing Accounts Receivable

A prospective buyer asked the current owner of a business about the value of her accounts receivable. The owner's business records showed $101,000 in receivables. But when the prospective buyer aged the accounts and multiplied them by his estimated collection probabilities, he discovered their real value:

Age of Accounts (days)	Amount ($)	Collection Probability (%)	Value ($)
0–30	40,000	95	38,000
31–60	25,000	88	22,000
61–90	14,000	70	9,800
91–120	10,000	40	4,000
121–150	7,000	25	1,750
151–plus	5,000	10	500
Total	101,000		78,050

Had he blindly accepted the seller's book value of these accounts receivable, this prospective buyer would have overpaid nearly $25,000 for them!

When one buyer was considering purchasing an existing business, his research showed that a substantial volume of accounts receivable were well past due. Further investigation revealed that the company and its largest customer were locked in a nasty dispute over outstanding account balances. The buyer decided to withdraw his preliminary offer.

The Business May Be Overpriced Each year, many people purchase businesses at prices far in excess of their value, which can impair the companies' ability to earn a profit and generate a positive cash flow. If a buyer accurately values a business's accounts receivable, inventories, and other assets, he or she will be in a better position to negotiate a price that will allow the business to be profitable. Making payments on a business that was overpriced is a millstone around the new owner's neck, making it difficult to keep the business afloat.

Although most buyers do not realize it, the price they pay for a company typically is not as crucial to its continued success as the terms on which they make the purchase. Of course, wise business buyers will try to negotiate a fair and reasonable price, but they are often equally interested in the more specific terms of the deal. For instance, how much cash they must pay out and when, how much of the price the seller is willing to finance and for how long, the interest rate at which the deal is financed, and other such terms can make or break a deal from the buyer's perspective. A buyer's primary concern is making sure that the terms of the deal do not endanger the company's future financial health and that they preserves the company's cash flow.

LEARNING OBJECTIVES
2. Define the steps involved in the right way to buy a business.

The Steps in Acquiring a Business

Buying an existing business can be risky if approached haphazardly. Studies show that more than 50 percent of all business acquisitions fail to meet the buyer's expectations. To avoid costly mistakes, an entrepreneur-to-be should follow a logical, methodical approach:

- Analyze your skills, abilities, and interests to determine what kind(s) of businesses you should consider.
- Prepare a list of potential candidates.
- Investigate those candidates and evaluate the best one(s).
- Explore financing options.
- Ensure a smooth transition.

Analyze Your Skills, Abilities, and Interests

The first step in buying a business is *not* searching out potential acquisition candidates. Every entrepreneur considering buying a business should begin by conducting a self-audit to determine the ideal business for him or her. The primary focus is to identify the type of business *you* will be happiest and most successful owning. Consider, for example, the following questions:

- What business activities do you enjoy most? Least? Why?
- Which industries or markets offer the greatest potential for growth?
- Which industries interest you most? Least? Why?
- What kind of business do you want to buy?
- What kinds of businesses do you want to *avoid*?
- What do you expect to get out of the business?
- How much time, energy, and money can you put into the business?
- What business skills and experience do you have? What skills and experience do you lack?
- How easily can you transfer your skills and experience to other types of businesses? In what kinds of businesses would that transfer be easiest?
- How much risk are you willing to take?

- Are you willing and able to turn around a struggling business?
- What size company do you want to buy?
- Is there a particular geographic location you desire?

Answering these and other questions beforehand will allow you to develop a list of criteria a company must meet to become a purchase candidate. Addressing these issues early in the process will also save a great deal of time, trouble, and confusion as you wade through a multitude of business opportunities. The better you know yourself and your skills, competencies, and interests, the more likely you will be to find and manage a successful business.

Prepare a List of Potential Candidates

Once you know what your goals are for acquiring a business, you can begin your search. Do *not* limit yourself to only those businesses that are advertised as being "for sale." In fact, the **hidden market** of companies that might be for sale but are not advertised as such is one of the richest sources of top-quality businesses. Many businesses that can be purchased are not publicly advertised but are available either through the owners or through business brokers and other professionals. Although they maintain a low profile, these hidden businesses represent some of the most attractive purchase targets a prospective buyer may find.

hidden market
Low-profile companies that might be for sale but are not advertised as such.

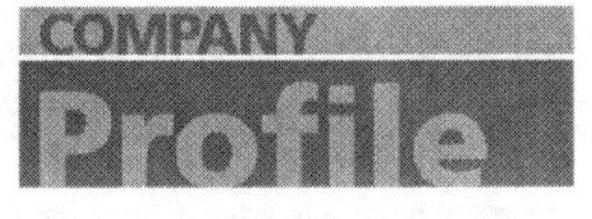

B.W. Burdette and Sons

When brothers Art and Allan McCraw, two enterprising college graduates, returned to their hometown, they approached the owners of B.W. Burdette and Sons, a local hardware store that had been founded by the current owners' father 80 years earlier, about buying the business. The company was not listed for sale, but because they were familiar with the business, the McCraws knew that the current owners might be interested in selling. After several months of due diligence and negotiations, the young entrepreneurs closed the deal. They have since expanded the business to include two more locations, expanded its market reach, and increased its profitability many times over.

How can you tap into this hidden market of potential acquisitions? Typical sources include the following:

- Business brokers
- Bankers
- Accountants
- Investment bankers
- Industry contacts—suppliers, distributors, customers, insurance brokers, and others
- "Networking"—social and business contact with friends and relatives
- Knocking on the doors of businesses you would like to buy (even if they're not advertised as being "for sale")
- Trade associations
- Newspapers and trade journals listing businesses for sale

In recent years, the World Wide Web also has become an important tool for entrepreneurs looking to buy businesses. In the past, the market for businesses was highly fragmented and unstructured, making it difficult for entrepreneurs to conduct an organized, thorough search for companies that might meet their purchase criteria. Today, hundreds of business brokers have established Web sites that list thousands of companies for sale in practically every industry imaginable, enabling entrepreneurs to search the entire country for that perfect business from the comfort of their own homes. Using the Web, potential buyers can eliminate the companies that do not suit them and can conduct preliminary research on those that look most promising. The more opportunities an entrepreneur has to find and evaluate potential acquisitions, the greater the likelihood of finding a match that meets his or her criteria.

Investigate and Evaluate Candidate Businesses and Evaluate the Best One

Finding the right company requires patience. Although some buyers find a company after only a few months of looking, the typical search takes much longer, sometimes as much as two or three years. Once you have a list of prospective candidates, it is time to do your homework. The next step is to investigate the candidates in more detail:

- What are the company's strengths? Weaknesses?
- Is the company profitable? What is its overall financial condition?
- What is its cash flow cycle? How much cash will the company generate?
- Who are its major competitors?
- How large is the customer base? Is it growing or shrinking?
- Are the current employees suitable? Will they stay?
- What is the physical condition of the business, its equipment, and its inventory?
- What new skills must you learn to be able to manage this business successfully?

Determining the answers to these and other questions addressed in this chapter will allow a prospective buyer to develop a list of the most attractive prospects and to prioritize them in descending order of attractiveness. This process also will make the task of valuing the business much easier.

A.M.E.'s Uniforms

When Mark Forst and his father decided to leave the corporate life and go into business for themselves, they knew that they wanted to buy an existing business rather than start their own. "We wanted a company that could use better marketing and service, one that we could take from the local to the national level," says Forst. Forst spent weeks poring over the business listings in Fort Lauderdale newspapers and hired a business broker to help uncover potential purchase candidates. One day he noticed a listing in the newspaper for a business called Rip's Uniforms that specialized in providing uniforms for postal workers. Forst and his father thought the asking price of $100,000 was reasonable, and they began researching the industry. Their research was encouraging. They discovered that the uniform supply industry had solid growth rates and that although a number of local uniform distributors were scattered across the United States, only five operated on a national level. Forst and his father began the due diligence process, talking with the small company's owners, studying the industry, and interviewing the company's vendors and its sole employee. They even conducted market research, talking with postal workers to glean ideas about how they could win them as customers and integrating what they learned into their business plan for the company. Their research of the company revealed that Rip's Uniforms had much more debt and far less inventory than the current owners believed, but the Forsts still believed in the company's potential. Using the information they had gathered, the Forsts purchased Rip's Uniforms after they were able to whittle the purchase price down to just $10,000. They renamed the company A.M.E.'s Uniforms, and sales, which now top $3 million annually, are growing so fast that the company has made *Inc.* magazine's list of the 500 fastest-growing small companies twice.[6]

Explore Financing Options

Placing a value on an existing business (a topic you will learn more about later in this chapter) represents a major hurdle for many would-be entrepreneurs. The next challenging task in closing a successful deal is financing the purchase. Although financing the purchase of an existing business usually is easier than financing a new one, some traditional lenders shy away from deals involving the purchase of an existing business. Those that are willing to finance business purchases normally lend only a portion of the value of the assets, and buyers often find themselves searching for alternative sources of funds. Fortunately, most business buyers have access to a ready source of financing: the seller.

Seller financing often is more flexible, faster, and easier to obtain than loans from traditional lenders.

Once a seller finds a suitable buyer, he or she typically will agree to finance anywhere from 25 to 80 percent of the purchase price. Usually, a deal is structured so that the buyer makes a sizeable down payment to the seller, who then finances a note for the balance. The buyer makes regular principal and interest payments over 5 to 10 years—perhaps with a larger balloon payment at the end—until the note is paid off. The terms and conditions of such a loan are a vital concern to both buyer and seller. They cannot be so burdensome that they threaten the company's continued existence; that is, the buyer must be able to make the payments to the seller out of the company's cash flow. At the same time, the deal must give the seller the financial security he or she is seeking from the sale. Defining reasonable terms is the result of the negotiation process between the buyer and the seller.

Anywhere Shoe Company

Tim Johnstone's experience in conducting due diligence for his former employer gave him an advantage when he was considering buying Anywhere Shoe Company, a Seattle-based maker and distributor of professional footwear. Johnstone's thorough analysis of the company revealed several factors that caused him concern, including a wrongful termination lawsuit filed by a former employee. Consequently, these discoveries caused him to assign a lower value to the business than the seller's asking price. Johnstone's offer included a "holdback" clause that allowed him to deduct from the purchase price the value of any undisclosed claims against Anywhere. To avoid paying off the seller at the expense of the security of the company's financial future, he also stipulated that the payout the seller was to receive would be based on the company's financial performance. Finally, Johnstone's terms required the seller to finance 55 percent of the purchase price. Initially, the owner balked at the terms but agreed to them rather than risk losing a viable buyer. "If we had not used seller financing, the deal probably wouldn't have come together," says Johnstone. His foresight paid off when, 14 months after the purchase, he discovered that a customer had filed a lawsuit against the company before he had signed the contract to buy the business. "Having seller financing gives you some protection that you otherwise might not have," says Johnstone. "It turned out to be the smartest thing I ever did."[7]

Ensure a Smooth Transition

Once the parties strike a deal, the challenge of making a smooth transition immediately arises. No matter how well planned the sale is, there are *always* surprises. For instance, the new owner may have ideas for changing the business—sometimes radically—that cause a great deal of stress and anxiety among employees and the previous owner. Charged with such emotion and uncertainty, the transition phase is always difficult and frustrating—and sometimes painful. To avoid a bumpy transition, a business buyer should do the following:

- Concentrate on communicating with employees. Business sales are fraught with uncertainty and anxiety, and employees need reassurance.
- Be honest with employees. Avoid telling them only what they want to hear. Share with the employees your vision for the business in the hope of generating a heightened level of motivation and support.
- Listen to employees. They have first-hand knowledge of the business and its strengths and weaknesses and usually can offer valuable suggestions for improving it.
- Consider asking the seller to serve as a consultant until the transition is complete. The previous owner can be a valuable resource, especially to an inexperienced buyer.

Table 7.2 describes 15 steps potential buyers should take to increase the probability that the businesses they buy are the right ones for them.

TABLE 7.2 Fifteen Steps to Buying the Company That's Right for You

1. *Make sure you shouldn't be starting a company instead.* You should have solid reasons for buying a company rather than starting one—and you should know what they are.
2. *Determine the kind of business you want—and whether you're capable of running it.* This requires an unflinching assessment of your strengths, weaknesses, personality, and goals.
3. *Consider the lifestyle you want.* What are you expecting from the business? Money? Freedom? Flexibility?
4. *Consider the location you want.* What part of the country (or world) do you want to live in?
5. *Reconsider lifestyle again.* You may own this business for a long, long time; it had better be one you enjoy.
6. *Cozy up to lenders in advance.* Visit potential lenders long before you need to borrow any money. Develop a rapport with them.
7. *Prepare to sell yourself to the seller.* You're buying their "baby," and they'll want to make sure you're the right person.
8. *Once you've defined the kind of business you're after, find the right company.* Three major sources of potential candidates are (1) the network of business people and advisers in the area, (2) business brokers specializing in companies of the size or type you want to buy, and (3) businesses that technically are not for sale but are very attractive.
9. *Choose the right seller.* Is he or she honest? What's the *real* reason he or she is selling the business?
10. *Do your research before agreeing to a price.* Ask lots of questions and get the facts to help you estimate the company's value.
11. *Make sure your letter of intent is specific.* It should establish deadlines, escape clauses, payment terms, confidentiality, and many other key issues.
12. *Don't skimp on due diligence.* Don't believe everything you see and hear; a relentless investigation will show whether the seller is telling the truth. Not all of them are.
13. *Be skeptical.* Don't fall in love with the deal; look for reasons *not* to buy the company.
14. *Don't forget to assess the employees.* You're not just buying a company; you're also buying the people who go with it.
15. *Make sure the final price reflects the company's real value.* Don't lower your chances of success by paying too much for the business.

Source: Adapted from Jay Finegan, "The Insider's Guide," *Inc.*, October 1991, pp 26–36.

Buying Dad's Business

Brian Schraff's father started an advertising agency for technology companies in 1976, and Brian joined the company after graduating from college in 1982. In 1996, Brian and a co-worker, Rick Roelofs, approached the elder Schraff with an offer to buy the company. "We have a completely different management philosophy in terms of the way we want to fund and capitalize the business and grow it," they told him. Their idea for increasing the company's revenue was to create a variety of services—from public relations to Internet services—around each client, which would require an investment in technology and in staff. The approach was a far cry from the business philosophy Schraff's father employed: keep costs low.

Because Schraff's father really had not wanted to sell the business, the young men knew they had to work hard if they were going to close the deal. Their proposal included seller financing; they would make an initial down payment and then pay Schraff's father the balance of the purchase price over several years out of the company's cash flow. The elder Schraff wanted to be sure that the company would remain financially sound enough to make all of the future payments. In addition, says Brian, "my Dad was like any other entrepreneur.

He's got a lot of pride, and he had built something really great. So it was difficult for him to let go of that."

As the parties began negotiating the sale of the business, it became apparent that one of the biggest stumbling blocks was the value of the business. "For us, it wasn't an emotional issue," recalls Brian. "It was 'What would it cost us to start this thing up ourselves?' As founder, my father had a lot of blood, sweat, and tears in the agency. He [believed] that the market price should me much more—at least 100 percent more—than we thought it should be."

Brian, his father, and Roelofs went on a retreat to try to come to an agreement over the sale of the company. Brian had received some shares of ownership in the company, and that was the key to making a deal that was acceptable to everyone. "It came down to my saying, 'I want out of the company. I want to sell my shares back to you for the price you want me to buy your shares for.' Once my father said, 'There's no way I would pay you that for your shares,' we were able to come back with, 'What would you pay me, and why wouldn't that be a good price for me to pay you?'"

With buyers and seller having come to an agreement on price, the deal moved forward. Brian and Roelofs made Brian's father chief financial officer of the new company and began to make the changes they had envisioned for the agency. "It really became a team effort to make sure that the transition was working," says Brian. Today, Brian's father serves as a high-level account manager for the company's technology clients, but he no longer is involved in the management of the company on a daily basis. Brian and Roelofs have increased the agency's annual billings to more than $5 million since buying it.

In hindsight, Brian realizes that he should have conducted the deal to buy the agency from his father differently, in particular, taking steps to remove some of the emotion from the process. Buying a business is difficult enough, but the difficulty is compounded when a father–son relationship is involved.

1. Evaluate the way in which Brian Schraff went about buying his father's business. What did he do right? What did he do wrong?
2. Work with a team of your classmates to develop a list of recommendations that would have made the process go faster and more smoothly. Write a brief report (no more than one page) summarizing your recommendations and the logic behind them.

Source: Adapted from Brian Schraff, "Buyout," *Inc.*, June 2001, pp. 52–53.

Evaluating an Existing Business—The Due Diligence Process

LEARNING OBJECTIVES
3. Explain the process of evaluating an existing business.

When evaluating an existing business, a buyer can quickly feel overwhelmed by the tremendous number and complexity of the issues involved. Therefore, a smart buyer will assemble a team of specialists to help investigate a potential business opportunity. This team is usually composed of a banker, an accountant familiar with the particular industry, an attorney, and perhaps a small business consultant or a business broker. The cost of assembling a team can range from $3,000 to $20,000, but most buyers agree that using a team significantly lowers the likelihood of making a bad purchase. Because making a bad purchase will cost many times the cost of a team of experts, most buyers see it as a wise investment. It is important for a buyer to trust the members of the business evaluation team. With this team assembled, the potential buyer is ready to explore the business opportunity by examining five critical areas:

1. Why does the owner want to sell?
2. What is the physical condition of the business?
3. What is the potential for the company's products or services?
4. What legal aspects should be considered?
5. Is the business financially sound?

due diligence
the process of investigating the details of a company that is for sale to determine the strengths, weaknesses, opportunities, and threats facing it.

Evaluating these five areas of a business is known as performing **due diligence**. A prospective buyer should never consider purchasing a business without conducting the necessary due diligence to learn about the strengths, weaknesses, opportunities, and threats facing the company. "There are so many ugly stories," explains Robert Strang, president of Strang Hayes Consulting, a firm that specializes in helping prospective buyers through the due diligence process. Strang Hayes discovered that the CEO of a company that one of its clients was considering purchasing had hidden five sexual harassment lawsuits that had been filed against him. Another search revealed that the business another buyer was considering purchasing had been banned from doing business in Florida, which was a major market for the prospective buyer.[8] The message is clear: Those buyers who neglect thorough due diligence do so at their own peril.

Why Is The Business for Sale?

Every prospective business buyer should investigate the *real* reason the business owner wants to sell. A study by DAK Group and Rutgers University found that the most common reason that owners of small businesses cite for selling their companies is to reduce the risk of having most of their personal assets tied up in their businesses (see Figure 7.1).[9] Their goal is to cash out their business investments and diversify into other types of assets. Many owners tell buyers that they have become bored or burned out and want to move on to other business ventures, but is that really the case? Note that market competition and external pressures are the next-most-common reasons owners give for selling their companies.

Smart business buyers know that the biggest and most unpleasant surprises can crop up outside the company's financial records and may never appear on the spreadsheets designed to analyze a company's financial position. For instance, a business owner might be looking to sell his or her business because a powerful new competitor is about to move into the market, a major highway rerouting will cause customer traffic to evaporate, the lease agreement on the ideal location is about to expire, or the primary customer base is declining. Every prospective buyer should investigate thoroughly any reason a seller gives for wanting to sell a business.

Businesses do not last forever, and smart entrepreneurs know when the time has come to sell. Some owners consider their behavior ethical only if they do not make false or misleading statements. Buyers should not expect to get a full disclose of the whole story behind the reasons for a business being offered for sale. In most business sales, the buyer bears the responsibility of determining whether the business is a good value. The best way to do that is to get out into the local community, talk to people, and ask a lot of questions. Visiting local business owners may reveal general patterns about the area and its overall vitality. The local Chamber of Commerce also may have useful information. Suppliers, customers, and even competitors may be able to shed light on why a business is up for sale. By combining this information with an analysis of the company's financial records, a potential buyer should be able to develop a clear picture of the business and its real value.

FIGURE 7.1

Reasons Business Owners Plan to Sell Their Companies

Source: DAK Group and Whitcomb Center for Research and Financial Services at Rutgers University.

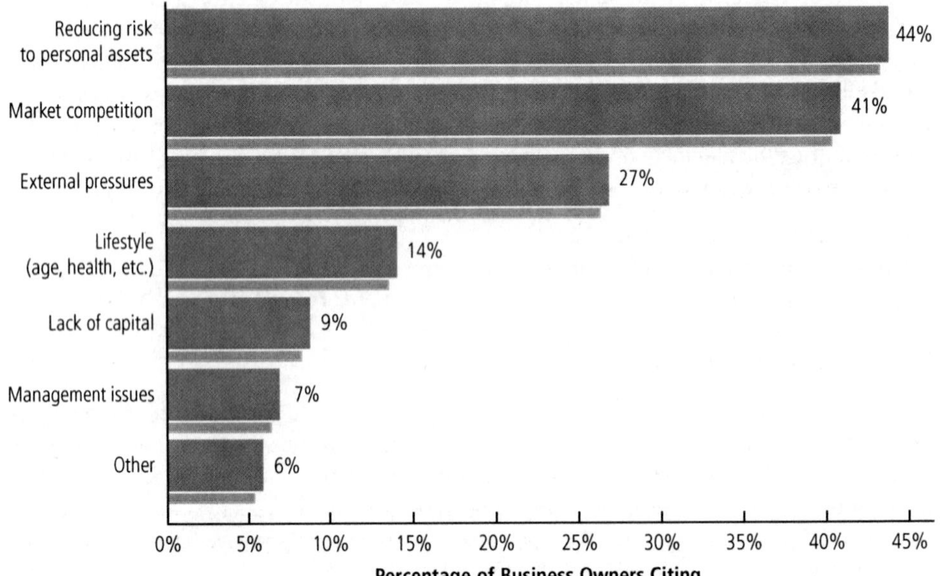

The Condition of the Business

What Is the Physical Condition of the Business? A prospective buyer should evaluate the business's assets to determine their value. Are they reasonably priced? Are they obsolete? Will they need to be replaced soon? Do they operate efficiently? The potential buyer should check the condition of both the equipment and the building. It may be necessary to hire a professional to evaluate the major components of the building—its structure and its plumbing, its electrical, and heating, and cooling systems, and other elements. Unexpected renovations are rarely inexpensive or simple and can punch a gaping hole in a buyer's financial plans.

How fresh is the company's inventory? Is it consistent with the image the new owner wants to project? How much of it would the buyer have to sell at a loss? A potential buyer may need to get an independent appraisal to determine the value of the company's inventory and other assets because the current owner may have priced them far above their actual value. These items typically comprise the largest portion of a business's value, and a potential buyer should not accept the seller's asking price blindly. Remember: *Book value is not the same as market value*. Usually, a buyer can purchase equipment and fixtures at substantially lower prices than book value. Value is determined in the marketplace, not on a balance sheet.

Other important factors that the potential buyer should investigate include the following:

Accounts receivable. If the sale includes accounts receivable, the buyer should check their quality before purchasing them. How creditworthy are the accounts? What portion of them is past due? How likely is it they can be collected? By aging the accounts receivable, a buyer can judge their quality and determine their value. (Refer to Table 7.1).

Lease arrangements. Is the lease included in the sale? When does it expire? What restrictions does it have on renovation or expansion? The buyer should determine *beforehand* what restrictions the landlord has placed on the lease and negotiate any change prior to purchasing the business.

Business records. Well-kept business records can be a valuable source of information and can tell a prospective buyer a lot about the company's pattern of success (or lack of it). Typically, buyers should expect to see financial statements documenting revenues and net income, operating budgets, and cash flow statements for at least five years. Sales and earnings forecasts from the seller for at least three years also can be helpful when trying to determine the value of a business.

Unfortunately, many business owners are sloppy record keepers. Consequently, the potential buyer and his or her team may have to reconstruct some critical records. It is important to verify as much information about the business as possible. For instance, does the owner have customer mailing lists? These lists can be a valuable marketing tool for a new business owner. Has the owner created an operations manual outlining the company's policies and procedures?

Intangible assets. Does the sale include any intangible assets such as trademarks, patents, copyrights, or goodwill? How long do patents have left to run? Is the trademark threatened by lawsuits for infringement? Does the company have logos or slogans that are unique or widely recognized? Determining the value of such intangibles is much more difficult than computing the value of the tangible assets.

Location and appearance. The location and the overall appearance of a business are important factors for a prospective buyer to consider. What had been an outstanding location in the past may be totally unacceptable today. Even if the building and equipment are in good condition and are fairly priced, the business may be located in a declining area. What other businesses operate in the surrounding area? Every buyer should consider the location's suitability not only for the present but also for several years into the future.

Table 7.3 offers a checklist of items every business buyer should investigate before closing a deal.

TABLE 7.3 A Business Buyer's Checklist

Buildings, Furnishings, and Fixtures

Every buyer should get a list of all of the fixed assets included in the purchase and then determine their condition, their age, their usefulness, and their value.

Inventory

Inventory may be the biggest part of a business sale, and it can be one of the trickiest parts of the deal. What inventory is on hand? What is its condition? How salable is it? What is its value? (Remember not to confuse *book* value with *market* value.) What is the company's merchandise return policy? How high is its return rate?

Financial Statements

Although small business owners are notoriously poor record keepers, a business buyer must have access to a company's financial statements for the last five years. This is the only way a buyer can judge the earning power of a company. The most reliable financial statements are those that have been audited by a certified public accountant. Comparing financial ratios against industry standards found in reports from RMA and Dun & Bradstreet can reveal important patterns.

Tax Returns

A good accountant should be able to reconcile the owner's or company's tax returns with its financial statements.

Sales Records

A prospective buyer should determine sales patterns by getting a monthly breakdown by product categories, sales representatives, cash versus credit, and any other significant factor for the company for three years. It is also a good idea to identify the company's top 10 customers and review their purchases over the last three years. What percentage of total sales did these 10 customers account for?

Accounts Receivable

Age the company's accounts receivable to see how many are current and how many are past due. Identify the top 10 accounts and check their credit ratings.

Accounts Payable

Conduct an analysis similar to the one for accounts receivable for the company's accounts payable. Past-due accounts are an indication that a business is experiencing cash flow difficulties.

Legal Documents

A prospective buyer should investigate all significant contracts (especially long-term ones) a company has with vendors, suppliers, distributors, lenders, employees, unions, customers, landlords, and others. Can the current owner assign the rights and obligations of these existing contracts to the buyer? If the company is incorporated, it is wise to check the articles of incorporation (or its articles of organization and operating agreement if it is a limited liability company.)

Patents, Trademarks, and Copyrights

Reviewing the documentation for any patents, trademarks, and copyrights the company holds is vital.

Lawsuits

Is the company facing any lawsuits, either current or pending?

Liabilities

It is essential that the seller provide the buyer with a complete list of liabilities that are outstanding against the company, including accounts and notes payable, loans, liens by creditors against business assets, lawsuits, and others.

Advertising and Sales Literature

A business buyer should study the company's advertising and sales literature to get an idea of the image it is projecting to its customers and the community. Talking to customers, suppliers, bankers, attorneys, and other local business owners will provide clues about the company's reputation.

TABLE 7.3 *Contiunued*

Organization Chart

Current employees can be a vital asset to a business buyer if they are willing to stay after the sale. Ask the seller to develop an organization chart showing the company's chain of command, and get copies of employees' job descriptions so you can understand who is responsible for which duties.

Insurance Coverage

Evaluate the types and amounts of insurance coverage the company currently has, including Workers' Compensation. Is it sufficient? If not, will you be able to obtain the necessary coverage at a reasonable price?

Sources: Adapted from "Look Before You Buy," Business Resale Network, http://www.br-network.com/features/bybl.html; "Making an In-Depth Evaluation," Business Resale Network, http://www.br-network.com/features/bybl.html; Norm Brodsky, "Caveat Emptor," *Inc.*, August 1998, pp. 31–32; "Basics of Buying a Business," American Express Small Business Exchange, http://home3.americanexpress.com/smallbusiness/resources/starting/buybiz.html.

Products and Services

What Is the Potential for the Company's Products or Services? No one wants to buy a business with a shrinking customer base. A thorough market analysis helps a buyer to develop his or her own sales forecast for an existing business (in addition to the one he or she should ask the seller to prepare). This research will tell a prospective buyer whether to consider buying a particular business and may reveal important trends in the business's sales and customer base.

Customer Characteristics and Composition Before purchasing an existing business, a buyer should analyze both existing and potential customers. Discovering why customers buy from the business and developing a profile of the company's existing customer base can help the buyer to identify a company's strengths and weaknesses and discover how to market more effectively to them. A potential buyer should determine the answers to the following questions:

- Who are the company's customers? What are their race, age, gender, and income levels? What is their demographic profile?
- Why do they buy?
- What do customers want the business to do for them? What needs are they satisfying when they make a purchase?
- How often do customers buy? Do they buy in seasonal patterns?
- How loyal are present customers?
- Is it practical to attract new customers at a reasonable cost?
- Does the business have a well-defined customer base? Is it growing? Do these customers come from a large geographic area or do they all live near the business?

Analyzing the answers to these questions can help a potential buyer to create and implement a more powerful marketing plan. Most likely he or she will try to keep the business attractive to existing customers while changing some features of its marketing plan to attract new ones.

Competitor Analysis A potential buyer must identify the company's direct competition—those businesses in the immediate area that sell the same or similar products or services. The potential profitability and survival of the business may well depend on the behavior of these competitors. Important factors to consider are the number of competitors and the intensity of the competition. How many competitors have opened in recent years? How many have closed in the last five years? What caused them to fail? Has the market already reached the saturation point? Being a latecomer in an already saturated market is not the pathway to long-term success.

When evaluating the competitive environment, a prospective buyer should address other questions:

- Which competitors have survived and what characteristics have led to their success?
- How do competitors' sales volumes compare with those of the business under consideration?
- What unique services do competitors offer?
- How well organized and coordinated are competitors' marketing efforts?
- What are the competitors' reputations?
- What are the strengths and weaknesses of the company's primary competitors? Which competitor is strongest?
- What competitive edge does each rival have?
- How can you gain market share in this competitive environment?

Legal Aspects

What Legal Aspects Should You Consider? Business buyers must be careful to avoid several legal pitfalls as they negotiate the final deal. The biggest potential legal traps include liens, bulk transfers, contract assignments, covenants not to compete, and ongoing legal liabilities.

lien
a creditor's claim against an asset.

Liens. The key legal issue in the sale of any asset is typically the proper transfer of good title from seller to buyer. However, because most business sales involve a collection of assorted assets, the transfer of a good title is more complex. Some business assets may have a **lien** (creditors' claim) against them, and unless the lien is satisfied before the sale, the buyer must assume it and is financially responsible for it. One way to reduce this potential problem is to include a clause in the sales contract stating that any liability not shown on the balance sheet at the time of sale remains the responsibility of the seller. A prospective buyer should have an attorney thoroughly investigate all of the assets for sale and their lien status before buying any business.

bulk transfer
protects the buyer of a business's assets from the claims unpaid creditors might have against those assets.

Bulk transfers. To protect against surprise claims from the seller's creditors after purchasing a business, the buyer should meet the requirements of a **bulk transfer** under Article 6 of the Uniform Commercial Code. Suppose that an owner owing many creditors sells his business to a buyer. The seller, however, does not use the proceeds of the sale to pay his debts to business creditors. Instead, he pockets them to use for his own benefit. Without the protection of a bulk transfer, those creditors could make claim to the assets that the buyer purchased in order to satisfy the previous owner's debts (within six months). To be effective, a bulk transfer must meet the following criteria:

- The seller must give the buyer a signed, sworn list of existing creditors.
- The buyer and the seller must prepare a list of the property included in the sale.
- The buyer must keep the list of creditors and the list of property for six months.
- The buyer must give written notice of the sale to each creditor at least 10 days before he or she takes possession of the goods or pays for them (whichever is first).

By meeting these criteria, a buyer acquires free and clear title to the assets purchased, which are not subject to prior claims from the seller's creditors. Because Article 6 can create quite a burden on a business buyer, 16 states have repealed it, and more may follow. About a half-dozen states have revised Article 6 to make it easier for buyers to notify creditors. Under the revised rule, if a business has more than 200 creditors, the buyer may notify them by public notice rather than by contacting them individually.

Contract assignments. Buyers must investigate the rights and the obligations they would assume under existing contracts with suppliers, customers, employees, lessors, and others. To continue the smooth operation of the business, the buyer must assume the rights of the seller under many existing contracts. Assuming these rights and obligations requires the seller to assign existing contracts to the new owner. For example, the current owner may have 4 years left on a 10-year lease and will need to assign this contract to the buyer. To protect her or his interest, the buyer (who is the assignee) should notify the other party involved in the contract of the assignment. In the previous example, the business buyer should notify the landlord promptly of the lease assignment from the previous owner.

Generally, the seller can assign any contractual right to the buyer, unless the contract specifically prohibits the assignment or the contract is personal in nature. For instance, loan contracts sometimes prohibit assignments with a **due-on-sale clause.** These clauses require the buyer to pay the full amount of the remaining loan balance or to finance the balance at prevailing interest rates. Thus, the buyer cannot assume the seller's loan (which may be at a lower interest rate than the prevailing rate on a loan). In addition, a seller usually cannot assign her or his credit arrangements with suppliers to the buyer because they are based on the seller's business reputation and are personal in nature. If such contracts are crucial to the business operation and cannot be assigned, the buyer must renegotiate new contracts. A prospective buyer also should evaluate the terms of any other unique contracts the seller has, including exclusive agent or distributor contracts, real estate leases, financing and loan arrangements, and union contracts.

due-on-sale clause
loan contract provision that prohibits a seller from assigning a loan arrangement to the buyer. Instead, the buyer is required to finance the remaining loan balance at prevailing interest rates.

Covenants not to compete. One of the most important and most often overlooked legal considerations for a prospective buyer is negotiating a **covenant not to compete** (or a **restrictive covenant** or a **noncompete agreement**) with the seller. Under a restrictive covenant, the seller agrees not to open a new, competing store within a specific time period and geographic area of the existing one. (The covenant should be negotiated with the *owner*, not with the corporation, because if the corporation signs the agreement, the owner may not be bound.) However, the covenant must be a part of a business sale and must be reasonable in scope in order to be enforceable. Although some states place limitations on the enforceability of restrictive covenants, business buyers should insist on the seller signing one. Without this protection, a buyer may find his or her new business eroding beneath his or her feet. For instance, suppose that Bob purchases a tire business from Alexandra, whose reputation in town for selling tires in unequaled. If Bob fails to negotiate a restrictive covenant, nothing can stop Alexandra from opening a new shop next to his old one and keeping all of his customers, thereby driving Bob out of business. A reasonable covenant in this case might restrict Alexandra from opening a tire store within a three-mile radius for three years. Every business buyer should negotiate a covenant not to compete with the seller.

covenant not to compete
an agreement between a buyer and a seller in which the seller agrees not to compete with the buyer within a specific time and geographic area.

To be enforceable, a restrictive covenant must be reasonable in geographic scope and in duration, must protect a legitimate business interest (such as a company's goodwill), and must be tied to a contract for the sale of an existing business (i.e., no "free-standing" restrictive covenants that restrain trade).

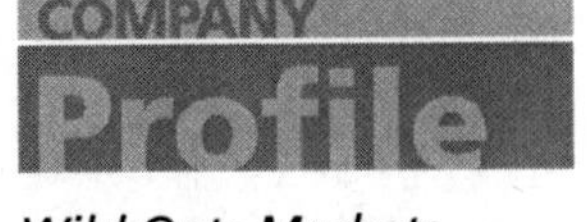

Wild Oats Markets

After launching Wild Oats Markets as a single store in Boulder, Colorado, Mike Gilliland turned the company into a national chain with $1 billion in annual sales. After selling out, Gilliland launched Sunflower Natural Markets, a seven-store discount natural food chain located in the Southwest. Gilliland's former company filed a lawsuit against him, claiming that launching the business was a violation of the restrictive covenant he had signed. A court enforced the noncompete agreement, forcing Gilliland to sell his shares in Sunflower Natural Markets to his former partners. Once the time limit on the restrictive covenant expired, Gilliland rejoined Sunflower Natural Markets and opened other stores.[10]

Ongoing legal liabilities. Finally, a potential buyer must look for any potential legal liabilities the purchase might expose. These typically arise from three sources: (1) physical premises, (2) product liability claims, and (3) labor relations. First, the buyer must examine the physical premises for safety. Are employees at risk because of asbestos or some other hazardous material? If the business is a manufacturing operation, does it meet Occupational Safety and Health Administration (OSHA) and other regulatory agency requirements? One entrepreneur who purchased a retail business located in a building that once housed a gasoline service station was quite surprised when the Environmental Protection Agency informed him that he would have to pay for cleaning up the results of an old, leaking gas tank that still sat beneath the property. Even though he had no part in running the old gas station and did not know the leaking tank was there, he was responsible for the cost of the cleanup. Removing the tank and cleaning up the site cost him several thousand dollars that he had not budgeted.

product liability lawsuits lawsuits that claim a company is liable for damages and injuries caused by the products it makes or sells.

Second, the buyer must consider whether existing products contain defects that could result in **product liability lawsuits,** which claim that a company is liable for damages and injuries caused by the products or services they make or sell. Existing lawsuits might be an omen of more to follow. In addition, the buyer must explore products that the company has discontinued because he or she might be liable for them if they prove to be defective. The final bargain between the parties should require the seller to guarantee that the company is not involved in any product liability lawsuits.

Third, what is the relationship between management to employees? Does a union contract exist? The time to discover sour management–labor relations is before the purchase, not after.

If the buyer's investigation reveals potential legal liabilities, it does not necessarily eliminate the business from consideration. Insurance coverage can shift such risks from the potential buyer, but the buyer should check to see whether the insurance will cover lawsuits resulting from actions predating the purchase.

Financial Soundness of the Business

A prospective buyer must analyze the financial records of a target business to determine its condition. He or she shouldn't be afraid to ask an accountant for help. Accounting systems and methods can vary tremendously from one type of business to another and can be quite confusing to a novice. Current profits can be inflated by changes in the accounting procedure or in the method for recording sales. For the buyer, the most dependable financial records are audited statements, those prepared by a CPA firm in accordance with generally accepted accounting principles (GAAP). Unfortunately, audited records do not exist in many small companies that are for sale. In some cases, a potential buyer has to hire an accountant to construct reliable financial statements because the owner's accounting and record keeping is so sloppy.

When evaluating the financial status of any business prospect, buyers must remember that any investment in a company should produce a reasonable salary for themselves, an attractive return on the money they invest, and enough to cover the amount they must borrow make the purchase. Otherwise, it makes no sense to purchase the business. Because most investors know that they can earn at least eight percent per year by investing wisely in the stock market, they expect any business they buy to earn at least that amount plus an extra return that reflects the additional risk of buying a business. Many owners expect to earn a return of at least 15 percent to 30 percent on the amount invested in their businesses.

Buyers also must remember that they are purchasing the future profit potential of an existing business. To evaluate the firm's profit potential, they should review past sales, operating expenses, and profits as well as the assets used to generate those profits. They must compare current balance sheets, income statements, and statements of cash flow with previous ones and then develop a set of projected statements for the next two to five years. Sales tax records, income tax returns, and financial statements are valuable sources of information.

Are profits consistent over the years, or are they erratic? Is this pattern typical in the industry, or is it a result of unique circumstances or poor management? Can the business survive with serious fluctuations in revenues, costs, and profits? If these fluctuations are the result of poor management, can a new owner turn the business around?

Some of the financial records that a potential buyer should examine include the following:

Income statements and balance sheets for the past three to five years. It is important to review data from several years because creative accounting techniques can distort financial data in any single year. Even though buyers are purchasing the future profits of a business, they must remember that many businesses intentionally keep net income low to minimize the owners' tax bills. Low earnings should prompt a buyer to investigate their causes.

Income tax returns for the past three to five years. Comparing basic financial statements with tax returns can reveal discrepancies of which the buyer should be aware. Some small business owners engage in **skimming** from their businesses—taking money from sales without reporting it as income. Owners who skim will claim their businesses are more profitable than their tax returns show. Although such underreporting is illegal and unethical, it is surprisingly common. Buyers should *not* pay for undocumented, "phantom" earnings a seller claims exist. In fact, buyers should consider whether they want to buy a business from someone who admits to doing business unethically.

skimming
taking money from sales without reporting it as income.

Owner's compensation (and that of relatives). The owner's compensation is especially important in small companies; and the smaller the company is, the more important it will be. Although many companies do not pay their owners what they are worth, others compensate their owners lavishly. The buyer must consider the impact of fringe benefits—company cars, insurance contracts, country club memberships, and the like. It is important to adjust the company's income statements for the salary and fringe benefits that the seller has paid himself or herself and others.

Cash flow. Most buyers understand the importance of evaluating a company's profitability, but fewer recognize the necessity of analyzing its cash flow. They assume that if earnings are adequate, there will be sufficient cash to pay all of the bills and to fund an attractive salary for them. *That is not necessarily the case!* Before agreeing to a deal, prospective buyers should sit down with an accountant and convert the target company's financial statements into a cash flow forecast. This forecast must take into account not only existing debts and obligations, but also any modifications the buyer would make in the business, including necessary capital expenditures. It must also reflect the repayment of any financing the buyer arranges to purchase the company, whether it is through the seller or a traditional lender. Will the company generate enough cash to be self-supporting? How much cash will it generate for you?

A potential buyer must look for suspicious deviations from normal (in either direction) for sales, expenses, profits, cash flow, assets, and liabilities. Have sales been increasing or decreasing? Is the equipment really as valuable as it is listed on the balance sheet? Are advertising expenses unusually high or low? How is depreciation reflected in the financial statements?

This financial information gives a buyer the opportunity to verify the seller's claims about a company's performance. Sometimes, however, an owner will take short-term actions that produce a healthy financial statement but weaken the company's long-term health and profit potential. For example, a seller might lower expenses and increase earnings by gradually eliminating equipment maintenance or boost sales by selling to marginal businesses that will never pay their bills. Techniques such as these artificially inflate earnings, but a well-prepared buyer should be able to see through them.

Finally, a potential buyer should walk away from a deal—no matter how good it may appear on the surface—if the present owner refuses to disclose the company's financial records or any other operating information the buyer needs to make an informed decision. If that is the case, says Marc Kramer, author of *Small Business Turnaround*, "don't walk—run—away."[11]

Buying an existing business is a process filled with potential missteps along the way. The expression "Let the buyer beware" should be the prospective buyer's mantra

FIGURE 7.2

The Acquisition Process

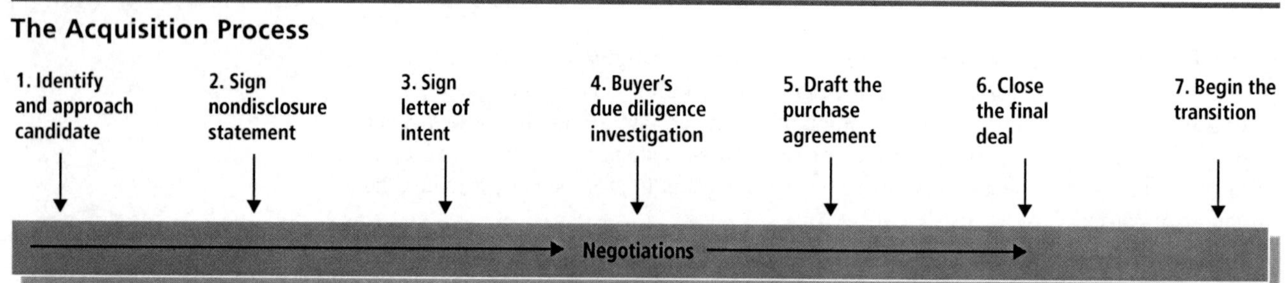

1. Approach the candidate. If a business is advertised for sale, the proper approach is through the channel defined in the ad. Sometimes buyers will contact business brokers to help them locate potential target companies. If you have targeted a company in the "hidden market," an introduction from a banker, accountant, or lawyer often is the best approach. During this phase, the seller checks out the buyer's qualifications, and the buyer begins to judge the quality of the company.
2. Sign a nondisclosure document. If the buyer and the seller are satisfied with the results of their preliminary research, they are ready to begin serious negotiations. Throughout the negotiation process, the seller expects the buyer to maintain strict confidentiality of all of the records, documents, and information he or she receives during the investigation and negotiation process. The nondisclosure document is a legally binding contract that ensures the secrecy of the parties' negotiations.
3. Sign a letter of intent. Before a buyer makes a legal offer to buy the company, he or she typically will ask the seller to sign a letter of intent. The letter of intent is a nonbinding document that says that the buyer and the seller have reached a sufficient "meeting of the minds" to justify the time and expense of negotiating a final agreement. The letter should state clearly that it is nonbinding, giving either party the right to walk away from the deal. It should also contain a clause calling for "good faith negotiations" between the parties. A typical letter of intent addresses terms such as price, payment terms, categories of assets to be sold, and a deadline for closing the final deal.
4. Buyer's due diligence. While negotiations are continuing, the buyer is busy studying the business and evaluating its strengths and weaknesses. In short, the buyer must "do his or her homework" to make sure that the business is a good value.
5. Draft the purchase agreement. The purchase agreement spells out the parties' final deal! It sets forth all of the details of the agreement and is the final product of the negotiation process.
6. Close the final deal. Once the parties have drafted the purchase agreement, all that remains to making the deal "official" is the closing. Both buyer and seller sign the necessary documents to make the sale final. The buyer delivers the required money, and the seller turns the company over to the buyer.
7. Begin the transition. For the buyer, the real challenge now begins: making the transition to a successful business owner!

Source: Adapted from Price Waterhouse, *Buying and Selling: A Company Handbook* (New York: Author, 1993), pp. 38–42; Charles F. Claeys, "The Intent to Buy," *Small Business Reports*, May 1994, pp. 44–47.

throughout the entire process. However, by following the due diligence procedure described in this section, buyers can lower dramatically the probability of getting "burned" with a business that does not suit their personalities or one that is in on the verge of failure. Figure 7.2 illustrates the sequence of events leading up to a successful negotiation with a seller.

LEARNING OBJECTIVES
4. Describe the various techniques for determining the value of a business.

Methods for Determining the Value of a Business

Business valuation is partly an art and partly a science. Part of what makes establishing a reasonable price for a privately held business so difficult is the wide variety of factors that influence its value: the nature of the business, its position in the market or industry, the outlook for the market or industry, the company's financial status, its earning capacity, any intangible assets it may own (e.g., patents, trademarks, or copyrights), the value of other similar publicly held companies, and many other factors.

Computing the value of the company's tangible assets normally poses no major problem, but assigning a price to the intangibles, such as goodwill, almost always creates controversy. **Goodwill** represents the difference in the value of an established business and one that has not yet built a solid reputation for itself. The buyer is willing to pay extra only for those intangible assets that produce additional income. The seller, however, believes that goodwill is a measure of the hard work, sacrifice, and long hours invested in building the business, something for which he or she expects to be paid—often quite handsomely.

goodwill
the difference in the value of an established business and one that has not yet built a solid reputation for itself.

Potential buyers also must recognize the role that the seller's ego can play in the business valuation process. Norm Brodsky, who owns a successful document storage business, explains:

> As a group, we [entrepreneurs] tend to have fairly large egos, which isn't entirely bad. You need one to make a business grow . . . But our egos can get us into trouble when it comes to putting a dollar value on something we've created. We generally take the highest valuation we've heard for a company somewhat like ours—and multiply it.[12]

So, how can the buyer and the seller arrive at a fair price? There are few hard and fast rules in establishing the value of a business, but the following guidelines are helpful:

- The wisest approach is to compute a company's value using several techniques and then to choose the one that makes the most sense.
- The deal must be financially feasible for both parties. The seller must be satisfied with the price received for the business, but the buyer cannot pay an excessively high price that would require heavy borrowing and would strain his or her cash flows from the outset.
- The potential buyer must have access to the business records.
- Valuations should be based on facts, not fiction.
- No surprise is the best surprise. Both parties should commit to dealing with one another honestly and in good faith.

The main reason that buyers purchase existing businesses is to get their future earning potential. The second -most- common reason is to obtain an established asset base; it is much easier to buy assets than to build them. Although evaluation methods should take these characteristics into consideration, too many business sellers and buyers depend on rules of thumb that ignore the unique features of small companies. Often, these rules of thumb are based on multiples of a company's net earnings or sales and vary by industry.

The next section describes three basic techniques and several variations on them for determining the value of a hypothetical business, Lewis Electronics.

Balance Sheet Techniques: Net Worth = Assets − Liabilities

Balance Sheet Technique The **balance sheet technique** is one of the most commonly used methods of evaluating a business, although it is not highly recommended because it oversimplifies the valuation process. This method computes the company's net worth or owner's equity (Net worth = Total assets − Total liabilities) and uses this figure as the value. The problem with this technique is that it fails to recognize reality: Most small businesses have market values that exceed their reported book values.

balance sheet technique
a method of valuing a business based on the value of the company's net worth (net worth = total assets − total liabilities).

The first step is to determine which assets are included in the sale. In most cases, the owner has some personal assets that he or she does not want to sell. Professional business brokers can help the buyer and the seller arrive at a reasonable value for the collection of assets included in the deal. Remember that net worth on a financial statement will likely differ significantly from actual net worth determined in the marketplace. Figure 7.3 shows the balance sheet for Lewis Electronics. Based on this balance sheet, the company's net worth is \$266,091 − \$114,325 = \$151,766.

Variation: Adjusted Balance Sheet Technique A more realistic method for determining a company's value is to adjust the book value of net worth to reflect *actual* market value—the so-called **adjusted balance sheet technique.** The values reported on a company's books may either overstate or understate the true value of assets and liabilities. Typical assets in a business sale include notes and accounts receivable, inventories, supplies, and fixtures. If a buyer purchases accounts receivable, he or she should estimate the likelihood of their collection and adjust their value accordingly (refer to Table 7.1).

adjusted balance sheet technique
a method of valuing a business based on the *market value* of the company's net worth (net worth = total assets − total liabilities).

FIGURE 7.3

Balance Sheet for Lewis Electronics

Lewis Electronics
Balance Sheet
June 30, 200X

Assets			
Current Assets:			
Cash		$ 11,655	
Accounts Receivable		15,876	
Inventory		56,523	
Supplies		8,574	
Prepaid Insurance		5,587	
Total Current Assets			$ 98,215
Fixed Assets:			
Land		$ 24,000	
Buildings	$ 141,000		
Less Accumulated Depreciation	51,500	89,500	
Office Equipment	$ 12,760		
Less Accumulated Depreciation	7,159	5,601	
Factory Equipment	$ 59,085		
Less Accumulated Depreciation	27,850	31,235	
Trucks and Autos	$ 28,730		
Less Accumulated Depreciation	11,190	17,540	
Total Fixed Assets			$ 167,876
Total Assets:			$ 266,091
Liabilities			
Current Liabilities:			
Accounts Payable		$ 19,497	
Mortgage Payable (current portion)		5,215	
Salaries Payable		3,671	
Note Payable		10,000	
Total Current Liabilities			$ 38,383
Long-Term Liabilities:			
Mortgage Payable		$ 54,542	
Note Payable		21,400	
Total Long-Term Liabilities			$ 75,942
Total Liabilities			$ 114,325
Owners' Equity			
Owners' Equity			$ 151,766
Total Liabilities and Owners' Equity			$ 266,091

In manufacturing, wholesale, and retail businesses, inventory is usually the largest asset in the sale. Taking a physical inventory count is the best way to determine accurately the quantity of goods to be transferred. The sale may include three types of inventory, each having its own method of valuation: raw materials, work-in-process, and finished goods. The buyer and the seller must arrive at a method for evaluating the inventory.

First-in-first-out (FIFO), last-in-first-out (LIFO), and average costing are three frequently used techniques, but the most common methods use the cost of last purchase and the replacement value of the inventory. Before accepting any inventory value, the buyer should evaluate the condition of the goods. One young couple purchased a lumberyard without sufficiently examining the inventory. After completing the sale, they discovered that most of the lumber in a warehouse they had neglected to inspect was warped and was of little value as building material. The bargain price they paid for the business turned out not to be the good deal they had expected.

To avoid problems, some buyers insist on having a knowledgeable representative on an inventory team count the inventory and check its condition. Nearly every sale involves merchandise that cannot be sold, but by taking this precaution, a buyer minimizes the chance of being stuck with worthless inventory. Fixed assets transferred in a sale might include land, buildings, equipment, and fixtures. Business owners frequently carry real estate and buildings at values well below their actual market value. Equipment and fixtures, depending on their condition and usefulness, may increase or decrease the true value of the business. Appraisals of these assets on insurance policies are helpful guidelines for establishing market value. In addition, business brokers can be useful in determining the current market value of fixed assets. Some brokers use an estimate of what it would cost to replace a company's physical assets (less a reasonable allowance for depreciation) to determine value. For Lewis Electronics, the adjusted net worth is $274,638 − $114,325 = $160,313 (see the adjusted balance sheet in Figure 7.4), indicating that some of the entries in its books did not accurately reflect true market value.

Business evaluations based on balance sheet methods suffer one major drawback: they do not consider the future earning potential of the business. These techniques value assets at current prices and do not consider them as tools for creating future profits. The next method for computing the value of a business is based on its expected future earnings.

Earnings Approach

The buyer of an existing business is essentially purchasing its future income. The **earnings approach** focuses on the future income potential of a business and assumes that a company's value depends on its ability to generate consistent earnings over time. In other words, the earnings approach recognizes that assets derive their *real* value from the income they produce in the future. There are three variations of the earnings approach.

earnings approach
a method of valuing a business that recognizes that a buyer is purchasing the future income (earning) potential of a business.

Variation 1: Excess Earnings Method This method combines the value of a business's existing assets (minus its liabilities) and an estimate of its future earnings potential to determine its selling price. One advantage of this technique is that it offers an estimate of goodwill. Goodwill is an intangible asset that often creates problems in a business sale. In fact, the most common method of valuing a business is to compute its tangible net worth and then to add an often arbitrary adjustment for goodwill. In essence, goodwill is the difference between an established, successful business and one that has yet to prove itself. It is based on the company's reputation and its ability to attract customers. A buyer should not accept blindly the seller's arbitrary adjustment for goodwill because it is likely to be inflated. The *real* value of a company's goodwill lies in its financial value to the buyer, not in its emotional value to the seller.

The excess earnings method provides a consistent and realistic approach for determining the value of goodwill. It measures goodwill by the amount of profit the business earns above that of the average firm in the same industry (its "extra earning power"). It also assumes that the owner is entitled to a reasonable return on the company's adjusted tangible net worth.

Step 1 **Compute adjusted tangible net worth.** Using the adjusted balance sheet method of valuation, the buyer should compute the firm's adjusted tangible net worth. Total tangible assets (adjusted for market value) minus total liabilities yields adjusted tangible net worth. In the Lewis Electronics example, adjusted tangible net worth is $274,638 − $114,325 = $160,313 (refer to Figure 7.4).

FIGURE 7.4

Balance Sheet for Lewis Electronics, Adjusted to Reflect Market Value

Lewis Electronics
Adjusted Balance Sheet
June 30, 200X

		Assets	
Current Assets:			
Cash		$ 11,655	
Accounts Receivable		10,051	
Inventory		39,261	
Supplies		7,492	
Prepaid Insurance		5,587	
Total Current Assets			$ 74,046
Fixed Assets:			
Land		$ 36,900	
Buildings	$ 177,000		
Less Accumulated Depreciation	51,500	125,500	
Office Equipment	$ 11,645		
Less Accumulated Depreciation	7,159	4,486	
Factory Equipment	$ 50,196		
Less Accumulated Depreciation	27,850	22,346	
Trucks and Autos	$ 22,550		
Less Accumulated Depreciation	11,190	11,360	
Total Fixed Assets			$ 200,592
Total Assets			$ 274,638
		Liabilities	
Current Liabilities:			
Accounts Payable		$ 19,497	
Mortgage Payable (current portion)		5,215	
Salaries Payable		3,671	
Note Payable		10,000	
Total Current Liabilities			$ 38,383
Long-Term Liabilities:			
Mortgage Payable		$ 54,542	
Note Payable		21,400	
Total Long-Term Liabilities			$ 75,942
Total Liabilities			$ 114,325
		Owners' Equity	
Owners' Equity			$ 160,313
Total Liabilities and Owners' Equity			$ 274,638

opportunity cost the cost of the next best alternative choice; the cost of giving up one alternative to get another.

Step 2 Calculate the opportunity costs of investing in the business. **Opportunity cost** represents the cost of forgoing a choice. If a buyer chooses to purchase the assets of a business, he or she cannot invest that money elsewhere. Therefore, the opportunity cost of the purchase would be the amount that the buyer could earn by investing the same amount *in a similar-risk investment.*

There are three components in the rate of return used to value a business: (1) the basic, risk-free return, (2) an inflation premium, and (3) the risk allowance for investing in the particular business. The basic, risk-free return and the inflation premium are reflected in investments such as U.S. Treasury bonds. To determine the appropriate rate of return for investing in a business, a buyer must add to this base rate a factor reflecting the risk of purchasing the company. The greater the risk, the higher will be the rate of return. A normal-risk business typically translates into a rate of return in the 20 to 25 percent range. In the Lewis Electronics example, the opportunity cost of the investment is $160,313 × 25% = $40,078.

The second part of the buyer's opportunity cost is the salary that he or she could earn working for someone else. For the Lewis Electronics example, if the buyer purchases the business, he or she must forgo the $25,000 salary that could be earned working elsewhere. Adding these amounts together yields a total opportunity cost of $65,078.

Step 3 **Project net earnings.** The buyer must estimate the company's net earnings for the upcoming year before subtracting the owner's salary. Averages can be misleading, so the buyer must be sure to investigate the trend of net earnings. Have they risen steadily over the last five years, dropped significantly, remained relatively constant, or fluctuated wildly? As you learned earlier in this chapter, past income statements provide useful guidelines for estimating earnings. In the Lewis Electronics example, the prospective buyer and the buyer's accountant project net earnings for the upcoming year to be $74,000.

Step 4 **Compute extra earning power.** A company's extra earning power is the difference between forecasted earnings (Step 3) and total opportunity costs (Step 2). Many small businesses that are for sale do not have extra earning power (i.e., excess earnings), and they show marginal or no profits. The extra earning power of Lewis Electronics is $74,000 − $65,000 = $8,922.

Step 5 **Estimate the value of intangibles.** The owner can use the business's extra earning power of the business to estimate the value of its intangible assets—that is, its goodwill. Multiplying the extra earning power by a years-of-profit figure yields an estimate of the intangible assets' value. The years-of-profit figure for a normal-risk business ranges from three to four. A very high risk business may have a years-of-profit figure of just one, whereas a well-established firm might warrant a years-of-profit figure of seven. For Lewis Electronics, the value of intangibles (assuming normal risk) would be $8,922 × 3 = $26,766.

Step 6 **Determine the value of the business.** To determine the value of the business, the buyer simply adds together the adjusted tangible net worth (Step 1) and the value of the intangibles (Step 5). Using this method, we find that the value of Lewis Electronics is $160,313 + $26,766 = $187,079.

The buyer and the seller should consider the tax implications of including in the purchase the value of goodwill and the value of a covenant not to compete. Because the *buyer* can amortize both the cost of goodwill and a restrictive covenant over 15 years, the tax treatment of either would be the same for him or her. However, the *seller* would prefer to have the amount of the purchase price in excess of the value of the assets allocated to goodwill, which is a capital asset. The gain on the capital asset would be taxed at the lower capital gains rates. If that same amount were allocated to a restrictive covenant (which is negotiated with the seller personally, not the business), the seller must treat it as ordinary income, which would be taxed at regular rates that are higher than the capital gains rates.

Variation 2: Capitalized Earnings Approach A variation of the earnings approach capitalizes expected net earnings to determine the value of a business. As you learned earlier in this chapter, buyers should prepare their own pro forma income statements and should ask the seller to prepare one also. Many appraisers use a five-year weighted average of past sales (with the greatest weights assigned to the most recent years) to estimate sales for the upcoming year.

Once again, a buyer must evaluate the risk of purchasing the business to determine the appropriate rate of return on the investment. The greater the perceived risk, the higher is the return that the buyer requires. Risk determination is always somewhat subjective, but it is necessary for proper evaluation.

capitalized earnings approach
a method of valuing a business that divides estimated earnings by the rate of return the buyer could earn on a similar-risk investment.

The **capitalized earnings approach** divides estimated net earnings (*after* subtracting the owner's reasonable salary) by the rate of return that reflects the risk level. For Lewis Electronics, the capitalized value (assuming a reasonable salary of $25,000) is

$$\frac{\text{Net earnings (after deducting owner's salary)}}{\text{Rate of return}} = \frac{\$74{,}000 - \$25{,}000}{25\%} = \$196{,}000$$

Clearly, firms with lower risk factors are more valuable (a 10 percent rate of return would yield a value of $499,000 for Lewis Electronics) than are those with higher risk factors (a 50 percent rate of return would yield a value of $99,800). Most normal-risk businesses use a rate-of-return factor ranging from 20 to 25 percent. The lowest risk factor that most buyers would accept for any business is around 15 percent.

Variation 3: Discounted Future Earnings Approach This variation of the earnings approach assumes that a dollar earned in the future is worth less than that same dollar today. Therefore, using this approach, the buyer estimates the company's net income for several years into the future and then discounts these future earnings back to their present value. The resulting present value is an estimate of the company's worth because it reflects the company's future earning potential stated in today's dollars.

The reduced value of future dollars represents the cost of the buyers' giving up the opportunity to earn a reasonable rate of return by receiving income in the future instead of today, a concept known as the time value of money. To illustrate the importance of the time value of money, consider two $1 million sweepstake winners. Rob wins $1 million in a sweepstakes, but he receives it in $50,000 installments over 20 years. If Rob invested every installment at 15 percent interest, he would have accumulated $5,890,505.98 at the end of 20 years. Lisa wins $1 million in another sweepstakes, but she collects her winnings in one lump sum. If Lisa invested her $1 million today at 15 percent, she would have accumulated $16,366,537.39 at the end of 20 years. The difference in their wealth is the result of the time value of money.

discounted future earnings approach
a method of valuing a business that forecasts a company's earnings several years into the future and then discounts them back to their present value.

The **discounted future earnings approach** includes five steps:

STEP 1. PROJECT FUTURE EARNINGS FOR FIVE YEARS INTO THE FUTURE One way is to assume that earnings will grow by a constant amount over the next five years. Perhaps a better method is to develop three forecasts—an optimistic, a pessimistic, and a most likely—for each year and then find a weighted average using the following formula, which weights the most likely forecast four times as heavily as either the optimistic or pessimistic forecasts:

Forecasted earnings for year i

$$= \frac{\text{Optimistic earnings for year } i + 4(\text{Most likely forecast for year } i) + (\text{Pessimistic forecast for year } i)}{6}$$

For Lewis Electronics, the buyer's forecasts (in dollars) are as follows:

Year	Pessimistic	Most Likely	Optimistic	Weighted Average
XXX1	65,000	74,000	92,000	75,500
XXX2	74,000	90,000	101,000	89,167
XXX3	82,000	100,000	112,000	99,000
XXX4	88,000	109,000	120,000	107,333
XXX5	88,000	115,000	122,000	111,667

Buyers must remember that the farther into the future they forecast, the less reliable their estimates will be.

STEP 2. DISCOUNT THESE FUTURE EARNINGS AT THE APPROPRIATE PRESENT VALUE RATE The rate that the buyer selects should reflect the rate he or she could earn on a similar-risk investment. Because Lewis Electronics is a normal-risk business, the buyer chooses a present value rate of 25 percent.

Year	Income Forecast (Weighted Average) ($)	Present Value Factor (at 25%)*	Net Present Value ($)
XXX1	75,500	0.8000	60,400
XXX2	89,167	0.6400	57,067
XXX3	99,000	0.5120	50,688
XXX4	107,333	0.4096	43,964
XXX5	111,667	0.3277	36,593
Total			248,712

*The appropriate present value factor can be found by looking in published present value tables, by using a calculator or computer, or by solving the formula

$$\text{Present value factor} = \frac{1}{(1 + k)^t}$$

where k is the rate of return and t is the year ($t = 1, 2, 3, \ldots, n$).

STEP 3. ESTIMATE THE INCOME STREAM BEYOND FIVE YEARS One technique suggests multiplying the fifth year income by 1 ÷ rate of return. For Lewis Electronics, the estimate is

$$\text{Income beyond year 5} = \$111{,}667 \times \frac{1}{25\%} = \$446{,}668$$

STEP 4. DISCOUNT THE INCOME ESTIMATE BEYOND FIVE YEARS USING THE PRESENT VALUE FACTOR FOR THE SIXTH YEAR For Lewis Electronics

$$\text{Present value of income beyond year 5} = \$446{,}668 \times 0.2622 = \$117{,}116$$

STEP 5. COMPUTE THE TOTAL VALUE OF THE BUSINESS Add the present value of the company's estimated earnings for years 1 through 5 (Step 2) and the present value of its earnings from year 6 on (Step 4):

$$\text{Total value} = \$248{,}712 + \$117{,}116 = \$365{,}828$$

The primary advantage of this technique is that it evaluates a business solely on the basis of its future earning potential, but its reliability depends on making forecasts of future earnings and on choosing a realistic present value rate. In other words, a company's present value is tied to its future performance, which is not always easy to project. The discounted cash flow technique is especially well suited for valuing service businesses (whose asset bases are often very thin) and for companies experiencing high growth rates.

Market Approach

The **market approach (or price/earnings approach)** uses the price/earnings (P/E) ratios of similar businesses listed on a stock exchange to establish the value of a company. A buyer must use businesses in the same industry whose stocks are publicly traded to get a meaningful comparison. A company's price/earnings ratio is the price of one share of its common stock in the market divided by its earnings per share (after deducting preferred stock dividends). To get a representative P/E ratio, a buyer should average the P/Es of as many similar businesses as possible.

market approach
a method of valuing a business that uses the price/earnings (P/E) ratio of similar, publicly held companies to determine value.

To compute the company's value, the buyer multiplies the average price/earnings ratio by the private company's estimated earnings. For example, suppose that the buyer found four companies comparable to Lewis Electronics but whose stock is publicly traded. Their price/earnings ratios are

Company 1	3.3
Company 2	3.8
Company 3	4.7
Company 4	4.1
Average P/E ratio	3.975

Using this average P/E ratio produces a value of $294,150:

$$\text{Value} = \text{Average PE ratio} \times \text{Estimated net earnings} = 3.975 \times \$74{,}000 = \$294{,}150$$

The biggest advantage of the market approach is its simplicity. However, this method does have several disadvantages, including the following:

Necessary comparisons between publicly traded and privately owned companies. Because the stock of privately owned companies is not as liquid as that of publicly held companies, the P/E ratio used is often subjective and lower than that of publicly held companies.

Unrepresentative earnings estimates. A private company's net earnings may not realistically reflect its true earning potential. To minimize taxes, owners usually attempt to keep earnings low and rely on fringe benefits and bonuses to make up the difference.

Finding similar companies for comparison. Often, it is extremely difficult for a buyer to find comparable publicly held companies when estimating the appropriate P/E ratio.

Applying the after-tax earnings of a private company to determine its value. If a prospective buyer is using an after-tax P/E ratio from a public company, he or she also must use the after-tax earnings from the private company.

Despite its drawbacks, the market approach is useful as a general guide to establishing a company's value.

Which of these methods is best for determining the value of a small business? Simply stated, there is no single best method. Valuing a business is partly an art and partly a science. Use of these techniques will yield a range of values. Buyers should look for values that might cluster together and then use their best judgment to determine a reasonable offering price. Table 7.4 summarizes the valuation techniques covered in this chapter.

TABLE 7.4 What's It Worth? A Summary of Business Valuation Techniques

Balance Sheet Technique

Book value of net worth = Total assets − Total liabilities
= $266,091 − $114,325 = $151,766

Variation: Adjusted Balance Sheet Technique

Net worth adjusted to reflect market value = $274,638 − $114,325 = $160,313

Earnings Approach

Variation 1: Excess Earnings Method

Step 1: Adjusted tangible net worth = $274,638 − $114,325 = $160,313

Step 2: Opportunity costs = Opportunity cost of investing + salary forgone
= $160,313 × 25% + 25,000 = $65,078

Step 3: Estimated net earnings = $74,000

TABLE 7.4 Contiunued

Step 4: Extra earning power = Estimated net earnings − Total opportunity costs
= $74,000 − $65,078 = $8,922

Step 5: Value of intangibles (goodwill) = Extra earning power × Years of profit figure
= $8,922 × 3 = $26,766

Step 6: Value of business = Tangible net worth + Value of intangibles
= $160,313 + 26,766 = $187,079

Variation 2: Capitalized Earnings Approach

$$\text{Value} = \frac{\text{Net Earnings (after deducting owner's salary)}}{\text{Rate of return on a similar-risk investment}}$$

$$= \frac{\$74{,}000 - \$25{,}000}{25\%} = \$196{,}000$$

Variation 3: Discounted Future Earnings Approach

Step 1: Project future earnings:

Year	Pessimistic	Most Likely	Optimistic	Weighted Average*
XXX1	$65,000	$ 74,000	$ 94,000	$ 75,500
XXX2	$74,000	$ 90,000	$101,000	$ 89,167
XXX3	$82,000	$100,000	$112,000	$ 99,000
XXX4	$88,000	$109,000	$120,000	$107,333
XXX5	$88,000	$115,000	$122,000	$111,667

$$\text{*Weighted average} = \frac{\text{Pessimistic} + 4(\text{Most likely}) + \text{Optimistic}}{6}.$$

Step 2: Discount future earnings using the appropriate present value factor:

Year	Forecasted Earnings	Present Value Factor	Net Present Value
XXX1	$ 75,500	0.8000	$ 60,400
XXX2	$ 89,167	0.6400	$ 57,067
XXX3	$ 99,000	0.5120	$ 50,688
XXX4	$107,333	0.4096	$ 43,964
XXX5	$111,667	0.3277	$ 36,593
Total			$248,712

Step 3: Estimate income stream beyond 5 Years:

$$\text{Income stream} = \text{Fifth-year forecasted income} \times \frac{1}{\text{Rate of return}}$$

$$= \$111{,}667 \times \frac{1}{25\%}$$

$$= \$446{,}668$$

Step 4: Discount income stream beyond 5 years using sixth-year present value factor:

Present value of income stream = $446,668 × 0.2622 = $117,116

Step 5: Compute total value:

Total value = $248,712 + $117,116 = $365,828

Market Approach

Value = Estimated earnings × Average price/earnings ratio of representative companies
= $74,000 × 3.975 = $294,150

Which value is correct? *Remember:* There is no best method of valuing a business. These techniques provide only estimates of a company's worth. The particular method used depends on the unique qualities of the business and the special circumstances surrounding the sale.

LEARNING OBJECTIVES
5. Understand the seller's side of the buyout decision and how to structure the deal.

Understanding the Seller's Side

A recent study by DAK Group and Columbia University's Lang Center for Entrepreneurship reports that 64 percent of the owners of closely held companies expect to sell their businesses within three years.[13] For entrepreneurs, few events are more anticipated—and more emotional—than selling their businesses. Selling their companies often produces vast personal wealth and a completely new lifestyle, and this newly gained wealth offers freedom and the opportunity to catch up on all the things the owners missed out on while building their businesses. Yet, many entrepreneurs who sell out experience a tremendous void in their lives, a "separation anxiety" that is the result of their lives having revolved around the businesses they created and nurtured for so many years. For these business owners, their companies were the focal point of their lives in their communities and were an essential part of their identities. When they sell their companies, a primary concern for many entrepreneurs is preserving the reputation, culture, and principles on which they built and operated the company. Will the new owner display the same values in managing the business? Can the company founder cope with the inevitable changes the new owner will make to the business?

California Pizza Kitchen

Seven years after founding the California Pizza Kitchen, Rick Rosenfield and Larry Flax were surprised when Pepsico offered to buy a majority stake in their company for $100 million. The soft drink giant kept Rosenfield and Flax on as co-chairmen but relieved them of any daily operating and decision-making duties and replaced them with a more experienced CEO, Fred Hipp. Hipp's strategy for the company was quite different from that of the founders, who had built the company on the basics: quality ingredients, upscale locations, and steady growth. When Hipp's decisions pushed the company toward financial ruin, Pepsico brought Rosenfield and Flax back in to save it. They closed underperforming outlets, upgraded the remaining ones, and introduced interesting new menu items designed to appeal to California Pizza Kitchen's core customers.[14]

Some business brokers differentiate between "financial buyers" and "strategic buyers." Financial buyers, usually individuals, see buying a business as a way to generate income for themselves and their families. Their primary concern is the company's ability to generate profits and positive cash flow in the future. Strategic buyers, often other businesses or even competitors, view buying a company as part of a larger picture, a piece in a strategic puzzle that gives them an advantage such as access to a new, fast-growing market, a unique product, or a new technological innovation. "Financial buyers typically will pay a lower price because they have a 'fire sale' mentality," says Andy Agrawal, a partner in an investment banking firm. "You need to find strategic buyers and paint a picture for them," he advises. "Show the strategic buyer how one plus one equals three."[15]

La Brea Bakery

Nancy Silverton sold 80 percent of LaBrea Bakery to the Irish food company IAWS Group but managed to maintain "artistic integrity" over the breads the company sells.

Nancy Silverton, who in 1989 co-founded a restaurant, Campanille, and a bakery, La Brea Bakery, with her husband in Los Angeles, managed to find a strategic buyer for La Brea bakery in the Irish food giant IAWS Group, which recently purchased 80 percent of the company for $68.5 million. When Silverton decided to sell, La Brea was generating annual profits of $9.4 million on sales of more than $50 million, primarily because the company had developed a unique flash-freezing process that allowed it to ship its breads almost anywhere without damaging its flavor and texture. (Celebrity chef Wolfgang Puck, who serves Silverton's bread at his star-studded Spago restaurant in Los Angeles, says, "Nobody's bread is as good as hers.") IAWS Group already had a par-baked operation in Europe and wanted to gain access to the premium bread market in the United States.

La Brea Bakery's established network of customers and its unique flash-freezing process were a perfect match for this strategic buyer's needs. As part of the deal, Silverton even managed to maintain "artistic integrity" over the breads the company sells.[16]

Selling a business involves developing a plan that maximizes the value of the business. Before selling her business, an entrepreneur must ask himself or herself some important questions: Do you want to walk away from the business completely, or do you plan to stay on after the sale? If you decide to stay on, how involved do you want to be in running the company? How much can you realistically expect to get for the business? Is this amount of money sufficient to maintain your desired lifestyle? Rather than sell the business to an outsider, should you be transferring ownership to your kids or to your employees? Who are the professionals—business brokers, accountants, attorneys, tax advisers—you will need to help you to close the sale successfully? How do you expect the buyer to pay for the company? Are you willing to finance at least some of the purchase price?

Sellers who have answered these fundamental questions are prepared to move forward with the sale of their companies.

You Be the Consultant

Seller's Remorse

In 1961, Larry Freeman went into his family's business, Freeman Sales Agency, like his father and his grandfather before him. The company served as a manufacturer's representative for makers of shampoos, lotions, and creams. Larry's father died in 1967, leaving Larry and his younger brother, Richard, both in their 20s, in charge of the family business. By the early 1970s, the ambitious, hard-working brothers had moved the company from just selling other manufacturers' cosmetics to producing and marketing their own line of products, some of which proved to be cutting edge at the time. For instance, the brothers launched one of the first shampoos made with all organic ingredients.

By 1984, Freeman Cosmetics, as the company was now known, was generating sales of $5 million but was losing money. Richard decided to leave the company, and Larry brought in his son, Mark, to help him run the business. The father–son team began to rebuild the company, introducing a string of new products made with oatmeal, avocadoes, and apples packaged in colorful bottles that appealed to young buyers. In 1991, Larry's sister, Jill, joined the business and found her niche in marketing. Mark had a knack for developing international markets and was busy building the Freeman's international division. Larry focused on building long-term relationships with the company's customers and guiding its social responsibility efforts. "A business is more than a business," he says. "It's a platform to do other things." For instance, in 1994, Freeman Cosmetics opened a 165,000-square-foot factory that created jobs for 300 people in South Central Los Angeles.

Since its beginning, Freeman's growth has been steady and methodical, funded solely by the company's cash flow. Larry never had brought in a dime of outside financing. By 1998, however, Freeman's sales, which had climbed to $70 million, were growing so fast that the company could no longer generate sufficient cash to fuel the growth. Larry contacted an investment banker to explore external financing options for the company and included a very explicit edict: "Do not bring me a buyer. I do not want to sell this [company]."

Ignoring Larry's decree, the investment banker brought a handful of enticing offers to Larry and the other family members involved in the business. Several family members had serious doubts about selling the company, but they all changed their minds when they began to see the offers. Dial, Inc., the consumer products giant, was offering the family $80 million for Freeman Cosmetics—far more than any of them had ever imagined they could get for their family business.

Everyone except Larry was ready to sell. He didn't need the money, and he wanted his grandchildren to have a chance to run the family business one day. Not wanting to stand in the way of his children, however, Larry reluctantly agreed to sell Freeman Cosmetics to Dial. After the closing, the family members escaped to a bathroom, where they hugged one another and cried.

The deal called for Larry to be president of Dial's personal care division, which included the newly acquired Freeman's Cosmetics. Just six weeks after closing the deal, however, Dial's chairman called Larry and told him, "Stay home; collect your checks." Larry and the rest of the Freeman clan could only stand by and watch Dial run their business. Unfortunately, the decisions Dial executives were making were running the once successful company straight into the ground. For instance, Dial managers cut Freeman's product line by one-third, closed the factory in South Central Los Angeles, and cut R&D expenditures. Sales began to slide, and the Freemans walked away in disgust from employment contracts with Dial valued at $2.5 million. "I was watching Dial destroy what it took me 25 years to build," Larry recalls.

After three years, Dial sold its personal care division, including Freeman Cosmetics, for $12 million to the Hathi Group, which was no better at running the business than Dial was. When Hathi declared bankruptcy in September 2003, the Freemans bought back their business for $10 million. Larry, Mark, and Jill are back at their same desks handling much the same areas they managed before the sale. Yet the new Freeman Cosmetics is quite different from the company they sold years ago. Instead of the vertically integrated business with 400 employees, the company is a lean, 25-person sales and marketing company that outsources all of its manufacturing to other factories. That does not concern Mark, however, who says that manufacturing never was one of the family's strengths.

The Freemans are focusing on their company's growth, knowing that if they did it once before, they can do it again. What happens down the road once they reach their goals? "It may be that ten years from now someone makes us an offer so big that we have to take it again," says Larry with a big smile, sounding as if he already is trying to convince himself that it would be the right thing to do.

1. Why do many entrepreneurs who sell their businesses suffer from seller's remorse? Use the Web to research entrepreneurs who have sold their businesses. What emotional issues do they face after the sale?
2. Referring to entrepreneurs who sell their companies, Eugene Muscat, director of the Gellert Foundation Family Business Center at the University of San Francisco, says, "If you were a business owner and then all of a sudden all you are is just a rich person, that's a big fall from grace." What does he mean? Do you agree? How does this tendency affect entrepreneurs?
3. Could the Freemans have done anything differently to avoid the problems they encountered when they sold their family business? Write a brief report (no more than one page) summarizing your recommendations and the logic behind them.

Source: Adapted from David Whitford, "Buying Back Their Name," *Inc.*, February 2004, pp. 57–60.

Structuring the Deal

Next to picking the right buyer, planning the structure of the deal is one of the most important decisions a seller can make. Entrepreneurs who sell their companies without considering the tax implications of the deal may wind up paying the IRS as much as 70% of the proceeds in the form of capital gains and other taxes. A skilled tax adviser or financial planner can help business sellers to legally minimize the bite various taxes take out of the proceeds of the sale. When it comes to exit strategies, entrepreneurs have the following options available to them.

Exit Strategies

Straight Business Sale A straight business sale often is best for those entrepreneurs who want to step down and turn over the reins of the company to someone else.

Folio Inc.

After graduating from a community college, Paul Hanlon, then 22, took a job earning minimum wage plus commissions for a company selling portable pop-up displays for use in trade shows. Five years later, Hanlon borrowed $47,000 to buy the company for just the cost of its inventory. Over the next decade, Hanlon, who renamed the company Folio Inc., expanded its product line and landed big-name clients such as Reebok, Oracle, and GE. When he was 39, Hanlon decided to sell Folio and retire and become an author and a motivational speaker when he received an offer for $20 million.[17]

In straight business sales, owners must decide whether to sell the assets of the business or transfer ownership to the buyer through a sale of company stock. Which choice is best for the seller and the buyer depends on the form of ownership. In an S corporation, the seller does not care if it the transaction is through stock or assets because the tax considerations are the same. Owners of C corporations are far better off selling stock rather than selling assets. Buyers will generally prefer to acquire the "hard" assets of the business, thus, avoiding any potential hidden liabilities. Despite these concerns, more than 90 percent of business sales involve a sale of shares of stock.[18]

Business Sale with an Agreement from the Founder to Stay on Sometimes business owners want to sell their companies but stay on to operate them. Doing so enables an entrepreneur to avoid concentrating his or her personal wealth in a single asset—the business—and to stay involved in managing the company he or she founded.

Compendit Inc.

Kevin McDonald co-founder of Compendit Inc., a consulting business specializing in enterprise resource planning, recently sold his firm to a larger company in the consulting business, Inforte Corporation, for $6 million and stayed on as executive vice-president and general manager. Inforte simply integrated Compendit into its corporate structure as a division, allowing McDonald's company to stay intact. Most of the company's 54 employees also stayed on. Although now subject to a corporate hierarchy, McDonald takes a philosophical view. "As an entrepreneur, I have always worked for my team, my customers, my wife, the bank . . . What's one more boss?"[19]

Although this scenario sounds like the ideal solution for entrepreneurs who are seeking more free time without stepping away entirely from the companies they built, it does not always prove to be. Accustomed to being in control, making the key decisions, and calling all of the shots, entrepreneurs who sell out with an agreement to stay on often have great difficulty relinquishing control of the company to the new owner. The situation is particularly difficult when the new owner makes decisions that jeopardize the company's future, forcing the founder to stand by and watch the business spiral slowly downward toward failure.

Meade Instruments

That's exactly what happened to John Diebel, who, in 1972 founded Meade Instruments as a small telescope maker and distributor while working as an engineer at Hughes Aircraft. In 1986, having built Meade into a successful company with annual sales of nearly $14 million, Diebel sold out to Harbor Group, a St. Louis-based leveraged buyout firm, but agreed to stay on as president to manage the company. It was a move he began to regret almost immediately. The new owners cut R&D spending and new product development efforts, imposed a rigid structure on the previously nimble company, and demanded endless reports from Diebel. "John was used to reporting to himself," says Meade's former chief operating officer. "If he had a good idea, he wanted to do it. He didn't want to make a plan." Within five years of the sale, the new owner had pushed the once successful company to the brink of bankruptcy. That's when Diebel stepped in and repurchased the company for just $1,000 and the assumption of $2.4 million in existing debt. Diebel has since rebuilt Meade and restored it to profitability, making his ownership stake worth more than $30 million.[20]

Form a Family Limited Partnership Entrepreneurs also can transfer their businesses to their children but still maintain control over them by forming a family limited partnership. The entrepreneur takes the role of the general partner, and the children become limited partners in the business. The general partner keeps just 1% of the company, but the partnership agreement gives him or her total control over the business. The children own 99% of the company but have little or no say over how to run the business. Until the founder decides to step down and turn over the reins of the company to the next generation, he or she continues to run the business and, with proper planning, can set up significant tax savings when the ultimate transfer of power takes place.

Sell a Controlling Interest Sometimes business owners sell a majority interest in their companies to investors, competitors, suppliers, or large companies, retain a portion of the ownership themselves, and agree to stay on after the sale as managers or consultants.

Happ Controls

That's just the kind of deal Frank Happ, who worked his way up the ranks at a company that made coin-operated games before purchasing the business, was able to negotiate with Pfingsten Partners, a private equity firm in Deerfield, Illinois. After purchasing the business in 1986, Happ bought out several competitors, expanded into the business of distributing games, and brought his two children into the business. When Happ reached his late 50s, he decided to sell the company, which had reached annual sales of $68 million. He considered a straight business sale but instead decided to sell a controlling interest in Happ Controls to Pfingsten Partners for eight times the company's earnings and retain 8.2 percent of the business. Happ now works just 30 days a year for the company (where he reports to his son, whom Pfingsten Partners named president), leaving him plenty of time to play golf and watch his grandchildren grow up.[21]

Restructure the Company Another way for business owners to cash out gradually is to replace the existing corporation with a new one formed with other investors. The owner essentially is performing a leveraged buyout of his or her own company. For example, assume that you own a company worth $15 million. You form a new corporation with $12 million borrowed from a bank and $3 million in equity: $1.5 million of your own equity and $1.5 million in equity from an investor who wants you to stay on with the business. The new company buys your company for $15 million. You net $13.5 in cash ($15 million minus your $1.5 million equity investment) and still own 50 percent of the new leveraged business (see Figure 7.5).[22]

Sell to an International Buyer In an increasingly global marketplace, small U.S. businesses have become attractive buyout targets for foreign companies. Foreign buyers—mostly European—buy more than 1,000 U.S. businesses each year. England leads the list of nations acquiring U.S. companies, but China is coming on strong.

FIGURE 7.5

Restructuring a Business for Sale

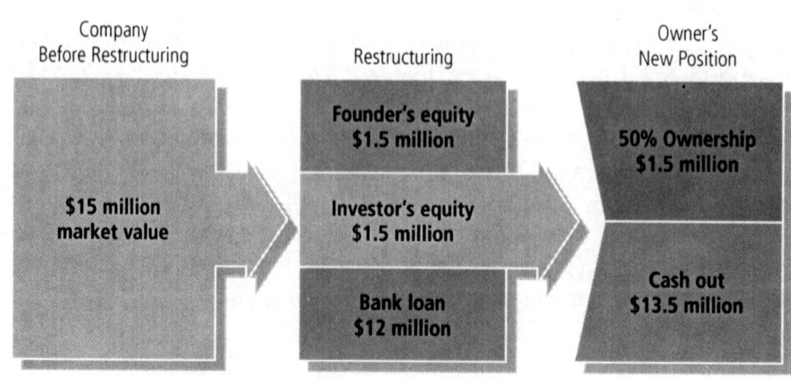

Adams Pressed Metals

Robert Parker, owner of Adams Pressed Metals, a small, family-owned company in Galesburg, Illinois, that makes stamped metal parts, saw his company struggle when John Deere, his largest customer, began buying parts from Tri-Star International, a Chinese manufacturer. Transforming a significant threat into a substantial opportunity, Parker negotiated a deal with Tri-Star to sell a majority interest in the family-run business for $1 million. Tri-Star recognized that Adams Pressed Metals had a solid reputation among its customer base, access to important distribution channels, and a skilled workforce. "Adams will provide Tri-Star with a U.S. platform to expand its global operations," says Parker. "We saved 40 jobs, and [Tri Star] got American know-how in sales."[23]

As Robert Parker's experience shows, it is not unusual in today's global economy to find companies across the globe with substantial financial resources looking to acquire small businesses in the United States. In many instances, foreign companies buy U.S.-based companies to gain access to a lucrative, growing market. They look for a team of capable managers, whom they typically retain for a given time period. They also want companies that are profitable, stable, and growing. Selling to foreign buyers can have disadvantages, however. They typically purchase 100 percent of a company, thereby making the previous owner merely an employee. Relationships with foreign owners also can be difficult to manage due to cultural and philosophical differences.

Use a Two-Step Sale For owners wanting the security of a sales contract now but not wanting to step down from the company's helm for several years, a two-step sale may be ideal. The buyer purchases the business in two phases—getting 20 to 70 percent today and agreeing to buy the remainder within a specific time period. Until the final transaction takes place, the entrepreneur retains at least partial control of the company.

Establish an Employee Stock Ownership Plan (ESOP) Some owners cash out by selling to their employees through an **employee stock ownership plan (ESOP).** An ESOP is a form of employee benefit plan in which a trust created for employees purchases their employer's stock. Here's how an ESOP works: The company transfers shares of its stock to the ESOP trust, and the trust uses the stock as collateral to borrow enough money to purchase the shares from the company. The company guarantees payment of the loan principal and interest and makes tax-deductible contributions to the trust to repay the loan (see Figure 7.6). The company then distributes the stock to employees' accounts based using a predetermined formula. In addition to the tax benefits an ESOP offers, the plan permits the owner to transfer all or part of the company to employees as gradually or as suddenly as preferred.

employee stock ownership plan (ESOP)
an employee benefit plan in which a trust created for employees purchases stock in their employer's company.

To use an ESOP successfully, a small business should be profitable (with pre-tax profits exceeding $100,000) and should have a payroll of more than $500,000 a year. Generally, companies with fewer than 15 to 20 employees do not find ESOPs beneficial. For companies that prepare properly, however, ESOPs offer significant financial and managerial benefits. Owners get great flexibility in determining their retirement schedules. An ESOP allows all parties involved to benefit, and the transfer of ownership can be timed to meet the entrepreneur's personal and financial goals.

Table 7.5 offers tips to help business sellers prepare their companies for sale to get maximum value from them.

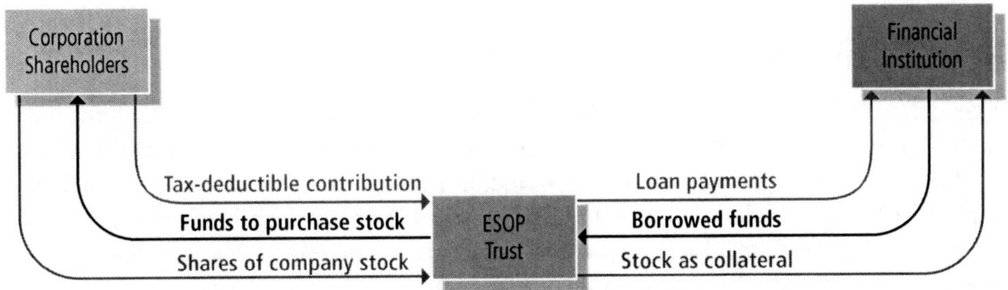

FIGURE 7.6

A Typical Employee Stock Ownership Plan (ESOP)

Source: Corey Rosen, "Sharing Ownership with Employees," *Small Business Reports*, December 1990, p. 63. © 1990 Corey Rosen. Used with permission.

TABLE 7.5 Preparing Your Company for Sale: How to Maximize Its Value

David Lobel, managing partner in a private equity firm that has purchased dozens of small companies, says that getting a company into shape to sell "can't be done overnight, but it can be done." What steps can business sellers take to prepare their companies for sale so that they can get maximum value from them? The following tips will help.

1. *Clean up the company's financial records.* Too many business owners are careless about keeping their books in pristine condition. A common excuse is "I'm too busy running my business to worry about keeping up with all of those financial records." However, a company's financial records are the raw materials from which potential buyers will establish the price they are willing to pay for a company. Make your company's financial records as tidy and as transparent as possible.
2. *Catch up on basic housekeeping.* People who are selling their houses know that cleaning and organizing their homes and eliminating clutter can add to the appeal—and to the price—of their houses. The same is true for businesses. Clean up all of the clutter that tends to build up over time, spruce up the physical appearance of the place, and put things in their proper places.
3. *Stop running personal expenses through the company.* Some business owners seek to minimize their company's tax bills by running personal expenses—for instance, gas for the family car—through the company. Tricks such as these make buyers nervous.
4. *Prepare a customer list for prospective buyers.* Buyers want to know that a company's sales will continue after they close the deal. Providing a list of important customers, including details such as how long each one has been buying from the company, how much each one has spent, key contacts (if business customers are involved), and the quality of the relationship, will add value to your business.
5. *Prepare a list of your company's key suppliers.* Which ones are most reliable? What kinds of contracts does your company have with them?
6. *Be prepared to show prospective buyers how much it costs to deliver your product or service to a customer.* Buyers want to know that the company's cost estimates are realistic.
7. *Prepare an employee policy manual.* The manual should include a job analysis for each position in the company, complete with a job description and job specifications. What rules of expected behavior does the company have?
8. *Prepare a document that describes how all of the machinery and equipment in the business works.* A list of service and repair contacts also is important.
9. *Consider removing from the payroll family members who are not essential to the operation of the business.* Many small businesses include family members whose contributions to the company are minimal.
10. *Take the time to conduct a business valuation at least every two years.* In many cases, when prospective buyers approach business owners with unsolicited offers for their companies, the entrepreneurs have no basis for making a deal because they have never taken the time to determine the value of their businesses. Seeing what makes up the real value in your business might enable you to operate it more effectively.
11. *Be prepared to stay on after the sale to help the new owner through the transition period.* In many instances, the business founder and his or her knowledge is the most important asset a company has.
12. *Take the steps listed here at least three years before you plan to sell your company. Remember:* It takes time to prepare a company for sale.

Sources: Adapted from Jim Melloan, "Sales Tips," *Inc.*, August 2004, p. 72; Laura Rich, "Seller's Market," *Inc.*, May 2005, pp. 39–42.

LEARNING OBJECTIVES
6. Understand how the negotiation process works and identify the factors that affect it.

Negotiating the Deal

Although determining the value of a business for sale is an important step in the process of buying a business, it is not the final one. The buyer must sit down with the seller to negotiate the actual selling price for the business and, more important, the terms of the deal. The final deal the buyer strikes depends, in large part, on his or her negotiating skills. The first "rule" of negotiating a deal is to avoid confusing price with value. *Value* is what the business is actually worth; *price* is what the buyer agrees to pay. In a business sale, the party who is the better bargainer usually comes out on top. The buyer seeks to:

- Get the business at the lowest possible price.
- Negotiate favorable payment terms, preferably over time.
- Get assurances that he or she is buying the business that he or she thinks he or she is getting.
- Avoid putting the seller in a position to open a competing business.
- Minimize the amount of cash paid up front.

The seller is looking to:

- Get the highest price possible for the business.
- Sever all responsibility for the company's liabilities.
- Avoid unreasonable contract terms that might limit his or her future opportunities.
- Maximize the cash he or she gets from the deal.
- Minimize the tax burden from the sale.
- Make sure the buyer will be able to make all future payments.

One factor that makes the process of negotiating the purchase of a business challenging is that many business founders overestimate the value of their companies because of all of the "sweat equity" they have poured into their businesses over the years. One entrepreneur recalls a negotiation he was involved in for the potential purchase of a rival's business. The company had \$4 million in sales but had incurred losses of more than \$1 million in the previous two years, owed more than \$2.5 million in unpaid bills, and had no machinery that was less than 30 years old. Much to the prospective buyer's amazement, the owner was asking \$4 million for the business![24] To deal with this reality, buyers must understand the negotiation process.

Factors Affecting the Negotiation Process

Before beginning negotiations, a buyer should take stock of some basic issues. How strong is the seller's desire to sell? Is the seller willing to finance part of the purchase price? What terms does the buyer suggest? Which ones are most important to him or her? Is it urgent that the seller close the deal quickly? What deal structure best suits your needs? What are the tax consequences for both parties? Will the seller sign a restrictive covenant? Is the seller willing to stay on with the company for a time as a consultant? What general economic conditions exist in the industry at the time of the sale? Sellers tend to have the upper hand in good economic times, and buyers will have an advantage during recessionary periods in an industry.

The Negotiation Process

On the surface, the negotiation process appears to be strictly adversarial. Although each party may be trying to accomplish objectives that are at odds with those of the opposing

"To be a successful negotiator, you'll need courage, cunning, and stamina. If that doesn't work, try rock, paper, scissors."

party, the negotiation process does not have to turn into a nasty battle of wits with overtones of "If you win, then I lose." The negotiation process will go much more smoothly and much faster if both parties work to establish a cooperative relationship based on honesty and trust from the outset. A successful deal requires both parties to examine and articulate their respective positions while trying to understand the other party's position. Recognizing that neither of them will benefit without a deal, both parties must work to achieve their objectives while making certain concessions to keep the negotiations alive.

To avoid a stalled deal, a buyer should go into the negotiation with a list of objectives ranked in order of priority. Once you have developed your list of priorities, it is useful to develop what you perceive to be the seller's list of priorities. That requires learning as much as possible about the seller. Knowing which terms are most important (and which are least important) to you and to the seller enables you to make concessions without "giving away the farm" and without getting bogged down in "nit-picking," which often leads to a stalemate. If, for instance, the seller insists on a term that the you cannot agree to, you can explain why and then offer to give up something in exchange. You also should identify the one concrete objective that sits at the top of that list, the one thing you absolutely must come away from the negotiations with. The final stage of preparing for the actual negotiation is to study your list and the one you developed based on your perceptions of the seller to determine where the two mesh and where they conflict. The key to a successful negotiation is to use this analysis to look for areas of mutual benefit and to use them as the foundation for the negotiation.

Hands on ... How to

Become a Successful Negotiator

Buying or selling a business always involves a negotiation, and so do many other business activities, whether an entrepreneur is dealing with a bank, a customer, or a vendor. "Everyone negotiates something everyday," says Roger Fisher and William Ury in their book, *Getting to Yes*. "All of us negotiate many times a day." That's why negotiating skills are among the most important skills that entrepreneurs can learn. How can you become a more successful negotiator? The following advice will help.

Negotiating the purchase of a business can test the will, patience, and stamina of any entrepreneur. What steps can entrepreneurs take to "get to yes?"

1. ***Prepare.*** Good negotiators know that the formula for a successful negotiation is 90 percent preparation and 10 percent bargaining. What you do—or don't do—before the actual negotiation ever begins is a primary determinant of how successful your negotiation will be. The key is to learn as much as possible about the party with whom you will be negotiating, the issues that are most important to him or her, and his or her likely positions on those issues. Leo Riley, president of a training and consulting firm, says, "Knowledge of their hobbies, families, dietary habits, religious beliefs, and [other traits] can be used as ice breakers or to avoid making embarrassing mistakes."

Your preparation for a negotiation also should include a statement of the outcome you desire from the negotiation. "Write down exactly what your goals are and then edit this description furiously until it is laser-focused and precise," advises John Patrick Nolan, a negotiation specialist. Then you should write down what you think your *counterpart's* goals from the negotiation are. This encourages you to look at the negotiation from a different perspective and can be a valuable and revealing exercise.

2. ***Remember the difference between a "position" and an "interest."*** The outcome a person wants from a negotiation is his or her position. What is much more important, however, is his or her interest, the reason behind the position he or she hopes to achieve. Focusing strictly on their positions usually leads two parties into a win–lose mentality in a negotiation, in which they try to pound one another into submission. When the parties involved in a negotiation focus on their *interests* rather than on their *positions*, however, they usually discover that there are several different solutions that both will consider acceptable and reasonable.

   The Parable of the Orange provides an excellent lesson on the difference between the two. Two parties each want an orange, but there is only one orange. After much intense negotiating, the two agree to cut the orange in half. As it turns out, however, one party wanted only the rind of the orange to make cookies, and the other party wanted the orange to make orange juice. If the parties involved in the negotiation had focused on their interests and taken a problem-solving approach, they each could have gotten exactly what they wanted from the negotiation!

3. ***Develop the right mindset.*** Inexperienced negotiators see a negotiation as a zero-sum, win–lose game. "If you win, then I lose." Entrepreneurs who want or need to maintain ongoing relationships with the other party (e.g., buying a business from the company founder, whom you want to convince to stay on through a transition period to help you learn the business) must see negotiations in a different light. Their goal is to work toward a mutually beneficial agreement that both parties consider to be fair and reasonable.

   Successful negotiations almost always involve compromise on both sides, which means that *neither* party gets *everything* that he or she wanted. "Sometimes the best deal you are going to get won't leave you jumping with joy," says Mike Staver, a negotiation consultant. In other words, successful negotiators see a negotiation not just as deal making but also as problem solving.

4. ***Always leave yourself an escape hatch.*** In any negotiation, you should be prepared to walk away without making a deal. Doing so, however, requires you to define what negotiation experts call a best alternative to a negotiated agreement (BATNA), which is the next-best alternative to a negotiated agreement. You cannot determine whether a negotiated agreement is suitable unless you know what your alternatives are, and one alternative (although not always the best one) is to walk away from the negotiation without an agreement—your BATNA. One writer explains, "You may never need [your BATNA], but just knowing it's in your back pocket gives you peace of mind. Without one, you can become anxious, appear desperate, and settle for a less-than-ideal solution."

   Having a BATNA increases your power in a negotiation, but you should use that power judiciously. Do not use your BATNA as a threat to coerce an agreement. In addition, don't kill the deal just because you can. Instead, use your BATNA as the baseline against which you measure your negotiated alternatives.

5. ***Keep your emotions in check.*** Negotiations can become emotionally charged, especially if those involved allow their egos to enter into the process. It is always best to abide by the Golden Rule of Negotiating: Treat others the way you want to be treated in the negotiation. Be fair but firm. If the other party forgets the Golden Rule of Negotiating, remember that you can always walk away from the negotiation and fall back on your BATNA.

6. ***Sometimes it's best to remain silent.*** A common mistake many people make in the negotiation process is talking too much. Not only does remaining silent allow you to listen to the other party, but it also encourages the other party to make the first offer. Some people are disconcerted

by prolonged periods of silence and begin talking, only to erode the strength of their negotiation base.

Sources: Adapted from Rhonda Abrams, "Know What You Need before Starting to Negotiate a Deal," *Greenville News Business*, May 29, 2005, p. 8; "Negotiating to Resolve Conflict," Fed Ex Small Business Center, January 22, 2003, www.mysmallbizcenter.com/rawdoc.asp?docID=7169&temp=6378; Scott Smith, "Negotiate from Strength," *Success*, July/August 2000, pp. 74–75; Susan St. John, "Five Steps to Better Negotiating," *E-Merging Business*, Fall–Winter 2000, pp. 212–214; Rob Walker, "Take It or Leave It: The *Only* Guide to Negotiating You Will *Ever* Need, *Inc.*, August 2003, pp. 75–82.

Chapter Summary by Learning Objectives

1. Understand (A) the advantages and (B) the disadvantages of buying an existing business.

The *advantages* of buying an existing business include the following: A successful business may continue to be successful; the business may already have the best location; employees and suppliers are already established; equipment is installed and its productive capacity known; inventory is in place and trade credit established; the owner hits the ground running; the buyer can use the expertise of the previous owner; and the business may be a bargain.

The disadvantages of buying an existing business include the following: An existing business may be for sale because it is deteriorating; the previous owner may have created ill will; employees inherited with the business may not be suitable; its location may have become unsuitable; equipment and facilities may be obsolete; change and innovation are hard to implement; inventory may be outdated; accounts receivable may be worth less than face value; and the business may be overpriced.

2. Define the steps involved in the right way to buy a business.

Buying a business can be a treacherous experience unless the buyer is well prepared. The right way to buy a business is to analyze your skills, abilities, and interests to determine the ideal business for you; prepare a list of potential candidates, including those that might be in the "hidden market"; investigate and evaluate candidate businesses and evaluate the best one; explore financing options before you actually need the money; and, finally, ensure a smooth transition.

3. Explain the process of evaluating an existing business.

Rushing into a deal can be the biggest mistake a business buyer can make. Before closing a deal, every business buyer should investigate five critical areas: (1) Why does the owner wish to sell? Look for the *real* reason. (2) Determine the physical condition of the business. Consider both the building and its location. (3) Conduct a thorough analysis of the market for your products or services. Who are the present and potential customers? Conduct an equally thorough analysis of competitors, both direct and indirect. How do they operate and why do customers prefer them? (4) Consider all of the legal aspects that might constrain the expansion and growth of the business: Did you comply with the provisions of a bulk transfer? Negotiate a restrictive covenant? Consider ongoing legal liabilities? (5) Analyze the financial condition of the business, looking at financial statements, income tax returns, and especially cash flow.

4. Describe the various techniques for determining the value of a business.

Placing a value on a business is partly an art and partly a science. There is no single "best" method for determining the value of a business. The following techniques (with several variations) are useful: the balance sheet technique (adjusted balance sheet technique); the earnings approach (excess earnings method, capitalized earnings approach, and discounted future savings approach); and the market approach.

5. Understand the seller's side of the buyout decision and how to structure the deal.

Selling a business takes time, patience, and preparation to locate a suitable buyer, strike a deal, and make the transition. Sellers must always structure the deal with tax consequences in mind. Common exit strategies include a straight business sale, a business sale with an agreement for the founder to stay on, forming a family limited partnership, selling a controlling interest in the business, restructuring the company, selling to an international buyer, using a two-step sale, and establishing an employee stock ownership plan (ESOP).

6. Understand how the negotiation process works and identify the factors that affect it.

The first rule of negotiating is to never confuse price with value. In a business sale, the party who is the better negotiator usually comes out on top. Before beginning negotiations, a buyer should identify the factors that are affecting the negotiations and then develop a negotiating strategy. The best deals are the result of a cooperative relationship between the parties based on trust.

Discussion Questions

1. What advantages can an entrepreneur who buys a business gain over one who starts a business from scratch?
2. How would you go about determining the value of the assets of a business if you were unfamiliar with them?
3. Why do so many entrepreneurs run into trouble when they buy an existing business? Outline the steps involved in the *right* way to buy a business.
4. When evaluating an existing business that is for sale, what areas should an entrepreneur consider? Briefly summarize the key elements of each area.
5. What is goodwill? How should a buyer evaluate a business's goodwill?
6. What is a restrictive covenant? Is it fair to ask the seller of a travel agency located in a small town to sign a restrictive covenant for one year covering a 20-square-mile area? Explain.
7. How much negative information can you expect the seller to give you about the business? How can a prospective buyer find out such information?
8. Why is it so difficult for buyers and sellers to agree on a price for a business?
9. Which method of valuing a business is best? Why? What advice would you offer to someone who is negotiating to buy a business about determining its value?
10. Outline the different exit strategy options available to a seller.
11. One entrepreneur who recently purchased a business advises buyers to expect some surprises in the deal no matter how well prepared they may be. He says that potential buyers must build some "wiggle room" into their plans to buy a company. What steps can a buyer take to ensure that he or she has sufficient "wiggle room"?

Business Plan Pro

Business PlanPro

This chapter has addressed acquiring an existing business. If this is your situation, determine whether the company has a business plan. If so, how recent is that plan? Is it representative of the current state of the organization? Do you have access to other historical information including the financial statements such as the profit and loss, balance sheet and cash flow statements? These documents may be a valuable resource to help you to better understand the business you may purchase.

Business Plan Exercises

On the Web

If the business has a Web site, review that site to assess the "online personality" of the business and to gather as much information as you can about the business. Does it match what you have learned about the business through the owner and other documents you have reviewed? Do a search for the business name and the owners' names on the Web. You may find that Google.com offers the most robust results. Note what you find and, again, determine if this information correlates with information from other sources.

Sample Plans

Review the executive summaries of these ongoing business plans through the Sample Plan Browser in Business Plan Pro:

- Machine Tooling
- Salvador's Sauces
- Sample Software Company
- Take Five Sports Bar
- Web Solutions, Inc.

Scan the table of contents and find the section of the plan with information on the company's past performance. What might this historical information tell you about the future potential of the venture? Which of these businesses would you expect to present the greatest profit potential based on their past performance? Which business represents the greatest risk based on these same criteria? How might this impact its purchase price?

In the Software

If the company that you are considering to buy has a business plan, enter this information into Business Plan Pro. First, select the "Existing" business plan option in the opening window. If you have access to an electronic version of company's plan you are considering purchasing, you can copy and paste text from a word processing document directly into Business Plan Pro by using the "Paste Special" option and then selecting the option "Without Formatting." This step will help to keep your formatting in order. Go to the "Company Summary" section and include the results of the due diligence process. The financial statements of the business, including the balance sheet, profit and loss, and cash flow statements for the last three years will be valuable historical data. This will set a baseline for you as you enter sales and expense scenarios into this plan. This process may help you to better assess the business's future earning potential and its current value.

Building Your Business Plan

One of advantages of using Business Plan Pro is the ease of creating different financial scenarios for your business. This can be an excellent way to explore multiple "what if" options. Once your business is in motion, updating the plan during the fiscal year and on an annual basis can be a quick and easy process. This will be an efficient way to keep your plan current and, by saving each of these files based on the date, for example, offer an excellent historical perspective of your business.

Beyond the Classroom . . .

1. Ask several new owners who purchased existing businesses the following questions:
   A. How did you determine the value of the business?
   B. How close was the price paid for the business to the value assessed prior to purchase?
   C. What percentage of the accounts receivable was collectible?
   D. How accurate were their projections concerning customers (sales volume and number of customers, especially)?
2. Visit a business broker and ask him or her how he or she brings a buyer and seller together. What does he or she do to facilitate the sale? What methods does he or she use to determine the value of a business?
3. Invite an attorney to speak to your class about the legal aspects of buying a business. How does he or she recommend a business buyer protect himself or herself legally in a business purchase?

Chapter 7
Building a Powerful Marketing Plan

- Describing the principles of building a guerrilla marketing plan and explaining the benefits of preparing one
- Explaining how small businesses can pinpoint their target markets
- Discussing the role of market research in building a guerrilla marketing plan and outlining the market research process
- Discussing how a small business can build a competitive edge in the marketplace using guerrilla marketing strategies
- Discussing the marketing opportunities the WWW offers entrepreneurs
- Discussing the 'Four Ps' of marketing and their role in building a successful marketing strategy

A multidimensional study of the key determinants of effective SME marketing activity: Part 1

Jimmy Hill
Northern Ireland Centre for Entrepreneurship, University of Ulster at Jordanstown, Newtownabbey, Northern Ireland

Keywords *Small to medium-sized enterprises, Marketing, Entrepreneurialism, Personal selling, Competences*

Abstract *This monograph is the consequence of a variety of experiences. It reflects an interest in SMEs and entrepreneurship stretching back almost 17 years from the author's days in the fresh food industry. It reflects knowledge from a series of studies and projects in which the author has been engaged since commencement of an academic career in 1990. In particular, it reflects the findings of a five-year piece of doctoral research that the author conducted with 57 firms in Ireland and the UK between 1995-1999. The study seeks to identify the key determinants of SME marketing activity. The research objectives focused on determining a framework of marketing competencies for SMEs, the extent of formal marketing processes practised, and how SME marketing decisions are made. Further research objectives emerged (these were inductive in nature) that focused on determining the extent of the sales orientation in SMEs and on gaining insights into the use and character of the contact networks of the individuals who manage such enterprises. A syncretised qualitative methodology was developed for the study. The research approach was both deductive and inductive. The analytical strategy adopted a range of tools but was predominantly characterised by data reduction through detailed coding and the development of strict frameworks for analysis. The findings identified a spectrum of marketing competencies for SMEs. It existed at three levels – foundation, transitional and operational. It was shown that the sales orientation of SMEs is what determines their marketing character. A core spectrum of SME sales competencies was identified. It showed significant overlap with the marketing competency spectrum. It was concluded that, since the sales orientation determines the marketing competencies, it also shapes the marketing character of SMEs. The sample firms engaged in significant formal marketing practice, most notably marketing planning. Marketing practice and decisions were characterised by significant usage of personal contact networks. Contact networks were also rooted in a strong sales orientation. It was clear that many marketing decisions that are ostensibly operational in character become strategic or eventually effect strategic change in the marketing practices of SMEs. A holistic model of SME marketing was developed. The model is an integrated complex of the elements of SME marketing examined. Whilst the holistic model developed is entrepreneurial in character, it depicts the SME as a much more sophisticated marketing entity than has been suggested in any previous research.*

Introduction

The small to medium-sized firm agenda

Zimmerer and Scarborough (1994) stated that this century would dawn with the greatest number of small businesses ever and, as predicted, over the past 17 years, new small to medium-sized enterprises (SMEs) have been identified by most western governments as significant components of economic strategies

International Journal of Entrepreneurial Behaviour & Research, Vol. 7 No. 5, 2001, pp. 171-204. © MCB University Press, 1355-2554 for job and wealth creation (Holmund and Kock, 1998; Kuratko and Hodgetts, 1995; Hodgetts and Kuratko, 1995; Birley and Westhead, 1989).

Since the late 1970s and, in particular, since the publication of Birch's (1979) evidence that between 1969 and 1976 66 per cent of the increase in employment in the USA was in firms with fewer than 20 employees, there has been considerable interest in the role of the SME in economic regeneration in general, and the creation of employment opportunities in particular. It has been estimated that more than half of the USA's economic growth came from industries that had not existed a decade ago (Valry, 1999). It is imperative that, to remain competitive, governments and firms need to accept the crucial need to nurture innovation and the entrepreneurial qualities of its workforces.

In the UK, where unemployment consequent upon industrial readjustment has been particularly marked, considerable government assistance has been provided to encourage new firm formation and to create what has been termed "an enterprise culture". Given all of these conditions, academic researchers have been slowly turning their attention to the small to medium-sized enterprises' (SMEs) research agenda. Nancarrow *et al.* (1999) noted that, while other industrialised countries, for example, the USA and Japan, stimulated and exploited independent inventors to a greater degree, the UK showed limitations in capitalising on the innovations from this pool of talent.

Previous research

Birley and Westhead (1989) indicate that previous research on small firms has explored the relationship between their origins and the personal characteristics of the founders (Westhead, 1988), the traits of owner-managers (Brockhaus, 1982; Kets de Vries, 1977), small business growth (Storey *et al.*, 1987), the role of the "incubator" organisation in the founding of growth-orientated firms (Cooper, 1989), managerial characteristics and the financial performance of small businesses (Filley and Aldag, 1988). In essence, what Birley and Westhead have indicated above all else is that traditionally such research has tended towards the macro-economic and policy perspectives of SME research.

Since the late 1980s, however, the tenor of research work in the area of small to medium-sized enterprises has changed. There has been for example, a growth in research at, what is now termed the marketing/entrepreneurship interface, that has spawned many research studies that examine aspects of both the marketing and entrepreneurship disciplines. These studies have also addressed how they interface in the context of the SME (Hills *et al.*, 1997; Hills and Mohan-Neill, 1994; Hills, 1987). Previous work tended to concentrate on the characteristics of the entrepreneur (Boag and Dastmalchian, 1988 and Abdner, 1988) or on the small firm itself (Bamberger, 1989; Scott and Bruce, 1987). In essence, entrepreneurial marketing defines the role of the entrepreneur as "fundamental" in marketing and organisational activities, so that flexibility in marketing was important to suitably adapt its principles and practices to the activities of SMEs. In contrast, marketing-entrepreneurship emphasises the importance of marketing and its pivotal role in helping to transform the entrepreneurial activities of SMEs into effective and competitive businesses. In practice there are cross-overs between these two emerging fields. Today the key difference is an increased understanding of the importance of carrying out quality research into every aspect of small firms' activities. Given their importance to economic prosperity and acceptance of the reality that most large firms have their beginnings in small entrepreneurial enterprises, there has been a growing demand for good quality SME research.

It is Storey (1994), however, who is most predominant amongst those who highlight the need for such research. In particular, he is concerned with researchers making theoretical as well as empirical contributions. Citing Wynarczyk *et al.* (1993), he argues that too often the large-firm model is taken as given and the small firm is assumed to be a "scaled-down" version of a large firm.

Moreover, today it is widely accepted that small businesses are not just "little big businesses". Rather it is acknowledged that small to medium-sized businesses have their own particular characteristics which affect the way they operate and which largely determine their preoccupations and concerns (Carson and Cromie, 1989). The argument is that theorists need to study the characteristics of small firms, other than size, and consider the implications of these across all of the functional areas of the business.

Leppard and McDonald (1991) stated that the omnipresence of the owner-manager has a significant impact on every aspect of the marketing activities of SMEs. This reinforced the notion that any examination of the marketing activities of small firms needs to take account, not only of the inherent characteristics of such enterprises, but also of the entrepreneurial characteristics of their owner-managers. Such studies also pointed clearly to the need for further research into understanding how small firms actually go about their marketing activities.

The management competency aspect

This enhanced understanding of SMEs, and of the way in which SME owner-managers manage such enterprises, only partly influenced the selection of the study objectives. The other source of influence came from the research and development activities of general management. In general management theory there was a marked growth in interest in the area of management competency, driven by the work of Klemp (1980), Boyatzis (1982), Pearson (1989), Boak (1991), Silver (1991), Constable and McCormick (1991), and Handy (1987).

The marketing competency aspect

Tacit in the competency literature was the notion that, in all spheres of management, marketing management, just like general management, is simply a process involving analysis, planning, implementation and control. There were few direct references to marketing management competencies and those that existed offered little of significance in the area of marketing practice (Middleton and Long, 1990).

A conceptual marketing competency spectrum

Consequently a review and synthesis of the competency literature were undertaken and this enabled the development of a spectrum of generic management competencies. This spectrum was then examined in respect of a review of the key characteristics of marketing management and a literature-based conceptual speculation of marketing management competencies was developed. This comprised vision, creativity, leadership, communication, motivation, initiative, intuition, adaptability, analytical abilities and judgement.

A conceptual small firms' marketing competency spectrum

Further refinement of this marketing management spectrum was undertaken on the basis of a further review of the literature on entrepreneurship, small firm entrepreneurship, small firm characteristics, and small firm marketing dimensions. This enabled the development of a conceptual speculation of a small firms' marketing competency spectrum. This comprised knowledge, experience, communication and judgement. As a consequence of this literature work a focus of the subsequent exploratory research was to test the small firms' marketing competency spectrum. The initial focus of the exploratory research was therefore to test the conceptual speculation outlined above and to explore and attempt to identify a spectrum of SME owner-manager or entrepreneurial marketing competencies.

The exploratory research programme was qualitative in nature and had a specific focus on key aspects of marketing management. It also sought to address the concept and importance of marketing; finding and keeping customers; assessing market opportunities; beating the competition; sourcing new product ideas; developing and utilising marketing networks; developing appropriate marketing competencies and co-ordinating and integrating the company's total marketing effort. A particular dimension of this programme focused on competency learning. The framework of competencies identified in this research phase was distilled by the researchers into a core set which corroborated the a priori literature-based speculation of knowledge, communication, experience and judgement.

With regard to the initial research focus these studies raised some important questions about the nature of competencies associated with effective marketing in SMEs and with the nature of marketing decision making in such firms. The following two key issues emerged:

(1) The studies suggested that competencies are not stand-alone entities but interactions between, and clusters of, other competency elements. In the observable performance of any particular SME marketing activity, one competency will be dominant.

(2) The research suggested that competencies are task and environment specific.

The emergence of a dominant competency at any given time is a reflection not only of individual ability but also of the nature of the particular task being undertaken, the particular organisational environment and the wider marketing environment. Furthermore, the research suggested that competencies have an interactive dimension, although this is often dependent on the nature of the particular marketing activity being undertaken. Third, and most significantly, all of the exploratory research pointed firmly to the existence of a particular type of marketing activity which can be associated with SMEs. Whether this is entrepreneurial marketing or SME marketing needs further investigation.

SME marketing or entrepreneurial marketing?

It is important to make a few comments about the nature of entrepreneurial marketing and how it might differ from SME marketing. Much of the fairly limited literature in respect of small firms' marketing points to a brand of marketing which is unique to small firms (Carson *et al.*, 1995; Mackintosh and Tynan, 1994; Carson, 1993; Carson and Cromie, 1989). Such literature suggests that existing conventional or formal marketing approaches are inappropriate for small firms, as small firms are "different". On reflection an outcome of the exploratory research phase was that what one was evidencing was marketing that was different but not necessarily marketing that was heavily influenced by the founding entrepreneur/owner-manager, as suggested in the small firms' marketing literature. In some instances this was the case but in other family succession businesses or SMEs that were part of a larger holding company the entrepreneurial influence was more muted. What was evident was a type of marketing that bore the hallmarks of its entrepreneurial antecedents but was equally characterised by other aspects. Indeed, in some circumstances the founding entrepreneur was no longer there.

More significantly, the exploratory research hinted, for example, at the use of personal contact networks, a strong selling focus, a strong awareness of some aspects of formal marketing as the key characteristics of what can be termed SME marketing. Key personnel in the SMEs examined appeared to exhibit characteristically entrepreneurial behaviour in the absence of a founding entrepreneur/owner-manager. These aspects of SME marketing are not well documented or researched and consequently formed the basis of this study.

In summary, the exploratory research suggested the existence of a core spectrum of small firm marketing competencies. Moreover, the exploratory research led to a series of competency spectra for examination and testing in the main empirical gathering phase of the research. Most importantly, it sharpened the research focus by raising a question about the scope, nature and character of entrepreneurial marketing in relation to SME marketing. The outcomes shaped the study objectives, although the inductive aspect of the research process meant that the original research objectives were expanded to address other important areas which emerged in the data-gathering phases and from the first cut analysis of the data.

Aims and objectives

The overall aims of this study, therefore, are to identify the key determinants of SME marketing, to deepen the fairly limited understanding of the way in which such enterprises actually carry out their marketing activities, to identify what factors influence and shape the character of their marketing and to evaluate the extent of the entrepreneurial character of their marketing. The specific research objectives are:

(1) Through a longitudinal, in-depth study to establish a definitive framework of marketing competencies which determine effective marketing in SMEs and to compare this with the competency framework suggested in the exploratory research.

(2) To establish the extent of the sales orientation in SMEs and to gain insight into its role in shaping SME marketing activities.

(3) To measure the extent to which formal and conventional marketing planning processes are practised by SMEs.

(4) To establish the use and nature of personal contact networks in the marketing practices of SMEs and to gain some insight into how contact networks might be used to enhance marketing decisions of both an operational and a strategic nature.

(5) To examine the ways in which SME decision makers actually go about making marketing decisions.

(6) To develop a holistic model of marketing in SMEs.

Literature review

Introduction

The literature review which develops the underlying theoretical structure for this research is broken up into two sections. The first of these sections reviews the foundation literatures of small firms' research and entrepreneurship. It is in the context of these literature areas that the nature of small firms' marketing can be fully understood. The second presents a review of the small firms' marketing literature and the other immediate literature disciplines of relevance to the research topics.

Small to medium-sized enterprises

Much of the literature which is concerned with SMEs and small firms is inextricably linked with the entrepreneurship dimensions (Geursen, 1995). In many cases the terms "small firm owner-manager" and "entrepreneur" are used interchangeably but of late there has been some effort amongst researchers to draw distinctions between the two (Fulop, 1991). It is perhaps appropriate therefore to begin with the thorny and contentious issue of actually defining the small firm.

Defining the small firm. Gore *et al.* (1992, p. 115), state that "Like the proverbial elephant the small firm is one of those things that is recognised when seen but difficult to define." Storey (1994) notes that there is no single, uniformly acceptable definition of a small firm. He offers an explanation for this, though noting that a small firm in an industry like petrochemicals, for example, is likely to have much higher levels of capitalisation, sales and possibly employment, than a small firm in the car repairs trade. What this means is that definitions ". . . that relate to 'objective' measures of size, such as number of employees, sales turnover, profitability, net worth etc., when examined at sectoral level, mean that in some sectors all firms may be regarded as small, while in other sectors there are possibly no firms which are small" (Storey, p. 9). In spite of such an understanding of the nature of small firms the definitions that do exist tend to focus on such objective measures.

The most widely accepted definition is still one based on the ideas of the Bolton Committee (1971). They identify three important characteristics that are likely to have a strong effect on management and decision making within a small firm. The Bolton Committee (1971) formulated what they called an "economic" definition and a "statistical" definition. The economic definition suggests that small firms meet the following criteria:

- they have a relatively small share of their marketplace;
- they are managed by owners or part-owners in a personalised way, and not through the medium of a formalised management structure;
- they are independent, in the sense of not forming part of a larger enterprise.

Wynarczyk *et al.* (1993) discuss key aspects that differentiate small and large firms. These are uncertainty, innovation and evolution. There is no doubt that uncertainty is a feature of the smaller enterprise that is characterised by limited resources. In summary, it is clear that there exists no one uniformly satisfactory definition of a small firm or SME. It is also clear that the definitions arrived at by the Bolton Commission are no longer particularly appropriate and have been constantly affected by regional variation.

Two other aspects worthy of consideration are the need to examine the difference between entrepreneurs and small business owners, and the nature of the SME environment.

Entrepreneurs or small business owners? According to Hodgetts and Kuratko (1995) the terms "small business owner" and "entrepreneur" are sometimes used interchangeably. While there are situations that encompass both, they note the importance of recognising differences in the titles.

In summary, entrepreneurs are deemed to have a different focus and drive from small business managers.

The SME environment. Carson *et al.* (1995) suggest that the small scale of SME operations means that such ventures have little impact on their surroundings and have limited power to modify environmental forces to their advantage. This means that, in economic terms, they merely accept their industry's price and that their output has no impact on the overall market for their goods or services. In addition, small firms are usually the weaker partner in marketing channel relationships and their wider influence in the marketplace is generally quite restricted.

The external factors need to be considered from a micro as well as a macro perspective. They are recognised as dynamic but with their impact changing over time. The critical observation about external influences is that their application to the formation of new ventures is not necessarily the same as their application to their likelihood of survival. Indeed, Storey (1994) notes that some factors which are crucial to the setting-up of a small business may not be such a significant consideration in whether or not it survives (see also Dana, 1992; 1999; d'Amboise, 1992; Ragab, 1992).

Summary. SMEs play an increasingly important role in many economies. Whilst it is important to recognise the proliferation of SMEs, it also must be recognised that they are different from large firms. Their unique characteristics do not always endow them with great influence in their markets but nonetheless it must be recognised that their size often can afford them competitive advantage. It is also clear that organisational structures in small firms are much less rigid, sophisticated and complex than in large firms. This means that the more fluid arrangements that prevail in small firms do not inhibit the creativity and flexibility which are necessary for continued success.

Entrepreneurship

The second important aspect of the foundation literature is the field of entrepreneurship. Any understanding of small to medium-sized enterprises cannot conceivably be divorced from consideration of the entrepreneurial dimensions.

Churchill and Lewis (1983) note that entrepreneurship is one of the youngest paradigms in the management sciences. They assert that, as with all young paradigms, it has emerged by using the methods and theories of other sciences such as business, economics, psychology, sociology and, to a lesser degree, politics. This youthful dimension to the paradigm also means that researchers schooled in the theories and methods of other sciences or indeed arts have endowed this discipline with its diversity of character.

The concept of entrepreneurship. Entrepreneurship is about change and the roles people play to bring it about. It is about innovation and doing new things which improve the circumstances of an enterprise. It is best understood as a process, the constituents of which are the entrepreneur, his/her persistent search for opportunities and his/her efforts to marshal the resources she/he needs to exploit them (Kao, 1991; Timmons, 1990). It can occur either in a new venture start-up or within an established enterprise (Lessem, 1986).

Furthermore, developments in the social, technological and economic circumstances in which the entrepreneurial enterprise operates have an impact upon it (Leppard and McDonald, 1991; Piercy and Morgan, 1989/1990).

The essential thesis of the above studies is that the entrepreneur is central to the entrepreneurial process. He/she is the driving force behind it. Without his/her commitment, energy and ambition it would not happen. However, given the central role he/she plays in it, it is amazing to note the lack of any agreed definition or clear understanding in the literature, of who the entrepreneur is or what he/she does (Cunningham and Lischeron, 1991). It depends, it seems, on the individual researcher's personal perspective and approach as to how the entrepreneur and entrepreneurship are ultimately interpreted and defined.

Definitions of entrepreneurship. What is accepted is that entrepreneurship is defined in many ways. It is also widely accepted that, as a consequence of the persistent search for a universally acceptable definition, our understandings of the entrepreneur are inextricably linked to an understanding of entrepreneurship. Bygrave (1989a,b), however, throws a cautionary note in to the definition debate, adding that the essence of entrepreneurship is merely a change of state. Importantly, he adds, it is a holistic process that cannot be analysed by reducing it to its individual parts. In spite of Bygrave's caveat the literature is replete with such fractured characterisations.

Kuratko and Hodgetts (1995) postulate that the contemporary entrepreneur is the aggressive catalyst for change in the world of business. He or she is an independent thinker who dares to be different against a background of common events.

Indeed, the classical Schumpeterian view that entrepreneurs are leaders of and major contributors to the process of creative destruction still finds much contemporary support. It ties in with Kirzner (1979), for example, who like the classical theorists also stresses that entrepreneurs perceive profit opportunities and initiate actions to fill currently unsatisfied needs or to do more efficiently what is already being done.

Vesper (1980) draws on this later 1965 Schumpeterian stance that posits what is now a fairly typical view of entrepreneurship – that is, someone who has an idea for a venture, implements it and then nurtures the venture for the rest of his or her life. In many ways Vesper's work is like the Janus of the entrepreneurship literature in that it looks backwards and forwards, thus becoming the essential link between the classical and contemporary positions. Stevenson and Gumpert (1985) discard the notion that entrepreneurship is an all-or-none trait that some people or organisations possess and others do not. They, on the other hand, suggest viewing entrepreneurship in the context of a range of behaviour.

Creativity is highlighted by Zimmerer and Scarborough (1994, p. 4), who define an entrepreneur as "... a person who creates a new business in the face of risk and uncertainty for the purpose of achieving profit and growth by identifying opportunities and assembling the necessary resources to capitalise on those opportunities." Whilst this might be debatable and whatever the veracity of such assertions, it is clear that today an entrepreneur is seen as an innovator or developer who recognises and seizes opportunities and converts those opportunities into workable or marketable ideas. Entrepreneurs add value through time, effort, money or skills and assume the risks of the competitive marketplace to implement these ideas. Entrepreneurs realise reward from such creative effort (Cunningham and Lischeron, 1991; Stevenson and Gumpert, 1985; Leibenstein, 1968).

The entrepreneurial process. In their classic article, "Theorizing about entrepreneurship", Bygrave and Hofer (1991, p. 13) make a strong statement about the problems caused by researchers' inability to agree on a definition of entrepreneurship. They state that "Good science has to begin with good definitions". The point they make is simply how can researchers know what they are studying, if they cannot define that which they are observing? They, in arriving at two working definitions of entrepreneurship, shift their focus from "the characteristics and functions of the entrepreneur" and the myriad definitions of what constitutes an entrepreneur and focus instead on the nature and characteristics of the "entrepreneurial process". They then suggest that the entrepreneurial processes involve all the functions, activities and actions associated with perceiving opportunities and the creation of organisations to pursue them. They go as far as to define the entrepreneur as someone who perceives an opportunity and creates an organisation to pursue it.

Amit *et al.* (1993) also recognise the wide range of fields that constitute the entrepreneurial process. These include, they suggest, decision sciences, economics, management, sociology and psychology. In addition, they state, like others, that there is no consensus among researchers as to the exact meaning of entrepreneurship and the role of entrepreneurs. Recognising the need for working definitions of both the entrepreneur and entrepreneurship, however, they suggest that entrepreneurs can be categorised into those who are profit-seeking, either working individually or in a corporate setting, and those who are not profit-seeking, working in charitable, government and other not-for-profit organisations. They do, however, add that with respect to business it is worth making the distinction that the entrepreneurial process is one of endowing resources with new wealth-creating capacity. Indeed, Drucker (1985) stresses that such an endowment is central to any conceptualisation of entrepreneurship and the entrepreneurial process itself.

What this means is that entrepreneurship can be defined as the "process" of extracting profits from new, unique and valuable combinations of resources in an uncertain environment. Amit *et al.* (1993, p. 817) add weight to such assertions, stating that "Entrepreneurs are individuals who innovate, identify and create business opportunities, assemble and co-ordinate new combinations of resources (i.e. production functions), so as to extract the most profits from their innovations in an uncertain environment."

Amit *et al.* (1993) are particularly critical of general equilibrium frameworks as a means of understanding entrepreneurship. Such frameworks, they suggest, assume that all potential entrepreneurs are equally able and suggest that, at equilibrium, the less risk-averse individuals become entrepreneurs. This leads us to a brief consideration of entrepreneurial characteristics.

Entrepreneurial characteristics. The entrepreneurial characteristics and the social construction of the personality are also widely discussed in the literature. These aspects are relevant here, because, as Birley and Westhead (1991) suggest, the formation and growth of new business are a complex process and many factors associated with this process can only be identified by in-depth investigation at the micro level of the new business and the new business founders. The entrepreneurial characteristics of greatest relevance to this research are risk (Hisrich, 1988; Casson, 1982; Swayne and Tucker, 1973), motivation (Herron *et al.*, 1992; LaFuente and Salas, 1989), need for achievement (Johnson, 1990; Begley and Boyd, 1987; McClelland, 1961), an internal *locus* of control (Amit *et al.*, 1993; Cunningham and Lischeron, 1991; and Sexton and Bowman, 1985), tolerance of ambiguity (Low and MacMillan, 1988), and leadership (Johnstone and Kirby, 1992; Peters, 1987).

In summary, it is clear that the concept of entrepreneurship is still an emergent discipline. It is as dynamic as the entrepreneur him/herself. Whilst debate will ensue in respect of acceptable definitions and the scope of the entrepreneurial process, what is of relevance here is ways in which the companies in this research exhibited entrepreneurial characteristics and, consequently, the way in which these characteristics impacted on the activities and managerial style of the SMEs in the study. The companies in this research all have strong entrepreneurial antecedents. Several of the companies are still under the control of the founding entrepreneur. To understand how this might impact on the data it is important to be aware of the major themes in the entrepreneurship literature. Furthermore, there is no meaningful research examining this aspect of entrepreneurship and how it affects the marketing activities of the SME. This study will address this literature gap.

It is now crucial to look briefly at those literature areas relevant to the prespecified and emergent research topics and objectives. The first of these is small firms' marketing.

Small firms' marketing

In a debate on small firms' marketing activities, Rhys (1989) suggests that the small firm pursues its marketing function in a way which aims at insulating it as much as possible from direct competition with more efficient producers. He points out that, as a consequence, small firms are left with strategic options such as exploiting niches left by larger firms (see also Stasch and Ward, 1989).

Though the basic tenets and principles of marketing are universally and equally applicable to both large and small businesses, academic research into such firms has been addressed only relatively recently (Davis *et al.*, 1985). Cannon (1991) makes the point that research into small businesses has been a little thin on the ground. Davis and Klassen (1991) note that there is currently insufficient knowledge about marketing in small businesses. Hills (1987) has been more precise in his criticism, insinuating that there is an absence of an appropriate small business marketing theory, specifically related to the understanding and knowledge of strategic marketing. Dodge *et al.* (1994) and Caird (1992) found that the most prevalent problems were a lack of knowledge about the marketplace and marketing planning.

Matthews and Scott (1995) note that minimal empirical attention has been given to the antecedents of strategic or operational planning in small firms. Consequently, the question of why some small firms plan and others do not becomes especially relevant. They state that it is the resource constraints of both small and growth-oriented entrepreneurial firms which will prevent them from maintaining planning activity in the face of increasing uncertainty (see also Patterson, 1986). Scase and Goffee (1982) take the view that generally life in the small firm is based on day-to-day survival rather than following a well thought-out marketing plan (see also Bronislaw and Waart, 1988). This means that, when conditions of uncertainty prevail, small firms will focus on doing, instead of engaging in formal strategic planning. In such circumstances actions tend to be based on intuition (Bhide, 1994).

The evolution of marketing and staged models of marketing growth. Another key area of the small firms' marketing literature is that which charts the growth of SMEs and examines their life cycles. Greiner (1972) and subsequently Adizes (1989) were at the forefront of such studies. They both adopted general growth models to study the business activities of firms. These examined the various stages of development and growth through which the entrepreneurial firm goes and, in addition, they provide insight into what sort of obstacles to growth and development such firms typically encounter. Others, such as Churchill and Lewis (1983) and Scott and Bruce (1987), have also developed growth models but these have concentrated on a depiction of the business activities of small firms. Such models concentrate on the types of problems encountered and the subsequent business activities and marketing behaviour of the small business or owner-manager to overcome the difficulties.

The competency debate

The next major literature influence to consider that is of relevance here is the area of managerial competence. Competence became the buzz-word of the 1980s in the jargon-ridden sphere of management development (Rothwell, 1986). Much of the early research on the competence issue alludes to its roots in classical management theory, whilst much of the current research to a large extent still centres on the issue of competence definition. Other studies, however, have sought to develop and define competency frameworks that govern more effective management practice. What competencies are needed, for example, to be effective at planning or for conducting any key management function? How much of a competency is capable of being taught and learned and how much is innate in the individual concerned? This section will examine the key themes that emerge from the competency literature that are of relevance to marketing and entrepreneurial marketing competency.

Competency definition. It is important to address the definition theme. Collin (1989, p. 20) states that "Given the central role of the concept of competence in the present debate on management performance, it is surprising that little attention seems to have been paid so far to its definition." She notes, for instance, that there is even an unexplained variation in the terms used by contemporary writers in the field, with competency used by Boyatzis (1982), Klemp (1980), Mangham and Silver (1986), Prideaux and Ford (1988), adding that Kolb *et al.* (1986) and Raven (1986) refer to both competency and competence, with Constable (1988) using competence/competences.

One broadly accepted definition of competence, however, is that it is an underlying characteristic of a person which results in effective and/or superior performance in a job (Klemp, 1980) or, as advocated by Boyatzis (1982), an effective mix of motives, traits, skills, aspects of one's self-image or social role, or body of knowledge used by an individual (see also Burgoyne, 1989).

Competency frameworks. The second key theme to emerge from the literature is the issue of competency frameworks. Successive studies of managerial competency have resulted in the generation of competency frameworks (Boak, 1991; Townroe and Mallalieu, 1991; Kotter, 1990; Pearson, 1989; Jacobs, 1989; Albanese, 1989; Boyatzis, 1982) comprising what the specific researchers see as the key competencies required for effective management.

Much of the framework literature and research tends, however, to take the form of syntheses and reviews of prior framework research. Take, for example, Dulewicz (1989) who reviews the work of Glaze (1989), Jacobs (1989), Greatrex and Phillips (1989), Jackson (1989) and Cockerill (1989) and develops a framework clustered into competencies associated with middle managers into intellectual, interpersonal, adaptability and results orientation. Thomas (1991), however, focuses his competency research on what he defines as the key management skills. Whilst these both take a strategic and operational viewpoint, others such as Katz (1955) had taken a singular focus to the development of a competency domain model, in his case focusing on the skills of an effective administrator.

More specifically here, it is vital to consider the role of marketing competency and what the literature offers on this important topic.

Marketing competency. There is little in the literature relating to which competencies are most appropriate for marketing (Carson, 1993). Marketing is on the offensive and future-focused in character and very much about initiating as much as reacting to continuous change opportunities. The literature offers some consideration as to which competencies are appropriate for marketing (although what is offered considers competencies from a management or decision-making perspective). Middleton and Long (1990, p. 325), for example, in their literature review offer nothing of significance in the area of marketing skills, stating "... it became clear that there was a dearth of well articulated and considered thought on the issues of marketing skills." Recurrent marketing management competencies, arising from an analysis of their research, are: with respect to marketing attributes, communication, creativity, imagination and initiative; with respect to management attributes, analytical, organisational and planning skills; with respect to personality attributes, motivation, resilience and entrepreneurship.

Hardy (1992) develops an interesting dimension to the competency debate, when he suggests that every manager is a member of the marketing team and needs marketing skills, knowledge and orientation. Hardy also makes the link between competency models, which he describes as descriptions of required abilities in individual managers or groups of managers. He adds that a set of required competencies can be derived from a description of the challenges that are expected to confront these managers in the future. He outlines typical marketing challenges that face organisations and develops a core set of marketing competencies, which he divides into general skills, sub-skills, knowledge, orientation (including values and standards) and fostering vision, creativity and pathfinding. General skills are described as identification and solution of marketing problems, use of problem-solving frameworks, for example, marketing environment analysis, and evaluation of options. Sub-skills include identification of market opportunity, creatively viewing and analysing markets, assessing competitors and markets, predicting market channel behaviour, managing market information, forecasting, financial analysis and organisational analysis.

Indeed, Middleton and Long (1990) address the marketing skills issue from the perspective of marketing education and training. They conclude that the attributes which have been identified elsewhere in reference to management skills are broadly the same as those which they have identified as desirable marketing skills in their research context. Their extensive review of the literature draws on the work of Thomas (1991), Cowell (1987), Kotler (1988), Gallagher (1985). They summarise this work and present a table of a classification of attributes broken down under the three headings of skills, attitudes, and a motley array of others which they classify as difficult to operationalise.

It could be argued, however, that such competency spectra are too descriptive and cumbersome for use in describing entrepreneurial or SME marketing management competencies. The thesis here is that there exists in the SME a generic set of marketing competencies which are influenced by the owner-manager, founding entrepreneur. Such competencies tend to be entrepreneurial in character.

Entrepreneurial competency. Martin and Staines (1994) note that, aside from the other well documented shortcomings and restrictions under which small firms operate, managerial experience, skills and personal qualities are often cited in the business press as the main reasons why firms in the small firm sector fail. Ray (1993) makes the important assertion that, in order to understand why some individuals become entrepreneurs and some entrepreneurs are relatively more successful than others, three key elements must be addressed. These are the entrepreneur's personality or attributes, the entrepreneur's background and experience, and the entrepreneur's skills, including how they learn.

Significantly, he notes that it is perhaps not so easy to identify entrepreneurial skills. The key conclusion from Ray's study is, however, that the entrepreneurial personality is important in shaping a venture, yet there is no ideal type of personality or marginal set of attributes that guarantees success for a new venture.

The entrepreneurial orientation, distinctive marketing competencies and organisational performance are discussed by Smart and Conant (1994). They conclude that an entrepreneurial orientation is positively and significantly related to distinctive marketing competencies and organisational performance. In particular, the study makes a link with the work of Hills and LaForge (1992), where they suggest that the entrepreneurial orientation has six dimensions. These are:

(1) the propensity to take risks;

(2) a tendency to engage in strategic planning activities;

(3) an ability to identify customer needs and wants;

(4) a level of innovation;

(5) the ability to persevere in making your vision of the business a reality; and

(6) the ability to identify new opportunities.

Cunningham and Licheron (1991) identified six schools of thought on entrepreneurship as a framework for understanding the growing literature in this area. This reflects two aspects of a competency: skills and traits. Moreover, Lessem (1986) in his research amongst practising entrepreneurs identified the following competencies: imaginative (developing vision), intuitive (market recognition and harnessing its potential), authoritative (providing structure, organisation), wilful (acquiring resources), flexible (planning for change for the future), social (animating people, motivation, communication) and physical (action-orientated, energy, physical activity). This lends itself to an understanding of the influence of entrepreneurial characteristics in shaping entrepreneurial marketing management competencies.

Bygrave (1989a,b) highlights innovation, risk taking, experience, creativity, commitment, resource management, leadership, vision, team building and implementation as crucial entrepreneurial competencies. Gartner (1989) supports the presence of many of these competencies in his conceptual framework for describing the phenomenon of new venture creation. In particular, he notes risk taking, experience and control. Kuratko and Hodgetts (1995) also consider the research literature in this area and derive a list of desirable skills and competencies encompassing commitment, opportunity seeking, ability to solve problems, control, risk taking, creativity, innovativeness, self-confidence and team-building ability, communication, networking and delegation.

One indisputable conclusion from the literature is that there is strong evidence to support the existence of frameworks of competencies that appear to be more appropriate in the entrepreneurial firm/SME context. Foremost amongst these are the competencies of experience, knowledge, communication, judgement and intuition (see Table I).

Summary. Both a major and A significant conclusion resulting from the literature is that many of the core generic managerial competencies are equally if not more applicable in the context of marketing. This is a fluid situation, however, and, as acknowledged by Boyatzis (1982), the interchangeability and emphasis on particular skills will vary and depend on the specific situation in which a particular task is being performed.

Another key conclusion from the competency literature is that whilst analysing questions of managerial competence and successful performance can be frustratingly elusive (Silver, 1991), a great deal seems to be known about managerial competence. This knowledge in the logic of Polanyi (1967) is tacit and defies intimacy of definition. This has meant that, in attempting to accurately define and describe management competency, researchers, theorists, management educators and trainers have developed incremental, stepwise analyses of the concept. In summary, over-analysis has impaired our understanding of competency.

Sales and personal selling

The key emergent focus of this research was sales and personal selling. It is critical, therefore, to review the relevant aspects of this mushrooming literature.

Sales competency frameworks. Williams and Seminerio (1985) generated an extensive list of salesperson attributes comprising: thoroughness and follow-through; knowledge of the product line; willingness to go into bat for the buyer within the supplier's firm; market knowledge and willingness to keep the buyer posted; imagination in applying his products to the buyer's needs; knowledge of the buyer's product lines; diplomacy in dealing with operating departments; preparation for well planned sales calls; regularity of sales calls and technical

Table I. Entrepreneurial competencies

Experience	Maclaren *et al.* (1997); Carson *et al.* (1994, 1995); Schon (1983); Luckmann (1982)
Knowledge	Pye (1991); Polanyi (1967)
Communication	Hill and McGowan (1996); Carson *et al.* (1995); Hill and Fallis (1995); Mole *et al.* (1993); Penley *et al.* (1991); Schuler (1979); Mintzberg (1973)
Judgement and intuition	Brownlie and Spender (1995); Allinson and Hayes (1996); Lank and Lank (1995); Hall (1994); Johnson (1993); Pye (1991); Benderly (1989); Harper (1988); Hogarth (1987); Agor (1984); Levinson and Rosenthal (1984); Mintzberg (1979); Ornstein (1972)

education. Phillips (1988) also stresses such abilities as effective communication, relationship building, influencing and the ability to conduct a natural sales conversation. Flynn (1992) and Weilbaker (1990) offer a range of skills that are viewed as being important to effective personal selling. These include product knowledge, professionalism, selling skills, appearance, courtesy, manners, honesty, reliability and clarity.

Considering the main framework literature enables the development of Table II, summarising the key personal selling competencies.

Personal selling and the small firm. A final literature theme of particular significance in this study is that of personal selling in the small firm. Dart and Pendleton (1984) suggest that most textbooks, educational establishments and researchers direct their thinking towards the promotional activities of large organisations and write that these are not easily adapted to suit small firms. Indeed, there is something of a dearth of published research into entrepreneurial small firms' use of promotion in general and in respect of personal selling in particular, yet Borden (1964), Jackson and Parasuraman (1986) and Nilson (1994) all feel that small firms mainly use personal selling to communicate with their target audience.

Hodgetts and Kuratko (1995) also write that the art and science of selling are important to the survival of every small business. They note that the owner-manager cannot do all of the selling and must have help. Carson *et al.* (1995) suggest that, as a small firm grows, its ability to cope with change is determined by new sales. These new sales may come from existing markets and customers and/or from new markets. The key issue is Carson *et al.*'s (1995)

Creativity and leadership	Glisan and Hawes (1990); Futrell (1989); Ingram and LaForge (1989); Slesinski (1989)
Leadership	Jolson *et al.* (1993)
Trust	Ali and Birley (1999) Macintosh *et al.* (1992); Szymanski (1987); Moine (1982)
Persuasion	Dion *et al.* (1995); Callahan (1992); Milliman and Fugate (1988); Hawes *et al.* (1989); Swan and Nolan (1985); Jolson (1984); Dwyer *et al.* (1987); Shapiro (1987); Michaels and Day (1985); Funkhouser (1984)
Knowledge	Leong *et al.* (1989); Szymanski (1987); Leigh (1987); Weitz *et al.* (1986)
Motivation	Simintiras and Cadogan (1994); Chowdhury (1993); Hart *et al.* (1989); Ryans and Weinberg (1981); Churchill *et al.* (1985); Mitchell (1978)
Interpersonal communication	Lawson and Ward (quoted in Younger, 1992); Webster (1968)
Relational communication	Soldow and Thomas (1984); Weitz (1981)

Table II. Personal selling competencies

contention that, in order to generate these new sales, the SME must employ some form of marketing activity, most probably a combination of products, price, promotion and distribution. The implication here is that, whilst there is an emphasis on personal selling in the SME, to sell effectively the small firm owner/manager/decision maker must draw on other marketing variables.

Personal contact networks

The data-gathering phases in tandem with a degree of "ongoing analysis" suggested that personal contact networks and the way in which these were used were an important aspect of the way in which SMEs do business. It is necessary therefore to examine the key themes in the contact network literature of relevance to this study. Moreover, the relevance of personal contact networks to this research in a more general sense is that it also represents one of the emergent research tracks from the work at the marketing/entrepreneurship interface.

Indeed, it was Szarka (1990, p. 10) who stated, by way of drawing management researchers' attention to the issue of personal contact networking, that "The rapid development and the widespread nature of the networking phenomenon have been attracting considerable attention in the management literature". If this statement is considered in a temporal sense, then the veracity of this assertion is without question. One only needs to consider the work of Aldrich and Whetten (1981) on organisations and networks; Birley (1985) in her examination of networks in the entrepreneurial process; Jarillo (1988) and Levenson (1986), who explore the area of strategic networks and strategic collaboration; and Thorelli (1986), who investigates the relationship between markets and hierarchies. Since Szarka's observation the number of studies has increased with Cromie and Birley (1994), examining the role of community brokers in the information and development of business ventures; Coviello and Munro (1995) and Hansen (1995), who suggest a direct link between networking and the growth of the organisation; Joyce *et al.* (1995), who note that networks are primarily used for information trading; and, finally, Carson *et al.* (1995), who explore the use of personal contact networks in the development of what they describe as an entrepreneurial marketing style in SMEs.

Given the stated importance and role of personal contact networks in a generic sense and the idea that they play an important role in SMEs in particular, it is apposite to define precisely what is meant by a personal network.

Defining a personal contact network. In terms of providing a backdrop to the issues of network definition Yanagida (1992, p. 364) states:

> Networks have the breadth and depth to accommodate all things, and the more we come to know them, the more strange and wondrous they seem.

This in many respects encapsulates the myriad aspects of network definition. Indeed, defining a network is a predominant theme of the network literature. In this research Hill and McGowan (1996) define a personal contact network as the relationships or alliances which individuals develop or, indeed, may seek to develop between themselves and others in their society (see also Dubini and Aldrich, 1991; Aldrich and Zimmer, 1986; Johannisson, 1986).

Entrepreneurial contact networks. The research in the area of contact networks, in particular that which has emerged from the marketing/entrepreneurship interface, has to a large extent focused on what is termed the entrepreneurial network. The network, it is suggested, characterises the SME. In particular, Hill and McGowan (1996), Shaw (1999) and Brito (1999) provide examples of typical entrepreneurial networks. It is worth considering this briefly, as it serves to demonstrate other relevant aspects of the network literature. In a typical entrepreneurial network they indicate that the focal entrepreneur is at the centre, with "direct" ties to individuals such as those identified by Cromie and Birley (1994). Importantly, they note that the entrepreneur has the potential to exercise an "indirect" tie with individuals outside the existing network, through careful use of the direct ties (Dubini and Aldrich, 1991; Granovetter, 1982). Cromie and Birley (1994, p. 68) also add that basically networking is "knowing who is likely to have up to date information, the people with the most ingenuity, the financiers who might support a new idea, finding out how customers might react to a new service or product and convincing others that the new idea has business potential, and being able to access these in a transparent way. A characteristic of entrepreneurial networks is the way in which they are lodged in the entrepreneur him- or herself. In essence, the argument predominantly advocated in the literature is that what characterises entrepreneurial personal contact networks is the entrepreneur's use of their personal resource of "whom they know". The literature also asserts that, for the entrepreneur, the personal contact network is a natural phenomenon, not a planned process (Dubini and Aldrich, 1991).

Without doubt the literature presents us with many aspects of the personal contact phenomena. These are best summarised in Table III.

Summary. The personal contact network issue is undoubtedly a major part of how entrepreneurial firms do business. There appears to be a strong relationship between the presence of strong personal contact networks and the level or existence of entrepreneurial effort. The use of contact networks as a peculiarly entrepreneurial resource seems to be becoming a more widely accepted wisdom with a particular emphasis on enhancing decision-making quality. This research will seek to expand knowledge in this vital area and to

Table III. The key dimensions of entrepreneurial personal contact networks

Networks and the entrepreneurial decision-making process	Barkham *et al.* (1996); Hill and McGowan (1996); Ostgaard and Birley (1994); Carson (1993); Butler and Hansen (1981)
Networks as an entrepreneurial resource in the SME	Johannisson (1995a,b); Curran *et al.* (1993); Cromie and Birley (1994); Dubini and Aldrich (1991); Aldrich and Zimmer (1986)

assess in particular the inter-relationships between proactive network use and personal selling.

The methodology for the study

This research was conducted under the auspices of the qualitative paradigm. Therefore, a range of qualitative research methods was adopted. This research approach was appropriate for a number of reasons. These are detailed below:

- This research approach recognizes the diversity of disciplines and concomitant characteristics that comprise the marketing-entrepreneurship interface in the context of the entrepreneurial small firm.
- Experience from the literature, research and practice suggests that existing approaches for researching in the entrepreneurial small firms are inappropriate.
- To research in entrepreneurial small firms and the key entrepreneurial personnel in such firms suggests an epistemological approach, which dictates a minimisation of the distance between the researcher and the entrepreneur.

Most prior research into small firms has its roots in positivist thinking. Without seeking to devalue such prior research, it is suggested here that such approaches may not yield a rich understanding of the key issues affecting small firms' marketing. Positivism, as followed in the traditional scientific route to developing knowledge, is manifested in the processes of proving or disproving hypotheses with quantitative measurement of variables. A more appropriate methodology was required for the research reported in this paper in order to understand and explain the meanings and complexities resulting from the in-depth interviews with the sampled firms. The focus for the research in this paper had leanings towards, but was not rooted in, the phenomenological tradition, because the observer, that is the interviewer, "was not part of that being observed".

There is a need, therefore, for an approach to research in the entrepreneurially owner-managed small firm that reflects its individual and unique characteristics and circumstances and the personalities active within it (Bygrave, 1989a,b; Chell *et al.*, 1991; Hofer and Bygrave, 1992). There is an ethnographic orientation to such research, so as to fully comprehend the issues affecting firms and personalities within firms peculiar to the individual SME.

Consequently, the qualitative approach applied here is based on several important assumptions. The first of these is the ontological positioning. The position here is that the only reality is that which is actually constructed by individuals involved in any research situation, that is those of the researcher(s), those individuals being investigated and the reader or audience interpreting a study. Thus multiple realities exist in any given situation. As Healey and Perry (2000) put it, "ontology is the reality that researchers investigate, epistemology is the relationship between that reality and the researcher". The epistemological issue for the research simply describes the nature of the relationship between the researcher and the subjects of the research. Given our understanding of the small firm and the impact of small firm and entrepreneurial characteristics on the marketing management and marketing development in such firms, the epistemological stance meant "researcher immersion in the small firms in the sample."

Therefore, taking consideration of all of the small firm management, marketing and entrepreneurial characteristics, and the impact of these on the selection of a research methodology, a syncretised approach was developed. Such an approach is particularly appropriate to qualitative enquiry, being an in-depth study of a specific situation or phenomenon.

Given the influences of inductivism and the qualitative paradigm on this research, the selection of methods and approaches offers several traditions. These range from case studies (Yin, 1994; Stake, 1994; Gummesson, 1991), action research (Gummesson, 1991; Argyris, 1973), grounded theory (Strauss and Corbin, 1990; Glaser and Strauss, 1967). Indeed, Tesch (1990; 1994), for example, offers as many as 20 types of qualitative methods and Creswell (1994) offers ethnography, grounded theory, case study and phenomenological studies. Patton (1990) and Bogdan and Taylor (1975) also present various methods for consideration. In summary, the array of methods available within the qualitative paradigm is extensive. What they all agree, however, is that qualitative research requires more than one data-gathering instrument and works best when borrowing from various methods to accommodate the situations which arise in the research context.

Given the particular a priori research focuses of this research, a methodological approach is required which also allows scope for the development of a fuller understanding of the pertinent phenomena. A review of extant research approaches, therefore, further vindicates the selection of a qualitative methodology. Furthermore, as outlined above, a review of existing qualitative methodologies indicated that, whilst many of them were useful for small firms' research, no single one seemed wholly appropriate.

It is argued that what is needed is a methodology which uses no one qualitative data gathering instrument, but instead borrows from several qualitative methods. This does not imply incommensurability of research paradigms but simply means that a syncretised methodology within a constructivist ontology is proposed.

The methodological approach focused on four main data-gathering instruments. These were:

(1) non-participant observation (mostly in the early stages);

(2) participant observation (after a period of immersion in the research settings and a clear acceptance by actors in the settings);

(3) in-depth discussions (with prespecified and emergent informants); and

(4) archival methods (although these were limited, and of questionable value).

Other methodological aids were employed. These included keeping a field log journal and an ethnographic diary. Given the research paradigm adopted, the researcher role was also significant.

The sample

Fifty-seven companies were eventually included in this sample. The companies and the informants were all located within the agrifood sector in Ireland and the UK. At the outset of this research process 12 companies were identified as prespecified discussants. The other companies and informants emerged throughout the research process, as new dimensions to the research developed and as ongoing analysis generated new aspects for examination. Since I had personal experience in this sector, it meant that access to key players was made easier. It also meant that I was familiar with the language, practices and customs of the various parts of the industry. This meant that I could get more quickly to meaningful data. It also brought with it certain biases but there is no doubt that a knowledge of the industry is paramount to effective insights.

Instrumentation

It was decided that the research, in keeping with the qualitative paradigm, should be allowed to evolve in an inductive manner. A decision was therefore made to minimise prior instrumentation. The key reasons for this are as follows. Predesigned and structured instruments blind the researcher to the research setting. What, for example, if the a priori instrumentation has omitted to examine the most important phenomena in the field? Prespecified instrumentation means that they will most likely be overlooked or at best misrepresented. Prior instrumentation is usually context-stripped. It is designed with regard to universality of application. This disregards the important fact that qualitative research lives and breathes through context. The simple axiom that the particularities produce the generalities and not the reverse must not be forgotten. This means that all that is needed at the start is some orienting questions, some headings for observations and a tentative document analysis pro forma. Below is an outline of the guiding topics for orienting questions:

- selling and the sales function;
- marketing mix variables;
- sourcing and buying;
- personal strengths and weaknesses;
- understanding markets;
- competition;
- service and quality;
- family business aspects;

- marketing planning;
- understanding customers;
- gathering and using information;
- understanding the firm's environment;
- problems encountered in developing their businesses; and
- how they dealt with/overcame obstacles to growth and development.

These topic areas constituted a tentative framework only. In line with the inductive nature of the research approach, the topics were addressed in all sorts of order. New topics emerged as the research progressed.

Data analysis

The data-gathering phases generated substantial amounts of usable and actionable data. Where possible discussions were audio-recorded and in all cases copious notes were made. In the observation phase "ethnographer's bladder" was a marked complaint! All of the discussions were transcribed and coded for purposes of analysis using a framework based on key topic areas (Miles and Huberman, 1994). Codes were constantly refined in tandem with ongoing analysis. These data were analysed using the discussion topics as frameworks for analysis. Observation notes were coded and analysed in the same manner. A degree of description and analysis of sequences of events across and within cases was employed to ensure rigour in theory development from the various respondents and respondent companies (Eisenhardt, 1990). As suggsted by Yin (1994), pattern-matching logic was also used to compare empirically based with predicted patterns in some instances. This enabled the generation of further research propositions that were in turn tested against the empirical findings. It is worth noting also that some of these constructs, from which the propositions were derived, were based on existing and accepted literatures.

Conclusion

This part of the monograph sought to set the scene, so to speak, and to bring together the wide-ranging but key literature areas of relevance to the study. The findings will be discussed within the context of these literatures. This section also sought to stress the perceived value of adopting the qualitative paradigm in small business and entrepreneurship research. The value of this approach is rooted in trying to see the world from the entrepreneurial perspective.

The second part of this monograph reports on the findings. It details the a priori and emergent issues. In particular, it enables some cogent commentary on the conventional wisdoms surrounding our understanding of small firms' marketing. It throws up sales as the preeminent aspect of the entrepreneurial small firm scenario and allows for the development of a comprehensive model of marketing in such firms.

References and further reading

Abdner, J. (1988), "The spirit of entrepreneurship", *Journal of Small Business Management*, January, Vol. 20 No. 1, pp. 1-5.

Adizes, I. (1989), *Corporate Life Cycles: How and Why Corporations Grow and Die and What to Do About it*, Prentice-Hall, Englewood Cliffs, NJ.

Agor, W.H. (1984), *Intuitive Management: Integrating Right and Left Brain Management Skills*, Prentice-Hall, Englewood Cliffs, NJ.

Albanese, R. (1989), "Competency-based management education", *Journal of Management Development*, Vol. 8 No. 2, pp. 66-70.

Aldrich, H. and Whetten, D.A. (1981), "Organisation sets, action sets and networks", in Nystrom, P.C. and Starbuck, W.H. (Eds), *Handbook of Organisational Design, Vol. 1*, OUP, London, pp. 385-408.

Aldrich, H. and Zimmer, C. (1986), "Entrepreneurship through social networks", in Sexton, D. and Sinclair (Eds), *The Art and Science of Entrepreneurship*, Ballinger, New York, NY, pp. 3-25.

Ali, H. and Birley, S. (1999), "Integrating deductive and inductive approaches in a study of new ventures and customer perceived risk", *Qualitative Market Research: An International Journal*, Vol. 2 No. 2, pp. 103-10.

Allinson, C. and Hayes, J. (1996), "The cognitive style index: a measure of intuition-analysis for organisational research", *Journal of Management Studies*, Vol. 33 No. 1, pp. 119-35.

Amit, R., Glosten, L. and Muller, E. (1993), "Challenges to theory development in entrepreneurship research", *Journal of Management Studies*, Vol. 30 No. 5, September, pp. 816-33.

Argyris, C. (1973), *Intervention Theory and Method*, Addison-Wesley, Reading, MA.

Bamberger, I. (1989), "Developing competitive advantage in small and medium-sized firms", *Long Range Planning*, Vol. 22 No. 5, pp. 80-9.

Barkham, R., Gudgin, Hart, M. and Hanvey, E. (1996), *The Determinants of Small Firm Growth: An Inter-regional Study in the United Kingdom 1986-1990*, Regional Studies Association, JKP, Athenaeum Press, Gateshead.

Begley, T.M. and Boyd, D.P. (1987), "Psychological characteristics associated with performance in entrepreneurial firms and smaller businesses", *Journal of Business Venturing*, Winter, pp. 79-93.

Benderly B.L. (1989), ". . .the abrupt, electrical flash of intuition", *Psychology Today*, September, pp. 36-40.

Bhide, A. (1994), "How entrepreneurs craft strategies that work", *Harvard Business Review*, March-April, pp. 150-61.

Birch, D. (1979), *The Job Generation Process*, MIT Program on Neighborhood and Regional Change, Cambridge, MA.

Birley, S. (1985), "The role of networks in the entrepreneurial process", *Journal of Business Venturing*, Vol. 1, pp. 107-17.

Birley, S. and Westhead., P. (1989), "Growth and performance contrasts between types of small firms", paper presented at the EIASM 3rd Workshop on Entrepreneurship Research.

Birley, S. and Westhead, P. (1991), "The effect of assisted area status on the profile of new firms", paper read at RENT V Conference, Vaxjo University, Vaxjo, November.

Boag, D. and Dastmalchian, D. (1988), "Market vulnerability and the design and management of the marketing function in small firms", *Journal of Small Business Management*, October, Vol. 20 No. 4, pp. 37-44.

Boak, G. (1991), *Developing Managerial Competencies – The Management Learning Contract Approach*, Pitman Publishing, London.

Bogdan, R. and Taylor, S.J. (1975), *Introduction to Qualitative Methods*, John Wiley, New York, NY.

Bolton Committee (1971), *Report of the Committee of Enquiry on Small Firms*, Cmnd 4811, HMSO, London.

Borden, N.H. (1964), "The concept of the marketing mix", *Journal of Advertising Research*, June, pp. 2-7.

Boyatzis, R.E. (1982), *The Competent Manager: A Model for Effective Performance*, John Wiley, New York, NY.

Brito, C. (1999), "Issue-based nets: a methodological approach to the sampling issue in industrial networks research", *Qualitative Market Research: An International Journal*, Vol. 2 No. 2, pp. 92-102.

Brockhaus, R. (1982), "The psychology of the entrepreneur", in Kent, C.A., Sexton, D.L. and Vesper, K.H. (Eds), *Encyclopedia of Entrepreneurship*, Prentice-Hall, Englewood Cliffs, NJ.

Bronislaw, J.V. and Waart, E. (1988), "Marketing planning for improved performance: a comparative analysis", Department of Marketing, Georgia State University, Atlanta, GA, pp. 29-30.

Brownlie, D. and Spender, J.C. (1995), "Managerial judgement in strategic marketing: some preliminary thoughts", *Management Decision*, Vol. 33 No. 6, pp. 39-50.

Butler, J.E. and Hansen, G.S. (1991), "Network evolution, entrepreneurial success and regional development", *Journal of Entrepreneurship and Regional Development*, Vol. 3, pp. 1-16.

Burgoyne, B. (1989), "Creating the management portfolio: building on competency approaches to management development", *Management Education and Development*, Vol 20 Part 1, pp. 56-61.

Bygrave, W.D., (1989a), "The entrepreneurship paradigm (I): a philosophical look at its research methodologies", *Entrepreneurship Theory and Practice*, Vol. 14 No. 1, Fall, pp. 7-26.

Bygrave, W.D. (1989b), "The entrepreneurship paradigm (II): chaos and catastrophes among quantum jumps?", *Entrepreneurship Theory and Practice*, Vol. 14 No. 2, Winter, pp. 7-30.

Bygrave, W.D. and Hofer, C.W. (1991), "Theorising about entrepreneurship", *Entrepreneurship Theory and Practice*, Winter, pp. 12-22.

Caird, S. (1992), "Problems with the identification of enterprise competencies and the implications for assessment and development", *Management Education and Development*, Vol. 23 Part 1, pp. 6-17.

Callahan, M.R. (1992), "Tending the sales relationship", *Training and Development*, December, pp. 31-6.

Cannon, T. (1991), "Marketing in small business", in Baker, M.J. (Ed), *The Marketing Book*, 2nd ed., Butterworth-Heinemann, London.

Carson, D.J. (1993), "A philosophy of marketing education in small firms", *Journal of Marketing Management*, Vol. 9 No. 2, pp. 189-205.

Carson, D.J. and Cromie, S. (1989), "Marketing planning in small enterprises: a model and some empirical evidence", *Journal of Marketing Management*, Vol. 5 No. 1, Summer, pp. 33-51.

Carson, D.J., Hill, J. and McGowan, P. (1994), "In pursuit of entrepreneurial marketing management competencies", in Hills, G.E. and Mohan-Neill, S.T. (Eds), *Research at the Marketing/Entrepreneurship Interface*, AMA, University of Illinois at Chicago, Chicago, IL, pp. 76-9.

Carson, D.J., Cromie, S., McGowan, P. and Hill, J. (1995), *Marketing and Entrepreneurship in SMEs: An Innovative Approach*, Prentice-Hall, London.

Casson, M. (1982), *The Entrepreneur, an Economic Theory*, Oxford Press.

Chell, E., Haworth, J.M. and Brearley, S.A. (1991), *The Entrepreneurial Personality: Concepts, Cases and Categories*, Routledge, London.

Chowdhury, J. (1993), "The motivational impact of sales quotas on effort", *Journal of Marketing Research*, Vol. 30, February, pp. 28-41.

Churchill, G.A. Jr, Ford, N.M., Hartley, S.W. and Walker, O.C. Jr (1985), "The determinants of salesperson performance: a meta analysis", *Journal of Marketing Research*, Vol. 22, May, pp. 103-18.

Churchill, N.C. and Lewis, V.L. (1983), "The five stages of small business growth", *Harvard Business Review*, May-June, pp. 30-49.

Cockerill, T. (1989), "The kind of competence for rapid change", *Personnel Management*, Vol. 21 No. 9, September, pp. 52-6.

Collin, A. (1989), "Managers' competence: rhetoric, reality and research", *Personnel Review*, Vol. 18 No. 6, pp. 20-5.

Constable, C.J. (1988), *Developing the Competent Manager in a UK Context*, report for the Manpower Services Commission, Manpower Services Commission, Sheffield.

Constable, C.J. and McCormick, R. (1991), "The current provision of management education and training in the UK", in Silver, M. (Ed.), *Competent to Manage*, Routledge, London, pp. 49-53.

Cooper, A.C. (1989), "The role of incubator organisations in the founding of growth-orientated firms", *Journal of Business Venturing*, Vol. 5, pp. 75-86.

Coviello, N. and Munro, H.J. (1995), "Growing the entrepreneurial firm: networking for international market development", *European Journal of Marketing*, Vol. 29 No. 7, pp. 49-61.

Cowell, D.W. (1987), *Some Insights into the Background and Training of Marketing Executives in the UK*, Plymouth Business School, Plymouth.

Creswell, J.W. (1994), *Research Design: Qualitative and Quantitative Approaches*, Sage, London.

Cromie, S. and Birley, S. (1994), "Relationships among small business support agencies", *Journal of Entrepreneurship and Regional Development*, Vol. 6, pp. 301-14.

Cunningham, B.J. and Lischeron, J. (1991), "Defining entrepreneurship", *Journal of Small Business Management*, Vol. 29 No. 1, pp. 45-61.

Curran, J., Jarvis, R., Blackburn, R. and Black, S. (1993), "Networks and small firms: constructs, methodological strategies and some findings", *International Small Business Journal*, Vol. 11 No. 2, pp. 13-24.

d'Amboise, G. (1992), "Empirical research on SMEs: the last ten years in Canada", *Proceedings of International Council for Small Business, 37th World Conference*, Toronto, June, pp. 135-57.

Dana, L.P. (1992), "Towards market economies and entrepreneurship: the Yugopluralist model", in *Enterprising in Partnership with the Environment, Proceedings of The International Council for Small Business, 37th World Conference*, Toronto, pp. 292-305.

Dana, L.P. (1999), "From local to international networks", in Dana, L.P. (Ed.), *International Entrepreneurship: An Anthology*, Nan Yang Technical University, Singapore, pp. 187-200.

Dart, J. and Pendleton, L.L. (1984), "The role of advertising agencies in entrepreneurship education", *Journal of Small Business Management*, Vol. 22 No. 2, April, pp. 38-44.

Davis, C.D., Hills, G.E. and LaForge, R.W. (1985), "The marketing/small enterprise paradox", *International Small Business Journal*, Vol. 3, Spring, pp. 31-42.

Davis, C.H. and Klassen, M.L. (1991), "What entrepreneurs need to know: are we researching it?", in Hills, G.E. and LaForge, R.W. (Eds), *Research at the Marketing/Entrepreneurship Interface*, AMA, University of Illinois at Chicago, Chicago, IL, pp. 107-18.

Dion, P., Easterling, D. and Miller, S.J. (1995), "What is really necessary in successful buyer/seller relationships?", *Industrial Marketing Management*, Vol. 24, pp. 1-9.

Dodge, H., Fullerton, S. and Robbins, J. (1994), "Stage of the organisational life cycle and competition as mediators of problem perception for small businesses", *Strategic Management Journal*, Vol. 15, pp. 121-34.

Drucker, P.F. (1985), "The discipline of innovation", *Harvard Business Review*, May-June, pp. 67-72.

Dubini, P. and Aldrich, H. (1991), "Personal and extended networks are central to the entrepreneurial process", *Journal of Business Venturing*, Vol. 6, pp. 305-13.

Dulewicz, V. (1989), "Assessment centres as the route to competence", *Personnel Management*, November, Vol. 21 No. 11, pp. 56-9.

Dwyer, R.F., Schurr, P. and Oh, S. (1987), "Developing buyer-seller relationships", *Journal of Marketing*, Vol. 51, April, pp. 11-27.

Eisenhardt, K.M. (1990), "Speed and strategic choice: how managers accelerate decision making", *California Management Review*, Spring, pp. 39-54.

Fetterman, D.M. (1989), *Ethnography: Step by Step*, Sage, Newbury Park, CA.

Filley, A.C. and Aldag, R.A. (1988), "Venture age and growth within organisation types", *Frontiers of Entrepreneurship Research*, Boston, MA, pp. 77-8.

Flynn, D. (1992), "Ireland's second-rate sales staff", *Business and Finance*, 26 March, pp. 13-17.

Fulop, L. (1991), "Middle managers: victims or vanguards of the entrepreneurial movement?", *Journal of Management Studies*, Vol. 28 No. 1, January, pp. 25-44.

Funkhouser, G.R. (1984), "A practical theory of persuasion based on behavioral science approaches", *Journal of Personal Selling and Sales Management*, November, pp. 17-25.

Futrell, C.M. (1989), *Fundamentals of Selling*, 2nd ed., Irwin, Homewood, IL.

Gallagher, S. (Ed.) (1985), *Sales and Marketing Casebook*, Hobsons Ltd, Cambridge.

Gartner, W.B. (1989), "'Who is the entrepreneur?' is the wrong question", *Journal of Entrepreneurship Theory and Practice*, Vol. 13 No. 4, Summer, pp. 49-56.

Geursen, G.M. (1995), "The parental relationship: a suggested theory for conceptualising structures in small business for decisions, relationships and stress avoidance", paper presented to The UIC/AMA Research Symposium on Marketing and Entrepreneurship, Melbourne, July.

Glaser, B. and Strauss, A. (1967), *The Discovery of Grounded Theory: Strategies for Qualitative Research*, Aldine, Chicago, IL.

Glaze, T. (1989), "Cadbury's dictionary of competence", *Personnel Management*, July-August, pp. 44-8.

Glisan, G.B. and Hawes, J.M. (1990), "Selecting creative people for sales positions", *Industrial Marketing Management*, Vol. 19, pp. 331-7.

Gore, C., Murray, K. and Richardson, B. (1992), *Strategic Decision Making*, Cassell, London.

Granovetter, M. (1982), "The strength of weak ties: a network theory revisited", in Marsden, P.V. and Lin, N. (Eds), *Social Structure and Network Analysis*, Sage, Beverly Hills, CA, pp. 105-30.

Greatrex, J. and Phillips, P. (1989), "Oiling the wheels of competence", *Personnel Management*, Vol. 21 No. 8, August, pp. 36-9.

Greiner, L.L. (1972), "Evolution and revolution as organizations grow", *Harvard Business Review*, Vol. 50 No. 4, July-August, pp. 37-46.

Gummesson, E. (1991), *Qualitative Methods in Management Research*, Sage, Newbury Park, CA.

Hall, R. (1994), "Judgement and hyper-reality", *Journal of General Management*, Vol. 19 No. 4, Summer, pp. 41-51.

Handy, C. (1987), *The Making of Managers*, National Economic Development Office, CBI/BIM, London.

Hansen, E.L. (1995), "Entrepreneurial networks and new organisation growth", *Entrepreneurship Theory and Practice*, Vol. 11 No. 4, Summer, pp. 7-19.

Hardy, K.G. (1992), "Marketing competencies for every manager", *Business Quarterly*, Winter, pp. 51-3.

Harper, S.C. (1988), "Intuition: what separates executives from managers", *Business Horizons*, September-October, pp. 13-19.

Hart, S.H., Moncief, W.C. and Parasuraman, A. (1989), "An empirical investigation of salespeople's performance, effort and selling method during a sales contest", *Journal of the Academy of Marketing Science*, Vol. 17 No. 1, Winter, pp. 29-39.

Hawes, J.M., Mast, K.E. and Swan, J.E. (1989), "Trust-earning perceptions of sellers and buyers", *Journal of Personal Selling and Sales Management*, Vol. IX, Spring, pp. 1-8.

Healey, M. and Perry, C. (2000), "Comprehensive criteria to judge validity and reliability of qualitative research within the realism paradigm", *Qualitative Market Research: An International Journal*, Vol. 3 No. 3, pp. 118-26.

Herron, L., Sapienza, H.J. and Smith-Cook, D. (1992), "Entrepreneurship theory from an interdisciplinary perspective", *Entrepreneurship Theory and Practice*, Spring, pp. 5-12.

Hill, J. and Fallis, A. (1995), "An investigation into the scope and nature of marketing management competencies for entrepreneurial decision making in small firms", in Hills, G.E., Muzyka, D.F., Omura, G.S. and Knight, G.A. (Eds), *Research at the Marketing/Entrepreneurship Interface*, American Marketing Association, University of Illinois at Chicago, Chicago, IL, pp. 137-56.

Hill, J. and McGowan, P. (1996), "Marketing development through networking: a competency based approach for small firm entrepreneurs", *Journal of Small Business and Enterprise Development*, Vol. 3 No. 3, pp. 148-57.

Hills, G.E. (1987), "Marketing and entrepreneurship research issues: scholarly justification?", in Hills, G.E. (Ed.), *Research at the Marketing/Entrepreneurship Interface*, United States Association for Small Business and Entrepreneurship, Marietta, GA.

Hills, G.E. and LaForge, R.W. (1992), "Research at the marketing interface to advance entrepreneurship theory", *Entrepreneurship Theory and Practice*, Vol. 16, Spring, pp. 91-100.

Hills, G.E. and Mohan-Neill, S.T. (Eds) (1994), *Research at the Marketing/Entrepreneurship Interface*, University of Illinois at Chicago, Chicago, IL.

Hills, G.E., Giglierano, J.J. and Hultman, C.M. (Eds) (1997), *Research at the Marketing/Entrepreneurship Interface*, University of Illinois at Chicago, Chicago, IL.

Hisrich, R.D. (1988), "The entrepreneur in N. Ireland: characteristics, problems and recommendations for the future", *Journal of Small Business Management*, Vol. 26, July, pp. 32-9.

Hodgetts, R.M. and Kuratko, D.F. (1995), *Effective Small Business Management*, 5th ed., Dryden, Fort Worth, TX.

Hofer, C.W. and Bygrave, W.D. (1992), "Researching entrepreneurship." *Journal of Entrepreneurship Theory and Practice*, Spring, pp. 91-100.

Hogarth, R.M. (1987), *Judgement and Choice*, John Wiley & Sons, Chichester.

Holmund, M. and Kock, S. (1998), "Relationships and the internationalisation of Finnish small and medium-sized companies", *International Small Business Journal*, Vol. 16 No. 64, July-September, pp. 46-63.

Ingram, T.N. and LaForge, R.W. (1989), *Sales Management: Analysis and Decision Making*, Dryden Press, Chicago, IL.

Jackson, L. (1989), "Turning airport managers into high-fliers", *Personnel Management*, Vol. 21 No. 10, pp. 80-5.

Jackson, R.W. and Parasuraman, A. (1986), "The *Yellow Pages* as an advertising tool for small businesses", *American Journal of Small Business*, Spring, pp. 29-35.

Jacobs, R. (1989), "Getting the measure of management competence", *Personnel Management*, Vol. 21 No. 6, pp. 32-7.

Jarillo, J.C. (1988), "When small is not enough: how to save entrepreneurs from themselves", *European Management Journal*, Vol. 6 No. 4, pp. 325-9.

Johannisson, B. (1986), "Network strategies: management technology for entrepreneurship and change", *International Small Business Journal*, Vol. 5, pp. 19-30.

Johannisson, B. (1995a), "Paradigms and entrepreneurial networks – some methodological challenges", *Entrepreneurship and Regional Development*, Vol. 7 No. 3, pp. 215-31.

Johannisson, B. (1995b), "Entrepreneurial networking in the Scandanavian context – theoretical and empirical positioning", *Journal of Entrepreneurship and Regional Development*, Vol. 7, pp. 189-92.

Johnson, B.R. (1990), "Toward a multidimensional model of entrepreneurship: the case of achievement motivation and the entrepreneur", *Entrepreneurship Theory and Practice*, Spring, pp. 39-54.

Johnson, V. (1993), "Intuition in decision making", *Successful Meetings*, Vol. 42 Part 2, pp. 148-53.

Johnstone, H. and Kirby, D. (1992), "Small firms and the recovery of the economic environment in Britain", in *Enterprising in Partnership with the Environment, Proceedings of International Council for Small Business*, (abstract only), Toronto, June, p. 669.

Jolson, M.A. (1984), "Selling assertively", *Business Horizons*, September-October, pp. 71-7.

Jolson, M.A., Dubinsky, A.J., Yammarino, F.J. and Comer, L.B. (1993), "Transforming the salesforce with leadership", *Sloan Management Review*, Spring, pp. 95-106.

Joyce, P., Woods, A. and Black, S. (1995), "Networks and partnerships: managing change and competition", *Journal of Small Business and Enterprise Development*, Vol 2 No. 1, March, pp. 11-18.

Kao, J.J. (1991), *The Entrepreneurial Organisation*, Prentice-Hall International, Englewood Cliffs, NJ.

Katz, R. (1955), "The skills of an effective administrator", *Harvard Business Review*, Vol. 33 No. 1, pp. 33-42.

Kets de Vries, M.F.R. (1977), "The entrepreneurial personality: a person at the crossroads", *Journal of Management Studies*, Vol. 14, pp. 34-57.

Kirzner, I.M. (1979), *Perception, Opportunity, and Profit: Studies in the Theory of Entrepreneurship*, Chicago University Press, Chicago, IL.

Klemp, G.O. Jr (Ed.) (1980), *The Assessment of Occupational Competence*, Report to the National Institute of Education, Washington DC.

Kolb, D., Lublin, S., Spoth, J. and Baker, R. (1986), "Strategic management development: using experiential learning theory to assess and develop managerial competencies", *Journal of Management Development*, Vol. 5 No. 3, pp. 13-24.

Kotler, P. (1988), *Marketing Management: Analysis, Planning, Implementation and Control*, Prentice-Hall International, London.

Kotter, J.P. (1990), "What leaders really do", *Harvard Business Review*, May-June, pp. 103-11.

Kuratko, D.F. and Hodgetts, R.M. (1995), *Entrepreneurship: A Contemporary Approach*, 3rd ed., The Dryden Press, Fort Worth, TX.

LaFuente, A. and Salas, V. (1989), "Types of entrepreneurs and firms: the case of new Spanish firms", *Strategic Management Journal*, Vol. 10, pp. 17-30.

Lank, A.G. and Lank, E.A. (1995), "Legitimizing the gut feel: the role of intuition in business", *Journal of Managerial Psychology*, Vol. 10 No. 5, pp. 18-23.

Leibenstein, K. (1968), "Entrepreneurship and development", *American Economic Review*, Vol. 38 No. 2, pp. 72-83.

Leigh, T.W. (1987), "Cognitive selling scripts and sales training", *Journal of Personal Selling and Sales Management*, Vol. 7, August, pp. 39-48.

Leong, S.M., Busch, P.S. and John, D.R. (1989), "Knowledge bases and salesperson effectiveness: a script-theoretic analysis", *Journal of Marketing Research*, Vol. 26, May, pp. 164-78.

Leppard, J. and McDonald, M.H. (1991), "Marketing planning and corporate culture: a conceptual framework", *Journal of Marketing Management*, Vol. 7 No. 3, pp. 213-35.

Lessem, R. (1986), *Enterprise Development*, Gower, Aldershot.

Levenson, I. (1986), "The phenomenon of strategic collaboration", *Directors and Boards*, Vol. 10 No. 4 , Summer, pp. 20-3.

Levinson, H. and Rosenthal, S. (1984), *CEO: Corporate Leadership in Action*, Basic Books, New York, NY.

Low, M.B. and Macmillan, I.C. (1988), "Entrepreneurship: past research", *Journal of Management*, Vol. 14 No. 2, pp. 139-61.

Luckmann, T. (1982), "Individual action and social knowledge", in von Cranach, M. and Harre, R. (Eds), *The Analysis of Action*, Cambridge University Press, Cambridge.

McClelland, D.C. (1961), *The Achieving Society*, Van Nostrand, Princeton, NJ.

Macintosh, G., Anglin, K.A., Szymanski, D.M. and Gentry, J.W. (1992), "Relationship development in selling: a cognitive analysis", *Journal of Personal Selling and Sales Management*, Vol. XII No. 4, Fall, pp. 23-34.

Mackintosh, S. and Tynan, C. (1994), "Assessing marketing planning in small firms using a focus group methodology", in *Marketing: Unity in Diversity, Proceedings of the Marketing Education Group Conference*, University of Ulster, Vol. 2, pp. 587-96.

Maclaren, P., McGowan, P. and Hill, J. (1997), "Marketing education for small firm entrepreneurs: a work-based learning approach", *Marketing Education Review*, Special Issue on "Research at the marketing/entrepreneurship interface", Vol. 17 No. 3, pp. 39-46.

Mangham, I.L. and Silver, M.S. (1986), *Management Training: Context and Practice*, School of Management, University of Bath, Bath.

Martin, G. and Staines, H. (1994), "Managerial competences in small firms", *Journal of Management Development*, Vol. 13 No. 7, pp. 23-34.

Matthews, C.H. and Scott, S.G. (1995), "Uncertainty and planning in small and entrepreneurial firms: an empirical assessment", *Journal of Small Business Management*, October, pp. 34-53.

Michaels, R.E. and Day, R.L. (1985), "Measuring customer orientation of salespeople: a replication with industrial buyers", *Journal of Marketing Research*, Vol. 22, November, pp. 443-6.

Middleton, B. and Long, G. (1990), "Marketing skills: critical issues in marketing education and training", *Journal of Marketing Management*, Vol. 5 No. 3, pp. 325-43.

Miles, M.B. and Huberman, A.M. (1994), *Qualitative Data Analysis*, Sage, Thousand Oaks, CA.

Milliman, R.E. and Fugate, D.L. (1988), "Using trust-transference as a persuasion technique: an empirical field investigation", *Journal of Personal Selling and Sales Management*, August, pp. 1-8.

Mintzberg, H. (1973), *The Nature of Managerial Work*, Prentice-Hall, Englewood Cliffs, NJ.

Mintzberg, H. (1979), *The Structuring of Organisations*, Prentice-Hall, Englewood Cliffs, NJ.

Mitchell, T.R. (1978), *People in Organizations: Understanding Their Behavior*, McGraw-Hill, New York, NY.

Moine, D.J. (1982), "To trust, perchance to buy", *Psychology Today*, August, pp. 51-4.

Mole, V., Dawson, S., Winstanley, D. and Sherval, J. (1993), "Researching managerial competences", paper presented to British Academy of Management Annual Conference, Milton Keynes, September.

Nancarrow, C., Attlee, C. and Wright, L.T. (1999), "Weaknesses in the marketing and the sdoption of independent inventions with implications for international competitiveness", *Journal of Enterprising Culture*, Vol. 7 No. 3, September, pp. 233-56.

Nilson, T.H. (1994), *Chaos Marketing: How to Win in a Turbulent World*, McGraw-Hill, London.

Ornstein, R.E. (1972), *The Psychology of Consciousness*, Penguin, London.

Ostgaard, T.A. and Birley, S. (1994), "Strategy – a strategic or coincidental match?", *Journal of Small Business Venturing*, Vol. 9, pp. 281-305.

Patterson, R. (1986), "Strategic planning for small business", in Gardner, J.R., Rachin, R. and Sweeney, A., (Eds), *Handbook of Strategic Planning*, John Wiley, New York, NY, pp. 242-51.

Patton, M.Q. (1990), *Qualitative Evaluation and Research Methods*, Sage, Beverly Hills, CA.

Pearson, A.F. (1989), "Six basics for general managers", *Harvard Business Review*, July-August, pp. 94-9.

Penley, L.E., Alexander, E.R., Jernigan, I.E. and Henwood, C.I. (1991), "Communication abilities of managers: the relationship to performance", *Journal of Management*, Vol. 17 No. 1, pp. 57-76.

Peters, T.J. (1987), *Thriving on Chaos*, Macmillan, London.

Phillips, C.P. (1988), "The not-so-sweet sound of sales talk", *Training*, September, pp. 56-62.

Piercy, N. and Morgan, N. (1989/1990), "Internal marketing strategy: leverage for managing marketing-led strategic change", *Irish Marketing Review*, Vol. 4 No. 3, pp. 11-27.

Polanyi, M. (1967), *The Tacit Dimension*, Garden City, NY.

Prideaux, G. and Ford, J.E. (1988), "Management development: competencies, contracts, teams and work-based learning", *Journal of Management Development*, Vol. 7 No. 1.

Pye, A. (1991), "Management competence: the flower in the mirror and the moon on the water", in Silver, M. (Ed.), *Competent to Manage: Approaches to Management Training and Development*, Routledge, London.

Ragab, M. (1992), "The business environment of the 1990s: implications for entrepreneurship", in *Enterprising in Partnership with the Environment, Proceedings International Council for Small Business 37th World Conference*, Toronto, pp. 670-84.

Raven, J. (1986), "Fostering competence", in Burgess, T. (Ed.), *Education for Capability*, NFER-Nelson, Windsor.

Ray, D.M. (1993), "Understanding the entrepreneur: entrepreneurial attributes, experience and skills", *Entrepreneurship and Regional Development*, Vol. 5, pp. 345-57.

Rhys, G. (1989), "Smaller car firms – will they survive?", *Long Range Planning*, Vol. 22 No. 5, pp. 22-9.

Rothwell, R. (1986), "The role of small firms in technological innovation", in Curran, J., Stanworth, J. and Watkins, D. (Eds), *The Survival of the Small Firm*, Vol. 2, Gower, Aldershot.

Ryans, A.B. and Weinberg, C.B. (1981), "Salesforce management: integrating research advances", *California Management Review*, Vol. 24 No. 1, reprinted in Enis, B.M., Cox, K.K. and Mokwa, M.P. (Eds), *Marketing Classics: A Selection of Influential Articles*, 8th ed., Prentice-Hall, Englewood Cliffs, NJ (1995), pp. 528-45.

Scase, R. and Goffee, R. (1982), *The Entrepreneurial Middle Class*, Croom Helm, London.

Schon, D.A. (1983), *The Reflective Practitioner*, Basic Books, New York, NY.

Schuler, R.S. (1979), "A role perception transaction process model for organizational communication-outcome relationships", *Organisational Behavior and Human Performance*, Vol. 23, pp. 268-91.

Scott, M. and Bruce, R. (1987), "Five stages of growth in small businesses", *Long Range Planning*, Vol. 20 No. 3, pp. 45-52.

Sexton, D.L. and Bowman, N. (1985), "The entrepreneur: a capable executive and more", *Journal of Business Venturing*, Winter, pp. 129-40.

Shaw, E. (1999), "A guide to the qualitative research process: evidence from a small firm study", *Qualitative Market Research: An International Journal*, Vol. 2 No. 2, pp. 59-70.

Silver, M. (1991), *Competent to Manage: Approaches to Management Training and Development*, Routledge, London.

Simintiras, A.C. and Cadogan, J.W. (1994), "An experimental analysis of the impact of a behaviour modification programme on salespersons' effort and performance behaviours", in *Marketing Unity and Diversity, Proceedings of the Marketing Education Group Annual Conference*, University of Ulster, Coleraine, pp. 843-53.

Slesinski, R.A. (1989), "Applied creativity: quantum leaps for sales and sales training", *Sales and Marketing Training*, Vol. 3, pp. 6-8.

Smart, D.T. and Conant, J.S. (1994), "Entrepreneurial orientation, distinctive marketing competencies and organizational performance", *Journal of Applied Business Research*, Vol. 10 No. 3, pp. 28-38.

Soldow, G.F. and Thomas, G.P. (1984), "Relational communication: form versus content in the sales interaction", *Journal of Marketing*, Winter, Vol. 48, pp. 84-93.

Stake, R.E. (1994), "Case studies", in Denzin, N.K. and Lincoln, Y.S. (Eds), *Handbook of Qualitative Research*, Thousand Oaks, CA, pp. 236-47.

Stasch, S.F. and Ward, J.L. (1989), "Evaluating aggressive marketing strategies for smaller-share firms", *Marketing Intelligence & Planning*, Vol. 7 No. 7/8, pp. 4-15.

Stevenson, H.H. and Gumpert, D.E. (1985), "The heart of entrepreneurship", *Harvard Business Review*, March-April, pp. 85-94.

Storey, D.J. (1994), *Understanding the Small Business Sector*, Routledge, London.

Storey, D.J., Keasey, K., Watson, R. and Wynarczyk, P. (1987), *The Performance of Small Firms*, Croom Helm, London.

Strauss, A. and Corbin, J. (1990), *Basics of Qualitative research: Grounded Theory Procedures and Techniques*, Sage, Newbury Park, CA.

Swan, J.E. and Nolan, J.J. (1985), "Gaining customer trust: a conceptual guide for the salesperson", *Journal of Personal Selling and Sales Management*, Vol. 5, November, pp. 39-48.

Swayne, C. and Tucker, W. (1973), *The Effective Entrepreneur*, General Learning Press, Morristown, NJ.

Szarka, J. (1990), "Networking and small firms", *International Small Business Journal*, Vol. 8 No. 2, pp. 19-33.

Szymanski, D.M. (1987), "Selling effectiveness: a declarative and categorical process perspective, unpublished dissertation, University of Wisconsin-Madison.

Tesch, R. (1990), *Qualitative Research: Analysis Types and Software Tools*, 1st ed., Falmer, New York, NY.

Tesch, R. (1994), *Qualitative Research: Analysis Types and Software Tools*, 2nd ed., Falmer, New York, NY.

Thomas, R.E. (1991), "Management competencies", in Silver, M. (Ed.), *Competent to Manage*, Routledge, London, pp. 221-27.

Timmons J.A (1990), *New Venture Creation: Entrepreneurship in the 1990s*, 3rd ed., Irwin, Homewood, IL.

Thorelli, H.B. (1986), "Networks: between markets and hierarchies", *Strategic Management Journal*, Vol. 7 No. 1, pp. 37-51.

Townroe, P.M. and Mallalieu, K. (1991), "Infrastructure for regional development advice and support to new small businesses", *Infrastructure and Regional Development*, R.W. Vickerman, London, pp. 43-60.

Valry, N. (1999), "Innovation in industry", *The Economist*, 20 February, Survey Insert.

Vesper, K. (1980), *New Venture Strategies*, Prentice-Hall, Englewood Cliffs, NJ.

Webster, F.E. Jr (1968), "Interpersonal communication and salesman effectiveness", *Journal of Marketing*, Vol. 32, July, pp. 7-13.

Weilbaker, D.C. (1990), "The identification of selling abilities needed for missionary type sales", *Journal of Personal Selling and Sales Management*, Vol. X, Summer, pp. 45-58.

Weitz, B.A. (1981), "Effectiveness in sales interactions: a contingency framework", *Journal of Marketing*, Vol. 45, pp. 85-103.

Weitz, B.A., Sujan, H. and Sujan, S. (1986), "Knowledge, motivation and adaptive behavior: a framework for improving selling effectiveness", *Journal of Marketing*, Vol. 50, pp. 174-91.

Westhead, P. (1988), "A typology of new manufacturing firm founders in Wales", Working Paper, No. 46, Cranfield School of Management, Cranfield.

Williams, A.J. and Seminerio, J. (1985), "What buyers like from salesmen", *Industrial Marketing Management*, Vol. 14, pp. 75-8.

Wynarczyk, P., Watson, R., Storey, D.J., Short, H. and Keasey, K. (1993), *The Managerial Labour Market in Small and Medium-Sized Enterprises*, Routledge, London.

Yanagida, I. (1992), "The business network: a powerful and challenging business tool", *The Journal of Business Venturing*, Vol. 7 No. 5, pp. 341-6

Yin, R.K. (1994), *Case Study Research: Design and Methods*, 2nd ed., Sage, Thousand Oaks, CA.

Younger, S.M. (1992), "Four by four: sales savvy for the 1990s", *Training and Development*, December, pp. 13-17

Zimmerer, T.W. and Scarborough, N.M. (1994), *Essentials of Small Business Management*, Macmillan, New York, NY.

A multidimensional study of the key determinants of effective SME marketing activity: Part 2

Jimmy Hill
Northern Ireland Centre for Entrepreneurship, University of Ulster at Jordanstown, Newtownabbey, Northern Ireland

Keywords *Small- to medium-sized enterprises, Marketing, Personal selling, Entrepreneurialism, Competences*

Abstract *This paper forms Part 2 of a monograph detailing a study that sought to examine the key determinants of SME marketing. It reports the key findings with respect to marketing competency in SMEs, explores the strong sales orientation of such firms, examines the nature and use of SME personal contact networks and considers to what extent formal marketing planning is practiced in such enterprises. New insights to these important areas of small firm research are presented. A new model of SME marketing competency is developed, depicting competencies at three levels, foundation, transitional and marketing in practice. The monograph concludes with a holistic interpretation of the data that enables the development of a new model of SME marketing.*

Introduction

This paper presents an interpretation of the key findings in respect of the five research issues presented in Part 1 of the monograph. It identifies and emphasises the key contributions of the research study. In addition, these contributions are considered within the context of the literature of the immediate disciplines. Implications for theory are considered, as are any revisions to existing theory.

It is first appropriate however to restate the five research issues identified in Part 1:

(1) Through a longitudinal, in-depth study to establish a definitive framework of marketing competencies which determine effective marketing, and to compare this with the competency framework suggested in the exploratory research.

(2) To establish the extent of the sales orientation in SMEs and to gain insight to its role in shaping SME marketing activities.

(3) To measure the extent to which formal and conventional marketing planning processes are practiced by SMEs.

(4) To establish the use and nature of personal contact networks in the marketing practices of SMEs and to gain some insight to how contact

International Journal of Entrepreneurial Behaviour & Research, Vol. 7 No. 6, 2001, pp. 211-235. 1355-2554 networks might be used to enhance marketing decisions of both an operational and strategic nature.

(5) To develop a holistic model of marketing in SMEs.

Interpretation of findings

SME marketing competencies

The major finding in respect of the first research objective is that there is a spectrum of competencies that can be associated with the practice of effective marketing in SMEs. This confirms the framework suggestions from the pilot work. This spectrum comprised experience, knowledge, communication, judgement and intuition. This is an important outcome as there has been no significant research work examining the nature of marketing competencies in SMEs (Carson, 1993). The literature offers some consideration as to which competencies are appropriate for marketing although this tends to be from a management decision-making perspective at a generic level (Middleton and Long, 1990; Hardy, 1992). Whilst an important contribution in respect of small firms' competencies has been made by Martin and Staines (1994), their work really only serves to reinforce the need for some larger scale empirical work in this field. Ray (1993) considers the competency aspect in respect of its contribution to the creation of an entrepreneurial individual but makes the key point that skills and competencies have not been empirically investigated. In addition, several interpretations can be made in respect of this spectrum, which serve to emphasise the importance of the contribution of the research in this area.

First, the experience competency is the most significant competency in the spectrum and it is one that permeates and characterises competence in every aspect of SMEs' activities. It is, however, seldom articulated. The presence of the competency is unquestionable in that it underpins every comment and action in the market place and much of what actually happens in SMEs in both a strategic and operational sense. The key assertion, therefore, is that experience is a foundation level competency without which competent marketing cannot occur. This assertion encapsulates the earlier assertions of Luckmann (1982) and Schon (1983), and actually develops the conclusion of MacLaren *et al.* (1997) that a management practitioner's ability must be seen as encompassing his/her total experience insofar as it can be drawn on for understanding and action. This research frames this conclusion within the context of marketing decision-making in the SME. The evidence to support the key role of experience is particularly strong in the way the competency, for example, is frequently linked to the judgement competency. Second, an interpretation with respect to experience would be that it is characteristic of firms that are particularly entrepreneurial. This assertion is founded on strong indications that experience is what makes or shapes a competency in opportunity identification. Experience enhances, sharpens and guides opportunistic instinct and hence influences major marketing decisions. The conclusions of studies to date in respect of entrepreneurship have frequently alluded to the role of "opportunity focus" (Ennis, 1999; Zimmerer and Scarborough, 1994; Stevenson and Gumpert, 1985; Vesper, 1980; Kirzner, 1979) but this has not been explicitly framed within the context of "quality" experience. The third key interpretation in respect of experience is that foundation level experience is "quality" experience, that is, the ability to learn from all manner of interaction with one's environment.

With regard to the competency of knowledge, also a foundation level competency, the key interpretation of the findings is that, as a consequence of the sales focus of SMEs, the need for technical/product knowledge is particularly dominant. This aspect of knowledge is particularly strong in respect of the industry specific situation of many of the research companies. This contribution is significant also in that research to date has paid insufficient attention to knowledge of this nature. This is a consequence of inadequate recognition of the strong sales orientation of SMEs. Wider marketing activity is rooted in the "quality" experience competency and is partly intuitive. A close link exists between knowledge born of experience and intuition. This assertion supports the seminal contention of Polanyi (1967, p. 61) who stated that such "tacit knowledge" is "that which dwells in our awareness of particulars while bearing on an entity which the particulars jointly constitute".

Communication is also a foundation level competency (see Hill and Fallis, 1995; and Penley *et al.*, 1991). Whilst internal and external communication capabilities are vital for competent marketing to occur, the key interpretation of the data indicates that the communication competency is a "set" of other competencies described here as the relational communications cluster. This cluster contributes to what is described as Level 2 marketing competencies. This cluster incorporates communication in a generic sense, but in particular, personality, relationship building, a long term perspective to relationship building, internal communication, trust, people skills, approachability, listening skills, adaptability, empathy and honesty. The reason for the emergence of the relational communications cluster can be attributed to the sales focus of the research companies. Such an assertion is an insightful development of the contention of Mole *et al.* (1993) that communication should be articulated in a tacit manner and is really a component part of other management areas.

Judgement is another foundation level competency. This adds to the significant statement of Hogarth (1987) that judgement, as a competency, is sacrosanct. This assertion builds on the recognition of Pye (1991) that much management success is dependent on sound judgement. A key interpretation here is that again this competency is dependent on "quality experience" and is particularly desirable in respect of routine marketing decision-making.

The final foundation competency is that of intuition. Intuition is dependent on "quality" experience and to a lesser degree objective knowledge (as opposed to product/technological/technical knowledge). Intuition significantly fashions the entrepreneurial character of SMEs, particularly in the way respondents with high levels of intuition can read market situations quickly and are less reliant on formal procedures to inform "on the hoof" decisions. The role of intuition should be framed against the backdrop of much research outlining the importance of intuition to effective management practice and business success. This research differs, however, in that it builds on the work of Agor (1984), Harper (1988), Lank and Lank (1995) and Hill and McGowan (1999) and asserts the importance of intuition as a key marketing competency within the context of the SME.

A significant theoretical contribution of this research is that the Level 1 foundation competencies underpin a spectrum of Level 2 competencies comprising vision, opportunity focus, relational communication and commitment. These competencies are particularly entrepreneurial in character. Vision, for example, really subsumes opportunity focus. It characterises informal articulations of the marketing planning process. An interpretation here though suggests that vision is perhaps consequent on a commitment to the marketing planning process. It is reasonable to conclude that whilst visioning in a future opportunities sense might be characteristically entrepreneurial, it is more likely to be consequent on experience gained from engaging in the formal marketing planning process. Similarly, the Level 2 competency of opportunity focus is equally consequent upon effective marketing planning. Marketing planning encourages both consideration of the status quo and stimulates thinking about future directions. It encourages environmental scanning and hence identification of opportunities.

Relational communication is a Level 2 competency comprising a cluster of other competency elements including personality, relationship building, internal company communications, trust, people skills, approachability, a long term approach to relationship building, listening skills, adaptability, empathy and honesty. These competency elements combine to comprise a set of Level 3 competencies which are much more operational in character.

Commitment is also a Level 2 competency. It reflects the importance attached to the sales and personal selling orientation of the SMEs in the research. Sales people characteristically need to be self-starters. Significantly though, interpretation of the findings on commitment pointed to the presence of a cluster of other feeder competencies including motivation, ambition, achievement, enthusiasm, self-confidence and aggression. These competency elements also combine to comprise a set of Level 3 competencies that are operational in character.

The three competency levels identified in the data are represented in Table I. Several interpretations pertain to the table. First, Levels 2 and 3 of marketing competency are dependent on the existence of a spectrum of lower level competencies. The higher the competency level, the more situation/task specific and operational in character the marketing activity is likely to be. This outcome raises questions about the link that exists between the level of competence and the stage of marketing development of the firm. Carson (1985) developed the work of Greiner (1972) and Adizes (1989) and suggested four discernible stages

Level 1 – foundation	Level 2 – transitional	Level 3 – marketing in practice: Relational communication	Level 3 – marketing in practice: Commitment
Experience	Vision	Personality	Motivation
Knowledge	Opportunity focus	Realtionship building	Ambition
Communication	Relational communication	People skills	Achievement
Judgement	Commitment	Internal communication	Enthusiasm
Intuition		Trust	Confidence
		Approachability	Aggression
		Listening skills	
		Adaptability	
		Empathy	
		Honesty	

Table I. Three levels of marketing competency in SMEs

in the evolution of marketing in small firms. He described Stage 2 as "Reactive selling" where as demand grows, marketing activity occurs usually in response to customer enquiries. The insight to the nature of competencies obtained here suggests that selling itself is the main trajectory of marketing evolution. The sales orientation becomes more dominant and sophisticated in parallel with increased marketing sophistication. Such increased sophistication and the stronger sales orientation is detectable in the increased level of manifest competencies. Such a conclusion also ties in with Stokes's (1995) assertion in respect of the marketing experience curve of the SME.

The most significant interpretation though is that the Level 3 marketing competencies are those clusters associated with the Level 2 competencies of commitment and relational communication clusters. These two competencies are also a consequence of the sales focus of SMEs. This does not mean that SMEs do nothing but sell. The evidence suggests that they engage in other marketing activities, for example planning, but that "marketing in practice" in SMEs is sales focused and driven by the need to make the sale. This does not have any discernible link to the stage of company development or company age as the life cycle research suggests (see Ennis, 1999). Another interpretation is that not only does the higher level of competency reflect a higher level of marketing sophistication but that it also reflects an SME that is entrepreneurial in character.

One other significant interpretation in respect of Table I is that whilst the extensive research work carried out in identifying competency frameworks tends to start with an extensive list of competencies and distil this down to a core set of generic competencies, this research has identified a core set of SME marketing competencies and worked outwards to an extended list of competencies (Level 3) which actually encapsulate marketing in practice in the SME. One cogent interpretation here would be that the Level 1 competencies are strategic and the Level 2 competencies are transitional or linking competencies that enable effective marketing to be filtered through to operational competencies at Level 3.

Other significant interpretations pertaining to the competency data, which support the contentions of the exploratory research, are that SME marketing competencies are not stand-alone entities. They are clusters of other competencies and skills. The highly interactive nature of SME competencies is clear when considering key marketing issues. Whilst this conclusion builds on the work of Boyatzis (1982), an interpretation of the data in the context of the SME would support an assertion that product/service, customer, market, industry trend specifics can all be assessed from the perspective of a competency in experience, knowledge, communication, judgement and intuition or some combination of these. What is important therefore is the way in which these Level 1 foundation competencies actually interact in relation to the resolution of specific marketing problems (see Figure 1). The interpretation here is that such clustering of competencies and the way in which such competencies interact mean that the predominant competency in any given marketing task situation depends on the marketing activity being undertaken and the specific marketing environment in which a specific action occurs. This conclusion supports exploratory research and the speculative contentions of Carson *et al.* (1994) as to the concept of competency inseparability. Figure 1 illustrates the interactive aspect to Level 1 competencies of experience, knowledge and judgement. It is suggested, therefore, that on the basis of this study that it is this inseparability of competencies that actually results in effective marketing performance as opposed to acknowledging the possession of any one marketing competency.

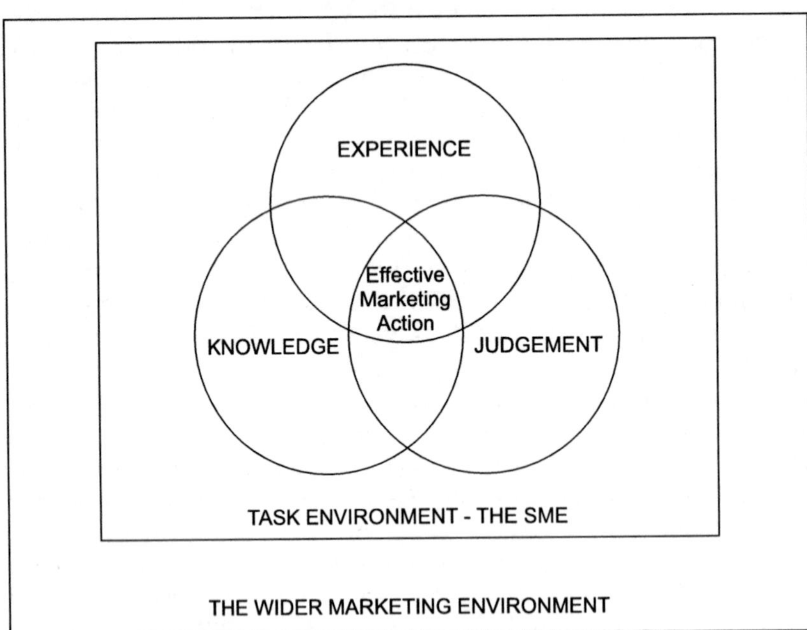

Figure 1.
A model of marketing competency inseparability

The sales orientation of SMEs

There was a strong sales orientation in all of the research companies and the data analysis allowed for the identification of three types of sales person operating within the SME context. These are the entrepreneurial sales person, the ambitious/career sales person and the long service sales person. Whilst there was evidence of all three types throughout the companies a significant finding is that the entrepreneurial sales person is the predominant type and is most representative of the type of selling activity practiced in SMEs. The interpretation here is that not only is a sales orientation a crucial area of SME strategy, but it is, as Comer and Dubinsky (1985) suggest, "the driving force behind many organisations today". Several other interpretations pertain to the entrepreneurial sales person.

The entrepreneurial sales person is loud, displays high levels of competency in commitment, is aggressive, opportunistic, highly motivated, and high in the competencies of vision, creativity and intuition. The entrepreneurial aspect to sales concurs with much of what the literature has to say about the entrepreneurial personality. Jarillo (1988) and Gartner (1989) describe a highly motivated individual, driven by the pursuit of opportunity, bubbling with creativity. The notion of an entrepreneurial sales person in the SME also relates to the idea espoused by Brockhaus and Horwitz (1986) that there are no significant differentiating features between entrepreneurs and small business owners or managers. The aspects of commitment, aggression, creativity and vision, for example, relate to the work of Bird and Jelinek (1988) who espouse the creative and visionary aspect of entrepreneurship, whereas commitment and aggression are particular features of "psychodynamic" models of the entrepreneurial personality (Kets de Vries, 1977). Whilst there are many similarities between the literature descriptions of the entrepreneur and the entrepreneurial sales person identified in the data, the key contribution of this finding is that an entrepreneurial type selling orientation is what characterises much of the marketing activities of SMEs. This relates to the Level 2 and 3 competencies discussed above.

Another interesting finding from this phase of the research is the positive impact of product quality on sales activity. Levels of sales person motivation increase significantly when the sales person has confidence in the product itself. The relationship between sales success and motivation is well documented (Chowdhury, 1993; Churchill *et al.*, 1985). Siminitirias and Cadogan (1994) note for example, that a dominant characteristic of most of the research undertaken in the sales setting is that sales behaviour is seen to be heavily dependent upon motivation. Whilst the literature recognises the importance of motivation to sales effectiveness there has been no study recognising the impact of product quality on the sales effort. This contribution, however, should take account of the contextual aspect of a large section of this data, that is, the agri-food sector, characterised to a large degree by traditional wholesale markets, where fresh quality produce is going to add a natural buzz to the sales effort.

The most significant finding from the data analysis though was that there clearly exists a core spectrum of personal competencies for selling in SMEs. This spectrum comprised knowledge, experience, judgement, communication ability, particularly a cluster of communication competencies focused on personal selling and a sales orientation, that is the relational communications cluster, commitment and confidence. The identification of a spectrum of sales competencies is not that surprising. Much work has been done in this area. Landmark studies such as those of Williams and Seminerio (1985), Phillips (1988), Weilbaker (1990), Hansen and Conrad (1991) and Flynn (1992) have all resulted in the generation of sales competency frameworks. The key issue here though is that not only does the spectrum of SME sale competencies concur for the most part with the generic frameworks, it bears a striking similarity with the spectrum of marketing competencies already identified as central to effective marketing in SMEs. The key interpretation, therefore, is that the reason that the sales competencies in SMEs are largely the same as the marketing competencies is a direct consequence of the predominant sales orientation of such firms. As suggested above, the Level 2 and Level 3 marketing competencies reflect an increased emphasis on sales irrespective of company demographics. This is a significant contribution to theory as although several studies have recognised the sales focus in SMEs, none has fully highlighted the significance of a selling orientation, nor indeed recognised how the sales orientation actually fashions the SME marketing competency spectrum.

One other interesting outcome in respect of sales competencies is the frequency of the interaction of the two competencies of knowledge and experience. The interpretation here is that knowledge is born of experience and that experience is the constructive and meaningful absorption of knowledge. In respect of personal selling the link between knowledge and experience is illustrated in Figure 2, the personal selling competency interaction continuum.

The important aspect of this continuum is that both experience and knowledge are vital competencies in respect of personal selling. In any given industry specific context, however, one or other will predominate. In respect of technical, product and industry problems, the competency of knowledge

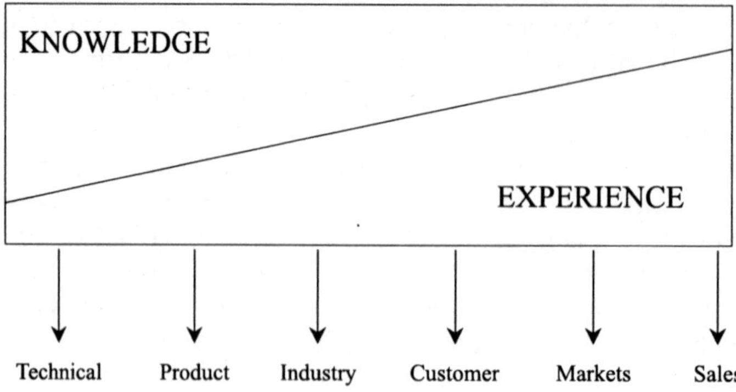

Figure 2.
The personal selling competency interaction continuum

dominates, whereas when it comes to dealing with markets, customers and making the sale, the value of "quality" experience is dominant. Effective selling in the SME, however, requires both competencies to some extent. Again, such an interpretation supports the contentions of the exploratory research.

Closely related to the competencies of knowledge and experience is the competency domain of judgement. Judgement is significant in that it was much more evident in respect of personal selling than it was in terms of marketing activities in a generic sense. The judgement competency is prevalent in this data in several ways. As identified by Hill and Fallis (1995), in their assertion that the judgement competency is key in the entrepreneurial decision-making process, the quality of good judgement is firmly embedded in a combination of other feeder competencies. These include the way in which sales people systematically gather and use market information discriminatingly, their capability to objectively analyse such information, the ability to analyse the results of their own actions and decisions and their ability to learn from experience in order to make better judgements in respect of key business decisions.

Another interesting and surprising finding of significance is that the data clearly recognises that sales people in SMEs, whilst sales driven, actually do focus to a large extent on the needs of the customer. Conventional textbook views suggest that a sales orientation focuses on the needs of the seller. In this research, however, a customer focus was facilitated through meaningful and sincere relationships with customers. This supports the contention of Jones (1996) who defines relationship marketing as the process of developing long-term, win-win relationships with valued customers, distributors, dealers and suppliers. He advocates what he calls relationship selling (see also Joshi and Stump, 1996 and Hall and Rao, 1993). Indeed, it was Levitt (1983, p. 111) who stated "... that the relationship between a seller and a buyer seldom ends when the sale is made ... The sale merely consummates the courtship. Then the marriage begins ...". The interpretation here is that the SME is perhaps especially adept at such consummation.

Marketing planning in SMEs

The findings with regard to marketing planning in this research enable several conclusions to be made. The first significant outcome is that companies did engage in fairly sophisticated marketing planning. There was some evidence of a non-planning culture in the operational practices of a few of the firms particularly, where opportunity focused individuals wielded much influence. All of the companies engaged in marketing planning with many committed to three year marketing plans. These plans were actually reviewed annually. The interpretation here is simple enough in that this dimension to their marketing reflects the professional influence of financial backers, government support agencies, company accountants and other backers. The more significant interpretation though is that in the respondent companies there was, in spite of such influences, a discernible commitment to planning. Respondents in this research clearly articulated an appreciation of its benefits and value.

As a general conclusion this contradicts previous studies into the nature of marketing planning in SMEs. Previous studies have argued that the marketing planning in SMEs is both under utilised and misunderstood (Mackintosh and Tynan, 1994; Dodge *et al.*, 1994; Watkins and Blackburn, 1986; Dunn *et al.*, 1986). Several reasons are offered to explain this shift towards an increased marketing orientation in such firms. First, most of the widely cited studies looking at marketing planning in small firms were carried out in the 1980s, and those that were conducted in the early and mid 1990s have tended to draw heavily on previous work, seeking to replicate or confirm the findings of such work rather than subject it to critical analysis. This research, however, reflects the status quo, in that today small firms are more likely to be populated with graduates with substantial theoretical knowledge of the tools and techniques of formal marketing. These graduates bring to SMEs new knowledge and put into practice the systems of planning that they have acquired. With practice they become good at this and gradually SMEs are growing in confidence in the marketing planning process. In addition, the typical constituents of a SME's formal network such as bankers, accountants and financial backers are demanding that SMEs produce formal plans that outline the direction in which the company is headed. They refuse to lend money unless there is evidence of an ongoing and realistic commitment to marketing planning. These two factors have impacted significantly on the marketing practices of such enterprises. In essence, environmental change has effected a change over a 15-year period in SME marketing practices. This has resulted in a gradual but clearly discernible shift to a higher level of marketing expertise and greater marketing competence in such firms.

The data indicated that not only did the firms engage in planning but that a particularly dominant aspect of planning was the issue of control and review of their activities. Much of the control was through formal reporting systems. Another significant aspect to control and review of their marketing was that the companies actually did take corrective action. It emerged that the firms continually sought ways to improve their marketing activities. This suggests a proactive aspect to marketing planning in SMEs which again contradicts much of what the literature states.

There are of course many small firms that do not engage in formal planning but the overwhelming evidence is that these are fast becoming the minority. This conclusion supports the assertion of Matthews and Scott (1995), that not only do small firms plan, but entrepreneurial firms engage in even more sophisticated planning. It also concurs with the view of Stokes (1995), in his description of the marketing paradox, that on the one hand marketing is regarded as the preserve of the large firm yet small firms are often the personification of the marketing concept.

One final interpretation in respect of a commitment to formal planning is that the commitment appears to be less related to the stage of a small firm's life cycle as described by Churchill and Lewis (1983), and Carson (1985; 1990). Carson (1990) suggests that there are four discernible stages in the evolution of marketing in the small firm. Notably he states that Stage 4, which he describes as integrated, proactive marketing, is the stage of firm evolution where the firm emerges with more sophisticated marketing planning and where the various elements of the marketing mix are coordinated into longer-term strategies. This research indicates that the types of marketing activity described in Carson's stages model are just as readily identifiable at any stage of a firm's life cycle. The assertion here is that whilst Stage 4 is a clear recognition of those firms that do engage in marketing planning, the first three stages are simply manifestations of marketing in practice or what Carson describes as operational marketing. A new contribution emerging from this work, therefore, is that the types of marketing described in the stages model are just as readily detectable at any stage of a firm's life cycle. They do not signify a lack of commitment to the planning process and any such assertion would appear from the evidence in this study to be speculative.

What can be concluded though, which supports Carson's research, is that the operational focus of marketing planning is very much in evidence. The nature of the businesses of the firms, the frenetic environments in which they operated dictated an operational focus. In addition, the methodology adopted here drew heavily on observational methods. Discussions and questionnaires conducted or administered by researchers tend to focus on marketing in practice dimensions. It is to be expected, therefore, that much data would point to operational issues. A further interesting aspect of this study, however, is that this informal aspect to marketing planning drew heavily on informal contact networks. The operationalisation of planning was clearly enhanced through the use of personal contacts.

Another important interpretation that emerged from the data is that SMEs display a propensity to plan in respect of their promotional activities. One of the main reasons for a commitment to promotional planning is as a direct consequence of relationships with other members of the firm's total distribution channel, for example, customers and suppliers. Formal alliances with such channel members were indisputably strategic. The implication, therefore, is that much of the marketing planning in SMEs is actually shaped by the marketing plans of customers and suppliers and vice versa. This particular aspect is quite novel and has not received any attention in the small firm's marketing literature. Integration of marketing channels has been addressed in the context of larger firms but there has not been any research focus on SMEs. It does, however, complement the assertions of Watkins and Blackburn (1986) and Kitchen and Proctor (1995) that the reasons why small firms are in any way responsive to marketing at all can be traced to a range of environmental factors. In this research the environment in which the small firm operates, particularly channel members in their microenvironments, constitutes a major influence on their marketing planning activity.

It would appear therefore that SMEs are focused and strategic in their marketing orientation. In addition, the opportunity focus so characteristic of the entrepreneurial firm is enhanced through such a commitment to planning and, rather surprisingly, in no way diluted. It is also important to note that many of the individuals who contributed to this data had no direct responsibility for developing the companies' marketing plans. Their roles tended to be operational. It is reasonable to infer therefore, that marketing planning is perhaps even more prevalent than the data suggests. One final point of summary would be that the industry specific aspect of the data brings with it settings that are operationally contextual. This creates an image of marketing planning activity as predominantly operationally focused. This however, is an erroneous deduction because it is only the dynamics of the industry specific aspects in this phase of the data that creates this impression. The food sector is a frenetic business environment constantly buffeted and shaped by industry and environmental dynamics. Consequently, it is logical that an operational focus should be very evident, even if unrepresentative, of the actual picture.

Personal contact networking

The first point with regard to personal contact networks is that the data analysis illustrated that they play a significant role in the marketing activities of SMEs. The SMEs in this study showed a strong tendency to use networks freely. Since Szarka (1990) drew management researchers' attention to the issue of PCNs there has been considerable work examining this phenomenon in all manner of organisations. Much of this work has focused on strategic networks and strategic collaboration (Jarillo, 1988) but a range of studies has considered the role of networks in the entrepreneurial process (Birley, 1985) and in the context of the small firm (Coviello and Munro, 1995; Carson *et al.*, 1995). Whilst this research supports the contentions of this work it still makes a worthwhile contribution to our understanding of how such networks operate. The SMEs in this study, for example, showed a strong tendency to use contact networks freely. Indeed, a reasonable interpretation from this research would be that all manner of decision-making in respect of marketing activities was distinctly characterised by the use of networks. It can be concluded, therefore, that using personal networks enhances the quality of marketing decisions in SMEs. This concurs with the conclusions of Webster (1992) and Hill and McGowan (1996) that contact networks actually enhance and add quality to marketing decisions in SMEs.

An interesting outcome of this research was a particular recognition that the personal selling environment is also strongly characterised by the frequent use of personal networks. Networks in the selling circumstance were characterised by high levels of trust. This supports previous studies of Jarillo (1988) and Szarka (1990). Bird (1989) also stated, for example, that networks require reciprocity, which is giving as well as receiving. An interesting contribution to theory here is that whilst the literature is replete with studies which stress the social interaction dimension to sales (Ruth, 1997), there is little evidence to suggest that informal or formal contact networks are a means to facilitate such interaction. The interpretation here is that if buyer-seller communication is enhanced through increased use of networks then the firm's offering can best be tailored to the unique needs of each market segment.

Previous studies (Coviello and Munro, 1995) have indicated that SMEs tend to use networks informally. Hill and McGowan (1996) addressed this aspect and advocated the need to create a competency in networking capability in SMEs. This study however provides an interesting insight in that it indicates that SMEs actually see serious value in their formal networks. A clear conclusion from the data was that formal networks are deemed a necessity. They are the *de facto* operating system of the firm. In spite of their entrepreneurial character and the literature assertions as to their proclivity towards informality the SMEs displayed significant maturity in their implicit and explicit appreciation of the value of such entities. They attempted to manage their networks to gain business advantage through better quality information for example, and to gain a better understanding of customer needs and wants, increased awareness of changes in the supply channel and a greater understanding of competitor activity.

The research however threw up a strange paradox in respect of the value of the SMEs' formal networks. There was a definite desire on behalf of the research companies not only to actively engage their formal network but to informalise such networks. The efforts of the companies in this research were firmly focused on moving contacts as speedily as possible along a continuum from formal to informal. In this sense there is evidence to indicate that engaging in personal contact networking overlaps considerably with aspects of relationship marketing and the competency cluster of relational communication. It therefore represents many of the characteristics associated with effective personal selling. The important distinction though is that within the companies in this study there is both an implicit and explicit appreciation of the value of the networks that exist. The data suggests that informal networks form an important influence on the decision-making processes of the SME.

Another interesting aspect to emerge is the extent to which this data supports previous studies as to the use of personal contact networks for information gathering. Joyce *et al.* (1995) and Szarka (1990) stress the value of contact networks in information trading. Whilst the constituent members of such networks often belong to the informal or formal contacts of the information seeker the networks themselves differ in that they have a total information seeking character. As a consequence they often lapse into one-way information flows. It can be suggested, therefore, that this information gathering aspect is the sole reason for the existence of many personal contact networks in the first place. In this respect they have been classified as occasional networks or networks that are machiavellian in character.

An interesting interpretation in respect of contact networks in this research was that such networks are, in spite of their informality, context bounded. The further removed from the actual context of the network, for example in the agrifood sector, in the fruit and vegetable wholesale markets, then the weaker the actual network ties. In a similar vein, the data supported the notion that contact networks are heavily invested in the individual. They cannot be passed on or inherited. A person can be introduced to another individual's contacts but this does not mean that they can activate the network to which they belong. Networks cease when the individual leaves the context in which the network actually exists. Some personal friends will of course remain but the network make-up becomes defunct.

In terms of conducting specific marketing activity there is evidence to indicate the extensive use of networks for price related activities. Price setters almost instinctively know precisely what information to look for and where in the network to go for this. This is also an important contribution to our understanding of the way in which networks are used and no major work has looked at the role of networks in relation to the performance of specific marketing mix activities.

One new insight to SME networking is detectable in a network type that has not received any research attention. This is categorised here as a "virtual network". Such a network type is again particularly prevalent in the fruit and vegetable wholesale markets. This network type is different in that its constituent parts are not necessarily the actors of the usual formal or informal contact network. The constituent parts are just as likely to be aspects of the marketing context and environment. An experienced fruit and vegetable market trader, for example, can walk on to the fruit market in the morning and within minutes can determine what sort of day's trading lies ahead. Constituent parts of such a network might be the weather, the pace of initial trade, the political climate, brief conversations with early customers or delivery men, a phone call or any number of contact points, only some of which are capable of being observed. An interpretation here is that such a network of contact points serves to enhance some intuitive knowledge grounded in "quality" experience. This type of network has not been addressed in the research literature.

Given the underlying marketing decision-making theme that permeates all aspects of this study it was important to briefly consider the findings with respect to this aspect.

Marketing decision-making in SMEs

The first conclusion in respect of marketing decision-making in the research companies is that the majority of the decisions taken are operationally focused. The observable side of marketing in SMEs is simply the operationalisation of strategic marketing decisions, in other words very much the tactical implementation of marketing planning. An important interpretation here is that studies which examine the marketing activities of SMEs and that conclude that SMEs tend to be very operationally focused are inaccurate if they are over concentrating on one dimension of such firms' activities. Such an operational focus does not in any way negate the importance of such decisions. Indeed, the conclusion serves to reinforce the assertion of Drucker (1967) that managerial decisions may be made as a matter of routine with the manager perhaps not even realising that he is making them. Drucker notes that even routine decisions may affect the future existence of the enterprise and require years of systematic analysis. An important interpretation here would be that SME decision-making can, as Simon (1960) suggested, be defined as a continuum ranging from routine programmed decisions to unpredictable, non-programmed or intuitive decisions. It is suggested here that non-programmed and intuitive decisions are entrepreneurial in character.

Another interpretation from the data in respect of marketing decision-making would be the influence that the level of risk involved has on the very nature of SME decision-making. Risk taking has long been associated with the entrepreneurial personality. Hisrich (1988), for example, defines the entrepreneur in terms as one who takes social, psychological and financial risks to create something new, to achieve independence and financial rewards. Others discuss the risk-taking dimension of the entrepreneurial personality, such as Newton (1991), Sexton and Bowman (1985) and Casson (1982). What these studies do not do, however, is show that the high risk in terms of marketing decision-making means more joint/shared marketing decisions will occur. This contradicts a popular view (Carson, 1985; 1990) that decision-making in small firms tends to be impulsive, haphazard and *ad hoc*. Decisions are shared in most instances and the higher the level of complexity of the decision then the more consultation will be engaged in.

It is noteworthy that joint marketing decisions are characteristic of the SME. These are implicit in the strategic alliances which the respondent companies engaged in. This formal decision-making, however, is secondary to ongoing consultation with a clearly identifiable set of people. The interpretation here is that SME decision-makers engage constituents of their contact networks to enhance or augment their decision-making quality. Whilst in the main the contacts, in terms of decision-making, tend to be informal, in certain circumstances they will be formal. In general, it can be said that much joint decision-making takes place in and as a consequence of the total distribution channel.

Finally, risk was especially detectable in two specific activities of the SMEs in this research. These were the buying process and the setting of prices. This might however be a reflection of the context of these decisions. The food supply sector is particularly price sensitive and fussy in its buying habits. There is no loyalty, with even what would be termed loyal customers, exhibiting a tendency to shop around.

This finding again illustrates the important role relational communication has, not only in terms of facilitating contact network development and maintenance, but also in terms of enhancing the marketing decision-making processes of SMEs.

A holistic interpretation of the data

Each "a priori" and emergent research objective provided valuable insight to an important aspect of SME marketing. Specifically, insight and understanding was gained in respect of the core marketing competencies, the strong sales orientation and the sales competencies of such firms. In addition, insight and understanding were gained in respect of the nature and use of personal contact networks in SMEs and the character of their marketing decision-making processes.

The key holistic interpretation therefore is that SME marketing is shaped by a range of influencing elements and that whilst each individually gives some insight to SMEs, it is only by considering these elements holistically that a true picture of SME marketing can be established.

The marketing competency aspect of this study highlighted a core spectrum of key marketing competencies. The strong sales orientation and the resultant focus on personal selling emerge as significant factors. A further outcome from these two sections is recognition and definition of the overlap between the key marketing competencies and the sales competencies of the sample firms. The overlap is significant but is largely evident in the two Level 2 competency clusters of "relational communication" and "commitment". These clusters not only determine the Level 3 competencies of "marketing in practice" but shape and are shaped by a propensity to engage in personal contact networking and also by the sales orientation of the firms. These Level 3 competencies (see Table I) in turn impact on the nature of marketing decision-making in SMEs and the nature of marketing decisions influences sales. The sales orientation in turn helps to determine the core SME competencies. The key elements of SME marketing, which were discussed, impact on each other in a circular way.

In summary, it is an integrated and holistic set of activities that characterises and determines SME marketing. A holistic model of SME marketing was developed (see Figure 3) which draws together the key determinants of SME marketing as identified in this research. The model illustrates SME marketing as an integrated whole. Each component element of the model impacts on and is impacted on by other elements. The model illustrates how SME marketing is determined by a core spectrum of marketing competencies. This core competency spectrum is largely determined by the strong sales and personal selling orientation of such companies. In particular, sales and marketing are both characterised by Level 3 marketing competencies, which are consequent on the presence of the Level 2 transitional competencies of "relational communication" and "commitment". It is these Level 2 and 3 competencies that enable effective personal contact networking to occur and an effective selling orientation and sales competencies are dependent on effective networking. The strong sales orientation means that the marketing decision-making behaviour of SMEs tends to be operational in character. Similarly, the strong sales orientation, since it is dependent on effective personal contact networking, determines the Level 2 and 3 marketing competencies that in turn determine the SME marketing competency spectrum. In every way therefore,

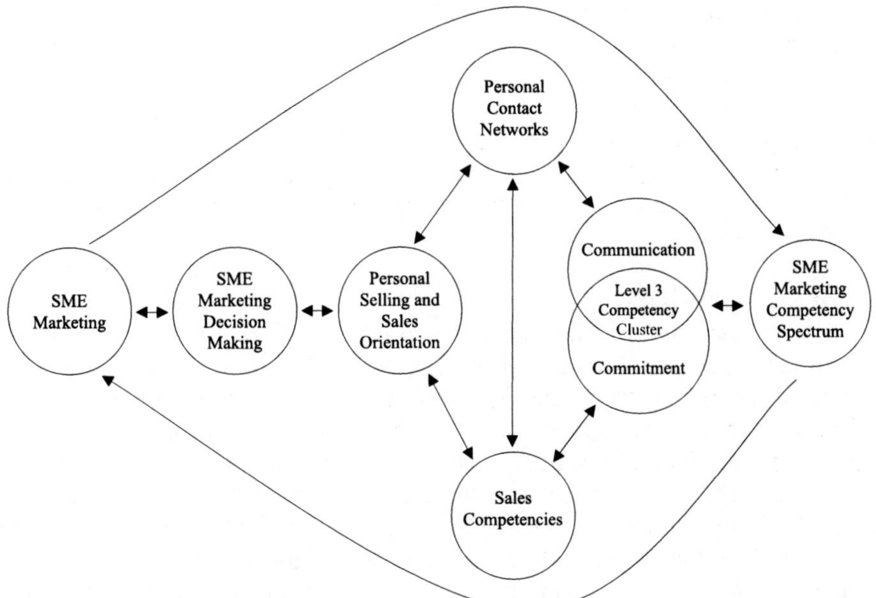

Figure 3.
A holistic model of SME marketing

the elements are interdependent. Each element helps to determine the character of the other elements in some way.

It is impossible to determine a starting point. It is simply an integrated whole and to fully understand the character of SME marketing means that all of the elements must be viewed in such a holistic manner. The model is neither overwhelmingly entrepreneurial nor a reflection of conventional marketing. In a sense if the disciplines of marketing and entrepreneurship are viewed as parent disciplines of SME marketing then the character of SME marketing has inherited the genes of both. The emphasis may, dependent on the circumstances and context of any one SME, be on a particular element or elements of the model, but the interrelated and integrative aspect will always be evident.

The holistic model of SME marketing is in itself a major contribution to theory. Whilst SME marketing has been addressed in several textbooks and formed the subject of several research studies, no study has depicted such a holistic perspective. Each of the elements and some limited combinations thereof have been examined but no study has looked at a comprehensive range of elements in such a holistic manner.

This model, for example, incorporates and embraces the sales orientation as a key determinant of SME marketing. It does not attempt to shunt the sales focus into the general "box of activities" which are the preserve of the promotional "P" of the marketing mix. It instead, links the SME and entrepreneurial sales orientation to personal contact networking, to a set of three core marketing competency spectra which determine and overlap with a spectrum of sales competencies. It clearly illustrates how SME marketing decision-making reflects an operational character as a consequence of these elements but also reflects a clear recognition of the too often unnoticed strategic significance of such decisions.

In summary, it is an integrated and holistic set of activities that characterises and determines SME marketing. The individual determinants of such marketing, whilst capable of providing insights such as those detailed in this monograph, are so much more meaningful and insightful when considered in a holistic sense.

Major contributions

This study has examined the nature of marketing in SMEs in significant depth over an extended period of time. It sought to provide an in-depth and detailed picture of the key determinants of marketing in such enterprises. Aside from the exploratory work detailed in Part 1 of this monograph, the research objectives drew on an extensive range of literature sources to determine the initial research objectives. These initially were focused on determining a definitive framework of marketing competencies for SMEs, determining the extent to which formal and conventional marketing processes are practiced by SMEs and examining ways in which SME decision-makers actually go about making marketing decisions. As a consequence of the inductive aspect of the work two further research objectives emerged which focused on determining the extent of the sales orientation in SMEs and gaining insight to the use and character of the contact networks of the individuals who manage such enterprises.

To realise these objectives a post positivist research methodology was established which was firmly characterised by the qualitative paradigm. The research approach was both deductive and inductive but justified in the context of the research companies and the research respondents, as detailed in Part 1.

The key contributions of the research were as follows. First, the research confirmed that there exists a clear spectrum of SME marketing competencies as suggested in the exploratory research. This competency spectrum comprised three levels. Level 1 is composed of a core set of foundation competencies best described as strategic in focus. Level 2 competencies are like transitional linkage competencies that are manifest in a core set of Level 3 competencies that are required for effective marketing in practice in the SME. Not only is this a new insight but the fact that competencies actually filter out from Level 1 to Level 3 and not vice versa is a significant new contribution to our understanding of the nature of marketing competency in such firms.

Another significant contribution of this research has been to gain new insight to the importance of the sales orientation of SMEs. Previous research has considered the sales orientation as a significant aspect of marketing perhaps, but has failed to really recognise the fundamental significance of sales in the SME context. It is not some adjunct of marketing or part of the paraphernalia of the promotions mix but the central tenet of marketing in such enterprises. This contribution is reinforced by the determination of a core spectrum of sales competencies in SMEs. These show significant overlap with the marketing competency spectrum and thus it can be concluded that it is the sales orientation which actually determines the marketing competency spectrum and hence the marketing character of such firms.

A further contribution of this study was to recognise that SMEs do engage in formal and conventional marketing practices, notably marketing planning. Traditionally the literature has insinuated that the balance of SME marketing is tilted in all respects towards a strong operational focus. The previous research studies are right in their recognition of the extent of the operational focus but erroneous in the importance accorded to such activities. Largely as a consequence of methodologies employed in previous studies, there has been insufficient recognition of the reality that the operational focus is simply the manifestation of Level 3 marketing competencies, that is the filtering through to marketing practice of immense strategic marketing effort and marketing plans that are often quite comprehensive.

A further contribution of this research, in respect of personal contact networks, was a clear determination of their extensive use in SMEs. Much of this use is rooted in a strong sales orientation, a fact overlooked by previous SME studies. Some relational selling literature has regarded networks to a limited extent in the context of the larger firm but no one has considered their importance to sales and personal selling in the SME. Other points of significance are that contact networks in SMEs are forever moving on a continuum from formal to informal. The evidence clearly shows that the research respondents sought to informalise the formal contact networks.

Another contribution in respect of contact networks was the recognition of what has been dubbed here as the "virtual network". This type of network is clearly significant in the context of the SME but is disregarded by the literature. In summary, it clearly emerged that contact networks are a means by which SME decision-making can actually add quality to all manner of marketing decisions.

With regard to the particular processes of marketing decision-making in SMEs several points emerged as significant. First, the SME respondents made lots of what are determined as routine decisions. What is disregarded is the extent to which seemingly routine decisions actually become strategic or effect strategic change in the marketing practices of the SME. In addition, it is clear that the higher the risk attached to a marketing decision then the more a marketing decision-maker will consult his or her contact network. The entrepreneurial orientation of the SMEs in this research is predominant and it seems that such risk aversion is at variance with what the literature has to say in terms of risk and entrepreneurial behaviour. This, therefore, is a significant new insight.

Given the nature of the qualitative methodology it is perhaps apposite to make a few comments as to its efficacy and general suitability to this research. The methodology was extremely effective. It allowed for close examination of the predetermined research phenomena as well as allowing new and important research issues to emerge. The most important contribution with respect to the research methodology in this study is that whilst the research was conducted and information gathered under the auspices of a constructivist paradigm the analysis was more conformist. This little internal paradox of research positions presented no difficulties other than bouts of what can best be described as researcher guilt on account of being a little unfaithful to the constructivist paradigm. It did work effectively however, and makes an interesting and worthwhile contribution to the range of available research methodologies for investigating marketing phenomena in SMEs.

The most significant contribution of the research has been the development of a holistic model of SME marketing. This marketing is an integrated complex of the variables detailed above and is representative of marketing that is entrepreneurial in character. There is the temptation to dub this marketing as entrepreneurial marketing but to do so would conjure up images of chaotic and haphazard activities. SMEs are clearly more measured and polished in respect of their marketing activities. They are of course inheritors of significant entrepreneurial characteristics and manifest themselves in much of what they do. The model therefore simply illustrates that what this study identified was not entrepreneurial marketing but SME marketing.

Implications for SME policy and practice

This study enables certain conclusions to be made with regard to issues of policy and practice for SMEs.

The first implication concerns government bodies with a remit to develop marketing in SMEs. As a consequence of this research it could be argued that standard and conventional marketing training programmes will have limited effect and their value would be short lived. The recommendation here is for programmes aimed at developing and enhancing core competencies in SME personnel and thereby releasing or facilitating enhanced marketing skills in the process.

Similarly, there needs to be a stronger recognition of the sales orientation of SMEs. There is insufficient recognition of the extent to which sales influences the character of SME marketing. This study does not regard this sales orientation as problematic for the development of such enterprises. On the contrary it recommends that the sales orientation be fully embraced by government bodies, management educators and academic researchers seeking to improve the marketing fortunes of SMEs.

Whilst there has been some recognition in the literature of the value of using personal contact networks to enhance and add value to SME marketing decisions there has been a general failure by SME policy makers to fully recognise the important role that networks play in their development. Hill and McGowan (1996), for example, stressed the need to develop a competency in personal contact networking for small firms. The implication here is that SMEs have got to recognise and be taught to recognise the value of contact networks. Training programmes are required which take account of the SME circumstance, perhaps something along the lines of work-based learning, which will facilitate the development of a networking competency.

A further implication from this work is that SMEs that recognise the value of conventional marketing practice such as the marketing planning process need to be encouraged to continue in their development and use of such formal marketing practices. Marketing practitioners and educators need to realise that the circumstances of the SME are as suitable for the application and use of formal marketing techniques as any other enterprise.

A final implication for the academic research community is that when investigating or studying marketing phenomena within the SME context a qualitative methodology is effective. What is important is getting in close to the companies and close to the research respondents and to be able to observe SMEs over time. The qualitative approach used here was effective in this respect. Traditionally, SME policy makers have tended to use quantitative surveys to examine the activities of SMEs. Consequently, it is suggested here that they add a range of qualitative methods to their methodological toolbox.

Future research directions

This study has extended and contributed to the literature and theories that exist in respect of the nature of marketing in SMEs. As it is the first to develop a holistic model comprising the elements presented in Figure 2 some of the aspects are not as tightly defined as perhaps desirable. Further research is required in several areas.

First, the holistic model should be tested across a range of industry sectors. This would allow for some determination on the possible effect of the characteristics of the agri-food sector on the model itself.

Second, although the firms selected for this research were international in terms of some aspects of their activities it would be interesting to verify the model through an international study. This would determine the extent of the impact of culture, if any, on SME marketing style.

Third, further research is required to clarify the linkage between sales and marketing competencies in SMEs and how such competencies relate to entrepreneurial competency frameworks? Future research needs to consider in what ways might such competencies help to determine whether a sales, a marketing or an entrepreneurial orientation predominates in the SME.

Fourth, it would be important to examine the competency model presented in Table I in the context of life cycle models of the SME. Can, for example, a relationship be established between the various levels of marketing competency and stage of the firm's life cycle or are life cycle models relevant at all when determining the nature of SME marketing?

Fifth, some clinical research focused on how to develop the key foundation marketing competencies would be useful. There is an urgent need to determine effective means of developing competent marketing managers and marketing decision-makers in SMEs. Some experimentation with work-based approaches, evaluated through qualitative methods would appear to be a useful starting point for such research. Similarly, work-based programmes aimed at developing a competency in contact networking would be useful. Longitudinal studies into the efficacy of such approaches would make a valuable contribution to marketing education.

Summary

In this research study an in-depth and longitudinal investigation of the nature of SME marketing was undertaken. The research agenda was both deductive and inductive. The initial research objectives were expanded as a consequence of the inductive character of the research. Consequently, the study ended up focusing on the following areas. These were marketing competencies in SMEs, the sales orientation of SMEs, the nature and use of personal contact networks in SMEs, the nature of marketing planning in SMEs and finally, decision-making in SMEs. The research issues were fully investigated and the insights provided allowed for the development of a holistic model of SME marketing. This model provides a range of new insights to the nature of SME marketing.

References

Adizes, I. (1989), *Corporate Lifecycles: How and Why Corporations Grow and Die and What to Do About It*, Prentice-Hall, Englewood Cliffs, NJ.

Agor, W.H. (1984), *Intuitive Management: Integrating Right and Left Brain Management Skills*, Prentice-Hall, Englewood Cliffs, NJ.

Bird, B.J. (1989), *Entrepreneurial Behavior*, Scott Foreman, Glenview, Illinois, pp. 295-8.

Bird, B. and Jelinek, M. (1988), "The operation of entrepreneurial intentions", *Entrepreneurship Theory and Practice*, Winter, pp. 21-9.

Birley, S. (1985), "The role of networks in the entrepreneurial process", *Journal of Business Venturing*, Vol. 1, pp. 107-17.

Boyatzis, R.E. (1982), *The Competent Manager: A Model for Effective Performance*, John Wiley, New York, NY.

Brockhaus, R.H., Sr and Horwitz, P.S. (1986), "The psychology of the entrepreneur," in Sexton, D.L. and Smilor, R.W. (Eds), *The Art and Science of Entrepreneurship*, Ballinger, Cambridge, pp. 25-48.

Carson, D.J. (1985), "The evolution of marketing in small firms", *European Journal of Marketing*, Vol. 19 No. 5, pp. 7-16.

Carson, D.J. (1990), "Some exploratory models for assessing small firms' marketing performance (a qualitative approach)", *European Journal of Marketing*, Special issue, Vol. 24 No. 11.

Carson, D.J. (1993), "A philosophy of marketing education in small firms", *Journal of Marketing Management*, Vol. 9 No. 2, pp. 189-205.

Carson, D.J., Cromie, S., McGowan, P. and Hill, J. (1995), *Marketing and Entrepreneurship in SMEs: An Innovative Approach*, Prentice-Hall, London.

Carson, D.J., Hill, J. and McGowan, P. (1994), "In pursuit of entrepreneurial marketing management competencies", in Hills, G.E. and Mohan-Neill, S.T. (Eds), *Research at the Marketing/Entrepreneurship Interface*, AMA, University of Illinois at Chicago, Chicago, IL, pp. 76-9.

Casson, M. (1982), *The Entrepreneur, An Economic Theory*, Oxford Press.

Chowdhury, J. (1993), "The motivational impact of sales quotas on effort", *Journal of Marketing Research*, Vol. 30, February, pp. 28-41.

Churchill, N.C. and Lewis, V.L. (1983), "The five stages of small business growth", *Harvard Business Review*, May-June, pp. 30-49.

Churchill, G.A., Jr, Ford, N.M., Hartley, S.W. and Walker, O.C., Jr (1985), "The determinants of salesperson performance: a meta analysis", *Journal of Marketing Research*, Vol. 22, May, pp. 103-18.

Comer, J.M. and Dubinsky, A.J. (1985), *Managing the Successful Sales Force*, D.C. Heath, Lexington, MA.

Coviello, N. and Munro, H.J. (1995), "Growing the entrepreneurial firm: networking for international market development", *European Journal of Marketing*, Vol. 29 No. 7, pp. 49-61.

Dodge, H., Fullerton, S. and Robbins, J. (1994), "Stage of the organisational life cycle and competition as mediators of problem perception for small businesses", *Strategic Management Journal*, Vol. 15, pp. 121-34.

Drucker, P.F. (1967), *The Effective Executive*, Pan, London.

Dunn, M., Birley, S. and Norburn, D. (1986), "The marketing concept and the smaller firm", *Marketing Intelligence and Planning*, Vol. 4 No. 3, pp. 3-11.

Ennis, S. (1999), "Growth and the small firm: using causal mapping to assess the decision-making process – a case study", *Qualitative Market Research: An International Journal*, Vol. 2 No. 2, pp. 147-60.

Flynn, D. (1992), "Ireland's second rate sales staff", *Business and Finance*, 26 March, pp. 13-17.

Gartner, W.B. (1989), "Who is the entrepreneur? Is the wrong question", *Journal of Entrepreneurship Theory and Practice*, Vol. 13 No. 4, Summer, pp. 49-56.

Greiner, L.L. (1972), "Evolution and revolution as organizations grow", *Harvard Business Review*, Vol. 50 No. 4, July-August, pp. 37-46.

Hall, M.C. and Rao, C.P. (1993), "An integration of buyer-seller relationships and perceived risk in industrial marketing", in the *Proceedings of AMA Summer Educators' Conference*, pp. 19-20.

Hansen, C.P. and Conrad, K.A. (1991), "Issues in the selection and development of professional salespeople", Hansen, C.P. and Conrad, K.A. (Eds), *A Handbook of Psychological Assessment in Business*, Quorum Books, New York, NY, pp. 170-81.

Hardy, K.G. (1992), "Marketing competencies for every manager", *Business Quarterly*, Winter, pp. 51-3.

Harper, S.C. (1988), "Intuition: what separates executives from managers", *Business Horizons*, September-October, pp. 13-19.

Hill, J. and Fallis, A. (1995), "An investigation into the scope and nature of marketing management competencies for entrepreneurial decision making decision making in small firms", in Hills, G.E., Muzyka, D.F., Omura, G.S. and Knight, G.A. (Eds), *Research at the Marketing/Entrepreneurship Interface*, American Marketing Association, University of Illinois at Chicago, Chicago, IL, pp. 137-56.

Hill, J. and McGowan, P. (1996), "Marketing development through networking: a competency based approach for small firm entrepreneurs", *Journal of Small Business and Enterprise Development*, Vol. 3 No. 3, pp. 148-57.

Hill, J. and McGowan, P. (1999), "Small business and enterprise development: questions about research methodology", *International Journal of Entrepreneurial Behaviour and Research*, Vol. 5 No. 1, pp. 5-18.

Hisrich, R.D. (1988), "The entrepreneur in N. Ireland: characteristics, problems and recommendations for the future", *Journal of Small Business Management*, July, Vol. 26, pp. 32-9.

Hogarth, R.M. (1987), *Judgement and Choice*, John Wiley and Sons, Chichester.

Jarillo, J.C. (1988), "When small is not enough: how to save entrepreneurs from themselves", *European Management Journal*, Vol. 6 No. 4, pp. 325-9.

Jones, E. III (1996), "A model of vendor loyalty in a buyer-seller relationship", in Droge, C., Catalone, R., Gordon, P.J. and Kellerman, B.J. (Eds), *Enhancing Knowledge Development in Marketing, The Proceedings of the AMA Summer Educators' Conference*, Vol. 7, pp. 128-9.

Joshi, A.W. and Stump, R.L. (1996), "Supplier opportunism: antecedents and consequences in buyer-seller relationships", in Droge, C., Catalone, R., Gordon, P.J. and Kellerman, B.J. (Eds), *Enhancing Knowledge Development in Marketing, The Proceedings of the AMA Summer Educators' Conference*, Vol. 7, pp. 129-35.

Joyce, P., Woods, A. and Black, S. (1995), "Networks and partnerships: managing change and competition", *Journal of Small Business and Enterprise Development*, Vol. 2 No. 1, March, pp. 11-18.

Kets De Vries, M.F.R. (1977), "The entrepreneurial personality: a person at the crossroads", *Journal of Management Studies*, Vol. 14, pp. 34-57.

Kirzner, I.M. (1979), *Perception, Opportunity, and Profit: Studies in the Theory of Entrepreneurship*, Chicago University Press, Chicago, IL.

Kitchen, P.J. and Proctor, R.A. (1995), "Adjusting to change: how small firms might get around the (potential) marketing myopia problem", *Journal of Small Business and Enterprise Development*, Vol. 2 No. 1, March, pp. 3-10.

Lank, A.G. and Lank, E.A. (1995), "Legitimizing the gut feel: the role of intuition in business", *Journal of Managerial Psychology*, Vol. 10 No. 5, pp. 18-23.

Levitt, T. (1983), *The Marketing Imagination*, The Free Press, New York, NY.

Luckmann, T. (1982), "Individual action and social knowledge", Von Cranach, M. and Harre, R. (Eds), *The Analysis of Action*, Cambridge University Press, Cambridge.

Mackintosh, S. and Tynan, C. (1994), "Assessing marketing planning in small firms using a focus group methodology", *Marketing: Unity in Diversity, Proceedings of The Marketing Education Group Conference*, University of Ulster, Coleraine, Vol. 2, pp. 587-96.

MacLaren, P., McGowan, P. and Hill, J. (1997), "Marketing education for small firm entrepreneurs: a work-based learning approach", *Marketing Education Review*, Special Issues on Research at the Marketing/Entrepreneurship Interface, Vol. 17 No. 3, pp. 39-46.

Martin, G. and Staines, H. (1994), "Managerial competences in small firms", *Journal of Management Development*, Vol. 13 No. 7, pp. 23-34.

Matthews, C.H. and Scott, S.G. (1995), "Uncertainty and planning in small and entrepreneurial firms: an empirical assessment", *Journal of Small Business Management*, October, pp. 34-53.

Middleton, B. and Long, G. (1990), "Marketing skills: critical issues in marketing education and training", *Journal of Marketing Management*, Vol. 5 No. 3, pp. 325-43.

Mole, V., Dawson, S., Winstanley, D. and Sherval, J. (1993), "Researching managerial competences," paper presented to British Academy of Management Annual Conference, Milton Keynes, September.

Newton, D. (1991), "Schumpeterian entrepreneurship versus intracorporate entrepreneurship: a differentiation based on risk transfer and assignment vesting", *Proceedings of Enterprising in Partnership with the Environment, International Council for Small Business*, Toronto, pp. 487-506.

Penley, L.E., Alexander, E.R., Jernigan, I.E. and Henwood, C.I. (1991), "Communication abilities of managers: the relationship to performance", *Journal of Management*, Vol. 17 No. 1, pp. 57-76.

Phillips, C.P. (1988), "The not-so-sweet sound of sales talk", *Training*, September, pp. 56-62.

Polanyi, M. (1967), *The Tacit Dimension*, Garden City, New York, NY.

Pye, A. (1991), "Management competence: the flower in the mirror and the moon on the water", in Silver, M. (Ed.), *Competent to Manage: Approaches to Management Training and Development*, Routledge, London.

Ray, D.M. (1993), "Understanding the entrepreneur: entrepreneurial attributes, experience and skills", *Entrepreneurship and Regional Development*, Vol. 5, pp. 345-57.

Ruth, A.G. (1997), "Human resource development in a pharmaceutical sales force", unpublished PhD dissertation, Fairfax University.

Schon, D.A. (1983), *The Reflective Practitioner*, Basic Books, New York, NY.

Sexton, D.L. and Bowman, N. (1985), "The entrepreneur: a capable executive and more", *Journal of Business Venturing*, Winter, pp. 129-40.

Simintiras, A.C. and Cadogan, J.W. (1994), "An experimental analysis of the impact of a behaviour modification programme on salespersons' effort and performance behaviours", *Marketing Unity and Diversity, Proceedings of the Marketing Education Group Annual Conference*, University of Ulster, Coleraine, pp. 843-53.

Simon, H.A. (1960), *The New Science of Management Decision*, Harper and Row, New York, NY.

Stevenson, H.H. and Gumpert, D.E. (1985), "The heart of entrepreneurship", *Harvard Business Review*, March-April, pp. 85-94.

Stokes, D. (1995), *Small Business Management: An Active-Learning Approach*, DP Publications Ltd, London.

Szarka, J. (1990), "Networking and small firms", *International Small Business Journal*, Vol. 8 No. 2, pp. 19-33.

Vesper, K. (1980), *New Venture Strategies*, Prentice Hall, Englewood Cliffs, NJ.

Watkins, T. and Blackburn, B. (1986), "The role of marketing in the small firm: evidence from a regional survey", *Marketing Intelligence and Planning*, Vol. 4 No. 4, pp. 26-38.

Webster, F.E. Jr (1992), "The changing role of marketing in the corporation", *Journal of Marketing*, Vol. 56, October, pp. 1-17.

Weilbaker, D.C. (1990), "The identification of selling abilities needed for missionary type sales", *Journal of Personal Selling and Sales Management*, Vol. X, Summer, pp. 45-58.

Williams, A.J. and Seminerio, J. (1985), "What buyers like from salesmen", *Industrial Marketing Management*, Vol. 14, pp. 75-8.

Zimmerer, T.W. and Scarborough, N.M. (1994), *Essentials of Small Business Management*, Macmillan, New York, NY.

Chapter 13

Marketing Competencies for Entrepreneurs

Objectives	**388**
Introduction	**389**
Management competency defined	**389**
Marketing competency defined	**389**
Entrepreneurial marketing competency defined	**390**
Judgement competency	**391**
Experience competency	**391**
Knowledge competency	**392**
Communication competency	**392**
Other predominant competencies	**393**
The nature of competencies	**394**
Entrepreneurial marketing management competency development	**395**
Summary	**400**
Learning questions	**400**

Objectives

After reading this chapter the reader will have an understanding of the scope and nature of entrepreneurial marketing management competencies in the SME context. In addition, the reader will be introduced to an approach to marketing competency development which takes account of the factors that characterize the entrepreneurial small firm scenario.

Introduction

This chapter begins with a brief review of our definitions of management, marketing and entrepreneurial marketing competencies. In particular, it examines the entrepreneurial marketing management competency spectrum as posited in Chapter 7 and explores how the elements of this spectrum impact on and manifest themselves in the marketing activities of SMEs. In addition the chapter explores the nature of these entrepreneurial marketing competencies, looking at such issues as competency interactions, in particular how certain competencies are interrelated and may be even interdependent. It addresses competency development and the sub-components and sub-elements that make up various competencies. Having explored the nature and makeup of entrepreneurial competencies we subsequently address the dimension of entrepreneurial marketing competency development in the SME context. In particular, the focus of such competency development seeks to create means by which the small firm entrepreneur can engage in the self-development of marketing competencies.

Management competency defined

Management competency has been defined by Boyatzis[1] as 'an underlying characteristic of a person which results in effective and/or superior performance in a job'. In addition, this text has acknowledged a definition of management competency which stresses competent management behaviour that is observable and demonstrable. A competent manager is an effective manager and management competencies are therefore the relevant qualities and management skills that lead to effective job performance. In relation to skills, it is worth restating that a management skill implies an ability which can be developed, not necessarily inborn, and which is manifested in performance, not merely in potential. This is an important aspect and one to which we shall return, given that this chapter also suggests an approach to competency development.

There are many management competency spectra and Chapter 7 presented a synthesis of these. It is worth noting that the range of competency frameworks available suggests that there is no general agreement in the field of management science about competency definition. What the existence of such frameworks does do, however, is suggest that there may be tasks and techniques common to all managers, but that these need to be applied to specific individual circumstances and situations before their appropriateness as descriptions of managerial competency can be assessed.

Marketing competency defined

If a management competency is the skill or ability that leads to observable and demonstrable effective and/or superior job performance, then a competent marketing manager is someone who possesses the relevant qualities and management skills that lead to effective performance of an enterprise's marketing activities. There is undoubtedly a varying degree of overlap in relation to the competencies required for the effective performance of both management and marketing tasks. The extent of this overlap will depend on the scope of management decisions for which the marketing manager has responsibility and how this impacts on other functional areas of the enterprise. It will also depend on a range of factors, including the background of the person performing the task, the task itself and the organizational environment.

Since marketing management focuses on decision-making in relation to an enterprise's marketing activities, we need to readdress briefly those general management competencies that are most appropriate for the marketing management function. We have debated this issue fully in an examination of management and marketing competencies in Chapter 7, where we suggested that there is a marketing management competency spectrum which is more appropriate to and consistent with good and effective marketing management decision-making. This spectrum of marketing competencies comprises vision, creativity, leadership, communication, motivation, initiative, intuition, adaptability, analytical skills and judgement. In essence, what is recognized is that many of the core generic management competencies are equally if not more applicable in the context of marketing.

Entrepreneurial marketing competency defined

So far we have explored the nature and characteristics of entrepreneurs and how these characteristics impact on the marketing activities of entrepreneurial owner-managed SMEs. Small firm characteristics have also been considered and the way these affect SME marketing activities has been examined. Consideration of such parameters enables the postulation of a set of marketing management competencies that would appear to be more suited to effective and/or superior marketing management decision-making in the SME context. As a consequence, in Chapter 7 it was suggested that there was an entrepreneurial marketing management spectrum dominated by the competencies of judgement, experience, knowledge and communication. To this spectrum we can add other entrepreneurial marketing management competencies such as motivation, planning and vision. Such a spectrum, it is argued, should be viewed as an integrative mix of attributes which, when used in a balanced way, will lead to improved decision-making in relation to the marketing activities of entrepreneurial owner-managed SMEs.

What is important here is to take a closer look at each of the entrepreneurial marketing management competencies within the spectrum and to establish the extent to which they manifest themselves in respect of SME marketing activities and, in particular, in respect of SME owner/managers' marketing decision-making.

Judgement competency

The judgement competency is crucial in the entrepreneurial marketing management decision-making processes. Entrepreneurs make marketing decisions based on a high degree of personal judgement. The competency is usually detectable in relation to marketing decisions affecting issues such as opportunity analysis, customer dimensions, product ranges and levels of service provided, etc. Inherent in this competency, for example, is the ability to identify a market opportunity and to be able to assess such an opportunity in the light of scarce company resources and perhaps to weigh up this opportunity against other attractive alternatives that might present themselves.

For many entrepreneurs however, judgement in respect of marketing decision-making seems to come as second nature, based on hunch, intuition and experience from finding themselves in similar circumstances over a number of years in the business. Therefore, SME entrepreneurs often exhibit high levels of product knowledge when it comes to making decisions about product modifications, for example, or customizing products or services for particular clients.

It can be seen that judgement, therefore, is closely related to the competency dimensions of experience and knowledge and many combinations of and interrelationships between these competencies are frequently evident and reflected through the manifestation of this particular competency in the marketing decisions of entrepreneurial SMEs. These dimensions will be explored below.

Experience competency

Experience is a key entrepreneurial competency. Although experience tends to be a dominant competency in the context of entrepreneurial marketing activity it is more usual for the competencies of experience, judgement and knowledge to be used together. A good example is that in times of heavy workload and pressure accurate prioritization of customers' orders without fear of customer dissatisfaction can occur. This entails a high level of knowledge of one's business, the firm's ability to satisfy customers and the ability to make sound judgements in such a scenario. Thus it is clear that these two important competency dimensions combine quite comfortably under the banner competency of experience.

The experience competency is usually evident in relation to a particular field of business – knowledge of who the main players are, for example. A more important aspect of the competency in relation to marketing is apparent in a high level of entrepreneurial confidence that individuals' wealth of experience enables them to predict how customers might react in certain circumstances, whether favourably or unfavourably. This type of expression of a key competence is refreshing in that it illustrates something more than an awareness of experience, being indicative of an ability to use, enhance and enrich experience through proactive marketing activity.

This asserts that the experience competency has a dynamic dimension in so far as it can constantly be refined and enriched with each experience. Indeed, one can contend that with the benefit of prior experience many entrepreneurial owner/managers are competent to deal with many marketing decisions, especially in relation to recurring events.

Knowledge competency

Knowledge is the fourth of our entrepreneurial marketing management competencies. Knowledge here refers in particular to knowledge of products and service ranges, markets, competitors, industry activity, emerging market trends and customers. It is fair to contend also that this competency is an essential dimension of the entrepreneurial marketing decision-making process. Typical SME entrepreneurs are highly competent to discuss their individual product ranges or to elaborate on each market segment in which they operate. SME entrepreneurs are generally competent to discuss markets, not only in geographical terms but also in terms of product usage and the breakdowns of each individual product line. They will talk knowledgeably about competitors and competitor activity. The key issue, however, is the fact that possessing this knowledge enables them to be more effective in relation to entrepreneurial marketing management decisions.

Evidence also indicates that entrepreneurs often attach importance to possessing the knowledge competency through an expression of their own shortcomings in aspects of marketing such as promotion or setting prices. Such individuals, it is suggested, feel less competent to take marketing decisions or engage in marketing activities in these areas about which they are less knowledgeable.

Communication competency

Communication is an essential competency for entrepreneurial marketing. The competency can be viewed from the two dimensions of communication in the SME context, that is, internal and external dimensions. Internally, the competency of communication is typically evident in the emphasis on staff and levels of staff awareness, staff confidence and entrepreneurial confidence. Externally, the key indicators of entrepreneurial style marketing communication emphasize customers, markets, suppliers, competitors and, of course, the formal actors of the entrepreneur's personal contact network. It is worth mentioning that both internal and external communications in SMEs can be viewed in many cases as proactive uses of the entrepreneur's personal contact network.

Entrepreneurs generally place a high degree of emphasis on the need for good communications internally and externally. Differences in the degree of emphasis are usually detectable though, and are generally dependent on the background of the individual entrepreneur. Those entrepreneurs who exhibit a strong sales orientation place more importance on external communications, especially those with customers. Others place a high value on internal communications and typically emphasize the need for healthy interaction with and among their staff. Such SME owner/managers believe that this proactive use of internal communications leads to improved business performance through better staff relations and see good internal relations as a mechanism for gathering vital information on key activities, for key marketing decisions and to stimulate innovation.

Finally, it can be asserted that communication is vital in relation to the whole process of entrepreneurial marketing decision-making. It can be argued, however, that when one considers the nature of communication in respect of SME marketing activities, it may depend on a range of component skills – e.g. knowledge, confidence, the ability to listen and to use simple and uncomplicated language, and the ability to use experience, judgement and knowledge. These sub-elements of the communication competency are notable; recognizing their existence is important in that such an understanding of competency makeup and building blocks can be used to aid entrepreneurial self-development of expertise.

Other predominant competencies

Additional entrepreneurial marketing management competencies such as motivation, planning and vision need to be examined briefly in terms of how they are evident in SME marketing activity.

> *Motivation.* Motivation is a vital entrepreneurial marketing management competency. As discussed in Chapter 6, entrepreneurs are a highly motivated group. Such motivation, however, manifests itself as job satisfaction, confidence, stamina, commitment, energy, a positive attitude and an unusually high level of task orientation in relation to performance of marketing activities.
>
> *Planning.* The ability to plan is also an important entrepreneurial competency. It is worth noting, however, that more so than any other competency planning can be broken down easily into component parts. Sub-elements can be identified as comprising organizing, opportunity analysis, implementation skills, analytical ability, judgement, experience, intuition, motivation, adaptability, etc. The planning competency, in other words, is a constellation of the other competencies discussed above.
>
> *Vision.* This is a key entrepreneurial marketing management competency. Entrepreneurship after all is characterized by vision and closely allied to the future focus dimensions of the entrepreneurial personality. Vision, in addition, is closely linked to judgement and planning, but it can none the less be viewed as a stand-alone competence. Typical entrepreneurial statements such as 'You always have to look ahead' typify this competency. In other instances vision is linked to innovation and creativity and the propensity to identify, grasp and exploit market opportunities or other opportunities for company development.

It is not being suggested here that entrepreneurial marketing management competencies are confined to those key issues addressed above. Such spectra, however, comprise many of the same elements and sub-elements as those discussed in this text.

The nature of competencies

We can now make a number of key points. First, there is a high level of interaction between the various competencies highlighted. The degree, level and extent of such interactions however, depends closely on the particular entrepreneurial marketing competencies in question and the nature of the specific marketing tasks to be undertaken.

In addition, our examination of marketing competency enables us to suggest, with a high degree of certainty, that entrepreneurial marketing competencies tend to be found in clusters or constellations with one particular competency dimension being dominant. The dominant competency will once again be dependent on the nature of the specific task being performed. These observations are critical to our understanding of marketing competency, especially so when considering issues pertaining to entrepreneurial marketing competency development. Each of these observations is therefore amplified below.

Competency interaction

An examination of entrepreneurial marketing competencies quickly supports the contention that they are not stand-alone entities. The highly interactive nature of entrepreneurial marketing competencies is clear when considering key marketing management issues. Take, for example, a few key marketing issues such as products, services, customers, markets, industry trends and specifics. These can all be assessed from the perspectives of knowledge, experience, judgement, etc. What is important is that the competencies must interact in relation to these marketing issues.

In certain circumstances issues relating to product/service and job specifics may lie largely in the competency domain of knowledge, whereas the parameters of market, industry activity and trends may largely lie in the domain of experience in other circumstances. Some specific parameters, however, are not indicative of any particular competence but rather are much more characteristic of the interaction between the two (or more) dimensions. This suggests that the ability to perform effective marketing activities in certain areas depends on having several key competencies.

Competency clusters

In assessing appropriate interactions of competencies it is useful to consider that competencies tend to be manifest in clusters of other competencies and skills. Indeed, each of the component parts of any entrepreneurial competency could be broken down into further clusters of competencies with the same key sub-elements recurring frequently (see Figure 13.1).

In this illustration the entrepreneurial marketing competency of judgement is the dominant one, but it does not stand alone in that it is closely related to the competencies of experience, knowledge, intuition, analytical skills and information

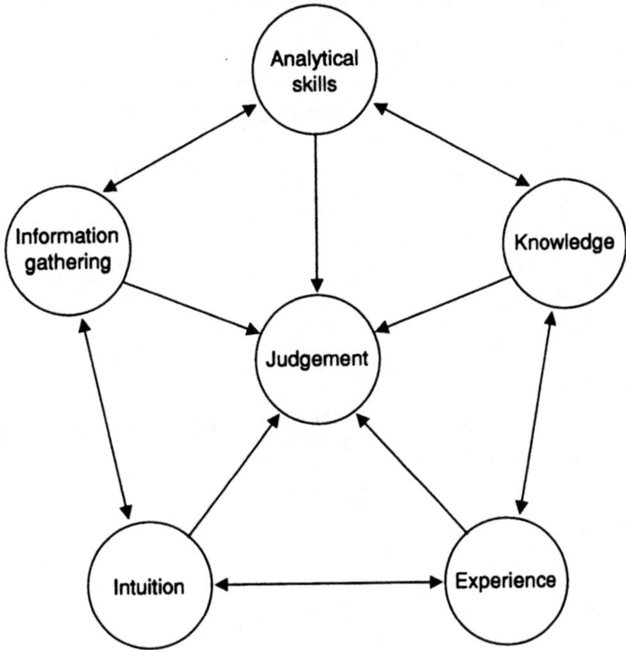

Figure 13.1 The 'judgement' cluster.

gathering. If the competency of knowledge was examined in the same way, then some of the competency elements, experience and information gathering for example, would undoubtedly recur. Such is the evidence of clusters of competencies interacting, that it is reasonable to assert that the predominant competency in any particular cluster depends on the marketing activity being undertaken and the specific environment in which an action occurs. This is illustrated in Figure 13.2, where we can see that the competencies of experience, knowledge and judgement are inseparable. This inseparability of competencies, it is suggested, is what actually results in effective performance of a specific job as opposed to acknowledging the possession of any one competency.

Having looked at the nature of entrepreneurial marketing management competency it is time to turn our attention to how these abilities might be developed in SME entrepreneurs.

Entrepreneurial marketing management competency development

First, it is important to accept that entrepreneurs and SME owner/managers have an inherent, common-sense knowledge of the marketing concept which can be realized

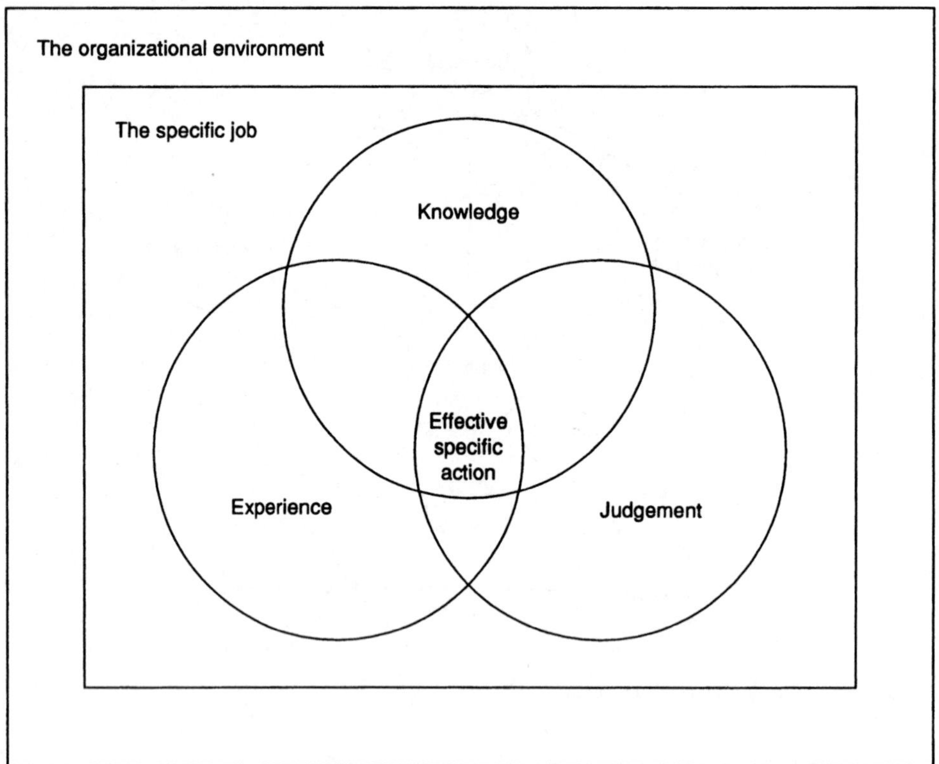

Figure 13.2 Competency inseparability.

through enhanced competency skills in marketing management. In addition, we must consider the nature of entrepreneurs and acknowledge that entrepreneurs engage in marketing, which is often implicit, often sophisticated but nearly always informal and not in line with the conventions of formal marketing. This means that there may be underlying dimensions of the entrepreneur which facilitate the self-development of these dimensions into marketing management competencies. Acknowledging this and having considered the nature of entrepreneurial marketing competencies and examined the nature of competency interactions and clusters, some suggestions can be made about ways in which these competencies can be developed. Account must be taken of these issues in addition to the issues already discussed; any focus on approaches to marketing competency development as a consequence need to be suitably tailored and sympathetic.

There have been many attempts to address competency development. A review of these techniques, however, suggests their inappropriateness for marketing management competency development. Nevertheless, one important dimension arising from previous work in this area is that it is clear that before developing competencies within any organizational system, the competencies needed must be identified and determined. It is also clear that the competencies to be developed are usually related to effective performance of a particular job within a specific organizational environment. Therefore, to be certain of effective competence development, competency frameworks need to be applicable to all jobs, job families and similar jobs with similar demands within the particular organization or enterprise. First and foremost, however, entrepreneurs must learn to recognize the competency that they wish to develop and understand how having this competency gives rise to effective and/or superior job performance.

The most effective approaches to marketing competency development in the entrepreneurial context, consequently, are rooted in some dimension of entrepreneurial self-assessment. This is important if individuals are to accept and acknowledge areas for personal development. Without self-assessment the entrepreneur is incapable of self-development as there is no self-recognition of competency weaknesses. In essence this means that entrepreneurs need to be able to recognize their own strengths and weaknesses in relation to marketing before being able to develop marketing skills in a positive way.

For self-development to occur in respect of marketing performance, entrepreneurs need to examine their own strengths and weaknesses when they carry out aspects of the enterprise's marketing activities. Some entrepreneurs, for example, regard themselves as very adept when dealing with customers; they pride themselves on the quality of such relationships. Others think of themselves as expert or highly qualified and capable as regards production processes and the quality of such processes. Others might regard themselves as having excellent judgement when it comes to making key marketing decisions and believe that such judgement is rooted in a vast reservoir of personal knowledge and experience.

On the other hand, some SME entrepreneurs readily recognize their own weaknesses. Experience indicates that those activities that entrepreneurs do not perform well are activities that they will tend to avoid in the day-to-day management of their enterprises. Specific to this discussion, some entrepreneurs regard themselves as weak in respect of various aspects of marketing activity. Some individuals feel that they do not communicate well with staff or customers. Others feel that they do not have a grasp of the financial side of their businesses; this might be rooted in self-doubt about their own analytical skills.

Entrepreneurial competency development, however, needs to go further than simply recognizing one's strengths and weaknesses and requires that the SME owner/manager fully explores these dimensions. This demands the entrepreneur to examine each strength and weakness thoroughly and examine the constituent and component elements of each. In other words, entrepreneurs must ask themselves why they are strong or weak at certain marketing activities. This enables them to focus on those sub-elements and aspects of each self-assessed strength which will be vital if they are subsequently to effect entrepreneurial marketing management competency development. Such a process is illustrated below in the case of an entrepreneur who, when exploring his own weaknesses, classes himself as a weak communicator. In particular, he classes himself as incompetent in relation to communicating with staff, customers and markets. When examining his strengths, however, he reckons that he possesses sound judgement, particularly in relation to decisions affecting the marketing development of his enterprise.

If one takes the two competencies being highlighted here – communication and judgement – and examines these in more detail (see Figure 13.3), it becomes clear that both are closely interrelated to a series of other competencies, competency sub-elements, characteristics and traits. In the case of communication the competency elements of information gathering, analytical skills and experience are evident. In the case of judgement the competency elements of discernment, experience and knowledge are evident.

What such a breakdown illustrates is that possessing the competencies of judgement and communication requires borrowing from other competencies/characteristics and traits such as experience, decision-making and judgement. By breaking down these two competencies it becomes clear that there is considerable overlap between the two. The entrepreneur needs to focus on these areas of commonality. By doing this in the manner illustrated in Figure 13.3, entrepreneurs will recognize that they possess abilities they did not know they had. They move from a state of being unconscious/competent to being conscious/competent.

In this example an immediate impact on the entrepreneurs' ability to communicate can be effected. In this illustration their ability to exercise sound judgement in

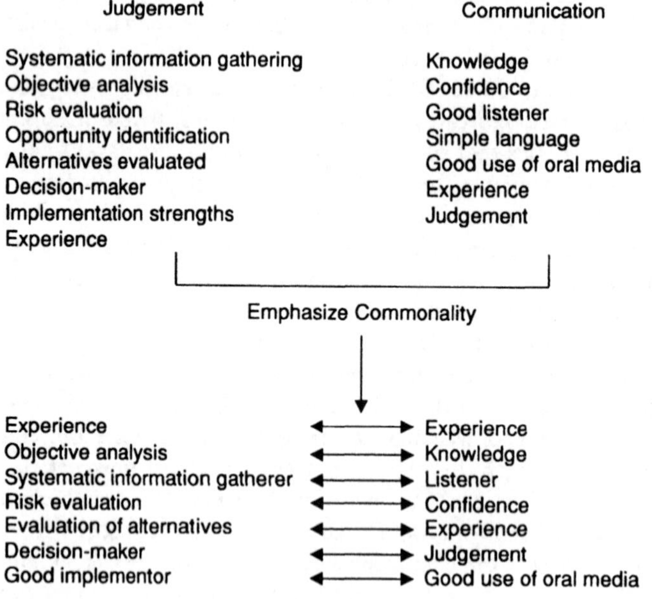

Figure 13.3 Entrepreneurial competency development.

relation to risk evaluation can be advocated as the potential catalyst for increasing personal confidence. Additionally, personal experience is common to the possession of sound judgement and to the ability to communicate; consequently, entrepreneurs are helped to realize that by concentrating on common strengths they can proactively address apparent weaknesses. This does not mean an immediate conversion of a former weakness into an entrepreneurial strength, but none the less it should still be viewed as a big stride forward in personal competency development. Much, of course, depends on the specific marketing management decision in question.

If, for example, an entrepreneur is considering the decision to launch an existing product into a new market, such a decision undoubtedly requires judgement (which in our example entrepreneurs possess) and the component elements of communication (which they feel that they do not possess). Experience is common to the possession of both competencies, objective analysis is not all that different from knowledge, systematic information gathering is allied to good listening skills, risk evaluation requires experience, making marketing decisions takes sound judgement and aspects of implementation of marketing activities require good use of oral media. Entrepreneurs realize that they actually do possess strengths of which they were unaware. These strengths allow entrepreneurs to begin to develop the sub-elements of the communication competency. Indeed, recognizing these competency sub-elements in the first place is a crucial step in their subsequent development. Here we see that by focusing and concentrating on natural strengths associated with judgement, entrepreneurs are actually honing their communication skills and abilities.

Through the application of the process as outlined above, entrepreneurs are helped to realize that all they need to do to develop their weaknesses is focus their strengths on developing the weaker areas. In this case the complementary skills are evident. These are experience, the ability to gather information, good decision-making ability and sound risk evaluation. Moreover, experience has shown that entrepreneurs are quick to realize and grasp an opportunity and do something positive if it will enable them to make better decisions – in this case more effective marketing decisions.

Other illustrations include recognizing that the vision competency in marketing may be developed by consideration of new domestic or international market opportunities; the creativity competency may be developed by consideration of new products and promotional ideas; and the communication competency may stimulate and enhance the company's message.

This approach touches on other issues relevant to the competency development debate. First, such competency breakdowns are dynamic in the sense that the composition of each breakdown changes and varies as a consequence of the specific marketing decision being taken. The competency sub-elements in the communication competency might vary from a circumstance of developing a sales lead to a situation involving information gathering in respect of competitors' activities.

This approach reinforces the other issues pertaining to the competency development debate. For example, it is clear from the illustration that competencies are highly interactive entities and that an emphasis on any particular dimension of competency will depend on the nature of the marketing decision being taken. Another issue which resurfaces here is the cluster aspect of competencies.

Summary

It is clear that a framework of marketing competencies exists which is more appropriate for marketing management decision-making in the entrepreneurial owner-managed SME. These key entrepreneurial marketing management competencies have been identified as judgement, experience, knowledge and communication. We can also comment on the nature of these competencies in that they are not stand-alone entities but interactions between, *and* clusters of, other competency elements. In the observable performance of any particular entrepreneurial marketing activity, one competency will be dominant. The competency that dominates will reflect the marketing activity being undertaken. In making a sale, for instance, one would anticipate the predominance of the communication competency in any cluster, whereas experience might come to the fore in, say, product development.

We also acknowledge that marketing competency can be developed. In an entrepreneurial circumstance a self-assessment and advancement approach to marketing competency development is offered.

The important conclusion, however, is acknowledgement of the existence of key entrepreneurial marketing management competencies and an acceptance that these can be developed. In an entrepreneurial owner-managed SME, therefore, self-development approaches to improving the competencies outlined in the entrepreneurial marketing management spectrum can result in effective and/or superior performance of the SME's marketing activities. If the SME entrepreneur focuses on using natural strengths and abilities to develop areas of personal weakness in respect of marketing, better company performance will follow. Essentially what is being offered is a means by which SME entrepreneurs can proactively develop key aspects of their marketing.

Learning questions

1. Select two marketing management competencies from the spectrum offered in this chapter. What are the ways in which these competencies interact in respect of the performance of a particular marketing activity?
2. How can entrepreneurs use the component elements of the judgement competency to develop their ability to analyze market opportunities?
3. What is the appropriateness of self-assessment and development approaches to marketing competency development in SMEs?

Notes and references

1. Boyatzis, R. E. (1992) *The Competent Manager*, New York: John Wiley.

Further reading

Quinn, R. E., Faerman, S. R., Thompson, M. P. and McGrath, M. R. (1990) *Becoming a Master Manager*, New York: John Wiley.

Whetten, D. A. and Cameron, K. S. (1991) *Developing Management Skills*, 2nd edition, London: HarperCollins.

2 Sales Strategies

Objectives

After studying this chapter, you should be able to:

1. Understand and appreciate the differences between sales and marketing strategies
2. Appreciate where the key marketing concepts fit into the planning process
3. Identify component parts of the communications mix
4. Differentiate between objectives, strategies and tactics

Key Concepts

- branding
- budget
- external audit
- internal audit
- promotional mix
- push and pull strategies
- PEST/PESTLE/STEEPLE analysis
- sales forecast
- sales planning process
- SWOT analysis
- TOWS matrix

2.1 Sales and Marketing Planning

To be effective, sales activities need to take place within the context of an overall strategic marketing plan. Only then can we ensure that our sales efforts complement, rather than compete with, other marketing activities. Accordingly, sales strategies and management are afforded a more holistic perspective and tend to cover the whole organisation. Hence, the current general consensus is that sales strategies and tactics may only be arrived at, implemented and assessed against a framework of company-wide objectives and strategic planning processes. Before discussing sales strategies and tactics, the nature and purpose of strategic market plans and the place of selling in these plans is outlined and discussed.

2.2 The Planning Process

The nature of the **sales planning process** is outlined in Figure 2.1. This process can be likened to that of operating a domestic central heating system.We first determine the temperature required, timing, etc. (setting objectives) and procedures which must be followed to make sure that this is achieved (determining operations). Next we have to implement appropriate procedures, including ensuring that the necessary resources are available (organisation). At this stage we can commence operation of the system (implementation). Finally, we need to check how the system is operating, in particular the temperature level that has been reached (measuring results). Any deviations in required temperature are then reported and corrected through the thermostatic system (re-evaluation and control).

This planning process can be described through the acronym MOST which describes the process from the general to the specific: mission, objective, strategy, tactics.

2.3 Establishing Marketing Plans

There is no universal way of establishing an ideal marketing plan; neither is the process simple in practice because every planning situation is unique. Conceptually, however, the process is straightforward, consisting a series of logical steps. The marketing plan (Figure 2.2) can be portrayed as a hierarchy consisting of three levels:

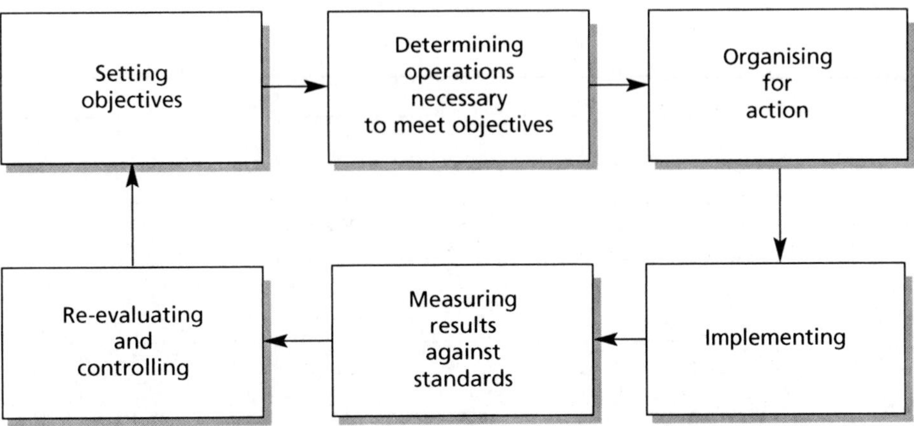

Figure 2.1 The planning process

- Objectives: Where do we intend to go? (*goals*)
- Strategies: How do we intend to get there? (*broadly descriptive*)
- Tactics: The precise route to be taken (*detailed*)

Business definition (corporate mission or goal)

As a prerequisite to the determination of marketing plans, careful consideration should be given to defining (or redefining) the overall role or mission of the business. This issue is best addressed by senior management's asking and answering the question: 'What business are we in?' The definition of the role of a business should be in terms of what customer needs are being served by a business rather than in terms of what products or services are being produced. For example, the manufacturer of microcomputers might define the company as being in the business of rapid problem-solving. In the automobile industry, companies might define their business as being the provision of transport, conferring status, etc., rather than manufacturing cars.

This process of business definition is important. Not only does it ensure that a company thinks in terms of its customers' wants and needs, but also in terms of the planning process, it forms a focusing mechanism for more detailed aspects that follow.

Situation analysis/marketing audit

The precise content of this step in preparing the marketing plan will vary from company to company, but will normally consist of a marketing analysis and an analysis of strengths/weaknesses, opportunities and threats (SWOT).

Market analysis (or marketing audit)

Examples of data and analysis required under the **internal audit** include:

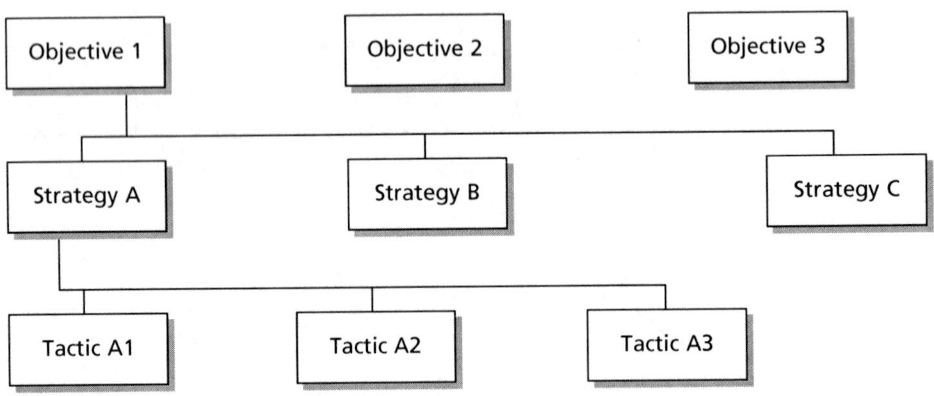

Figure 2.2 Hierarchy of the marketing plan

1 Current and recent size and growth of market. In the multi-product company this analysis needs to be made in total, by product/market and by geographical segment.

2 Analysis of customer needs, attitudes and trends in purchasing behaviour.

3 Current marketing mix.

4 Competitor analysis, including an appraisal of:

- current strategy
- current performance, including market share analysis
- their strengths and weaknesses
- expectations as to their future actions.

As well as analysing existing competition, potential new entrants should be appraised.

The **external audit** consists of an analysis of broad macro-environment trends – Political, Economic, Socio-cultural and Technological (**PEST**) – that might influence the future of the company's products. This original description was first extended to SLEPT with the introduction of Legal factors, and then to **PESTLE** with the introduction of Environmental factors and now to **STEEPLE** with the introduction of Ecological factors.

Application of PEST analysis to Corus

Corus examined its construction strategy in light of the external environment to identify future market needs. By linking Corus competencies and technical knowledge to future market needs, Corus aims to develop products that give the company a competitive advantage in construction. PEST analysis is a powerful tool that can be used to help analyse the external construction environment. This analysis involves examining the current situation with regard to the following factors:

Political
UK government policy and EU directives, for example, planning and environmental issues, including sustainability, affect the construction industry.

Economic
The health of the economy and interest rates affect demand for commercial and residential property. The UK government is using taxation as a means to encourage improving environmental performance, e.g. The Climate Change Levy, Aggregates and Landfill taxes. The construction industry is increasingly interested in whole life costs of buildings, which include initial capital costs, operating and maintenance costs – understanding how better design can improve all these costs.

Social
Changes in the birth/divorce rates and the average number of people living in a household affect the demand for housing. Increasing crime, ageing population,

(continued on following page)

and people's well-being are part of the social dimension. Research shows that the highest number of disagreements amongst neighbours is due to car parking.

Technology
New construction technologies affect working practices, for example in the building industry, constructing more component systems in factories rather than on building sites.

PEST analysis can be extended to SLEPT through the addition of Legal factors including legislation that regulates industry. A PESTLE analysis is extended further and includes two additional factors.

Legislation
UK and European governments believe the construction industry is highly fragmented and the only way to improve the performance of the industry in terms of safety and environmental performance is to increase legislation.

Environmental
Two of the main issues here are meeting the Kyoto Agreement in reduction of carbon dioxide from the burning of fossil fuels and waste going to land fill.

Note: When using PESTLE as a tool for analysis it is possible to get overlap between a specific issue which can be put into two sections. What is important is to identify the changes and to understand the impact those changes will have on the construction industry.

The factors identified in the analysis are concerned with the current situation. However, it is essential to plan for the future through forecasting events over the next 20 years using factors from the PESTLE analysis. This is partly due to the need to have accreditation for products. This is a testing regime carried out by an independent body against relevant UK/International standards and building regulations. On successful outcomes of the tests, a performance certification is issued for the specific product in the specific application – generally stating structural, fire, acoustic, thermal and durability performance of the product. This is important as the construction industry is generally conservative and hence, to introduce a new product, it is essential to have third party validation that the product will perform as the manufacturer states. Achieving this accreditation can take up to two years and it then takes a substantial amount of time to develop the product for today's construction industry.

The process of forecasting future events is known as Road Mapping. It allows Corus to understand changes in PESTLE factors over time and identify how these affect the construction industry and link product developments to these changes. It also allows Corus to identify market opportunities, develop products to meet these and identify which existing technologies can manufacture them.

Source: *http://www.thetimes100.co.uk/case_study* with permission

Both internal and external audits are deliberate and detailed coverage of the internal and external elements that have been described. It can be carried out by people within marketing or from other departments and, most importantly, they must have the backing of top management as they are central to both the marketing planning and corporate planning horizons of the company.

Analysis of strengths/weaknesses, opportunities and threats

Here management must make a realistic and objective appraisal of *internal* company strengths and weaknesses in the context of potential *external* opportunities and threats (**SWOT analysis**). Opportunities for the future of a business and threats to it stem primarily from factors outside the direct control of a company and in particular from trends and changes in those factors which were referred to earlier as the macro-environment – namely political, economic, socio-cultural and technological factors. It is important to recognise that the determination of what constitutes an opportunity/threat, and indeed the appraisal of strengths and weaknesses, must be carried out concurrently. An 'apparent' strength, for example, a reputation for quality, becomes a real strength only when it can be capitalised on in the marketplace.

A SWOT analysis is not a lengthy set of statements; it is simply a number of bullet points under each heading. It should be short and uncomplicated as it is from the SWOT that marketing strategies are generated.

Statement of objectives

On the basis of the preceding steps, the company can now determine specific objectives and goals that it wishes to achieve. These objectives, in turn, form the basis for the selection of marketing strategies and tactics.

A company may have several objectives. Although marketing objectives usually tend to support business objectives, business and marketing objectives may also be one and the same. It should be pointed out that there are several types of objectives, such as financial and corporate objectives. Additionally, objectives may be departmental or divisional. However, regardless of the type or format, each objective requires its own strategy.

Objectives are needed in a number of areas – production objectives, financial objectives, etc. In a market driven company, marketing objectives are the most important as they reflect customer needs and how the company can satisfy these. In a market driven company, marketing plans come first in the overall corporate planning process. The objectives of other areas must then be consistent with marketing objectives. In addition to this element of consistency, objectives should be expressed unambiguously, preferably quantitatively, and with an indication of the time span within which the objectives are planned to be achieved. The acronym SMART describes the requirement for such objectives: Specific, Measurable, Achievable, Realistic and Time related.

This time span of planned activities often gives rise to some confusion in planning literature. Marketing plans are often categorised as being short range, intermediate range and long range. The confusion arises from the fact that there is no accepted definition of what constitutes the appropriate time horizon for each of these categories. What is felt to comprise long-term planning in one company (say five to ten years) may be considered intermediate in another. It is suggested that the different planning categories are identical in concept, although clearly different in detail. Furthermore, the different planning categories are ultimately related to each other – achieving long-term objectives requires first that intermediate and short-term objectives be met. The following criteria are necessary for setting objectives:

1 *Ensure objectives focus on results*

   - Because the effects of marketing activity are essentially measurable, sales and marketing strategies should enable the quantification of marketing achievement.

2 *Establish measures against objectives*

   - Return on investment.

3 *Where possible have a single theme for each objective*

   - Imprecise objectives such as 'reduce customer defections by 20 per cent through best-in-class service' are not acceptable. There are at least two objectives here and each should be quantified.

4 *Ensure resources are realistic*

   - Best practice: attempt to answer common marketing problems through the use of test and roll-out plans.
   - Because testing enables roll-out costs to be estimated reasonably accurately, this should ensure that campaign running costs are realistic. (Of course, overheads or labour cost may not be.)

5 *Ensure marketing objectives are integral to corporate objectives*

   - This is indisputable, because there will be a serious mismatch if corporate objectives differ from marketing objectives, e.g. general corporate objectives suggest expansion into new member countries of the European Union, and specific marketing objectives only include current members of the EU.

Example of establishing an objective

Saga Holidays – Meeting the needs of empty nesters

Saga Holidays was set up to provide holidays for people with a high proportion of leisure time, people defined as either 'retired' or 'empty nesters'. The holidays would be outside school holidays and other peak periods.

Original objective: Sell long-stay holidays and cruises

Success: Negotiating strength

But what were their options for business expansion?

Either 1 Sell holidays to other market sectors.

Or 2 Sell other products and services to established customers.

So what did Saga do?

Instead of expanding out of a profitable market segment into less profitable segments, Saga met other needs of the retired/empty nester market by selling insurance, savings and other suitable products. The business is thus now defined as a *retired market service provider* rather than merely a *specialist holiday organisation.*

Saga followed what Michael Porter would term a Focus Business Strategy as opposed to a differentiation strategy or cost leadership strategy.

In today's competitive market, it is not uncommon for companies to diversify their product offering to an established customer base. With customer acquisition, customer service and database management costs already met, this may indeed be the most profitable expansion option.

Saga offers a practical example of 'WHAT WOULD OUR CUSTOMERS WANT TO BUY FROM US NEXT?'

A most important document in a company is the annual marketing plan, which the sales manager plays a key part in preparing. The remainder of this chapter discusses planning in the context of the preparation of this annual document.

Determine sales and market potential and forecast sales

A critical stage in the development of marketing plans is the assessment of market and sales potential followed by the preparation of a detailed **sales forecast.** Market potential is the maximum possible sales available for an entire industry during a stated period of time. Sales potential is the maximum possible portion of that market which a company could reasonably hope to achieve under the most favourable conditions. Finally, the sales forecast is the portion of the sales potential that the company estimates it will achieve. The sales forecast is an important step in the preparation of company plans. Not only are the marketing and sales functions directly affected in their planning considerations by this forecast, but other departments, including production, purchasing and human resource management, will use the sales forecast in their planning activities. Sales forecasting, therefore, is a prerequisite to successful planning and is considered in detail in Chapter 16.

Generating and selecting strategies

Once marketing objectives have been defined and market potential has been assessed, consideration should be given to the generation and selection of strategies. Broadly, strategies encompass the set of approaches that the company will use to achieve its objectives.

This step in the process is complicated by the fact that there are often many alternative ways in which each objective can be achieved. Although several strategies may be evaluated, only one strategy can be employed, hence giving rise to the formula: one strategy per objective. For example, an increase in sales revenue of

10 per cent can be achieved by increasing prices, increasing sales volume at the company level (increasing market share) or increasing industry sales. At this stage it is advisable, if time consuming, to generate as many alternative strategies as possible. In turn, each of these strategies can be further evaluated in terms of their detailed implications for resources and in the light of the market opportunities identified earlier. Finally, each strategy should be examined against the possibility of counter-strategies on the part of competitors.

The vignette that follows was provided by PR Artistry and concerns one of their clients, MCRL. It provides an illustration of how the planning process is implemented through the application of what the company has termed GOSPA.

GOSPA for MCRL

GOSPA is a corporate performance management process that implements and produces measurable results. It stands for *Goals, Objectives, Strategies, Plans and Actions*.

Using this process improves communication, control, morale, measurement and performance through a set of easy to implement steps. It gives management a structure for business planning, change, restructuring, measurement and consistent communication after an initial short training period. It is appropriate for organisations both large and small.

Goals in relation to press relations for MCRL in Europe

G1 To build a strong brand and market for MCRL by raising awareness in the press and amongst potential customers within the retail sector in the UK, France, Italy and Germany

G2 For MCRL to be an immediate shortlist choice as a supplier to the 'Enterprise Service Bus' in terms of content integration and digital media/store-innovation projects within retailers in the UK, France, Italy and Germany

Objectives

O1 Implement a regular press release service, issuing a target of one release per month per country to a specific target press list concentrating on quality rather than volume starting January 2007

O2 Produce articles and opinion pieces for the target press using James Pemberton, Michael Jaszczyk and Mike Camerling to position MCRL as the company that provides the technology for retailers to adopt what is next in retail starting January 2007

O3 Produce additional case studies of customers to illustrate how MCRL applications can benefit customers, in-store staff, operations and IT departments starting January 2007

O4 Monitor forward feature opportunities in target publications, contributing relevant and authoritative material whenever possible beginning December 2006

O5 Provide a coordinated approach to the press in the UK, France, Italy and Germany

Strategies

S1 To target three distinct audiences within retailers – marketing, operations and IT. To agree key messages for each of these audiences e.g. for IT to give advice and guidance as to how to provide the 'Enterprise Service Bus' concept

S2 For Mary Phillips of PR Artistry to work with James Pemberton of MCRL to produce an opinion piece per quarter for proactive placement with the retail press

S3 To build a selected list of target publications in each country and a target list of freelance writers in the retail sector. Possibly three sub-lists dealing with the three target audiences mentioned in S1

S4 Proactively identify and target forward features in the target press on a continuous basis, making submissions wherever possible

Plans for January, February, March

P1 Produce Media lists for each country

P2 Prioritise the first six press releases for each country:

- Metro – shopping list management
- HIT – PSA in use since July at Dohle Retail Group
- Wincor Nixdorf partner release regarding Retail Management System (RMS)
- PSA uses Flash MX for the first time
- Retail Framework to integrate with Portable Shopping Systems (PSS) to by-pass Point of Sale (POS)
- MCRL and RMS certified SIF (Store Integration Framework) by IBM

P3 Write and issue the first three press releases

P4 Agree and prioritise the first two opinion pieces – possible topics:

- MCRL provide the infrastructure necessary for retailers to benefit from the next wave of in-store systems, including in-store digital media, kiosks, PSA, PDA and intelligent scales
- Digital Signage – MCRL shows the right approach to get meaningful ROI metrics and a sustainable and manageable solution. 'There's more to it than just hanging a few screens with TV commercials'
- Flash comes of age to make the shopping experience easier and more fun

P5 Write and get the first two articles placed

Actions

A1 Meeting in Paris on 9 December – MCRL, PRA and MN

A2 PRA to write the first press release and then PRA and MN to introduce MCRL to the target press

A3 Agree topic for the first opinion piece

Source: *http://www.gospaplanning.com* with permission

Examples of strategies

We begin by supposing that the objective is to maximise profit from dealings with established customers.

Strategy 1: Targeting

To the marketer, targeting is equivalent to segmentation. A segmentation/targeting strategy may be based on any or all of the following:

- value (high or low consumption, value of goods purchased)
- customer preference (telephone/email ordering service, type of products/services purchased)
- lifestage (status of relationship between supplier and customer: active/lapsed/dormant customer/months since last purchase)

At this point it is important to emphasise that:

- segments must be potentially profitable
- segments are not mutually exclusive
- segments are not stable

Hence, a consumer may fall into more than one segment or different segments at different times. If the segment requires a special effort to reach or appeal to it, then it must have sufficient potential purchasing power to justify the effort.

Strategy 2: Pricing

In line with the classic marketer's approach, the following pricing strategies may be adopted:

- make short-term tactical reductions
- establish price premiums
- elevate perceived quality

Thus, the classic principle of elevating the perceived quality of a brand so that it can command a higher selling margin may be adopted. Additionally, a discount has more value if the worth of what is being discounted is understood.

Discounting is of course prevalent in all marketing. In Fast Moving Consumer Goods (FMCG) markets it tends to be driven by competitive or retailer pressures. Often, tactical cuts are seen as defensive.

Strategy 3: Customer retention

Because advanced technology enables suppliers to track the progress of an enquirer or customer, focus is increasingly shifting from mere product profitability to the profitability of customer relationships. However, customer profitability will be determined by:

- the cost of acquisition
- the losses of customers or would-be customers at various key stages in the relationship

Key stages in the customer relationship could be revised as:

- enquiry
- conversion to customer
- repeat purchase
- up-trade
- threatened dormancy
- recovery

The probability of loss usually declines with the length of the relationship. In consumer markets (but not in business markets) most often the duration of a relationship outweighs rate of spending in determining the lifetime value of the relationship. Here, a customer database will not only facilitate measurement of this relationship, but more importantly enable corrective action to be undertaken more easily. Thus, an offer may be triggered to prevent the customer 'going dormant'. Consequently, if the customer fails to respond and does go dormant, further offers may be made to recover the customer and re-start the relationship/recovery.

Additionally, there could be a customer development and retention strategy, which could provide the means to retain customers. There may be a retention strategy based on customer care and a development strategy based on sales promotion.

From this list of alternative strategies a choice must be made with regard to the broad marketing approach which the company considers will be the most effective in achieving objectives. This must then be translated into a strategy statement which must be communicated to and agreed with all those managers who will influence its likely degree of success or failure. Once again, the specific contents of such a strategy statement will vary between companies, but as an example a strategy statement might encompass the following areas:

1 A clear statement of marketing objectives.

2 A description of the choice of strategies for achieving these objectives.

3 An outline of the broad implications of the selected strategies with respect to the following key areas in marketing:

   - target market
   - positioning
   - marketing mix
   - marketing research.

At this stage the strategy statement should give a clear and concise indication of where the major marketing efforts of the company will be focused. Once this has been discussed and agreed we can progress to the next step of preparing a detailed plan of action.

There are many tools available for generating strategic options, the most popular of which are the Boston Matrix and the GE/McKinsey Matrix. A description and application of such tools is more appropriate to corporate strategy and strategic marketing planning texts and not within the sphere of this text. However, analysis using the product life-cycle concept and diffusion of innovations is appropriate in this context and these have been discussed in Chapter 1. SWOT analysis is a useful method of generating strategies. A number of stages are necessary:

1 Evaluate the influence of environmental factors (STEEPLE/PEST) on the company.

2 Make a diagnosis about the future.

3 Consider company strengths and weaknesses in relation to all key areas of the company.

4 Develop strategic options.

For example, in Figure 2.3 let us consider the case of a specialist, low-volume UK sports car producer.

Strategic possibilities using SWOT analysis

As an illustration, here are two strategic possibilities for the sports car producer mentioned in Figure 2.3: use existing strong, well-established brand to raise production levels through automation to market to other European countries (S1, S2, W1, W2, O2, T2). Raise the basic price (S4, W3, O1, T1, T2).

This is an application of the use of SWOT matrix which in essence takes elements of SWOT and brings them together to form marketing strategies. It was first proposed by Weihrich in 1982.[1]

Preparing the marketing programme

The strategy statement prepared in the previous section provides the input for the determination of the detailed programme required to implement these strategies. The first step in the preparation of this programme is the determination of the mar-

Strengths	Weaknesses
1 Well-established brand name 2 In business since 1920 3 Cult following 4 Low price 5 Consistently good press reviews	1 Production only semi-automated 2 Maximum production 30 units per week 3 Long waiting list 4 Only sold in UK, USA, Germany, Holland, Belgium and Scandinavia
Opportunities	**Threats**
1 USA market can take twice their allocation 2 Other European countries would like to purchase	1 Some purchasers not prepared to wait 2 Other volume manufacturers now producing niche models like this

Figure 2.3 SWOT matrix for a sports car producer

keting mix. Detailed decisions must be made with respect to product policy, pricing, promotion and distribution. Care should be exercised to ensure that the various elements of the marketing mix are integrated, i.e. that they work together to achieve company objectives in the most effective manner.

At this stage of the planning process what has previously been an outline plan for guiding decision-making becomes a detailed operational plan and this section is inevitably the lengthiest part of the planning document. It is on the basis of this part of the plan that day-to-day marketing activities and tactics of the company will be organised, implemented and assessed.

Allocating resources – budgeting

Having made detailed decisions with respect to the elements of the marketing mix, the next step is to assemble a **budget** for each of these elements. In most companies limited resources ensure that managers from the different functional areas have to compete for these scarce resources. It is likely that much discussion will take place between those responsible for each element of the marketing mix. In addition it may be found that initial marketing objectives, strategies and detailed plans for the marketing programme to achieve the forecast level of sales may, in the light of financial and other resource constraints, be unrealistic. In this event modifications to the original plan may have to be made.

It should be noted that at this stage an estimate can be made of both costs and revenues and a forecast profit and loss statement prepared.

Implementation

The procedure so far should have resulted in the preparation of a detailed document setting out what is to be done, when it will be done, who is responsible and estimated costs and revenues, as well as agreed time frames for the various activities in the plan. Once approved, details of the marketing plan should be communicated to everyone involved. This communication is an essential and sometimes neglected aspect of marketing planning. Many companies have elaborate marketing plans that are not implemented because key people have not been informed or have not agreed the proposed plan.

Control

Finally, the plan should contain an outline of the control mechanisms that will be applied. This should include details of major objectives and key parameters in the measurement of the degree of success in achieving the objectives, enabling corrections and modifications to be made as the plan unfolds. This control part of the marketing plan should specify what is to be measured, how it is to be measured and what data are required for measurement. It may also include details of what action is to be taken in the light of deviations from the plan. This contingency planning is a key feature of any planning process, recognising as it does that plans need to be flexible in order to accommodate possible unforeseen or unpredictable changes in the market. The overall marketing planning process is summarised in Figure 2.4.

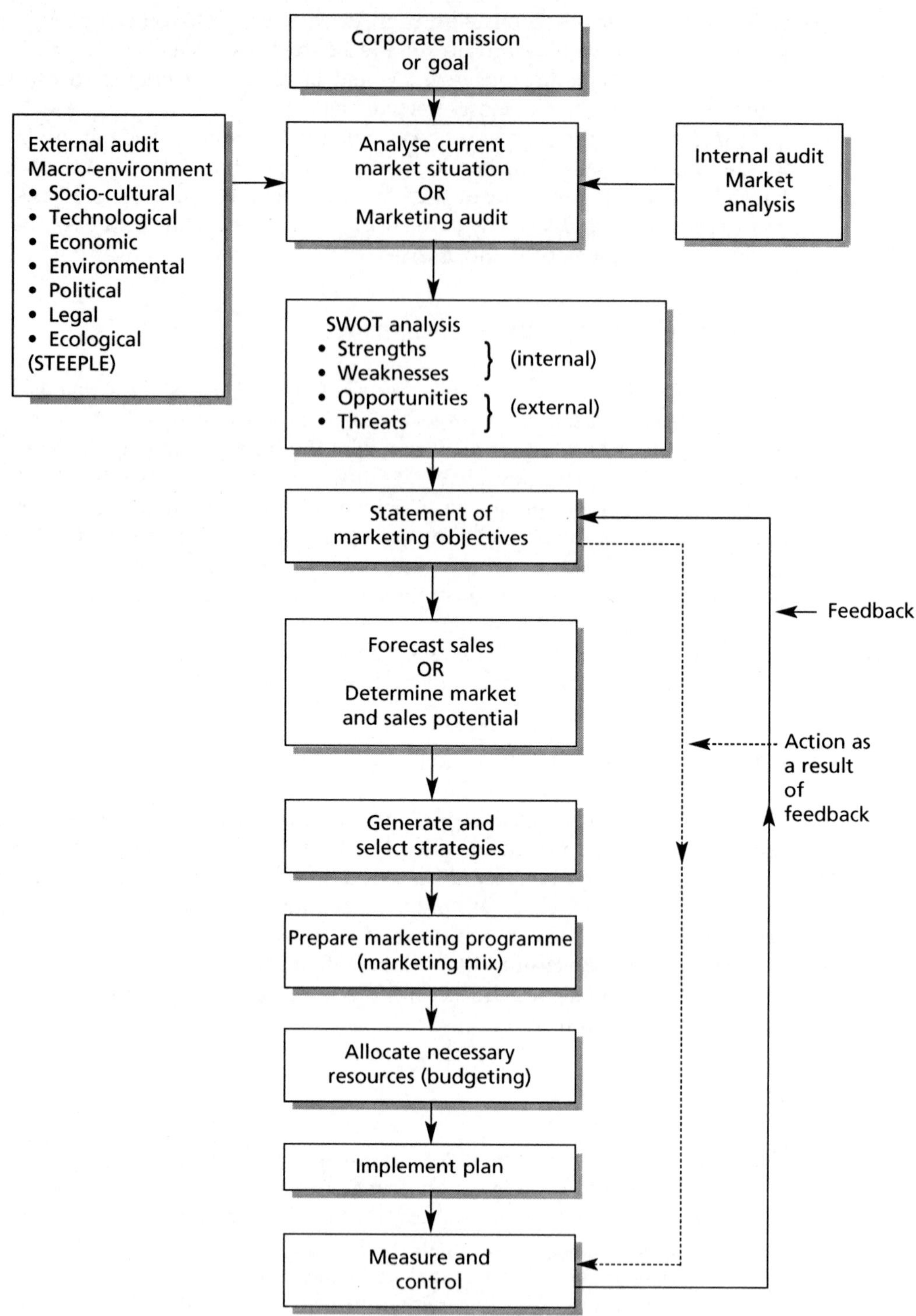

Figure 2.4 An overview of the marketing planning process

2.4 The Place of Selling in the Marketing Plan

We have examined how marketing plans are prepared. The sales function has an important role to play in this process and we now look at the nature of this role and, in particular, the contribution that the sales function makes to the preparation of the marketing plan and how the sales function itself is influenced by the marketing plan.

Contribution of the sales function

Throughout the planning process alternative courses of action need to be identified and decisions taken as to which of these alternatives is the most appropriate. Contingency planning measures like these involve identifying alternatives and choosing between them, which requires accurate and timely information. A key role of the sales function in the planning process is the provision of such information. This becomes clearer if we examine some of the stages in the planning process where the sales function can make a valuable contribution:

(a) analysis of current market situation (marketing audit)

(b) determining sales potential/sales forecasting

(c) generating and selecting strategies

(d) budgeting, implementation and control

Toyota

By constantly finding out what its customers will want to buy next, Toyota has achieved profitable line extension and replacement. In fact, by being able to make additional low-cost sales to its established customers, Toyota has not only achieved sustainable competitive advantage through customer retention, but is also in a stronger position to invest in expansion.

Analysis of current market situation (marketing audit)

The proximity of the sales function to the marketplace places it in a unique position to contribute to the analysis of the current market situation facing the company. In particular, sales is often well placed to contribute to the analysis of customer needs and trends in purchasing behaviour. The sales manager can also make a valuable contribution with respect to knowledge about competitors and their standing in the marketplace. This informational role of sales managers should not be ignored because, through the salesforce, they are ideally equipped to provide up-to-date, accurate information based on feedback from customers.

Determining sales potential/sales forecasting

As we later see in Chapter 16, an important responsibility of the sales manager is the preparation of sales forecasts for use as the starting point for business planning. Short-, medium- and long-term forecasts by the sales manager form the basis for allocating company resources in order to achieve anticipated sales.

Generating and selecting strategies

Although decisions about appropriate marketing strategies to adopt rest with marketing management, the sales manager must be consulted and should make an input to this decision. Again, the sales function is ideally placed to comment on the appropriateness of any suggested strategies.

The sales manager should actively encourage sales staff to comment upon the appropriateness of company marketing strategies. The field salesforce are at the forefront of tactical marketing and can more realistically assess how existing target markets will respond to company marketing initiatives. Indeed, the fact that there are front-line people who benefit from the most contact with customers should not be overlooked.

Budgeting, implementation and control

Preparation of the sales forecast is a necessary precursor to detailed marketing plans. The sales forecast is also used in the preparation of the sales budget.

On the basis of the sales forecast, the sales manager must determine what level of expenditure will be required to achieve the forecasted level of sales. The important thing to remember about this budget is that it is the cornerstone of the whole budgeting procedure in a company. Not only the activities of the sales department, but also production, human resource management, finance and research and development will be affected by this budget. Because of this importance, sales budgets are considered in detail in Chapter 16. At this stage it is sufficient to note that in preparing the sales budget the sales manager must prepare an outline of the essential sales activities required to meet the sales forecast, together with an estimate of their costs. The precise contents of the annual sales budget will vary between companies, but normally include details of salaries, direct selling expenses, administrative costs and commissions and bonuses.

Having agreed the sales budget for the department, the sales manager must assume responsibility for its implementation and control. In preparing future plans, an important input is information on past performance against budget and, in particular, any differences between actual and budgeted results. Such 'budget variances', both favourable and unfavourable, should be analysed and interpreted by the sales manager as an input to the planning process. The reasons for budget variances should be reported, together with details of any remedial actions that were taken and their effects.

Influence of marketing plan on sales activities: strategies and tactics

Any planning process is effective only to the extent that it influences action. An effective marketing planning system influences activities, both strategic and tactical, throughout the company. The classical marketing approach favours the inside-out planning model proposed by Schultz, Tannenbaum and Lauterborn[2] (Figure 2.5).

However, the reverse outside-in planning model is becoming more and more popular. Figure 2.6 shows an outside-in planning sequence, starting with a calculation of the cost per sale to current customers, then to lapsed customers and prospects on the database, and finally to new customers. The cost-per-sale calculations determine the sales target in each case.

This process is followed by a strategy for each discrete segment. A product may not, for example, be offered to each segment at the same price. Similarly, types of communication will be different for each segment.

Both the segment strategy and the content of communications will, ideally, be tested against reasonable alternatives. The most successful alternatives on testing will then be rolled out to the remaining population in each segment.

Although the inside-out model is financially driven, it is much less safe than the customer-oriented planning model. Perhaps this influence is most clearly seen through decisions relating to the marketing programme or marketing mix. Sales strategies are most directly influenced by planning decisions on the promotional element of the marketing mix. Here we will consider briefly the notion of a 'mix' of promotional tools, outlining the considerations in the choice of an appropriate mix and the implications for sales strategies. In particular, the important and often misunderstood relationship between advertising and selling is explained and discussed. We conclude this section by examining briefly the nature of sales tactics.

The promotional mix

Earlier in this chapter we suggested that an important facet of marketing planning is the preparation of a marketing programme, the most important step in this preparation being the determination of the marketing mix – product, price, distribution

Figure 2.5 Inside-out planning model

Figure 2.6 Outside-in planning model

and promotion. As selling is only one element in the promotion part of this mix, it is customary to refer to the **promotional mix** (or more correctly the communications mix) of a company. This traditional promotional mix is made up of four major elements:

1 Advertising.

2 Sales promotion.

3 Publicity/public relations.

4 Personal selling.

To these traditional elements can now be added:

5 Direct marketing.

6 Interactive/internet marketing.

In most companies all four traditional elements can contribute to company sales, but a decision has to be made as to where to place the emphasis. This decision is made at the planning stage. In addition, it is important that the elements of the promotional mix work together to achieve company objectives. An important planning task of management is the co-ordination of promotional activities.

Several factors influence the planning decision as to where to place emphasis within the promotional mix. In some firms the emphasis is placed on the salesforce with nearly all promotional budget being devoted to this element of the mix. In others, advertising or sales promotion is seen as being much more efficient and productive than personal selling. Perhaps the most striking aspect of the various promotional tools is the extent to which they can be substituted for each other. Companies within the same industry differ markedly in where they place the promotional emphasis. This makes it difficult to be specific about developing the promotional mix within a particular company. As a guide, some of the more important factors influencing this decision are now outlined.

1 *Type of market*. In general, advertising and sales promotion play a more important role in the marketing of consumer products, whereas personal selling plays the major role in industrial marketing. The reasons for this stem from differences between industrial and consumer marketing, which are outlined in Chapter 3. An obvious contrast is the marketing of fast-moving consumer goods (FMCG) with the marketing of often highly technical, expensive capital goods to industry. Despite this, it is a mistake to conclude that advertising does not have a role to play in the marketing of industrial products. Indeed, the contribution of advertising is often undervalued by sales personnel and discounted as a waste of company resources. The relationship between advertising and sales is considered later in this chapter.

The 'new' promotional mix increasingly involves e-commerce possibilities and this is highlighted through developments in this field and numbers of companies using this facility. In addition, the use of freephone facilities is also making communication easier and cost-free to the potential customer. These more contemporary issues are highlighted in the two vignettes that follow.

E-commerce is made e-asy with new site

PSICommerce is a new e-commerce package designed by PSINet to open up the world of global trading to small and medium businesses. It claims to make merchandising on the web a simple and cost-effective process.

The PSICommerce basic package costs from £125 for SMEs to register and get the package components to be connected to the internet. An ongoing connection charge starts at £100 a month.

A Government Competitiveness White Paper says UK e-commerce transactions are currently worth around $US4.5 billion. Growth over the next three years could reach $US47 billion, with 70–80 per cent of e-commerce revenues expected to involve small and medium sized enterprises, either in business-to-business or business-to-consumer roles.

Valerie Holt, Managing Director of PSINet UK and Vice President of Europe, said SMEs' appetite for e-commerce was rapidly developing. But adoption of it was being throttled because of fear of costs related to the technical complexities of developing and building an internet 'shop' and integrating to the credit card payment systems.

'The benefits of the package will allow any small business to instantly trade globally on the internet. They may have only 2 or 30 clients worldwide but the internet enables them, by negating location, to overcome the physical barrier to trade,' said Holt.

Source: *www.psi.commerce.com*

Benefits to business of marketing numbers

Many companies do not realise that telephone numbers can be an effective marketing tool in terms of generating revenue and increasing customer bases. Research shows that marketing numbers can increase calls by up to 300 per cent. Patrick Naughton of Telecom One has suggested a number of benefits when using marketing numbers and has given a number of questions to be asked when weighing up the pros and cons:

- Are you trying to increase awareness of the company, products and services?
- Are you trying to improve the quality of your customer service?
- Are you trying to broaden the reach of your business?
- Do you already have a solid customer base and want to generate a new revenue stream?

The facilities that are available include:

Freephone (0800/0808) – customers can reach you free of charge; you pay 8p per minute.

Local rate or Lo-call (0845/0844) – customers pay 8p per minute weekdays, 4p evenings, and 2p at weekends, regardless of where in the country they call from.

National rate (0870/0871) – a single, location independent number. Calls are the same cost as local rate calls. Customers pay national rate charges and your business benefits by revenue generated from every call you receive.

Gold numbers – a memorable number that will stick in a customer's memory. It is likely to be used more frequently than others and thus generate more business.

Alphanumeric numbers – dialling a word in place of a number, e.g. 0800 BUSINESS (can only be used in countries that have this facility).

Websites *www.theidm.com* (Institute of Direct Marketing) *www.telecom1.com* and *www.oftel.com*.

Source: *www.whattobuyforbusiness.co.uk* Edition 252, March 2002

2 *Stage in the buying process*. In Chapter 3 it is suggested that for both industrial and consumer products it is useful to consider the stages through which the prospective purchaser passes en route to making a purchase decision. Although there are a number of ways in which this process may be conceptualised, essentially it consists of the potential purchaser moving from a position of being unaware of a company and/or its products, to being convinced that its products or services are the most appropriate to the buyer's needs. The sequential nature of this process is shown in Figure 2.7.

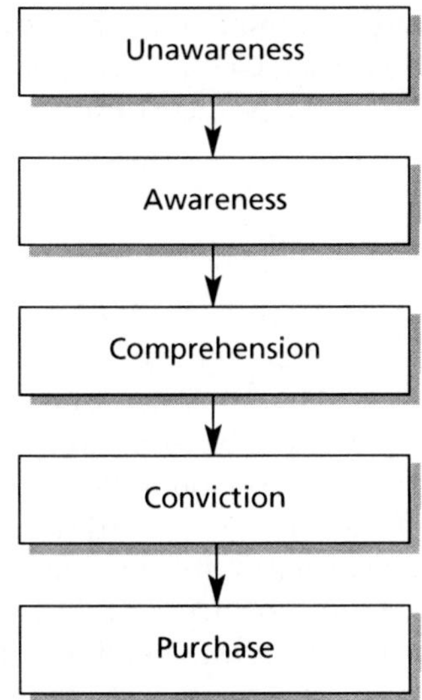

Figure 2.7 Stages in the buying process

For a given outlay, advertising and publicity are more effective in the earlier stages of moving potential purchasers through from unawareness to comprehension. Personal selling is more cost effective than other forms of promotional activity at the conviction and purchase stages. This is not to suggest that 'cold calling' is not an important area of sales activity but, as we see later, such cold calling is rendered much more effective if the customer is already aware of the company's products.

3 *Push versus pull strategies.* One of the most important determinants in the choice of promotional mix is the extent to which a company decides to concentrate its efforts in terms of its channels of distribution. This can perhaps be best illustrated if we contrast a push strategy with that of a pull strategy:

A **push strategy** is one in which the focus of marketing effort is aimed at pushing the product through the channel of distribution. The emphasis is to ensure that wholesalers and retailers stock the product in question. The idea is that if channel members can be induced to stock a product they in turn will be active in ensuring that your product is brought to the attention of the final customer. In general a push strategy entails a much greater emphasis on personal selling and trade promotion in the promotional mix.

A pull strategy relies much more heavily on advertising to promote the product to the final consumer. The essence of this approach is based on the notion that if sufficient consumer demand can be generated for a product this will result in final consumers asking retailers for the product. Retailers will then ask wholesalers for the product, who will contact the producer. In this way the product is 'pulled' through the channel by creating consumer demand via assertive advertising. (Channel management is considered in detail in Chapter 10 and in particular the diminishing role of wholesalers is examined.)

4 *Stage in the product life-cycle.* Chapter 1 introduced the concept of the product life-cycle. There is evidence to suggest that different promotional tools vary in their relative effectiveness over the various stages of this cycle. In general,

advertising and sales promotion are most effective in the introduction and growth stages of the life-cycle, whereas it is suggested that the emphasis on personal selling needs to increase as the market matures and eventually declines.

Co-ordinating promotional efforts: the relationship between advertising and selling

In discussing factors affecting choice of promotional tools, it may have appeared that to some extent these tools are mutually exclusive – for example, one chooses to concentrate either on advertising or personal selling. This is not the case. The relationship between the various promotional tools, including personal selling, should be complementary and co-ordinated. Perhaps this obvious point would not need to be stressed were it not for the fact that often this complementary relationship is misunderstood. Nowhere is this misunderstanding more evident than in the relationship between advertising and selling.

It is unfortunate that many sales managers and their salesforces believe that expenditure on advertising is a waste of company resources. Very rarely, they argue, does a customer purchase simply because a product is advertised, particularly where that customer is an industrial purchaser. Because of this, the argument continues, the money 'wasted' on advertising would be better spent where it will have a direct and immediate effect – on the salesforce. Increasingly, evidence suggests the notion that advertising money is wasted in industrial markets is misplaced. Among the functions that advertising can perform in such markets are the following:

1 Corporate advertising can help to build the reputation of a company and its products.

2 Advertising is particularly effective in creating awareness among prospective clients. The sales representative facing a prospect who is unaware of the company or product faces a much more difficult selling task than the representative who can build on an initial awareness.

3 Advertising can aid the sales representative in marketing new products by shouldering some of the burden of explaining new product features and building comprehension.

4 Advertising using return coupons may be used to open up new leads for the salesforce.

Overall, by far the greatest benefit of advertising in industrial markets is seen, not through a direct effect on sales revenue, but in the reduction of overall selling costs. Evidence suggests that, given adequate frequency, this reduction in selling costs to customers exposed to advertising may be as high as 30 per cent. Conversely, non-advertisers may find themselves at a disadvantage. The cost of selling to customers exposed to competitors' advertising may be increased by as much as 40 per cent.

In marketing consumer goods, **branding** and brand image are very important and advertising is generally thought to be the most effective promotional tool. However, personal selling and a well-trained salesforce can contribute significantly to increased market penetration by influencing stockists to allocate more shelf space to company products and persuading new dealers to stock them.

At all times, sales and advertising should be co-ordinated to achieve company objectives. It is important for sales personnel to be informed about company advertising campaigns. This advertising should be utilised in selling, the advertising theme being reinforced in the sales presentation.

From sales strategies to tactics

We have seen that a number of factors influence the setting for sales strategies. It was suggested that this influence is most direct in determining the relative emphasis to be given to sales activities in overall company and promotional strategy. Sales strategies are of course also influenced by the marketing and sales objectives specified in the marketing plan. As an illustration, a marketing objective of increased market share may mean that the sales manager has to ensure that sales in the forthcoming year increase by 10 per cent. Furthermore, the planning document should specify the route or strategy by which this objective will be accomplished, e.g. 'Additional sales effort is to be targeted on the opening of new accounts'. Sales objectives and strategies, therefore, also stem directly from the planning process, after consulation and agreement with relevant personnel.

However, not all researchers support the merits of relationship marketing, and opposing this outlook, Shaw[3] argues: 'Marketers must stop their obsession with loving customers since it has become a distraction from the basics of selling and tracking the origins of sale success.' Having agreed these strategic guidelines, a more detailed set of activities must be built into the planning process. The sales manager must determine the specific actions required to achieve sales goals, i.e. tactics.

Tactics encompass the day-to-day activities of the sales function in the achievement of marketing and sales objectives. Tactics also include actions which need to be taken in response to unexpected short-term events in the marketplace, for example, a special promotional effort by a competitor. The relationship between objectives, strategies and tactics is shown in Figure 2.8.

Tactical decisions represent the 'fine tuning' of sales activities and encompass many decision areas covered in greater detail elsewhere; for example, the deployment of sales personnel – territory design and planning (Chapter 15) – can be considered a tactical aspect of sales. Similarly, the design of incentive systems (Chapter 15) should form part of a tactical plan, designed to accomplish sales goals within the framework of sales strategies.

The importance of tactics should not be underestimated; even the best-formed strategies fail for want of proper tactics. As an example of the use and importance

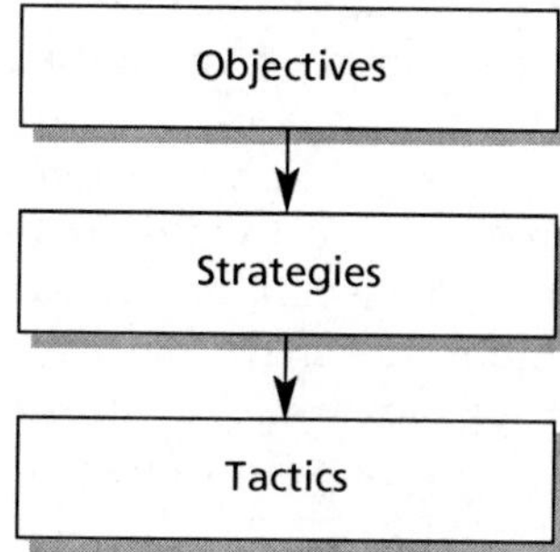

Figure 2.8 The relationship between objectives, strategies and tactics

of tactics in selling, we consider briefly an aspect of purchasing which is of vital interest to many companies, namely brand/supplier loyalty.

Brand/supplier loyalty

If we examine the purchase of products and services over time, we find that often the purchasing sequence of individuals indicates that they repeatedly buy the same brand of a product or, if the product is an industrial one, they consistently buy from a particular supplier. For such individuals, if we imagine that the brand or supplier in question is called X, the purchasing sequence would be as shown below:

Purchase occasion	1	2	3	4	5	6
Brand purchased/supplier	X	X	X	X	X	X

There is no doubt that brand/supplier loyalty does exist. Moreover, the cultivation of such loyalty among customers often accounts for a significant part of tactical marketing and sales effort, representing, as it does, a substantial market asset to a company.

By favouring a longer term perspective, such a cultivation of customer loyalty complements traditional brand-building techniques. Indeed, as Martin[4] insists, customer relationships with brands help insulate brands from competitors, 'the customer-brand linkage can be viewed as an important subset of relationship marketing'.

Additionally, while Reichheld and Schefter[5] also support this theory when they claim 'a large group of customers are influenced primarily by brand' and that these customers 'are looking for stable long-term relationships', Curtis[6] succinctly summarises that 'customers need to feel that they are part of a brand's crusade'.

Before considering the part that sales tactics can play in this process of cultivating brand loyalty, it is important to explain precisely what is meant by brand loyalty. This apparently simple notion gives rise to some misunderstanding.

Let us return to the purchasing sequence just shown. Although we have suggested that such a sequence is associated with a brand-loyal customer, the existence of such an array of purchases for a customer does not, of itself, constitute evidence that this customer *is* brand loyal. There are a number of possible explanations for this purchasing behaviour. One such explanation might be that this customer concentrates much of his or her purchasing in one particular retail outlet and it so happens that this particular retail outlet only stocks brand X of this product, i.e. the customer exhibits loyalty, but to the store, rather than the brand. Another possible explanation is that this customer pays little regard to the particular brand or supplier; s/he is not consciously brand loyal at all, but rather has simply slipped into the habit of purchasing this brand and cannot be bothered to switch. In this second example it is true to say that the customer must be reasonably satisfied with the brand being purchased consistently. If this were not the case, or the customer became dissatisfied, s/he would then make the decision to switch. Nevertheless, the fact is that this is not true brand loyalty.

True brand or supplier loyalty exists when customers make a conscious decision to concentrate their purchases on a particular brand because they consider that supplier or brand superior to others. There may be a number of reasons/bases for such perceived superiority, e.g. superior quality, better delivery and after-sales services, the availability of credit, or some combination of these or other factors. In discussing possible reasons for brand/supplier loyalty, we enter the realms of motives, perceptions, attitudes, etc, and more complex behavioural areas discussed in Chapter 3.

The concept of brand/supplier loyalty is a difficult one and care should be taken in interpreting the often conflicting evidence for its causes. Nevertheless, there are some indications that the salesperson can play a key role in helping to establish brand/supplier loyalty amongst a company's customers. One of the reasons for this is that learning theory suggests we have a tendency to repeat experiences that give us pleasure and to avoid those that do not. Among the most powerful and lasting impressions that serve as a source of pleasure or displeasure in purchasing activities are experiences in the face-to-face encounters with sales staff. Favourable attitudes and behaviour of sales personnel in dealing with their customers can contribute significantly to the creation of brand/supplier loyalty.

2.5 Conclusions

A framework for sales strategies and tactics has been established. We have seen that these are developed and operated within the framework of marketing planning. The sales function makes a valuable contribution to the establishment of marketing plans, providing, as it does, key data on customers, markets, competitors, sales forecasts and budgets. In turn, selling activities are directly influenced by decisions taken at the marketing planning stage. In the meantime, the increasingly essential role of databases should not be ignored.

We have looked at planning decisions for the marketing programme or marketing mix and, specifically, at the communications mix in a company. Factors such as type-of-product market, steps in the buying process, push versus pull strategies and stage in the product life-cycle have all been shown to influence promotional and consequently sales strategies.

Finally, we examined sales tactics, the relationship between advertising and selling, and the important area of brand/supplier loyalty. It was shown that advertising plays a key role in aiding the sales effort, reducing selling costs and easing the sales task. Brand/supplier-loyal customers are a valuable asset to any company and the salesforce is central to the establishment and maintenance of such customer loyalty.

References

1 Weihrich, H. (1982) 'The TOWS matrix – a tool for situational analysis', *Long Range Planning*, 15(2), pp. 54–66.

2 Schultz, D.E., Tannenbaum, S.I. and Lauterborn, R.F. (1993) *Integrated Marketing Communications*, NTC Business Books, Lincolnwood, IL.

3 Shaw, R. (1999) 'Customers are about sales, not false friendships', *Marketing*, January, p. 20.

4 Martin, C.L. (1998) 'Relationship marketing: a high-involvement product attribute approach', *Journal of Product & Brand Management*, 7(1), pp. 6–26.

5 Reichheld, F. and Schefter, P. (2000) 'E-Loyalty', *Harvard Business Review*, July/August, pp. 105–13.

6 Curtis, J. (2000) 'Get some decent exposure', *Revolution*, 12 July, pp. 32–6.

Practical Exercise

Welsh Lamb & Beef Promotions Ltd

Welsh Lamb & Beef Promotions Ltd (WLBP) was established by a group of like-minded Welsh livestock farmers who believe that Welsh lamb and beef have a reputation for excellence that needs to be promoted to a wide consumer audience.

The company is now one of the UK's largest farmer co-operatives with over 7,500 farmer members, and is dedicated to the promotion and marketing of branded, farm-assured Welsh lamb and beef in target markets worldwide. WLBP believes that livestock farming is of significant commercial importance to rural Wales, with the preservation of the family farm critical to the maintenance of Welsh culture and the scenic beauty of the Welsh countryside.

Wales is a land famous for its mountains, lakes, valleys, history, legends and song. For centuries it has been home to native Welsh sheep breeds. They have thrived on natural grassland available all year round. Welsh lamb is considered to have a good colour and a sweet, succulent flavour. The unique reputation and qualities enjoyed by the product worldwide come from traditional husbandry methods and feeding the animals on abundant grazing. The character of Welsh lamb arises from the influence of the traditional hardy Welsh breeds from the mountains, providing good quality breeding stock that forms the basis of lowland flocks.

Welsh lamb provides the consumer with a natural, versatile, tender, succulent meat with the distinct flavour of Wales. Welsh lamb (Cig Oen Cymru) together with the Welsh lamb dragon logo, is a guarantee of consistent high quality.

Welsh beef, however, is the hidden treasure of Wales and has now established its own identity (Cig Eidion Cymru). The foundation of this brand is the high quality of Welsh stock. With over 86 per cent of the land down to grass, Welsh beef farmers are renowned for their ability to convert quality grassland into top quality beef. The alluvial soils of the Welsh valleys are rich in minerals that are perfect for producing the finest quality beef. Cattle thrive in this unspoilt environment, producing beef that is succulent and of the highest standard. Its unique character arises from the influence of traditional beef breeds that dominate Welsh herds and from the topography of the country, coupled with the expertise of livestock farmers that has been handed down over generations.

Welsh producers were hit hard by the ban imposed during the foot-and-mouth crisis, but WLBP are confident that old markets are being reclaimed and new ones created. 'The export market has always been very important,' says Linda Jones, spokeswoman for WLBP. 'Before foot-and-mouth we were exporting £100 million of Welsh branded lamb, mainly to Spain and Southern Europe, and added to this was £10 million worth of beef, mainly to the Netherlands.'

Despite the heavy blow of the export ban, consumers and buyers on the continent have retained their enthusiasm for Welsh meat, if events since the ban was lifted towards the end of 2001 are anything to go by. 'We've been out of the market for a year, but within a week after the ban had been lifted they wanted Welsh lamb,' says Linda Jones. 'In December 2001 we met the Eroski group of Spanish buyers and they want Welsh beef as well as lamb.' The recovery of Welsh beef into export markets will take longer than Welsh lamb as a result of the 'Date Based Export Scheme'.

An application has been lodged with the EU to give Welsh lamb and beef the status of 'Protected Geographical Indication' – similar to that given to champagne.

Meanwhile, representatives of the group have been meeting with buyers across Europe to promote Welsh meat. Don Thomas, managing director of WLBP, said, 'The effort placed on the recovery of our valuable export markets must not be underestimated. It is vital for the long term commercial security of rural Wales that we re-establish the export of Welsh meat in key European countries as soon as possible. The reputation of Welsh meat in these target European markets needs to be reaffirmed.' He went on to say, 'A branded product will prevail in the export market, not a commodity. It is now important that the industry works together to exploit these opportunities with vigour. We can now positively implement our commercial strategies with existing and new customers to recover these vital export markets.'

In a UK context, Safeway's latest promotion for Welsh lamb backs up suggestions that supermarkets are taking home-produced meat more seriously following the foot-and-mouth crisis. A ten-week campaign, launched on 6 June 2002, specifically promotes Welsh lamb in-store. Dennis Hobbs, Sales Director of Safeway's dedicated lamb supplier, H M Bennett, says, 'We hope this major initiative will give Safeway customers the opportunity to support farmers by buying more lamb and the rural economy by visiting the countryside.'

Four years after Safeway's launch of Welsh mountain lamb, the first of the regional meat marketing campaigns by the multiples, it is clear that consumer demand has been more enthusiastic than anticipated. The campaign was more than just an in-store promotion. It required the creation of a new supply chain as the Welsh industry's infrastructure for procurement, killing and distribution of hill lambs to major retailers was inadequate and unstable. But according to Safeway category manager, Kelly Hathway, 'Our lamb initiatives have gone from strength to strength since we launched Welsh mountain lamb.'

Source: Adapted from articles by Paul Carey and Thomos Livingstone in *The Western Mail*, 17/5/02, pp. 3, 5; a news item in *The Grocer*, 15/6/02, p. 23; *www.welshlambandbeef.co.uk*

Discussion Questions

Acting as an external marketing consultant to WLBP, prepare a report for management that:

1 Provides strategic guidelines for promoting WLBP products both in the UK and internationally following the foot-and-mouth crisis. Justify reasons for including the various elements of the communications mix that you have suggested.

2 Suggest how other multiples like Safeway, which is now actively promoting WLBP products, can now be persuaded to promote WLBP products.

Practical Exercise

Auckland Engineering plc

Jim Withey, Sales Manager for Auckland Engineering plc, a well-established engineering company in the Midlands, received the following memo from D C Duncan, his recently appointed Marketing Director.

Memo
To: J Withey, Sales Manager
From: D C Duncan, Marketing Director
Date: 16 January 2006
Subject: Preparation of annual marketing plan

You will recall that at our series of preliminary meetings to discuss future marketing plans for the company I suggested that I was unhappy with the seemingly haphazard approach to planning. Accordingly, you will recall it was agreed between departmental heads that each would undertake to prepare a formal input to next month's planning meeting.

At this stage I am not seeking detailed plans for each product market, rather I am concerned that you give thought to how your department can contribute to the planning process. Being new to the company and its product/markets, I am not fully up to date on what has been happening to the market for our products, although as we all know our market share at 35 per cent is down on last year. I would particularly like to know what information your department could contribute to the analysis of the situation.

To help in your analysis I have summarised below what came out of our first planning meetings.

1 **Business definition.** It was agreed that the business needs redefining in customer terms. An appropriate definition for our company would be: 'Solutions to engine component design and manufacturing problems'.

2 **SWOT analysis**

Our main *strengths* are:

- Excellent customer awareness and an image of reliability and quality.
- Salesforce is technically well qualified.

- Manufacturing flexibility second to none – we respond quickly and effectively to individual customer needs.

Our main *weaknesses* are:

- Prices approximately 10 per cent above industry average.
- Spending higher proportion of turnover on advertising than most main competitors.
- Salesforce not skilled in generating new leads.

Our major *opportunities* are:

- Some major competitors having difficulty keeping customers because of quality and delivery problems.
- Recent legislation means research and development programme on new TDIX component, emphasising lower exhaust emission levels, should prove advantageous.
- Recent and forecast trends in the exchange rate should help export marketing efforts.
- Buyers in the industry seem prone to switching suppliers.

Our major *threats* are:

- Our largest customer threatening to switch owing to our higher average prices.
- Apart from TDIX programme, we have not been keeping pace with rapid technological change in the industry.
- Some major export markets are threatened by possibility of import restrictions.

3 **Objectives**

Financial

- To increase return on capital employed by 5 per cent.
- Net profit in the forthcoming year to be £4 million.

Marketing

- Sales revenue to be increased to £35 million in the forthcoming year.

4 **Marketing strategy**

Target markets

- Major manufacturers of diesel engines worldwide.

Positioning

- Highest engineering quality and after-sales service in supply of specialist low-volume diesel engine components.

I would welcome your comments on my analysis, together with any views on the appropriateness of the objectives I have set.

For the next meeting I suggest that as sales manager you give some thought as to where the relative emphasis should be placed in our promotional effort. As I have mentioned, we seem to be spending an excessive amount on advertising compared with our competitors. Perhaps you could give me your thoughts on this, as I understand you were in favour of raising our advertising budget from 1 per cent to 2 per cent of turnover last year. As you are aware, from a limited budget, we must decide where to place the relative emphasis in our communications mix. Perhaps you can indicate what you feel are the major considerations in this decision.

Discussion Questions

1 Give a brief outline of ways the sales manager can contribute to the marketing planning process at Auckland Engineering.

2 Looking at Duncan's analysis of the previous meeting, what issues/problems do you see that are of relevance to the activities of the salesforce?

3 How would you respond to Duncan's comments on the promotional mix and in particular to his comments about the level of advertising expenditure?

4 What is the logic in conducting a SWOT analysis in this context?

Practical Exercise

Flying high

Graham Keddie, appointed Managing Director late 2004, believes the magnetic effect of attracting two low-cost airlines has now succeeded in putting East Midlands Airport (EMA) firmly on the map. It has been a long-held view that EMA suffered from an identity problem; situated on the fringes of three major cities – Birmingham, Nottingham and Leicester. However, the announcement that 210,545 people flew from the airport in April 2005 – an incredible increase of 47.4 per cent on the previous year – shows that a point has clearly been proved.

Many passengers came from outside the region and one of the attractions has been the cheap flights with Go and bmibaby. Graham Keddie has started to fulfill the seemingly unlimited potential of EMA. Those living in the huge catchment area can now fly from their local airport to the destination of their choice. There is more than enough room for Go and bmibaby to thrive at EMA. There has been no need for a winner in the battle for supremacy and both airlines report that sales have exceeded expectations.

It has been a challenge for the airport because the dramatic increase in passengers came virtually overnight, but the workforce has put in a tremendous amount of work to make things go smoothly. In the long term a new terminal will need to be built, and plans are being worked upon but will take years to complete the entire project.

Keddie has said that the breakthrough has been made and proved what people have been claiming for many years. However, he feels there is still a lot more potential to be fulfilled. Suddenly people want to do business with the airport and that is good news for the many people who want to travel from EMA.

The international scheduled market showed an increase of 135.3 per cent in April 2005 compared to 12 months ago, with Malaga as the most popular destination. Domestic scheduled flights also experienced a large upturn with passengers increasing 30.6 per cent year on year – due entirely to the launch of the Go service between EMA and Edinburgh.

Source: Adapted from article originally in *Flightscene News Magazine of East Midlands Airport*, 50, Summer 2002.

Discussion Questions

1 Suggest a general outline marketing planning strategy for 12 months ahead for Graham Keddie.

2 What part should the sales function play when drawing up a detailed 12 months operational marketing plan for EMA?

3 Discuss the pros and cons of providing a long-term marketing plan, given the relative volatility of the market.

Examination Questions

1 Explain the differences between marketing strategies and sales strategies.

2 What is the relationship between objectives, strategies and tactics?

3 Discuss the component parts of the communications mix.

4 What is the relationship between SWOT analysis and the SWOT matrix?

5 What is meant by contingency planning and when is it required in the marketing planning process?

Chapter 8

E-Commerce and the Entrepreneur

- Discussing the benefits of selling on the WWW
- Understanding the factors an entrepreneur should consider before launching into e-commerce
- Explaining the 12 myths of e-commerce
- Discussing the basic approaches to e-commerce
- Evaluating the effectiveness of the company's website

12 Internet and IT Applications in Selling and Sales Management

Objectives

After studying this chapter you should be able to:

1. Understand how a range of information technology developments have altered the selling and sales management functions
2. Understand how the internet impacts sales and marketing
3. Know how information technology can enable customer relationship management
4. Recognise the different generations of salesforce automation (SFA) software
5. Understand the specific information technology applications in retail selling and marketing
6. Discuss some of the newer technology trends relating to sales and sales management

Key Concepts

- customer relationship management
- customer relationship quality (CRQ)
- e-commerce
- extranets
- information technology
- intranets
- salesforce automation (SFA)

Developments in information technology are having profound effects on the way products are sold and the nature of selling and sales management activities. The chapter begins by providing a general overview of important developments in information technology (IT) and electronic commerce (e-commerce). The impact of the internet is then discussed before explaining the nature and effect of customer relationship management on selling and sales management. Salesforce effectiveness and salesforce automation (SFA) are then examined, followed by a brief look at specific developments and applications as well as some of the newer technology trends.

12.1 The Internet and e-Commerce Revolution

The changing nature of the salesforce

Information technology, the internet and electronic commerce (e-commerce) have each had a major impact on salesforce productivity and management. The extent to which such technology developments have affected salespeople's jobs can be gauged by the boxed account of a national account manager for a major company.

A sales practitioner's perspective

Over the last 15 years the role of information technology has rapidly explored nearly every possible avenue of our working and social lives from the emergence of ATMs to personal computers, domestic appliances and the wealth of information that is held about us as individuals whenever we make a transaction.

During my ten years' experience of field-based sales, many changes have occurred. I will now give a few examples of how communication methods have changed and how more efficient methods of operation have developed.

First, not so long ago most communication was by landline telephone and letter. This was followed by the fax and pagers. Then mobile phones and email arrived and communication between businesspeople became almost instantaneous.

Second, in the arena of a traditional salesperson, the raising of letters confirming arrangements, quotations, etc., passed in the post and several weeks were often needed to conclude simple transactional business deals. These have been replaced first by fax but now by email and web-based purchasing. In addition, the role of the secretary in this is becoming obsolete as the majority of salespeople generate their own letters from standard templates and quotation software.

In purely transactional purchases, customers can produce their own quotations by specifying certain criteria on a web-based purchasing system. The various fields are entered and the system automatically produces a quotation, which is legally binding on the company.

Within industrial sales many changes have occurred through technology. Historically, knowledge was power and the salesperson or sales engineer would know nearly everything about the customer-facing side of the relationship. Customer records were often randomly completed and 'deals or agreements' could often be verbal or have an unwritten verbal amendment. This was a potential cause for conflict, particularly if the personnel changed. On average people would change every three years in a typical industrial sales role.

With the introduction of IT, laptops and PDAs, much of this information can now be accessed not only by salespeople and their line managers but anyone

(continued on following page)

within the company who may have a requirement to be aware of what has been agreed previously with the customer (e.g. customer service, technical support, finance and logistics).

One of the major advantages of this is that any contact with the customer is entered into their file so everyone is fully aware of conversations, comments and offers made. These systems are becoming more commonplace, particularly in larger firms trying to manage their customer information more efficiently and with less reliability on memory or paper records.

Customer relationship management (CRM) is becoming commonplace in a wide range of sales related areas, including banks, industrial sales, catalogues and even taxi firms where a log of all previous transactions, enquiries, purchasing profiles and other communications is kept. In the most complex systems, details about a customer preference for hobbies, family anniversaries, pet likes or dislikes can be logged to assist in creating a more familiar relationship between individuals in the sales process.

The belief, where this is applied correctly, is that the customer can contact or be contacted by the company with an almost seamless approach. Questions about invoices, technical issues and quotations can be fielded by a whole range of employees within the organisation. However all this information needs to be gathered, entered and managed and the onus of this task often falls to the field salesperson in addition to getting the order.

These CRM systems offer great advantages in managing customers and identifying micro-segments within the overall customer base for highly focused marketing campaigns and promotions. These systems are now also capable of identifying and creating actual profit and loss statements on individual accounts, and the efficiency with which the salesperson and the company as a whole deals with each individual customer.

In effect a customer can be rated not only on the traditional basis of revenue generation but on actual net profit generated. This takes into account the level of service that is required to maintain the business from sales calls to technical services, discounts, and all the little extras that can often be given away in order to get the initial sale but then continue to cost the company for years afterwards.

The advantage of this mechanism is that expensive resources are not exhausted purely on the pet customer or the difficult customer but available to those who are in reality the lifeblood of the company. It also allows the salesperson to compile a service offering (or scale of offering) for individual clients which is in proportion to their current and potential worth to the organisation as a whole. This requires a great deal of trust from the parent company, as the salesperson needs to know the profitability of accounts and product lines. However, the potential advantage of the salesperson running their area as their own business and seeing business as more than just the sale on offer at a particular time has proven its worth within the added value sales arena.

The increased efficiency of sales resources utilising these types of IT systems I believe is proven in the field, but with them comes an additional level of responsibility and workload in managing them.

In summary, technology in all its facets has impacted greatly on today's working environment. In some cases it has replaced people; in others it has assisted not necessarily in reducing the overall workload but in increasing the time spent on profitable activities, reducing time on mundane tasks and increasing efficiencies.

There are only so many hours in a day and it is the responsibility of each company and their employees to find and utilise methods, devices and technologies to enable them to work smarter in today's environment.

Source: A perspective given by Mr Paul Miller, National Account Manager, BP Castrol Ltd. Part of BP Amoco Plc.

Paul Miller's account is typical of the changes that have taken place in sales and sales management over the last decade or more. The growth in the adoption of the internet in sales and marketing during this period has been phenomenal.

The rise of electronic commerce

One key capability of the internet is the ability to conduct and support electronic commerce (**e-commerce**), a term that is used mainly in connection with business-to-business (B2B) commerce, as opposed to its business-to-consumer (B2C) counterpart. Although the first wave of growth of internet usage was in the B2C domain, the B2B area is now between five and ten times larger.[1] E-commerce is any trading activity that is carried out over an electronic network such as the internet. As such it is not unique to the internet. For example, banks have been conducting business electronically for decades.

Electronic data interchange (EDI) has also allowed customers to place orders and suppliers to send invoices electronically for many years. However, the growth of internet use has seen an accompanying expansion of e-commerce through this medium. The boxed case study discusses how e-commerce has contributed to the success of Federal Express, Cisco, Dell and GE. This should not mislead anyone into believing that success on the internet is guaranteed. For every success story there are hundreds of expensive e-commerce failures. Poor website design, reluctance to conduct transactions through a new medium, problems with the adoption of common standards, difficulties with the integration of back-end systems and security fears are all barriers that hinder the faster adoption of e-commerce by consumers and businesses alike.

E-commerce in action

Internet-based e-commerce began in the mid-1990s when companies like Federal Express, Cisco, Dell and GE started to focus on online sales, customer service and

(continued on following page)

procurement. These companies recognised the advantages of the internet as a more flexible alternative to electronic data interchange (EDI). It allowed them to expand their electronic trading to smaller organisations and transactions now started to flow on the internet. The terminology changed also – people began to use terms like 'e-business', 'e-commerce' and 'business-to-business' (B2B) as the use of the internet increased as a networking mechanism. A good example is Siemens, the German giant with an annual procurement budget of around €35bn. The company buys all sorts of materials, from metals and plastics to pencils and desks, and spreads these over a dozen global divisions in sectors ranging from semiconductors and telecommunications to transportation and medicine. In 2002, 76 per cent of Siemens' procurement was offline and 24 per cent online. Of the online purchases, 90 per cent were conducted via EDI, the transfer of data between different companies using networks, and the remainder via the web. The reason for the high EDI usage is simply that this electronic service is still widespread in some industries, particularly vehicle manufacturing. The goal is to process 50 per cent of all purchases electronically by 2006, with at least half of these web-based.

Source: Based on O'Connor, J., Galvin, E. and Evans, M. (2004) *Electronic Marketing – Theory and Practice for the 21st Century*, Financial Times Prentice Hall, Harlow.

E-commerce can take place at four levels (see Figure 12.1).[2]

Publish

This is the provision of information to the customer electronically. It is one-way communication that may involve annual reports, press releases, information on products and services, recruitment opportunities and advertising. Sometimes

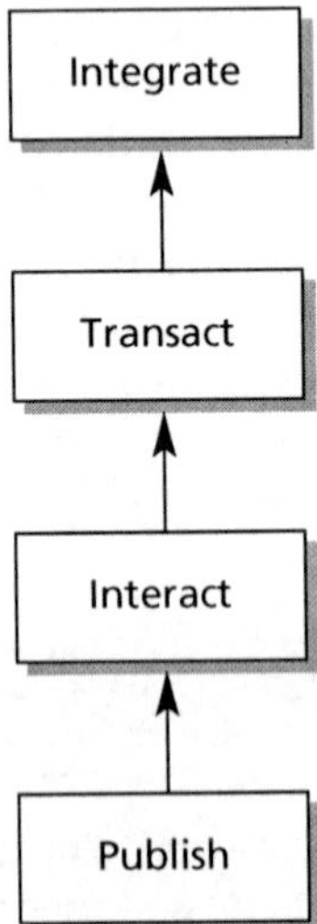

Figure 12.1 Four levels of e-commerce

referred to as 'brochureware', it is little more than the establishment of an online presence and has little to do with selling.

Interact

The next level refers to interactive engagement with the user on the internet. For example, Dell's website provides online technical support services including e-mail links to online technical support representatives. Again, this has little to do with sales but does provide an additional layer of functionality to the 'publish' level.

Transact

The third level of e-commerce allows goods and services to be bought and sold over the internet. Reaching this level can be costly in terms of initial investment, and although operating costs should be lower than more traditional ways of conducting business, usually costs need to be driven down in other areas of the business for cost savings overall to fall.

Integrate

The highest level of e-commerce is where integration of the computer system and processes of traders is achieved to create a strong, formalised relationship. This may involve the establishment of a business-to-business **extranet**, which is an electronic network linking companies to their trading partners. Extranets allow partners to exchange information such as that relating to ordering, delivery and invoicing in a secure environment. For example, Mobil's extranet allows the oil company to accept orders from 300 distributors globally.

The real impact of the internet on selling and sales management

To date, most of the commentary on the impact of the internet and information technology on sales and sales management has been anecdotal, offering exaggerated speculative forecasts of its future potential. Consequently, 'despite one view contending that the internet will become a major new retail format, replacing the traditional dominance of fixed location stores, little academic research exists to either disprove or support the claims of Internet penetration by retailers'.[3] Nonetheless, the internet channel continues to gain an increasing proportion of both B2C and B2B sales transactions.

With electronic commerce showing enormous potential to take over a significant share of sales, there has been an increasing need for companies to provide services that can reach individual users with different information profiles and levels of expertise.[4] Indeed, the internet has not only become a powerful tool, transforming the fundamental dynamics behind social and business interactions, but also more importantly, seems to be growing in both popularity and profitability.[5]

However, the application of the internet on selling and sales management remains a relatively new discipline with the potential to revolutionise the way companies build brands, sell products or services and develop relationships.

Although still in its infancy, this discipline represents a considerable ground for research with a fast pace of development. Nonetheless, as pointed out by some authors, few companies seem to have a focused strategy, let alone a clear understanding of this phenomenon.[6]

It should also be pointed out that while the initial objective of websites was to provide information, today increasing emphasis is being placed on the setting of lasting relationships between companies and customers.[7] As Martin suggests: 'The focus of marketing efforts are (and should be) shifting from marketing mix manipulation for the purpose of immediate exchange transactions to those that focus on longer-term exchange relationships.'[8] Accordingly, by developing a marketing strategy continuum focusing on steps to enable organisations to move from transaction cost marketing to relationship marketing, Grönroos not only complements Martin's argument, but further supports Scott's view that: 'Relationship marketing moves the dyadic exchange associated with personal selling from a short-term transaction orientation to a lifelong process where immediate closings must be postponed on the basis of more effectively meeting customer needs.'[9]

Not all researchers support the merits of this process and, opposing this outlook, Shaw argues: 'Marketers must stop their obsession with loving customers since it has become a distraction from the basics of selling and tracking the origins of sales success.'[10]

Nevertheless the internet has the potential to affect selling and sales management in many ways.

Building customer-centric selling arenas

The increasing use of the internet as a marketing and sales medium increases the power of the consumer by increasing the availability of comparative price information and the diversity of purchasing options. Customer focus not only compels management to realise the firm's primary responsibility of serving the customer, but also to recognise that customer knowledge is key to achieving market orientation.[11] As a result of this many organisations have successfully integrated strategies, tactics and web technologies to cement relationships with customers online.[12]

A major tool in creating customer-centric selling arenas is the emergence of extranets. These are secure sites accessible only to certain people and/or organisations. They allow transactions between buyer and seller to take place without the need for the involvement of expensive salespeople. Customers are able to log on to make routine purchases, allowing salespeople to focus on building customer relationships, developing customised solutions for customers and prospecting for new business. These business-to-business sites improve sales productivity and allow salespeople to build customer loyalty.[13]

Another internet-based selling arena is the open market catalogue site. These sites provide customers with product and price information and allow them to purchase from the site, rather like purchasing from a direct mail catalogue. The best known example is the online bookseller Amazon (www.amazon.com, www.amazon.co.uk, etc.).

Focusing on the right customer

Because the internet enables access to any online customer at any time and anywhere in the world, companies may be tempted to try to attract as many potential customers as possible. However, several authors warn against this lack of focus and advocate the necessity for companies to adhere to the principles of sales and marketing management such as targeting. For instance, Van Niekerk, Berthon and Davies stress that 'the temptation to be everything to everyone must be vigorously guarded against' and that 'a tighter focus on the specific target audience needs to be paramount'.[14]

When using the internet it is important that the organisation's website is designed to achieve a specific set of objectives and provides a focus, rather than just being a vehicle for promoting the company in general terms. These objectives can relate to servicing current customers when making purchases, cross-selling company products, encouraging new customers or building greater loyalty amongst existing customers. A method of encouraging response is to make a specific product or service offering or to ask for a website evaluation.

It is of course important that the website is simple to access, load and navigate with appropriate links. If it contains icons or banners to gain attention at the beginning, then these should not be used deeper in the site as they might prove to be distractions.

Data can be captured from those who respond to website offerings in terms of frequency of ordering, size of orders, types of purchase made, methods of payment, etc. This will provide a clearer picture of customers who can be profiled, segmented and targeted more easily along the lines suggested.

Creating quality in communications

The general consensus seems to be that the internet and its related technologies allow for swifter information exchange and more consistent communications.[15] However, researchers such as Reichheld and Schefter warn that 'with the freedom to do more comes the temptation to do too much'.[16]

Given the plethora of information now available, it is becoming increasingly important that evidence presented to the customer is kept to a manageable proportion.

Understanding buyer behaviour patterns

A study on consumer behaviour by Long and Schiffman clearly concludes: 'it pays to understand customers'.[17] Nonetheless, we still do not have a complete understanding of how users actually interact with the internet. Two factors seem critical to predicting consumer behaviour on the internet. The first factor questions whether the buyer builds a relationship with a selected vendor or searches for a different electronic vendor for each transaction. While the first pattern of behaviour will undoubtedly create an opportunity for the seller to tune regular offerings and promote loyalty, the second pattern precludes stable relationships. The other critical factor lies in the scope of the goods and services linking buyer and seller. Thus, the consumer is expected either to search for the provider of the best individual goods and services or favour a search for the best provider of a collection of goods and services.[18]

Based on these suggested patterns of behaviour, companies operating in varied industries will arguably find themselves in one or more of four competitive landscapes: Opportunity Spot, Opportunity Store, Loyal Link and Loyal Chains.

Opportunity spot occurs when purchasers exhibit no loyalty whatsoever. Each purchase is likely to be from a different supplier with no 'one-stop' shopping for a bundle of goods occurring. They may buy a ticket from British Airways one day and from United the next. When consumers show no loyalty or relationship continuity to brands or stores, but use intermediaries to put together bundles of goods, *opportunity store* markets occur. They may use Amazon.com one day and Buy.com another.

For *loyal links* to occur, consumers must show continuity when choosing vendors and services providers, although they may have no inclination to buy 'packages'. Consumers may be loyal to American Express for their credit card but see no reason to use that company for insurance. Consumers buying in categories that are described as *loyal chains* have preferred providers on whom they rely for a range of services and products. For example, Merrill Lynch might be used to help choose stocks, remind the consumers to write a will and arrange guardians for their children. Each type of consumer behaviour has marketing implications. For opportunity spot and opportunity store consumers, price is likely to be a key marketing mix variable. However, for loyal link markets the objective will be to retain the best customers through a careful blend of service and price. Dell Computers is an example of a company attempting to succeed in such a market. In practice, though, many companies have little information of the behaviour of their customers beyond sales figures and website hit rates.

Changing approaches to brand management

The internet is changing traditional approaches to brand management. While images and allusions are used to communicate branding messages in traditional marketing, on the internet product features and the provision of information are needed as a basis for branding as some consumers scan alternative product offerings and outlets for bargains. Furthermore, as consumers gain more experience of using the internet, they are more likely to search for alternative sources of information and to be less reliant on product branding.[19] Branding may become less dominant in consumer choice but still important.

Pricing

The internet makes the process of searching for the lowest price a simple task. Therefore, one prediction is that brands will have to become more price competitive to survive in the new electronic world. However, Reichheld and Schefter claim that 'contrary to common perception, the majority of on-line customers are not out to score the absolute lowest price ... Price does not rule the web; trust does'.[20] A contrary view is presented by Sinha who believes that 'cost transparency may weaken customer loyalty and create perceptions of price unfairness by encouraging dispassionate comparisons of price and features'.[21]

Creating interactive opportunities with consumers

The interactive opportunities afforded by the internet not only offer information about buyers' current tastes and preferences, but can also provide information about their potential needs and future market trends through marketing research.[22] It therefore represents a valuable source of new product ideas. The key is not only to design brands to be interactive, but also to equip customers with the ability and willingness to interact.[23]

Building customer relationships

Advances in information technology present new opportunities and challenges to establish, build and manage customer relationships. In fact, interactive communication is increasingly being hailed as the conductor to relationships, which cannot only drive brand value but more importantly provide up-to-date information on customers' needs and thoughts. For example, increasingly interactive databases have become the platform from which companies are tailoring the targeting of their messages to attract and retain customers. This is discussed in more detail in Chapter 11. Regarding the internet, the growth of email campaigns (as a replacement for direct mail) and extranets as forms of external communications and the growing complexity of intranet systems to facilitate internal communications show how information technology can aid (if done with care) buyer–seller relationships.

Performance measurement

Developments in information technology have increased the scope to collect, analyse and exploit customer information. The internet offers companies unprecedented opportunities for understanding their customers in depth and for customising offerings to meet their preferences. However, not only does the average website achieve less than 30 per cent of its full sales potential with each customer, but 'fewer than 20 per cent of companies even track customer retention rigorously let alone try to systematically learn from customer defection patterns'.[24] This lack of analysis means that strengths and weaknesses in past performance are not identified and opportunities to improve future performance are missed. Supporting this outlook, Kenny and Marshal argue that companies are so fixated on building web capacity and increasing their visitor counts, click-throughs and online sales that they overlook opportunities to cross-sell and upsell with a result that purchase value per customer is lower than it should be.[25] There is, therefore, considerable scope for improving the measurement of the effectiveness of websites and the information they provide.

12.2 Customer Relationship Management

Customer relationship management is a term for methodologies, technologies and e-commerce capabilities used by firms to manage customer relationships.[26] In particular, CRM software packages aid the interaction between customer and company, enabling the company to co-ordinate all the communication effort so that the customer is presented with a unified message and image. CRM companies offer a range of information technology-based services such as call centres, data analysis and website management. One basic principle behind CRM is that company personnel have a single-customer point of view of each client.[27] As customers are now using multiple channels more frequently, they may buy one product from a salesperson and another from a website. A website may provide product information which is used to buy the product from a distributor. Interactions between customer and company may take place through the salesforce, call centres, websites, email, fax services or distributors. Therefore it is crucial that no matter how customers contact a company, front-line staff have instant access to the same data about them such as their details and past purchases. This usually means consolidation of the many databases held by individual company departments into one centralised database that can be accessed by all relevant staff on a computer screen.

A model of customer management

Customer relationship management is much more than simply the technology. A good perspective of the CRM process is provided by the QCi Customer Management Model (see Figure 12.2). This model can be used by companies to understand how well they are managing their customers.[28] The model also shows the supporting role that IT plays in managing customers and sales relationships. Each of the elements of the QCi model will now be discussed.

Analysis and planning

Effective CRM begins by understanding the value, attitudes and behaviour of various customers and prospects. Once this has been achieved customers and prospects should be segmented so that planning activity can be as effective as possible. The planning will focus on such areas as the cost-effective retention and acquisition of customers. The boxed case history describes how a CRM system can be used to segment and target customers.

How CRM software can aid segmentation and targeting

A financial services company markets several financial service products and wants to identify new segments within its existing customer base for a cross-selling strategy. It wants to cross-sell Account Type A to those who have already purchased Account Type B. Through the application of CRM software, the company can easily identify those customers who have already purchased various of the company's products.

The company could target all those who have *not* bought A, but this would undervalue customer and transactional data as an asset. In addition, the company would also want the highest return on marketing investment. It is increasingly important to be accountable in terms of return on investment (ROI). So, instead the company could use this CRM software to interrogate existing customers who have both A and B accounts. Data mining can identify what makes these customers different from others and what makes them more or less likely to take both products. Transactional data can also be analysed for recency, frequency and monetary value (RFM) and long-term

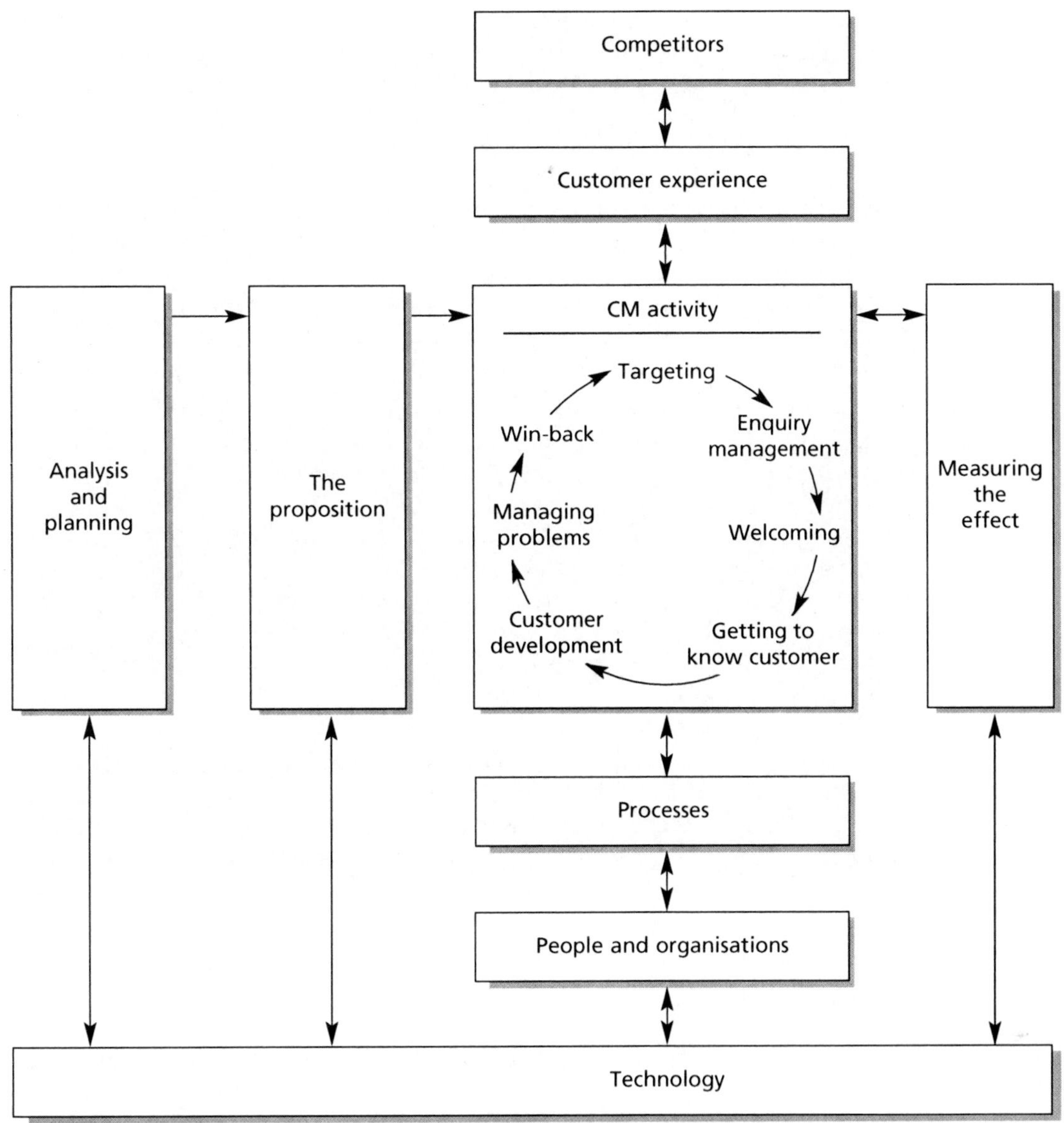

Figure 12.2 The QCi Customer Management Model
Source: From Foss, B. and Stone, M. (2001) *Successful Customer Relationship Marketing*, Kogan Page: London.

value (LTV) analyses. These are two important metrics in data-driven marketing and many software packages such as the one demonstrated here include algorithms for these further metrics. The results might show that the 'best' existing A and B account-holding customers come mainly from areas classified as blue-collar owners, high-income families, suburban semis, and low-rise council MOSAIC groups, income over £35,000, married, and aged in the 40 to 60 band.

However, the fullest benefit from existing customer data comes from looking at all the attributes together. The easiest way to achieve this is via CHAID,

(continued on following page)

which in this case is an integral component of the software being used and of most similar packages. CHAID (Chi-Squared Automatic Interaction Detection) is a form of cluster analysis which categorises individuals into groups based upon their characteristics. Here, various customer and transactional attributes have been investigated to see which best explain the characteristics of customers who have both A and B accounts. A 'tree' structure represents different 'hot and cold branches' through the data. Each branch represents a different level of importance in explaining who the A and B customers are. Each attribute is assessed and the most important or 'significant' forms the first split. Taking the entire customer base in this instance, 26 per cent of all customers have both A and B accounts.

By following the 'hottest branch', the company can understand the characteristics possessed by those customers who have purchased both A and B account types. Further branches of the CHAID tree might cascade down to even more segments based on whichever variables prove to be significant. Space prevents showing further stages here, but assume the analysis produced 60 target segments. Each of these would have significant and different characteristics. Targeting could be done on a 'test' basis in which a sample from each might be targeted and those with better response rates could then be targeted with the full 'roll-out' campaign. Also, each could be targeted with different treatments, according to whatever gender, age, marital status or geodemographic characteristic might underpin the 'creative' element.

Source: Based on a description of the Viper CRM software system owned by Smartfocus and provided by Martin Evans, Senior Teaching Fellow, Cardiff Business School. Thanks are given to Smartfocus for providing this example of their VIPER CRM software.

Proposition

Once segments of customers are identified and understood, the proposition to each segment needs to be defined and appropriate value-based offers planned. The proposition will be defined in terms of such issues as price, brand and service, and should drive the experience which the customer can expect when dealing with the organisation, its products and distributors. The proposition must then be communicated to both the customers and the people responsible for delivering it.

Information and technology

Information and technology provide the foundations for the whole model. Data needs to be collected, stored, analysed and used in a way that provides information which is consistent with the CRM strategy, the way people work and the way customers want to access the company. Technology enables an organisation to acquire, analyse and use vast amounts of data involved in managing customers. It needs to deliver the right information to the relevant people at the right time so that they can achieve their role in managing customers.

People and organisation

An organisation's front-line staff need to be recruited, trained, developed and motivated to deliver high standards of customer relations. Key elements are an organisational structure that supports effective customer management, role identification, training requirements and resources, and employee satisfaction.

Process management

In an environment where customer contact can take place at several different points, process can be difficult to implement and manage. Nevertheless, clear and consistent processes for managing customer relations need to be developed and reviewed in the light of changing customer requirements.

Customer management activity

This concerns the implementation of the plans and processes to deliver the proposition(s) to target segment(s) and involves the following:

1. *Targeting customer and prospect groups* with clear propositions (see earlier case history).
2. *Enquiry management*: this starts as soon as an individual expresses an interest and continues through qualification, lead handling and outcome reporting.
3. *Welcoming*: this covers new customers and those upgrading their relationship.It ranges from simple 'thank you' messages to sophisticated contact strategies.
4. *Getting to know*: customers need to be persuaded to give information about themselves. The information needs to be stored, updated and used. Useful information includes attitude and satisfaction information and relationship 'healthchecks'.
5. *Customer development*: decisions need to be made regarding which customers to develop through higher levels of relationship management activity and which to maintain or drop.
6. *Managing problems*: this involves early problem identification, complaint handling and 'root cause' analysis to spot general issues that have the potential to cause problems for many customers.
7. *Win-back*: activities include understanding reasons for loss, deciding which customers to try to win back, and developing win-back programmes that offer lost customers the chance to return and good reason to do so.

Customer experience

External measurement of customer experiences needs to take place and includes satisfaction tracking, loyalty analysis and mystery shopping.

Competitors

The strengths and weaknesses of competitors need to be monitored and the company's performance on the above issues evaluated in the light of the competition.

Measuring the effect

This final element occurs after the sale has been made and the service delivered. A core part of the CRM proposition is to ensure that customers' expectations are either met or exceeded, to the extent that those customers may become loyal and repeat purchasers in the future, and ambassadors or advocates to other potential customers. It sounds easy but, as mentioned earlier in this chapter, surprisingly few companies attempt to measure and manage customer retention in a systematic fashion. This is a subject we will pick up again in the next section.

CRM in selling and sales management

Customer retention and account management are sales activities that can be supported today by IT in a relatively sophisticated fashion. As the boxed example shows, the type of CRM technology available to today's sales managers can provide both a strategic overview of how well a company's portfolio of customers is being managed, and operational reports to guide individual sales managers to nurture their customers more effectively.

Getting a deep-insight into your customers

Most customer surveys miss the point. They don't account for the customer's feelings and trust. Furthermore, they are designed in a way that fail to capture the changing needs of customers. Let me start by clearing up a misunderstanding. I don't wish to play with semantics, but it is important to highlight the difference between Customer Loyalty and Customer Retention. Customer Loyalty is an elusive and intangible concept that cannot be measured and consequently *cannot* be *managed.* However, customer retention is a tangible concept that can be measured. If it can be measured, it *can* be *managed*! However, customer retention is a complex process.

Our research shows that the most important factor in customer retention is the measure of *Customer Relationship Quality (CRQ).* This is an assessment of six factors, each of which can be measured:

- *the overall quality* of the firm's products or services,
- *customer satisfaction* (general assessment of what the firm does),
- *leading edge* (comparison with its competitors),
- *service performance* (reliability, responsiveness and customer care),
- *trust,* and
- *relationship commitment* (an intellectual and emotional link with a firm or a brand that reinforces one's self-identity).

We help customers measure and manage CRQ on an ongoing basis. We are also pragmatic enough to understand that sales directors need more operational measures to monitor the performance of their sales or account managers. At Deep-insight, we provide 'account manager packs' that provide an assessment of CRQ across different customer portfolios. That helps the sales director identify under-performing (and over-performing) sales managers, and helps the individual sales manager to identify the actions he or she needs to take on specific accounts to improve the quality of the relationship with (and future sales from!) that customer.

Online assessment tools like ours provide results within days, not weeks or months. More important, because the assessment takes only 12 minutes to complete, we get response rates of up to 75%. In other words, today's technology allows you to check the pulse of ALL your customers regularly, not just a small sample. Sales directors love that, because they can get regular and speedy feedback that allows them to take remedial action where necessary.

Source: A perspective from Dr Pierre Chenet, founder of the customer retention company Deep-insight (www.deep-insight.com).

Chenet's perspective is an example of true CRM in selling and sales management – attempting to gain a real understanding of, and insight into, the relationships that companies have with their customers. Armed with these insights, sales directors and account managers can focus on what they really need to do in order to make the next sale to these customers.

In the next section, we examine some of the more tactical uses of technology in the sales process. Note that much of what is described as salesforce automation (SFA) is an attempt at reducing the cost and improving the productivity of the salesperson. This is very important from a commercial perspective, but should not be confused with the true CRM activities described above, which are focused on the customer rather than the salesperson.

12.3 Improving Salesforce Effectiveness

Automating the salesforce

While sales representatives traditionally operated with limited technology support, in recent times, technology has been used to improve productivity. This technology, typically using laptop computers, is often referred to as salesforce automation (SFA).

Technology can increase the overall professionalism of salespeople as they work through the sales cycle with potential customers. Some of the benefits provided by this type of laptop software application include:

- Freeing salespeople from routine office administrative tasks, enabling them to spend more time with customers.

- Providing better customer service because the salesperson has immediate access to information such as stock levels or quotations.
- Capturing information that allows management to measure and monitor sales performance.
- Helping to create and manage sales opportunities so that a greater proportion is converted into sales.

The important caveat here is that salesforce productivity issues cannot be solved completely by technology. Selecting salespeople with the right skills, training them and motivating them with good incentives are also critical to salesforce productivity.

Three generations of salesforce automation (SFA) software

Salesforce automation software has developed through a series of different generations over the past decade.

Generation 1: Personal information and contact management

The first generation involved equipping the salesforce with laptops and other types of computing and data storage devices. At first, these machines contained the typical office productivity applications such as spreadsheets and word processors. Before long, salespeople clearly saw the value of Personal Information Managers (PIMs) and over time, these applications became tied into the other personal productivity applications on the PC. Products such as ACT!, Goldmine, and Maximizer were designed to help a salesperson manage contacts and time, and increase their selling effectiveness. Powerful time and contact management tools that had not existed previously were quickly developed and implemented.

Generation 2: The networked salesforce

As managers realised that this technology was helpful to their field sales representatives, they began to wonder how they might also harness this information for corporate purposes. The 'second generation' SFA tools were essentially networked versions of the first, connecting the contacts database and personal productivity tools of the salesforce to the corporate network. This was usually accomplished via data replication, by plugging the laptop into a phone-line, typically at night. While sales representatives retained their interest in time and contact management, these tools offered them little if any additional advantage over the first generation, although some were much smaller, more portable and lighter than their predecessors.

Generation 3: Technology-enabled selling

Technology-enabled selling is the name give to the latest generation of SFA tools. Technology-enabled sales systems incorporate a much richer variety of functions to help salespeople acquire and close more business, including some combination of the following:

- *Lead management.* The ability for sales to receive leads from marketing and other departments.
- *Opportunity management.* This organises all information around a sales opportunity to give a complete view of the sales cycle, co-ordinate schedules and resources, and bring the sales process to closure.
- *Account management.* The ability to track successfully closed opportunities. This can also track business contacts through companies, subsidiaries, branch offices, departments, etc. with multiple addresses and contacts.
- *Proposal management.* The ability of the salesforce to produce on-the-spot, customised, accurate product configurations and proposals. It is critically important for complex product and service sales opportunities.
- *Win/loss reporting.* The ability to evaluate wins, losses and return on investment objectively. It allows people and companies to learn and improve their sales and customer support processes.

There are literally hundreds of different software solutions aimed at the salesforce automation market. Some well-known US packages are shown in Table 12.1 below.

12.4 Other Applications of IT in Sales

Optimising sales territories

Another area of opportunity is the allocation of sales territories to particular salespeople. This can be an inefficient manual process that can be automated using statistical techniques to optimise the ratio of time spent with clients to time spent on the road. Zoltners and Lorimer (2000)[30] believe that many salesforces are losing millions of dollars each year because of sales territory imbalances. They cite a study of 4,800 sales territories from 18 companies in four different industries where more

Table 12.1 Well-known US salesforce automation (SFA) software packages

SFA solutions aimed at large enterprises	SFA solutions aimed at small–medium enterprises
Amdocs/Clarify (www.amdocs.com)	Pivotal (www.pivotal.com)
E.piphany (www.epiphany.com)	Onyx Software (www.onyx.com)
Firepond (www.firepond.com)	Interact Commerce (www.saleslogix.com)
J.D. Edwards (www.jdedwards.com)	
Oracle (www.oracle.com)	
PeopleSoft (www.peoplesoft.com)	
SAP (www.sap.com)	
Siebel Systems (www.siebel.com)	

Source: Gartner Research (2002).[29]

than half of the territories were imbalanced because they were either too large or too small. They also note that there are very real obstacles that prevent companies from optimising their sales territories:

- Salesforces resist change.
- Salesforce incentives and compensation plans can work against achieving the best alignment.
- Realignment is a cumbersome task.
- Data required for alignment is often not readily available.

These are the internal difficulties associated with any changes to existing sales territories. The realignment or optimisation of sales territories can also be problematic and confusing for customers. Zoltners and Lorimer believe that sales territory alignment is one of the most frequently overlooked areas of salesforce productivity and provide a methodology for overcoming the obstacles that includes obtaining buy-in from the salesforce and making territory decisions based on accurate data.

The boxed case shows an example of one implementation of territory management software.

IT applications in territory management

In the past, sales managers drew sales territory boundaries using a map, a thick felt pen, lots of pins and years of experience. The result was highly inefficient territories. At best this approach led to lots of unnecessary driving and at worst it meant lost sales as some areas were less well served than they should have been. Today software packages such as CACI Fieldforce Planning's *Insite Fieldforce* provide computerised territory planning. The package calculates the best possible balance of workloads and drive times to create efficient territories that allow the salesforce to spend less time driving and more time face-to-face with customers.

Territories are normally built around the locations of the salespeople – their home addresses or the local offices from which they travel – and the number of territories requested will be the number of salespeople in post. If more salespeople are to be recruited, extra 'floating locations' can be added and the package will work out the optimum location for each one. Alternatively, all territories can be based around floating locations to identify the best location for all salespeople. By default, territories of equal workload are produced. Account is taken of the greater time spent driving in more rural territories in Scotland, mid-Wales, East Anglia, Devon and Cornwall. Allowance is also taken of the distribution of calls around the sales base. For example, in one territory calls over an hour's drive time from the salesperson's home may be widely scattered while in another they may be concentrated in three towns where several calls can be made on the same day to reduce the total time spent driving. In this way efficient territories based on both drive time and workload can be designed.

A companion software package, *CallSmart*, allows sales calls to be placed in the best sequence to minimise drive time. It takes into account many factors such as call locations, call cycles, visit restrictions, fieldforce locations and driving times. It will deal with single and multiple frequency calls and plan tomorrow's visits or a set of call cycles for the next year. There are two versions of software, one allowing head office to plan calls and the other for use on the field salesperson's laptop.

The most efficient call sequence is achieved by using a matrix of drive times to and from any postcode. The package can then make the most efficient choice of when to plan each call. Call sequences can be viewed on a map to reassure users that the chosen plan is sensible, logical and efficient.

Source: Based on Shaw, M. and Williams, C. (1999) 'Putting territories on the map', *Journal of Targeting, Measurement and Analysis*, 8(2), pp. 135–52; www.caci.co.uk/ppf-insitefieldforce.htm; www.caci.co.uk/pff-callscheduling.htm

Geographic Information Systems (GIS) and Global Positioning Satellite (GPS) systems

One of the critical steps in realigning salesforce territories is the creation of an accurate territory database. Companies need to spend a significant amount of time creating, evaluating and verifying the geographic data that drive territory alignment decisions. In many Western countries, commercially-available geographic information systems (GIS) contain very good geographic data, based on detailed ZIP code or postal code information, to identify sales targets in metropolitan areas down to street level. CACI's *Insite Fieldforce* system (see box 'IT applications in territory management') is one example of a GIS that can be used for resource planning, territory planning and call scheduling.

In other countries where good geographic data are less easily available, the process is not so straightforward. Zoltners and Lorimer discuss the application of global positioning satellite (GPS) technology for creating the geographic account database. In one case in the Dominican Republic, a consumer products company equipped its salesforce with GPS readers. Salespeople stood at each account location and recorded account details (such as account name) while the GPS system captured the exact coordinates of the account location from satellite signals overhead. It took approximately one month to create an electronic database of the exact locations for over 20,000 accounts. Moreover, the salesforce also accepted the territory realignment process more readily because they were intimately involved in the data gathering activities.

Other sales support applications

Recruitment and selection

Recruitment and selection decisions can also be facilitated by IT applications. Specific software packages have been developed to assess the suitability of sales personnel. Packages assess candidates on the basis of key attributes for a salesperson, for example, intellect, motivation and sales ability. Some packages provide a suite of skill areas which can be selected according to the nature of the sales job and may include prospecting, lead qualification, handling objections, presentation skills, closing the sale, telephone technique and time management.

Such software packages can also be used in relation to the current sales team to diagnose underperformance and to identify training and motivational needs. For example, a sales manager can identify skills weaknesses and therefore focus on the area (e.g. presentation skills) in most need of attention. In relation to motivation, a manager can determine whether status is more important than money and adjust incentives accordingly.

Training

Implementation of *training* can also be assisted by IT. Computer-based training (CBT) packages can be used to deliver knowledge and develop skills in managing information. In particular, new product information can be delivered in this way. The software can be used to present information and challenge the salesperson to remember key points or to monitor knowledge levels. Some companies such as those in financial services (e.g. insurance) require their salespeople to achieve a minimum score before they are allowed to sell. A key advantage of computer-based training software is that it can be used at times and locations to suit the company and user. There has been growing interest in multimedia training packages. As more and more portable computers have CD-ROMs and training organisations install multimedia labs, this application has grown.

Sales forecasting

Computers have been used for *sales forecasting* purposes for many years. For example, the statistical software package SPSS can be used to forecast future sales using sophisticated techniques such as regression analysis. This takes account of variables such as advertising spend, disposable income and relative price levels to predict future sales. Without the power of the computer, the calculations would be time consuming, tiresome and prone to error.

Applications in retail sales and marketing

Some of the greatest changes in e-commerce have taken place within the field of retailing. This has major implications for the way in which business is conducted between suppliers and retailers, as described in the box below.

The changing relationship between supplier and retailer

The area of the relationship between a supplier and a retailer in the grocery industry has for a long time been a relationship built on personal contact. The personal contact between the salesforce of the supplier and representatives for the retailers (from store managers and 'upwards') has been the foundation of business relationships in the grocery sector. In recent years, the size of the salesforces have decreased, and more and more communication is done electronically between supplier and retailer. This is especially true in countries like the UK, where different forms of extranet, proprietary-nets based on internet technology, is increasingly the contact point between suppliers and retailers.

Source: Johansson, U. (2000) 'Consequences of information technology on supplier-retailer relationships in the grocery industry: a comparative study of Sweden and the UK', available at www.lri.lu.se/lifs/projects/it.htm

Johansson describes how suppliers access information on their sales and stocks, including promotions, with the retailers. He cites Safeway (now taken over by Morrisons), the fourth largest grocery retailer in the UK, which is linked to 500 of its suppliers, including all major ones, through the company's Supplier Information System (SIS). Tesco, the market leader in the UK, has its own system while Asda is argued to be even more advanced given that it is owned and operated by Wal-Mart, a retailer that builds its success largely on the use of state of the art information technology.

Suppliers need to be fully conversant with the technology employed by their trade customers and ensure their strategy and systems are consistent with their customer's approach. Suppliers need to be sensitive to the impact their own actions can have on a customer's technology and should take advantage of opportunities to assist the customer through the sharing of information and technological resources.

The pace of change in retailing continues to accelerate. Much of this change has been as a consequence on investment and focus on information technology by retailers of all sizes and made possible by falling infrastructure costs, such as the internet, which makes using data possible and cost effective.

We have already examined the role of electronic data interchange (EDI) applications in the retail industry. The following paragraphs give a brief insight into other applications used in the retail industry by both suppliers and retailers.

Supply chain management

Much of the drive for investment being made by retailers is to increase the efficacy of data relating to stock to allow efficiencies to be made in supply chain management. Supply chain management is the concept of the provision of products from suppliers' production lines to their sale at the retailers' tills. Supply chain management drives profitability as it ensures retailers and suppliers are focused on ensuring the right products are available in the right quantities at the right times to meet their individual customers' requirements. Accurate and real time data are the enablers for this.

Retailers are increasingly aware of the benefit of having collaborative relationships with their suppliers and are now making this data available to their suppliers, usually through web-based technology such as secure intranets and extranets. This allows the supplier to see the same data as their customers at the same time. Through the use of algorithm-based software packages both parties are able to use this data to manage the supply chain. Production and supply are harmonised to in-store demand, facilitating the concept of demand management. This can have the mutual benefits of sales being maximised, as stock-outs are reduced and lower levels of stock in the supply chain produce cost savings.

Retailers have taken the lead in this investment and thus now hold the balance of power in dealings with suppliers as they now possess more up-to-date and relevant real time data than their suppliers. This obviously gives a commercial advantage when negotiating with suppliers.

Electronic point of sale (EPOS) and electronic funds transfer at point of sale (EFTPOS)

Data is captured at the moment a product's unique bar code is scanned through at the till. Advances in technology have significantly aided the scope for data analysis. In addition to the original scanner-related data on sales rate, stock levels, stock turn, price and margin, retailers now have information about the demographics, socio-economic and lifestyle characteristics of consumers. They can also assess the impact of a whole host of variables, e.g. price, promotions, advertising, position in store, shelf position and number of facings. This information drives their choice of product mix, allocation of shelf space and promotional tactics. Some retailers also use customer loyalty cards as a means to capture data which can be analysed, allowing the retailer to engage in one-to-one marketing initiatives, e.g. information on new products and offers of discounts to retain customers.

EPOS has certainly changed the relationship between buyer and seller. Before the availability of scanner data, the trading relationship depended on information provided by manufacturers from retail audits, information that was at least several weeks old. More detailed, accurate and timely data from scanner systems gives the retailer significant bargaining power. Not surprisingly, therefore, information finds itself on the negotiating agenda. Manufacturers do buy EPOS data from their customers, but they can also trade the information and capabilities they have in exchange for it. Market knowledge is still the manufacturer's forte and this national market picture is of great use to the retailer. Additionally, armed with the retailer's EPOS data, the manufacturer could deliver well-targeted trade marketing programmes beneficial to both sides. In true trade marketing spirit, co-operation is the overall preferred approach.

EPOS depends on the inclusion of bar codes on all products to be scanned. This impacts directly on the manufacturer/supplier who should ensure that all packs carry a bar code and that the bar codes for any new line listings or promotional packs are entered into the customer's system before any goods are shipped.

Space management systems

Maximising the sales and profitability of selling space is critical. One of the reasons for retailers investing in supply chain management is to reduce the amount of storage space required in-store, allowing sales areas to be increased. To ensure the right amount of product is kept in-store and featured on the shelf, retailers use space management systems to construct virtual plannograms, which should maximise sales that can be achieved from each metre of selling space. To better understand the implications of these software packages on their products, suppliers have not only bought packages but also set up departments which specialise in space management. Opportunities exist for their proactive use by manufacturers, particularly in situations where the retailer is short of resources; importantly manufacturers can put themselves forward as produce category specialists. In the soft drinks sector, Coca-Cola Schweppes Beverages (CCSB) acts as the category specialist. A key function of the trade marketing role at CCSB is to advise the retail trade on the allocation of space to the soft drinks category in totality. An example of a software package that can accomplish this is *Nielsen's Spaceman.* Recently, however, retailers have become concerned that some suppliers may use this technology to favour their products at the expense of competitors at the key point of purchase.

Direct product profitability

Maximising the profitability of every product is critical in many areas of retailing where price figures highly in the marketing mix.

The output from direct product profitability (DPP) systems can affect retailer decisions on product stocking, store position, pricing and even trading terms demanded. It is vital therefore that the manufacturer understands DPP and the extent to and manner in which individual retailers use it.

DPP replaces gross margin as a much more accurate measure of a product's contribution to total company overhead and profit. It takes account of the fact that products differ with respect to the amount of resource they use, such as the amount of transport costs, warehouse and back-of-store space, staff handling time, share of shelf space, even head office costs. As a minimum, the manufacturer needs to be aware of how the retailer is using DPP and have sufficient expertise to question the results of the retailer's analysis. For example, a product with low DPP may still be essential to a retailer's success if it generates in-store customer flow, and if deleting it would lead to a loss of customers.

It can be used by manufacturers and retailers to examine the costs at their individual ends of the distribution chain, and by both to estimate the costs and profits in the other's field for use in negotiation. In some instances manufacturers have taken the lead in introducing DPP and in doing so have capitalised on the potential gains for both sides. Procter & Gamble (USA) claims it would modify its packaging, trading terms and other variables on the basis of DPP analysis. Proactive use of DPP by manufacturers works best with actual cost data from the retailer; without this only standard retail industry data can be used. In fact, to continue a theme already begun, manufacturer–retailer co-operation in the sharing of data is the preferred strategy in order to maximise gains for both parties.

Category management

Technology also enables category management. Scanning technology delivers information at a level of detail that allows customised merchandising strategies (tailored product assortments, space allocations, pricing, promotions) to be devised for categories or types of store. Furthermore, sophisticated computer modelling programs allow such marketing programmes to be pre-tested before they are implemented.

Retailers will best respond to those manufacturers who establish themselves as experts in the category and share their data on product sales, consumer behaviour and competitor activity with them. Manufacturers can add this data to their knowledge, analyse and identify significant consumer and category trends and use this to make strategic recommendations to the retailer on ranging, merchandising, products and promotions that will increase the overall profitability of the category. This, of course, presumes the adoption by the manufacturer of the relevant technology and applications, but the gains to the proactive manufacturer are substantial.

12.5 Other Trends

The wireless revolution

One significant trend in recent years is the move towards wireless technology, freeing the salesperson from his or her desk and allowing greater freedom to spend time with customers. Signorini (2001)[31] defines four areas into which the majority of these wireless data applications fall:

- *Field sales*. These include product inventory and pricing systems, access to customer account information, and real-time ordering.
- *Mobile office*. These include email, personal information management (PIM), access to corporate intranets and human resources systems.
- *Fleet management*. These solutions include despatch applications for courier companies, call scheduling systems for taxis and vans, location-tracking applications for managing the utilisation of large fleets of trucks, routing and mapping systems.
- *Field service*. These include the scheduling of work orders in the service and repair industry, access to customer records and information while on-site, financial services applications such as insurance claims handling and assessing, and access to national databases while 'on the road'.

Field sales constitute the single biggest use of wireless technology, accounting for more than a quarter of all applications in large organisations.[32] Wireless sales technology is typically used in one of two ways:

- The salesperson has a laptop computer that can be synchronised with head office by connecting a mobile phone to the laptop.
- The salesperson uses a personal digital assistant (PDA) that can transmit sales information to, and receive sales reports from, head office.

Although handheld devices are cheaper than laptops, it may well be the case that the overall cost per salesperson increases as a result of the introduction of mobile technology. If sales representatives retain their laptops, rather than replacing them with PDAs, then costs will certainly increase. There is also the potential for higher costs associated with the relative immaturity of some of the underlying technologies and standards.

Outsourcing of sales management applications

Another development worth noting is the trend towards outsourcing of sales management applications to specialist third parties. The business model can often be compelling, as many smaller companies do not have the resources to host their own salesforce applications. By using third parties, they avoid the need to develop and maintain their own software and sales systems. Their salespeople can gain access to the software using a standard internet browser and the data is then transferred to the company's database. One of the best examples of this is Salesforce.com (www.salesforce.com).

12.6 Conclusions

This chapter has explored the new developments in information technology that have impacted selling and sales management. Information technology is helping companies such as Wal-Mart, GE and Dell Computers to sell efficiently and effectively to customers. The internet is allowing customers to search for product and price information more easily than ever before, and to buy directly without the need for salespeople or distributors.

Developments in information technology such as email, fax and mobile phones are improving the communications links between salespeople, customers and head office. They are also bringing pressure on salespeople who are now expected to respond faster because of the speed at which these new technologies operate.

Customer relationship management software is allowing companies to understand the quality of their customer relationships better than they could historically. CRM software also provides company staff with access to the same data about the customer and so can respond in a unified way. This usually means the consolidation of the many databases held by individual departments into a centralised database that can be accessed by all relevant staff.

Sales management has also benefited from these developments. Salesforce automation (SFA) software has helped to increase the productivity of the salesperson, while IT is also employed to support territory management, journey planning, recruitment and selection, training, sales forecasting, salesforce size and evaluation systems.

Finally, an in-depth look at how IT has affected retail selling and marketing has identified applications in the areas of supply chain management, EPOS, space management systems, direct product profitability and category management.

References

1 Sharma, A. (2002) 'Trends in internet-based business-to-business marketing', *Industrial Marketing Management*, 31, pp. 77–84.

2 O'Connor, J. and Galvin, E. (1998) 'Creating value through e-commerce', *Financial Times Management*, FT Prentice Hall, London.

3 Hart, C. *et al.* (2000) 'Retailer adoption of the internet – implications for retail marketing', *European Journal of Marketing*, 34(8), pp. 954–74.

4 Aberg, J. and Shahmehri, N. (2000) 'The role of human web assistants in e-commerce: an analysis and a usability study', *Internet Research*, 10(2), pp. 114–25.

5 Birch, A., Gerbert, P., Schneider, D., OC&C and the McKenna Group (2000) *The Age of E-Tail*, Capstone Publishing, Tulsa, US; Chaffey, D., Mayer, R., Johnston, K. and Ellis-Chadwick, F. (2000) *Internet Marketing*, Pearson Education, Harlow; Evans, P. and Wurster, T.S. (2000) *Blown to Bits: How the New Economics of Information Transforms Strategy*, Harvard Business School Press, Boston; Simeon, R. (1999) 'Evaluating domestic and international web strategies', *Internet Research: Electronic Networking Applications and Policy*, 9(4), pp. 297–308.

6 See Cannon (2000) op. cit.; and Chaffey et al. (2000) op. cit.

7 Zineldin, M. (2000) 'Beyond relationship marketing: technologicalship marketing', *Marketing Intelligence and Planning*, 18(1), pp. 9–23.

8 Martin, C.L. (1998) 'Relationship marketing: a high-involvement product attribute approach', *Journal of Product and Brand Management*, 7(1), pp. 6–26.

9 Grönroos, C. (1994) 'Quo vadis, marketing? Toward a relationship marketing paradigm', *Journal of Marketing Management*, 10, pp. 347–60; Scott, M.P. (1995) 'Relationship selling', *Executive Excellence*, 12(1), p. 18.

10 Shaw, R. (1999) 'Customers are about sales, not false friendships', *Marketing*, January, p. 20.

11 Gummesson, E. (1996) 'Relationship marketing and imaginary organisations: a synthesis', *European Journal of Marketing*, 30(2), pp. 31–44.

12 Reichheld, F. and Schefter, P. (2000) 'E-loyalty', *Harvard Business Review*, July–August, pp. 105–13.

13 Shoemaker, M.E. (2001) 'A framework for examining IT-enabled market relationships', *Journal of Personal Selling and Sales Management*, 21(2), pp. 177–85.

14 Van Niekerk, D.N.R., Berthon, J.P. and Davies, T. (1999) 'Going with the flow', *Internet Research: Electronic Networking Applications and Policy*, 9(2), pp. 109–16.

15 Schwartz, D.G. (2000) 'Concurrent marketing analysis: a multiagent model for product, price, place, and promotion', *Marketing Intelligence and Planning*, 18(1), pp. 24–30.

16 Reichheld and Schefter (2000) op. cit.

17 Long, M.M. and Schiffman, L.G. (2000) 'Consumption values and relationships: segmenting the market for frequency program', *Journal of Consumer Marketing*, 17(3), pp. 214–32.

18 Clemons, E. and Row, M. (2000) 'Behaviour is key to web retailing strategy', *Financial Times*, p. 24.

19 Ward, M.R. and Lee, M.J. (2000) 'Internet shopping, consumer search and product branding', *Journal of Product and Brand Management*, 9(1), pp. 6–20.

20 Reichheld and Schefter (2000) op. cit.

21 Sinha, I. (2000) 'Cost transparency: the net's real threat to prices and brands', *Harvard Business Review*, March–April, pp. 43–55.

22 Li, T., Nicholls, J.A.F. and Roslow, S. (1999) 'The relationship between market-driven learning and new product success in export markets', *International Marketing Review*, 16(6), pp. 476–503.

23 Martin, C.L. (1998) 'Relationship marketing: a high-involvement product attribute approach', *Journal of Product and Brand Management*, 7(1), pp. 6–26.

24 Reichheld and Schefter (2000) op. cit.

25 Kenny, D. and Marshal, J.F. (2000) 'Contextual marketing: the real business of the internet', *Harvard Business Review*, November–December, pp. 119–25.

26 Foss, B. and Stone, M. (2001) *Successful Customer Relationship Marketing*, Kogan Page, London.

27 Dempsey, J. (2001) 'An elusive goal leads to confusion', *Financial Times Information Technology Supplement*, 17 October, p. 4.

28 See Foss and Stone (2001) op. cit.; and Woodcock, N., Starkey, J., Stone, J., Weston, P. and Ozimek, J. (2001) *State of the Nation II: 2002, An Ongoing Global Study of How Companies Manage Their Customer*, QCi Assessment Ltd, West Byfleet.

29 Close, W. and Eisenfeld, B. (2002). 'CRM sales suites: 1H02 magic quadrant,' *Gartner Research Note M-14-7938*, 1 March.

30 Zoltners, A. and Lorimer, S. (2000). 'Sales territory alignment: an overlooked productivity tool', *Journal of Personal Selling & Sales Management*, Summer.

31 Signorini, E. (2001) *The Enterprise Wireless Data Application Opportunity: A Segmentation Analysis*, The Yankee Group, December.

32 Yankee Group (2001) *Wireless Connectivity to the Enterprise: 2001 Survey Analysis*, The Yankee Group, March.

Practical Exercise

Computer assisted sales process (CASP)

Buying a car is a highly involved and lengthy process when compared to most other retail purchasing experiences. Today's car buyers are armed with far more information and can choose to buy vehicles online if they wish. However, the majority of customers still choose to buy a car through the traditional dealer network, despite the buying process remaining unchanged during the industry's 100-year history and surveys which suggest that customers view the process negatively. The motor manufacturers have started to address this issue by providing their dealership networks with more sophisticated tools aimed at improving customer handling and enhancing the consumer experience. One of these tools has been the computer assisted sales process (CASP). The CASP systems are usually designed with the following features:

A salesperson's diary assists in operating a controlled sales process, appointments for test drives, meeting with customers, vehicle handovers and follow-up calls to customers. The system encourages salespeople to collect prospect information such as name and contact details, what vehicle the customer currently has and what they like about it. The system automatically connects to the dealer management system and updates details of customers that are already held from previous car purchases or interactions with other departments in the dealership.

An electronic brochure guides the salesperson and customer through a structured presentation, allowing the customer to configure a car of their choice, which is then displayed on screen and includes vehicle model, engine size, colour and trim selection and factory options.

The CASP system also provides product reviews collected and added by the brand and marketing teams and also competitor vehicle comparisons – one of the weakest areas of salespeople's knowledge.

Following a test drive, the CASP can collect customer feedback on the driving experience. This aids constructive reflection for the customer, provides a 'closing' aid for the salesperson, and also provides an effective feedback mechanism for the manufacturer on the performance of their vehicles.

Should the customer have a vehicle to trade in, the system provides an on-screen part exchange price which adds an element of 'believability' for the customer and helps to provide a better trade-in price for the dealer.

The system also integrates into the manufacturer's national vehicle stock locator to source the customer's desired vehicle. Alternatively, if not available, it can place an order directly with the factory.

The finance presenter calculates and presents the various financing options and once chosen, it also credit checks the customer via a connection to the manufacturer's credit company. The system provides and prints either a comprehensive proposal with graphic images or an order confirmation document.

Finally, should the customer wish to make any amendments to a factory order, this can be done online from the salesperson's terminal.

In summary, the CASP should provide the customer with a coherent and clear process for buying a car, with the salesperson gaining the correct information to provide customers with the product or service they require.

Source: Written by Jim Saker, Professor of Retail Management, Loughborough University Business School. Gary Reed, Lecturer, Loughborough University Business School. Vicky Story, Lecturer, Loughborough University Business School.

Discussion Question

What do you see as the advantages and disadvantages from the point of view of the customer and also the salesperson?

Practical Exercise

Understanding customer value creation

The Customer Management Model (developed by QCi) described in this chapter may be used to analyse the contribution that customer management can make to the organisation. Adding value for stakeholders is an important aspect of a business proposition (e.g. improving share value, employability, etc.) but measuring this is usually not well performed and often results in poor understanding of critical success factors. Customer value is usually measured relative to what they have to pay either directly or indirectly (e.g. costs, taxation, etc.). In many cases, stakeholder and customer value are closely related. It is therefore important that organisations seek to enhance value to the customer which is only achievable through the 'value chain', that is, all parties involved in meeting the needs of customers. It is important to recognise and retain those customers that help the organisation shape its business proposition appropriately, to align its people, processes and infrastructure.

This exercise will get you thinking about how value is created and destroyed by organisations through the different activities they typically engage in to manage customers. Imagine you are a senior manager for a large organisation (pick a company with which you are familiar). For each of the following areas, list a couple of points under the headings: 'Value is created by' – 'Value is destroyed by'. For example:

Analysis and planning	Creating value through insight, knowledge and effective planning.
Value is created by	Understanding which customers you want to manage. Retaining those who are worth retaining.
Value is destroyed by	A lack of customer knowledge and insight. A mismatch of costs to revenues.
Proposition	Creating value through a proposition which helps you find, keep and develop those customers you want to manage.
People and organisation	Creating value through effective people and partners.
Processes	Creating value by being customer-centric.
Information and technology (including data)	Creating value through efficiency, service and intelligence.
Measurement	Creating value through understanding performance.

Customer experience	Creating value through understanding the customer experience.
Customer management activities	Creating value through excellent acquisition, retention, development and recovery activities.

This exercise will give you a list of factors that can be applied to the business in order to help you understand how effective and efficient they are at customer management.

Source: This exercise was prepared by Tracy Harwood, Senior Lecturer in Marketing, De Montfort University. Michael Starkey, Senior Lecturer in Marketing, De Montfort University.

Examination Questions

1 Choose five technological changes that have impacted selling and sales management. What effect have they had on selling and sales management practices?

2 What is e-commerce? E-commerce can take place at four levels. Discuss each of the four levels.

3 Discuss four ways that the internet has affected selling and sales management practices.

4 What is customer relationship management? Discuss how each of the elements of the QCi Customer Management Model can be used to understand how well customers are being managed.

Chapter 9
Integrated Marketing Communications and Pricing Strategies

- Describing the basis of a marketing communications plan
- Describing the operational elements of a marketing communications plan
- Describing the advantages and disadvantages of the different elements of communications
- Describing the effective pricing strategies
- Explaining major pricing policies

Chapter 15

The entrepreneurial marketing plan

Objectives 468
Introduction 469
Underlying factors 469
The framework for developing entrepreneurial marketing 469
Devising the entrepreneurial marketing plan 470
Developing a statement of the entrepreneurial marketing plan 471
Beating the competition 471
Marketing information for SMEs 473
Knowing customer expectations 474
Marketing tools for SMEs 476
An integrated marketing plan 478
The marketing plan in relation to the market 479
Summary 479

Objectives

After reading this chapter the reader will have a clear understanding of how to develop an entrepreneurial marketing plan. The reader will appreciate the scope and parameters of an entrepreneurial marketing plan and the processes involved in devising it. The chapter is linked to a series of worksheets in Appendix A, which will allow the reader to build an entrepreneurial marketing plan that is unique to the individual enterprise.

Introduction

We have argued throughout this text that formal management approaches and techniques are inappropriate for entrepreneurs and SMEs. This is not to say that entrepreneurs do not manage, nor is it to say that some aspects of management approaches and techniques cannot be utilized for the benefit of an SME. Indeed, we have acknowledged that entrepreneurs take decisions just like any other managers, but that they do so in a way that is unique to them. Similarly, we have recognized that entrepreneurs do perform marketing, albeit in a way that is uniquely influenced by the entrepreneur. Remember also that we stated in Chapter 1 that the link shared by marketing and entrepreneurship is, in fact, management. The essence of our conclusion is that, while entrepreneurs may manage, take decisions and carry out a form of marketing, such management and marketing may be inefficient and most certainly could be improved. But how can this be done? What steps can an entrepreneur follow in order to develop a *usable* and *meaningful* marketing plan?

Underlying factors

When developing an entrepreneurial marketing plan it is important that it conforms to existing constraints and conditions. A whole range of constraints and conditions have been repeatedly referred to throughout this text, but we can distil them down to certain basic underlying factors. These encompass the following.

Any entrepreneurial marketing plan must take account of the inherent characteristics of marketing, which are about a positive approach to doing business in a changing environment and which takes as its focus the customer. Equally, the inherent characteristics of entrepreneurship must also be taken into account; these can be summarized as opportunistic exploitation of a change environment. Having debated these characteristics in some depth, we can say with some confidence that the characteristics of marketing and entrepreneurship are closely related, if not similar. This conclusion is confirmed when we set both dimensions in the context of SMEs, primarily in relation to the inherent resource constraints of SMEs but also by the fact that they have a limited impact on their market because of these resource constraints.

The framework for developing entrepreneurial marketing

In the context of the inherent and fundamental characteristics mentioned above, we have devoted this section of this text to setting out a framework for developing entrepreneurial marketing. As the reader will know, the key aspects of this framework are the notion of adaptation of management and particularly marketing approaches and techniques, and the application of new concepts. When we advocate adaptation of marketing approaches we are implicitly arguing that there is a proven merit in the formal or traditional approaches of marketing. If we take account of the inherent characteristics of entrepreneurship and SMEs, then we must adapt these proven concepts.

We have illustrated how this can be done in relation to aspects of marketing planning and decision-making, as these are most relevant to the ultimate aim of this text. The new concepts that we have concentrated on are, of course, the development, value and use of marketing competencies and marketing networks. These are chosen because they are inherent to good management practice and performance in the case of competencies, and implicit to the entrepreneurial decision-making processes in the case of networks.

There is one other underlying factor which we must recognize before we set out the process of developing an entrepreneurial marketing plan. Consider that we have repeatedly used the term context in connection with the adaptation process and in relating management and marketing concepts to SMEs. It is of primary importance that any marketing activity, whether entrepreneurial or otherwise, should be set in the context in which it is occurring if that marketing is to be truly effective and meaningful. So our description of the importance of moving general marketing concepts, approaches and techniques towards the situation specific of an actual marketing circumstance must be adhered to if entrepreneurial marketing is to be successful. Of course, situation-specific aspects are most likely to be implicitly inherent in entrepreneurial marketing because this is something that an entrepreneur will do naturally. Remember, we stated that entrepreneurs address issues that are of primary importance to themselves or their business. By doing this they are addressing the situation specific and therefore introducing a degree of context. However, we cannot rely on this happening intuitively; we must proactively and explicitly ensure that we take full account of all the factors that influence the situation specific. Therefore, an entrepreneur must not only take account of the type of marketing circumstance that pertains to the enterprise but also such factors as the inherent characteristics of industry, competition, market profiles, product differentiation, etc. Only by a proper and full assessment of *all* factors relating to a situation specific will entrepreneurial marketing be set in context.

Devising the entrepreneurial marketing plan

The entrepreneurial marketing plan will have as its foundations the individual's competency abilities and his/her use of the marketing network. Determination and techniques of application of these concepts have been described in detail in Chapters 13 and 14. Suffice to say here that the entrepreneur will have given consideration to the range of marketing competencies and determined his or her personal strengths and weaknesses in relation to them. It is implicit in developing the entrepreneurial marketing plan that entrepreneurs *know* their competency strengths and know how to use them to minimize competency weaknesses. By using these strong marketing competencies the entrepreneur will enhance the entrepreneurial marketing plan.

Similarly, it is assumed that a personal marketing network will have been identified by the entrepreneur. This will be made up of those individuals who can offer the best possible advice and guidance on aspects of marketing in relation to the SME. The network will be utilized proactively in the development of the entrepreneurial marketing plan. That is, the entrepreneur will purposefully and actively seek advice and guidance by presenting ideas and problems to individuals within the network, with a view to refining and finalizing the plan after carefully considering their response.

It has been assumed that the entrepreneur will make provisional decisions about the plan by naturally utilizing his or her marketing competencies; then, having determined an outline plan, will allow the marketing network to comment on and assess the viability of its proposals. If necessary, this process can be repeated until the entrepreneur is confident that the plan is appropriate and workable. This is an ongoing process: constant refinement and realignment of marketing activities in anticipation of, or in reaction to, market changes are natural aspects of the process.

Developing a statement of the entrepreneurial marketing plan

Having determined appropriate marketing competencies and networks and how best these can be developed and used, our task is to complete the framework by marrying them with the adaptation of marketing approaches and techniques.

Let us remind ourselves that the adaptation of marketing techniques must be done in the context of SMEs. SMEs do not operate in a vacuum, they exist in an interactive environment which can be hostile or friendly. When competitiveness is seen as hostility, entrepreneurs often perceive themselves to be under a major threat, and in such cases feel they cannot compete with the seemingly greater resources of the competition. This is particularly true in relation to larger companies. If there is substance to these comments, what can entrepreneurial SMEs do to compete effectively with strong competition?

Beating the competition

To beat the competition we must appreciate and understand, not only the inherent characteristics of SMEs but also the potential marketing advantages they might have over the competition in general and larger companies in particular. In order to determine these advantages, we must appreciate how they can be used to beat the competition through entrepreneurial marketing.

We have discussed elsewhere the inherent characteristics of SMEs as incorporating size, limited resources, flexibility, limited marketing expertise, lack of finance, a narrow product base, credibility and innovativeness. This is not an exhaustive list; there are undoubtedly many more characteristics that may need to be taken into account. However, we have tried, in Chapter 6, to encompass all factors by considering the characteristics from a marketing perspective and summarizing them as limited resources – including finance, marketing knowledge, time, etc.; lack of specialist expertise – because entrepreneurs tend to be generalists rather than specialists in any one field, including marketing; and limited impact on the market – because of fewer orders and customers, and as a consequence less of a presence in any industry or geographical area.

While these limitations may exist it does not mean that SME characteristics will not lead to or allow some marketing advantages. Marketing advantages might include: personal touch and more personal contact and service; specialist offers; employee loyalty; better/quicker delivery; flexibility; quicker decision-making; direct access to the top decision-maker; more intimate knowledge of the customer; local image, etc. While this too is not an exhaustive list, it is still extensive and impressive from a competitive viewpoint. The challenge is for an entrepreneur to give careful consideration to the advantages that offer the best opportunities for beating the competition.

A typical list of characteristics that might enable an SME to beat its competition at marketing might include:

- Consistent quality in relation to product, delivery and after-sales, all of which might lead to a good reputation.
- Personalized product/service.
- Flexibility of operations.
- Quick response, leading to speedy operations, opportunism and marketing innovation.
- Local market knowledge allowing greater impact in local markets.

There are substantial advantages in knowing the marketing characteristics of SMEs and evaluating them in such a way as to allow SMEs to compete favourably with large companies and competition in general. Readers may wish to consider how to beat the competition for themselves by completing worksheets 1.1–1.3 in Appendix A.

While there may be attractions in making a list of competitive advantages such as those outlined above, it is important that the entrepreneur does not forget the constraints and limitations imposed on marketing activity. Therefore, if entrepreneurs are to realize the benefits of marketing activity they must concentrate on those key issues that will enable this to occur. Having acknowledged this, an entrepreneurial SME may do well to concentrate on key customers and the best marketing opportunities in key market segments while positioning its strengths against the competition's weaknesses. These are issues which will be addressed later in this planning process.

Marketing information for SMEs

We live in an information age. Businesses in general are deluged with data on all aspects of their operations. Information put to good use will lead to knowledge, which in turn will enhance decision-making. However, as many entrepreneurs will agree, it can often feel as if there is too much information available across a wide spectrum of activity. Prior knowledge will enable the entrepreneur to assess what is good information and what is marginal to his/her needs. But regardless of prior knowledge, it is important that the entrepreneur knows where to get information and how to acquire it and use it to best advantage. We shall consider these issues while recognizing the inherent constraints and limitations of SMEs' marketing.

The key dimensions of marketing information in relation to SMEs are:

- Sources of marketing information in terms of *who* can provide it and *where* it can be found.
- The methods that can be employed to gather information.
- How information can be utilized and organized.

Readers may wish to answer these questions by completing worksheets 2.1–2.3 in Appendix A.

Completion of these worksheets will have generated a wide variety of sources of marketing information and methods for gathering and using it. The primary sources of marketing information of use to SMEs are likely to incorporate the following items:

- Media publications for general observation and awareness.
- Media editors and marketing information departments for specific information.
- Government sources and publications.
- Widely known and accepted consumer preferences.
- Industry key informants and trend-setters.
- Competitors.
- Customers.
- Suppliers.
- Internal information from sales profiles and employees.

This list is by no means exhaustive; there will be several other sources of information, many of which will be peculiar to specific markets and industries. For SMEs the most immediate problem is how to gather information within their inherent constraints. The question is: Which are the best low-cost, information-gathering techniques that an SME can effectively employ? These can be listed as follows:

- *Recording information from the environment.* This can generally be found in the popular media by referring to competitive activities, industry trends, economic changes, political decisions, new developments in the market, and so on.
- *Observation.* This can be done intuitively by maintaining an awareness of events surrounding an SME's activities. The references listed above can also be enhanced and enriched by general observation.
- *Information from key informants.* These informants are likely to be customers, suppliers, competitors' customers, employees, etc. The information gathered can be of a general

nature such as described above, or highly specific in terms of information about a competitor's products or views on an entrepreneur's own company and its products.

- *Internal record systems.* Such information can provide sales profiles; potential sources of enquiries, customer enquiries, and general requests.

There are many other techniques for gathering information; indeed, SMEs often devise techniques uniquely suited to their particular circumstances. Two points to emphasize are (1) that information gathering is a continual process and should be viewed as an integral part of normal marketing activity whether sophisticated or not; and (2) information should be gathered from as wide a variety of sources as possible. The principle here is that reliance on one or a few sources of information may be dangerous and certainly carries a greater risk of giving a misleading signal than information which indicates a strong signal but which is gathered from a wide range of sources.

Knowing customer expectations

One of the cornerstones of marketing is to satisfy customers by providing products or services which meet their expectations. It goes without saying that an SME's offerings must match its customers' expectations. However, these expectations can sometimes be very complex and diverse. What an SME must do is find out as much as possible about its customers. This means knowing precisely who they are and precisely what motivates them. Also, it means knowing how they like to make purchases and why they purchase from one source and not another. In particular, an SME should know its customers' expectations in relation to the performance of its products or services, and how this might compare with other competitive products or services. In other words, an SME must consider *why* a potential customer buys one firm's products or services in preference to another firm's products or services.

To this end it is important to consider the customers' perception of the SME's products or services; that is, to consider the product or service from the *customer's* perspective as opposed to the firm's perspective.

An SME must have a thorough understanding of how customers think and evaluate this with a view to providing what the customers want; in other words, satisfying customers through the firm's products or services. Let us attempt this by considering the following aspects.

Customer definition of an SME's product or service

In arriving at a conclusion to this definition we must consider *how a potential customer thinks*. To do this we must understand the importance of customer needs and expectations. These may cover a wide spectrum of issues, including economic factors revolving around price, availability, acceptability and convenience; and psychological or emotional factors such as value for money, the image of the firm and its products or services, impressions or expectations of how a product or service performs, and needs and wants in general.

It is possible to test how well an SME's customers are known by comparing a definition of a firm's product from the entrepreneur's view with *why* customers should buy this product. Often the answers vary considerably, because the entrepreneur sees the product from the perspective of features while the customer sees the product from the perspective of benefits in use. It is the latter that are important and must be the focus of the marketing and sales message, since it is *how the customer thinks* that is important. How can an entrepreneur bridge the divide and think like the customer? One way is to follow a simple process. This involves defining your product/service as though you were explaining it to someone else. Readers may wish to do this for themselves by completing worksheets 3.1–3.3 in Appendix A. An examination of the definition may involve discarding any of the following statements:

- The product is special, unique, different, the only one available, superior, etc.
- The price is good, cheap, better, etc.
- The quality is good, better, superior, etc.

A restatement of definitions *only* in relation to customer expectations may be necessary. That is, definitions should *only* include statements that *customers* would make or consider when buying the product or service.

Determining who the customers really are

One reason for defining a product or service from the customers' perspective is to help determine precisely *who* the customers are. The following questions may help to answer this:

- How many are there approximately?
- Are they increasing, declining or static in number?
- How old or how long established are they?
- Where are they situated?
- How much do they spend annually on your kind of product or service?
- Have they any special features or characteristics, and if so what are they?
- Has their behaviour changed over the past *x* years, and if so in what way?

Worksheets 4.1–4.4 in Appendix A offer the reader the opportunity to answer these questions for themselves.

Why should customers buy an enterprise's products?

Once an entrepreneur has determined who his/her customers are and defined the company's product/service in customer terms, it is possible to combine these two considerations and determine the reasons *why* potential customers should buy the company's products/services. It is sometimes useful to ask the question 'Why should customers buy my products?' and then seek qualification and justification for the

Table 15.1 Why should customers buy your products/services?

Is it because:
• You are better than the competition? If yes, how and why? • Your products/services are unique? If yes, in what way? • You are the only supplier? If yes, were there ever any other suppliers? What happened to them and why? Are there likely to be any other suppliers in the future? If yes, where will they come from? • You know your customers personally? If yes, how did you get to know them? • Your customer likes you? If yes, why and in what way? • You are convenient to your customer? If yes, how and why is this important? • You delivery quickly? If yes, how can you do this and how important is it to deliver quickly? • You are better priced than others? If yes, in what way and why? • You are reliable and dependable? If so, how and why?

answer by asking 'Is it because?' questions. Table 15.1 lists potential 'Is it because?' questions which cover most aspects of customer expectations. Worksheet 4.5 in Appendix A allows the reader to formulate some answers.

It is easy to appreciate that there are many answers to these very important questions, but it is imperative that the answers are known in as much detail as possible. The more precisely these answers are known the more certainty there is that an SME will be in control of its marketing. If these answers are not known, then it is highly likely that an SME will *not* be in control of its marketing and therefore be at considerable risk of competitor dominance. Also, by answering these questions the entrepreneur can go a long way towards constructing a marketing plan. *Knowing why* customers respond to different aspects of a firm's marketing activity allows an entrepreneur to strengthen the performance of these activities. Let us expand on these questions and consider how we can examine the major tools of marketing in relation to SMEs.

Marketing tools for SMEs

The actual tools of marketing employed by an SME are those that are most appropriate for the individual enterprise. Thus the tools used and the emphasis given in this use are likely to be *unique* to an enterprise and its marketing. What we shall give here is a broad description of tools of marketing considered from the perspective of an SME, the way in which these tools interact and the different emphasis that can be given to them are outlined in several case studies in Appendix B.

The process for determining appropriate marketing for an SME is simply to consider each marketing tool in three ways:

1. Make a list of the different ways in which particular marketing tools can be performed. The process at this stage is not judgemental, but simply to brainstorm as many ways or methods in which a particular function of marketing can be performed. The object is to create a comprehensive list of methods and by so doing stimulate consideration of issues which have previously been ignored or missed through too narrow a focus.

2. Evaluate the list of ways and methods in relation to the actual SME and determine the *best methods* that would serve the company most effectively. This means taking account of the market and *customer knowledge* gleaned from the previous considerations and exercises. By doing so the entrepreneur will not only be determining, with reasonable certainty, which are the best methods for the enterprise, but also will have the opportunity of assessing the *viability* of the various methods. In considering this it is useful to restrict these to a manageable number within the resources of the enterprise; therefore, it is unlikely that more than five methods can be justified. Indeed, there may be some benefits in this restriction as it forces a tight assessment to be made.
3. Having determined the best methods of marketing activity for the enterprise it is important that these are put to good and effective use. This requires an articulation not only of how marketing activities will be used but also a plan of the sequence in which they will be employed. In doing this the enterprise will have developed a coordinated and cohesive plan of marketing.

These three steps should be taken in relation to each important area of marketing. Thus the process might resemble something like the following:

Promotion and publicity decisions (Worksheets 5.1–5.3)

- Make a list of ways/methods of promoting and publicizing your businesses products/services.
- Make a list of the five *best* viable ways/methods for promoting and publicizing your business and justify these.
- Describe how the five best ways/methods you have chosen can *actually be used and implemented.* Your description should explain the *sequence* in which they might be used/implemented.

Distribution decisions (Worksheets 6.1–6.3)

- Make a list of factors that can be taken into account when distributing products. In other words, how do you distribute your goods?
- Make a list of the five best ways/methods for distributing your products and justify your choice.
- Describe how the five best ways/methods you have chosen can actually be used and implemented. Your description should explain the *sequence* in which they might be used/implemented.

Pricing decisions (Worksheets 7.1–7.3)

- Make a list of factors that can be taken into account when setting price. That is, how do you set price?
- Make a list of the five best ways/methods of setting price and justify your choice.
- Describe how the five best ways/methods you have chosen can actually be used and implemented. Your description should explain the *sequence* in which they might be used/implemented.

Selling decisions (Worksheets 8.1–8.3)

- Make a list of factors that can be taken into account when selling your products/services. That is, how do you sell your products/services?

- Make a list of the five best ways/methods of selling and justify your choice.
- Describe how the five best ways/methods you have chosen can actually be used and implemented. Your description should explain the *sequence* in which they might be used/implemented.

An integrated marketing plan

Having evaluated and justified your decisions in relation to each of the important aspects of marketing activity, it is now important to evaluate each one in relation to all the others. This means going through the process outlined in Figure 15.1.

The value of this exercise is that it enables integration and cohesiveness throughout the whole of the marketing activity.

Describe your marketing activity by considering each aspect of marketing in relation to all other aspects. That is, consider how decisions in relation to each aspect impact upon all other aspects and how these aspects must match.

Consider the impact of:

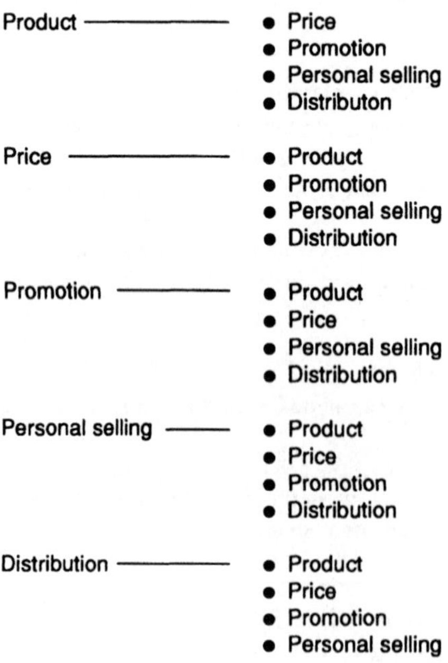

Figure 15.1 Summary of a marketing strategy.

The marketing plan in relation to the market

So far we have gone through a process that has allowed us to give considered thought to knowing the market and knowing customers, and using this knowledge to determine marketing variables and how these integrate. What we must do now is assess these decisions against the market and assess how they will stand up to market forces. In planning terms this means evaluating the enterprise's marketing variables in relation to the company's strengths and weaknesses and the opportunities and threats emanating from the market. In formal marketing terms this means doing a SWOT analysis. Strengths and weaknesses should be evaluated against competitors, opportunities and threats in the market. Short- and long-term opportunities, and the enterprise's strengths and weaknesses and threats, should be evaluated against competitors and market trends, as well as against the enterprise's strengths and weaknesses. Worksheets 9.1–9.4 allow the reader to go through this process.

After consideration of all the aspects described in this planning process the entrepreneur will be in a position to describe the enterprise's marketing environment and its situation and position within this marketing environment accurately. The entrepreneur will also be able to define the products and services accurately and describe *how* each of the marketing variables integrates with the others. Worksheets 10.1–10.3 allow the reader to make this statement.

On completion of this final step in the process we will have completed what we have termed an 'entrepreneurial marketing plan'. In fact, the final three worksheets *are* the plan.

The discipline of going through this process will have considerably enhanced the company's marketing profile. But there will have been much greater benefits accruing which can be summarized as:

- The substantial learning experience of the process in itself.
- The amount of knowledge gleaned with respect to marketing issues.
- The ability to do marketing.

Perhaps the most important benefit is that the SME will have a marketing plan that is built on the foundation of entrepreneurial, marketing and SME characteristics that is entirely compatible with the unique characteristics of the firm. The benefits of operating to such a plan will be found in the enhanced performance of the firm.

Summary

This chapter has been concerned with implementing a framework for developing entrepreneurial marketing. The chapter represents the culmination of entrepreneurial marketing decision-making in that it offers the opportunity to articulate the thought processes surrounding the application of competencies and networks in the form of an action plan for entrepreneurial marketing. The reader will now understand marketing thought processes which are suited to SMEs and, if desired, will have completed a unique entrepreneurial marketing plan.

10 | Pricing Strategies

The price is what you pay; the value is what you receive. —Anonymous

Learning Objectives

On completion of this chapter, you will be able to:

1. Discuss the relationships among pricing, image, competition, and value.
2. Describe effective pricing techniques for introducing new products or services and for existing ones.
3. Explain the pricing methods and strategies for (A) retailers, (B) manufacturers, and (C) service firms.
4. Describe the impact of credit on pricing.

Setting prices is a business decision governed by both art and science—with a measure of instinct thrown in for good measure. Setting prices for their products and services requires entrepreneurs to balance a multitude of complex forces, many of them working in opposite directions. Entrepreneurs must determine prices for their goods and services that will draw customers and produce a profit. Unfortunately, many small business owners set prices without enough information about their cost of operations and the nature of their customers. Price is an important factor in building long-term relationships with customers, and haphazard pricing techniques can confuse and alienate customers and endanger a small company's profitability. Setting prices is not only one of the toughest decisions small business owners face, but it also is one of the most important. Research by the consulting firm McKinsey and Company shows that proper pricing strategies have far greater impact on a company's profits than corresponding reductions in fixed or variable costs.[1] Improper pricing has destroyed countless businesses whose owners mistakenly thought their prices were high enough to generate a profit when, in fact, they were not.

Timeless Message

After working with a consultant, Jeff Trott, founder of Timeless Message, a company that sells bottles with greeting messages inside them, raised its prices from an average of $30 per bottle to $60 per bottle. The company had underestimated both its costs and the market value of its products. The price increase resulted in a brief sales dip, but, according to Trott, "We started making a profit for the first time in four years. It was like we had been shipping a ten-dollar bill out the door with each order."[2]

Pricing decisions cut across every aspect of a small company, influencing everything from its marketing and sales efforts to its operations and strategy. Price is the monetary value of a product or service in the marketplace; it is a measure of what the customer must give up to obtain various goods and services. Price also is a signal of a product's or service's value to an individual, and different customers assign different values to the same goods and services. From an entrepreneur's viewpoint, price must be compatible with customers' perceptions of value. "Pricing is not just a math problem," says one business writer. "It's a psychology test."[3] The psychology of pricing is an art much more than it is a science. It focuses on creating value in the customer's mind but recognizes that value is what the customer perceives it to be. In many cases, customers look to a product's or service's price for clues about value. Consider the following examples, which illustrate the sometimes puzzling connection between price and perceived value:

- In the ultra-premium segment of the watch industry, Rolex, Cartier, Patek Philippe, Chopard, Toric, Blancpain, and Corum are legendary brands of handmade watches that sell at prices ranging from $10,000 to $50,000. To some people, owning one of these watches is a hallmark of financial success, even though they are less accurate at keeping time than a $10 quartz-driven Timex.[4]
- To establish a niche in the beer market, microbrewers in the United States began producing small batches of high-quality beer in the European style, focusing on ales, porters, and stouts rather than the lagers the giant brewers were selling. Moving even farther upscale in the beer market (which has seen relatively flat sales compared to a 63 percent increase in wine sales since 1991), small brewers are marketing premium craft beers with all of the cachet of wine—at premium prices, of course. In addition to its 18.5 percent alcohol content and $16 per bottle price, Dogfish Head Brewery's Fort Beer has a raspberry flavor, and the company suggests that connoisseurs drink it from a champagne flute. Microbrewer Samuel Adams makes the world's most expensive beer. Its Utopia, made from special malts and yeast, sells for $100 per bottle. Because the company produces just 8,000 bottles a year, some bottles of Utopia have fetched as much as $200 on eBay![5]
- The Renaissance Pen Company markets fountain pens made from gold and platinum and encrusted with diamonds selling for as much as $230,000. It also sells a pen that contains the crystallized DNA of Abraham Lincoln for only $1,650.[6]

As you can see, setting higher prices sometimes can *increase* appeal of a product or service ("If you charge more, you must be worth it"). Value for these products is not found in their superior technical performance but in their scarcity and uniqueness and the resulting image they create for the buyer. Although an entrepreneur must recognize the shallow depth of the market for such ultra-luxury items, the ego-satisfying ownership of limited-edition watches, pens, cars, jewelry, and other items is the psychological force supporting the premium price strategy.

Three Potent Forces: Image, Competition, and Value

LEARNING OBJECTIVES
1. Discuss the relationships among pricing, image, competition, and value.

Price Conveys Image

A company's pricing policies communicate important information about its overall image to customers. For example, the prices charged by a posh men's clothing store reflect a completely different image from those charged by a factory outlet. Customers look at prices to determine what type of store they are dealing with. High prices frequently convey the idea of quality, prestige, and uniqueness to customers. "People bring a whole set of equations with them when they make a purchase, and one of the values for most people is that high price equals quality," says Rob Docters, a pricing expert.[7] Accordingly, when developing a marketing approach to pricing, entrepreneurs must establish prices that are compatible with what customers expect and are willing to pay. Too often, small business owners *underprice* their goods and services, believing that low prices are the only way they can achieve a competitive advantage. A study by the Copernicus consulting firm found that only 15 to 35 percent of customers consider price to be the chief criterion when selecting a product or service.[8]

A common pricing mistake small business owners make is failing to recognize the extra value, convenience, service, and quality they give their customers—all things many customers are willing to pay for. These companies fall into the trap of trying to compete solely on the basis of price when they lack the sales volume—and, hence, the lower cost structures—of their larger rivals. It is a recipe for failure. "People want quality," says one merchant selling upscale goods at upscale prices. "They want value. But if you lower prices, they think that you are lowering the value and lowering the quality."[9] Lowering prices may be a dangerous cycle that can destroy a business. A study of businesses in multiple industries by Rafi Mohammed, author of *The Art of Pricing*, found that those companies that raised prices by 1 percent saw their profits increase 11 percent. Those that raised their prices by 10 percent realized profit increases of 100 percent![10] The study does not imply that businesses have free rein to raise prices to any level, but it does suggest that many companies could raise their prices enough to improve their financial results significantly if they can convince customers that their products offer superior value.

In the crowded soft drink market, the battle for market share often boils down to price competition among the industry giants Coca-Cola and Pepsi. However, some small companies have managed to carve out niches in the soft drink market with higher-priced specialty products that are made with all-natural ingredients, offer exotic flavors, or provide some other appealing twist.

Healthy Beverage Company

By emphasizing the uniqueness of their organic green tea-soda combination drink, Eric Schnell and Steven Kessler, co-founders of Steaz Green Tea Soda, are able to charge a premium price over regular carbonated drinks.

In 2002, Eric Schnell and Steven Kessler introduced the Steaz Green Tea Soda line as part of their new business, the Healthy Beverage Company, as a nutritious alternative to regular carbonated soft drinks. Their lightly carbonated beverage contains green tea (touted by many health care professionals for its antioxidant properties) and sugar cane juice and is certified as "organic" by the U.S. Department of Agriculture. Marketing their tea-soda combination as a healthy beverage alternative to conventional soft drinks allows the company to charge $1.50 for a 12-ounce bottle, a healthy price premium over standard carbonated drinks.[11]

One key to setting prices properly is based on understanding a company's target market, the customer groups at which the small company is aiming its goods or services. Target market, business image, and pricing strategy are closely related.

Sway and Cake and TBC

When Tamara Donaghy-Bates launched Sway & Cake, a Seattle, Washington, retail store selling women's clothing, her target audience was young professional women in their late 20s to late 30s who are looking for something other than traditional styles. Donaghy-Bates describes the clothing she sells in Sway & Cake as "funky" and "flirty"—trendy, fashion-forward styles that are common in metropolitan areas such as New York or Los Angeles but are hard to find in conservative towns such as Seattle. Her upscale pricing strategy is geared toward her target audience, and it works; her company's first-year sales exceeded $800,000. Working with customers every day in the shop provided Donaghy-Bates with clear insight into her customers' fashion preferences, and she soon saw an opportunity to tap into another target audience with a different pricing strategy: students and young women in their early to mid 20s. To reach this group of customers, Donaghy-Bates opened TBC (To Be Continued) in Seattle as a lower-cost outlet for similar styles of clothing that she sells in Sway & Cake. In fact, nearly half of the merchandise sold in TBC is clothing that did not sell in Sway & Cake and has been marked down at a significant discount, sometimes as much as 50 or 60 percent off the normal retail price. TBC's remaining merchandise is new, lower priced, and aimed at a younger audience. Customers have responded to both stores' pricing strategies and merchandise mix, and combined sales for the two stores have grown well beyond the $1 million mark.[12]

Competition and Pricing

When setting prices, entrepreneurs should take into account their competitors' prices, but they should *not* automatically match or beat them. Although price is an important factor in the purchase decision, it is not the only consideration for shoppers. Two factors are vital to studying the effects of competition on the small company's pricing policies: the location of the competitors and the nature of the competing goods and services. In most cases, unless a company can differentiate the quality and the quantity of extras it provides, it must match the prices charged by nearby competitors for identical items. For example, if a self-service station charges a nickel more per gallon for gasoline than does another self-service station across the street, customers will simply go across the street to buy. Without the advantage of a unique business image—quality of goods sold, value of services provided, convenient location, favorable credit terms—a small company must match local competitors' prices or lose sales. Although the prices that distant competitors charge are not nearly as critical to the small business as are those of local competitors, it can be helpful to know them and to use them as reference points. Before matching any competitor's prices, however, small business owners should consider the rival's motives. The competition may be establishing its price structure based on a unique set of criteria and a totally different strategy. Blindly matching competitors' prices can lead a company to financial ruin, and companies that set their prices this way typically do so because they perceive themselves in a position of strategic weakness.

The nature of the competitors' goods and services also influences a company's pricing policies. Entrepreneurs must monitor competitors' prices on products that are identical to or are close substitutes for those they sell and then strive to keep their prices in line with them. For example, the local sandwich shop should consider the hamburger restaurant, the taco shop, and the roast beef shop as competitors because they all serve fast foods. Although none of them offers the identical menu of the sandwich shop, they are all competing for the same quick-meal dollar. Of course, if a small business can differentiate its products by creating a distinctive image in customers' minds or by offering superior service, quality, convenience, or speed, it can charge prices higher than those of its competitors. Because competitors' prices can have a dramatic impact on a small company's prices, entrepreneurs should make it a habit to monitor their rivals' prices, especially on identical items.

Yosha Enterprises

When Anthony Shurman launched Yosha Enterprises in 2002, a company that markets liquid breath mints, he established a price of $1.99 for a 36-mint package. Later, in response to competitors' prices, he lowered the price to $1.79 and then to $1.69 per pack. Momints contained more mints than any of the competing brands, but customers failed to recognize that benefit, and based their purchase decisions on the package price. When Shurman recently rolled out Momints at a regional chain of grocery stores, he cut the size of the pack to the industry standard 28 mints and set a price of 99 cents. "Our sales went up 350 percent," he says. Yosha generates $3 million in annual revenue, and Shurman believes that he can sell even more mints at the lower 99-cent price.[13]

Generally, entrepreneurs should avoid head-to-head price competition with other firms that can more easily achieve lower prices through lower cost structures. For instance, most locally owned drugstores cannot compete with the prices of large national drug chains. However, many local drugstores operate successfully by using nonprice competition; these stores offer more personalized service, free delivery, credit sales, and other extras that the chains have eliminated. Nonprice competition can be an effective strategy for a small business in the face of larger, more powerful enterprises, especially because there are many dangers in experimenting with price changes. Price shifts cause fluctuations in sales volume that a small company may not be able to tolerate. In addition, frequent price changes may damage a company's image and its customer relations.

Attempting to undercut competitors' prices may lead to a price war, one of the most deadly games a small business can play. Price wars can eradicate companies' profit margins and scar an entire industry for years. "Many entrepreneurs cut prices to the point of unprofitablility just to compete," says one business writer. "In doing so, they open the door to catastrophe. Less revenue often translates into lower quality, poorer service, sloppier salesmanship, weaker customer loyalty, and financial disaster."[14] Price wars usually begin when one competitor thinks he or she can achieve higher volume instantaneously by lowering prices. Rather than sticking to their strategic guns, competitors believe they must follow suit.

Entrepreneurs usually overestimate the power of price cuts, however. Sales volume rarely increases enough to offset the lower profit margins of a lower price. A business with a 25 percent gross profit margin that cuts its price by 10 percent would have to *triple* its sales volume just to break even. In a price war, a company may cut its prices so severely that it is impossible to achieve the volume necessary to offset the lower profit margins. Even when price cuts work, their effects often are temporary. Customers lured by the lowest price usually have almost no loyalty to a business. The lesson: The best way to survive a price war is to stay out of it by emphasizing the unique features, benefits, and value your company offers its customers.

Focus on Value

Ultimately, the "right" price for a product or service depends on one factor: the value that it provides for a customer. There are two aspects of value, however. Entrepreneurs may recognize the *objective* value of their products and services, which is the price customers would be willing to pay if they understood perfectly the benefits that a product or service delivers for them. Unfortunately, few, if any, customers can see a product's or a service's true objective value; instead, they see only its *perceived* value, which determines the price they are willing to pay for it. Research into purchasing decisions has revealed a fundamental problem that adds to the complexity of a business owner's pricing decision: People faced with pricing decisions often act irrationally. In one classic study, researchers asked shoppers if they would travel an additional 20 minutes to save $5 on a calculator that costs $15; most said they would. When asked the same question about a $125 jacket, most of the shoppers said no, even though they would be saving the exact same amount of money! "People make [purchasing] decisions piecemeal, influenced by the context of the choice," says Richard Thaler, who won a Nobel Prize for his work in behavioral economics.[15]

Note that value does not necessarily correspond to low price, however. Businesses that underprice their products and services or run special discount price promotions may be short-circuiting the value proposition they are trying to build and communicate to their customers. Customers may respond to price cuts, but companies that rely on them to boost sales risk undermine the perceived value of their products and services. In addition, once customers grow accustomed to buying products and services during special promotions, the habit can be difficult to break. They simply wait for the next sale. Some companies in the auto industry have faced this problem as customers accustomed to buying autos with large rebates postpone buying new cars until automakers offer them special incentives. The result has been fluctuating sales and a diminished value of those automotive brands.

One of the most important determinants of customers' response to a price is whether they perceive the price to be a fair exchange for the value they receive from the product or service. The good news is that companies can influence through marketing and other efforts customers' perception of value. "The price you get for a product is a function of what it's truly worth—and how good a job you do communicating that value to the end user," says one entrepreneur.[16] Indeed, setting a product's or a service's price is another way a company can communicate value to its customers. For most shoppers, three reference points define a fair price: the price they have paid for the product or service in the past, the prices competitors charge for the same or similar product or service, and the costs a company incurs to provide the product or service. The price that customers have paid in the past for an item serves as a baseline reference point, but people often forget that inflation causes a company's costs to rise from year to year. Therefore, it is important for business owners to remind customers periodically that they must raise prices to offset the increased cost of doing business. "Over time, costs always go up," says Norm Brodsky, owner of a successful document storage company. "I'd rather raise prices a little every year or with every new contract than be forced to demand a big increase down the road."[17]

As we have seen already, companies often find it necessary to match competitors' prices on the same or similar items unless they can establish a distinctive image in customers' minds. One of the most successful strategies for companies facing direct competition is to differentiate their products or services by adding value for customers and then charging for it. For instance, a company might offer faster delivery, a longer product warranty, extra service, or something else that adds value to an item for its customers and allows the business to charge a higher price.

Perhaps the least understood of the three reference points is a company's cost structure. Customers often underestimate the costs businesses incur to provide products and services, whether it is a simple cotton T-shirt on a shelf in a beach-front shop or a life-saving drug that may have cost hundreds of millions of dollars and many years to develop. They forget that business owners must make or buy the products they sell, market them, pay their employees, and cover a host of other operating expenses, ranging from health care to legal fees. Entrepreneurs facing rapidly rising costs in their businesses should consider the following strategies:

- ***Communicate with customers.*** Rather than hide bad news from customers, let them know what is happening. When the owner of a wholesale coffee business saw coffee bean prices escalate because of bad weather in key coffee-producing countries, he included copies of news articles in a letter he sent to customers explaining his company's price increases.
- ***Focus on improving efficiency in the company.*** One way to lessen the impact of rising costs in one area of a business is to look for ways to cut costs in other areas. Improving operating efficiency may not offset totally the increased costs of doing business, but it will help dampen their effects.
- ***Consider absorbing the cost increases.*** When Norm Brodsky, owner of the document storage company mentioned earlier, saw his competitors add a fuel surcharge to their customers' bills to offset steep increases in gas prices, he decided *not* to add a fuel surcharge. Then, he used the pricing decision to attract new accounts, telling them, "We have found other ways besides a surcharge to deal with the problem. When we say the price [of our contract] is fixed for five years, we mean it, and you can count on it." Brodsky also used the fuel surcharge issue to build loyalty among his existing customers, something he is certain will pay off in the future.[18]

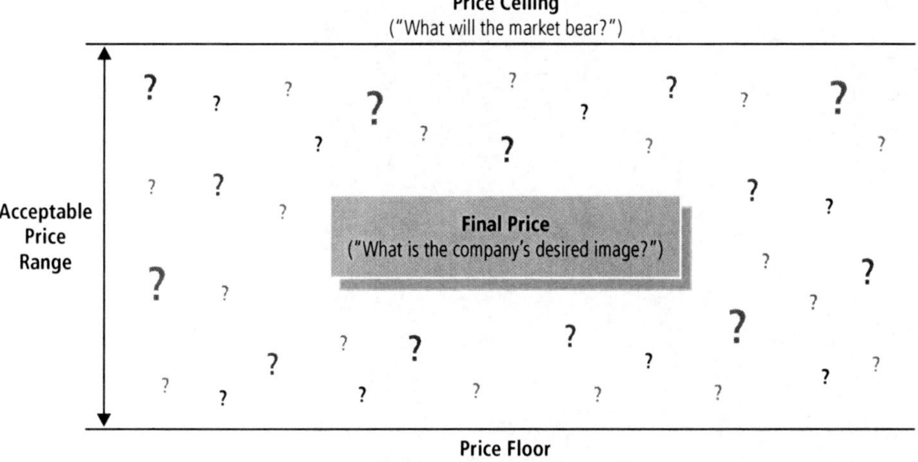

FIGURE 10.1

Pocket Price Waterfall

- ***Emphasize the value your company's product or service delivers to customers.*** Customers have a tendency to forget the benefits and value a business provides unless an entrepreneur periodically reminds them.
- ***Anticipate rising costs and try to lock in prices early.*** By tracking coffee and tea prices on commodities exchanges every day, the owner of a small coffee and tea shop was able to anticipate price increases for her raw materials and committed early on to purchase 125,000 pounds of coffee at a fixed price for one year. When coffee prices doubled, she saved more than $80,000.

Setting prices with an emphasis on value is more important than trying to choose the ideal price for a product. In fact, for most products there is an acceptable price range, not a single ideal price. This price range is the area between the price ceiling defined by customers in the market and the price floor established by the company's cost structure. An entrepreneur's goal is to position the company's prices within this acceptable price range. The final price that business owners set depends on the desired image they want to create for the business in their customers' minds—discount, middle-of-the-road, or prestige (see Figure 10.1).

Setting appropriate prices requires more than just choosing a number based solely on intuition. Rather, proper pricing policies require information, facts, and analysis. The factors that small business owners must consider when determining the final price for goods and services include the following:

- Product or service costs
- Market factors—supply and demand
- Sales volume
- Competitors' prices
- A company's competitive advantage
- Economic conditions
- Business location
- Seasonal fluctuations
- Psychological factors
- Credit terms and purchase discounts
- Customers' price sensitivity
- Desired image

Although business owners may not be able to charge the ideal price for a product or service, they should set the price high enough to cover their costs and earn a reasonable profit but low enough to attract customers and generate an adequate sales volume.

After the terrorist attacks in 2001 dampened attendance at Broadway, theaters cut their prices. As audiences returned, theaters were able to raise their ticket prices. Even though they charge more than $100 per ticket, popular shows such as *Wicked* (featuring here Idina Menzel (l) as Elpheba and Kristin Chenoweth (r) as Glinda) play to sold out houses almost every night.

Furthermore, the right price today may be completely inappropriate tomorrow because of changing market and competitive conditions. Broadway shows, which had suffered steep sales declines in the wake of the terrorist attacks in 2001, recently pushed ticket prices above the $100 level as audiences returned and shows began selling out once again. *Monty Python's Spamalot* was the first hit show to push through the psychological $100 price ceiling, but long-running *Mamma Mia!* and *Wicked* quickly followed suit. The decisions were based on the fact that all three shows were playing to sold-out houses almost every night of the week, but theater managers were quick to point out that customers could still buy standing-room-only tickets for as little as $20.[19]

For many businesses, the pricing decision has become more challenging because the World Wide Web gives customers access to incredible amounts of information about the prices of items ranging from cars to computers. Increasingly, customers are using the Web to find the lowest prices available. To maintain their profitability, companies have responded with **customized or dynamic pricing,** in which they set different prices on the same products and services for different customers using the information they have collected about their customers. For instance, a first-time customer making a purchase at an online store may pay a higher price for an item than a regular customer who shops there frequently pays for that same item. AllState Insurance Company relies on a huge database of statistical research that includes information ranging from customers' driving records and their age to their credit scores and whether they pay their bills on time to determine the prices it charges for insurance coverage. AllState's credit-derived premiums have enabled the company to go from a system that established prices using three broad-based categories to one that divides customers into nearly 400 categories, each with its own price point. Since implementing the dynamic pricing strategy, AllState's sales and profitability have climbed significantly.[20]

customized or dynamic pricing
a pricing technique that sets different prices on the same products and services for different customers using the information that a company collects about its customers.

Pricing Strategies and Tactics

2. Describe effective pricing techniques for introducing new products or services and for existing ones.

There is no limit to the number of variations in pricing strategies and tactics. This wide variety of options is exactly what allows the small business manager to be so creative. This section examines some of the more commonly used tactics under a variety of conditions. Pricing always plays a critical role in a firm's overall strategy; pricing policies must be compatible with a company's total marketing plan and the image it plans to create in the marketplace.

Introducing a New Product

Entrepreneurs are often apprehensive to set the price of a new product when they have no precedent on which to base their decisions. If the new product's price is excessively high, it is in danger of failing because of low sales volume. However, if its price is too low, the product's sales revenue might not cover costs. In addition, the company runs the risk of establishing the product's perceived value at a low level. The management consulting firm McKinsey and Company claims that 80 to 90 percent of the pricing problems on new products are the result of companies setting prices that are too low.[21] When pricing any new product, the owner should try to satisfy three objectives:

1. ***Getting the product accepted.*** No matter how unusual a product is, its price must be acceptable to a company's potential customers. The acceptable price range for a new product depends, in part, on the product's position:
   - Revolutionary products are so new and unique that they transform existing markets. The acceptable price range for revolutionary products tends to be rather wide, but the businesses introducing them must be prepared to make an investment in educating customers about them.
   - Evolutionary products offer upgrades and enhancements to existing products. The acceptable price range for evolutionary products is not a wide as it is for revolutionary products. Companies that introduce evolutionary products with many new features at prices that are too low may initiate a price war.
   - Me-too products, as the name suggests, offer the same basic features as existing products on the market. The acceptable price range for these products is quite narrow, and many companies introducing them find themselves left with me-too pricing strategies that are the same or similar to those of their competitors.
2. ***Maintaining market share as competition grows.*** If a new product is successful, competitors will enter the market, and the small company must work to expand or at least maintain its market share. Continuously reappraising the product's price in conjunction with special advertising and promotion techniques helps to retain a satisfactory market share.
3. ***Earning a profit.*** Obviously, a small firm must establish a price for the new product higher than its cost. Entrepreneurs should not introduce a new product at a price below cost because it is much easier to lower a price than to increase it once the product is on the market. Pricing their products too low is a common and often fatal mistake for new businesses; entrepreneurs are tempted to underprice their products and services when they enter a new market to ensure their acceptance or to gain market share quickly. Doing so, however, sets customers' value expectations at low levels as well, and that can be a difficult perception to overcome.

Calder & Calder Promotions

Linda Calder, owner of Calder & Calder Promotions, a company that produces trade shows, knows how difficult it can be to raise prices. When she launched her company, Calder decided to set her price below the average price of competing trade show production companies because she thought that would give her a competitive edge. "My fee was so low . . . I sold out but did not make a profit," she says. Realizing her mistake, Calder raised prices in her second year, but her customers balked. Her sales fell by 50 percent.[22]

Entrepreneurs have three basic strategies to choose from when establishing a new product's price: a penetration pricing strategy; a skimming pricing strategy; and a sliding-down-the-demand-curve strategy.

Market Penetration If a small business introduces a product into a highly competitive market in which a large number of similar products are competing for acceptance, the product must penetrate the market to be successful. To gain quick acceptance and extensive distribution in the mass market, entrepreneurs should consider introducing the product at a low price. In other words, it should set the price just above total unit cost to develop a wedge in the market and quickly achieve a high volume of sales. The resulting low profit margins tend to discourage competitors from entering the market with similar products.

In most cases, a penetration pricing strategy is used to introduce relatively low-priced goods into a market where no elite segment and little opportunity for differentiation exists. The introduction is usually accompanied by heavy advertising and promotional techniques, special sales, and discounts. Entrepreneurs must recognize that penetration pricing is a long-range strategy; until customers accept the product, profits are likely to be small. If the strategy works and the product achieves mass market penetration, sales volume will increase, and the company will earn adequate profits. The objectives of the penetration strategy are to break into the market quickly, generate a high sales volume as soon as possible, and build market share. Many consumer products, such as soap, shampoo, and light bulbs, are introduced through penetration pricing strategies.

Majesco

Majesco, a small company that competes against many industry giants in the video game business, uses a penetration pricing strategy for most of the games it sells. The company releases 5 to 10 new games each year, and 80 percent of them are "bargain titles," targeted for sale in retailers' discount bins, where they are priced from $9.99 to $19.99. "There's not much competition in the value-game market," explains company co-founder Jesse Sutton. Because the average cost of producing budget games is far below that of creating premium games with sophisticated graphics, Majesco can break even on sales of just 15,000 to 50,000 units for its budget games compared to 200,000 to 1 million units for premium games. One of the company's most popular titles, *Hypersonic Extreme,* has sold more than 170,000 units, earning the company a solid profit.[23]

Skimming A skimming pricing strategy often is used when a company introduces a new product into a market with little or no competition. Sometimes the firm employs this tactic when introducing a product into a competitive market that contains an elite group that is able to pay a higher price. Here a firm uses a higher-than-normal price in an effort to quickly recover the initial developmental and promotional costs of the product. Start-up costs usually are substantial due to intensive promotional expenses and high initial production costs. The idea is to set a price well above the total unit cost and to promote the product heavily to appeal to the segment of the market that is not sensitive to price. Such a pricing tactic often reinforces the unique, prestigious image of a store and projects a quality image of the product. Another advantage of this technique is that the manager can correct pricing mistakes quickly and easily. If the firm sets a price that is too low under a penetration strategy, raising the price can be very difficult. If a firm using a skimming strategy sets a price too high to generate sufficient volume, it can always lower the price. Successful skimming strategies require a company to differentiate its products or services from those of the competition, justifying the above-average price.

Sliding Down the Demand Curve One variation of the skimming price strategy is called sliding down the demand curve. Using this tactic, the small company introduces a product at a high price. Then, technological advances enable the firm to lower its costs quickly and to reduce the product's price before its competition can. By beating other businesses in a price decline, the small company discourages competitors and gradually, over time, becomes a high-volume producer. High-definition television sets are a prime

"Too pricey? Perhaps you wish to see something in macaroni and spray paint?"

example of a product introduced at a high price that quickly cascaded downward as companies forged important technological advances and took advantage of economies of scale. When they were first introduced in 1999, high-definition TVs sold for $19,000; today, they are priced at $1,000 or less.

Sliding is a short-term pricing strategy that assumes that competition will eventually emerge. Even if no competition arises, however, the small business almost always lowers the product's price to attract a larger segment of the market. Nonetheless, the initial high price contributes to a rapid return of start-up costs and generates a pool of funds to finance expansion and technological advances.

Pricing Established Goods and Services

Each of the following pricing tactics or techniques can become part of the toolbox of pricing tactics entrepreneurs can use to set prices of established goods and services.

Odd Pricing Although studies of consumer reactions to prices are mixed and generally inconclusive, many small business managers use the technique known as **odd pricing.** These managers prefer to establish prices that end in odd numbers such as 5, 7, or 9 because they believe that merchandise selling for $12.69 appears to be much cheaper than the item priced at $13.00. Psychological techniques such as odd pricing are designed to appeal to certain customer interests, but research on their effectiveness is mixed. Some studies show no benefits from using odd pricing, but others have concluded that the technique can produce significant increases in sales.

odd pricing
a pricing technique that sets prices that end in odd numbers to create the psychological impression of low prices.

Price Lining **Price lining** is a technique that greatly simplifies the pricing function by pricing different products in a product line at different price points, depending on their quality, features, and cost. Under this system, entrepreneurs stock merchandise in several different price ranges, or price lines. Each category of merchandise contains items that are similar in appearance but that differ in quality, cost, performance, or other features. For example, most music and video stores use price lines for their CDs and DVDs to make it

price lining
a technique that greatly simplifies the pricing function by pricing different products in a product line at different price points, depending on their quality, features, and cost.

easier for customers to select items and to simplify inventory planning. Many lined products appear in sets of three—good, better, and best—at prices designed to satisfy different market segment needs and incomes. Price lining can boost a store's sales because it makes goods available to a wide range of shoppers, simplifies the purchase decision for customers, and allows them to keep their purchases within their budgets.

leader pricing
a technique that involves marking down the normal price of a popular item in an attempt to attract more customers who make incidental purchases of other items at regular prices.

Leader Pricing **Leader pricing** is a technique in which a retailer marks down the customary price (i.e., the price consumers are accustomed to paying) of a popular item in an attempt to attract more customers. The company earns a much smaller profit on each unit because the markup is lower, but purchases of other merchandise by customers seeking the leader item often boost sales and profits. In other words, the incidental purchases that consumers make when shopping for the leader item boost sales revenue enough to offset a lower profit margin on the leader. Grocery stores frequently use leader pricing. For instance, during the holiday season, stores often use turkeys as a price leader, knowing that they will earn higher margins on the other items shoppers purchase with their turkeys.

zone pricing
a technique that involves setting different prices for customers located in different territories because of different transportation costs.

delivered pricing
a technique in which a firm charges all of its customers the same price regardless of their location.

FOB-Factory
a pricing method in which a company sells merchandise to customers on the condition that they pay all shipping costs.

Geographic Pricing Small businesses whose pricing decisions are greatly affected by the costs of shipping merchandise to customers across a wide range of geographic regions frequently employ one of the geographic pricing techniques. For these companies, freight expenses comprise a substantial portion of the cost of doing business and may cut deeply into already narrow profit margins. One type of geographic pricing is **zone pricing,** in which a small company sells its merchandise at different prices to customers located in different territories. For example, a manufacturer might sell at one price to customers east of the Mississippi and at another to those west of the Mississippi. The U.S. Postal Service's varying parcel post charges offer a good example of zone pricing. The company must be able to show a legitimate basis (e.g., differences in selling or transporting costs) for the price discrimination or risk violating Section 2 of the Clayton Act.

Another variation of geographic pricing is uniform **delivered pricing,** a technique in which a firm charges all of its customers the same price regardless of their location, even though the cost of selling or transporting merchandise varies. The firm calculates the proper freight charges for each region and combines them into a uniform fee. The result is that local customers subsidize the company's charges for shipping merchandise to distant customers.

A final variation of geographic pricing is **FOB-Factory,** in which a company sells its merchandise to customers on the condition that they pay all shipping costs. In this way, the company can set a uniform price for its product and let each customer cover the freight costs.

opportunistic pricing
a pricing method that involves charging customers unreasonably high prices when goods or services are in short supply.

Opportunistic Pricing When products or services are in short supply, customers are willing to pay more for products they need. Some businesses use such circumstances to maximize short-term profits by engaging in price gouging. Many customers have little choice but to pay the higher prices. **Opportunistic pricing** may backfire, however, because customers know that unreasonably high prices mean that a company is exploiting them. For example, after a devastating Los Angeles earthquake, one convenience store jacked up prices on virtually every item, selling small bottles of water for $8 each. Neighborhood residents had no choice but to pay the higher prices. After the incident, many customers remembered the store's unfair prices and began to shop elsewhere. The convenience store's sales slipped and never recovered.

discounts or markdowns
reductions from normal list prices.

Discounts Many small business managers use **discounts or markdowns**—reductions from normal list prices—to move stale, outdated, damaged, or slow-moving merchandise. A seasonal discount is a price reduction designed to encourage shoppers to purchase merchandise before an upcoming season. For instance, many retail clothiers offer special sales on winter coats in midsummer. Some firms grant purchase discounts to special groups of customers, such as senior citizens or students, to establish a faithful clientele and to generate repeat business. For example, one small drugstore located near a state

One of the most common tactics for selling slow-moving merchandise is the markdown.

university offered a 10 percent student discount on all purchases and was quite successful in developing a large volume of student business.

multiple-unit pricing
a technique offering customers discounts if they purchase in quantity.

Multiple-unit pricing is a promotional technique that offers customers discounts if they purchase in quantity. Many products, especially those with relatively low unit value, are sold using multiple pricing. For example, instead of selling an item for 50 cents, a small company might offer five for $2.

bundling
a pricing method that involves grouping together several products or services, or both, into a package that offers customers extra value at a special price.

Bundling Many small businesses have discovered the marketing benefits of **bundling,** grouping together several products or services, or both, into a package that offers customers extra value at a special price. For instance, many software manufacturers bundle several computer programs (such as a word processor, spreadsheet, database, presentation graphics, and Web browser) into "suites" that offer customers a discount over purchasing the same packages separately. Fast food outlets often bundle items into "meal deals" that customers can purchase at lower prices than if they bought the items separately.

Recognizing that each fall the 15 million students who set out for college spend more than $210 million to furnish and decorate their dormitory rooms and apartments, one retailer began offering a line of bundled products aimed squarely at this target audience. The company's Dorm Room line includes Kitchen in a Box, a set of between 46 and 80 starter pieces that are suitable for equipping an empty kitchen. One set that is priced at $80 includes pieces that would cost $140 if purchased separately. The company's Bath in a Box includes oversized towels that are convenient for dorm life and a laundry bag with handy instructions for washing clothes for students who have not yet mastered the art of sorting clothes.[24]

optional product pricing
a technique that involves selling the base product for one price but selling the options or accessories for it at a much higher markup.

Optional-product pricing involves selling the base product for one price but selling the options or accessories for it at a much higher markup. Automobiles are often sold at a base price with each option priced separately. In some cases, the car is sold with some of the options "bundled" together, as explained previously.

Kettler

Kettler, a German company that makes upscale tricycles, uses an optional-product pricing strategy that more closely mimics BMW than Babies "R" Us. A basic model of its most popular tricycle, The Navigator, starts at $70, but a host of options ranging from a seat belt ($15.99) to a little red bell ($5.99) quickly pushes the price to $150 or more, far above the price of an average tricycle. Despite Kettler's premium prices, parents who want only the best for their children are snapping up the company's high-quality tricycles fast enough that its sales are growing at nearly 20 percent a year.[25]

captive-product pricing
a technique that involves selling a product for a low price and charging a higher price for the accessories that accompany it.

Captive-product pricing is a pricing strategy in which the base product is not functional without the appropriate accessory. King Gillette, the founder of Gillette, taught the business world that the real money is not in selling the razor (the product) but in selling the blades (the accessory)! Most companies in the desktop printer business use this technique. They introduce a printer at a low initial price and then price replacement cartridges so that they earn high margins on them. Manufacturers of electronic games also rely on captive-product pricing, earning lower margins on the game consoles and substantially higher margins on the game cartridges.

byproduct pricing
a technique in which the revenues from the sale of byproducts allow a company to be more competitive in its pricing of the main product.

Byproduct pricing is a technique in which the revenues from the sale of byproducts allow a company to be more competitive in its pricing of the main product. For years, sawmills thought that the bark from the trees they processed was a nuisance. Now it is packaged and sold to gardeners who use the bark chips for ground cover. Zoos across the globe offer one of the most creative examples of byproduct pricing, packaging once-worthless exotic animal droppings and marketing it as fertilizer under the clever name "Zoo Doo."

Suggested Retail Prices Many manufacturers print suggested retail prices on their products or include them on invoices or in wholesale catalogs. Small business owners frequently follow these suggested retail prices because this eliminates the need to make a pricing decision. Nonetheless, following prices established by a distant manufacturer may create problems for the small firm. For example, a haberdasher may try to create a high-quality, exclusive image through a prestige pricing policy, but manufacturers may suggest discount outlet prices that are incompatible with the small firm's image. Another danger of accepting the manufacturer's suggested price is that it does not take into consideration a small company's cost structure or competitive situation. A manufacturer cannot force a business to accept a suggested retail price or require a business to agree not to resell merchandise below a stated price because this would be a violation of the Sherman Antitrust Act and other legislation.

Pricing for Value

After spending 15 years as an executive in the textile industry and 3 years as an elementary school teacher, Jeannette Doellgast made a major career move. With her husband and business partner, Alam El Din, she purchased the Plumbush Inn, a bed-and-breakfast (B&B) located in the scenic town of Cold Spring, New York. Shortly after taking over the inn, which had been in business for 30 years, Doellgast and El Din realized that they needed to raise the prices they charged for both the rooms they rented and the meals they served in their dining area. "It was a risk," says Doellgast. Most of their customers were regulars, so the couple took the time to explain the new pricing policy with each one. A few customers were displeased, but most accepted the price increases without complaint. The increases have put the Plumbush Inn in a much stronger financial position. Revenues have climbed to $1.25 million, and profits are up.

As they considered their pricing options, Doellgast and El Din spent time defining the image they wanted the inn to have and the target customers they wanted to attract. In the end, they defined the inn as a B&B where couples could go for a romantic escape rather than one where a family with children might stop for inexpensive lodging on their way to some vacation destination. Doellgast says that once they settled on the image they wanted to create, the price increases were essential. "A richer experience costs more money to provide," she explains. The meals in the Plumbush Inn dining room are a perfect example. "We are a slow dining experience," says Doellgast. "We don't buy anything frozen. Everything is fresh, which makes a difference in the price." The chef also uses organic products, which typically cost more, but diners appreciate the fine dining experience they get at the inn. Even the customers who initially complained about the price increases have returned and are satisfied because they now receive a higher level of service. "People bring with them a whole set of equations when they make a purchase, and one of the values for most people is that high price equals quality," explains pricing expert Rob Docters. "Pricing is not just about cost," he says. It's about value."

Before establishing their new pricing structure, Doellgast and El Din researched their competitors' prices. Their competitors' prices were a consideration in making their own pricing decisions, but the primary factors were the image they wanted to create for the Plumbush Inn and the customers they were targeting. "Pricing is an art, but it's not only about pricing," says Deollgast. It's about differentiating yourself and deciding what your niche [is] and what the value of your niche [is]. If you build your business around low price, somebody is going to come in next week and undercut you. [In that case], you really haven't established your market."

What steps can entrepreneurs take when it comes to setting prices the right way? The following tips will help:

- Know your costs, including the direct and the indirect costs, of providing your product or service.
- Don't set your price below your costs. "We lose money on every unit we sell, but we make up for it in volume" is a business philosophy that never works.
- Price increases are easier to accomplish when a company faces fewer competitors. The more intense the competition, the more difficult it is to raise prices.
- If you need to raise prices shortly after launching your business, try to soften the blow by bundling products and services to create more value for customers.
- Assign someone in your company to track competitors' prices regularly (at least monthly) and to present the results on a timely basis.
- Do not blindly follow your competitors' pricing strategies.
- Base your pricing on the value that your product or service offers customers. Remember that sometimes the most valuable components of a product or service are intangible.
- Define the image you want to create for your business and use your pricing strategy to communicate that image to your customers and to position your company in the market.

1. Why do many entrepreneurs underprice their goods and services, especially when they first get into business? Discuss the connection between the prices a company establishes for its goods and services and the image it creates for the company.
2. What is the impact of these pricing errors on a small company? What steps can entrepreneurs take to avoid this problem?

Sources: Geoff Williams, "Name Your Price," *Entrepreneur*, September 2005, pp. 108–115; Bridget McCrea, "When Is the Price Right? Effective Pricing Is Crucial to Remain Competitive and Move Product," *Black Enterprise*, July 2004, pp. 78–79.

Pricing Strategies and Methods for Retailers

LEARNING OBJECTIVES
3A. Explain the pricing methods and strategies for retailers.

As customers have become more price-conscious, retailers have changed their pricing strategies to emphasize value. This value/price relationship allows for a wide variety of highly creative pricing and marketing practices. As discussed previously, delivering high levels of recognized value in products and services is one key to retail customer loyalty.

Markup

The basic premise of a successful business operation is selling a good or service for more than it costs. The difference between the cost of a product or service and its selling price is called **markup (or markon).** Markup can be expressed in dollars or as a percentage of either cost or selling price:

markup (or markon) the difference between the cost of a product or service and its selling price.

$$\text{Dollar markup} = \text{Retail price} - \text{Cost of the merchandise}$$

$$\text{Percentage (of retail price) markup} = \frac{\text{Dollar markup}}{\text{Retail price}}$$

$$\text{Percentage (of cost) markup} = \frac{\text{Dollar markup}}{\text{Cost of unit}}$$

For example, if a man's shirt costs \$15 and a business owner plans to sell it for \$25, the markup would be as follows:

$$\text{Dollar markup} = \$25 - \$15 = \$10$$
$$\text{Percentage (of retail price) markup} = \$10 \div \$25 = 40\%$$
$$\text{Percentage (of cost) markup} = \$10 \div \$15 = 66.67\%$$

Notice that the cost of merchandise used in computing markup includes not only the wholesale price of the merchandise, but also any incidental costs (e.g., selling or transportation charges) that the retailer incurs and a profit minus any discounts (quantity, cash) that the wholesaler offers.

Once a business owner has a financial plan, including sales estimates and anticipated expenses, he or she can compute the firm's initial markup. The initial markup is the *average* markup required on all merchandise to cover the cost of the items, all incidental expenses, and a reasonable profit:

$$\text{Initial dollar markup} = \frac{\text{Operating expenses} + \text{Reductions} + \text{Profits}}{\text{Net sales} + \text{Reductions}}$$

In this calculation, operating expenses include the cost of doing business, such as rent, utilities, and depreciation, and reductions include employee and customer discounts, markdowns, special sales, and the cost of stockouts.

For example, if a small retailer forecasts sales of \$380,000, expenses of \$140,000, and \$24,000 in reductions, and he or she expects a profit of \$38,000, the initial markup percentage is calculated as follows

$$\text{Initial markup percentage} = \frac{\$140{,}000 + \$24{,}000 + \$38{,}000}{\$380{,}000 + \$24{,}000} = 50\%$$

This retailer thus knows that an average markup of 50 percent is required to cover costs and generate an adequate profit.

Some businesses employ a standard markup on all of their merchandise. This technique, which is usually used in retail stores carrying related products, applies a standard percentage markup to all merchandise. Most stores find it much more practical to use a flexible markup, which assigns various markup percentages to different types of products. Because of the wide range of prices and types of merchandise they sell, department stores frequently rely on a flexible markup. It would be impractical for them to use a standard markup on all items because they have such a divergent cost and volume range. For instance, the markup percentage for socks is not likely to be suitable as a markup for washing machines.

Once an owner determines the desired markup percentage, he or she can compute the appropriate retail price. Knowing that the markup of a particular item represents 40 percent of the retail price gives

$$\begin{aligned} \text{Cost} &= \text{retail price} - \text{markup} \\ &= 100\% - 40\% \\ &= 60\% \text{ of retail price} \end{aligned}$$

Assuming that the cost of the item is \$18.00, the retailer can rearrange the percentage (of retail price) markup formula:

$$\text{Retail price} = \text{Dollar cost} \div \text{Percentage of retail price}$$

The retailer computes a price as follows:

$$\text{Retail price} = \$18.00 \div 0.60 = \$30.00$$

Thus, the owner establishes a retail price of \$30.00 for the item using a 40 percent markup.

Finally, retailers must verify that the retail price they have calculated is consistent with their planned initial markup percentage. Will it cover costs and generate the desired profit?

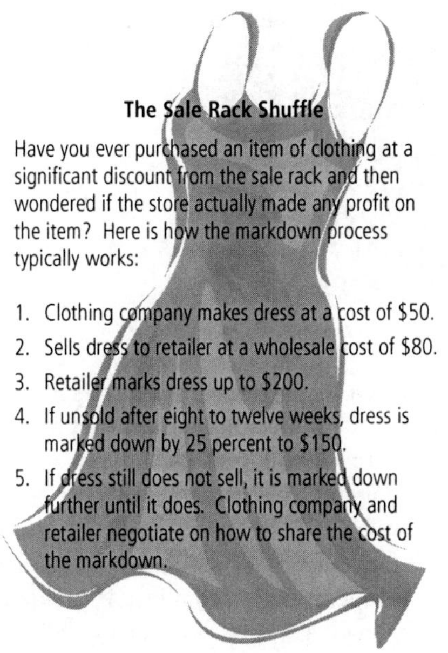

The Sale Rack Shuffle

Have you ever purchased an item of clothing at a significant discount from the sale rack and then wondered if the store actually made any profit on the item? Here is how the markdown process typically works:

1. Clothing company makes dress at a cost of $50.
2. Sells dress to retailer at a wholesale cost of $80.
3. Retailer marks dress up to $200.
4. If unsold after eight to twelve weeks, dress is marked down by 25 percent to $150.
5. If dress still does not sell, it is marked down further until it does. Clothing company and retailer negotiate on how to share the cost of the markdown.

FIGURE 10.2

Sample Pocket Price Band

Is it congruent with the firm's overall price image? Is the final price in line with the company's strategy? Is it within an acceptable price range? How does it compare to the prices charged by competitors? And, perhaps most important, are the customers willing and able to pay this price? Figure 10.2 explains the mathematics of markups—and markdowns—at the retail level.

Follow-the-Leader Pricing

Some small companies make no effort to be price leaders in their immediate geographic areas and simply follow the prices that their competitors establish. Entrepreneurs wisely monitor their competitors' pricing policies and individual prices by reviewing their advertisements or by hiring part-time or full-time comparison shoppers. However, some retailers use this information to establish "me-too" pricing policies, which eradicate any opportunity to create a special price image for their businesses. Although many retailers must match competitors' prices on identical items, maintaining a follow-the-leader pricing policy may not be healthy for a small business because it robs the company of the opportunity to create a distinctive image in its customers' eyes.

Below-Market Pricing

Some small businesses choose to create a discount image in the market by offering goods at below-market prices. By setting prices below those of their competitors, these firms hope to attract a sufficient level of volume to offset the lower profit margins. Many retailers using a below-market pricing strategy eliminate most of the extra services that their above-market-pricing competitors offer. For instance, these businesses trim operating costs by cutting out services like delivery, installation, credit granting, and sales assistance. Below-market pricing strategies can be risky for small companies because they require them to constantly achieve high sales volume to remain competitive.

Pricing Concepts for Manufacturers

LEARNING OBJECTIVES
3B. Explain the pricing methods and strategies for manufacturers.

For manufacturers, the pricing decision requires the support of accurate, timely accounting records. The most commonly used pricing technique for manufacturers is cost-plus pricing. Using this method, a manufacturer establishes a price that is composed of direct materials, direct labor, factory overhead, selling and administrative costs, plus the desired profit margin. Figure 10.3 illustrates the cost-plus pricing components.

FIGURE 10.3

Cost-Plus Pricing Components

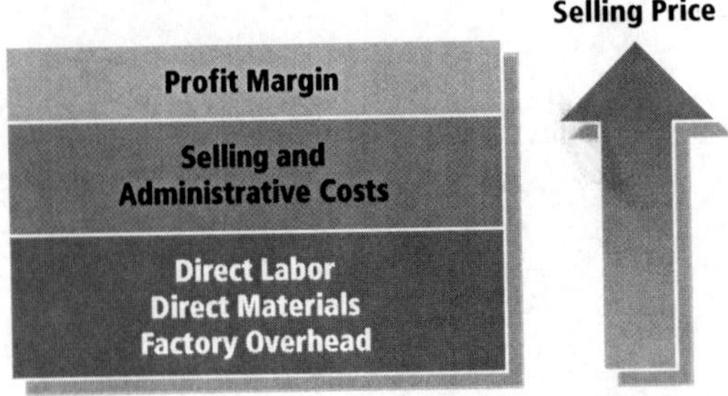

The main advantage of the cost-plus pricing method is its simplicity. Given the proper cost accounting data, computing a product's final selling price is relatively easy. In addition, because they add a profit onto the top of their companies' costs, manufacturers are guaranteed the desired profit margin. This process, however, does not encourage the manufacturers to use their resources efficiently. Even if the company fails to employ its resources in the most effective manner, it will still earn a reasonable profit, and thus there is no motivation to conserve resources in the manufacturing process. Finally, because manufacturers' cost structures vary so greatly, cost-plus pricing fails to consider the competition (and market forces) sufficiently. Despite its drawbacks, the cost-plus method of establishing prices remains prominent in many industries such as construction and printing.

Direct Costing and Price Formulation

absorption costing
the traditional method of product costing in which all manufacturing and overhead costs are absorbed into the product's total cost.

variable (or direct) costing
a method of product costing that includes in the product's cost only those costs that vary directly with the quantity produced.

One requisite for a successful pricing policy in manufacturing is a reliable cost accounting system that can generate timely reports to determine the costs of processing raw materials into finished goods. The traditional method of product costing is called **absorption costing** because all manufacturing and overhead costs are absorbed into a finished product's total cost. Absorption costing includes direct materials, direct labor, plus a portion of fixed and variable factory overhead in each unit manufactured. Full absorption financial statements are used in published annual reports and in tax reports and are very useful in performing financial analysis. However, full absorption statements are of little help to manufacturers when determining prices or the impact of price changes.

A more useful technique for managerial decision making is **variable (or direct) costing,** in which the cost of the products manufactured includes only those costs that vary directly with the quantity produced. In other words, variable costing encompasses direct materials, direct labor, and factory overhead costs that vary with the level of the firm's output of finished goods. Those factory overhead costs that are fixed (rent, depreciation, insurance) are *not* included in the costs of finished items. Instead, they are considered to be expenses of the period.

A manufacturer's goal when establishing prices is to discover the combination of selling price and sales volume that covers the variable costs of producing a product and contributes toward covering fixed costs and earning a profit. The problem with using full-absorption costing for this is that it clouds the true relationships among price, volume, and costs by including fixed expenses in unit cost. Using a direct costing basis yields a constant unit cost for the product no matter what volume of production. The result is a clearer picture of the price/volume/costs relationship.

The starting point for establishing product prices is the direct cost income statement. As Table 10.1 indicates, the direct cost statement yields the same net income as does the full-absorption income statement. The only difference between the two statements is the format. The full-absorption statement allocates costs such as advertising, rent, and utilities according to the activity that caused them, but the direct cost income statement separates expenses into their fixed and variable components. Fixed expenses remain constant regardless of the production level, but variable expenses fluctuate according to production volume.

When variable costs are subtracted from total revenues, the result is the manufacturer's contribution margin—the amount remaining that contributes to covering fixed expenses and earning a profit. Expressing this contribution margin as a percentage of total

TABLE 10.1 Full-Absorption versus Direct-Cost Income Statement

Full-Absorption Income Statement		
Sales revenue		$ 790,000
Cost of goods sold		
Materials	250,500	
Direct labor	190,200	
Factory overhead	120,200	560,900
Gross profit		$ 229,100
Operating expenses		
General and administrative	66,100	
Selling	112,000	
Other	11,000	
Total operating expenses		189,100
Net income (before taxes)		$ 40,000
Direct-Cost Income Statement		
Sales revenue (100%)		$ 790,000
Variable costs		
Materials	250,500	
Direct labor	190,200	
Variable factory overhead	13,200	
Variable selling expenses	48,100	
Total variable costs (63.54%)		502,000
Contribution margin (36.46%)		288,000
Fixed costs		
Fixed factory overhead	107,000	
Fixed selling expenses	63,900	
General and administrative	66,100	
Other fixed expenses	11,000	
Total fixed expenses (31.39%)		248,000
Net income (before taxes) (5.06%)		$ 40,000

revenue yields the company's contribution margin. Computing the contribution percentage is a critical step in establishing prices through the direct costing method. This manufacturer's contribution percentage is 36.5 percent.

Computing the Break-Even Selling Price

The manufacturer's contribution percentage tells what portion of total revenues remains after covering variable costs to contribute toward meeting fixed expenses and earning a profit. This manufacturer's contribution margin is 36.5 percent, which means that variable costs absorb 63.5 percent of total revenues. In other words, variable costs make up 63.5 percent ($1.00 - 0.365 = 0.635$) of the product's selling price. Suppose that this manufacturer's variable costs include the following:

Material	$2.08/unit
Direct labor	$4.12/unit
Variable factory overhead	$0.78/unit
Total variable cost	$6.98/unit

The minimum price at which the manufacturer would sell the item for is $6.98. Any price below this would not cover variable costs. To compute the break-even selling price for this product, we find the selling price using the following equation:

$$\text{Selling price} = \frac{\text{Profit} + (\text{Variable cost per unit} \times \text{Quantity produced}) + \text{Total fixed cost}}{\text{Quantity produced}}$$

To break even, the manufacturer assumes \$0 profit. Suppose that his plans are to produce 50,000 units of the product and that fixed costs will be \$110,000. The break-even selling price is as follows:

$$\text{Break-even selling price} = \frac{\$0 + (\$6.98 \text{ per unit} \times 50{,}000 \text{ units}) + \$110{,}000}{50{,}000 \text{ units}}$$

$$= \frac{\$459{,}000}{50{,}000 \text{ units}}$$

$$= \$9.18 \text{ per unit}$$

Thus, \$2.20 (\$9.18/unit − \$6.98/unit) of the \$9.18 break-even price contributes to meeting fixed production costs. But suppose the manufacturer wants to earn a \$50,000 profit. Then the selling price is calculated as follows:

$$\text{Selling price} = \frac{\$50{,}000 + (\$6.98 \text{ per unit} \times 50{,}000 \text{ units}) + \$110{,}000}{50{,}000 \text{ units}}$$

$$= \frac{\$509{,}000}{50{,}000 \text{ units}}$$

$$= \$10.18 \text{ per unit}$$

Now the manufacturer must decide whether customers will purchase 50,000 units at \$10.18. If not, he or she must decide either to produce a different, more profitable product or to lower the selling price. Any price above \$9.18 will generate some profit, although less than that desired. In the short run, the manufacturer could sell the product for less than \$9.18 if competitive factors so dictated, but not below \$6.98 because this would not cover the variable cost of production.

Because the manufacturer's capacity in the short run is fixed, pricing decisions should be aimed at employing these resources most efficiently. The fixed costs of operating the plant cannot be avoided, and the variable costs can be eliminated only if the firm ceases offering the product. Therefore, the selling price must be at least equal to the variable costs (per unit) of making the product. Any price above this amount contributes to covering fixed costs and providing a reasonable profit.

Of course, over the long run, the manufacturer cannot sell below total costs and continue to survive. So, selling price must cover total product cost—both fixed and variable—and generate a reasonable profit.

Hands on ... How to

Calculate Your Company's Pocket Price Band

When entrepreneurs make pricing decisions, they usually look at the retail price or the invoice price they charge. Doing so, however, may be misleading if the company offers significant "off-invoice" discounts such as cash discounts for paying early, quantity discounts for large purchases, special promotional discounts, and others. These invoice leakages mean that a business is getting less, sometimes far less, than the retail or

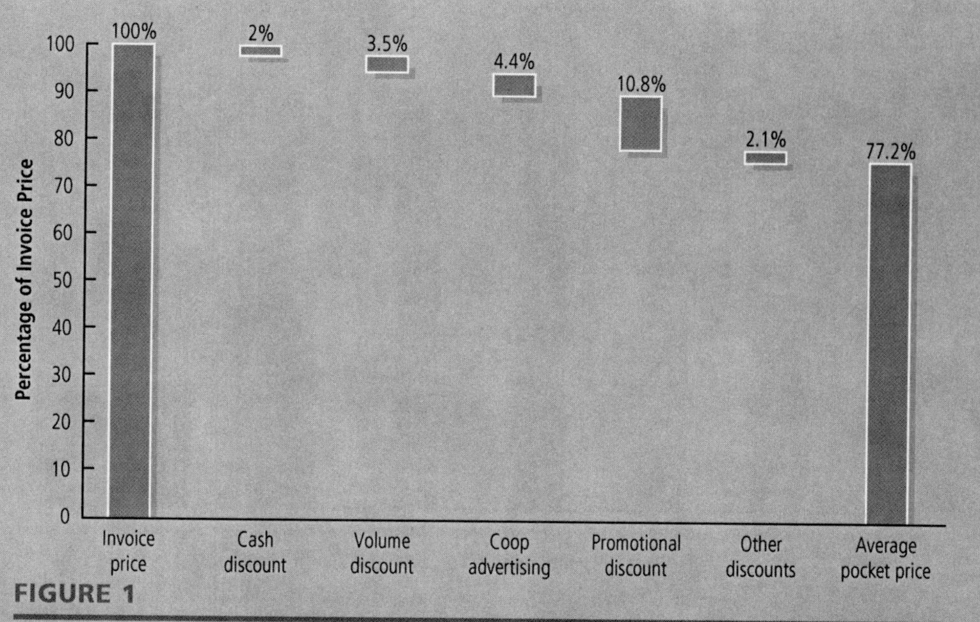

FIGURE 1

What Determines Price?

invoice price listed. In some cases, a company's pocket price, the price it receives for a product or a service after deducting all discounts and purchase incentives, is far below the listed retail or invoice price. The impact of these discounts can be significant. Research by the consulting firm McKinsey and Company shows that a decrease of one percent in a typical company's average prices will reduce its operating profits by eight percent if all other factors remain constant.

How are discounts affecting your business? To find out, you need to estimate your company's pocket price waterfall and its pocket price band (see Figure 1). The pocket price waterfall starts with a company's invoice or retail price on the far left of the diagram and then shows how much every discount or incentive the company offers its customers reduces that price. In the example in Figure 1, this small manufacturer offers a cash discount for early payment that shaves 2.0 percent off of the retail price, a 3.5 percent discount for companies whose purchases exceed a particular volume, a cooperative advertising program (in which it splits the cost of advertising its products with retailers) that amounts to 4.4 percent, and periodic promotional discounts to move products that average 10.8 percent. Other discounts the company offered customers further reduced its pocket price. In the end, the company's average pocket price is 77.2 percent of the listed invoice price.

Not every customer qualifies for every discount, however. The type and the amount of the discount vary from one customer to another; the pocket prices they pay can vary a good deal. Therefore, it is important to estimate the width of the company's pocket price band, which shows the percentage of sales accounted for by each pocket price (shown as a percentage of the listed invoice or retail price) (see Figure 2). In this example, pocket prices that are 90 percent or more of the company's invoice price account for just 28.3 percent of its total revenue. Conversely, pocket prices that are 80 percent or less of its invoice price make up 46.2 percent of its total revenue. The final step in the process is to identify the individual customers that make up each segment of the company's pocket price band.

A wide pocket price band is not necessarily bad. It simply shows that some customers generate much higher pocket prices than others. When a band is wide, small changes in its shape can produce big results for a company. If an entrepreneur can increase sales at the upper end of the band while reducing or even dropping those at the lower end of the band, both the company's revenues and profits will climb. If a company's price band is narrow, an entrepreneur has less room to maneuver prices, changing the shape of the band is more difficult, and any changes the entrepreneur can make tend to have less impact on the company's sales and revenues.

When one lighting company calculated its pocket price band, managers were surprised at its width. Once managers realized how big a dent discounts were putting in its revenues and profits, they worked with the sales force to realign the company's discount structure. Some of the company's smallest accounts had been getting the largest discounts, despite their small volume of purchases. Managers also focused on boosting

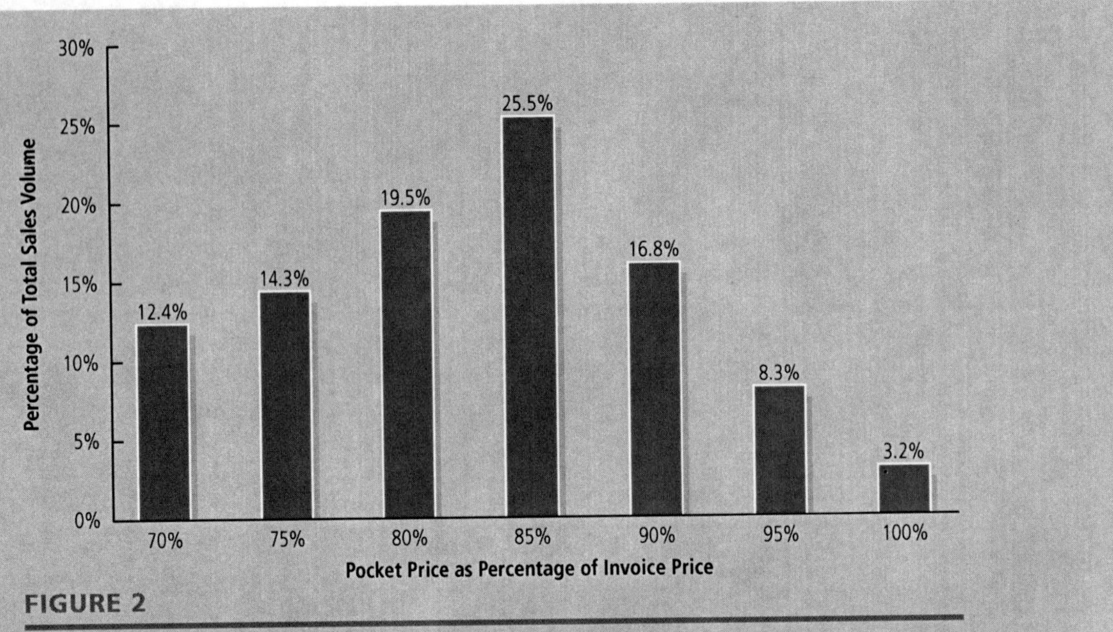

FIGURE 2

The Mathematics of Markups and Markdowns

sales to those accounts that were producing the highest pocket prices. These changes resulted in the company's average pocket price rising by 3.8 percent and its profits climbing 51 percent.

Discounts tend to work their way into a company's pricing structure gradually over time, often one transaction at a time, especially if an entrepreneur gives sales representatives latitude to negotiate prices with customers. Few companies make the effort to track these discounts, and, as a result, few companies realize the impact that discounts have on their profitability. By monitoring their companies' pocket price waterfall and the resulting pocket price band, entrepreneurs can improve significantly the revenue and the profits they generate.

Sources: Michael V. Marn, Eric V. Roegner, and Craig C. Zawada, "The Power of Pricing," The McKinsey Quarterly, Number 1, 2003, www.mckinseyquarterly.com.

LEARNING OBJECTIVES
3C. Explain the pricing methods and strategies for service firms.

Pricing Strategies and Methods for Service Firms

A service firm must establish a price based on the materials used to provide the service, the labor employed, an allowance for overhead, and a profit. As in the manufacturing operation, a service business must have a reliable, accurate accounting system to keep a tally of the total costs of providing the service. Most service firms base their prices on an hourly rate, usually the actual number of hours required to perform the service. Some companies, however, base their fees on a standard number of hours, determined by the average number of hours needed to perform the service. For most firms, labor and materials comprise the largest portion of the cost of the service. To establish a reasonable, profitable price for service, the small business owner must know the cost of materials, direct labor, and overhead for each unit of service. Using these basic cost data and a desired profit margin, an owner of the small service firm can determine the appropriate price for the service.

Consider a simple example for pricing a common service—television repair. Ned's T.V. Repair Shop uses the direct costing method to prepare an income statement for exercising managerial control (see Table 10.2). Ned estimates that he and his employees spent about 12,800 hours in the actual production of television service. Therefore, total cost per productive hour for Ned's T.V. Repair Shop comes to the following:

$$\$172{,}000 \div 12{,}800 \text{ hours} = \$13.44/\text{hour}$$

TABLE 10.2 Direct-Cost Income Statement, Ned's T.V. Repair Shop

Sales revenue		$199,000
Variable expenses		
Labor	52,000	
Materials	40,500	
Variable factory overhead	11,500	
Total variable expenses		104,000
Fixed expenses		
Rent	2,500	
Salaries	38,500	
Fixed overhead	27,000	
Total fixed expenses		68,000
Net income		$ 27,000

Now Ned must add in an amount for his desired profit. He expects a net operating profit of 18 percent on sales. To compute the final price he uses the following equation:

$$\text{Price per hour} = \text{Total cost per productive hour} \times \frac{1.00}{1.00 - \text{Net profit target as percentage of sales}}$$

$$= \$13.44 \times 1.219$$

$$= \$16.38 \text{ per hour}$$

A price of $16.38 per hour will cover Ned's costs and generate the desired profit. The wise service shop owner computes his cost per production hour at regular intervals throughout the year. Rapidly rising labor costs and material prices dictate that the service firm's price per hour be computed even more frequently. As in the case of the retailer and the manufacturer, Ned must evaluate the pricing policies of competitors, and decide whether his price is consistent with his firm's image.

Of course, the price of $16.38 per hour assumes that each job requires the same amount of materials. If this is not a valid assumption, Ned must recalculate the price per hour *without* including the cost of materials:

$$\text{Cost per productive hour} = \frac{\$172.000 - \$40{,}500}{12{,}800 \text{ hours}}$$

$$= \$10.27 \text{ per hour}$$

Adding in the desired 18 percent net operating profit on sales gives

$$\text{Price per hour} = \frac{\$10.27}{\text{hour}} \times \frac{1.00}{1.00 - 0.18}$$

$$= \frac{\$10.27}{\text{hour}} \times 1.219$$

$$= \$12.52 \text{ per hour}$$

Under these conditions, Ned would charge $12.52 per hour plus the actual cost of materials used and any markup on the cost of material. A repair job that takes four hours to complete would have the following price:

Cost of service (4 hours × $12.52/hour)	$50.08
Cost of materials	$21.00
Markup on material (20%)	$4.20
Total price	$75.28

Concepts in Success

Finding the right price for his business and event planning service was a problem facing Joshua Estrin, founder of Concepts in Success. Initially, Estrin established a reasonable annual salary for himself and then set the price for each project as a percentage of that salary. Because that system required him to spend excessive amounts of time documenting details of every expense for his clients, Estrin soon switched to an hourly rate that exceeded $100 per hour. Now that he has more experience, Estrin charges for the services that Concepts in Success offers using set price points that depend on the services his clients choose. Estrin's pricing policy is working. His company now generates $1 million in annual revenue and counts several major corporations, including American Express, Hertz, and PepsiCo, among its clients.[26]

You Be the Consultant

Pricing Web Services

Kerry Pinella, a recent business graduate of a small private college, started her career working for a large multinational computer software maker as a sales representative. After two years in sales, Kerry applied for a position on a development team that was working on software applications for the World Wide Web. Kerry thrived on the team atmosphere and learned the technical aspects of the new assignment very quickly. Not only did her team bring their project in on budget, but it also completed it slightly ahead of schedule. Team members give much of the credit for the project's success to Kerry's unofficial role as team leader. Her work ethic and relentless pursuit of quality inspired other team members.

After Kerry's team completed their project, however, Kerry had a hard time recapturing the thrill and excitement of developing the World Wide Web software. Subsequent projects simply could not measure up to the "magic" of that first assignment. After talking with several of the members of that software team, Kerry discovered that they felt the same way. Before long, Kerry and two of her former team members left the company to launch their own computer consulting company, Web Consultants. Having worked on the forefront of the Web's commercialization, Kerry and her partners saw the potential it had for revolutionizing business. Their company would specialize in developing , designing, and maintaining Web sites for clients. In their first year of business, Web Consultants accepted jobs from virtually anybody who wanted a Web site. Although they experienced some growing pains, Web Consultants quickly earned a reputation for producing quality work on time and became more selective in the jobs it bid on.

Halfway into their second year of operation, the partners planned a weekend retreat at a nearby resort so they could get away, review their progress, and plan for the future. As they reviewed their latest financial statements, one of the questions that kept popping up dealt with pricing. Were Web Consultant's pricing policies appropriate? Its sales were growing twice as fast as the industry average, and the company's bid-winning ratio was well above that of practically all of its competitors. For the current year, sales were up, but Web Consultants' net profits were virtually the same as they had been in their first year.

Pulling the records from a computer database for each job they had completed since founding the company, they found that the partners and their employees had spent 22,450 hours developing projects for their clients at a total cost of $951,207. "We were shooting for a net profit of 25 percent on sales," Kerry reminded her partners, "but we so far, our net profit margin is just 7.7 percent, only one-third of our target."

"Maybe we could increase our profits if we increased our sales," offered one partner.

The partners began to wonder whether their price of $45 per hour was appropriate. Admittedly, they had been so busy completing projects for clients that they had not kept up with what their competitors were charging. Nor had they been as diligent in analyzing their financial statements as they should have been.

As Kerry closed the cover on her laptop computer, she looked at her partners and asked, "What should Web Consultant's hourly price be?"

1. Help Kerry answer the question she posed.
2. What factors should Kerry and her partners consider when determining Web Consultant's final price?
3. Is the company's current price too low? If so, what signals could have alerted Kerry and her partners?

The Impact of Credit on Pricing

LEARNING OBJECTIVES
4. Describe the impact of credit on pricing.

Consumers crave convenience when they shop, and one of the most common conveniences they demand is the ability to purchase goods and services on credit. Small businesses that fail to offer credit to their customers lose sales to competitors who do. However, companies that do sell on credit incur additional expenses for offering this convenience. Small companies have three options for selling to customers on credit: credit cards, installment credit, and trade credit.

Credit Cards

Credit cards have become a popular method of payment among customers, who now make 30 percent of personal consumption expenditures with credit cards. Approximately 73 percent of the adult U.S. population uses credit cards to make purchases, and the average U.S. household has 17 credit cards carrying an average interest rate of 18.9 percent a year.[27] The number of credit cards in circulation in the United States exceeds 1.5 billion, an average of more than 8.5 cards per person! Customers use credit cards to make purchases of more than $2.2 trillion a year, an amount equal to about 20 percent of the total U.S. gross domestic product. The average amount a household charges to credit cards in a year now exceeds $15,000.[28] Studies have found that accepting credit cards increases the probability, speed, and magnitude of customer spending. In addition, surveys show that customers rate businesses offering credit options higher on key performance measures such as reputation, reliability, and service.[29] In short, accepting credit cards broadens a small company's customer base and closes sales that it would normally lose if customers had to pay in cash.

Increasingly, customers are using credit cards to pay for micropurchases, those costing less than $5. The research company Gartner Inc. predicts that by 2020, the average American adult will make more than 20 micropurchases per month on either debit or credit cards. To make sure that they capture their share of those small purchases, fast food restaurants now accept credit and debit cards. As a result, quick-service restaurants have seen sales climb rapidly and the average transaction time drop. For instance, average sales have risen from $5 to $7 since McDonald's began accepting debit and credit cards, and the cashless transactions have shaved seven seconds off the average service time. Customers now purchase more than $37 billion worth of fast food on their debit and credit cards a year.[30]

The convenience of credit cards is not free to business owners, however. Companies must pay to use the system, typically one to six percent of the total credit card charges, which they must factor into the prices of their products or services. They also pay a transaction fee of 5 to 25 cents per charge. Given customer expectations, small businesses cannot drop major cards, even when the big credit card companies raise the fees that merchants must pay. Fees operate on a multistep process. On a typical $100 Visa or MasterCard purchase, a processing bank buys the credit card slip from the retailer for $98.25. Then, that bank sells the slip to the bank that issued the card for about $98.49. The $1.75 discount from the purchase price is called the **interchange fee,** the fee that banks collect from retailers whenever customers use a credit or a debit card to pay for a purchase. A study by Morgan Stanley estimates that the average interchange fees for Visa and MasterCard transactions will increase from 1.75 percent to 1.86 percent in 2010.[31] Before it can accept credit cards, a business must obtain merchant status from either a bank or an independent sales organization (ISO).

interchange fee
the fee that banks collect from retailers whenever customers use a credit or a debit card to pay for a purchase.

In 2003, the first time in history, shoppers used credit and debit cards more often than cash or checks to make retail purchases.[32] As debit cards have become more widely used, many small businesses are equipping their stores to handle debit card transactions, which act as electronic checks, automatically deducting the purchase amount immediately from a customer's checking account. The equipment is easy to install and to set up, and the cost to the company is negligible. The payoff can be big, however, in the form of increased sales and decreased losses due to bad checks. "How can you possibly lose when you're offering customers another avenue for purchasing merchandise?" says Mark Knauff, who recently installed a debit card terminal in his guitar shop.[33]

Online merchants face one major challenge when customers pay by credit card. Because there is no actual signature captured during the transaction, some customers later deny that they made the purchase and dispute the charge. These chargebacks represent a significant threat to online merchants. First Data Corporation, the largest credit card processor in the United States, says that 1.25% of all Internet transactions are charged back, compared with just 0.33% of catalog transactions by telephone and mail and 0.14% of storefront retail transactions.[68] New computer software is attempting to reduce this fraud by checking whether customers' shipping addresses match their billing addresses.

Installment Credit

Small companies that sell big-ticket consumer durables, such as major appliances, cars, and boats, frequently rely on installment credit to support their sales efforts. Because very few customers can purchase such items in a single lump-sum payment, small businesses finance them over an extended time. The time horizon may range from just a few months to 30 or more years. Most companies require customers to make an initial down payment for the merchandise and then finance the balance for the life of the loan. The customer repays the loan principal plus interest on the loan. One advantage of installment loans for a small business is that the owner retains a security interest as collateral on the loan. If a customer defaults on the loan, the owner still holds the title to the merchandise. Because installment credit absorbs a small company's cash, many rely on financial institutions such as banks and credit unions to provide installment credit. When a company has the financial strength to "carry its own paper," the interest income from the installment loan contract often yields more than the initial profit on the sale of the product. For some businesses, such as furniture stores, this traditionally has been a major source of income.

Trade Credit

Companies that sell small-ticket items frequently offer their customers trade credit, that is, they create customer charge accounts. The typical small business bills its credit customers each month. To speed collections, some offer cash discounts if customers pay their balances early; others impose penalties on late payers. Before deciding to use trade credit as a competitive weapon, the small business owner must make sure that the firm's cash position is strong enough to support the additional pressure.

Chapter Summary by Learning Objective

1. Discuss the relationships among pricing, image, competition, and value.

Setting prices for their products and services requires entrepreneurs to balance a multitude of complex forces. When it comes to setting prices, three forces are particularly important: image, competition, and value. A company's pricing policies communicate important information about its overall image to customers. A company's prices must be consistent with the image it projects to its customers. When setting prices, entrepreneurs should take into account their competitors' prices, but they should *not* automatically match or beat them. The "right" price for a product or service also depends on the value that it provides for customers.

2. Describe effective pricing techniques for introducing new goods or services and for existing ones.

Pricing a new product is often difficult for the small business manager, but it should accomplish three objectives: getting the product accepted; maintaining market share as the competition grows; and earning a profit. Generally, there are three major pricing strategies used to introduce new products into the market: penetration, skimming, and sliding down the demand curve.

Pricing techniques for existing products and services include odd pricing, price lining, leader pricing, geographic pricing, opportunistic pricing, discounts, and suggested retail pricing.

3. Explain the pricing methods and strategies for (A) retailers, (B) manufacturers, and (C) service firms.

Pricing for the retailer means pricing to move merchandise. Markup is the difference between the cost of a product or service and its selling price. Most retailers compute their markup as a percentage of retail price, but some retailers put a standard markup on all their merchandise; more frequently, they use a flexible markup.

A manufacturer's pricing decision depends on the support of accurate cost accounting records. The most common technique is cost-plus pricing, in which the manufacturer charges a price that covers the cost of producing a product plus a reasonable profit. Every manufacturer should calculate a product's break-even price, the price that produces neither a profit nor a loss.

Service firms often suffer from the effects of vague, unfounded pricing procedures, and frequently charge the going rate without any idea of their costs. A service firm must set a price based on the cost of materials used, labor involved, overhead, and a profit. The proper price reflects the total cost of providing a unit of service.

4. Describe the impact of credit on pricing.

Offering consumer credit enhances a small company's reputation and increases the probability, speed, and magnitude of customers' purchases. Small firms offer three types of consumer credit: credit cards, installment credit, and trade credit (charge accounts).

Discussion Questions

1. How does pricing affect a small firm's image?
2. What competitive factors must the small firm consider when establishing prices?
3. Describe the strategies a small business could use in setting the price of a new product. What objectives should the strategy seek to achieve?
4. Define the following pricing techniques: odd pricing, price lining, leader pricing, geographic pricing, and discounts.
5. Why do many small businesses use the manufacturer's suggested retail price? What are the disadvantages of this technique?
6. What is a markup? How is it used to determine individual price?
7. What is a standard markup? A flexible markup?
8. What is cost-plus pricing? Why do so many manufacturers use it? What are the disadvantages of using it?
9. Explain the difference between full-absorption costing and direct costing. How does absorption costing help a manufacturer determine a reasonable price?
10. Explain the technique for a small service firm setting an hourly price.
11. What benefits does a small business get by offering customers credit? What costs does it incur?

Business Plan Pro

Business PlanPro

As the chapter describes, setting the price of your products and services and understanding your break-even point are major elements of your business plan. Resources and information are available within Business Plan Pro that may help you to better understand the impact that pricing will have on your business.

Business Plan Exercises

On the Web

Do some competitive pricing research on the Web. Search for products and services that are similar to what you are offering and list their price points. Check to see that you are making parallel comparisons of these products. For example, are you considering the entire price, which may include shipping, handling, complementary products, and other attributes that will influence the final price to the customer? Do you consider these businesses to be direct competitors? If not, why? What does this information tell you about your price point? Does your price point coincide with your stated business strategy?

In the Software

Open your business plan and locate the "Break Even" section under "Financial Plan." Follow the instructions and enter the information that will enable to you to determine your break-even point. This will require you to have estimated figures for your fixed costs, variable costs, and price. Once you have entered that information, look at the break-even point shown in units and revenue. Based on what you find, is this break-even point realistic? How long do you expect it would take to reach your break-even point? Is this timeframe acceptable? Now, increase your price by 10%. What does this do to your break-even point? You may want to experiment with your break-even point by entering different price points and costs to see the impact price will have on the break-even point when you will begin making a profit.

Building Your Business Plan

Go to the "Sales Forecast" table under the "Sales Strategy" section. An optional wizard will appear that you may select to help you through the process, or you can enter your information directly on the worksheet. If you have not done so yet, enter your price information in that section. Work through the rest of the table as you estimate your direct unit costs. The instructions and examples will assist you through that process.

Beyond the Classroom . . .

1. Interview a successful small retailer and ask the following questions: Do they seek a specific image through their prices? What type of outlet do you consider the retailer to be? What role do their competitors play in their pricing strategy? Do they use specific pricing techniques such as odd pricing, price lining, leader pricing, or geographic pricing? How are discounts calculated? What markup percentage does the firm use? How are prices derived? What are their cost structures?
2. Select an industry that has several competing small firms in your area. Contact these firms and compare their approaches to determining prices. Do prices on identical or similar items differ? Why?

Chapter 10
Crafting a Winning Business Plan

- Introducing the importance of business planning for an entrepreneurial venture
- Discussing the nature and elements of a solid business plan
- Examining the key dimensions that influence a firm's business planning process
- Relating some of the benefits of business planning
- Understanding the keys to making an effective business plan presentation

CHAPTER 19

The business plan: an entrepreneurial tool

Chapter overview

A business plan is an essential tool for the entrepreneur. This chapter explores the role of the business plan and the kind of information it should include. It considers the way a business plan can help the venture by guiding analysis, creating a synthesis of new insights, communicating the potential of the venture to interested parties, and promoting management action. It also describes the Pyramid Principle: a method of structuring the business plan to produce an effective and influential communication tool. The chapter concludes by looking at the ways in which business planning can increase the flexibility and responsiveness of the venture.

19.1 Planning and performance

Key learning outcome

A recognition of the influence of formal planning activity on the performance of the entrepreneurial venture.

Entrepreneurs, like many other managers, are often called upon to prepare formal, written plans. They may do this of their own accord or it may be at the instigation of external investors such as venture capitalists or banks. The picture of entrepreneurs 'locked away' writing formal business plans sits ill at ease with the image of them as dynamic individuals actively pursuing their business interests. Many entrepreneurs object to preparing plans because they feel their time would be better spent pushing the venture forward. They claim that they already know what is in the plan and that no one else will read it.

This objection highlights an important point in that developing a plan demands time, energy and (often) hard cash. It ties up both the entrepreneur and the business's staff. A business plan represents an *investment* in the venture. It must be justified as an investment, that is, in terms of the return it offers the business. The relationship between formal planning and business performance has been the subject of numerous statistical studies; however, no clear picture has emerged. The correlation between *formal* planning and performance is generally weak so it is not possible to say with certainty that formal planning will improve the performance of a particular business. As a result, there has been something of a reaction against formal planning in recent years, especially in relation to smaller businesses. As noted in the previous chapter, Mintzberg (1994) has offered a profound criticism of at least a narrow approach to planning. However, a recent study by Perry (2001) indicated a negative correlation between planning and failure rates for small businesses in the USA. Formal planning was not found to be a common activity, but businesses that had planned were less likely to fail than those that had not. Schneider (1998) provides a general defence of planning for the smaller business.

However, the poor statistical correlation should not be taken to mean that performance is unaffected by planning. Statistical studies usually compare 'planning activity' (the definition of this varies between studies) against performance measured in financial or growth terms. Inevitably, these studies must reduce a complex organisational phenomenon to simple variables. Planning is not an easily defined, isolated activity. Rather, it is an activity embedded in both the wider strategy process of the organisation and the control strategy of the entrepreneur. Financial performance is important but it is not the only measure of achievement which motivates the entrepreneur. The entrepreneur may compromise financial gains in order to achieve less tangible benefits. They may even *plan* to make this compromise. Intuitively it seems the case that a good plan will lead to an improved performance and, equally, that a bad one will lead the business astray. There is also the problem of distinguishing between the existence of a plan and whether that plan is actually *implemented*.

Statistical studies of planning and performance also face the issue of causation; that is, when two things seem to correlate, how can we be sure which is the cause and which the effect? It may be that the variation in performance observed is not so much due to the mere existence of planning as to the *quality* of the planning. It has even been suggested that planning does not lead to performance, but rather that a good performance allows managers the time and money to indulge in planning.

The planning/performance debate reflects the problems to be encountered in teasing out cause-and-effect relationships in a system as complex and subject to as many variables as an entrepreneurial venture. In short, then, it is impossible to give a straight yes or no answer to questions like: 'Should entrepreneurs produce a formal plan?' or 'Should entrepreneurs formalise the way their organisation plans?' Overgeneralisation is unwise. The decision to engage in formal planning, like most other decisions the entrepreneur faces, must be made in the light of what is best for the individual venture, the way it operates and the specific opportunities it faces. Planning, if it is approached in a way which is right for the venture and is aimed at addressing the right issues, would seem to offer a number of benefits. The remainder of this chapter examines the decision to create a formal plan, explores the ways in which it might benefit the business and suggests ways in which the plan might be structured.

19.2 The role of the business plan

Key learning outcome

An understanding of how the business plan works as a management tool.

The activity of creating a formal business plan consumes both time and resources. If it is to be undertaken, and undertaken well, there must be an appreciation of the way in which the business plan can actually be made to work as a tool for the business. In principle, there are four mechanisms by which a business plan might aid the performance of the venture.

As a tool for analysis

A business plan contains information. Some of this information will be that used as the basis for articulating and refining the entrepreneur's vision, for generating the mission statement and for developing a strategy content and strategy process for the venture. The structure of the business plan provides the entrepreneur with an effective checklist of the information they must gather in order to be sure the direction for their venture is both achievable and rewarding (see Schneider, 1998, for a development of this point). Creating the plan guides and disciplines the entrepreneur in gathering this information. Hills (1985) emphasises that the level of background market research in entrepreneurs' plans is usually quite low, but investment in market research can have a high payoff, not least in making demand planning more effective. Wyckham and Wedley (1990) demonstrate the value of the plan in distinguishing feasible from unfeasible ventures.

As a tool for synthesis

Once data have been gathered and analysed in a formal way then the information generated must be used to provide a direction for the venture. The information must be integrated with, and used to refine, the entrepreneur's vision and used to support the development of a suitable mission and strategy. The planning exercise acts to *synthesise* the entrepreneur's vision with a definite plan of action in a unified way. This synthesis converts the vision into a strategy for the venture, and then into the actions appropriate to pursuing that strategy.

As a tool for communication

The business plan provides a vehicle for communicating the potential of the venture, the opportunities it faces and the way it intends to exploit them in a way which is concise, efficient and effective. This may be of value in communicating with both internal and external stakeholders. The plan may draw internal people together and give them a focus for their activities. The business plan is particularly important as a tool for communicating with potential investors, gaining their interest and attracting them to the venture.

As a call to action

The business plan is a call to action. It provides a detailed list of the activities that must be undertaken, the tasks that must be performed and the outcomes that must be achieved if the entrepreneur is to convert their vision into a new world. The plan may also call upon formal project management techniques such as critical path analysis in order to organise, prioritise and arrange tasks in a way which makes the best use of scarce resources.

The four ways in which the planning exercise contributes to the success drive of the venture do not operate in isolation. They underpin and support each other and the performance of the venture (Figure 19.1). Together they define not only the plan that should be developed for the venture, but also the way the venture should engage in planning.

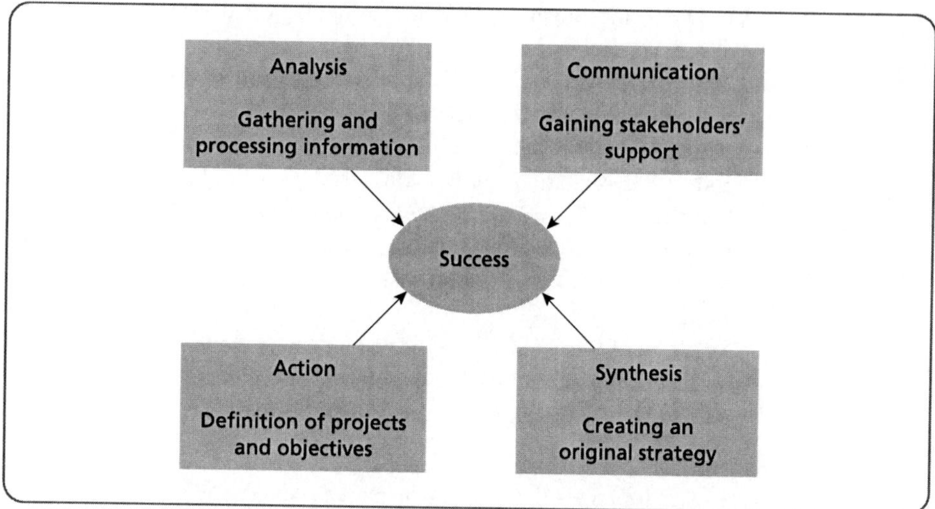

Figure 19.1 Planning: analysis, communication, synthesis and action

19.3 What a business plan should include

> **Key learning outcome**
>
> An appreciation of the type of information to be included in a business plan.

There are no hard and fast rules about what a business plan should include since a business plan must be shaped to reflect the needs and requirements of the venture it represents. The entrepreneur and the management team will have their own preferences. The information included will depend on what stage the venture is at: the plan for a new venture may be more exhaustive than the ongoing yearly plan for one which is quite well established. Importantly, the plan will reflect the information required by the audience to whom the plan is directed as well as the action the entrepreneur desires from them. Financial backers may dictate both the format the business plan must take and the information it should include.

The type and scope of information that might be included in a fairly exhaustive business plan are set out below.

Mission

- *The mission for the venture* – the formal mission statement that defines the business, what it is, what it is aiming to deliver, to whom, why it makes a difference and what it aspires to achieve.

Overview of key objectives

- *Financial objectives* – the turnover and profit targets for the period of the plan; the growth desired over the previous period.
- *Strategic objectives* – achievements in the market and gains to be made in market position.

The market environment

- *Background to the market* – i.e. how the market is defined; the size of the market; major market sectors and niches; overall growth rate; key trends and developments in consumer behaviour and buying habits; and technological developments in the product, service delivery and operations.

- *Competitors* – key competitors, their strengths and weaknesses; competitors' strategy and likely reaction to the venture's activity.
- *Competitive conditions* – the basis of competition in the market; the importance of price, product differentiation and branding; the benefits to be gained from positioning.
- *Competitive advantage of the venture* – the important strengths of the venture relative to competitors; sources of competitive advantage.
- *Definition of product offerings* – the products/services that the business will offer to the market.
- *Definition of target markets* – the way in which the market is split into different sectors; the dimensions of the market important for characterising the sectors; and the market sectors that will be priority targets for the business.

Strategy

- *Product strategy* – the way in which the product/service will be differentiated from competitors (e.g. features, quality, price); why this will be attractive to customers.
- *Pricing strategy* – how the product/service will be priced relative to competitors (e.g. offer of a premium, discounting); means of establishing price; promotional pricing and price cutting; pricing policy and margins to be offered to intermediaries.
- *Distribution strategy* – the route by which the product/service will be delivered to the customer; intermediaries (wholesalers, distributors, retailers) who will be partners in distribution; strategy for working with distributors; policy for exporting and international marketing if appropriate.
- *Promotional strategy* – approaches to informing the customer (and intermediaries) about the product/service; advertising message, means and media; sales activity and approach to selling; sales promotions (including price promotions); public relations activity.
- *Networking* – relationship between the organisation and other organisations in the network; use of the network to create and support competitive advantage.

Financial forecasts

- *Income* – revenues from trading activity; structure of the capital provided by investors.
- *Routine expenditure* – expenditure on salaries, raw materials and consumables; payment of interest on debt.
- *Capital expenditure* – major investment in new assets; how these assets will enhance performance.
- *Cash flow* – difference between revenues and expenditure by period; cash flow reflects the liquidity of the business and its ability to fund its activities. If income is more than expenditure then cash flow is positive. If expenditure is more than income then cash flow is negative.

Activity

- *Major projects* – the key projects that will drive the venture forward and deliver the objectives, e.g. new product developments, sales drives, launches with distributors and advertising campaigns.

People

- *Key players in the venture* – the individuals behind the venture; the skills and experience they will contribute to the business; evidence of their achievements; personal profiles and CVs.

The list above reflects a 'traditional' structure of a business plan that is related in many planning guides. However, a list is just an account of what should be included, not necessarily an instruction on the order in which it is presented. Section 19.6 considers a more effective way of structuring the plan. The information included in the business plan will depend on how it is intended to use the plan and to whom it will be communicated. The business need not be restricted to a single version of the plan, and it may prove advantageous to use different formats for different audiences. A detailed and exhaustive 'master' plan may act as a source for the rapid, and informed, production of such specific plans.

19.4 Business planning: analysis and synthesis

Key learning outcome

An appreciation of how business planning facilitates analysis of the venture's potential and a synthesis of its strategy.

Effective planning requires information. Information is all around us but it rarely comes for free. Information has a cost: this may be relatively low – a trip to the local library perhaps – or it may be very expensive – commissioning a major piece of market research, for example. Even if it has no direct cost, gathering and analysing information takes time. Hence information must be gathered with an eye to how it will be used. The benefits to be gained from having the information must justify its cost.

Information is used to manage uncertainty. Having information means that uncertainty is reduced, which in turn reduces the risk of the venture and improves the prospects of its success. Essentially, the entrepreneur is interested in answering the following questions:

- What are the customer's fundamental needs in relation to the product category? (What benefits does the product offer? What problems do customers solve with the product?)
- How does the market currently serve those needs? (What products are offered? What features do they have?)
- In what way(s) does the market fail to serve those needs? (Why are customers left dissatisfied? How often are they left dissatisfied?)
- How might customer needs be better served? (How might the product on offer be improved?)

Marketing, as a discipline, offers a number of techniques to develop these answers. In addition, the entrepreneur must ask:

- How does the better way being advocated add up as a real business opportunity?
- What risks are likely to be present in pursuing such an opportunity?

These final two points are critical. Developing an answer to these questions, and understanding the decisions they involve, will be explored fully through the development of the *strategic window* in Part 5 of this book.

Planning certainly supports strategy development but it is not *equivalent* to it. Mintzberg (1994) observes that planning is about *analysis*; it is about breaking down information to spot opportunities and possibilities. Strategy, on the other hand, is about *synthesis*; it is about bringing the capabilities of the business to bear on the opportunity in a way which is creative and original. Developing answers to the questions listed above is the analysis part of the equation. Reconciling them into a workable, rewarding strategy is the synthesis part. This synthesis must include both the strategy *content* and the *process* to deliver it.

In order to synthesise an original strategy the entrepreneur must address the following questions:

- How will the venture address the needs of the customer? (What is the nature of the opportunity that has been identified?)
- Why will the venture's offerings serve those needs better than those of competitors? (What is the *innovation*? Why is it valuable?)
- How will demand be stimulated? (This involves issues of communication, promotion and distribution.)
- Why can the entrepreneur's business deliver this in a way that competitors cannot? (What will be the *competitive advantage* that the business enjoys? What will it be able to do that its competitors cannot do that is valuable for its customers?)
- What is it about the business that enables them to do this? (What are the *competences* and *capabilities* of the business?)
- Why will competitors be unable to imitate them? (In what way(s) is the competitive advantage *sustainable*?)

Planning helps the business by first demanding an analysis of information about the market, customers and competitors. This information provides a sure basis for decision making. Planning goes on to help the business by synthesis, that is, by integrating the information into a strategy. This strategy gives the venture a shape and a direction. It forms the basis for plans and projects which offer definite actions for the people who make up the venture and those who support it to follow. Thus information is valuable because it links the analysis of opportunity with the synthesis of strategy in a planning framework (Figure 19.2).

19.5 Business planning: action and communication

> **Key learning outcome**
>
> An appreciation of how the business plan may be used as a communication tool and as a call to action.

Communication is not just about passing on information. It is an attempt to elicit a particular *response* from someone. In business, it is not only what we want people to *know* that matters; it is also what we want them to *do*. The ways the business plan functions both as a piece of communication and as a recipe for action are closely interrelated.

The business plan is a communication that relates in a succinct way a precise and unambiguous account of the venture *and* what it aims to achieve. It defines the decisions the entrepreneur has made in relation to the opportunity that has been identified; the way the opportunity will be exploited; the value the entrepreneur aims to create as a result of exploiting it; the resources that will be needed in order to progress the venture; the risks those resources will be exposed to; and the projects the entrepreneur will undertake with the resources they receive.

These decisions are communicated with the intention of gaining support for the venture. The entrepreneur will be particularly interested in communicating with and influencing the following groups of people.

Figure 19.2 Factors governing investment in market information

Investors

The business plan relates not only the potential of the venture and the rewards it offers to investors but also the risks that it entails. It is also an opportunity for the entrepreneur to convince the investor of the skills the entrepreneur has, and to make the investor feel confident that the goods can be delivered. Numerous studies have found that the quality of the business plan and the effectiveness of its communication are critical factors in gaining investors' interest and support. See, for example, the studies by Macmillan *et al.* (1985, 1987), Knight (1994) and Mason and Harrison (1996). This is an issue we shall revisit in Chapter 20.

Employees

Employees make their own investment in the business by committing themselves to it. The business plan can give them confidence in the future of the venture. It will also specify the key projects that need to be undertaken, so defining individual objectives and the way in which the role the individual plays fits with the goals of the organisation as a whole. Jan Carlzon, the entrepreneur who turned around the failing Scandinavian Airline Systems (SAS) in the early 1980s, issued each of the organisation's 20,000 employees with a plan which outlined the vision and strategy he had devised. This plan became known as the 'little red book'.

Employee commitment does not come simply from letting people in on the plan. Letting them get involved in *creating* it in the first place is also a sure way to gain their support.

Important customers

A customer may face a cost in taking on a new supplier. Moving between suppliers demands the time and attention of managers. In some cases there may need to be a direct investment in new equipment so that the products can be used. If the product is new, the customer may have to learn to use it, for example staff may need additional training. The customer may be willing to face these costs if the benefits offered by the new product are high enough. They will resist, however, if they have doubts about the long-term viability of the supplier. Sharing the business plan with them is an effective way of giving them confidence in the entrepreneurial venture and encouraging them to make the necessary commitment. Customers are usually flattered to be asked to become involved with the venture in this way. Therefore, for a new venture, communicating the business plan as well as the product offering can be an important part of the selling strategy.

Major suppliers

Suppliers may also need to make an investment if they wish to supply the venture. This may take the form of dedicated selling and support activity and may even involve developing bespoke products. Although the venture offers the prospect of new business, suppliers will, like the venture's customers, resist making the investment if they harbour doubts about the long-term viability of the venture. Again, the business plan may be used to give them the confidence to make an investment of time and resources on behalf of the venture.

In short, the business plan is a communication tool which can be used by the venture to help build the network of relationships which will be critical to its long-term success.

19.6 Structuring and articulating the business plan: the Pyramid Principle

> **Key learning outcome**
>
> An appreciation of Barbara Minto's Pyramid Principle technique for structuring and articulating in business communication, and how it can be applied to create an influential business plan.

A business plan is not just a repository for facts and statements. It is a business *communication*. And like any form of human communication its impact and influence are determined by *how* things are said as well as *what* is said. The organisation of ideas is as important as the ideas themselves. The structuring of the business plan considered in the section 19.3 places emphasis on the information that must be communicated rather than on the case that the business plan is attempting to make. The impact of the business plan on key decision makers (particularly, but not exclusively, potential investors) will depend on the way in which information is *delivered* as well as the information itself. Effective business communications work with, rather than against, the cognitive processes that human decision makers adopt. The ideas to be explored in this section are based on the work of Barbara Minto (1996), a management consultant who has studied business communication styles and their effectiveness in depth. These ideas are not restricted just to business plans but are effective with any business communication (written or verbal).

(I am not ashamed to admit I use them for structuring academic papers.) Barbara Minto's book *The Pyramid Principle* is highly recommended to those who wish to explore these ideas in more depth.

Minto's central idea is based on discoveries in cognitive psychology about the way in which humans store and manage information and then use it to support decision making. It is clear that we human beings are actually quite inefficient information processors. When presented with a lot of information, we inevitably simplify it. We are, at best, able to store between five and nine pieces of information at any one time. From any one communication we only take away one or two key ideas. Further, we do not store information in our brains in a linear way, one idea after another. Rather, we build hierarchies of information in which facts are connected in a network of linkages. Minto suggests that we can use all of these facts to construct communications that will be more effective and influential.

First, she suggests, we should consider the *one* key message the recipient will take away, what she refers to as the 'key point'. Given that the recipient is likely to take away only one 'big idea', we should aim to control what that is, rather than let the recipient do it for themself. Second, we should order information in a way that builds a hierarchy (a pyramid) of understanding under our control rather than deliver the information linearly and assume that the recipient will order it in the way we would wish. In other words, we should take active control of the process of 'translating' both from the idea network to its written (linear) form and back again.

Minto's ideas provide useful insights into the preparation of effective business plans. First, the key point or 'big idea'. It is important to recognise what we want the recipients of the plan to *do*, rather than what we would wish them to *know*. Communication transfers information, but this is the means to the end of eliciting action, not an objective in itself. What we wish a recipient of a business plan to do depends on who the recipient is. If an investor, then we hope they will provide the investment requested. If a potential employee, then the key point will be 'work for me'; a customer: 'buy from me', and so on. We must then put in place supporting ideas (ideally five to eight) that lay out a case for that big idea. Moving down the pyramid, we should then develop *arguments* that justify the supporting ideas. Finally, at the bottom of the pyramid, we must provide evidence that backs up the arguments.

Table 19.1 illustrates such a structure for a business plan aimed at investors. Six supporting ideas are entered, reflecting the series of questions an investor would wish to see answered. These are the supporting questions I often use, but I would not claim this version is definitive. Other supporting questions may also be appropriate and arguments may be articulated differently.

With this pyramid structure in place, the next step is to construct the business plan around it. The pyramid must be converted into a linear flow of narrative while retaining a feel for the underlying pyramid structure. Minto suggests that using headings and sub-headings to indicate different levels of the pyramid is a good way of doing this, and this approach works for a business plan. The headings should be short and to the point and be used to highlight the pyramid structure. They should not be thought of as informative in their own right. The plan has the overall structure shown in Figure 19.3.

An illustration of the process in action is as follows. The first step is to construct an introduction. The introduction serves two purposes. First, it is an invitation to the recipient to read the plan and to engage them. (Don't forget, the majority of business plans sent to

Table 19.1 Pyramid structure of business plan

Key point
Invest in this venture!

Supporting questions					
1. Is there a gap in the market for this product/service?	2. Does this market have potential?	3. Why will this innovation fill that gap?	4. Can this innovation be delivered profitably and at acceptable risk?	5. Does the venture have a long-term future?	6. Are the proposers the right people to deliver it?
Arguments					
Individuals have these needs in relation to this product category Current offerings fail to meet these needs satisfactorily Recent developments in the product category still leave these needs unmet	Assumptions about market definition Demand in this sector is high and is likely to grow Market conditions offer potential to new entrants	This innovation meets customer needs better than anything currently on offer. It offers unique and attractive benefits This innovation is new and original Technological and organisational capabilities are in place to effect delivery to market	Pricing is sufficient to cover unit production costs Long-term profits will sustain necessary investment Distribution route is available Promotional plans have been thought through and costed Risk has been assessed and its management considered	Venture has a sustainable competitive advantage It is delivering something of value; it is doing so in a unique way; competitors can be fended off Advantage will be gained in terms of costs, strategic assets, innovation capabilities, reputation and/or organisational architecture Options for future expansion have been considered	Managerial experience, capabilities and motivation
Evidence					
Primary and secondary customer research Competitor analysis Product evaluation	Rationale for market definition Market research: market size, growth rate and structure Existing supply structure PEST analysis	Primary and secondary customer research Product testing and trials Evidence of technical and organisational capabilities	Costing data and financial projections Assumptions about output volumes, prices, costs and demand conditions Competitor costs and investment benchmarks Evaluation of promotional plans and distribution routes Scenario analysis	Strategic analysis of venture and competitors Explanation as to why competitive advantage will be gained and sustained	Managers' CVs Evidence of relevant experience, qualifications, sector knowledge and previous successes Evidence supporting leadership abilities

Main heading: Introduction

Main heading: Supporting question 1
Sub-heading: *Argument 1 – Evidence 1*
Sub-heading: *Argument 2 – Evidence 2*
Sub-heading: *Argument 3 – Evidence 3*
etc.

Main heading: Supporting question 2
Sub-heading: *Argument 1 – Evidence 1*
Sub-heading: *Argument 2 – Evidence 2*
Sub-heading: *Argument 3 – Evidence 3*
etc.

Main heading: Supporting question 3
Sub-heading: *Argument 1 – Evidence 1*
Sub-heading: *Argument 2 – Evidence 2*
Sub-heading: *Argument 3 – Evidence 3*
etc.

Main heading: Summary

Figure 19.3 Organising the pyramid structure

venture capitalists are dismissed without being fully read. If attention is not captured in the first few paragraphs, it never will be.) Second, it may be used to lay out the structure of the case to be made for the venture. As a first move, the introduction should put in place the big idea. A good opening would be:

Introduction

This plan proposes a new business venture that offers a major and attractive investment opportunity.

The next step is to relate the supporting arguments in a succinct manner. (Do not be tempted to overexpand on the ideas at this stage; this will come later.)

It will outline an innovative product (service) that offers unique benefits to customers in a way superior to existing competitors in a market with significant potential. The experienced management team leading the venture is confident that the venture has long-term potential, will be financially sound, and will gain and sustain an advantage over existing competitors.

At this stage, it is important that the recipient is guided in developing a mental image of the business concerned. Too often with business plans the reader is left to fit together pieces of information about the business from different parts of the plan. This takes effort that the reader may not be willing to invest. They may simply reject the plan. Even if they do put in that effort, the picture built is not under the proposer's control. A good way to take control is to relate the venture's mission. Articulating the mission was considered in Chapter 17.

The venture's mission

Following this, the venture's key objectives (financial, market, growth) can be related.

Key objectives

With the introduction in place, the plan can then expand, argue for and give evidence to support the claims made. Each supporting idea is dealt with in turn. For example, the first supporting question is, 'Is there a gap in the market for this product?'. Again, following the Pyramid Principle, the opportunity should be taken to map out the structure of the arguments to follow.

The market gap

There is a significant gap in the market for the new product (service). Customer expectations are high and existing products are not meeting requirements. Recent developments in the product category have not significantly delivered on these expectations.

Now sub-headings can be used to detail each argument in turn and provide evidence for it.

Customer needs and expectations

Customers have high expectations about what this product category should offer. In particular, they feel that it should . . .

Now is the opportunity to support these claims with evidence, for example:

This is confirmed by independent market research using focus groups . . .

And then on to the second argument under this supporting question:

Customers' attitudes to products already available

Purchases in this product category are significant [introduce evidence on market size here]. The market is buoyant [introduce evidence on market growth rate here]. While customers do express some satisfaction with current offerings, they have a number of criticisms that add up to a clear opportunity for a new product. Research with focus groups and a telephone survey of a large sample of buyers indicate that the key failings are . . .

And then on to the third argument

Recent developments in the product category

Development of new products in this category is relatively active. X and Y have both launched new products. While these have been relatively successful, they do not address the fundamental failings of the category as seen by customers. Our research indicates . . . [evidence]

Once the first supporting question has been addressed, then the second can be explored in the same way. Then the third.

Another example: the venture's long-term potential (supporting question 5 in Table 19.1):

Long-term profitability and growth

We believe the business will have long-term potential and will be able to hold its position against follower competitors.

Now lay out the arguments:

As has been illustrated, the venture is offering a product with unique benefits to a large number of buyers. These benefits are unique and are not matched by any existing product [may re-summarise evidence here]. This valuable uniqueness is protectable.

Detail the argument on the last point, depending on particular sources of competitive advantage:

This will be achieved by:

- *access to unique and valuable resources;*
- *a lower cost structure;*
- *faster and more effective innovation;*
- *a better reputation than competitors; and/or*
- *performance enhanced through organisational and network architecture.*

(Refer to Chapter 25 for a full discussion of these sources of competitive advantage.)

Once this process is complete, a summary can be used to close the plan and encapsulate its ideas in the mind of the recipient. Aim to repeat the key point and the supporting questions once again:

Summary

This plan has highlighted a major investment opportunity. It demonstrates . . . [lay out supporting questions again].

The objective of the summary is to provide a final reinforcement of the key point, 'Invest in me!', not to summarise everything in the plan. Don't be tempted to go through the arguments and evidence again.

This approach gives a business plan a quite different structure to the 'list structure' discussed in section 19.3. For a start, there is no one section that relates all the market research. Market research is introduced when and where it is needed to back up a claim. So the reader's attention is being drawn to facts that matter, when they matter, rather than as a mass of data, which the reader will not be able to absorb or directly relate to the case for investment being made. Considerations on strategy are integrated with discussion of market opportunity, not separated.

Here are a few points by way of a summary. First, at each stage in the pyramid, summarise the structure below that will follow. Second, it will be recognised that given the number of supporting ideas, arguments and evidence, not much needs to be said at each stage. Do not be tempted to overexpand on points made. If a section is longer than a couple of paragraphs, it is probably better to go back to the pyramid and split the ideas. Third, do not worry too much about repetition. My experience with entrepreneurs introduced to the Pyramid Principle is that they feel they are being repetitious and saying the same thing over and over again. This reflects the fact we value originality. However, the value of a business plan is its effectiveness in engendering support, not its literary qualities. In any case, readers do not find the pyramid structure repetitious, just highly informative and impactful.

19.7 Strategy, planning and flexibility

Key learning outcome

An understanding of how planning may be used to make the business responsive, rather than rigid, in the face of opportunity and uncertainty.

Many entrepreneurs are suspicious of formal planning. They may see the written plan as restrictive, and feel that it reduces their room for manoeuvre. They may be concerned that by defining future actions they limit their options. However, these suspicions are ill founded. If approached in the right way, planning increases, rather than restricts, flexibility. The right sort of strategy can make the business more, not less, responsive.

Focus on ends rather than means

Goals should be given priority over plans. It is what the business aims to achieve that matters. It may be that there is more than one way in which the business can reach its objectives. If so, all the possibilities should be explored. Not all are likely to be equally attractive and one route may be given priority. However, a knowledge of the alternatives allows for contingency plans to be made and an alternative course can be followed if some routes become blocked.

Challenge assumptions

What are the assumptions on which the plan is based? For example, what assumptions have been made in measuring the size of markets and the venture's rate of growth, in determining how attractive the innovation is to customers and in gauging the strengths of competitors? How sensitive is the plan to these assumptions? What will happen if they are wrong? How can the plan be 'immunised' against poor assumptions by building in contingencies for when they are wrong?

Model scenarios

What are the likely outcomes if the plan is implemented? How certain are these outcomes? In the face of uncertainty, what is likely to be the *best* of all possible worlds and what is likely to be the *worst*? What is the *most likely* outcome? Determine what scenarios will result if an *optimistic*, a *pessimistic* and a *realistic* attitude is taken to the outcomes that are expected (particularly in relation to income and expenditure). How will the business fare in the face of each eventuality? How exposed is the business if the pessimistic scenario comes about? Has it (or can it get) the resources to manage the optimistic? Furthermore, have investors been made party to all scenarios, not just the best?

Create strategic flexibility

At the end of the day, a strategy is just a way of doing things. Strategic flexibility is a way of doing things well when faced with uncertainty. It involves actively responding to outcomes and adjusting activity, not just blindly following set plans. Strategic flexibility comes from questioning moves. For example, can the product or service be modified in the light of consumer responses to it (*positive* as well as negative)? If one target market is proving hard to break into, can an alternative one be approached? Can costs be managed in response to demand (for example, how exposed is the business to fixed costs)? If some relationships in the network prove to be less valuable than expected, can new relationships be built quickly?

Leave space to learn

The way in which entrepreneurs and their businesses meet opportunities and respond to challenges is dependent on how they see the world, the knowledge that they have and their range of skills. All these factors must evolve through learning. The entrepreneur must constantly question the business. Are the underlying assumptions still valid? Is this still the best way to do things? Success does not speak for itself and it is important to question why a particular outcome is a success. What was done right? In what way might the business have been even *more* successful? What were the failings? How might they be avoided next time?

Learning is an active process. The good business plan identifies and highlights those areas where learning can take place. In short, a good strategy should be about flexibility, about enabling the business to take advantage of opportunities as they take shape, and to manage the unexpected. It is not about setting a rigid course of action.

Summary of key ideas

- There is no simple correlation between investment in planning and business performance, although there is evidence that planning may be important in small business survival.
- A business plan can help the entrepreneurial venture by:
  - ensuring that a full analysis of the situation and the environment has been undertaken;
  - encouraging the synthesis of insights to generate a vision and a strategy;
  - acting as a call to action;
  - being a medium for communication with both internal and external stakeholders.
- Barbara Minto's Pyramid Principle can be adopted to produce impactful and influential business plans.
- A well-defined business plan will increase the venture's flexibility, not impair it.
- The level of formality in planning will be influenced by the level of investment in the start-up, the involvement of external stakeholders (especially, but not exclusively, investors), the availability and cost of information, external support, and the entrepreneur's personal style.

Research themes

Impact of pyramid structuring

Using the framework in Table 19.1, obtain information for four business plans (aim for 2,000–3,000 word descriptions, a typical length for a business plan). These may be imaginary, based on case studies, or based on real business plans you have access to. For each of the four data sets, construct two different versions of the plan. For the first, deliver information in a pyramid format with the 'big idea' up front and then a supporting idea, its argument and then its evidence, then on to the next supporting idea followed by its argument and evidence, and so on until all supporting ideas have been covered. For the second version, deliver the information linearly, starting with the 'big idea', then all the supporting ideas, then all the arguments, then all the evidence. Take a sample of decision makers (fellow students would be ideal). Split them into two equal groups and offer each group the four plans, two pyramidally structured and two linearly structured. Switch the ordering between the two groups. Have each subject rate the four business plans in terms of their attractiveness as investment opportunities. This could be by ranking, or on a Likert scale (e.g. would definitely invest, may invest, probably would not invest, would definitely not invest, etc.). Compare the ratings across the two different structures. Does pyramid structuring make the plan more attractive?

Information acquisition from business plans

This is a variation on the theme of the project above and might be included with it. Using the described method, create four business plans with linear and pyramid structures. Set up a comprehension test for subjects who have read the plans. This might include questions about the venture's products, its target markets, how it will gain competitive advantage, the capabilities of the management team, and so forth. Centre these on the supporting questions and arguments within them. I suggest about 10 questions in total. A multi-choice format will make analysis easier. If Barbara Minto's reading of cognitive psychology is correct (and there is a lot of evidence to suggest it is), then individuals should achieve better comprehension from the pyramid structure than from the linear. Let the subjects (again, fellow students would be ideal) read the plans (set a time limit, say 15 minutes) and then take the plan away so the subject cannot refer back to it. Then present the comprehension test (again, set a time limit). Analysis should concentrate on the comprehension scores and how they correlate with plan structure. Is the prediction borne out?

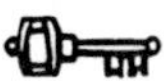

Key readings

Now quite old, but nonetheless the debate is still current and the points raised are still valid:

Thurston, P.H. (1983) 'Should smaller companies make formal plans?', *Harvard Business Review*, Sept./Oct., pp. 162–88.

Looking towards a resolution by rethinking the role, form and function of the business plan for the small and entrepreneurial venture:

Ames, M.D. (1994) 'Rethinking the business plan paradigm: bridging the gap between plan and plan execution', *Journal of Small Business Strategy*, Vol. 5, No. 1, pp. 69–76.

Suggestions for further reading

Ackelsburg, R. (1985) 'Small businesses do plan and it pays off', *Long Range Planning*, Vol. 18, No. 5, pp. 61–7.

Allaire, Y. and Firsirotu, M. (1990) 'Strategic plans as contracts', *Long Range Planning*, Vol. 23, No. 1, pp. 102–15.

Bhide, A. (1994) 'How entrepreneurs craft strategy', *Harvard Business Review*, Mar./Apr., pp. 150–61.

Bracker, J.S., Keats, B.W. and Person, J.N. (1988) 'Planning and financial performance among small firms in a growth industry', *Strategic Management Journal*, Vol. 9, pp. 591–603.

Chakravarthy, B.S. and Lorange, P. (1991) 'Adapting strategic planning to the changing needs of a business', *Journal of Organisational Change Management*, Vol. 4, No. 2, pp. 6–18.

Cooper, A.C. (1981) 'Strategic management: new ventures and small business', *Long Range Planning*, Vol. 14, No. 5, pp. 39–45.

Grieve Smith, J. and Fleck, V. (1988) 'Strategies of new biotechnology firms', *Long Range Planning*, Vol. 21, No. 3, pp. 51–8.

Hamel, G. and Prahalad, C.K. (1993) 'Strategy as stretch and leverage', *Harvard Business Review*, Mar./Apr., pp. 75–84.

Harari, O. (1994) 'The hypnotic danger of competitive analysis', *Management Review*, Vol. 83, No. 8, pp. 36–8.

Higgins, J.M. (1996) 'Innovate or evaporate: creative techniques for strategists', *Long Range Planning*, Vol. 29, No. 3, pp. 370–80.

Hills, G.E. (1985) Market analysis and the business plan: venture capitalists' perceptions', *Journal of Small Business Management*, Vol. 23, pp. 38–46.

Hopkins, W.E. and Hopkins, S.A. (1994) 'Want to succeed? Get with the plan!', *Journal of Retail Banking*, Vol. XVI, No. 3, pp. 26–31.

Kim, W.C. and Mauborgne, R. (2000) 'Knowing a winning business idea when you see one', *Harvard Business Review*, Sept./Oct., pp. 129–38.

Knight, R.M. (1994) 'Criteria used by venture capitalists: a cross-cultural analysis', *International Small Business Journal*, Vol. 13, No. 1, pp. 26–37.

Macmillan, I.C., Siegel, R. and Subba Narashima, P.N. (1985) 'Criteria used by venture capitalists to evaluate new venture proposals', *Journal of Business Venturing*, Vol. 1, pp. 119–28.

Macmillan, I.C., Zeeman, L. and Subba Narashima, P.N. (1987) 'Effectiveness of criteria used by venture capitalists in the venture screening process', *Journal of Business Venturing*, Vol. 2, pp. 123–38.

McKiernan, P. and Morris, C. (1994) 'Strategic planning and financial performance in UK SMEs: does formality matter?' *British Journal of Management*, Vol. 5, Special Issue, pp. S31–41.

Mason, C. and Harrison, R. (1996) 'Why "business angels" say no: a case study of opportunities rejected by an informal investor syndicate', *International Small Business Journal*, Vol. 14, No. 2, pp. 35–51.

Minto, B. (1996) *The Pyramid Principle*. London: FT Pitman.

Mintzberg, H. (1994) *The Rise and Fall of Strategic Planning*. London: Prentice Hall.

Perry, S.C. (2001) 'The relationship between written business plans and the failure of small business in the US', *Journal of Small Business Management*, Vol. 39, No. 3, pp. 201–8.

Schneider, T.W. (1998) 'Building a business plan: a good business plan will not ensure success, but the lack of one is a formula for failure', *Journal of Property Management*, Vol. 63, No. 6, pp. 1–2.

Schwenk, C.R. and Shrader, C.B. (1993) 'Effects of formal planning on financial performance in small firms: a meta-analysis', *Entrepreneurial Theory and Practice*, Vol. 17, No. 3, pp. 53–64.

Shuman, J.C., Shaw, J.J. and Sussman, G. (1985) 'Strategic planning in smaller rapid growth companies', *Long Range Planning*, Vol. 18, No. 6, pp. 48–53.

Waalewijn, P. and Segaar, P. (1993) 'Strategic management: the key to profitability in small companies', *Long Range Planning*, Vol. 26, No. 2, pp. 24–30.

Wyckham, R.G. and Wedley, W.C. (1990) 'Factors related to venture feasibility analysis and business plan preparation', *Journal of Small Business Management*, Vol. 28, No. 4, pp. 48–59.

Selected case material

CASE 19.1

20 January 2006 

The entrepreneur who wants to give it all away

BEN KING

So you have made half a billion dollars and you have paid for a trip to space. What on earth do you do next? Some might consider politics, others would sit back and enjoy a life of leisure. But for technology entrepreneur and cosmonaut Mark Shuttleworth the next battle was to take on the might of Microsoft on its core territory: the desktop.

He has developed a complete suite of software for personal computers that handles everything from the inner workings to word processing. It is called Ubuntu, named after one of the founding principles of post-apartheid South Africa, the country where he was born. In both the Zulu and Xhosa languages, it means 'humanity to others'.

The project is based on Linux, the free operating system written largely by volunteers and widely used by businesses, governments and other organisations to run servers,

CASE 19.1 CONT.

the computers that sit at the heart of networks. Ubuntu is meant to take this complex but powerful system and make it easy for non-technical people to use. Hence the project's mission statement: 'Linux for human beings'.

Although the technology behind it may be very different, a computer running Ubuntu looks much like one running Microsoft's Windows. The interface is based on similar menus, icons and windows, and users can surf the internet with the popular Firefox browser, or edit documents and spreadsheets with OpenOffice.

Instead of the largely blue world of Windows XP, Ubuntu is predominantly brown. Some quirky features hint at its African origin, such as the little burst of drumming that rings out when an application opens. Each new version of Ubuntu is known not just by the usual number, but an animal codename, such as Warty Warthog or Breezy Badger.

Less than two years after launch, Ubuntu has established itself as a favourite among the hundreds of different Linux-based operating systems. Ubuntu is top by some distance on a popularity chart for different flavours of Linux compiled by the website, DistroWatch. Exact numbers are hard to come by, but estimates put the number of computers running Ubuntu at up to 6m and doubling every eight months.

Unlike some of the other leading Linux projects, such as Linspire, Novell and Red Hat, Ubuntu is distributed free. Users can download it and use it without paying at all, and Mr Shuttleworth's company, Canonical, will even post a free installation compact disc to anyone who requests it.

This is possible because of Mr Shuttleworth's vast fortune. He made $575m (£327m) selling his internet company, Thawte Consulting, in 1999, and invests about $10m a year in Ubuntu. It is unlikely to make him any money, at least not for several years. Canonical sells support and related services for Ubuntu, but Mr Shuttleworth has no firm idea about when it will make a profit.

He launched the project because he believes he is in the vanguard of a revolution. 'It is very high risk,' he says. 'It is not a sensible business model. But shaping the digital platform of the future is an incredibly interesting position to be in.'

He has certainly created a powerful and effective desktop software package. From its commitment to freedom to its quirky public image, Ubuntu has many appealing features and considerable momentum. However, to continue growing at the current rate, it will need to expand beyond its existing technology-savvy base to embrace people with no prior experience of Linux.

Linux consultant and author Tom Adelstein thinks it is still hard for such people to use. 'From a usability point of view, Ubuntu is ahead of the others, I think. But it is still in the Linux bag – you have to be computer literate to use it. Microsoft is still far ahead on that.' Likewise, many buyers will be put off by the fact that a number of programs, notably games, are not available for Linux systems.

Few of those target users would install an operating system themselves. So a key stage in Ubuntu's growth will be persuading PC makers to sell machines with Ubuntu already installed. Some computer makers already ship PCs with Linux suites such as Linspire.

Smaller PC makers, competing at the lower end of the market, are particularly interested in free software, as it helps them to cut their prices. Small companies account for one-third of the global market, according to research company IDC, and Mr Shuttleworth is soon to visit Taiwan to open negotiations with some of them.

Corporate and government desktops may also be fertile ground for growth. A survey by Forrester, the research company, found that

30 per cent of companies in North America are considering switching some or all of their desktops to Linux.

Among those changing is Google, which has developed its own version of Ubuntu, called Goobuntu. Mr Shuttleworth says he is also in talks with the city government in Munich about creating an edition of Ubuntu for them.

This ability to customise Linux is a big selling point, and Canonical is developing an easy way for corporations to design and maintain specific versions of Ubuntu to suit their exact needs.

Although a stock-market darling such as Google may seem an excellent reference customer, it has an intense rivalry with Microsoft so it is keener than average to try alternatives to Windows. Other organisations will need more convincing reasons to adopt Ubuntu. Being free is clearly an advantage and Linux advocates argue that the security and robustness of Linux products are superior to those of Windows, although these issues are hotly debated.

Mr Shuttleworth has managed to rally one important group around his standard: developers. Canonical has just 50 staff, but Ubuntu has attracted many thousands of engineers at partner companies, as well as volunteers and students, who do most of the work of extending and improving the software.

The Ubuntu community has a reputation for friendliness – which is important when you are not being paid. Also, many developers who dislike the increasing commercialisation of other Linux projects are attracted by Ubuntu's commitment to remaining free.

However, selling Ubuntu beyond the circle of geeky initiates will require a massive marketing and education process, and even Mr Shuttleworth's deep pockets are no match for the budgets of Microsoft and Apple. He hopes that the virtues of a free, open operating system will sell themselves.

'My instinct tells me that free software is going to be a significant force on the desktop,' he says. 'Whether that is an Apple Mac-like force of 3–5 per cent; or whether that is a Linux in the data centre [on servers] force, that is 50 per cent and growing really, really fast – I don't know.'

With no serious business plan, it would be easy to dismiss Ubuntu as the plaything of a whimsical hobbyist that will not go far beyond the geek fraternity. Can a Breezy Badger really be a serious challenge to a titan like Microsoft?

During his interview with the *Financial Times*, Mr Shuttleworth sits across his chair with both legs on the armrest, as if it were a hammock – not something you imagine Larry Ellison, Oracle's chief executive, doing.

But he has an impressive record, and you certainly cannot question his dedication. He is currently on a gruelling three-week world tour in his private jet, promoting Ubuntu and making contacts in Croatia, Pakistan, India, China, Indonesia and Kenya. After that, he plans to 'unwind' by meeting other enthusiasts for free software in, of all places, the war-torn republic of Sierra Leone.

For some, Mr Shuttleworth just seems to be having too much fun to be taken seriously. But Linux has surprised many people before – there is nothing a geek finds more fun than turning a whole industry on its head.

Source: Ben King, 'The entrepreneur who wants to give it all away', *Financial Times*, 20 January 2006, p. 13.

CASE 19.2

15 September 2005 

Mediobanca to target perceptions

ADRIAN MICHAELS

Mediobanca outlined the next phase of its internal revolution this week, in the process driving reforms in the structure of Italian capitalism.

The powerful investment bank, founded after the Second World War, has been the most influential in Italian business for decades. It has been at the centre of a web of cross-shareholdings and directorships in which a few businesses and people used their limited capital to look after each other's interests and maintain their positions. It helped provide crucial stability through numerous upheavals.

Mediobanca, though, was not often seen as a great investment opportunity in its own right by outside investors who thought it could be seen as the sum of the parts of its equity holdings.

But the bank has been trying to change perceptions and focus investor minds on the earnings potential of its banking activities. It had already separated its equity investment portfolio into 'strategic' and 'non-strategic' holdings.

Now it has transferred responsibility for almost all the holdings to its wholesale banking division and said there would be a €1.5bn ($1.8bn) reduction in capital allocated to the equity portfolio.

Only holdings in insurer Generali and RCS, the media group which runs *Corriere della Sera*, one of Italy's most respected newspapers, are not being transferred. Mediobanca owns 14 per cent of both RCS and Generali.

Mediobanca's holdings in a large number of other Italian companies, including Telecom Italia, Pirelli and Fiat, might now be regarded as less stable than in the past, particularly since they are being treated as 'for sale' under new accounting rules.

But investments in companies already classified as non-strategic could go first. They include defence company Finmeccanica and financial groups Mediolanum and Fondiaria SAI.

Alberto Nagel, the bank's co-general manager, said some holdings were still untouchable, including those in TI and Fiat. All the same, analysts saw the announcement as seismic.

Matteo Ramenghi, analyst at UBS, said Mediobanca's first approach to investors last year 'was a very bold statement; this one is more so: it is a push to the evolution of the entire Italian system'.

The Italian market is opening up all the time, but it is still maturing compared with other countries in western Europe or the US. This year has seen some dramatic posturing against the old establishment, as epitomised by Mediobanca.

A group of younger entrepreneurs has been taking large shareholdings in companies which are part of Mediobanca's sphere of influence, including the investment bank itself. Stefano Ricucci is now the largest single shareholder in RCS and has not ruled out a takeover bid.

A number of establishment members have been visibly riled by the challenge which has increased the reputation of the Italian market for volatility and rumour and comes amid a banking scandal which also involves Mr Ricucci among others.

It is curious then that Mediobanca may soon be increasing speculation about the shareholder composition of some important companies.

But the bank sees the step as important in promoting its future shape. In the process it may help to open up Italy's market.

Source: Adrian Michaels, 'Mediobanca to target perceptions', *Financial Times*, 15 September 2005, p. 30.

Discussion points

1. In what ways might a business plan improve Ubuntu's chances of success?
2. If you were one of the young entrepreneurs mentioned, how would you see a business plan helping you? What key pieces of information would you include in one?

4 | Conducting a Feasibility Analysis and Crafting a Winning Business Plan

A good beginning makes a good end. —Proverb

In preparing for battle, I have always found that plans are useless, but planning is indispensable.
—Dwight Eisenhower

Learning Objectives

On completion of this chapter, you will be able to:

1. Discuss the steps involved in subjecting a business idea to a feasibility analysis.
2. Explain why every entrepreneur should create a business plan, as well as the benefits of developing a plan.
3. Describe the elements of a solid business plan.
4. Explain the "five Cs of credit" and why they are important to potential lenders and investors reading business plans.
5. Describe the keys to making an effective business plan presentation.

For many entrepreneurs, the easiest part of launching a business is coming up with an idea for a new business concept or approach. As you learned in Chapter 2, entrepreneurs do not lack creativity and are responsible for some of the world's most important innovations. Business success, however, requires much more than just a great new idea. Once entrepreneurs develop an idea for a business, the next step is to subject it to a feasibility analysis to determine whether they can transform the idea into a viable business. A **feasibility analysis** is the process of determining whether an entrepreneur's idea is a viable foundation for creating a successful business. Its purpose is to determine whether a business idea is worth pursuing. If the idea passes the feasibility analysis, the entrepreneur's next step is to build a solid business plan for capitalizing on the idea. If the idea fails to pass muster, the entrepreneur drops it and moves on to the next opportunity. He or she has not wasted valuable time, money, energy, and other resources creating a full-blown business plan, or worse, launching a business that is destined to fail because it is based on a flawed concept. Although it is impossible for a feasibility study to guarantee an idea's success, conducting a study reduces the likelihood that entrepreneurs will spend too much of their time pursuing fruitless business ventures.

feasibility analysis
the process of determining whether an entrepreneur's idea is a viable foundation for creating a successful business.

A feasibility study is *not* the same as a business plan; both play important, but separate, roles in the start-up process. A feasibility study answers the question, "Should we proceed with this business idea?" Its role is to serve as a filter, screening out ideas that lack the potential for building a successful business, *before* an entrepreneur commits the necessary resources to building a business plan. A feasibility study primarily is an investigative tool. It is designed to give an entrepreneur a picture of the market, sales, and profit potential of a particular business idea. Will a ski resort located here attract enough customers to be successful? Will customers in this community support a sandwich shop with a retro rock-n-roll theme? Can we build the product at a reasonable cost and sell it at a price customers are willing and able to pay? Does this entrepreneurial team have the ability to implement the idea successfully?

A business plan, on the other hand, is a planning tool for transforming an idea into reality. It builds on the foundation of the feasibility study but provides a more comprehensive analysis than a feasibility study. It functions primarily as a planning tool, taking an idea that has passed the feasibility analysis and describing how to turn it into a successful business. Its primary goals are to guide entrepreneurs as they launch and operate their businesses and to help them acquire the necessary financing to launch.

Feasibility studies are particularly useful when entrepreneurs have generated multiple ideas for business concepts and must winnow their options down to the best choice. They enable entrepreneurs quickly to explore the practicality of each of several potential paths for transforming an idea into a successful business venture. Sometimes the result of a feasibility study is the realization that an idea simply won't produce a viable business, no matter how it is organized. In other cases, a study shows an entrepreneur that the business idea is a sound one but must be organized in a different fashion to be profitable.

Conducting a Feasibility Analysis

LEARNING OBJECTIVES
1. Discuss the steps involved in subjecting a business idea to a feasibility analysis.

A feasibility analysis consists of three interrelated components: an industry and market feasibility analysis, a product or service feasibility analysis, and a financial feasibility analysis (see Figure 4.1).

Industry and Market Feasibility Analysis

When evaluating the feasibility of a business idea, entrepreneurs find a basic analysis of the industry and targeted market segments a good starting point. The focus in this phase is twofold: (1) to determine how attractive an industry is overall as a "home" for a new business, and (2) to identify possible niches a small business can occupy profitably.

The first step in assessing industry attractiveness is to paint a picture of the industry with broad strokes, assessing it from a "macro" level. Answering the following questions will help:

- How large is the industry?
- How fast is it growing?

FIGURE 4.1

Elements of a Feasibility Analysis

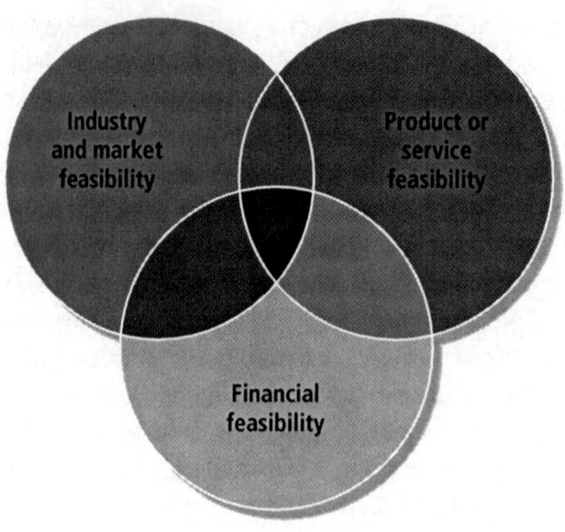

- Is the industry as a whole profitable?
- Is the industry characterized by high profit margins or razor-thin margins?
- How essential are its products or services to customers?
- What trends are shaping the industry's future?
- What threats does the industry face?
- What opportunities does the industry face?
- How crowded is the industry?
- How intense is the level of competition in the industry?
- Is the industry young, mature, or somewhere in between?

Addressing these questions helps entrepreneurs to determine whether the potential exists for sufficient demand for their products and services.

five forces model
a model that recognizes the power of five forces—rivalry among competing firms, bargaining power of suppliers, bargaining power of buyers, threat of new entrants, and threat of substitute products or services—on an industry.

A useful tool for analyzing an industry's attractiveness is the **five forces model** developed by Michael Porter of the Harvard Business School (see Figure 4.2). Five forces interact with one another to determine the setting in which companies compete and hence the attractiveness of the industry: (1) The rivalry among the companies competing in the industry, (2) the bargaining power of suppliers to the industry, (3) the bargaining power of buyers, (4) the threat of new entrants to the industry, and (5) the threat of substitute products or services.

Rivalry Among Companies Competing in the Industry The strongest of the five forces in most industries is the rivalry that exists among the businesses competing in a particular market. Much like the horses running in the Kentucky Derby, businesses in a market are jockeying for position in an attempt to gain a competitive advantage. When a company

FIGURE 4.2

The Five Forces Model of Competition

Source: Adapted from Michael E. Porter, "How Competitive Forces Shape Strategy," *Harvard Business Review*, Vol. 57, No. 2, March–April 1979, pp. 137–145.

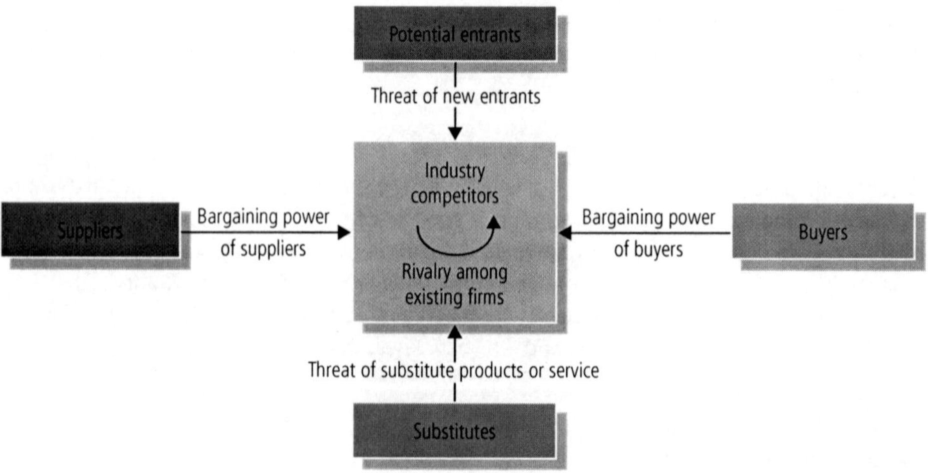

creates an innovation or develops a unique strategy that transforms the market, competing companies must adapt or run the risk of being forced out of business. This force makes markets a dynamic and highly competitive place. Generally, an industry is more attractive when the following conditions hold:

- The number of competitors is large or, at the other extreme, quite small (fewer than five).
- Competitors are not similar in size or capability.
- The industry is growing at a fast pace.
- The opportunity to sell a differentiated product or service is present.

Bargaining Power of Suppliers to the Industry The greater the leverage that suppliers of key raw materials or components have, the less attractive is the industry. For instance, because they supply the chips that serve as the "brains" of PCs and because those chips make up a sizeable portion of the cost of a computer, chip makers such as Intel and Advanced Micro Devices (AMD) exert a great deal of power over computer manufacturers such as Dell, Hewlett-Packard, and Gateway. Generally, an industry is more attractive when the following conditions hold:

- Many suppliers sell a commodity product to the companies in it.
- Substitute products are available for the items suppliers provide.
- Companies in the industry find it easy to switch from one supplier to another or to substitute products (i.e., "switching costs" are low).
- The items suppliers provide the industry account for a relatively small portion of the cost of the industry's finished products.

Bargaining Power of Buyers Just as suppliers to an industry can be a source of pressure, buyers also have the potential to can exert significant power over a business, making it less attractive. When the number of customers is small and the cost of switching to competitors' products is low, buyers' influence on companies is high. Famous for offering its customers low prices, Wal-Mart, the largest company in the world, is also well known for applying relentless pressure to its 21,000 suppliers for price concessions, which it almost always manages to get.[1] Generally, an industry is more attractive when the following conditions hold:

- Industry customers' "switching costs" to competitors' products or to substitutes are relatively high.
- The number of buyers in the industry is large.
- Customers demand products that are differentiated rather than purchase commodity products that they can obtain from any supplier (and subsequently can pit one company against another to drive down price).
- Customers find it difficult to gather information on suppliers' costs, prices, and product features—something that is becoming much easier for customers in many industries to do by using the World Wide Web.
- The items companies sell to the industry account for a relatively small portion of the cost of their customers' finished products.

Threat of New Entrants to the Industry The larger the pool of potential new entrants to an industry, the greater is the threat to existing companies in it. This is particularly true in industries in which the barriers to entry, such as capital requirements, specialized knowledge, access to distribution channels, and others, are low. Generally, an industry is more attractive to new entrants when the follow conditions hold:

- The advantages of economies of scale are absent. Economies of scale exist when companies in an industry achieve low average costs by producing huge volumes of items (e.g., computer chips).
- Capital requirements to enter the industry are low.
- Cost advantages are not related to company size.

- Buyers are not extremely brand-loyal, making it easier for new entrants to the industry to draw customers away from existing businesses.
- Governments, through their regulatory and international trade policies, do not restrict new companies from entering the industry.

Threat of Substitute Products or Services Substitute products or services can turn an entire industry on its head. For instance, many makers of glass bottles have closed their doors in recent years as their customers—from soft drink bottlers to ketchup makers—have switched to plastic containers, which are lighter, less expensive to ship, and less subject to breakage. Printed newspapers have seen their readership rates decline as new generations of potential readers turn to online sources of news that are constantly updated. Generally, an industry is more attractive when the following conditions hold:

- Quality substitute products are not readily available.
- The prices of substitute products are not significantly lower than those of the industry's products.
- Buyers' cost of switching to substitute products is high.

After surveying the power these five forces exert on an industry, entrepreneurs can evaluate the potential for their companies to generate reasonable sales and profits in a particular industry. In other words, they can answer the question, "Is this industry a good home for my business?" Table 4.1 provides a matrix that allows entrepreneurs to assign quantitative scores to the five forces influencing industry attractiveness. Note that the lower the score for an industry, the more attractive it is.

The next step in assessing an industry is to identify potentially attractive niches that exist in it. As you learned in Chapter 2, many small businesses prosper by sticking to niches in a market that are too small to attract the attention of large competitors. Occupying an industry niche enables a business to shield itself to some extent from the power of the five forces. The key questions entrepreneurs address here are, "Can we identify a niche that is large enough to produce a profit? Or can we position our company uniquely in the market to differentiate it from the competition in a meaningful way?"

TABLE 4.1 Five Forces Matrix

Assign a value to rate the importance of each of the five forces to the industry on a 1 (not important) to 5 (very important) scale. Then assign a value to reflect the threat that each force poses to the industry. Multiply the importance rating in column 2 by the threat rating in column 3 to produce a weighted score. Add the weighted scores in column 3 to get a total weighted score. This score measures the industry's attractiveness. The matrix is a useful tool for comparing the attractiveness of different industries.

Minimum Score = 5 (Very attractive)
Maximum Score = 125 (Very unattractive)

Force	Importance (1 to 5)	Threat to Industry (1 to 5)	Weighted Score Col 2 × Col 3
Rivalry among companies competing in the industry	5	5	25
Bargaining power of suppliers in the industry	2	2	4
Bargaining power of buyers	2	4	8
Threat of new entrants to the industry	3	4	12
Threat of substitute products or services	4	3	12
		Total	61

*Scale of importance from 1 = not important to 5 = very important. Scale of threat to the industry from 1 = low, 3 = medium, to 5 = high.

Entrepreneurs who have designed successful focus or differentiation strategies for their companies can exploit these niches to their advantage.

Questions entrepreneurs should address in this portion of the feasibility analysis include the following:

- Which niche in the market will we occupy?
- How large is this market segment, and how fast is it growing?
- What is the basis for differentiating our product or service from competitors?
- Do we have a superior business model that will be difficult for competitors to reproduce?

Dell Inc.

In 1984, Michael Dell, founder of Dell Inc., created a superior business model that revolutionized the retail computer industry and toppled the industry leader, IBM, a company that many industry experts thought was invincible when it came to selling personal computers. Dell transformed the industry by designing a business model based on selling customized PCs directly to consumers without using retail outlets. The impact on the company's fortunes was significant; higher inventory turnover rates, increased customer satisfaction levels, and higher profit margins than the industry average were just some of the benefits Dell experienced. Dell's model really showed its muscle with the advent of the Web; today, Dell, the industry leader with nearly 35 percent market share in PCs, sells an average of $135 million worth of computers online each day![2]

One technique for gauging the quality of a company's business model involves **business prototyping,** in which entrepreneurs test their business models on a small scale before committing serious resources to launch a business that might not work. Business prototyping recognizes that every business idea is a hypothesis that needs to be tested before an entrepreneur takes it to full scale. If the test supports the hypothesis and its accompanying assumptions, it is time to launch a company. If the prototype flops, the entrepreneur scraps the business idea with only minimal losses and turns to the next idea.

business prototyping a process in which entrepreneurs test their business models on a small scale before committing serious resources to launch a business that might not work.

Little Earth Productions Inc.

Before entrepreneurs Ava DeMarco and Robert Brandegee launched Little Earth Productions, Inc., a company that makes fashion accessories (such as this purse) from recycled license plates, bottle caps, hubcaps, and other material, they used business

Before they launched Little Earth Productions, Inc., a company that makes distinctive fashion accessories such as belts, handbags, and wallets from recycled bottle caps, license plates, tires, hubcaps, and other items, entrepreneurs Ava DeMarco and Robert Brandegee used business prototyping to test their unique concept. "We had a gut feeling about recycled fashion accessories, and the research we did confirmed our instincts," says DeMarco. "Before we invested a lot of time and money, we took a look at the market to make certain we were targeting the right buyers and offering products they wanted and could afford." Their first move was to set up booths displaying their unique products at various arts and crafts festivals in their local community, Pittsburgh,

prototyping to test their concept. The lessons they learned selling their products at arts and crafts festivals allowed them to hone their idea into a successful business.

Pennsylvania. They were able to get face to face with buyers, learn what appealed to them, and find out what they were like—all important steps to building a successful business. They learned, for instance, that their primary customers were people in their teens to mid-30s who appreciated the recycling aspect of the company's products but were more interested in its distinctive fashion-forward accessories. "It was a good way to watch people use our products," says DeMarco. "We also got a lot of good feedback on price and comments on how our products worked or didn't work for them." Using the information they had gathered from the festivals, DeMarco and Brandegee refined their business concept and rented a booth at a big industry trade show in Miami, where they came away with more than $24,000 worth of orders.[3]

The World Wide Web makes business prototyping practical, fast, and easy. Entrepreneurs can test their ideas by selling their products on established sites such as eBay or by setting up their own Web sites to gauge customers' response. Frank Ross, a home-based entrepreneur who dropped out of corporate America, operates three successful online businesses. Before launching them, however, he tested his business concepts on eBay. Ross explains:

> If you're considering selling a product line online as your home-based business, there is really no better place to test a market than eBay. It's considerable trouble to set up a Web site, and it can be expensive if your product fails. (I've made that mistake.) If you want to be sure you have a viable, salable product line prior to going to the trouble and expense of setting up a Web site, try selling on eBay. For the price of a few listings, you will be able to tell very quickly what kind of market you have for your potential Web store, and it may also help you weed out any problems you had not thought of.[4]

You Be the Consultant

A Circus Strategy

With its innovative, off-the-wall acts, dramatic staging, and talented staff of performers and engineers, Cirque du Soleil (French for "Circus of the Sun") has built a successful strategy that gives it a unique position in the entertainment market.

When visitors arrive at the company headquarters of Cirque du Soleil (French for "Circus of the Sun") in Montreal, Quebec, the 27-foot-long clown shoe is the first hint that the company it houses is quite unique. Indeed, Cirque du Soleil is one of the most successful entertainment companies in the world, and its success is due to the differentiation strategy that the company executes with the same precision that its world-class acrobats demonstrate in their performances. All 15 of the productions the company has created since its founding in 1984 have been huge successes, a particularly impressive record when considering the fact that 9 of 10 Broadway shows fail to earn back the money originally invested in them. Five Cirque shows tour the globe accompanied by their own custom-designed 2,500-seat tents; four others play in permanent locations in Las Vegas and Orlando. Even though ticket prices range from $45 to $150, Cirque manages to sell 97 percent of available seats for its shows. Although it uses the word "circus" in its name, Cirque is a far cry from the traditional traveling circus with its ringmaster, clowns, tightrope walkers, and daredevils. Cirque shows feature the same types of performers as traditional circuses, but it combines them in innovative, off-the-wall acts with New Age music, surreal costumes, and dazzling staging to create some of the most memorable and entertaining shows on the planet. For example, in its show called *O*, trapeze artists swing high above the stage before diving into a huge, 25-foot-deep on-stage lake that disappears in seconds with the help of a hydraulically powered pump designed by the company's team of talented engineers. Cirque du Soleil's strategy incorporates five key components that enable it to hold a unique position in the entertainment market:

1. ***Meticulous brand management.*** Cirque is a hotbed of creativity, and managers guard the brand carefully. Shows have a long gestation period (about three years) to ensure quality and distinctiveness. "Each show is a new member of the family, and we never want twins," says Daniel Gauthier, co-founder of Cirque.
2. ***Acquisition of world-class talent.*** At the heart of every show are the performers, and Cirque constantly patrols the world in search of the best. The company has 12 full-time talent scouts who travel the globe searching out performers whom they add to the company's database (the largest of its kind in the world) of 20,000 potential recruits. The scouts have recruited performers from such far-flung places as the Olympic games, the Moscow Circus school, a Mongolian elementary school, and the Imperial Orgy erotic arts festival in New York City.
3. ***Stringent cost control.*** Top managers meet with creative directors to set a budget and an opening date for each new show and then step back and let the directors work their creative magic. The directors can spend the budget—typically $10 to $25 million—in any way they choose, and company president Daniel Lamarre says that no director has ever come back to ask for more money. "Cirque allows you to approach shows with the artistic priority first," explains Franco Dragone, who led the creative teams for six of Cirque's nine current productions.
4. ***Investment in research and development (R&D).*** To make certain that its shows are different from those of other entertainment companies and stimulating to its target audience (which is very upscale, college-educated, and heavily populated by women), Cirque invests heavily in R&D. As a percentage of sales, the company spends on R&D twice what the average U.S. corporation spends, and it shows on stage—from the unusual props performers use and waterproof makeup invented by Cirque cosmetologists to the evaporating indoor lake and an elaborate on-stage blizzard. The technology keeps audiences mesmerized, wondering what is coming next.
5. ***Concerted efforts in opportunity recognition and strategic planning.*** Cirque managers intentionally have kept the company growing at a controlled pace. Building on the company's ability to transform itself in each of its unique shows, managers are considering expanding Cirque's circle of influence. "We define ourselves as a creative content provider," explains Lamarre. In the future, managers are planning to take Cirque's creative approach into new industries such as television, hotels, restaurants, and nightclubs. "Whether you are an innkeeper or a restaurateur, you are entertaining on some level," says Lyn Heward, president of the creative content division (and a former competitive gymnastics coach). Ideas being batted around for a Cirque resort include a Las Vegas resort that would feature New Age music, brightly colored furniture, and theatrical lighting throughout the building. Lamarre envisions jugglers serving as waiters. "We want to challenge our creative people to work in new mediums," he says.

Questions

1. How has Cirque du Soleil redefined the industry in which it competes with its differentiation strategy? What benefits does the company reap from having done so?
2. Use the Web to learn more about Cirque du Soleil's unique approach to the entertainment industry. Select one of the projects the company is considering as part of its strategy for the future (television show, hotel, restaurants, and nightclubs). Work with a team of your classmates to brainstorm ideas for applying Cirque's unique approach to entertainment to the project you selected.
3. How would you define the company's core competencies? Given these core competencies, can you spot other opportunities Cirque might be able to exploit?
4. What threats does the company's strategies pose?

Source: Adapted from Geoff Keighley, "The Phantasmagoria Factory," *Business 2.0*, January/February 2004, pp. 103–107.

Product or Service Feasibility Analysis

product or service feasibility analysis
an analysis that determines the degree to which a product or service idea appeals to potential customers and indentifies the resources necessary to produce the product or provide the service.

Once entrepreneurs discover that sufficient market potential for their product or service idea actually exists, they sometimes rush in with their exuberant enthusiasm ready to launch a business without actually considering whether they can actually produce the product or provide the service at a reasonable cost. A **product or service feasibility analysis** determines the degree to which a product or service idea appeals to potential customers and identifies the resources necessary to produce the product or provide the service. This portion of the feasibility analysis addresses two questions:

- Are customers willing to purchase our goods and services?
- Can we provide the product or service to customers at a profit?

To answer these questions, entrepreneurs need feedback from potential customers. Getting that feedback might involve engaging in primary research such as customer surveys and focus groups, gathering secondary customer research, building prototypes, and conducting in-home trials.

primary research
information that an entrepreneur collects first-hand and analyzes.

secondary research
information that has already been compiled and is available for use, often at a very reasonable cost or sometimes even free.

Conducting **primary research** involves collecting data first-hand and analyzing it; **secondary research** involves gathering data that have already been compiled and are available, often at a very reasonable cost or sometimes even free. In both types of research, gathering both quantitative and qualitative information is important to drawing accurate conclusions about a product's or service's market potential. Primary research techniques include the following:

Customer surveys and questionnaires. Keep them short. Word your questions carefully so that you do not bias the results, and use a simple ranking system (e.g., a 1-to-5 scale, with 1 representing "definitely would not buy" and 5 representing "definitely would buy"). Test your survey for problems on a small number of people before putting it to use. Web surveys are inexpensive, easy to conduct, and provide feedback fast. Monster.com, the online job search company, recently conducted an online survey of 30,000 customers and integrated the results from the survey into every aspect of the company's operation. "The survey results impact policy, process, product development and marketing efforts," says Chip Henry, Monster.com's, vice president, voice of the customer (note the unique job title). "There's nothing in the company that isn't touched as a result of the surveys."[5]

Focus groups. A **focus group** involves enlisting a small number of potential customers (usually 8 to 12) to give feedback on specific issues about a product or service (or the business idea itself). Listen carefully for what focus group members like and don't like about your product or service as they tell you what is on their minds. The founders of one small snack food company that produced apple chips conducted several focus groups to gauge customers' acceptance of the product and to guide many key business decisions, ranging from the product's name to its packaging. Once again, consider creating virtual focus groups on the Web; one small bicycle retailer conducts 10 online focus groups each year at virtually no cost and gains valuable marketing information from them. Feedback from online customers is fast, convenient, and real-time.

Secondary research, which is usually less expensive to collect than primary data, includes the following sources:

Trade associations and business directories. To locate a trade association, use *Business Information Sources* (University of California Press) or the *Encyclopedia of Associations* (Gale Research). To find suppliers, use *The Thomas Register of American Manufacturers* (Thomas Publishing Company) or *Standard and Poor's Register of Corporations, Executives, and Industries* (Standard and Poor Corporation). *The American Wholesalers and Distributors Directory* includes details on more than 18,000 wholesalers and distributors.

Direct mail lists. You can buy mailing lists for practically any type of business. *The Standard Rates and Data Service (SRDS) Directory of Mailing Lists* (Standard Rates and Data) is a good place to start looking.

Demographic data. To learn more about the demographic characteristics of customers in general, use *The Statistical Abstract of the United States* (Government Printing Office). Profiles of more specific regions are available in *The State and Metropolitan Data Book* (Government Printing Office). *The Sourcebook of Zip Code Demographics* (CACI, Inc.) provides detailed breakdowns of the population in every zip code in the country. *Sales and Marketing Management's Survey of Buying Power* (Bill Communications) has statistics on consumer, retail, and industrial buying. *Demographics USA* provides users with one of the most extensive collections of demographic and marketing data available. It contains more than 1,700 pages of useful reports, which range from business characteristics and retail sales by merchandise line to buying power indices and detailed demographics by county and by zip code.

Census data. The Bureau of the Census publishes a wide variety of reports that summarize the wealth of data found in its census database, which is available at most libraries and at the Census Bureau's Web site (http://www.census.gov).

Forecasts. The *U.S. Global Outlook* traces the growth of 200 industries and gives a five-year forecast for each one. Many government agencies, including the Department of Commerce, offer forecasts on everything from interest rates to the number of housing starts. A government librarian can help you to find what you need.

Market research. Someone may already have compiled the market research you need. *The FINDex Worldwide Directory of Market Research Reports, Studies, and Surveys* (Cambridge Information Group) lists more than 10,600 studies available for purchase. Other directories of business research include *Simmons Study of Media and Markets* (Simmons Market Research Bureau Inc.) and the *A.C. Neilsen Retail Index* (A.C. Neilsen Company).

Articles. Magazine and journal articles pertinent to your business are a great source of information. Use the *Reader's Guide to Periodical Literature*, the *Business Periodicals Index* (similar to the *Reader's Guide* but focuses on business periodicals), and *Ulrich's Guide to International Periodicals* to locate the ones you need.

Local data. Your state department of commerce and your local chamber of commerce will very likely have useful data on the local market of interest to you. Call to find out what is available.

World Wide Web. Most entrepreneurs are astounded at the marketing information that is available on the World Wide Web (WWW). Using one of the search engines, you can gain access to a world of information—literally!

Prototypes One of the most effective ways to gauge the viability of a product is to build a prototype of it. A **prototype** is an original, functional model of a new product that entrepreneurs can put into the hands of potential customers so that they can see it, test it, and use it. Prototypes usually point out potential problems in a product's design, giving inventors the opportunity to fix them even before they put the prototype into customers' hands. The feedback customers give entrepreneurs based on prototypes often leads to design improvements and new features, some of which the entrepreneurs might never have discovered on their own. Makers of computer software frequently put prototypes of new products into customers' hands as they develop new products or improve existing ones. Known as *beta tests*, these trials result in an iterative design process in which software designers collect feedback from users and then incorporate their ideas into the product for the next round of tests.

prototype
an original, functional model of a new product that entrepreneurs can put into the hands of potential customers so they can see it, test it, and use it.

Trac Tool Inc.

Entrepreneur Shawn Donegan teamed up with inventor Mike Puczkowski to launch Trac Tool Inc., a Cleveland, Ohio–based business that markets Speed Rollers, a paint application system aimed at professional paint contractors. Puczkowski's invention features an airless paint pump that feeds paint onto one of two rollers, eliminating the need to dip the rollers into a paint tray and making the system four to five times faster than using traditional rollers. Donegan and Puczkowski built several models of the system before they had a prototype that worked. Early prototypes pointed out several problems the entrepreneurs had to fix, including a valve that could handle only a fraction of the pressure that a typical airless system delivers and coupling joints that leaked paint. "Once we redesigned the components, we tested them thoroughly," says Donegan. "We wanted to ensure worker safety and product quality before proceeding." They used the prototype to conduct focus groups with paint contractors, industry experts, and property managers to get feedback on the product and its features. The response from the focus groups was very positive, leading Donegan and Puczkowski to launch Trac Tool Inc., which now generates more than $3 million in sales of the Speed Rollers system.[6]

Existing companies can benefit from creating prototypes as well. As their business grew, Ava DeMarco and Robert Brandegee, founders of Little Earth Productions, changed their approach to developing new products. "When we first started out, we designed new products two weeks before a trade show and hoped people would buy them," says DeMarco. Today, the company creates a small number of prototypes, places them in half a dozen or so retail stores, and tests customers' responses to them. "The feedback lets us know if we're on the right track with a new product before we invest time and money," explains DeMarco.[7]

in-home trial
a research technique that involves sending researchers into customers' homes to observe them as they use the company's product or service.

In-Home Trials One technique that reveals some of the most insightful information into how customers actually use a product or service is also the most challenging to coordinate: in-home trials. An **in-home trial** involves sending researchers into customers' homes to observe them as they use the company's product or service.

Intuit

Intuit, the software company that produces popular programs such as Quicken, QuickBooks, and TurboTax, was one of the first companies to adopt in-home trials as part of its product development process in 1989. In the company's follow-me-home program, software engineers hang around a retail store, waiting for customers to buy an Intuit product. They then ask to go into customers' homes, where they watch how customers install and use the software and listen to their suggestions in a natural setting. Intuit has adapted the program to its call centers, where customers call with questions about Intuit software. Software managers and product engineers periodically sit at call center employees' desks, looking for ways to improve the employees' ability to serve customers more effectively. The company also combs through blogs and Intuit online communities, looking for comments and feedback about its software products. The process works; the latest version of Quicken included 121 customer-recommended improvements.[8]

Financial Feasibility Analysis

The final component of a feasibility analysis involves assessing the financial feasibility of a proposed business venture. At this stage of the process, a broad financial analysis is sufficient. If the business concept passes the overall feasibility analysis, an entrepreneur should conduct a more thorough financial analysis when creating a full-blown business plan. The major elements to be included in a financial feasibility analysis include the initial capital requirement, estimated earnings, and the resulting return on investment.

Capital Requirements Just as a Boy Scout needs fuel to start a fire, an entrepreneur needs capital to start a business. Some businesses require large amounts of capital, but others do not. Typically, service businesses require less capital to launch than manufacturing or retail businesses. Start-up companies often need capital to purchase equipment, buildings, technology, and other tangible assets as well as to hire and train employees, promote their products and services, and establish a presence in the market. A good feasibility analysis will provide an estimate of the amount of start-up capital an entrepreneur will need to get the business up and running. For instance, Shawn Donegan and Mike Puczkowski needed $150,000 to launch Trac Tool Inc. and bring the Speed Rollers paint system to market. They spent most of that start-up capital to develop and test the prototype and to introduce the product at the Painting and Decorating Contractors of America trade show.[9]

You will learn more about finding sources of business funding, both debt and equity, in Chapter 13, "Sources of Financing: Debt and Equity."

Estimated Earnings In addition to producing an estimate of the start-up company's capital requirements, an entrepreneur also should forecast the earning potential of the proposed business. Industry trade associations and publications such as the *RMA Annual Statement Studies* offer guidelines on preparing sales and earnings estimates. From these, entrepreneurs can estimate the financial results they and their investors can expect to see from the business venture.

Return on Investment The final aspect of the financial feasibility analysis combines the estimated earnings and the capital requirements to determine the rate of return the venture is expected to produce. One simple measure is the rate of return on the capital invested, which is calculated by dividing the estimated earnings the business yields by the amount of capital invested in the business. Although financial estimates at the feasibility analysis stage typically are rough, they are an important part of the entrepreneur's ultimate "go/no go" decision about the business ventures. A venture must produce an attractive rate of return relative to the level of risk it requires. This risk–return tradeoff means that the higher the level of risk a prospective business involves, the higher the rate of return it must provide to the entrepreneur and investors. Why should an entrepreneur take on all of the risks of starting and running a business that produces a mere three or four percent rate of return when he or she could earn that much in a risk-free investment at a bank or other financial institution? You will learn more about developing detailed financial forecasts for a business start-up in Chapter 10, "Creating a Successful Financial Plan."

Wise entrepreneurs take the time to subject their ideas to a feasibility analysis like the one described here, whatever outcome it produces. If the study suggests that transforming the idea into a viable business is not feasible, the entrepreneur can move on to the next idea, confident that he or she has not wasted valuable resources launching a business destined to fail. If the analysis shows that the idea has real potential as a profitable business, the entrepreneur can pursue it, using the information gathered during the feasibility analysis as the foundation for building a sound business plan. We now turn our attention to that process.

How a Ruined Shirt Launched a Successful Venture

A simple trip to the dry cleaners changed Robert Byerley's career path. When the Dallas businessman picked up his clothes, he discovered that the cleaner had ruined one of his $100 dress shirts. He would have been satisfied if the owner of the cleaner had offered to replace his shirt, but he did not. He didn't even apologize to Byerley, and that's when Byerley decided to do something about it.

Although the Dallas market was crowded with dry cleaning establishments, Byerley left his corporate job to launch Bibbentuckers, a dry cleaning operation that offers Dallas residents better quality and better service at higher prices than other dry cleaning establishments. He suspected that a segment of the market would be willing to pay premium prices for a cleaner that offered convenient locations, superior quality and service, and extra amenities. Byerley didn't rely on his instincts alone, however. Before starting Bibbentuckers, Byerley did plenty of research and put together a business plan to guide his entrepreneurial venture.

He started with the vision he had for his business. One night when he couldn't sleep, Byerley began listing the characteristics he wanted his dry cleaners to exhibit. Based on his negative experience with his former dry cleaner, Byerley listed "standing behind our work" first. He listed nine other items, including a drive-up service with curbside delivery, a computerized system that would track clothes through the entire process and would use bar code scanners to read customers' cleaning preferences, and a cleaning process that used the most current, environmentally friendly equipment and materials.

The one item that was not on his list: low prices. "The things I wanted in a perfect dry cleaner were incompatible with a discount operation," he explains.

Byerley's next step was to research the industry and the market potential for his venture. He spent a solid week in the library, where he learned all about the dry cleaning industry, a $16 billion-a-year business dominated by small independent operators who competed primarily on the basis of price. He also discovered that dry cleaning establishments accounted for a large number of customer complaints with the Better Business Bureau. The number one complaint? "Cleaners didn't stand behind what they did," says Byerley with a smile. He also learned about legislation that was about to take effect that would change the way cleaners handled their cleaning solvents.

As he assembled his plan, Byerley realized he could use his environmentally friendly approach to cleaning as a marketing tool, something that very few operators were doing. He researched the existing competition in Dallas and discovered that several dry cleaners were taking a premium approach to the market. Realizing that he had to differentiate his business from his competitors, Byerley gave his outlets a unique and appealing design. The free-standing stores' professionally appointed décor included attractive awnings and drive-through lanes as well as television screens and free refreshments. "I wanted a place that people would feel comfortable leaving their best clothes, a place that paired five-star service with an establishment that didn't look like a dry cleaner," he says.

One key question to be answered, of course, was "Would customers be willing to pay for quality, service, and convenience?" To find out, Byerley hired a marketing firm and conducted focus groups of potential customers who discussed everything from the look of the company's buildings to its name. Byerley even took clothes to the 15 best cleaners in town and let the members of the focus groups critique them to learn exactly what customers' expectations were. His goal was to exceed their expectations.

After synthesizing all of his research into a plan, Byerley launched Bibbentuckers in the Dallas suburb of Plano. From his research, he knew that the typical dry cleaner generates $250,000 in revenue a year. Byerley knew his research and planning had paid off when his first store was on track to surpass $1 million in sales in its first year and began earning a profit after just four months. He opened two more stores before stepping out of the daily operation of the company to serve as chairman of the board. He is now involved in another business start-up, and he and his co-founders are taking the same fastidious approach to researching the industry and the business before they are ready to launch. In fact, a team of 13 people has already spent a year researching the venture to be sure they get it right the first time.

1. Why is it important for entrepreneurs to research their industry and markets before launching a business? Why do so many fail to do so?
2. Suppose that a close friend is considering launching a new restaurant (or some other type of business you choose). What type of research would you advise your friend to conduct? Where would you suggest your friend look for the information he or she needs?
3. Refer to Question 2. How would you advise your friend to get feedback from potential customers about his or her business concept?

Source: Adapted from Ann Zimmerman, "Do the Research," *Wall Street Journal*, May 9, 2005, pp. R3–R4.

LEARNING OBJECTIVES
2. Explain why every entrepreneur should create a business plan, as well as the benefits of developing a plan.

Why Develop a Business Plan?

Any entrepreneur who is in business or is about to launch a business needs a well-conceived and factually based business plan to increase the likelihood of success. For decades, research has proven that companies that engage in business planning outperform those that do not. Unfortunately, studies also show that small companies are especially lackadaisical in their approach to developing business plans. Many entrepreneurs never take the time to develop plans for their businesses; unfortunately, the implications of the lack of planning are all too evident in the high failure rates that small companies experience.

business plan
a written summary of an entrepreneur's proposed business venture, its operational and financial details, its marketing opportunities and strategy, and its managers' skills and abilities.

A **business plan** is a written summary of an entrepreneur's proposed business venture, its operational and financial details, its marketing opportunities and strategy, and its managers' skills and abilities. There is no substitute for a well-prepared business plan, and there are no shortcuts to creating one. The plan serves as an entrepreneur's road map on the journey toward building a successful business. It describes the direction the company is taking, what its goals are, where it wants to be, and how it's going to get there. The plan is written proof that an entrepreneur has performed the necessary research, has studied the business opportunity adequately, and is prepared to capitalize on it with a sound business model. In short, a business plan is an entrepreneur's best insurance against launching a business destined to fail or mismanaging a potentially successful company.

A business plan serves three essential functions. First and most important, it guides an entrepreneur by charting the company's future course of action and devising a strategy for success. The plan provides a battery of tools—a mission statement, goals, objectives, market analysis, budgets, financial forecasts, target markets, and strategies—to help entrepreneurs lead a company successfully. It gives managers and employees a sense of direction, but only if everyone is involved in creating, updating, or altering it. As more team members become committed to making the plan work, the plan takes on special meaning. It gives everyone targets to shoot for, and it provides a yardstick for measuring actual performance against those targets, especially in the crucial and chaotic start-up phase. Creating a plan also forces entrepreneurs to subject their ideas to the test of reality. Can this business idea actually produce a profit?

The second function of the business plan is to attract lenders and investors. Too often small business owners approach potential lenders and investors without having prepared to sell themselves and their business concept. Simply scribbling a few rough figures on a note pad to support a loan application is not enough. Applying for loans or attempting to attract investors without a solid business plan rarely attracts needed capital. Rather, the best way to secure the necessary capital is to prepare a sound business plan, which enables an entrepreneur to communicate to potential lenders and investors the potential the business opportunity offers. Entrepreneurs must pay attention to details because they are germane to their sales presentations to potential lenders and investors. The quality of the firm's business plan weighs heavily in the decision to lend or invest funds. It is also potential lenders' and investors' first impression of the company and its managers. Therefore, the finished product should be highly polished and professional in both form and content.

A business plan must prove to potential lenders and investors that a venture will be able to repay loans and produce an attractive rate of return. Entrepreneur and author Neal Stephenson, who started several high-tech companies before focusing on a writing career, explains his experience writing a business plan:

> As I was trying to write my plan, something came into focus for me that should have been obvious from the very beginning. I was proposing to borrow a lot of money from strangers and gamble it on doing something. If it didn't work, these people would lose their money, which is a very sobering prospect. It really shakes you up and makes you think very hard about what it is you are doing . . . . We're using other people's real money, and those people could get hurt.[10]

Building a plan forces a potential entrepreneur to look at his or her business idea in the harsh light of reality. It also requires the entrepreneur to assess the venture's chances of success more objectively. A well-assembled plan helps prove to outsiders that a business idea can be successful. To get external financing, an entrepreneur's plan must pass three tests with potential lenders and investors: (1) the reality test, (2) the competitive test, and (3) the value test. The first two tests have both an external and an internal component:

> ***Reality test.*** The external component of the reality test revolves around proving that a market for the product or service really does exist. It focuses on industry attractiveness, market niches, potential customers, market size, degree of competition, and similar factors. Entrepreneurs who pass this part of the reality test prove in the marketing portion of their business plan that there is strong demand for their business idea.
>
> The internal component of the reality test focuses on the product or service itself. Can the company *really* build it for the cost estimates in the business plan? Is it truly different from what competitors are already selling? Does it offer customers something of value?

Competitive test. The external part of the competitive test evaluates the company's relative position to its key competitors. How do the company's strengths and weaknesses match up with those of the competition? Do these reactions threaten the new company's success and survival?

The internal competitive test focuses on management's ability to create a company that will gain an edge over existing rivals. To pass this part of the competitive test, a plan must prove the quality, skill, and experience of the venture's management team. What other resources does the company have that can give it a competitive edge in the market?

Value test. To convince lenders and investors to put their money into the venture, a business plan must prove to them that it offers a high probability of repayment or an attractive rate of return. Entrepreneurs usually see their businesses as good investments because they consider the intangibles of owning a business—gaining control over their own destinies, freedom to do what they enjoy, and other factors; lenders and investors, however, look at a venture in colder terms: dollar-for-dollar returns. A plan must convince lenders and investors that they will earn an attractive return on their money.

The same business basics that investors have employed for decades to evaluate the financial potential of a new venture are still valid today, although during the dot-com craze in the late 1990s, many entrepreneurs and investors lost site of the importance of practical, profitable business models. The collapse of many of those dot-com companies at the beginning of the twenty-first century proved that unrealistic "smoke and mirror" assumptions are no substitute for sound business basics. "Those businesses had full tech staffs and fat marketing budgets," says one business writer, "but a lot of them went belly up because their business plans were no better than the Titanic's plans for dealing with icebergs."[11]

Today what matters most are realistic financial projections based on research and reasonable assumptions. A new venture must have both a long-term strategic vision and a practical focus on operations. In their business plans, entrepreneurs must be able to communicate clearly an understanding of the following issues:

- Cost of raw materials and supplies
- Unit labor costs
- Market-determined selling prices and gross profit margins
- Break-even point for their businesses[12]

Sometimes the greatest service a business plan provides an entrepreneur is the realization that "it just won't work." The time to find out a potential business idea won't succeed is in the planning stages *before* an entrepreneur commits significant resources to a venture. In other cases it reveals important problems to overcome before launching a company.

The real value in preparing a business plan is not so much in the plan itself as it is in the *process* an entrepreneur goes through to create the plan. Although the finished product is useful, the process of building a plan requires an entrepreneur to subject his or her idea to an objective, critical evaluation. What the entrepreneur learns about his or her company, its target market, its financial requirements, and other factors can be essential to making the venture a success. This process allows the entrepreneur to replace "I think's" with more "I know's" and to make mistakes on paper, which is much cheaper than making them in reality. Simply put, building a business plan reduces the risk and uncertainty in launching a company by teaching the entrepreneur to do it the right way!

Third, a business plan is a reflection of its creator. It should demonstrate that the entrepreneur has thought seriously about the venture and what will make it succeed. Preparing a solid plan demonstrates that the entrepreneur has taken the time to commit the idea to paper. Building a plan also forces the entrepreneur to consider both the positive and the negative aspects of the business. A detailed and thoughtfully developed business plan makes a positive first impression on those who read it. In most cases, potential lenders and investors read a business plan before they ever meet with the entrepreneur behind it. Sophisticated investors will not take the time to meet with an entrepreneur whose business plan fails to reflect a serious investment of time and energy. They know that an entrepreneur who lacks this discipline to develop a good business plan likely lacks the discipline to run a business.

The business plan should reflect the fire and passion an entrepreneur has for the venture. For this reason an entrepreneur cannot allow others to prepare the business plan for him or her because outsiders cannot understand the business nor envision the proposed company as well as the entrepreneur can. The entrepreneur is the driving force behind the business idea and is the one who can best convey the vision and the enthusiasm he or she has for transforming that idea into a successful business. In addition, because the entrepreneur will make the presentation to potential lenders and investors, he or she must understand every detail of the business plan. Otherwise, an entrepreneur cannot present it convincingly, and in most cases the financial institution or investor will reject it. Investors want to feel confident that an entrepreneur has realistically evaluated the risk involved in the new venture and has a strategy for addressing it. Furthermore, as you can expect, they also want to see proof that a business will be profitable and produce a reasonable return on their investment.

Perhaps the best way to understand the need for a business plan is to recognize the validity of the "two-thirds rule," which says that only two-thirds of the entrepreneurs with a sound and viable new business venture will find financial backing. Those who do find financial backing will only get two-thirds of what they initially requested, and it will take them two-thirds longer to get the financing than they anticipated. The most effective strategy for avoiding the two-thirds rule is to build a business plan!

The Elements of a Business Plan

LEARNING OBJECTIVES
3. Describe the elements of a solid business plan.

Smart entrepreneurs recognize that every business plan is unique and must be tailor-made. They avoid the off-the-shelf, "cookie-cutter" approach that produces look-alike plans. The elements of a business plan may be standard, but the way entrepreneurs tell their stories should be unique and reflect their enthusiasm for the new venture. If this is a first attempt at writing a business plan, it may be very helpful to seek the advice of individuals with experience in this process. Accountants, business professors, attorneys, and consultants with Small Business Development Centers can be excellent sources of advice in creating and refining a plan. (For a list of Small Business Development Center locations, see the Small Business Administration's Web SBDC Web page at http://www.sba.gov/SBDC/.) Entrepreneurs also can use business planning software available from several companies to create their plans. Some of the most popular programs include Business Plan Pro (Palo Alto Software), BizPlan Builder (Jian Tools), PlanMaker (Power Solutions for Business), and Plan Write (Business Resources Software). These planning packages help entrepreneurs to organize the material they have researched and gathered, and they provide helpful tips on plan writing and templates for creating financial statements. These planning packages produce professional-looking business plans, but entrepreneurs who use them face one drawback: the plans they produce often look the same, as if they came from the same mold. That can be a turn-off for professional investors, who see hundreds of business plans each year.

Initially, the prospect of writing a business plan may appear to be overwhelming. Many entrepreneurs would rather launch their companies and "see what happens" than invest the necessary time and energy defining and researching their target markets, defining their strategies, and mapping out their finances. After all, building a plan is hard work! However, it is hard work that pays many dividends, not all of which are immediately apparent. Entrepreneurs who invest their time and energy in building plans are better prepared to face the hostile environment in which their companies will compete than those who do not. Earlier, we said that a business plan is like a road map that guides an entrepreneur on the journey to building a successful business. If you were making a journey to a particular destination through unfamiliar, harsh, and dangerous territory, would you rather ride with someone equipped with a road map and a trip itinerary or with someone who didn't believe in road maps or in planning trips, destinations, and layovers? Although building a business plan does not *guarantee* success, it *does* raise an entrepreneur's chances of succeeding in business.

A business plan typically ranges from 25 to 40 pages in length. Shorter plans usually are too sketchy to be of any value, and those much longer than this run the risk of never getting used or read! This section explains the most common elements of a business plan. However, entrepreneurs must recognize that, like every business venture, every business plan is unique. An entrepreneur should view the following elements as a starting point for building a plan and should modify them as needed to better tell the story of his or her new venture.

Title Page and Table of Contents

A business plan is a professional document and should contain a title page with the company's name, logo, and address as well as the names and contact information of the company founders. Many entrepreneurs also include on the title page the copy number of the plan and the date on which it was issued.

Business plan readers appreciate a table of contents that includes page numbers so that they can locate the particular sections of the plan in which they are most interested.

Executive Summary

To summarize the presentation to each potential financial institution or investors, the entrepreneur should write an executive summary. It should be concise—a maximum of two pages—and should summarize all of the relevant points of the business venture. The executive summary is a synopsis of the entire plan, capturing its essence in a capsulized form. It should briefly describe the following:

- The company's business model and the basis for its competitive edge.
- The company's target market(s) and the benefits its products or services will provide customers.
- The qualifications of the founders and key employees.
- The key financial highlights (e.g., sales and earnings projections, capital required, rates of return on the investment, and when any loans will be repaid).

The executive summary is a written version of what is known as "the elevator pitch." Imagine yourself on an elevator with a potential lender or investor. Only the two of you are on the elevator, and you have that person's undivided attention for the duration of the ride, but the building is not very tall! To convince the investor that your business is a great investment, you must boil your message down to its essence—key points that you can communicate in just a matter of one or two minutes.

The executive summary *must* capture the reader's attention. If it misses the mark, the chances of the remainder of the plan being read are minimal. A well-developed, coherent summary introducing the financial proposal establishes a favorable first impression of the entrepreneur and the business and can go a long way toward obtaining financing. Although the executive summary is the first part of the business plan, it should be the last section written.

Vision and Mission Statement

As you learned in Chapter 3, a mission statement expresses in words an entrepreneur's vision for what his or her company is and what it is to become. It is the broadest expression of a company's purpose and defines the direction in which it will move. It anchors a company in reality and serves as the thesis statement for the entire business plan. Every good plan captures an entrepreneur's passion and vision for the business, and the mission statement is the ideal place to express them.

Company History

The owner of an existing small business who is creating a business plan should prepare a brief history of the operation, highlighting the significant financial and operational events in the company's life. This section should describe when and why the company was formed, how it has evolved over time, and what the owner envisions for the future. It should highlight the successful accomplishment of past objectives such as developing prototypes, earning patents, achieving market-share targets, or securing long-term customer contracts. This section also should describe the company's current image in the marketplace.

Business and Industry Profile

To acquaint lenders and investors with the industry in which a company competes, an entrepreneur should describe it in the business plan. This section should provide the reader with an overview of the industry or market segment in which the new venture will operate. Industry data such as market size, growth trends, and the relative economic and competitive strength of the major firms in the industry all set the stage for a better understanding of the viability of the new product or service. Strategic issues such as ease of market entry and exit, the ability to achieve economies of scale or scope, and the existence of cyclical or seasonal economic trends further help readers to evaluate the new venture. This part of the plan also should describe significant industry trends and key success factors as well as an overall outlook for its future. Information about the evolution of the industry helps the reader to comprehend its competitive dynamics. The *U.S. Industrial Outlook Handbook* is an excellent reference that profiles a variety of industries and offers projections for future trends in them. Another useful resource of industry and economic information is the *Summary of Commentary on Current Economic Conditions*, more commonly known as the Beige Book. Published eight times a year by the Federal Reserve, the Beige Book provides detailed statistics and trends in key business sectors and in the overall economy. It offers valuable information on topics ranging from tourism and housing starts to consumer spending and wage rates. Entrepreneurs can find this wealth of information at their fingertips on the Web at http://www.federalreserve.gov/FOMC/BeigeBook/2005/.

This portion of the plan also should describe the existing and anticipated profitability of the industry. Any significant entry or exit of firms or consolidations and mergers should be discussed in terms of their impact on the competitive behavior of the market. The entrepreneur also should mention any events that have significantly affected the industry in the last 10 years.

This section should contain a statement of the company's general business goals and then work down to a narrower definition of its immediate objectives. Together they should spell out what the business plans to accomplish and how, when, and who will do it. **Goals** are broad, long-range statements of what a company plans to achieve in the future that guide its overall direction. In other words, they address the question, "What do I want my company to look like in three to five years?"

goals
broad, long-range statements of what a company plans to achieve in the future that guide its overall direction.

Objectives, on the other hand, are short-term, specific performance targets that are attainable, measurable, and controllable. Every objective should reflect some general business goal and should include a technique for measuring progress toward its accomplishment. To be meaningful, an objective must have a time frame for achievement. Both goals and objectives should relate to the company's basic mission (see Figure 4.3).

objectives
short-term specific performance targets that are attainable, measurable, and controllable.

FIGURE 4.3

The Relationships among Mission, Goal, and Objectives

Business Strategy

Another important part of a business plan is the owner's view of the strategy needed to meet—and beat—the competition. In the previous section, the entrepreneur defined *where* to take the business by establishing goals and objectives. This section addresses the question of *how* to get there—business strategy. Here an entrepreneur must explain how he or she plans to gain a competitive edge in the market and what sets the business apart from the competition. The entrepreneur should comment on how he or she plans to achieve business goals and objectives in the face of competition and government regulation and should identify the image that the business will try to project. An important theme in this section is what makes the company unique in the eyes of its customers. One of the quickest routes to business failure is trying to sell "me-too" products or services that offer customers nothing new, better, bigger, faster, more convenient, or different from existing products or services.

First Penthouse

After moving to London, entrepreneurs Annika and Håkan Olsson came up with the idea of adding modular penthouses to existing flat-roof buildings. Building a business plan convinced the couple that a market existed for their unique product, one that adds value for both landlords and tenants.

While renovating their top-floor apartment in Stockholm, Sweden, civil engineers Håkan and Annika Olsson came up with a unique idea for creating high-quality modular penthouses that could be manufactured in factories and installed atop existing flat-roof buildings. When the couple moved to London, they purchased aerial photographs of the city and marked all of the flat-roof buildings in red ink. "We knew we had a good business idea when the whole picture was red," says Håkan. After conducting more research and building a business plan, the Olssons launched First Penthouse, a company specializing in rooftop development. Their business model adds value both for tenants, who get ritzy penthouse living quarters where none existed before, and for landlords, whose property values are enhanced by the addition of the modular penthouses. First Penthouse offers the convenience of one-day installation of its penthouses and guarantees no disturbances to existing residents. Like most entrepreneurs, the Olssons had to overcome obstacles, including banks that were hesitant to extend credit "because the idea was so new," says Håkan. (To get the capital they needed, the Olssons used angel financing, a topic you will learn more about in Chapter 13, when they convinced a wealthy friend to put up most of the $400,000 they needed to create and install the first penthouse.) To convince balking regulators, the Olssons agreed to use special "quiet" tools and to place soundproof mats over the roofs on which they worked. Sales of the company's penthouses are growing, and the Olssons are planning to take their concept into other large urban markets around the world, including New York City.[13]

The strategy section of the business plan should outline the methods the company can use to satisfy the key success factors required to thrive in the industry. If, for example, a strong, well-trained sales force is considered critical to success, the owner must devise a plan of action for assembling one. The foundation for this part of the business plan comes from the material in Chapter 3, "Designing a Competitive Business Model and Building a Solid Strategic Plan."

Description of the Firm's Product or Service

An entrepreneur should describe the company's overall product line, giving an overview of how customers use its goods or services. Drawings, diagrams, and illustrations may be required if the product is highly technical. It is best to write product and service descriptions in a jargon-free style so that laypeople can understand them. A statement of a product's position in the product life cycle might also be helpful. An entrepreneur should include a summary of any patents, trademarks, or copyrights protecting the product or service from infringement by competitors. Finally, it is helpful provide an honest comparison the company's product or service with those of competitors, citing specific advantages or improvements that make the company's goods or services unique and indicating plans for creating the next generation of goods and services that will evolve from the present product line.

The emphasis of this section should be on defining the unique characteristics of the company's products or services and the *benefits* customers get by purchasing them, rather than on just a "nuts and bolts" description of the *features* of those products or services. A **feature** is a descriptive fact about a product or service ("An ergonomically designed, more comfortable handle"). A **benefit** is what a customer gains from the product or service feature ("Fewer problems with carpal tunnel syndrome and increased productivity"). Advertising legend Leo Burnett once said, "Don't tell the people how good you make the goods; tell them how good your goods make them."[6] This part of the plan must describe how a business will transform tangible product or service *features* into important, but often intangible, customer *benefits*—for example, lower energy bills, faster access to the Internet, less time writing checks to pay monthly bills, greater flexibility in building floating structures, shorter time required to learn a foreign language, or others. Remember: Customers buy benefits, *not* product or service features.

feature
a descriptive fact about a product or service.

benefit
what a customer gains from the product or service.

Manufacturers should describe their production process, strategic raw materials required, sources of supply they will use, and their costs. They should also summarize the production method and illustrate the plant layout. If the product is based on a patented or proprietary process, a description (including diagrams, if necessary) of its unique market advantages is helpful. It is also helpful to explain the company's environmental impact and how the entrepreneur plans to mitigate any negative environmental consequences the process may produce.

Swash

As the value of the automobiles Americans drive has increased, so has their desire to maintain the value of their cars by keeping them showroom clean. Some 75,000 car washes operate across the United States, but they vary drastically in terms of service and quality. Matthew Lieb and Chris Jones saw the opportunity to offer a superior car wash service and created Swash, a state-of-the art, no-muss, no-fuss car wash in which customers select the services they want to purchase at an ATM-like machine and remain in their comfort of their vehicles. Cleaning services are delivered by software-controlled equipment that never lays a brush on the car and the process is environmentally friendly from start to finish—all in just five minutes.[14]

Stressing unique features such as these to investors can help to differentiate a product or process from those of competitors.

Marketing Strategy

One crucial concern of entrepreneurs and the potential lenders and investors who finance their companies is whether there is a real market for the proposed good or service. Every entrepreneur must therefore describe the company's target market and its characteristics. Defining the target market and its potential is one of the most important—and most challenging—parts of building a business plan. Creating a successful business depends on an entrepreneur's ability to attract real customers who are willing and able to spend real money to buy its products or services. Perhaps the worst marketing error an entrepreneur can commit is failing to define his or her target market and trying to make the business "everything to everybody." Small companies usually are much more successful when focusing on a specific market niche where they can excel at meeting customers' special needs or wants.

One technique for identifying potential target markets is to list all of the features your company's product or service provides and then translate those features into a list of benefits (refer to the previous section). The next step is to develop a list of the types of people who need or could use those benefits. Be creative, and let your mind roam free. Once you have identified potential target markets, you can begin to research them to narrow the list down to the most promising one or two. Those are the markets your company should pursue.

One growing and evolving target market for small businesses is teenagers. By 2010, the number of teens will grow to 35 million (that's nearly 12 percent of the U.S. population), but even more important than their numbers is this group's purchasing power. According to Teenage Research Unlimited, teens spend $170 billion a year, an amount larger than the gross domestic products of Finland, Portugal, and Greece![15] Because they are not tied down with mortgage and car payments, most of teenagers' spending is discretionary, an appealing fact for many savvy entrepreneurs looking to connect with this target market. The teen market also is important to businesses because teenagers exert strong influence over family purchases and tend to be early adopters of products and services that set societal trends. (Who were the early adopters of iPods? Teens.) "Young consumers are a very important market," explains Mike Gatti, a top manager at the Retail Advertising and Marketing Association. "Young people have their own money and make their own buying decisions, and they are growing more important as society changes. Parents are getting more time starved, and they treat their children more like adults than previous generations of parents did."[16]

Firefly Mobile, a cell phone company based in Lincolnshire, Illinois, markets its Firefly cell phone squarely at kids, billing it as "the mobile phone for mobile kids." Recognizing that kids today could use cell phones to keep in touch with the important people in their lives, company founder Don Deubler came up with the idea for a cell phone tailored specifically for kids, one that is easier to use than a cell phone designed for adults and would give parents more control over its use. Working directly with kids, Deubler came up with a clever design. For instance, the Firefly has no keypad like a traditional cell phone. Instead, it has just five simple buttons, and parents can program the phone to make and accept calls for up to 20 numbers of their choice (avoiding teenage pranks such as calling Australia to see what the temperature is). The Firefly is proving to be popular with dual-career couples with hectic schedules and with parents who are concerned about their children's safety. To make the phone appealing to the kids using it, Firefly has incorporated cool colors, lights, sounds, and animations (with input from customers) into its design.[17]

Defining a company's target market involves using the techniques described in more detail in Chapter 6, "Building a Marketing Plan," but a business plan should address the following questions:

- Who are my target customers (age, gender, income level, and other demographic characteristics)?
- Where do they live, work, and shop?
- How many potential customers are in my company's trading area?
- Why do they buy? What needs and wants drive their purchase decisions?
- What can my business do to meet those needs and wants better than my competitors?
- Knowing my customers needs, wants, and habits, what should be the basis for differentiating my business in their minds?

Proving that a profitable market exists involves two steps: showing customer interest and documenting market claims.

Showing Customer Interest An entrepreneur must be able to prove that his or her target customers need or want his or her good or service and are willing to pay for it. Two of the most reliable techniques involve building a working prototype of a product so that customers can see how it works and producing a small number of products so that customers can actually use them. An entrepreneur might offer a prototype or an actual product to several potential customers to get written testimonials and evaluations to show investors. Another way to get useful feedback is to sell the product to several customers at a discount. This would prove that there are potential customers for the product and would allow demonstrations of the product in operation. Getting a product into customers' hands early in the process is also an excellent way to get valuable feedback that can lead to significant design improvements and increased sales down the road.

Documenting Market Claims Too many business plans rely on vague generalizations such as, "This market is so huge that if we get just 1 percent of it, we will break even in 8 months." Statements such as this are not backed by facts and usually reflect an entrepreneur's unbridled optimism. In most cases, they are also unrealistic! Market share determination is not obtained by a "shoot from the hip" generalization; on the contrary, sophisticated investors expect to see research that supports the claims an entrepreneur makes about the market potential of a product or service.

Providing facts about the sales potential of a product or service requires market research. Results of market surveys, customer questionnaires, and demographic studies lend credibility to an entrepreneur's frequently optimistic sales projections. (You will learn more about market research techniques and resources in Chapter 7, "Building a Guerrilla Marketing Plan.")

Spin Clean

To gather data for their business plan, Joe Robertson and Dave Dudley decided to put their invention, the Spin Clean, a device that uses water pressure to clean swimming pool filters quickly and easily, into customers' hands and get their responses. After refining the design with several prototypes, Robertson and Dudley built a small number of the products and convinced seven nearby pool supply stores to carry them. The Spin Clean sold out quickly, and the entrepreneurs had the facts to prove that their product had real sales potential.[18]

One of the goals of this section of the business plan is to lay the foundation for the financial forecasts that come later in the plan. A start-up company's financial forecasts must be based on more than just wishful thinking. As much as possible, they should be built on research and facts. Many entrepreneurs build financial models for their potential business by applying information collected from trade or professional associations, local chambers of commerce, articles in magazines and newspapers, market studies conducted by themselves or others, government agencies, and, of course, the Web. With the availability of this volume of information, the sales, cost, and net income projections in a business plan should be a great deal more accurate than sketchy estimates scribbled on the backs of napkins.

This section of the business plan should address the following topics:

Advertising. Once an entrepreneur defines her or his company's target market, she or he can design a promotion and advertising campaign to reach those customers most effectively and efficiently. Which media are most effective in reaching the target market? How will they be used? How much will the promotional campaign cost? How can the company benefit from publicity?

Market size and trend. How large is the potential market? Is it growing or shrinking? Why? Are the customer's needs changing? Are sales seasonal? Is demand tied to another product or service?

Location. For many businesses, choosing the right location is a key success factor. For retailers, wholesalers, and service companies, the best location usually is one that is most convenient to their target customers. By combining census data and other market research with digital mapping software, entrepreneurs can locate sites with the greatest concentrations of their customers and the least interference from competitors. Which specific sites put the company in the path of its target customers? Do zoning regulations restrict the use of the site? For manufacturers, the location issue often centers on finding a site near its key raw materials or near its major customers. Using demographic reports and market research to screen potential sites takes the guesswork out of choosing the ideal location for a business.

Pricing. What does the product or service cost to produce or deliver? What is the company's overall pricing strategy? What image is the company trying to create in the market? Will the planned price support the company's strategy and desired image? (See Figure 4.4.) Can it produce a profit? How does the planned price compare to those of similar products or services? Are customers willing to pay it? What price tiers

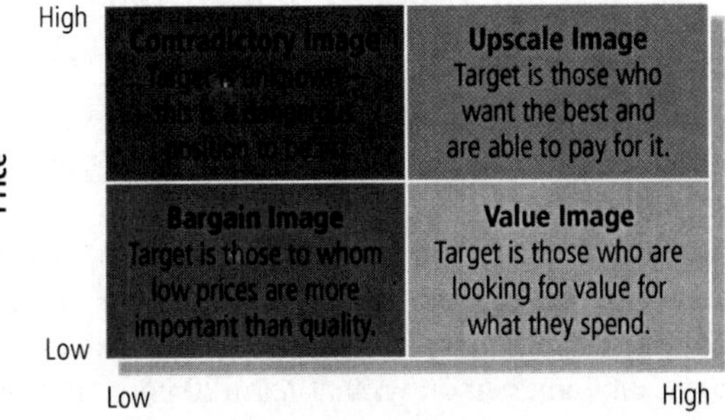

FIGURE 4.4

The Links among Pricing, Perceived Quality, and Company Image

exist in the market? How sensitive are customers to price changes? Will the business sell to customers on credit? Will it accept credit cards?

Distribution. How will the product or service be distributed? What is the average sale? How many sales calls does it take to close a sale? What are the incentives for salespeople? What can the company do to make it as easy as possible for customers to buy?

This portion of the plan also should describe the channels of distribution that the business will use (mail, in-house sales force, sales agent, retailers). The owner should summarize the firm's overall pricing and promotion strategies, including the advertising budget, media used, and publicity efforts. The company's warranties and guarantees for its products and services should be addressed as well.

Competitor Analysis

An entrepreneur should discuss the new venture's competition. Failing to assess competitors realistically makes entrepreneurs appear to be poorly prepared, naive, or dishonest, especially to potential lenders and investors. An analysis of each significant competitor should be presented. Entrepreneurs who believe they have no competitors are only fooling themselves and are raising a huge red flag to potential lenders and investors. Gathering information on competitors' market shares, products, and strategies is usually not difficult. Trade associations, customers, industry journals, marketing representatives, and sales literature are valuable sources of data. This section of the plan should focus on demonstrating that the entrepreneur's company has an advantage over its competitors. Who are the company's key competitors? What are their strengths and weaknesses? What are their strategies? What images do they have in the marketplace? How successful are they? What distinguishes the entrepreneur's product or service from others already on the market, and how will these differences produce a competitive edge? This section of the plan should demonstrate that the firm's strategies are customer focused.

Paper Mojo

Frustrated with her job as a Web-site designer, Shelly Gardner-Alley decided to launch an e-commerce business with her husband. The couple did not have a particular product in mind, so they invested considerable time in researching markets that would be most suitable for e-commerce and would allow them to differentiate their business from the competition. They finally settled on an online business selling high-end, decorative paper from all over the world—ranging from silk paper from Japan to translucent vellum from France—at prices ranging from $2 to $16 per sheet. Before launching their business, Paper Mojo, one of their first tasks was to study their competition. Gardner-Alley discovered that most companies lacked extensive product lines, and she decided to use that as one differentiating point for her business. As a former Web-site designer, Gardner-Alley also noted that the few companies that did have broad product lines suffered from poorly designed Web sites that made shopping a chore for customers. A well-designed Web site that would be easy to navigate became another basis for differentiating her company from the competition. Paper Mojo's sales took off after Gardner-Alley submitted the site to search engine Yahoo!, which featured the new business in a newsletter. Gardner-Alley's extensive research and the decision to build her business model on a platform of outperforming the competition in ways that directly benefit customers are paying off.[19]

Description of the Management Team

The most important factor in the success of a business venture is the quality of its management, and financial officers and investors weigh heavily the ability and experience of the company's managers in their financing decisions. Thus, a plan should describe the qualifications of business officers, key directors, and any person with at least 20 percent ownership in the company. *Remember: Lenders and investors prefer experienced managers.*

A management team with industry experience and a proven record of success goes a long way in adding credibility to the new venture.

Inkwell Fine Arts, LLC

When Jason Henry, Anil Nair, and Heath Seymour wrote the business plan for their company, Inkwell Fine Arts, LLC, a company that sells customized, high-quality art prints to interior designers over the Web, they emphasized the diverse and complementary backgrounds of their management team as well as their business experience. Seymour, an artist, manages the artistic and creative aspects of the business, Henry handles daily operations, and Nair oversees the Web site and the information technology components. With the three founders working in tandem, Inkwell Fine Arts is able to offer interior designers prints made to their specifications—the exact size, colors, and medium they need to decorate a client's living or work space.[20]

Résumés in a plan should summarize each key person's education, work history (emphasizing managerial responsibilities and duties), and relevant business experience. When compiling a personal profile, an entrepreneur should review the primary reasons for small business failure (refer to Chapter 1) and show how the management team will use its skills and experience to avoid them. Entrepreneurs should not cover up previous business failure, however. Failing in business no longer has a terrible stigma attached to it. In fact, many investors are suspicious of entrepreneurs who have never experienced a business failure.

When considering investing in a business, lenders and investors look for the experience, talent, and integrity of the people who will breathe life into the plan. This portion of the plan should show that the company has the right people organized in the right fashion for success. One experienced private investor advises entrepreneurs to remember the following:

- Ideas and products don't succeed; people do. Show the strength of your management team. A top-notch management team with variety of proven skills is crucial.
- Show the strength of key employees and how you will retain them. Most small companies cannot pay salaries that match those at large businesses, but stock options and other incentives can improve employee retention.
- A board of directors or advisers consisting of industry experts lends credibility and can enhance the value of the management team.[21]

Plan of Operation

To complete the description of the business, the owner should construct an organizational chart identifying the business's key jobs and the qualifications of the people occupying them. Assembling a management team with the right stuff is difficult, but keeping it together until the company is established may be harder. Thus, the entrepreneur should describe briefly the steps taken to encourage important officers to remain with the company. Employment contracts, shares of ownership, and perks are commonly used to keep and motivate such employees.

Finally, a description of the form of ownership (partnership, joint venture, S Corporation, LLC) and of any leases, contracts, and other relevant agreements pertaining to the business is helpful. (You will learn more about this topic in Chapter 5, "Organizational Issues and Forms of Ownership.")

Pro Forma (Projected) Financial Statements

One of the most important sections of the business plan is an outline of the proposed company's financial statements—the "dollars and cents" of the proposed venture. In fact, one survey found that 74 percent of bankers say that financial documentation is the most important aspect of a business plan for entrepreneurs seeking loans.[22] For an existing business, lenders and investors use past financial statements to judge the health of the company and its ability to repay loans or generate adequate returns; therefore, an owner should supply copies of the firm's financial statements from the last three years. Ideally, these statements should be audited by a certified public accountant because most financial institutions prefer that extra reliability, although a financial review of the statements by an accountant sometimes may be acceptable.

Whether assembling a plan for an existing business or for a start-up, an entrepreneur should carefully prepare monthly projected (or pro forma) financial statements for the operation for the next year (and for two more years by quarter) using past operating data, published statistics, and research to derive three sets of forecasts of the income statement, balance sheet, cash forecast (always!), and a schedule of planned capital expenditures. (You will learn more about creating projected financial statements in Chapter 10, "Creating a Successful Financial Plan.") The forecasts should cover pessimistic, most likely, and optimistic conditions to reflect the uncertainty of the future. When in doubt, be up front and include some contingencies for any costs that you are unsure about.

It is essential that all three sets of forecasts be realistic. Entrepreneurs must avoid the tendency to "fudge the numbers" just to make their businesses look good. Lenders and investors compare these projections against published industry standards and can detect unrealistic forecasts. In fact, some venture capitalists automatically discount an entrepreneur's financial projections by as much as 50 percent. After completing these forecasts, an entrepreneur should perform a break-even analysis and a ratio analysis on the projected figures.

It is also important to include a statement of the *assumptions* on which these financial projections are based. Potential lenders and investors want to know how an entrepreneur derived forecasts for sales, cost of goods sold, operating expenses, accounts receivable, collections, accounts payable, inventory, taxes, and other items. Spelling out realistic assumptions gives a plan more credibility and reduces the tendency to include overly optimistic estimates of sales growth and profit margins. Greg Martin, a partner in the venture capital company Redpoint Ventures, says, "I have problems with start-ups making unrealistic assumptions—how much money they need or how quickly they can ramp up revenue. Those can really kill a deal for me."[23]

In addition to providing valuable information to potential lenders and investors, projected financial statements help entrepreneurs to run their businesses more effectively and more efficiently after the start-up. They establish important targets for financial performance and make it easier for an entrepreneur to maintain control over routine expenses and capital expenditures.

The Loan or Investment Proposal

The loan or investment proposal section of the business plan should state the purpose of the financing, the amount requested, and the plans for repayment or, in the case of investors, an attractive exit strategy. When describing the purpose of the loan or investment, an entrepreneur must specify the planned use of the funds. General requests for funds using terms such as "for modernization," "working capital," or "expansion" are unlikely to win approval. Instead, entrepreneurs should use more detailed descriptions such as "to modernize production facilities by purchasing five new, more efficient looms that will boost productivity by 12 percent" or "to rebuild merchandise inventory for fall sales peak, beginning in early summer." Entrepreneurs should state the precise amount requested and include relevant backup data, such as vendor estimates of costs or past production levels. Entrepreneurs should not hesitate to request the amount of money needed but should not inflate the amount, anticipating the financial officer to "talk them down." Remember: Lenders and investors are normally very familiar with industry cost structures.

Another important element of the loan or investment proposal is the repayment schedule and exit strategy. A lender's main consideration in granting a loan is the reassurance that the applicant will repay, whereas an investor's major concern is earning a satisfactory rate of return. Financial projections must reflect a company's ability to repay loans and produce adequate returns. Without this proof, a request for funding stands little chance of being approved. It is necessary for the entrepreneur to produce tangible evidence showing the ability to repay loans or to generate attractive returns. "Plan an exit for the investor," advises the owner of a financial consulting company. "Generally, the equity investor's objective with early stage funding is to earn a 30% to 50% annual return over the life of the investment. To enhance the investor's interest in your enterprise, show how they can 'cash out' perhaps through a public offering or acquisition."[24]

Finally, an entrepreneur should have a timetable for implementing the proposed plan. He or she should present a schedule showing the estimated start-up date for the project and noting any significant milestones along the way. Entrepreneurs tend to be optimistic, so document how and why the timetable of events is realistic.

It is beneficial to include an evaluation of the risks of a new venture. Evaluating risk in a business plan requires an entrepreneur to walk a fine line, however. Dwelling too much on everything that can go wrong will discourage potential lenders and investors from financing the venture. Ignoring the project's risks makes those who evaluate the plan tend to believe an entrepreneur to be naïve, dishonest, or unprepared. The best strategy is to identify the most significant risks the venture faces and then to describe the plans the entrepreneur has developed to avoid them altogether or to overcome the negative outcome if the event does occur.

There is a difference between a *working* business plan—the one the entrepreneur is using to guide the business—and the *presentation* business plan—the one he or she is using to attract capital. Although coffee rings and penciled-in changes in a working plan don't matter (in fact, they're a good sign that the entrepreneur is actually using the plan), they have no place on a plan going to someone outside the company. A plan is usually the tool that an entrepreneur uses to make a first impression on potential lenders and investors. To make sure that impression is a favorable one, an entrepreneur should follow these tips:

- Realize that first impressions are crucial. Make sure the plan has an attractive (not necessarily expensive) cover.
- Make sure the plan is free of spelling and grammatical errors and "typos." It is a professional document and should look like one.
- Make it visually appealing. Use color charts, figures, and diagrams to illustrate key points. Don't get carried away, however, and end up with a "comic book" plan.
- Include a table of contents with page numbers to allow readers to navigate the plan easily. Reviewers should be able to look through a plan and quickly locate the sections they want to see.
- Make it interesting. Boring plans seldom get read.
- A plan must prove that the business will make money. In one survey of lenders, investors, and financial advisors, 81 percent said that, first and foremost, a plan should prove that a venture will earn a profit.[25] Start-ups do not necessarily have to be profitable immediately, but sooner or later (preferably sooner), they must make money.
- Use computer spreadsheets to generate financial forecasts. They allow entrepreneurs to perform valuable "what if" (sensitivity) analysis in just seconds.
- *Always* include cash flow projections. Entrepreneurs sometimes focus excessively on their proposed venture's profit forecasts and ignore cash flow projections. Although profitability is important, lenders and investors are much more interested in cash flow because they know that's where the money to pay them back or to cash them out comes from.
- The ideal plan is "crisp," long enough to say what it should but not so long that it is a chore to read.
- Tell the truth. Absolute honesty is always critical when preparing a business plan.

Hands on ... How to

Write a Plan That Will Win You Money

At first, writing a business plan may seem like a daunting task, but like most big projects, the key to success is to take one step at a time. Often the toughest part is getting started! Entrepreneurs who take the time to research and write a business plan discover that, even though the plan itself is extremely useful for launching and managing their businesses and for raising capital, the real value lies in the *process* they go through to create the plan. Preparing a plan gives them a solid foundation from which to run their companies.

Another important use for a business plan is in raising the capital entrepreneurs need to launch their companies, a task that often proves to be quite challenging. How can you write a plan that will attract the capital you need to launch your business? The following tips will help.

Tip #1. Know your audience. As you write your plan, keep in mind your audience. Remember that potential lenders, private investors, venture capitalists, and other potential sources of funds receive hundreds of business plans a year. Most of them fail in two key areas: capturing the reader's attention in a compelling way and spelling out how the business offers customers a product or service that is different or better in some way. Writing a business plan requires entrepreneurs to walk a fine line between being optimistic about the business's market potential and realistically laying out the challenges and the risks involved. None of this matters, of course, if your executive summary fails to hook the reader in the first place. Be sure to invest plenty of time in honing the executive summary so that it communicates the basic business concept and its benefits in just a few sentences or paragraphs.

Tip #2. Know the elements of a business plan. The business plan outline and discussion in this chapter provide you with all of the elements a sound plan should contain. However, the way in which you organize and present them is up to you. Remember that because each entrepreneur and each business idea are unique, each business plan also should be unique. Don't fall into the "cookie-cutter" trap. Cover the topics potential lenders and investors expect to see, but do it in your own style and in a way that is appropriate for your business.

Tip #3. Recognize the importance of strategy to your business success. Experienced lenders and investors know that the real key to building a successful company lies in creating and then executing a sound business strategy. Don't give short shrift to explaining your company's strategy for gaining a competitive edge in the plan. Experienced lenders and investors know that's how a company achieves a sustainable record of success. Too often, entrepreneurs focus on creating financial forecasts without describing the strategies that will enable them to achieve those numbers.

Tip #4. Be thorough but not excessive. Potential lenders and investors want proof that entrepreneurs have done their homework—analyzing the industry, researching their target markets, studying the competition, and covering other important elements of a plan. However, they don't want to wade through a lengthy tome to understand the essence of your business idea. Stay focused as you write, and limit your plan to no more than 40 pages if possible.

Tip #5. Be sure your financial forecasts are realistic. Experienced lenders and investors know that entrepreneurs tend to be optimists and that the financial projections they produce for their business plans also are optimistic. One of the fastest paths to having your business plan rejected is to include financial forecasts that are so optimistic that they are unreasonable. You may want to ask an accountant, a banker, or some other financial expert to review your financial forecasts before presenting your plan to potential lenders and investors.

Tip #6. Explain the exit strategy. Investors, in particular, are in the business of investing in start-up businesses for one reason: to make money when they cash out their ownership in the business. Any plan aimed at potential investors should explain how the company intends for investors to get their money back—preferably with a big return on their investments. Will the company make an initial public offering? Will it look to be bought out by a larger business? Potential lenders want to see evidence that the company will generate sufficient cash flow to be able to repay loans on time.

What Lenders and Investors Look for in a Business Plan

LEARNING OBJECTIVES
4. Explain the "five Cs of credit" and why they are important to potential lenders and investors reading business plans.

Banks usually are not a new venture's sole source of capital because a bank's return is limited by the interest rate it negotiates, but its risk could be the entire amount of the loan if the new business fails. Once a business is operational and has established a financial track record, however, banks become a regular source of financing. For this reason the small business owner needs to be aware of the criteria lenders and investors use when evaluating the creditworthiness of entrepreneurs seeking financing. Lenders and investors refer to these criteria as the **five Cs of credit**: capital, capacity, collateral, character, and conditions.

five Cs of credit
criteria lenders and investors use to evaluate the creditworthiness of entrepreneurs seeking financing: capital, capacity, collateral, character, and conditions.

Capital

A small business must have a stable capital base before any lender is willing to grant a loan. Otherwise the lender would be making, in effect, a capital investment in the business. Most banks refuse to make loans that are capital investments because the potential for return on the investment is limited strictly to the interest on the loan, and the potential loss would probably exceed the reward. In fact, the most common reasons that banks give for rejecting small business loan applications are undercapitalization and too much debt. Banks expect a small company to have an equity base of investment by the owner(s) that will help to support the venture during times of financial strain, which are common during the start-up and growth phases of a business. Lenders and investors see capital as a risk-sharing strategy with entrepreneurs.

Capacity

A synonym for capacity is cash flow. Lenders and investors must be convinced of the firm's ability to meet its regular financial obligations and to repay loans, and that takes cash. In Chapter 9, we will see that more small businesses fail from lack of cash than from lack of profit. It is possible for a company to be showing a profit and still have no cash—that is, to be technically bankrupt. Lenders expect small businesses to pass the test of liquidity, especially for short-term loans. Potential lenders and investors examine closely a small company's cash flow position to decide whether it has the capacity necessary to survive until it can sustain itself.

Collateral

Collateral includes any assets an entrepreneur pledges to a lender as security for repayment of a loan. If the company defaults on the loan, the lender has the right to sell the collateral and use the proceeds to satisfy the loan. Typically, banks make very few unsecured loans (those not backed by collateral) to business start-ups. Bankers view the entrepreneurs' willingness to pledge collateral (personal or business assets) as an indication of their dedication to making the venture a success. A sound business plan can improve a banker's attitude toward a venture.

Character

Before extending a loan to or making an investment in a small business, lenders and investors must be satisfied with an entrepreneur's character. The evaluation of character frequently is based on intangible factors such as honesty, integrity, competence, polish, determination, intelligence, and ability. Although the qualities judged are abstract, this evaluation plays a critical role in the decision to put money into a business or not.

Lenders and investors know that most small businesses fail because of incompetent management, and they try to avoid extending loans to high-risk entrepreneurs. A solid business plan and a polished presentation by the entrepreneur can go far in convincing the banker of the owner's capability.

Conditions

The conditions surrounding a funding request also affect an entrepreneur's chances of receiving financing. Lenders and investors consider factors relating to a business's operation such as potential growth in the market, competition, location, strengths, weaknesses, opportunities, and threats. Again, the best way to provide this relevant information is in a business plan. Another important condition influencing the banker's decision is the shape of the overall economy, including interest rate levels, inflation rate, and demand for money. Although these factors are beyond an entrepreneur's control, they still are an important component in a banker's decision.

The higher a small business scores on these five Cs, the greater its chance will be of receiving a loan. The wise entrepreneur keeps this in mind when preparing a business plan and presentation.

LEARNING OBJECTIVES
5. Describe the keys to making an effective business plan presentation.

Making the Business Plan Presentation

Lenders and investors are favorably impressed by entrepreneurs who are informed and prepared when requesting a loan or investment. When attempting to secure funds from professional venture capitalist or private investors, the written business plan almost always precedes the opportunity to meet face to face. Typically, an entrepreneur's time for presenting her or his business opportunity will be quite limited. (When presenting a plan to a venture capital forum, the allotted time is usually no more than 15 to 20 minutes, and at some forums, the time limit is a mere 5 or 6 minutes.). When the opportunity arises, an entrepreneur must be well prepared. It is important to rehearse, rehearse, and then rehearse more. It is a mistake to begin by leading the audience into a long-winded explanation about the technology on which the product or service is based. Within minutes most of the audience will be lost; and so is any chance the entrepreneur has of obtaining the necessary financing for her or his new venture.

The Presentation

Dick Bardow sat quietly in his car, pondering why he had failed to convince Pat Guinn, managing partner of Next Century Venture Capital, to provide the start-up capital he needed to launch the business that would present his new high-tech medical invention. Bardow had spent the past three-and-a-half years researching and developing the concept, and now that he had a product in hand, he was ready to take it to the market. The idea for Bardow's new venture had been simmering for many years during his stints as a researcher for a major medical lab and as a technical advisor for a medical products company. Bardow had learned a great deal about use of the end product in his technical job, which he took after earning a Master's degree in Biomedical Engineering. But it was during his tenure at the medical lab that Bardow saw the importance of staying on the cutting edge of technology in the field of medicine. He also saw the tremendous profit potential of successful medical products.

Driving home, Bardow replayed his meeting with Guinn in his mind. "How could those venture capitalists have missed the tremendous opportunity right in front of them?" he mused. During his 45-minute meeting with Guinn and her staff, Bardow had spent 30 minutes explaining how the technology had evolved over time, how he had developed the product, and why it was technologically superior to anything on the market. "I've got them where I want then, now," he remembers thinking. "They can't help but see the incredible power of this technology." Throughout his corporate career, Bardow had earned a reputation for his ability to explain abstract ideas and highly technical concepts to his fellow scientists. Over the years, he had made dozens of presentations at scientific professional meeting, all of which were well received.

Bardow had to admit, however, that he was puzzled by all of the questions Guinn had asked him toward the end of their meeting. They weren't at all what he was expecting! "She never asked a single question about my product, its design, the technology behind it, or the patent I have pending," he muttered. He remembered her questioning him about a "market analysis" and how and to whom he planned to market his product. "How foolish!" he thought. "You can't forecast exact sales for a new product. Once this product is on the market and the medical industry sees what it can do, we'll have all the sales we'll need—and more." Bardow was convinced that Guinn simply didn't understand that new, innovative products create their own markets. "I've seen it dozens of times," he said. Dick was beginning to believe that venture capital firms were too focused on revenues, profits, and return on investment. "Don't they know that those things are outcomes?" he thought. "They come . . . in time."

1. Identify the possible problems with Dick Bardow's presentation of his business plan to Pat Guinn and the other venture capitalists.
2. Should potential lenders and investors evaluate new ventures that are based on cutting-edge technology differently from other business ventures? Explain.
3. List at least five suggestions you would make to Dick Bardow to improve his business plan and his presentation of it.

Helpful tips for making a business plan presentation to potential lenders and investors include the following:

- Demonstrate enthusiasm about the venture, but don't be overemotional.
- Know your audience thoroughly, and work to establish a rapport with them.
- "Hook" investors quickly with an up-front explanation of the new venture, its opportunities, and the anticipated benefits to them.
- Hit the highlights; specific questions will bring out the details later. Don't get caught up in too much detail in early meetings with lenders and investors.
- Keep your presentation simple by limiting it to the two or three (no more) major points you must get across to your audience.
- Avoid the use of technological terms that will likely be above most of the audience. Do at least one rehearsal before someone who has no special technical training. Tell that person to stop you anytime he or she does not understand what you are talking about. When this occurs (and it likely will) rewrite that portion of your presentation.
- Use visual aids. They make it easier for people to follow your presentation, but do not make the visual aids the "star" of the presentation. They should merely support and enhance your message.
- Close by reinforcing the nature of the opportunity. Be sure you have sold the benefits the investors will realize when the business is a success.
- Be prepared for questions. In many cases, there is seldom time for a long "Q&A" session, but interested investors may want to get you aside to discuss the details of the plan.
- Follow up with every investor to whom you make a presentation. Don't sit back and wait; be proactive. They have what you need—investment capital. Demonstrate that you have confidence in your plan and have the initiative necessary to run a business successfully.

You Be the Consultant

Battle of the Plans

In 1984, two MBA students at the University of Texas thought that an experience to teach entrepreneurship in the same comprehensive way that "moot court" competitions taught law would be a good idea. They approached some of their professors and soon launched Moot Corp., the country's first business plan competition in which students competed not only for pride but also for start-up capital to launch their businesses. In 1989, the Massachusetts Institute of Technology started the MIT $10K (now $50K) Entrepreneurship Competition, and many other colleges and universities have followed suit with business plan competitions of their own. "In the 1980s and even in the 1990s, putting on a competition like this was a radical concept," says Randy Swangard, director of the New Venture Championship, a business plan competition started in 1991 at Lundquist College.

Today dozens of colleges and universities across the United States sponsor business plan competitions, and it is not uncommon for the winners to attract impressive amounts of venture capital from judges. "I have been amazed at the quality of the plans and the companies coming out of these competitions," says Steve Kaplan of the University of Chicago. One student team that recently won the $20,000 first prize at the University of Pennsylvania's Wharton Business Plan Competition spotted an opportunity in the health care industry based on the research of team leader Dhavel Gosalia, a doctoral student in bioengineering. The team's plan for FibrinX is based on the fact that fish blood clots more readily than mammalian blood. FibrinX plans to market a tissue sealant derived from the blood plasma of the Atlantic salmon that stimulates and enhances the human body's natural blood-clotting process for treating patients with serious injuries or those undergoing surgery. Because fish show no tendencies for transmitting blood-borne diseases such as AIDS and hepatitis, FibrinX's product offers another key advantage: safety.

One winning team at Harvard's business plan competition also went on to launch the company for which they created the plan, Chemdex, an e-commerce site that buys and sells life science products. The young entrepreneurs raised $13 million from one of the nation's best-known venture capital firms and later made a public stock offering . . . and it was only a *runner-up* in the competition! The winning company was an Internet consulting company named Zefer that attracted $100 million in start-up capital, the largest private funding ever for an Internet start-up.

Faculty and students alike find the idea of business plan competitions appealing because they provide an all-encompassing educational experience. As they prepare their plans, students learn a comprehensive set of business skills, ranging from conducting industry and market research and assembling a new venture team to developing realistic financial forecasts and writing mission statements. They also learn valuable skills as they present their plans to panels of judges that often comprise successful entrepreneurs, bankers, venture capitalists, and other business heavy-hitters. "If you want to launch an entrepreneurship program at your business school," advises Gary Cadenhead, director of Moot Corp., "it makes sense to start a business plan competition because students learn topics such as intellectual property and trademarks, venture capital, and guerrilla marketing." Two valuable lessons that often come from business plan competitions are that it takes more than just a good idea to build a successful business venture and that building a business is hard work.

One of the largest business plan competitions is the Venture Bowl, founded by entrepreneur and venture capitalist David Geliebter. Open to any start-up team with a member who is a part-time or full-time student at any college or university in North America, Venture Bowl offers big prize money: $500,000 for first place, $250,000 for second place, and $125,000 each for two third-place finishers. In one recent Venture Bowl competition, Harvard University students Michelle Crames and Jeff Norton beat out hundreds of challengers to take the first-place prize with their business plan for Lean Forward Media, an interactive media company that holds the exclusive home entertainment rights to the Choose Your Own Adventure® series of children's books. "Venture Bowl has been an extraordinary experience for us," says Norton. "It gave us the opportunity to showcase ourselves and our company to a stellar group of judges who provided invaluable advice." Since winning the competition, Crames and Norton have launched Lean Forward with the goal of adapting to DVD the popular books' idea of allowing readers to determine the ending by making decisions for the main character ("you") along the way. "Lean Forward Media is a wonderful example of the entrepreneurial spirits that exists on America's campuses," says Geliebter.

According to one business writer, "Business plan competitions remind would-be entrepreneurs that success requires a solid business plan even more than a bountiful bank balance. Once students have truly learned that business basic, they're not only better prepared to play the entrepreneurial game, they're more likely to end up as winners."

1. If your school does not already have a business plan competition, work with a team of your classmates in a brainstorming session to develop ideas for creating one. What would you offer as a prize? How would you finance the competition? Whom would you invite to judge it? How would you structure the competition?
2. Use the World Wide Web to research business plan competitions at other colleges and universities across the nation. Using the competitions at these schools as benchmarks and the ideas you generated in Question 1, develop a format for a business plan competition at your school.
3. Assume that you are a member of a team of entrepreneurial students competing in a prestigious business plan competition. Outline your team's strategy for winning the competition.

Sources: Adapted from Tricia Bisoux, "Winning Ways," *BizEd*, September/October 2004, pp. 26–32; Suzanne Isack, "Search for Next Google on America's College Campuses," The National Institute for Entrepreneurship, May 12, 2004, pp.1–2; Nichole L. Torres, "Planning for Gold," *Entrepreneur B.Y.O.B.*, November 2004, pp. 112–118; Marc Ballon, "MIT Springboard Sends Internet Company Aloft," *Inc.*, December 1998, pp. 23–25; MIT $50K Entrepreneurship Competition, http://www.50k.mit.edu/; Alex Frankel, "Battle of the Business Plans," *Forbes ASAP*, August 23, 1999, pp. 22–24; Michael Warshaw, "The Best Business Plan on the Planet," *Inc.*, August 1999, pp. 80–90; "Eight Great Business Plans, But Only One Is the Winner," Knowledge@Wharton, May 5, 2005, http://www.knowledge.wharton.upenn.edu/index.cfm?fa=printArticle&ID=1190.

Conclusion

Although there is no guarantee of success when launching a business, the best way to insure against failure is create a business plan. A good plan serves as an entrepreneurial strategic compass that keeps a business on course as it travels into an uncertain future. In addition, a solid plan is essential to raising the capital needed to start a business; lenders and investors demand it. It is absolutely essential for the business plan to be built on facts and realistic assumptions. Nothing destroys an entrepreneur's credibility faster than a document or presentation that lacks substance and is viewed by potential investors as a complete fabrication or an exercise in wishful thinking.

Business Plan Format

Although every company's business plan will be unique, reflecting its individual circumstances, certain elements are universal. The following outline summarizes these components:

I. Executive Summary (not to exceed two pages)
- **A.** Company name, address, and phone number
- **B.** Name, address, and phone number of all key people
- **C.** Brief description of the business, its products and services, and the customer problems they solve
- **D.** Brief overview of the market for your products and services
- **E.** Brief overview of the strategies that will make your firm a success
- **F.** Brief description of the managerial and technical experience of key people
- **G.** Brief statement of the financial request and how the money will be used
- **H.** Charts or tables showing highlights of financial forecasts

II. Vision and Mission Statement
- **A.** Entrepreneur's vision for the company
- **B.** "What business are we in?"
- **C.** Values and principles on which the business stands
- **D.** What makes the business unique? What is the source of its competitive advantage?

III. Company History (for existing businesses only)
- **A.** Company founding
- **B.** Financial and operational highlights
- **C.** Significant achievements

IV. Business and Industry Profile
- **A.** Industry analysis
  - **1.** Industry background and overview
  - **2.** Significant trends
  - **3.** Growth rate
  - **4.** Key success factors in the industry
- **B.** Outlook for the future stages of growth (start-up, growth, maturity)
- **C.** Company goals and objectives
  - **1.** Operational
  - **2.** Financial
  - **3.** Other

V. Business Strategy
- **A.** Desired image and position in market
- **B.** SWOT analysis
  - **1.** Strengths
  - **2.** Weaknesses
  - **3.** Opportunities
  - **4.** Threats
- **C.** Competitive strategy
  - **1.** Cost leadership
  - **2.** Differentiation
  - **3.** Focus

VI. Company Products and Services
- **A.** Description
  - **1.** Product or service features
  - **2.** Customer benefits
  - **3.** Warranties and guarantees
  - **4.** Uniqueness
- **B.** Patent or trademark protection
- **C.** Description of production process (if applicable)
  - **1.** Raw materials
  - **2.** Costs
  - **3.** Key suppliers
- **D.** Future product or service offerings

VII. Marketing Strategy
- **A.** Target market
  - **1.** Complete demographic profile
  - **2.** Other significant customer characteristics
- **B.** Customers' motivation to buy
- **C.** Market size and trends
  - **1.** How large is the market?
  - **2.** Is it growing or shrinking? How fast?

- **D.** Advertising and promotion
  - **1.** Media used—reader, viewer, listener profiles
  - **2.** Media costs
  - **3.** Frequency of usage
  - **4.** Plans for generating publicity
- **E.** Pricing
  - **1.** Cost structure
    - **a.** Fixed
    - **b.** Variable
  - **2.** Desired image in market
  - **3.** Comparison against competitors' prices
- **F.** Distribution strategy
  - **1.** Channels of distribution used
  - **2.** Sales techniques and incentives

VIII. Location and Layout

- **A.** Location
  - **1.** Demographic analysis of location versus target customer profile
  - **2.** Traffic count
  - **3.** Lease/rental rates
  - **4.** Labor needs and supply
  - **5.** Wage rates
- **B.** Layout
  - **1.** Size requirements
  - **2.** Americans with Disabilities Act compliance
  - **3.** Ergonomic issues
  - **4.** Layout plan (suitable for an Appendix)

IX. Competitor Analysis

- **A.** Existing competitors
  - **1.** Who are they? Create a competitive profile matrix.
  - **2.** Strengths
  - **3.** Weaknesses
- **B.** Potential competitors: companies that might enter the market
  - **1.** Who are they?
  - **2.** Impact on your business if they enter

X. Description of Management Team

- **A.** Key managers and employees
  - **1.** Their backgrounds
  - **2.** Experience, skills, and know-how they bring to the company
- **B.** Résumés of key managers and employees (suitable for an Appendix)

XI. Plan of Operation

- **A.** Form of ownership chosen and reasoning
- **B.** Company structure (organization chart)
- **C.** Decision-making authority
- **D.** Compensation and benefits packages

XII. Financial Forecasts (suitable for an Appendix)

- **A.** Financial statements
  - **1.** Income statement
  - **2.** Balance sheet
  - **3.** Cash flow statement
- **B.** Break-even analysis
- **C.** Ratio analysis with comparison to industry standards (most applicable to existing businesses)

XIII. Loan or Investment Proposal
- **A.** Amount requested
- **B.** Purpose and uses of funds
- **C.** Repayment or "cash-out" schedule (exit strategy)
- **D.** Timetable for implementing plan and launching the business

XIV. Appendices—Supporting documentation, including market research, financial statements, organization charts, resumes, and other items.

Chapter Summary by Learning Objectives

1. Discuss the steps involved in subjecting a business idea to a feasibility analysis.

A feasibility analysis consists of three interrelated components: an industry and market feasibility analysis, a product or service feasibility analysis, and a financial feasibility analysis. The goal of the feasibility analysis is to determine whether an entrepreneur's idea is a viable foundation for creating a successful business.

2. Explain why every entrepreneur should create a business plan, as well as the benefits of developing a plan.

A business plan serves two essential functions. First and most important, it guides the company's operations by charting its future course and devising a strategy for following it. The second function of the business plan is to attract lenders and investors. Applying for loans or attempting to attract investors without a solid business plan rarely attracts needed capital

Preparing a sound business plan clearly requires time and effort, but the benefits greatly exceed the costs. Building the plan forces a potential entrepreneur to look at her or his business idea in the harsh light of reality. It also requires the owner to assess the venture's chances of success more objectively. A well-assembled plan helps prove to outsiders that a business idea can be successful.

The *real* value in preparing a business plan is not so much in the plan itself as it is in the process the entrepreneur goes through to create the plan. Although the finished product is useful, the process of building a plan requires an entrepreneur to subject her or his idea to an objective, critical evaluation. What the entrepreneur learns about the company, its target market, its financial requirements, and other factors can be essential to making the venture a success.

3. Describe the elements of a solid business plan.

Although a business plan should be unique and tailor-made to suit the particular needs of a small company, it should cover these basic elements: an executive summary, a mission statement, a company history, a business and industry profile, a description of the company's business strategy, a profile of its products or services, a statement explaining its marketing strategy, a competitor analysis, owners' and officers' résumés, a plan of operation, financial data, and the loan or investment proposal.

4. Explain the "five Cs of credit" and why they are important to potential lenders and investors reading business plans.

Small business owners needs to be aware of the criteria bankers use in evaluating the credit-worthiness of loan applicants—the five Cs of credit: capital, capacity, collateral, character, and conditions.

Capital—Lenders expect small businesses to have an equity base of investment by the owner(s) that will help to support the venture during times of financial strain.

Capacity—A synonym for capacity is cash flow. The bank must be convinced of the firm's ability to meet its regular financial obligations and to repay the bank loan, and that takes cash.

Collateral—Collateral includes any assets the owner pledges to the bank as security for repayment of the loan.

Character—Before approving a loan to a small business, the banker must be satisfied with the owner's character.

Conditions—The conditions—interest rates, the health of the nation's economy, industry growth rates, and so on—surrounding a loan request also affect the owner's chance of receiving funds.

5. Describe the keys to making an effective business plan presentation.

Lenders and investors are favorably impressed by entrepreneurs who are informed and prepared when requesting a loan or investment.

Tips include: Demonstrate enthusiasm about the venture, but don't be overemotional; "hook" investors quickly with an up-front explanation of the new venture, its opportunities, and the anticipated benefits to them; use visual aids; hit the highlights of your venture; don't get caught up in too much detail in early meetings with lenders and investors; avoid the use of technological terms that will likely be above most of the audience; rehearse your presentation before giving it; close by reinforcing the nature of the opportunity; and be prepared for questions.

Discussion Questions

1. Explain the steps involved in conducting a feasibility analysis.
2. Why should an entrepreneur develop a business plan?
3. Describe the major components of a business plan.
4. How can an entrepreneur seeking funds to launch a business convince potential lenders and investors that a market for the product or service really does exist?
5. How would you prepare to make a formal presentation of your business plan to a venture capital forum?
6. What are the 5 Cs of credit? How does a potential lender use them to evaluate a loan request?

Business Plan Pro

Business PlanPro This chapter on the creation of a successful business plan is designed to test your business concept. The following exercises will assist you in validating or challenging your business concept. You will also begin to work through the situation analysis part of your plan to better understand your market. Be as objective as possible as you work through these exercises. Rely on your ability to gather information and make realistic assessments and projections as the exercises require.

Business Plan Exercises

On the Web

Go to http://www.prenhall.com/scarborough to the Business Plan Resource tab. If you have not done this yet, find the Standard Industry Classification (SIC) Code associated with your industry. You will find a link in the SIC Code information that will connect you to a resource to help you do that. Explore the information and links that are available to you on that site to learn more about the size of the industry and its growth, trends, and issues. Based on the industry you have selected and the associated SIC code, apply Porter's five forces model. Consider the five forces—the bargaining power of buyers, the power of suppliers, the threat of new entrants, the threat of substitute products, and the level of rivalry. Again, you will find additional information on Porter's five forces model in the "Strategy" section of this same site. Look for information on the Web that may assist you with this analysis. Based on this information, how attractive do you consider this industry? How would you assess the opportunity this industry presents? Does this information encourage you to become involved in this industry, or does it highlight significant challenges?

In the Software

Your text may have come with Business Feasibility Analysis Pro. This software is designed to take you through the essential steps of assessing the feasibility of your business concept. It addresses the overall feasibility of your product or service, helps you to conduct an industry assessment, reviews your management skills, and steps through a preliminary financial analysis. The software provides "feedback" based on your input through four components of the feasibility analysis with a numerical assessment. You can then export this information directly into Business Plan Pro.

Business Plan Pro will also be a good resource to help you assess the feasibility of your business concept in the areas of product, service, market organization, and financial feasibility. For example, you can enter the initial capital requirements for the business in the start-up and expenses section. Your sales forecast will help to predict the revenue that may be generated, and this will help to determine your return on investment. If you have these estimates available, enter those into your plan. Based on that information, refer to the Profit and Loss statement. At what point, if any, does that statement indicate that your venture will begin generating a profit based on those forecasts and expenses. In what year does that occur? Do you find that amount of time acceptable? If you are seeking investors, will they find that timeframe acceptable? Is the return on investment promising, and does this venture merit taking on the associated level of risk? We will talk more about these sections of your plan as you progress through the chapters.

Sample Plans

Review the start-up sample plans called "IntelliChild.com" and "Fantastic Florals."

1. What was the total amount of the start-up investment for each of these plans?
2. At one point—in months or years—did the plan indicate that it would begin making a profit?
3. What was the total profit that was projected in the year following this point?
4. Based on the break-even point, which of these ventures do you find most attractive?
5. Based the projections by year three, which plan appears to offer the greatest financial potential?
6. How does the scale and potential of these two opportunities compare to those in your plan?

Building Your Business Plan

Review the information in Market Analysis section. Continue to build your information in this section based on the outline. Now, go to Sales Strategy section and you will find information to help you to project your expenses. You may enter your numbers in the table itself or use the Wizard that will pop up to assist you with this process. You can manipulate the visual graph to build that forecast based on a visual growth curve or enter the actual data. If your business is a start-up venture, your expenses will include those figures along with your ongoing expense projections. At this point, don't worry about the accuracy of your projection. Enter data into the software; you can change those numbers at any time. Look at the Profit and Loss statement. Do you find that acceptable? At what point in time will your business begin making a profit?

As you build your plan, you will want to check to see that the outline and structure of your plan are a good fit to tell your story. Although the outline in Business Plan Pro is not identical to the outline presented in the chapter, by "right clicking" on the outline, you can move, add, and delete any topic you choose to modify the plan you create.

Beyond the Classroom . . .

1. Contact a local entrepreneur who recently launched a business. Did he or she prepare a business plan before starting the company? Why or why not? If the entrepreneur did not create a plan, is he or she considering doing so now? If the entrepreneur did create a plan, what benefits did he or she gain from the process? How long did it take to complete the plan? How did he or she put the plan to use during the start-up phase? Does he or she intend to keep the business plan updated? What advice does he or she have to offer another entrepreneur about to begin writing a business plan?
2. Interview a local banker who has experience in making loans to small businesses. Ask him or her the following questions.
   - **A.** How important is a well-prepared business plan?
   - **B.** How important is a smooth presentation?
   - **C.** How does the banker evaluate the owner's character?
   - **D.** How heavily does the bank weigh the five Cs of credit?
   - **E.** What percentage of small business owners are well prepared to request a bank loan?
   - **F.** What are the most common reasons the bank rejects small business loan applications?
3. Interview a small business owner who has requested a bank loan or an equity investment from external sources. Ask him or her these questions:
   - **A.** Did you prepare a written business plan before approaching the financial officer?
   - **B.** If the answer is "yes," did you have outside or professional help in preparing it?
   - **C.** How many times have your requests for additional funds been rejected? What reasons were given for the rejection?

11 Creating a Successful Financial Plan

Volume is vanity; profitability is sanity. —Brad Skelton

It is better to solve problems than crises. —John Guinther

Learning Objectives

On completion of this chapter, you will be able to:

1. Understand the importance of preparing a financial plan.
2. Describe how to prepare the basic financial statements and use them to manage a small business.
3. Create projected (pro forma) financial statements.
4. Understand the basic financial statements through ratio analysis.
5. Explain how to interpret financial ratios.
6. Conduct a break-even analysis for a small company.

LEARNING OBJECTIVES
1. Understand the importance of preparing a financial plan.

financial management
a process that provides entrepreneurs with relevant financial information in an easy-to-read format on a timely basis; it allows entrepreneurs to know not only how their businesses are doing financially, but also why they are performing that way.

Fashioning a well-designed, logical financial plan as part of a comprehensive business plan is one of the most important steps to launching a new business venture. Entrepreneurs who fail to develop workable strategies for earning a profit within a reasonable time eventually will suffer the ultimate business penalty: failure. Potential lenders and investors demand a realistic financial plan before putting their money into a start-up company. More important, a financial plan is a vital tool that helps entrepreneurs to manage their businesses more effectively, steering their way around the pitfalls that cause failures. Proper **financial management** requires putting in place a system that provides entrepreneurs with relevant financial information in an easy-to-read format on a timely basis; it allows entrepreneurs to know not only *how* their businesses are doing financially, but also *why* their companies are performing that way. The information in a small company's financial records is one resource to which competitors have no access. Smart entrepreneurs recognize this and put their companies' numbers to work for them so that they can make their businesses more successful. "Salted away in your accounting records are financial alerts, ways to trim costs, and tips on where profit is hiding," explains one business writer.[1]

Unfortunately, failure to collect and analyze basic financial data is a common mistake among entrepreneurs. According to one survey, one-third of all entrepreneurs run their companies *without any kind of financial plan.*[2] Another study found that only 11 percent of small business owners analyzed their financial statements as part of the managerial planning and decision-making process.[3] To reach profit objectives, entrepreneurs must be aware of their firms' overall financial position and the changes in financial status that occur over time. Most accounting experts advise entrepreneurs to use one of the popular computerized small business accounting programs such as QuickBooks, Peachtree Accounting, Small Business Accounting, Netsuite, and others to manage routine record-keeping tasks. Working with an accountant to set up the system at the outset and then having a trained employee enter the transactions is most efficient for most businesses. These programs make analyzing a company's financial statements, preparing reports, and summarizing data a snap.

This chapter focuses on some very practical tools that will help entrepreneurs to develop a workable financial plan, keep them aware of their company's financial plan, and enable them to plan for profit. They can use these tools to help them anticipate changes and plot an appropriate profit strategy to meet them head on. These profit-planning techniques are not difficult to master, nor are they overly time consuming. We will discuss the techniques involved in preparing projected (pro forma) financial statements, conducting ratio analysis, and performing break-even analysis.

Basic Financial Statements

LEARNING OBJECTIVES
2. Describe how to prepare the basic financial statements and use them to manage a small business.

Before we begin building projected financial statements, it would be helpful to review the basic financial reports that measure a company's financial position: the balance sheet, the income statement, and the statement of cash flows. The level of financial sophistication among small business owners may not be high, but the extent of financial reporting among small businesses is. Most small businesses regularly produce summary financial information, almost all of it in the form of these traditional financial statements.

The Balance Sheet

balance sheet
a financial statement that provides a snapshot of a business's financial position, estimating its worth on a given date; it is built on the fundamental accounting equation: Assets = Liabilities + Owner's equity.

current assets
assets such as cash and other items to be converted into cash within one year or within the company's normal operating cycle.

The **balance sheet** takes a "snapshot" of a business's financial position, providing owners with an estimate of its worth on a given date. Its two major sections show the assets the business owns and the claims creditors and owners have against those assets. The balance sheet is usually prepared on the last day of the month. Figure 11.1 shows the balance sheet for Sam's Appliance Shop for the year ended December 31, 200X.

The balance sheet is built on the fundamental accounting equation: Assets = Liabilities + Owner's equity. Any increase or decrease on one side of the equation must be offset by an increase or decrease on the other side; hence the name *balance sheet.* It provides a baseline from which to measure future changes in assets, liabilities, and equity. The first section of the balance sheet lists the company's assets (valued at cost, not actual market value) and shows the total value of everything the business owns. **Current assets** consist of cash and

FIGURE 11.1

Balance Sheet, Sam's Appliance Shop

Assets		
Current Assets		
Cash		$49,855
Accounts Receivable	$179,225	
Less Allowance for Doubtful Accounts	$6,000	$173,225
Inventory		$455,455
Prepaid Expenses		$8,450
Total Current Assets		$686,985
Fixed Assets		
Land		$59,150
Buildings	$74,650	
Less Accumulated Depreciation	$7,050	$67,600
Equipment	$22,375	
Less Accumulated Depreciation	$1,250	$21,125
Furniture and Fixtures	$10,295	
Less Accumulated Depreciation	$1,000	$9,295
Total Fixed Assets		$157,170
Intangibles (Goodwill)		$3,500
Total Assets		$847,655
Liabilities		
Current Liabilities		
Accounts Payable		$152,580
Notes Payable		$83,920
Accrued Wages/Salaries Payable		$38,150
Accrued Interest Payable		$42,380
Accrued Taxes Payable		$50,820
Total Current Liabilities		$367,850
Long-Term Liabilities		
Mortgage		$127,150
Note Payable		$85,000
Total Long-Term Liabilities		$212,150
Owner's Equity		
Sam Lloyd, Capital		$267,655
Total Liabilities and Owner's Equity		$847,655

items to be converted into cash within one year or within the normal operating cycle of the company, whichever is longer, such as accounts receivable and inventory, and **fixed assets** are those acquired for long-term use in the business. Intangible assets include items such as goodwill, copyrights, and patents that, although valuable, are not tangible.

The second section shows the business's **liabilities**—the creditors' claims against the company's assets. **Current liabilities** are those debts that must be paid within one year or within the normal operating cycle of the company, whichever is longer, and **long-term liabilities** are those that come due after one year. This section of the balance sheet also shows the **owner's equity,** the value of the owner's investment in the business. It is the balancing factor on the balance sheet, representing all of the owner's capital contributions to the business plus all accumulated (or retained) earnings not distributed to the owner(s).

fixed assets
assets acquired for long-term use in a business.

liabilities
creditors' claims against a company's assets.

current liabilities
those debts that must be paid within one year or within the normal operating cycle of a company.

long-term liabilities
liabilities that come due after one year.

owner's equity
the value of the owner's investment in the business.

The Income Statement

income statement (profit and loss statement or "P&L") a financial statement that represents a "moving picture" of a business, comparing its expenses against its revenue over a period of time to show its net profit (or loss).

cost of goods sold the total cost, including shipping, of the merchandise sold during the accounting period.

The **income statement (profit and loss statement or "P&L")** compares expenses against revenue over a certain period of time to show the firm's net profit (or loss). The income statement is a "moving picture" of a firm's profitability over time. The annual P&L statement reports the bottom line of the business over the fiscal/calendar year. Figure 11.2 shows the income statement for Sam's Appliance Shop for the year ended December 31, 200X.

To calculate net profit or loss, an entrepreneur records sales revenues for the year, which includes all income that flows into the business from sales of goods and services. Income from other sources (rent, investments, interest) also must be included in the revenue section of the income statement. To determine net sales revenue, owners subtract the value of returned items and refunds from gross revenue. **Cost of goods sold** represents the total cost, including shipping, of the merchandise sold during the accounting period. Manufacturers, wholesalers, and retailers calculate cost of goods sold by adding purchases

FIGURE 11.2

Income Statement, Sam's Appliance Shop

Net Sales Revenue		$1,870,841
Credit Sales	$1,309,589	
Cash Sales	$561,252	
Cost of Goods Sold		
Beginning Inventory, 1/1/xx	$805,745	
+ Purchases	$939,827	
Goods Available for Sale	$1,745,572	
– Ending Inventory, 12/31/xx	$455,455	
Cost of Goods Sold		$1,290,117
Gross Profit		$580,724
Operating Expenses		
Advertising	$139,670	
Insurance	$46,125	
Depreciation		
Building	$18,700	
Equipment	$9,000	
Salaries	$224,500	
Travel	$4,000	
Entertainment	$2,500	
Total Operating Expenses		$444,495
General Expenses		
Utilities	$5,300	
Telephone	$2,500	
Postage	$1,200	
Payroll Taxes	$25,000	
Total General Expenses		$34,000
Other Expenses		
Interest Expense	$39,850	
Bad Check Expense	$1,750	
Total Other Expenses		$41,600
Total Expenses		$520,095
Net Income		$60,629

to beginning inventory and subtracting ending inventory. Service-providing companies typically have no cost of goods sold because they do not carry inventory.

Net sales revenue minus cost of goods sold results in a company's gross profit. Dividing gross profit by net sales revenue produces the **gross profit margin,** a percentage that every small business owner should watch closely. If a company's gross profit margin slips too low, it is likely that it will operate at a loss (negative net income). Many business owners whose companies are losing money mistakenly believe that the problem is inadequate sales volume; therefore, they focus on pumping up sales at any cost. In many cases, however, the losses their companies are incurring are the result of an inadequate gross profit margin, and pumping up sales only deepens their losses! Repairing a poor gross profit margin requires a company to raise prices, cut manufacturing or purchasing costs, refuse orders with low profit margins, or add new products with more attractive profit margins. Monitoring the gross profit margin over time and comparing it to those of other companies in the same industry are important steps to maintaining a company's long-term profitability.

gross profit margin
gross profit divided by net sales revenue.

Skelton Tomkinson

After evaluating his company's gross profit margin, Brad Skelton, managing director of Skelton Tomkinson, a contract shipper based in Brisbane, Australia, decided to raise prices with the intent of driving away the company's least profitable customers so he could focus on a niche in shipping heavy machinery. Although sales dropped a significant amount initially, they have since rebounded to $20 million per year. The company's niche strategy and its focus on growing its "bottom line" (profits) rather than its "top line" (sales) have paid off handsomely in terms of profitability; Skelton Tomkinson's profits have climbed 98 percent![4]

Operating expenses include those costs that contribute directly to the manufacture and distribution of goods. General expenses are indirect costs incurred in operating the business. "Other expenses" is a catch-all category covering all other expenses that do not fit into the other two categories. Total revenue minus total expenses gives the net income (or loss) for the accounting period. Comparing a company's current income statement to those of prior accounting periods often reveals valuable information about key trends and a company's progress toward its financial goals.

operating expenses
those costs that contribute directly to the manufacture and distribution of goods.

The Statement of Cash Flows

The **statement of cash flows** show the changes in the firm's working capital from the beginning of the year by listing both the sources and the uses of those funds. Many small businesses never need to prepare such a statement, but in some cases creditors, investors, new owners, or the IRS may require this information.

statement of cash flows
a financial statement showing the changes in a company's working capital from the beginning of the year by listing both the sources and the uses of those funds.

To prepare the statement, the owner must assemble the balance sheets and the income statements summarizing the present year's operations. The owner begins with the company's net income for the period (from the income statement), then adds the sources of the company's funds—borrowed funds, owner contributions, decreases in accounts receivable, increases in accounts payable, decreases in inventory, depreciation, and any others. Depreciation is listed as a source of funds because it is a noncash expense that has already been deducted as a cost of doing business. Because the owner has already paid for the item being depreciated, however, its depreciation is a source of funds. Next the owner subtracts the uses of these funds—plant and equipment purchases, dividends to owners, repayment of debt, increases in accounts receivable, decreases in accounts payable, increases in inventory, and so on. The difference between the total sources and the total uses is the increase or decrease in working capital. By investigating the changes in their companies' working capital and the reasons for them, owners can create a more practical financial action plan for the future of the enterprise.

These financial statements are more than just complex documents used only by accountants and financial officers. When used in conjunction with the analytical tools described in the following sections, they can help entrepreneurs to map a firm's financial future and actively plan for profit. Mere preparation of these statement is not enough, however; owners and employees must *understand and use* the information contained in them to make the business more effective and efficient.

You Be the Consultant

CFO-of-the-Day

At 23 years old and just out of college, Maria Mantz had worked for Development Counsellors International (DCI), a New York City public relations firm, for only five months. Yet here she was shuffling spreadsheets and waiting to present the company's monthly financial report to 30 of her colleagues. As she approached the podium, her nervousness abated. "Several accounts had quite an increase in May," she began, pointing out revenue tables she had included in the handouts. She then gestured to a flip chart and asked, "Does anyone know what the five clients listed here have in common?"

"They're all performance-based accounts," said one account executive, referring to clients whose fees are based on performance.

"Right," Mantz replied. "In fact, 20 percent of our billings for May came from performance-based accounts. Is this a good thing or a bad thing?"

The group began to discuss the question, and then Mantz finished her presentation. It was exactly what Andrew Levine, DCI's president, was hoping to see. Levine's goal is to have every DCI employee—from receptionists to president—understand the company's financial statements by presenting them to their colleagues. Each month, a different employee has the responsibility of leading the company's monthly financial meeting to go over the numbers. The CFO-of-the-day provides a breakdown of revenues and expenses, points out trends, launches discussions about everything from cost cutting to energy conservation, and fields questions. At the end of the session, the CFO-of-the-day reveals DCI's bottom line, showing whether the company met its profit goal for the month. It's an important number because every time DCI's retained earnings increases by $100,000, 30 percent of it is distributed among employees in their next paychecks.

DCI, with annual revenues of nearly $4.5 million, began the CFO-of-the-day program in 1996 and has been profitable ever since. In addition to the company's outstanding financial performance, Levine says employee tenure is longer than before the program began—an average of five years, compared to just two and one-half years before. Customer retention rates also are up.

Levine introduced the concept soon after taking over the company from his father, who founded DCI in 1960. Long before the term "open-book management," which refers to business owners sharing the financial results of their companies' performances with employees, was ever coined, Levine began practicing the concept. There was only one problem with the monthly meetings: Employees were bored. "Most of our staffers were poor at math, and here I was talking about statistics and ratios," he says. At one meeting, Levine asked his employees how to calculate a company's profit, and only one worker, receptionist Sergio Barrios, knew the answer. "It was mind-boggling," recalls Levine.

That's when the idea for the CFO-of-the-day hit him. Why not require employees to present the company's financial report at the monthly meetings? To do that, each worker at least would have to learn the basics of financial management. Levine appointed Barrios, the receptionist, as the first CFO-of-the-day, and she did a terrific job of explaining the company's financial statements in a way that any layperson could understand them. Since then, the program has transformed even the most unlikely employees, including Mantz, into financial wizards.

When she first joined the company, Mantz watched her co-workers master DCI's financial statements and soon realized that she could as well. The day before the monthly financial meeting, Mantz spent an hour going over the monthly financial statements with Levine and DCI's controller, Carrie Nepo. Nepo walked Mantz through the financial statements, allowing her to ask questions along the way. The three talked about trends that would form the basis for good discussions at the meeting. Mantz then took four spreadsheets and spent another hour reviewing the company's financial statements on her own. The next morning, Mantz performed a "dress rehearsal" of her presentation before Levine and Nepo before making her presentation to her co-workers that afternoon.

"It's a good way to learn how things add up," says Mantz. "I understand things much better now that I've done it." One benefit is that employees see exactly how their daily decisions and actions have an impact on the company's financial performance—and on their own compensation. Levine sees evidence that employees care more about revenues and expenses when they understand their impact on the company's financial statements and when they have a stake in the company's profits. DCI's profit-sharing program is integrally linked to the success of its open-book management style. Levine keeps things simple, using the analogy of a bucket being filled with sand. Every time DCI's profits reach the brim, employees receive 30 percent of the bucket in their next checks.

DCI reaps other benefits as well. "I'm a new, young employee," says Mantz. "I'm being trained not only as a PR executive but also as a business executive."

1. Use the resources of the World Wide Web to research open-book management. Discuss the benefits of open-book management for the companies using it and for employees of those companies.
2. What factors are necessary to the success of an open-book management program such as the one DCI uses? What are the risks associated with open-book management?
3. Why don't more small businesses use open-book management?

Source: Adapted from Nadine Heintz, "Everyone's a CFO," *Inc.*, September 2005, pp. 42–44.

Creating Projected Financial Statements

LEARNING OBJECTIVES
3. Create projected (pro forma) financial statements.

Creating projected financial statements helps the small business owner to transform business goals into reality. Budgets answer such questions as: What profit can the business expect to earn? If the owner's profit objective is x dollars, what sales level must the company achieve? What fixed and variable expenses can be expected at that level of sales? The answers to these and other questions are critical in formulating a functional financial plan for the small business.

This section will focus on creating projected income statements and balance sheets for a small start-up. These projected (or pro forma) statements are a crucial component of every business plan because they estimate the profitability and the overall financial condition of a company in the future. They are an integral part of convincing potential lenders and investors to provide the financing needed to get the company off the ground (the topic of Chapter 13). In addition, because these statements project a company's financial position through the end of the forecasted period, they help entrepreneurs to plan the route to improved financial strength and healthy business growth. To be useful, however, these forecasts must be *realistic*! "A business plan is not complete until it contains a set of financial projections that are not only inspiring but also logical and defensible," says one business writer.

Because an established business has a history of operating data from which to construct pro forma financial statements, the task is not nearly as difficult as it is for the beginning business. When creating pro forma financial statements for a brand-new business, an entrepreneur typically relies on published statistics summarizing the operation of similar-size companies in the same industry. These statistics are available from a number of sources (described later), but this section draws on information found in the Risk Management Association's (RMA) *Annual Statement Studies*, a compilation of financial data on nearly 200,000 companies across more than 700 industries organized by Standard Industrial Classification (SIC) Code and North American Industry Classification System (NAICS).

Pro Forma Statements for the Small Business

One of the most important tasks confronting the entrepreneur launching a new enterprise is to determine the amount of funding needed to begin operation as well as the amount required to keep the company going through its initial growth period until it can generate positive cash flow. The amount of money needed to begin a business depends on the type of operation, its location, inventory requirements, sales volume, and many other factors. However, every new firm must have enough capital to cover all start-up costs, including funds to rent or buy plant, equipment, and tools, as well as pay for advertising, wages, licenses, utilities, and other expenses. In addition, entrepreneurs must maintain a reserve of capital to carry the company until it begins to generate positive cash flow. Too often entrepreneurs are overly optimistic in their financial plans and fail to recognize that expenses initially exceed income (and cash outflow exceeds cash inflow) for most small firms. This period of net losses (and negative cash flow) is normal and may last from just a few months to several years. During this time, entrepreneurs must be able to pay the company's regular bills, meet payrolls, maintain adequate levels of inventory, take advantage of cash discounts, grant customers credit, and meet their personal financial obligations.

The Pro Forma Income Statement Although they are projections, financial forecasts must be based in reality; otherwise the resulting financial plan is nothing more than a hopeless dream. When creating a projected income statement, an entrepreneur has two options: to develop a sales forecast and work down or set a profit target and work up. Developing a realistic sales forecast for a business startup is not always easy, but with creativity and research it is possible. Talking with owners of existing businesses in the industry (outside of the local trading area, of course) can provide meaningful insight into the sales levels a company can expect to generate during its early years. For a reasonable fee, entrepreneurs can access published aggregated financial statistics that industry trade associations collect on the companies in their industries. Other organizations, such as the RMA and Dun & Bradstreet, publish useful financial information for a wide range of industries. Web searches and trips to the local library will produce the desired information. Interviews with potential customers and test marketing an actual product or service also can reveal the number of customers a company can expect to attract. Multiplying the number of customers by projected prices yields a revenue estimate. One method for checking the accuracy of a sales revenue estimate is to calculate the revenue other companies in the same industry generate per employee and compare it to your own projected revenue per employee. A value that is out of line with industry standards is not likely to be realistic.

Many entrepreneurs prefer the other method of creating a projected income statement, targeting a profit figure and then "working up" to determine the sales level they must achieve to reach it. Of course, it is important to compare this sales target against the results of the marketing plan to determine whether it is realistic. The next step is to estimate the expenses that the business will incur in securing those sales. In any small business, the annual profit must be large enough to produce a return for time the owners spend operating the business plus a return on their investment in the business.

An entrepreneur who earns less in his or her own business than he or she could earn working for someone else must weigh carefully the advantages and disadvantages of choosing the path of entrepreneurship. Why be exposed to all of the risks, sacrifices, and hard work of beginning and operating a small business if the rewards are less than those of remaining in the secure employment of another? Although there are many nonfinancial benefits of owning a business, the net profit after taxes a company generates should be at least as much as an entrepreneur could earn by working for someone else.

An adequate profit must also include a reasonable return on the owner's total investment in the business. The owner's total investment is the amount contributed to the company at its inception plus any retained earnings (profits from previous years funneled back into the operation). If a would-be owner has $70,000 to invest and can invest it in securities and earn 10 percent, he or she should not consider investing it in a business venture that would yield only 3 percent.

An entrepreneur's target income is the sum of a reasonable salary for the time spent running the business and a normal return on the amount invested in the firm. Determining how much this should be is the first step in creating the pro forma income statement.

An entrepreneur then must translate this target profit into a net sales figure for the forecasted period. To calculate net sales from a target profit, the entrepreneur can use published industry statistics. Suppose an entrepreneur wants to launch a small retail bookstore and has determined that his target net income is $30,000. Statistics gathered from RMA's *Annual Statement Studies* show that the typical bookstore's net profit margin (net profit ÷ net sales) is 7.3 percent. Using this information, he can compute the sales level required to produce a net profit of $30,000:

$$\text{Net profit margin} = \frac{\text{Net profit}}{\text{Net sales (annual)}}$$

$$7.3\% = \frac{\$30{,}000}{\text{Net sales (annual)}}$$

$$\text{Net sales} = \frac{\$30{,}000}{0.073} = \$410{,}959$$

Now this entrepreneur knows that to make a net profit of $30,000 (before taxes), he must achieve annual sales of $410,959. To complete the projected income statement, the owner simply applies the appropriate statistics from *Annual Statement Studies* to the annual sales figure. Because the statistics for each income statement item are expressed as percentages of net sales, he merely multiplies the proper percentage by the annual sales figure to obtain the desired value. For example, cost of goods sold usually comprises 61.4 percent of net sales for the typical small bookstore. So the owner of this new bookstore expects his cost of goods sold to be the following:

$$\text{Cost of goods sold} = \$410{,}959 \times 0.614 = \$252{,}329$$

The bookstore's complete projected income statement is shown as follows:

Net sales	(100%)	$410,959
− Cost of goods sold	(61.4%)	$252,329
Gross profit margin	(38.6%)	$158,630
− Operating expenses	(31.3%)	$128,630
Net profit (before taxes)	(7.3%)	$ 30,000

At this point, the business appears to be a lucrative venture. But remember: this income statement represents a sales goal that the owner may not be able to reach. The next step is to determine whether this required sales volume is reasonable. One useful technique is to break down the required annual sales volume into *daily* sales figures. Assuming the store will be open six days per week for 50 weeks (300 days), we see that the owner must average $1,370 per day in sales:

$$\begin{aligned}\text{Average daily sales} &= \$410{,}959/300 \text{ days}\\ &= 1{,}370 \text{ day}\end{aligned}$$

This calculation gives the owner a better perspective of the sales required to yield an annual profit of $30,000.

To determine whether the profit expected from the business will meet or exceed the target income, the entrepreneur should also create an income statement based on a realistic sales estimate. The previous analysis shows an entrepreneur the sales level needed to reach a desired profit. But what happens if sales are lower? Higher? The entrepreneur requires a reliable sales forecast using the market research techniques described in Chapter 6.

Suppose, for example, that after conducting a marketing survey of local customers and talking with nearby business owners, the prospective bookstore operator projects annual sales for the proposed business to be only $385,000. The entrepreneur must take this expected sales figure and develop a pro forma income statement:

Net Sales	(100%)	$385,000
− Cost of Goods Sold	(61.4%)	$236,390
Gross Profit Margin	(38.6%)	$148,610
− Operating Expenses	(31.3%)	$ 83,505
Net Profit (before taxes)	(7.3%)	$ 28,105

Based on sales of $385,000, this entrepreneur should expect a net income (before taxes) of $28,105. If this amount is acceptable as a return on the investment of time and money in the business, he should proceed with his planning.

At this stage in developing the financial plan, the owner should create a more detailed picture of the venture's expected operating expenses. One common method is to use the operating statistics data found in *Dun & Bradstreet's Cost of Doing Business* reports. These booklets document typical selected operating expenses (expressed as a percentage of net sales) for 190 different lines of businesses. Contacting potential vendors, suppliers, and providers to get estimates of expenses increases the accuracy of the expected expenses on a projected income statement. One entrepreneur who was preparing a business plan for the launch of an upscale women's clothing store contacted local utility companies, insurance agencies, radio and television stations, and other vendors to get estimates of her utility, insurance, advertising, and other general expenses.

To ensure that no business expenses have been overlooked in preparing the business plan, entrepreneurs should list all of the expenses they will incur and have an accountant review the list. Sometimes in their estimates of expenses entrepreneurs neglect to include salaries for themselves, which immediately raises a red flag among lenders and investors. Without drawing a salary, how will an entrepreneur pay his or her personal bills? At the other extreme, lenders and investors frown on exorbitantly high salaries for owners of business start-ups. Typically, salaries are not the best use of cash in a start-up; one guideline is to draw a salary that is about 25 to 30 percent below the market rate for a similar position (and to make adjustments from there if conditions warrant). In addition, as the company grows, executive salaries should be among the *last* expenses to be increased. Reinvesting the extra money back into the company for essentials will accelerate its growth rate even more.

Smart Furniture

When Stephen Culp created the financial plan for his company, Smart Furniture, he decided to draw no salary for the first three years in business, choosing instead to live off of his savings. He invested that money in the business, and it paid off.

Stephen Culp, who in 2001 started Smart Furniture, a Chattanooga, Tennessee-based modular furniture company, drew no salary at all for his first three years in business, choosing instead to live very frugally off of his personal savings. Culp planned his company this way from the outset, using the money he could have drawn as his salary to hire two employees who played key roles in tripling the company's sales in just three years. "It's a prioritization of cash flow," explains Culp. "If I can survive on cereal and take all that cash that I would have spent on a more extravagant lifestyle and put it back into the company, it increases my chances of success." Culp's plan called for attracting venture capital to accelerate his company's growth, and he knew that he would have to include a salary for himself before approaching venture capital firms. Culp researched the industry and talked with colleagues to determine a reasonable salary, discounted that number by 30 percent, and came up with a salary of less than $100,000. "I'm still trying to show investors that I'm in this for the long haul," he says.[5]

Figures 11.3 and 11.4 show two useful forms designed to help entrepreneurs estimate both monthly and start-up expenses. Totals derived from this list of expenses should approximate the total expense figures calculated from published statistics. Naturally, entrepreneurs should be more confident in their own list of expenses because they reflect their company's particular set of circumstances.

The Pro Forma Balance Sheet In addition to projecting a small company's net profit or loss, an entrepreneur must develop a pro forma balance sheet outlining the fledgling firm's assets and liabilities. Most entrepreneurs' primary concern is profitability because, on the surface, the importance of a business's assets is less obvious. In many cases, small companies begin their lives on weak financial footing because entrepreneurs fail to

Worksheet No. 2
Estimated Monthly Expenses

Your estimate of monthly expenses based on sales of $ _______ per year.
Your estimate of how much cash you need to start your business (see column 3).
What to put in column 2. (These figures are typical for one kind of business. You will have to decide how many months to allow for in your business.)

Item	Column 1	Column 2	Column 3
Salary of owner-manager	$	$	2 times column 1
All other salaries and wages			3 times column 1
Rent			3 times column 1
Advertising			3 times column 1
Delivery expense			3 times column 1
Supplies			3 times column 1
Telephone and telegraph			3 times column 1
Other utilities			3 times column 1
Insurance			Payment required by insurance company
Taxes, including Social Security			4 times column 1
Interest			3 times column 1
Maintenance			3 times column 1
Legal and other professional fees			3 times column 1
Miscellaneous			3 times column 1
Starting Costs You Have to Pay Only Once			Leave column 2 blank
Fixtures and equipment			Fill in worksheet 3 and put the total here
Decorating and remodeling			Talk it over with a contractor
Installation of fixtures and equipment			Talk to suppliers from whom you buy these
Starting inventory			Suppliers will probably help you estimate this
Deposits with public utilities			Find out from utilities companies
Legal and other professional fees			Lawyer, accountant, and so on
Licenses and permits			Find out from city offices what you have to have
Advertising and promotion of opening			Estimate what you'll use
Accounts receivable			What you need to buy more stock until credit customers pay
Cash			For unexpected expenses or losses, special purchases, etc.
Other			Make a separate list and enter total
Total Estimated Cash You Need To Start		$	Add up all the numbers in column 2

FIGURE 11.3

Anticipated Expenses

Source: U.S. Small Business Administration, *Checklist for Going into Business.* (Small Marketers Aid No. 71) (Washington, DC, 1982), pp. 6–7.

FIGURE 11.4

Anticipated Expenditures for Fixtures and Equipment

Source: U.S. Small Business Administration, *Checklist for Going into Business* (Small Marketers Aid No. 71) (Washington, DC: Author, 1982), pp. 6–7.

Worksheet No. 3
List of Furniture, Fixtures, and Equipment

Leave out or add items to suit your business. Use separate sheets to list exactly what you need for each of the items below.	If you plan to pay cash in full, enter the full amount below and in the last column.	If you are going to pay by installments, fill out the columns below. Enter in the last column your down payment plus at least one installment.			Estimate of the cash you need for furniture, fixtures, and equipment.
		Price	Down payment	Amount of each installment	
Counters	$	$	$	$	$
Storage shelves, cabinets					
Display stands, shelves, tables					
Cash register					
Safe					
Window display fixtures					
Special lighting					
Outside sign					
Delivery equipment if needed					
Total furniture, fixtures, and equipment (Enter this figure also in worksheet 2 under "Starting Costs You Have to Pay Only Once.")					$

determine their firms' total asset requirements. To prevent this major oversight, entrepreneurs should prepare a projected balance sheet listing every asset their businesses will need and all the claims against these assets.

Assets. Cash is one of the most useful assets the business owns; it is highly liquid and can quickly be converted into other tangible assets. But how much cash should a small business have at its inception? Obviously, there is no single dollar figure that fits the needs of every small firm. One practical rule of thumb, however, suggests that a company's cash balance should cover its operating expenses (less depreciation, a noncash expense) for at least one inventory turnover period. Using this guideline, the cash balance for the small bookstore is calculated as follows:

Operating expenses = \$158,630 (from projected income statement)
Less: depreciation (1.4% of annual sales*) of \$5,753
Equals: cash expenses (annual) = \$152,877
Annual inventory turnover ratio* = 3.6 times per year

$$\text{Cash requirement} = \frac{\text{Cash expenses}}{\text{Average inventory turnover ratio}}$$

$$= \frac{\$152{,}877}{3.6}$$

$$= \$42{,}466$$

*From Risk Management Association, *Annual Statement Studies.*

Notice the inverse relationship between the small firm's average turnover ratio and its cash requirement. The smaller the number of inventory turns a company generates, the higher is its cash requirement.

Another decision facing the entrepreneur is how much inventory the business should carry. A rough estimate of the inventory requirement can be calculated from the information found on the projected income statement and from published statistics:

$$\text{Cost of goods sold} = \$252{,}329 \text{ (from projected income statement)}$$

$$\text{Average inventory turnover} = \frac{\text{Cost of goods sold}}{\text{Inventory level}} = 3.6 \text{ times per year}$$

Substituting, we obtain

$$3.6 \text{ times per year} = \frac{\$252{,}329}{\text{Inventory level}}$$

Solving for the inventory level gives

$$\text{Inventory level} = \$70{,}091$$

Entrepreneurs can use the planning forms shown in Figures 11.3 and 11.4 to estimate fixed assets (land, building, equipment, and fixtures). Suppose the estimate of fixed assets is as follows:

Fixtures	$27,500
Office equipment	4,850
Computers/cash register	3,125
Signs	6,200
Miscellaneous	1,500
Total	**$43,175**

Liabilities. To complete the projected balance sheet, the owner must record all of the small firm's liabilities—the claims against its assets. The bookstore owner was able to finance 50 percent of the inventory and fixtures ($48,796) through suppliers and has a short-term note payable in the amount of $3,750. The only other major claim against the firm's assets is a note payable to the entrepreneur' father-in-law for $40,000. The difference between the company's assets ($157,532) and its total liabilities ($92,546) represents the owner's investment in the business (owner's equity) of $64,986.

The final step is to compile all of these items into a projected balance sheet, as shown in Figure 11.5.

Assets		Liabilities	
Current Assets		**Current Liabilities**	
Cash	$ 42,466	Accounts Payable	$ 48,796
Inventory	70,091	Note Payable	3,750
Miscellaneous	1,800		
Total Current Assets	$114,357	Total Current Liabilities	$ 52,546
Fixed Assets		**Longs-Term Liabilities**	
Fixtures	$ 27,500	Note Payable	$ 40,000
Office Equipment	4,850		
Computer/Cash Register	3,125	Total Liabilities	$ 92,546
Signs	6,200		
Miscellaneous	1,500		
Total Fixed Assets	$ 43,175	**Owner's Equity**	$ 64,986
Total Assets	$157,532	**Total Liabilities and Owner's Equity**	$157,532

FIGURE 11.5

Projected Balance Sheet for a Small Bookstore

Source: U.S. Small Business Administration, *Checklist for Going into Business* (Small Marketers Aid No. 71) (Washington, DC: Author, 1982), p. 12.

You Be the Consultant

The Choice Is Yours

It's a common trap that catches many entrepreneurs: the pursuit of growth at all costs. Rather than see the many contributions their businesses make to the local community and the accomplishments they have achieved, entrepreneurs often have a nagging sense of inadequacy. No matter how successful they may appear to be, it's never quite enough. After 19 years in business, Jay Goltz, the owner of highly successful picture framing business with $7 million in sales and 75 employees, compared his business to those of Richard Branson and Michael Dell and concluded that his company was "dinky." That set him off on a drive for growth, diversification, and expansion that nearly ruined his personal life and put his successful business in peril. Then, at a retirement party for one of his employees, the guest of honor turned to Goltz in front of everyone and thanked him for all he had done for her and her co-workers over the years. It was then that Goltz realized that he did not have to build a billion-dollar company like Dell's and Branson's to be considered a success. He had made a difference in the lives of many people and in the local community. "Having calm, controlled growth is good," he says. Now approaching 50, Goltz says that rather than having a midlife crisis, "I'm having midlife contentment. For me, happiness is not about building a $110 million company."

Focusing on growing the top line (revenue) can cause small companies to make sacrifices on its bottom line (profits). "Bigger is better—that's the old Holy Grail," says Paul Schaye, a manager at an investment banking firm. "It gets you bragging rights at the bar, but those bragging rights are what drives people to do crazy things." Sharon Anderson Wright, owner of Half Price Books, has managed to avoid the siren's song of growth at whatever cost. Wright has continued the same simple formula for success with the business that her mother, Pat Anderson, followed when she opened the first Half Price Books in an abandoned laundromat in 1972. Unlike so many bookstores that offer cappuccinos and biscotti in well-lit stores that take an almost antiseptic approach to selling books, Wright's formula relies on stores that are not always well organized but have lots of "personality" and are staffed by friendly, knowledgeable employees who love books. As the company's name implies, Half Price Books also sells used books at very low prices. The combination of low prices, friendly service, and long-time, knowledgeable employees keeps customers coming back regularly. "Our cash cow is our repeat customers," says Wright. "The last thing we want to do is grow too fast and become impersonal."

Wright now has 79 stores in 11 states, and the company generates $120 million a year in revenues. Half Price Books could grow much faster, but Wright has held back on the reins of growth. The company is profitable and debt-free, and sales are climbing as demand for used books is growing rapidly. Whereas Barnes and Noble and Borders typically open 40 new stores a year, Wright chooses to open 6 or 8 new stores in carefully selected locations. The company's target customer is middle-aged with an average annual income of $50,000 and has a college degree. When Wright considers a location for a new store, she looks for sites that have high concentrations of customers that fit this profile.

Wright routinely turns down offers from other companies to buy Half Price Books, and she pays for the company's expansion out of retained earnings, refusing to borrow money to finance growth. If Half Price Books grew any faster, she reasons, she would have to borrow money and then reflect the cost of the borrowed funds in the form of higher prices for the books she sells. "We were raised as kids to do only the things that we could afford," says Wright. "Why would I run my company any differently?"

When Wright is considering opening a new store, she does so only if a long-time manager will move and set up the store. Not only does this policy cut training costs, but it also complements Wright's management philosophy. She promotes from within and provides full-time employees health insurance, regular training programs, and a profit-sharing plan. Fast growth is not an enticement to Wright and other entrepreneurs of her ilk. These visionary entrepreneurs prefer to grow steadily at their own manageable pace and to define their success in terms of satisfied customers, dedicated employees, and profitable companies.

1. Why is it so easy for entrepreneurs to fall into the high-growth trap, even when growing fast may have negative repercussions on their companies?

2. What benefits do entrepreneurs such as Jay Goltz and Sharon Anderson Wright experience by choosing to pursue profitability over sales growth? What are the costs of such a strategy?
3. Research the companies listed on the *Inc.* 500 list of the fastest-growing companies in the United States from two to five years ago. Find the most recent listing of the *Inc.* 500 list. How many of the companies from the past appear on the current list? Use *Inc.* magazine and the resources of the World Wide Web to research some of the companies that appeared on the earlier list but that are missing from the current list. What happened to them? What lessons can entrepreneurs learn from their stories?

Source: Adapted from Bo Burlingham, "There's a Choice," *Inc.*, February 2006, pp. 80–89; Ellyn Spragins and Verne Harnish, "Size Doesn't Matter—Profits Do," *FSB*, March 2004, pp. 37–42.

Ratio Analysis

LEARNING OBJECTIVES
4. Understand the basic financial statements through ratio analysis.

Once an entrepreneur has the business up and running with the help of a solid financial plan, the next step is to keep the company moving in the right direction with the help of proper financial controls. Establishing these controls—and using them consistently—is one of the keys to keeping a business vibrant and healthy. "If you don't keep a finger on the pulse of your company's finances, you risk making bad decisions," explains one business writer. "You could be in serious financial trouble and not even realize it."[6]

A smoothly functioning system of financial controls is essential to achieving business success. Such a system can serve as an early warning device for underlying problems that could destroy a young business. According to one writer:

"A company's financial accounting and reporting systems will provide signals, through comparative analysis, of impending trouble, such as:

- Decreasing sales and falling profit margins.
- Increasing corporate overheads.
- Growing inventories and accounts receivable.

These are all signals of declining cash flows from operations, the lifeblood of every business. As cash flows decrease, the squeeze begins:

- Payments to vendors become slower.
- Maintenance on production equipment lags.
- Raw material shortages appear.
- Equipment breakdowns occur.

All of these begin to have a negative impact on productivity. Now the downward spiral has begun in earnest. The key is hearing and focusing on the signals."[7]

What are these signals, and how does an entrepreneur go about hearing and focusing on them? One extremely helpful tool is ratio analysis. **Ratio analysis,** a method of expressing the relationships between any two elements on financial statements, provides a convenient technique for performing financial analysis. When analyzed properly, ratios serve as barometers of a company's financial health. "You owe it to yourself to understand each ratio and what it means to your business," says one accountant. "Ratios point out potential trouble areas so you can correct them before they multiply."[8] Ratio analysis allows entrepreneurs to determine whether their companies are carrying excessive inventory, experiencing heavy operating expenses, overextending credit, taking on too much debt, and managing to pay their bills on time and to answer other questions relating to the efficient and effective operation of the overall business. Unfortunately, few business owners actually use ratio analysis; one study discovered that only 27 percent of small business owners compute financial ratios and use them in managing their businesses.[9]

ratio analysis
a method of expressing the relationship between any two accounting elements that allows business owners to analyze their companies' financial performances.

Clever business owners use financial ratio analysis to identify problems in their businesses while they are still problems and not business-threatening crises. Tracking these ratios over time permits an owner to spot a variety of red flags that are indications of these problem areas. This is critical to business success because business owners cannot solve problems they do not know exist!

COMPANY Profile

Atkinson-Baker & Associates

At Atkinson-Baker & Associates, a Los Angeles court-reporting service, every one of the firm's 50 employees is responsible for tracking every day a key financial statistic relating to his or her job. CEO Alan Atkinson-Baker believes that waiting until the month's end to compile financial ratios takes away a company's ability to respond to events as they happen. "Employees have statistics for their jobs, and it helps them see how well they are producing," he says. Because the statistics are linked directly to their jobs, employees quickly learn which numbers to track and how to compile or to calculate them. "Each day everybody reports their statistics," explains Atkinson-Baker. "It all goes into a computer . . . and we keep track of it all." A spreadsheet summarizes the calculations and generates 27 graphs so managers can analyze trends in a meeting the following morning. One rule the company developed from its financial analysis is "Don't spend more today than you brought in yesterday." Atkinson-Baker explains, "You can never run into trouble as long as you stick to that rule." He also notes that effective financial planning would be impossible without timely data. "When we have had problem areas, the statistics have helped us catch them before they become a bigger problem," he says.[10]

Business owners also can use ratio analysis to increase the likelihood of obtaining loans. By analyzing their financial statements with the use of ratios, business owners can anticipate potential problems and identify important strengths in advance. And loan officers *do* use ratios to analyze the financial statements of companies applying for loans, comparing them against industry averages and looking for trends over time.

How many ratios should the small business manager monitor to maintain adequate financial control over the firm? The number of ratios that an owner could calculate is limited only by the number of accounts on a firm's financial statements. However, tracking too many ratios only creates confusion and saps the meaning from an entrepreneur's financial analysis. The secret to successful ratio analysis is *simplicity*, focusing on just enough ratios to provide a clear picture of a company's financial standing.

Twelve Key Ratios

In keeping with the idea of simplicity, we will describe 12 key ratios that will enable most business owners to monitor their companies' financial positions without becoming bogged down in financial details. This chapter presents explanations of these ratios and examples based on the balance sheet and the income statement for Sam's Appliance Shop shown in Figures 11.1 and 11.2. We will group them into four categories: liquidity ratios, leverage ratios, operating ratios, and profitability ratios.

liquidity ratios
tell whether a small business will be able to meet its short-term obligations as they come due.

Liquidity Ratios **Liquidity ratios** tell whether a small business will be able to meet its short-term financial obligations as they come due. These ratios can forewarn a business owner of impending cash flow problems. A small company with solid liquidity not only is able to pay its bills on time, but it also has enough cash to take advantage of attractive business opportunities as they arise. The primary measures of liquidity are the current ratio and the quick ratio.

current ratio
measures a small firm's solvency by indicating its ability to pay current liabilities out of current assets.

1. ***Current ratio.*** The **current ratio** measures a small firm's solvency by indicating its ability to pay current liabilities (debts) from current assets. It is calculated in the following manner:

$$\text{Current ratio} = \frac{\text{Current assets}}{\text{Current liabilities}} = \frac{\$686{,}985}{\$367{,}850} = 1.87{:}1$$

Sam's Appliance Shop has $1.87 in current assets for every $1 it has in current liabilities.

Current assets are those that an owner expects to convert into cash in the ordinary business cycle, and normally include cash, notes/accounts receivable, inventory, and any other short-term marketable securities. Current liabilities are those short-term obligations that come due within one year, and include notes/accounts payable, taxes payable, and accruals.

The current ratio is sometimes called the *working capital ratio* and is the most commonly used measure of short-term solvency. Typically, financial analysts suggest that a small business maintain a current ratio of at least 2:1 (i.e., two dollars of current assets for every one dollar of current liabilities) to maintain a comfortable cushion of working capital. Generally, the higher a company's current ratio, the stronger is its financial position; a high current ratio, however, does not guarantee that a company is using its assets in the most profitable manner. For example, a business may be have an abundance of accounts receivable (many of which may not even be collectible) or may be overinvesting in inventory.

With its current ratio of 1.87, Sam's Appliance Shop could liquidate its current assets at 53.5% (1 ÷ 1.87 = 0.535) of its book value and still manage to pay its current creditors in full.

2. ***Quick ratio.*** The current ratio sometimes can be misleading because it does not show the quality of a company's current assets. As we have already seen, a company with a large number of past-due receivables and stale inventory could boast an impressive current ratio and still be on the verge of financial collapse. The **quick ratio (acid test ratio)** is a more conservative measure of a company's liquidity because it shows the extent to which its most liquid assets cover its current liabilities. This ratio includes only a company's "quick assets," excluding the most illiquid asset of all—inventory. It is calculated as follows:

quick ratio (acid test ratio) a conservative measure of a firm's liquidity, measuring the extent to which its most liquid assets cover its current liabilities.

$$\text{Quick ratio} = \frac{\text{Quick assets}}{\text{Current liabilities}}$$
$$= \frac{\$686{,}985 - \$455{,}455}{\$367{,}850}$$
$$= 0.61{:}1$$

Sam's Appliance Shop has 63 cents in quick assets for every $1 of current liabilities.

Quick assets include cash, readily marketable securities, and notes/accounts receivables, assets that can be converted into cash immediately if needed. Most small firms determine quick assets by subtracting inventory from current assets because they cannot convert inventory into cash quickly. Moreover, inventory is the asset on which losses are most likely to occur in case of liquidation.

The quick ratio is a more specific measure of a firm's ability to meet its short-term obligations and is a more rigorous test of its liquidity. It expresses capacity to pay current debts if all sales income ceased immediately. Generally, a quick ratio of 1:1 is considered satisfactory. A ratio of less than 1:1 indicates that the small firm is overly dependent on inventory and on future sales to satisfy short-term debt. A quick ratio of greater than 1:1 indicates a greater degree of financial security.

Leverage Ratios **Leverage ratios** measure the financing supplied by a firm's owners against that supplied by its creditors; they are a gauge of the depth of a company's debt. These ratios show the extent to which an entrepreneur relies on debt capital (rather than equity capital) to finance operating expenses, capital expenditures, and expansion costs. As such, it is a measure of the degree of financial risk in a company. Generally, small businesses with low leverage ratios are less affected by economic downturns, but the returns for these firms are lower during economic booms. Conversely, small firms with high leverage ratios are more vulnerable to economic slides because their debt loads demolish cash flow; however, they have greater potential for large profits.

leverage ratios measure the financing supplied by a firm's owners against that supplied by its creditors; they are a gauge of the depth of a company's debt.

Over the last decade, American businesses have relied increasingly on debt financing to fuel their growth and expansion. Nonfinancial businesses in the United States have $4.97 trillion in outstanding debt, double the amount in 1995.[11]

Ironbound Heat Treating Company

John Ross, owner of Ironbound Heat Treating Company, a metal heat-treating company that was profitable on sales of $4 million, experienced severe problems with his company's debt load as a result of a combination of unfortunate events. By focusing on a niche, Ross' company was growing rapidly, but the loss of a big customer caused revenue to dip. Then Ironbound had to spend $1 million to replace a steel furnace that was crucial to its operation. The company's debt ratios skyrocketed, causing it to spin out of control. Rather than declare bankruptcy, Ross worked with a business credit counseling company to renegotiate his company's payments on the debt, giving it some breathing room. To get the business back on track, Ross decided to sell it to a larger company, Metal Improvement Company, which agreed to pay off all of Ironbound's debt as part of the deal.[12]

debt ratio
measures the percentage of total assets financed by a company's creditors compared to its owners.

3. ***Debt ratio.*** A small company's **debt ratio** measures the percentage of total assets financed by its creditors compared to its owners. The debt ratio is calculated as follows:

$$\text{Debt ratio} = \frac{\text{Total debt (or liabilities)}}{\text{Total assets}}$$

$$= \frac{\$367{,}850 + \$212{,}150}{\$847{,}655}$$

$$= 0.68{:}1$$

Creditors have claims of 68 cents against every $1 of assets that Sam's Appliance Shop owns.

Total debt includes all current liabilities and any outstanding long-term notes and bonds. Total assets represent the sum of the firm's current assets, fixed assets, and intangible assets. A high debt ratio means that creditors provide a large percentage of a company's total financing and, therefore, bear most of its financial risk. Owners generally prefer higher leverage ratios; otherwise, business funds must come either from the owners' personal assets or from taking on new owners, which means giving up more control over the business. In addition, with a greater portion of a firm's assets financed by creditors, the owner is able to generate profits with a smaller personal investment. Creditors, however, typically prefer moderate debt ratios because a lower debt ratio indicates a smaller chance of creditor losses in case of liquidation. To lenders and creditors, high debt ratios mean a higher risk of default.

According to a senior analyst at Dun & Bradstreet's Analytical Services, "If managed properly, debt can be beneficial because it's a great way to have money working for you. You're leveraging your assets, so you're making more money than you're paying out in interest." However, excessive debt can be the downfall of a business. "As we pile up debt on our personal credit cards our lifestyles are squeezed," he says. "The same thing happens to a business. Overpowering debt sinks thousands of businesses each year."[13]

debt to net worth (debt to equity) ratio
expresses the relationship between the capital contributions from creditors and those from owners and measures how highly leveraged a company is.

4. ***Debt to net worth ratio.*** A small firm's **debt to net worth (debt to equity) ratio** also expresses the relationship between the capital contributions from creditors and those from owners and measures how highly leveraged a company is. This ratio reveals a company's capital structure by comparing what the business "owes" to "what it is worth." It is a measure of the small firm's ability to meet both its creditor and owner obligations in case of liquidation. The debt to net worth ratio is calculated as follows:

$$\text{Debt to net worth ratio} = \frac{\text{Total debt (or liabilities)}}{\text{Tangible net worth}}$$

$$= \frac{\$367{,}850 + \$212{,}150}{\$267{,}655 - \$3{,}500}$$

$$= 2.20{:}1$$

Sam's Appliance Shop owes creditors $2.20 for every $1 of equity that Sam owns.

Total debt is the sum of current liabilities and long-term liabilities, and tangible net worth represents the owners' investment in the business (capital + capital stock + earned surplus + retained earnings) less any intangible assets (e.g., goodwill) the firm owns.

The higher this ratio, the more leverage a business is using and the lower the degree of protection afforded creditors if the business should fail. A higher debt to net worth ratio also means that the firm has less capacity to borrow; lenders and creditors see the firm as being "borrowed up." Conversely, a low ratio typically is associated with a higher level of financial security, giving the business greater borrowing potential.

As a company's debt to net worth ratio approaches 1:1, the creditors' interest in the business approaches that of the owners'. If the ratio is greater than 1:1, creditors' claims exceed those of the owners', and the business may be undercapitalized. In other words, the owner has not supplied an adequate amount of capital, forcing the business to be overextended in terms of debt.

5. ***Times interest earned ratio.*** The **times interest earned ratio** is a measure of a small firm's ability to make the interest payments on its debt. It tells how many times a company's earnings cover the interest payments on the debt it is carrying. This ratio measures the size of the cushion a company has in covering the interest cost of its debt load. The times interest earned ratio is calculated as follows:

times interest earned ratio measures a small firm's ability to make the interest payments on its debt.

$$\text{Times interest earned ratio} = \frac{\text{Earnings before interest and taxes (EBIT)}}{\text{Total interest expense}}$$

$$= \frac{\$60{,}629 - \$39{,}850}{\$39{,}850}$$

$$= 2.52{:}1$$

Sam's Appliance Shop's earnings are 2.5 times greater than its interest expense.

EBIT is the firm's profit *before* deducting interest expense and taxes; the denominator measures the amount the business paid in interest over the accounting period.

A high ratio suggests that the company would have little difficulty meeting the interest payments on its loans; creditors see this as a sign of safety for future loans. Conversely, a low ratio is an indication that the company is overextended in its debts; earnings will not be able to cover its debt service if this ratio is less than one. "I look for a [times interest earned] ratio of higher than three-to-one," says one financial analyst, "which indicates that management has considerable breathing room to make its debt payments. When the ratio drops below one-to-one, it clearly indicates management is under tremendous pressure to raise cash. The risk of default or bankruptcy is very high."[14] Many creditors look for a times interest earned ratio of at least four-to-one to six-to-one before pronouncing a company a good credit risk.

Although low to moderate levels of debt can boost a company's financial performance, trouble looms on the horizon for businesses whose debt loads are so heavy that they must starve critical operations, research and development, customer service, and others just to pay interest on the debt. Because their interest payments are so large, highly leveraged companies find that they are restricted when it comes to spending cash, whether on an acquisition, normal operations, or capital spending.

Debt is a powerful financial tool, but companies must handle it carefully—just as a demolitionist handles dynamite. And, like dynamite, too much debt can be deadly. Unfortunately, some companies have pushed their debt loads beyond the safety barrier (see Figure 11.6) and are struggling to survive.

Tri-Star Industries

Rick Sapio, CEO of Tri-Star Industries, a hardware distributor in Chicago, put his company on the fast-growth track and took on loads of debt to pay for it. With the company solidly profitable ($2 million) on sales of $10 million, Sapio borrowed more money to acquire another company for $4 million. Within a year of the acquisition, Tri-Star's sales had climbed, but it was losing $1.4 million a year, and Sapio had to sell the business to pay off the debt the company had accumulated. "We'd be sitting on $12 to $14 million in retained earnings right now if I had been satisfied with a $10 million company," says Sapio regretfully.[15]

Like dynamite, debt financing can be a powerful tool, but companies must handle it carefully, or it can be deadly.

Managed carefully, debt can boost a company's performance and improve its productivity. Its treatment in the tax code also makes debt a much cheaper means of financing growth than equity. When companies with AA financial ratings borrow at, say, 8 percent, the after-tax cost is about 5.75 percent (because interest payments to lenders are tax deductible); equity financing often costs twice that.

Table 11.1 describes how lenders view liquidity and leverage.

operating ratios
help an entrepreneur evaluate a small company's overall performance and indicate how effectively the business employs its resources.

Operating Ratios **Operating ratios** help an entrepreneur evaluate a small company's overall performance and indicate how effectively the business employs its resources. The more effectively its resources are used, the less capital a small business will require. These five operating ratios are designed to help entrepreneurs spot those areas they must improve if their business is to remain competitive.

average inventory turnover ratio
measures the number of times its average inventory is sold out, or turned over, during an accounting period.

6. ***Average inventory turnover ratio.*** A small firm's **average inventory turnover ratio** measures the number of times its average inventory is sold out, or turned over, during the accounting period. This ratio tells the owner whether an entrepreneur is managing inventory properly. It apprises the owner of whether the business inventory

FIGURE 11.6

The Right Amount of Debt Is a Balancing Act

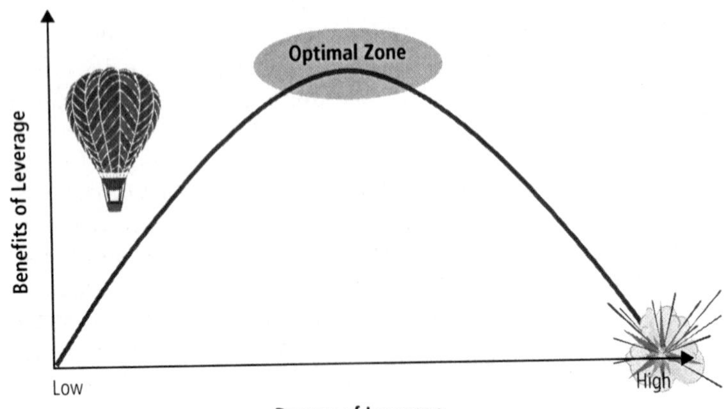

TABLE 11.1 How Lenders View Liquidity and Leverage

	Liquidity	Leverage
Low	If chronic, this is often evidence of mismanagement. It is a sign that the owner has not planned for the company's working capital needs. In most businesses characterized by low liquidity, there is usually no financial plan. This situation is often associated with last minute or "Friday night" financing.	This is a very conservative position. With this kind of leverage, lenders are likely to lend money to satisfy a company's capital needs. Owners in this position should have no trouble borrowing money.
Average	This is an indication of good management. The company is using its current assets wisely and productively. Although they may not be impressed, lenders feel comfortable making loans to companies with adequate liquidity.	If a company's leverage is comparable to that of other businesses of similar size in the same industry, lenders are comfortable making loans. The company is not overburdened with debt and is demonstrating its ability to use its resources to grow.
High	Some lenders look for this because it indicates a most conservative company. However, companies that constantly operate this way usually are forgoing growth opportunities because they are not making the most of their assets.	Businesses that carry excessive levels of debt scare most lenders off. Companies in this position normally will have a difficult time borrowing money unless they can show lenders good reasons for making loans. Owners of these companies must be prepared to sell lenders on their ability to repay.

Source: Adapted from David H. Bangs, Jr., *Financial Troubleshooting* (Dover, NH: Upstart Publishing Company, 1992), p. 124.

is understocked, overstocked, or obsolete. The average inventory turnover ratio is calculated as follows:

$$\text{Average inventory turnover ratio} = \frac{\text{Cost of goods sold}}{\text{Average inventory}}$$
$$= \frac{\$1{,}290{,}117}{(\$805{,}745 + \$455{,}455)/2}$$
$$= 2.05 \text{ times per year}$$

Sam' Appliance Shop turns its inventory about two times a year, or once every 178 days.

Average inventory is the sum of the value of the firm's inventory at the beginning of the accounting period and its value at the end of the accounting period, divided by 2.

This ratio tells an entrepreneur how fast merchandise is moving through the business and helps him or her to balance the company's inventory on the fine line between oversupply and undersupply. To determine the average number of days units remain in inventory, the owner can divide the average inventory turnover ratio into the number of days in the accounting period (e.g., 365 days ÷ average inventory turnover ratio). The result is called *days' inventory* (*or average age of inventory*). Auto dealerships often use the average age of inventory as a measure of their performance.

An above-average inventory turnover indicates that the small business has a healthy, salable, and liquid inventory and a supply of quality merchandise supported by sound pricing policies. A below-average inventory turnover suggests an illiquid inventory characterized by obsolescence, overstocking, stale merchandise, and poor purchasing procedures.

Tiger Imports Group

Frank Toledano, president of Tiger Imports Group, a Highpoint, North Carolina business that imports high-end Italian leathers, relies on the inventory turnover ratio to know when to discontinue one of the company's 100 different styles of leather. Toledano's suppliers require a minimum purchase of $10,000, and with sales of $5 million, Tiger Imports cannot afford to tie up valuable cash in product lines that move slowly. When the inventory turnover ratio of a particular type of leather begins to slow, Toledano does not reorder it and moves on to other, faster-selling lines.[16]

A healthy average inventory turnover ratio means that inventory is moving through a business at a brisk pace. If a company's average inventory turnover ratio is too low, it will experience a buildup in inventory.

Businesses that turn their inventories more rapidly require a smaller inventory investment to produce a particular sales volume. That means that these companies tie up less cash in inventory that idly sits on shelves. For instance, if Sam's could turn its inventory *four* times each year instead of just *two*, the company would require an average inventory of just $322,529 instead of the current level of $630,600 to generate sales of $1,870,841. Increasing the number of inventory turns would free up more than $308,000 in cash currently tied up in excess inventory! Sam's would benefit from improved cash flow and higher profits.

The inventory turnover ratio can be misleading, however. For example, an excessively high ratio could mean that the firm has a shortage of inventory and is experiencing stockouts. Similarly, a low ratio could be the result of planned inventory stockpiling to meet seasonal peak demand. Another problem is that the ratio is based on an inventory balance calculated from two days out of the entire accounting period. Thus, inventory fluctuations due to seasonal demand patterns are ignored, which may bias the resulting ratio. There is no universal, ideal inventory turnover ratio. Financial analysts suggest that a favorable turnover ratio depends on the type of business, its size, its profitability, its method of inventory valuation, and other relevant factors. For instance, the typical supermarket turns its inventory on average about 16 times a year, but a jewelry store averages just 1.5 to 2 inventory turns a year.

average collection period ratio (days sales outstanding, DSO)
measures the number of days it takes to collect accounts receivable.

7. ***Average collection period ratio.*** A small firm's **average collection period ratio (days sales outstanding, DSO)** is a measure of the average number of days it takes to collect accounts receivable. To compute the average collection period ratio, you must first calculate the firm's receivables turnover. Given that Sam's *credit* sales for the year

were $1,309,589 (out of the total sales of $1,870,841), then the company's receivables turnover ratio is as follows:

$$\text{Receivables turnover ratio} = \frac{\text{Credit sales}}{\text{Accounts receivables}} = \frac{\$1{,}309{,}589}{\$179{,}225} = 7.31 \text{ times/year}$$

Sam's Appliance Shop turns over its receivables 7.31 times per year. This ratio measures the number of times the firm's accounts receivable turn over during the accounting period. The higher the firm's receivables turnover ratio, the shorter the time lag is between the sale and the cash collection.

Use the following to calculate the firm's average collection period ratio:

$$\text{Average collection period ratio} = \frac{\text{Days in accounting period}}{\text{Receivables turnover ratio}} = \frac{365 \text{ days}}{7.31 \text{ times/year}} = 50.0 \text{ days}$$

The lower a company's average collection period, the faster it is collecting its receivables. Sam's Appliance Shop's accounts receivable are outstanding for an average of 50 days. Typically, the higher a firm's average collection period ratio, the greater is its chance of incurring bad debt losses.

One of the most useful applications of the collection period ratio is to compare it to the industry average and to the firm's credit terms. Such a comparison will indicate the degree of the small company's control over its credit sales and collection techniques. A healthy collection period ratio depends on the industry in which a company operates. For instance, a study by REL Consultancy Group found that the average collection period for companies selling technology hardware is 69 days; for retailers of food, it is just 10 days.[17] Perhaps the most meaningful analysis is comparing the collection period ratio to a company's credit terms. One rule of thumb suggests that a company's collection period ratio should be no more than one-third greater than its credit terms. For example, if a small company's credit terms are net 30, its average collection period ratio should be no more than 40 days. A ratio greater than 40 days indicates poor collection procedures.

Slow payers represent a great risk to many small businesses. Many entrepreneurs proudly point to rapidly rising sales only to find that they must borrow money to keep their companies going because their credit customers are paying their bills in 45, 60, or even 90 days instead of the desired 30. Slow receivables are a real danger because they usually lead to a cash crisis that threatens a company's survival. Table 11.2 shows how to calculate the savings associated with lowering a company's average collection period ratio.

8. ***Average payable period ratio.*** The converse of the average collection period, the **average payable period ratio,** is a measure of the average number of days it takes a company to pay its accounts payable. Like the average collection period, it is measured in days. To compute this ratio, we first calculate the payables turnover ratio. Sam's payables turnover ratio is as follows:

average payable period ratio
measures the number of days it takes a company to pay its accounts payable.

$$\text{Payables turnover ratio} = \frac{\text{Purchases}}{\text{Accounts payable}} = \frac{\$939{,}827}{\$152{,}580} = 6.16 \text{ times/year}$$

TABLE 11.2 How Lowering Your Average Collection Period Can Save You Money

Too often, entrepreneurs fail to recognize the importance of collecting their accounts receivable on time. After all, collecting accounts is not as glamorous or as much fun as generating sales. Lowering a company's average collection period ratio, however, *can* produce tangible—and often significant—savings. The following formula shows how to convert an improvement in a company's average collection period ratio into dollar savings:

$$\text{Annual savings} = \frac{\text{Credit sales} \times \text{Annual interest rate} \times \text{Number of days average collection period is lowered}}{365}$$

where

Credit sales = Company's annual credit sales in dollars

Annual interest rate = Interest rate at which the company borrows money

Number of days average collection period is lowered = Difference between the previous year's average collection period ratio and the current one

Example:

Sam's Appliance Shop's average collection period ratio is 50 days. Suppose that the previous year's average collection period ratio was 58 days, an 8-day improvement. The company's credit sales for the most recent year were $1,309,589. If Sam borrows money at 8.75%, this 8-day improvement has generated savings for Sam's Appliance Shop of

$$\text{Savings} = \frac{\$1{,}309{,}589 \times 8.75\% \times 8 \text{ days}}{365 \text{ days}} = \$2{,}512$$

By collecting his accounts receivable just 8 days faster on the average, Sam has saved his business more than $2,512! Of course, if a company's average collection period ratio rises, the same calculation will tell the owner how much that costs.

Source: Adapted from "Days Saved, Thousands Earned," *Inc.*, November 1995, p. 98.

To find the average payable period, we use the following computation:

$$\begin{aligned}\text{Average payable period} &= \frac{\text{Days in accounting period}}{\text{Payables turnover ratio}}\\ &= \frac{365 \text{ days}}{6.16 \text{ times/year}}\\ &= 59.3 \text{ days}\end{aligned}$$

Sam's Appliance Shop takes an average of 59 days to pay its accounts with suppliers.

An excessively high average payables period ratio indicates the presence of a significant amount of past-due accounts payable. Although sound cash management calls for a business owner to keep his or her cash as long as possible, slowing payables too drastically can severely damage the company's credit rating. Ideally, the average payable period would match (or exceed) the time it takes to convert inventory into sales and ultimately into cash. In this case, the company's vendors would be financing its inventory and its credit sales. Amazon.com reaps the benefits of this situation; it does not pay its vendors until after it collects from its customers.[18]

One of the most meaningful comparisons for this ratio is against the credit terms suppliers offer (or an average of the credit terms offered). If the average payable ratio slips beyond vendors' credit terms, it is an indication that the company is suffering from a sloppy accounts payable procedure or from cash shortages, and its credit rating is in danger. If this ratio is significantly lower than vendors' credit terms, it may be a sign that the firm is not using its cash most effectively.

We will see the impact that these three operating ratios—inventory turnover, accounts receivable, and accounts payable have on a small company's cash flow in the next chapter.

9. ***Net sales to total assets ratio.*** A small company's **net sales to total assets ratio (total asset turnover ratio)** is a general measure of its ability to generate sales in relation to its assets. It describes how productively the firm employs its assets to produce sales revenue. The total assets turnover ratio is calculated as follows:

net sales to total assets (total asset turnover) ratio measures a company's ability to generate sales in relation to its asset base.

$$\text{Total assets turnover ratio} = \frac{\text{Net sales}}{\text{Net total assets}}$$
$$= \frac{\$1{,}870{,}841}{\$847{,}655}$$
$$= 2.21:1$$

Sam's Appliance Shop is generating $2.21 in sales for every dollar of assets.

The denominator of this ratio, net total assets, is the sum of all of a company's assets (cash, inventory, land, buildings, equipment, tools, and everything it owns) less depreciation. This ratio is meaningful only when compared to that of similar firms in the same industry category. A total assets turnover ratio below the industry average indicates that a small firm is not generating an adequate sales volume for its asset size.

An excessively low net sales to assets ratio indicates that a small firm is not employing its assets efficiently or profitably. On the other hand, an extremely high ratio may indicate an inadequate level of assets to maintain a suitable level of sales, which puts creditors in a more vulnerable position. Monitoring this ratio over time is very helpful in maintaining a sufficient asset base as a small business grows.

Profitability Ratios **Profitability ratios** indicate how efficiently a small company is being managed. They provide the owner with information about a company's bottom line; in other words, they describe how successfully the firm is using its available resources to generate a profit.

profitability ratios indicate how efficiently a small company is being managed.

10. ***Net profit on sales ratio.*** The **net profit on sales ratio (profit margin on sales or net profit margin)** measures a company's profit per dollar of sales. The computed percentage shows the portion of each sales dollar remaining after deducting all expenses. The profit margin on sales is calculated as follows:

net profit on sales ratio (profit margin on sales or net profit margin) measures a company's profit per dollar of sales.

$$\text{Net profit on sales ratio} = \frac{\text{Net profit}}{\text{Net sales}}$$
$$= \frac{\$60{,}629}{\$1{,}870{,}841}$$
$$= 3.24\%$$

For every dollar in sales Sam's Appliance Shop generates, Sam keeps 3.24 cents in profit.

Many small business owners believe that a high profit margin on sales is necessary for a successful business operation, but this is a myth. To evaluate this ratio properly, an entrepreneur must consider a firm's asset value, its inventory and receivables turnover ratios, and its total capitalization. For example, the typical small supermarket earns an average net profit of only one or two cents on each dollar of sales, but, as we have seen, its inventory turnover ratio is 16 times a year. If a company's profit margin on sales is below the industry average, it may be a sign that its prices are too low, that its costs are excessively high, or both.

Avidian Technologies

James Wong, co-founder and CEO of Avidian Technologies, a software provider based in Bellevue Washington, monitors the company's net profit margin closely. Avidian Technologies' average annual growth rate has averaged 400 percent for several years, and Wong knows that such fast-paced growth can wreak havoc on a successful company's bottom line. He monitors the company's cash flow daily and never allows its net profit margin to dip below 15 percent. Wong's attentiveness has paid off for Avidian.

Despite its rapid growth rate, the company has no significant debt and has taken on no outside investors. "I've learned that profitability takes conscious effort," says Wong. "If you just keep growing, for growth's sake, you won't be nearly as profitable."[19]

A natural reaction to low profitability ratios is to embark on a cost-cutting effort. Although minimizing costs can improve profitability, entrepreneurs must be judicious in their cost cutting, taking a strategic approach rather than imposing across-the-board cuts. Cutting costs in areas that are vital to operating success—such as a retail jeweler cutting its advertising expenditures—can inhibit a company's ability to succeed and can lead to failure. For instance, choosing to lay off workers, a common reaction at many companies facing financial challenges, often backfires. Not only does a company risk losing talented workers and the knowledge they have built up over time, but research also shows that repeated rounds of layoffs destroy the morale and the productivity of the remaining workers.[20] In other cases, entrepreneurs on cost-cutting vendettas alienate employees and sap worker morale by eliminating nitpicking costs that affect employees adversely and really do not save much money. The owner of one company thought he would save money by eliminating the free coffee the company provided for its workers. Employee productivity took a hit, however, when workers began taking trips several times a day to a nearby coffee shop. "What a wonderful productivity enhancer!" says one former employee sarcastically.[21]

If a company's net profit on sales ratio is excessively low, the owner first should check the gross profit margin (net sales minus cost of goods sold expressed as a percentage of net sales). Of course, a reasonable gross profit margin varies from industry to industry. For instance, a service company may have a gross profit margin of 75 percent, while a manufacturer's may be 35 percent. The key is to know what a reasonable gross profit margin is for your particular business. If this margin slips too low, it puts a company's future in immediate jeopardy. An inadequate gross profit margin cannot cover all of a company's business expenses and still be able to generate a profit.

Monitoring the net profit margin is especially important for fast-growing companies in which sales are climbing rapidly. Unbridled growth can cause expenses to rise faster than sales, eroding a company's net profit margin. Success can be deceptive: Sales are rising, but profits are shrinking. Ideally, a company reaches a point at which it achieves **operating leverage,** a situation in which increases in operating efficiency mean that expenses as a percentage of sales revenues flatten or even decline. As a result, the company's net profit margin will climb as it grows.

operating leverage
a situation in which increases in operating efficiency mean that expenses as a percentage of sales revenue flatten or even decline.

Mutuals.com

In 1994, when Rick Sapio launched Mutuals.com, a mutual fund advisory and account management service, he was able to raise $14 million in equity capital from private and institutional investors. That largess and the ease with which he raised it gave Sapio an excuse for ignoring the importance of operating leverage. "We were not accountable to being a profitable company at the beginning," he says, "and our energies weren't focused on [analyzing] expenses. We were looking only at revenue." Even though Mutuals.com's sales were growing at an average of 113% a year, the company lost money consistently. Sapio decided to get serious about controlling costs. Every day at 4:37 p.m. just after the markets close, Sapio and his top managers gather to assess the company's financial results for that day, and each person is responsible for reporting one revenue item and one expense item. "Every line item on our financial statement has a name attached to it," says Sapio. Since 1999, the company's revenues have increased 190 percent and expenses are actually dropping about 4 percent a year, producing a solid net profit margin of 15 percent.[22]

net profit to assets ratio
measures how much profit a company generates for each dollar of assets that it owns.

11. *Net profit to assets ratio.* The **net profit to assets ratio (return on assets ratio)** tells how much profit a company generates for each dollar of assets that it owns. This ratio describes how efficiently a business is putting to work all of the assets it owns to generate

a profit. It tells how much net income an entrepreneur is squeezing from each dollar's worth of the company's assets. It is calculated as follows:

$$\text{Net profit to assets ratio} = \frac{\text{Net profit}}{\text{Total assets}}$$
$$= \frac{\$60,629}{\$847,655}$$
$$= 7.15\%$$

Sam's Appliance shop earns a return of 7.15 percent on its asset base. This ratio provides clues about the asset intensity of an industry. Return on assets ratios that are below 5 percent are indicative of asset-intense industries that require heavy investments in assets to stay in business (e.g., manufacturing and railroads). Return on assets ratios that exceed 20 percent tend to occur in asset-light industries such as business or personal services—for example, advertising agencies and computer services. A net profit to assets ratio that is below the industry average suggests that a company is not using its assets very efficiently to produce a profit. Another common application of this ratio is to compare it to the company's cost of borrowed capital. Ideally, a company's return on assets ratio (ROA) should exceed the cost of borrowing money to purchase those assets. Companies that experience significant swings in the value of their assets over the course of a year often use an average value of the asset base over the accounting period to get a more realistic estimate of this ratio.

12. ***Net profit to equity ratio.*** The **net profit to equity ratio (return on net worth ratio)** measures the owners' rate of return on investment (ROI). Because it reports the percentage of the owners' investment in the business that is being returned through profits annually, it is one of the most important indicators of a firm's profitability or a management's efficiency. The net profit to equity ratio is computed as follows:

net profit to equity ratio (return on net worth ratio) measures the owners' rate of return on investment.

$$\text{Net profit to equity ratio} = \frac{\text{Net profit}}{\text{Owner's equity (or net worth)}}$$
$$= \frac{\$60,629}{\$267,655}$$
$$= 22.65\%$$

Sam is earning 22.65 percent on the money he has invested in this business.

This ratio compares profits earned during the accounting period with the amount the owner has invested in the business during that time. If this interest rate on the owners' investment is excessively low, some of this capital might be better employed elsewhere.

YOU Be the Consultant

All Is Not Paradise in Eden's Garden: Part 1

Joe and Kaitlin Eden, co-owners of Eden's Garden, a small nursery, lawn, and garden supply business, have just received their year-end financial statements from their accountant. At their last meeting with their accountant, Shelley Edison, three months ago, the Edens had mentioned that they seemed to be having trouble paying their bills on time. "Some of our suppliers have threatened to put us on 'credit-hold,'" said Joe.

"I think you need to sit down with me very soon and let me show you how to analyze your financial statements so you can see what's happening in your business,"

Edison told them at that meeting. Unfortunately, that was the beginning of Eden's Garden's busy season, and the Edens were so busy running the company that they never got around to setting a time to meet with Shelley.

"Now that business has slowed down a little, perhaps we should call Shelley and see what she can do to help us understand what our financial statements are trying to tell us," said Kaitlin.

"Right. Before it's too late to do anything about it," said Joe, pulling out the following financial statements.

Balance Sheet, Eden's Garden

Assets		
Current Assets		
Cash		$6,457
Accounts receivable		
Less allowance for	$29,152	
doubtful accounts	$3,200	$25,952
Inventory		$88,157
Supplies		$7,514
Prepaid expenses		$1,856
Total current assets		$129,936
Fixed Assets		
Land		$59,150
Buildings	$51,027	
Less accumulated depreciation	$2,061	$48,966
Autos	$24,671	
Less accumulated		
depreciation	$12,300	$12,371
Equipment	$22,375	
Less accumulated depreciation	$1,250	$21,125
Furniture and fixtures	$10,295	
Less accumulated depreciation	$1,000	$9,295
Total fixed assets		$150,907
Intangibles (goodwill)		$0
Total assets		$280,843
Liabilities		
Current Liabilities		
Accounts payable		$54,258
Notes payable		$20,150
Credit line payable		$8,118
Accrued wages/salaries payable		$1,344
Accrued interest payable		$1,785
Accrued taxes payable		$1,967
Total current liabilities		$87,622
Long-Term Liabilities		
Mortgage		$72,846
Note payable		$47,000
Total long-term liabilities		$119,846
Owner's equity		
Sam Lloyd, capital		$73,375
Total liabilities and owner's equity		$280,843

Income Statement, Eden's Garden

Net sales revenue*		$689,247
Cost of Goods Sold		
Beginning inventory, 1/1/xx	$78,271	
+ purchases	$403,569	
Goods available for sale	$481,840	
− ending inventory, 12/31/xx	$86,157	
Cost of goods sold		$395,683
Gross profit		$293,564
Operating Expenses		
Advertising	$22,150	
Insurance	$9,187	
Depreciation		
Building	$26,705	
Autos	$7,895	
Equipment	$11,200	
Salaries	$116,541	
Uniforms	$4,018	
Repairs and maintenance	$9,097	
Travel	$2,658	
Entertainment	$2,798	
Total operating expenses		$212,249
General Expenses		
Utilities	$7,987	
Telephone	$2,753	
Professional fees	$3,000	
Postage	$1,892	
Payroll taxes	$11,589	
Total general expenses		$27,221
Other Expenses		
Interest expense	$21,978	
Bad check expense	$679	
Miscellaneous expense	$1,248	
Total other expenses		$23,905
Total expenses		$263,375
Net income		$30,189

*Credit sales represented $289,484 of this total.

1. Assume the role of Shelley Edison. Using the financial statements for Eden's Garden, calculate the 12 ratios covered in this chapter.
2. Do you see any ratios that, on the surface, look suspicious? Explain.

Interpreting Business Ratios

LEARNING OBJECTIVES
5. Explain how to interpret financial ratios.

Ratios are useful yardsticks when measuring a small firm's performance and can point out potential problems before they develop into serious crises. But calculating these ratios is not enough to ensure proper financial control. In addition to knowing how to calculate these ratios, entrepreneurs must understand how to interpret them and apply them to managing their businesses more effectively and efficiently.

Hi-Shear Technology Inc.

With the help of financial ratios, Linda Nespole, a top manager at Hi-Shear Technology Inc., an aerospace subcontracting company in Torrance, California, noticed the company's performance beginning to slip. Given the signals her analysis revealed, she immediately devised a strategy to restore Hi-Shear's financial position, focusing first on cost-cutting measures. Simply charting the company's major costs led Nespole to discover leaking water pipes and inefficient lighting that were driving up costs unnecessarily. Some basic repairs lowered utility costs significantly, and a new, more efficient lighting system paid for itself in just six months. Nespole's cost-saving attitude took hold throughout the entire company, and soon all 125 employees were finding ways to keep costs down—from switching long-distance carriers to cutting the cost of its 401(k) retirement plan by 30 percent.[23]

Not every business measures its success with the same ratios. In fact, key performance ratios vary dramatically across industries and even within different segments of the same industry. Entrepreneurs must know and understand which ratios are most crucial to their companies' success and focus on monitoring and controlling those. Sometimes business owners develop ratios and measures that are unique to their own operations to help them achieve success. Known as **critical numbers,** these indicators measure key financial and operational aspects of a company's performance. When these critical numbers are headed in the right direction, a business is on track to achieve its objectives. The owner of a delivery company breaks his business into four categories and tracks critical numbers for each one. Every Monday morning, he gets a report comparing the previous week's critical numbers to those of the previous 28 weeks and the same week for the previous three years. "In 30 seconds, I can see what's going on in every part of my delivery business," he says. "I get another sheet for my storage business because I need to track a different set of numbers there, but the idea is the same."[24] Examples of critical numbers at other companies include the following:

critical numbers indicators that measure key financial and operational aspects of a company's performance; when these numbers are moving in the right direction, a business is on track to reach its objectives.

- The gross profit margin of a manufacturer of pallets.
- Sales per labor hour at a supermarket.
- The number of new boxes put into storage each week in a records storage business. "Tell me how many new boxes came in during [a particular week]," says Norm Brodsky, owner of a successful records storage company, "and I can tell you our overall sales figure for [that week] within one or two percent of the actual figure."[25]
- Food costs as a percentage of sales for a restaurant. When rising cheese prices pushed food costs as a percentage of sales to 40 percent at Mark Parry's pizza restaurant, he was forced to raise prices. "We're not set to [earn] a profit when we're [operating] at 40 percent food costs," says Parry.[26]
- The utilization ratio, billable hours as a percentage of total hours worked at an Internet service provider.
- The load factor, the percentage of seats filled with passengers, at an airline.[27]

Critical numbers may be different for two companies who compete in the same industry. The key is knowing what *your* company's critical numbers are, monitoring them, and then driving them in the right direction. That requires communicating the importance of these critical numbers to employees and giving them feedback on how well the business is achieving them.

One California retail chain established the daily customer count and the average sale per customer as its critical numbers. The company organized a monthly contest with prizes and posted charts tracking each store's performance. Soon, employees were working hard to improve their stores' performances over the previous year and to outdo other stores in the chain. The healthy rivalry among stores boosted the company's performance significantly.[28]

Another valuable way to use ratios is to compare them with those of similar businesses in the same industry. By comparing the company's financial statistics to industry averages, an entrepreneur is able to locate problem areas and maintain adequate financial controls. "By themselves, these numbers are not that meaningful," says one financial expert of ratios, "but when you compare them to [those of] other businesses in your industry, they suddenly come alive because they put your operation in perspective."[29]

The principle behind calculating these ratios and comparing them to industry norms is the same as that of most medical tests in the health care profession. Just as a healthy person's blood pressure and cholesterol levels should fall within a range of normal values, so should a financially healthy company's ratios. A company cannot deviate too far from these normal values and remain successful for long. When deviations from "normal" do occur (and they will), a business owner should focus on determining the cause of the deviations (see Table 11.3). In some cases, such deviations are the result of sound business decisions, such as taking on inventory in preparation for the busy season, investing heavily in new technology, and others. In other instances, however, ratios that are out of the normal range for a particular type of business are indicators of what could become serious problems for a company. Properly used, ratio analysis can help owners to identify potential problem areas in their businesses early—*before* they become crises that threaten their very survival.

Several organizations regularly compile and publish operating statistics, including key ratios, that summarize the financial performance of many businesses across a wide range of industries. The local library should subscribe to most of these publications:

Risk Management Association. Founded in 1914, the Risk Management Association publishes its *Annual Statement Studies*, showing ratios and other financial data for more than 700 different industrial, wholesale, retail, and service categories that are organized by North American Industry Classification System (NAICS) and Standard Industrial Classification (SIC) code.

Dun & Bradstreet, Inc. Since 1932, Dun & Bradstreet has published *Key Business Ratios*, which covers 22 retail, 32 wholesale, and 71 industrial business categories. Dun & Bradstreet also publishes *Cost of Doing Business*, a series of operating ratios compiled from the IRS's *Statistics of Income*.

Vest Pocket Guide to Financial Ratios. This handy guide, published by Prentice Hall, gives key ratios and financial data for a wide variety of industries.

Industry Spotlight. Published by Schonfeld & Associates, this publication, which can be customized for any one of more than 150 industries, contains financial statement

TABLE 11.3 Putting Your Ratios to the Test

When comparing your company's ratios to your industry's standards, ask the following questions:

1. Is there a significant difference in my company's ratio and the industry average?
2. If so, is this a *meaningful* difference?
3. Is the difference good or bad?
4. What are the possible causes of this difference? What is the most likely cause?
5. Does this cause require that I take action?
6. What action should I take to correct the problem?

Source: Adapted from George M. Dawson, "Divided We Stand," *Business Start-Ups*, May 2000, p. 34.

data and key ratios from more than 95,000 tax returns. *Industry Spotlight* also provides detailed financial information for both profitable companies and those with losses.

Bank of America. Periodically, the Bank of America publishes many documents relating to small business management, including the *Small Business Reporter*, which details costs of doing business ratios.

Trade Associations. Virtually every type of business is represented by a national trade association, which publishes detailed financial data compiled from its membership. For example, owners of small supermarkets could contact the National Association of Retail Grocers or check the *Progressive Grocer,* its trade publication, for financial statistics relevant to their operations.

Government Agencies. Several government agencies (the Federal Trade Commission, Interstate Commerce Commission, Department of Commerce, Department of Agriculture, and Securities and Exchange Commission) offer a great deal of financial operating data on a variety of industries, although the categories are more general. In addition, the IRS annually publishes *Statistics of Income,* which includes income statement and balance sheet statistics compiled from income tax returns. The Census Bureau also publishes the *Census of Business*, which gives a limited amount of ratio information.

What Do All of These Numbers Mean?

Learning to interpret financial ratios just takes a little practice. This section will show you how it's done by comparing the ratios from the operating data already computed for Sam's to those taken from RMA'*s Annual Statement Studies.* (The industry median is the ratio falling exactly in the middle when sample elements are arranged in ascending or descending order.)

Sam's Appliance Shop	Industry Median

Liquidity ratios. These tell whether a small business will be able to meet its maturing obligations as they come due.

1. Current ratio = 1.87:1 — 1.50:1

   Sam's Appliance Shop falls short of the rule of thumb of 2:1, but its current ratio is above the industry median by a significant amount. Sam's should have no problem meeting its short-term debts as they come due. By this measure, the company's liquidity is solid.

2. Quick ratio = 0.63:1 — 0.50:1

   Again, Sam's is below the rule of thumb of 1:1, but the company passes this test of liquidity when measured against industry standards. Sam's relies on selling inventory to satisfy short-term debt (as do most appliance shops). If sales slump, the result could be liquidity problems for Sam's. Sam should consider building a cash reserve as a precautionary measure.

Leverage ratios. These measure the financing supplied by a firm's owners against that supplied by its creditors and serve as a gauge of the depth of a company's debt.

3. Debt ratio = 0.68:1 — 0.64:1

   Creditors provide 68 percent of Sam's total assets, very close to the industry median of 64 percent. Although Sam's does not appear to be overburdened with debt, the company might have difficulty borrowing additional money, especially from conservative lenders.

4. Debt to net worth ratio = 2.20:1 — 1.90:1

   Sam's Appliance Shop owes creditors \$2.20 for every \$1.00 the owner has invested in the business (compared to \$1.90 in debt to every \$1.00 in equity for the typical business). Although this is not an exorbitant amount of debt, many lenders and creditors will see Sam's as "borrowed up." The company's borrowing capacity is limited because creditors' claims against the business are more than twice those of the owners. Sam should consider increasing his owner's equity in the business through retained earnings or by paying down some of the company's debt.

5. Times interest earned ratio = 2.52:1 2.0:1

Sam's earnings are high enough to cover the interest payments on its debt by a factor of 2.52, slightly better than the typical firm in the industry, whose earnings cover its interest payments just two times. Sam's Appliance Shop has a cushion (although a small one) in meeting its interest payments.

Operating ratios. These evaluate the firm's overall performance and show how effectively it is putting its resources to work.

6. Average inventory turnover ratio = 2.05 times/year 4.0 times/year

Inventory is moving through Sam's at a very slow pace, *half* that of the industry median. The company has a problem with slow-moving items in its inventory and, perhaps, too much inventory. Which items are they, and why are they slow-moving? Does Sam need to drop some product lines? Sam must analyze his company's inventory and reevaluate his inventory control procedures.

7. Average collection period ratio = 50.0 days 19.3 days

Sam's Appliance Shop collects the average account receivable after 50 days (compared with the industry median of 19 days), more than two and one-half times longer. A more meaningful comparison is against Sam's credit terms; if credit terms are net 30 (or anywhere close to that), Sam's has a dangerous collection problem, one that drains cash and profits and demands *immediate* attention! He must implement the cash management procedures you will learn about in Chapter 12.

8. Average payable period ratio = 59.3 days 43 days

Sam's payables are nearly 40 percent slower than those of the typical firm in the industry. Stretching payables too far could seriously damage the company's credit rating, causing suppliers to cut off future trade credit. This could be a sign of cash flow problems or a sloppy accounts payable procedure. This problem also demands *immediate* attention. Once again, Sam must implement proper cash management procedures to resolve this problem.

9. Net sales to total assets ratio = 2.21:1 2.7:1

Sam's Appliance Shop is not generating enough sales, given the size of its asset base. This could be the result of a number of factors—improper inventory, inappropriate pricing, poor location, poorly trained sales personnel, and many others. The key is to find the cause . . . *Fast!*

Profitability ratios. These measure how efficiently a firm is operating and offer information about its bottom line.

10. Net profit on sales ratio = 3.24% 7.6%

After deducting all expenses, 3.24 cents of each sales dollar remains as profit for Sam's—less than half the industry median. Sam should check his company's gross profit margin and investigate its operating expenses, checking them against industry standards and looking for those that are out of balance.

11. Net profit to assets ratio = 7.15% 5.5%

Sam's generates just a return of 7.15% for every $1 in assets, which is 30 percent above the industry average. Given his asset base, Sam is squeezing an above-average return out of his company. This could be an indication that Sam's is highly profitable; however, given the previous ratio, this is unlikely. It is more likely that Sam's asset base is thinner than the industry average.

12. Net profit to equity ratio = 22.65% 12.6%

Sam's Appliance Shop's owners are earning 22.65 percent on the money they have invested in the business. This yield is nearly twice that of the industry median,

"This one pretty much sums it up."

and, given the previous ratio, is more a result of the owners' relatively low investment in the business than an indication of its superior profitability. Sam is using O.P.M. (Other People's Money) to generate a profit in his business.

When comparing ratios for their individual businesses to published statistics, small business owners must remember that the comparison is made against averages. An entrepreneur should strive to achieve ratios that are at least as good as these average figures. The goal should be to manage the business so that its financial performance is above average. As they compare their company's financial performance to those covered in the published statistics, they inevitably will discern differences between them. They should note those items that are substantially out of line from the industry average. However, a ratio that varies from the average does not *necessarily* mean that the small business is in financial jeopardy. Instead of making drastic changes in financial policy, entrepreneurs must explore *why* the figures are out of line.

Petra Group

Greg Smith, CEO of Petra Group, a systems integrator with $1.5 million in annual sales, once gave little thought to comparing his company's financial performance against industry standards. Then, Petra Group's sales flattened and Smith's company faced the prospect of losing money for the first time. Smith worked with an accounting firm, using information from the Risk Management Association and a nonprofit organization that provides similar studies, to analyze his company's financial position. Comparing his numbers to industry statistics, Smith quickly saw that his payroll expenses for his 15-person company were too high to allow the company to generate a profit. He also discovered that Petra Group's debt ratio was too high. To restore his company's financial strength, Smith reduced his staff by two and began relying more on temporary employees and independent contractors. He realigned Petra Group's financing, reducing the company's line of credit from $100,000 to just $35,000. The analysis also revealed several strengths for the company. For instance, the company's average collection period was 36.5 days, compared to an industry average of 73 days. Smith continues to use ratio comparisons to make key decisions for his company, and he credits the initial financial analysis with getting his company back on the track to profitability.[30]

FIGURE 11.7

Trend Analysis of Ratios

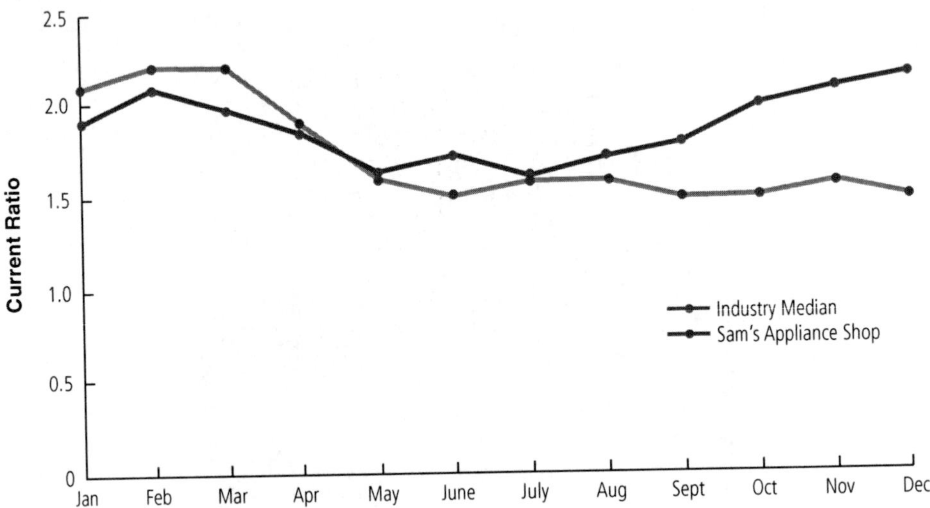

In addition to comparing ratios to industry averages, owners should analyze their firms' financial ratios over time. By themselves, these ratios are "snapshots" of a company's financial position at a single instant; but by examining these trends over time, an entrepreneur can detect gradual shifts that otherwise might go unnoticed until a financial crisis is looming (see Figure 11.7).

You Be the Consultant

All Is Not Paradise in Eden's Garden: Part 2

Remember Joe and Kaitlin Eden, co-owners of Eden's Garden? Assume the role of Shelley Edison, their accountant. Tomorrow, you have scheduled a meeting with them to review their company's financial statements and to make recommendations about how they can improve their company's financial position. Use the following worksheet to summarize the ratios you calculated earlier in this chapter. Then, compare them against the industry averages from the Risk Management Association's *Annual Statement Studies.*

Ratio Comparison

Ratio	Eden's Garden	Garden Supply Industry Median*
Liquidity Ratios		
Current ratio		1.4
Quick ratio		0.5
Leverage Ratios		
Debt ratio		0.6
Debt to net worth ratio		1.8
Times interest earned ratio		2.6
Operating Ratios		
Average inventory turnover ratio		5.6
Average collection period ratio		9 days
Average payable period ratio		17 days
Net sales to total assets ratio		3.0
Profitability Ratios		
Net profit on sales ratio		7.5%
Net profit to asset ratio		9.1%
Net profit to equity ratio		15.0%

*Risk Management Association's *Annual Statement Studies*.

1. Analyze the comparisons you have made of Eden's Garden's ratios with those from the Risk Management Association. What "red flags" do you see?
2. What might be causing the deviations you have observed?
3. What recommendations can you make to the Edens to improve their company's financial performance in the future?

Break-Even Analysis

LEARNING OBJECTIVES
6. Conduct a break-even analysis for a small company.

Another key component of every sound financial plan is a break-even analysis. A small company's **break-even point** is the level of operation (sales dollars or production quantity) at which it neither earns a profit nor incurs a loss. At this level of activity, sales revenue equals expenses, that is, the firm "breaks even." By analyzing costs and expenses, an entrepreneur can calculate the minimum level of activity required to keep the firm in operation. These techniques can then be refined to project the sales needed to generate the desired profit. Most potential lenders and investors will require entrepreneurs to prepare a break-even analysis to assist them in evaluating the earning potential of the new business. In addition to its being a simple, useful screening device for financial institutions, break-even analysis can also serve as a planning device for the small business owner. It occasionally will show a poorly prepared entrepreneur just how unprofitable a proposed business venture is likely to be.

break-even point
the level of operation (sales dollars or production quantity) at which a company neither earns a profit nor incurs a loss.

Calculating the Break-Even Point

A small business owner can calculate a firm's break-even point by using a simple mathematical formula. To begin the analysis, the owner must determine fixed costs and variable costs. **Fixed expenses** are those that do not vary with changes in the volume of sales or production (e.g., rent, depreciation expense, interest payments). **Variable expenses,** on the other hand, vary directly with changes in the volume of sales or production (e.g., raw material costs, sales commissions).

fixed expenses
expenses that do not vary with changes in the volume of sales or production.

variable expenses
expenses that vary directly with changes in the volume of sales or production.

Some expenses cannot be neatly categorized as fixed or variable because they contain elements of both. These semivariable expenses change, although not proportionately, with changes in the level of sales or production (electricity is one example). These costs remain constant up to a particular production or sales volume, and then climb as that volume is exceeded. To calculate the break-even point, an entrepreneur must separate these expenses into their fixed and variable components. A number of techniques can be used (which are beyond the scope of this text), but a good cost accounting system can provide the desired results.

Here are the steps an entrepreneur must take to compute the break-even point using an example of a typical small business, the Magic Shop:

Step 1 Determine the expenses the business can expect to incur. With the help of a budget, an entrepreneur can develop estimates of sales revenue, cost of goods sold, and expenses for the upcoming accounting period. The Magic Shop expects net sales of $950,000 in the upcoming year, with a cost of goods sold of $646,000 and total expenses of $236,500.

Step 2 Categorize the expenses estimated in Step 1 into fixed expenses and variable expenses. Separate semivariable expenses into their component parts. From the budget, the owner anticipates variable expenses (including the cost of goods sold) of $705,125 and fixed expenses of $177,375.

Step 3 Calculate the ratio of variable expenses to net sales. For the Magic Shop, this percentage is $705,125 ÷ $950,000 = 74 percent. So the Magic Shop uses $0.74 out of every sales dollar to cover variable expenses, leaving $0.26 as a contribution margin to cover fixed costs and make a profit.

Step 4 Compute the break-even point by inserting this information into the following formula:

$$\text{Break-even sales (\$)} = \frac{\text{Total fixed cost}}{\text{Contribution margin expressed as percentage of sales}}$$

For the Magic Shop,

$$\text{Break-even sales (\$)} = \frac{\$177{,}375}{0.26}$$
$$= \$682{,}212$$

Thus, the Magic Shop will break even with sales of $682,212. At this point, sales revenue generated will just cover total fixed and variable expense. The Magic Shop will earn no profit and will incur no loss. We can verify this with the following calculations:

Sales at break-even point	$ 682,212
− Variable expenses (74% of sales)	−504,837
Contribution margin	177,375
− Fixed expenses	−177,375
Net profit (or net loss)	$ 0

Adding in a Profit

What if the Magic Shop's owner wants to do *better* than just break even? His analysis can be adjusted to consider such a possibility. Suppose the owner expects a reasonable profit (before taxes) of $80,000. What level of sales must the Magic Shop achieve to generate this? He can calculate this by treating the desired profit as if it were a fixed cost. In other words, he modifies the formula to include the desired net income:

$$\text{Sales (\$)} = \frac{\text{Total fixed expenses} + \text{Desired net income}}{\text{Contribution margin expressed as a percentage of sales}}$$

$$= \frac{\$177{,}375 + \$80{,}000}{0.26}$$

$$= \$989{,}904$$

To achieve a net profit of $80,000 (before taxes), the Magic Shop must generate net sales of $989,904.

Break-Even Point in Units

Some small businesses may prefer to express the break-even point in units produced or sold instead of in dollars. Manufacturers often find this approach particularly useful. The following formula computes the break-even point in units:

$$\text{Break-even volume} = \frac{\text{Total fixed costs}}{\text{Sales price per unit} - \text{Variable cost per unit}}$$

For example, suppose that Trilex Manufacturing Company estimates its fixed costs for producing its line of small appliances at, $390 000. The variable costs (including materials, direct labor, and factory overhead) amount to $12.10 per unit, and the selling price per unit is $17.50. So, Trilex computes its contribution margin in the following way:

$$\text{Contribution margin} = \text{price per unit} - \text{variable cost per unit}$$

$$= \$17.50 \text{ per unit} - \$12.10 \text{ per unit}$$

$$= \$5.40 \text{ per unit}$$

So, Trilex's break-even volume is as follows:

$$\text{Break-even volume} = \frac{\text{Total fixed costs}}{\text{Per unit contribution margin}}$$

$$= \frac{\$390{,}000}{\$5.40 \text{ per unit}}$$

$$= 72{,}222 \text{ units}$$

To convert this number of units to break-even sales dollars, Trilex simply multiplies it by the selling price per unit:

$$\text{Break-even sales} = 72{,}222 \text{ units} \times \$17.50 \text{ per unit} = \$1{,}263{,}889$$

Trilex could compute the sales required to produce a desired profit by treating the profit as if it were a fixed cost:

$$\text{Sales (units)} = \frac{\text{Total fixed costs} + \text{Desired net income}}{\text{Per unit contribution margin}}$$

For example, if Trilex wanted to earn a $60,000 profit, its required sales would be:

$$\text{Sales (units)} = \frac{\$390{,}000 + \$60{,}000}{\$5.40 \text{ per unit}} = 83{,}333 \text{ units}$$

which would require 83,333 units × $17.50 per unit = $1,458,328 in sales.

Constructing a Break-Even Chart

The following steps outline the procedure for constructing a graph that visually portrays the firm's break-even point (that point where revenues equal expenses):

Step 1 On the horizontal axis, mark a scale measuring sales volume in dollars (or in units sold or some other measure of volume). The break-even chart for the Magic Shop shown in Figure 11.8 uses sales volume in dollars because it applies to all types of businesses, departments, and products.

Step 2 On the vertical axis, mark a scale measuring income and expenses in dollars.

Step 3 Draw a fixed expense line intersecting the vertical axis at the proper dollar level parallel to the horizontal axis. The area between this line and the horizontal axis represents the firm's fixed expenses. On the break-even chart for the Magic Shop shown in Figure 11.8, the fixed expense line is drawn horizontally beginning at $177,375 (point *A*). Because this line is parallel to the horizontal axis, it indicates that fixed expenses remain constant at all levels of activity.

Step 4 Draw a total expense line that slopes upward beginning at the point where the fixed-cost line intersects the vertical axis. The precise location of the total expense line is determined by plotting the total cost incurred at a particular sales volume. The total cost for a given sales level is found by using the following formula:

Total = Fixed expenses + Variable expenses expressed as a % of sales
× Sales level expenses

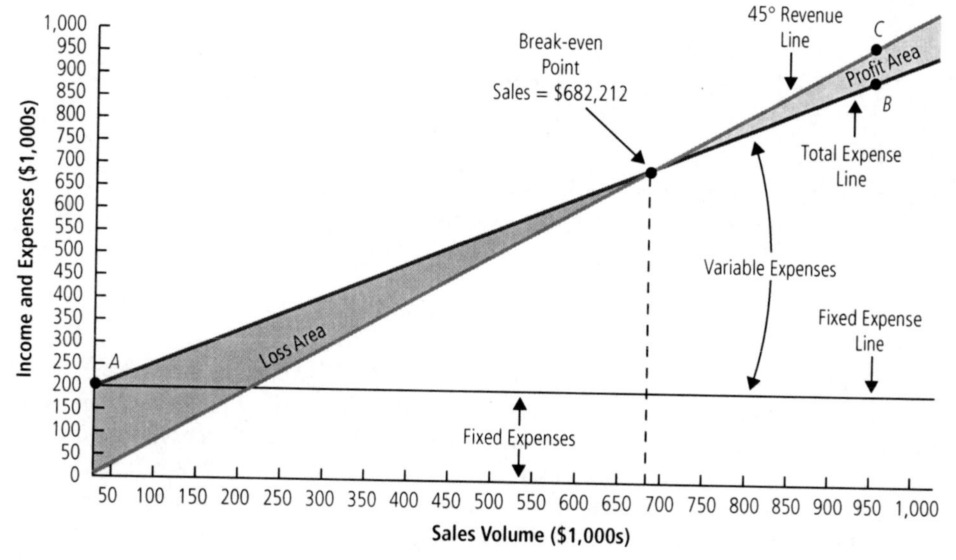

FIGURE 11.8

Break-Even Chart for the Magic Shop

At an arbitrarily chosen sales level of $950,000, the Magic Shop's total costs would be as follows:

$$\text{Total expenses} = \$177{,}375 + (0.74 \times \$950{,}000)$$
$$= \$880{,}375$$

Thus, the Magic Shop's total cost is $880,375 at a net sales level of $950,000 (point *B*). The variable-cost line is drawn by connecting points *A* and *B*. The area between the total cost line and the horizontal axis measures the total costs the Magic Shop incurs at various levels of sales. For example, if the Magic Shop's sales are $850,000, its total costs will be $806,375.

Step 5 Beginning at the graph's origin, draw a 45-degree revenue line showing where total sales volume equals total income. For the Magic Shop, point *C* shows that sales = income = $950,000.

Step 6 Locate the break-even point by finding the intersection of the total-expense line and the revenue line. If the Magic Shop operates at a sales volume to the left of the break-even point, it will incur a loss because the expense line is higher than the revenue line over this range. This is shown by the triangular section labeled Loss Area. On the other hand, if the firm operates at a sales volume to the right of the break-even point, it will earn a profit because the revenue line lies above the expense line over this range. This is shown by the triangular section labeled Profit Area.

You Be the Consultant

Where Do We Break Even?

Anita Dawson is doing some financial planning for her music store. Based on her budget for the upcoming year, Anita is expecting net sales of $495,000. She estimates that cost of goods sold will be $337,000 and that other variable expenses will total $42,750. Using the previous year as a guide, Anita anticipates fixed expenses of $78,100.

Anita recalls an earlier meeting with her accountant, who mentioned that her store had already passed the break-even point eight and one-half months into the year. She was pleased, but really didn't know how the accountant had come up with that calculation. Anita is considering expanding her store into a vacant building next to her existing location and taking on three new product lines. The company's cost structure would change, adding another $66,000 to fixed costs and $22,400 to variable expenses. Anita believes the expansion could generate additional sales of $102,000.

She wonders what she should do.

1. Calculate Anita's break-even point without the expansion plans. Draw a break-even chart.
2. Compute the break-even point assuming that Anita decides to expand.
3. Would you recommend that Anita expand her business? Explain.

Using Break-Even Analysis

Break-even analysis is a useful planning tool for the potential small business owner, especially when approaching potential lenders and investors for funds. It provides an opportunity for integrated analysis of sales volume, expenses, income, and other relevant factors. Break-even analysis is a simple, preliminary screening device for the entrepreneur faced with the business start-up decision. It is easy to understand and use. With just a few calculations, the small business owner can determine the effects of various financial strategies on the business operation. It is a helpful tool for evaluating the impact of changes in investments and expenditures. Greg Smith, for instance, knows that Petra Group's break-even point is $23,000 per week, and he compares sales to that figure every week.[31]

Calculating the break-even point for a start-up business is important because it tells an entrepreneur the minimum volume of sales required to stay in business in the long run.

PowerNap Sleep Centers

Steev RamsDell, founder of PowerNap Sleep Centers, tested his unique business concept—providing spaces for weary travelers to catch a nap—at the Boca Raton International Airport. "We do much more than just give people a place to rest," says RamsDell. "It's like a mini-vacation." The company's DreamSuites are decorated in various themes, including Asian Mist and Tropical Isle. Amenities include aromatherapy, massage tables, recordings of nature sounds, and alarm clocks, and the price is 70 cents per minute. Before setting up a subsidiary, minneNAPolis, in the Mall of America, the largest mall in the United States, located in Bloomington, Minnesota, RamsDell calculated that he would have to sell $700 of nap time to tired shoppers to break even. Given the mall's 4.3 miles of retail stores and attractions, RamsDell thinks he will hit his break-even point quickly. "We're appealing to people who shop all day until they're tired," explains RamsDell.[32]

Break-even analysis does have certain limitations. It is too simple to use as a final screening device because it ignores the importance of cash flows. In addition, the accuracy of the analysis depends on the accuracy of the revenue and expense estimates. Finally, the assumptions pertaining to break-even analysis may not be realistic for some businesses. Break-even calculations assume the following: fixed expenses remain constant for all levels of sales volume; variable expenses change in direct proportion to changes in sales volume; and changes in sales volume have no effect on unit sales price. Relaxing these assumptions does not render this tool useless, however. For example, the owner could employ nonlinear break-even analysis using a graphical approach.

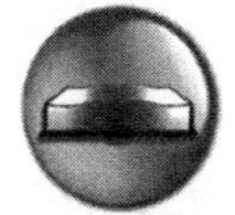

Chapter Summary by Learning Objectives

1. Understand the importance of preparing a financial plan.

Launching a successful business requires an entrepreneur to create a solid financial plan. Not only is such a plan an important tool in raising the capital needed to get a company off the ground, but it also is an essential ingredient in managing a growing business.

Earning a profit does not occur by accident; it takes planning.

2. Describe how to prepare the basic financial statements and use them to manage a small business.

Entrepreneurs rely on three basic financial statements to understand the financial conditions of their companies:

1. ***The balance sheet.*** Built on the accounting equation Assets = Liabilities + Owner's equity (Capital), it provides an estimate of the company's value on a particular date.
2. ***The income statement.*** This statement compares the firm's revenues against its expenses to determine its net profit (or loss). It provides information about the company's bottom line.
3. ***The statement of cash flows.*** This statement shows the change in the company's working capital over the accounting period by listing the sources and the uses of funds.

3. Create projected (pro forma) financial statements.

Projected financial statements are a basic component of a sound financial plan. They help the manager plot the company's financial future by setting operating objectives and by analyzing the reasons for variations from targeted results. In addition, the small business in search of start-up funds will need these pro forma statements to present to prospective lenders and investors. They also assist in determining the amount of cash, inventory, fixtures, and other assets the business will need to begin operation.

4. Understand the basic financial statements through ratio analysis.

The 12 key ratios described in this chapter are divided into four major categories: *liquidity ratios*, which show the small firm's ability to meet its current obligations; *leverage ratios*, which tell how much of the company's financing is provided by owners and how much by creditors; *operating ratios*, which show how effectively the firm uses its resources; *and profitability ratios,* which disclose the company's profitability.

Many agencies and organizations regularly publish such statistics. If there is a discrepancy between the small firm's ratios and those of the typical business, the owner should investigate the reason for the difference. A below-average ratio does not necessarily mean that the business is in trouble.

5. Explain how to interpret financial ratios.

To benefit from ratio analysis, the small company should compare its ratios to those of other companies in the same line of business and look for trends over time.

When business owners detect deviations in their companies' ratios from industry standards, they should determine the cause of the deviations. In some cases, such deviations are the result of sound business decisions; in other instances, however, ratios that are out of the normal range for a particular type of business are indicators of what could become serious problems for a company.

6. Conduct a break-even analysis for a small company.

Business owners should know their firm's break-even point, the level of operations at which total revenues equal total costs; it is the point at which companies neither earn a profit nor incur a loss. Although just a simple screening device, break-even analysis is a useful planning and decision-making tool.

Discussion Questions

1. Why is developing a financial plan so important to an entrepreneur about to launch a business?
2. How should a small business manager use the 12 ratios discussed in this chapter?
3. Outline the key points of the 12 ratios discussed in this chapter. What signals does each give the manager?
4. Describe the method for building a projected income statement and a projected balance sheet for a beginning business.
5. Why are pro forma financial statements important to the financial planning process?
6. How can break-even analysis help an entrepreneur planning to launch a business?

Business Plan Pro

Business PlanPro

One of the significant advantages Business Plan Pro offers is the efficient creation of pro forma financial statements including the balance sheet, profit and loss statement, and cash flow statement. Once you enter the revenues, expenses, and other relevant figures, your financial statements are done! This can save an incredible amount of time, and the format is one that is commonly recognized and respected by bankers and investors. The simplicity of this process also enables you to create "what if" scenarios based on various levels of anticipated revenues and expenses simply by saving versions of your business plan under unique file names.

Business Plan Exercises

On the Web

Go to http://www.bplans.com/bc/# or use the link at http://www.prenhall.com/scarborough under the Business Plan Resource tab, Finance and Business Calculators. Here you will find a collection of online tools including a Break Even Calculator. Open this tool and enter the information it requests—the average per unit revenue, the average per unit cost, and the estimated monthly fixed costs you anticipate. This tool will calculate your break-even point in units and revenue. Change the data and observe the difference it makes in your break-even point. What does this tell you about the level of risk that you may experience based on the most realistic projections you can make?

In the Software

Select a sample plan that you have found to be interesting. Go to the "Financial Plan" section and look at their financial statements within the text of the business plan. Notice how the statements are organized. Month-to-month detail is provided for at least the first year with annual totals for subsequent years. Also note the associated tables and graphics that appear within the financial plan. Graphics can be excellent communication tools, particularly when you are communicating information about financial trends and comparisons.

Building Your Business Plan

Review all information that you have within the "Financial Plan" section of your business plan. Add any "Important Assumptions" to this section as you deem necessary. This is a good place to make notes and comments to test or further research any of these assumptions. If you are in the start-up stage, capture the costs that you expect will be incurred to launch your business. The "Investment Offering" may appear, based on your choice in the Plan Wizard, and you can complete that information. Review your information for your break-even analysis and then review the financial statements including your profit and loss, cash flow, and balance sheet statements.

This chapter identifies 12 key business ratios. Based on your projections, determine each of those ratios. Compare them to industry standard ratios. Most, if not all, of these ratios are available through Business Plan Pro's "ratio" section, the final topic in the "Financial Plan" section.

Ratio Analysis

	Your Projected Ratio	Industry Ratio	Variance
1. Current ratio	______	______	______
2. Quick ratio	______	______	______
3. Debt ratio	______	______	______
4. Deb to net worth ratio	______	______	______
5. Times interest earned ratio	______	______	______
6. Average inventory turnover ratio	______	______	______
7. Average collection period ratio	______	______	______
8. Average payable period ratio	______	______	______
9. Net sales to total assets ratio	______	______	______
10. Net profit on sales ratio	______	______	______
11. Net profit to assets ratio	______	______	______
12. Net profit to equity ratio	______	______	______

If you notice significant differences in these comparisons, determine why those variances exist. Might this be telling you something about the reality of your projections, or is this just due to the stage and differences of your business compared to the larger industry? These ratios can be excellent tools for helping you to question, test, and validate your assumptions and projections. Good business planning, solid projections, and a thorough analysis of these ratios can help you to launch a more viable business with greater certainty of the outcome.

Beyond the Classroom . . .

1. Ask the owner of a small business to provide your class with copies of the firm's financial statements (current or past).
   - Using these statements, compute the 12 key ratios described in this chapter.
   - Compare the company's ratios with those of the typical firm in this line of business.
   - Interpret the ratios and make suggestions for operating improvements.
   - Prepare a break-even analysis for the owner.
2. Find a publicly held company of interest to you that provides its financial statements on the Web. You can conduct a Web search using the company's name or you can find lists of companies at the Securities and Exchange Commission's EDGAR database at http://www.sec.gov/cgi-bin/srch-edgar or you can visit the Report Gallery at AnnualReports.com at http://www.reportgallery.com/. Analyze the company's financial statements by calculating the 12 ratios covered in this chapter and compare these ratios to industry averages found in RMA's *Annual Statement Studies* or Dun & Bradstreet's *The Cost of Doing Business* reports. Do you spot any problem areas? Strengths? What recommendations can you make to improve the company's financial position? What do you project the company's future to be?

Chapter 11
Managing Entrepreneurial Growth

- Discussing the five stages of a typical life cycle
- Exploring the elements involved with an entrepreneurial firm
- Surveying the ways that entrepreneurs build adaptive firms
- Examining the transformation from an entrepreneurial style to a managerial style
- Identifying the key factors that play a major role during the growth stage
- Introducing the steps useful for breaking through the growth wall

Chapter 11

Entrepreneurial management

Objectives	**615**
Introduction	**616**
The entrepreneurial new venture	**616**
Influences on the entrepreneurial effort	**617**
The challenge of entrepreneurial growth	**618**
Keeping SME management simple	**618**
Ability to manage growth	**619**
Maintaining entrepreneurship	**619**
Pressures for change	**621**
The transformation characterized	**622**
The threat to entrepreneurship in the growing venture	**622**
Implications for management	**623**
Conclusions	**625**
Summary	**626**
Learning questions	**626**

Objectives

After reading this chapter the reader will have an overview of the pioneering SME. We shall consider some of the factors that determine whether or not an SME continues to be entrepreneurial, and the reader will have an insight into the impact of being entrepreneurial on the SME. The chapter aims to give the reader an appreciation of the implications of managing an entrepreneurial enterprise and defines an entrepreneurial management approach.

Introduction

In Chapter 5 the issues pertinent to managing an SME were discussed. Some of the focus was on the characteristics of the SME, the turbulence of the environment in which SMEs operate, their relative lack of power in such circumstances and the necessary management practices. In Chapter 4 we discussed the concept of entrepreneurship and the numerous approaches that help us to understand entrepreneurial managers.

The entrepreneurial firm, though, can be distinguished from any other SME by its consistent focus on opportunity and its commitment to continuous innovation and change. However, any enterprise will be entrepreneurial only because its management is consistently entrepreneurial. In terms of its character and culture the enterprise reflects the personality and behaviour of its management. As in lifecycle models though, entrepreneurship can emerge, grow, mature and decline. The challenge of managing in an entrepreneurial small firm is to plan and organize to maintain that entrepreneurial effort to develop an entrepreneurial character within the enterprise that once initiated becomes a force in itself, driving the enterprise along a path of change and growth.

In this chapter we shall discuss how this focus on opportunities and the commitment to continuous innovation and change impacts on the SME. We consider what the implications are for managing such an enterprise. Some further thoughts on entrepreneurial management, considered first in Chapter 5 are offered in conclusion.

The entrepreneurial new venture

Lifecycle models give us a useful framework for characterizing the entrepreneurial SME and for understanding what makes it entrepreneurial. When a new venture is launched, the action is entrepreneurial, the period is pioneering. An opportunity in the marketplace has been identified and action taken to recruit the resources needed to exploit it.

These early stages are characterized by informality in relations between actors in the enterprise, by limitless energy on their part, and a high tolerance of the equally high levels of uncertainty and attendant risk that pervade these pioneering days in particular. Yet there is boundless zeal on the part of those involved and a determination to succeed. There is little structure, few specialist skills and extensive role ambiguity, with people in the company prepared to do any job. The new venture will have little in the way of resources, be they plans, skilled people, finance or current and accurate sources of information, the latter being especially critical for effective decision-making at this stage. Control and communications will tend to be highly informal, unstructured and based on the existence of strong personal relationships and on the charisma and even the magnetism of the founding entrepreneur. This will be reflected in leadership style, which in this pioneering stage will tend to be highly centralized, personalized and authoritarian in character. The founding entrepreneur is likely to experience problems with delegation and the sharing of the enterprise with others, so great is the need at this time for independence in the management of the new venture.[1]

Luckily, though, there will be few customers and the new venture will be operating in only a small number of localized markets, with few products, so the management of this new venture will be relatively simple. The founding entrepreneur alone makes the decisions on how to take the enterprise forward. The founder is involved in everything to do with the running of the business and is of necessity a generalist when it comes to managing the new venture. While the firm remains small and simple in terms of activity in its chosen market the founder can continue to play 'small business' and even make a reasonable living. So long as the enterprise does not appear to be so successful so as to attract the predatory attention of potential competitors, then all should continue well. The challenge to new business owners is keeping the business ticking over at an acceptable level to meet their material and personal needs.

Whether owner-managers who wish to contain their enterprise to a definite size, either in terms of number of employees or level of turnover, are still entrepreneurial is open to debate. One approach we suggest to understanding an individual's *degree* of commitment to entrepreneurship is to consider the degree of entrepreneurship on a continuum (see Figure 11.1). This commitment reflects their focus on opportunity and their willingness to accept the impact on them and on their enterprise of successfully managing that opportunity. The continuum suggests that some SME owners are reluctantly entrepreneurial, are, or indeed may become, essentially resistant to change, accepting it only because they must. At the other extreme the individual entrepreneur is represented as proactively keen to pursue any opportunity and to acquire and manage whatever resources are necessary to exploit it fully. Somewhere in between the individual's commitment to entrepreneurial activity can be seen as a response to opportunities that present themselves.

Influences on the entrepreneurial effort

As the enterprise begins to grow it will need to maintain an entrepreneurial character. Whether or not this happens depends wholly on the entrepreneur. It is the entrepreneur's attitude to growth and her/his appreciation of the impact that successful growth will have on the new enterprise that will be the crucial determining factors.

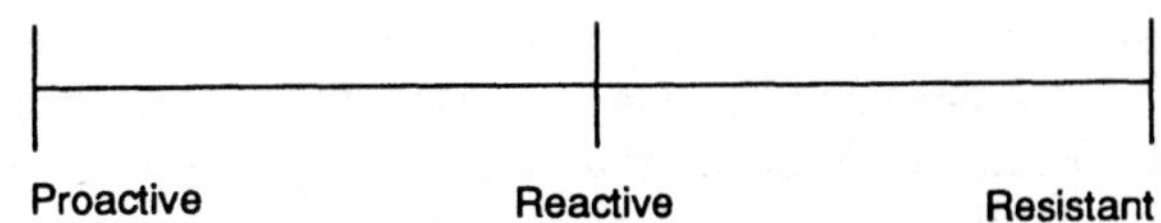

Figure 11.1 Entrepreneurial continuum.

A number of issues will have a bearing on their decision to remain proactively entrepreneurial or to exercise a degree of control over the amount of growth and change that the enterprise undergoes. First, SME owners may desire to remain independent and maintain ownership of their enterprise. Second, they may be driven, after the initial taxing effort to launch the venture, by an impulse to simplify life by keeping the enterprise small and more easily manageable. Thus they may attempt to limit the number of customers with whom they deal. As a consequence, the number of employees and external associates can be kept to a minimum. Keeping the business small will also mean that the informal rules defining the nature of relationships with people inside and outside the venture can be kept simple. The level of uncertainty and risk too can be kept to more manageable levels. Third, SME owners may harbour a genuine concern about their ability to manage successfully in a fast-growing, increasingly complex enterprise.

The challenge of entrepreneurial growth

Owner/managers' desire to maintain ownership of their enterprise and to remain independent operators will have a significant bearing on their commitment to growth. However, the individual owner/managers can never embody all the skills, the know-how and know-who, nor have access to all the resources necessary to expand the small firm on a continuous basis. Real entrepreneurial growth in an enterprise is only possible when entrepreneurs share their vision of the enterprise's potential with others who can bring to the venture new ideas, specialist skills, energy and commitment that make the achievement of that vision a real possibility. In return for their involvement, such people want to have a say in how the venture develops and grows.

The degree to which owner/managers want their enterprise to grow and develop will be reflected in their preparedness to share the management of their enterprise with others, both from within and outside the enterprise, who can help in a material way. This will have implications for the style of management in the enterprise, recruitment policies and teambuilding activities, the generation and maintenance of an appropriate climate that encourages entrepreneurship, and the development of relationships beyond the enterprise.[2]

Keeping SME management simple

The pioneering stage of the new business venture is recognized as the most chaotic, uncertain and risky period, with only a third of enterprises surviving beyond the first eighteen months. Not surprisingly, many owner/managers, having got beyond this period and established a viable business of sorts are reluctant to expose themselves or their enterprises to further risk and uncertainty by seeking ever more growth. The often overwhelming temptation is to keep life simple by keeping the business small.

Thus, the number of external rules and regulations and the level of risk and uncertainty are kept to acceptable and tolerable limits.

Ability to manage growth

Growth will have an impact on the small firm. It will change the nature of the informal roles and relationships that characterized the very early pioneering days and increase the level of complexity in terms of the rules and regulations needed to control more efficiently the increasingly larger enterprise. Many small business owners feel a genuine concern about their ability to manage in such rapidly changing, increasingly complex circumstances, in particular when they have to give leadership and guidance to employees who may have higher levels of current, specialist knowledge and training than the owner/manager. The problem is how they can manage these people and maintain an entrepreneurial thrust, which may often appear to be detrimental to the more formal backgrounds of the new staff.

Maintaining entrepreneurship

Continued entrepreneurship is not enough, though, for potential growth if this means simply 'more of the same'. The energies, the vision, the competencies required to address the challenges of starting a new venture differ substantially from those required to take that venture on to a consistently growth-oriented track. What is needed if the pioneering enterprise is to have any real chance for growth is a maturing entrepreneurship which, while remaining opportunity-focused and innovative, is professionally competent in managing the growing enterprise, in giving leadership, in sharing a vision of its potential and in building an entrepreneurial team to achieve it.

Such entrepreneurship will be unconstrained by debates about ownership but will see in growth a potential for a different type of independence, one built on an increasingly strengthened profile and competitive position in an industry and marketplace. It will be undaunted by the complex challenges that attend growth from both inside and outside the enterprise, indeed it will seek to tackle them in a typically positive and innovative way. Finally, it will be an entrepreneurship that will have developed the necessary professional management skills that will relieve the lead entrepreneurs of any lingering concerns they might have regarding their personal ability to manage the growing enterprise beyond its pioneering stage.

The stages of entrepreneurship beyond the pioneering stage can be illustrated as a lifecycle (see Figure 11.2). The key elements of the model are the entrepreneurial effort, the entrepreneurial scenario and the return on the entrepreneurial effort. The model seeks to represent the relationships between these elements and give a basis for understanding the challenge of maintaining the entrepreneurial effort. This, we suggest, is reflected in the energy, zeal and level of commitment of the individual to

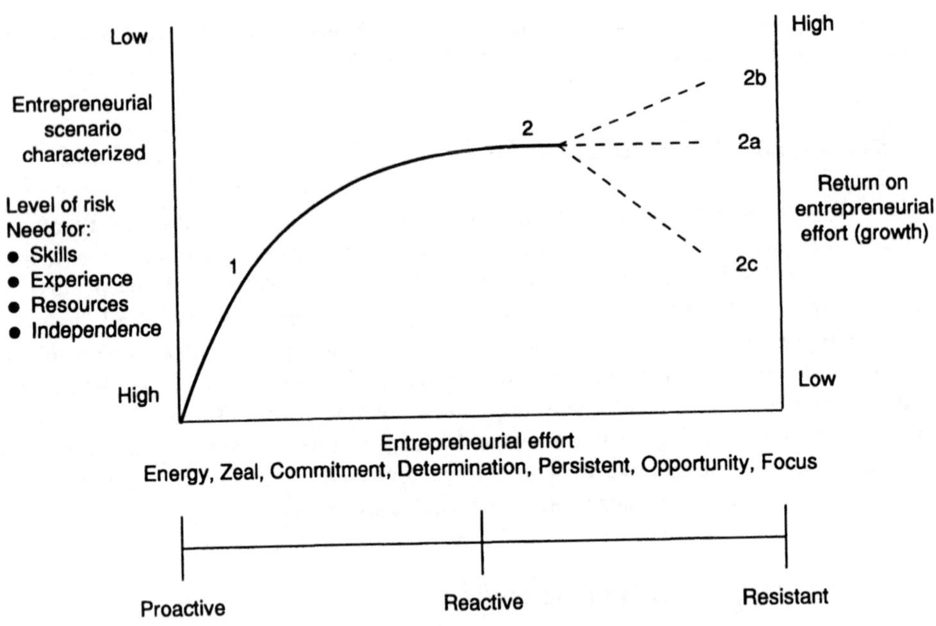

Figure 11.2 Entrepreneurial effort over the lifecycle of an enterprise.

establishing and building an enterprise by constantly focusing on market opportunities and innovative activity. The entrepreneurial scenario is characterized by the level of risk, uncertainty and chaos attending the launch of the new venture and the individual's need for skills, knowledge, experience and personal independence, not to mention adequate resources to launch the venture. Finally, the return on entrepreneurial effort reflects the degree to which the venture develops and grows over time as a consequence of the entrepreneur's efforts and changing circumstances.

From the model let us consider three points. At point (1) the entrepreneurial effort is highest at the outset of the venture and the entrepreneurial scenario is probably at its most adverse. The level of risk and uncertainty too is high, as are individuals' needs for skills and experience. Their desire to maintain their independence will be particularly significant at this time too. Their need for resources is also going to be high, as indeed will be their difficulties in gaining access to them. The return on entrepreneurial efforts in these early days is at its lowest. Yet entrepreneurs have a vision of how things might be and they are hungry enough proactively to seek ways to fulfil their ambitions.

At point (2) the model suggests that towards the late growth/early maturity stage, the level of entrepreneurial effort has arrived at a mid-point. The circumstances here are characterized by relatively low risk and a degree of sophistication and professionalism in the management of the enterprise. Access to resources is less problematic, the enterprise has a presence in the marketplace so it is easier to acquire whatever is needed for any new innovations. Individual entrepreneurs now are more reactive in their outlook. They and the enterprise may be less hungry for change and new opportunities, which characterized the early days. The return on current entrepreneurial effort is more than satisfactory and life for the entrepreneur is rewarding. Why spoil it?

As with lifecycle models generally we have a framework for gaining an insight into the options facing the SME at this time. To take action to extend the maturity stage (at point 2a), to seek to bring the enterprise on to a venture renewal track (at point 2b) or to do nothing and, in an entrepreneurially dynamic environment, risk losing everything (at point 2c).

Pressures for change

The truly entrepreneurial enterprise does not stand still. Constantly in search of new opportunities, entrepreneurs' focus primarily on the external environment of customers, competitors and markets – after all, the growth of any enterprise is achieved through effective action in the markets for its products. The successful pursuit and exploitation of opportunities emanating from the external market, however, will have an impact on the existing SME by creating pressure for internal change.

In recent times research has sought to spotlight the crucial importance for managers of adopting strategies for the internal market similar to those adopted so successfully in the company's external markets. There can be little doubt, though, that the successful implementation of marketing strategies in the organization's external market will impact on the existing organization bringing about changes of all kinds; for example, in the way resources are allocated, how information is communicated, the roles people play and in the very structures needed to ensure the continuous and successful delivery of externally focused marketing strategies.[3]

Any failure to manage these change processes and maintain a good fit between what is happening in the firm's external and internal environments will undermine the successful implementation of those strategies for growth. Once again, change and the management of change as a consequence of successfully adopting and implementing marketing-led strategies are key issues and lie at the heart of understanding the entrepreneurial energies at work within the enterprise. They are critical to understanding the challenge of management in the entrepreneurial small firm. These entrepreneurial energies force a transition or transformation in the fabric of the organization and a consequential change in the way things are done by the people who work there, including the lead entrepreneur.[4]

The transformation characterized

The entrepreneurial enterprise goes through a transformation with each successfully implemented, marketing-led growth strategy. In the pioneering stages the company is close to its few customers. Relationships, communications systems and decision-making are all informal. There is a great deal of ambiguity about the roles and tasks people play in the enterprise, control systems and accountability are unclear, the level of specialist or management skills are limited and the fortunes of the enterprise remain firmly under the personal guidance of the founder entrepreneur, who is the sole source of entrepreneurial thinking and energy. Chaos and unpredictability typify these early days.[5]

However, with each success comes pressure for change, forcing a transformation on the new venture and the people in it. This period will be characterized by a rapid succession of dilemmas or challenges which will have implications for the ongoing management of the enterprise. First, there will be the sense that the challenges confronting the growing venture are getting too big and that things are getting out of hand. As a consequence increasing pressure is exerted on existing communication systems and organization structures. The pressure also begins to open up gaps in the skills mix of the existing staff members and exposes deficits in the lead entrepreneur's management competencies. Increasing confusion emerges and not a little resentment over people's roles and responsibilities during the transition. Crisis management, 'fire-fighting', and an increasing loss of focus characterize this period, leading to pressures for new systems, clear structures, more formal controls and greater accountability. And with the emergence of specialist skills comes pressure too for increased decentralization and a greater sharing of power.

The threat to entrepreneurship in the growing venture

One possible victim of entrepreneurial success is the culture within the enterprise for entrepreneurship itself. The successful application of pressure for greater stability in the venture as a reaction to constant change undermines the acceptability of change as part of the emerging culture. In addition any strict definition or clarification of people's roles and tasks in the venture, reinforced by the emergence of specialist functions and supporting structures (with implied routes for promotion), undermines the early culture of collaboration and the sharing of ideas. The new commitment to tighter operating mechanisms and control systems compromises the potential for initiative and reduces the scope of people in the enterprise to take risks, to act entrepreneurially.

Implications for management

With mounting pressure for greater stability and structure in the enterprise, the lead entrepreneur faces a fundamental management challenge in order somehow to maintain the entrepreneurial character of the venture and to ensure it remains focused on opportunity and growth. This can only be done if founding entrepreneurs are prepared to share the management of their enterprises with the people who work for them and if they create a climate within the enterprise that is essentially entrepreneurial in that it encourages those employees within it to be opportunity focused and innovative too.

Specifically, they must give leadership, they must provide vision and develop it in others in the enterprise, they must build and manage entrepreneurial teams and provide appropriate organizational structures in the enterprise to facilitate their work. They must plan for change and act as a catalyst in the enterprise to ensure that things do happen, that goals are clearly identified and action is taken to achieve them. Ultimately, they must acquire the appropriate skills to manage the changes occurring in their enterprise, and gain access, through effective networking, to the necessary resources to implement them.[6]

Giving leadership

SME owner/managers must play the critical and pivotal role of the lead entrepreneur in the enterprise. Therefore, they must provide vision and direction to those working in the enterprise and such structure as is needed, without crushing initiative, to ensure things get done. They must build entrepreneurial teams within the enterprise and encourage members to be creative and innovative in the resolution of problems or the exploitation of opportunities. They must protect the innovative, empower colleagues, secure resources and encourage a climate within the enterprise, as it grows, that is tolerant and committed to planned change.

Providing vision

As lead entrepreneurs, the owners of growing SMEs must provide a focus for those working for them and a vision of the venture's longer-term direction, notwithstanding the twists and turns that characterize its progress *en route*. They also need to encourage those who work with them to accept ownership of that vision and to identify their own progress and development over the longer run with this vision.

Building entrepreneurial teams

Building entrepreneurial teams within the growing enterprise is a further critical management activity of lead entrepreneurs within the entrepreneurial small firm. As the enterprise undergoes a transformation the attendant pressures highlight the growing skills deficit within it. New specialist skills, undoubtedly considered unnecessary in the pioneering days, are now urgently needed as the challenges facing the growing enterprise become more complex. Identifying the nature of such gaps and selecting and recruiting the best possible people available to fill them becomes an essential activity for management in the entrepreneurial SME if it is to remain entrepreneurial. Critical too are the steps taken to create an environment within the enterprise which encourages those carefully selected people to stay with it as it continues to develop and grow. Good people don't stay in an organization long if their value is not recognized and rewarded. Consequently, the entrepreneurial manager has a key role to play in motivating entrepreneurial people within the SME, in empowering them and encouraging them to take initiatives and in offering protection to the very innovative, who consistently challenge and disturb the status quo.

Providing structure

Organization structures are often seen as the very antithesis of entrepreneurial activity and potential, however, the provision of some sort of loose structure in the enterprise becomes essential as it grows. The lead entrepreneur must play a core role in this critical activity if the innovative efforts of the people within the enterprise are not to be misdirected and squandered.

Furthermore, with constant and rapid growth, confusion and resentment can begin to build as people employed in the organization, both original employees and new recruits, become increasingly unclear about their changing roles and the nature of the relationships that exist between them. The pressure will mount for clearer definitions of people's relationships with each other within the organization.

The provision of some structure clarifies the roles and responsibilities of people in the venture, ensuring an integration, balance and direction to their activities. People know what is expected of them and where their efforts contribute to the continued progress of the enterprise.

Planning for change

The truly entrepreneurial enterprise strives to anticipate change opportunities and to become increasingly proactive in its commitment to innovation and continual renewal. Dissatisfaction with the status quo, therefore, characterizes the culture of the business, and the entrepreneurial manager plays the central role in nurturing and maintaining an environment within the enterprise which sustains such a culture. Planning for and managing change within the enterprise becomes as fundamental a part of the manager's thinking as the very definition of what business the company is in.

It calls for practice in creative problem-solving and imagination in decision-making, for experimentation and adaptability and the involvement of everyone in the enterprise in the pursuit and accommodation of continuous change.

Ensuring things happen

The innovative owner/manager in the entrepreneurial SME plays the key management role of ensuring things get done within the enterprise. As a primary catalyst they must be able to commit considerable time and effort to the development of the enterprise and to be able to draw from those working with them comparable levels of effort and commitment. The lead entrepreneurs must act as role models; indeed, within the enterprise they must be energetic, adventurous, action-oriented but able to manage the attendant stress of such a commitment to achieving goals in a positive way.

Acquiring skills and resources

The management of a truly entrepreneurial SME means managing an enterprise which is, by design, experiencing continued growth and development. This growth is a consequence of the management's opportunity focus and continuous commitment to innovation and change. In the pioneering period, when customers and employees were few in number and the demand for resources was small, relationships were relatively uncomplicated and simple to manage. The entrepreneur worked with employees on the shopfloor and managed the strategic progress of the small firm by the 'seat of his pants', gut feeling and intuition. He/she saw an opportunity, felt it could work and pursued it. He/she was happiest at the cutting edge of operations in the enterprise, doing things, solving problems, looking up now and then to see how – and, indeed, where – things were going.

Relationships within and beyond the enterprise become more complex as it grows in size, in terms of the numbers and types of customers, markets and products it addresses and the type of skilled people it must employ or be in contact with if it is to remain entrepreneurial. The lead entrepreneur must be prepared to change role within the enterprise, from one who is at the sharp end of innovative activity in the business to one who manages it in others, giving focus and guidance to those doing it.

Conclusions

To give leadership, sell a vision, develop and motivate entrepreneurial teams, encourage an opportunity focus in others and maintain the entrepreneurial effort of the enterprise calls for a whole new array of competencies. To manage effectively in the entrepreneurial SME business owners must seek to develop these in themselves. This critical issue of developing entrepreneurial competencies, and in particular the planned management of personal contact networks, is extensively developed in Chapters 14 and 15 as innovative responses to managing in the entrepreneurial marketing-oriented SME.

Summary

In this chapter we have considered the entrepreneurial small and medium-sized enterprise, how it might be considered to be entrepreneurial and how it might differ from SMEs which are not. The primary focus was the propensity of the SME to seek out opportunities for change and to accommodate the impact of those changes on its culture, structure, roles, relationships and control mechanisms. The characteristics of the entrepreneurial scenario, the entrepreneurial effort and the return on entrepreneurial effort highlight the implications of managing in such a dynamic environment. Effective management in these conditions has implications for management styles, orientations and competencies.

Learning questions

1. What is an entrepreneurial SME?
2. In what ways does the entrepreneurial SME differ from one that is not?
3. Discuss the likely impact on the pioneering new venture of a continued commitment to entrepreneurship.
4. What are the key characteristics of the entrepreneurial transformation?
5. What factors determine whether or not an SME remains entrepreneurial?
6. Discuss the implications for the entrepreneur of managing this entrepreneurial transformation.

Notes and references

1. Timmons, J. (1990) *New Venture Creation*, Chicago: Richard Irwin.
2. Kao, J. J. (1990) *The Entrepreneurial Organization*, Englewood Cliffs, NJ: Prentice Hall.
3. Piercy, N. (1992) *Marketing Led Strategic Change*, London: Butterworth-Heinemann.
4. Miner, J. B. (1990) 'Entrepreneurs, high growth entrepreneurs and managers: Contrasting and overlapping motivational patterns', *Journal of Business Venturing* 5, pp. 221–34.
5. Stewart, V. (1983) *Change: The challenge of management*, Maidenhead: McGraw-Hill.
6. Lessem, R. (1986) *Enterprise Development*, Aldershot: Gower.

Further reading

Greiner, L. E. (1972) 'Evolution and revolution as organizations grow', *Harvard Business Review*, July–August, pp. 64–73.

Moss, Kanter, R. (1985) *The Change Masters*, London: Unwin.

Scott, M. and Bruce, R. (1987) 'Five stages of growth in small business', *Long Range Planning* **20** (3), pp. 45–52.

Chapter 12
Contemporary Issues in Entrepreneurship

- Introducing the new international developments that have expanded opportunities for the global market
- Examining how entrepreneurs can take advantage of importing opportunities
- Exploring the entrepreneurial benefits of exporting
- Setting forth the five key steps for entering the international marketplace
- Describing four basic steps to follow when buying a business
- Explaining the importance of valuation
- Considering the characteristics of family business
- Considering female entepreneurs and minority entrepreneurs

Chapter 14

Networks for entrepreneurs and entrepreneurial marketers

Objectives	**629**
Introduction	**629**
Defining a personal contact network (PCN)	**630**
Why PCNs are particularly entrepreneurial	**630**
Entrepreneurial networks as a process	**631**
The importance of entrepreneurial marketing networks	**633**
Entrepreneurial networking	**635**
Factors determining the quality and potential of the entrepreneur's PCN	**636**
Developing entrepreneurial marketing networks	**639**
Relationships between organizations	**640**
Rationale for inter-organizational relationships (IORs)	**640**
Examples of IORs	**643**
Forming IORs – the process	**644**
Relations between enterprise support agencies	**646**
Summary	**647**
Learning questions	**647**

Objectives

After reading this chapter, the reader will have covered the following objectives:

- To introduce the reader to the types of network available to entrepreneurs.
- To discuss the entrepreneurial nature of personal contact networks (PCNs).
- To investigate the particular significance of PCNs for marketing in an SME.
- To discuss those factors that determine the quality and potential of an individual entrepreneur's PCN.
- To consider the implications for the entrepreneur of developing his/her PCN.
- To introduce inter-organizational relationships (IORs) as a logical development from personal contacts.
- To examine the conditions that encourage IORs.
- To study models of IOR formation.
- To consider examples of inter-firm collaboration.

Introduction

Business people regularly make contact with numerous associates; these may include suppliers, customers, opinion-formers, competitors, government agencies, etc., and this allows them to conduct their business. However, while a business owner may initially set up unilateral contacts with others, as associations develop, the focal business person's contacts will, in all probability, make further contacts among themselves. The focal entrepreneur's suppliers may, for example, begin to supply others in the network. Therefore, networks encompass the totality of the associations or links between individuals, groups and organizations in a given social system, and it is likely that any modification in the nature of the contact between two or more associates will have a corresponding influence on other associations within the network.

In a business context associations can be instrumental, political, affective or normative. Entrepreneurs interact regularly with people and businesses in their environment to acquire resources, initiate action and dispose of marketable goods, and these exchanges have an essential economic component. However, these instrumental connections often create dependencies between individuals and they impact on the power of the interacting parties. In this situation highly dependent individuals will try to improve their own situation by persuading or putting pressure on others to modify their behaviour. Current relationships may also encourage friendship bonds and a sharing of values or beliefs between the parties. These bonds of affection can have a considerable impact on the way in which people conduct their business. In general, the frequency, nature and type of relationship between individuals or organizations influences the manner in which business is carried out between them.[1]

While networks generally define the type and totality of relationships between people and organizations, personal contact networks (PCNs) are seen as particularly relevant in the context of the entrepreneurial SME with its centralized, independent and personalized style of management. Personal contacts are also significant for marketing in the entrepreneurial SME from its pioneering days of intuitive marketing through subsequent periods of greater structure and control when marketing might be described as sophisticated. Such contacts play a critical role in maintaining the entrepreneurial efforts of those managing the enterprise's development and ensuring its continued commitment to opportunity and change.

With further development and maturity many organizations begin to consider the possibility of more permanent associations with their personal contacts. The complexity and volatility of the organizational world in recent years, coupled with a lack of resources in difficult economic times, has encouraged many firms to consider the benefits of working with their contact organizations and not against them. These inter-organizational relationships can lead to improved customer care, a sharing of information and a reduction in the costs of developing new products and services.

Defining a personal contact network (PCN)

A PCN can be defined as the relationships or alliances which individuals develop, or may seek to develop, between themselves and others. Individual behaviour is strongly influenced by the social context within which it takes place and not in isolation from it. Individuals may play a focal or central role in building both formal and informal relationships with people within their environs who are useful in assisting them to develop an enterprise in which they have a personal interest. The relationships that they establish and develop are unique to those individuals given their central role within it. Such a network is not a tangible asset that can be sold to another interested party; rather, it is intrinsically lodged in individuals themselves and in the personalized way they have nurtured and developed their relationships with those who form a part of their network of contacts.

Why PCNs are particularly entrepreneurial

PCNs are uniquely useful for entrepreneurs since the pioneering small firm is wholly dependent on the owner/manager for its direction and focus. Management in such an enterprise is characterized as being largely independent, highly centralized and highly personalized. Ideas for growth and development, its direction and how it is to be achieved, including the identification of the necessary resources, remain solidly the responsibility of the lead entrepreneur, who struggles to make and maintain a fit between the many components of the entrepreneurial process. To do so requires the sensitive use of entrepreneurial contacts in order to obtain the necessary knowledge and information. Entrepreneurs' use of personal contacts lends itself particularly well to this typically entrepreneurial way of doing business, which is largely unstructured, unplanned, intuitive, non-linear and time-compressed. Entrepreneurs' PCNs are aptly characterized by a high degree of informality and lack of planning which surrounds the management of the PCN and by its natural, almost subconscious development and use. Such personal networks act as a lubricant to the often overheated, chaotic and almost frenzied process by which the lead entrepreneur seeks to orchestrate that fit between an opportunity identified and the resources needed to exploit it.[2]

Entrepreneurs' personal contacts provide them with a source of accurate information and dependable guidance in a turbulent and dynamic environment. Because of the limited time, size and no track record they need to be able to access the support, information and guidance necessary for their enterprise's continued entrepreneurial development. Even with successful entrepreneurial action, which often forces the pioneering enterprise along an uncertain and risky transformational path towards growth, the need for personal networks remains strong. Such a transformation is often characterized by a rapid succession of dilemmas and challenges which change the character and culture of the firm and the roles and relationships of people working within it. Lead entrepreneurs play a critical role in effecting this transformation. Their decision to go for growth (or not) and what steps to take to achieve it will depend on their appreciation, understanding and acceptance of the most likely impact that growth will have on the enterprise and their role in it. The increasing complexities that attend such growth underline the central role of maintaining a dynamic network of personal contacts.

Entrepreneurial networks as a process

Entrepreneurial networking may be seen, therefore, as an activity in which the entrepreneurially oriented SME owners build and manage personal relationships with particular individuals in their surroundings. These are likely to be people who may be influential in determining the degree to which their enterprise is likely to become and remain committed to innovation, development and growth. The focus of entrepreneurial networking in the first place lies in providing entrepreneurs with a consistent supply of ideas for new products or markets which offer them and their enterprises real possibilities for sustainable growth.

In addition to providing them with insights into possible new opportunities they provide them with a means of accessing the resources necessary to exploit them. More often than not, though, entrepreneurs' need for resources exceeds their ability to acquire them. Entrepreneurs regularly pursue a number of opportunities and continuously evaluate their likelihood of real success. They must make tentative, short-term contracts for the supply of resources and, therefore need lots of likely backers who are prepared to support them in the expectation that they can realize an outstanding opportunity.

Accessing resources is no mean undertaking for someone with a vision or opportunity that might be exploited, but little understanding of how to do it. The shopping list of requisite resources can be extensive. Alongside finance, physical resources such as plant and equipment and additional human assets are essential. Lead entrepreneurs rarely possess all the skills and know-how needed to develop the firm; there will be gaps in any individual's portfolio of skills and teams are an effective means of filling this gap. Finding those resources and persuading those who own them to place them at the disposal of the entrepreneur is a critical aspect of networking. In making the fit between an opportunity and the necessary resources lead entrepreneurs need to employ all their persuasive and political skills to encourage people who are more powerful than they are to part with their valuable resources.[3]

An approach to networking which parallels this process is proposed by William Biemans. The elements of the approach include 'actors', 'activities' and 'resources'. Actors may be individuals, groups or organizations who perform activities and control resources. The activities they perform are categorized as transformational (activities that change resources through the use of other resources) and transactional (activities which link resources to each other). The resources in question are any human, physical or financial assets needed and acquired to carry out an activity. To make such processes work requires particular types of contacts to obtain the necessary knowledge and information and assets. These are issues which we shall consider in greater detail later in this chapter, when we look at factors determining the quality and potential of the entrepreneur's PCN.[4]

One final point worth addressing in relation to this process of entrepreneurial networking is that it is important to recognize that an entrepreneur's networks change and evolve in response to the increasing complexity attendant on entrepreneurially driven growth and development. The literature suggests that as the enterprise moves from launch, to new venture start-up through to becoming an established business with a recognized profile in its marketplace, the nature of its networking changes. The initial near-total dependence on social networks gives way to more business-focused networking and finally to strategic networking. The importance of broad social and inter-organizational networks are recognized as important for successful new venture start-ups and for their subsequent development.[5]

We must recognize that as the small entrepreneurial firm itself develops and grows, so too will the nature and character of the networks and networking within the enterprise and outside it. In its early days marketing in the small firm is conducted in a very chaotic, intuitive manner, but there is normally continued commitment to entrepreneurial development. As the enterprise develops, marketing activities move increasingly towards a greater level of sophistication. This has implications for the way in which entrepreneurs manage their networking activity. As they are urged to develop a competency in the planned construction of networks, so too it seems they must develop an ability in what might be called a planned approach to deconstruction too. As with most social systems, networks have lifecycles and they need to be maintained and renewed constantly. However, if they become obsolete, networks must be discarded.

The importance of entrepreneurial marketing networks

Marketing in an entrepreneurial SME has been discussed above in detail and it was suggested that the practice very much reflects the personality of the entrepreneur, that it is highly informal and *ad hoc*, relying, certainly in the early days, on the intuitive skills of the entrepreneur. This early unsophisticated marketing approach is seen as largely reactive in character. In addition, the enterprise they are developing emerges characteristically as one with a limited capability in obtaining quality information for effective decision-making and future planning, particularly in the area of marketing. With limited capability for processing information and with limited margins for absorbing errors, should plans not go accordingly, one can understand why much planning and decision-making are perceived by many small business owners as esoteric exercises more relevant to larger organizations than their own. However, identifying sustainable market opportunities and finding the resources to support them requires entrepreneurial contacts who can provide the necessary information and guidance. It also requires a confidence in networking practice to sell the vision of a venture idea, with a perhaps otherwise uncertain future, to potential, usually financial, backers. For the entrepreneurial manager of a small or medium-sized enterprise this is a challenge indeed. With a limited profile in the marketplace, an inherent desire for independence and to manage the business their own way, persuading others to put up the necessary resources to fund a venture requires sensitive political skills. Finding the right backers who can help or who know who can is important, as is finding information about that unique opportunity.[6]

Need for information

To succeed, the entrepreneurial SME owners need information on what is happening in the market to allow them to distil those opportunities that non-entrepreneurs fail to notice, to establish their likely potential and to ascertain the best way to exploit them fully. For example, entrepreneurs need information about what their customers want, what changes are happening in their market and how best to create and maintain a competitive advantage.

Conventional marketing wisdom in response to a company's need for quality information for effective decision-making and planning, emphasizes the importance of a planned programme in marketing research focusing on both secondary and primary sources of information. Any cursory consideration of the sources available indicates that there is any amount of material and, perhaps, paradoxically, that is the problem. As indicated above, the entrepreneurial small firm owner's approach to managing the enterprise might best be characterized as chaotic and opportunistic. The availability of time is one further resource which is often in short supply. Most entrepreneurial small firm owners who are characteristically action-oriented, simply do not seem to have the time, even if they have the skill, to search for appropriate data to uncover quality information for planning or decision-making. The challenge is to glean from the vast array of data those highly pertinent nuggets of information which pertain directly to the issue in hand. Gathering the data creates its own problems since information overload soon begins to make an impact.

Entrepreneurial small firm owners attempt to gather and absorb as much as possible 'on the hoof' as it were, given the many other demands for their attention and then, unless some better way of gathering information is available, an impromptu decision will be taken. However, decisions made in such circumstances and in such a way, against a backdrop of limited margins for error, greatly increase the level of risk attendant in the decision-making process. This makes it difficult to convince likely financial backers to support the business. Characteristically, entrepreneurs are moderate risk-takers, but decisions made on incomplete information, at best (or at worst on erroneous information) because the entrepreneur has little time, or like as not skill in planning for the necessary intelligence, must be suspect.

Successful entrepreneurial growth brings its own challenges. The advent of additional new products to the existing portfolio, the entry of the company into new markets, the introduction of new customers to the company's product add new complexities to managing the developing enterprise. The need for new and different types of information and ways of processing it increases. The entrepreneur needs to seek a more effective way of managing in these circumstances.

Need for confirmation

In addition to a regular and, from the entrepreneurs' point of view, more manageable supply of good quality, relevant information, entrepreneurs need a means to redress any doubt about the quality of decisions made. Entrepreneurs seek some means of confirming the validity of the decisions they are making, to establish their accuracy in so far as that can be done. So much is at stake: the future of the venture and the livelihood of the entrepreneur and those employed in the enterprise.

Consider the following scenario. The entrepreneur is planning to introduce a new product idea into the existing portfolio of products; the market has been particularly volatile and this opportunity has presented itself; it seems to offer real scope to develop the business. But it is going to cost a lot in terms of time, personnel and money. Should the entrepreneur go ahead? In such circumstances a decision like this is not easy to make, particularly when the firm has attained some reasonable degree of success in the past. Why risk what has been achieved? The ever-threatening 'comfort factor' lurks to undermine the continued entrepreneurial effort.[7]

The entrepreneur is often seen as a socially marginal person, one who is, to some extent, outside the cultural confines of the community. The entrepreneur seeks recognition through acceptance, perhaps in communities which revere professionalism, education and job security, where pressure in the environment is opposed to too much change and very much in favour of stability and predictable routine.

In general, entrepreneurs do not have all the skills needed to manage and develop their enterprises successfully. Any personal and honest analysis of their managerial strengths and weaknesses will tell them pretty quickly that this is so. Any comparison with the skills needed to manage and grow the enterprise will quickly identify the gaps that exist and that will need to be plugged if the venture is to continue to be successfully entrepreneurial. For example, an SME owner may have a background in engineering or production and have identified a product opportunity on which the enterprise has been built. But the ability to market the product may be relatively weak. In response and in a bid to develop the business, entrepreneurs may embark on a programme of focused technology transfer to compensate for and develop answers to marketing problems confronting the enterprise in its early stages. While things remain simple they may even be able to continue in this vein. As the enterprise expands and complexity increases they are faced with the need to update their marketing competencies, along with so many other necessary skills. But there are numerous pressures, not least lack of time. They might consider employing a professional marketing person, but perhaps the enterprise isn't large enough to afford that yet; then there is the question of sharing part of the enterprise with this emerging middle management. But it is largely recognized that teams build enterprises, lone entrepreneurs make a living. To grow, the business needs the entrepreneur to think in terms of a 'team'. A possible solution to the immediate problem of filling the gaps opening up in the required portfolio of competencies is for the entrepreneur to use a PCN and develop an 'entrepreneurial team' of contacts, on this occasion, outside the enterprise itself.

The critical point here is that the approach is planned for and worked through. The literature abounds with commentary on the specific weakness of entrepreneurial small firm owners in the area of marketing. The planned management of the entrepreneur's PCN offers an approach to addressing that weakness without necessarily compromising the entrepreneur's need for independence, in a way that is not time-consuming, while the relationship is mutually beneficial and perfectly legitimate.

Entrepreneurial networking

Confronted by the need for information and concerned to validate, if possible, a course of action, typical entrepreneurial SME owners seek feedback from people they know well. Any information about, and an endorsement of, an adopted position sustains morale and builds confidence. But entrepreneurs' approach to this networking activity reflects, to a critical degree, the chaotic, largely unplanned approach that characterizes their approach to managing and marketing their enterprises. Communication with members of their network will often be largely unplanned, opportunistic, highly informal and unstructured. It will be direct and verbal, focused on a specific issue of current importance to entrepreneurs and their enterprises.

An entrepreneur seeking to develop a new product or market, for example, will seek information from the network about the opportunity and its potential and/or the resources needed to exploit such a chance. They will formulate a decision on how to make progress with that opportunity, based on the feedback received, and may well return to the network members for confirmation of the value and validity of the chosen path. But as we suggested earlier, the entrepreneur will probably commit only limited time to this exercise, giving little thought to the approach being taken, who is consulted, why and to what end. However, once relationships have been established and seen to be of value, the sophistication in the way they are used may develop.

Entrepreneurial managers' preference is likely to be for face-to-face data collection, with the result that they employ their personal contact networks when gathering market information. It is through the continued use of those networks that they can further refine and develop the data collected and distil from it the intelligence needed to make decisions. The quality and potential of an entrepreneur's PCN is a function of a number of factors, which suggests that the entrepreneur needs to adopt an approach to networking which is better thought out and considered. The entrepreneur needs to be able to develop relations with people who are knowledgeable, empathetic, experienced, well connected and willing to help. We consider what some of those factors might be in the following section.

Factors determining the quality and potential of the entrepreneur's PCN

There are a number of important characteristics which define an entrepreneur's network. Foremost among these are density, reachability and diversity.

The density of the network refers to the number of contacts that exist between people in the network.

Allied to this is the degree of reachability that exists in the network, and this refers to the existence of 'pathways' between two people and the ease with which people in a network can make contact with one another. They may be direct, in that they define immediate and significant relationships with people who can have a particular impact on the enterprise, or indirect in that they define relationships with people outside the immediate network but contactable through it. The strength of the link in any network depends on the geographical, psychological and cultural distances between the two actors involved, how often the relationship is used, how mature it is, the degree of trust and the nature of past experiences between the two parties.

Diversity refers to the number of different sources from which information or assistance might be drawn and reflects the backgrounds of people in the network, their skills, knowledge, experience, additional access opportunities, and the like. The strength of these characteristics in any given network will ultimately determine the richness of the information being distilled from the network and the value of the advice and guidance available from its members. To network effectively, therefore, an individual must give thoughtful consideration to these issues and how they might best be managed. We look at some of these issues in more detail below.[8]

Characterizing personal contact networks

The entrepreneurial small firm owner needs to be able to access what we might describe as 'rich' information. By this we mean information that is current, accurate, focused, manageable and validated. Rich information is very much a function of the properties or characteristics of the source from which it has been acquired and the methods used to gather it. In an entrepreneurial contact network the focal person is the entrepreneurial SME owner and the network comprises those persons with whom the owner has *direct* relationships. *Direct ties* depict immediate and significant relationships with people who can have a particular direct impact on the enterprise. In addition there are *indirect ties*, which define relationships with people outside the immediate network but who can, if their role becomes significant, be contacted through it. Figure 14.1 outlines this property more clearly.

The entrepreneur is the focal person in the network with direct contacts with A, B, C and D. We said that they should be significant in terms of their relationship with the entrepreneur, and by significant we mean that they should be people who are knowledgeable about business issues generally and perhaps the entrepreneurs' industry in particular. They will be experienced in business, with a reputation or profile among people in the industry; they will have influence with the entrepreneur, people the entrepreneur can trust and in whose views, comments and guidance the

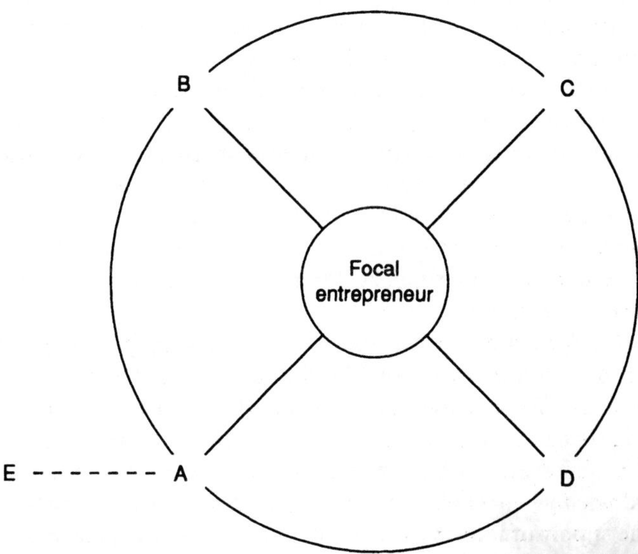

Figure 14.1 Entrepreneurial contact network.

entrepreneur has confidence. The entrepreneur, however, has an indirect tie with E through his direct association with A. Any decision to draw E into the direct network will be a function of many issues, not least the significance of such contacts to all parties concerned.

Let us look at this in more detail by considering a related and arguably complementary property of networking, the issue of *strong and weak ties*. Whether a tie between contacts in a network is strong or weak reflects the nature and consequent strength of the bond between the actors involved. The *strongest ties* are with people who share affection: family members, very close friends and relatives. These are people who are close to the entrepreneur; they know and care for one another. They have played a meaningful part in the entrepreneur's life for a very long time, often over a lifetime, and share a range of experiences and emotions. These emotions and interactions are vital in holding relationships together. Such relationships might be seen as largely unconditional, in that the actors give and receive without any recognizable or definable preconditions or expectations of reciprocity. These types of relationships are rooted in mutual respect and affection and are common in family and social relationships. These are the ultimate network for the lonely, otherwise marginal personality who is setting up an enterprise and who will need all the moral support and confidence-boosting available, particularly when things go wrong.

However, such non-business relationships need to be differentiated from the more commercially rooted relationships. As mentioned above, when introducing the idea of *direct ties* the entrepreneurial small firm owner needs to build *strong ties* with people who can give the information and confirmation needed to make decisions for the development of the enterprise. Additionally, though, these contacts may be bonded together by ties of mutual trust and confidence, mutual support and the valid expectation of reciprocity. The more people in the network are known to each other, usually over a long period of time, the stronger the ties between them. Such a network reflects the family/community network, although it can be argued that the former is more planned and the latter is more natural in evolution and development. *Weak ties* in a network, however, will be made up of casual acquaintances with people who are unlikely to know one another; however, the maintenance and nurturing of these ties is essential for an effective network. Where the entrepreneur relies solely on existing strong direct ties where everyone is known to each other and is mutually dependent on each other for support, information and guidance, we have what is called a *high density network*.

The opportunity in such a network for new thinking beyond the norms of the existing group of members is potentially limited as members endorse and support each other's views. The potential for a version of 'group think' must be strong. For a network to be truly useful it needs to have access to diverse opinions and varying perspectives. This introduces a further property of networks, the need for *diversity*. For a personal network to be effective, it needs a relative balance between strong and weak ties if the supply of information and the prospects of guidance and confirmation are to be rich and valuable.[9]

So the density of the network refers to the degree of interconnectedness between people in the network. Diversity refers to the number of different sources from which information or assistance might be drawn and reflects the backgrounds of the people in the network, their skills, knowledge, experience, and the like. The third key characteristic of networks introduced above is the degree of *reachability* that exists in the network. Howard Aldrich and Catherine Zimmer refer to the existence of pathways between two people and the ease with which people in the network may make contact with one another. For example, in Figure 14.1 the reachability between the entrepreneur as the focal person and E is very much a function of the strength of the tie not only between the entrepreneur and contact A but between A and E and A's willingness to act as a go-between. This introduces an additional characteristic of developing networks, particularly wider social networks: *the networking broker*. The entrepreneurial small business owner operates within some context or contexts, be it an industry sector or, say, a community or wider social system. Membership of this system bestows an identity and with it a legitimacy or standing, the strength of which is crucial for the usefulness of networking opportunities. *Networking brokers* play a significant role in any social system by linking the entrepreneurial PCN with people outside it who have complementary interests, by transferring information or resources and generally facilitating the interests of people not otherwise directly related to one another. A in Figure 14.1, for example, might be such a person.

Developing entrepreneurial marketing networks

What the entrepreneurial owner/manager requires is a competency in building networks which have the characteristics described. This needs to be done in a way that reflects the maturing character of the enterprise and the increasing complexities that attend effective entrepreneurial action. This necessarily poses a significant challenge to recognize the critical importance of networks to maintaining the entrepreneurial effort of the enterprise and to develop an approach to networking that is increasingly rational rather than wholly natural, that is more planned than unstructured and that is more formal than totally informal in character.

The entrepreneur must recognize, in adopting a more rational approach to network development and management, the importance of building quality into the potential of the networks. Entrepreneurs must thoughtfully seek appropriate levels of diversity and density in their relations with others and think strategically about the issue of reachability. David Carson[10] points out that entrepreneurs' personal contact networks provide them with one mechanism for developing a common-sense approach to marketing. He suggests that what is required is for them to use it consciously and proactively to help them make key marketing planning decisions to resolve problems. This ultimately is the challenge facing the entrepreneurial networker.

Relationships between organizations

We have noted that organizational leaders contact one another regularly, that the networks of personal contacts are extremely useful in gathering information about opportunities and resources and that the friendships which develop provide important support for individuals. They can test out their ideas on informed listeners and discuss matters of mutual benefit. However, in recent years organizations have been developing more formal associations and joint research projects, marketing alliances and systematic comprehensive associations between manufacturers are commonplace.[11] In contrast with these developments classical economists argue strongly in favour of independent firms which operate in a competitive market. Their basic argument is that competitive market forces are an effective mechanism for regulating the contact between organizations. In essence if organization (1) believes that an association with organization (2) will yield a greater return on investment than a linkage with venture (3), then (1) and (2) will develop their relationship, at least until such times that linking with a new organization will yield a greater rate of return. Contacts are made and exchanges occur so long as they facilitate the maximization of profit. However, we saw in Chapter 9 that this competitive, dog eat dog situation can produce some unwanted results. In the UK and US automobile industries in the 1970s, manufacturers demanded ever-cheaper parts from their suppliers and threatened that they would change suppliers if cost-cutting could not be achieved. Suppliers responded to these demands by cutting prices but with disastrous consequences for quality. We saw also in Chapter 9 that manufacturers, aware that fickle customers in a competitive world will quickly shift their loyalty to another product in pursuit of economic advantage, are concerned to build lasting relationships with customers. When we recognize that the customers for many firms are other organizations rather than the general public, we can see that permanent associations between transforming and client organizations are a distinct possibility.

While not denying that many sectors of the economy function in a competitive world it has been pointed out that organizations have always been embedded in semi-permanent networks of other organizations – sometimes called organization sets – which supply raw materials and act as markets and that these associations are a source of stability in a turbulent world.[12] However, inter-organizational relationships (henceforth referred to as IORs) are more common nowadays and we shall explore the reasons for this increase in collaboration.

Rationale for inter-organizational relationships (IORs)

Several authors have argued that many organizations do not have the resources they need to accomplish their objectives and that in these situations there is an incentive to cooperate to acquire the necessary resources.[13] For example, two organizations may have an interest in developing a new product but discover that, independently, they do not have sufficient money. However, by cooperating and pooling their financial resources they discover that the development process can be completed to the benefit of both parties. Similar arguments apply with non-financial resources. For example, two firms may develop a new service but find that the market is insufficient to occupy staff from both organizations fully. In this situation they can compete and let the winner take all, or share the work among staff from both organizations to the benefit of both ventures. It has been suggested that when organizations seek opportunities in their environment but discover that they cannot command sufficient resources to realize the opportunity, they begin to seek collaborative associations which will allow them to gain access to requisite resources.[14]

The situation just described is particularly relevant for small firms, restricted as they often are by limited resources. For example, a recent research study in Sweden showed that many businesses involved outsiders fully in the process of developing their new products.[15]

New knowledge and technologies

The need to marshall resources often gives rise to inter-organizational collaboration, but Alter and Hage suggest that recent events have given an even greater impetus to this trend. A key factor is the pace of change in today's world; it has been so rapid that it has revolutionized industrial structures. In a traditional market a firm might buy the best scientific and marketing talent and nurture a new product in the expectation that, even in a competitive market, its new product would provide them with an advantage over the competition for some time. However, if we consider areas such as microelectronics, biotechnology and genetic engineering, new knowledge emerges so quickly that today's new invention is superseded by an even newer product in a short time. This presents huge problems for innovative firms.

They can be sure that their competitors have similar or more advanced scientific and market information and that the lifecycle of their new product will be short. Speed, flexibility and responsiveness are the necessary attributes for the modern innovative firm and recent research confirms that collaborative associations with other organizations, including former competitors, are the only viable ways to acquire the necessary knowledge, share the developmental costs and spread the risks of new product development. They must also share the benefits. If not, competitive pressures will re-emerge.[16]

The organizational arrangements that can deliver these outcomes are not large, vertically and horizontally integrated, bureaucracies; indeed, these firms are rapidly removing their former acquisitions and creating smaller, organically structured work constellations which are linked in collaborative networks. Many small firms are flexible and responsive but they have a serious disadvantage – their decision-making is centralized and focused on the owner/manager. The generation of new knowledge, ideas, processes, etc. requires independent thought from experts to whom decision-making has been decentralized. Assuming that fiercely independent entrepreneurs can be persuaded to decentralize, the organizational form which can encompass flexibility, responsiveness, creativity and specialized expertise is the systemic network of small specialized knowledge-based firms.

Adaptive efficiency

Changes in technological knowledge can influence the supply of goods or services, but equally important changes are taking place in the marketplace. Customers are increasingly sophisticated and demanding and want quality goods and services geared to their specific needs. Alter and Hage point out that in previous decades efficiency was associated with the ability to produce large quantities of standard goods at low cost. Large bureaucratic performance organizations perfected the production of cars, televisions and the like, and this approach was referred to as 'Fordism'.[17] These authors argue that in today's world 'adaptive efficiency' is required. Customers want goods which are competitively priced but they are prepared to pay a premium for individualized, good quality goods and services. Cooperation between networks of small niche firms allows them to derive some of the benefits of large combined output along with the capacity to meet special customer needs and to modify products to meet the particular needs of customers. There is considerable research evidence to show that small firms are likely to act conjointly with others by entering into cooperative market agreements.[18]

Trust

Classical theories of economics assume that if people pursue their own self-interest, an invisible hand will guide economic activity for the general benefit of society. Organizations in the market are supposed to base their interactions on economic criteria only and to distrust those with whom they do business. Safety for individual firms is provided by the large number of competing suppliers and buyers. If one supplier seeks a disproportionate advantage a producer will simply engage a new supplier.

If a producer is to enter into an exclusive agreement with suppliers, customers or even competitors, then it is vital that a high degree of trust exists between the parties. Trust is a fragile commodity. It takes time for it to develop and a single action can destroy it forever. However, in spite of traditional economic theory there is considerable evidence that trust is part and parcel of business activity. Without it participants would constantly have to look over their shoulders and there is increasing evidence from Europe that relations between suppliers, manufacturers and customers in industrial markets are characterized by 'cooperation, trust and loyalty'.[19]

In addition, far from confirming that nice guys always finish last, research has shown that the most effective strategy for managing on-going exchanges is one of reciprocity. In other words, it is best for one party to start an exchange in a cooperative mode and to continue to do so as long as the other party cooperates. If the other person takes an uncooperative stance, the first person should retaliate immediately and only return to a cooperative mode if the other person does so.

Numerous trials on this kind of interactive exchange show that reciprocity is the most beneficial strategy for both parties.[20] Research into problem-solving and negotiation shows that, if the parties adopt a collaborative stance, they can often arrive at innovative solutions to problems that are beneficial to both sides. These outcomes are more effective than grudging compromises which merely split the difference between the demands of each party.

Bureaucratic organizations rely on a small group of thinkers and experts to design organizational practices and on a mass of unthinking workers to complete activities and tasks mechanically. However, in the newer innovative and complex ventures, which are likely to form IORs, highly educated individuals who will challenge the status quo are required. Fortunately, as a result of higher education for larger numbers of students, a tendency for people in modern societies to appreciate different cultures and values, and an increase in international travel, many countries have a pool of people with the skills to function effectively in complex, problem-solving organizations.

In general, new notions of efficiency, rapid changes in knowledge and markets and a highly educated populace who are prepared to trust their colleagues support the formation of collaborative IORs. While we started our discussion on IORs by emphasizing collaboration to acquire additional resources we have seen that significant changes in organizational environments can increase communication between organizations as they explore threats and possibilities for working together.

Examples of IORs

Our discussion to date has been quite general and we feel that we should present some examples of extensive IORs. One of the most developed systems of IORs occurs in sections of the Japanese motor industry. Major manufacturers like Honda and Toyota involve their suppliers fully in the design of components and in resolving the problems they encounter with the final product – the car. When parts malfunction they are not declared as rejects: they prompt a joint investigation by supplier and assembler to try to ensure that the difficulty does not arise again. Any cost savings that are made are shared between the suppliers and the manufacturers and prices for components are set collaboratively. In effect, suppliers and manufacturers operate as if they were part of the same organization and because the needs of the suppliers are being met they have every incentive to carry on cutting costs, improving quality and delivering parts to the manufacturer just-in-time.[21]

In Europe the completion of the integrated market in 1992 prompted several organizations to form IORs to allow them to share information, costs and markets to make them globally competitive. For example, DAF and Bava, two Dutch bus manufacturers, joined forces and then invited firms from Britain and Denmark to collaborate with them. Phillips, the Dutch giant, stated in 1990 that as part of their business strategy to increase competitiveness they would reduce the extent of their vertical integration and increase their cooperation with other organizations.[22]

Public services such as health and welfare have been decentralized in the United States since the 1950s but initial evaluations reported many problems. Services were fragmented and duplication was common. However, financial pressure on agencies and an insistence that there be no duplication of effort created a situation where agencies (1) cooperated to make the best of available financial resources, (2) specialized in the services they provided, and (3) developed client referral systems to meet the needs of clients with multiple problems. These developments reflect those that have occurred in many service areas in the United States and elsewhere and some of the most intricate IORs are to be found in the service sector.[23]

Forming IORs – the process

We have argued that a number of environmental variables have increased the likelihood of IOR formation, but it should be noted that environmental conditions do not determine organizational structures; they are determined by senior managers. The decision of a manager to enter into an IOR will, in all probability, be influenced by the factors discussed above, but s/he will have to be committed to the idea personally before interaction takes place. Andrew Van de Ven argues that a number of conditions must be met before senior managers will enter an IOR.[24] When entrepreneurs feel that they might want to collaborate with another organization to acquire resources or exploit an opportunity, they will need to know about the capabilities and activities of neighbouring organizations. They will have to develop some awareness of their strengths and weaknesses, the organizational culture and their goals. Most of this awareness will develop through communication with people who have information about the likely contact organization, most particularly personal contacts within the target organization. If contacts have known one another for a long time and if the parties are on good terms personally, this will speed up the flow of information. Personal contacts are important for this purpose but so is geographical proximity. Research indicates that organizations are more likely to make contact with a neighbouring organization than a distant one.[25]

Before an IOR becomes a reality there will have to be a measure of agreement among the participants on the ends they are pursuing and on the means of achieving them. Distinct organizations are likely to have distinct goals, but to work conjointly they will have to arrive at a joint decision on means and ends. This will entail discussion, understanding of each other's position and a degree of accommodation. If moderate consensus does not emerge it is unlikely that an IOR will come into being. We need to emphasize, once again, the importance of communication between the parties in developing an awareness of one another's capabilities and desires and in seeking agreement on collective goals. An effective personal network is indispensable for this purpose.

Communication, awareness and consensus are important but so is the business sector of the parties. Some authors suggest that organizations that provide very similar or very dissimilar services are unlikely to collaborate. In the former instance they will compete for a greater market share while in the latter they will pursue their own ends in their niche market. Andrew Van de Ven suggests, therefore, that collaboration is most likely among ventures with moderately similar domains. Others argue that cooperation is most likely when the collaborators are highly differentiated. In the latter case, however, the customers or clients served by the collaborating organizations will require a variety of services, and organizations will route clients to those providing additional assistance.[26]

If these conditions are suitable, then a degree of cooperation will emerge between agencies. This can range from tenuous links in which information is pooled and exchanged, through joint agreements on procurement or marketing to the fully integrated production network where the separate organizations behave like semi-autonomous divisions in a divisionalized organization. In all cases there will be exchange of one or more of the following: (1) friendship, (2) information, (3) resources and (4) products/services. Without these flows it is doubtful if an IOR will continue. In analyzing IORs it is important to be aware of the intensity and direction of flows. These variables allow us to recognize the leaders and followers.

If relationships continue for some time, the pattern of interaction and flows will stabilize and the IOR will develop recognizable structured elements. The major structural features are formalization, centralization and complexity. Formal IORs exist when agreements are concrete and written down. Centralization occurs when joint decisions are made by a small number of people such as a coordinating committee. Complexity refers to the number of agencies whose efforts have to be integrated. In general, increasing participating units increases IOR complexity.

When structural features emerge they indicate that there is a degree of permanence in the IOR but Alter and Hage point out that IORs can be vulnerable. If one or more parties pursue their own ends at the expense of the collectivity an IOR may well break up. If an IOR is to continue, it is important that the parties agree, and continue to agree, on means of achieving goals, on the capacities of the participating organizations and on the contribution each can make to the overall goal(s). In reality, just as departments within single organizations specialize, so organizations within an IOR develop particular abilities which should complement those of other ventures.

Power is another matter which must be monitored in an IOR. IORs comprise horizontally linked organizations and it is important that decisions are made jointly and that no organization begins to control proceedings. If this occurs, it is likely that the IOR will end. We must appreciate, however, that it is not easy to achieve power-sharing among independent ventures. With the best will in the world there will be many disagreements about activities, procedures and objectives. It is vital, therefore, that key individuals in a network develop the skills of negotiation, bargaining and compromise to allow them to find creative solutions to the problems they will face as a network of organizations.[27]

Relations between enterprise support agencies

To complete our discussion we shall illustrate some of the matters we have been examining with the help of a recent case study of inter-agency collaboration between small business support agencies.[28] This text has been addressing matters of importance to entrepreneurial SMEs but it is widely recognized that they experience many difficulties. As a result most governments provide support for SMEs, and in Northern Ireland this assistance is provided by approximately eighty state, semi-state and private enterprises offering advice, training, financial assistance, etc. While this support is welcome, some people believe that there is duplication of effort among agencies. When we examine the environment of these enterprise supporters we find that they are not well financed and are clear candidates for the pooling of financial resources. In addition, we find that following the huge increase in knowledge about SMEs in recent decades and the demand by small firms for customized assistance, enterprise supporters are increasingly responsive to and innovative when providing services to their clients. An additional factor is the high level of educational attainment of our enterprise supporters. If we review those conditions favouring IORs above, it would appear that conditions are suitable for collaboration.

Turning to the process of IOR formation we find that, because of the small geographical size of Northern Ireland and government-sponsored conferences, the enterprise supporters have a keen awareness about their fellow supporters and there is regular and effective communication among them. Given the level of communication and awareness among organizations we might have predicted a high level of consensus among agencies but this is not the case. There was only a modest level of consensus on the goals of enterprise support policy and the means of achieving objectives. On domain similarity we find that the agencies have a mean score on this variable of 2.7, where 2 means that respondents think their domain is similar to that of other contact agencies to a 'little extent' and 3 indicates they are similar 'to some extent'. Since agency domains are neither very similar nor very dissimilar this would suggest that there would be a considerable flow of resources between agencies.

As it turns out there is only a modest level of exchange between the agencies. In general, there is little exchange of tangible resources such as money, equipment or personnel; a little more willingness to trade clients and advice; and they are even more content to exchange social support and promote their organizations collaboratively.

The enterprise supporters' environment was quite conducive for integrated network formation but it did not happen and few IOR structural dimensions, such as the centralization and formalization of procedures and decision-making, emerged. In spite of favourable conditions the key decision-makers within agencies decided to act largely independently. This points to the importance of the willingness of the parties to create IORs.

Summary

Many associations in life are unplanned and coincidental and arise through social activity. Even in a business context associations may emerge in a subconscious and reactive manner. However, the planned development of networks, in a thoughtful and proactive way, may offer a useful addition to the pool of competencies needed by small firm owners. In contrast with managers in bureaucracies, who act as the custodians of resources under their control, entrepreneurs actively seek resources to capitalize on their business ideas. In their quest for information, resources and customers, entrepreneurs simultaneously explore many possibilities and a range of contacts, who are knowledgeable about these and related matters, are indispensable for the growth-oriented entrepreneur. Business know-how is essential for successful venturing but without large numbers of specialized employees who are expert in business functions, the entrepreneur needs to know who to turn to for expertise, assistance or information.

As organizations mature they often recognize that loosely coupled connections with others are not sufficient for continued business success. In the increasingly turbulent and complex business world of the late twentieth century permanent alliances between organizations are becoming necessary to acquire new knowledge, develop new markets and share the expense of purchasing scarce resources. In many spheres of endeavour permanent systemic networks of organizations, not autonomous firms, are seen as the structural formation which will guarantee the continued competitiveness of business organizations.

Learning questions

1. Discuss the two main networking approaches available to the entrepreneurial SME owner.
2. In what ways are the personal contact networks (PCNs) of the SME owner particularly entrepreneurial?
3. Evaluate the significance of PCNs to the practice of marketing in the SME?
4. Discuss the factors that will determine the quality and potential of the individual entrepreneur's PCN.
5. Discuss the implication for the entrepreneur of developing the PCN.
6. It has been contended that in a modern business environment independent firms are unable to maintain sustained growth. What are your views on this matter?
7. Comment on those influences from outside and inside organizations which might stimulate the formation of IORs.

Notes and references

1. See Johannisson, B. (1986) 'Network strategies: Management technology for entrepreneurship and change', *International Small Business Journal* 5, pp. 19–30; and

Mastenbroek, W. F. G. (1993), *Conflict Management and Organisation Development*, Chichester: John Wiley.
2. Dubini, P. and Aldrich, H. (1991) 'Personal and extended networks are central to the entrepreneurial process', *Journal of Business Venturing* **6**, pp. 305–13.
3. Stephenson, H. H. and Gumpert, D. E. (1991) 'The heart of entrepreneurship', in W. A. Sahlman and H. H. Stephenson (eds.), *The Entrepreneurial Venture*, Boston, MA: Harvard Business School.
4. Biemans, W. G. (1992) *Managing Innovation within Networks*, London: Routledge.
5. Butler, J. E. and Hansen, G. S. (1991) 'Network evolution, entrepreneurial success, and regional development', *Journal of Entrepreneurship and Regional Development* **3**, pp. 1–16.
6. MacMillan, I. C. (1991) 'The politics of new venture management', in Sahlman and Stephenson (1991), *op. cit.*, pp. 160–70.
7. Drucker, P. F. (1985) *Innovation and Entrepreneurship*, London: Heinemann, argues that a successful current product inhibits the drive for innovation.
8. See Aldrich, H. and Zimmer, C. (1986) 'Entrepreneurship through social networks', in D. A. Sexton and R. W. Smilor (eds.), *The Art and Science of Entrepreneurship,* Cambridge, MA: Ballinger, for an excellent analysis of network characteristics.
9. Granovetter, M. (1982) 'The strength of weak ties: A network theory revisited', in P. V. Marsden and N. Lin (eds.), *Social Structure and Network Analysis,* Beverely Hills, CA: Sage, pp. 105–30.
10. Carson, D. (1993) 'A philosophy of marketing education in small firms', *Journal of Marketing Management* **9**, pp. 189–204.
11. See, for example, Jarillo, J. C. (1993) *Strategic Networks – Creating the Borderless Organisation*, Oxford: Butterworth/Heinemann; Gadde, L. E. and Hakaanson, H. (1993) *Professional Purchasing*, London: Routledge; and Biemans (1992), *op. cit.*
12. See Evan, W. M. (1976) 'An organisation-set model of interorganisational relations', in W. M. Evan (ed.) *Inter-Organisational Relations*, Middlesex: Penguin Books, pp. 78–90 and Trist, E. (1983), 'Referent organisations and the development of inter-organisational domains', *Human Relations* **36**, pp. 269–84 for a discussion on the stabilizing influence of networks.
13. See Alter, C. and Hage, J. (1993) *Organizations Working Together*, Newbury Park, CA: Sage.
14. Van de Ven, A. H. (1976) 'On the nature, formation and maintenance of relations among organisations', *Academy of Management Review* **1**, pp. 24–36.
15. Hakaanson, H. (1990) 'Technological collaboration in industrial networks', *European Management Journal* **8**, pp. 371–9.
16. Lambourghini, B. (1982) 'The impact on the enterprise', in G. Friedrichs and A. Schaff (eds.) *Micro-electronics and Society*, London: Pergamon; Powell, W. W. (1990), 'Neither market nor hierarchy: Network forms of organisation', in L. L. Cummings and B. M. Staw (eds.), *Research in Organizational Behaviour*, Greenwich, CT: JAI Press; Alter and Hage (1993), *op. cit.*; Biemans (1992), *op. cit.*
17. Hollingsworth, J. R. (1991) 'The logic of coordinating American manufacturing sectors', in J. L. Campell, J. R. Hollingsworth and L. N. Lindberg, *The Governance of the American Economy*, New York: Cambridge University Press.
18. Pollack, A. (1992) 'Technology without borders raises big questions for U.S.', *The New York Times*, 1 January, p. 1.
19. Biemens (1992) *op. cit.*, p. 79.
20. Axlerod, R. (1984) *The Evolution of Cooperation*, New York: Basic Books.
21. See the discussion in Alter and Hage (1993) *op. cit.*, pp. 7–10 on cooperation in the Japanese and other motor industries.
22. See Biemens (1992) *op. cit.*, pp. 82–4 for examples of inter-firm cooperation in Europe.
23. See Alter and Hage (1993) *op. cit.*, pp. 10–12 for details of public sector cooperation.

24. Van de Ven, A. H. and Ferry, D. (1980) *Measuring and Assessing Organisations*, New York: John Wiley.
25. Schermerhorn, J. R. (1975) 'Determinants of interorganizational cooperation', *Academy of Management Journal* 18, pp. 846–56.
26. See Van de Ven (1976) *op. cit.* on domain similarity.
27. See Alter and Hage (1993) *op. cit.*, pp. 78–80 for a discussion on the necessary conditions for the continuation of IORs. See also Van de Ven and Ferry (1980), *op. cit.*
28. Cromie, S. and Birley, S. (1994) 'Relationships among small business support agencies', *Entrepreneurship and Regional Development*, 6, pp. 301–14.

Further reading

Andersson, P. and Soderlund, M. (1988) 'The network approach to marketing', *Irish Marketing Review* 3, pp. 63–8.

Gummesson, E. (1987) 'The new marketing – Developing long-term interactive relationships', *Long Range Planning* 20, pp. 10–20.

Entrepreneurship Today

Chapter 1

Learning Objectives

- $ To become aware of the way in which entrepreneurship emerged as a leading economic force during the 1980s and 1990s.
- $ To appreciate the nature of the U.S. economy undergoing important changes early in this new century.
- $ To see that countries around the world have discovered entrepreneurship as a source of economic vitality.
- $ To comprehend that a small business has what it takes to compete successfully with much larger organizations.

During the 1980s and the 1990s, we saw historic changes in the world economy. These changes were part of what is called the *new world order*. At its heart have been transformations in the way in which business is conducted. Technology is assuming an increasingly important role; service industries are steadily growing; world competition is more open and spirited than ever; and outsourcing—once an obscure staffing strategy—has become a household word as thousands of jobs have been eliminated in industry after industry. Another of these landmark changes is the unparalleled rise in entrepreneurship, which has become a major source of vitality in today's world economy.

In this text, we provide an introduction to entrepreneurship. We explore the issue of **who** is an entrepreneur, considering personality traits of the individual as we examine the question "What is an entrepreneur?" We then explore the issue of **how**, as we describe the three primary routes into independent business ownership.

Also addressed are the unique problems and opportunities entrepreneurship poses for women and minority members. Next we describe the growing importance of home-based businesses, new product development as a basis for establishing new ventures, and the opportunities and problems presented by international markets.

Before we deal with any of those topics, however, we describe the spread of entrepreneurship. As you will see, while it has had a surprisingly strong impact on economies around the globe, entrepreneurship is most robust and pervasive here in the United States. We explain why so much interest in entrepreneurship has developed in recent years and why that level of interest is likely to continue. Our early focus is on the United States, after which we broaden our view, looking at the diversified textures and shapes of entrepreneurship around the world.

ENTREPRENEURSHIP IN THE UNITED STATES

Entrepreneurship is flourishing in many places around the world; here in the United States, new venture creation has been the chief source of economic vigor for the last several years. We have benefited from the emergence of a new spirit of entrepreneurship, the reasons for which we will explore in this section. This exploration should be placed in the context of how our economy has evolved during the past 40 to 50 years.

Industry Structure

Fortune 500 – a listing of the 500 largest firms in the country.

The year was 1955. World War II had ended 10 years before and the country had experienced a decade of rapid economic growth. **Fortune** had established its list of the country's 500 largest firms and much interest centered on who topped the list. (It was General Motors, with nearly $10 billion in sales and 575,000 employees.)[1] The interest in our industrial giants continued, with most observers concluding that size meant strength, and through strength these giants had established positions that were unassailable.

In contrast to the excitement surrounding big business, the attitude toward entrepreneurship seemed to be indifference. Very few universities offered studies in this area, and few books were written on the topic. In 1955 there were approximately 4.5 million small businesses in the United States.[2] The country's population was 165 million, which meant that there was one small business for every 38 people.[3] It was about that time that an interesting trend started, and since then small business has become an increasingly important part of our lives.

By 1965 the population had increased to 194 million, but the number of small businesses had increased at an even faster rate to 6.7 million, or one for every 29 people.[4] By 1975 it was one for every 26. In 2000, the U.S. population was approximately 280 million; the number of small businesses was estimated by the SBA's Office of Advocacy at about 22 million.[5] Using these figures, the ratio had fallen to one small business for every 12.7 people, approximately one-third of what it had been in 1955.

The steady decline in the number of people per small business—or conversely, the increase in the number of small businesses serving the population—emphasizes the growing significance of small business in our nation's economy. This trend is perhaps impossible to explain completely because it reflects so many societal trends or conditions, but two factors deserve special mention because of their impact on our economy.

First, competition from foreign companies became significant during the 1960s, and by the end of that decade, the United States was importing nearly as much as it exported. Change was rapid for many of our large markets by the end of the 1970s. In automobiles, electronics, industrial equipment, clothing, and construction and agricultural machinery, the changes were particularly unsettling for our domestic producers. They were losing market share to competitors who operated differently from "old-line" members. This industry shake-up meant problems for traditional competitors, but it brought opportunities for its smaller, more agile members.

Second, the late 1970s marked another watershed in the country's economic history: the start of deregulation. It drastically changed many areas, such as trucking, airlines, and the communications and financial industries. Outstanding among deregulation's many profound changes was the entry of many small firms into industries that for years had been dominated by giant companies.

Both factors—foreign competition and deregulation—were disruptive; they changed the structure of much of American industry and in the process provided many entrepreneurs with the opportunity they needed. These opportunities continue and entrepreneurship continues to flourish. In 1996 our economy set a record of nearly 850,000 new business incorporations; 1997 was even better with 884,000. Since those banner years the figure has dropped to a still robust level of approximately 600,000.[6]

Just how big a role entrepreneurship plays in our economy, as suggested in the number of start-ups, seems to be a matter of opinion and the method of counting used. The estimates vary widely. Dun & Bradstreet, using an extremely conservative approach to counting, includes businesses only as they begin to compete actively in the marketplace; the estimate for 2000 was about 130,000 start-ups. The U.S. Small Business Administration, using census data, pegs its estimate at nearly 600,000, as mentioned previously. Finally, an Omaha company, New Business USA, gathers data on new business permits, new incorporations, and so on. Its figures for 2000 show more than 900,000 home-based and 600,000 commercial-site businesses, totaling more than 1,500,000 start-ups.

Two other gradual, but potentially profound, changes have contributed to the wave of entrepreneurship. One is organizational in nature, the other is broader.

Organizational strategies and the practice of downsizing Since the start of the Industrial Revolution, large organizations have been the most important source of economic stability for the nation and have provided boundless opportunities for individuals. Managers, unskilled workers, professionals, and highly trained technicians have all experienced the comfort of knowing that hard work and loyalty to the employer would bring bright career prospects and a secure retirement.

Employees were rewarded with improved earnings and benefits linked to the success of the organization. Employees thought, "If I work hard for the company, the company will take good care of me." For countless people, that was the American Dream, and for years it was real.

As our country's economic landscape has changed, so have the assumptions underlying the relationship between the organization and the individual. Many people who used to believe that their ability and dedication to their employer protected them from job loss have learned they were wrong. Massive layoffs, or downsizing programs, have become commonplace, even in good times. As Table 1–1 indicates, despite the robust performance of the economy during the first quarter of 1998, some prominent firms announced staff reductions. The period covered in the table was selected not because it was unusually active in job losses, but because it was a typical slice of business life in the late 1990s. For any other week the results would likely be much the same.

Downsizing – the practice of firms by which they systematically and substantially reduce the number of people they employ to achieve a reduction in costs.

A sampling from a time of economic slowdown (August 2001) not too surprisingly shows even greater job losses. See Table 1–2. It seems that in good times and in times of uncertainty, layoffs continue. Why is this pattern of job reduction so pervasive and persistent? Two types of answers are frequently given.

The first explanation is that organizational survival is at stake. In order to compete in today's market, firms must cut costs to the lowest level possible, and this means that staffing is kept at an absolute minimum. Any company that has more people than it needs is headed for trouble. Support for this explanation can be found in changes in markets as they become more open to international competition and subject to the constant pressure from producers in third-world countries. Every organization with costs beyond those of its competition faces serious disadvantages and an uncertain future. Procter & Gamble chairman Edwin L. Artzt, commenting on his firm's reduction from 106,000 to 93,000 employees, said, "We must slim down to stay competitive. The consumer wants better value. Our competitors are getting leaner and quicker, and we are simply going to have to run faster to stay ahead."[7]

The second explanation is that it is less a matter of need than one of greed on the part of top managers. Those holding this view cite the fact that the bonus plans of many executives are typically based on cost improvements, which are generally achievable only through massive reductions in payroll expenditures.

TABLE 1–1 Workforce reduction announcements during the first week of June 1998

DATE	COMPANY	NUMBER
June 2	Data General, Westboro, MS Kemet, Greenville, SC	400 worldwide 540 United States 900 Mexico
June 3	American Standard, Piscataway, NJ	Texas plant closed Operations sent to Mexico
June 4	Handleman, Troy, MI	900–1,000—10% of workforce
June 5	Motorola, Chicago	15,000 worldwide
June 6	Diebold, North Canton, OH	600 worldwide—9% of workforce

Source: The New York Times, "Company News," section C, dates given.

TABLE 1–2 Workforce reduction announcements during the last week of August 2001

DATE	COMPANY	NUMBER
August 28	Deere & Company, Moline, IL	2,000
August 28	Toshiba, Tokyo	19,000—10% of workforce
August 29	Gateway, San Diego	5,000—25% of workforce
August 29	Honeywell, Minneapolis	700
August 29	Otis Elevator, Farmington, CT	500–600
August 30	Corning, Corning, NY	1,000
August 31	Hitachi, Tokyo	14,700—5% of workforce
August 31	Charles Schwab, San Francisco	2,400

Source: The New York Times, "Business Day" section, dates given.

They point to the fact that some of the biggest layoffs occur in firms that report healthy financial results.

Important support for this view can be found in a report issued by DRI/McGraw-Hill, an economic consulting firm.[8] A study done by the company found that corporate profits rose 11 percent in 1994, after increasing 13 percent in 1993. During 1994, however, corporate America cut 516,069 jobs. This was nearly as many as were laid off in 1991, which marked the deepest point of the most recent previous recession.

Societal change The end of jobs? Some writers claim that our economy has developed to the point where the job is no longer the best way to accomplish the things that need to be done. They contend that jobs were a societal invention that provided the needed human resource element to allow the Industrial Revolution to proceed. Up to that point in history, people didn't have, or need, jobs as we define them today. What the Industrial Revolution made necessary, the post-industrial society does not need. We now have the technology to run large production facilities—the kind that used to employ thousands of workers—with a skeleton crew. This is what one observer had in mind when he said, "The plant of the future will have only two employees: a man and a dog. The man will be there to feed the dog and the dog will be there to see that the man doesn't touch the equipment."

Post-industrial society – a country where large-scale businesses are declining in importance.

Whatever the plant of the future may look like, today's large organizations do not hesitate in eliminating jobs, and they are slow in establishing new ones, frequently choosing to have current employees work overtime instead. As a result, large firms no longer generate jobs as they once did. For example, between 1979 and 1993, total employment in Fortune 500 manufacturing firms dropped from 16.2 million to 11.5 million, a decrease of nearly one-third. This pattern of job loss in big companies has meant that any expansion in the number of jobs in our economy has been in the small business arena. Indeed, most analysis of job generation indicate that in recent years, the source of job creation is much more likely to have been a small firm rather than a large one.

Consequences for the Individual

Regardless of which explanation for corporate job loss is most accurate, the fact is working for a large organization no longer seems to provide the kind of security and career opportunities it once did. Consequently, it should come as no surprise that many people are looking for a new route to take in the world of work. For growing numbers of people, that new route is entrepreneurship, and today that route has greater accessibility than ever. Just as the restructuring described earlier resulted in massive job losses—and continues to do so—the changes have led to unprecedented opportunities for small business.

Underemployed – being in a job that requires skill and knowledge below your capabilities.

The new economic face of America includes large numbers of capable unemployed, or underemployed, managers for whom the chances of regaining a comparable position in a large organization are slim. For many of these people, the appeal of making it on their own is easy to understand. They have talent, experience, drive, and contacts but nonetheless find themselves without a job. The need for productive channels for these managers to be able to make their contribution is clear; entrepreneurship is that channel for many.

Even for people who have not been directly touched by layoffs or by the uncertainties and pressures associated with corporate downsizing, the lure of the independence of entrepreneurship is strong. According to *Inc.* magazine, the number of universities and colleges offering courses or programs in entrepreneurship has increased to its current level of well beyond 1,000 from about 150 in 1979. Beyond the dramatic increase in the numbers of programs and courses, entrepreneurship education has grown in the ways in which it is offered. As Illustration Capsule 1-1 shows, some of the nation's leading entrepreneurship programs, as ranked in a 2004 survey conducted by *Forbes* magazine and *The Princeton Review*, go to great lengths to provide experiences, incentives, and opportunities to help start an entrepreneurial career.

ILLUSTRATION CAPSULE 1-1

TOMORROW ENTREPRENEURS

While some communities and regions—Seattle, Austin, Boston, Silicon Valley—are seen as hotbeds for business start-ups, many other locations around the country have vibrant programs for developing and encouraging young people interested in starting a business. Listed here are the to ten top-ranked university programs in entrepreneurship in a 2004 survey conducted by *Forbes* magazine and *The Princeton Review.* Notice the diverse and creative features of the programs and the way in which they prepare students to launch a business.

#1 – University of North Carolina — Chapel Hill
Programs include the Carolina Entrepreneurial Initiative, the Carolina Entrepreneurship Club, Students in Free Enterprise, and the Carolina Launch Program.

#2 – University of Notre Dame
Students may work the IrishAngels, a network of university alums from around the world, representing a variety of industries and markets.

#3 – Louisiana State University and A&M College
Independent studies, geared toward exploring a business idea or developing a feasibility study, are offered.

#4 – Northeastern University
Through its Entrepreneurship Center the university provides a business plan competition and co-op program opportunities.

#5 – Indiana University — Bloomington
The Young Entrepreneurs Association sponsors projects and internships; the university provides experiential learning through the Start-up Training Assistance Research Center.

#6 – Carnegie Mellon University
Students participate in activities offered by the Undergraduate Entrepreneurship Association, Students in Free Enterprise, Innovation Works, Pittsburgh Life Science Greenhouse, and Pittsburgh Digital Greenhouse.

#7 – Syracuse University
The university's Orange Hatchery is a student incubator, accommodating eight student ventures. In addition, the school sponsors the Syracuse Business Plan, which awards $40,000 to student-initiated ventures.

#8 – University of Arizona
Students work in teams with large and small corporations to identify new markets and opportunities for existing technologies and products, then develop business plans for commercialization.

#9 – University of Iowa
The school's entrepreneurial center provides coordination of a mentor program and runs the Wellmark Venture Capital Fund, which serves students, faculty, and area entrepreneurs.

#10 – University of New Hampshire
Entrepreneurship students are given the chance to operate the campus's convenience store, and can participate in the High Tech internship program.

Source: 2004 Survey of University Entrepreneurship Programs; *Forbes* magazine and *The Princeton Review*.

THE GLOBAL SCENE

While it may be true that by almost any measure the United States has the most vibrant entrepreneurship of any of the world's economies, by no means does it have a monopoly. The advantages of widespread entrepreneurial activity have not gone unnoticed by economic planners in countries around the globe, and recent years have seen the initiation of many programs to encourage small business formation. China was a traditional opponent of any economic ideas that even hinted of capitalism, and yet it, like many countries with socialist traditions, has seen entrepreneurship emerge as a major force in its economy. See Illustration Capsule 1-2.

ILLUSTRATION CAPSULE 1-2

ROADS TO ENTREPRENEURSHIP IN CHINA

Some historic movements start in barely noticeable ways. Years ago, the village elders of Xiangyang, an obscure town in the southwestern part of China, decided to remove a sign that designated the town as a "people's commune." The move came as a result of a 1978 decision by the country's leaders to allow communities to change from communes to "townships." Although the elders took more than a year to respond to the opportunity, Xiangyang was the first community to do so and thereby set in motion some profound changes. In the years following World War II, the Communist government had banned private commerce, so the move toward establishing free markets required considerable political courage. The first Xiangyang businesses to be involved in the transformation were in agriculture; the success there led to changes in other industries, particularly in the emergence of individual private enterprise. By the 1980s entrepreneurship was changing the country. In 1984 an authority on modern China, Orville Schell, wrote the book *To Get Rich Is Glorious: China in the Eighties*. Not everyone has been able to get rich, of course, but the possibility of doing so has energized, and continues to energize, enough people to have made a significant difference in the nation's economic fortunes.

In recent years China's ability to compete internationally has created considerable unrest in overseas markets. For example, *BusinessWeek,* in its December 6, 2004, cover story, identified the "three scariest words" in U.S. industry as "the China price." Manufacturing companies are told that their price is too high. To keep selling to an aggressive retailer, which insists on lowest prices from its suppliers, U.S. manufacturers often turn away from domestic plants and to offshore outsourcing. China's industrial might, based on many profound cost advantages and threatening to transform international business, prompted *The New York Times Magazine* to speculate that we have entered the "The China Century."

Often overlooked in the analysis of China's ability to compete is a strong entrepreneurial urge in many of its people. *Inc.* magazine gives as an example of this urge the case of a woman from the Zhejiang province, Hong Dongyang. She started as a school teacher but began making socks in the 1970s. She did well and therefore decided to open a roadside stand, calling her modest enterprise, "Zhejiang Stocking Company." Her success did not go unnoticed and her efforts were copied by others in the province. Many others—today 8,000 companies—in the province produce 8 billion pairs of socks, or one-third of the world's supply.

Sources: Tony Walker, "Communing with the Future," *Financial Times Weekend,* May 30/May 31, 1998, I; Orville Schell, *To Get Rich Is Glorious: China in the Eighties* (New York: Pantheon Books, 1984); Ted C. Fishman, "How China Will Change Your Business," *Inc.*, March 2005; Ted C. Fishman, "The China Bind," *The New York Times Magazine*, July 4, 2004.

The wave of interest in entrepreneurship has also made its way around the world. This interest has been particularly strong in organizations whose objective is to improve the economic life of underdeveloped nations. The World Bank has had a role in each of the following projects:

$ In Rio de Janeiro, 36,000 students are being given training to enhance their computer and literacy skills, with the objective of developing entrepreneurs capable of starting small information technology businesses.

$ In the African country of Niger, marketing and entrepreneurial skills are taught to farmers to bolster their independence.

$ Various forms and applications of information technology are being used in Bangladesh to develop entrepreneurship. Cellular telephones, for example, are provided to individuals who in turn sell calls and services in rural areas that do not have a traditional communications infrastructure.

$ The government of Peru and the World Bank are engaged in a program to develop "entrepreneurial capacity" in indigenous and Afro-Peruvian peoples.

$ In Guatamala, a program called MicroNet, sponsored by the government, Microsoft, and the World Bank, is helping people develop entrepreneurial skills to allow them to start their own businesses. The goal is 25,000 starts annually.

$ The Enterprise Incubator Project in Armenia provides assistance to emerging businesses, particularly those in information technology. Furthermore, entrepreneur grants cover initial business investment costs.

$ The Malawi Entrepreneurship Program was established to aid in food distribution in response to the country's severe drought problems.

Of all the institutional efforts to nurture small business, none has had more dramatic results than that of an economist from Bangladesh. His idea was simple: provide financing to the poor so that they can become self-sufficient entrepreneurs. Muhammad Yunus founded the Grameen Bank, because, as he says, "Capital does not need to be the handmaiden only of the rich." See Illustration Capsule 1-3 for a description of the bank and its remarkable accomplishments.

ILLUSTRATION CAPSULE 1-3

ENTREPRENEURSHIP IN A CHANGING ENVIRONMENT

Muhammed Yunus's idea for Grameen Bank came 20 years ago when he visited one of Bangladesh's desperately poor villages. It was obvious to him that the village's people, especially the women, needed loans to let them start their own businesses, and it was just as obvious that they were not going to get them from conventional banking circles. The warnings Mr. Yunus had heard from traditional bankers that the Grameen poor people would not repay their loans did not trouble him, so he started a "micro-credit for micro-enterprises" program at his Grameen Bank.

The program has grown impressively. Small loans have been made to 2 million families in 35,000 villages in Bangladesh, incredible numbers by any standard. Not only is there impressive volume in terms of customers, but the repayment record is outstanding, with a rate of over 90 percent.

The success of the program has led to an extension to the beggars of Bangladesh, and they too have vindicated Mr. Yunus's belief in them. Like the village women, they have improved their lives and have repaid their loans faithfully.

More recently microenterprise programs have been established in Haiti and Bolivia. Both show the same kinds of remarkable results, most notably repayment rates of 97 percent. The Haiti program, established in 1997, has grown at an annual rate of 73 percent and has women as 68 percent of its borrowers. The Bolivian program has 60 percent women in its borrower ranks and attracts primarily marginalized low-income members of the population.

Continued

Continued

Mr. Yunus's faith in the creditworthiness of the poor people of the world was well founded, and as a result, countless numbers of poor people, primarily women, from around the world have achieved a level of financial and personal success they would otherwise have not experienced.

Sources: Patrick E. Tyler, "Banker Is Star at Parley on Women," *The New York Times*, September 14, 1995, A7; David Bornstein, "The Barefoot Bank with Cheek," *Atlantic Monthly*, December 1995, 40–47.

ENTREPRENEURSHIP IN A CHANGING ENVIRONMENT

Perhaps the most powerful element of today's environment is change. Although it is more dramatic in some sectors of our economy than in others, none is immune to its threat. Change is everywhere, and according to most observers, it will continue to accelerate. It has important implications for entrepreneurs, and we will examine two of its aspects: changes in markets and the emergence of new markets.

Changes in Markets

A tactic commonly used when a company's management feels the pressure of competitors using aggressive pricing is to reduce costs to the lowest possible levels. As we noted in discussing downsizing, the target of these cost reduction efforts is frequently the workforce. Fewer people on the payroll obviously means lower costs, but the need to produce the product or provide the service remains. Many firms have handled this dilemma by having an outside supplier perform the tasks. They are engaging in outsourcing.

Outsourcing – the practice of using outside firms to perform tasks that could be performed internally.

Outsourcing has become an increasingly common practice, an opportunity for small firms. The tasks performed by the victims of downsizing usually have to be taken care of, and small companies are typically used to do so. Consequently, as big firms experience threats, small firms are given opportunities.

In addition to receiving such outsourcing requests, small businesses can also compete in markets where size and scope are required to compete effectively, by themselves contracting with outsiders to provide services. Using this method in the extreme, an individual can enter into alliances with a variety of suppliers to design a product, produce it, and even market it. The relationship, or alliance, between the company and supplier continues until the contract requirements are met, after which the relationship ceases to exist. Should a new opportunity emerge, a new set of alliances is formed. By creating such relationships to cover all the tasks needed to bring the product to market, the entrepreneur can enter markets that otherwise would have been out of reach. The term for a business that operates this way is *virtual organization*, a firm that operates as though it has all of the customary parts of an ongoing business, when in fact it may consist of only the entrepreneur and a file of contacts for establishing relationships.

Virtual organization – a company that does not have the internal resources needed to compete, choosing rather to form alliances with other firms to perform the necessary tasks.

Another change taking place in markets is one of continued fragmentation, or the development of niches. The population of the United States is so large that for almost any product, the overall size of the market would preclude small businesses from competing effectively. Within markets, however, are small groups of customers looking for a unique set of attributes in a product; these groups constitute a niche. Many niches are too small to interest large firms and therefore provide small firms with opportunities. Benefiting from these opportunities requires focusing on a clearly defined niche in the market, understanding exactly the expectations of the customer in that niche, and filling those expectations.

Fragmentation of market – when markets become divided into unique and distinctive parts.

New Markets

For the past 20 years or so, many firms have tried to take advantage of the opportunities provided by a heightened concern for our environment. Wide arrays of goods and services, marketed under the "green" label and ranging from recycled paper goods to environmentally friendly lawn care products, now compete for our dollars. The green market provides opportunities that small firms may be particularly well suited to address.

Green markets – those that develop in response to our society's concerns for our physical environment.

They typically bring to the market a fresher image and a more convincing case than do many of the old-line firms whose reputations have been tarnished in this area. See Illustration Capsule 1-4.

Illustration Capsule 1-4

THE GREENING OF ENTREPRENEURSHIP

While big business seems anxious to promote its efforts to save the planet, many ambitious plans remain just that: plans. Companies learn that the market isn't large enough, or that entering it may require turning its back on its old customers, or that more study is needed, and so on. These obstacles seem to be less formidable to small business. Here are two examples of entrepreneurs who have established companies that are making money while making a difference.

In the town of Sebastopol, California, entrepreneur Gary Starr is determined to use his product, the electric bicycle, to accomplish something that the big automobile manufacturers do not seem willing to tackle. Mr. Starr would like to reduce our nation's dependence on the internal-combustion engine. He has developed the ZAP bike, which provides supplemental power to help the rider negotiate hills and to provide a higher cruising speed. He hopes that after a period of using the ZAP, the owner will be ready to move up to an electric car, and when that happens, his company will sell that vehicle as well.

In the early 1980s John Schaeffer founded his "hippie hardware store," Real Goods, in Willetts, California. The firm's early years were, at best, modestly successful. In 1986, however, Mr. Schaeffer started a mail-order operation with hopes of increasing sales from $18,000 to $1 million by 2000. His projection was not very accurate: the firm sold $18.3 million in 1996. The firm sells environmentally friendly goods, including energy-efficient and renewable items and some rather unusual items such as ultrasonic toothbrushes and Zen alarm clocks. The company catalog has established itself as a premier purveyor of environmentally friendly items not only with consumers—7 million copies were printed last year—but with the sources of the items as well. Now inventors and developers of new "green" items seek out Mr. Schaeffer for inclusion in the catalog.

Source: Marc Reisner, "Green Expectations," *The Amicus Journal*, Summer 1998, 19–23.

Marketplace – a physical location where buyers and sellers meet.

Market space – the techniques, machines, and processes that allow buyers and sellers to transact business electronically.

As the World Wide Web develops, we will see a change in the way commerce is conducted. This change has been called the transformation from "marketplace" (meaning physical business activities) to "market space" (business done electronically). Predictions of how this new technology-driven process will develop are always hazardous, but it seems likely that some of the major players will be companies we have not heard of, and many of them will be companies that have not even been started. Among the ingredients for success in this kind of embryonic industry are insights as to what it takes to serve customers who have not yet been identified, and the inspiration to follow through on those insights. Someone with those characteristics will move us in the direction toward market space from marketplace, and that someone is likely to be an entrepreneur rather than a manager with a large company.

The Competitive Advantages of Small Business

Competitive advantage – a characteristic of a business that allows it to compete successfully.

Regardless of whether it is an upheaval in existing markets or the emergence of a new one, small businesses have important advantages that allow them to succeed. One is their responsiveness to conditions and trends in the market, which comes from a close relationship with customers and therefore a thorough understanding of their needs. For many entrepreneurs the relationship with the customer is a personal one, and that means being the first to learn of changes in preferences that will affect the market. Not only does such a relationship give the entrepreneur the chance to learn from the customer, but it also gives the entrepreneur the chance to reverse the communication process: to give the customer the message that he or she matters to the business. Large companies spend considerable amounts of money and energy to learn from the customer and to send messages of concern; for small firms, both learning and showing concern are natural parts of the process of doing business. Successful small businesses never lose sight of that.

Another factor that distinguishes the successful small business from the typical large company is its ability to innovate. The independence of an entrepreneurial company allows it to move quickly when something changes or a new opportunity arises. While many large firms recognize the need to change directions quickly, most seem to be burdened with procedures and administrative controls that slow things down, no matter what the sense of urgency might be. This ability of small businesses to innovate can take on many forms, including product innovation (new features, improvements), process innovation (improvements to how production is carried out), and service innovation (offering something new to serve the market). Regardless of its form, innovation enables small business to compete successfully.

Closely related to innovation is flexibility. For many successful small businesses, a change requested (or even hinted at) by the customer or a new product feature developed by a competitor typically becomes a call for action that leads to new ways of doing things or modifications to the product line. The reasons for this flexibility are both attitudinal and practical. Entrepreneurs know that responding to the customer is important enough to deal with the disruption brought on by change; it "goes with the territory." As a practical matter, small companies tend to invest less than many big firms in expensive, single-purpose machines, large inventory levels, and rigid production tools and techniques. As a result, they can change what they do, or the way they do it, with far less difficulty.

Taken together, these characteristics—responsiveness, the ability to innovate, and flexibility—provide a small business with what it takes to compete in a rapidly changing environment. But clearly the entrepreneur, the individual, is at the core of any success achieved by the small company. Chapter 2 describes that individual.

SMALL BUSINESS AND THE BUSINESS PLAN

One of the most important documents needed by entrepreneurs is a business plan. In this text we discuss the topics important to small business owners and then address each of these topics in the business plan section in the second half of the text. The topics mentioned—competitive advantage, innovative ideas, and markets to be served—must be described in detail in the business plan. This helps the entrepreneur to develop the business concept and shows bankers and investors that the entrepreneur has carefully thought through the business idea.

SUMMARY

Here in the United States entrepreneurship has had profound effects on our economy since the years after World War II. During the 1990s and the first years of the new century, we have witnessed a continuation in the number of independent small businesses relative to our population. Some reasons for this increasing popularity of small business include the manner in which large firms have dealt with their economic imperatives, competition from overseas companies, and the spread of many forms of technology that make it possible for small firms to compete effectively with large ones. Recent years have brought the recognition that entrepreneurship can be an important source of vitality in countries whose economies are still developing.

DISCUSSION QUESTIONS

1. What are the major reasons for entrepreneurship becoming so important in our economy?
2. What are the two leading explanations for the massive job losses that have characterized the nation's largest firms in recent years?
3. Will the concept of a job become obsolete?
4. Give some examples of the sources of strength of the entrepreneurial movement in different countries.
5. What is outsourcing, and how has it given a boost to entrepreneurship?
6. Define market space and explain how it represents an opportunity for entrepreneurs.

ENDNOTES

1. "The Fortune Directory," *Fortune*, July 1955, 2.
2. *2004–2005 Statistical Abstract of the United States* (Washington, DC: U.S. Department of Commerce, Bureau of the Census), 734.
3. Ibid.
4. *1970 Statistical Abstract of the United States* (Washington, DC: U.S. Department of Commerce, Bureau of the Census), 468.
5. *2004–2005 Statistical Abstract of the United States* (Washington, DC: U.S. Department of Commerce, Bureau of the Census), 716.
6. "TAPEWATCH," *The Wall Street Journal*, May 4, 1995, 1.
7. Ibid.
8. Jennifer Click, "Downsizing Continues As Profits Climb," *HRMagazine*, July 1995, 14.